The Adventures
in Literature Program

Adventures for Readers: Book 1
Test Booklet
Steps to Better Reading: Book 1*
Teacher's Manual
Many Voices 7, a long-play record

Adventures for Readers: Book 2
Test Booklet
Steps to Better Reading: Book 2*
Teacher's Manual
Many Voices 8, a long-play record

Adventures in Reading
Test Booklet
Steps to Better Reading: Book 3*
Teacher's Manual
Many Voices 9, a two-record
(long-play) album

Adventures in Appreciation
Test Booklet
Steps to Reading Literature: Book 1*
Teacher's Manual
Many Voices 10A, a long-play record
Many Voices 10B, a long-play record
of *Julius Caesar*

Adventures in American Literature
Test Booklet
Steps to Reading Literature: Book 2*
Teacher's Manual
Many Voices 11, a two-record
(long-play) album

Adventures in English Literature
Test Booklet
Steps to Reading Literature: Book 3*
Teacher's Manual
Many Voices 12A, a long-play record
Many Voices 12B, a long-play record
of *Macbeth*

* Programed Instruction

ADVENTURES

in American
Literature

LAUREATE
EDITION

EDMUND FULLER

B. JO KINNICK

Series Editor: MARY RIVES BOWMAN
Reading Consultant: HERBERT POTELL

Harcourt, Brace & World, Inc.

New York   Chicago   Atlanta   Dallas   Burlingame

EDMUND FULLER is an author, editor, critic, and teacher. Among his works are two novels, *Brothers Divided* and *A Star Pointed North,* and two critical studies, *George Bernard Shaw: Critic of Western Morale* and *Man in Modern Fiction.* His reviews and articles appear in the New York *Times Book Review,* the *Saturday Review,* the *American Scholar,* and the Chicago Tribune *Magazine of Books.* He has taught comparative literature at Columbia University, and is presently a member of the English Department at Kent School in Kent, Connecticut, In addition to his co-editorship of *Adventures in American Literature,* Mr. Fuller is general editor of the Adventures in Good Books Series.

B. JO KINNICK attended the University of Iowa (B.A.) and the University of California (M.A.); she now teaches American literature and creative writing at Oakland High School, Oakland, California. She has been a member of various educational organizations and has served as president of the Central California Council of Teachers of English; in addition, she has been active as a poet for a number of years. Her poems have appeared in numerous magazines, including the *Saturday Review,* the *Saturday Evening Post,* and the *English Journal.* A collection of her poetry, *Time Is the Stream,* was published in 1961.

The Series Editor, MARY RIVES BOWMAN, holds degrees in English from the University of Texas (B.A.) and the University of Chicago (M.A.) and has also engaged in graduate study in English at the University of Colorado and at East Texas State College. She has been active in various professional organizations and has devoted much of her time to the training and supervision of high school English teachers. Miss Bowman is co-editor of three earlier editions of *Adventures in American Literature* and of two editions of *Adventures for Readers,* Books 1 and 2.

HERBERT POTELL is reading co-ordinator and teacher of English at New Utrecht High School, Brooklyn, New York. A graduate of Brooklyn College, he has done graduate work in English at Columbia University and the College of the City of New York. He is a member of the International Reading Association and has served as reading consultant on two other editions of the Adventures in Literature Series. In addition, he is co-author of the ninth and tenth grade books in the Adventures in Literature Companion Series — *Adventures for Today* and *Adventures in Living.*

FRONTISPIECE: *an oil painting of the American eagle by the artist* W. F. Vaché. *This painting was hung over the door of President Lincoln's cabin on the steamer* River Queen. (Courtesy, The Home Insurance Company.)

Artists who have contributed to the illustration of this book are: Robert Shore, Harvey Dinnerstein, Marilyn Miller, Lawrence Bjorklund, Donald Bolognese, Joseph Weishar, Aldren Watson, and Raphael Palacios.

Contents

Modern Nonfiction

Modern Poetry

Modern Drama

Part 2 The Growth of
American Literature

The Colonial Time

The Making of a Nation

The American Imagination Awakens

TWO MAJOR NOVELISTS

New England's Golden Years

FOUR NEW ENGLAND POETS

Growth and Conflict

THE ADVANCING FRONTIER

THE WAR BETWEEN THE STATES

Time of Change

NEW DIRECTIONS IN POETRY

WHAT IS

AN AMERICAN?

O VER THE COURSE OF TWO CENTURIES, the question has been
asked again and again: What is an American? The fascination of it,
the element that makes it just as lively a query today as it was two
hundred years ago, is the fact that the American, like everyone else in the world
but perhaps more intensely than most, is constantly changing and developing.
Parts of the earliest answers remain true, but new conditions demand
consideration. Each generation of Americans has, in its own way, reviewed
the question and stated the answer.

One of the earliest answers — and still a memorable one — was made by
Hector St. John de Crèvecœur, who was born in France in 1735, spent some time
in England, and emigrated to America in 1765. He settled on a farm in what
is now New York state and remained until 1780, the late years of the American
Revolution. While he was here, he wrote a book called *Letters from an American
Farmer*. It was published first in England in 1782, and in America, at
Philadelphia, in 1793. The book was not reprinted until more than a hundred
years later, in 1904. De Crèvecœur died in France in 1813, unaware that the
world would someday acclaim his modest book to be a classic. The English
essayist William Hazlitt said that the author of the *Letters* was one of the three
great North American writers of the eighteenth century. Whether or not this
judgment still stands, the fact is that De Crèvecœur uniquely caught the spirit
of this new land: he saw the American as a man and citizen, and as a
forerunner of free people everywhere. The clarity and directness of his vision
brings to us, American readers of today, remembrance of our origins and a thrill
of recognition.

FROM *Letters from an American Farmer*

What then is the American, this new man? He is either a European, or
the descendant of a European, hence that strange mixture of blood, which you
will find in no other country. I could point out to you a family whose grandfather
was an Englishman, whose wife was Dutch, whose son married a French

woman, and whose present four sons have now four wives of different nations. *He* is an American, who, leaving behind him all his ancient prejudices and manners, receives new ones from the new mode of life he has embraced, the new government he obeys, and the new rank he holds. He becomes an American by being received in the broad lap of our great Alma Mater. Here individuals of all nations are melted into a new race of men, whose labors and posterity will one day cause great changes in the world. Americans are the Western pilgrims, who are carrying along with them that great mass of arts, sciences, vigor, and industry which began long since in the East; they will finish the great circle. The Americans were once scattered all over Europe; here they are incorporated into one of the finest systems of population which has ever appeared, and which will hereafter become distinct by the power of the different climates they inhabit. The American ought therefore to love this country much better than that wherein either he or his forefathers were born. Here the rewards of his industry follow with equal steps the progress of his labor; his labor is founded on the basis of nature, *self-interest;* can it want a stronger allurement? Wives and children, who before in vain demanded of him a morsel of bread, now, fat and frolicsome, gladly help their father to clear those fields whence exuberant crops are to arise to feed and to clothe them all. . . . The American is a new man, who acts upon new principles; he must therefore entertain new ideas, and form new opinions.

A European, when he first arrives, seems limited in his intentions, as well as in his views; but he very suddenly alters his scale; two hundred miles formerly appeared a very great distance, it is now but a trifle; he no sooner breathes our air than he forms schemes, and embarks in designs he never would have thought of in his own country. There the plenitude of society confines many useful ideas, and often extinguishes the most laudable schemes which here ripen into maturity. Thus Europeans become Americans.

But how is this accomplished in that crowd of . . . people who flock here every year from all parts of Europe? I will tell you; they no sooner arrive than they immediately feel the good effects of that plenty of provisions we possess: they fare on our best food, and they are kindly entertained; their talents, character, and peculiar industry are immediately inquired into; they find countrymen everywhere disseminated, let them come from whatever part of Europe. Let me select one as an epitome of the rest; he is hired, he goes to work, and works moderately; instead of being employed by a haughty person, he finds himself with his equal, placed at the substantial table of the farmer, or else at an inferior one as good; his wages are high, his bed is not like that bed of sorrow on which he used to lie: if he behaves with propriety, and is faithful, he is caressed, and becomes, as it were, a member of the family. He begins to feel the effects of a sort of resurrection; hitherto he had not lived, but simply vegetated; he now feels himself a man, because he is treated as such; the laws of his own country had overlooked him in his insignificancy; the laws of this cover him with their mantle. Judge what an alteration there must arise in the mind and thoughts of this man; he begins to forget his former servitude and dependence, his heart involuntarily swells and glows; this first swell inspires him with those new thoughts which constitute an American. What love can he entertain for a country where his existence was a burthen to him? If he is a generous, good man, the love of this new adoptive parent will sink deep into his heart. He looks around, and sees many a prosperous person, who but a few years before was as poor as himself. This encourages him much; he begins to form some little scheme, the first, alas, he ever formed in his life. If he is wise, he thus spends two or three years, in which time he acquires knowledge, the use of tools, the modes of working the lands, felling trees, etc. This prepares the foundation of a good name, the most useful acquisition he can make. He is encouraged, he has gained friends; he is advised and directed, he feels bold, he purchases some land; he gives all the money he has brought over, as well as what he has earned, and trusts to the God of harvests for the discharge of the rest. His good name procures him credit. He is now possessed of the deed, conveying to him and his posterity the fee simple and absolute property of two hundred acres of land, situated on such and such a river. . . . If he is a good man, he forms schemes of future prosperity; he proposes to educate his children better than he has been educated himself; he thinks of future modes of conduct, feels an ardor to labor he never felt before.

How happy are we here, in having fortunately escaped the miseries which attended our fathers, how thankful ought we to be that they reared us in a land where sobriety and industry never fail to meet with the most ample rewards! You have, no doubt, read several histories of this continent, yet there are a thousand facts, a thousand explanations overlooked. Authors will certainly convey to you a geographical knowledge of this country; they will acquaint you with the eras of the several settlements, the foundations of our towns, the spirit of our different charters, etc., yet they do not sufficiently disclose the genius of the people, their various customs, their modes of agriculture, the innumerable resources which the industrious have of raising themselves to a comfortable and easy situation. Few of these writers have resided here, and those who have have not pervaded every part of the country, nor carefully examined the nature and principles of our association. It would be a task worthy of a speculative genius to enter intimately into the situation and characters of the people . . . and surely history cannot possibly present any subject more pleasing to behold. Sensible how unable I am to lead you through so vast a maze, let us look attentively for some small unnoticed corner; but where shall we go in quest of such a one? Numberless settlements, each distinguished by some peculiarities, present themselves on every side; all seem to realize the most sanguine wishes that a good man could form for the happiness of his race. It is always a refreshing spectacle to me, when in my review of the various component parts of this immense whole, I observe the labors of its inhabitants singularly rewarded by nature; when I see them emerged out of their first difficulties, living with decency and ease, and conveying to their posterity that plentiful subsistence which their fathers have so deservedly earned.

— Hector St. John de Crèvecœur

The changes which De Crèvecœur predicted America would produce began at the very time he was writing. Though he withdrew from the New World during its struggle for independence, he had seen, and captured in words, the vision of freedom, of opportunity, of boundless frontiers, of fresh thought, and of mingled contributions from many backgrounds. These were the elements, among others, that formed the American.

The question, What is an American? has found a continuing answer in two ways: through deeds and through words. The actions of the people of America have shaped an answer in each of the eras of our history. Thus far, the answers have been bold and often great. The question is being answered today in a world changed more vastly than De Crèvecœur could have imagined. Another answer is to be found in our literature. De Crèvecœur speaks of a time when few writers had described the young country. But there followed writers of all kinds of literature who did precisely what De Crèvecœur regards as so important: disclosed "the genius of the people, their various customs . . . ," examined "the nature and principles of our association," and entered "intimately into the situation and characters of the people. . . ."

Our writers have produced in their total work a definition and description of the American. This was rarely their first, or conscious, purpose. Literature is always a personal, individual expression. It has many purposes but only one source: the vision of the artist. Yet the total, complex figure of the American emerges from the works of our writers. You will see it in the cross section of American writing in the pages that follow. Men of faith speak of their quest for religious freedom. Statesmen speak of their determination to establish and maintain liberty and justice. Poets celebrate the moods and prospects of American life. Historians, biographers, and social critics describe and analyze the long way we have come, not sparing our mistakes and faults. Essayists and philosophers weigh the values that guide us. Novelists, short-story writers, and playwrights tell us, as Thornton Wilder does in the play *Our Town*, ". . . this is the way we were in our growing up and in our marrying . . . and in our living and in our dying."

These things, and more, are what literature is about. That is why literature is one of our best means of understanding who and what we are. American literature, a vigorous, varied, and magnificent body of writing, brings a living and growing answer to the question: What is an American?

Part I

Modern American Literature

MODERN FICTION

MODERN NONFICTION

MODERN POETRY

MODERN DRAMA

Modern Fiction

Fiction is one of the most basic and ancient of human pleasures. The storyteller has been with us for as long as the human race has memories. Stories can be told in poetry or prose. The epic poet or novelist may spin them out to great length. The drama acts out its stories before our eyes; the opera sings its tales; the ballet dances them.

Of all the forms of fiction, the short story is the one to which our country made the most important early contributions. An American writer, Edgar Allan Poe, first defined and wrote in this form, fashioning stories that gained international admiration. The short story has continued to attract the abilities of our finest writers. The stories that follow, all written by Americans during the past few decades, will suggest the variety and range of this popular form of fiction.

Guide to Reading Short Stories

Before you can fully appreciate and understand the short story, you should be able to recognize some of its important characteristics. You should know how the parts of a story combine to form a whole and how much each part contributes toward the total effect. In other words, you should learn to read critically. In ordinary usage you may associate "criticism" with unfavorable comment, but this is not the real meaning of the word. In literature — in any of the arts — criticism means appraisal, evaluation, and appreciation. As you learn to read critically, you will develop your ability to recognize good writing, and you will increase your enjoyment of the best literature.

ACTION

In simplest terms, a story is an account of something that happened: The "something that happens" is the *action*. In most stories the action is more than just a series of unrelated incidents; rather, the action is organized into a *plot*. The plot is the plan, the blueprint of the story. The basis of every plot is a struggle or conflict, with the opposing forces so evenly balanced that the reader is in doubt about the outcome. Generally the opposing forces are persons or groups of persons, though many fine stories have been written about other kinds of conflict, such as the struggle of an individual against the forces of nature, and some of our best stories are purely psychological; the conflict centers about ideas or attitudes. The turning point of the plot, the point at which the reader can foresee the outcome of the struggle, is called the *climax*.

CHARACTER

Character is as basic as action. These two story elements are linked inseparably. Action reveals character, and character determines action. Action leads to changes in character, and changes in character in turn lead to new kinds of action. In many modern stories character *is* the action, for very little happens except in the mind of the chief character.

In a short story, descriptions of characters cannot be long. The few sentences that can be spared to present a character must be keenly illuminating. A gifted writer will often sketch his characters while showing them in action, so that the plot develops while the reader is forming his impression of the persons involved. The finest writing generally presents subtle and complex characters. Some stories emphasize action more than character, but even in this kind of fiction, character must seem realistic, though not necessarily complex. To create a successful story, the author must convince the reader that the actions and motives of his characters are those of living people.

POINT OF VIEW

A story must be told from a *point of view*. This is the position from which the action and characters are seen by the author. Fundamentally, there are two ways of telling a story: through the *first person* ("I said," "I did") or the *third person* ("he said," "he did"), but there are varieties of these two methods. The first-person narrative may represent the voice of the main character, or it may simply be that of a minor character who observes the action. First-person narration, regardless of how it is used, has the advantage of speaking directly to the reader, but it limits the author in that he can reveal only what the narrator could be expected to know. The narrator, for example, cannot tell us what the other characters are thinking.

Third-person narration allows the author to reveal more knowledge than any single character in the story could possess. The author may even tell what many of the characters are thinking. This treatment is called the *omniscient* ("all-knowing") point of view, and its obvious advantage is that it allows the author the greatest freedom in telling a story, since no restriction is placed on the information he may reveal.

Occasionally the author will employ third-person narration, but he will tell of events only as they appear to the eyes of one of the characters in the story. This *limited* point of view has both the advantages and limitations of first-person narration: it can intensify our identification with a specific character, and it can present a situation vividly and realistically, but it restricts the knowledge that the author may reveal.

SETTING

The *setting* of a story — the specific time and place of the events — is rarely a dominant element. Setting is stressed in only two kinds of fiction: the local-color story, which focuses on the interesting peculiarities of a particular region, and historical fiction, which concentrates on a specific era. Even where setting is not dominant, however, it can still be important. In stories that attempt to create a special mood, setting can be used to build up atmosphere; the descriptive details can give an emotional coloring to the entire story. Another frequent use of setting is to create an impression of reality. Stories of fantasy will often be given a realistic setting in order to help make the strange events more believable.

STYLE

Style refers to the author's use of language, his selection of words, his ways of expressing himself. One writer may use as many figures of speech as a poet; another may employ a host of adjectives and adverbs; another may write a sparse, direct prose. Style helps determine the *tone* of a story. Whether the tone is light or serious, comic or tragic, it will be created by the author's use of particular words or phrases. As you read, watch for the effects of style, and try to determine how the author's use of language creates a particular tone.

RAY BRADBURY

The Flying Machine

A glorious day . . . a peaceful ancient land . . . a man soars in the air, birdlike. Here is what seems to be a gently beautiful fairy tale, like Hans Christian Andersen's story of a Chinese Emperor and a mechanical nightingale. But Bradbury, as usual, has a surprise for us. Happy scene, joyous news — or *is* it?

STYLE TAILORED FOR EFFECT. Ray Bradbury is skillful at adapting his writing style to create a particular effect. As you read, try to see what effect the author is trying to create and in what ways the style contributes to that effect. Notice that he likes to suggest ideas indirectly and quietly.

In THE year A.D. 400, the Emperor Yuan held his throne by the Great Wall of China, and the land was green with rain, readying itself toward the harvest, at peace, the people in his dominion neither too happy nor too sad.

Early on the morning of the first day of the first week of the second month of the new year, the Emperor Yuan was

sipping tea and fanning himself against a warm breeze, when a servant ran across the scarlet and blue garden tiles, calling, "Oh, Emperor, Emperor, a miracle!"

"Yes," said the Emperor, "the air is sweet this morning."

"No, no, a miracle!" said the servant, bowing quickly.

"And this tea is good in my mouth, surely that is a miracle."

"No, no, Your Excellency."

"Let me guess then — the sun has risen and a new day is upon us. Or the sea is blue. That now is the finest of all miracles."

"Excellency, a man is flying!"

"What?" The Emperor stopped his fan.

"I saw him in the air, a man flying with wings. I heard a voice call out of the sky, and when I looked up, there he was, a dragon in the heavens with a man in its mouth, a dragon of paper and bamboo, colored like the sun and the grass."

"It is early," said the Emperor, "and you have just wakened from a dream."

"It is early, but I have seen what I have seen! Come, and you will see it too."

"Sit down with me here," said the Emperor. "Drink some tea. It must be a strange thing, if it is true, to see a man fly. You must have time to think of it, even as I must have time to prepare myself for the sight."

They drank tea.

"Please," said the servant at last, "or he will be gone."

The Emperor rose thoughtfully. "Now you may show me what you have seen."

They walked into a garden, across a meadow of grass, over a small bridge, through a grove of trees, and up a tiny hill.

"There!" said the servant.

The Emperor looked into the sky.

And in the sky, laughing so high that you could hardly hear him laugh, was a man; and the man was clothed in bright papers and reeds to make wings and a beautiful yellow tail, and he was soaring all about like the largest bird in a universe of birds, like a new dragon in a land of ancient dragons.

The man called down to them from high in the cool winds of morning. "I fly! I fly!"

The servant waved to him. "Yes, yes!"

The Emperor Yuan did not move. Instead, he looked at the Great Wall of China now taking shape out of the farthest mist in the green hills, that splendid snake of stones which writhed with majesty across the entire land. That wonderful wall which had protected them for a timeless time from enemy hordes and preserved peace for years without number. He saw the town, nestled to itself by a river and a road and a hill, beginning to waken.

"Tell me," he said to his servant, "has anyone else seen this flying man?"

"I am the only one, Excellency," said the servant, smiling at the sky, waving.

The Emperor watched the heavens another minute and then said, "Call him down to me."

"Ho, come down, come down! The Emperor wishes to see you!" called the servant, hands cupped to his shouting mouth.

The Emperor glanced in all directions while the flying man soared down the morning wind. He saw a farmer, early in his fields, watching the sky, and he noted where the farmer stood.

The flying man alit with a rustle of paper and a creak of bamboo reeds. He came proudly to the Emperor, clumsy in his rig, at last bowing before the old man.

"What have you done?" demanded the Emperor.

"I have flown in the sky, Your Excellency," replied the man.

"What have you done?" said the Emperor again.

"I have just told you!" cried the flier.

"You have told me nothing at all." The Emperor reached out a thin hand to touch the pretty paper and the bird-like keel of the apparatus. It smelled cool, of the wind.

"Is it not beautiful, Excellency?"

"Yes, too beautiful."

"It is the only one in the world!" smiled the man. "And I am the inventor."

"The only one in the world?"

"I swear it!"

"Who else knows of this?"

"No one. Not even my wife, who would think me mad with the sun. She thought I was making a kite. I rose in the night and walked to the cliffs far away. And when the morning breezes blew and the sun rose, I gathered my courage, Excellency, and leaped from the cliff. I flew! But my wife does not know of it."

"Well for her, then," said the Emperor. The sun was full in the sky now, and the smell of the grass was refreshing. The Emperor, the servant, and the flier paused within the huge garden.

The Emperor clapped his hands. "Ho, guards!"

The guards came running.

"Hold this man."

The guards seized the flier.

"Call the executioner," said the Emperor.

"What's this!" cried the flier, bewildered. "What have I done?" He began to weep, so that the beautiful paper apparatus rustled.

"Here is the man who has made a certain machine," said the Emperor, "and yet asks us what he has created. He does not know himself. It is only necessary that he create, without knowing why he has done so, or what this thing will do."

The executioner came running with a sharp silver ax. He stood with his naked, large-muscled arms ready, his face covered with a serene white mask.

"One moment," said the Emperor. He turned to a nearby table upon which sat a machine that he himself had created. The Emperor took a tiny golden key from his own neck. He fitted this key to the tiny, delicate machine and wound it up. Then he set the machine going.

The machine was a garden of metal and jewels. Set in motion, birds sang in tiny metal trees, wolves walked through miniature forests, and tiny people ran in and out of sun and shadow, fanning themselves with miniature fans, listening to the tiny emerald birds, and standing by impossibly small but tinkling fountains.

"Is it not beautiful?" said the Emperor. "If you asked me what I have done here, I could answer you well. I have made birds sing, I have made forests murmur, I have set two people to walking in this woodland, enjoying the leaves and shadows and songs. That is what I have done."

"But, oh, Emperor!" pleaded the flier, on his knees, the tears pouring down his face. "I have done a similar thing! I have found beauty. I have flown on the morning wind. I have looked down on all the sleeping houses and gardens. I have smelled the sea and even seen it, beyond the hills, from my high place. And I have soared like a bird; oh, I cannot say how beautiful it is up there, in the sky, with the wind about me, the wind blowing me here like a feather, there like a fan, the way the sky smells in the morning! And how free one feels! That is beautiful, Emperor, that is beautiful too!"

"Yes," said the Emperor sadly, "I know it must be true. For I felt my heart move with you in the air, and I wondered: What is it like? How does it feel? How do the distant pools look from so high? And how my house and servants? Like ants? And how the distant towns not yet awake?"

"Then spare me!"

"But there are times," said the Emperor, more sadly still, "when one must lose a little beauty if one is to keep what little beauty one already has. I do not fear you, yourself, but I fear another man."

"What man?"

"Some other man who, seeing you, will build a thing of bright papers and bamboo like this. But the other man will have an evil face and an evil heart, and the beauty will be gone. It is this man I fear."

"Why? Why?"

"Who is to say that someday just such a man, in just such an apparatus of paper and reed, might not fly in the sky and drop huge stones upon the Great Wall of China?" said the Emperor.

No one moved or said a word.

"Off with his head," said the Emperor.

The executioner whirled his silver ax.

"Burn the kite and the inventor's body, and bury their ashes together," said the Emperor.

The servant retreated to obey.

The Emperor turned to his hand servant, who had seen the man flying. "Hold your tongue. It was all a dream, a most sorrowful and beautiful dream. And that farmer in the distant field who also saw, tell him it would pay him to consider it only a vision. If ever the word passes around, you and the farmer die within the hour."

"You are merciful, Emperor."

"No, not merciful," said the old man. Beyond the garden wall he saw the guards burning the beautiful machine of paper and reeds that smelled of the morning wind. He saw the dark smoke climb into the sky. "No, only very much bewildered and afraid." He saw the guards digging a tiny pit wherein to bury the ashes. "What is the life of one man against those of a million others? I must take solace from that thought."

He took the key from its chain about his neck and once more wound up the beautiful miniature garden. He stood looking out across the land at the Great Wall, the peaceful town, the green fields, the rivers and streams. He sighed. The tiny garden whirred its hidden and delicate machinery and set itself in motion; tiny people walked in forests, tiny foxes loped through sun-speckled glades in beautiful shining pelts, and among the tiny trees flew little bits of high song and bright blue and yellow color, flying, flying, flying in that small sky.

"Oh," said the Emperor, closing his eyes, "look at the birds, look at the birds!"

FOR DISCUSSION

1. What does the Emperor's response to the word "miracle" tell us about his attitude toward life?

2. Why does the Emperor say that they must have time to "think of" and "prepare . . . for" the sight of the flying machine? What does this reaction suggest about haste?

3. Why do you think Bradbury says the inventor was "laughing so high" rather than flying so high?

4. Why does the Emperor twice ask, "What have you done?"

5. The Emperor says of the inventor, "It is only necessary that he create, without knowing why he has done so, or what the thing will do." According to the Emperor's belief, who should be held responsible for the consequences of an invention? Who would be the judge of the value of an invention?

6. The Emperor fears the consequences of the flying machine. Are his fears realistic? Do you think the Emperor succeeds in justifying the death of the inventor?

YOUR OWN WRITING

The Emperor seems to suggest that man should confine his inventive talents to making elaborate toys. In a short composition of your own, argue for or against the statement that some inventions should be forcibly suppressed to avoid future dangers.

THE AUTHOR

RAY BRADBURY (b. 1920) spent his early years in Waukegan, Illinois, and moved with his family to Los Angeles in 1934. At the age of twelve, he began writing for his own amusement, and on graduation from high school in 1938, he worked only at jobs that left him time to write. In 1940 he sold his first story, and by 1942 he was able to quit all work but writing. By 1953 he had had 170 stories published and many radio and television plays performed.

Because Bradbury's work is highly imaginative, his early publication was confined to science fiction and fantasy magazines. But the freshness and power of his stories attracted discriminating critics, and soon his narratives were appearing in general magazines and repeatedly in the collections of "best stories" of the year. Some good collections of his stories are *The Martian Chronicles*, *The Illustrated Man*, *Fahrenheit 451*, and *The Golden Apples of the Sun*.

As the Artist Sees It ➤

On the facing page is an oil painting by Robert Shore based on the climax of "The Flying Machine." Notice that the flying machine ("colored like the sun and the grass") stands between the Emperor and the Great Wall of China, presenting symbolically the conflict in the Emperor's mind.

CONRAD RICHTER

Early Marriage

With only a younger brother to accompany her, Nancy Belle had to ride across two hundred miles of Apache country to marry her man. This story will convince you that pioneer women were courageous.

FOLLOWING CHARACTERIZATION. Observe how Richter develops character in this story. As you read, notice the ways in which you come to know Nancy Belle and Rife.

For two days the leathery face of Asa Putman had been a document in cipher to anyone who could read the code. Since Saturday but one traveler had passed his solitary post, a speck of adobe and picket corrals lost on the vast, sandy stretch of the Santa Ana plain. Far as the eye could see from his doorway, the rutted El Paso trail — unfenced, gutterless, innocent of grading, gravel, culverts, or telephone poles, imprinted only by iron tires, the hoofs of horses and oxen, sheep and cattle, and the paw of the loping lobo wolf — lay with dust unraised.

Ordinarily, there were freighters with cracking whips and trailers rumbling on behind. Army trains to and from the forts set up their tents for the night beyond the springs. The private coaches of Santa Fe and Colorado merchants, of cattle kings and government officials, stopped long enough for the Putman children to admire the ladies, the magnificent woodwork, and the luxurious cushions inside. Trail herds of gaunt red steers bawled for the water in the earthen tank, and pairs and companies of horsemen rode up and down.

But since Saturday not even a solitary buckboard[1] from the far settlements in the Cedar country had called for supplies or letters. Only a girl from the Blue Mesa had ridden in for her and her neighbors' mail. She had eaten dinner with the Putnams, refused to stay overnight, and started her long ride home.

A stranger from the East would have spoken about the stillness, the deadly waiting, and asked uneasily why Uncle Gideon hadn't come as promised. But

[1] **buckboard:** a horse-drawn vehicle with seats cushioned by a long, springy frame between the axles.

in the Putman household it was not mentioned.

Asa deliberately busied himself about the post, filling the bin beneath the counter with navy beans and green coffee, leafing through the packet of letters in the drawer, and making a long rite out of feeding the occupants of the picket corrals — four horses of which were fresh for the next stage.

Rife, just turned fifteen, carried water and gathered cow chips in an old hide dragged by a rope to his saddle horn. Ignacita,[1] the Mexican housekeeper, spat sharply on her heavy irons in the torrid kitchen and kept glancing over her shoulder and out of the open door and windows.

And Nancy Belle, going on seventeen, packed and repacked the high, iron-bound trunk that her father had bought for her at Santa Fe and sang softly to herself in the way that women sang fifty and sixty years ago.

Saturday she was being married at Gunstock, two hundred miles away — five days' journey in a wagon, four in a saddle or buckboard.

For six months she had thought of little else. The almanac fell apart at June as naturally as her mother's Bible did at the Twenty-third Psalm. So often had she run her finger down the page that anyone might tell from the worn line of type the very day she and Stephen Dewee would be man and wife. The Dewees lived four hundred miles west across the territory in the Beaverhead country. She and Stephen were taking a mountain ranch near his people, and for the wedding they had compromised on Gunstock, nearly equidistant from both families and convenient to friends scattered up and down the Rio Grande.

She had lighted a candle in the dusk, when a figure appeared reluctantly in her doorway. Asa Putman had never been at ease in his daughter's bedroom.

[1] Ignacita (ĕg·nä·sē′tä).

A tall, rawhide man in an unbuttoned sagging vest, he was visibly embarrassed by any furnishings that suggested refinement. Invariably he kept his hat on in the house. He had it on now, a flat top and a flat brim, not so much like the Western hats you see now. Nancy Belle knew that her mother's people had never forgiven him for bringing his young wife and their two small children to this lonely post, at the mercy of outlaws and the worse Apaches.

Tonight she could see that something bothered him. He gave her a sidewise glance, so sharp and characteristic.

"I don't expect, Nancy Belle, you could put off your weddin'?"

The girl stood quietly gazing at him with a face like the tintype[2] of her mother. But under her sedate gray dress, with tight waist and full skirts to the instep, she had frozen. She looked much older than her years. Her air of gentlefolk and her wide-apart gray eyes came from her mother. But the chin, tipped up with resolute fearlessness, was her father's.

"No, papa!" Her two clear words held all the steady insistence of the desert.

"I figured how you'd feel," he nodded, avoiding her eyes. "I just wanted to put it up to you. I'd a' covered the *jornada*[3] on foot to be on time at my own weddin', but I didn't have to count on Gideon to hold me up."

"Are you telling me, papa, that you can't go to Gunstock tomorrow?" Her voice remained quiet, but a coldness had seized her. Of all the people she had visualized at her wedding, the one next to Stephen she could least spare was the tall, grave figure of her father.

"I reckon I kind of can't, Nancy Belle," he said soberly. "Rife could tend

[2] **tintype** (or **ferrotype**): an early kind of photograph made on a thin iron plate.
[3] *jornada* (hôr·nä′dä): a journey, often used in the Southwest for a long stretch of desert country.

to the stage all right and do the feedin'. But they's men come to this post no boy can handle." He shifted his position. "I figured once on closin' up the post till I got back. But the stage is comin' and the mail. And the freighters count on me for feed and grub. Then I got to protect my own property and the mail and freight for the Cedar country that's in the storage room."

"I know," Nancy Belle said steadily. "I can get to Gunstock all right."

Far back in her father's assaying eyes, she fancied she saw a glint of pride.

"You're pretty nigh a woman now, Nancy Belle. And Rife's a good slice of a man. It's a straight trail to the Rio Grande, once you turn at the old post. Both you and Rife's been over it before. Of course, I'd like to be at the weddin', but the boy can tell me about it." He went to the window. "Rife!" he called.

Nancy Belle's brother came in presently. A slight boy, with his father's blue eyes, he seldom made a fuss over anything, even when he shot a stray duck on the tank or when they braked down the last cedar hill into Santa Fe with all the open doors of the plaza shops in sight. And when his father told him now, he showed neither enthusiasm nor regret — merely straightened.

"Sure. I can take you, Nancy Belle," he said.

Something pulled under his sister's tight basque.[1] She remembered the long miles they would have in the wagon, the camps at lonely places, the ugly shadow ever hovering over the outposts of this frontier country, and the blight that, since Saturday, seemed to have fallen on the trail. Her eyes swam. Now, at the last minute, she yielded.

"If you'll let me ride, papa, I'll wait another day for Uncle Gideon," she promised.

Her father's eyes moved to the ruf-

fled red calico curtains at the shadeless windows.

"I don't hardly count on Gideon comin' any more, Nancy Belle. Besides, it's too long in the saddle to Gunstock — especially for a girl to get married. You'd be plumb wore out, and you wouldn't have your trunk. You couldn't get dressed for your weddin'."

He turned thoughtfully and went out, Rife close behind. Nancy Belle could hear her father's tones, slow and grave, coming from near one of the picket corrals.

It was too far to catch the words; but when they came in, she saw that her brother's features looked a little pale under the tan.

"You better get some sleep, Nancy Belle," her father said. "You and Rife are startin' before daylight. If Gideon comes, I'll ride after."

They had scarcely gone from the room when Ignacita came in from the kitchen, her black eyes glittering over a pile of freshly starched white in her arms.

"Nancy Belle, chinita—"[2] she whispered, plucking at the girl's sleeve. "You don't say to your papacito[3] I talk to you! I have promise I don't scare you. But I can't see you go so far in the wilderness alone, pobrecita![4] Sometimes people go safe from one place to the other, oh, sí![5] But sometimes, chinita, they don't come back! You have not the oldness like Ignacita. Ay, I tell you these old eyes have seen men and women quartered from a tree like sheep or maybe tied over a stove like I don't have the words to say to you."

Nancy Belle did not answer except to lay, one by one, the ironed pieces in her

---

[1] basque (băsk): a fitted jacketlike shirt or blouse.

[2] chinita (shē-nē'tà): a term of endearment.

[3] papacito (pä'pä-sē'tō): "little" papa, a familiar, affectionate form.

[4] pobrecita (pō'brá-sē'tà): poor little one, another familiar form.

[5] sí (sē): yes.

trunk — a bride's muslin underwear trimmed with red and blue feather stitching; long petticoats stiffly flounced with ruffles, and nightgowns long in the sleeve and high in the neck, with ruffles at wrist and throat. The Mexican woman went on hoarsely. The girl folded away her winter's cashmere dress, buttoned up the front and with a white fichu.[1] She unwrapped and wrapped again in crumpled white tissue the red slippers the old gentleman on the stage had sent her as a wedding present from Philadelphia.

When Ignacita had left, she opened her keepsake box covered with colored shells. The mirror on the inside lid turned back a face as calm as the little golden clouds that hung of an evening over the east to catch the desert sunset. But after she had undressed and put on her nightdress, for a long time she was aware of the soft pound of her heart faintly swaying the bed on its rawhide springs.

At the first sound of Ignacita's hand on the kitchen stove, Nancy Belle sprang out of bed. She dressed on the brown pool of burro skin, the only carpet on her adobe floor. Through the west window she could see the morning star burning like a brilliant candle. It hung, she told herself, over Gunstock and the Beaverhead, where Stephen, at this moment, in their new log ranch house, lay thinking about her.

They ate in the kitchen by lamplight. She had never been so conscious of every detail — the great white cups and saucers, the familiar steel knives, the homey smell of the scorched paper lampshade, the unreadable eyes of her father, Rife, and Ignacita.

Asa Putman himself carried out the trunk. There was already hay in the wagon, a gunny sack of oats, food in a canned-tomato box and utensils in another, a water keg, bedroll tied in a

wagon sheet, an ax, a bridle, and her own sidesaddle, made to order over a man's tree.[2] Her eyes caught the gleam of a rifle leaning up against the seat in the lantern light. Tethered to the rear of the wagon stood her saddle mare, Fancy, with pricked-up ears. She was going along to their new ranch home. Nancy Belle felt that she was still among intimate things, but outside the little circle of light lay darkness and the unknown.

When she said good-by to her father, he kissed her — something he had not done for years.

"You haven't changed your mind, Nancy Belle?" he asked.

She climbed quickly up over the wheel to the spring seat of the wagon before he might see that she was crying. Rife swung up like a monkey on the other side and pushed the rifle into the crevice behind the seat cushion. The lines tautened and the wagon lurched.

"*Dios* go with you safe to your husband, Nancy Belle!" she heard Ignacita cry after her.

The morning star had set. They moved into a world of silent blackness. Nancy Belle could not see how the horses remained on the trail. When she looked back, the only light in all these square miles of black, unfriendly earth was the yellow window of her father's post.

It was almost a vision, golden and faraway, like all beautfiul things. She didn't trust herself to look again.

Two hours later the wagon was a lonely speck of boat rocking in an illimitable sage-green sea beneath the sun. The canvas wagon sheet fastened over the bows was a kind of sail, and eastward the sandy water did not stop rolling till it washed up at the foot of the faintly blue ramparts of the distant Espiritu Range.

[1] **fichu** (fĭsh'oo): a kind of kerchief of muslin or lace, worn about the neck.

[2] **tree**: saddletree, the wooden frame of a saddle.

Just before they turned west on the cross trail to the Rio Grande, a heavy wagon with a yoke of oxen in front and a cow behind toiled round the crumbling adobe walls of the old, abandoned posthouse. A bearded man and a thin woman with a white face sat on the seat. She held a baby in her arms, and three black-eyed children peered from under the wagon sheet.

The bearded man saluted and stopped his willing team. Rife did likewise. The woman spoke first. Her tongue was swift and slightly acid.

"You better turn around and follow us if you want to save your hair!" she called. "Yesterday a sheepherder told us he saw — "

A sharp word from the bearded man caused her to relapse into sullen silence. He asked Rife where he might be going, then climbed down to the trail and said he wanted to talk to him a little. The boy followed reluctantly behind his wagon. Nancy Belle could hear the bearded man's tones coming slow and grave like her father's, while the woman made silent and horribly expressive lip language.

Rife came back, walking stiffly. The bearded man climbed up beside the woman.

"They got to go on," he told her in a low tone, then saluted with his whip. "Good luck, boy! And you, miss!"

Rife raised his whip in stiff acknowledgment. The wagons creaked apart. Nancy Belle saw in front of her the trail to the Rio Grande, little more than a pair of wheel tracks that lost itself on the lonely plain. Rife seemed relieved that she did not ask what the bearded man had said. But it was enough for her not to be able to forget the woman's fearful signs and mouthings and the horror in the curious eyes of the staring children.

Sister and brother talked very little. Nancy Belle saw her brother's eyes keep sweeping the country, scanning the horizons. Bunches of bear grass that might have been feathers pinioned his blue gaze, and clumps of cane cactus that seemed to hold pointing gun barrels. At arroyos [1] thick with *chamiso* [2] and Apache plume she could see his feet tighten on the footboard. Once he pulled out the rifle, but it was only a herd of antelopes moving across the desert page.

They camped for the night when the sun was still high. Nancy Belle asked no questions as the boy drove far off the trail into a grassy *cañada*. [3] She sang softly to herself as she fried the salt side bacon and put the black coffeepot to boil.

Rife hobbled Anton Chico and the Bar X horse and staked out Fancy close to the wagon.

She pretended not to notice when, before dark, he poured earth on the fire till not a spark or wisp of smoke remained. Out of one eye she watched him climb the side of the *cañada* and stand long minutes sweeping the country from the ridge, a slight, tense figure against the sullen glow of the sunset.

"It's all right," he said when he came down. "You can go to bed."

"What's all right?" she asked him.

"The horses," he said, turning away, and Nancy Belle felt a stab of pain that so soon this boy must bear a man's responsibilities and tell a man's lies.

She prayed silently on her blankets spread on the hay in the wagon box, and lay down with her head on the sidesaddle, her unread Testament in her hand. She heard Rife unroll his camp bed on the ground beneath the wagon. It was all very strange and hushed without her father. Just to feel the Testament in her hand helped to calm her, and to remember the day at the post when she had first met Stephen.

[1] arroyos (ă·roi'ōz): small, often dry, gullies or channels.
[2] *chamiso* (chà·mē'sō): a semidesert shrub.
[3] *cañada* (kä·nyä'dä): an open glade between mountains or ridges.

Her father had never let her come in contact with the men of the trail. Always, at the first sign of dust cloud on the horizon, he would tell both children to heap up the chip box, fill the water buckets and carry saddles and bridles into the house. But this day Asa Putman and Rife had gone to Fort Sumner. And to Nancy Belle, Uncle Gideon could seldom say no.

It had been a very hot day. She had been sitting in the shade of the earthen bank of the tank, moving her bare feet in the cool water, watching the ripples in the hot south wind. The leaves of the cottonwoods clashed overhead, and she heard nothing until she looked up, and there was a young man on a blue-gray horse with dust clinging to his hat brim and mustache. His eyes were direct as an eagle's. Firm lines modeled his lean face. But what she noticed most at the time was the little bow tie on his dark shirt.

Instantly she had tucked her bare, wet legs under her red dress. Her face burned with shame, but the young stranger talked to her about her father coolly, as if she, a girl of fifteen, had not been caught barefooted. Then he did what in her mind was a noble thing. When Uncle Gideon came out, he magnificently turned his back for her to run into the house and pull on shoes and stockings.

She thought of Stephen constantly next day and the next. She had grown a little used to the journey without her father now — the still, uncertain nights under the wagon sheet, sitting, lying, listening, waiting; the less uncertain days with the sun on the endless spaces; her never-quiet perch on the high spring seat under the slanted bow; the bumps, creaks, and lumberings of the wagon; the sand sifting softly over the red, turning wheels; all afternoon the sun in their faces; ahead the far haze and heat waves in which were still lost Gunstock and the Rio Grande. Almost

she had forgotten the bearded man with the oxen, and the curious, detached horror in the eyes of his children.

Since morning of the third day, their progress had been slower. The trail seemed level, except for the heavy breathing of the horses. But when Nancy Belle glanced back, she could see the steady grade they had been climbing. Abruptly, in midafternoon, she found that the long, blue Espiritu Range had disappeared, vanished behind a high pine-clad hill which was its southernmost beginning. It was like the lizard that swallowed itself, a very real lizard. At this moment they were climbing over the lizard's tail.

"Cedars!" Rife said briefly, pointing with the whip to dark sprawling growths ahead.

"You breathe deep up here!" Nancy Belle drank in the light air.

Rife took a sniff, but his blue eyes never ceased to scan the high, black-thatched hill under whose frowning cliff they must pass.

"Soon we can see the Gunstock Mountains," Nancy Belle said.

"And Martin Cross's cabin," Rife nodded. "It's the last water to the Rio Grande."

"He's a nice old man," Nancy Belle ventured casually. "It would be nice to camp by his cabin tonight and talk."

The boy inclined his head. After a few moments he started to whistle softly. At the first cedar Nancy Belle leaped off the moving wagon and climbed back with an evergreen branch. The twig, crushed in her hand, smelled like some store in Santa Fe.

They gained the summit. A breeze was sweeping here from the southwest, and the horses freshened. But Rife had suddenly stopped whistling and Nancy Belle's sprig of cedar lay on her lap. The frowning cliff of the pine-clad hill was still there. But Martin Cross's cabin had turned to a desolate mound of ashes. As they stared, a gust of wind sent wisps of smoke scurrying from the mound, and a red eye opened to watch them from the embers. Nancy Belle felt an uncontrollable twitching in the hair roots at the base of her scalp.

Where Martin Cross's eastbound wheel tracks met the trail, Rife reluctantly halted the horses and wet his air-dried lips.

"The water keg's dry, and the horses. If papa was here, he'd drive over."

"I'm the oldest." Nancy Belle found her voice steady. "I'll ride over. There might be something we can do."

The boy rose quickly. His eyes seemed to remember something his father had said.

"You can drive the wagon over if I wave."

He had thrown her the lines and slipped back through the canvas-covered tunnel of wagon box, picking up Fancy's bridle and the rifle. Barebacked he rode toward the smoldering ashes at the foot of that frowning hill. The chestnut mare's tail and mane streamed like something gold in the wind.

When she looked back to the trail, her eyes were pinioned by a light object in the wheel track ahead of the Bar X horse. It was a long gray feather. Instantly she told herself that it had come from some wild turkey Martin Cross had shot, and yet never had air anywhere become so suddenly horrible and choking as in this canyon.

Rife did not signal her to drive over. She saw him come riding back at full speed. The mare was snorting. As he stopped her at the wagon, her chestnut head kept turning back toward what had once been a cabin. Rife slipped the lead rope about her neck and climbed into the seat with the rifle in his hands.

"The water — you wouldn't want it!" he said thickly. His cheeks, she noticed, were the color of *yeso*.[1]

"Rife" — Nancy Belle touched his

[1] *yeso* (yā′sō): gypsum, used to whitewash the walls of pioneer houses in the Southwest.

arm when she had driven down the canyon — "what did you see at the cabin?"

The boy sat deaf and rigid beside her, eyes staring straight ahead. She saw that his young hands were still tortured around the barrel of his rifle.

Far down on the pitch-dark mesa she stopped the horses in the trail and listened. There were no stars, not a sound but the flapping of the wagon sheet in the wind and the clank of coffeepot and water bucket under the wagon. Half standing on the footboard, she guided the team off the trail in the intense blackness. Her swift hands helped the trembling boy stake out the mare and hobble the team. They did not light a lantern. Rife declined to eat. Nancy Belle chewed a few dry mouthfuls.

The wind came drawing out of the blackness with a great draft. It hissed through the grass, sucked and tore at the wagon sheet, and whistled through the spokes and brake rigging. Rife did not take his bedroll under the wagon tonight. He drew the ends of the wagon sheet together and lay down in the wagon box near his sister. For a long time they were silent. When she heard his heavy breathing, she lifted the rifle from his chest.

The storm grew. Sand began pelting against the canvas and sifted into the wagon box. An invisible cloud of choking dust found its way into eyes, mouth, ears, and lungs. Nancy Belle laid down the rifle a moment to pull a blanket over the face of the boy. He tossed and muttered pitifully, but he slept on.

Magically the rain, when it came, stopped the sand and dust. The girl drank in the clean-washed air. At daylight she slipped out to the ground. The mesa, stretching away in the early light, touched here and there with feathers of mist, would have been beautiful except for a sharp new loneliness. The horses were gone!

At her exclamation, Rife appeared from the wagon box. His shame at having slept through the night was quickly overshadowed by their misfortune.

Together they found where Fancy's stake had been pulled out and dragged. Yards farther on they could tell by Anton Chico's tracks that his hobbles had parted.

Nancy Belle made her brother come back to the wagon and stuff his pockets with cold biscuits and antelope jerky. She said she would have a hot breakfast ready when he returned. The horses, perhaps, were just down in some draw where they had drifted with the wind.

When he had gone with the rifle, she filled the coffeepot from a clearing water hole in the nearest arroyo. She fried potatoes and onions in the long-handled skillet. And when he did not come, she set fresh biscuits in the Dutch oven. Each biscuit held a square of salt side bacon in its top, and as it baked, the fat oozed down and incased it in a kind of glazed tastiness.

At noon she thought she heard a shot. Nowhere could she see him on the endless sweep of mesa. By late afternoon she was still alone. She read her Testament and wondered how many women over the world had read it in hours like this. Sitting in the shadow of the wagon, facing the direction in which he had gone, she looked up every few minutes. But all her eyes could find were cloud shadows racing across the lonely face of the mesa. All she could hear were the desolate cries from the unseen lark sparrows.

Darkness, stillness settled down on the empty land. She climbed back into the wagon and sat on the chuck box, hands rigid on her knees. Again and again she convinced herself that the horses could not have been driven off or she would have seen the drivers' tracks. When wild, sharp barks shattered the stillness and set wires jerking in her limbs, she talked to herself steadily, but a little meaninglessly, of the post — on and on as the darkness was filled with the ringing and counter-ringing of shrill, cracked yappings — not long tones like a dog's, but incredibly short syllables rising, rising in a mad eternal scale and discord.

"I wish Papa had given me two of the chairs," she repeated. "Mamma said they were post oak from Texas. She said they had got white from scrubbing. I liked the laced rawhide seats with the hair left on. It made them soft to sit on. The seats in the parlor were black. And the ones in the kitchen were red. But I liked the brockle [1] one in my room best."

The insane din around the wagon had become terrific. There were only two or three of the animals, Nancy Belle guessed, but they threw their voices and echoes together to make a score.

"When I was little, I liked to go in the storage room," her voice went on, scarcely intelligible to her own ears. "It was dark and cool, and smelled of burlap and kerosene and whisky, and sweetish with brown sugar. I can see the fat sacks of green coffee. And the round tins of kerosene had boards on the side. The flour sacks were printed: 'Rough and Ready' in red letters. Mamma once used to make our underwear out of the sacking. I can smell the salt side bacon in the gunny sacks."

She could tell from the sounds that one of the animals was running insanely back and forth near the wagon tongue. She had never noticed before that they yelped both when breathing in and out. Suddenly came silence. It warned her. Instinctively she felt for the ax.

"Nancy Belle!" a boy's far, anxious voice called from the darkness.

She hallooed and leaned out over the tailboard. Three shadowy forms were coming across the mesa in the starlight.

[1] **brockle:** brown or black markings on a white background.

Never had horses looked so good.

"Were you scared?" Rife greeted. "Anything bother you?"

"Nothing," Nancy Belle said. "Just coyotes."

"I had to give Fancy her head after it got dark." He slid wearily to the ground. "She brought us straight back to the wagon."

Nancy Belle had wanted to put her arms around her brother. Now she hugged the mare instead. Rife ate fresh biscuits and a tin plate of cold potatoes. He drank several tin cups of coffee. Nancy Belle had slipped the oats-laden, gunny-sack *morrals* [1] over the horses' heads.

"I had to walk halfway to the mountain," Rife said.

"Just help hitch up; then you can sleep all night," she promised.

It rained again heavily toward midnight. Flashes of lightning lit the drenched plain. For minutes at a time, quivering fingers of blue phosphorescence stood on the ears of the toiling horses. At dawn Nancy Belle still held the reins as the mud-splashed wagon crawled through a world bathed in early purple splendor.

Four days they had been crossing a hundred and seventy miles of desolate plain. Now the end waited in sight. To the west lay a land broken and tumbled by a mighty hand. Hill shouldered hill and range peered over range, all indescribably violet except where peaks tipped by the unseen sun were far-off flaming towers of copper.

It was a new land, her promised land, Stephen's land, Nancy Belle told herself, where nobody burned cow chips, but snapping cedar and pine, where cold water ran in the wooded canyons, and the eye, weary of one flat circle the horizon round, had endless geometric designs to refresh the retina.

She sang softly as the wagon lumbered to the edge of a long, shallow valley, brown and uninhabited, running north and south, and desolate except for a winding ribbon that was white with sky and narrowly bordered with green.

"Rife!" Nancy Belle cried. "The Rio Grande!"

An hour afterward they pulled out of the sun into the shade of the long cottonwood *bosque.* [2] Nancy Belle wasn't singing now. Where she remembered wide sandbars glistening with sky and tracked by waterfowl, a chocolate-red flood rolled. Where had been the island, tops of tule and scrub willow swung to and fro with the current.

Anton Chico and the Bar X horse stopped of their own accord in the trail, ears pricked forward at the swirling brown wash. While Rife turned the three horses loose to graze, Nancy Belle silently fried bacon and made coffee. When she had washed skillet and tin dishes in the river, the boy had wired the wagon box to the brake rigging. Now he was tying securely one end of his rope to the center of the coupling pole under the wagon. The other end she knew he would fasten to the inadequate upper horn of the sidesaddle.

"I wouldn't mind the river if I just had my own saddle," he mourned.

They hitched up the team silently. Rife cinched the sidesaddle on Fancy and straddled it, the single stirrup useless to a man. Nancy Belle climbed into the wagon and picked up the lines. The other bank looked as far away as the Espiritu Range from the post. She wanted to say something to her brother — some last word, in case they didn't make it. But all she did was cluck her tongue to the horses.

Gingerly, one slow foot at a time, the team moved down the trail into the water.

"Give 'em their heads!" Rife called from the right rear.

Nancy Belle held a rein in each hand.

[1] *morrals:* feed bags.

[2] *bosque* (bôs'kȧ): a wood or grove.

The red channel water came to the wagon tongue, covered it, reached the horses' bellies. The team wanted to stop. Nancy Belle swung her whip, a stick tipped with a long rawhide lash. The wagon went on. The collars of both horses kept dipping, but never entirely out of sight. Still barely wading, the slow team reached the firmer footing of the island.

Two thirds of the river still rolled in front of the wagon. The west bank did not seem to have grown much closer, but the east bank behind them had moved far away. The team had to be whipped into the violent current. The water churned white through the wagon wheels. Suddenly both horses appeared to stumble and drop out of sight. Their heads came up wildly, spray blowing from their nostrils. The muddy water hid their legs, but by their bobbing motions Nancy Belle knew that they were swimming.

"Keep 'em pointed up the river!" Rife shouted.

Already she felt the wagon floating. It swung downstream with the current; then Rife's rope from Fancy's saddle snubbed it. The team was snorting with every breath. The Bar X horse swam high in the water, his withers and part of his back out of the chocolate current. But all she could see of Anton Chico were his nose and ears.

Down between her ankles she saw water in the wagon box. She thought of the hemstitched sheets at the bottom of her trunk, the towels and pillowcases crocheted with shell lace. Her blue velvet corduroy dress was probably wet already, and all the cunning print aprons with dust caps to match. River water couldn't hurt the little yellow creamer, sugar bowl, and covered butter dish that had been her mother's. And the gingham dresses could be washed. What worried her were her wedding dress and the keepsake box, especially the tintypes, one of which was Rife in a child's suit edged with black braid,

his brand-new hat on his knee.

An older Rife was shouting something behind her now. She couldn't catch the words. Then she found what it was. The neck and withers of Anton Chico raised suddenly out of the water and both horses were scrambling up the steep bank below the ford. Only quick work with the lines saved the wagon from turning over. Safe and blowing on the high bank, the dripping horses shook themselves like puppies.

Nancy Belle couldn't go on until she had opened the trunk and appraised the damage. Rife unsaddled Fancy and drove on with the refreshed team. Behind his slight back in the wagon box, the girl changed to her blue velvet corduroy, which was hardly wet at all. Then she combed her hair and rolled into a cranny of her trunk the old felt hat that had been too large for her father.

A half-dozen riders met the wagon some miles down the Gunstock Canyon. All of them, Nancy Belle noticed, carried guns. Stephen wore a new white shirt and a gray hat with curled brim she had not seen before. He stood in his stirrups and swung her down in front of him on the saddle, where he kissed her. She had never felt his lips press into such a straight line.

"Papa couldn't come," she said. "So Rife brought me."

She felt Stephen's rigid arm around her.

"We just got in from the Beaverhead ourselves."

"He means they never get any news out in the Beaverhead or he'd 'a' come further east to meet you!" Uncle Billy Williams put in. He had a lovable, squeaky voice. "The Apaches been breakin' loose again. Funny you didn't hear anything over in your country."

Nancy Belle gave him an inscrutable look with her gray eyes. Uncle Billy pulled out his bandanna and blew his nose.

"They got my old friend Judge

Hower and his wife and kid in a buggy on the Upper Espiritu. The man that found what they did to 'em, they say, cried like a baby."

"That's all right, Uncle Billy," Stephen said in a gentle voice.

Nancy Belle glanced at Rife. Her brother's face looked gray, the eyes staring as when he had ridden in the late afternoon sunlight from the smoking ashes of Martin Cross's cabin.

Nearly fifty people, gathered in the big parlor upstairs at the hotel, greeted Nancy Belle. An old man whose young black eyes twinkled out of a bearded face said he was glad to see that she had her "hair on straight." Rife stopped with the trunk before driving to the livery, and Stephen's mother showed Nancy Belle to a room to dress.

The guests stopped talking when she came into the parlor in her white wedding dress. Her basque came to a point in the front and back. It fitted like a glove. The silk underskirt came to her instep, and the ruffled overskirt to her knees. She had parted her hair from side to side and brushed the bangs down on her forehead. She felt very light-headed. The wagon still seemed to be jerking under her.

She glimpsed Rife gazing at her, a rapt expression in his reticent blue eyes. She was glad to see that he had brushed his hair. The brass swinging lamp had been lighted and the dark woodwork of the parlor festooned [1] with evergreen branches. White streamers from the wall met in a papier-mâché [2] bell in one corner. She noticed two children peering eagerly from the dark hall.

Stephen came to her, very straight in a long coat and stand-up collar with a black tie. He led her up beneath the papier-mâché bell. In a sibilant, church-like whisper, the Gunstock preacher made sure of her full name. Then he

coughed and began the ceremony. He had a deep voice, but Nancy Belle didn't hear all of the service. Her mind kept going back to a tall, grave man in a lonely adobe post on the wide Santa Ana plain. And after she had said "I do," her lips moved, but she was not praying for Stephen, her husband.

FOR DISCUSSION

1. Trace the steady building up of suspense from the first indications at the post that something was wrong. Why did the family never discuss these signs of trouble?

2. At what point were Nancy Belle and Rife in greatest danger? When was her courage nearest the breaking point?

3. How can you tell that the father had thought long and hard about Nancy Belle's journey before suggesting that she postpone it? What evidence of real devotion between the two did you find?

4. What behavior of Rife's showed that his father had warned him of danger? Review the responsibility and hard work demanded of this boy of fifteen.

5. Compare this realistic story with the kind of "Western" that one generally finds on TV. How do the two differ? Would you have preferred an actual encounter with Apaches in the story? What would probably have been the outcome of the meeting?

FOLLOWING THE CHARACTERIZATION

Did you come to know Nancy Belle and Rife: (1) through their actions, (2) through what they said, (3) through what others said about them, or (4) through what the author said about them? Which of these methods were used most often?

The Setting of "Early Marriage" ➤

On the facing page is a photograph of the Rio Grande River, showing the approximate area of the final scenes of "Early Marriage." The photograph was taken almost a hundred years after the events of the story, but the character of the land has changed little in that time.

---

[1] festooned: decorated.
[2] papier-mâché (pā′pĕr·mǎ·shā′): a hard substance made of paper pulp.

CONRAD RICHTER (b. 1890), a native of Pennsylvania, followed a long and difficult road to reach the top rank of our writers of early American life. At fifteen he finished high school and went to work driving teams, pitching hay, serving behind the counter in stores and in a bank before landing his first job as a reporter. When he began to sell his fiction, he moved to New Mexico, where half a day in the saddle can take one back a hundred years in time. From the recollections of old settlers and from books, he gleaned his intimate knowledge of early times. Four of Richter's novels trace the westward progress of pioneering Americans: *The Sea of Grass* (1937), *The Trees* (1940), *The Fields* (1946), and *The Town* (1950), for which he was awarded a Pulitzer prize in 1951. In *The Light in the Forest* (1953) he shows the settlers as they appeared to the Indians during the struggle for the new land. This later novel is considered one of Richter's finest.

ERNEST HEMINGWAY

Old Man at the Bridge

To fighting men war may be a vast drama, with the prize, victory for a cherished cause, balanced against the risk of death. But what of simple people who know nothing of larger causes and only suffer dislocation, loss, and misery?

UNDERSTANDING SYMBOLS IN STORIES. In modern fiction the effect of a story is frequently heightened by the use of symbols. Some simple object may stand for complex ideas or emotions associated with it. To a pioneer housewife, for example, a silver teapot brought from her old home may symbolize all that she left behind, and its loss can be taken as a sign that the old ties are broken. A person can be a symbol, too, and represent a whole group of people sharing similar traits or facing similar problems. You will get the full force of this story only if you see the old man as such a symbol, as one among the millions of victims of war. Watch for symbols, too, of the kind of life the old man will not know again.

An old man with steel-rimmed spectacles and very dusty clothes sat by the side of the road. There was a pontoon bridge across the river; and carts, trucks, and men, women, and children were crossing it. The mule-drawn carts staggered up the steep bank from the bridge, with soldiers helping push against the spokes of the wheels. The trucks ground up and away, heading out of it all, and the peasants plodded along in the ankle-deep dust. But the old man sat there without moving. He was too tired to go any farther.

It was my business to cross the bridge, explore the bridgehead beyond, and find out to what point the enemy had advanced. I did this and returned over the bridge. There were not so many carts now and very few people on foot, but the old man was still there.

"Where do you come from?" I asked him.

"From San Carlos," he said, and smiled.

That was his native town and so it gave him pleasure to mention it and he smiled.

"I was taking care of animals," he explained.

"Oh," I said, not quite understanding.

"Yes," he said, "I stayed, you see, taking care of animals. I was the last one to leave the town of San Carlos."

He did not look like a shepherd nor a herdsman, and I looked at his black dusty clothes and his gray dusty face and his steel-rimmed spectacles and said, "What animals were they?"

"Various animals," he said, and shook his head. "I had to leave them."

I was watching the bridge and the African-looking country of the Ebro [1] Delta, and wondering how long now it would be before we would see the enemy, and listening all the while for the first noises that would signal that ever-mysterious event called contact, and the old man still sat there.

"What animals were they?" I asked.

"There were three animals altogether," he explained. "There were two goats and a cat, and then there were four pairs of pigeons."

"And you had to leave them?" I asked.

"Yes. Because of the artillery. The captain told me to go because of the artillery."

"And you have no family?" I asked, watching the far end of the bridge where a few last carts were hurrying down the slope of the bank.

"No," he said, "only the animals I stated. The cat, of course, will be all right. A cat can look out for itself, but I cannot think what will become of the others."

"What politics have you?" I asked.

"I am without politics," he said. "I am seventy-six years old. I have come twelve kilometers [2] now and I think now I can go no further."

"This is not a good place to stop," I said. "If you can make it, there are trucks up the road where it forks for Tortosa." [3]

"I will wait a while," he said, "and then I will go. Where do the trucks go?"

"Toward Barcelona," [4] I told him.

"I know no one in that direction," he said, "but thank you very much. Thank you again very much."

He looked at me very blankly and tiredly, then said, having to share his worry with someone, "The cat will be all right, I am sure. There is no need to be unquiet about the cat. But the others. Now what do you think about the others?"

---

[1] **Ebro** (ā'brō): a river in northeastern Spain, along which battles were fought during the Spanish Civil War of the 1930's.

[2] **twelve kilometers:** about seven and one-half miles.

[3] **Tortosa** (tôr·tō'sä).

[4] **Barcelona** (bär'sĕ·lō'nä).

"Why, they'll probably come through it all right."

"You think so?"

"Why not?" I said, watching the far bank where now there were no carts.

"But what will they do under the artillery when I was told to leave because of the artillery?"

"Did you leave the dove cage unlocked?" I asked.

"Yes."

"Then they'll fly."

"Yes, certainly they'll fly. But the others. It's better not to think about the others," he said.

"If you are rested I would go," I urged. "Get up and try to walk now."

"Thank you," he said and got to his feet, swayed from side to side and then sat down backward in the dust.

"I was taking care of animals," he said dully, but no longer to me. "I was only taking care of animals."

There was nothing to do about him. It was Easter Sunday and the Fascists were advancing toward the Ebro. It was a gray overcast day with a low ceiling so their planes were not up. That and the fact that cats know how to look after themselves was all the good luck that old man would ever have.

FOR DISCUSSION

1. What is really uppermost in the soldier's mind as he talks with the old man? Tell the significance of the details that he notes in between parts of the conversation.

2. Is the dramatic effect of this incident heightened or lessened by the information that the old man has "no politics"? Why does he keep repeating that he was only looking after animals?

3. Tell what you think happens to the old man and to his animals. How can you tell what the narrator expects to happen to them?

4. Do you think the validity of this tiny image of war is limited to the place, the time, or the kinds of weapons involved?

THE SYMBOLS IN THE STORY

1. Explain why the situation of this one old man is a typical part of war. Ernest Hemingway saw much of war, including its spectacular aspects. Why do you think he felt that this simple incident was worth recording?

2. The animals in this story can also be regarded as symbols. Tell what you think they may represent.

THE AUTHOR

ERNEST HEMINGWAY (1898–1961) was born and grew up in Oak Park, Illinois. Following graduation from high school, he began working for the Kansas City *Star,* where the experience he gained as a reporter helped form his terse and clear style of writing. Hemingway was a man of wide interests and varied experiences. His early novel *The Sun Also Rises* (1926) concentrates on the lives of a small group of Englishmen and Americans living in Paris during the 1920's. His next, *A Farewell to Arms* (1929), draws on his experience as an ambulance driver with an Italian combat unit during World War I. Hemingway's participation in the Spanish Civil War resulted in his writing *For Whom the Bell Tolls* (1940), which some consider his finest novel.

Deep-sea fishing held such attraction for him that for many years he made his home in Cuba, the scene of his novelette *The Old Man and the Sea.* Another of his foremost interests was bullfighting. It is the subject of *Death in the Afternoon* (1932).

In 1954 Ernest Hemingway became the fifth American to receive the Nobel prize for literature.

Hemingway's World ➤

Hemingway's writing ranged over a wide variety of scenes and subjects. Paris (center left) was the setting of his first success, *The Sun Also Rises;* bullfighting also forms an important part of that novel. Hunting and fishing scenes occur in Hemingway's earliest stories as well as his later works. Hemingway himself appears in the photographs at the upper right and bottom of the page.

JOHN STEINBECK

Flight

"A boy gets to be a man when a man is needed," said Mama Torres. And she was right. The events of one night changed a gangling boy into a man before he set out on his lonely flight into the mountains.

RESPONDING TO THE SETTING. The location Steinbeck chose for this story vitally influences the nature of the people and the course of events. But he uses the background with even greater skill to enhance the emotional effect. His descriptions are brief, but full of clear detail and subtle emotional color. Spur your imagination to register all the impressions of the country, and you will feel that you are actually taking part in Pepé's desperate struggle for survival.

Aʙᴏᴜᴛ fifteen miles below Monterey, on the wild coast, the Torres family had their farm, a few sloping acres above a cliff that dropped to the brown reefs and to the hissing white waters of the ocean. Behind the farm the stone mountains stood up against the sky.

The farm buildings huddled like the clinging aphids [1] on the mountain skirts, crouched low to the ground as though the wind might blow them into the sea. The little shack, the rattling, rotting barn were gray-bitten with sea salt, beaten by the damp wind until they had taken on the color of the granite hills. Two horses, a red cow and a red calf, half a dozen pigs and a flock of lean, multicolored chickens stocked the place. A little corn was raised on the sterile slope, and it grew short and thick under the wind, and all the cobs formed on the landward sides of the stalks.

Mama Torres, a lean, dry woman with ancient eyes, had ruled the farm for ten years, ever since her husband tripped over a stone in the field one day and fell full length on a rattlesnake. When one is bitten on the chest there is not much that can be done.

Mama Torres had three children, two undersized black ones of twelve and fourteen, Emilio [2] and Rosy, whom Mama kept fishing on the rocks below the farm when the sea was kind and when the truant officer was in some dis-

[1] aphids (ā'fĭdz): small insects that live on plants and suck their juices.
[2] Emilio (ä·mēl'yō).

tant part of Monterey County. And there was Pepé,[1] the tall smiling son of nineteen, a gentle, affectionate boy, but very lazy. Pepé had a tall head, pointed at the top, and from its peak coarse black hair grew down like a thatch all around. Over his smiling little eyes Mama cut a straight bang so he could see. Pepé had sharp Indian cheekbones and an eagle nose, but his mouth was as sweet and shapely as a girl's mouth, and his chin was fragile and chiseled. He was loose and gangling, all legs and feet and wrists, and he was very lazy. Mama thought him fine and brave, but she never told him so. She said, "Some lazy cow must have got into thy father's family, else how could I have a son like thee." And she said, "When I carried thee, a sneaking lazy coyote came out of the brush and looked at me one day. That must have made thee so."

Pepé smiled sheepishly and stabbed at the ground with his knife to keep the blade sharp and free from rust. It was his inheritance, that knife, his father's knife. The long heavy blade folded back into the black handle. There was a button on the handle. When Pepé pressed the button, the blade leaped out ready for use. The knife was with Pepé always, for it had been his father's knife.

One sunny morning when the sea below the cliff was glinting and blue and the white surf creamed on the reef, when even the stone mountains looked kindly, Mama Torres called out the door of the shack, "Pepé, I have a labor for thee."

There was no answer. Mama listened. From behind the barn she heard a burst of laughter. She lifted her full long skirt and walked in the direction of the noise.

Pepé was sitting on the ground with his back against a box. His white teeth glistened. On either side of him stood the two black ones, tense and expectant.

1 Pepé (pā·pā′).

Fifteen feet away a redwood post was set in the ground. Pepé's right hand lay limply in his lap, and in the palm the big black knife rested. The blade was closed back into the handle. Pepé looked smiling at the sky.

Suddenly Emilio cried, "Ya!"

Pepé's wrist flicked like the head of a snake. The blade seemed to fly open in mid-air, and with a thump the point dug into the redwood post, and the black handle quivered. The three burst into excited laughter. Rosy ran to the post and pulled out the knife and brought it back to Pepé. He closed the blade and settled the knife carefully in his listless palm again. He grinned self-consciously at the sky.

"Ya!"

The heavy knife lanced out and sunk into the post again. Mama moved forward like a ship and scattered the play.

"All day you do foolish things with the knife, like a toy baby," she stormed. "Get up on thy huge feet that eat up shoes. Get up!" She took him by one loose shoulder and hoisted at him. Pepé grinned sheepishly and came halfheartedly to his feet. "Look!" Mama cried. "Big lazy, you must catch the horse and put on him thy father's saddle. You must ride to Monterey. The medicine bottle is empty. There is no salt. Go thou now, Peanut! Catch the horse."

A revolution took place in the relaxed figure of Pepé. "To Monterey, me? Alone? Sí, Mamá."

She scowled at him. "Do not think, big sheep, that you will buy candy. No, I will give you only enough for the medicine and the salt."

Pepé smiled. "Mama, you will put the hatband on the hat?"

She relented then. "Yes, Pepé. You may wear the hatband."

His voice grew insinuating. "And the green handkerchief, Mama?"

"Yes, if you go quickly and return with no trouble, the silk green handkerchief will go. If you make sure to take off the handkerchief when you eat so no spot may fall on it."

"Sí, Mama. I will be careful. I am a man."

"Thou? A man? Thou art a peanut."

He went into the rickety barn and brought out a rope, and he walked agilely enough up the hill to catch the horse.

When he was ready and mounted before the door, mounted on his father's saddle that was so old that the oaken frame showed through torn leather in many places, then Mama brought out the round black hat with the tooled leather band, and she reached up and knotted the green silk handkerchief about his neck. Pepé's blue denim coat was much darker than his jeans, for it had been washed much less often.

Mama handed up the big medicine bottle and the silver coins. "That for the medicine," she said, "and that for the salt. That for a candle to burn for the papá. That for *dulces* [1] for the little ones. Our friend Mrs. Rodriguez [2] will give you dinner and maybe a bed for the night. When you go to the church, say only ten paternosters [3] and only twenty-five Ave Marias. [4] Oh! I know, big coyote. You would sit there flapping your mouth over Aves all day while you looked at the candles and the holy pictures. That is not good devotion to stare at the pretty things."

The black hat, covering the high pointed head and black thatched hair of Pepé, gave him dignity and age. He sat the rangy horse well. Mama thought how handsome he was, dark and lean and tall. "I would not send thee now alone, thou little one, except for the medicine," she said softly. "It is not good to have no medicine, for who

knows when the toothache will come, or the sadness of the stomach. These things are."

"*Adiós,* Mama," Pepé cried. "I will come back soon. You may send me often alone. I am a man."

"Thou art a foolish chicken."

He straightened his shoulders, flipped the reins against the horse's shoulder, and rode away. He turned once and saw that they still watched him, Emilio and Rosy and Mama. Pepé grinned with pride and gladness and lifted the tough buckskin horse to a trot.

When he had dropped out of sight over a little dip in the road, Mama turned to the black ones, but she spoke to herself. "He is nearly a man now," she said. "It will be a nice thing to have a man in the house again." Her eyes sharpened on the children. "Go to the rocks now. The tide is going out. There will be abalones [5] to be found." She put the iron hooks into their hands and saw them down the steep trail to the reefs. She brought the smooth stone metate [6] to the doorway and sat grinding her corn to flour and looking occasionally at the road over which Pepé had gone. The noonday came and then the afternoon, when the little ones beat the abalones on a rock to make them tender and Mama patted the *tortillas* to make them thin. They ate their dinner as the red sun was plunging down toward the ocean. They sat on the doorsteps and watched a big white moon come over the mountaintops.

Mama said, "He is now at the house of our friend Mrs. Rodriguez. She will give him nice things to eat and maybe a present."

Emilio said, "Someday I, too, will ride to Monterey for medicine. Did Pepé come to be a man today?"

[1] *dulces* (dōōl'säs): sweets.
[2] Rodriguez (rô·drē'gäs).
[3] ten paternosters (pä'tẽr·nŏs'tẽrz): ten repetitions of the Lord's Prayer. The Latin word means "Our Father."
[4] Ave Marias (ä'vå mä·rē'äz): prayers to the Virgin Mary, beginning "Hail, Mary."

[5] abalones (ăb'á·lō'nêz): large rock-clinging shellfish.
[6] metate (må·tä'tä): a stone used in Spanish North America and by the Indians of the southwestern United States for grinding cereal seeds.

Mama said wisely, "A boy gets to be a man when a man is needed. Remember this thing. I have known boys forty years old because there was no need for a man."

Soon afterward they retired, Mama in her big oak bed on one side of the room, Emilio and Rosy in their boxes full of straw and sheepskins on the other side of the room.

The moon went over the sky and the surf roared on the rocks. The roosters crowed the first call. The surf subsided to a whispering surge against the reef. The moon dropped toward the sea. The roosters crowed again.

The moon was near down to the water when Pepé rode on a winded horse to his home flat. His dog bounced out and circled the horse, yelping with pleasure. Pepé slid off the saddle to the ground. The weathered little shack was silver in the moonlight and the square shadow of it was black to the north and east. Against the east the piling mountains were misty with light; their tops melted into the sky.

Pepé walked wearily up the three steps and into the house. It was dark inside. There was a rustle in the corner.

Mama cried out from her bed. "Who comes? Pepé, is it thou?"

"Sí, Mama."

"Did you get the medicine?"

"Sí, Mama."

"Well, go to sleep, then. I thought you would be sleeping at the house of Mrs. Rodriguez." Pepé stood silently in the dark room. "Why do you stand there, Pepé? Did you drink wine?"

"Sí, Mama."

"Well, go to bed then and sleep out the wine."

His voice was tired and patient, but very firm. "Light the candle, Mama. I must go away into the mountains."

"What is this, Pepé? You are crazy." Mama struck a sulfur match and held the little blue burr until the flame spread up the stick. She set light to the candle on the floor beside her bed. "Now, Pepé, what is this you say?" She looked anxiously into his face.

He was changed. The fragile quality seemed to have gone from his chin. His mouth was less full than it had been, the lines of the lips were straighter, but in his eyes the greatest change had taken place. There was no laughter in them any more, nor any bashfulness. They were sharp and bright and purposeful.

He told her in a tired monotone, told her everything just as it had happened. A few people came into the kitchen of Mrs. Rodriguez. There was wine to drink. Pepé drank wine. The little quarrel — the man started toward Pepé and then the knife — it went almost by itself. It flew, it darted before Pepé knew it. As he talked, Mama's face grew stern, and it seemed to grow more lean. Pepé finished. "I am a man now, Mama. The man said names to me I could not allow."

Mama nodded. "Yes, thou art a man, my poor little Pepé. Thou art a man. I have seen it coming on thee. I have watched you throwing the knife into the post, and I have been afraid." For a moment her face had softened, but now it grew stern again. "Come! We must get you ready. Go. Awaken Emilio and Rosy. Go quickly."

Pepé stepped over to the corner where his brother and sister slept among the sheepskins. He leaned down and shook them gently. "Come, Rosy! Come, Emilio! The Mama says you must arise."

The little black ones sat up and rubbed their eyes in the candlelight. Mama was out of bed now, her long black skirt over her nightgown. "Emilio," she cried. "Go up and catch the other horse for Pepé. Quickly, now! Quickly." Emilio put his legs in his overalls and stumbled sleepily out the door.

"You heard no one behind you on the road?" Mama demanded.

"No, Mama. I listened carefully. No one was on the road."

Mama darted like a bird about the room. From a nail on the wall she took a canvas water bag and threw it on the floor. She stripped a blanket from her bed and rolled it into a tight tube and tied the ends with string. From a box beside the stove she lifted a flour sack half full of black stringy jerky. "Your father's black coat, Pepé. Here, put it on."

Pepé stood in the middle of the floor watching her activity. She reached behind the door and brought out the rifle, a long 38–56, worn shiny the whole length of the barrel. Pepé took it from her and held it in the crook of his elbow. Mama brought a little leather bag and counted the cartridges into his hand. "Only ten left," she warned. "You must not waste them."

Emilio put his head in the door. "'*Qui 'st 'l caballo,*[1] Mama."

"Put on the saddle from the other horse. Tie on the blanket. Here, tie the jerky to the saddle horn."

Still Pepé stood silently watching his mother's frantic activity. His chin looked hard, and his sweet mouth was drawn and thin. His little eyes followed Mama about the room almost suspiciously.

Rosy asked softly, "Where goes Pepé?"

Mama's eyes were fierce. "Pepé goes on a journey. Pepé is a man now. He has a man's thing to do."

Pepé straightened his shoulders. His mouth changed until he looked very much like Mama.

At last the preparation was finished. The loaded horse stood outside the door. The water bag dripped a line of moisture down the bay shoulder.

The moonlight was being thinned by the dawn, and the big white moon was near down to the sea. The family stood by the shack. Mama confronted Pepé. "Look, my son! Do not stop until it is dark again. Do not sleep even though you are tired. Take care of the horse in order that he may not stop of weariness. Remember to be careful with the bullets — there are only ten. Do not fill thy stomach with jerky or it will make thee sick. Eat a little jerky and fill thy stomach with grass. When thou comest to the high mountains, if thou seest any of the dark watching men, go not near to them nor try to speak to them. And forget not thy prayers." She put her lean hands on Pepé's shoulders, stood on her toes and kissed him formally on both cheeks, and Pepé kissed her on both cheeks. Then he went to Emilio and Rosy and kissed both of their cheeks.

Pepé turned back to Mama. He seemed to look for a little softness, a little weakness in her. His eyes were searching, but Mama's face remained fierce. "Go now," she said. "Do not wait to be caught like a chicken."

Pepé pulled himself into the saddle. "I am a man," he said.

It was the first dawn when he rode up the hill toward the little canyon which let a trail into the mountains. Moonlight and daylight fought with each other, and the two warring qualities made it difficult to see. Before Pepé had gone a hundred yards, the outlines of his figure were misty; and long before he entered the canyon, he had become a gray, indefinite shadow.

Mama stood stiffly in front of her doorstep, and on either side of her stood Emilio and Rosy. They cast furtive glances at Mama now and then.

When the gray shape of Pepé melted into the hillside and disappeared, Mama relaxed. She began the high, whining keen[2] of the death wail. "Our beautiful — our brave," she cried. "Our protector, our son is gone." Emilio and Rosy moaned beside her. "Our beauti-

---

[1] '*Qui 'st 'l caballo* (kĕst'l kä·bä′yō): Here is the horse. (Colloquial Spanish.)

[2] **keen:** a lamentation or dirge for the dead.

ful — our brave, he is gone." It was the formal wail. It rose to a high piercing whine and subsided to a moan. Mama raised it three times and then she turned and went into the house and shut the door.

Emilio and Rosy stood wondering in the dawn. They heard Mama whimpering in the house. They went out to sit on the cliff above the ocean. They touched shoulders. "When did Pepé come to be a man?" Emilio asked.

"Last night," said Rosy. "Last night in Monterey." The ocean clouds turned red with the sun that was behind the mountains.

"We will have no breakfast," said Emilio. "Mama will not want to cook." Rosy did not answer him. "Where is Pepé gone?" he asked.

Rosy looked around at him. She drew her knowledge from the quiet air. "He has gone on a journey. He will never come back."

"Is he dead? Do you think he is dead?"

Rosy looked back at the ocean again. A little steamer, drawing a line of smoke, sat on the edge of the horizon. "He is not dead," Rosy explained. "Not yet."

Pepé rested the big rifle across the saddle in front of him. He let the horse walk up the hill and he didn't look back. The stony slope took on a coat of short brush so that Pepé found the entrance to a trail and entered it.

When he came to the canyon opening, he swung once in his saddle and looked back, but the houses were swallowed in the misty light. Pepé jerked forward again. The high shoulder of the canyon closed in on him. His horse stretched out its neck and sighed and settled to the trail.

It was a well-worn path, dark soft leaf-mold earth strewn with broken pieces of sandstone. The trail rounded the shoulder of the canyon and dropped steeply into the bed of the stream. In the shallows the water ran smoothly, glinting in the first morning sun. Small round stones on the bottom were as brown as rust with sun moss. In the sand along the edges of the stream the tall, rich wild mint grew, while in the water itself the cress,[1] old and tough, had gone to heavy seed.

The path went into the stream and emerged on the other side. The horse sloshed into the water and stopped. Pepé dropped his bridle and let the beast drink of the running water.

Soon the canyon sides became steep and the first giant sentinel redwoods guarded the trail, great round red trunks bearing foliage as green and lacy as ferns. Once Pepé was among the trees, the sun was lost. A perfumed and purple light lay in the pale green of the underbrush. Gooseberry bushes and blackberries and tall ferns lined the stream, and overhead the branches of the redwoods met and cut off the sky.

Pepé drank from the water bag, and he reached into the flour sack and brought out a black string of jerky. His white teeth gnawed at the string until the tough meat parted. He chewed slowly and drank occasionally from the water bag. His little eyes were slumberous and tired, but the muscles of his face were hard-set. The earth of the trail was black now. It gave up a hollow sound under the walking hoofbeats.

The stream fell more sharply. Little waterfalls splashed on the stones. Five-fingered ferns hung over the water and dripped spray from their finger tips. Pepé rode half over his saddle, dangling one leg loosely. He picked a bay leaf from a tree beside the way and put it into his mouth for a moment to flavor the dry jerky. He held the gun loosely across the pommel.

Suddenly he squared in his saddle, swung the horse from the trail and

---

[1] cress (or water cress): an edible white-flowered plant that grows in clear running water.

kicked it hurriedly up behind a big redwood tree. He pulled up the reins tight against the bit to keep the horse from whinnying. His face was intent and his nostrils quivered a little.

A hollow pounding came down the trail, and a horseman rode by, a fat man with red cheeks and a white stubble beard. His horse put down his head and blubbered at the trail when it came to the place where Pepé had turned off. "Hold up!" said the man, and he pulled up his horse's head.

When the last sound of the hoofs died away, Pepé came back into the trail again. He did not relax in the saddle any more. He lifted the big rifle and swung the lever to throw a shell into the chamber, and then he let down the hammer to half cock.

The trail grew very steep. Now the redwood trees were smaller and their tops were dead, bitten dead where the wind reached them. The horse plodded on; the sun went slowly overhead and started down toward the afternoon.

Where the stream came out of a side canyon, the trail left it. Pepé dismounted and watered his horse and filled up his water bag. As soon as the trail had parted from the stream, the trees were gone and only the thick brittle sage and manzanita [1] and chaparral [2] edged the trail. And the soft black earth was gone, too, leaving only the light tan broken rock for the trail bed. Lizards scampered away into the brush as the horse rattled over the little stones.

Pepé turned in his saddle and looked back. He was in the open now: he could be seen from a distance. As he ascended the trail the country grew more rough and terrible and dry. The way wound about the bases of great square rocks. Little gray rabbits skittered in the brush. A bird made a monotonous high creaking. Eastward the bare rock mountaintops were pale and powder-dry under the dropping sun. The horse plodded up and up the trail toward a little V in the ridge which was the pass.

Pepé looked suspiciously back every minute or so, and his eyes sought the tops of the ridges ahead. Once, on a white barren spur, he saw a black figure for a moment; but he looked quickly away, for it was one of the dark watchers. No one knew who the watchers were, nor where they lived, but it was better to ignore them and never to show interest in them. They did not bother one who stayed on the trail and minded his own business.

The air was parched and full of light dust blown by the breeze from the eroding mountains. Pepé drank sparingly from his bag and corked it tightly and hung it on the horn again. The trail moved up the dry shale hillside, avoiding rocks, dropping under clefts, climbing in and out of old water scars. When he arrived at the little pass he stopped and looked back for a long time. No dark watchers were to be seen now. The trail behind was empty. Only the high tops of the redwoods indicated where the stream flowed.

Pepé rode on through the pass. His little eyes were nearly closed with weariness, but his face was stern, relentless, and manly. The high mountain wind coasted sighing through the pass and whistled on the edges of the big blocks of broken granite. In the air, a red-tailed hawk sailed over close to the ridge and screamed angrily. Pepé went slowly through the broken jagged pass and looked down on the other side.

The trail dropped quickly, staggering among broken rock. At the bottom of the slope there was a dark crease, thick with brush, and on the other side of the crease a little flat, in which a grove of oak trees grew. A scar of green grass cut across the flat. And behind the flat another mountain rose, desolate with dead rocks and starving little black bushes.

---

[1] **manzanita** (măn′zȧ·nē′tȧ): shrubs.
[2] **chaparral** (chăp′ȧ·răl′): a thicket of shrubs or dwarf trees.

Pepé drank from the bag again, for the air was so dry that it encrusted his nostrils and burned his lips. He put the horse down the trail. The hoofs slipped and struggled on the steep way, starting little stones that rolled off into the brush. The sun was gone behind the westward mountain now, but still it glowed brilliantly on the oaks and on the grassy flat. The rocks and the hillsides still sent up waves of the heat they had gathered from the day's sun.

Pepé looked up to the top of the next dry withered ridge. He saw a dark form against the sky, a man's figure standing on top of a rock, and he glanced away quickly not to appear curious. When a moment later he looked up again, the figure was gone.

Downward the trail was quickly covered. Sometimes the horse floundered for footing, sometimes set his feet and slid a little way. They came at last to the bottom where the dark chaparral was higher than Pepé's head. He held up his rifle on one side and his arm on the other to shield his face from the sharp brittle fingers of the brush.

Up and out of the crease he rode, and up a little cliff. The grassy flat was before him, and the round comfortable oaks. For a moment he studied the trail down which he had come, but there was no movement and no sound from it. Finally he rode out over the flat, to the green streak, and at the upper end of the damp he found a little spring welling out of the earth and dropping into a dug basin before it seeped out over the flat.

Pepé filled his bag first, and then he let the thirsty horse drink out of the pool. He led the horse to the clump of oaks, and in the middle of the grove, fairly protected from sight on all sides, he took off the saddle and the bridle and laid them on the ground. The horse stretched his jaws sideways and yawned. Pepé knotted the lead rope about the horse's neck and tied him to a sapling among the oaks where he

could graze in a fairly large circle.

When the horse was gnawing hungrily at the dry grass, Pepé went to the saddle and took a black string of jerky from the sack and strolled to an oak tree on the edge of the grove, from under which he could watch the trail. He sat down in the crisp dry oak leaves and automatically felt for his big black knife to cut the jerky, but he had no knife. He leaned back on his elbow and gnawed at the tough strong meat. His face was blank, but it was a man's face.

The bright evening light washed the eastern ridge, but the valley was darkening. Doves flew down from the hills to the spring, and the quail came running out of the brush and joined them, calling clearly to one another.

Out of the corner of his eye Pepé saw a shadow grow out of the bushy crease. He turned his head slowly. A big spotted wildcat was creeping toward the spring, belly to the ground, moving like thought.

Pepé cocked his rifle and edged the muzzle slowly around. Then he looked apprehensively up the trail and dropped the hammer again. From the ground beside him he picked an oak twig and threw it toward the spring. The quail flew up with a roar and the doves whistled away. The big cat stood up; for a long moment he looked at Pepé with cold yellow eyes, and then fearlessly walked back into the gulch.

The dusk gathered quickly in the deep valley. Pepé muttered his prayers, put his head down on his arm and went instantly to sleep.

The moon came up and filled the valley with cold blue light, and the wind swept rustling down from the peaks. The owls worked up and down the slopes looking for rabbits. Down in the brush of the gulch a coyote gabbled. The oak trees whispered softly in the night breeze.

Pepé started up, listening. His horse had whinnied. The moon was just slipping behind the western ridge, leaving the valley in darkness behind it. Pepé sat tensely gripping his rifle. From far up the trail he heard an answering whinny and the crash of shod hoofs on the broken rock. He jumped to his feet, ran to his horse and led it under the trees. He threw on the saddle and cinched it tight for the steep trail, caught the unwilling head and forced the bit into the mouth. He felt the saddle to make sure the water bag and the sack of jerky were there. Then he mounted and turned up the hill.

It was velvet-dark. The horse found the entrance to the trail where it left the flat, and started up, stumbling and slipping on the rocks. Pepé's hand rose up to his head. His hat was gone. He had left it under the oak tree.

The horse had struggled far up the trail when the first change of dawn came into the air, a steel grayness as light mixed thoroughly with dark. Gradually the sharp snaggled edge of the ridge stood out above them, rotten granite tortured and eaten by the winds of time. Pepé had dropped his reins on the horn, leaving direction to the horse. The brush grabbed at his legs in the dark until one knee of his jeans was ripped.

Gradually the light flowed down over the ridge. The starved brush and rocks stood out in the half-light, strange and lonely in high perspective. Then there came warmth into the light. Pepé drew up and looked back, but he could see nothing in the darker valley below. The sky turned blue over the coming sun. In the waste of the mountainside, the poor dry brush grew only three feet high. Here and there, big outcroppings of un-rotted granite stood up like moldering houses. Pepé relaxed a little. He drank from his water bag and bit off a piece of jerky. A single eagle flew over, high in the light.

Without warning Pepé's horse screamed and fell on its side. He was almost down before the rifle crash echoed up from the valley. From a hole behind the struggling shoulder, a stream of bright crimson blood pumped and stopped and pumped and stopped. The hoofs threshed on the ground. Pepé lay half stunned beside the horse. He looked slowly down the hill. A piece of sage clipped off beside his head and another crash echoed up from side to side of the canyon. Pepé flung himself frantically behind a bush.

He crawled up the hill on his knees and one hand. His right hand held the rifle up off the ground and pushed it ahead of him. He moved with the instinctive care of an animal. Rapidly he wormed his way toward one of the big outcroppings of granite on the hill above him. Where the brush was high he doubled up and ran; but where the cover was slight he wriggled forward on his stomach, pushing the rifle ahead of him. In the last little distance there was no cover at all. Pepé poised and then he darted across the space and flashed around the corner of the rock.

He leaned panting against the stone. When his breath came easier he moved along behind the big rock until he came to a narrow split that offered a thin section of vision down the hill. Pepé lay on his stomach and pushed the rifle barrel through the slit and waited.

The sun reddened the western ridges now. Already the buzzards were settling down toward the place where the horse lay. A small brown bird scratched in the dead sage leaves directly in front of the rifle muzzle. The coasting eagle flew back toward the rising sun.

Pepé saw a little movement in the brush far below. His grip tightened on the gun. A little brown doe stepped daintily out on the trail and crossed it and disappeared into the brush again. For a long time Pepé waited. Far below he could see the little flat and the oak trees and the slash of green. Suddenly his eyes flashed back at the trail again. A quarter of a mile down there had been a quick movement in the chaparral. The rifle swung over. The front sight nestled in the V of the rear sight. Pepé studied for a moment and then raised the rear sight a notch. The little movement in the brush came again. The sight settled on it. Pepé squeezed the trigger. The explosion crashed down the mountain and up the other side, and came rattling back. The whole side of the slope grew still. No more movement. And then a white streak cut into the granite of the slit and a bullet whined away and a crash sounded up from below. Pepé felt a sharp pain in his right hand. A sliver of granite was sticking out from between his first and second knuckles and the point protruded from his palm. Carefully he pulled out the sliver of stone. The wound bled evenly and gently. No vein or artery was cut.

Pepé looked into a little dusty cave in the rock and gathered a handful of spider web, and he pressed the mass into the cut, plastering the soft web into the blood. The flow stopped almost at once.

The rifle was on the ground. Pepé picked it up, levered a new shell into the chamber. And then he slid into the brush on his stomach. Far to the right he crawled, and then up the hill, moving slowly and carefully, crawling to cover and resting and then crawling again.

In the mountains the sun is high in

its arc before it penetrates the gorges. The hot face looked over the hill and brought instant heat with it. The white light beat on the rocks and reflected from them and rose up quivering from the earth again, and the rocks and bushes seemed to quiver behind the air.

Pepé crawled in the general direction of the ridge peak, zigzagging for cover. The deep cut between his knuckles began to throb. He crawled close to a rattlesnake before he saw it, and when it raised its dry head and made a soft beginning whir, he backed up and took another way. The quick gray lizards flashed in front of him, raising a tiny line of dust. He found another mass of spider web and pressed it against his throbbing hand.

Pepé was pushing the rifle with his left hand now. Little drops of sweat ran to the ends of his coarse black hair and rolled down his cheeks. His lips and tongue were growing thick and heavy. His lips writhed to draw saliva into his mouth. His little dark eyes were uneasy and suspicious. Once when a gray lizard paused in front of him on the parched ground and turned its head sideways, he crushed it flat with a stone.

When the sun slid past noon he had not gone a mile. He crawled exhaustedly a last hundred yards to a patch of high sharp manzanita, crawled desperately, and when the patch was reached he wriggled in among the tough gnarly trunks and dropped his head on his left arm. There was little shade in the meager brush, but there was cover and safety. Pepé went to sleep as he lay and the sun beat on his back. A few little birds hopped close to him and peered and hopped away. Pepé squirmed in his sleep and he raised and dropped his wounded hand again and again.

The sun went down behind the peaks and the cool evening came, and then the dark. A coyote yelled from the hillside. Pepé started awake and looked about with misty eyes. His hand was swollen and heavy; a little thread of pain ran up the inside of his arm and settled in a pocket in his armpit. He peered about and then stood up, for the mountains were black and the moon had not yet risen. Pepé stood up in the dark. The coat of his father pressed on his arm. His tongue was swollen until it nearly filled his mouth. He wriggled out of the coat and dropped it in the brush, and then he struggled up the hill, falling over rocks and tearing his way through the brush. The rifle knocked against stones as he went. Little dry avalanches of gravel and shattered stone went whispering down the hill behind him.

After a while the old moon came up and showed the jagged ridgetop ahead of him. By moonlight Pepé traveled more easily. He bent forward so that his throbbing arm hung away from his body. The journey uphill was made in dashes and rests, a frantic rush up a few yards and then a rest. The wind coasted down the slope, rattling the dry stems of the bushes.

The moon was at meridian when Pepé came at last to the sharp backbone of the ridgetop. On the last hundred yards of the rise no soil had clung under the wearing winds. The way was on solid rock. He clambered to the top and looked down on the other side. There was a draw like the last below him, misty with moonlight, brushed with dry struggling sage and chaparral. On the other side the hill rose up sharply and at the top the jagged rotten teeth of the mountain showed against the sky. At the bottom of the cut the brush was thick and dark.

Pepé stumbled down the hill. His throat was almost closed with thirst. At first he tried to run, but immediately he fell and rolled. After that he went more carefully. The moon was just disappearing behind the mountains when he came to the bottom. He crawled into the heavy brush, feeling with his fingers for water. There was no water in the bed of the stream, only damp earth.

Pepé laid his gun down and scooped up a handful of mud and put it in his mouth, and then he spluttered and scraped the earth from his tongue with his finger, for the mud drew at his mouth like a poultice. He dug a hole in the stream bed with his fingers, dug a little basin to catch water; but before it was very deep his head fell forward on the damp ground and he slept.

The dawn came and the heat of the day fell on the earth, and still Pepé slept. Late in the afternoon his head jerked up. He looked slowly around. His eyes were slits of weariness. Twenty feet away in the heavy brush a big tawny mountain lion stood looking at him. Its long thick tail waved gracefully; its ears were erect with interest, not laid back dangerously. The lion squatted down on its stomach and watched him.

Pepé looked at the hole he had dug in the earth. A half inch of muddy water had collected in the bottom. He tore the sleeve from his hurt arm, with his teeth ripped out a little square, soaked it in the water and put it in his mouth. Over and over he filled the cloth and sucked it.

Still the lion sat and watched him. The evening came down but there was no movement on the hills. No birds visited the dry bottom of the cut. Pepé looked occasionally at the lion. The eyes of the yellow beast drooped as though he were about to sleep. He yawned and his long thin red tongue curled out. Suddenly his head jerked around and his nostrils quivered. His big tail lashed. He stood up and slunk like a tawny shadow into the thick brush.

A moment later Pepé heard the sound, the faint far crash of horses' hoofs on gravel. And he heard something else, a high whining yelp of a dog.

Pepé took his rifle in his left hand and he glided into the brush almost as quietly as the lion had. In the darkening evening he crouched up the hill toward the next ridge. Only when the dark came did he stand up. His energy was short. Once it was dark he fell over the rocks and slipped to his knees on the steep slope, but he moved on and on up the hill, climbing and scrambling over the broken hillside.

When he was far up toward the top, he lay down and slept for a little while. The withered moon, shining on his face, awakened him. He stood up and moved up the hill. Fifty yards away he stopped and turned back, for he had forgotten his rifle. He walked heavily down and poked about in the brush, but he could not find his gun. At last he lay down to rest. The pocket of pain in his armpit had grown more sharp. His arm seemed to swell out and fall with every heartbeat. There was no position lying down where the heavy arm did not press against his armpit.

With the effort of a hurt beast, Pepé got up and moved again toward the top of the ridge. He held his swollen arm away from his body with his left hand. Up the steep hill he dragged himself, a few steps and a rest, and a few more steps. At last he was nearing the top. The moon showed the uneven sharp back of it against the sky.

Pepé's brain spun in a big spiral up and away from him. He slumped to the ground and lay still. The rock ridgetop was only a hundred feet above him.

The moon moved over the sky. Pepé half turned on his back. His tongue tried to make words, but only a thick hissing came from between his lips.

When the dawn came, Pepé pulled himself up. His eyes were sane again. He drew his great puffed arm in front of him and looked at the angry wound. The black line ran up from his wrist to his armpit. Automatically he reached in his pocket for the big black knife, but it was not there. His eyes searched the ground. He picked up a sharp blade of stone and scraped at the wound, sawed at the proud flesh and then squeezed the green juice out in big drops. Instantly he threw back his head and whined like a dog. His whole right side shuddered at the pain, but the pain cleared his head.

In the gray light he struggled up the last slope to the ridge and crawled over and lay down behind a line of rocks. Below him lay a deep canyon exactly like the last, waterless and desolate. There was no flat, no oak trees, not even heavy brush in the bottom of it. And on the other side a sharp ridge stood up, thinly brushed with starving sage, littered with broken granite. Strewn over the hill there were giant outcroppings, and on the top the granite teeth stood out against the sky.

The new day was light now. The flame of the sun came over the ridge and fell on Pepé where he lay on the ground. His coarse black hair was littered with twigs and bits of spider web. His eyes had retreated back into his head. Between his lips the tip of his black tongue showed.

He sat up and dragged his great arm into his lap and nursed it, rocking his body and moaning in his throat. He threw back his head and looked up into the pale sky. A big black bird circled nearly out of sight, and far to the left another was sailing near.

He lifted his head to listen, for a familiar sound had come to him from the valley he had climbed out of; it was the crying yelp of hounds, excited and feverish, on a trail.

Pepé bowed his head quickly. He tried to speak rapid words but only a thick hiss came from his lips. He drew a shaky cross on his breast with his left hand. It was a long struggle to get to his feet. He crawled slowly and mechanically to the top of a big rock on the ridge peak. Once there, he arose slowly, swaying to his feet, and stood erect. Far below he could see the dark brush where he had slept. He braced his feet and stood there, black against the morning sky.

There came a ripping sound at his feet. A piece of stone flew up and a bullet droned off into the next gorge. The hollow crash echoed up from below. Pepé looked down for a moment and then pulled himself straight again.

His body jarred back. His left hand fluttered helplessly toward his breast. The second crash sounded from below. Pepé swung forward and toppled from the rock. His body struck and rolled over and over, starting a little avalanche. And when at last he stopped against a bush, the avalanche slid slowly down and covered up his head.

FOR DISCUSSION

1. Tell three impressions you get of the Torres family life from the first few paragraphs, with details to support each impression. What admirable qualities do you find in Mama?

2. Why was getting Pepé off to Monterey a good bridge between the opening scenes and the flight?

3. How did Pepé's behavior on his return from Monterey and on his flight support Mama's idea of what changes a boy into a man?

4. Do you think Mama and Pepé chose the right way of meeting the situation? Why, or why not? Compare the careful preparations for Pepé's flight with the happenings at home after his departure. How did these two scenes affect the suspense in the rest of the story?

5. Is the story more or less interesting because you never see the pursuers or know anything about them? What was the first indication of real danger? Trace the happenings that make Pepé's situation increasingly hopeless. Explain why the ending does or does not satisfy you.

RESPONDING TO THE SETTING

1. What details in the opening sentences showed the isolation in which the Torres family lived? How did this isolation influence the events of the story?

2. Find places in which the moon is used to show the passing of time. Is this more effective than a mere statement of the time? Why? Why not?

3. Try to recall without looking at the story again the changing nature of the country through which Pepé rode. How did these changes harmonize with his chances of escape?

4. Why were the stretches beyond the timber an effective background for the events of Pepé's last two days? What harmony can you find between the scene of his death and the manner of his death?

5. What differences would result if this basic plot had a large city as background, with the Torres home in a slum?

THE AUTHOR

JOHN STEINBECK (b. 1902) can fill his California stories with authentic local color, for he was born at Salinas, has lived on the Monterey peninsula and in the California valley country, and attended college at Stanford. During the depression of the 30's, working as a fruit-packer, hod carrier, painter, and reporter, he gained both a wide knowledge of people and a deep sympathy for those who lived close to poverty.

His affectionate portrayal of the varied down-and-outers of *Tortilla Flat* (1935) first gained him recognition; and *The Grapes of Wrath* (1939), his novel of dust-bowl victims struggling for survival as migratory workers, won the Pulitzer prize and firmly established his reputation, even though the book stirred much controversy.

Steinbeck's skill as a writer of dialogue helped him to turn several of his books into successful plays, notably *Of Mice and Men, The Moon Is Down,* and *Pipe Dream.*

Steinbeck's other novels include *East of Eden* (1952) and his latest work, *The Winter of Our Discontent* (1961).

As the Artist Sees It ➔

On the facing page are three major scenes from John Steinbeck's "Flight," drawn in pen and ink by Harvey Dinnerstein. The sketches concentrate on the important steps in the plot of the story. Do you feel that the artist has also succeeded in capturing the somber tone of Steinbeck's "Flight"?

JAMES THURBER

The Secret Life
of Walter Mitty

Do you occasionally escape the daily grind by slipping into a secret life of adventure and acclaim? Doesn't everyone? Typically, James Thurber tells an amusing tale of Walter Mitty's escape; and, also typically, Thurber's keen observation of human nature provokes thought long after the laughter dies away.

OBSERVING STRUCTURE. A skillful arrangement of the sequence of episodes contributes to the strong impact of this story. Be alert for the sudden shifts that make its structure effective and unusual.

W<small>E'RE</small> going through!" The Commander's voice was like thin ice breaking. He wore his full-dress uniform, with the heavily braided white cap pulled down rakishly over one cold gray eye. "We can't make it, sir. It's spoiling for a hurricane, if you ask me." "I'm not asking you, Lieutenant Berg," said the Commander. "Throw on the power lights! Rev her up to 8,500! We're going through!" The pounding of

the cylinders increased: ta-pocketa-pocketa-pocketa-*pocketa-pocketa*. The Commander stared at the ice forming on the pilot window. He walked over and twisted a row of complicated dials. "Switch on No. 8 auxiliary!" he shouted. "Switch on No. 8 auxiliary!" repeated Lieutenant Berg. "Full strength in No. 3 turret!" shouted the Commander. "Full strength in No. 3 turret!" The crew, bending to their various tasks in the huge, hurtling eight-engined navy hydroplane, looked at each other and grinned. "The Old Man'll get us through," they said to one another. "The Old Man ain't afraid of Hell! . . ."

"Not so fast! You're driving too fast!" said Mrs. Mitty. "What are you driving so fast for?"

"Hmm?" said Walter Mitty. He looked at his wife, in the seat beside him, with shocked astonishment. She seemed grossly unfamiliar, like a strange woman who had yelled at him in a crowd. "You were up to fifty-five," she said. "You know I don't like to go more than forty. You were up to fifty-five." Walter Mitty drove on toward Waterbury in silence, the roaring of the SN-202 through the worst storm in twenty years of navy flying fading in the remote, intimate airways of his mind. "You're tensed up again," said Mrs. Mitty. "It's one of your days. I wish you'd let Dr. Renshaw look you over."

Walter Mitty stopped the car in front of the building where his wife went to have her hair done. "Remember to get those overshoes while I'm having my hair done," she said. "I don't need overshoes," said Mitty. She put her mirror back into her bag. "We've been all through that," she said, getting out of the car. "You're not a young man any longer." He raced the engine a little. "Why don't you wear your gloves? Have you lost your gloves?" Walter Mitty reached in a pocket and brought out the gloves. He put them on, but after she had turned and gone into the building and he had driven on to a red light, he took them off again. "Pick it up, brother!" snapped a cop as the light changed, and Mitty hastily pulled on his gloves and lurched ahead. He drove around the streets aimlessly for a time, and then he drove past the hospital on his way to the parking lot.

. . . "It's the millionaire banker, Wellington McMillan," said the pretty nurse. "Yes?" said Walter Mitty, removing his gloves slowly. "Who has the case?" "Dr. Renshaw and Dr. Benbow, but there are two specialists here, Dr. Remington from New York and Dr. Pritchard-Mitford from London. He flew over." A door opened down a long, cool corridor and Dr. Renshaw came out. He looked distraught and haggard. "Hello, Mitty," he said. "We're having the devil's own time with McMillan, the millionaire banker and close personal friend of Roosevelt. Obstreosis [1] of the ductal tract. Tertiary. Wish you'd take a look at him." "Glad to," said Mitty.

In the operating room there were whispered introductions: "Dr. Remington, Dr. Mitty. Dr. Pritchard-Mitford, Dr. Mitty." "I've read your book on streptothricosis," said Pritchard-Mitford, shaking hands. "A brilliant performance, sir." "Thank you," said Walter Mitty. "Didn't know you were in the States, Mitty," grumbled Remington. "Coals to Newcastle, bringing Mitford and me up here for a tertiary." "You are very kind," said Mitty. A huge, complicated machine, connected to the operating table, with many tubes and wires, began at this moment to go pocketa-pocketa-pocketa. "The new anesthetizer is giving away!" shouted an intern. "There is no one in the East who knows how to fix it!" "Quiet, man!" said Mitty, in a low, cool voice. He sprang to the machine, which was now going pocketa-pocketa-queep-pocketa-queep. He began fingering delicately a row of glistening dials. "Give me a fountain pen!" he snapped. Someone handed him a fountain pen. He pulled a faulty piston out of the machine and inserted the pen in its place. "That will hold for ten minutes," he said. "Get on with the operation." A nurse hurried over and whispered to Renshaw, and Mitty saw the man turn pale. "Coreopsis [2] has set in," said Renshaw nervously. "If you would take over, Mitty?" Mitty looked at him and at the craven figure of Benbow, who drank, and at the grave, uncertain faces of the two great specialists. "If you wish," he said. They slipped a white gown on him; he adjusted a mask and drew on thin gloves; nurses handed him shining . . .

"Back it up, Mac! Look out for that Buick!" Walter Mitty jammed on the brakes. "Wrong lane, Mac," said the parking-lot attendant, looking at Mitty closely. "Gee. Yeh," muttered Mitty. He began cautiously to back out of the lane marked "Exit Only." "Leave her sit there," said the attendant. "I'll put her away." Mitty got out of the car. "Hey, better leave the key." "Oh," said

[1] **Obstreosis** (probably ŏb′strē·ō′sĭs): Mitty makes up a technical-sounding word.

[2] **Coreopsis** (kō′rē·ŏp′sis): a real word, but it is the name of a flower of the aster family.

Mitty, handing the man the ignition key. The attendant vaulted into the car, backed it up with insolent skill, and put it where it belonged.

They're so darn cocky, thought Walter Mitty, walking along Main Street; they think they know everything. Once he had tried to take his chains off, outside New Milford, and he had got them wound around the axles. A man had had to come out in a wrecking car and unwind them, a young, grinning garageman. Since then Mrs. Mitty always made him drive to a garage to have the chains taken off. The next time, he thought, I'll wear my right arm in a sling; they won't grin at me then. I'll have my right arm in a sling and they'll see I couldn't possibly take the chains off myself. He kicked at the slush on the sidewalk. "Overshoes," he said to himself, and he began looking for a shoe store.

When he came out into the street again, with the overshoes in a box under his arm, Walter Mitty began to wonder what the other thing was his wife had told him to get. She had told him twice before they set out from their house for Waterbury. In a way he hated these weekly trips to town — he was always getting something wrong. Kleenex, he thought, Squibb's, razor blades? No. Toothpaste, toothbrush, bicarbonate, carborundum, initiative and referendum? He gave it up. But she would remember it. "Where's the what's-its-name?" she would ask. "Don't tell me you forgot the what's-its-name." A newsboy went by shouting something about the Waterbury trial.

. . . "Perhaps this will refresh your memory." The District Attorney suddenly thrust a heavy automatic at the quiet figure on the witness stand. "Have you ever seen this before?" Walter Mitty took the gun and examined it expertly. "This is my Webley-Vickers 50.80," he said calmly. An excited buzz ran around the courtroom. The Judge rapped for order. "You are a crack shot with any sort of firearms, I believe?" said the District Attorney, insinuatingly. "Objection!" shouted Mitty's attorney. "We have shown that the defendant could not have fired the shot. We have shown that he wore his right arm in a sling on the night of the fourteenth of July." Walter Mitty raised his hand briefly, and the bickering attorneys were stilled. "With any known make of gun," he said evenly, "I could have killed Gregory Fitzhurst at three hundred feet *with my left hand.*" Pandemonium broke loose in the courtroom. A woman's scream rose above the bedlam, and suddenly a lovely, dark-haired girl was in Walter Mitty's arms. The District Attorney struck at her savagely. Without rising from his chair, Mitty let the man have it on the point of the chin. "You miserable cur!". . .

"Puppy biscuit," said Walter Mitty. He stopped walking, and the buildings of Waterbury rose up out of the misty courtroom and surrounded him again. A woman who was passing laughed. "He said 'Puppy biscuit,'" she said to her companion. "That man said 'Puppy biscuit' to himself." Walter Mitty hurried on. He went into an A & P, not the first one he came to but a smaller one farther up the street. "I want some biscuit for small, young dogs," he said to the clerk. "Any special brand, sir?" The greatest pistol shot in the world thought a moment. "It says 'Puppies Bark for It' on the box," said Walter Mitty.

His wife would be through at the hairdresser's in fifteen minutes, Mitty saw in looking at his watch, unless they had trouble drying it; sometimes they had trouble drying it. She didn't like to get to the hotel first; she would want him to be there waiting for her as usual. He found a big leather chair in the lobby, facing the window, and he put the overshoes and the puppy biscuit on the floor beside it. He picked up an old copy of *Liberty* and sank down into the chair. "Can Germany Conquer the World Through the Air?" Walter Mitty looked at the pictures of bombing planes and of ruined streets.

. . . "The cannonading has got the wind up in young Raleigh, sir," said the sergeant. Captain Mitty looked at him through tousled hair. "Get him to bed," he said wearily, "with the others. I'll fly alone." "But you can't, sir," said the sergeant anxiously. "It takes two men to handle that bomber and the Archies are pounding hell out of the air. Von Richtman's circus is between here and Saulier." "Somebody's got to get that ammunition dump," said Mitty. "I'm going over. Spot of brandy?" He poured a drink for the sergeant and one for himself. War thundered and whined around the dugout and battered at the door. There was a rending of wood, and splinters flew through the room. "A bit of a near thing," said Captain Mitty carelessly. "The box barrage is closing in," said the sergeant. "We only live once, Sergeant," said Mitty, with his faint, fleeting smile. "Or do we?" He poured another brandy and tossed it off. "I never see a man could hold his brandy like you, sir," said the sergeant. "Begging your pardon, sir." Captain Mitty stood up and strapped on his huge Webley-Vickers automatic. "It's forty kilometers through hell, sir," said the sergeant. Mitty finished one last brandy. "After all," he said softly, "what isn't?" The pounding of the cannon increased; there was the rat-tat-tatting of machine guns, and from somewhere came the menacing pocketa-pocketa-pocketa of the new flame throwers. Walter Mitty walked to the door of the dugout humming "Auprès de ma blonde." He turned and waved to the sergeant. "Cheerio!" he said. . . .

Something struck his shoulder. "I've been looking all over this hotel for you," said Mrs. Mitty. "Why do you have to hide in this old chair? How did you expect me to find you?" "Things close in," said Walter Mitty vaguely. "What?" Mrs. Mitty said. "Did you get the what's-its-name? The puppy bis-cuit? What's in that box?" "Overshoes," said Mitty. "Couldn't you have put them on in the store?" "I was thinking," said Walter Mitty. "Does it ever occur to you that I am sometimes thinking?" She looked at him. "I'm going to take your temperature when I get you home," she said.

They went out through the revolving doors that made a faintly derisive whistling sound when you pushed them. It was two blocks to the parking lot. At the drugstore on the corner she said, "Wait here for me. I forgot something. I won't be a minute." She was more than a minute. Walter Mitty lighted a cigarette. It began to rain, rain with sleet in it. He stood up against the wall of the drugstore, smoking. . . . He put his shoulders back and his heels together. "To hell with the handkerchief," said Walter Mitty scornfully. He took one last drag on his cigarette and snapped it away. Then, with that faint, fleeting smile playing about his lips, he faced the firing squad; erect and motionless, proud and disdainful, Walter Mitty the Undefeated, inscrutable to the last.

FOR DISCUSSION

1. Why is this story amusing? Why is it also serious? Can you compare the situation with any in real life that make you laugh, but also have their serious side?

2. What is the common factor in all Mitty's imaginary adventures? Compare the imaginary Mitty with the real one. How are the two related?

3. Give examples to show how a trivial detail in Mitty's real life can be a springboard to the secret one. Are any details carried back into the real life from the secret one? Do you think Thurber has a sound knowledge of everyday psychology? Justify your answer.

4. Cite incidents and remarks that show what sort of person Mitty's wife is. To what extent is she responsible for Mitty's need to escape to daydreams?

OBSERVING STRUCTURE

Point out the places in the story where each new incident begins and ends. Show how the author makes the various transitions from Mitty's real to his imaginary life.

BUILDING YOUR VOCABULARY

Reversing the meaning of a word by use of the prefixes *un-* or *in-* has long been familiar to you, and you have probably realized that *dis-* in its original sense of "away from" often has the same effect, as in *disarm* and *distrust*. Less common words often yield up their meaning if you know that the prefix *an-* (sometimes merely *a-*), meaning "not," "without," has the same effect. The *anesthetizer* which Mitty miraculously repairs shows how a knowledge of word parts enables you to arrive at exact meanings. The root *esthet*, common in *aesthetic*, means "feeling," especially of the senses. With the prefix *an-*, the two suffixes *-ize*, "to make," and *-er*, "the one or thing that does," round out the full meaning of the word.

THE AUTHOR

JAMES THURBER (1894–1961) was born, brought up, and educated in Ohio, but there is no local flavor in his writing. His men and women and, for that matter, his famous dogs, are universal in their traits and in their appeal. Both his cartoons and his writing show him as a humorist without bitterness, who tempered his mockery with sympathy as he recounted the struggles and the foibles of modern man. Like his drawings, his stories and essays have a deceptive air of casualness, the fruit of painstaking care and multiple rewriting.

After working for several newspapers, in 1926 Thurber joined the staff of the *New Yorker;* he was a regular contributor until his death. *Thurber Carnival* (1945) collects cartoons, stories, and essays from his earlier books; more recent volumes are *The Beast in Me and Other Animals* (1948) and *Thurber Country* (1954). He also collaborated with actor Elliot Nugent in writing the Broadway success *The Male Animal*. He wrote books for children, too, notably *The Thirteen Clocks* (1950) and *The Wonderful O* (1957). In 1959 a successful musical revue, *A Thurber Carnival*, was based upon selections from his cartoons and writings.

A Trio of Thurber Cartoons →

When Thurber's cartoons began to appear in the *New Yorker*, mothers began flooding the magazine with children's drawings. Thurber wrote all of them the same letter: "Your son can certainly draw as well as I can. The only trouble is he hasn't been through as much."

Thurber's characters, whether men, women, dogs, or rabbits, always seem to have been through a great deal. Like Walter Mitty, the characters in Thurber's cartoons appear to be fighting a constant, and losing, battle with a series of overwhelming, petty circumstances. There are small victories, however: a rabbit finds a new good-luck charm, a fencer enjoys a slight lapse of etiquette, and if things start to close in, even for a Walter Mitty, a dog sled is sometimes handy for getting away from it all.

James Thurber claimed that humor is a serious thing. "I like to think of it as one of our greatest national resources . . . A professor of mine once said that if a thing cannot stand laughter, it is not a good thing; and we must not lose in this country the uses of laughter."

"*I wear it for luck.*"

"*Touché!*"

"*Mush!*"

WILLA CATHER

The Sculptor's Funeral

The body of a man has been brought back to his home town. What manner of man had he been? A friend and pupil who accompanies the coffin has one view of him; the people of the little town have another. From their different attitudes, can we piece together the truth about the dead man? Can we learn the truth about the living?

A GROUP of the townspeople stood on the station siding of a little Kansas town, awaiting the coming of the night train, which was already twenty minutes overdue. The snow had fallen thick over everything; in the pale starlight the line of bluffs across the wide, white meadows south of the town made soft, smoke-colored curves against the clear sky. The men on the siding stood first on one foot and then on the other, their hands thrust deep into their trousers pockets, their overcoats open, their shoulders screwed up with the cold; and they glanced from time to time toward the southeast, where the railroad track wound along the river shore. They conversed in low tones and moved about restlessly, seeming uncertain as to what was expected of them. There was but one of the company who looked as if he knew exactly why he was there, and he kept conspicuously apart; walking to the far end of the platform, returning to the station door, then pacing up the track again, his chin sunk in the high collar of his overcoat, his burly shoulders drooping forward, his gait heavy and dogged. Presently he was approached by a tall, spare, grizzled man clad in a faded Grand Army [1] suit, who shuffled out from the group and advanced with a certain deference, craning his neck forward until his back made the angle of a jackknife three quarters open.

"I reckon she's a-goin' to be pretty late again tonight, Jim," he remarked in a squeaky falsetto.[2] "S'pose it's the snow?"

"I don't know," responded the other man with a shade of annoyance, speak-

"The Sculptor's Funeral" Reprinted from *Youth and the Bright Medusa* by Willa Cather by permission of Alfred A. Knopf, Inc. Copyright 1904, 1932 by Willa Cather.

[1] **Grand Army:** The Grand Army of the Republic (or G.A.R.), an organization of veterans of the War Between the States.

[2] **falsetto** (fôl·sĕt′ō): a high-pitched tone of voice.

ing from out an astonishing cataract [1] of red beard that grew fiercely and thickly in all directions.

The spare man shifted the quill toothpick he was chewing to the other side of his mouth. "It ain't likely that anybody from the East will come with the corpse, I s'pose," he went on reflectively.

"I don't know," responded the other, more curtly than before.

"It's too bad he didn't belong to some lodge or other. I like an order funeral myself. They seem more appropriate for people of some repytation," the spare man continued, with an ingratiating concession in his shrill voice, as he carefully placed his toothpick in his vest pocket. He always carried the flag at the G.A.R. funerals in the town.

The heavy man turned on his heel, without replying, and walked up the siding. The spare man rejoined the uneasy group. "Jim's ez full ez a tick, ez ushel," he commented commiseratingly.

Just then a distant whistle sounded, and there was a shuffling of feet on the platform. A number of lanky boys, of all ages, appeared as suddenly and slimily as eels wakened by the crack of thunder; some came from the waiting room, where they had been warming themselves by the red stove, or half asleep on the slat benches; others uncoiled themselves from baggage trucks or slid out of express wagons. Two clambered down from the driver's seat of a hearse that stood backed up against the siding. They straightened their stooping shoulders and lifted their heads, and a flash of momentary animation kindled their dull eyes at that cold, vibrant scream, the world-wide call for men. It stirred them like the note of a trumpet; just as it had often stirred the man who was coming home tonight, in his boyhood.

The night express shot, red as a rocket, from out the eastward marshlands and wound along the river shore under the long lines of shivering poplars that sentineled the meadows, the escaping steam hanging in gray masses against the pale sky and blotting out the Milky Way. In a moment the red glare from the headlight streamed up the snow-covered track before the siding and glittered on the wet, black rails. The burly man with the disheveled red beard walked swiftly up the platform toward the approaching train, uncovering his head as he went. The group of men behind him hesitated, glanced questioningly at one another, and awkwardly followed his example. The train stopped, and the crowd shuffled up to the express car just as the door was thrown open, the man in the G.A.R. suit thrusting his head forward with curiosity. The express messenger appeared in the doorway, accompanied by a young man in a long ulster [2] and traveling cap.

"Are Mr. Merrick's friends here?" inquired the young man.

The group on the platform swayed uneasily. Philip Phelps, the banker, responded with dignity: "We have come to take charge of the body. Mr. Merrick's father is very feeble and can't be about."

"Send the agent out here," growled the express messenger, "and tell the operator to lend a hand."

The coffin was got out of its rough box and down on the snowy platform. The townspeople drew back enough to make room for it and then formed a close semicircle about it, looking curiously at the palm leaf [3] which lay across the black cover. No one said anything. The baggage man stood by his truck, waiting to get at the trunks. The engine panted heavily, and the fireman dodged in and out among the wheels with his yellow torch and long oilcan, snapping the spindle boxes. The young Boston-

[1] **cataract** (kăt′*a*·răkt): waterfall.

[2] **ulster:** overcoat.
[3] **palm leaf:** a symbol of achievement.

ian, one of the dead sculptor's pupils, who had come with the body, looked about him helplessly. He turned to the banker, the only one of that black, uneasy, stoop-shouldered group who seemed enough of an individual to be addressed.

"None of Mr. Merrick's brothers are here?" he asked uncertainly.

The man with the red beard for the first time stepped up and joined the others. "No, they have not come yet; the family is scattered. The body will be taken directly to the house." He stooped and took hold of one of the handles of the coffin.

"Take the long hill road up, Thompson, it will be easier on the horses," called the liveryman as the undertaker snapped the door of the hearse and prepared to mount to the driver's seat.

Laird, the red-bearded lawyer, turned again to the stranger: "We didn't know whether there would be anyone with him or not," he explained. "It's a long walk, so you'd better go up in the hack." He pointed to a single battered conveyance, but the young man replied stiffly: "Thank you, but I think I will go up with the hearse. If you don't object," turning to the undertaker, "I'll ride with you."

They clambered up over the wheels and drove off in the starlight up the long, white hill toward the town. The lamps in the still village were shining from under the low, snow-burdened roofs; and beyond, on every side, the plains reached out into emptiness, peaceful and wide as the soft sky itself, and wrapped in a tangible, white silence.

When the hearse backed up to a wooden sidewalk before a naked, weather-beaten frame house, the same composite, ill-defined group that had stood upon the station siding was huddled about the gate. The front yard was an icy swamp, and a couple of warped planks, extending from the sidewalk to the door, made a sort of rickety foot-bridge. The gate hung on one hinge, and was opened wide with difficulty. Steavens, the young stranger, noticed that something black was tied to the knob of the front door.

The grating sound made by the casket, as it was drawn from the hearse, was answered by a scream from the house; the front door was wrenched open, and a tall, corpulent woman rushed out bareheaded into the snow and flung herself upon the coffin, shrieking: "My boy, my boy! And this is how you've come home to me!"

As Steavens turned away and closed his eyes with a shudder of unutterable repulsion, another woman, also tall, but flat and angular, dressed entirely in black, darted out of the house and caught Mrs. Merrick by the shoulders, crying sharply: "Come, come, mother; you mustn't go on like this!" Her tone changed to one of obsequious [1] solemnity as she turned to the banker: "The parlor is ready, Mr. Phelps."

The bearers carried the coffin along the narrow boards, while the undertaker ran ahead with the coffin rests. They bore it into a large, unheated room that smelled of dampness and disuse and furniture polish, and set it down under a hanging lamp ornamented with jingling glass prisms and before a "Rogers group" [2] of John Alden and Priscilla, wreathed with smilax.[3] Henry Steavens stared about him with the sickening conviction that there had been a mistake and that he had somehow arrived at the wrong destination. He looked at the clover-green Brussels,[4] the fat plush upholstery, among the hand-painted

---

[1] **obsequious** (ŏb·sē′kwĭ·ŭs): fawning; servilely flattering.

[2] "**Rogers group**": Plaster reproductions of statuette groups by John Rogers, often with historical or sentimental themes, were common in late nineteenth-century American homes.

[3] **smilax**: a delicate twining plant with green leaves.

[4] **Brussels**: a patterned carpet.

china plaques and panels and vases, for some mark of identification — for something that might once conceivably have belonged to Harvey Merrick. It was not until he recognized his friend in the crayon portrait of a little boy in kilts and curls, hanging above the piano, that he felt willing to let any of these people approach the coffin.

"Take the lid off, Mr. Thompson; let me see my boy's face," wailed the elder woman between her sobs. This time Steavens looked fearfully, almost beseechingly, into her face, red and swollen under its masses of strong, black, shiny hair. He flushed, dropped his eyes, and then, almost incredulously, looked again. There was a kind of power about her face — a kind of brutal handsomeness, even; but it was scarred and furrowed by violence, and so colored and coarsened by fiercer passions that grief seemed never to have laid a gentle finger there. The long nose was distended and knobbed at the end, and there were deep lines on either side of it; her heavy, black brows almost met across her forehead, her teeth were large and square, and set far apart — teeth that could tear. She filled the room; the men were obliterated, seemed tossed about like twigs in an angry water, and even Steavens felt himself being drawn into the whirlpool.

The daughter — the tall, rawboned woman in crepe, with a mourning comb in her hair which curiously lengthened her long face, sat stiffly upon the sofa, her hands, conspicuous for their large knuckles, folded in her lap, her mouth and eyes drawn down, solemnly awaiting the opening of the coffin. Near the door stood a mulatto woman, evidently a servant in the house, with a timid bearing and an emaciated face pitifully sad and gentle. She was weeping silently, the corner of her calico apron lifted to her eyes, occasionally suppressing a long, quivering sob. Steavens walked over and stood beside her.

Feeble steps were heard on the stairs, and an old man, tall and frail, odorous of pipe smoke, with shaggy, unkempt gray hair and a dingy beard, tobacco stained about the mouth, entered uncertainly. He went slowly up to the coffin and stood rolling a blue cotton handkerchief between his hands, seeming so pained and embarrassed by his wife's orgy of grief that he had no consciousness of anything else.

"There, there, Annie, dear, don't take on so," he quavered timidly, putting out a shaking hand and awkwardly patting her elbow. She turned and sank upon his shoulder with such violence that he tottered a little. He did not even glance toward the coffin, but continued to look at her with a dull, frightened, appealing expression, as a spaniel looks at the whip. His sunken cheeks slowly reddened and burned with miserable shame. When his wife rushed from the room, her daughter strode after her with set lips. The servant stole up to the coffin, bent over it for a moment, and then slipped away to the kitchen, leaving Steavens, the lawyer, and the father to themselves. The old man stood looking down at his dead son's face. The sculptor's splendid head seemed even more noble in its rigid stillness than in life. The dark hair had crept down upon the wide forehead; the face seemed strangely long, but in it there was not that repose we expect to find in the faces of the dead. The brows were so drawn that there were two deep lines above the beaked nose, and the chin was thrust forward defiantly. It was as though the strain of life had been so sharp and bitter that death could not at once relax the tension and smooth the countenance into perfect peace — as though he were still guarding something precious, which might even yet be wrested from him.

The old man's lips were working under his stained beard. He turned to the lawyer with timid deference: "Phelps and the rest are comin' back to set up with Harve, ain't they?" he asked. "Thank'ee, Jim, thankee." He brushed the hair back gently from his son's forehead. "He was a good boy, Jim; always a good boy. He was ez gentle ez a child and the kindest of 'em all — only we didn't none of us ever onderstand him." The tears trickled slowly down his beard and dropped upon the sculptor's coat.

"Martin, Martin! Oh, Martin! come here," his wife wailed from the top of the stairs. The old man started timorously: "Yes, Annie, I'm coming." He turned away, hesitated, stood for a moment in miserable indecision; then reached back and patted the dead man's hair softly, and stumbled from the room.

"Poor old man, I didn't think he had any tears left. Seems as if his eyes would have gone dry long ago. At his age nothing cuts very deep," remarked the lawyer.

Something in his tone made Steavens glance up. While the mother had been in the room, the young man had scarcely seen anyone else; but now, from the moment he first glanced into Jim Laird's florid face and bloodshot eyes, he knew that he had found what he had been

heartsick at not finding before — the feeling, the understanding, that must exist in someone, even here.

The man was red as his beard, with features swollen and blurred by dissipation, and a hot, blazing blue eye. His face was strained — that of a man who is controlling himself with difficulty — and he kept plucking at his beard with a sort of fierce resentment. Steavens, sitting by the window, watched him turn down the glaring lamp, still its jangling pendants with an angry gesture, and then stand with his hands locked behind him, staring down into the master's face. He could not help wondering what link there had been between the porcelain vessel and so sooty a lump of potter's clay.

From the kitchen an uproar was sounding; when the dining-room door opened, the import of it was clear. The mother was abusing the maid for having forgotten to make the dressing for the chicken salad which had been prepared for the watchers. Steavens had never heard anything in the least like it; it was injured, emotional, dramatic abuse, unique and masterly in its excruciating cruelty, as violent and unrestrained as had been her grief of twenty minutes before. With a shudder of disgust, the lawyer went into the dining room and closed the door into the kitchen.

"Poor Roxy's getting it now," he remarked when he came back. "The Merricks took her out of the poorhouse years ago; and if her loyalty would let her, I guess the poor old thing could tell tales that would curdle your blood. She's the mulatto woman who was standing in here a while ago, with her apron to her eyes. The old woman is a fury; there never was anybody like her. She made Harvey's life a hell for him when he lived at home; he was so sick ashamed of it. I never could see how he kept himself sweet."

"He was wonderful," said Steavens slowly, "wonderful; but until tonight I have never known how wonderful."

"That is the eternal wonder of it, anyway; that it can come even from such a dung heap as this," the lawyer cried, with a sweeping gesture which seemed to indicate much more than the four walls within which they stood.

"I think I'll see whether I can get a little air. The room is so close I am beginning to feel rather faint," murmured Steavens, struggling with one of the windows. The sash was stuck, however, and would not yield, so he sat down dejectedly and began pulling at his collar. The lawyer came over, loosened the sash with one blow of his red fist, and sent the window up a few inches. Steavens thanked him, but the nausea which had been gradually climbing into his throat for the last half hour left him with but one desire — a desperate feeling that he must get away from this place with what was left of Harvey Merrick. Oh, he comprehended well enough now the quiet bitterness of the smile that he had seen so often on his master's lips!

Once when Merrick returned from a visit home, he brought with him a singularly feeling and suggestive bas-relief[1] of a thin, faded old woman, sitting and sewing something pinned to her knee; while a full-lipped, full-blooded little urchin, his trousers held up by a single gallows,[2] stood beside her, impatiently twitching her gown to call her attention to a butterfly he had caught. Steavens, impressed by the tender and delicate modeling of the thin, tired face, had asked him if it were his mother. He remembered the dull flush that had burned up in the sculptor's face.

The lawyer was sitting in a rocking chair beside the coffin, his head thrown back and his eyes closed. Steavens looked at him earnestly, puzzled at the line of the chin, and wondering why a man should conceal a feature of such distinction under that disfiguring shock of beard. Suddenly, as though he felt the young sculptor's keen glance, Jim Laird opened his eyes.

"Was he always a good deal of an oyster?"[3] he asked abruptly. "He was terribly shy as a boy."

"Yes, he was an oyster, since you put it so," rejoined Steavens. "Although he could be very fond of people, he always gave one the impression of being detached. He disliked violent emotion; he was reflective, and rather distrustful of himself — except, of course, as regarded his work. He was sure enough there. He distrusted men pretty thoroughly and women even more, yet somehow without believing ill of them. He was determined, indeed, to believe the best; but he seemed afraid to investigate."

"A burnt dog dreads the fire," said the lawyer grimly, and closed his eyes.

Steavens went on and on, reconstructing that whole miserable boyhood. All this raw, biting ugliness had been the portion of the man whose mind was to become an exhaustless gallery of beautiful impressions — so sensitive that the mere shadow of a poplar leaf flickering against a sunny wall would be etched and held there forever. Surely, if ever a man had the magic word in his finger tips, it was Merrick. Whatever he touched, he revealed its holiest secret; liberated it from enchantment and restored it to its pristine[4] loveliness. Upon whatever he had come in contact with, he had left a beautiful record of the experience — a sort of ethereal signature; a scent, a sound, a color that was his own.

Steavens understood now the real tragedy of his master's life; neither love

---

[1] bas-relief (bä′rē·lēf′): a type of sculpture in which the figures are a part of the background and project only slightly from it; a coin is an example of one type of relief.

[2] gallows (găl′ŭs): suspender (colloquial).

[3] oyster: a shy, quiet person (slang).

[4] pristine (prĭs′tēn): uncorrupted.

nor wine, as many had conjectured; but a blow which had fallen earlier and cut deeper than anything else could have done — a shame not his, and yet so unescapably his, to hide in his heart from his very boyhood. And without — the frontier warfare; the yearning of a boy, cast ashore upon a desert of newness and ugliness and sordidness, for all that is chastened and old, and noble with traditions.

At eleven o'clock the tall, flat woman in black announced that the watchers were arriving, and asked them to "step into the dining room." As Steavens rose, the lawyer said dryly: "You go on — it'll be a good experience for you. I'm not equal to that crowd tonight; I've had twenty years of them."

As Steavens closed the door after him, he glanced back at the lawyer, sitting by the coffin in the dim light, with his chin resting on his hand.

The same misty group that had stood before the door of the express car shuffled into the dining room. In the light of the kerosene lamp, they separated and became individuals. The minister, a pale, feeble-looking man with white hair and blond chin whiskers, took his seat beside a small side table, and placed his Bible upon it. The Grand Army man sat down behind the stove and tilted his chair back comfortably against the wall, fishing his quill toothpick from his waistcoat pocket. The two bankers, Phelps and Elder, sat off in a corner behind the dinner table, where they could finish their discussion of the new usury law [1] and its effect on chattel [2] security loans. The real-estate agent, an old man with a smiling, hypocritical face, soon joined them. The coal and lumber dealer and the cattle shipper sat on opposite sides of the hard

coal burner, their feet on the nickelwork. Steavens took a book from his pocket and began to read. The talk around him ranged through various topics of local interest while the house was quieting down. When it was clear that the members of the family were in bed, the Grand Army man hitched his shoulders and, untangling his long legs, caught his heels on the rounds of his chair.

"S'pose there'll be a will, Phelps?" he queried in his weak falsetto.

The banker laughed disagreeably, and began trimming his nails with a pearl-handled pocketknife.

"There'll scarcely be any need for one, will there?" he queried in his turn.

The restless Grand Army man shifted his position again, getting his knees still nearer his chin. "Why, the ole man says Harve's done right well lately," he chirped.

The other banker spoke up. "I reckon he means by that Harve ain't asked him to mortgage any more farms lately, so as he could go on with his education."

"Seems like my mind don't reach back to a time when Harve wasn't bein' edycated," tittered the Grand Army man.

There was a general chuckle. The minister took out his handkerchief and blew his nose sonorously. Banker Phelps closed his knife with a snap. "It's too bad the old man's sons didn't turn out better," he remarked with reflective authority. "They never hung together. He spent money enough on Harve to stock a dozen cattle farms, and he might as well have poured it into Sand Creek. If Harve had stayed at home and helped nurse what little they had, and gone into stock on the old man's bottom farm, they might all have been well fixed. But the old man had to trust everything to tenants and was cheated right and left."

"Harve never could have handled stock none," interposed the cattleman.

---

[1] usury (ū'zhŏŏ·rĭ) law: a law regulating the amount of interest that may be charged on a loan. In modern usage the term usury means an excessive rate of interest.

[2] chattel: any item of property except real estate.

"He hadn't it in him to be sharp. Do you remember when he bought Sander's mules for eight year olds, when everybody in town knew that Sander's father-in-law give 'em to his wife for a wedding present eighteen years before, an' they was full-grown mules then?"

The company laughed discreetly, and the Grand Army man rubbed his knees with a spasm of childish delight.

"Harve never was much account for anything practical, and he shore was never fond of work," began the coal and lumber dealer. "I mind the last time he was home; the day he left, when the old man was out to the barn helpin' his hand hitch up to take Harve to the train, and Cal Moots was patchin' up the fence; Harve, he come out on the step and sings out, in his ladylike voice: 'Cal Moots, Cal Moots! Please come cord my trunk.'"

"That's Harve for you," approved the Grand Army man. "I kin hear him howlin' yet, when he was a big feller in long pants and his mother used to whale him with a rawhide in the barn for lettin' the cows git foundered in the cornfield when he was drivin' 'em home from pasture. He killed a cow of mine that-a-way onct — a pure Jersey and the best milker I had, an' the ole man had to put up for her. Harve, he was watchin' the sun set acrost the marshes when the anamile got away."

"Where the old man made his mistake was in sending the boy East to school," said Phelps, stroking his goatee and speaking in a deliberate, judicial tone. "There was where he got his head full of nonsense. What Harve needed, of all people, was a course in some first-class Kansas City business college."

The letters were swimming before Steavens' eyes. Was it possible that these men did not understand, that the palm on the coffin meant nothing to them? The very name of their town would have remained forever buried in the postal guide had it not been now

and again mentioned in the world in connection with Harvey Merrick's. He remembered what his master had said to him on the day of his death, after the congestion of both lungs had shut off any probability of recovery, and the sculptor had asked his pupil to send his body home. "It's not a pleasant place to be lying while the world is moving and doing and bettering," he had said with a feeble smile, "but it rather seems as though we ought to go back to the place we came from, in the end. The townspeople will come in for a look at me; and after they have had their say, I shan't have much to fear from the judgment of God!"

The cattleman took up the comment. "Forty's young for a Merrick to cash in; they usually hang on pretty well. Probably he helped it along with whisky."

"His mother's people were not long lived, and Harvey never had a robust constitution," said the minister mildly. He would have liked to say more. He had been the boy's Sunday-school teacher, and had been fond of him; but he felt that he was not in a position to speak. His own sons had turned out badly, and it was not a year since one of them had made his last trip home in the express car, shot in a gambling house in the Black Hills.

"Nevertheless, there is no disputin' that Harve frequently looked upon the wine when it was red, also variegated,[1] and it shore made an oncommon fool of him," moralized the cattleman.

Just then the door leading into the parlor rattled loudly, and everyone started involuntarily, looking relieved when only Jim Laird came out. The Grand Army man ducked his head when he saw the spark in his blue, bloodshot eye. They were all afraid of Jim; he was a drunkard, but he could twist the law to suit his client's needs as no other man in all western Kansas could do, and there were many who tried. The lawyer closed the door behind him, leaned back against it, and folded his arms, cocking his head a little to one side. When he assumed this attitude in the courtroom, ears were always pricked up, as it usually foretold a flood of withering sarcasm.

"I've been with you gentlemen before," he began in a dry, even tone, "when you've sat by the coffins of boys born and raised in this town; and, if I remember rightly, you were never any too well satisfied when you checked them up. What's the matter anyhow? Why is it that reputable young men are as scarce as millionaires in Sand City? It might almost seem to a stranger that there was some way something the matter with your progressive town. Why did Ruben Sayer, the brightest young lawyer you ever turned out, after he had come home from the university as straight as a die, take to drinking and forge a check and shoot himself? Why did Bill Merrit's son die of the shakes in a saloon in Omaha? Why was Mr. Thomas' son, here, shot in a gambling house? Why did young Adams burn his mill to beat the insurance companies, and go to the pen?"

The lawyer paused and unfolded his

[1] variegated (vâr′ĭ·ĕ·gāt′ĕd): multicolored.

arms, laying one clenched fist quietly on the table. "I'll tell you why. Because you drummed nothing but money and knavery into their ears from the time they wore knickerbockers; because you carped away at them as you've been carping here tonight, holding our friends Phelps and Elder up to them for their models, as our grandfathers held up George Washington and John Adams. But the boys were young, and raw at the business you put them to, and how could they match coppers with such artists as Phelps and Elder? You wanted them to be successful rascals; they were only unsuccessful ones — that's all the difference. There was only one boy ever raised in this borderland between ruffianism and civilization who didn't come to grief, and you hated Harvey Merrick more for winning out than you hated all the other boys who got under the wheels. Lord, Lord, how you did hate him! Phelps, here, is fond of saying that he could buy and sell us all out any time he's a mind to; but he knew Harve wouldn't have given a tinker's dam for his bank and all his cattle farms put together; and a lack of appreciation, that way, goes hard with Phelps.

"Old Nimrod thinks Harve drank too much; and this from such as Nimrod and me!

"Brother Elder says Harve was too free with the old man's money — fell short in filial consideration, maybe. Well, we can all remember the very tone in which brother Elder swore his own father was a liar, in the county court; and we all know that the old man came out of that partnership with his son as bare as a sheared lamb. But maybe I'm getting personal, and I'd better be driving ahead at what I want to say."

The lawyer paused a moment, squared his heavy shoulders, and went on: "Harvey Merrick and I went to school together, back East. We were dead in earnest, and we wanted you all to be proud of us some day. We meant to be great men. Even I, and I haven't lost my sense of humor, gentlemen, I meant to be a great man. I came back here to practice, and I found you didn't in the least want me to be a great man. You wanted me to be a shrewd lawyer — oh, yes! Our veteran here wanted me to get him an increase of pension, because he had dyspepsia; [1] Phelps wanted a new county survey that would put the widow Wilson's little bottom farm inside his south line; Elder wanted to lend money at five per cent a month, and get it collected; and Stark here wanted to wheedle old women up in Vermont into investing their annuities [2] in real-estate mortgages that are not worth the paper they are written on. Oh, you needed me hard enough, and you'll go on needing me!

"Well, I came back here and became the damned shyster you wanted me to be. You pretend to have some sort of respect for me; and yet you'll stand up and throw mud at Harvey Merrick, whose soul you couldn't dirty and whose hands you couldn't tie. Oh, you're a discriminating lot of Christians! There have been times when the sight of Harvey's name in some Eastern paper has made me hang my head like a whipped dog; and, again, times when I liked to think of him off there in the world, away from all this hog wallow, climbing the big, clean upgrade he'd set for himself.

"And we? Now that we've fought and lied and sweated and stolen, and hated as only the disappointed strugglers in a bitter, dead little Western town know how to do, what have we got to show for it? Harvey Merrick wouldn't have given one sunset over your marshes for all you've got put together, and you know it. It's not for me to say why, in

---

[1] **dyspepsia** (dĭs·pĕp′shá): indigestion.
[2] **annuities** (ă·nū′ĭ·tĭz): an amount of money received yearly, usually from investments or trust funds.

---

the inscrutable wisdom of God, a genius should ever have been called from this place of hatred and bitter waters; but I want this Boston man to know that the drivel he's been hearing here tonight is the only tribute any truly great man could have from such a lot of sick, sidetracked, burnt-dog, land-poor sharks as the here-present financiers of Sand City — upon which town may God have mercy!"

The lawyer thrust out his hand to Steavens as he passed him, caught up his overcoat in the hall, and had left the house before the Grand Army man had time to lift his ducked head and crane his long neck about at his fellows.

Next day Jim Laird was drunk and unable to attend the funeral services. Steavens called twice at his office, but was compelled to start East without seeing him. He had a presentiment that he would hear from him again, and left his address on the lawyer's table; but if Laird found it, he never acknowledged it. The thing in him that Harvey Merrick had loved must have gone underground with Harvey Merrick's coffin; for it never spoke again, and Jim got the cold he died of driving across the Colorado mountains to defend one of Phelps's sons, who had got into trouble out there by cutting government timber.

FOR DISCUSSION

This story is a stark example of that school of writing called *realism*. As realistic art must often do, it offers an unappealing and critical view of certain elements of human nature. The story is built around two essential conflicts. It contrasts the bleak existence of a remote, late-frontier town with the sense of a broader, more cultured world, and it shows a dramatic picture of the gap that separates the perceptive and sensitive person from the crass and dull. Miss Cather has taken sides in these conflicts: her choice of details, and the accumulated power of those details, particularly in many of the descriptive passages, clearly indicates where her sympathies lie. The author makes a judgment about certain characters in "The Sculptor's Funeral," and she wants the reader to share this judgment, to agree with her attitude. Let us examine a few of the ways by which Miss Cather accomplishes her purpose.

1. The first few paragraphs rapidly and strongly establish the basic mood of the story. What is that mood? Point out some of the details which help create it.

2. Miss Cather works with minutely realistic details combined for an overwhelming effect. Take any one of her long descriptive passages and pick out details of a kind that you might not find in less realistic stories.

3. How do the several references to James Laird's beard seem appropriate to the quality of his character? How is he like Harvey Merrick? How different?

4. What is meant by "He could not help wondering what link there had been between the porcelain vessel and so sooty a lump of potter's clay"? Who is the "porcelain vessel"? Who is the "sooty lump of potter's clay"? Why is it appropriate for Henry Steavens to use this kind of figurative language?

5. Read the detailed description of the furnishings and decorations of the house. What does the taste shown in the furnishings tell us about the sculptor in relation to his background?

6. We are told that the sculptor's face looked "as though he were still guarding something precious and holy which might even yet be wrested from him." What is that "something"? Against what had he guarded it?

7. The sculptor had anticipated what his funeral would be like. Explain his words: ". . . after they have had their say, I shan't have much to fear from the judgment of God." What do you think of his choice to be buried in this town?

8. Can you point to examples, like Merrick, of individuals in conflict with a materialistic society — one that believes that the only important values are those that can be measured in terms of money?

YOUR OWN WRITING

The pattern of this story is a familiar one — the central figure is dead, and the reader learns about him only through the memories and comments of the other characters. Write a character sketch of Harvey Merrick. Take into consideration both the opinions of the townspeople and the attitudes of Merrick's friends, but your judgment and description of him should be based on all available evidence, including perhaps your personal experience. Support your opinions by quotations from the story.

THE AUTHOR

WILLA CATHER (1873–1947), though born in Virginia, grew up in Nebraska. The West and the passing frontier of the prairies are among her main themes. She came East and was for a time a magazine editor, but she gave up this work to return to her beloved region and devote herself to writing. Both as novelist and short-story writer she is one of our foremost literary figures. Among her novels, perhaps the finest are *O Pioneers* (1913), *My Ántonia* (1918), *Death Comes for the Archbishop* (1927), and *Shadows on the Rock* (1931).

As the Artist Sees It ➤

Reproduced on the facing page is an interpretation of the setting of "The Sculptor's Funeral." The water color is by Marilyn Miller. Do you feel that the painting reflects the qualities of the town as they are revealed in the story?

STEPHEN VINCENT BENÉT

The Devil and Daniel Webster

The devil seldom meets his match. But the great American orator Daniel Webster, so they say, was a worthy opponent for the grim stranger.

THE AUTHOR'S TONE. Your acceptance of this story hinges on identifying the author's tone. Very early you learn what the tone is. See whether you can describe it when you have finished the tale.

I T'S A STORY they all tell in the border country, where Massachusetts joins Vermont and New Hampshire.

Yes, Dan'l Webster's dead — or, at least, they buried him. But every time there's a thunderstorm around Marshfield,[1] they say you can hear his rolling voice in the hollows of the sky. And they say that if you go to his grave and speak loud and clear, "Dan'l Webster — Dan'l Webster!" the ground'll begin to shiver and the trees begin to shake.

[1] **Marshfield:** a small town southeast of Boston, where Webster had a farm, and where he spent most of his private life.

"The Devil and Daniel Webster" from *Selected Works of Stephen Vincent Benét,* published by Rinehart & Company, Inc. Copyright, 1936 by Stephen Vincent Benét. Reprinted by permission of Brandt & Brandt.

And after a while you'll hear a deep voice saying, "Neighbor, how stands the Union?" Then you better answer: the Union stands as she stood, rock-bottomed and copper-sheathed, one and indivisible, or he's liable to rear right out of the ground. At least, that's what I was told when I was a youngster.

You see, for a while, he was the biggest man in the country. He never got to be President, but he was the biggest man. There were thousands that trusted in him right next to God Almighty, and they told stories about him and all the things that belonged to him that were like the stories of patriarchs and such. They said when he stood up to speak, stars and stripes came right out in the sky, and once he spoke against a river and made it sink into the ground. They said when he walked the woods with his fishing rod, Killall, the trout would jump out of the streams right into his pockets, for they knew it was no use putting up a fight against him; and, when he argued a case, he could turn on the harps of the blessed and the shaking of the earth underground. That was the kind of man he was, and his big farm up at Marshfield was suitable to him. The chickens he raised were all white meat down through the drumsticks, the cows were tended like children, and the big ram he called Goliath [1] had horns with a curl like a morning-glory vine and could butt through an iron door. But Dan'l wasn't one of your gentlemen farmers; he knew all the ways of the land, and he'd be up by candlelight to see that the chores got done. A man with a mouth like a mastiff, a brow like a mountain, and eyes like burning anthracite — that was Dan'l Webster in his prime. And the biggest case he argued never got written down in the books, for he argued it against the devil, nip and tuck, and no holds barred. And this is the way I used to hear it told:

There was a man named Jabez Stone, lived at Cross Corners, New Hampshire. He wasn't a bad man to start with, but he was an unlucky man. If he planted corn, he got borers; [2] if he planted potatoes, he got blight. [3] He had good enough land, but it didn't prosper him; he had a decent wife and children, but the more children he had, the less there was to feed them. If stones cropped up in his neighbor's field, boulders boiled up in his; if he had a horse with the spavins, [4] he'd trade it for one with the staggers [5] and give something extra. There's some folks bound to be like that, apparently. But one day Jabez Stone got sick of the whole business.

He'd been plowing that morning and he'd just broke the plowshare on a rock that he could have sworn hadn't been there yesterday. And, as he stood looking at the plowshare, the off horse began to cough — that ropy kind of cough

that means sickness and horse doctors. There were two children down with the measles, his wife was ailing, and he had a whitlow [6] on his thumb. It was about the last straw for Jabez Stone. "I vow," he said, and he looked around him kind of desperate — "I vow it's enough to make a man want to sell his soul to the devil! And I would, too, for two cents!"

Then he felt a kind of queerness come over him at having said what he'd said; though, naturally, being a New Hampshireman, he wouldn't take it back. But, all the same, when it got to be evening and, as far as he could see, no notice had been taken, he felt relieved in his mind, for he was a religious man. But notice is always taken, sooner or later, just like the Good Book says. And, sure enough, the next day, about suppertime, a soft-spoken, dark-dressed stranger drove up in a handsome buggy and asked for Jabez Stone.

Well, Jabez told his family it was a lawyer, come to see him about a legacy. But he knew who it was. He didn't like the looks of the stranger, nor the way he smiled with his teeth. They were white teeth, and plentiful — some say they were filed to a point, but I wouldn't vouch for that. And he didn't like it when the dog took one look at the stranger and ran away howling, with his tail between his legs. But having passed his word, more or less, he stuck to it, and they went out behind the barn and made their bargain. Jabez Stone had to prick his finger to sign, and the stranger lent him a silver pen. The wound healed clean, but it left a little white scar.

After that, all of a sudden, things began to pick up and prosper for Jabez Stone. His cows got fat and his horses sleek, his crops were the envy of the neighborhood, and lightning might strike all over the valley, but it wouldn't

[1] **Goliath** (gô·lī′ăth): a famous giant in the Bible (I Samuel, 17), slain by the young David.

[2] **borers:** a corn-destroying insect.

[3] **blight:** a plant disease.

[4] **spavins** (spăv′ĭnz): a disease of the leg bone that causes a horse to limp.

[5] **staggers:** a disease that causes a horse to reel or fall down.

[6] **whitlow:** an inflamed sore.

strike his barn. Pretty soon, he was one of the prosperous people of the county; they asked him to stand for selectman,[1] and he stood for it; there began to be talk of running him for state senate. All in all, you might say the Stone family was as happy and contented as cats in a dairy. And so they were, except for Jabez Stone.

He'd been contented enough, the first few years. It's a great thing when bad luck turns; it drives most other things out of your head. True, every now and then, especially in rainy weather, the little white scar on his finger would give him a twinge. And once a year, punctual as clockwork, the stranger with the handsome buggy would come driving by. But the sixth year, the stranger lighted, and, after that, his peace was over for Jabez Stone.

The stranger came up through the lower field, switching his boots with a cane — they were handsome black boots, but Jabez Stone never liked the look of them, particularly the toes. And, after he'd passed the time of day, he said, "Well, Mr. Stone, you're a hummer! It's a very pretty property you've got here, Mr. Stone."

"Well, some might favor it and others might not," said Jabez Stone, for he was a New Hampshireman.

"Oh, no need to decry your industry!" said the stranger, very easy, showing his teeth in a smile. "After all, we know what's been done, and it's been according to contract and specifications. So when — ahem — the mortgage falls due next year, you shouldn't have any regrets."

"Speaking of that mortgage, mister," said Jabez Stone, and he looked around for help to the earth and the sky, "I'm beginning to have one or two doubts about it."

"Doubts?" said the stranger, not quite so pleasantly.

<hr>

[1] **selectman:** one of a board of officers chosen annually in some New England towns to transact public business.

"Why, yes," said Jabez Stone. "This being the U.S.A. and me always having been a religious man." He cleared his throat and got bolder. "Yes, sir," he said, "I'm beginning to have considerable doubts as to that mortgage holding in court."

"There's courts and courts," said the stranger, clicking his teeth. "Still, we might as well have a look at the original document." And he hauled out a big black pocketbook, full of papers. "Sherwin, Slater, Stevens, Stone," he muttered. "I, Jabez Stone, for a term of seven years — Oh, it's quite in order, I think."

But Jabez Stone wasn't listening, for he saw something else flutter out of the black pocketbook. It was something that looked like a moth, but it wasn't a moth. And as Jabez Stone stared at it, it seemed to speak to him in a small sort of piping voice, terrible small and thin, but terrible human.

"Neighbor Stone!" it squeaked. "Neighbor Stone! Help me! I beg you, help me!"

But before Jabez Stone could stir hand or foot, the stranger whipped out a big bandanna handkerchief, caught the creature in it, just like a butterfly, and started tying up the ends of the bandanna.

"Sorry for the interruption," he said. "As I was saying — "

But Jabez Stone was shaking all over like a scared horse.

"That's Miser Stevens' voice!" he said, in a croak. "And you've got him in your handkerchief!"

The stranger looked a little embarrassed.

"Yes, I really should have transferred him to the collecting box," he said with a simper, "but there were some rather unusual specimens there and I didn't want them crowded. Well, well, these little contretemps[2] will occur."

<hr>

[2] **contretemps** (kôn′trĕ-tän′): an embarrassing situation. Note Stone's pronunciation of the word in the next paragraph.

"I don't know what you mean by contertan," said Jabez Stone, "but that was Miser Stevens' voice! And he ain't dead! You can't tell me he is! He was just as spry and mean as a woodchuck, Tuesday!"

"In the midst of life —"[1] said the stranger, kind of pious. "Listen!" Then a bell began to toll in the valley, and Jabez Stone listened, with the sweat running down his face. For he knew it was tolled for Miser Stevens and that he was dead.

"These long-standing accounts," said the stranger with a sigh; "one really hates to close them. But business is business."

He still had the bandanna in his hand, and Jabez Stone felt sick as he saw the cloth struggle and flutter.

"Are they all as small as that?" he asked hoarsely.

"Small?" said the stranger. "Oh, I see what you mean. Why, they vary." He measured Jabez Stone with his eyes, and his teeth showed. "Don't worry, Mr. Stone," he said. "You'll go with a very good grade. I wouldn't trust you outside the collecting box. Now, a man like Dan'l Webster, of course — well, we'd have to build a special box for him, and even at that, I imagine the wingspread would astonish you. He'd certainly be a prize. I wish we could see our way clear to him. But, in your case, as I was saying —"

"Put that handkerchief away!" said Jabez Stone, and he began to beg and to pray. But the best he could get at the end was a three years' extension, with conditions.

But till you make a bargain like that, you've got no idea of how fast four years can run. By the last months of those years, Jabez Stone's known all over the state and there's talk of running him for governor — and it's dust and ashes in his mouth. For every day, when he gets up, he thinks, "There's one more night gone," and every night when he lies down, he thinks of the black pocketbook and the soul of Miser Stevens, and it makes him sick at heart. Till, finally, he can't bear it any longer, and, in the last days of the last year, he hitches up his horse and drives off to seek Dan'l Webster. For Dan'l Webster was born in New Hampshire, only a few miles from Cross Corners, and it's well known that he has a particular soft spot for old neighbors.

It was early in the morning when he got to Marshfield, but Dan'l was up already, talking Latin to the farm hands and wrestling with the ram, Goliath, and trying out a new trotter and working up speeches to make against John C. Calhoun.[2] But when he heard a New Hampshireman had come to see him, he dropped everything else he was doing, for that was Dan'l's way. He gave Jabez Stone a breakfast that five men couldn't eat, went into the living history of every man and woman in Cross Corners, and finally asked him how he could serve him.

Jabez Stone allowed that it was a kind of mortgage case.

"Well, I haven't pleaded a mortgage case in a long time, and I don't generally plead now, except before the Supreme Court," said Dan'l, "but if I can, I'll help you."

"Then I've got hope for the first time in ten years," said Jabez Stone, and told him the details.

Dan'l walked up and down as he listened, hands behind his back, now and then asking a question, now and then plunging his eyes at the floor, as if they'd bore through it like gimlets.[3] When Jabez Stone had finished, Dan'l puffed out his cheeks and blew. Then he turned to Jabez Stone, and a smile

---

[1] The remainder of this quotation is "we are in death." It is part of the burial service in the *Book of Common Prayer*.

[2] **Calhoun:** the great orator for the South, as Webster was for the North.

[3] **gimlets:** small tools used for drilling.

broke over his face like the sunrise over Monadnock.[1]

"You've certainly given yourself the devil's own row to hoe, Neighbor Stone," he said, "but I'll take your case."

"You'll take it?" said Jabez Stone, hardly daring to believe.

"Yes," said Dan'l Webster. "I've got about seventy-five other things to do and the Missouri Compromise[2] to straighten out, but I'll take your case. For if two New Hampshiremen aren't a match for the devil, we might as well give the country back to the Indians."

Then he shook Jabez Stone by the hand and said, "Did you come down here in a hurry?"

"Well, I admit I made time," said Jabez Stone.

"You'll go back faster," said Dan'l Webster, and he told 'em to hitch up Constitution and Constellation to the carriage. They were matched grays with one white forefoot, and they stepped like greased lightning.

Well, I won't describe how excited and pleased the whole Stone family was to have the great Dan'l Webster for a guest, when they finally got there. Jabez Stone had lost his hat on the way, blown off when they overtook a wind, but he didn't take much account of that. But after supper he sent the family off to bed, for he had most particular business with Mr. Webster. Mrs. Stone wanted them to sit in the front parlor, but Dan'l Webster knew front parlors and said he preferred the kitchen. So it was there they sat, waiting for the stranger, with a jug on the table between them and a bright fire on the hearth — the stranger being scheduled to show up on the stroke of midnight, according to specification.

Well, most men wouldn't have asked for better company than Dan'l Webster and a jug. But with every tick of the clock Jabez Stone got sadder and sadder. His eyes roved round, and though he sampled the jug, you could see he couldn't taste it. Finally, on the stroke of 11:30, he reached over and grabbed Dan'l Webster by the arm.

"Mr. Webster, Mr. Webster!" he said, and his voice was shaking with fear and a desperate courage. "For God's sake, Mr. Webster, harness your horses and get away from this place while you can!"

"You've brought me a long way, neighbor, to tell me you don't like my company," said Dan'l Webster, quite peaceable, pulling at the jug.

"Miserable wretch that I am!" groaned Jabez Stone. "I've brought you a devilish way, and now I see my folly. Let him take me if he wills. I don't hanker after it, I must say, but I can stand it. But you're the Union's stay and New Hampshire's pride! He mustn't get you, Mr. Webster! He mustn't get you!"

Dan'l Webster looked at the distracted man, all gray and shaking in the firelight, and laid a hand on his shoulder.

"I'm obliged to you, Neighbor Stone," he said gently. "It's kindly thought of. But there's a jug on the table and a case in hand. And I never left a jug or a case half finished in my life."

And just at that moment there was a sharp rap on the door.

"Ah," said Dan'l Webster, very coolly, "I thought your clock was a trifle slow, Neighbor Stone." He stepped to the door and opened it. "Come in!" he said.

The stranger came in — very dark and tall he looked in the firelight. He was carrying a box under his arm — a black, japanned[3] box with little air holes in the lid. At the sight of the box, Jabez Stone gave a low cry and shrank into a corner of the room.

---

[1] **Monadnock** (mô·năd'nŏk): the highest mountain in southern New Hampshire.

[2] **Missouri Compromise:** an act passed by Congress in 1820 in an attempt to settle the dispute about slavery in the newly formed Western states.

[3] **japanned:** laquered.

"Mr. Webster, I presume," said the stranger, very polite, but with his eyes glowing like a fox's deep in the woods.

"Attorney of record for Jabez Stone," said Dan'l Webster, but his eyes were glowing too. "Might I ask your name?"

"I've gone by a good many," said the stranger carelessly. "Perhaps Scratch will do for the evening. I'm often called that in these regions."

Then he sat down at the table and poured himself a drink from the jug. The liquor was cold in the jug, but it came steaming into the glass.

"And now," said the stranger, smiling and showing his teeth, "I shall call upon you, as a law-abiding citizen, to assist me in taking possession of my property."

Well, with that the argument began — and it went hot and heavy. At first, Jabez Stone had a flicker of hope, but when he saw Dan'l Webster being forced back at point after point, he just sat scrunched in his corner, with his eyes on that japanned box. For there wasn't any doubt as to the deed or the signature — that was the worst of it. Dan'l Webster twisted and turned and thumped his fist on the table, but he couldn't get away from that. He offered to compromise the case; the stranger wouldn't hear of it. He pointed out the property had increased in value, and state senators ought to be worth more; the stranger stuck to the letter of the law. He was a great lawyer, Dan'l Webster, but we know who's the King of Lawyers, as the Good Book tells us, and it seemed as if, for the first time, Dan'l Webster had met his match.

Finally, the stranger yawned a little. "Your spirited efforts on behalf of your client do you credit, Mr. Webster," he said, "but if you have no more arguments to adduce, I'm rather pressed for time — " and Jabez Stone shuddered.

Dan'l Webster's brow looked dark as a thundercloud. "Pressed or not, you shall not have this man!" he thundered. "Mr. Stone is an American citizen, and no American citizen may be forced into the service of a foreign prince. We fought England for that in '12[1] and we'll fight all hell for it again!"

"Foreign?" said the stranger. "And who calls me a foreigner?"

"Well, I never yet heard of the dev — of your claiming American citizenship," said Dan'l Webster with surprise.

"And who with better right?" said the stranger, with one of his terrible smiles. "When the first wrong was done to the first Indian, I was there. When the first slaver put out for the Congo, I stood on her deck. Am I not in your books and stories and beliefs, from the first settlements on? Am I not spoken of, still, in every church in New England? 'Tis true the North claims me for a Southerner, and the South for a Northerner, but I am neither. I am merely an honest American like yourself — and of the best descent — for, to tell the truth, Mr. Webster, though I don't like to boast of it, my name is older in this country than yours."

"Aha!" said Dan'l Webster, with the veins standing out in his forehead. "Then I stand on the Constitution! I demand a trial for my client!"

"The case is hardly one for an ordinary court," said the stranger, his eyes flickering. "And, indeed, the lateness of the hour — "

"Let it be any court you choose, so it is an American judge and an American jury!" said Dan'l Webster in his pride. "Let it be the quick[2] or the dead; I'll abide the issue!"

"You have said it," said the stranger, and pointed his finger at the door. And with that, and all of a sudden, there was a rushing of wind outside and a noise of footsteps. They came, clear and distinct, through the night. And yet, they were not like the footsteps of living men.

[1] '12: the War of 1812 was partially caused by the impressing of Americans into the British navy.

[2] quick: living.

STEPHEN VINCENT BENÉT   67

"In God's name, who comes by so late?" cried Jabez Stone, in an ague of fear.

"The jury Mr. Webster demands," said the stranger, sipping at his boiling glass. "You must pardon the rough appearance of one or two; they will have come a long way."

And with that the fire burned blue and the door blew open and twelve men entered, one by one.

If Jabez Stone had been sick with terror before, he was blind with terror now. For there was Walter Butler, the Loyalist, who spread fire and horror through the Mohawk Valley in the times of the Revolution; and there was Simon Girty, the renegade, who saw white men burned at the stake and whooped with the Indians to see them burn. His eyes were green, like a cata-mount's, and the stains on his hunting shirt did not come from the blood of the deer. King Philip [1] was there, wild and proud as he had been in life, with the great gash in his head that gave him his death wound, and cruel Governor Dale,[2] who broke men on the wheel. There was Morton of Merry Mount, who so vexed the Plymouth Colony, with his flushed, loose, handsome face and his hate of the godly. There was Teach, the bloody pirate, with his black beard curling on his breast. The Reverend John Smeet, with his strangler's hands and his Geneva gown,[3] walked as daintily as he had to the gallows. The red print of the rope was still around his neck, but he carried a perfumed handkerchief in one hand. One and all, they came into the room with the fires of hell still upon them, and

[1] **King Philip:** an Indian chief who organized an uprising against the white settlers in 1675, and was killed the following year.

[2] **Dale:** English Deputy-Governor of Virginia, 1611–1616, whose severe laws caused the colonists to call these the "years of slavery."

[3] **Geneva gown:** minister's robe.

the stranger named their names and their deeds as they came, till the tale of twelve was told. Yet the stranger had told the truth — they had all played a part in America.

"Are you satisfied with the jury, Mr. Webster?" said the stranger mockingly, when they had taken their places.

The sweat stood upon Dan'l Webster's brow, but his voice was clear.

"Quite satisfied," he said. "Though I miss General Arnold from the company."

"Benedict Arnold is engaged upon other business," said the stranger, with a glower. "Ah, you asked for a justice, I believe."

He pointed his finger once more, and a tall man, soberly clad in Puritan garb, with the burning gaze of the fanatic, stalked into the room and took his judge's place.

"Justice Hathorne is a jurist of experience," said the stranger. "He presided at certain witch trials once held in Salem. There were others who repented of the business later, but not he."

"Repent of such notable wonders and undertakings?" said the stern old justice. "Nay, hang them — hang them all!" And he muttered to himself in a way that struck ice into the soul of Jabez Stone.

Then the trial began, and, as you might expect, it didn't look anyways good for the defense. And Jabez Stone didn't make much of a witness in his own behalf. He took one look at Simon Girty and screeched, and they had to put him back in his corner in a kind of swoon.

It didn't halt the trial, though; the trial went on, as trials do. Dan'l Webster had faced some hard juries and hanging judges in his time, but this was the hardest he'd ever faced, and he knew it. They sat there with a kind of glitter in their eyes, and the stranger's smooth voice went on and on. Every time he'd raise an objection, it'd be "Objection sustained," but whenever

Dan'l objected, it'd be "Objection denied." Well, you couldn't expect fair play from a fellow like this Mr. Scratch.

It got to Dan'l in the end, and he began to heat, like iron in the forge. When he got up to speak, he was going to flay that stranger with every trick known to the law, and the judge and jury too. He didn't care if it was contempt of court or what would happen to him for it. He didn't care any more what happened to Jabez Stone. He just got madder and madder, thinking of what he'd say. And yet, curiously enough, the more he thought about it, the less he was able to arrange his speech in his mind.

Till, finally, it was time for him to get up on his feet, and he did so, all ready to bust out with lightnings and denunciations. But before he started, he looked over the judge and jury for a moment, such being his custom. And he noticed the glitter in their eyes was twice as strong as before, and they all leaned forward. Like hounds just before they get the fox, they looked, and the blue mist of evil in the room thickened as he watched them. Then he saw what he'd been about to do, and he wiped his forehead, as a man might who's just escaped falling into a pit in the dark.

For it was him they'd come for, not only Jabez Stone. He read it in the glitter of their eyes and in the way the stranger hid his mouth with one hand. And if he fought them with their own weapons, he'd fall into their power; he knew that, though he couldn't have told you how. It was his own anger and horror that burned in their eyes; and he'd have to wipe that out or the case was lost. He stood there for a moment, his black eyes burning like anthracite. And then he began to speak.

He started off in a low voice, though you could hear every word. They say he could call on the harps of the blessed when he chose. And this was just as simple and easy as a man could talk. But he didn't start out by condemning or reviling. He was talking about the

things that make a country a country, and a man a man.

And he began with the simple things that everybody's known and felt — the freshness of a fine morning when you're young, and the taste of food when you're hungry, and the new day that's every day when you're a child. He took them up and he turned them in his hands. They were good things for any man. But without freedom, they sickened. And when he talked of those enslaved, and the sorrows of slavery, his voice got like a big bell. He talked of the early days of America and the men who had made those days. It wasn't a spread-eagle speech, but he made you see it. He admitted all the wrong that had ever been done. But he showed how, out of the wrong and the right, the suffering and the starvations, something new had come. And everybody had played a part in it, even the traitors.

Then he turned to Jabez Stone and showed him as he was — an ordinary man who'd had hard luck and wanted to change it. And, because he'd wanted to change it, now he was going to be punished for all eternity. And yet there was good in Jabez Stone, and he showed that good. He was hard and mean, in some ways, but he was a man. There was sadness in being a man, but it was a proud thing too. And he showed what the pride of it was till you couldn't help feeling it. Yes, even in hell, if a man was a man, you'd know it. And he wasn't pleading for any one person any more, though his voice rang like an organ. He was telling the story and the failures and the endless journey of mankind. They got tricked and trapped and bamboozled, but it was a great journey. And no demon that was ever foaled could know the inwardness of it — it took a man to do that.

The fire began to die on the hearth and the wind before morning to blow. The light was getting gray in the room when Dan'l Webster finished. And his words came back at the end to New Hampshire ground, and the one spot of land that each man loves and clings to. He painted a picture of that, and to each one of that jury he spoke of things long forgotten. For his voice could search the heart, and that was his gift and his strength. And to one, his voice was like the forest and its secrecy, and to another like the sea and the storms of the sea; and one heard the cry of his lost nation in it, and another saw a little harmless scene he hadn't remembered for years. But each saw something. And when Dan'l Webster finished, he didn't know whether or not he'd saved Jabez Stone. But he knew he'd done a miracle. For the glitter was gone from the eyes of judge and jury, and, for the moment, they were men again, and knew they were men.

"The defense rests," said Dan'l Webster, and stood there like a mountain. His ears were still ringing with his speech, and he didn't hear anything else till he heard Judge Hathorne say, "The jury will retire to consider its verdict."

Walter Butler rose in his place and his face had a dark, gay pride on it.

"The jury has considered its verdict," he said, and looked the stranger full in the eye. "We find for the defendant, Jabez Stone."

With that, the smile left the stranger's face, but Walter Butler did not flinch.

"Perhaps 'tis not strictly in accordance with the evidence," he said, "but even the damned may salute the eloquence of Mr. Webster."

With that, the long crow of a rooster split the gray morning sky, and judge and jury were gone from the room like a puff of smoke and as if they had never been there. The stranger turned to Dan'l Webster, smiling wryly. "Major Butler was always a bold man," he said. "I had not thought him quite so bold. Nevertheless, my congratulations, as between two gentlemen."

"I'll have that paper first, if you please," said Dan'l Webster, and he took it and tore it into four pieces. It was queerly warm to the touch. "And now," he said, "I'll have you!" and his hand came down like a bear trap on the stranger's arm. For he knew that once you bested anybody like Mr. Scratch in fair fight, his power on you was gone. And he could see that Mr. Scratch knew it too.

The stranger twisted and wriggled, but he couldn't get out of that grip. "Come, come, Mr. Webster," he said, smiling palely. "This sort of thing is ridic — ouch! — is ridiculous. If you're worried about the costs of the case, naturally, I'd be glad to pay — "

"And so you shall!" said Dan'l Webster, shaking him till his teeth rattled. "For you'll sit right down at that table and draw up a document, promising never to bother Jabez Stone nor his heirs or assigns [1] nor any other New Hampshireman till doomsday! For any hades we want to raise in this state, we

---

[1] assigns: persons who inherit money or property.

can raise ourselves, without assistance from strangers."

"Ouch!" said the stranger. "Ouch! Well, they never did run very big to the barrel, but — ouch! — I agree!"

So he sat down and drew up the document. But Dan'l Webster kept his hand on his coat collar all the time.

"And, now, may I go?" said the stranger, quite humble, when Dan'l'd seen the document was in proper and legal form.

"Go?" said Dan'l, giving him another shake. "I'm still trying to figure out what I'll do with you. For you've settled the costs of the case, but you haven't settled with me. I think I'll take you back to Marshfield," he said, kind of reflective. "I've got a ram there named Goliath that can butt through an iron door. I'd kind of like to turn you loose in his field and see what he'd do."

Well, with that the stranger began to beg and to plead. And he begged and he pled so humble that finally Dan'l, who was naturally kindhearted, agreed to let him go. The stranger seemed terrible grateful for that and said, just to show they were friends, he'd tell Dan'l's fortune before leaving. So Dan'l agreed to that, though he didn't take much stock in fortunetellers ordinarily.

But, naturally, the stranger was a little different. Well, he pried and he peered at the lines in Dan'l's hands. And he told him one thing and another that was quite remarkable. But they were all in the past.

"Yes, all that's true, and it happened," said Dan'l Webster. "But what's to come in the future?"

The stranger grinned, kind of happily, and shook his head. "The future's not as you think it," he said. "It's dark. You have a great ambition, Mr. Webster."

"I have," said Dan'l firmly, for everybody knew he wanted to be President.

"It seems almost within your grasp," said the stranger, "but you will not attain it. Lesser men will be made President and you will be passed over."

"And, if I am, I'll still be Daniel Webster," said Dan'l. "Say on."

"You have two strong sons," said the stranger, shaking his head. "You look to found a line. But each will die in war and neither reach greatness."

"Live or die, they are still my sons," said Dan'l Webster. "Say on."

"You have made great speeches," said the stranger. "You will make more."

"Ah," said Dan'l Webster.

"But the last great speech you make will turn many of your own against you," said the stranger. "They will call you Ichabod; [1] they will call you by other names. Even in New England some will say you have turned your coat and sold your country, and their voices will be loud against you till you die."

"So it is an honest speech, it does not matter what men say," said Dan'l Webster. Then he looked at the stranger and their glances locked.

"One question," he said. "I have fought for the Union all my life. Will I see that fight won against those who would tear it apart?"

"Not while you live," said the stranger, grimly, "but it will be won. And after you are dead, there are thousands who will fight for your cause, because of words that you spoke."

"Why, then, you long-barreled, slab-sided, lantern-jawed, fortunetelling note-shaver!" said Dan'l Webster, with a great roar of laughter, "be off with you to your own place before I put my mark on you! For, by the thirteen original colonies I'd go to the Pit itself to save the Union!"

And with that he drew back his foot

[1] Ichabod (ik'a̸·bŏd): the title of Whittier's poem criticizing Webster's speech of March 7, 1850. Webster had denounced the Abolitionists. Because of his speech many Northerners considered Webster a traitor. Ichabod is a Hebrew name meaning "where is the glory?" or "the glory is departed."

for a kick that would have stunned a horse. It was only the tip of his shoe that caught the stranger, but he went flying out of the door with his collecting box under his arm.

"And now," said Dan'l Webster, seeing Jabez Stone beginning to rouse from his swoon, "let's see what's left in the jug, for it's dry work talking all night. I hope there's pie for breakfast, Neighbor Stone."

But they say that whenever the devil comes near Marshfield, even now, he gives it a wide berth. And he hasn't been seen in the state of New Hampshire from that day to this. I'm not talking about Massachusetts or Vermont.

FOR DISCUSSION

1. How does the first description of Webster prepare you for fantastic events later in the story? How does the author's style give a folklore tone to the story?
2. Summarize the troubles that provoked Jabez Stone's threat to sell his soul to the devil. Why did he hope for a while that nothing would come of his remark? Why wouldn't he take it back?
3. Describe the stranger who came to close the deal. What details confirmed Stone's suspicion as to his identity?
4. How was Stone's life affected by his secret compact with the stranger? What means did he use to try to dodge the compact? Why did he fail? What happening filled him with terror? Why did Webster agree to take his case?
5. On what grounds did the stranger claim American citizenship? What criticism of some American policies of the past is implied? Is it justified? What facts made the case go against Webster at first?
6. How is suspense increased by the entrance of the jury? Why was the judge particularly well chosen for the stranger's side of the case? What indicates that the court procedure was unfair?
7. What made Webster change the tone of his final speech? Why was it a masterpiece of appeal to such a jury?

THE TONE OF THE STORY

Much of the total effect of this tale stems from the author's tone. How would you describe that tone? Would you call it serious or humorous? Perhaps you can think of a better description. How soon were you able to identify the tone?

BUILDING YOUR VOCABULARY

Patriarchs (page 62) is made up of two word parts that you will meet over and over again. The first comes from the Latin and Greek words for "father," and *arch* means leader or chief, therefore ruler. We find this form also in *–archy* at the end of words. What sort of rule is a *monarchy?* The patriarchs referred to are the old Biblical chiefs. What would a *matriarch* be? Your *patrimony* is your inheritance from whom? Which ranks higher, a bishop or an *archbishop?*

THE DEVIL AND THE ARTS

Selling one's soul to the devil is a familiar theme not only in literature but in drama, opera, and ballet. Since the puppet shows of the sixteenth century, the devil has appeared under various names; for example, as Mephistopheles in Marlowe's play *The Tragicall History of Dr. Faustus* (1588?) and in the German poet Goethe's drama *Faust* (1831). Gounod's opera *Faust* (1859) is still widely performed.

Washington Irving was the first American to use the idea of bargaining with the devil in the short story "The Devil and Tom Walker" (page 495).

The Visual Arts ➤

The devil has also been the subject of some excellent pictorial art. At the top of the facing page is a reproduction of "The Flight of Tom Walker," an oil painting by the American artist John Quidor (1801–1881). At the lower right is an engraving of Faust and Mephistopheles by the French artist Ferdinand Delacroix (1799–1863). The illustration at the lower left is from an edition of John Bunyan's book *The Life and Death of Mr. Badman.* The engraving is by the nineteenth-century English artist Louis Rhead.

STEPHEN VINCENT BENÉT (1898–1943), son of an army officer, was born in Pennsylvania and later lived in Georgia and California. He began writing in his youth; he had published one volume of verse before he entered Yale and another before his graduation. For the next few years he supported himself by writing novels and short stories. While studying at the Sorbonne in Paris, he met and married Rosemary Carr, an American journalist, with whom he shared the authorship of *A Book of Americans*. Benét's five novels are overshadowed by the success of his short stories. "The Devil and Daniel Webster" quickly became a classic and has been made into a motion picture, a one-act play, and an opera. He was one of our best-known poets. His masterpiece is the book-length narrative poem *John Brown's Body*, which won the Pulitzer prize in 1929.

WALLACE STEGNER

The Wolfer

Grimness — in man, beast, and the elements — is the primary quality of this story. It is a powerful picture of a brutal country and of a man brutalized by it. We never see that man directly — we only hear about him — yet he and his terrible dog are vivid to us. The story is not pretty, not pleasant in the ordinary sense. It is written for the sake of stark power in painting a bleak landscape and a bleak life.

Yes, I saw a good deal of it, and I knew them all. It was my business to, and in those days it wasn't hard to know nearly every man between Willow Bunch and Fort Walsh, even the drifters; the women you could count on your two thumbs. One was Molly Henry at the T-Down Bar, the other was Amy Schulz, living up on Oxarart Creek. I knew Schulz, too, and his miserable boy. At least I had seen him a good many times, and stopped with him a half-dozen times at one or another shack when I was out on patrol, and at least that many times had come within an ace of being eaten by his hound. Probably I knew him better than most people did, actually. Friends — that's another matter. He was about as easy to be friendly with as a wolverine.

Summers, he camped around in the Cypress Hills, hunting, but in winter he used the shacks that the cattle outfits maintained out along the Whitemud, on the patrol trail between the Hills and Wood Mountain. Two of them, at Stonepile and Pinto Horse Butte, were abandoned Mounted Police patrol posts

"The Wolfer" by Wallace Stegner. Originally in the October, 1959 issue of *Harper's* Magazine. © 1959 by Wallace Stegner. Reprinted by permission of Brandt & Brandt.

— abandoned in the sense that no constables were stationed there, though we kept the barracks stocked with emergency supplies and always cut and stacked a few tons of prairie wool [1] there in the fall. Both Schulz and I used the barracks now and then, for he as a wolfer and I as a Mountie covered pretty much the same territory. If the truth were known, I kept pretty close tab on him in my patrol book, because I was never entirely sure, after Amy left him, that he wouldn't go back up on Oxarart Creek and shoot her.

Probably I wronged him. I think he was glad to get rid of Amy; it freed him to be as wild as the wolves he hunted, with his snuffling, adenoidal boy for a slave and daily killing for occupation and his staghound for friend and confidant. They were a pair: each was the only living thing that liked the other, I guess, and it was a question which had the edge in savagery. Yet love, too, of a kind. I have heard him croon and mutter to that thing, baby-talk, in a way to give you the creeps.

Whenever I found Schulz at Stonepile or Pinto Horse, I picked an upper bunk; if the hound got drooling for my blood in the night, I wanted to be where he'd at least have to climb to get at me. There was no making up to him — he was Schulz's, body and soul. He looked at every other human being with yellow eyes as steady as a snake's, the hackles lifting between his shoulders and a rumble going away down in his chest. I'd hear him moving in the dark shack, soft and heavy, with his nails clicking on the boards. He wore a fighting collar studded with brass spikes, he stood as high as a doorknob at the shoulder, and he weighed a hundred and forty pounds. Schulz bragged that he had killed wolves single-handed. The rest of the pack, Russian wolfhounds and Russian-greyhound crosses, slept in the sta-

ble and were just dogs, but this staghound thing, which Schulz called Puma, was the physical shape of his own savagery: hostile, suspicious, deadly, unwinking. I have seen him stand with a foolish, passive smile on his face while that monster put his paws up on his shoulders and lapped mouth and chin and eyes with a tongue the size of a coal shovel.

He was a savage, a wild man. He hated civilization — which meant maybe two hundred cowpunchers and Mounties scattered over ten thousand square miles of prairie — but it was not civilization that did him in. It was the wild, the very savagery he trusted and thought he controlled. I know about that too, because I followed the last tracks he and his hound made in this country.

My patrol books would show the date. As I remember, it was toward the end of March 1907. The patrol was routine — Eastend, Bates Camp, Stonepile, the Warholes, Pinto Horse Butte, Wood Mountain, and return — but nothing else was routine that winter. With a month still to go, it was already a disaster.

Since November there had been nothing but blizzards, freezing fogs, and cold snaps down to forty below. One chinook [2] — and that lasted only long enough to melt everything to mush, whereupon another cold snap came on and locked the country in a four-inch shell of ice. A lot of cattle that lay down that night never got up: froze in and starved there.

That time, just about Christmas, I passed the Warholes on a patrol and found a *métis* [3] named Big Antoine and twenty of his Indian relatives trapped and half-starved. They had made a run for it from Wood Mountain toward Big Stick Lake when the chinook blew up,

---

[1] **prairie wool:** probably white sage, useful as forage for animals.

[2] **chinook** (shǐ·no͞ok′): a warm, moist wind.

[3] *métis* (mā′tēs′): a half-breed.

and got caught out. When I found them, they hadn't eaten anything in two weeks except skin-and-bone beef that had died in the snow; they were seasoning it with fat from coyotes, the only thing besides the wolves that throve.

A police freighter got them out before I came back on my next trip. But the cowpunchers out in the range shacks were by that time just about as bad off. For weeks they had been out every day roping steers frozen into the drifts, and dragging them free; or they had been floundering around chasing cattle out of the deep snow of the bottoms and out onto the benches where the wind kept a little feed bare. They had got them up there several times, but they hadn't kept them there. The wind came across those flats loaded with buckshot, and the cattle turned their tails to it and came right back down to starve. At one point the two Turkey Track boys stationed at Pinto Horse had even tried to make a drag of poles, and drag bare a patch of hillside for the cattle to feed on. All they did was kill off their ponies. When I came by in March, they had given up and were conducting a nonstop blackjack game in the barracks, and laying bets whether the winter would last till August or whether it would go right on through and start over.

We had a little poker game that night. Whenever the talk died, we could hear, through the logs and sod of the shack, the heavy hunting song of wolves drawn down from the hills for the big barbecue. It was a gloomy thing to hear. Say what you want about cowpunchers, they don't like failing at a job any better than other people. And they were sure failing. In November there had been close to 70,000 head of cattle on that Whitemud range. At a conservative guess, half of them were dead already. If we didn't get a chinook in the next week, there wouldn't be a cow alive come spring.

I quit the game early to get some sleep, and for a joke pushed the deck over toward Curly Withers for a cut. "Cut a chinook," I said. He turned over the jack of diamonds. Then we went to the door for a look-see, and everything was wooled up in freezing fog, what nowadays they call a whiteout. You could have cut sheep out of the air with tin shears. "Some chinook," Curly said.

In the morning there was still no wind, but the air was clear. As I turned Dude down the trail and looked back to wave at the Turkey Track boys, I had the feeling they were only six inches high, like carved figures in a German toy scene. The shack was braced from eaves to ground with icicles; the sky behind the quiver of heat from the stovepipe jiggled like melting glass. Away down in the southeast, low and heatless, the sun was only a small painted dazzle.

It seemed mean and cowardly to leave those boys out there. Or maybe it was just that I hated to start another day of hard, cold riding through all that death, with nobody to talk to. You can feel mighty small and lonesome riding through that country in winter, after a light snowfall that muffles noises. I was leading a packhorse, and ordinarily there is a good deal of jingle and creak and sound of company with two ponies, but that morning it didn't seem my noises carried ten feet.

Down in the river trough everything was still and white. Mainly the channel had a fur of frozen snow on it, but here and there were patches of black slick ice full of air bubbles like quarters and silver dollars. Depending on how the bends swung, drifts sloped up to the cutbanks or up to bars overgrown with snow-smothered rose bushes and willows. I crossed the tracks of three wolves angling upriver, side by side and bunched in clusters of four: galloping. They must have been running just for the heck of it, or else they had sighted an antelope or deer. They didn't have to gallop to eat beef.

Without wind, it wasn't bad riding, though when I breathed through my mouth, the aching of my teeth reminded me that under the Christmas frosting the world was made of ice and iron. Now a dead steer among the rose bushes, untouched by wolves or coyotes. I cut a notch in a tally stick, curious about how many I would pass between Pinto Horse and Eastend. Farther on, a bunch of whitefaces lying and standing so close together they had breathed frost all over one another. If they hadn't been such skeletons, they would have looked like farmyard beasts in a crèche.[1] They weren't trapped or frozen in, but they were making no move to get out — only bawled at me hopelessly as I passed. Two were dead and half drifted over. I cut two more notches.

In three hours I cut a good many more, one of them at a big wallow and scramble near the mouth of Snake Creek, where wolves had pulled down a steer since the last snowfall. The blood frozen into the snow was bright as paint, as if it had been spilled only minutes before. Parts of the carcass had been dragged in every direction.

Those wolves rubbed it in, pulling down a beef within a half mile of where Schulz and his boy were camped at Stonepile. I wondered if he had had any luck yet — he hadn't had any at all last time I saw him — and I debated whether to stop with him or go on to Bates and heat up a cold shack. The decision was for Bates. It was no big blowout to spend a night with the Schulzes, who were a long way from being the company the T-Down and Turkey Track boys were, and who besides were dirtier than Indians. Also I thought I would sleep better at Bates than I would at Stonepile, in an upper bunk with my hand on a gun while that hound prowled around in the dark

[1] crèche (krĕsh): a representation of the manger at Bethlehem.

and rumbled every time I rolled over. Sure Schulz had it trained, but all he had hold of it with was his voice; I would have liked a chain better.

Just to make a check on Stonepile for the patrol book, I turned up Snake Creek, and a little after noon I came up the pitch from the bottoms and surprised the Schulz boy standing bare-armed before the barracks door with a dishpan hanging from his hand. The dishpan steamed, his arm steamed, the sunken snow where he had flung the dishwater steamed. I was quite pleased with him, just then; I hadn't known he and his old man ever washed their dishes. He stood looking at me with his sullen, droop-lipped, watchful face. Down in the stable the wolfhounds began to bark and whine and howl. I saw nothing of Schulz or the big hound.

"Howdy, Bud," I said. "How's tricks?"

He was sure no chocolate-box picture. His gray flannel shirt was shiny with grease, his face was pimply, long black hair hung from under the muskrat cap that I had never seen off his head. I think he slept in it, and I'll guarantee it was crawling. He never could meet a man's eyes. He said, looking past me, "Hello, constable."

I creaked down. Dude pushed me from behind, rubbing the icicles off his nose. "Pa not around?" I said.

Something flickered in his eyes, a wet gray gleam. One eye-socket and temple, I saw, were puffy and discolored — about a three-day-old black eye. He touched one cracked red wrist to his chapped mouth and burst out, "Pa went out yesterday and ain't come back!" His eyes hunted mine and ducked away instantly. "And Puma got out!" he said — wailed, almost.

At that moment I wouldn't have trusted him a rope length out of my sight. He looked sneakily guilty; he had that black eye which could only be a souvenir from Daddy; he had fifteen years of good reasons for hating his old man. If Schulz and his hound were really missing, I had the conviction that I would find them dry-gulched and stuffed through the ice somewhere. Not that I could have blamed young Schulz too much. In the best seasons his old man must have been a bearcat to live with. In this one, when he had hunted and trapped all winter and never got a single wolf, he was a crazy man. The wolves walked around his traps laughing — they fed much too well to be tempted. They sat just out of rifle shot and watched him waste ammunition. And though he had the best pack of dogs in that country, he hadn't been able to run them for months because of the weather and the deep snow. Out on the flats the dogs could have run, but there were no wolves there; they were all down in the bottoms hobnobbing with the cattle. The last time I had passed through, Schulz had talked to me half the night like a man half crazed with rage: red-faced, jerky-voiced, glassy-eyed. To make his troubles worse, he had headaches, he said; "bunches" on his head. A horse had fallen on him once.

So in a winter of complete hard luck, who made a better whipping boy than that sullen son of his? And who more likely, nursing his black eye and his grievance, to lie behind the cabin or stable and pot his father as he came up the trail?

It was a fine theory. Pity it wasn't sound. I told young Schulz to hold it while I turned the horses into the police haystack, and while I was down there, I got a look around the stable and corrals. No bodies, no blood, no signs of a fight. Then up in the barracks, in the hot, close, tallowy-mousy room with muskrat and marten pelts on bows of red willow hanging from the ceiling and coyote and lynx hides tacked on the wall, and three spirals of last-year's flypaper, black with last year's flies, moving in the hot air above the stove, I began asking him questions and undid all my nice imaginary murder.

I even began to doubt that anything would turn out to be wrong with Schulz or his hound, for it became clear at once that if Schulz was in trouble, he was in trouble through some accident, and I didn't believe that the Schulzes had accidents. They might get killed, but they didn't have accidents. It was about as likely that he would freeze, or get lost, or fall through a rapid, or hurt himself with a gun, as it was that a wolf would slip and sprain his ankle. And if you bring up those bunches on his head, and the horse that he said fell on him, I'll bet you one thing. I'll bet you the horse got hurt worse than Schulz did.

Still, he was missing, and in that country and that weather it could be serious. He had left the barracks the morning before, on foot but carrying snowshoes, to check on some carcasses he had poisoned down by Bates Camp. Usually he didn't use poison because of the dogs. Now he would have baited traps with his mother, or staked out his snuffling boy, if he could have got wolves that way. He shut the wolfhounds in the stable and the staghound in the barracks and told the boy to keep them locked up. The staghound especially had to be watched. He was used to going everywhere with Schulz, and he might follow him if he were let out.

That was exactly what he did do. Young Schulz kept him in the barracks — it would have been like being caged with a lion — until nearly dark, when he went down to the stable to throw some frozen beef to the other dogs. He slid out and slammed the door ahead of the staghound's rush. But when he came back, he wasn't so lucky. The dog was waiting with his nose to the crack, and when it opened, he threw his hundred and forty pounds against the door and was gone. No one but Schulz would have blamed the boy — ever try to stop a bronc from coming through a corral gate, when you're there on foot and he's scared and ringy and wants to come?

You get out of the way or you get trom-pled. That hound would have trompled you the same way. But Schulz wouldn't think of that. The boy was scared sick of what his father would do to him if and when he came back.

I thought that since the hound had *not* come back, he obviously must have found Schulz. If he had found him alive and unhurt, they would be back togeth-er before long. If he had found him hurt, he would stay with him, and with any luck I could find them simply by following their tracks. I asked the boy if he was afraid to stay alone two or three days, if necessary. He wasn't — it was exactly the opposite he was scared of. Also I told him to stay put, and not get in a panic and take off across a hun-dred miles of open country for Malta or somewhere; I would see to it that his old man laid off the horsewhip. Some-body — his old man, or me, or some-body — would be back within three days at the latest.

He stood in the doorway with his arms still bare, a tough kid actually, a sort of wild animal himself, though of an unattractive kind, and watched me with those wet little gleaming eyes as I rode off down Snake Creek.

I couldn't have had better trailing. The light snow two nights before had put a nice firm rippled coating over ev-ery old track. When I hit the river, the channel was perfectly clean except for Schulz's moccasin tracks, and braided in among them the tracks of the hound. A wolf makes a big track, especially with his front feet — I've seen them nearly six inches each way — but that staghound had feet the size of a plate, and he was so heavy that in deep snow, even a packed drift, he sank way down. So there they went, the companionable tracks of a man and his dog out hunt-ing. If I hadn't known otherwise, I would have assumed that they had gone upriver together, instead of six hours apart.

The day had got almost warm. Under the north bank the sun had thawed an occasional rooty dark spot. I kneed Dude into a shuffle; the packhorse dragged hard and then came along. I could have followed that trail at a lope.

It led me four miles up the river's me-anders before I even had to slow down, though I cut four more notches in the tally stick and saw two thin does and a buck flounder away from the ford be-low Sucker Creek, and took a snapshot with the carbine at a coyote, fatter than I ever saw a coyote, that stood watch-ing me from a cutbank. My bullet kicked snow at the cutbank's lip, and he was gone like smoke. Then a mile above Sucker Creek I found where Schulz had put on his snowshoes and cut across the neck of a bend. The hound had wallowed after him, leaving a trail like a horse.

The drifts were hard-crusted under the powder, but not hard-crusted enough, and the horses were in to their bellies half the time. They stood heav-ing while I got off to look at a little tentlike shelter with fresh snow shov-eled over it. The hound had messed things up some, sniffing around, but he had not disturbed the set. Looking in, I found a marten in a No. 2 coyote trap, caught around the neck and one front leg. He wasn't warm, but he wasn't quite frozen either. I stuffed marten and trap into a saddlebag and went on.

The trail led out of the river valley and up a side coulee,[1] where among thin red willows a spring came warm enough from the ground to stay unfro-zen for several feet. The wolfer had made another marten set there, and then had mushed up onto the bench and northwest to a slough[2] where tules[3] whiskered up through the ice

---

[1] **coulee:** a small valley.
[2] **slough** (sloo): a swampy creek.
[3] **tules** (too′lēz): large bulrushes.

and a half-dozen very high muskrat houses rose out of the clear ice farther out.

At the edge of the slough, I got off and followed where man and hound had gone out on the ice. Where the ice was clear, I could see the paths the rats make along the bottom. For some reason this slough wasn't frozen nearly as deep as the river, maybe because there were springs or because of organic matter rotting in the water. The Royal Society [1] will have to settle that sometime. All I settled was that Schulz had chopped through the ice in two places and set coyote traps in the paths, and had broken through the tops of three houses to make sets inside. He had a rat in one of the house sets. Since I seemed to be running his trapline for him, I put it in the other saddlebag.

Nothing, surely, had happened to Schulz up to here. The hound had been at every set, sniffing out the trail. That would have been pretty late, well after dark, when the fog had already shut off the half moon. It occurred to me as I got back on Dude and felt the icy saddle under my pants again that I would not have liked to be out there on that bare plain to see a wild animal like that hound go by in the mist, with his

[1] **Royal Society:** an English society which conducts scientific investigations.

nose to his master's track.

From the slough the trail cut back to the river; in fifteen minutes I looked down onto the snowed-over cabin and buried corrals of Bates Camp. There had been nobody stationed in it since the T-Down fed its last hay almost two months before. No smoke from the stovepipe, no sign of life. My hope that I would find the wolfer holed up there, so that I could get out of the saddle and brew a pot of tea and eat fifty pounds or so of supper, went glimmering. Something had drawn him away from here. He would have reached Bates about the same time of day I reached it — between two and three in the afternoon — for though he was a tremendous walker, he could not have covered eight miles, some of it on snowshoes, and set seven traps, in less than about four hours. I had then been on his trail more than two hours and pushing it hard.

I found that he hadn't gone near the shack at all, but had turned down toward the corrals, buried so deep that only the top pole showed. Wading along leading the horses, I followed the web tracks to the carcass of a yearling shorthorn half dug out of the snow.

There were confusing tracks all around — snowshoes, dog, wolf. The shorthorn had died with his tongue out, and a wolf had torn it from his head. The carcass was chewed up some, but not scattered. Schulz had circled it about six feet away, and at one place deep web tracks showed where he had squatted down close. I stood in the tracks and squatted too, and in front of me, half obscured by the dog's prints, I saw where something had rolled in the snow. Snagged in the crust was a long gray-black hair.

A wolf, then. This was one of the poisoned carcasses, and a wolf that rolled might be sick. Squatting in the quenched afternoon, Schulz would have come to his feet with a fierce grunt, darting his eyes around the deceptive shapes of snow and dusk, and he would not have waited a second to track the wolf to his dying place. The coyotes he ran or shot, and the marten and muskrat he trapped when nothing better offered, were nothing to him; it was wolves that made his wild blood go, and they had cheated him all winter.

For just a minute I let myself yearn for the cabin and a fire and a hot meal. But I still had an hour and a half of light good enough for trailing — about what Schulz himself had had — and after that maybe another half hour of deceptive shadows, ghostly moonlight, phosphorescent snow, and gathering mist and dark. If he had got hurt somehow chasing the wolf, he might have survived one night; he couldn't possibly survive two. So I paused only long enough to put the packhorse in the stable and give him a bait of oats, and to light a fire to take a little of the chill out of the icy shack. Then I set the damper and took out on the trail again.

It was like a pursuit game played too long and complicated too far, to the point of the ridiculous — like one of these cartoons of a big fish swallowing a smaller fish swallowing a smaller fish swallowing a small fish. There went the sick wolf running from the heat of the strychnine in his own guts, and after him the wolfer, implacable in the blue-white cold, and after him the great hound running silently, hours behind but gaining, loping hard down the river ice or sniffing out the first marten set. There went wildness pursued by hate pursued by love, and after the lot of them me, everybody's rescuer, everybody's nursemaid, the law on a tired horse.

Schulz never did catch up with that wolf. Probably it had never been sick at all, but had rolled in the snow in sassy contempt. Up on the bench its tracks broke into the staggered pairs that showed it was trotting, and after a half mile or so another set of wolf tracks came in from the west, and the two went off together in the one-two-one of an easy lope.

Schulz quit, either because he saw it was hopeless or because the light gave out on him. I could imagine his state of mind. Just possibly, too, he had begun to worry. With darkness and fog and the night cold coming on, that open flat, bare of even a scrap of sagebrush, was no place to be. In an hour the freak windlessness could give way to a blizzard; a wind right straight off the North Pole, and temperatures to match, could light on him with hardly a warning, and then even a Schulz could be in trouble.

Above me, as I studied his tracks where he broke off the chase, a chip of moon was pale and blurry against a greenish sky; the sun over the Cypress Hills was low and strengthless. It would go out before it went down. And I was puzzled by Schulz. He must have been lost; he must have looked up from his furious pursuit and his furious reading of failure, and seen only misty dusk, without landmarks, moon, stars, anything, for instead of heading back for the river and the cabin, he started straight eastward across the plain. So did I, because I had to.

It took him about a mile to realize his mistake, and it was easy to read his mind from his footprints, for there out in the middle of the empty snowflats, they milled around a little and made an eloquent right angle toward the south. Probably he had felt out his direction from the drifts, which ran like shallow sea waves toward the southeast. I turned after him thankfully. But he hadn't gone back to Bates, and he hadn't gone back downriver to Stonepile. So where *had* he gone? I worked the cold out of my stiff cheeks, and flapped my arms to warm my hands, and kicked old Dude into a tired trot across the packed flats.

In twenty minutes I was plowing down into the river valley again. The sun was blurring out, the bottoms were full of shadows the color of a gun barrel, the snow was scratched with black willows. I judged that I was not more than a mile upriver from Bates. The plowing web tracks and the wallowing trail of the hound went ahead of me through deep drifts and across the bar onto the river ice, and coming after them I saw under the opposite cutbank the black of a dead fire.

I stopped. There was no sign of life, though the snow, I could see, was much tracked. I shouted: "Schulz?" and the sound went out in that white desolation like a match dropped in the snow. This looked like the end of the trail, and because it began to look serious, and I didn't want to track things up until I got a chance to study them, I tied the horse in the willows and circled to come into the bend from below. When I parted the rose bushes to slide down onto the ice, I looked straight down on the body of Schulz's hound.

Dead, he looked absolutely enormous. He lay on his side with his spiked collar up around his ears. I saw that he had been dragged by it from the direction of the fire. He had bled a great deal from the mouth, and had been bleeding as he was dragged, for the snow along the drag mark had a filigree of red. On the back of his head, almost at his neck, was a frozen bloody patch. And along the trough where the body had been dragged came a line of tracks, the unmistakable tracks of Schulz's moccasins. Another set went back. That was all. It was as clear as printing on a page. Schulz had dragged the dead dog to the edge of the bank, under the overhanging bushes, and left him there, and not come back.

I tell you, I was spooked. My hair stood on end, I believe, and I know I looked quickly all around, in a fright that I might be under somebody's eyes or gun. On the frozen river there was not a sound. As I slid down beside the

hound, I looked both ways in the channel, half expecting to see Schulz's body too, or somebody else's. Nothing. Clean snow.

The hound's body was frozen rock-hard. His mouth was full of frozen blood, and the crusted patch on the back of his neck turned out to be a bullet hole, a big one. He had been shot in the mouth, apparently by a soft-nosed bullet that had torn the back of his head off. And no tracks, there or anywhere, except those of Schulz himself. I knew that Schulz never used any gun but a .22, in which he shot long rifle cartridges notched so they would mushroom and tear a big internal hole and stop without making a second puncture in the hide. If he had shot the hound — and that was totally incredible, but who else could have? — a .22 bullet like that would not have gone clear through brain and skull and blown a big hole out the other side unless it had been fired at close range, so close that even in fog or half-dark the wolfer must have known what he was shooting at.

But I refused to believe what my eyes told me must be true. I could conceive of Schulz shooting his son, and I had already that day suspected his son of shooting *him*. But I could not believe that he would ever, unless by accident, shoot that dog. Since it didn't seem he could have shot it accidentally, someone else must have shot it.

It took me ten minutes to prove to myself that there were no tracks around there except the wolfer's. I found those, in fact, leading on upriver, and since I had looked at every footprint he made from Stonepile on, I knew these must be the ones he made going out. Instead of going home, he went on. Why?

Under the cutbank, in front of the fire, I found a hard path beaten in the snow where Schulz had walked up and down many times. The fire itself had never been large, but it had burned a long time; the coals were sunk deeply into the snow and frozen in their own melt. Schulz had evidently stayed many hours, perhaps all night, keeping the little fire going and walking up and down to keep from freezing. But why hadn't he walked a mile downriver and slept warm at Bates?

I might have followed to try to find out, but the light was beginning to go, and I was too cold and tired to think of riding any more of that crooked river that night. Still, just thinking about it gave me an idea. In any mile, the Whitemud ran toward every point of the compass, swinging and returning on itself. If Schulz had hit it after the fog closed in thick, he would have known that Bates lay downriver, but how would he know which way was downriver? There were no rapids in that stretch. There would have been no landmarks but bends and bars endlessly repeating, changing places, now on the right and now on the left. Some of the bends were bowknots that completely reversed their direction.

That might answer one question, but only one. I put myself in the path he had made, and walked up and down trying to see everything just as he had. I found the mark where he had stuck his rifle butt-down in the snow, probably to leave his arms free for swinging against the cold. There were hound tracks on the path and alongside it, as if the dog had walked up and down with him. At two places it had lain down in the snow off to the side.

That answered another question, or corroborated what I had guessed before: Schulz couldn't have shot the hound not knowing what it was; it had been there with him for some time.

Standing by the fire, I looked back at the deep tracks where Schulz, and after him the hound, had broken down off the bar onto the ice. The hound's tracks led directly to the fire and the path. I walked the path again, searching every foot of it. I found only one thing more: just where the path went along a streak

of clear ice, where ice and snow joined in a thin crust, there were the deep parallel gouges of claws, two sets of them, close together. Would a heavy hound, rearing to put its front paws on a man's shoulders and its happy tongue in a man's face, dig that way, deeply, with its hind claws? I thought it would.

I stood at the spot where I thought Schulz and the hound might have met, and again studied the tracks and the places where the hound had lain down. In front of one of them was a light scoop, just the rippled surface taken off the new snow. Made by a tongue lapping? Maybe. By pure intensity of imagining, I tried to reconstruct what might have happened. Suppose it went this way:

Suppose he fumbled down to the river with the visibility no more than fifty or a hundred feet, and could not tell which way it ran. The fact that he had lost himself up on the bench made that not merely possible, but probable. A fire, then, until daylight let him see. Willows yielded a little thin fuel, the tiny heat along leg or backside or on the turned stiff hands made the night bearable. But caution would have told anyone as experienced as Schulz that the night was long and fuel short — and at Pinto Horse the night before, the thermometer had stood at fifteen below. He would have had to keep moving, the rifle stuck in a drift and his arms flailing and the felt cap he wore pulled down to expose only his eyes and mouth — a figure as savage and forlorn as something caught out of its cave at the race's dim beginning.

The sound of hunting wolves would have kept him company as it had kept us company in our social poker game, and it would have been a sound that for many reasons he liked less than we did. Except for that dark monotone howling, there would have been no sound in the shrouded bend except the creak of his moccasins and the hiss of the fire threatening always to melt itself out — no other sound unless maybe the grating of anger in his own aching head, an anger lonely, venomous, and incurable, always there like the pressure of those "bunches" on his skull. I could imagine it well enough, too well. For the first time, that day or ever, I felt sorry for Schulz.

Endless walking through frozen hours; endless thinking; endless anger and frustration. And then — maybe? — the noise of something coming, a harsh and terrifying noise smashing in on his aloneness, as something big and fast plowed through the snowy brush and came scraping and sliding down the bank. Schulz would have reached the gun in one leap (I looked, but could find no sign to prove he had). Assuming he did: while he crouched there, a wild man with his finger on the trigger and his nerves humming with panic, here came materializing out of the white darkness a great bony shape whining love.

And been shot as it rushed up to greet Schulz, shot in the moment of fright when the oncoming thing could have been wolf or worse? It would have been plausible if it hadn't been for those hound tracks that went up and down along the path on the ice, and that place where the toenails had dug in as if the hound had reared to put its paws on the wolfer's shoulders. If there was ever a time when Schulz would have welcomed the hound, greeted it, talked to it in his mixture of baby talk, questions, and grunts of endearment, this would have been the time. The coming of the dog should have made the night thirty degrees warmer and hours shorter.

Surely the hound, having pursued him for ten miles or so, would have stuck close, kept him company in his pacing, stood with him whenever he built up the fire a little and warmed his feet and hands. But it had walked up and down the path only two or three times. Twice it had lain down. Once, perhaps, it had lapped up snow.

And this hound, following Schulz's tracks with blind love — and unfed all day, since it had escaped before the Schulz boy could feed it — had passed, sniffed around, perhaps eaten of, the carcass of the yearling at Bates Camp. Suppose Schulz had looked up from his stiff pacing and seen the hound rolling, or feverishly gulping snow. Suppose that in the murk, out of the corner of his eye, he had seen it stagger to its feet. Suppose, in the flicker of the fire, its great jaws had been opening and closing and that foam had dripped from its chops. Suppose a tight moment of alarm and disbelief, a tableau of freezing man and crazed hound, the deadliest creature and his deadly pet. Suppose it started toward him. Suppose the wolfer spoke to it, and it came on; yelled his peremptory command of "Charge!" which usually dropped the dog as if it had been poleaxed — and the hound still came on. Suppose he yelled a cracking yell, and the hound lumbered into a gallop, charging him. The spring for the gun, the mitt snatched off between the teeth, the stiffened finger pulling the trigger, a snapshot from the waist: Schulz was a good shot, or a lucky one; he had had to be.

Suppose. I supposed it, I tell you, in a way to give myself gooseflesh. By the vividness of imagination or the freakishness of the fading light, the hound's tracks arranged themselves so that only those decisive, final ones were clear. They led directly from one of the places where it had lain down to the bloody scramble where it had died, and if I read them right, they came at a scattering gallop. Standing in the path, Schulz would have fired with the hound no more than thirty feet away. Its momentum had carried it in a rolling plunge twenty feet closer. I stepped it off. When Schulz, with what paralysis in his guts and shaking in his muscles, lowered his gun and went up to the dead pet that his own poison had turned into an enemy, he had only three steps to go.

I went over to the hound and took off his collar, evidence, maybe, or a sort of souvenir. Dude was drooping in the willows with his head down to his knees. It was growing dark, but the fog that had threatened was evidently not going to come on; the moon's shape was in the sky.

What Schulz had done after the shooting of the hound was up for guesses. He had had to stay through the night until he knew which way was which. But then he had made those tracks upriver — whether heading for the T-Down for some reason, or wandering out of his head, or simply, in disgust and despair, starting on foot out of the country.

I would find out tomorrow. Right now it was time I got back to camp. When I led Dude down onto the ice and climbed on, the moon had swum clear, with a big ring around it. There was no aurora; the sky behind the thin remaining mist was blue-black and polished. Just for a second, when I took off a mitt and reached back to unbuckle the saddlebag and put the hound's collar inside, I laid my hand on the marten, stiff-frozen under soft fur. It gave me an unpleasant shock, somehow. I pulled my hand away as if the marten might have bitten me.

Riding up the channel, I heard the wind beginning to whine under the eaves of the cutbanks, and a flurry of snow came down on me, and a trail of drift blew eastward ahead of me down the middle of the ice. The moon sat up above me like a polished brass cuspidor in a high-class saloon, but that could be deceptive; within minutes the rack of another storm could be blowing it under.

Then I rode out into an open reach, and something touched my face, brushed it, and was gone, then back again. The willows shuddered in a gust. Dude's head came up, and so did mine, because that wind blew out of hundreds of miles of snowy waste as if it wafted across orange groves straight from Florida: instantly, in its first breath, there was a promise of incredible spring. I have felt the beginnings of many a chinook; I never felt one that I liked better than that one.

Before I reached Bates, I was riding with my earlaps up and my collar open. I had heard a willow or two shed its load of snow and snap upright. The going under Dude's feet was no longer the squeaky dryness of hard cold, but had gone mushy.

By morning the coulees and draws would be full of the sound of water running under the sagged and heavied drifts; the rims of the river valley and patches of watery prairie might be worn bare and brown. There might be cattle on their feet again, learning again to bawl, maybe even working up toward the benches, because this was a wind they could face, and the prairie wool that had been only inches below their feet all winter would be prickling up into sight. Something — not much but something — might yet be saved out of that winter.

That night I went to bed full of the sense of rescue, happy as a boy scenting spring, eased of a long strain, and I never thought until morning, when I looked out with the chinook still blowing strong and saw the channel of the Whitemud running ten inches of water on top of the ice, that now I wouldn't be able to follow to their end the single line of tracks, by that time pursuing nothing and unpursued, that led upriver into ambiguity. By the time I woke up, Schulz's last tracks were on their way toward the Milk and the Missouri in the spring breakup; and so was his last fire; and so, probably, was the body of his great hound; and so, for all I or anyone else ever found out, was he.

FOR DISCUSSION

1. Discuss the character of the mounted policeman who tells the story. Our only way of knowing him is through his actions and attitudes. Point out some of the passages that tell us about him. What are some of the important traits of his character?

2. The mounted policeman says of Schulz, "He hated civilization . . . but it was not civilization that did him in. It was the wild, the very savagery he trusted and thought he controlled." In your opinion, what does the statement mean? This remark could apply directly to Schulz's trust in his dog, but could it also mean something more general?

3. Consider the phrase "under the Christmas frosting the world was made of ice and iron." Can you relate this figure of speech to the story as a whole? Consider also the statement that from a distance the cowboys looked "like carved figures in a German toy scene." Is the appearance of the story's natural setting sometimes deceptive? Does the mounted policeman realize the true nature of the setting despite its appearance?

YOUR OWN WRITING

In a brief essay, describe the character of Schulz, comparing him to the mounted policeman who tells the story. How did Schulz become what he was? He lacks a number of specific traits of the policeman's character. Point them out by reference to the text of the story. How important are these specific traits (or the lack of them) in marking the differences between the two men?

REALISM AND NATURALISM

"The Wolfer," like "The Sculptor's Funeral," can be called a *realistic* story. Stegner's story might also be considered an example of *naturalism* in fiction. These terms have special meanings in literary criticism. Realism almost defines itself. It means an attempt to be true to the realities of life ("the way things really are") without fantasy, or romance, or any other modifying quality. A naturalistic story adds to its realism of technique a particular idea about the nature of man and his behavior. It is an idea called *determinism*, which suggests that man has little or no choice in the kind of person he becomes or the kinds of actions he performs. It supposes that all such things — character, behavior, beliefs — are determined by some single thing or a combination of things: heredity, environment, or economic level, to name just three of numerous possible influences. Thus naturalism, including as it does the notion of determinism, often has a tendency to deny man's freedom of will.

Realism is concerned with the way the elements of a story are chosen and handled. *Naturalism* is concerned with an attitude, a philosophy that the author wishes to express.

Do you think that Schulz is responsible for his own character, or is he solely a product of his environment? How does the character of the mounted policeman help you answer this question?

THE AUTHOR

WALLACE STEGNER (b. 1909) is a native of Iowa. He has been a teacher of English at colleges in many parts of the country and has been for some time a professor at Stanford University in California, where he directs the creative writing program. During this academic career he has also earned a prominent place as a writer of short stories, novels, and nonfiction. Among his novels are *Remembering Laughter* (1937) and *The Big Rock Candy Mountain* (1943). His nonfiction includes *Beyond the Hundredth Meridian* (1954), the story of John Wesley Powell, first explorer of the Grand Canyon. Stegner has spoken of his "rather overbearing sense of place." We may take this to mean that he is intensely responsive to the effect and mood of the setting or background in which a story is cast.

American Art and Artists ➤

On the facing page is a detail from "The Scout," an oil painting by the American artist Frederic Remington (1861–1909). The stark qualities that distinguish "The Wolfer" can also be seen in the work of this Western painter.

SINCLAIR LEWIS

The Hack Driver

Here is an early short story by a man who became one of our foremost novelists in the 1920's. It is the experience of an eager, hopeful city boy — a fledgling lawyer — on what appears to be a simple mission to a small town. But the young man meets with some unexpected difficulties.

W HEN I graduated from law school I wanted to climb, socially and financially. I wanted to be famous, and dine at large houses with men who shuddered at Common People who don't dress for dinner. Oh, I was a fine young calf! I even planned a rich marriage. Imagine then how I felt when, after taking honors [1] and becoming fifteenth assistant clerk in the magnificent law firm of Hodgins, Hodgins, Berkman, and Taupe, I was set not at preparing briefs [2] but at serving summonses! Like a cheap private detective! Like a mangy sheriff's officer! They told me I had to begin that way, and, holding my nose, I feebly went to work. I was kicked out of actresses' dressing rooms, and from time to time I was righteously beaten by large and indignant litigants. [3] I came to know, and still more to hate, every dirty and shadowy corner of the city. I thought of fleeing to my home town, where I could at once become a full-fledged attorney-at-law. I rejoiced one day when they sent me out forty miles or so to a town called New Mullion, to serve a summons on one Oliver Lutkins. This Lutkins had worked in the Northern Woods, and he knew the facts about a certain timberland boundary agreement; we needed him as a witness, and he had dodged service.

When I got off the train at New Mullion, my sudden affection for sweet and

[1] **taking honors:** those who achieve high academic standing in college graduate with "honors."

"The Hackdriver" from *Selected Short Stories of Sinclair Lewis* by Sinclair Lewis. Copyright 1923 by Sinclair Lewis. Reprinted by permission of Doubleday and Company, Inc.

[2] **briefs:** concise statements of the facts of a legal case.

[3] **litigants** (lĭt′ĭ-gănts): persons involved in a lawsuit.

simple villages was dashed by the look of the place, with its mud-gushing streets and its rows of shops either paintless or daubed with a sour brown. Though it must have numbered eight or nine thousand inhabitants, New Mullion was as littered as a mining camp. There was one agreeable-looking man at the station — the expressman. He was a person of perhaps forty, red-faced, cheerful, thick; he wore his overalls and denim jumper as though they belonged to him; he was quite dirty and very friendly, and you knew at once that he liked people and slapped them on the back out of pure, easy affection.

"I want," I told him, "to find a fellow named Oliver Lutkins."

"Him? I saw him 'round here 'twa'n't an hour ago. Hard fellow to catch, though — always chasing around on some phony business or other. Probably trying to get up a poker game in the back of Fritz Beineke's harness shop. I'll tell you, boy — any hurry about locating Lutkins?"

"Yes. I want to catch the afternoon train back." I was as impressively secret as a stage detective.

"I'll tell you. I've got a hack. I'll get the old bone-shaker, and we can drive around together and find Lutkins. I know most of the places he hangs out."

He was so frankly friendly, he so immediately took me into the circle of his affection, that I glowed with the warmth of it. I knew, of course, that he was drumming up business, but his kindness was real, and if I had to pay hack fare in order to find my man, I was glad that the money would go to this good fellow. I got him down to two dollars an hour; he brought from his cottage, a block away, an object like a black piano box on wheels.

He didn't hold the door open, certainly he didn't say, "Ready, sir." I think he would have died before calling anybody "sir." When he gets to heaven's gate, he'll call St. Peter "Pete," and I imagine the good saint will like it. He remarked,

"Well, young fellow, here's the handsome equipage,"[1] and his grin — well, it made me feel that I had always been his neighbor. They're so ready to help a stranger, those villagers. He had already made it his own task to find Oliver Lutkins for me.

He said, and almost shyly: "I don't want to butt in on your private business, young fellow, but my guess is that you want to collect some money from Lutkins — he never pays anybody a cent; he still owes me six bits on a poker game I was fool enough to get into. He ain't a bad sort of a Yahoo,[2] but he just naturally hates to loosen up on coin of the realm. So if you're trying to collect any money off him, we better kind of, you might say, creep up on him and surround him. If you go asking for him — anybody can tell you come from the city, with that trick fedora[3] of yours — he'll suspect something and take a sneak. If you want me to, I'll go into Fritz Beineke's and ask for him, and you can keep out of sight behind me."

I loved him for it. By myself I might never have found Lutkins. Now, I was an army with reserves. In a burst I told the hack driver that I wanted to serve a summons on Lutkins; that the fellow had viciously refused to testify in a suit where his knowledge of certain conversation would clear up everything. The driver listened earnestly — and I was still young enough to be grateful at being taken seriously by any man of forty. At the end he pounded my shoulder (very painfully) and chuckled: "Well, we'll spring a little surprise on Br'er Lutkins."

"Let's start, driver."

[1] equipage (ĕk'wĭ-pĭj): a vehicle, usually a coach or a carriage.
[2] Yahoo: one of a race of brutes having the form of men, in the fourth book of Jonathan Swift's satire *Gulliver's Travels*. It is used here colloquially to mean a stupid, clumsy person.
[3] fedora: a type of felt hat.

"Most folks around here call me Bill. Or Magnuson, William Magnuson, fancy carting and hauling."

"All right, Bill. Shall we tackle this harness shop — Beineke's?"

"Yes, jus' likely to be there as anywheres. Plays a lot of poker, and a great hand at bluffing." Bill seemed to admire Mr. Lutkins' ability as a scoundrel; I fancied that if he had been sheriff, he would have caught Lutkins with fervor and hanged him with affection.

At the somewhat gloomy harness shop we descended and went in. The room was odorous with the smell of dressed leather. A scenty sort of man, presumably Mr. Beineke, was selling a horse collar to a farmer.

"Seen Nolly Lutkins around today? Friend of his looking for him," said Bill, with treacherous heartiness.

Beineke looked past him at my shrinking, alien self; he hesitated, and owned: "Yuh, he was in here little while ago. Guess he's gone over to the Swede's to get a shave."

"Well, if he comes in, tell him I'm looking for him. Might get up a little game of poker. I've heard tell that Lutkins plays these here immoral games of chance."

"Yuh, I believe he's known to sit in on Authors,"[1] Beineke growled.

We sought the barbershop of "the Swede." Bill was again good enough to take the lead, while I lurked at the door. He asked not only the Swede but two customers if they had seen Lutkins. The Swede decidedly had not; he raged: "I ain't seen him, and I don't want to, but if you find him, you can just collect the dollar thirty-five he owes me!" One of the customers thought he had seen Lutkins "hiking down Main Street, this side of the hotel."

"Well, then," Bill concluded, as we labored up into the hack, "his credit at

the Swede's being ausgewent,[2] he's probably getting a scrape at Heinie Gray's. He's too darn lazy to shave himself."

At Gray's barbershop we missed Lutkins by only five minutes. He had just left — presumably for the poolroom. At the poolroom it appeared that he had merely bought a "pack" of cigarettes and gone on. Thus we pursued him, just behind him but never catching him, for an hour, till it was past one and I was hungry. Village-born as I was and in the city often lonely for good coarse country wit, I was so delighted by Bill's cynical opinions on the barbers and clergymen and doctors and draymen of New Mullion that I scarcely cared whether I found Lutkins or not.

"How about something to eat?" I suggested. "Let's go to a restaurant and I'll buy you a lunch."

"Well, I ought to go home to the old woman. I don't care much for these restaurants — ain't but four of 'em, and they're all rotten. Tell you what we'll do. Like nice scenery? There's an elegant view from Wade's Hill. We'll get the old woman to put us up a lunch — she won't charge you but half a dollar, and it'd cost you that for a greasy feed at the café — and we'll go up there and have a Sunday school picnic."

I knew that my friend Bill was not free from guile; I knew that his hospitality to the Young Fellows from the City was not altogether a matter of brotherly love. I was paying him for his time; in all I paid him for six hours (including the lunch hour!) at what was then a terrific price. But he was no more dishonest than I, who charged the whole thing up to the Firm, and it would have been worth paying him myself to have his presence. His country serenity, his natural wisdom, was a refreshing bath to the city-twitching

[1] **Authors:** a polite parlor game played with a set of special cards.

[2] **ausgewent:** Bill makes up a German-sounding word, meaning "used up."

youngster. As we sat on the hilltop, looking across orchards and a creek which slipped among the willows, he talked of New Mullion, gave a whole gallery of portraits. He was cynical yet tender. Nothing had escaped him, yet there was nothing, no matter how ironically he laughed at it, which was beyond his understanding and forgiveness. In ruddy color he painted the rector's wife who, when she was most in debt, most loudly gave the responses of what he called the "Episcopalopian church." He commented on the boys who came home from college in "ice-cream pants," and on the lawyer who, after years of torrential argument with his wife, would put on either a linen collar or a necktie, but never both. He made them live. In that day I came to know New Mullion better than I did the city and to love it better.

If Bill was ignorant of universities and of urban ways, yet much had he traveled in the realm of jobs. He had worked on railroad section gangs, in harvest fields and contractors' camps, and from his adventures he had brought back a philosophy of simplicity and laughter. He strengthened me. Nowadays, thinking of Bill, I know what people mean . . . when they yearn over "real he-men."

We left the placid place of orchards and resumed the search for Oliver Lutkins. We could not find him. At last Bill cornered a friend of Lutkins and made him admit that "he guessed Oliver's gone out to his ma's farm, three miles north."

We drove out there, mighty with strategy.

"I know Oliver's ma. She's a terror. She's a cyclone," Bill sighed. "I took a trunk out for her once, and she pretty near took my hide off because I didn't treat it like it was a crate of eggs. She's somewheres about nine feet tall and four feet thick and quick's a cat, and she sure manhandles the Queen's English. I'll bet Oliver has heard that some-

body's on his trail, and he's sneaked out there to hide behind ma's skirts. Well, we'll try bawling her out. But you better let me do it, boy. You may be great at Latin and geography, but you ain't educated in cussing." We drove into a poor farmyard; we were faced by an enormous and cheerful old woman. My guardian stockily stood before her and snarled, "Remember me? I'm Bill Magnuson, the expressman. I want to find your son Oliver. Friend of mine here from the city got a present for him."

"I don't know anything about Oliver, and I don't want to," she bellowed.

"Now you look here. We've stood for just about enough plenty nonsense. This young man is the attorney general's provost,[1] and we got legal right to search any and all premises for the person of one Oliver Lutkins."

Bill made it sound terrific, and the amazon seemed impressed. She retired into the kitchen, and we followed. From the low old range, turned by years of heat into a dark silvery gray, she snatched a sadiron,[2] and she marched on us, clamoring, "You just search all you want to — providin' you don't mind getting burnt to a cinder." She bellowed, she swelled, she laughed at our nervous retreat.

"Let's get out of this. She'll murder us," Bill groaned and, outside: "Did you see her grin? She was making fun of us. Can you beat that for nerve?"

We did, however, make adequate search. The cottage had but one story. Bill went around it, peeking in at all the windows. We explored the barn and the stable; we were reasonably certain that Lutkins was not there. It was nearly time for me to catch the afternoon train, and Bill drove me to the station. On the way to the city, I worried very little over my failure to find Lutkins. I was too absorbed in the thought of Bill Magnuson. Really, I considered return-

[1] **provost** (prŏv′ŭst): officer.
[2] **sadiron** (săd′ī′ẽrn): a flatiron.

ing to New Mullion to practice law. If I had found Bill so deeply and richly human, might I not come to love the yet uncharted Fritz Beineke and the Swede barber and a hundred other slow-spoken, simple, wise neighbors? I saw a candid and happy life beyond the neat earnings of universities and law firms. I was excited, as one who has found a treasure.

But if I did not think much about Lutkins, the office did. I found them in a state, next morning; the suit was ready to come to trial; they had to have Lutkins; I was a disgrace and a fool. That morning my eminent legal career almost came to an end. The chief did everything but commit mayhem; he somewhat more than hinted that I would do well at ditchdigging. I was ordered back to New Mullion, and with me they sent an ex-lumber-camp clerk who knew Lutkins. I was rather sorry, because it would prevent my loafing again in the gorgeous indolence of Bill Magnuson.

When the train drew in at New Mullion, Bill was on the station platform, near his dray. What was curious was that the old dragon, Lutkins' mother, was there talking to him, and they were not quarreling but laughing.

From the car steps I pointed Bill out to the lumber-camp clerk, and in young hero worship I murmured: "There's a fine fellow, a real man."

"Meet him here yesterday?" asked the clerk.

"I spent the day with him."

"He help you hunt for Oliver Lutkins?"

"Yes, he helped me a lot."

"He must have! He's Lutkins himself!"

But what really hurt was that, when I served the summons, Lutkins and his mother laughed at me as though I were a bright boy of seven, and with loving solicitude they begged me to go to a neighbor's house and take a cup of coffee.

"I told 'em about you, and they're dying to have a look at you," said Lutkins joyfully. "They're about the only folks in town that missed seeing you yesterday."

FOR DISCUSSION

1. Why does the narrator call himself "a young calf"?

2. As you look back, can you point out some clues to the story's surprise?

3. This story reverses the old formula of the country boy fooled by the city slicker. Locate passages that emphasize this reversal.

4. The entire town seems to enter spontaneously into the hoax. What does this tell us about the townspeople?

5. How does "the hack driver" describe the character of Oliver Lutkins? What sort of man is Oliver Lutkins? How does the narrator feel about him?

6. At the time the story takes place, what sort of person is the narrator? As an older person recalling the story, how has he changed?

RECOGNIZING ALLUSIONS

The phrase "much had he traveled in the realm of jobs" is a sly paraphrase of the opening line of John Keats's famous sonnet "On First Looking into Chapman's Homer": "Much have I travel'd in the realms of gold." Why do you suppose Lewis makes this remote allusion? What does it contribute to those who recognize it?

Scenes from Lewis Novels →

On the facing page, Lawrence Bjorkland has sketched, in pen and ink, scenes from four Lewis novels that you may wish to add to your personal reading list. At the top, George F. Babbitt (from *Babbitt*) is shown addressing the Booster's Club of Zenith; next, "Main Street," from the novel of that name; next, Dr. Martin Arrowsmith (from *Arrowsmith*) is pictured at the beginning of his medical career; last, from *Dodsworth*, Sam Dodsworth and his wife are shown on their way to Europe.

FOUR LEWIS NOVELS

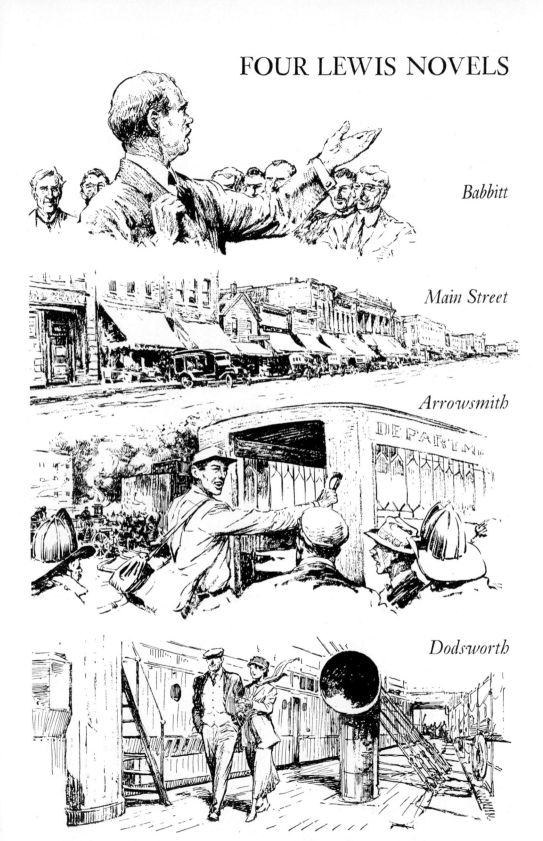

Babbitt

Main Street

Arrowsmith

Dodsworth

THE AUTHOR

SINCLAIR LEWIS (1885–1951) was born in Sauk Center, Minnesota, and used that town as the barely disguised setting of his most famous novel, *Main Street* (1920). His books often satirized Midwestern life, yet even with the acidity of some of his work, Lewis showed that he had a deep affection for his roots. He was himself much like some of the people he portrayed. His novel *Babbitt* (1922) put its title into our dictionaries as a word to identify the type of man its chief character,

George F. Babbitt, represents. *Arrowsmith* (1925), one of his most popular books, is about a doctor who makes medical research his chosen field. *Dodsworth* (1929) and *It Can't Happen Here* (1935) both were successfully adapted for the theater. His other novels include *Elmer Gantry* (1927), *Cass Timberlane* (1945), and *World So Wide* (1951). In 1930 Lewis became the first American to receive the Nobel prize for literature. He died in Italy in 1951. Mark Schorer's *Sinclair Lewis: An American Life* (1961) is an extensive study of Lewis' career.

WALTER VAN TILBURG CLARK

The Portable Phonograph

Bleak prairie with a threatening sky darkening into night is the background for this story. All about, the earth is slowly healing from the deep wounds of war. Civilization is gone. . . . Many writers have experimented with this situation. Walter Van Tilburg Clark presents one of the most profound consequences of such a catastrophe: the loss of those things in life that help to make us civilized, the sum of which we call culture.

"The Portable Phonograph" by Walter Van Tilburg Clark. Yale Review, 1942. Reprinted by permission of Random House, Inc.

GRASPING THE MEANING OF THE STORY. To experience the full impact of "The Portable Phonograph," the reader must project himself into a possible future that haunts the minds of many men — especially those at the heads of nations. The author tells us the most important things here by indirection. The men in this story suffer from a great hunger. But it is not hunger for food or for any other physical thing. Try to share what they feel by imagining yourself in their place. Use the full power of your imagination to picture the setting, the characters, and the situation of the story.

THE red sunset, with narrow, black cloud strips like threats across it, lay on the curved horizon of the prairie. The air was still and cold, and in it settled the mute darkness and greater cold of night. High in the air there was wind, for through the veil of the dusk, the clouds could be seen gliding rapidly south and changing shapes. A queer sensation of torment, of two-sided, unpredictable nature, arose from the stillness of the earth air beneath the violence of the upper air. Out of the sunset, through the dead, matted grass and isolated weed stalks of the prairie, crept the narrow and deeply rutted remains of a road. In the road, in places, there were crusts of shallow, brittle ice. There were little islands of an old oiled pavement in the road too, but most of it was mud, now frozen rigid. The frozen mud still bore the toothed impress of great tanks, and a wanderer on the neighboring undulations might have stumbled, in this light, into large, partially filled-in and weed-grown cavities, their banks channeled and beginning to spread into badlands. These pits were such as might have been made by falling meteors, but they were not. They were the scars of gigantic bombs, their rawness already made a little natural by rain, seed, and time. Along the road there were rakish remnants of fence. There was also, just visible, one portion of tangled and multiple barbed wire still erect, behind which was a shelving ditch with small caves, now very quiet and empty, at intervals in its back wall. Otherwise there was no structure or remnant of a structure visible over the dome of the darkling earth, but only, in sheltered hollows, the darker shadows of young trees trying again.

Under the wuthering [1] arch of the high wind, a V of wild geese fled south. The rush of their pinions sounded brief-

[1] **wuthering**: rushing, blustering.

ly, and the faint, plaintive notes of their expeditionary talk. Then they left a still greater vacancy. There was the smell and expectation of snow, as there is likely to be when the wild geese fly south. From the remote distance, toward the red sky, came faintly the protracted howl and quick yap-yap of a prairie wolf.

North of the road, perhaps a hundred yards, lay the parallel and deeply intrenched course of a small creek, lined with leafless alders and willows. The creek was already silent under ice. Into the bank above it was dug a sort of cell, with a single opening like the mouth of a mine tunnel. Within the cell there was a little red of fire, which showed dully through the opening, like a reflection or a deception of the imagination. The light came from the chary burning of four blocks of poorly aged peat, which gave off a petty warmth and much acrid smoke. But the precious remnants of wood, old fence posts and timbers from the long-deserted dugouts, had to be saved for the real cold, for the time when a man's breath blew white, the moisture in his nostrils stiffened at once when he stepped out, and the expansive blizzards paraded for days over the vast open, swirling and settling and thickening till the dawn of the cleared day when the sky was a thin blue-green and the terrible cold, in which a man could not live for three hours unwarmed, lay over the uniformly drifted swell of the plain.

Around the smoldering peat four men were seated cross-legged. Behind them, traversed by their shadows, was the earth bench, with two old and dirty army blankets, where the owner of the cell slept. In a niche in the opposite wall were a few tin utensils which caught the glint of the coals. The host was rewrapping in a piece of daubed burlap four fine, leather-bound books. He worked slowly and very carefully, and at last tied the bundle securely with a piece of grass-woven cord. The other three looked intently upon the process, as if a great significance lay in it. As the host tied the cord, he spoke. He was an old man, his long, matted beard and hair gray to nearly white. The shadows made his brows and cheekbones appear gnarled, his eyes and cheeks deeply sunken. His big hands, rough with frost and swollen by rheumatism, were awkward but gentle at their task. He was like a prehistoric priest performing a fateful ceremonial rite. Also his voice had in it a suitable quality of deep, reverent despair, yet perhaps at the moment, a sharpness of selfish satisfaction. "When I perceived what was happening," he said, "I told myself, 'It is the end. I cannot take much; I will take these.'

"Perhaps I was impractical," he continued. "But for myself, I do not regret, and what do we know of those who will come after us? We are the doddering remnant of a race of mechanical fools. I have saved what I love; the soul of what was good in us is here; perhaps the new ones will make a strong enough beginning not to fall behind when they become clever."

He rose with slow pain and placed the wrapped volumes in the niche with his utensils. The others watched him with the same ritualistic gaze.

"Shakespeare, the Bible, *Moby Dick*, the *Divine Comedy*," one of them said softly. "You might have done worse, much worse."

"You will have a little soul left until you die," said another harshly. "That is more than is true of us. My brain becomes thick, like my hands." He held the big, battered hands, with their black nails, in the glow to be seen.

"I want paper to write on," he said. "And there is none."

The fourth man said nothing. He sat in the shadow farthest from the fire, and sometimes his body jerked in its rags from the cold. Although he was still young, he was sick and coughed often. Writing implied a greater future than he now felt able to consider.

The old man seated himself laboriously, and reached out, groaning at the movement, to put another block of peat on the fire. With bowed heads and averted eyes, his three guests acknowledged his magnanimity.

"We thank you, Doctor Jenkins, for the reading," said the man who had named the books.

They seemed then to be waiting for something. Doctor Jenkins understood, but was loath to comply. In an ordinary moment he would have said nothing. But the words of *The Tempest*, which he had been reading, and the religious attention of the three, made this an unusual occasion.

"You wish to hear the phonograph," he said grudgingly.

The two middle-aged men stared into the fire, unable to formulate and expose the enormity of their desire.

The young man, however, said anxiously, between suppressed coughs, "Oh, please," like an excited child.

The old man rose again in his difficult way, and went to the back of the cell. He returned and placed tenderly upon the packed floor, where the firelight might fall upon it, an old portable phonograph in a black case. He smoothed the top with his hand, and then opened it. The lovely green-felt-covered disc became visible.

"I have been using thorns as needles," he said. "But tonight, because we have a musician among us"—he bent his head to the young man, almost invisible in the shadow—"I will use a steel needle. There are only three left."

The two middle-aged men stared at him in speechless adoration. The one with the big hands, who wanted to write, moved his lips, but the whisper was not audible.

"Oh, don't!" cried the young man, as if he were hurt. "The thorns will do beautifully."

"No," the old man said. "I have become accustomed to the thorns, but they are not really good. For you, my young friend, we will have good music tonight.

"After all," he added generously, and beginning to wind the phonograph, which creaked, "they can't last forever."

"No, nor we," the man who needed to write said harshly. "The needle, by all means."

"Oh, thanks," said the young man. "Thanks," he said again in a low, excited voice, and then stifled his coughing with a bowed head.

"The records, though," said the old man when he had finished winding, "are a different matter. Already they are very worn. I do not play them more than once a week. One, once a week, that is what I allow myself.

"More than a week I cannot stand it; not to hear them," he apologized.

"No, how could you?" cried the young man. "And with them here like this."

"A man can stand anything," said the man who wanted to write, in his harsh, antagonistic voice.

"Please, the music," said the young man.

"Only the one," said the old man. "In the long run, we will remember more that way."

He had a dozen records with luxuriant gold and red seals. Even in that light the others could see that the threads of the records were becoming worn. Slowly he read out the titles, and the tremendous, dead names of the composers and the artists and the orchestras. The three worked upon the names in their minds, carefully. It was difficult to select from such a wealth what they would at once most like to remember. Finally, the man who wanted to write named Gershwin's "New York."

"Oh, no!" cried the sick young man, and then could say nothing more because he had to cough. The others understood him, and the harsh man withdrew his selection and waited for the musician to choose.

The musician begged Doctor Jenkins to read the titles again, very slowly, so that he could remember the sounds. While they were read, he lay back against the wall, his eyes closed, his thin, horny hand pulling at his light beard, and listened to the voices and the orchestras and the single instruments in his mind.

When the reading was done, he spoke despairingly. "I have forgotten," he complained; "I cannot hear them clearly.

"There are things missing," he explained.

"I know," said Doctor Jenkins. "I thought that I knew all of Shelley by heart. I should have brought Shelley."

"That's more soul than we can use," said the harsh man. "*Moby Dick* is better.

"We can understand that," he emphasized.

The Doctor nodded.

"Still," said the man who had admired the books, "we need the absolute if we are to keep a grasp on anything.

"Anything but these sticks and peat clods and rabbit snares," he said bitterly.

"Shelley desired an ultimate absolute," said the harsh man. "It's too much," he said. "It's no good; no earthly good."

The musician selected a Debussy [1] nocturne. The others considered and approved. They rose to their knees to watch the Doctor prepare for the playing, so that they appeared to be actually in an attitude of worship. The peat glow showed the thinness of their bearded faces, and the deep lines in them, and revealed the condition of their garments. The other two contin-

[1] **Debussy** (dĕ·bü′sē′): Claude Debussy, a French composer, 1862–1918.

occurred rapid sequences of tragically heightened recollection. He heard nothing but what was there. At the final, whispering disappearance, but moving quietly so that the others would not hear him and look at him, he let his head fall back in agony, as if it were drawn there by the hair, and clenched the fingers of one hand over his teeth. He sat that way while the others were silent, and until they began to breathe again normally. His drawn-up legs were trembling violently.

Quickly Doctor Jenkins lifted the needle off, to save it and not to spoil the recollection with scraping. When he had stopped the whirling of the sacred disc, he courteously left the phonograph open and by the fire, in sight.

The others, however, understood. The musician rose last, but then abruptly, and went quickly out at the door without saying anything. The others stopped at the door and gave their thanks in low voices. The Doctor nodded magnificently.

"Come again," he invited, "in a week. We will have the 'New York.'"

When the two had gone together, out toward the rimed [1] road, he stood in the entrance, peering and listening. At first, there was only the resonant boom of the wind overhead, and then far over the dome of the dead, dark plain, the wolf cry lamenting. In the rifts of clouds, the Doctor saw four stars flying. It impressed the Doctor that one of them had just been obscured by the beginning of a flying cloud at the very moment he heard what he had been listening for, a sound of suppressed coughing. It was not nearby, however. He believed that down against the pale alders he could see the moving shadow.

With nervous hands he lowered the piece of canvas which served as his door, and pegged it at the bottom. Then quickly and quietly, looking at the piece of canvas frequently, he

ued to kneel as the old man carefully lowered the needle onto the spinning disc, but the musician suddenly drew back against the wall again, with his knees up, and buried his face in his hands.

At the first notes of the piano, the listeners were startled. They stared at each other. Even the musician lifted his head in amazement, but then quickly bowed it again, strainingly, as if he were suffering from a pain he might not be able to endure. They were all listening deeply, without movement. The wet, blue-green notes tinkled forth from the old machine, and were individual, delectable presences in the cell. The individual, delectable presences swept into a sudden tide of unbearably beautiful dissonance, and then continued fully the swelling and ebbing of that tide, the dissonant inpourings, and the resolutions, and the diminishments, and the little, quiet wavelets of interlude lapping between. Every sound was piercing and singularly sweet. In all the men except the musician, there

---

[1] **rimed:** frosted.

slipped the records into the case, snapped the lid shut, and carried the phonograph to his couch. There, pausing to stare at the canvas and listen, he dug earth from the wall and disclosed a piece of board. Behind this there was a deep hole in the wall into which he put the phonograph. After a moment's consideration, he went over and reached down his bundle of books and inserted it also. Then, guardedly, he once more sealed up the hole with the board and the earth. He also changed his blankets, and the grass-stuffed sack which served as a pillow, so that he could lie facing the entrance. After carefully placing two more blocks of peat upon the fire, he stood for a long time watching the stretched canvas, but it seemed to billow naturally with the first gusts of a lowering wind. At last he prayed, and got in under his blankets, and closed his smoke-smarting eyes. On the inside of the bed, next the wall, he could feel with his hand the comfortable piece of lead pipe.

FOR DISCUSSION

1. Discuss the characters of the men in the story. Are they similar in any way? How does each react to the situation in which he finds himself?

2. What is meant by "We are the doddering remnants of a race of mechanical fools"?

3. Discuss the four books the man has preserved. "You might have done worse . . . ," someone says. Was this a good selection? Why? Would you propose any substitutions? If so, offer a good reason for your changes.

4. Who says, "You will have a little soul left until you die"? What does he mean?

5. Explain Dr. Jenkins' precautions as he prepares to sleep. Who is the threat? Why? Considering the characters of the men, do you think the threat is believable?

6. Imagine yourself in such a situation: the collapse and loss of culture. What

would you value most? What would you miss most? Do many of us fully appreciate the cultural heritage we enjoy?

7. Discuss the statement: "We need the absolute if we are to keep a grasp on anything." Look up the word *absolute* in a dictionary. From among its several meanings, which do you think is appropriate to the quotation and the "harsh man's" reply?

YOUR OWN WRITING

In a short essay, write character sketches of the four men in the story. The characters of "The Portable Phonograph" are not minutely described, but the author is careful to distinguish them from each other. Point out how he does so.

THE AUTHOR

WALTER VAN TILBURG CLARK (b. 1909) has been associated with Western scenes in his literary career. His first novel, *The Ox-Bow Incident* (1940), made an immediate reputation for him and was the start of a new trend toward greater seriousness, both psychological and social, in Western stories. It was made into an excellent film. *The Track of the Cat* (1949), the story of a lone man on a panther hunt in the mountains, displays the knowledge of nature and hunting that he shares with his exact contemporary, Wallace Stegner. The present story, a change in some respects from his usual vein, is one of many collected in the volume called *The Watchful Gods* (1950).

WILLIAM FAULKNER

Two Soldiers

In accepting the Nobel prize of 1950, Faulkner stated his creed as a writer: It is the writer's privilege to help his fellow man by "lifting his heart, by reminding him of the courage and honor and hope and pride and compassion and pity and sacrifice which have been the glory of his past."

THE POINT OF VIEW. As soon as you find that a story is told in the first person, you can make a quick adjustment that will pay dividends in understanding and enjoyment. Get yourself mentally inside the narrator as quickly as possible, and take in from his point of view all that happens. Pick up bits of information about this central character and his relationship to the other people in the story and to the special situation from which the action springs.

M E AND PETE would go down to Old Man Killegrew's and listen to his radio. We would wait until after supper, after dark, and we would stand outside Old Man Killegrew's parlor window, and we could hear it because Old Man

Killegrew's wife was deaf, and so he run the radio as loud as it would run, and so me and Pete could hear it plain as Old Man Killegrew's wife could, I reckon, even standing outside with the window closed.

And that night I said, "What? Japanese? What's a pearl harbor?" and Pete said, "Hush."

And so we stood there, it was cold, listening to the fellow in the radio talking, only I couldn't make no heads nor tails out of it. Then the fellow said that would be all for a while, and me and Pete walked back up the road to home, and Pete told me what it was. Because he was nigh twenty and he had done finished the Consolidated [1] last June and he knowed a heap: about them Japanese dropping bombs on Pearl Harbor and that Pearl Harbor was across the water.

"Across what water?" I said. "Across that Government reservoy up at Oxford?"

"Naw," Pete said. "Across the big water. The Pacific Ocean."

We went home. Maw and pap was already asleep and me and Pete laid in

---

[1] **Consolidated:** the consolidated high school.

bed, and I still couldn't understand where it was, and Pete told me again — the Pacific Ocean.

"What's the matter with you?" Pete said. "You're going on nine years old. You been in school now ever since September. Ain't you learned nothing yet?"

"I reckon we ain't got as fer as the Pacific Ocean yet," I said.

We was still sowing the vetch [1] then that ought to been all finished by the fifteenth of November, because pap was still behind, just like he had been ever since me and Pete had knowed him. And we had firewood to git in, too, but every night me and Pete would go down to Old Man Killegrew's and stand outside his parlor window in the cold and listen to his radio; then we would come back home and lay in bed and Pete would tell me what it was. That is, he would tell me for a while. Then he wouldn't tell me. It was like he didn't want to talk about it no more. He would tell me to shut up because he wanted to go to sleep, but he never wanted to go to sleep.

He would lay there, a heap stiller than if he was asleep, and it would be something, I could feel it coming out of him, like he was mad at me, or like he was worried about something, and it wasn't that neither, because he never had nothing to worry about. He never got behind like pap, let alone stayed behind. Pap give him ten acres when he graduated from the Consolidated, and me and Pete both reckoned pap was durn glad to get shut of at least ten acres, less to have to worry about himself; and Pete had them ten acres all sowed to vetch and busted out and bedded for the winter, and so it wasn't that. But it was something. And still we would go down to Old Man Killegrew's every night and listen to his radio, and they was at it in the Philippines now, but General MacArthur was holding um. Then we would come back home

[1] vetch: a plant of the same family as peas and beans, used as a winter cover crop.

and lay in the bed, and Pete wouldn't tell me nothing or talk at all. He would just lay there still as an ambush and when I would touch him, his side or his leg would feel hard and still as iron, until after a while and I would go to sleep.

Then one night — it was the first time he had said nothing to me except to jump on me about not chopping enough wood at the wood tree where he was cutting — he said, "I got to go."

"Go where?" I said.

"To that war," Pete said.

"Before we even finish gettin' in the firewood?"

"Firewood, heck," Pete said.

"All right," I said. "When we going to start?"

But he wasn't even listening. He laid there, hard and still as iron in the dark. "I got to go," he said. "I jest ain't going to put up with no folks treating the Unity States that way."

"Yes," I said. "Firewood or no firewood, I reckon we got to go."

This time he heard me. He laid still again, but it was a different kind of still.

"You?" he said. "To a war?"

"You'll whup the big uns and I'll whup the little uns," I said.

Then he told me I couldn't go. At first I thought he just never wanted me tagging after him, like he wouldn't leave me go with him when he went sparking them girls of Tull's. Then he told me the army wouldn't leave me go because I was too little, and then I knowed he really meant it and that I couldn't go nohow noways. And somehow I hadn't believed until then that he was going himself, but now I knowed he was and that he wasn't going to leave me go with him a-tall.

"I'll chop the wood and tote the water for you-all then!" I said. "You got to have wood and water!"

Anyway, he was listening to me now. He wasn't like iron now.

He turned onto his side and put his hand on my chest because it was me that was laying straight and hard on my back now.

"No," he said. "You got to stay here and help pap."

"Help him what?" I said. "He ain't never caught up nohow. He can't get no further behind. He can sholy take care of this little shirttail of a farm while me and you are whupping them Japanese. I got to go too. If you got to go, then so have I."

"No," Pete said. "Hush now. Hush." And he meant it, and I knowed he did. Only I made sho from his own mouth. I quit.

"So I just can't go then," I said.

"No," Pete said. "You just can't go. You're too little, in the first place, and in the second place — "

"All right," I said. "Then shut up and leave me go to sleep."

So he hushed then and laid back. And I laid there like I was already asleep, and pretty soon he was asleep and I knowed it was the wanting to go to the war that had worried him and kept him awake, and now that he had decided to go, he wasn't worried any more.

The next morning he told maw and pap. Maw was all right. She cried.

"No," she said, crying, "I don't want him to go. I would rather go myself in his place, if I could. I don't want to save the country. Them Japanese could take it all and keep it, so long as they left me and my family and my children alone. But I remember my brother Marsh in that other war. He had to go to that one when he wasn't but nineteen and our mother couldn't understand it then any more than I can now. But she told Marsh if he had to go, he had to go. And so, if Pete's got to go to this one, he's got to go to it. Jest don't ask me to understand why."

But pap was the one. He was the feller. "To the war?" he said. "Why I don't see a bit of use in that. You ain't old enough for the draft, and the country ain't being invaded. Our President in Washington, D.C., is watching the conditions and he will notify us. Besides, in that other war your ma just mentioned, I was drafted and sent clean to Texas and was held there nigh eight months until they finally quit fighting. It seems to me that that, along with your Uncle Marsh who received a actual wound on the battlefields of France, is enough for me and mine to have to do to protect the country, at least in my lifetime. Besides, what'll I do for help on the farm with you gone? It seems to me I'll get mighty far behind."

"You been behind as long as I can remember," Pete said. "Anyway I'm going. I got to."

"Of course he's got to go," I said. "Them Japanese — "

"You hush your mouth!" maw said, crying. "Nobody's talking to you! Go and get me a armful of wood! That's what you can do!"

So I got the wood. And all the next day, while me and Pete and pap was getting in as much wood as we could in that time because Pete said how pap's idea of plenty of wood was one more stick laying against the wall that maw ain't put on the fire yet, maw was getting Pete ready to go. She washed and mended his clothes and cooked him a shoe box of vittles. And that night me and Pete laid in the bed and listened to her packing his grip and crying, until after a while Pete got up in his nightshirt and went back there, and I could hear them talking, until at last maw said, "You ought to go, and so I want you to go. But I don't understand it, and I won't never, and so don't expect me to." And Pete come back and got into bed again and laid again still and hard as iron on his back, and then he said, and he wasn't talking to me, he wasn't talking to nobody: "I got to go. I just got to."

"Sho you got to," I said. "Them Japanese — " He turned over hard, he kind of surged over onto his side, looking at me in the dark.

"Anyway, you're all right," he said. "I expected to have more trouble with you than with all the rest of them put together."

"I reckon I can't help it neither," I said. "But maybe it will run a few years longer and I can get there. Maybe someday I will jest walk in on you."

"I hope not," Pete said. "Folks don't go to wars for fun. A man don't leave his maw crying just for fun."

"Then why are you going?" I said.

"I got to," he said. "I just got to. Now you go on to sleep. I got to ketch that early bus in the morning."

"All right," I said, "I hear tell Memphis is a big place. How will you find where the army's at?"

"I'll ask somebody where to go to join it," Pete said. "Go on to sleep now."

"Is that what you'll ask for? Where to join the army?" I said.

"Yes," Pete said. He turned onto his back again. "Shut up and go to sleep."

We went to sleep. The next morning we et breakfast by lamplight because the bus would pass at six o'clock. Maw wasn't crying now. She jest looked grim and busy, putting breakfast on the table while we et it. Then she finished packing Pete's grip, except he never wanted to take no grip to the war, but maw said decent folks never went nowhere, not even to a war, without a change of clothes and something to tote them in. She put in the shoe box of fried chicken and biscuits and she put the Bible in, too, and then it was time to go. We didn't know until then that maw wasn't going to the bus. She jest brought Pete's cap and overcoat, and still she didn't cry no more, she jest stood with her hands on Pete's shoulders and she didn't move, but somehow, and just holding Pete's shoulders, she looked as hard and fierce as when Pete had turned toward me in the bed last night and tole me that anyway I was all right.

"They could take the country and keep the country, as long as they never bothered me and mine," she said. Then she said, "Don't never forget who you are. You ain't rich and the rest of the world outside of Frenchman's Bend never heard of you. But your blood is good as any blood anywhere, and don't you never forget it."

Then she kissed him, and then we was out of the house, with pap toting Pete's grip whether Pete wanted him to or not. There wasn't no dawn even yet, not even after we had stood on the highway by the mailbox awhile. Then we seen the lights of the bus coming and I was watching the bus until it come up and Pete flagged it, and then, sho enough, there was daylight — it had started while I wasn't watching. And now me and Pete expected pap to say something else foolish, like he done before, about how Uncle Marsh getting wounded in France and that trip to Texas pap had taken in 1918 ought to be enough to save the Unity States in 1942, but he never. He done all right too. He jest said, "Good-by, son. Always remember what your ma told you and write her whenever you find the time." Then he shaken Pete's hand, and Pete looked at me for a minute and put his hand on my head and rubbed my head durn nigh hard enough to wring my neck off and jumped into the bus, and the feller wound the door shut and the bus began to hum; then it was moving, humming and grinding and whining louder and louder; it was going fast, with two little red lights behind it that never seemed to get no littler, but jest seemed to be running together until pretty soon they would touch and jest be one light. But they never did, and then the bus was gone, and even like it was, I could have pretty nigh busted out crying, nigh to nine years old and all.

Me and pap went back to the house. All that day we worked at the wood tree, and so I never had no good chance until about middle of the afternoon. Then I taken my slingshot and I would have liked to took all my bird eggs, too, because Pete had give me his collection and he holp me with mine, and he would like to git the box out and look at them as good as I would, even if he was nigh twenty years old. But the box was too big to tote a long ways and have to worry with, so I just taken the shikepoke [1] egg, because it was the best un, and wropped it up good into a matchbox and hid it and the slingshot under the corner of the barn. Then we et supper and went to bed, and I thought then how if I would 'a' had to stayed in that room and that bed like that even for one more night, I jest couldn't 'a' stood it. Then I could hear pap snoring, but I never heard no sound from maw, whether she was asleep or not, and I don't reckon she was. So I taken my shoes and drapped them out the window, and then I clumb out like I used to watch Pete do when he was still jest seventeen and pap wouldn't leave him out, and I put on my shoes and went to the barn and got the slingshot and the shikepoke egg and went to the highway.

It wasn't cold, it was jest durn confounded dark, and that highway stretched on in front of me like, without nobody using it, it had stretched out half again as fer just like a man does when he lays down, so that for a time it looked like full sun was going to ketch me before I had finished them twenty-two miles to Jefferson. But it didn't. Daybreak was jest starting when I walked up the hill into town. I could smell breakfast cooking in the cabins and I wished I had thought to brought me a cold biscuit, but that was too late now. And Pete had told me Memphis was a piece beyond Jefferson, but I never knowed it was no eighty miles. So I stood there on that empty square, with daylight coming and coming and the street lights still burning and that Law [2] looking down at me, and me still

<hr>

[1] **shikepoke** (or **shitepoke**): a heron.
[2] **Law:** colloquial for a policeman.

eighty miles from Memphis, and it had took me all night to walk jest twenty-two miles, and so, by the time I got to Memphis at that rate, Pete would 'a' done already started for Pearl Harbor.

"Where do you come from?" the Law said. And I told him again. "I got to git to Memphis. My brother's there."

"You mean you ain't got any folks around here?" the Law said. "Nobody but that brother? What are you doing way off down here and your brother in Memphis?"

And I told him again, "I got to git to Memphis. I ain't got no time to waste talking about it and I ain't got time to walk it. I got to git there today."

"Come on here," the Law said.

We went down another street. And there was the bus, jest like when Pete got into it yestiddy morning, except there wasn't no lights on it now and it was empty. There was a regular bus dee-po like a railroad dee-po, with a ticket counter and a feller behind it, and the Law said, "Set down over there," and I set down on the bench, and the Law said, "I want to use your telephone," and he talked into the telephone a minute and put it down and said to the feller behind the ticket counter, "Keep your eye on him. I'll be back as soon as Mrs. Habersham can arrange to get herself up and dressed." He went out. I got up and went to the ticket counter.

"I want to go to Memphis," I said.

"You bet," the feller said. "You set down on the bench now. Mr. Foote will be back in a minute."

"I don't know no Mr. Foote," I said. "I want to ride that bus to Memphis."

"You got some money?" he said. "It'll cost seventy-two cents."

I taken out the matchbox and unwropped the shikepoke egg. "I'll swap you this for a ticket to Memphis," I said.

"What's that?" he said.

"It's a shikepoke egg," I said. "You never seen one before. It's worth a dollar. I'll take seventy-two cents fer it."

"No," he said, "the fellers that own that bus insist on a cash basis. If I started swapping tickets for bird eggs and livestock and such, they would fire me. You go and set down on the bench now, like Mr. Foote — "

I started for the door, but he caught me, he put one hand on the ticket counter and jumped over it and caught up with me and reached his hand out to ketch my shirt. I whupped out my pocketknife and snapped it open.

"You put a hand on me and I'll cut it off," I said.

I tried to dodge him and run at the door, but he could move quicker than any grown man I ever see, quick as Pete almost. He cut me off and stood with his back against the door and one foot raised a little, and there wasn't no other way to get out. "Get back on that bench and stay there," he said.

And there wasn't no other way out. And he stood against the door. So I went back to the bench. And then it seemed like to me that dee-po was full of folks. There was that Law again, and there was two ladies in fur coats and their faces already painted. But they still looked like they had got up in a hurry and they still never liked it, a old one and a young one, looking down at me.

"He hasn't got an overcoat!" the old one said. "How in the world did he ever get down here by himself?"

"I ask you," the Law said. "I couldn't get nothing out of him except his brother is in Memphis and he wants to get back up there."

"That's right," I said. "I got to git to Memphis today."

"Of course you must," the old one said. "Are you sure you can find your brother when you get to Memphis?"

"I reckon I can," I said. "I ain't got but one and I have knowed him all my life. I reckon I will know him again when I see him."

The old one looked at me. "Some-

how he doesn't look like he lives in Memphis," she said.

"He probably don't," the Law said. "You can't tell though. He might live anywhere, overhalls or not. This day and time they get scattered overnight from hope to breakfast; boys and girls, too, almost before they can walk good. He might have been in Missouri or Texas either yestiddy, for all we know. But he don't seem to have any doubt his brother is in Memphis. All I know to do is send him up there and leave him look."

"Yes," the old one said.

The young one set down on the bench by me and opened a hand satchel and taken out a artermatic writing pen and some papers.

"Now, honey," the old one said, "we're going to see that you find your brother, but we must have a case history for our files first. We want to know your name and your brother's name and where you were born and when your parents died."

"I don't need no case history neither," I said. "All I want is to git to Memphis. I got to git there today."

"You see?" the Law said. He said it almost like he enjoyed it. "That's what I told you."

"You're lucky, at that, Mrs. Habersham," the bus feller said. "I don't think he's got a gun on him, but he can open that knife fast enough to suit any man."

But the old one just stood there looking at me.

"Well," she said. "Well. I really don't know what to do."

"I do," the bus feller said. "I'm going to give him a ticket out of my own pocket, as a measure of protecting the company against riot and bloodshed. And when Mr. Foote tells the city board about it, it will be a civic matter and they will give me a medal too. Hey, Mr. Foote?"

But nobody paid him no mind. The old one still stood looking down at me. She said, "Well," again. Then she taken a dollar from her purse and give it to the bus feller. "I suppose he will travel on a child's ticket, won't he?"

"Wellum," the bus feller said, "I just don't know what the regulations would be. Likely I will be fired for not crating him and marking the crate Poison. But I'll risk it."

Then they were gone. Then the Law come back with a sandwich and give it to me.

"You're sure you can find that brother?" he said.

"I ain't yet convinced why not," I said. "If I don't see Pete first, he'll see me. He knows me, too."

Then the Law went out for good, too, and I et the sandwich. Then more folks come in and bought tickets, and then the bus feller said it was time to go, and I got into the bus just like Pete done, and we were gone.

I seen all the towns. I seen all of them. When the bus got to going good, I found out I was jest about wore out for sleep. But there was too much I hadn't never saw before. We run out of Jefferson and run past fields and woods, then we would run into another town and out of that un and past fields and woods again, and then into another town with stores and gins [1] and water tanks, and we run along by the railroad for a spell and I seen the signal arm move, and then some more towns, and I was jest about plumb wore out for sleep, but I couldn't resk it. Then Memphis begun. It seemed like, to me, it went on for miles. We would pass a patch of stores and I would think that was sholy it and the bus would even stop. But it wouldn't be Memphis yet and we would go on again past water tanks and smokestacks on top of the mills, and if they was gins and saw-mills, I never knowed there was that many and I never seen any that big, and where they got enough cotton and logs to run um I don't know.

Then I seen Memphis. I knowed I was right this time. It was standing up into the air. It looked like about a dozen whole towns bigger than Jefferson was set up on one edge in a field, standing up into the air higher than ara [2] hill in all Yoknapatawpha [3] County. Then we was in it, with the bus stopping every few feet, it seemed like to me, and cars rushing past on both sides of it and the streets crowded with folks from ever'where in town that day, until I didn't see how there could 'a' been nobody left in Mis'sippi a-tall to even sell me a bus ticket, let alone write out no case histories. Then the bus stopped. It was another bus dee-po, a heap bigger than the one in Jefferson. And I said, "All right. Where do folks join the army?"

[1] gins: machines for separating cotton lint from the seeds.

[2] ara: any.

[3] Yoknapatawpha (yŏk′nă·pă·tá′fá): Faulkner's imaginary county in Mississippi.

"What?" the bus feller said.

And I said it again, "Where do folks join the army?"

"Oh," he said. Then he told me how to get there. I was afraid at first I wouldn't ketch on how to do in a town as big as Memphis. But I caught on all right. I never had to ask but twice more. Then I was there, and I was durn glad to git out of all them rushing cars and shoving folks and all that racket fer a spell, and I thought, it won't be long now, and I thought how if there was any kind of a crowd there that had done already joined the army, too, Pete would likely see me before I seen him. And so I walked into the room. And Pete wasn't there.

He wasn't even there. There was a soldier with a big arrerhead on his sleeve, writing, and two fellers standing in front of him, and there was some more folks there, I reckon. It seems to me I remember some more folks there.

I went to the table where the soldier was writing, and I said, "Where's Pete?" and he looked up and I said, "My brother. Pete Grier. Where is he?"

"What?" the soldier said. "Who?"

And I told him again. "He joined the army yestiddy. He's going to Pearl Harbor. So am I. I want to ketch him. Where you-all got him?" Now they were all looking at me, but I never paid them no mind. "Come on," I said. "Where is he?"

The soldier had quit writing. He had both hands spraddled out on the table. "Oh," he said. "You're going, too, hah?"

"Yes," I said. "They got to have wood and water. I can chop it and tote it. Come on. Where's Pete?"

The soldier stood up. "Who let you in here?" he said. "Go on. Beat it."

"Durn that," I said. "You tell me where Pete — "

I be dog if he couldn't move faster than the bus feller even. He never come over the table, he come around it, he was on me almost before I knowed it, so that I jest had time to jump back and whup out my pocketknife and snap it open and hit one lick, and he hollered and jumped back and grabbed one hand with the other hand and stood there cussing and hollering.

One of the other fellers grabbed me from behind, and I hit at him with the knife, but I couldn't reach him.

Then both of the fellers had me from behind, and then another soldier come out of a door at the back. He had on a belt with a britching strop [1] over one shoulder.

"What's this?" he said.

"That little kid cut me with a knife!" the first soldier hollered. When he said that I tried to git at him again, but both them fellers was holding me, two against one, and the soldier with the britching strop said, "Here, here. Put your knife up, feller. None of us are armed. A man don't knife-fight folks that are barehanded." I could begin to hear him then. He sounded jest like Pete talked to me. "Let him go," he said. They let me go. "Now what's all the trouble about?" And I told him. "I see," he said. "And you come up to see if he was all right before he left."

"No," I said. "I come to — "

But he had already turned to where the first soldier was wropping a handkerchief around his hand.

"Have you got him?" he said. The first soldier went back to the table and looked at some papers.

"Here he is," he said. "He enlisted yestiddy. He's in a detachment leaving this morning for Little Rock." He had a watch stropped on his arm. He looked at it. "The train leaves in about fifty minutes. If I know country boys, they're probably all down there at the station right now."

"Get him up here," the one with the britching strop said. "Phone the station. Tell the porter to get him a cab. And you come with me," he said.

[1] britching strop: breeching strap, which is part of a rude harness; this is the boy's impression of the soldier's Sam Browne belt.

It was another office behind that un, with jest a table and some chairs. We set there while the soldier smoked, and it wasn't long; I knowed Pete's feet soon as I heard them. Then the first soldier opened the door and Pete come in. He never had no soldier clothes on. He looked jest like he did when he got on the bus yestiddy morning, except it seemed to me like it was at least a week, so much had happened, and I had done had to do so much traveling. He come in and there he was, looking at me like he hadn't never left home, except that here we was in Memphis, on the way to Pearl Harbor.

"What in durnation are you doing here?" he said.

And I told him, "You got to have wood and water to cook with. I can chop it and tote it for you-all."

"No," Pete said. "You're going back home."

"No, Pete," I said. "I got to go too. I got to. It hurts my heart, Pete."

"No," Pete said. He looked at the soldier. "I jest don't know what could have happened to him, lootenant," he said. "He never drawed a knife on anybody before in his life."

He looked at me. "What did you do it for?"

"I don't know," I said. "I jest had to. I jest had to git here. I jest had to find you."

"Well, don't you never do it again, you hear?" Pete said. "You put that knife in your pocket and you keep it there. If I ever again hear of you drawing it on anybody, I'm coming back from wherever I am at and whup the fire out of you. You hear me?"

"I would pure cut a throat if it would bring you back to stay," I said. "Pete," I said. "Pete."

"No," Pete said. Now his voice wasn't hard and quick no more, it was almost quiet, and I knowed now I wouldn't never change him. "You must go home. You must look after maw, and I am depending on you to look after my ten

acres. I want you to go back home. To-day. Do you hear?"

"I hear," I said.

"Can he get back home by himself?" the soldier said.

"He come up here by himself," Pete said.

"I can get back, I reckon," I said. "I don't live in but one place. I don't reckon it's moved."

Pete taken a dollar out of his pocket and give it to me. "That'll buy your bus ticket right to our mailbox," he said. "I want you to mind the lootenant. He'll send you to the bus. And you go back home and you take care of maw and look after my ten acres and keep that durn knife in your pocket. You hear me?"

"Yes, Pete," I said.

"All right," Pete said. "Now I got to go." He put his hand on my head again. But this time he never wrung my neck. He just laid his hand on my head a minute. And then I be dog if he didn't lean down and kiss me, and I heard his feet and then the door, and I never looked up and that was all, me setting there, rubbing the place where Pete kissed me and the soldier throwed back in his chair, looking out the window and coughing. He reached into his pocket and handed something to me without looking around. It was a piece of chewing gum.

"Much obliged," I said. "Well, I reckon I might as well start back. I got a right fer [1] piece to go."

"Wait," the soldier said. Then he telephoned again and I said again I better start back, and he said again, "Wait. Remember what Pete told you."

So we waited, and then another lady come in, old, too, in a fur coat, too, but she smelled all right, she never had no artermatic writing pen nor no case history neither. She come in and the soldier got up, and she looked around quick until she saw me, and come and

---

[1] **fer**: far.

put her hand on my shoulder light and quick and easy as maw herself might 'a' done it.

"Come on," she said. "Let's go home to dinner."

"Nome,"[1] I said. "I got to ketch the bus to Jefferson." *look keep bus in bus*

"I know. There's plenty of time. We'll go home and eat dinner first."

She had a car. And now we was right down in the middle of all them other cars. We was almost under the busses, and all them crowds of people on the street close enough to where I could have talked to them if I had knowed who they was. After a while she stopped the car. "Here we are," she said, and I looked at it, and if all that was her house, she sho had a big family. But all of it wasn't. We crossed a hall with trees growing in it and went into a little room without nothing in it but a Negro dressed up in a uniform a heap shinier than them soldiers had, and the Negro shut the door, and then I hollered, "Look out!" and grabbed, but it was all right; that whole little room jest went right on up and stopped and the door opened and we was in another hall, and the lady unlocked a door and we went in, and there was another soldier, an old feller, with a britching strop, too, and a silver-colored bird on each shoulder.

"Here we are," the lady said. "This is Colonel McKellogg. Now, what would you like for dinner?"

"I reckon I'll jest have some ham and eggs and coffee," I said.

She had done started to pick up the telephone. She stopped. "Coffee?" she said. "When did you start drinking coffee?"

"I don't know," I said. "I reckon it was before I could remember."

"You're about eight, aren't you?" she said.

"Nome," I said. "I'm eight and ten months. Going on eleven months."

[1] "Nome": contraction of "no ma'am."

She telephoned then. Then we set there and I told them how Pete had jest left that morning for Pearl Harbor and I had aimed to go with him, but I would have to go back home to take care of maw and look after Pete's ten acres, and she said how they had a little boy about my size, too, in a school in the East. Then a Negro, another one, in a short kind of shirttail coat, rolled a kind of wheelbarrer in. It had my ham and eggs and a glass of milk and a piece of pie, too, and I thought I was hungry. But when I taken the first bite I found out I couldn't swallow it, and I got up quick.

"I got to go," I said.

"Wait," she said.

"I got to go," I said.

"Just a minute," she said. "I've already telephoned for the car. It won't be but a minute now. Can't you drink the milk even? Or maybe some of your coffee?"

"Nome," I said. "I ain't hungry. I'll eat when I git home." Then the telephone rung. She never even answered it.

"There," she said. "There's the car." And we went back down in that 'ere little moving room with the dressed-up Negro. This time it was a big car with a soldier driving it. I got into the front with him. She give the soldier a dollar. "He might get hungry," she said. "Try to find a decent place for him."

"O.K., Mrs. McKellogg," the soldier said.

Then we was gone again. And now I could see Memphis good, bright in the sunshine, while we was swinging around it. And the first thing I knowed, we was back on the same highway the bus run on this morning — the patches of stores and them big gins and saw-mills, and Memphis running on for miles, it seemed like to me, before it begun to give out. Then we was running again between the fields and woods, running fast now, and except for that soldier, it was like I hadn't never been to Memphis a-tall. We was going fast now. At this rate, before I knowed it we would be home again, and I thought about me riding up to Frenchman's Bend in this here big car with a soldier running it, and all of a sudden I begun to cry. I never knowed I was fixing to, and I couldn't stop it. I set there by that soldier, crying. We was going fast.

FOR DISCUSSION

1. Human relationships make the basis of most good stories. How would you describe the relationship between Pete and his brother? Give some specific action or remark to support each point in your description.

2. What outside event, affecting the relationship of the brothers, provoked the happenings in this story?

3. What would usually happen to a small boy who set out to make such a trip? How did this boy defeat the usual methods of getting him straight back home?

4. Recall each person who dealt with the boy on his trip to Memphis. Who came nearest to being unkind to him? What treatment did he receive that was positively kind? What was the one time Pete was really stern with him? Why?

5. How was Pete's farewell in Memphis different from the one that took place when he boarded the bus? Give reasons for the difference.

A BOY'S POINT OF VIEW

1. What did you learn about the boy, his family, and his general background from the very first paragraph? What details did you fill in later?

2. Give examples of humor in the story that arise entirely from the boy's telling it. Tell how he described at least three things that were new to him. Recall details of his reports on people to show that he was observant, even though inexperienced.

3. What difference would it have made in the story if Pete had told it, instead of the little brother?

THE AUTHOR

WILLIAM FAULKNER (1897–1962) spent most of his life in Oxford, Mississippi, which is often identified with the "Jefferson" of his novels. But his fellow townsmen did not appreciate this distinction for Faulkner's recurrent theme was that the South has declined from the aristocratic splendor of former days, as shown in *The Sound and the Fury* (1929) and *Light in August* (1932). During World War I, he served in France with the British Royal Air Force, and this background appears in his novel *A Fable*, winner of the National Book Award for 1954.

Faulkner's books are not easy reading, for he often told his stories through illiterate characters, and his style is marked by long, involved sentences. But the tremendous emotional effectiveness and deep sense of reality which he developed won him a place in the front ranks of American novelists. In 1950 he was awarded the Nobel prize for literature, the fourth American to be so honored.

The Faulkner Range ➤

The photographs on the facing page depict the sense of Southern history that dominates Faulkner's major novels: the bayou today looks exactly as it did in the early 1700's; the plantation home appears much as it did in the 1840's; modern Atlanta completes the range of 250 years of Southern history.

SHIRLEY JACKSON

The Lottery

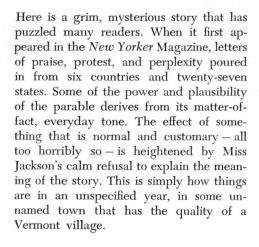

Here is a grim, mysterious story that has puzzled many readers. When it first appeared in the *New Yorker* Magazine, letters of praise, protest, and perplexity poured in from six countries and twenty-seven states. Some of the power and plausibility of the parable derives from its matter-of-fact, everyday tone. The effect of something that is normal and customary — all too horribly so — is heightened by Miss Jackson's calm refusal to explain the meaning of the story. This is simply how things are in an unspecified year, in some unnamed town that has the quality of a Vermont village.

THE morning of June 27th was clear and sunny, with the fresh warmth of a full-summer day; the flowers were blossoming profusely, and the grass was richly green. The people of the village began to gather in the square, between the post office and the bank, around ten o'clock; in some towns there were so many people that the lottery took

two days and had to be started on June 26th, but in this village, where there were only about three hundred people, the whole lottery took only about two hours, so it could begin at ten o'clock in the morning and still be through in time to allow the villagers to get home for noon dinner.

The children assembled first, of course. School was recently over for the summer, and the feeling of liberty sat uneasily on most of them; they tended to gather together quietly for a while before they broke into boisterous play, and their talk was still of the classroom and the teacher, of books and reprimands. Bobby Martin had already stuffed his pockets full of stones, and the other boys soon followed his example, selecting the smoothest and roundest stones; Bobby and Harry Jones and Dickie Delacroix — the villagers pronounced this name "Dellacroy" — eventually made a great pile of stones in one corner of the square and guarded it against the raids of the other boys. The girls stood aside, talking among themselves, looking over their shoulders at the boys, and the very small children rolled in the dust or clung to the hands of their older brothers or sisters.

Soon the men began to gather, surveying their own children, speaking of planting and rain, tractors and taxes. They stood together, away from the pile of stones in the corner, and their jokes were quiet, and they smiled rather than laughed. The women, wearing faded house dresses and sweaters, came shortly after their menfolk. They greeted one another and exchanged bits of gossip as they went to join their husbands. Soon the women, standing by their husbands, began to call to their children, and the children came reluctantly, having to be called four or five times. Bobby Martin ducked under his mother's grasping hand and ran, laughing, back to the pile of stones. His father spoke up sharply, and Bobby came quickly and took his place between his father and his oldest brother.

The lottery was conducted — as were the square dances, the teen-age club, the Halloween program — by Mr. Summers, who had time and energy to devote to civic activities. He was a round-faced, jovial man, and he ran the coal business; and people were sorry for him, because he had no children and his wife was a scold. When he arrived in the square, carrying the black wooden box, there was a murmur of conversation among the villagers, and he waved and called, "Little late today, folks." The postmaster, Mr. Graves, followed him, carrying a three-legged stool; and the stool was put in the center of the square, and Mr. Summers set the black box down on it. The villagers kept their distance, leaving a space between themselves and the stool, and when Mr. Summers said, "Some of you fellows want to give me a hand?" there was a hesitation before two men, Mr. Martin and his oldest son, Baxter, came forward to hold the box steady on the stool while Mr. Summers stirred up the papers inside it.

The original paraphernalia for the lottery had been lost long ago, and the black box now resting on the stool had been put into use even before Old Man Warner, the oldest man in town, was born. Mr. Summers spoke frequently to the villagers about making a new box, but no one liked to upset even as much tradition as was represented by the black box. There was a story that the present box had been made with some pieces of the box that had preceded it, the one that had been constructed when the first people settled down to make a village here. Every year, after the lottery, Mr. Summers began talking again about a new box, but every year the subject was allowed to fade off without anything's being done. The black box grew shabbier each year; by now it was no longer completely black but splintered badly along one side to show the original wood color, and in some places faded or stained.

Mr. Martin and his oldest son, Baxter, held the black box securely on the stool until Mr. Summers had stirred the papers thoroughly with his hand. Because so much of the ritual had been forgotten or discarded, Mr. Summers had been successful in having slips of paper substituted for the chips of wood that had been used for generations. Chips of wood, Mr. Summers had argued, had been all very well when the village was tiny, but now that the population was more than three hundred and likely to keep on growing, it was necessary to use something that would fit more easily into the black box. The night before the lottery, Mr. Summers and Mr. Graves made up the slips of paper and put them into the box, and it was then taken to the safe of Mr. Summers' coal company and locked up until Mr. Summers was ready to take it to the square next morning. The rest of the year, the box was put away, sometimes one place, sometimes another; it had spent one year in Mr. Graves's barn and another year underfoot in the post office, and sometimes it was set on a shelf in the Martin grocery and left there.

There was a great deal of fussing to be done before Mr. Summers declared the lottery open. There were the lists to make up — of heads of families, heads of households in each family, members of each household in each family. There was the proper swearing-in of Mr. Summers by the postmaster, as the official of the lottery; at one time, some people remembered, there had been a recital of some sort, performed by the official of the lottery, a perfunctory, tuneless chant that had been rattled off duly each year; some people believed that the official of the lottery used to stand just so when he said or sang it; others believed that he was supposed to walk among the people; but years and years ago this part of the ritual had been allowed to lapse. There had been, also, a ritual salute, which the official of the lottery had had to use in addressing each person who came up to draw from the box, but this also had changed with time, until now it was felt necessary only for the official to speak to each person approaching. Mr. Summers was very good at all this; in his clean white shirt and blue jeans, with one hand resting carelessly on the black box, he seemed very proper and important as he talked interminably to Mr. Graves and the Martins.

Just as Mr. Summers finally left off talking and turned to the assembled villagers, Mrs. Hutchinson came hurriedly along the path to the square, her sweater thrown over her shoulders, and slid into place in the back of the crowd. "Clean forgot what day it was," she said to Mrs. Delacroix, who stood next to her, and they both laughed softly. "Thought my old man was out back stacking wood," Mrs. Hutchinson went on, "and then I looked out the window and the kids was gone, and then I remembered it was the twenty-seventh and came a-running." She dried her hands on her apron, and Mrs. Delacroix said, "You're in time, though. They're still talking away up there."

Mrs. Hutchinson craned her neck to see through the crowd and found her husband and children standing near the front. She tapped Mrs. Delacroix on the arm as a farewell and began to make her way through the crowd. The people separated good-humoredly to let her through; two or three people said, in voices just loud enough to be heard across the crowd, "Here comes your Mrs., Hutchinson," and "Bill, she made it after all." Mrs. Hutchinson reached her husband, and Mr. Summers, who had been waiting, said cheerfully, "Thought we were going to have to get on without you, Tessie." Mrs. Hutchinson said, grinning, "Wouldn't have me leave m'dishes in the sink, now, would you, Joe?" and soft laughter ran through the crowd as the people stirred back into position after Mrs. Hutchinson's arrival.

"Well, now," Mr. Summers said soberly, "guess we better get started, get this over with, so's we can go back to work. Anybody ain't here?"

"Dunbar," several people said. "Dunbar, Dunbar."

Mr. Summers consulted his list. "Clyde Dunbar," he said. "That's right. He's broke his leg, hasn't he? Who's drawing for him?"

"Me, I guess," a woman said, and Mr. Summers turned to look at her. "Wife draws for her husband," Mr. Summers said. "Don't you have a grown boy to do it for you, Janey?" Although Mr. Summers and everyone else in the village knew the answer perfectly well, it was the business of the official of the lottery to ask such questions formally. Mr. Summers waited with an expression of polite interest while Mrs. Dunbar answered.

"Horace's not but sixteen yet," Mrs. Dunbar said regretfully. "Guess I gotta fill in for the old man this year."

"Right," Mr. Summers said. He made a note on the list he was holding. Then he asked, "Watson boy drawing this year?"

A tall boy in the crowd raised his hand. "Here," he said. "I'm drawing for m'mother and me." He blinked his eyes nervously and ducked his head as several voices in the crowd said things like "Good fellow, Jack," and "Glad to see your mother's got a man to do it."

"Well," Mr. Summers said, "guess that's everyone. Old Man Warner make it?"

"Here," a voice said, and Mr. Summers nodded.

A sudden hush fell on the crowd as Mr. Summers cleared his throat and looked at the list. "All ready?" he called. "Now, I'll read the names — heads of families first — and the men come up and take a paper out of the box. Keep the paper folded in your hand without looking at it until everyone has had a turn. Everything clear?"

The people had done it so many times that they only half listened to the directions; most of them were quiet, wetting their lips, not looking around. Then Mr. Summers raised one hand high and said, "Adams." A man disengaged himself from the crowd and came forward. "Hi, Steve," Mr. Summers said, and Mr. Adams said, "Hi, Joe." They grinned at one another humorlessly and nervously. Then Mr. Adams reached into the black box and took out a folded paper. He held it firmly by one corner as he turned and went hastily back to his place in the crowd, where he stood a little apart from his family, not looking down at his hand.

"Allen," Mr. Summers said. "Anderson. . . . Bentham."

"Seems like there's no time at all between lotteries any more," Mrs. Delacroix said to Mrs. Graves in the back row. "Seems like we got through with the last one only last week."

"Time sure goes fast," Mrs. Graves said.

"Clark. . . . Delacroix."

"There goes my old man," Mrs. Delacroix said. She held her breath while her husband went forward.

"Dunbar," Mr. Summers said, and Mrs. Dunbar went steadily to the box while one of the women said, "Go on, Janey," and another said, "There she goes."

"We're next," Mrs. Graves said. She watched while Mr. Graves came around from the side of the box, greeted Mr. Summers gravely, and selected a slip of paper from the box. By now, all through the crowd there were men holding the small folded papers in their large hands, turning them over and over nervously. Mrs. Dunbar and her two sons stood together, Mrs. Dunbar holding the slip of paper.

"Harburt. . . . Hutchinson."

"Get up there, Bill," Mrs. Hutchinson said, and the people near her laughed.

"Jones."

"They do say," Mr. Adams said to Old Man Warner, who stood next to him, "that over in the north village they're talking of giving up the lottery."

Old Man Warner snorted. "Pack of crazy fools," he said. "Listening to the young folks, nothing's good enough for them. Next thing you know, they'll be wanting to go back to living in caves, nobody work any more, live *that* way for a while. Used to be a saying about 'Lottery in June, corn be heavy soon.' First thing you know, we'd all be eating stewed chickweed and acorns. There's always been a lottery," he added petulantly. "Bad enough to see young Joe Summers up there joking with everybody."

"Some places have already quit lotteries," Mrs. Adams said.

"Nothing but trouble in that," Old Man Warner said stoutly. "Pack of young fools."

"Martin." And Bobby Martin watched his father go forward. "Overdyke. . . . Percy."

"I wish they'd hurry," Mrs. Dunbar said to her older son. "I wish they'd hurry."

"They're almost through," her son said.

"You get ready to run tell Dad," Mrs. Dunbar said.

Mr. Summers called his own name and then stepped forward precisely and selected a slip from the box. Then he called, "Warner."

"Seventy-seventh year I been in the lottery," Old Man Warner said as he went through the crowd. "Seventy-seventh time."

"Watson." The tall boy came awkwardly through the crowd. Someone said, "Don't be nervous, Jack," and Mr. Summers said, "Take your time, son."

"Zanini."

After that, there was a long pause, a breathless pause, until Mr. Summers, holding his slip of paper in the air, said, "All right, fellows." For a minute, no one moved, and then all the slips of paper were opened. Suddenly, all the women began to speak at once, saying, "Who is it?" "Who's got it?" "Is it the Dunbars?" "Is it the Watsons?" Then the voices began to say, "It's Hutchinson. It's Bill." "Bill Hutchinson's got it."

"Go tell your father," Mrs. Dunbar said to her older son.

People began to look around to see the Hutchinsons. Bill Hutchinson was standing quiet, staring down at the paper in his hand. Suddenly, Tessie Hutchinson shouted to Mr. Summers, "You didn't give him time enough to take any paper he wanted. I saw you. It wasn't fair!"

"Be a good sport, Tessie," Mrs. Delacroix called, and Mrs. Graves said, "All of us took the same chance."

"Shut up, Tessie," Bill Hutchinson said.

"Well, everyone," Mr. Summers said, "that was done pretty fast, and now we've got to be hurrying a little more to get done in time." He consulted his next list. "Bill," he said, "you draw for the Hutchinson family. You got any other households in the Hutchinsons?"

"There's Don and Eva," Mrs. Hutchinson yelled. "Make *them* take their chance!"

"Daughters draw with their husbands' families, Tessie," Mr. Summers said gently. "You know that as well as anyone else."

"It wasn't *fair*," Tessie said.

"I guess not, Joe," Bill Hutchinson said regretfully. "My daughter draws with her husband's family, that's only fair. And I've got no other family except the kids."

"Then, as far as drawing for families is concerned, it's you," Mr. Summers said in explanation, "and as far as drawing for households is concerned, that's you, too. Right?"

"Right," Bill Hutchinson said.

"How many kids, Bill?" Mr. Summers asked formally.

"Three," Bill Hutchinson said. "There's Bill, Jr., and Nancy, and little Dave. And Tessie and me."

"All right, then," Mr. Summers said. "Harry, you got their tickets back?"

Mr. Graves nodded and held up the slips of paper. "Put them in the box, then," Mr. Summers directed. "Take

Bill's and put it in."

"I think we ought to start over," Mrs. Hutchinson said, as quietly as she could. "I tell you it wasn't *fair*. You didn't give him time enough to choose. *Everybody* saw that."

Mr. Graves had selected the five slips and put them in the box, and he dropped all the papers but those onto the ground, where the breeze caught them and lifted them off.

"Listen, everybody," Mrs. Hutchinson was saying to the people around her.

"Ready, Bill?" Mr. Summers asked, and Bill Hutchinson, with one quick glance around at his wife and children, nodded.

"Remember," Mr. Summers said, "take the slips and keep them folded until each person has taken one. Harry, you help little Dave." Mr. Graves took the hand of the little boy, who came willingly with him up to the box. "Take a paper out of the box, Davy," Mr. Summers said. Davy put his hand into the box and laughed. "Take just one paper," Mr. Summers said. "Harry, you hold it for him." Mr. Graves took the child's hand and removed the folded paper from the tight fist and held it while little Dave stood next to him and looked up at him wonderingly.

"Nancy next," Mr. Summers said. Nancy was twelve, and her school friends breathed heavily as she went forward, switching her skirt, and took a slip daintily from the box. "Bill, Jr.," Mr. Summers said, and Billy, his face red and his feet overlarge, nearly knocked the box over as he got a paper out. "Tessie," Mr. Summers said. She hesitated for a minute, looking around defiantly, and then set her lips and went up to the box. She snatched a paper out and held it behind her.

"Bill," Mr. Summers said, and Bill Hutchinson reached into the box and felt around, bringing his hand out at last with the slip of paper in it.

The crowd was quiet. A girl whis-pered, "I hope it's not Nancy," and the sound of the whisper reached the edges of the crowd.

"It's not the way it used to be," Old Man Warner said clearly. "People ain't the way they used to be."

"All right," Mr. Summers said. "Open the papers. Harry, you open little Dave's."

Mr. Graves opened the slip of paper, and there was a general sigh through the crowd as he held it up and everyone could see that it was blank. Nancy and Bill, Jr., opened theirs at the same time, and both beamed and laughed, turning around to the crowd and holding their slips of paper above their heads.

"Tessie," Mr. Summers said. There was a pause, and then Mr. Summers looked at Bill Hutchinson, and Bill unfolded his paper and showed it. It was blank.

"It's Tessie," Mr. Summers said, and his voice was hushed. "Show us her paper, Bill."

Bill Hutchinson went over to his wife and forced the slip of paper out of her hand. It had a black spot on it, the black spot Mr. Summers had made the night before with the heavy pencil in the coal-company office. Bill Hutchinson held it up, and there was a stir in the crowd.

"All right, folks," Mr. Summers said. "Let's finish quickly."

Although the villagers had forgotten the ritual and lost the original black box, they still remembered to use stones. The pile of stones the boys had made earlier was ready; there were stones on the ground with the blowing scraps of paper that had come out of the box. Mrs. Delacroix selected a stone so large she had to pick it up with both hands and turned to Mrs. Dunbar. "Come on," she said. "Hurry up."

Mrs. Dunbar had small stones in both hands, and she said, gasping for breath, "I can't run at all. You'll have to go ahead and I'll catch up with you."

The children had stones already, and

someone gave little Davy Hutchinson a few pebbles.

Tessie Hutchinson was in the center of a cleared space by now, and she held her hands out desperately as the villagers moved in on her. "It isn't fair," she said. A stone hit her on the side of the head.

Old Man Warner was saying, "Come on, come on, everyone." Steve Adams was in the front of the crowd of villagers, with Mrs. Graves beside him.

"It isn't fair, it isn't right," Mrs. Hutchinson screamed, and then they were upon her.

FOR DISCUSSION

For a long time Miss Jackson refused to discuss this story. Finally, some twelve years after it was written, she remarked to an interviewer that she had been on her way to the market one day when it occurred to her to wonder how it might be if human sacrifice were practiced in our society. Turning back home, she proceeded to write "The Lottery." If that seems like a strange history — well, it is a strange story. Now let us consider some of the ways in which the tale gains its effects.

1. What effect is gained by the opening description of June 27 with its warmth, flowers, and green grass? Can you think of any reason why Miss Jackson would specify the exact day of the month? Why do you think she does not state the year?

2. Notice that the lottery is taking place in other towns over an unspecified area. What is the effect of the remark that in this town they "could be through in time to allow the villagers to get home for noon dinner"?

3. What are some of the details that contribute most, even if indirectly, to the horror of the tale?

4. Discuss the attitude of Old Man Warner, who says, "There's *always* been a lottery." Consider his recollections and the old sayings he quotes. What is his opinion of the towns that have given up the lottery?

5. Does the way in which each member of the Hutchinson family makes the final drawing add to our understanding of the individuals? What is the effect of having Nancy and Bill, Jr., laugh at their own blank slips without thinking beyond?

UNDERLYING IDEAS

1. Mrs. Hutchinson's last words are: "It isn't fair, it isn't right." Discuss each of these remarks separately. Is there any difference between them?

2. We are never told directly why the lottery is being held, yet it is every reader's right to speculate about it. Can you suggest a reason for this dreadful annual act, now so old that its origins seem completely forgotten? Can you find some small hint in the story about a possible origin for the lottery? Why might such an activity continue even when there are no longer any reasons for it?

3. The lottery is imaginary — happily. But what may the story tell us about customs, practices, attitudes, and aspects of human nature that are quite real?

THE AUTHOR

SHIRLEY JACKSON (b. 1919) is a native of California. She came East to attend Syracuse University, and there met Stanley Edgar Hyman, now a well-known literary critic, whom she married. The Hymans live in Vermont, where he teaches at Bennington College. Miss Jackson's stories have appeared in many magazines, and she has also published a number of novels, including *The Bird's Nest* and *The Haunting of Hill House.* Much of her fiction is preoccupied with the mysterious and the supernatural. In a different vein are two delightful and funny books about life in the Hyman household with their four children: *Life Among the Savages* and *Raising Demons.*

As the Artist Sees It ➤

On the facing page is a water color by Donald Bolognese, interpreting the climax of "The Lottery." Do you think the artist has captured the mood of Shirley Jackson's stark story?

Comparing Stories and Techniques

Now that you have read the stories in this section and discussed the points mentioned in the Guide to Reading, you may find it useful to make some critical comparisons. Here you can re-examine the methods and materials of fiction and see some of the ways in which skillful writers create the effects of their stories.

ACTION

A short story rarely has a complicated plot because its length simply will not allow for any extended development of action. Within this limitation, however, there is room for a great deal of variety. You noticed, for example, that "Old Man at the Bridge" is almost plotless. Very little "happens" in the story: we simply learn of the plight of an old man who has gotten involved in a war. In contrast, both "The Devil and Daniel Webster" and "The Wolfer" have fairly intricate plots. In these stories, the plots are resolved only after a series of complications. "The Lottery" is a good example of the surprise ending; that is, the climax of the plot occurs at the very end of the story. "The Hack Driver" follows a similar pattern to gain an entirely different effect. In this case, the surprise ending is comic rather than shocking.

What other stories in this section would you characterize as almost plotless? Which stories have more complicated plots? Try to explain how the author's purpose for the story as a whole determined the treatment of plot in your examples.

CHARACTER

Fullness of characterization varies considerably in the twelve stories in this section. Consider the subtle, complex characterizations in Willa Cather's "The Sculptor's Funeral," and compare this treatment to the simple character "sketches" of "The Portable Phonograph." We learn more about even the minor figures of Cather's story — Banker Phelps, for instance — than we do about any of the men in "The Portable Phonograph." Or compare Heming-

way's "Old Man at the Bridge" to Bradbury's "The Flying Machine." Hemingway's pathetic old man, worried over the fate of his animals, appears to us as a more complete character than Bradbury's Emperor, no matter how important or imposing the latter may be. These simple characterizations are not necessarily weaknesses in "The Portable Phonograph" or "The Flying Machine." Notice that both stories have a point to make or a message to express. It would appear that a "message" story will not allow for much character development: if we became too concerned over the fate of the individuals, we might miss the point of the story.

How do the characterizations in "The Lottery" differ from those in "Two Soldiers"? How would you explain these different treatments of character? What effect does each treatment create?

POINT OF VIEW

"The Sculptor's Funeral" is told from an omniscient point of view. The author, and therefore the reader, knows virtually everything that can be known about the characters and events of the story. The best-informed person in the story could not have possessed all this knowledge. Willa Cather chose this method deliberately. Much of the effect of "The Sculptor's Funeral" hinges on our having a complete picture of the dead man and his two lives, and this picture can be presented only through an omniscient point of view.

"Two Soldiers" offers a good example of the first-person point of view. Much of the humor of the story is created through this treatment, as the reader sees familiar things through the eyes of an inexperienced boy. Consider, for example, the description of a Sam Browne belt as a "britching strop." Some serious effects are created through this treatment, as the reader learns how a distant war can directly affect a boy.

To see the importance of a particular point of view, ask yourself how the story would have been changed if "The Sculptor's Funeral" had been told in the first person by Mrs. Merrick or Jim Laird or Henry Steavens.

At certain important points in "Early Marriage," the reader is limited to Nancy Belle's point of view. Point out some situations in the story where the point of view becomes limited in this way. In what ways would "Early Marriage" have been different if the point of view had been omniscient throughout, if the reader could always possess more knowledge than Nancy Belle?

SETTING

In at least two of the stories you have read, "The Portable Phonograph" and "The Lottery," the setting is deliberately unspecified. The reasons for this treatment should be clear. Both stories represent general comments on situations that presumably could occur at any time and place. A specific setting would interfere with this universal quality. In contrast, notice how the specific setting of "The Devil and Daniel Webster" is used to create an effect of realism in a tale of fantasy.

Point out some other stories in which setting serves a definite purpose. In your examples, are time and place clearly specified or not? How does the treatment of setting affect the stories? Would you describe any of the stories in this unit as "local color"? That is, are there any stories in which the setting is the most important element?

STYLE

Style, the author's particular use of language, is one of the things that helps determine the *tone* of the story. That is, the writer will create a special tone through his choice of certain kinds of words and phrases. Notice, for example, the opening lines of "The Hack Driver":

. . . When I graduated from law school, I wanted to climb, socially and financially. I wanted to be famous, and dine at large houses with men who shuddered at Common People who don't dress for dinner.

The tone is humorous and somewhat self-critical. The narrator finds his youthful attitudes and ambitions silly. Observe how a great part of this effect is created by capitalizing "Common People." The next sentence establishes the humorous tone even more firmly:

Oh, I was a fine young calf!

Young calves are clumsy, comic figures, and the reader can guess that the narrator will also be a comic character. Notice how the tone would have been altered if the line had read, "Oh, I was a stupid young fool!" or "Oh, how blind I was then!"

"Flight" opens with what seems like a simple description of the setting, but many of the phrases help establish a specific tone:

About fifteen miles below Monterey, on the wild coast, the Torres family had their farm, a few sloping acres above a cliff that dropped to the brown reefs and to the hissing white waters of the ocean.

"Wild coast," "cliff . . . dropped to the brown reefs," "hissing white waters" — these are the important clues to the tone, the phrases that help create an atmosphere of seriousness or danger. The treatment continues with such phrases as "the farm buildings huddled . . . crouched low to the ground," "the rotting barn . . . beaten by the damp wind," "the sterile wind." Before we meet a single character in "Flight," we can guess that the story will be serious and possibly tragic.

Point out some of the effects of style in "The Portable Phonograph." What particular words or phrases help give a feeling of desolation?

How would you describe the tone of "The Secret Life of Walter Mitty"? Can you point out some of the ways in which James Thurber establishes the tone of the story? Point out the effects of style in some of the other stories in this unit. In each of your examples, show what methods the author has used to establish the tone.

An Analysis of a Single Story

As you have observed, "Old Man at the Bridge" displays little or no plot. Two men meet and talk for a few minutes, and that is all. Within the span of the story, however, there is a great deal of psychological and emotional development.

The story opens with straightforward description:

An old man with steel-rimmed spectacles and very dusty clothes sat by the side of the road.

The story, then, will concentrate on the old man; and the scene of war, flight, and dislocation will provide a setting.

The next passage is significant:

It was my business to cross the bridge, explore the bridgehead beyond, and find out to what point the enemy had advanced. I did this and returned over the bridge.

Here is an opportunity for action, for contact with the enemy, yet we are told nothing about the scouting foray, and we are not even told how close the enemy is. Nevertheless, we return to the old man with a sense of foreboding. In this connection, notice the effect of the phrase, "The trucks ground up and away, heading out of it all. . . ." The old man cannot get out.

The narrator begins questioning the old man, and eventually manages to piece together the refugee's story. Meanwhile we are never allowed to ignore the background that was established at the beginning.

"Various animals," he said, and shook his head. "I had to leave them."

I was watching the bridge and the African-looking country of the Ebro Delta and wondering how long now it would be before we would see the enemy, and listening all the while for the first noises that would signal that ever-mysterious event called contact, and the old man still sat there. . . .

"And you have no family?" I asked, watching the far end of the bridge where a few last carts were hurrying down the slope of the bank. . . .

"Why not?" I said, watching the far bank where now there were no carts.

The enemy is never far away. Now, the scene that a few moments ago was crowded with carts, soldiers, and refugees is left silent and deserted, waiting in ominous stillness for "that ever-mysterious event called contact."

Throughout the story, the narrator avoids telling the old man what both of them know: that the animals will be killed. In a sense the animals have two symbolic functions in the story. They represent the things that all refugees must leave behind when they flee, but they symbolize something else as well. If animals cannot survive, then neither can human beings. By the end of the story, we can guess that the old man will be killed. He tries to rise, but falls back to the ground, and "there was nothing to do about him."

The final paragraph adds an ironic note:

It was Easter Sunday and the Fascists were advancing toward the Ebro.

It is Easter Sunday, but war must go on. And the old man, who has no part in the war, "no politics," must suffer:

It was a gray overcast day with a low ceiling so their planes were not up. That and the fact that cats know how to look after themselves was all the good luck that old man would ever have.

In a short essay, analyze William Faulkner's "Two Soldiers," paying particular attention to the following questions. How does the use of the boy's point of view affect the story? Was the boy a good choice as the narrator? Why, or why not? What is the tone of the story? What words or phrases help establish the tone?

The Short Story in the Twentieth Century

You might enjoy reading more short stories by the writers represented in this section. The work of these writers has a range and variety that no single short story can reveal. ERNEST HEMINGWAY and WILLIAM FAULKNER particularly demand a wider acquaintance — they are masters of both the long and short forms of fiction. JAMES THURBER is an expert in the comic tale. WILLA CATHER, SINCLAIR LEWIS, and JOHN STEINBECK have also written many excellent short stories, although they are known primarily as novelists.

There are a host of other important short-story writers whose work you might sample. SHERWOOD ANDERSON influenced many writers with his realistic stories of life in a small Midwestern town. These were collected in a volume called *Winesburg, Ohio.*

The stories of F. SCOTT FITZGERALD offer a picture of the "Jazz Age" of the 1920's. With Ernest Hemingway, Fitzgerald is considered a representative of the "lost generation" — the group of writers who lived through the period of disillusion and disruption that followed World War I. Some of Fitzgerald's finest stories examine the effects of this troubled era on the wealthier classes of American society.

In some of his best stories, RING LARDNER brought a warm, perceptive humor to bear on the world of sports, especially baseball. The work of WILLIAM SAROYAN ranges from broad humor to touching pathos, sometimes in the same story.

Many outstanding writers have become identified with particular regions of the country. DOROTHY CANFIELD is noted for her Vermont stories. Many of KATHERINE ANNE PORTER's stories take place in the Southwest. MARJORIE KINNAN RAWLINGS is closely identified with Florida settings. WILBUR DANIEL STEELE treats a variety of scenes in his work, but many of his best stories take place in the Cape Cod region of New England.

There are many younger writers whose work in the short story has won attention. J. D. SALINGER writes with an effective blend of sophistication, humor, and piercing sadness. EUDORA WELTY, ELIZABETH ENRIGHT, HORTENSE CALISHER, and IRWIN SHAW all share this age's preoccupation with psychological fiction. PAUL HORGAN and JESSE STUART deal with more traditional subjects in their stories. JOHN COLLIER and JOHN CHEEVER bring the note of the weird or the macabre to much of their work, often adding a touch of sardonic humor.

One of the best ways to broaden your knowledge of the short story is by reading standard collections. Many short-story anthologies are available; some of the best are included in the following reading list. In addition to these standard collections, you should make a habit of reading two well-established annual publications, *The Best American Short Stories of 19–*, and the *O. Henry Memorial Award Prize Stories of 19–*. Through these two collections you can observe many of our newest writers make their bids for recognition. Since both collections began well over forty years ago, you can often trace the development of some of our finest writers by glancing through earlier editions in each series.

For Further Reading of Short Stories

COLLECTIONS

(Only those having a large proportion of American stories are given.)

Becker, M. L., *Golden Tales of Our America* (Dodd, Mead, 1929)

Canby, H. S. and R. Bailey, *The Book of the Short Story*, rev. ed. (Appleton-Century-Crofts, 1948)

Cerf, Bennett, *Modern American Short Stories* (World Publishing, 1945)

Conklin, Groff, *The Best of Science Fiction* (Crown, 1962, paperback)

Crane, Milton, *Fifty Great Short Stories* (Bantam Books, 1952, paperback)

Daly, Maureen, *My Favorite Stories* (Dodd, Mead, 1948)

Derleth, August, *Portals of Tomorrow, The Best Tales of Science Fiction and Other Fantasy* (Holt, Rinehart & Winston, 1954)

Fabricant, N. D. and H. Werner, *A Caravan of Music Stories* (Fell, 1947)

Foley, Martha, *Best American Short Stories, 1915–1960* (Houghton Mifflin, 1960)

Grayson, Charles, *Half a Hundred; Tales by Great American Writers* (Blakiston, 1945)

Havighurst, W., *Masters of the Short Story* (Harcourt, Brace & World, 1955)

Jensen, Paul, *The Fireside Book of Flying Stories* (Simon & Schuster, 1952)

Jessup, Alexander, *Representative Modern Short Stories* (Macmillan, 1944)

Kielty, B. A., *A Treasury of Short Stories* (Simon & Schuster, 1947)

O. Henry Memorial Award, *First Prize Stories, 1919–1960, from the O. Henry Memorial Awards* (Doubleday, 1960)

Schaefer, Jack, *Out West* (Houghton Mifflin, 1955)

Schramm, Wilbur, *Great Short Stories* (Harcourt, Brace & World, 1950)

Schweikert, H. C., *Short Stories* (Harcourt, Brace & World, 1947)

Shaw, H. L. and R. Davis, *Americans One and All* (Harper, 1947)

Sloane, William, *Stories for Tomorrow* (Funk, 1954)

Stern, Philip Van Doren, *The Pocket Book of Modern American Short Stories* (Pocket Library PL 24, 1959)

BY INDIVIDUAL AUTHORS

Benét, S. V., *Twenty-five Short Stories* (Sun Dial, 1943)

Cather, Willa, *Early Stories*, selected by Mildred Bennett (Dodd, Mead, 1957)

Fisher, Dorothy Canfield, *A Harvest of Stories* (Harcourt, Brace & World, 1956)

Welty, Eudora, *The Bride of Innesfallen* (Harcourt, Brace & World, 1955)

West, Jessamyn, *The Friendly Persuasion* (Harcourt, Brace & World, 1945)

(The following single stories are among the best by modern American writers. Each of these stories appears in numerous collections. If you have trouble finding a specific title, consult the *Index to Short Stories* compiled by Dorothy Cook and Isabel Monro.)

Anderson, Sherwood, "I'm a Fool"; "Sophistication"

Bradbury, Ray, "The Foghorn"; "The Fox and the Forest"

Faulkner, William, "The Bear"; "Race at Morning"

Hemingway, Ernest, "Big Two-hearted River"; "In Another Country"

Jackson, Shirley, "Charles"; "The Summer People"

Lardner, Ring, "Haircut"; "There Are Smiles"

Lewis, Sinclair, "The Man Who Knew Coolidge"; "Young Man Axelbrod"

O'Connor, Flannery, "Greenleaf"

Porter, Katherine Anne, "The Jilting of Granny Wetherall"

Rawlings, Marjorie K., "Gal Young 'Un"; "The Pelican's Shadow"

Richter, Conrad, "Doctor Hanray's Second Chance"

Stegner, Wallace, "The Blue-winged Teal"; "The Colt"

Steinbeck, John, "The Leader of the People"

Thurber, James, "The Unicorn in the Garden"

FOR LISTENING

James Thurber's "The Secret Life of Walter Mitty" has been recorded on *Many Voices* 5A.

The Novel

Novels are long works of prose fiction that may vary widely in style and in structure. In the scope of a novel, there is room, if the author wishes, for his own commentary about the events he relates, and there is room for materials that are factual or historical. For example, *Moby Dick*, Herman Melville's famous novel, contains many pages of information on whaling. One of the world's greatest novels, *War and Peace* by Leo Tolstoi, contains a long essay on history. In similar ways many modern novelists incorporate nonfictional material into their books.

It is no criticism of the fine and subtle art of the short story to say that opinion generally regards mastery of the novel as the highest goal and achievement in fiction. It is impossible to know American literature in depth, past or present, without wide reading in the novel. Since the length of novels will not permit their representation in a general collection, it is recommended that you read outside of class at least one novel and as many more as you can. The reading list on page 131 offers a sampling of some characteristic American novels.

The following section traces the development of the American novel from its earliest beginnings to modern times.

The Novel in America

In England, the novel grew in popularity throughout the eighteenth century, but it did not gain a similar following in America. Here, the important task of getting a nation organized and the hard work of extending settlements left little time for "light" reading. Fiction was considered frivolous, a waste of time. Too many other concerns needed attention.

This attitude persisted for a long time, but the first major American novelist, JAMES FENIMORE COOPER, 1789–1851 (page 492), won over some of the opposition by proving that novels could help Americans to appreciate their own history. Cooper's first book was an imitation of popular English novels, but Cooper himself was dissatisfied with the story and turned to the life he knew best, on the high seas,and along the frontier that lay just west of his early home in western New York. Cooper's series of five novels called *The Leatherstocking Tales* (published from 1823 to 1841) gave American fiction its first hero, the frontier scout and expert woodsman Natty Bumppo.

The next important American novelist did even more to win a firm place for the art. NATHANIEL HAWTHORNE, 1804–1864 (page 538), used the novel to search out profound moral truths underlying human behavior. He did this not by preaching but by allowing the truth to come out clearly through the lives of characters wrestling with inner conflicts. With Hawthorne's *The Scarlet Letter* (1850), the American novel gained a dimension of deeper seriousness.

This new depth was also explored by HERMAN MELVILLE, 1819–1891 (page 540), a friend of Hawthorne. Melville drew upon his experiences at sea and in the South Sea Islands for a number of remarkable novels, some of which were neglected in their own day but have fascinated modern readers. His *Moby Dick* (1851), almost completely ignored for seventy years after its publication, now ranks among the greatest of our novels.

At this point in our history, the novel, like most other forms of American literature, was a product of the Atlantic seaboard. However, the next major novelist, MARK TWAIN, 1835–1910 (page 698), grew up on the Mississippi River and began writing in the Far West. Millions of Americans know Tom Sawyer as well as any of the boys in their own neighborhood, and *Huckleberry Finn* (1884) today ranks as an American classic.

TWO IMPORTANT INFLUENCES

Before beginning to consider the novelists of the twentieth century, we must remind ourselves that many of our modern writers have developed their styles, forms, and attitudes under the influence of their immediate predecessors. The modern novel should be considered in its relationship to the literary movement in the latter part of the nineteenth century (see "New Directions in Prose," page 768). Two of the major writers of that period, STEPHEN CRANE and HENRY JAMES, greatly influenced the modern novel. Crane's *The Red Badge of Courage* (1895), with its direct and vivid prose, inspired the style of many modern writers. Henry James, whose writing career extended into this century, paved the way toward more penetrating and complex exploration of character and society.

THE MODERN NOVEL

Among our age's most important novelists are many versatile writers whose short stories, essays, or critical writings can be sampled in this volume.

In the early years of this century, three gifted women did major work in the novel. EDITH WHARTON, a New Yorker who was influenced by Henry James, wrote of the wealthy social "aristocracy" of American cities. *The House of Mirth* (1905) and *The Age of Innocence* (1920) are among her best novels of this type. *Ethan Frome* (1911), a stark story set in isolated New England farm country, is perhaps her best-known book, though one of her least typical.

ELLEN GLASGOW was a Virginian of distinguished family. Her favorite subject was the pattern of contrasts in the old and new South and the study of class relationships. *Barren Ground* (1925) and *Vein of Iron* (1935) are among her best books.

WILLA CATHER, perhaps the greatest of our women novelists, wrote predominantly of the West. Like Ellen Glasgow, Miss Cather was born in Virginia, but her youth was spent in Nebraska. She worked as a journalist and editor in New York, returning later to the Midwest. The Midwest and the Southwest are the settings of *O Pioneers!* (1913), *My Ántonia* (1918), and, perhaps her finest novel, *Death Comes for the Archbishop* (1927).

These three writers have since been followed by a number of distinguished women novelists. One of the most famous of the later writers is PEARL BUCK, who was awarded the Nobel prize in 1938. Her writing career has extended into the 1960's. Her best novel, *The Good Earth* (1931), portrays family life among Chinese farmers such as she knew in her youth in that country.

Of the writers who began their careers during and after World War I, SINCLAIR LEWIS stands out as one of the most important. His first major novel was *Main Street*, published in 1920. It was an intense, frank picture of life in a small town in the Midwest, and it marked the beginning of a series of satirical, realistic novels about modern American life. *Babbitt* (1922) pictured the failings of a certain type of businessman. *Arrowsmith* (1925) is about a doctor who wishes to devote his life to medical research but is criticized by his associates for his neglect of money-making opportunities. *Dodsworth* (1929), a novel about a retired American businessman in Europe, was made into a fine play by Lewis and the distinguished playwright Sidney Howard. Lewis' career ranged all the way to the early nineteen-fifties. He was awarded the Nobel prize in 1930.

JOHN DOS PASSOS reacted to World War I in a bitter novel called *Three Soldiers* (1921). In *Manhattan Transfer* (1925) he portrayed city life with new and effective techniques of storytelling. His methods reached their most extreme experimental form in a series of related novels that Dos Passos published during the 1930's. In these unusual works, which reflect the unrest and disorder of war, boom times, and depression, Dos Passos introduced newspaper headlines, news stories, biographical sketches, and many other devices not ordinarily used in fiction. As recently as 1961, in *Midcentury,* Dos Passos returned to some of these methods of bringing fiction close to the current events of an era.

One of the many labels pinned to the 1920's was the "Jazz Age." In some respects, it was a period of confusion and restlessness. F. SCOTT FITZGERALD caught the flavor of the age in his novel *This Side of Paradise* (1920). A later novel, *The Great Gatsby* (1925), which many consider his finest work, etched even more sharply the image of the "roaring twenties."

There still remain three major novelists who began their careers in the 1920's but whose work has extended well into the following decades.

THORNTON WILDER is noted primarily for his plays (page 365), yet he has written some particularly fine novels, including *The Bridge of San Luis Rey* (1927) and *The Ides of March* (1948).

ERNEST HEMINGWAY experienced war first as an ambulance driver and later as a war correspondent. He popularized the phrase "the lost generation" as a description of a group uprooted and demoralized by war. The phrase had originated with an American woman living in Paris, Gertrude Stein, whose odd experiments with prose style influenced not only the terse style of Hemingway but also the work of Thornton Wilder. Hemingway's novels include *The Sun Also Rises* (1926), *A Farewell to Arms* (1929), *For Whom the Bell Tolls* (1940), and *The Old Man and the Sea* (1952). In 1954 he was awarded the Nobel prize.

WILLIAM FAULKNER, another Nobel prize winner, has made his home region of Mississippi the setting of the major part of his work. Faulkner writes broodingly of the South from pre-Revolutionary days to the present, with many overlapping threads of time, place, and family, sometimes tracing a set of characters through as many as four novels. Among his foremost novels about the region he has called Yoknapatawpha County are *The Sound and the Fury* (1929), *As I Lay Dying* (1930), *Light in August* (1932), and *Intruder in the Dust* (1948).

Just on the threshold of a new decade, in 1929, appeared *Look Homeward, Angel*, which was acclaimed at once as the work of an outstanding novelist. Into this work and the others that followed, THOMAS WOLFE poured a stormy record of a young man groping his way toward maturity. His other novels are *Of Time and the River* (1935), *The Web and the Rock*, and *You Can't Go Home Again*. The last two were published after Wolfe's death in 1938.

JOHN STEINBECK published several novels before reaching substantial success with *Of Mice and Men* (1937), which was later adapted as a play. In 1940, Steinbeck was awarded the Pulitzer prize for *The Grapes of Wrath*. This novel, which is still regarded as his best work, portrays vividly the hard lot of people driven from their Oklahoma farms by the droughts that made a dust bowl of that region and forced the farmers to become migrant workers in California.

Other modern novelists who deserve attention include KENNETH ROBERTS, HERVEY ALLEN, WALTER D. EDMONDS, and CONRAD RICHTER, all of whom have re-created richly in fiction the early years of our national history. JAMES GOULD COZZENS has moved to the forefront among our novelists. MARJORIE KINNAN RAWLINGS, in *The Yearling* (1938) and other books, sensitively portrayed the life of inland Florida. JOHN P. MARQUAND was a noted satirist of modern American business and social life, as in *The Late George Apley* (1937). ROBERT PENN WARREN, also known as a poet and critic, has ranged in his novels from colonial times to the present day.

JOHN HERSEY, J. D. SALINGER, JOHN UPDIKE, and WILLIAM STYRON have gained important rank in the past few years.

Today the American literary scene is vigorous and flourishing, with a host of younger writers making their bids for attention. Time will sift them out relentlessly, holding some and dropping others into obscurity. The important thing is that vigor, ambition, and creative energy are still present in our writing, helping to fulfill one of literature's classic functions, that of challenging and testing the values of the times.

Guide to Reading the Novel

No matter what pattern your class follows in reporting on novels, you will find it especially valuable to fix certain information in your mind as you read.

The basic methods and materials of the novel are the same as those of the short story. Both the long and the short forms of fiction are constructed of the same elements and display many of the same characteristics. Action, character, point of view, setting, and style function in the novel as they do in the short story, though of course their use is sometimes more complex in the longer form. The major differences are that a novel has room for complex plot development and even for subplots and that character development can take place on a much larger scale. Unlike a short story, the novel can even portray the entire life of a character. With these exceptions, you should ask of a novel essentially the same questions you ask of a short story.

Is the major action of the novel organized into a clear and consistent plot? If there is a subplot, does it have a clear bearing on the main action? If there is little plot, does the action nevertheless form a pattern of development, or does it simply present a group of unconnected incidents?

How does the author create character? Does he describe the characters directly, or does he allow them to reveal themselves through their words and actions? Do the characters change in the course of the novel? Do the characters seem realistic — are their actions and motives those of living people?

Is the point of view consistent, or if it changes from time to time, are there good reasons for the changes? Why was the particular point of view selected? What is its effect?

How important is the setting of the novel? Is the setting detailed and specified, or is it left purposely vague? Why may it have been treated this way? (Remember that in the local-color novel and the historical novel, setting may assume major importance, but in other kinds of fiction, it usually serves a lesser purpose.)

Is the author's style involved and difficult or simple and clear? Is the language formal and exact or relaxed and conversational? What is the tone of the novel? Does the tone change at any time? What is the effect of the tone?

Of course, it would be impractical to stop after every sentence of a novel to ask these questions, but if you recall some of them from time to time during your reading, you will increase your understanding and appreciation of the novel.

MAKING A CRITICAL ESTIMATE

The exact type of report you give on your reading of novels will be determined by your own teacher, but you may want to try your hand at a critical estimate, which is perhaps the most valuable form of report.

First, open with a brief statement of the author's position in the history of our literature: when he lived, where he lived, his general reputation as a writer. Next, name the book you have read, and identify it as one of the author's early or later works and whether it is considered a typical example of his writing or perhaps as one of his best novels.

Then you have a choice of two good plans for the body of your report:

1. Make your main statement an answer to these two questions: In your opinion, what was the author's purpose in writing the novel? Did he succeed in carrying out his purpose?

Among the many purposes that govern the writing of novels are the following: to give the reader an escape from reality by means of fantasy or thrilling adventure; to entertain by presenting humorous incidents or characters; to present a picture of life in a specific place at a specific time (especially in historical and local-color novels); to present a study of a particular character; to satirize some social situation or group of people.

2. Examine in turn the action, characters, and setting of the novel. Tell which of the three elements seems most important to the author, and explain why. Then discuss briefly the other two and the way they are handled in the book. Finally, point out the effects of the particular point of view and the style. (You may find the list of questions on page 129 helpful in this kind of report.)

A good conclusion for either type of report is a statement of the kind of reader who would especially enjoy the novel. Members of your class will probably be sharing with you an interesting discovery — that as your experience with novels increases, you find the greatest enjoyment in those books that emphasize realistic character and action rather than mere plot.

FOR THE READING OF NOVELS

The novels in the following list are recommended both for their high quality and for their interest. Of course they represent only a sampling of American novels. Your teacher may suggest others that will especially appeal to you. A standard classified book list with short descriptions of each book, such as *Books for You* or *Your Reading* (reading lists for high school students published by the National Council of Teachers of English), can guide you to choices that will satisfy any of your special interests.

For the Reading of Novels

NINETEENTH-CENTURY NOVELS

*Crane, Stephen, *The Red Badge of Courage* (1895); a young soldier's introduction to war.

Ford, Paul Leicester, *Janice Meredith* (1899); a story about the American Revolution.

*Hawthorne, Nathaniel, *The Scarlet Letter* (1850); a study of sin and retribution in Puritan Boston.

Jackson, Helen Hunt, *Ramona* (1884); Indians in early California oppressed by American ranchers.

James, Henry, *Portrait of a Lady* (1881); the experiences of a young American woman living in Europe.

Johnston, Mary, *To Have and to Hold* (1899); romance in the early settlement at Jamestown.

*Melville, Herman, *Moby Dick* (1851); the famous symbolic search for a white whale.

Twain, Mark, *A Connecticut Yankee in King Arthur's Court* (1889); a modern man is transported into the age of chivalry.

Wallace, Lew, *Ben-Hur* (1880); a long feud between a young Jewish aristocrat and a Roman in the first century A.D.

TWENTIETH-CENTURY NOVELS

Boyd, James, *Drums* (Scribner, 1925); a young North Carolinian's part in the Revolution.

Cather, Willa, *Death Comes for the Archbishop* (Knopf, 1927); a courageous struggle to bring Christianity to the Indians of frontier New Mexico.

Churchill, Winston, *The Crisis* (Macmillan, 1901); the approaching War Between the States throws barriers between a young Northerner and his Southern sweetheart.

Clark, Walter Van Tilburg, *The Ox-Bow Incident* (Random House, 1940); a posse tracks down innocent men in Nevada in the eighties.

Edmonds, Walter D., *Wilderness Clearing* (Dodd, Mead, 1944); the struggle to hold the Northwest Territory for the Colonies. *Drums Along the Mohawk* (Little, Brown, 1936); a novel of the Revolutionary War.

Ferber, Edna, *Show Boat* (Doubleday, 1926); romance of the floating theaters on the Mississippi River. *Cimarron* (Grosset & Dunlap, 1929); the settlement of Oklahoma.

Guthrie, A. B., *The Big Sky* (Houghton Mifflin, 1947); an account of fur-trading days.

Hersey, John, *A Bell for Adano* (Knopf, 1944); an Italian village in World War II under a sympathetic American military governor.

Horgan, Paul, *A Distant Trumpet* (Farrar, Straus & Cudahy, 1960); war with the Indians in the 1880's.

La Farge, Oliver, *Laughing Boy* (Houghton Mifflin, 1929); story of a young Navajo of modern times.

Nordhoff, Charles B., and James N. Hall, *Mutiny on the Bounty* (Little, Brown, 1932); the heroism, brutalities, and tragedies of life on the old sailing vessels.

Rawlings, Marjorie Kinnan, *The Yearling* (Scribner, 1938); the affection and understanding between a boy and his father in Florida.

Roberts, Kenneth, *Arundel* (Doubleday, 1933); a secret expedition by Benedict Arnold against Quebec.

Stewart, George, *Storm* (Random House, 1945); a "biography" of a storm that affects the lives of millions.

Tarkington, Booth, *Alice Adams* (Grosset & Dunlap, 1937); the pathetic struggle of a young girl to live above her family's place in the community.

West, Jessamyn, *Cress Delahanty* (Harcourt, Brace & World, 1954); growing up on a California ranch.

*Wilder, Thornton, *The Bridge of San Luis Rey* (Boni, 1929); a five-part novel that traces the lives of five people killed in the fall of a bridge.

Wister, Owen, *The Virginian* (1902); America's favorite cowboy hero.

Wouk, Herman, *The Caine Mutiny* (Doubleday, 1951); an irrational captain provokes his officers to rebellion.

* Included in *Four American Novels*, eds., Edmund Fuller and Olga Achtenhagen (Harcourt, Brace & World, Inc., 1959). *Moby Dick* is abridged.

Modern Nonfiction

NONFICTION is a continuously popular kind of reading that has gained even greater favor in recent years. The many varieties of modern nonfiction include history, biography, news articles, formal and informal essays, book reviews, and columns on every conceivable subject. Perhaps the traditional American respect for facts helps explain the important position that nonfiction occupies in our day. Or it may be that the complexity of the modern world creates an ever-growing demand for news and information. Whatever the reasons, the appetite for nonfiction seems to grow stronger every day, and the variety of styles and subjects continually increases. The following pages offer a generous sampling of that variety.

Guide to Reading Nonfiction

THE THREE MAJOR TYPES OF NONFICTION

The types of nonfiction sometimes become like Huckleberry Finn's favorite meals, in which the food is all cooked together and, as Huck describes it, "things get mixed up, and the juice kind of swaps around and the things go better." When "things get mixed up" in this way, it is often difficult to distinguish between the various kinds of nonfiction. In general, however, nonfiction falls into the three broad classifications used in the following pages: essays and articles, appreciation and criticism, and history and biography. *Essays and articles* on general topics form by far the largest category, with the greater part of almost every popular magazine devoted to this type of writing. *Appreciation and criticism* of literature, theater, and the arts in general has gained a remarkably wide range of readers in this century. Reviews of motion pictures, books, and plays rank high in this category. *History and biography* have always been highly favored types of reading.

THE AUTHOR'S PURPOSE

Why did the author write this? This question is the first concern of the reader of nonfiction. The author may be presenting a generalization and supporting it with specific examples or evidence derived from the observations of experts. Or perhaps the author's purpose is to present the portrait of a man, his role in the modern world, his routines of living and working. Again, the author may be evaluating a work of art. Or he might be describing a historical event, its causes and results. Watch for the author's statement of his purpose in writing. It will usually occur early in the work.

ORGANIZATION — THE AUTHOR'S BLUEPRINT

Underlying all good writing there is a plan, a blueprint, and this blueprint can be followed by the reader. Some readers can note the major points and the supporting details in the first reading, while others do better to read the article through once and then look for the plan on a second reading. Writers of nonfiction often guide the reader with words that alert him to what is coming next: "for example," "that is," "on the other hand," "in contrast." Learn to pay attention to the author's signals.

STYLE — THE AUTHOR'S SIGNATURE

Another important hint to the reader of nonfiction is to get acquainted with the author. Try to fall in with the tone and mood of the piece so that you can discover the author's attitudes. Unless you discover his feelings toward his subject, you are unlikely to see it as he does even for the short time it takes you to read the piece.

Essays and Articles

American interest in the informative article is traditional. In the historical part of this book is the poem *Snow-Bound* by John Greenleaf Whittier. The family presented in the poem had been snowbound and shut off from news of the world for a week. They were reduced to reading the almanac, one novel, a few pamphlets, and one book of poetry. Then the storm was over; the village paper came, and the family members felt their horizons broadening. The news was so exciting to them that they felt "the pulse of life," and in the final line their feeling is summed up: "And all the world was ours once more."

"All the world was ours . . ." — the family's statement goes a long way toward explaining the popularity of the article. It is also possible that men who live in democracies like factual writing better than other men because self-governing men can act to shape facts and alter events. The sense of dignity and responsibility that a current fact brings to a man who can change it may explain the pleasure most Americans experience in reading the news and informative articles.

It is quite difficult to make a clear-cut distinction between the essay and the article. Most short pieces of modern nonfiction share characteristics of both types. There are, however, one or two obvious differences. While both the essay and the article are based on fact, the essay often emphasizes interpretation and opinion as well as the presentation of information. Of course the author of an article will sometimes interpret facts. When Betty Friedan writes about "The Coming Ice Age" on page 163, she is anxious to interpret the facts clearly for the reader, to explain the significance of the events she discusses. Yet she does not tell us exactly how she herself feels about the theory, whether she likes it or not. On the other hand, Thomas Wolfe, in "Circus at Dawn" on page 139, is determined to let the reader know exactly how he feels about the circus. The facts — the performers, the tent, the animals — are important, obviously, but what is more important is Wolfe's reaction to all this, the emotions that the circus creates in him.

Unlike the article, which usually tends to be impersonal, the essay leans heavily on the author's personal style of writing. The style of the essay may be as friendly and informal as Jesse Stuart's "If I Were Seventeen Again" (page 135), or it may concentrate on painting the mysterious mood of Rachel Carson's "The Hidden Pool" (page 144). In the essay, style is supreme.

ALL THE WORLD IS YOURS

In the following pages you will find a wide assortment of essays and articles. Some will bring smiles, and some will provoke serious thought. You will roam the country from the ranches of the Southwest to a village in New England. If you like people and ideas, and if you are curious about the world that lies beyond the reach of your own eyes and ears, these essays and articles will provide many an hour of satisfaction and pleasure.

JESSE STUART

If I Were Seventeen Again

Most of the readers of this book are seventeen, or a little more or a little less. Seventeen is a challenging age because it is an "alive" age. You do not need to be told how you feel at seventeen. You know. But you may be interested to learn what an American teacher and author imagines he would do if he were seventeen again. His conclusions may surprise you.

IF I were seventeen again, I would want to live on a Kentucky hill farm. I would want to grow up and live where there are trees, meadows, and streams.

If I couldn't live on a large farm, a few acres would do. But I would want space to hunt over, and a stream or lake nearby where I could fish. I would want to mow the meadows with a span of horses or mules, and haul the hay to the barn on a hay wagon. I believe the boy or girl who hasn't ridden on a hay wagon has missed something in his youth. If he hasn't smelled new-mown clover,

he has missed the finest wind a youth ever breathed.

In the spring of the year, if I were seventeen again, I'd want to take long walks into the woods. I'd want to get acquainted with all kinds of birds, how they build their nests and the kind of materials they use, what color and size eggs they lay—from the hoot owl to the chicken hawk and sparrow—and how and what they feed their young. I'd want to know all about the animals— foxes, possums, coons, rabbits, skunks, minks, weasels, groundhogs, and all others. I would want to know and I would find out what they ate, where they lived, what animals were friendly to each other and which were enemies. This is a world every teen-age boy should know. I've never seen one yet who didn't love the animal world. And I would protect each nondestructive animal, each nondestructive bird. I would want to know the hunting laws, abide by them, and help restock and protect the game so it would be here for the next seventeen-year-old when he came along.

I would also learn the names of wild flowers and plants that grow in the woods. I would also want to learn the

"If I Were Seventeen Again" by Jesse Stuart. Originally in *Country Gentleman*. Reprinted by permission of the author.

kinds of trees. I'd want to learn them so that when I touched the bark on the darkest nights I could identify the tree. I'd want to fox-hunt on April nights when the trees were leafing, and hear a pack of hounds running the fox all night. And I would want to own at least one hound dog and have him in the chase.

A boy seventeen who has not stood on a high hilltop under the stars or a bright moon and listened to the music of barking hounds has missed something really great. Stars, moon, a high hill, the loneliness of night, and barking hounds, is a wholesome enjoyment. It puts character in a young man. It gives him something he cannot get any place else. I used to write high school themes for my English class by lantern light or by moonlight as I listened for the hounds to come back into hearing distance.

In summer, if I were seventeen again, I wouldn't miss working on a farm. I wouldn't miss plowing and harrowing land, planting seeds in the ground and hoeing vegetables and plowing the young green corn. I would want to work without a shirt, work in shorts, and work barefooted, because the feel of loose, warm dirt to one's feet is a good thing in one's growth. I always hate to see a colt that has run barefooted over the pasture have to bow to steel shoes. His being shod is that grim reminder that his youth is ended.

I would, if I were back at seventeen, learn all I could about planting. I would want to be able, if I were cut away from all money-earning jobs or positions, to grow my food from the soil. I would want to specialize in growing one particular thing. And I'd want to specialize in growing a breed of cattle or a kind of hog, or rabbit, or chicken. And I would want pets too — a coon, groundhog, or squirrel. Or, I would want a pet hawk, such as I once had, that flew to the places where I fished and sat in a tree above me until I

flipped a minnow from the stream. Then, soon as he saw the minnow dangling, he would fly down and eat it.

If I were seventeen again, I'd try to build my body strong. I wouldn't drink anything intoxicating. I wouldn't smoke until I got my growth. I'd want to build my body so strong, that if I were ever forced to use my fists, it would have the force of a kicking mule. I'd want to have the strength, and did have at seventeen, to lift the end of small saw log or to carry a green crosstie or a turning plow or the hind carriage of a joltwagon. I'd want to be able to do these things whether I could or not. A young man rejoices in strength, and he can build strength by proper work and recreational exercises.

If I were back at seventeen, I'd want to find bees watering on the hot sand by some little stream, course them to their tree, cut the tree at night, and rob the bees. I'd want a few bee stings too. A boy who has never found a wild bee tree, robbed bees, and tasted wild honey has missed a lot in life.

And here is something I would definitely do. I'd go to high school. The boy who hasn't finished high school has missed something too. It doesn't matter whether he leads his class or not, whether he's the best athlete, or the most popular boy. I never had these honors and I failed three subjects in high school because I entered high school unprepared. But going to high school, taking different subjects under different teachers, knowing the boys and girls in my class and in the school is something I wouldn't miss. I would consider it enjoyment and recreation and not work to attend high school. I wish I could go over those four years again. It was never work. If I couldn't be the best athlete, I would still be one, if it were physically possible, even if I were one who was only substituted in an easy game. I'd try out for all kinds of athletics until I found the one game I could play best. But I wouldn't miss athletics. This builds men physically and teaches them sportsmanship and give and take.

I wouldn't want to ride a bus to school either, unless I lived too many miles away. One of the greatest track men I ever taught, one of the smallest and weakest boys I had in high school, refused to ride eight miles on a bus to school (sixteen miles a day), but instead he walked and ran to and from school with a wrist watch to check his time. He didn't let a boy on the track squad know what he was doing. In his first three years in high school, he didn't win a race. In his senior year he ran the fastest mile ever recorded in his school. His record still holds.

I would walk to school because it would build muscles in my legs, because I could breathe fresher air and my brain would be more alert in my studies. I could also meet people on my way, see trees, flowers, and animals; and all of these help in one's education.

And this is another way I used to get my themes. I'd sit down on my way to school and write a theme after I'd seen something that gave me an idea. There is a whole world of subjects one can get just walking to and from school.

If I were seventeen and hadn't already done so, I would identify myself with the church of my choice, and I would be there at least once each week. I received a shocking report once when I was pleading to a circuit judge for four of my schoolboys, who had disobeyed laws knowingly. Said the judge: "Ninety-six per cent of the young men that come before me don't go to church." These four boys, all from good families, hadn't attended any kind of religious services. So this is reason enough for one of seventeen to identify himself with some church.

I would be honest to the penny. If I borrowed a nickel from someone, I would pay it back. I would put myself into the rut of honesty, and I would follow through. Why build strong bodies at seventeen, bodies to stand the wear and tear of the years ahead, and stunt the great growth of our character? If I were to choose between a strong body, or strong, honest character, I'd take the latter. I'd want a reputation for honesty. I'd want to be able to go to my home-town bank and borrow, if need be, without anybody but myself signing the note. When a seventeen-year-old boy can do this, he has character. And if he has honesty, he will pay that note if it takes his hide.

If I were seventeen again, I would earn my own money, or most of it. I would take days of work for other people. And if and when I accepted a job for the other fellow, I would do it well. I would do it so well that he would want me to work for him again. I'd do it so well, others who had seen my work would want me to work for them. I would do the work so that I would rejoice at the finished product, so I could sleep contentedly at night — because we build character through work we do with our hands. Do work well at seventeen, and you'll be doing it well from then on.

If I were seventeen again, I would stand up for my convictions. I wouldn't be a follower of something I didn't believe and knew was wrong. No matter how popular the idea might be, I would hold out. I would be myself. I would be guided by what I thought was right. No one, no matter how much more powerful physically he was than I, would sway me. And it wouldn't be very long until several of my age would be following me. Popularity fades as often as the wind changes its course, but character never fades. In your schoolwork it is better to have C grades and A character than it is to have A grades and C character.

Seventeen may be the shortest year in your life. It was for me. It was a wonderful year, and like a Kentucky April it came too slowly and went too quickly. It was a great year for physical and mental growth. A year of beauty and spirit. All years to be alive are good years. But, really not too much happens before you are seventeen. You'll never feel again like you could turn the earth over to see what is under it. Most of us would trade fame, fortune, and achievements for what you have. So, hold seventeen and live seventeen, while you can.

FOR DISCUSSION

1. Why do you think Stuart felt such pleasure in helping plants and animals to grow?

2. Comment on Stuart's ideas about getting and holding a job. Do you agree or disagree?

3. Do you agree with Stuart that "In your schoolwork it is better to have C grades and A character than it is to have A grades and C character"? Explain the reasons for your answer.

4. Why does Stuart feel that it is important to have a reputation for honesty?

5. What activities might a seventeen-year-old living in a town or city substitute for Stuart's hunting, fishing, and walking in the woods?

6. Why does Stuart emphasize the importance of physical skills? Quote from the essay to support your answer.

THE AUTHOR

JESSE STUART (b. 1907) grew up on a fifty-acre mountain farm near Riverton, Kentucky. Stuart worked hard for the opportunity of a high school and college education, and later as a teacher and school principal he helped other young people get an education. As this essay suggests, Stuart loves the out-of-doors, and enjoys hunting, plowing, and planting. He is a man genuinely and proudly in love with his country, and his readers soon know it. In 1934 he published *Man with the Bull-Tongue Plow*, a collection of 703 sonnets, which reflect the beauty of his life on the mountain. His short stories have been published in dozens of American magazines, and he has fulfilled many a schoolboy's dream by revising several stories he wrote for English class assignments and selling them. He writes novels as well as poems, essays, articles, and short stories. His best-known prose works are probably *Taps for Private Tussie* (1943), a best seller, and *The Thread That Runs So True* (1949), the story of his own experiences as a teacher in mountain schools.

Stuart Country

Reproduced below is a photograph of Jesse Stuart on his farm in Kentucky, the area that provides a setting for most of his writing.

THOMAS WOLFE

Circus at Dawn

Is the circus larger than life? Are its performers "strange and romantic creatures"? If you have never watched its arrival with fascinated eyes, let Thomas Wolfe tell you what it was like.

THE CREATION OF A MOOD. Critics frequently note that Thomas Wolfe's style in such essays as "Circus at Dawn" and in many passages from his novels is more like poetry than prose. An important element in this poetic style is Wolfe's intense response to all that he sees and hears and touches and smells, and his ability to capture in words his feelings and sensations. Notice how each word helps create the mood of strange excitement as the author recalls a youthful experience of special charm.

THERE were times in early autumn — in September — when the greater circuses would come to town — the Ringling Brothers, Robinson's, and Barnum and Bailey shows, and when I was a route-boy on the morning paper, on those mornings when the circus would be coming in, I would rush madly

through my route in the cool and thrilling darkness that comes just before break of day, and then I would go back home and get my brother out of bed.

Talking in low excited voices we would walk rapidly back toward town under the rustle of September leaves, in cool streets just grayed now with that still, that unearthly and magical first light of day which seems suddenly to rediscover the great earth out of darkness, so that the earth emerges with an awful, a glorious sculptural stillness, and one looks out with a feeling of joy and disbelief, as the first men on this earth must have done, for to see this happen is one of the things that men will remember out of life forever and think of as they die.

At the sculptural still square where at one corner, just emerging into light, my father's shabby little marble shop stood with a ghostly strangeness and familiarity, my brother and I would "catch" the first streetcar of the day bound for the "depot" where the circus was — or sometimes we would meet someone we knew, who would give us a lift in his automobile.

Then, having reached the dingy, grimy, and rickety depot section, we would get out, and walk rapidly across the tracks of the station yard, where we could see great flares and steamings from the engines, and hear the crash and bump of shifting freight cars, the swift sporadic thunders of a shifting engine, the tolling of bells, the sounds of great trains on the rails.

And to all these familiar sounds, filled with their exultant prophecies of flight, the voyage, morning, and the shining cities — to all the sharp and thrilling odors of the trains — the smell of cinders, acrid smoke, of musty, rusty freight cars, the clean pine-board of crated produce, and the smells of fresh stored food — oranges, coffee, tangerines and bacon, ham, and flour and beef — there would be added now, with an unforgettable magic and familiarity, all the strange sounds and smells of the coming circus.

The gay yellow sumptuous-looking cars in which the star performers lived and slept, still dark and silent, heavily and powerfully still, would be drawn up in long strings upon the tracks. And all around them the sounds of the unloading circus would go on furiously in the darkness. The receding gulf of lilac and departing night would be filled with the savage roar of the lions, the murderously sudden snarling of great jungle cats, the trumpeting of the elephants, the stamp of the horses, and with the musty, pungent, unfamiliar odor of the jungle animals: the tawny camel smells, and the smells of panthers, zebras, tigers, elephants, and bears.

Then, along the tracks, beside the circus trains, there would be the sharp cries and oaths of the circus men, the magical swinging dance of lanterns in the darkness, the sudden heavy rumble of the loaded vans and wagons as they were pulled along the flats [1] and gondolas,[2] and down the runways to the

[1] **flats:** flatcars.

[2] **gondolas** (gŏn'dō-lāz): railroad cars with sides and ends, but without tops.

ground. And everywhere, in the thrilling mystery of darkness and awakening light, there would be the tremendous conflict of a confused, hurried, and yet orderly movement.

The great iron-gray horses, four and six to a team, would be plodding along the road of thick white dust to a rattling of chains and traces and the harsh cries of their drivers. The men would drive the animals to the river which flowed by beyond the tracks, and water them; and as first light came, one could see the elephants wallowing in the familiar river and the big horses going slowly and carefully down to drink.

Then, on the circus grounds, the tents were going up already with the magic speed of dreams. All over the place (which was near the tracks and the only space of flat land in the town that was big enough to hold a circus) there would be this fierce, savagely hurried, and yet orderly confusion. Great flares of gaseous circus light would blaze down on the seared and battered faces of the circus toughs as, with the rhythmic precision of a single animal — a human riveting machine — they swung their sledges at the stakes, driving a stake into the earth with the incredible instancy of accelerated figures in a motion picture. And everywhere, as light came, and the sun appeared, there would be a scene of magic, order, and of violence. The drivers would curse and talk their special language to their teams, there would be the loud, gasping, and uneven labor of a gasoline engine, the shouts and curses of the bosses, the wooden riveting of driven stakes, and the rattle of heavy chains.

Already in an immense cleared space of dusty beaten earth, the stakes were being driven for the main exhibition tent. And an elephant would lurch ponderously to the field, slowly lower his great swinging head at the command of a man who sat perched upon his skull, flourish his gray, wrinkled snout a time or two, and then solemnly wrap it around a tent pole big as the mast of a racing schooner. Then the elephant would back slowly away, dragging the great pole with him as if it were a stick of matchwood. . . .

Meanwhile, the circus food tent — a huge canvas top without concealing sides — had already been put up, and now we could see the performers seated at long trestled tables underneath the tent, as they ate breakfast. And the savor of the food they ate — mixed as it was with our strong excitement, with the powerful but wholesome smells of the animals, and with all the joy, sweetness, mystery, jubilant magic and glory of the morning and the coming of the circus — seemed to us to be of the most maddening and appetizing succulence of any food that we had ever known or eaten.

We could see the circus performers eating tremendous breakfasts, with all the savage relish of their power and strength: they ate big fried steaks, pork chops, rashers[1] of bacon, a half-dozen eggs, great slabs of fried ham and great stacks of wheat cakes which a cook kept flipping in the air with the skill of a juggler, and which a husky-looking waitress kept rushing to their tables on loaded trays held high and balanced marvelously on the fingers of a brawny hand. And above all the maddening odors of the wholesome and succulent food, there brooded forever the sultry and delicious fragrance — that somehow seemed to add a zest and sharpness to all the powerful and thrilling life of morning — of strong boiling coffee, which we could see sending off clouds of steam from an enormous polished urn, and which the circus performers gulped down, cup after cup.

And the circus men and women themselves — these star performers — were such fine-looking people, strong

[1] rashers: thin slices.

and handsome, yet speaking and moving with an almost stern dignity and decorum, that their lives seemed to us to be as splendid and wonderful as any lives on earth could be. There was never anything loose, rowdy, or tough in their comportment. . . .

Rather, these people in an astonishing way seemed to have created an established community which lived an ordered existence on wheels, and to observe with a stern fidelity unknown in towns and cities the decencies of family life. There would be a powerful young man, a handsome and magnificent young woman with blond hair and the figure of an Amazon,[2] and a powerfully built, thickset man of middle age, who had a stern, lined, responsible-looking face and a bald head. They were probably the members of a trapeze team — the young man and woman would leap through space like projectiles, meeting the grip of the older man and hurtling back again upon their narrow perches, catching the swing of their trapeze in mid-air, and whirling thrice before they caught it, in a perilous and beautiful exhibition of human balance and precision.

But when they came into the breakfast tent, they would speak gravely yet courteously to other performers, and seat themselves in a family group at one of the long tables, eating their tremendous breakfast with an earnest concentration, seldom speaking to one another, and then gravely, seriously, and briefly.

And my brother and I would look at them with fascinated eyes; my brother would watch the man with the bald head for a while and then turn toward me, whispering:

"D-d-do you see that f-f-fellow there with the bald head? W-w-well, he's the heavy man," he whispered knowingly. "He's the one that c-c-c-catches them!

[2] Amazon: a member of a legendary race of women warriors; used generally to describe a woman of great strength or size.

That f-f-fellow's got to know his business! You know what happens if he m-m-misses, don't you?" said my brother.

"What?" I would say in a fascinated tone.

My brother snapped his fingers in the air.

"Over!" he said. "D-d-done for! W-w-why, they'd be d-d-d-dead before they knew what happened. Sure!" he said, nodding vigorously. "It's a f-f-f-fact! If he ever m-m-m-misses it's all over! That boy has g-g-g-got to know his s-s-s-stuff!" my brother said. "W-w-w-why," he went on in a low tone of solemn conviction, "it w-w-w-wouldn't surprise me at all if they p-p-p-pay him s-s-seventy-five or a hundred dollars a week! It's a fact!" my brother cried vigorously.

And we would turn our fascinated stares again upon these splendid and romantic creatures, whose lives were so different from our own, and whom we seemed to know with such familiar and affectionate intimacy. And at length, reluctantly, with full light come and the sun up, we would leave the circus grounds and start for home.

And somehow the memory of all we had seen and heard that glorious morning, and the memory of the food tent with its wonderful smells, would waken in us the pangs of such a ravenous hunger that we could not wait until we got home to eat. We would stop off in town at lunchrooms and, seated on tall stools before the counter, we would devour ham-and-egg sandwiches, hot hamburgers, red and pungent at their cores with coarse, spicy, sanguinary [1] beef, coffee, glasses of foaming milk, and doughnuts, and then go home to eat up everything in sight upon the breakfast table.

[1] sanguinary (săng′gwĭ·nĕr′ĭ): rare.

FOR DISCUSSION

1. How does viewpoint affect the telling — how do the eager eyes of two excited boys make the persons and events described here seem "larger than life"?

2. Recall special sources of interest at each of the three circus scenes pictured here — at the depot, at the tent-raising, and at the food tent. Which did you find most vivid? Why?

THE CREATION OF A MOOD

1. What words early in the essay help create the special mood of excitement and strangeness that pervades the whole experience? How does the description of the town add effectiveness to the circus scenes? What details does Wolfe use to create this impression?

2. Skim back through the essay, and point out the words that give clear impressions of sounds, sights, and odors.

THE AUTHOR

THOMAS WOLFE (1900–1938) was born in Asheville, North Carolina. After graduating from the University of North Carolina, he went to Harvard to learn to write plays. Wolfe's wealth of words, however, demanded a very broad canvas. The novel form itself was scarcely broad enough, and, for Wolfe, trying to communicate in a play was, as one critic said, "like trying to put a strait jacket on a whale." Thomas Wolfe wrote short stories and several novels, passages of which sound like free verse and blank verse — full of imagery and haunting in their music. Trains appear so often in his works that they begin to take on the power of a symbol. *Look Homeward, Angel* (1929) was Wolfe's first novel, followed by *Of Time and the River* (1935). He died before the publication of his last two novels, *The Web and the Rock* and *You Can't Go Home Again*. The epitaph inscribed on his tombstone was taken from *The Web and the Rock*: "Death bent to touch his chosen son with mercy, love, and pity, and put the seal of honor on him when he died."

The Big Top ➤

The sights and sounds of the circus have held a special fascination for generations of Americans, including one of the most American of writers, Thomas Wolfe.

RACHEL CARSON

The Hidden Pool

A hidden cave is a delight to anyone who discovers it, but a hidden pool in a hidden cave at the edge of the sea presents even more adventures of sight and sound and touch. In this essay, selected from *The Edge of the Sea,* Rachel Carson imaginatively combines fact and mood as she draws the picture of a secret pool.

SOME of the most beautiful pools of the shore are not exposed to the view of the casual passer-by. They must be searched for — perhaps in low-lying basins hidden by great rocks that seem to be heaped in disorder and confusion, perhaps in darkened recesses under a projecting ledge, perhaps behind a thick curtain of concealing weeds.

I know such a hidden pool. It lies in a sea cave, at low tide filling perhaps the lower third of its chamber. As the flooding tide returns, the pool grows, swelling in volume until all the cave is water-filled and the cave and the rocks that form and contain it are drowned

beneath the fullness of the tide. When the tide is low, however, the cave may be approached from the landward side. Massive rocks form its floor and walls and roof. They are penetrated by only a few openings — two near the floor on the sea side and one high on the landward wall. Here one may lie on the rocky threshold and peer through the low entrance into the cave and down into its pool. The cave is not really dark; indeed on a bright day it glows with a cool green light. The source of this soft radiance is the sunlight that enters through the openings low on the floor of the pool, but only after its entrance into the pool does the light itself become transformed, invested with a living color of purest, palest green that is borrowed from the covering of sponge on the floor of the cave.

Through the same openings that admit the light, fish come in from the sea, explore the green hall, and depart again into the vaster waters beyond. Through those low portals the tides ebb and flow. Invisibly, they bring in minerals — the raw materials for the living chemistry of the plants and animals of the cave. They bring, invisibly again, the larvae [1] of many sea creatures — drifting, drifting in their search for a resting place. Some may remain and settle here; others will go out on the next tide.

Looking down into the small world confined within the walls of the cave, one feels the rhythms of the greater sea world beyond. The waters of the pool are never still. Their level changes not only gradually with the rise and fall of the tide, but also abruptly with the pulse of the surf. As the backwash of a wave draws it seaward, the water falls away rapidly; then with a sudden reversal the inrushing water foams and surges upward almost to one's face.

On the outward movement one can look down and see the floor, its details revealed more clearly in the shallowing water. The green crumb-of-bread sponge covers much of the bottom of the pool, forming a thick-piled carpet built of tough little feltlike fibers laced together with glassy, double-pointed needles of silica [2] — the spicules [3] or skeletal supports of the sponge. The green color of the carpet is the pure color of chlorophyll,[4] this plant pigment being confined within the cells of an alga [5] that are scattered through the tissues of the animal host. The sponge clings closely to the rock, by the very smoothness and flatness of its growth testifying to the streamlining force of heavy surf. In quiet waters the same species sends up many projecting cones; here these would give the turbulent waters a surface to grip and tear.

Interrupting the green carpet are patches of other colors, one a deep mustard yellow, probably a growth of the sulfur sponge. In the fleeting moment when most of the water has drained away, one has glimpses of a rich orchid color in the deepest part of the cave — the color of the encrusting coralline [6] algae.

Sponges and corallines together form a background for the larger tide-pool animals. In the quiet of ebb tide there is little or no visible movement even among the predatory starfish that cling to the walls like ornamental fixtures painted orange or rose or purple. A group of large anemones [7] lives on the wall of the cave, their apricot color vivid against the green sponge. Today all the anemones may be attached on the north wall of the pool, seemingly immobile and immovable; on the next spring tides when I visit the pool again, some of them may have shifted over to the west wall and there taken up their station, again seemingly immovable.

There is abundant promise that the anemone colony is a thriving one and will be maintained. On the walls and ceiling of the cave are scores of baby anemones — little glistening mounds of soft tissue, a pale, translucent brown. But the real nursery of the colony seems to be in a sort of antechamber opening into the central cave. There a roughly cylindrical space no more than a foot across is enclosed by high perpendicular rock walls to which hundreds of baby anemones cling.

On the roof of the cave is written a starkly simple statement of the force of the surf. Waves entering a confined space always concentrate all their tremendous force for a driving, upward leap; in this manner the roofs of caves are gradually battered away. The open portal in which I lie saves the ceiling of this cave from receiving the full force of such upward-leaping waves; nevertheless, the creatures that live there are exclusively a heavy-surf fauna. It is a

[1] larvae (lär′vē): the immature forms of certain animals and insects.

[2] silica: quartz or rock crystal.

[3] spicules (spĭk′ūlz): slender bodies of bony material.

[4] chlorophyll (klō′rō·fĭl): the green coloring matter of leaves and plants.

[5] alga (ăl′gȧ): a plant of the seaweed group.

[6] coralline: coral-like.

[7] anemones (ȧ·nĕm′ō·nēz): spongelike sea animals.

simple black and white mosaic — the black of mussel shells, on which the white cones of barnacles are growing. For some reason the barnacles, skilled colonizers of surf-swept rocks though they be, seem to have been unable to get a foothold directly on the roof of the cave. Yet the mussels have done so. I do not know how this happened but I can guess. I can imagine the young mussels creeping in over the damp rock while the tide is out, spinning their silk threads that bind them securely, anchoring them against the returning waters. And then in time, perhaps, the growing colony of mussels gave the infant barnacles a foothold more tenable than the smooth rock, so that they were able to cement themselves to the mussel shells. However it came about, that is the way we find them now.

As I lie and look into the pool, there are moments of relative quiet, in the intervals when one wave has receded and the next has not yet entered. Then I can hear the small sounds: the sound of water dripping from the mussels on the ceiling or of splashes losing themselves in the vastness of the pool and in the confused, murmurous whisperings that emanate from the pool itself — the pool that is never quite still.

Then as my fingers explore among the dark-red thongs of the dulse [1] and push away the fronds of the Irish moss that cover the walls beneath me, I begin to find creatures of such extreme delicacy that I wonder how they can exist in this cave when the brute force of storm surf is unleashed within its confined space.

Adhering to the rock walls are thin crusts of one of the bryozoans,[2] a form in which hundreds of minute, flask-shaped cells of a brittle structure, fragile as glass, lie one against another in regular rows to form a continuous crust.

The color is a pale apricot; the whole seems an ephemeral creation that would crumble away at a touch, as hoarfrost before the sun.

A tiny spiderlike creature with long and slender legs runs about over the crust. For some reason that may have to do with its food, it is the same apricot color as the bryozoan carpet beneath it; the sea spider, too, seems the embodiment of fragility.

Another bryozoan of coarser, upright growth, Flustrella, sends up little club-shaped projections from a basal [3] mat. Again, the lime-impregnated clubs seem brittle and glassy. Over and among them, innumerable little round-worms crawl with serpentine motion, slender as threads. Baby mussels creep in their tentative exploration of a world so new to them they have not yet found a place to anchor themselves by slender silken lines.

Exploring with my lens, I find many very small snails in the fronds of seaweed. One of them has obviously not been long in the world, for its pure white shell has formed only the first turn of the spiral that will turn many times upon itself in growth from infancy to maturity. Another, no larger, is nevertheless older. Its shining amber shell is coiled like a French horn and, as I watch, the tiny creature within thrusts out a bovine head and seems to be regarding its surroundings with two black eyes, small as the smallest pinpoints.

But seemingly most fragile of all are the little calcareous [4] sponges that here and there exist among the seaweeds. They form masses of minute, upthrust tubes of vaselike form, none more than half an inch high. The wall of each is a mesh of fine threads — a web of starched lace made to fairy scale.

I could have crushed any of these

[1] dulse (dŭls): a type of seaweed.
[2] bryozoans (brī′ō·zō′ănz): mosslike animals.

[3] basal: forming a base.
[4] calcareous (kăl·kâr′ė·ŭs): containing calcium.

fragile structures between my fingers, yet somehow they find it possible to exist here, amid the surging thunder of the surf that must fill this cave as the sea comes in. Perhaps the seaweeds are the key to the mystery, their resilient fronds a sufficient cushion for all the minute and delicate beings they contain.

But it is the sponges that give to the cave and its pool their special quality — the sense of a continuing flow of time. For each day that I visit the pool on the lowest tides of the summer, they seem unchanged — the same in July, the same in August, the same in September. And they are the same this year as last, and presumably as they will be a hundred or a thousand summers hence.

Simple in structure, little different from the first sponges that spread their mats on ancient rocks and drew their food from a primordial[1] sea, the sponges bridge the eons of time. The green sponge that carpets the floor of this cave grew in other pools before this shore was formed; it was old when the first creatures came out of the sea in those ancient eras of the Paleozoic,[2] 300 million years ago; it existed even in the dim past before the first fossil record, for the hard little spicules — all that remains when the living tissue is gone — are found in the first fossil-bearing rocks, those of the Cambrian period.

So, in the hidden chamber of that pool, time echoes down the long ages to a present that is but a moment.

As I watched, a fish swam in, a shadow in the green light, entering the pool by one of the openings low on its seaward wall. Compared with the ancient sponges, the fish was almost a symbol of modernity, its fishlike ancestry traceable only half as far into the past. And I, in whose eyes the images of the two were beheld as though they were contemporaries, was a mere newcomer whose ancestors had inhabited the earth so briefly that my presence was almost anachronistic.[3]

As I lay at the threshold of the cave thinking those thoughts, the surge of waters rose and flooded across the rock on which I rested. The tide was rising.

[3] anachronistic (á·năk'rô·nĭs'tĭk): out of the proper time sequence.

FOR DISCUSSION

1. Why are the waters of the hidden pool described as "never still"?

2. What does the author mean when she says, "On the roof of the cave is written a starkly simple statement of the force of the surf"?

3. How can delicate plants and animals live in a pool that is beaten by surf as the tide comes in?

4. What animal gives to the hidden pool its timeless quality? How does the entrance of a fish provide a contrast?

AN AUTHOR'S TECHNIQUE: APPEALS TO THE SENSES

Try to catalogue the sensory appeals of the essay. At the top of a sheet of paper, write *Sight — Sound — Touch*. Under each heading, put the words in the piece that appeal to the sense indicated. Some of your first entries may be "purest, palest green," "dripping," and "brittle."

THE AUTHOR

RACHEL CARSON (b. 1907) was born in Springdale, Pennsylvania, so far inland that until she graduated from college she never saw the sea, which as her favorite subject has contributed so greatly to her fame. She was an author early, however, selling a piece to a children's magazine when she was only twelve. She took degrees in zoology, taught, and was an aquatic biologist for the United States Fish and Wildlife Service. Her first book, *Under the Sea-Wind* (1941), grew from an essay written for the *Atlantic Monthly*. Her second was a nonfiction best seller and a winner of a National Book Award in 1951. It was entitled *The Sea Around Us.*

[1] primordial (prī·môr'dĭ·ăl): ancient.
[2] Paleozoic (pā'lê·ô·zō'ĭk).

J. FRANK DOBIE

The Heraldry of the Range

If the average American had to pick one symbol to represent the cowboy, he would probably choose six-guns or spurs or silver-trimmed saddles or high-heeled boots. But any real working rancher knows that the supreme symbol of his life is the cattle brand.

RELATING DETAILS TO MAIN POINTS. One distinction of a skillful reader is the ability to keep up with the main divisions of a piece of factual writing and to relate details to the main point they illustrate or support. As you read this article on cattle brands and the part they play in ranch life, you will find it easy to practice this skill of recognizing the principal topics and associating with each one the illustrations the writer provides.

THE other day a ranchman out in West Texas whose brand is T Half Circle announced that the United States Patent Office had registered it as a trade-mark. Since many cattle raisers nowadays sell their product by mail, the owner's brand on an animal being a guaranty of its standard breeding, other

"The Heraldry of the Range" by J. Frank Dobie. Reprinted by permission of the author.

cowmen are likely to have their brands registered as trade-marks. A brand is just that — a trade-mark — though it is also much more, and to it is attached all the sentiment and connotation once borne by coats of arms.

Primarily it is a means of identification, whether against thieves or among honest men, on the owner's home range or far away. If names and addresses were not so long, they would be branded on cattle. A brand is a seal that stands for a name; and somewhere, with name and address, every legal brand is recorded, just as with the purchaser's name are recorded the make and engine number of every automobile, somewhere.

Just when brands were introduced into the world it would be difficult to say. The claim has often been made that Cortes, conqueror of Mexico, originated branding in America. At Thebes, so it is said, a tomb twenty-five hundred years old has been uncovered bearing among other mural decorations the representation of a cow tied down and a man branding her with a geometric design. The tomb must have been that of an Egyptian cattle king. When Chaucer's pilgrims set out on their immortal journey from London to Canterbury more than five hundred years ago, some of them probably rode on rented horses. At least, horses kept for rent at that time were, says the great historian Jusserand — who cites authority for the statement — "branded in a prominent manner, so that unscrupulous travelers should not be tempted to quit the road and appropriate the steeds." In 1643, before the cattle industry in the Southwest was born, the New Haven, Connecticut, code stipulated how horses should be branded in order to prevent trouble between rival claimants of "horses running together in the woods."

But nowhere have brands been so important to people or so interwoven with their lives as on the ranges of western America. A ranchboy often learns the language of brands earlier than he learns the language of books.

When George Asa was a very small boy living on a big ranch near the Rio Grande, his father began one day to teach him the letters of the alphabet, drawing them on paper with a pencil. He drew A, and George Asa learned it; then B, and George Asa learned it. But when he drew a C and called it, George Asa refused to accept it as a letter.

"Aw, Daddy," he exclaimed, "you're trying to tease me now! That's not a letter at all. That's Mr. Cox's brand."

Mr. Cox was a neighboring ranchman whose brand, a big C, was familiar to George Asa before he knew one letter from another. As a ranchboy he was learning to read brands before he learned his A B C's.

At a one-teacher school out in the mesquite,[1] the Friday-afternoon session usually closed with recitations. A frequent recitation began with the well-known injunction to the little star:

---

[1] **mesquite** (měs·kēt′): a spiny tree or shrub of the Southwest; here, an area where such vegetation is common.

Twinkle, twinkle, little star!
How I wonder what you are,
Up above the world so high
Like a diamond in the sky.

One of the school urchins was the son of a rancher who ran the Diamond P brand — ◈. That was the only diamond the lad knew, and he confesses now that he used to study the stars by the hour, trying to catch one of them assuming the diamond shape so familiar to him on the sides of cows and at the hot end of a branding iron. He knew the language of brands better than he knew the language of jewels and poetry.

The brand gives its name to everything on the ranch. The chuck wagon of the Olmos — Elms — Ranch is seldom called the Olmos wagon but is almost invariably referred to as the "A Dot wagon," Λ being the ranch brand. The "cow crowd" working on the Withers range is customarily referred to not as the Withers outfit but as the "Pig Pen outfit"; the Pig Pen — made thus, ⌗ — being the Withers brand. A cowboy rides a "Double Circle horse," which is branded ◎. Another cowboy is "one of the Rocking Chair hands" because he works on the Rocking Chair — ⌐ — Ranch.

A ranch may be named for its owner, as the Kokernut Ranch; it may be named after a creek that runs through it, as the San Francisco Ranch; it may take its name from some other feature of nature, as the Seven Oaks Ranch. But the greater number of ranches by far take their names simply from the ranch brand: the JA Ranch — ꞁA — the Pitchfork — Ψ — the Hundred and One — IOI . Sometimes after a brand is no longer in use, some feature of the land keeps its name; although the great 7D outfit has quitted the Pecos forever, 7D Mountain keeps the brand as part of the language of the country.

The very owner of a ranch sometimes loses his name in his brand. There is

"Diamond and a Half Hud" of the plains, who signs his checks as W. D. Hudson and gives ⟨⟩ as his brand. Colonel B. H. Campbell, a prominent cowman of the Indian Territory who for a time managed the great XIT Ranch of Texas, gave for his brand B̅Q̅ . It was read as "Barbeque," and "Barbeque Campbell" became known where B. H. Campbell had never been heard of.

As a means of identification, the brand envelops all things else on the range. An incident related by Walter Billingsley, an old trail driver, well illustrates this fact.

In 1884 [he says] I took a herd of King Ranch steers from South Texas to Cheyenne, Wyoming. Everything went all right until we crossed the South Platte and reached Fort Sidney, Nebraska. While we held the herd a few miles out from town, I let a bunch of the boys go in to see the sights. Five of them laid out and did not report for work next morning. I rode in, found them, and fired them on the spot. I owed them one hundred and twenty dollars apiece. I had no money to pay them off, and I did not know a soul in Sidney.

My first move was to see the banker. Says I to him: "I'm trail boss for the King Ranch, owned by Captain Richard King and known from Canada to the Rio Grande. I've fired five of the sorriest cowboys that ever rode out of Texas. They are due six hundred dollars, and when they get it they will make you fine citizens and spend it all right here. I want to leave them with you, and I want to draw on Wright and Beverley at Dodge City for the six hundred dollars. Will you cash my draft?"

"Well," says the banker, "you look all right and I am satisfied you are all right, but can't you get someone to identify you?"

"I'm where I never was before and where I never expect to be again," I replied, "and I don't see a soul in town that I know."

The banker seemed awful anxious to accommodate me, and I sure did not want to hire those cowboys back just because I couldn't pay them off. I just wasn't going to give them the whip hand over me that way.

"Suppose you look around a little and see if you can't strike somebody you know," the banker concluded, "and then come back."

I went out. My mind was made up. I rounded up the men I'd fired and said, "Follow me and get your money."

We galloped to camp. "Load up and hitch up," I says to the cook, "and follow me."

Then I called the horse wrangler. "Drive up that *remuda* [1] of saddle horses," I says to him, "and follow the chuck wagon."

When we were all ready we struck a high trot for town, and a sight we must have made — me in the lead, those five sorry cowboys swinging after me, then the chuck wagon with six mules hitched to it, and then one hundred and fifty saddle horses with the *remudero* and a couple of other hands driving them. I drew up at the bank and the outfit halted.

"Come here!" I yelled to the banker, who was already at the door. "Come out here and look at my identification!"

He came a-laughing.

"Now," says I, "I guess you know what the King Ranch brand is — Running W on the side and K on the jaw. Well, there's one hundred and fifty saddle horses branded K W. There's a wagon with K W branded on the sideboards, branded on the chuck box, branded all over everything. Look at the cook's saddle on that near wheel mule, and you'll see K W on it. In fact, everything and everybody in this outfit is branded K W."

The banker was impressed all right. He shelled out the six hundred dollars right away. I paid off the quitters; they unsaddled right there, turned their horses into the *remuda*, took their bedding out of the wagon, and the Running W outfit rolled its tail on for Cheyenne.

The average cow hand is so conscious of brands that in season and out of season, appropriately and inappropriately, consciously and unconsciously, he brands whatever he comes across. He

[1] *remuda* (rĕ·mū′dȧ): all of the saddle horses belonging to the outfit.

whittles brands on sticks; he burns them into the planks of branding chutes, on pasture gates, on the anchor posts of windmill towers. He smears them with axle grease across the doors of barns and garages. He paints them with charcoal on the rock walls of canyons in which he has made a campfire. He carves them into his spur traps, leggings, and saddle — above all, into his boot tops. More pistols were etched with cattle brands than were ever notched for dead victims. Many a cook has stenciled the ranch coat of arms into the top crust of that gala-day treat — a wild-plum cobbler. Ranchboys are incorrigible when it comes to carving brands on their desks at school. They play ranch, and, with baling wire for running irons, brand oak balls, the sawed-off tips of horns, spools, and other objects used to represent cattle and horses.

An old-time, dyed-in-the-wool cowman took pride in nothing more than in his memory for brands, and good cowmen still take the same pride. There are hotel clerks who never forget a face, scholars who never falter on a date, and automobile salesmen who hold in mind the engine number of every car sold or inspected. One must marvel with Mark Twain at the memory of a trained Mississippi River steamboat pilot. But the memory of a top brandman surpasses any other kind of memory I have ever met or heard of. It is more than memory; it is an instinct for cattle. Still riding the range are men who can count a hundred head of mixed cattle as they string along, and then from memory classify them and give every brand correctly.

Some of the cattle inspectors operating today in stockyards and on the range can recognize, with only an occasional reference to their brand books, literally thousands of brands. They say that Lod Calohan, head inspector for the Texas and Southwestern Cattle Raisers' Association at the Kansas City stockyards, can tell what brand an animal had on it by tasting the beef.

Deciphering and remembering the letters, figures, curves, and other configurations that make up brands is not enough. The thoroughgoing rangeman is a master of brand nomenclature,[1] on the esoteric [2] principles of which somebody ought to write a grammar. Generally, be it said, brands read from top to bottom and from left to right. A majority of the cattle brands in use are so simple that nearly anyone, once he has mastered a few principles, can "call" them properly. The brand **H4** can be nothing else than "H Four"; *HD* will easily be conceived to be the "H Triangle." But only the initiated denominate ⊥ as "Lazy H," or Ɛ as "Crazy Three." Any letter "too tired to stand up" is "lazy"; though if it is merely in an oblique position and not on its back, it is "tumbling." ⊀ or ⊁ is "Tumbling T."

A letter with curves at the end is often said to be "running." The most noted illustration of this principle is the "Running W" brand — ∿ — of the million-acre King Ranch. A letter or figure with "wings" to it is "flying" — thus, **W** is the "Flying W."

Brands "walk," "drag," "swing," and "rock" as well as they "run" or "fly." *Ƒ* is the "Walking F," and **A** is the "Walking A." The projection at the bottom of the figure makes **Z** the "Drag Seven." L suspended from a curve — **T** — becomes the "Swinging L." Many brands are on rockers, as the "Rocking H" — **H**. But if the rocker is unjoined, then it is a half or quarter circle; so **H** is "H Half Circle." One of the most historic brands of the West is the "Rocking Chair" — **H**.

Sometimes a brand rests on a "bench," as **Y**, the "Y Bench." V-

[1] **nomenclature:** (nō′měn·klā′tûr): method of naming.

[2] **esoteric** (ěs′ō·těr′ĭk): mysterious; hidden from all but a few.

shaped prongs attached to some part of a letter make it forked. ⌇S is "Forked S," but ⅄ is not "Forked N"; it is "Forked Lightning."

A straight mark is usually called a "bar"; but if it is very long or leaning at an angle to the normal horizontal position, it is apt to be called a "slash." The / \ is called " Cut and Slash." ⌐ is "Bradded Dash." John Chisum, noted cowman of the Pecos, branded twenty thousand calves each year with a straight line running from shoulder to tail, and that "bar" was known all over the cattle country as the "Fence Rail." A brand burner added to it thus, ―o―, and the result was known both as "Knot on the Rail" and "Bug on the Rail." o—o might be "O Bar O," but it isn't. It is "Hobble O," for it resembles a pair of horse hobbles.

One time a rancher started a new brand made thus, ⑂. Somebody asked him what he called it. "*Quién sabe?*" [1] ("Who knows?") he replied. And as the "Quién Sabe" brand it was known ever afterward and was placed on tens of thousands of cattle. Looking through a mixed herd of cattle or a brand book, one might note many brands of apparently a *quién sabe* nature; but somehow the rangemen have usually found a name for the most nameless device.

Fanciful designs frequently have fanciful names that could never be guessed even by good cowmen not familiar with the local interpretation of the brand. For instance, ⌇ was known on the Colorado River in Texas as "Pot Hooks." When the owners moved their cattle to a new ranch several hundred miles to the southwest, the brand took the name of "Straddle Bug." A well-known brand was the "Gourd and Vine." It was run in this manner, ⌇, so as to cover the whole side of an animal; and while everybody called it "Gourd and Vine," no stranger would at first sight of it ever guess the name.

Many owners use their initials in brands and sometimes even spell out their names. John M. Doak took **DOK** for his brand. With elegant simplicity Mrs. Katie Barr spelled out her whole name in **KT**, "KT Bar." Jack Barber approached the sound of his last name with **B̄R̄**. Pete Coffin had both his jest and his name in ⑆. A man by the name of Hightower used **HI⌇⌇**. Napoleon Daniel embodied in a brand his nickname −**BONY**. Ingenious but a little puzzling was Mr. Float's brand − ⌇, which does spell FLOT.

Instead of telling the owner's name, a brand may suggest something of his biography. J. C. Studer was a blacksmith working for the Santa Fe Railroad when it was built across the Texas Panhandle. He fell in love with the country, invested his savings in land and cattle, and, out of respect for his trade, adopted an anvil − ⌇ − as his brand. One of the sea captains who used to sail in the Gulf of Mexico quit the sea for ranching; but he could not forget the old seafaring life, and his "Ship's Anchor" brand − ⌇ − was a tribute to the memory.

There are legendary tales about brands, as there are about everything else with which man has had a vital connection. One of the most widely known of these legends tells how the "Four Sixes" − **6666** − originated.

Back in the early days a young cowboy by the name of Burk Burnett, who was just getting his start in cattle, rode into the village of Fort Worth one morning bent on indulging his skill in the favorite game of the range − poker. At one of the many gaming tables, then wide open to the public, he invested in a sombrero full of chips. At first he lost heavily; then the game became variable; about midnight his luck had changed, and by daylight he had a barrelful of money.

---

[1] *Quién sabe?* (kyān sä′vä).

One of his opponents was desperate. "Burk," he said, "I'm broke, but I'll play my ranch and cattle against your pile."

"You've made a bet," was the reply.

On the deal Burk Burnett drew two sixes. He discarded three other cards, keeping the pair. Then he drew two more sixes. The four sixes won the ranch. Immediately, the story goes on, Burnett rebranded the cattle he had won with his lucky number — 6666. In time he increased his holdings until he had three hundred thousand acres in the Indian Territory stocked with Four Sixes cattle, besides an enormous ranch in North Texas. An oil field came in on his land and a boom city named Burkburnett sprang up. When his widow died, only a few years ago, she left several million dollars to Texas Christian University — probably the best poker hand that a Christian institution ever drew.

Whatever the facts, the poker story has fastened itself upon the imagination of thousands of recounters and will live for a long time.

No account of brands would be complete without consideration of the art of burning out brands. It was an art that reached the height of development during the days of open range, but it is by no means lost yet. Before the practice of counterbranding went out, a thief might void a brand by running a bar through it or by counterbranding the animal — as if it had been legitimately sold — and then putting his own brand on it. Again, he might rub out the owner's brand by taking a hot smoothing iron and burning all that part of an animal's hide covered by a brand. This was called blotching, or blotting. The result would be an enormous scar or blotch, through which the original lines were apt still to be visible. In any case, the blotch was evidence that the animal had been stolen, though not always could it be ascertained from whom stolen.

The most common practice by far was, and is yet, to run the original brand into something else.

One of the oldest chestnuts in the cow country is the "I See You Too" story. A ranchman somewhere started the IC brand. Before long he noticed that certain cattle in his herd wore the brand ICU. Not to be outdone, he did a little doctoring himself, and then the whole herd wore the ICU2 brand. Then there was the fellow who started with B4 for a brand. A longhorn neighbor presently claimed that cattle branded B4U were his. The king of brand alterers then rode in, and presently nobody could find on the range anything that was not branded B4U2.

If brands could always be added to so easily and if they could be subtracted from as well as added to, the problem of the brand burner would be much simpler; but in brands, as in Scripture, what is writ is writ. In addition to adding a fresh figure or mark to an old device, the brand burner must try to cover up his alterations. For instance, one cattle company gave ⅂P — "Seven P" — for a brand. A thief ran it into ⅂P — "Seven Up." But expert rangemen can usually detect such mutilations. The new part never has the same look as the old part that has been reburned.

The classic story of brand burning has, fittingly, to do with the largest ranch the United States of America has known, the XIT, the three million acres of which were granted by the State of Texas to the Capitol Syndicate in exchange for the present granite capitol building at Austin. Wherever men talk of brands — and that is wherever range cattle graze — the story of the "Star Cross burn" is told.

Range rustlers had tried and tried to figure out a way to turn XIT into another brand that would not give itself away. At last, so the yarn goes, a clever range rider solved the problem. He revealed his secret to no one; he never blurred a brand. He was an artist. Nevertheless, he was finally brought to trial. The evidence was conclusive that he had built up from nothing a herd of cattle branded "Star Cross" — ⚡ — but the prosecuting attorney was unable to inform the jury how XIT could be altered into that symbol. So the rustler was freed. The XIT people were helpless. They offered him five thousand dollars if he would tell them how he achieved the Star Cross and would quit burning it on their cattle. Then the legendary rustler told his secret.

Among the thousands of calves branded each year on the XIT Ranch, many of them had one or more of the letters imperfectly placed. The rustler looked for animals on which the T was slanting. When he found ⅩⅠ⅄ he easily ran it into ⅩⅠ⅄ .

Many brand burners have been clever, but probably not one of them ever gained anything by his cleverness. After all, a great majority of the rangemen have always been honest men, and among them brands on cattle have served well the purpose for which they were designed; that is, to identify and maintain ownership. On ranches, cattle are branded today by the millions, just as they were branded during the days of the open range.

If branding could be avoided, it would be avoided. Humane societies have protested against the practice; experiments have been conducted with chemical compositions purporting to make an indelible but painless mark. But no substitute has been found for branding. Anyhow, branding is not unduly cruel, and the resultant pain is of short duration. As long as there are ranches, there will be brands — and that will be until millions and millions of acres of rocks and arid soil are made fertile and moist. The heraldry of the range is not obsolete; it is not even obsolescent.[1]

    [1] obsolescent: going out of use.

FOR DISCUSSION

1. Tell of some attitudes of ranchers toward cattle brands to justify the statement that brands mean to them what coats of arms mean to members of noble families.

2. What do you think is the writer's purpose in this article? Can you cite evidence that the life of the cattle ranch is still high in interest for the American people?

3. What other professions does Dobie compare with that of the brandman, in the matter of memory?

4. Brands are often used as decorative motifs in buildings and house furnishings in the Southwest. Pick out some of the brands reproduced in this article that would make good decorative designs and suggest uses for them.

RELATING DETAILS TO MAIN POINTS

Write down the main points that Dobie makes in this discussion of cattle brands. Then recall all the details you can to support each of the main points.

THE AUTHOR

J. FRANK DOBIE (b. 1888) once complained that his school courses entirely neglected literature about the Southwest, where he grew up. Now he has reported so well the life he knew as a boy on a South Texas ranch that no course in American literature is complete without a sample from the saga.

A Vaquero of the Brush Country re-creates ranch life amid mesquite, chaparral, and cactus, very different from ranching on the open plains. Coronado's Children and Apache Gold and Yaqui Silver collect legends of the lost mines of Indian and Spanish times and of men who spend their lives with an old chart and a pickax in search of buried treasure. His other books include The Longhorns, The Mustangs, and The Song of the Coyote.

American Art and Artists ➤

Reproduced on the facing page is a detail from "Branding Cattle," an oil painting by the American artist Frederic Remington (1861–1909).

E. B. WHITE

Walden

(June, 1939)

E. B. White, perhaps our most skillful modern essayist, uses the style of the friendly letter in this informal essay. He pretends to address his letter to Henry Thoreau, the famous nineteenth-century writer who made Walden Pond near Concord, Massachusetts, one of America's memorable landmarks. A photograph of Walden Pond appears on page 161.

COMPARISON AND CONTRAST. Both the humor and the seriousness of White's essay depend upon the contrast between America in the mid-nineteenth century and the modern age. It will more than double your understanding and enjoyment of this selection to turn to page 584 and read, or re-read, the excerpts from Thoreau's *Walden* before you begin E. B. White's essay.

June, 1939

Miss Nims, take a letter
to Henry David Thoreau.

Dear Henry: I thought of you the other afternoon as I was approaching Concord, doing fifty on Route 62. That is a high speed at which to hold a phi-

losopher in one's mind, but in this century we are a nimble bunch.

On one of the lawns in the outskirts of the village, a woman was cutting the grass with a motorized lawn mower. What made me think of you was that the machine had rather got away from her, although she was game enough, and in the brief glimpse I had of the scene, it appeared to me that the lawn was mowing the lady. She kept a tight grip on the handles, which throbbed violently with every explosion of the one-cylinder motor, and as she steered around bushes and lurched along at a reluctant trot behind her impetuous servant, she looked like a puppy who had grabbed something that was too much for him. Concord hasn't changed much, Henry; the farm implements and the animals still have the upper hand.

I may as well admit that I was journeying to Concord with the deliberate intention of visiting your woods; for although I have never knelt at the grave of a philosopher nor placed wreaths on moldy poets, and have often gone a mile out of my way to avoid some place of historical interest, I have always wanted to see Walden Pond. The account which you left of your sojourn there is, you will be amused to learn, a document of increasing pertinence; each year it seems to gain a little headway, as the world loses ground. We may all be transcendental [1] yet, whether we like it or not. As our common complexities increase, any tale of individual simplicity (and yours is the best written and the cockiest) acquires a new fascination; as our goods accumulate, but not our well-being, your report of an existence without material adornment takes on a certain awkward credibility.

My purpose in going to Walden Pond, like yours, was not to live cheaply or to live dearly there, but to transact some private business with the fewest obstacles. Approaching Concord, doing forty, doing forty-five, doing fifty, the steering wheel held snug in my palms, the highway held grimly in my vision, the crown of the road now serving me (on the right-hand curves), now defeating me (on the left-hand curves), I began to rouse myself from the stupefaction which a day's motor journey induces. It was a delicious evening, Henry, when the whole body is one sense, and imbibes delight through every pore, if I may coin a phrase. Fields were richly brown where the harrow, drawn by the stripped Ford, had lately sunk its teeth; pastures were green; and overhead the sky had that same everlasting great look which you will find on page 144 of the Oxford pocket edition.[2] I could feel the road entering me, through tire, wheel, spring, and cushion; shall I not have intelligence with earth too? Am I not partly leaves and vegetable mold myself? — a man of infinite horsepower, yet partly leaves.

Stay with me on 62, and it will take you into Concord. As I say, it was a delicious evening. The snake had come forth to die in a bloody S on the highway, the wheel upon its head, its bowels flat now and exposed. The turtle had come up too to cross the road and die in the attempt, its hard shell smashed under the rubber blow, its intestinal yearning (for the other side of the road) forever squashed. There was a sign by the wayside which announced that the road had a "cotton surface." You wouldn't know what that is, but neither, for that matter, did I. There is a cryptic ingredient in many of our modern improvements — we are awed and pleased without knowing quite what we are enjoying. It is something to be traveling on a road with a cotton surface.

The civilization round Concord today is an odd distillation of city, village, farm, and manor. The houses, yards, fields look not quite suburban, not quite rural. Under the bronze beech and the blue spruce of the departed baron grazes the milch [3] goat of the heirs. Under the porte-cochère [4] stands the reconditioned station wagon; under the grape arbor sit the puppies for sale. (But why do men degenerate ever? What makes families run out?)

It was June and everywhere June was publishing her immemorial stanza; in the lilacs, in the syringa,[5] in the freshly edged paths and the sweetness of moist, beloved gardens, and the little wire wickets that preserve the tulips' front. Farmers were already moving the fruits of their toil into their yards, arranging the rhubarb, the asparagus, the strictly fresh eggs on the painted stands under the little shed roofs with the patent shingles. And though it was almost a hundred years since you had taken your ax and started cutting out your home on Walden Pond, I was interested to observe that the philosophi-

[1] **transcendental** (trăn′sĕn·dĕn′tăl): not concerned with practical matters or material things. For a fuller discussion of the term, especially as it applies to Thoreau, see pages 565–66.

[2] **Oxford pocket edition:** an edition of Thoreau's *Walden.*

[3] **milch:** giving milk.

[4] **porte-cochère** (pōrt′kō·shâr′): a carport.

[5] **syringa** (sĭ·rĭng′gȧ): a large white or cream flower.

cal spirit was still alive in Massachusetts: in the center of a vacant lot, some boys were assembling the framework of the rude shelter, their whole mind and skill concentrated in the rather inauspicious helter-skeleton of studs and rafters. They too were escaping from town, to live naturally, in a rich blend of savagery and philosophy.

That evening, after supper at the inn, I strolled out into the twilight to dream my shapeless transcendental dreams and see that the car was locked up for the night (first open the right front door, then reach over, straining, and pull up the handles of the left rear and the left front till you hear the click, then the handle of the right rear, then shut the right front but open it again, remembering that the key is still in the ignition switch, remove the key, shut the right front again with a bang, push the tiny keyhole cover to one side, insert key, turn, and withdraw). It is what we all do, Henry. It is called locking the car. It is said to confuse thieves and keep them from making off with the lap robe. Four doors to lock behind one robe. The driver himself never uses a lap robe, the free movement of his legs being vital to the operation of the vehicle; so that when he locks the car, it is a pure and unselfish act. I have in my life gained very little essential heat from lap robes, yet I have ever been at pains to lock them up.

The evening was full of sounds, some of which would have stirred your memory. The robins still love the elms of New England villages at sundown. There is enough of the thrush in them to make song inevitable at the end of day, and enough of the tramp to make them hang round the dwellings of men. A robin, like many another American, dearly loves a white house with green blinds. Concord is still full of them.

Your fellow townsmen were stirring abroad — not many afoot, most of them in their cars; and the sound which they made in Concord at evening was a rustling and a whispering. The sound lacks steadfastness and is wholly unlike that of a train. A train, as you know who lived so near the Fitchburg line, whistles once or twice sadly and is gone, trailing a memory in smoke, soothing to ear and mind. Automobiles, skirting a village green, are like flies that have gained the inner ear — they buzz, cease, pause, start, shift, stop, halt, brake, and the whole effect is a nervous polytone,[1] curiously disturbing.

As I wandered along, the toc-toc of Ping-pong balls drifted from an attic window. In front of the Reuben Brown house, a Buick was drawn up. At the wheel, motionless, his hat upon his head, a man sat, listening to Amos and Andy on the radio (it is a drama of many scenes and without an end). The deep voice of Andrew Brown, emerging from the car, although it originated more than two hundred miles away, was unstrained by distance. When you used to sit on the shore of your pond on Sunday morning, listening to the church bells of Acton and Concord, you were aware of the excellent filter of the intervening atmosphere. Science has attended to that, and sound now maintains its intensity without regard for distance. Properly sponsored, it goes on forever.

A fire engine, out for a trial spin, roared past Emerson's house, hot with readiness for public duty. Over the barn roofs the martins[2] dipped and chittered. A swarthy daughter of an asparagus grower, in culottes,[3] shirt, and bandanna, pedaled past on her bicycle. It was indeed a delicious evening, and I returned to the inn (I believe it was your house once) to rock with the old ladies on the concrete veranda.

Next morning early I started afoot

[1] **polytone:** combination of sounds.
[2] **martins:** small swallows.
[3] **culottes** (kü·lŏts′): a woman's garment, which looks like a skirt, but is divided like trousers.

for Walden, out Main Street and down Thoreau, past the depot and the Minuteman Chevrolet Company. The morning was fresh, and in a bean field along the way, I flushed an agriculturalist, quietly studying his beans. Thoreau Street soon joined Number 126, an artery of the State. We number our highways nowadays, our speed being so great we can remember little of their quality or character and are lucky to remember their number. (Men have an indistinct notion that if they keep up this activity long enough, all will at length ride somewhere, in next to no time.) Your pond is on 126.

I knew I must be nearing your woodland retreat when the Golden Pheasant lunchroom came into view — Sealtest ice cream, toasted sandwiches, hot frankfurters, waffles, tonics, and lunches. Were I the proprietor, I should add rice, Indian meal, and molasses [1] — just for old time's sake. The Pheasant, incidentally, is for sale: a chance for some nature lover who wishes to set himself up beside a pond in the Concord atmosphere and live deliberately, fronting only the essential facts of life on Number 126. Beyond the Pheasant was a place called Walden Breezes, an oasis whose porch pillars were made of old green shutters sawed into lengths. On the porch was a distorting mirror, to give the traveler a comical image of himself, who had miraculously learned to gaze in an ordinary glass without smiling. Behind the Breezes, in a sunparched clearing, dwelt your philosophical descendants in their trailers, each trailer the size of your hut, but all grouped together for the sake of congeniality. Trailer people leave the city, as you did, to discover solitude and in any weather, at any hour of the day or night, to improve the nick of time; but they soon collect in villages and get bogged deeper in the mud than ever.

The camp behind Walden Breezes was just rousing itself to the morning. The ground was packed hard under the heel, and the sun came through the clearing to bake the soil and enlarge the wry smile of cramped housekeeping. Cushman's bakery truck had stopped to deliver an early basket of rolls. A camp dog, seeing me in the road, barked petulantly. A man emerged from one of the trailers and set forth with a bucket to draw water from some forest tap.

Leaving the highway, I turned off into the woods toward the pond, which was apparent through the foliage. The floor of the forest was strewn with dried old oak leaves and *Transcripts*.[2] From beneath the flattened popcorn wrapper (*granum explosum*) peeped the frail violet. I followed a footpath and descended to the water's edge. The pond lay clear and blue in the morning light, as you have seen it so many times. In the shallows a man's waterlogged shirt undulated gently. A few flies came out to greet me and convoy me to your cove, past the No Bathing signs on which the fellows and the girls had scrawled their names. I felt strangely excited suddenly to be snooping around your premises, tiptoeing along watchfully, as though not to tread by mistake upon the intervening century. Before I got to the cove, I heard something which seemed to me quite wonderful: I heard your frog, a full, clear *troonk*, guiding me, still hoarse and solemn, bridging the years as the robins had bridged them in the sweetness of the village evening. But he soon quit, and I came on a couple of young boys throwing stones at him.

Your front yard is marked by a bronze tablet set in a stone. Four small granite posts, a few feet away, show where the house was. On top of the tablet was a pair of faded blue bathing

---

[1] rice, Indian meal, and molasses: the main ingredients of Thoreau's diet.

[2] **Transcripts**: The *Evening Transcript* was a Boston newspaper.

trunks with a white stripe. Back of it is a pile of stones, a sort of cairn,[1] left by your visitors as a tribute, I suppose. It is a rather ugly little heap of stones, Henry. In fact, the hillside itself seems faded, browbeaten; a few tall, skinny pines, bare of lower limbs, a smattering of young maples in suitable green, some birches and oaks, and a number of trees felled by the last big wind. It was from the bole [2] of one of these fallen pines, torn up by the roots, that I extracted the stone which I added to the cairn — a sentimental act in which I was interrupted by a small terrier from a nearby picnic group, who confronted me and wanted to know about the stone.

I sat down for a while on one of the posts of your house to listen to the bluebottles and the dragonflies. The invaded glade sprawled shabby and mean at my feet, but the flies were tuned to the old vibration. There were the remains of a fire in your ruins, but I doubt that it was yours; also two beer bottles trodden into the soil and become part of earth. A young oak had taken root in your house, and two or three ferns, unrolling like the ticklers at a banquet. The only other furnishings were a DuBarry pattern sheet,[3] a page torn from a picture magazine, and some crusts in wax paper.

Before I quit, I walked clear round the pond and found the place where you used to sit on the northeast side to get the sun in the fall, and the beach where you got sand for scrubbing your floor. On the eastern side of the pond, where the highway borders it, the State has built dressing rooms for swimmers, a float with diving towers, drinking fountains of porcelain, and rowboats for hire. The pond is in fact a State Preserve, and carries a twenty-dollar fine for picking wild flowers, a decree

signed in all solemnity by your fellow citizens Walter C. Wardwell, Erson B. Barlow, and Nathaniel I. Bowditch. There was a smell of creosote [4] where they had been building a wide wooden stairway to the road and the parking area. Swimmers and boaters were arriving; bodies plunged vigorously into the water and emerged wet and beautiful in the bright air. As I left, a boatload of town boys were splashing about in mid-pond, kidding and fooling, the young fellows singing at the tops of their lungs in a wild chorus:

Amer-ica, Amer-ica, God shed his grace on thee,
And crown thy good with brotherhood
From sea to shi-ning sea!

I walked back to town along the railroad, following your custom. The rails were expanding noisily in the hot sun, and on the slope of the roadbed, the wild grape and the blackberry sent up their creepers to the track.

The expense of my brief sojourn in Concord was:

Canvas shoes	$1.95	
Baseball bat	.25	⎫ gifts to
Left-handed fielder's		⎬ take back
glove	1.25	⎭ to a boy
Hotel and meals	4.25	
In all	$7.70	

As you see, this amount was almost what you spent for food for eight months. I cannot defend the shoes or the expenditure for shelter and food: they reveal a meanness and grossness in my nature which you would find contemptible. The baseball equipment, however, is the kind of impediment with which you were never on even terms. You must remember that the house where you practiced the sort of economy which I respect was haunted only by mice and squirrels. You never had to cope with a shortstop.

---

[1] cairn (kârn): a pile of stones raised as a memorial or landmark.
[2] bole: trunk.
[3] DuBarry pattern sheet: a dress pattern.

[4] creosote (krē′ȯ·sōt): tar.

A view of Walden Pond.

FOR DISCUSSION

1. What does White mean when he says, "Concord hasn't changed much, Henry; the farm implements and the animals still have the upper hand"?
2. Can you guess White's purpose in describing all the details of locking up the car? What aspect of modern life is he criticizing here?
3. In White's comparison of the sounds of trains and cars, which comes off better?
4. What aspects of nature at Walden seemed to bridge the years?
5. Do you think that White would be willing to change his times for those of Thoreau? Why? Why not?

SUBTLE WIT

A number of lines in White's essay will cause the alert reader to smile not just once but often. This subtle wit is worth examination. Can you suggest what, in each of the following lines, generates the humor?

"Although I have never knelt at the grave of a philosopher nor placed wreaths on moldy poets, and have often gone a mile out of my way to avoid some place of historical interest, I have always wanted to see Walden Pond."

". . . sound now maintains its intensity without regard for distance. Properly sponsored, it goes on forever."

"We number our highways nowadays, our speed being so great we can remember little of their quality or character and are lucky to remember their number. . . . Your pond is on 126."

"From beneath the flattened popcorn wrapper (*granum explosum*) peeped the frail violet."

YOUR OWN WRITING

White's technique — casting the essay in the form of a friendly letter — is not difficult to imitate. Try writing your own informal essay as a letter to some famous person of the past. Comment on the changes since his day in his country, his city or town, or in his particular business or profession. Try to introduce specific details and to keep the tone of the essay as friendly as a conversation between friends.

THE AUTHOR

E. B. WHITE (b. 1899) was born in Mt. Vernon, New York, and educated at Cornell University. He was a reporter on the Seattle *Times,* and later, in his native state, he wrote for the *New Yorker,* eventually becoming a staff member of that magazine. In 1929 he retired to live and write in Maine. He is well known for his children's stories, *Stuart Little* and *Charlotte's Web,* and for collections of essays, *One Man's Meat* (1944) and *The Second Tree from the Corner* (1954). *The Elements of Style,* a book on the principles of English composition, was written by William Strunk, Jr., one of White's teachers at Cornell Uni-

versity, and revised and expanded by White. It ranked high on the best-seller lists of 1959. White's reputation rests primarily on his distinguished prose, but he has also written some fine light verse, collected in *The Lady Is Cold.*

Walden Pond

Reproduced on page 161 is a photograph of Walden Pond, Massachusetts. The photograph was taken within recent years, but this particular area of Walden has remained much as it was in Henry Thoreau's day. This picture, and the smaller photograph on page 156, illustrate the difference between the old and new Walden that forms the basis for White's humorous letter to Thoreau.

BETTY FRIEDAN

The Coming
Ice Age

A True, Scientific Detective Story

One of the exciting features of the article is that it may speculate about the future as well as discuss the past. In either case, such speculation must be based on the author's investigation of facts or on the author's research of investigations made by others. In "The Coming Ice Age" Betty Friedan gathers evidence and clues discovered by two distinguished scientists. She brings to their hunt for truth a kind of detective-story suspense, which explains the subtitle that she gave to this article.

T HIS IS the story of two scientists who started five years ago — with a single radiocarbon clue from the ocean bottom and a wild hunch — to track down one of the earth's great unsolved mysteries: What caused the ancient Ice Ages? Their search led over many continents and seas, to drowned rivers and abandoned mountain caves, into far-removed branches of science. It took them down through recorded history,

from the stone tablets of primitive man to contemporary newspaper headlines.

These two serious, careful scientists — geophysicist[1] Maurice Ewing, director of Columbia University's Lamont Geological Observatory, and geologist[2]-meteorologist[3] William Donn — believe they have finally found the explanation for the giant glaciers, which four times during the past million years have advanced and retreated over the earth. If they are right, the world is now heading into another Ice Age. It will come not as sudden catastrophe, but as the inevitable culmination of a process that has already begun in northern oceans.

As Ewing and Donn read the evidence, an Ice Age will result from a slow warming and rising of the ocean that is now taking place. They believe that this ocean flood — which may submerge large coastal areas of the eastern United States and Western Europe — is going

[1] **geophysicist** (jĕ'ō-fĭz'ĭ-sĭst): one who studies the physics of the earth.
[2] **geologist** (jĕ-ŏl'ō-jĭst): a scientist who studies the earth and its history.
[3] **meteorologist** (mē'tĕ-ĕr-ŏl'ō-jĭst): a specialist in studies of atmosphere and weather.

to melt the ice sheet which has covered the Arctic Ocean through all recorded history. Calculations based on the independent observations of other scientists indicate this melting could begin within roughly one hundred years.

It is this melting of Arctic ice which Ewing and Donn believe will set off another Ice Age on earth. They predict that it will cause great snows to fall in the north — perennial unmelting snows which the world has not seen since the last Ice Age thousands of years ago. These snows will make the Arctic glaciers grow again, until their towering height forces them forward. The advance south will be slow, but if it follows the route of previous Ice Ages, it will encase in ice large parts of North America and Europe. It would, of course, take many centuries for that wall of ice to reach New York and Chicago, London and Paris. But its coming is an inevitable consequence of the cycle which Ewing and Donn believe is now taking place.

The coming of another Ice Age is an event serious scientists have never been able to predict from observable earth phenomena. For until Ewing and Donn postulated their new theory of Ice Ages (it was first published in *Science* in June 1956, and a second report appeared in May 1958), the very nature of the problem seemed to defy the kind of scientific understanding which makes prediction possible.

Scientists know that the glaciers which stand quiet in the Arctic today once covered America with a wall of ice up to two miles thick — its southern boundary extending from Long Island across New York, Pennsylvania, Ohio, Illinois, Wisconsin, Iowa, and the Dakotas to the Missouri River, with extensions into the Western mountain country . . . that it covered northern Europe, England, large parts of France and Germany . . . that it created the Great Lakes, the Hudson and St. Lawrence Rivers . . . that it moved moun-

tains, crashed down forests, destroyed whole species of life.

They also know that it is cold enough at the Arctic for glaciers to grow today, but almost no snow has fallen there in modern times. What caused those snows that built the Ice Age glaciers until their own height forced them to march, and what caused them finally to retreat? And why has the earth been swinging back and forth between Ice Ages and climate like today's for a million years, when before then the entire planet enjoyed a temperate climate with no extremes of hot or cold? Scientists could answer these questions only in terms of sudden catastrophe — a volcanic eruption, the earth's movement into a cloud of cosmic dust — and unpredictable catastrophes are not the concern of contemporary science. Few scientists had even worked on the problem in recent years.

It was only by a combination of lucky circumstance and persistent curiosity that Ewing and Donn as a team began working steadily on the Ice Age mystery. As director of Lamont Geological Observatory, located on top of the New York Palisades over the Hudson River, Ewing teaches theoretical geophysics and directs research in earthquake seismology, marine geology and biology, and oceanography.[1] Donn teaches geology at Brooklyn College and directs the research in meteorology at Lamont. Since the two men live twenty miles apart and were occupied all day, they would often meet at eleven at night in a deserted laboratory at Columbia University — midway between their homes — and work into the morning on the Ice Age trail.

The two men share the scientist's passion for pure search, no matter where it leads. Ewing, a tall and powerful Texan who speaks in a gentle voice, was white-haired before he was fifty, a

[1] **oceanography** (ō'shē-*á*-nŏg'r*á*-fĭ): the study of the ocean's geography and related subjects.

fact his friends attribute to the pace at which he has lived his life as a scientist. For a quarter century he has been leading expeditions over the ocean, often risking his life while pioneering new methods of investigating its secrets. In the early 1930's he founded a new science by dropping charges from a whale boat and using a seismograph [1] to identify the different layers of earth beneath the ocean. In 1955 he was given the navy's Distinguished Service award for devising the SOFAR (Sound Fixing and Ranging) method for rescuing men from ships and planes lost at sea.

Donn, New York City bred, is a slight, wiry meteorologist, who tames tidal waves with logarithms.[2] His mastery of the complex relationship between sea and weather complemented Ewing's knowledge of the depths of the oceans.

The original bits of information which set the two scientists onto the trail of the Ice Age Mystery first came to light on the decks of the three-masted schooner *Vema,* which Lamont Observatory uses for scientific exploration. In the summer of 1953, the ship traced a puzzling pattern on the ocean bottom which led from the Atlantic to the Gulf of Mexico and into the Caribbean Sea. The Columbia-Lamont crew were working with their newly perfected "deep-sea corer," a device which can bring up primeval sediment undisturbed through as much as 4,000 fathoms of water (24,000 feet) — just as it was deposited thousands of years ago.

This "corer" is a sharp-edged steel tube, two and a half inches in diameter and up to seventy feet in length. When it has been lowered from the ship to within fifteen feet of the sea bottom, a

trigger trips the holding mechanism, and the tube is punched by a weight into the sediment. The Lamont ocean expeditions have brought up cores as long as sixty feet — nearly two thousand of them — representing the successive deposits of thousands of years. As Ewing describes it:

"The entire record of the earth is there in the most undisturbed form it is possible to find anywhere — traces of the animals, rocks, and plants of successive ages preserved in the order in which they filtered down from the surface of the sea."

Only recently, radioactive isotope [3] techniques have made it possible to deduce when the sediment was deposited, and other things about the world from which it came. Scientists can now measure the radiocarbon in a sample of ocean-bottom mud — and know how long it has lain there. Radioactive carbon ceases to be replenished when removed from the atmosphere, and decays at a known rate. Chemists therefore calculate from the ratio of radiocarbon to ordinary carbon in a fossil shell whether it has been decaying for a thousand, five, or ten thousand years.

In these cores of mud from the Caribbean, the equatorial Atlantic, and the Gulf of Mexico that summer, the Lamont expedition kept seeing a strange sharp line. "About a foot below the floor of the ocean, the sediment suddenly changed from salmon pink to gray," Ewing said. "You could see it sharp as a razor when the cores were opened on the ship's deck. Others had reported this same line in the North Atlantic.

"When we put these cores to paleontological [4] laboratory tests back at Lamont, we found out what that razor-

---

[1] **seismograph** (sīz'mō·grȧf): an instrument that is ordinarily used to record earthquake shocks.

[2] **logarithms** (lŏg'ȧ·rĭth'mz): certain kinds of mathematical relations useful in calculating.

[3] **isotope** (ī'sō·tōp): a form of an element which differs slightly — in weight and behavior — from the original element.

[4] **paleontological** (pā'lė·ŏn'tō·lŏj'ĭ·kȧl): referring to the study of the life of ancient geological periods.

sharp line meant: at a certain time the ocean suddenly changed from cold to warm. The pink sediment contained shells of minute warm-water animals; the gray sediment, cold-water animals."

Back at Lamont, measurement of radiocarbon showed that this sudden warming took place throughout the length and breadth of the vast Atlantic Ocean — eleven thousand years ago. The cores showed virtually no change in temperature for ninety thousand years — except for this one sudden increase. Donn, Lamont's meteorological expert, was as mystified as Ewing.

"What happened eleven thousand years ago to heat the ocean?" they kept asking themselves at odd moments over the next year or so. "What could change the climate of the whole ocean so abruptly?"

Neither Ewing nor Donn can say precisely when the hunch came. The problem continued to tantalize them, as they traveled about the country attending meetings and doing field work. On the way back from Chicago, they may have watched the ice break up in the Delaware River. They recall reading a newspaper item about a big gambling jackpot on which day the ice would go out in the Yukon. The chain of thought seems obvious now: water freezing — ice going out — this is a sharp, abrupt change, the only sudden change that *can* happen to a body of water.

But oceans don't freeze. Ocean currents dissipate the cold — except, of course, in the small Arctic Ocean, which is almost entirely surrounded by land.[1]

"What would happen if the ice went out of the Arctic Ocean as it does in the Yukon or the Delaware?" Ewing and Donn remember wondering, as they went over the problem again, one day at Lamont.

[1] The important point here is the combination of the two factors — small size and enclosure. Neither condition alone would cause the ocean to freeze.

"Well, we figured the Arctic Ocean would get warmer. Because water would flow more freely between it and the Atlantic, dissipating the cold. And, of course, the Atlantic Ocean would get colder. But wait a minute . . . we saw it simultaneously. If the Arctic Ocean were open water, warmed by the Atlantic, warmer than the land around it, water would evaporate and fall as snow on the land. More snow on Greenland and northern Canada would make glaciers grow. Glaciers don't grow now because there is no open water in the Arctic to provide the moisture for snow.

"And suddenly we had the startling hunch that the Arctic Ocean *was open* during the Ice Age. And that it froze over only eleven thousand years ago. It was this freezing over of the Arctic Ocean which so suddenly warmed the Atlantic — and ended the Ice Age.

"That rather exciting ten minutes," they told me, "contradicted a whole lot of things we'd always taken for granted. Everyone has assumed that the Arctic Ocean, so covered with ice today, would be even colder and more completely frozen during an Ice Age.

"You get a lot of these wild ideas in our business. If one lasts five minutes, you begin to take it seriously. The more we thought about this one, the more it added up. It explained so many things that have always puzzled us.

"For, once you accept the radical idea that the Arctic was a warm open ocean at the time of the great continental glaciers, you can reconstruct a completely different weather pattern from the one we know today. As we worked it out, we could see a startling chain of cause and effect between the oceans and the glaciers themselves. We could see how the oceans would work as an actual 'thermostat' to keep the earth alternating between glacial ice ages and interglacial periods such as today.

"It all hinges on the fact that the North Pole is where it is — in the middle of the Arctic Ocean, which is almost completely surrounded by land except for a shallow 'sill' between Norway and Greenland opening into the Atlantic, and the insignificant Bering Strait. If the cold waters of the Arctic interchanged freely over this sill with the warm Atlantic water, the Arctic Ocean would not freeze over. Its moisture would build glaciers. (In the cold temperatures of the north, the moisture that evaporates from the open Arctic would all fall as snow — too much snow to melt in the short Arctic summer. When the rate at which snow accumulates exceeds the rate at which it melts, glaciers grow.) But as those glaciers grew, they would lock up so much ocean water that sea level would fall.

"We know that sea level was lowered between three hundred and four hundred feet at the peak of the last Ice Age. Now, most of that sill between Norway and Greenland is less than three hundred feet deep. At a certain point the glaciers would lower the sea level so much that the Arctic Ocean would be virtually cut off from the warmer Atlantic. The Arctic Ocean would then freeze over. And the glaciers, no longer fed by snow, would melt under the Arctic summer sun, restoring their water to the oceans. Then sea level would rise, until enough warm Atlantic water again flowed over that sill to melt the Arctic ice sheet, and start another glacial cycle."

Donn worked out a weather map of the world, with an open Arctic Ocean, warmer than surrounding lands. It showed a completely different storm pattern than exists today; more rain and snow in the Arctic, a wind pattern carrying more ocean moisture inland generally. It showed violent blizzards over eastern North America, which would spread more snow on the glaciers. Summers would become more like winters as the glacial wall advanced southward. Donn's weather map with the open Arctic even showed that there would be rain in today's deserts.

But they needed more proof for their theory. They had to track down the circumstantial evidence of what happened eleven thousand years ago; they had to find geological witnesses to confirm their reconstruction of the crime.

They embarked on the painstaking examination of the records of past Arctic explorers. There was little relevant data. One day, going through dusty old volumes of the *National Geographic*, they found a photograph of an Arctic beach — a beach that could have been made only by long years of pounding waves. There must have been open sea in the Arctic to make that beach.

Ewing took to sea in the *Vema* again. In the Gulf of Mexico, the Ice Age trail seemed to peter out altogether in a bottomless plain of flat, gray silt. The *Vema* took core after core below the Mississippi Delta without finding the crucial fossil lines.

"We couldn't even get to the bottom of it with our corers," Ewing recalls. "We were sure the Gulf must have changed from cold to warm just as the other oceans, but how could we prove it when there seemed to be no fossils at all in that endless gray layer? We suspected that the gray silt had come from the Mississippi and had spread over the floor of the Gulf by creeping along the bottom. If we could find a hill that stood well above the Gulf floor, the sediment on top of it would have come down undisturbed from the surface of the water and might contain the record of those temperature changes."

They nearly sailed over them — a cluster of hills rising a thousand feet off the ocean floor. There, instead of puzzling gray silt, they finally found the familiar, razor-sharp layers of glacial and interglacial fossils.

And that very gray silt which had obscured their trail turned out to be further proof that eleven thousand years ago was the date the Ice Age ended. For back at Lamont, radiocarbon measurement showed that the silt *stopped* sliding from the Mississippi just eleven thousand years ago. This meant that a great rise in sea level must have taken place at just that time. Drowned by the rising sea, the lower channels of the Mississippi River would retain their own sediment, losing the power to take it out to the deep central part of the Gulf. It was, almost certainly, the rise in sea level caused by the melting of the glaciers.

As the Lamont crew were pursuing this mystery in the sea, other scientists were unearthing new Ice Age clues on land. Atomic Energy Commissioner Willard F. Libby, the scientist who originated radiocarbon dating, found fossils of a forest at Two Creeks, Wisconsin, that had been first flooded and then overridden by the advancing ice. Radiocarbon dating proved that those trees, at one of the southern finger tips of the last glacial advance, were pushed over about eleven thousand years ago. (Previously, geologists thought the ice had disappeared long before that time.)

Then a series of dramatic clues were brought in by other geologists from caves in the cliffs above the dry Great Basin of Nevada and Utah. Several thousand feet above the basin are rock niches worn by the waves of glacial lakes — lakes created by the great rains that fell south of the Ice Age snows. Far below are caves, also worn by those waves, that were inhabited by man: the famous Fishbone Cave above the dry Winnemucca Lake in western Nevada and the Danger Cave above glacial Lake Bonneville in Utah.

The evidence showed that men moved into those caves shortly after the lake level suddenly dropped and exposed them. Remains were found of the nets and baskets they used to catch the fish of the now-vanished glacial lakes. Radiocarbon dating showed that men were living in those caves — brought above the water when the great glacial rains and snows stopped — approximately eleven thousand years

ago. And the time during which the glacial lakes dropped from those niches thousands of feet above on the cliffs, to the level of the lower caves, was dramatically short — only several hundred years. It was like the sudden change Ewing and Donn had observed in the ocean. The date was now established: eleven thousand years ago, plus or minus a few hundred years, the last Ice Age suddenly ended.

At the time the theory was constructed, there was no actual evidence from the Arctic Ocean itself to indicate it had ever been ice-free. Some months later Dr. A. P. Crary came back from the Arctic Ocean and sent his cores to Lamont. These cores indicated there had been minute animal life for thousands of years in the Arctic Ocean, which suddenly stopped — eleven millenniums ago. They also showed evidence of icebergs free to move in open water at the time Ewing and Donn think the Arctic was open.

Could men have lived on the shores of this ocean during the Ice Age? Were there human witnesses to the open Arctic sea?

"It was only by accident that we stumbled on a vital clue in a completely different branch of science," they told me. "We might have missed it altogether because of the compartmentalization [1] of science."

One day a colleague of Donn's happened to remark over coffee that he'd overheard an anthropologist [2] in the faculty room talking about some traces that had just been discovered of an ancient civilization around the Arctic.

Donn and Ewing started calling anthropologists. The evidence was uncertain, they learned, but some of it pointed strongly to well-established communities of man around the Arctic

[1] **compartmentalization:** division into separate compartments; used here to indicate extreme specialization.

[2] **anthropologist** (ăn′thrȯ·pŏl′ȯ·jĭst): a specialist in the study of man.

many thousands of years ago. In fact, the oldest flints showing man in America had been found recently in a band round the Arctic Circle, seldom straying south.

Anthropologists had been mystified. Even if a land bridge between Siberia and Alaska had existed then, why would man choose to use it to settle in the Arctic Circle, in the very heart of the intense polar cold, at temperature which was assumed to be even lower than today? Around that frozen Arctic Ocean, where would man have found the fish and game those flints suggested? Why would men have *stayed* there for centuries — unless, as Ewing and Donn now believe, the Arctic Ocean was open then, and its shores were a warm oasis compared with the glaciers to the south?

Ewing and Donn got another anthropologist out of bed late at night to question him further. He told them that, while anthropologists are still uncertain as to how and when man first *came* to America, they are pretty sure he suddenly started migrating south, in an explosive wave, about eleven thousand years ago.

Here, perhaps, were their human witnesses to the end of the Ice Age! The people who lived "beyond the north wind" on Arctic shores, behind the towering wall of ice, using their flint-tipped weapons on big game and fish that could not survive the cold Arctic temperatures of today. These men evidently came to America from Siberia when the glaciers had taken enough water from the sea to uncover the Siberian land bridge. They stayed for some centuries around the warm Arctic because the glaciers kept them from straying south. Then, eleven thousand years ago, they suddenly fled. If the Arctic Ocean suddenly froze over, they couldn't eat. Nor could they go back to Siberia because the great rise in sea level at the end of the Ice Age would once more submerge the land bridge.

And just at the time when they could no longer stay in the Arctic, paths opened in the great ice wall south of them. The melting glaciers permitted men to go south at last — in such a rapid wave that they reached the tip of South America in a few thousand years.

So anthropologists are now reconstructing their own mysteries in the light of Ewing and Donn's theory of Ice Ages — which California's authority on early man, Carl Sauer, calls "a major contribution to our understanding. . . . The old, simple belief that man waited at the threshold of the New World until the last ice sheet was gone has been proved wrong."

And, finally, human witnesses were tracked down in southern deserts. During this past year archaeologists [1] have brought back new evidence that the Sahara Desert was green and fertile and thriving with civilization when glaciers froze life in America and Europe. Ewing and Donn had deduced that an open Arctic Ocean would have caused rain in today's deserts. Now, from the caves of the Sahara, came ancient man's vivid drawings of the animals that he hunted on the once-grassy desert.

One big question remained which the new theory did not seem to answer: What started off the first Ice Age cycle?

"We know that during the past million years the world has swung back and forth between Ice Ages and weather like today's," Ewing and Donn told me. "Before then, the whole earth was much warmer. There were no zones of extreme heat or cold; palms and magnolias grew in Greenland, and coral around Iceland; subtropical plants thrived within eleven degrees of the North Pole. Why didn't the Arctic Ocean glacier 'thermostat' work then? What suddenly turned it on one million years ago?

"The answer, we believe, is that until a million years ago, the North Pole was

[1] **archaeologists** (är'kē-ŏl'ō-jĭsts): scientists who study the remains of past human life.

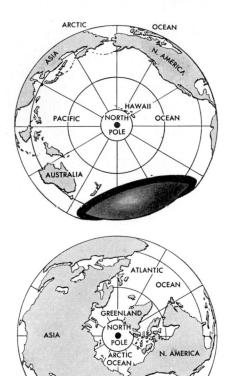

If the Ewing and Donn hypothesis is correct, the Ice Age cycle could have begun in the manner indicated by the two drawings, as a shift of the earth's crust brought the North Pole from the mid-Pacific to the landlocked Arctic Ocean.

not in that landlocked Arctic Ocean at all, but in the middle of the open Pacific, where there was no land on which snow and ice could accumulate, and ocean currents dissipated the cold.

"The idea of wandering poles may seem fantastic. But recently discovered magnetic evidence leads to the geological inference that the whole earth can shift its surface crust with respect to the interior. As the earth's crustal zone 'slides' over the interior, different points on the surface can be at the North or South Pole.

"Such a shift in the earth's crust, it is now believed, did take place before the

first Pleistocene [1] Ice Age, which began a million years ago. Before then, the magnetic record shows the North Pole in the middle of the Pacific, and the South Pole in the open southern Atlantic.

"An abrupt shift in the earth's crust carried the North Pole into the small and virtually landlocked Arctic, and the South Pole to the Antarctic continent, where the polar cold could not be dissipated by free ocean currents. That started the greatly contrasting zones of climate we know today — and the concentration of cold which finally froze the Arctic Ocean, to start the Ice Age cycles."

This would explain why the Ice Age glaciers have always marched from the Arctic. No ocean thermostat exists to turn on drastic glacial-interglacial cycles in the Antarctic. There, according to the theory, the Antarctic icecap has been building up continually since the South Pole shifted to that continent a million years ago — with only minor changes caused by the slight warming and cooling of the Atlantic in the glacial-interglacial cycles. This is confirmed by evidence from elevated beaches, which seems to indicate that maximum sea level has been dropping successively lower in each glacial era.

And as long as the poles stay where they are, the Ice Age cycles must continue.

Ewing and Donn realized that their theory had startling implications for the future. They have the scientist's distaste for the sensational, and carefully worked out the wording of the theory's formal conclusion: "The recent epoch can be considered as another interglacial stage." A number of scientists have tried to disprove their theory; so far they have been unsuccessful.

As Ewing and Donn read the glacial thermostat, the present interglacial

[1] **Pleistocene** (plīs′tô·sēn): one of the names used by scientists to distinguish geological periods.

stage is well advanced; the earth is now heading into another Ice Age. Certain signs, some of them visible to the layman as well as the scientist, indicate we may have been watching an Ice Age approach for some time without realizing what we were seeing.

Although scientists do not agree on its significance, they have observed an increasingly rapid warming and rising of the ocean in recent years. Warm water flowing north has driven the codfish off Cape Cod to Newfoundland; annual temperature has risen ten degrees in Iceland and Greenland; down here winters are warmer; the Hudson River no longer freezes over as it used to. It is part of the Ewing-Donn paradox that the next Ice Age will be preceded by such a warming of climate.

"We suspect that the ocean is already warm enough to melt the Arctic ice sheet," Ewing and Donn told me. "For some time it has remained at the highest temperature ever reached in the four previous interglacial stages." As climate becomes warmer, more and more glacial melt-water pours into the sea. The Atlantic has already risen three hundred feet since the glaciers of the last Ice Age started to melt away. Up until twenty-five years ago the U.S. Geodetic [1] Surveys indicated that sea level was rising six inches a century; in the past twenty-five years that rate has increased to two feet a century.

As sea level rises, more and more warm water pours over the Norway-Greenland sill, under the Arctic ice sheet. American, Russian, and Scandinavian scientists have observed a definite warming of the Arctic Ocean over the past fifty years and a consequent thinning of the ice sheet. At an international conference on Arctic sea ice in March 1958, scientists estimated that Arctic ice covers an area twelve per cent smaller than it did fifteen years

[1] **Geodetic** (jē'ȯ·dĕt'ĭk): referring to measurements of the earth's shape and size.

ago, and is forty per cent thinner. A layman might surmise that if this trend continues, the Arctic Ocean will be open and the Ice Age begin in another twenty years. Ewing and Donn are much more cautious about predictions.

"The rate at which our weather has been warming in recent years could be temporarily slowed down," they told me. "We don't know the exact rate at which the sea is now rising. We need long-term world-wide evidence, which the International Geophysical Year may give us, to assess accurately the changes that seem to be taking place in the ocean and the ice."

If the ocean continues to warm up at the present rate, Ewing and Donn think it is conceivable that there will be open water in the Arctic within about a hundred years. If they are right, for the first time in the history of the world, the victims of an Ice Age are going to see it coming. Television cameramen will be ranging all over the far north, covering the breakup of the Arctic ice sheet, looking for the first dirty summer slush. For the Ice Age will dawn, not in crashing glacial terror but in slush; as Ewing and Donn describe it, on a summer vacation up north, you will simply see a lot of dirty slush, winter's snow that for the first time in thousands of years didn't quite melt.

In many parts of America, at that time, the worry may not be ice, but water. Many scientists have speculated on the ocean flood that will be caused if the melting of glacial icecaps continues. Antarctic scientist Laurence Gould recently warned that "the return of only a few feet of thickness of ice as melt-water to the oceans would have serious effects in many places; and if all the ice were melted into the sea, its level would rise from 150 to 200 feet. All the world's seaports and some of its most densely populated areas would be submerged."

Ewing and Donn don't know how much higher the sea is going to rise before it melts the Arctic ice sheet. They say the ocean has already risen to the point where, if certain recent storms had occurred at high tide, it would have flooded New York and Boston subways. Donn is now working at Lamont on studies of long and short period changes in world sea level.

The ocean flood that brings about the Ice Age will not resemble the flash floods that have caused havoc in the East in recent years. It will build up slowly, and it will not flow away. The cities, industries, and military bases that are concentrated on both sides of the Atlantic may have to be evacuated. (Fortunately, Pacific coastlines are higher.)

It will probably be possible to protect New York and Washington by levees. Parts or all of New Orleans, Amsterdam, Rotterdam, and other cities are now protected by levees from high water, Ewing and Donn point out. Evidently, New York is in no danger of becoming a lost Atlantis,[1] drowned under the sea. If low-lying Brooklyn, Miami, Washington, New Orleans, or Amsterdam should become ghost cities, it will be because a decision will have been made long in advance of this slow-creeping flood to evacuate rather than build levees.

"According to our theory, with the melting of the Arctic ice sheet, the rise in sea level will stop," Ewing and Donn explained. Instead of adding water to the sea, the glaciers will begin taking it out.

For a long time after the ocean flood subsides, the only effect the Ice Age will have on us down here will be more rain. The new Arctic moisture that falls as snow on glaciers will increase both rain and snow here, swelling rivers and watering deserts. Then, gradually, our weather will cool. Icy winds will blow from the advancing glaciers; the great snows will fall farther and farther south.

[1] **Atlantis:** a legendary island which was supposed to have sunk beneath the ocean.

In several thousand years a two-mile ice sheet may cover the United States and Europe. If man finds no way to switch the glacial thermostat, there may well be a real-estate boom in the Sahara.

FOR DISCUSSION

1. What evidence led Donn and Ewing to decide that the temperature of the Atlantic Ocean changed suddenly?
2. How did the Arctic Ocean serve as a clue to the two scientists?
3. Why is it necessary for scientists to "get a lot of . . . wild ideas"? When do those ideas stop being "wild"?
4. How did the discoveries of anthropologists help to support speculation about a once-warm Arctic Ocean?

YOUR OWN WRITING: PROVING YOUR POINT

Imagine that in an article or expository paper you had just made Betty Friedan's assertion: "The two men share the scientist's passion for pure search, no matter where it leads." Try to support the claim that scientists do have a passion for search — another way of saying a passion for truth — no matter where it leads. Think of an example from your own knowledge of scientists in the present or the past, and relate the example in a paragraph.

THE AUTHOR

BETTY FRIEDAN graduated with honors from Smith College in Massachusetts, and then studied for a year at the University of California. She is married, has three children, and writes an occasional article when she has time to research the subject.

A Glacier ➤

On the facing page is a photograph of the huge Pettiwick glacier in Greenland. The walls of this glacier are over 200 feet high. The cracks near the edge are large enough to allow a helicopter to fly through; these cracks will eventually widen even more, and the smaller portions of the glacier will break away to form icebergs.

Appreciation and Criticism: Writers at Work

Appreciation and criticism are essentially the same. All worthwhile criticism attempts to renew or increase our possibilities for appreciation and enjoyment. The deepest pleasures of literature, whether fiction, nonfiction, poetry, or drama, come through appreciation — the shared experience, the shared emotion. Critical writing, when it is sensitive and perceptive, provides exactly this type of sharing. The following selections range from a comparison of the movie and the novel to a description of the playwright's problems, from a biographer's comments on libraries and librarians to an informal discussion of the methods of a short-story writer. Written by authors who engage in the very arts they evaluate, these selections provide new insight into the world of the writer.

MOSS HART

Playwrights at Work

When Moss Hart began his long and brilliant collaboration with George Kaufman — a collaboration that resulted in a number of Broadway hit plays — Hart was young, eager, and greatly awed by his famous teammate. The first result of this unusual partnership was the dazzling success *Once in a Lifetime* (1930). Moss Hart describes the beginning of the collaboration in this selection from his popular autobiography, *Act One*.

As the selection begins, Kaufman and Hart have just agreed to work together on Hart's manuscript of *Once in a Lifetime*. Kaufman's fame as a brilliant comic playwright seemed to offer Hart his first chance at success after years of poverty; but at the same time Kaufman's reputation for biting wit left Hart feeling uneasy and unsure of himself. He questions a friend about his new partner.

"Is THERE anything else I ought to know about Mr. Kaufman?" I asked.

Max Siegel [1] hesitated and laughed again. "There is, but if I started, you'd never make that eleven o'clock appointment tomorrow morning. Anyway, it's like marriage — nothing anybody tells you about it is really any help. You've got to live it out for yourself; and if I know George, you'll be living it out every day from now on. Get a good night's sleep — that's the best advice I can give you." We shook hands warmly, and I walked out into the bright October afternoon.

I stood for a moment outside the Music Box [2] and looked up at its columned façade with a new and proprietary interest, the contracts and the check rustling importantly in my pocket. There could be no doubt of it now; at last I was on my way.

The next morning at five minutes of eleven, I rang the bell of 158 East 63rd Street. The rather modest brownstone house was a little disappointing to my fancy of how a famous playwright should live, but the street was fashionable, and the maid who opened the door was a reassuring sight. She was in uniform, a starched white cap perched correctly on her head. More like it, I thought, as she held the door open for me to pass her. I walked in and glanced quickly down the hall at a dining room leading out into a little garden. There was a bowl of flowers on the polished table flanked by silver candlesticks. Just right, I told myself satisfactorily and looked inquiringly at the stairway.

"Mr. Kaufman is waiting for you," said the maid. "The top floor, just go right up."

I walked up the stairs and stopped briefly at the second landing to look at a drawing room and library divided by the stair well. Both rooms might have come straight out of the movies as far as my innocent eyes were concerned. I knew at once that my first goal the moment the money began to roll in, beyond the taking of taxicabs wherever and whenever I wanted to, would be to live like this. It was an illuminating and expensive moment.

The doors on the third floor — evidently bedrooms — were all tightly closed, and as I reached the fourth-floor landing, Mr. Kaufman stood awaiting me in the doorway of what turned out to be his own bedroom and study combined. After the elegance and style of the drawing room and library, this room was a great blow. It was a small, rather dark room, furnished sparsely with a studio couch, a quite ugly typewriter desk and one easy chair. It was hard for me to believe that a stream of brilliant plays had come out of this monklike interior. I am not certain what I expected the atelier [3] of Kaufman and Connelly [4] would be like, but it most certainly was the opposite of this. There was no hint of any kind that this room was in any way concerned with the theater. Not a framed photograph or program hung on its walls, and except for an excellent etching of Mark Twain, it might well have been, I thought regretfully, the bedroom and workroom of a certified public accountant. My initial disappointment was to deepen into an active loathing of that room, but at the moment, my eyes after the first quick look were focused on its occupant.

Mr. Kaufman was in the process of greeting me with what turned out to be his daily supply of enthusiasm so far as the social amenities were concerned; that is to say, one finger was being wearily lifted, and his voice was managing a tired "Hi." He had moved to the window after this display of cordial-

---

[1] **Max Siegel:** a theatrical producer.
[2] **the Music Box:** a New York theater.

[3] atelier (ăt′ĕl·yā): workshop (French).
[4] **Connelly:** Marc Connelly, a writer who occasionally collaborated with Kaufman.

ity and now stood with his back to the room and to me, staring out at the gardens of the houses on 62nd Street. I had not been asked to sit down, but I was too uncomfortable to remain standing, and after a moment of waiting, I sat down in the armchair and stared at his back. His arm now reached around his neck to scratch his ear, a gesture I was to come to recognize as a prelude to a rearrangement of a scene or the emergence of a new line; now he remained for a few moments engrossed in the movements of a large cat slowly moving along the garden fence as it contemplated a sparrow on one of the leafless trees. This back-yard spectacle seemed to hold him in deep fascination until the cat leaped up into the tree and the bird flew off, whereupon he turned from the window with a large sigh.

I looked at him, eager and alert, but there were still other things of moment that caught and held his attention before he addressed me directly. As he turned from the window, he spied two or three pieces of lint on the floor, and these he carefully removed from the carpet with all the deftness of an expert botanist gathering specimens for the Museum of Natural History. This task completed, he turned his eye toward a mound of sharpened pencils on the desk, found two whose points were not razor-sharp or to his liking, and ground them down in a pencil sharpener attached to the wall. In the process of doing so, he discovered some more lint at the side of the desk, and this, too, was carefully picked up, after which he held up and inspected a few sheets of carbon paper, found them still usable, and placed them neatly beside a pile of typewriter paper, which he neatly patted until all its edges were perfectly aligned. His eyes darted dolefully around the room again, seeming to be looking for something else — anything at all, it seemed to me! — to engage his attention, but the carpet being quite free of lint, his gaze finally came to rest on the armchair in which I sat, and he addressed me at last.

"Er . . ." he said, and began to pace rapidly up and down the room. This, too — the word "Er," used as a form of address and followed by a rapid pacing — I was to come to recognize as the actual start of a working session: a signal that lint-picking, cat-watching, and pencil-sharpening time was over and that he wanted my attention. During all the time we were engaged together on *Once in a Lifetime*, he never once addressed me by any other name but "Er," even in moments of stress or actual crisis. Perhaps he felt, being the innately shy and private person he was, that "Moss" was too intimate a name to call me; and to address me as "Mr. Hart" seemed a little silly, considering the difference in our ages and positions. But somehow or other I recognized at this first meeting that "Er" meant me and not a clearing of the throat, and I waited attentively until Mr. Kaufman stopped his pacing and stood in front of the armchair looking down at me.

"The trouble begins in the third scene of the first act," he said. "It's messy and unclear and goes off in the wrong direction. Suppose we start with that."

I nodded, trying to look agreeable and knowing at the same time; but this, like my disappointment with the workshop of the master, was my second blow of the morning. After the brilliant peroration on satire in the modern theater that I had heard from Jed Harris,[1] I had been looking forward with great eagerness to that first talk on playwriting by the celebrated Mr. Kaufman. I had expected to make mental notes on everything he said each day and put it all down every evening in a loose-leaf folder I had bought expressly for that purpose. But this flat, unvarnished statement that something was wrong with the third scene of the first act

[1] Jed Harris: a theatrical producer.

seemed to be all I was going to get, for Mr. Kaufman was already moving past me now on his way to the bathroom. I turned in my chair and looked at him as he stood by the washbasin and slowly and meticulously washed his hands, and I was struck then and forever afterward by the fact that his hands were what one imagines the hands of a great surgeon to be like.

This impression was further implemented by the odd circumstance that he invariably began the day's work by first washing his hands — a ritual that was, of course, unconscious on his part, but which he would sometimes perform two or three times more during each working session, usually at the beginning of attacking a new scene, as though the anatomy of a play were a living thing whose internal organs were to be explored surgically. I watched him dry his hands and forearms carefully — he took the trouble, I noticed, to undo the cuffs of his shirt and roll them up — and as he came back into the room, walked briskly toward the desk, and selected a pencil with just the right pointed sharpness, I was again startled by the inescapable impression that the pencil held poised over the manuscript in those long tensile [1] fingers was a scalpel.

The pencil suddenly darted down onto the paper and moved swiftly along the page, crossing out a line here and there, making a large X through a solid speech, fusing two long sentences into one short one, indicating by an arrow or a question mark the condensation or transference of a section of dialogue so that its point was highlighted and its emphasis sharpened; the operation was repeated with lightninglike precision on the next page and the next, until the end of the scene. Then he picked up the manuscript from the desk and brought it over to me.

"Just cutting away the underbrush," he said. "See what you think." I took the manuscript and read with astonishment. The content of the scene remained the same, but its point was unmuddied by repetition, and the economy and clarity with which everything necessary was now said gave the scene a new urgency. The effect of what he had done seemed to me so magical that I could hardly believe I had been so downright repetitive and verbose. I looked up from the manuscript and stared admiringly at the waiting figure by the desk.

Mr. Kaufman evidently mistook my chagrined and admiring silence for pique.[2] "I may have cut too deeply, of course," he said apologetically. "Is there something you want to have go back?"

"Oh, no," I replied hastily, "not a word. It's just wonderful now. Just great! I don't understand how I could have been so stupid. The scene really works now, doesn't it?"

It was Mr. Kaufman's turn to stare at me in silence for a moment, and he looked at me quizzically over the rims of his glasses before he spoke again. "No, it doesn't work at all," he said gently. "I thought the cuts would show you why it *wouldn't* work. He sighed and scratched his ear. "Perhaps the trouble starts earlier than I thought."

He took the play from my lap and placed it on the desk again. "All right. Page one — Scene One. I guess we might as well face it." He picked up a pencil and held it poised over the manuscript, and I watched fascinated and awestruck as the pencil swooped down on page after page.

If it is possible for a book of this sort to have a hero, then that hero is George S. Kaufman. In the months that followed that first day's work, however, my waking nightmare was of a glittering steel pencil suspended over my head that sometimes turned into a

[1] **tensile:** capable of becoming tense.

[2] **pique** (pēk): resentment, irritation.

scalpel, or a baleful stare over the rims of a huge pair of disembodied tortoise-shell glasses. I do not think it far-fetched to say that such success as I have had in the theater is due in large part to George Kaufman. I cannot pretend that I was without talent, but such gifts as I possessed were raw and undisciplined. It is one thing to have a flair for playwriting or even a ready wit with dialogue. It is quite another to apply these gifts in the strict and demanding terms of a fully articulated play so that they emerge with explicitness, precision, and form. All of this and a great deal more I learned from George Kaufman. And if it is true that no more eager disciple ever sat at the feet of a teacher, it is equally true that no disciple was ever treated with more infinite patience and understanding.

The debt I owe is a large one, for it could not have been easy for him to deal with some of my initial blunderings and gaucheries,[1] particularly in those first early days of our collaboration. He was not at heart a patient man or a man who bothered to tolerate or maintain the fiction of graceful social behavior in the face of other people's infelicities. In particular, easy admiration distressed him, and any display of emotion filled him with dismay; the aroma of a cigar physically sickened him. I was guilty of all three of these things in daily and constant succession, and since he was too shy or possibly too fearful of hurting my feelings to mention his distress to me, I continued to compound the felony day after day: filling the room with clouds of cigar smoke, being inordinately admiring of everything he did, and in spite of myself, unable to forbear, each evening before I left, the making of a little speech of gratitude or thanks. His suffering at these moments was acute, but I construed his odd behavior at these times

as being merely one more manifestation of the eccentricities that all celebrated people seem to have in such abundance. And the next morning, as I sat down, I would cheerfully light a cigar without pausing to wonder even briefly why Mr. Kaufman was walking as quickly and as far away from me as it was possible for him to get within the confines of that small room.

It did not occur to me, I cannot think why, to be either astonished or confounded by the fact that each time I rose from the armchair and came toward him to speak, he retreated with something akin to terror to the window and stood breathing deeply of such air as was not already swirling with blue cigar smoke. Nor could I understand why, after I fulsomely admired a new line or an acid turn of phrase that he had just suggested that seemed to me downright inspired, he would scratch his ear until I thought it would drop off and stare at me malignantly over the top of his glasses, his face contorted with an emotion that seemed too painful to find expression. Even his passion to remove each dead cigar butt from the room almost before my hand had reached the ashtray with it, and his obsession with keeping the windows wide open on even the most frigid days, did nothing to alert me to his suffering, and I was, seemingly, deaf as well as dense when his diatribes [2] against people who made speeches at each other took on added strength and fervor with each passing day.

I suppose his worst moment of the day came at my leave-taking, when he could sense another little speech coming on. I know now that he evolved various stratagems of his own to escape these eulogies, such as rushing into the bathroom and, with the water taps turned full on, calling out a good-by through the closed door, or going to the

[1] **gaucheries** (gō′shē·rēz′): awkward actions.

[2] **diatribes** (dī′á·trībz): angry, abusive remarks.

telephone and, with his back to me, hurriedly calling a number; but with something approximating genius, I nearly always managed to find the moment to have my say. He seldom escaped!

Mr. Kaufman spent a good deal of his time, particularly in the late afternoons, stretched out full length on the floor, and it was usually at one of these unwary moments when he was at his lowest ebb and stretched helplessly below me that I would stand over him and deliver my captivating compendium [1] of the day's work. Something like a small moan, which I misinterpreted as agreement, would escape from his lips, and he would turn his head away from the sight of my face, much the way a man whose arm is about to be jabbed with a needle averts his gaze to spare himself the extra pain of seeing the needle descend.

All unknowing and delighted with my eloquence, I would light a new cigar, puff a last fresh aromatic cloud of smoke down into his face, and cheerfully reminding him of the splendid ideas he had had for the scene we were going to work on tomorrow, I would take my leave. I have never allowed myself to think of some of the imprecations [2] that must have followed my retreating figure down the stairway, but if I was torturing Mr. Kaufman all unknowingly, the score was not exactly one-sided. Quite unaware that he was doing so, he was on his part providing me with a daily Gethsemane [3] of my own that grew more agonizing with each passing day, and though his suffering was of the spirit and mine was of the flesh, I think our pain in the end was about equal, for I was as incapable of mentioning my distress to him as he

was of mentioning his to me.

The cause of my agony was simple enough. Mr. Kaufman cared very little about food. His appetite was not the demanding and capricious one mine was — indeed, his lack of concern with food was quite unlike anyone else's I have ever known. The joys and pleasures of the table seemed simply to have passed him by in the way that a dazzling sunset must escape the color-blind. He apparently needed very little food to sustain him and cared even less when and how it was served. He had his breakfast at ten o'clock in the morning, and work was enough to nourish him thereafter until evening. His energy, unlike my own, seemed to be attached not to his stomach but to his brain; and his capacity for work, which was enormous, seemed to flourish and grow in ratio to the rattle of a typewriter.

True, every afternoon at about four o'clock, apparently as a concession to some base need he knew existed in other human beings but did not quite understand himself, tea would be brought in by the maid. Six cookies, no more and no less, and on gala occasions two slices of homemade chocolate cake would lie on a plate naked and shimmering to my hunger-glazed eyes; and, as I could sniff the tea coming up the stairs or hear the teacups rattling on the tray outside the door, my stomach would rumble so loudly and my ravenousness would be so mouth-watering that I would get up and walk about the room, pretending to stretch my arms and legs, in order to control myself, for it was all I could do not to grab and stuff the minute the maid set the tray down.

My predicament was further complicated by the fact that Mr. Kaufman was always scrupulously polite and devilishly insistent that I help myself first, and since I was only too aware that he took only a sip or two of tea and never more than one cookie, which

---

[1] **compendium:** summary.
[2] **imprecations** (ĭm′prė-kā′shŭnz): curses.
[3] **Gethsemane** (gĕth·sĕm′a·nė): the scene of the agony of Jesus; often used, as it is here, to indicate any place of suffering.

he absent-mindedly nibbled at, I could never bring myself to do more than slavishly follow his example for fear of being thought ill-mannered or unused to high life — until one day, maddened by hunger, I gobbled up every single cookie and the two slices of chocolate cake while he was in the bathroom washing his hands. Whether it was the mutely empty plate or my guilt-ridden and embarrassed face staring up at him as he approached the tea tray, I do not know; but from that day onward, little sandwiches began to appear, and tea-time, to my vast relief, was moved up an hour earlier.

Meanwhile, in spite of the separate and unwitting mortifications with which we daily afflicted each other, work proceeded with a grueling regularity and an unswerving disregard of endurance, health, well-being, or personal life that left me at first flabbergasted and then chastened and awestruck at his unrivaled dedication to the task in hand. It was a kind of unflagging industry and imperturbable concentration that anyone, not just myself, might well marvel at, for this eminently successful man labored each day quite as though our positions had been reversed and this were *his* first play, not mine; his great chance to make his mark as a Broadway playwright, not my own. There was an element of the demoniacal in his tireless search for just the right word to round a sentence into its proper unity, for the exact juxtaposition of words and movement that would slyly lead the audience along the periphery [1] of a scene to its turning point and then propel them effortlessly to its climax.

His ear for a comedic line was faultless and his zeal for the precise effect he wanted boundless. No moment, however small, seemed unimportant enough to escape his almost fierce attention, and his grasp of the play's latent values was immediate and com-

plete. My eyes and ears were opened anew each day to the thousand-and-one endless details that go to make up the subtle and infinitely fragile clockwork of a play's interior mechanism, and to the slow cultivation of its subsoil that gradually makes it blossom into something vital and alive. I watched and listened with the consecration of a yogi,[2] and yet, in awe of him though I was, it never occurred to me not to disagree when I thought he was wrong, whether on the reshaping of a scene or even on a newly coined line which he liked and I did not. This was not a special bravery on my part or some noble effort at keeping my own identity intact — it had simply never entered my mind to be timorous with him or to be in any way discomforted by his manner.

I was all the more amazed to discover later on that this gentle man with whom I had been at once thoroughly at ease and completely comfortable, this same kindly and understanding man at whose side I worked each day, could instantly succeed in disquieting the most formidable men in the theater or out of it and, by his mere presence in a room, frighten the daylights out of half the people there. There could be no doubt about the effect his presence created. Headwaiters cowered and the wits of the town watched their tongues as he loomed up in a doorway, the eyes over those tortoise-shell rims seeming to examine the room for a sign of the inept, the fake, or the pompous.

Famous raconteurs seemed to wither and dwindle under that penetrating glance, for he could puncture pretense or bombast with an acid verbal thrust that would be repeated with malicious glee in every corner of the so-called charmed circle before the sun set. Even such rugged specimens as New York taxi drivers or talkative barbers quailed

---

[1] **periphery** (pē·rĭf′ēr·ĭ): outer edge.

[2] **yogi:** a follower of yoga, a mental discipline characterized by the ability to concentrate on an object for long periods of time.

at his stare and were silent until he was safely deposited out of the cab or the chair, and so fearsome a practitioner of the art of discomfiture as Alexander Woollcott [1] admitted that George Kaufman was the one person who could always make him uncomfortable and ill at ease.

This side of him at first bewildered and astonished me. I never ceased being surprised at the startling and sometimes numbing effect he created among even the most seemingly secure and self-assured people, for unquestionably he did indeed intimidate even his close friends. But the result, though trying on the more timid of them, was not without its compensations. People took pains to be at their best with him, and just as a mediocre tennis player will sometimes play above his game when he is matched with a superior opponent, people were generally stimulated into their level best when he was about. It is my own guess that his somewhat terrifying manner, far from being any sort of pose, stemmed from the fact that he more than most men simply refused to resort to the banalities [2] of what usually passes for polite conversation; faced with some of the cant [3] and nonsense that a good deal of theater talk consists of, he allowed himself the luxury of saying exactly what came into his mind as the only proper answer to the extravagant claptrap and twaddle he was often forced to listen to. It is not difficult to acquire a reputation for asperity and irascibility, particularly if one has the courage to indulge this luxury as a matter of principle and it is accompanied by a tart and ready wit.

These he had and the audacity to use them, for unlike most of us, he was not

driven by a savage necessity to be liked. He cared little for the good opinion or the admiration of the special world he moved in and was a celebrated part of. He adhered strictly to his own standards and judgments, and they were stern ones. The most striking characteristic of the personality he presented to the world at large was an almost studied aloofness and indifference, and it struck me as remarkable how the world at large continually tried to break through this wall and win his approval on any terms he chose to make. Indifference can be a wonderful weapon — whether it is used as ammunition in a warfare between lovers or as a mask for timidity and shyness, for behind that mask of disdain and unconcern lay the diffident and modest man whom it never entered my mind to be afraid of.

Perhaps better than most, I came to know that this seeming indifference was the protective coloring of a temperament whose secret and inmost recesses held a deep reservoir of emotion; that it was the superficial exterior of a man who chose to reveal himself only to a very few, but whose emotions could be fervent and profound. I knew how quickly he could be seized and touched emotionally and how susceptible he was to the dark doubts that licked at other men's souls. Somehow or other, I do not know why, or quite understand how, I seemed to have managed from the very beginning to bypass both the façade and the legend and immediately to fall into a warmhearted and gay relationship in which he bore no resemblance to the tales I heard or to the scenes I witnessed of his cantankerous behavior with other people.

He was not, of course, without his own mischievous and annoying qualities, even for me. He could be willfully stubborn on small things with a dogged and inflexible obstinacy, and perversely fair and just on large issues to the point of exasperating saintliness; and he had an abundant share of inconsistent and

---

[1] **Alexander Woollcott:** a drama critic, journalist, and essayist, who was famous for his sharp wit.
[2] **banalities** (bá·năl′ĭ·tĭz): commonplace remarks.
[3] **cant** (kănt): meaningless professional jargon; insincere, hypocritical speech.

crotchety prejudices that extended over a wide area and included, most particularly and actively, waiters who never seemed to be able to take down his order correctly, people who tried to tell him jokes, and any fellow passenger he happened to find himself next to when he was in an elevator or on a train and who had the misfortune to recognize him and attempt to engage him in conversation. If I was with him at one of these awful moments, his churlishness would make me cringe and I would move away and pretend we were not together, but to my unfailing amazement it was always him they apologized to and me they glared at. Like "the man who came to dinner,"[1] whom he resembled in a muted way more than he ever suspected, he suffered daily from the gross inadequacies of the human race; but these failings, however infuriating, were seldom sufficient — after a small but satisfactory explosion of irritation — to keep him from walking toward the typewriter with alacrity. Nothing in the world, as far as I could tell, ever stopped him from doing that — and as he walked toward the desk, I would marshal my wits and try to think of a bright line to begin the day's work.

[1] "the man who came to dinner": the play of this name by Kaufman and Hart has as its central character Sheridan Whiteside, a witty, self-centered writer. Whiteside was modeled on Alexander Woollcott and to some extent, as Hart indicates, on Kaufman himself.

FOR DISCUSSION

1. What characteristics of George Kaufman's home fit Hart's mental picture of how a famous playwright should live? What features did not fit that picture?

2. What were the Kaufman mannerisms that Hart observed? How do you explain them?

3. What do you think of Kaufman's method of pointing out the weaknesses in Hart's play? Could his way be characterized best as kind, cruel, domineering, or intelligent? Justify your choice of adjective.

4. In the early days of the collaboration, what was Hart's outstanding contribution? What was Kaufman's?

5. In what ways did each collaborator torment the other without being aware of it?

6. In your opinion, why did Hart eventually come to feel at ease with a man who inspired terror, fear, and discomfort in so many persons from cab drivers to Alexander Woollcott?

THE AUTHOR

MOSS HART (1904–1961) was born in New York and educated in that city's public schools. He began his theatrical career by working with little-theater groups and directing a summer camp theater. His first New York play, *The Beloved Bandit*, was a failure, but *Once in a Lifetime*, his first play with George Kaufman, was a hit. The collaboration produced a number of other successes, among them *Face the Music* (1932), *As Thousands Cheer* (1933), *You Can't Take It with You*, the Pulitzer prize winning play of 1937, and *The Man Who Came to Dinner* (1939).

Hart worked alone on one of his most popular plays, the musical drama *Lady in the Dark*, written for the English star Miss Gertrude Lawrence. Hart's autobiography, *Act One*, from which "Playwrights at Work" is taken, was a best seller on nonfiction lists in 1959.

Director at Work ➤

Moss Hart's earliest successes were as a playwright, working either in collaboration with George Kaufman or alone. In later years, however, Hart also earned an excellent reputation as a director. During the 1940's he directed two popular comedies, *Junior Miss* and *Dear Ruth*; later, in 1954, Hart directed *Anniversary Waltz*. By far his greatest success as a director, however, came in 1957 with the famous musical *My Fair Lady*, written by Alan Jay Lerner and Frederick Loewe. On the facing page, Hart is shown directing the rehearsal of another Lerner-Loewe musical, *Camelot*, which opened on Broadway in 1960. On stage are the stars of the play, Richard Burton and Julie Andrews.

BUDD SCHULBERG

Why Write It
if You Can't Sell It
to Pictures?

What can a novel do for a story that a movie cannot? Plenty! says the man who reversed the usual procedure, writing a movie script first and then developing it into a novel.

Last summer I encountered a Hollywood producer who wanted to know if I was writing any fiction that might be adaptable to the movies. I told him I had devoted the past year to my waterfront novel. The rotund gentleman with a soft Viennese accent shook his head in concern for my apparent loss of common sense. "I never heard of such a thing," he said. "Why spend all that time on something that has no chance of being sold to the movies?"

I found it a little difficult to explain to this one-track-minded friend that after five years of prowling the New York waterfront, roaming the West Side and Jersey bars across from the docks, drinking beer with longshore families in the kitchens of their $26.50 per month railroad flats, and talking to har-

bor union leaders, waterfront priests, and Irish and Italian rank-and-file "insoigents,"[1] our film *On the Waterfront* left me with an irresistible conviction that there was still far more to say than could possibly be included in my screenplay for the picture.

Our picture won every possible prize and award from the Venice Festival to the Academy sweep, and yet I could not down a certain sense of frustration entirely separate from my pride in the effectiveness of the film. Surely my story could not have been placed in more artistic hands than Elia Kazan's and the film's main characters'; the Hell's Kitchen[2] fringe hoodlum named Terry Malloy could not have found a more sensitive interpreter than Marlon Brando. In many cases Kazan and Brando intensified the vitality and accuracy of what I had written. And yet, after my Oscar was perched securely on the mantelpiece, I could not overcome a growing conviction that my job as chronicler of waterfront people and waterfront

[1] "insoigents": insurgents, rebels against the established order.
[2] Hell's Kitchen: a lower West Side district of Manhattan formerly notorious for its gunmen and thieves.

"Why Write It if You Can't Sell It to Pictures?" by Budd Schulberg. Reprinted from the *Saturday Review*, September 3, 1955. Used by permission of the author.

tensions was not yet completed.

This feeling is an inevitable result of the fundamental difference between the two media I have used in coping with my waterfront experience: the motion picture and the novel. For the past fifteen years I have worked principally in the field of fiction, but because my father was for many years the head of a major film studio, and because I was raised in Hollywood, I may be something of a literary schizophrene.[1] As a novelist and part-time screen writer I confess to a live and continuing interest in both ways of storytelling. The novelist succumbing to Hollywood scenario-writing is an old, sad story, a downward path to unwisdom that haunts me. But as a believer in the art and power of the film, as well as a die-hard novelist, I see difference rather than conflict between the two forms, so long as authors do not confuse one with the other. One can go to Hollywood without succumbing to Hollywood, and one who is interested in writing truly can move back from the film into the novel, where he may find another, more ranging kind of aesthetic experience.

Actually, a filmplay seems to me related more closely to the short story than to the novel. At least its dramatic unity is closer. The difference is, of course, that a short story is tightly disciplined in form, writer-fulfilled in content. The screenplay is restricted in form. It is the director who has the opportunity to develop character and background through insight, so that the authorship of a film at best becomes a true director-writer co-creation. To take my *Waterfront* script as an example, its length (after much pruning) was 115 manuscript pages. The novel was five times as long. The film is an art of high points. I think of it as embracing five or six sequences, each one mounting to a climax that rushes the action

onward. The novel is an art of high, middle, and low points and, though I believe its form must never be overlooked, it's the sort of form you lock the front door against, knowing full well it will climb into one of the small back windows thoughtfully left open for it. The film does best when it concentrates on a single character. It tells *The Informer*[2] superbly. It tends to lose itself in the ramifications of *War and Peace*.[3] It has no time for what I call the essential digressions: the "digression" of complicated, contradictory character; the "digression" of social background. The film must go from significant episode to more significant episode in a constantly mounting pattern. It's an exciting form. But it pays a price for this excitement. It cannot wander as life wanders, or pause as life always pauses, to contemplate the incidental or the unexpected. The film has a relentless form. Once you set it up, it becomes your master, demanding and rather terrifying. It has its own tight logic, and once you stray from that straight and narrow path, the tension slackens — or, you might say, the air is let out of the balloon.

So, in the film *On the Waterfront* we followed the life line of Terry Malloy, a half-vicious hoodlum caught between the waterfront mob and the vaguest, anxious beginnings of a conscience. His brothers are to be found on New York's troubled West Side, or along Brooklyn's Gowanus Canal, or in the corrupt political-machine towns on the Jersey shore. Kazan and Brando, gifted and dedicated, did sensitive and brilliant things with this character, and I had written his dialogue carefully, with an ear to my wanderings along the riverfront. But the restricting form of

[1] schizophrene (skĭz′ô·frēn): a psychological term popularly used to mean a person with a "split" personality.

[2] *The Informer:* a novel by the Irish writer Liam (lēăm) O'Flaherty, which was made into a motion picture that won the Academy Award in 1935.

[3] *War and Peace:* a long novel by the Russian writer Leo Tolstoi.

He said — She said allowed no time to relate Terry to his background, to explore his mind with its groping efforts to shake off its sloth, to catch him off guard, so to speak. More important, the film's concentration on a single dominating character, brought close to the camera-eye, made it aesthetically inconvenient — if not impossible — to set Terry's story in its social and historical perspective. What I have tried to do in the novel is to use Terry as a single strand in a rope of intertwining fibers, in order to suggest the knotted complexities of the world of the waterfront that loops around New York, a lawless frontier almost unknown to the metropolitan citizenry.

During the 1952–1953 period when I was preparing the screenplay, I was fully aware that the wholesale crimes of the waterfront were not to be explained merely by the prominence of certain gentlemen from Sing Sing and Dannemora [1] in positions of authority on the docks. The shipping companies and the stevedore management had accepted — in some cases encouraged — the thugs for years, and in many cases city politicians were nothing less than partners of the longshore union racketeers. It was this unhealthy axis, I knew, that made it so difficult to bring any real democratic reform to the graft-ridden docks. I even discussed with my film collaborators scenes that would dramatize this civic blight. Those scenes were not eliminated through any cowardice or fear of censorship, as some critics have suggested. No, it was another tyrant, the ninety-minute feature form, that lopped off their heads.

But, thanks to our muse, the novel is a wide-angle lens, broader even than Cinerama, the real 3-D. The novel is the ideal medium for the development of social themes. The novel isn't a straight piece of string. It's a ball of twine. In the novel I found my opportunity to put Terry Malloy in proper focus. It only required retelling his story from another point of view, and with a different end in mind. I mean this literally and figuratively. Terry's decision, even his fate, became subordinated to the anxious balance and the fate of the waterfront as a whole. This demanded an entirely different ending, as well as fuller development of characters who were secondary figures in the film. So Father Barry, the "waterfront priest," is brought to stage center, is allowed to share the action with Terry and to dominate the thinking of the book. As a curate in a poor parish, he must take grave chances if he is to follow Christ. The film had no time for this sort of thing. The novel has not only time but the obligation to examine this with great care. This searching becomes, in fact, the stuff of the novel, and the violent action line of Terry Malloy is now seen for what it is, one of the many moral crises in the spiritual-social development of Father Barry.

In the great novels *Moby Dick, War and Peace, The Red and the Black,* [2] we see how the action and the ideas are able to flow together, with no violence one to the other. There you have the glory of the novel, the reason why, in this age of supercommunication, we should never forsake the novel. I am not so vain as to claim membership in that great company for my *Waterfront,* but in the tradition — from Stendhal to Steinbeck — I was able to work veins impossible in dramatic art. It was not only that, having gained a great deal of knowledge and indignation from men on the docks, I was able to speak out in a way not feasible on film. I was able also to speak *in,* to search the interior drama in the heart and mind of a cleric militant who dares apply the insights of his Savior to the

---

[1] **Sing Sing and Dannemora** (dăn'ĭ·mō'rå): New York state prisons.

[2] **The Red and the Black:** a novel by the French writer Stendhal (stăn'dâl').

dark and godless alleyways of the waterfront. Thus, regardless of the surprising popularity of our film, and regardless of the success or failure of my novel, I have already had my reward. I had had the privilege of friendship with a number of labor priests who were concerned for the inhumanity of the slavish "shape-up" [1] of men born to be free. Now I was able to create a figure in their image, to follow him into an Irish tenement wake, to take him for a solitary, mind-troubled walk along the river, where he can measure his religious convictions against the spiritually bankrupt atmosphere of a typical waterfront neighborhood. I can listen in on his private prayers as he kneels sleepless on the cold floor of his cell-like room in the rectory, and I can end not with a dramatic close-up of Marlon Brando, excellent in its own way, but with the deeper truth of inconclusiveness as this priest stands at night on the edge of the Hudson, weighing the martyrdom of Terry Malloy and thinking bitterly of the millions on millions in the great city who do not care, "Having eyes, they see not."

So, grateful as I was for the reception of our film, I am even more grateful to the limitless scope of the novel, which has given me the opportunity to try to sum up my hundreds of days and nights among a wonderful people, embattled, humorous, and perhaps tragically ensnared.

Maybe what I am trying to say is that a film must act, a book has time to think and wonder. There is the essential difference which keeps me, for all my love of movie-going and film-writing, still a confirmed novel writer and an enthusiastic novel reader. In the flush of TV spectaculars, wider and wider screeneramas, and all the rest of our frightful, fruitful mechanical advancements, the book is still the essential civ-

---

[1] "shape-up": a corrupt system of assigning jobs on the waterfront.

ilizing influence, able to penetrate the unknowns of human aspiration.

That's my answer, as simply as I know how to put it, to the Philistine [2] who asks, "Why write it if you can't sell it to pictures?"

---

[2] Philistine (fĭ·lĭs'tĭn): a person lacking in appreciation of cultural values.

FOR DISCUSSION

1. Review the circumstances that Schulberg mentions to prove that he has no grudge against the movies as a medium for telling a story. Why does he want to make this point clear?

2. How does the interest pattern of a motion picture affect the choice of incidents to be included?

3. What "essential digressions" can the novel include that cannot be put into a film?

4. Why does Schulberg feel that the novel can represent the waterfront situation more accurately by focusing the story on the priest rather than on Terry Malloy?

5. Collect the direct comparisons Schulberg makes between the special powers of the two media. Think of a movie you have seen that was made from a novel you have read, and illustrate Schulberg's meaning by comparing the treatment of the story in the two forms.

THE AUTHOR

BUDD SCHULBERG (b. 1914) has been shuttling back and forth across the continent most of his life. Born in New York City and educated in the East, he is also at home in Hollywood, where his father headed Paramount Studios.

He published his first novel before becoming a naval officer in World War II. Assigned to OSS, he won a commendation for gathering from German films photographic evidence of war crimes. His return to writing brought two more novels, *The Harder They Fall* and *The Disenchanted*, an outstanding novel of 1950. In 1954 he wrote the screenplay for *On the Waterfront*, and in 1955 he published the novel on the same subject.

THREE BOOK REVIEWS

The modern reader has learned to depend on the book review. From the hundreds of volumes that are published each year, book reviews help us select those few books that we will have time to read. Book reviews keep us informed on new ideas and new developments in every major field of interest. Many of our best modern writers contribute their talents to this important type of critical commentary. A good review provides entertainment as well as information, giving pleasure through its deft style of writing and its accurate, sometimes provocative, judgment of a work. Today, the book review is probably the most popular form of literary appreciation and criticism.

THE EXPERT READER REPORTS

The practiced book reviewer is a topflight reader and critic. He is fast and skillful in noting the author's purpose, observing the structure of the book, and recognizing tone and mood. The book reviewer is an *active* reader: he thinks and forms judgments as he reads. The veteran reviewer will often develop a consistent pattern in his reviews. First he may give information about the contents of the book. Then he may offer a considered criticism, evaluating the book according to his own standards of literary excellence.

You have a practical reason for observing both processes closely, for they can suggest ways for you to improve the quality of the many book reports you will make in school. From the reviewer's discussion of the contents of a book, you can get useful tips on presenting an economical summary of your own reading. From the critical portion of the review, you can learn standards of evaluation. As you develop independent judgment, you will become a more observant reader, responding to what you read with ideas of your own.

CARL CARMER

The Adventures of Natty Bumppo

Wʜᴇɴ Allan Nevins, professor of American history at Columbia University, was a boy in Illinois, he and his companions played at being the picturesque heroes whose exploits they

"The Adventures of Natty Bumppo" by Carl Carmer, from the *New York Times Book Review*, October 3, 1954. Reprinted by permission of the author.

had read in those five of James Fenimore Cooper's novels which portrayed the most popular of all American fictional figures, Natty Bumppo, known variously to his companions as Leatherstocking, Deerslayer, Hawkeye, Pathfinder and to "the Frenchers and the redskins on the other side of the Big

Lakes" as *la longue Carabine.*[1] Inspired by nostalgic memories, Mr. Nevins has now linked in this one volume, *Leatherstocking Saga*, the portions of these books which have pleased him most, omitting or briefly summarizing passages which do not concern Bumppo and such superfluities as reveal Cooper's affected mannerisms, lush sentimentalities, and painfully forced humor.

The books are wisely arranged, moreover, in the chronological sequence of Bumppo's life rather than the order in which they appeared in print. This may be somewhat confusing to the student of the development of Cooper as a writer, since *The Deerslayer,* in which Bumppo is at his youngest (in his early twenties) was published eighteen years after the first of the series, *The Pioneers,* which presented the hero in his seventies. The result of the editing and arrangement, however, is a unified and artistically highlighted portrait of the simple and noble master of forest lore whom readers from nearly all nations of the world have long regarded as the supreme characterization in American literature.

Cooper could well take for granted in 1823 the assumption by his readers that his unlettered sage of the forest was based on an existing American type. He acknowledged his debt to the widely known adventures of Daniel Boone, but near his home in Cooperstown lived old men who resembled the woodland sage he was planning to describe. One named David Shipman and one named Nathaniel Shipman were in no way related to each other, but each in many qualities fitted Cooper's descriptions of his famous hunter, and it may be that he made use of both, though to this day separate factions quarrel over which of them was the "original" of Natty Bumppo.

The character emerging from Cooper's pages as edited by Allan Nevins is an original in another sense, "untutored but noble-minded . . . a being of great purity of character but of as marked peculiarities." Most readers of Leatherstocking tales find their first admiration, as did Allan Nevins, for the scout's practical and intimate knowledge of life in the woods. Few can resist the appeal of a man who can "journey by the moss on the beeches" or set a backfire to save his companions from a flaming death, who knows that "grass is a treacherous carpet . . . but wood and stone take no print from a moccasin," or that a good hunter never overloads his gun because "a kicking rifle never carries a true bullet."

Add to the scout's knowledge of the forest utter fearlessness, even when Indians have bound him to the stake for burning, an affection for his deep-voiced hound dog, Hector, and calm assurance that his gun, Killdeer, "the long-barreled, true-grooved, soft-metaled rifle," is the most dangerous of all weapons, and you have a character that will not fade from the memory or the heart. From these attributes alone grew a popularity which resulted in an endless parade of imitative narratives in which the wise old man-of-the-woods played his familiar role.

In *The Prairie* Cooper tells of the death of Bumppo, who had sought his accustomed freedom in the woods of the ever-receding frontier. But the old man had too much blood in him to die. Other writers, less able than Cooper, gave him new names and made him a hero in adventure tales of prairie and desert.

When in 1860 Erastus Beadle of Cooperstown began to publish in New York his sensational dime novels, the number of replicas of Leatherstocking — Seth Jones, Kent the Ranger, Oregon Sol, Pete Shafer — grew apace. Nearly half of Beadle's orange-backed books of Western adventure contained such a character.

---

[1] *la longue Carabine* (là lôɴɢ kär'ä'bēn'): the long rifle (French).

So greatly loved was this "nature's gentleman" that those who would popularize living flesh-and-blood men gave them the attributes of Leatherstocking. Davy Crockett, half-history and half-legend, became another Hawkeye in coonskin cap and fringed buckskin, listening for the voices of his favorite hounds, Whirlwind and Growler, never missing his target with his long rifle, Betsy. Like Deerslayer, Crockett was an associate of ex-pirates and bee-hunters. Like Pathfinder he was a lover of justice and a champion of the rights of honest Indians.

Mr. Nevins decries the humor of the Leatherstocking tales and has removed by skillful editing many of Cooper's efforts to be funny. By so doing he has brought into sharper relief witty passages that compare more than favorably with the brag-and-boast humor-filled narratives that were to come. Many of early America's funniest anecdotes have to do with the cunning of the trader, and Cooper proves his hero an able precursor of T. C. Haliburton's Sam Slick and E. N. Westcott's David Harum [1] when he reports the sharp exchange between Iroquois warriors, who have taken two white prisoners, and Leatherstocking, who offers for their release a carved elephant from a recently discovered chess set. The Indians praise their captives, and the scout lists their faults and disparages their value so successfully that he convinces the savages that "a beast with two tails is well worth two such scalps."

At another tense bargaining, when asked by a villainous Indian if he will give his life for that of a kidnapped white girl, Leatherstocking refuses, then mildly suggests: "I might go into winter quarters now — at least six weeks before the leaves will turn, on condition you will release the maiden."

Scholars have apparently accepted Deerslayer's oft-stated assurance that "it don't become white blood to brag" and have not noted that the opinion does not hamper its holder. If they read for evidence of influence on the Davy Crockett, Mike Fink, dead-shot, ring-tailed roarer school of comic braggarts already aborning, they will not go unrewarded.

More important today than his influence on certain sections of our literary history are Cooper's observations as folklorist and poet. Through the scout's mouth he reports accepted folk talk of his time — "You burnt your powder to warm your nose," or "A crow would shed tears . . . to fly across this district" — and in his role as narrator, he describes turkey shoots, maple tappings, militia training days, materials that America has since approved in the writings of Ben Lucien Burman, Jesse Stuart, Stephen Vincent Benét, Marjorie Kinnan Rawlings, and many another.

As for poetry, Cooper said that Bumppo "felt, though it was unconsciously, like a poet." The author gave much of his own poetic expression the common touch by offering it in the unpretentious duds of an unlettered man's dialect, a device that many an American poet, from James Russell Lowell to Robert Frost, has adopted to advantage. Said Bumppo: "The echoes repeat pretty much all that is said and done on Glimmerglass in this calm summer weather. If a paddle falls, you hear of it sometimes ag'in and ag'in, as if the hills were mocking your clumsiness."

An accomplished American stylist recently described the admirers of Leatherstocking and his ilk contemptuously as "the cult of the sublimated [2] roughneck." Allan Nevins' inspired contriv-

---

[1] **Sam Slick** and **David Harum** were fictional characters of the 1800's; both were famous for their shrewd dealing and dry humor.

[2] **sublimated** (sŭb'lĭ·māt'ĕd): having directed the energy of an impulse from a lower to a higher aim.

ance has made answer. His peeling of the unessential has left a core of gold. As a result of Nevins' taste and skill, Cooper's genius has been so illuminated that it will need and receive many new and favorable appraisals.

FOR DISCUSSION

1. Tell two important steps Nevins took in making one book out of parts of five. What is the reviewer's opinion of the result? Explain why you do or do not expect this new arrangement of the adventures of Natty Bumppo to be as popular as the five original Cooper novels.

2. Describe Leatherstocking as he is reflected in this review. Mention at least three of his important traits, and illustrate each one with detailed information.

3. Examine the evidence given to support the reviewer's belief that Leatherstocking served as a model for a long line of favorite American heroes. Which points do you find most convincing? Explain your answers.

4. Carmer reveals several opinions of Cooper in the course of the review. Find them and compare them with the discussion of Cooper on pages 492–93. Be prepared to discuss the important points of agreement or disagreement that you discover.

BUILDING YOUR VOCABULARY

It is clear from context that the *"chronological* sequence" in which Leatherstocking's adventures are arranged in the new version means in the order in which they occurred, or "time" order. "Time" is the meaning of *chrono–*, a word root that crops up in many other useful terms. An *anachronism* is an error in the time sequence, such as describing Washington riding in an automobile. When you find *chron* in a word, you know the meaning relates to time. What is the meaning of: *chronic, chronicle, chronometer, synchronize?*

THE REVIEWER

CARL CARMER (b. 1893) has had a varied literary career, combining poetry, fiction, history, folklore, magazine editing, journalism, radio broadcasting, and a term as a military instructor. He spent his youth in New York state, where he now makes his home; but his work has taken him to Alabama, Oklahoma, and Louisiana.

His poetic bent is apparent not only in his volume of poems, *Deep South*, but in the titles of his novels — *Stars Fell on Alabama*, and *Dark Trees to the Wind*.

EDWARD WEEKS

Hemingway at His Best

"Hemingway at His Best" by Edward Weeks from the *Atlantic Monthly*, September 1952. Reprinted by permission of the *Atlantic Monthly*.

IN *The Old Man and the Sea,* Ernest Hemingway has returned to the stripped, lean, objective narrative so characteristic of him at his best. In his short novel of an aging but still resourceful Havana fisherman, there is not a waste word, not a single intrusion of the author or of a bystander who might be Hemingway. The old man, sage, tempered, and set apart by his age, has been cursed with eighty-four days of bad luck. Not a fish in that time; so the young boy who was his helper has been ordered by his parents to another and a luckier boat, and the old man must go out alone to farther, deeper waters, where the bigger marlin lie. The boy, Manolin, still helps him when the boats are ashore — helps him get his supper, picks up the fresh baits, and helps him carry the gear, the rolls of line in the basket, the harpoon and gaff, the mast with the furled sail, down to the water-side. So it is that the old man rows out in his skiff in the dark before dawn for the most taxing fight in his long life, a struggle with a giant marlin which is to break his luck for good.

Mr. Hemingway has stripped the story to the essentials of the old Cuban. Having no family, he has few wants; lust and liquor are behind him; in his little shack ashore he has but one meal a day and lives in that borderland between reverie and sleep. But on the sea it is different; he lives for fishing and he loves *la mar* [1] — "the old man always thought of her as feminine and as something that gave or withheld great favors, and if she did wild or wicked things, it was because she could not help them." To his fishing he brings the instinct and knowledge of a lifetime, great courage and cunning to make up for the youth he has lost.

The old man's response to the sea, the sureness with which he pierces its depth with line or sight, the incredible resourcefulness with which he hangs on to the giant marlin through days and nights, and the rage with which he tries to defend his prize from the sharks — these are the successive stages in a story which is beautiful in its description, and of clean, thrusting power in its pursuit. Here is none of the braggadocio [2] which made that other fisherman,

[1] la mar (là mâr): the sea (Spanish).
[2] braggadocio (brăg′a·dō′shĭ·ō): boasting.

Harry Morgan,[3] something less than believable. The old man and the boy are perfectly tuned to Hemingway's purpose: their affection and utterance are true to themselves as their philosophy is true to the sea. I have put this book on the top shelf of Mr. Hemingway's work, and i am grateful for it.

[3] Harry Morgan: the central character in Hemingway's novel *To Have and Have Not*.

FOR DISCUSSION

1. What quality of Hemingway's novel is most praised by the reviewer? Explain the meaning of "objective narrative," and find one hint that the reviewer does not always find Hemingway objective.

2. After telling much of the story, the reviewer breaks off in the midst of a crucial struggle. Why? What good rule for book reports is suggested by this example?

3. Tell two possible meanings of the reviewer's statement that the old man's struggle with the giant fish "is to break his luck for good."

4. Edward Weeks mentions a number of characteristics of *The Old Man and the Sea* that he finds typical of Hemingway at his best. Are these characteristics also apparent in Hemingway's short story "Old Man at the Bridge" (page 26)? Judging from the story, do you think that Weeks' remarks are accurate?

THE REVIEWER

EDWARD WEEKS (b. 1898) has been associated with the *Atlantic Monthly* for most of his adult life. After attending public school in Elizabeth, New Jersey, he attended college at Cornell and Harvard and went to England for graduate work at Cambridge University. After one year as a manuscript reader and book salesman for a New York publishing house, he joined the *Atlantic* staff as an associate editor. In 1927 he became editor of the Atlantic Monthly Press, and since 1938 he has been editor of the magazine. His regular comments on current literature appear in the department "The Atlantic Bookshelf."

JOHN P. MARQUAND

A Saga of Domestic Life

IT MAY very well be that the pursuit of happiness in the American home is more difficult today than it was, say, at the turn of the century — in spite of dishwashers, hair driers, detergents, vitamin pills, and television. It is certain at least that anyone who can write with genuine joy, gusto, and enthusiasm regarding the vicissitudes of home, husband, dogs, and children commands an enormous audience. This, of course, has been the deserved good fortune of Betty MacDonald ever since *The Egg and I*[1] appeared in 1945. She is a girl who seems to enjoy every moment of living, no matter how or where. She has coped with red-ink budgets, balky plumbing, and nothing in the kitchen but noodles. She has lived through dog fights, measles, and all the usual and unusual cataclysms[2] of nature. But even when domestic morale has sunk to the bottom of the barrel, she and everyone around her have had a wonderful time. Because of her ability to tell a good story, this *joie de vivre*[3] is communicated to all who read her pages.

[1] *The Egg and I:* a book about the adventures of newlyweds trying to run a chicken ranch.
[2] cataclysms (kăt′*á*·klĭz′mz): catastrophes.
[3] *joie de vivre* (zhwä′ dĕ vē′vr′): joy in living.

Her latest book is, in my opinion, her very best to date. *Onions in the Stew* is a homely title, but then it is a homely book, brimming over with incidents of everyday life — some which we have experienced ourselves, others which Betty MacDonald enables us to live vicariously[4] and with unalloyed delight.

Onions in the Stew is a saga of domestic life on Vashon[5] Island, which lies in Puget Sound within commuting distance of the city of Seattle, Washington. If one thinks that Vashon Island — complete with Betty MacDonald, her husband, Don, her daughters, Anne and Joan, and the family dog, Tudor — resembles anything in New York Harbor, he is in error. The American Northwest is still a land of rugged plenty that has not lost all its frontier quality. Its Douglas fir trees are not lumbered out yet; its shores are washed by the marrow-chilling North Pacific; its forests and farmlands are watered by almost constant winter rainfall. Mount Rainier, when you can see it through the rainclouds, broods over a world of plenty; and a perpetual conflict between nature and encroaching man lends life there a comedy value which only Betty MacDonald so far has been able to interpret. She knows that you can never

[4] vicariously (vī·kâr′ĭ·ŭs·lĭ): enjoying or suffering an experience through sympathetic participation with another person's experience.
[5] Vashon (văsh′ŭn).

tell exactly what nature may do in the vicinity of Seattle. Plant a sapling on your front lawn, and almost overnight it becomes a giant. If you are not careful with vines and shrubbery, they smother your house while your back is turned. Small fruits, particularly berries, grow in such lavish profusion that they threaten housewives with nervous breakdown. Deer and raccoon wander vaguely over lawns and gardens, and on the beaches are peculiar shellfish, including a clamlike creature known as a geoduck that can move through sand with the speed of an express train. Vashon Island is inhabited by many friendly and interesting neighbors; the MacDonald house can only be reached by beach or by trail; and the whole area seems to abound in dogs, all of whom appear to have incurred the intense dislike of Tudor.

Seeing these phenomena through the eyes of Mrs. MacDonald causes one to grow wiser in the ways of the Northwest — but never sadder. No one can tell a better story than she when it involves the ludicrous details that go into keeping a home together. It is impossible to forget the MacDonalds' pursuit of the washing machine which they thought was resting safely in a rowboat near their sea wall, or Tudor's classic fight with one of his bitterest enemies, or the family's capture of a geoduck. The variety of the MacDonald life is as abundant as Betty MacDonald's good nature. Aside from being consistently entertained, readers of *Onions in the Stew* will also gain a strong sense of inner satisfaction. In these days of war and rumors of war, when it is fashionable to write of emotional maladjustment and shattered homes, this book brings a warming note of cheer. It teaches us that happiness can flourish in very unexpected quarters as long as it is nourished by comradeship and love and humor, and that for some of us, at any rate, a lot is still right with the world.

FOR DISCUSSION

1. Describe the tone the review promises you will find in *Onions in the Stew*. Mention some happenings referred to in the review to which a different writer might give a decidedly different emotional tone. What conclusions can you draw about Betty MacDonald's personality?

2. What difficulties does Mrs. MacDonald encounter that stem from living on an island? from living in the Pacific Northwest?

3. What phrases does Marquand use to describe some trends in modern literature? How is this comment related to the book being reviewed? On the basis of this review, tell why you would or would not like to read some of Marquand's own novels.

THE REVIEWER

JOHN P. MARQUAND (1893–1960) was one of our foremost modern novelists. He was born in Wilmington, Delaware, but his family soon returned to the old sailing town of Newburyport, Massachusetts, and a farm that had been in the family for a hundred years. After graduation from Harvard, he spent only five years working as a journalist and an advertising copywriter before his fiction met with such success that he gave up other employment. From the start he sold profitably everything he wrote. When *The Late George Apley* won the Pulitzer prize in 1938, Marquand was firmly established among the major contemporary novelists. His other novels, especially *H. M. Pulham, Esq.*, *Point of No Return*, and *Melville Goodwin, U.S.A.*, continued his brilliant pictures of life in modern New England and New York. Two of his best novels became successful plays. *The Late George Apley* was dramatized by Marquand and George S. Kaufman; *Point of No Return* was dramatized by Paul Osborn.

REVIEWING THE REVIEWS

Collect from the three reviews statements that present the reviewer's judgment of the value of each book, and compare them. All three books are recommended by the reviewers, but for different reasons. What are the reasons in each case?

F. SCOTT FITZGERALD

Advice to a Young Writer

"Advice to a Young Writer" from "Memories of Fitzgerald" by George Jean Nathan, originally in the October, 1958 issue of *Esquire*. Reprinted by permission of Mrs. Frances Turnbull Kidder.

One of the finest novelists of this century, F. Scott Fitzgerald became famous while still in his twenties after the publication of his first novel, *This Side of Paradise*. The short stories and novels that followed increased his reputation for polished craftsmanship. The "Frances" whom Fitzgerald advises in this letter was a sophomore at Radcliffe College. She had asked for his honest opinion on one of several "Sketches of a Debutante" that she had written for her composition class, and Fitzgerald was kind enough to give a thoughtful and challenging answer. His own situation, when he took the time to be kind to this young student, was not a happy one. He was heavily in debt and burdened by personal difficulties. His stories were no longer selling. In desperation he had gone to Hollywood to write movie scripts. He lived there quietly: writing and observing. It was a Fitzgerald at the peak of his wisdom — if far from the height of his popularity — who wrote this penetrating letter. The postscript to the letter is like a postscript to the man: an added testimonial to his kindness, his intelligence, and his integrity.

November 9, 1938

Dear Frances:

I've read the story carefully and, Frances, I'm afraid the price for doing professional work is a good deal higher than you are prepared to pay at present. You've got to sell your heart, your strongest reactions, not the little minor things that only touch you lightly, the little experiences that you might tell at dinner. This is especially true when you *begin* to write, when you have not yet developed the tricks of interesting people on paper, when you have none of the technique which it takes time to learn. When, in short, you have *only* your emotions to sell.

This is the experience of all writers. It was necessary for Dickens to put into *Oliver Twist* the child's passionate resentment at being abused and starved that had haunted his whole childhood. Ernest Hemingway's first stories, *In Our Time*, went right down to the bottom of all that he had ever felt and known. In *This Side of Paradise* I wrote about a love affair that was still bleeding as fresh as the skin wound on a hemophile.[1]

[1] **hemophile** (hē′mô·fīl): a person suffering from a disease in which even the slightest cuts bleed profusely.

The amateur, seeing how the professional, having learned all that he'll ever learn about writing, can take a trivial thing such as the most superficial reactions of three uncharacterized girls and make it witty and charming — the amateur thinks he or she can do the same. But the amateur can only realize his ability to transfer his emotions to another person by some such desperate and radical expedient as tearing your first tragic love story out of your heart and putting it on pages for people to see.

That, anyhow, is the price of admission. Whether you are prepared to pay it or whether it coincides or conflicts with your attitude on what is "nice" is something for you to decide. But literature, even light literature, will accept nothing less from the neophyte.[1] It is one of those professions that wants the "works." You wouldn't be interested in a soldier who was only a *little* brave.

In the light of this, it doesn't seem worthwhile to analyze why this story isn't salable, but I am too fond of you to kid you along about it, as one tends to do at my age. If you ever decide to tell *your* stories, no one would be more interested than,

> Your old friend,
> *F. Scott Fitzgerald*

P.S. I might say that the writing is smooth and agreeable and some of the pages very apt and charming. You have talent — which is the equivalent of a soldier having the right physical qualifications for entering West Point.

[1] neophyte (nē'ō-fĭt): beginner.

FOR DISCUSSION

1. Explain what you think Fitzgerald means when he says that when you *begin* to write, "you've got to sell your heart."

2. If you have read *Oliver Twist* (or *David Copperfield*), tell the class what parts of each story reveal Dickens' resentment over injustices suffered in childhood.

3. How does Fitzgerald's sentence, "You wouldn't be interested in a soldier who was only a *little* brave," fit into the theme of his letter?

4. Why is the word "your" italicized in the last sentence of the letter?

5. What do you think of the "equivalent" that the author puts in his postscript? Can you suggest some of the necessary qualifications for a professional writer in addition to talent?

THE AUTHOR

F. SCOTT FITZGERALD (1896–1940) was named for Francis Scott Key, the author of "The Star-Spangled Banner," and "star-spangled" seems to describe his career. Born in St. Paul, Minnesota, Fitzgerald attended an Eastern private school and Princeton University. He left college to join the army in World War I. At the end of the war, after selling a short story, Fitzgerald plunged into the writing of his first novel, *This Side of Paradise* (1920).

His first novel contained many flaws, but the works that followed demonstrated Fitzgerald's increasing mastery of his art. Among his writings are a collection of short stories, *Tales of the Jazz Age* (1922), and three novels, *The Beautiful and Damned* (1921), *The Great Gatsby* (1925), and *Tender Is the Night* (1934). He died at 44 in Hollywood while working on what would probably have been his finest novel, *The Last Tycoon*. The book was published after his death in the form in which he left it.

CATHERINE DRINKER BOWEN

Salute
to Librarians

How does a famous biographer use the resources of a library in her research? How
long does it take to write a biography? Are
relatively unknown and often privately
printed books ever valuable to a biographer? What part can libraries and librarians play in the process of getting to know
a man who lived a generation or even centuries ago? In this chapter from *Adventures of a Biographer*, Catherine Drinker
Bowen answers these questions and offers
a number of other hints on using the library, as she gives a memorable salute to
librarians.

T HE pleasing condition known as
true love is seldom attained without
difficulty. Nowadays, I can declare with
truth that I am in love with librarians
— engaged in a perpetual, delightful affair of the heart with all public cus-
todians of books.

But in my early twenties, struggling
in library basements with bound volumes of newspapers or shuffling

through a jungle of card catalogues, I
was convinced that librarians existed
solely to keep people from reading
books. It is natural for young readers
to experience shyness in big city or university libraries; the presence of so
many books is at the same time exciting
and intimidating. The young scholar
longs for introduction, a knowledgeable hand to reach, point, act as intermediary between himself and all
those riches.

In early days I tried not to give
librarians any trouble, which was
where I made my primary mistake. Librarians like to be given trouble; they
exist for it; they are geared to it. For
the location of a mislaid volume, an
uncatalogued item, your good librarian
has a ferret's nose. Give her a scent and
she jumps the leash, her eye bright with
battle. But I did not know this. All unaware I used to make my way to those
block-long municipal buildings, hope
in my heart, and in my hand a list of
ten or fifteen books. Not books to read
in the library but to take home, where
I could copy at length, with time to
think about what I was copying. I did
not telephone beforehand and ask to
have my books ready at the desk. I

took my list and looked up the proper numbers in the card catalogue, re-checked each one, and carried the cards to the desk. The young woman would glance at the cards, and then she would say, "Only two books at a time can be taken from the circulation department, Miss." Black hatred would then well up in a heart that had been ready to love.

"*Shut not your doors to me proud libraries.*" Walt Whitman had said it, and the words gave comfort, letting me know the great had their troubles, too, in libraries. But I was puzzled. Why should there be a conspiracy to keep anyone away from books? The fault must lie in myself, perhaps in my lack of systematized training in research. This was long before I had met the professors or attended a conference of historians; there was still fixed in my mind the pleasing illusion that the possessor of a Ph.D. in history has before him a blazed trail, a path straight to the heart of his subject.

While I was working on the life of Tchaikovsky,[1] in 1938, a British musicologist happened to be a guest in my brother's house. I admired Professor Dent's books about musicians; I was sure that so famous a scholar could tell me how to proceed and that his experience would provide a magic formula for libraries, an open sesame [2] to those tall, imperious doors. I asked Mr. Dent point-blank how he went about his research. (I was too inexperienced to know this is not a question one asks of scholars.) "Do you use five-by-eight cards?" I said. "How do you start, for instance?"

Mr. Dent smiled. "How do *you* start?" he asked. "How do *you* do *your* research?"

"Me?" I said. "Oh, I just plunge

---

[1] **Tchaikovsky** (chĭ·kôf′skĭ): Peter Ilich Tchaikovsky, a Russian composer, 1840–1893.

[2] **open sesame** (sĕs′ả·mê): the words that opened the door of the robbers' den in the tale of *Ali Baba and the Forty Thieves.*

around in libraries."

Twenty-three years and five books later, I know that Mr. Dent answered me in the only way he could. On that tortuous, long journey there is indeed no sure trail, no shortcut. I went ahead, plunging and bucking my way through libraries or slinking defeated from some municipal encounter. I do not know how it is with other students of history. But looking back, it seems my every forward movement derived not from success but failure, from some humiliation suffered, inducing anger, the stubborn resolve to find what I knew was on the shelves and use it in my own way for better or for worse.

One day in the New York Public Library, I received a crushing rebuff. That the incident was due to my own ineptitude made it, as usual, no easier to bear. I had walked into the Slavonic Division and told the learned curator that I was writing a life of Tchaikovsky. Might I look around, not at the cards but at the shelved books, the titles? "You speak Russian, of course?" the curator asked, with a fine roll of the R. His question took me by surprise. Actually, I knew enough to read titles and find my way about. But I gave a cautious negative. No, I didn't speak the language.

The curator shrugged. "No Russian?" he said. "Then of what use to come to this room? What use to write a life of Peter Ilich Tchaikovsky?"

I turned tail and fled, too flustered to stop and explain that I had a Russian collaborator, and that we both knew quite well what we were doing. At the Pennsylvania Station I boarded the train for home. By the time we reached Princeton Junction I had recovered. People, I thought, should be thrusting books at me, not snatching them away! Moreover, it was high time I did something to resolve this feud between me and the charge-out ladies and gentlemen behind the desks. The train pulled into North Philadelphia, and it came to me with a redeeming flash that what I needed to study was not books, systems, "disciplines," but *librarians*.

I bought a large notebook, something I am apt to do in moments of stress. Perhaps every student does it; a clean, untouched notebook invites the bravest plans. On the outside of this one I wrote "Librarians and Libraries," and then I began making lists of the librarians I had encountered. After each name I wrote a brief and useful characterization. The lists were continued for years, they were made in all seriousness, meant only for business, and they far overflowed that first notebook. I have them today and reproduce some samples, unchanged except for the exclusion of one proper name:

Library of Congress. Mr. Shaw — Mr. Cole. Can find anything. For heaven's sake, don't forget your library number.
Harvard Archives. Mr. Lovett, wears glasses. Bright. Mr. Elkins, seventh floor, Widener. Head man. Cannot understand what I am trying to do, but helpful. Said, "You don't want *printed* material, do you?" No use telling him why I want it. Just give him the numbers.
Widener Library downstairs. Mr. X. . . . Old curmudgeon.[1] Hates women. Keep away from him. Find out name the little short one, desk, head of stairs. Sweet.
Massachusetts Historical Society. Mrs. Hitchcock, the nice one who knows Henry Adams. When he comes in the basement, she will notify me upstairs. Says better not let him catch me downstairs near the Adams Papers. Says he takes off his hearing aid to make it harder. Says don't be put down by this. Says just yell.

This last was written in the late 1940's, before the Adams Papers, a superb repository of historical material, were thrown open to scholars.[2] Mr. Henry Adams was custodian of the

---

[1] **curmudgeon** (kĕr·mŭj'ŭn): an ill-natured man.
[2] Publication of *The Adams Papers* began in 1961.

Papers, and only an occasional favored student was permitted a glimpse inside the room. Mr. Barnes's famous arcanum [3] of painting, near Philadelphia, was never more difficult to penetrate; I was forewarned to failure. Already there had been correspondence by mail and by messenger. At Mr. Adams' instance I had reduced my requests to specific queries. There were eight of these, carefully worded and typed; I had delivered them to Mr. Adams' office on State Street. What I wanted from the Adams Papers was modest enough; it had to do with John Adams at college, between 1751 and 1755. Adams' *Autobiography* had been printed nearly a century ago in what its editor called "fragments," opening with the year 1775; the Massachusetts Historical Society had printed a brief and still earlier "fragment" in which John Adams told of taking his entrance examinations for Harvard. It seemed to me there must be more, somewhere. Adams was deeply interested in education. Surely he would mention his teachers, his tutors? I counted on one more meeting with the curator of the Papers, here in the Historical Society. A last chance and I knew it.

I had been at work in the library for perhaps a week, when one morning Mrs. Hitchcock sent word that Mr. Henry Adams had entered the building and was on his way up in the elevator. The second floor of the Massachusetts Historical Society is a succession of handsome, open rooms that echo, with lofty doorways and marble floors. I stood perhaps ten steps from the elevator. Mr. Adams got out, took a startled look at me, and snatched a hearing button from each ear. My instinct was for retreat, but I advanced, and there in the open room gave tongue for a full half hour. Mr. Adams had my list; I had a carbon. We stood and I shouted. Finally Mr. Adams seized me by the

---

[3] **arcanum** (är·kā'nŭm): a secret room.

elbow. "Mrs. Bowen," he said, "I don't want to block your work. I don't want to be the cause of destroying your chapters, as you say I will. But you cannot have this material. It has never been printed. You know very well it has never been printed. *How do you know it is in the Adams Papers?*"

I told Mr. Adams I did not know, but that I had studied his ancestor for a long time, and such studies permitted one to infer that John Adams might have mentioned these matters in his *Autobiography*. I said that inference was the business of a biographer.

Mr. Adams' voice rose to a pitch of real distress. "Mrs. Bowen," he said, "I wish I had never laid *eyes* on you."

Something in the desperate pronunciation of the noun softened me; plainly, Mr. Adams' suffering was worse than mine. I gave up, and we parted in a mutual rush. Downstairs in the little retiring room I threw myself on the couch; the sound of my voice still rang in my ears. The entire Historical Society had been apprised [1] of my work, hopes, ambitions; right now I desired nothing so much as dignified anonymity. A Japanese girl was standing by the mirror, arranging her hair. "Excuse me," she said, "but are you writing a life of John Adams?"

I told the young woman she must know that by now. Everyone in the building must know it.

She smiled politely, but her next words startled me. "What was the old gentleman afraid of?" she said.

I went home to Philadelphia and fidgeted. How could I complete my chapter without that material? I was genuinely worried, in a condition of frustration, and I could not proceed. At the end of three weeks, on the day before Christmas, an envelope came in the mail, postmarked Boston. Inside, typed laboriously by Mr. Adams, was everything I had asked for. Plainly, he

had entered that sacred room, had found what I wanted, taken it down, and copied it line for line. What alchemy [2] melted his New England heart I do not know. I know only that a surge of relief and joy came over me; I can feel it now, some ten years afterward.

Since those hazardous days, matters have begun to run smoothly for me in libraries. Confronted by fifty thousand books, I have not lost my diffidence; perhaps it has increased. But I am not at all abashed in the presence of librarians. I can remember the day the tide began to turn. It was in the Pennsylvania Historical Society, at Thirteenth and Locust Streets, in Philadelphia. I was three quarters through my life of John Adams and needed some eighteenth-century broadsides to brighten my chapters on the Continental Congress. Research for my preceding book, on Justice Holmes, had been done in Boston and Washington; I was unfamiliar with the Pennsylvania Historical Society, and no one there knew me. I walked into the building and upstairs to the library, signed my name in the ledger, and went to the card catalogues by the window.

I had not gone through the A's when I felt a tap on my shoulder, and the librarian from the desk handed me a folded slip of paper. It was a note from the director, Richard Norris Williams. "Mrs. Bowen," it said, "would you like a quiet room to work in upstairs?"

I kept that message tacked above my desk for weeks. It cheered me, though I had not accepted Dr. Williams' kind offer because I like the genial commotion of the card catalogue room, the companionship of other readers, and the nearness of the books. In research libraries, one hesitancy remained, however, to plague me. It was brought on

[1] apprised: informed.

[2] alchemy (ăl'kê·mĭ): the ancient and medieval science of chemistry. One of the goals of the alchemist was to change common metals such as lead into gold or silver.

by the repeated question, put to me first by Mr. Elkins on the seventh floor of the Widener Library: "You don't want *printed* material,[1] do you?" That query, always phrased negatively by research librarians, still had power to put me down. Yet even this bogy [2] was shortly due for exorcism.[3] Again, I recall the day.

Because he is hunting for detail, the biographer finds his material, as I have said, in unlikely places, and this is true in libraries as well as in personal interviews or an out-of-door search conducted through the subject's home county or locale. Suppose one wants to find who was proprietor of a certain Philadelphia tavern, favored by John Adams in a hot July of 1775. The matter may be concealed in some quite ordinary volume, say the published memoirs of a cousin thrice removed, or in scattered notes on Philadelphia streets, compiled in the mid-nineteenth century by some finicky antiquarian and printed obscurely at his own expense.

A list of such publications is not impressive to scholars, accustomed as they are to primary or manuscript sources, and I was conscious of it. The incident that liberated me took place in the Free Library of Philadelphia. It began on that vast second floor, where I had gone to check my book numbers, carrying in my hand a list of just such titles as I have described — thirteen of them, each referring to material vital to my subject and discovered by me at the cost of much time and digging.

I had never used this public library, but the general reference collection is large, and it seemed likely the volumes would be here, rather than in a more specialized collection. I found my num-

A portrait of John Adams by Charles Willson Peale.

bers in the cards and took them to the librarian at the circulation desk. "Only two books at a time . . ." she began.

Two blades of grass to a cow, I told myself, would be as nourishing. I left my books on the desk and wandered off. In libraries it is not well to hurry. To the research worker, haste is fatal. The books have been where they are for a long time; they reveal themselves slowly, at their own pace.

Drifting downstairs in search of help, I came upon a door marked *Assistant Librarian in Charge of Research.* For a public library it was an odd, inviting title. I knocked and walked into a big square room, littered from floor almost to ceiling with the tools of the working scholar: bibliographies, dictionaries, encyclopedias, rare-book catalogues, and unanswered letters, no doubt from other librarians.

A young man with startling white hair rose from a table where he was writing. I told him my name and what had occurred upstairs. He seized my hand and wrung it, said I could have anything I wanted in the library, took my list, ran an eye over it, and remarked, all in one loud, welcoming breath, "Trash! Everything on this list

---

[1] *printed* material: as opposed to original material in manuscript. The librarian's confusion is explained in the paragraphs that follow.

[2] **bogy**: something that causes fear.

[3] **exorcism** (ĕk′sôr·sĭz′m): the act of driving off evil spirits.

is trash. My name is John Powell. What do you want with third-rate books like these?"— and was on the intercom telephone to start the wheels rolling.

It was the beginning of a lasting friendship. With this young man I could defend myself, and did. How dared a librarian condemn the contents of books he had not read! I demanded vigorously. These volumes contained letters printed nowhere else, notes from John Adams' daughter to her mother: "I have dined at General Knox's; [1] the General is not half so fat as he was." John Powell was himself a biographer; when the books came, he looked into them and made handsome retraction, adding that there is no material the biographer can afford to ignore, whether primary, tertiary, [2] or quinquagintal. [3]

History withholds so much! Thomas Carlyle [4] has said it with his usual violence and the hammering of his bold Germanic capitalizations. "Listening from a distance of Two Centuries, across the Death-chasms and the howling kingdoms of Decay, it is not easy to catch everything."

To catch everything? It is not easy to catch anything at all, or at least anything that will communicate in living terms across the centuries. The biographer is much in the position of a journalist who looks for news. Not for fillers or musty historical chestnuts that can be found in the textbooks, but for *biographical news*. Sometimes the biographer's news is gleaned from the mere titles of books. I well remember the summer morning when first I saw the Holmes family library. The books had recently been moved to the Library of

Congress, in Washington, and awaited settlement of Justice Holmes's will before being catalogued and arranged. A young librarian, shirt-sleeved against the heat, took me upstairs in a small staff elevator, led me down a corridor, unlocked a door, and beckoned me into a narrow, steel-walled room.

Stored and filed on shelves, tables, chairs, were the accumulated personal libraries of three generations of Holmeses, some six thousand volumes in all. Perhaps half were lawbooks; they filled two rooms; yellow library slips stuck out from the pages. Framed pictures, tied in stacks, lay along the floor, and there was a wooden box of china, each piece wrapped in tissue paper. At the door a table held a pile of dime thrillers in paperback, with lurid drama depicted on the covers; I wondered if they belonged here and which of the family had collected them.

Altogether it was an inspiring, dazzling, dusty sight. Here were books beloved of Wendells, Olivers, Jacksons, Holmeses, inscribed on flyleaves by donors and owners: "O. W. H., Jr., from his loving father and mother, Christmas, 1859." Here were Dr. Holmes's books on music, acquired no doubt when he was learning to play the violin in the 1850's. (A trying time for the family; the good Doctor considered fiddle playing to be a mere matter of time and application.) I noted the German edition of his *Autocrat of the Breakfast-Table . . . Der Tischdespot*. What a travesty of a title, and how had the Doctor felt when first he saw it?

Here were books I had myself been reared on: *The Dolly Dialogues*, Anstey's *Tinted Venus*, the many volumes of old Isaac D'Israeli's *Curiosities of Literature*. There were enough Latin books to stock a school — Mr. Epes Sargent Dixwell's own school, no doubt, where O. W. Holmes, Jr., had studied. And here was Mr. Dixwell's *Phaedrus*, [5] with

---

[1] **General Knox:** an American general who fought in the Revolutionary War.
[2] **tertiary** (tûr′shĭ·ĕr′ĭ): of the third rank; third-hand.
[3] **quinquagintal** (kwĭn′kwȧ·jĭn′tȧl): fiftieth-hand (a coined word).
[4] **Thomas Carlyle:** (1795–1881) a Scottish essayist and historian.

[5] **Phaedrus** (fē′drŭs): one of the dialogues of the Greek philosopher Plato.

a signed photograph of William Tyndall pasted in, dated 1877. Here also were the *Letters to a Young Physician, Just Entering upon Practice,* by James Jackson, M.D., LL.D. That would be Justice Holmes's grandfather, I thought, through the maternal line; he had dedicated his book to that excellent physician Dr. John C. Warren, professor of anatomy at Harvard. There was a chapter on "Somnambulism,[1] Animal Magnetism, and Insanity"; there was one on "Phthises,"[2] which recommended exercise in the open air, particularly horseback riding. The chapter "On Dyspepsy" went directly to the point: "I believe that very many persons are benefited from the juice of the grape, and I choose to say so. I love to tell the truth, even when it is unfashionable."

What a very sensible book, I told myself, and copied the sentences in my notes. "On entering the sick room," wrote Dr. Jackson, "the physician's deportment should be calm, sober without solemnity, civil without formality. He should abstain from all levity. He should never attract attention to himself. He should leave the room with an air of cheerfulness. . . ."

During all this time, the librarian had waited, sitting on a box by the door. I paused in my reading to tell him a person could learn more about the Holmeses, here in this little room, than in a dozen interviews with the Justice's friends and relatives. The librarian asked how long I expected to stay. "All day," I said. The librarian replied that he would have to stay with me; readers were not permitted in this room by themselves. I said I was sorry to take up his time. Following my usual procedure, I opened my brief case, took out paper and a dozen sharpened pencils, and laid them conveniently by. Then I removed

my hat and shoulder bag, produced from the latter a kitchen apron (library dust can begrime one's traveling clothes), and put it on.

The librarian watched. Then he smiled. "I think the library can assume this risk," he said quietly, and took his departure.

I never saw him again. But I remember that young man with gratitude. He led me where I wanted to go and showed me what I had come there to see, then took my measure and left me with the books.

Recently I heard a young lawyer say, "When I go into a really good library, things happen to me." For the librarians there could be no tastier compliment and none more true. Since I began to read in libraries some thirty years ago, times have changed and policies have altered. Modern librarians look on it as their business to make their shelves inviting. A librarian's policy depends, of course, on where he is placed. Among rare books, custodial care is of first importance, whereas in the public libraries of great cities, it is important to "get the titles off the shelves," whether or no the volumes fall apart from overwork.

But to the biographer, a scholarly librarian stands at times in the relation of editor. By tactful approach the librarian will discover the scheme of one's book, how widely one plans to explore certain phases of history, certain scenes and personalities. What he says can encourage expansion, a deeper treatment. He calls on the telephone or writes letters at strategic moments: "We are on the trail of that holograph[3] map (or that portrait or manuscript letter). We have written twice to England and enclose replies to date. We will surely track this item down. By the way, last night our Miss Y. found that 1607 edition of Cowell's *Interpreter*. Do you still want to take it home? . . . May we say your

[1] **Somnambulism** (sŏm·năm′bŭ·lĭz′m): the act of sleepwalking.
[2] **Phthises,** commonly **phthisis** (thĭ′sĭs): tuberculosis.

[3] **holograph:** a document in the handwriting of the author.

treatment of the Norwich episode is especially valuable, and we hope you will not give up but pursue it further."

In the five or six years it takes to write a biography, such expert, persistent interest is to the writer like food to the famished. The librarian has gone beyond the path of duty; he believes in one's book, and his involvement proves it. For lack of certain materials, the biographer may have deleted a telling episode. But the librarian's letter gives the writer heart. He fishes his chapter from the pile, inserts a blank page on which he scribbles, *Librarian X will supply material,* and arranges his narrative accordingly.

As it happens, I am especially dependent on librarians because my scheme of biography requires that I do the entire bulk of reading myself. Contrary to common practice, I do not engage research workers to go to libraries and read for me, or even to search for specific things. Such a helper, no matter how skillfully trained, may miss something on the way, some side picture, name, or incident vital to the illumination of my characters. Therefore I prefer to make the journey alone, though it may add years to my task.

I have known librarians over half the world. I think their praises are not often sung, and I am glad to sing them now. Wherever they are, I salute them and wish them joy of their work.

FOR DISCUSSION

1. How does Mrs. Bowen explain her early discomfort in libraries?

2. Discuss the questions of the curator of the Tchaikovsky material. Were his questions justified?

3. How does Mrs. Bowen begin her research for a biography? Why does she say, "To the research worker, haste is fatal"?

4. How could Mrs. Bowen feel so sure that John Adams had left more notes on his college years than had ever been printed?

5. Why did the librarian smile and leave

Mrs. Bowen alone with the personal library of the Holmes family the minute she put on a kitchen apron?

6. Is it possible that Mrs. Bowen's salute to librarians is more fervent than the tributes other biographers might pay them? Why? Why not?

7. Why is the library the most important tool for the biographer, the research worker, and the student? How would you go about gathering material from a library for a paper you wished to write? Do you think it sensible for a biographer or a student to keep notes on libraries and librarians? Why? Why not?

THE AUTHOR

CATHERINE DRINKER BOWEN (b. 1897) is a native of Pennsylvania. Her father, Henry Sturgis Drinker, was president of Lehigh University; her mother was a musician. Mrs. Bowen was educated in the Peabody Conservatory of Music, Baltimore, and at the Institute of Musical Art in New York. *Friends and Fiddlers* (1935), her first book, was a collection of essays that focused on music and musicians. In her second book, *Beloved Friend* (in collaboration with Barbara von Meck), she celebrated the friendship of Tchaikovsky and his patroness, Nadejda von Meck. Then Mrs. Bowen deserted music and musicians to write *Yankee from Olympus* (1944), her biography of Oliver Wendell Holmes, Jr. The book was four years in the writing, and it has been widely acclaimed for its excellence as a portrait of Justice Holmes. The next of Mrs. Bowen's biographical studies was *John Adams and the American Revolution* (1950) and the latest, *The Life and Times of Sir Edward Coke* (1955). *Adventures of a Biographer,* from which "Salute to Librarians" is taken, was published in 1959.

The Widener Library ➤

This photograph of the interior of the Widener Library of Harvard University shows where Mrs. Bowen did much of the research for her biography of John Adams, discussed in this selection. A photograph of the exterior of the library is reproduced on page 197.

History and Biography

We might say that history is about men in general, while biography is about men in particular. These very ancient literary forms remain distinctly different, yet their functions overlap, and each is often of great service to the other.

History attempts to record the truth about the actions of men in groups. The historian may confine himself to narrow ranges of time and place and to small groups of men, or he may seek to span years or even centuries, and encompass entire societies, races, or civilizations. Whatever the scope of his work, the historian aims to relate as accurately and completely as possible the events of an era.

The finest historians, from ancient Greece to modern times, have been men of letters. Their works are treasures of literature. Yet in its scholarly concern with fact, with accurate information, with precise truth, history can also be thought of as a science. Thus, the gathering of historical materials is essentially a scientific process, while the narration and interpretation of those materials is, in the best histories, an artistic process, often similar to the task of a novelist.

Biography focuses its attention upon the lives of specific men or women. Perhaps the finest comment about the art was that expressed by the greatest of ancient biographers, the Greek Plutarch:

> It was for the sake of others that I first commenced writing biographies; but I find myself proceeding . . . for my own; the virtues of those great men serving me as a sort of looking glass, in which I may see how to adjust and adorn my own life.

The relationship of biography and history is clear. We cannot understand the life of a man without having knowledge of the world in which he lived and the great events of his time. For this information, the biographer will often turn to the historian. He will depend on the historian to provide a detailed setting for the biographical study. In turn, the historian, no matter how broad his field, must give attention to those specific men and women who have played roles of critical importance in the great movements of a nation or an age. To understand such key figures, the historian may well depend on the work of the biographer.

The interplay of history and biography is clearly visible in the selections that follow. All of them deal with small units of history. Yet three of the selections (those by Douglas Southall Freeman, Carl Sandburg, and Samuel Eliot Morison) are taken from long, detailed biographies in which the study of a man is the primary aim. Another ("The Smart Ones Got Through") makes a perceptive comment about history in general while relating an exciting episode of the frontier, and much of the interest develops through vivid character sketches. Another ("The Beard of Joseph Palmer") provides a fine example of the brief biographical essay. In it we are given a portrait of a man, and through that portrait we learn a great deal about a particular period in our country's history.

GEORGE R. STEWART

The Smart Ones Got Through

This article describes a particular historical event and also makes an observation about history in general. The author offers an idea that may never have occurred to you: that a peculiar kind of fame — fame through dramatic failure — can overshadow an important success. Remember that this is not always the case. There are many dramatic successes enshrined in memory, while hosts of failures are forgotten. Perhaps the lesson is that if you hope to be remembered, whether you succeed or fail in a great venture, do it dramatically.

THE difference between "a historical event" and "a dramatic event" is well illustrated by the stories of the Stevens Party and the Donner Party. The former is historically important, and the pioneers who composed it brought the first wagons to California and discovered the pass across the Sierra Nevada that serves still as the chief route for railroad, highway, telephone, and airlines. The Donner Party, however, is of negligible impor-

"The Smart Ones Got Through" by George Stewart. Reprinted from *American Heritage,* The Magazine of History, with their permission.

tance historically, but the story has been told and retold, published and republished, because of its dramatic details of starvation, cannibalism, murder, heroism, and disaster. Against every American who knows of the one, a thousand must know of the other. As a kind of final irony, the pass discovered by the Stevens Party has come to be known as Donner Pass.

Yet actually the two parties had much in common. They were groups of Middle Westerners, native and foreign-born, migrating to California. Both included women and children, and traveled overland in ox-drawn covered wagons. Over much of the way, they followed the same route. Both were overtaken by winter, and faced their chief difficulties because of snow. Some of the Donner Party spent the winter in a cabin built by three members of the Stevens Party. One individual, Caleb Greenwood, actually figures in both stories.

The difference in the significance, however, springs from two differences in actuality. First, the Stevens Party set out in 1844, two years before the Donner Party; they were the trail breakers. Second, the Stevens Party was efficiently run, used good sense, had fairly good luck — in a word, was so successful that it got through without the loss of a single life. The Donner Party, roughly speaking, was just the opposite, and the upshot was that the casualty list piled up to 42, almost half of the total roster and nearly equaling the whole number of persons in the Stevens Party. The latter, incidentally, arrived in California more numerous by two than at the start because of babies born on the road.

The contrast between the parties is shown even in the nature of the sources of material available on them. No one bothered to record much about the non-dramatic Stevens Party, and we should have scarcely any details if it had not been for Moses Schallenberger, a lad of seventeen at the time of the actual events, who forty years later dictated to his schoolmarm daughter his memories of the journey. On the other hand, the story of the Donner Party is possibly the best-documented incident of any in the early history of the West. Its dramatic quality was such that everyone and his brother rushed in to tell what he knew about it or thought he knew about it, either at first or second hand, and publishers took it all.

Of course, this is still the everyday tale. Drive efficiently about your business, and no one ever hears of you. Scatter broken glass and blood over the highway, and a picture of the twisted wreck makes the front page. . . .

The Donner Party — to summarize briefly — was formed from family groups of other emigrant parties in July 1846, and set out by themselves from Little Sandy Creek, in what is now Wyoming, to reach California by the so-called Hastings Route. They lost much time, found the gateway to California blocked by snow, built cabins to winter it out, and ran short of food. Soon they were snowed in deeply, and began to die of starvation. A few escaped across the mountains on improvised snowshoes. Others were saved by the heroic work of rescue parties from the settlements in California. As the result of hardships, the morale of the party degenerated to the point of inhumanity, cannibalism, and possibly murder. Of 89 people — men, women, and children — involved with the misfortunes of the party, 47 survived, and 42 perished.

The Stevens Party left Council Bluffs on May 18, 1844. Before doing so, they performed what may well have been the act that contributed most to their final success — they elected Elisha Stevens to be their captain.

He was an unusual enough sort of fellow, that Stevens — about forty years old, with a big hawk nose and a peaked head; strange-acting, too. He seemed friendly enough, but he was solitary, having his own wagon but neither chick nor child. Born in South Carolina, raised in Georgia, he had trapped in the Rockies for some years, then spent a while in Louisiana, and now finally he was off for California, though no one knows why.

How such a man came to be elected captain is more than can be easily figured out. How did he get more votes than big-talking Dr. John Townsend, the only member of the party with professional status and of some education? Or more than Martin Murphy, Jr., who could muster kinsmen and fellow Irishmen numerous enough to make up a majority of votes? Perhaps Stevens was a compromise candidate between the native American and the Irish contingents that split the party and might well have brought quarrels and disaster. He had good experience behind him, indeed. And perhaps there was something about him that marked him for the natural leader of men that he apparently was. His election seems to me one of those events giving rise to the exclamation, "It makes you believe in democracy!"

Yes, he took the wagons through. If there were justice in history, his name would stand on the pass he found and conquered, and not merely on a little creek that runs into San Francisco Bay.

So they pushed off from the Missouri River that spring day, numbering 26 men, eight women, and about seventeen children. During the first part of the journey, they traveled in company with a larger party bound for Oregon. The swollen Elkhorn River blocked the way, but they emptied the wagons, ferried everything across in a waterproofed wagon bed, swam the cattle, and kept ahead. They chased buffalo, saw their first wild Indians at Fort Laramie. At Independence Rock they halted a week to rest the oxen, "make meat" by hunting buffalo, and allow Helen Independence Miller to be born. They were the first to take wagons across the Green River Desert by what was later known as Sublette's (or Greenwood's) Cutoff. On the cutoff they suffered from thirst, had their cattle stampede (but got them back), were scared by a Sioux war party (but had no real trouble). All this, of course, is mere routine for a covered-wagon journey, nothing to make copy of.

At Fort Hall they separated from the Oregon party. At Raft River, eleven wagons in the line, they left the Oregon Trail, and headed south and west, following the wheel tracks of an emigrant party that Joe Walker, the famous

mountain man, had tried to take to California the year before. Whether the people in the Stevens Party knew of his failure — the people got through, but the wagons were abandoned — is only one of the many details we do not know. Uneventfully and monotonously they followed his trail all the way to Humboldt Sink, a matter of 500 miles. Then, after careful scouting and on the advice of an intelligent Paiute chief, whom they called Truckee, they decided to quit following Walker and strike west.

From that point they were on their own, making history by breaking trail for the forty-niners, the Central Pacific, and U.S. 40. They made it across the Forty-Mile Desert with less trouble than might have been expected, considering that they were the first. Even so, the crossing took 48 hours, and the oxen were thirst-crazed by the time they approached the cottonwoods marking the line of a stream. The men of the party, with their usual good sense, unyoked the oxen some distance from the stream to prevent them from scenting water while still attached to the wagons and stampeding toward it. Thankful to their guide, the emigrants named the stream

The routes of the Donner and Stevens parties.

the Truckee, and prudently camped two days among its cottonwoods for rest and recuperation.

They knew no route, except to follow the river. The canyon got tighter and tighter until in places they merely took their wagons upstream like river boats. The oxen began to give out, hoofs softening because of being in the water so much. Now it came November, and a foot of snow fell. The oxen would have starved except for some tall rushes growing along the water.

Finally they came to where the river forked. Which way to go? They held "a consultation," which must have been close to a council of desperation. It was past the middle of November — snow two feet deep now, high mountain crags in view ahead, oxen footsore and gaunt, food low, womenfolks getting scared. But they were good men and staunch. They must have been — or we would have had the Donner story two years earlier.

Yes, there must have been some good men, and we know the names, if not much else about them. Old Caleb Greenwood, the trapper, was there, and he would have been heard with respect, though personally I do not cast him for the hero's part, as some do. Neither do I have much confidence in "Doc" Townsend, though his name is sometimes used to identify the whole party; he was full of wild ideas. But "Young" Martin Murphy, Irish as his name, was probably a good man, and so, I think, was Dennis Martin, Irish too. Then there was Hitchcock, whose Christian name has been lost because everyone has referred to him just as Old Man Hitchcock; he should have been valuable in the council, having been a mountain man in his day. But the one on whom I put my money is Stevens himself, who had taken them all the way, so far, without losing a man.

He or some other, or all of them together, worked out the plan, and it came out in the end as what we would call today a calculated risk, with a certain

hedging of the bets. Leave five wagons below the pass at what is now called Donner Lake, and three young men with them, volunteers, to build a cabin and guard the wagons and goods through the winter. Take six wagons ahead over the pass, and with them the main body including all the mothers and children. Up the other fork of the river, send a party of two women and four men, all young, well mounted, and well armed, prepared to travel light and fast and live off the country. Unencumbered they can certainly make it through somewhere; when they get to Sutter's Fort, they can have help sent back, if necessary.

So Captain Stevens and the main body took the six wagons ahead to the west, and with a heave and a ho, in spite of sheer granite ledges and ever-deepening snow, they hoisted those wagons up the pass, which is really not a pass so much as the face of a mountain. Even today, when you view those granite slopes, close to precipices, and imagine taking wagons up through the snow, it seems incredible.

Beyond the pass, some days' journey, they got snowed in, but by that time they were over the worst. On Yuba River they built a cabin to winter it out, and Elizabeth Yuba Murphy was born there. Eventually all of them, including E. Y. M., together with the wagons, got safely through to Sutter's.

As for the light-cavalry unit that took the other fork, they went up the stream, were the first white people on record to stand on the shore of Lake Tahoe, then turned west across the mountains. They suffered hardship, but got through.

That brings everybody in except the three young men who were with the wagons at the lake. They had built themselves a cabin, and were just settling down to enjoy a pleasant winter of hunting in the woods when snow started falling. Before long the cabin was up to the eaves, all game had disappeared, no man could walk. The three were left with two starving cows that they slaughtered, but they themselves were soon close to starving. They decided to get out of there fast, and so manufactured themselves crude snowshoes of the hickory strips that held up the canvases on the covered wagons.

One morning they set out — each with ten pounds of dried beef, rifle and ammunition, and two blankets. The snow was light and powdery, ten feet deep. The improvised snowshoes were heavy and clumsy, and exhausting to use. By evening the three had reached the summit of the pass, but young Moses Schallenberger, a mere gawky lad of seventeen, was sick and exhausted.

In the morning he realized that he could not make it through. Rather than impede his companions, he said good-by and turned back — with no expectation but death. The two others went on, and reached Sutter's Fort.

All in now but Moses Schallenberger! He had barely managed to make it back, collapsing at the very cabin and having to drag himself over the doorsill. He felt a little better the next day, forced himself to go out hunting on his snowshoes, saw nothing except fox tracks. Back at the cabin, "discouraged and sick at heart," he happened to notice some traps that Captain Stevens had left behind.

Next day he set traps, and during the night caught a coyote. He tried eating it, but found the flesh revolting, no matter how cooked. Still, he managed to live on that meat for three days, and then found two foxes in the traps. To his delight, the fox meat was delicious. This was about the middle of December. From then on, he managed to trap foxes and coyotes. He lived on the former, and hung the latter up to freeze, always fearing that he would have to eat another one, but keeping them as a reserve.

Alone in the snow-buried cabin, through the dim days and long nights of midwinter, week after week, assailed by fierce storms, often despairing of his life,

he suffered from deep depression. As he put it later, "My life was more miserable than I can describe," but he never lost the will to live. Fortunately he found some books that "Doc" Townsend had been taking to California, and reading became his solace. The two works that he later mentioned as having pored over were the poems of Byron,[1] and (God save the Mark!) [2] the letters of Lord Chesterfield.[3]

Thus the boy lived on, despondent but resolute, eating his foxes and hanging up his coyotes until he had a line of eleven of them. The weeks dragged along until it was the end of February, and still the snow was deep and the mountain winter showed no sign of breaking. Then, one evening a little before sunset, he was standing near the cabin, and suddenly saw someone approaching. At first he imagined it to be an Indian, but then he recognized his old comrade Dennis Martin!

Martin had traveled a long road since he went over the pass with the main body, in the middle of November. He had been picked up in the swirl of a California revolution and marched south almost to Los Angeles. Returning, he had heard of Schallenberger's being left behind and had come across the pass on snowshoes to see if he were still alive to be rescued.

Martin had lived for some years in Canada, and was an expert on snowshoes. He made a good pair for Schallenberger, and taught him their use. Thus aided, the lad made it over the pass without great difficulty. The last one was through!

[1] **Byron:** George Gordon (Lord Byron) an English poet, 1788–1824.
[2] **God save the Mark!:** an exclamation of surprise.
[3] **letters of Lord Chesterfield:** An English statesman and author, Lord Chesterfield (1694–1773) wrote a series of letters to his son, in which he outlined the conduct, manners, and duties required of a gentleman in fashionable eighteenth-century society.

The men of the party even went back the next summer, and brought out the wagons that had been left east of the pass. The only loss was their contents, taken by wandering Indians, except for the firearms, which the Indians considered bad medicine. . . .

If we return to the story that offers natural comparison with that of the Stevens Party, we must admit that the historical significance of the Donner Party is negligible. The road that the Donners cut through the Wasatch Mountains was useful to the Mormons when they settled by Great Salt Lake, but they would have got through without it. The Donners served as a kind of horrible example to later emigrants, and so may have helped to prevent other such covered-wagon disasters. That is about all that can be totaled up.

There is, of course, no use arguing. The Donner Party has what it takes for a good story, even a dog — everything, you might say, except young love. So, when I drive past the massive bronze statue of the Donner Memorial and up over the pass, I think of these folk who endured and struggled, and died or lived to produce what may be called the story of stories of the American frontier.

But as I drive over the pass, fighting the summer traffic of U.S. 40 or the winter blizzard, I also like to remember those earlier ones, to think of hawk-nosed Elisha Stevens; of Caleb Greenwood and "Old Man" Hitchcock; of gawky Moses Schallenberger, letting his comrades go on and facing death; of Mrs. Townsend, Moses' sister, riding her Indian pony with the horseback party; of Martin Murphy and fantastic "Doc" Townsend; of Dennis Martin who knew about snowshoes.

These are the ones who discovered the pass and took the wagons over, who kept out of emergencies or had the wit and strength to overcome them, who did not make a good story by getting into trouble, but made history by keeping out of trouble.

FOR DISCUSSION

1. Explain Stewart's distinction between a "historical event" and a "dramatic event." Reflect on the history you know, and see if you can point out other examples of these two categories. Remember that the distinction, though interesting, does not always exist. Many events can be both historically important and dramatic at the same time.

2. Do you think it was luck or ability that enabled the Stevens party to get through safely while the Donner party failed? Some people deny that there is such a thing as luck in matters of this kind. Consider the saying that luck favors the man who is ready. Point out some examples of how the Stevens party was prepared to take full advantage of its "luck."

3. Why does Stewart exclaim over Moses Schallenberger's reading material — the letters of Lord Chesterfield?

4. Do you agree with the sentiments Stewart feels when he drives through the Donner Pass? Or do you think the Donner party may have a just claim to the memorial?

FURTHER READING

If you would like to know more about ventures like these, you may find some interesting material in a work of history, Francis Parkman's *The Oregon Trail*, and a work of fiction, A. B. Guthrie's *The Way West*. There are several books on the Donner party, one of them, *Ordeal by Hunger*, by George R. Stewart himself.

THE AUTHOR

GEORGE R. STEWART (b. 1895) has written extensively, both in fiction and nonfiction. His first popular success was *Storm* (1941), a novel that has a storm as its "heroine" and that popularized the now universal practice of giving feminine names to hurricanes. *Fire* (1948) makes a forest fire the chief character. One of his best nonfiction works is *Names on the Land* (1945), a study of the many odd and interesting place names in this country, with their histories. His other nonfiction books include *U.S. 40* (1953) and *American Ways of Life* (1954).

STEWART H. HOLBROOK

The Beard of Joseph Palmer

Astonishing and disturbing things happened in a Massachusetts town, well over a hundred years ago, when one person ventured to be different from his neighbors in his appearance. Could a man become a martyr over the matter of his whiskers? It is sobering to see how rapidly a trifling matter exploded into a persecution.

THE BIOGRAPHICAL ESSAY. Here is a fine example of the biographical essay. It is a difficult form, for it challenges the writer to compress a man's life into a few short pages and still illuminate its central interest and significance. In this essay the biography reaches beyond the merely personal elements of one man's life and extends into social history. Old Joe Palmer's story has its humorous moments, but beneath the surface lie some significant comments on American principles of individual freedom.

Oₙₑ of the unsung but really great individualists who helped to make the United States a better and a safer place to live in was Joseph Palmer of Fitchburg

"The Beard of Joseph Palmer" by Stewart H. Holbrook. Reprinted from *The American Scholar,* Volume 13, Number 4, Autumn, 1944. Copyright © 1944 by the United Chapters of Phi Beta Kappa. By permission of the publishers.

and Harvard, Massachusetts, a man to be reckoned with in any discussion of the Bill of Rights. He is forgotten now, and this is bad forgetting, for Palmer was of a race of men that is now all but extinct. And his story, I think, is as heart-warming as it is improbable.

Palmer came to national attention because he was the victim of one of the strangest persecutions in history. Neither race nor religion played a part in Palmer's case, which with some reason might otherwise be termed *l'affaire Dreyfus* [1] of Fitchburg. It was brought about by the fact that Joe Palmer liked to wear a beard, one of the most magnificent growths ever seen in New England or, for that matter, in the United States; and what made this beard particularly heinous was that it was almost, if not

[1] *l'affaire Dreyfus* (là'fâr' drā'fŭs): "The Dreyfus Affair." Alfred Dreyfus was a French army officer who, in 1895, was unjustly convicted of treason and imprisoned. It was claimed that some of the army and court officials were prejudiced against Dreyfus because of his Jewish religion. When the French government failed to take action, the case attracted international attention, with protests pouring in from many countries. Finally, after some five years' delay and a change of government, Dreyfus was released and declared innocent.

quite, the only beard east of the Rocky Mountains, and possibly beyond.

One lone set of whiskers amid millions of smooth-shaven faces is something to contemplate, and Palmer paid dearly for his eccentricity. Indeed, one might say, with but little stretch of imagination and metaphor, that it was Joe Palmer who carried the Knowledge of Whiskers through the dark ages of beardless America. He was born almost a century too late and seventy-five years too soon to wear whiskers with impunity. He was forty-two years old in 1830, when he moved from his nearby farm into the hustling village of Fitchburg. He came of sturdy old Yankee stock. His father had served in the Revolution, and Joe himself had carried a musket in 1812. He was married and had one son, Thomas.

When the beard first made its appearance isn't of record, but Joe was wearing it when he came to Fitchburg, and here, because of it, he immediately became the butt of cruel jokes and derision and, in time, the victim of downright persecution. But before relating the violence caused by Palmer's famous beard, it is imperative — if one is to comprehend the proceedings at all — to trace briefly the history of whiskers in America up to the time of the Palmer beard.

This continent was explored by men of many nationalities, almost all of them wearing whiskers. About Columbus and Amerigo Vespucci we are uncertain, since there are no authenticated contemporary portraits of them. But after them came a host of beards. Cortes, Ponce de León, Cartier, Champlain, Drake, Raleigh, Captain John Smith, De Soto — all sported whiskers of varying length and style. Little wonder the Indians thought them gods.

Then came the Pilgrims and the Puritans, bearded almost to a man when they arrived at The Rock and elsewhere. But the beards of the first settlers didn't last. American whiskers were reduced gradually in size until they were scarcely more than mild goatees, and soon disappeared entirely. By 1720 at the latest, American colonists were wholly free of facial hair. Try to find a Copley [1] portrait, or a Ralph Earle [1] with a whisker in it. And the fighting men of the Revolution were beardless. Not a mustache or a suspicion of a mutton chop appeared on the faces of Washington, Gates, Greene, Knox. Even old John Stark and Israel Putnam were smooth-shaven, and so was the backwoods general Ethan Allen. It was the same with the other Patriots, and with the British also — Cornwallis, the Howes, Burgoyne. No signer of the Declaration had either beard or mustache.

And so it continued down the years. No President before Lincoln had any hair on his face. Until 1858 the cartoonists' conception of their own creature, Uncle Sam — otherwise much as he is today — was of a tall and lanky but smooth-shaven man. America did not really go hairy until the War Between the States was well under way.

Thus, when Joe Palmer came to town wearing a beard in 1830, whiskers had been virtually nonexistent for at least a hundred years. In spite of his hirsute [2] oddity, Palmer was an honest, kindly man and a good citizen, deeply religious but tolerant, and a man of many intellectual interests. He was also quite immovable when it came to principles, which in his case included the right to wear a full, flowing beard.

Everywhere he went, small boys threw stones and shouted at him and made life miserable for his son, Tom. Women sniffed and crossed to the other side of the street when they saw him coming. Often the windows of his modest home were broken by unknown rowdies. Grown men jeered at him openly. The Reverend George Trask, local pastor,

---

[1] **John Singleton Copley** (1738–1815) and **Ralph Earle** (1751–1801) were famous American portrait painters of the late eighteenth century.

[2] **hirsute** (hûr′sūt): shaggy.

took him to task for his eccentricity, but Joe replied with exact Scriptural reasons — nay, commands — for beard-wearing. Old Doctor Williams told Joe to his face that he should "be prosecuted for wearing such a monstrosity." And when Joe went to Boston to attend literary and reform meetings, huge crowds "followed him the length of Tremont Street, jeering." He was present at the celebrated Chardon Street Convention [1] in 1840, and one has no difficulty locating him in Emerson's comment on that gathering:

If the assembly was disorderly, it was picturesque. Madmen, madwomen, men with beards, Dunkers, Muggletonians, Come-outers, Groaners, Agrarians, Seventh-Day Baptists, Quakers, Abolitionists, Calvinists, Unitarians, and Philosophers — all came successively to the top, and seized their moment, if not their hour, wherein to chide, or pray, or preach, or protest.

By the time of this convention, Joe Palmer was a national character, made so by two events that had happened in quick succession in his home town of Fitchburg. In spite of the snubs of the congregation, Joe never missed a church service, but one Sunday he quite justifiably lost his usually serene temper. It was a Communion Sunday in 1830. Joe knelt with the rest, only to be publicly humiliated when the officiating clergyman ignored him, "passed him by with the communion bread and wine." Joe was cut to the quick. He rose up and strode to the communion table. He lifted the cup to his lips and took a mighty swig. Then: "I love my Jesus," he shouted in a voice loud with hurt and anger, "as well, and better, than any of you!" Then he went home.

A few days later, as he was coming out of the Fitchburg Hotel, he was seized by four men armed with shears, brush, soap,

[1] **Chardon Street Convention:** the meeting brought together various groups of religious and political reformers.

and razor. They told him that the sentiment of the town was that his beard should come off and they were going to do the job there and then. When Joe started to struggle, the four men threw him violently to the ground, seriously injuring his back and head. But Joe had just begun to fight. When they were about to apply the shears, he managed to get an old jackknife out of his pocket. He laid about him wildly, cutting two of his assailants in their legs, not seriously but sufficiently to discourage any barber work. When Joe stood up, hurt and bleeding, his gorgeous beard was intact.

Presently he was arrested, charged with "an unprovoked assault." Fined by Justice Brigham, he refused to pay. Matter of principle, he said. He was put in the city jail at Worcester, and there he remained for more than a year, part of the time in solitary confinement. Even here he had to fight for his whiskers, for once Jailor Bellows came with several men with the idea of removing the now-famous beard. Joe threw himself at them and fought so furiously that the mob retreated without a hair. He also successfully repulsed at least two attempts by prisoners to shave him.

In the jail Joe wrote letters which he smuggled out a window to his son, who took them to the Worcester *Spy*. They were published and soon were being widely copied by other newspapers. In his letters the bearded prisoner stated that he was in jail not for assault but because he chose to wear whiskers — which was unquestionably the case. He complained of the food, of the quarters, and of the lack of any religious life behind the bars. People all over Massachusetts read these letters. They began to talk, and even to reflect. It wasn't long before the sheriff came to realize that he had a Tartar [2] and possibly a martyr on his hands. He went to Joe and told him to run along home and forget it — the

[2] **Tartar (or Tatar):** a person from Tatary in Siberia; used in a general sense to indicate a captive who proves stronger than his captor.

fine and everything. No, said Joe. The jailor urged him to leave. His aged mother wrote him to come home. All in vain. Nothing could move the man who was now known as The Bearded Prisoner of Worcester.

Day after day he sat in his limbo, keeping an elaborate and pathetic journal of his persecutions. And time after time he told officers and worried magistrates that they had put him there, and they would have to take him out. "I won't walk one single step toward freedom!" he roared through the bars. Nor did he. He sat there in a chair like a whiskered Buddha until the desperate sheriff and jailors picked him up in his chair and carried him to the street.

Never again was violence attempted on Joe Palmer's beard, which by the time of his release, or rather his eviction, from jail, was a beard famous as far away as New York and Philadelphia. Free now, he soon became a minor figure in New England's intellectual ferment. A hater of slavery, he went to Boston often for the meetings of Parker and Garrison,[1] contributing both time and money to the movement for abolition. He met Emerson, Thoreau, Alcott, Channing, and these men found him an odd but staunch character, the possessor of much good sense. He loathed liquor as much as he did slavery, and was active at Temperance meetings. He visited the communities at Brook Farm and Hopedale.

When Bronson Alcott and family,[2] with Charles Lane and a few others, bought a farm in Harvard, near Fitchburg, named it Fruitlands, and attempted to found the Con-Sociate Family, Joe Palmer was vastly interested. He donated a lot of fine old furniture and up-to-date

farm implements to the colony. When he saw that Alcott's idiotic ideas about farming were going to bring famine to the group, he brought his own team and plow and turned up the soil. He was, in fact, the only sensible male in that wondrous experiment. (Joe Palmer appears in Louisa May Alcott's *Transcendental Wild Oats* as Moses White.)

Fruitlands had the distinction of being the worst-managed and shortest-lived of all American colonies. When the half-starved Alcotts and the others had moved away, Joe Palmer bought the farm and moved there with his wife and family. Here, for more than twenty years, he carried on a strange sort of community life of his own devising. He was widely known now and never lacked for company. Emerson and Thoreau visited him, and so did every reformer who passed through or operated in New England. The merely curious came to see the famous beard. The Palmers always had a pot of beans on the stove, plenty of bread in the butt'ry.[3] All were welcome to come and to stay, so long as they had no trace of liquor about them.

In place of persecution, Joe now found himself something of a hero. The years crept on, and with them his great beard grew even more famously, spreading like a willow. A photograph taken at about this time shows a growth that makes Walt Whitman seem a beardless youth in comparison. And at last, many years before he died, the whiskers of all America came into their fullest glory. This second coming of the beard was sudden, an almost instantaneous wilderness of hair that covered the face of male America.

One cannot know with certainty the reason for this sudden era of whiskers; it can only be recorded. Lincoln, when elected, was smooth-shaven, but, when inaugurated, wore a beard. Grant, the lieutenant, had worn a tiny mustache;

[1] **Theodore Parker** (1810–1860) and **William Lloyd Garrison** (1805–1879) were leading figures in the movement for abolition of slavery.
[2] For more information on the Alcott family and the farming communities of Brook Farm and Fruitlands, see pages 539 and 567.

[3] butt'ry (or buttery): storeroom.

Grant, the general, had a full beard. Robert E. Lee went smooth of face to war, and was presently full-bearded. In 1860 Jeff Davis was clean of chin. He was soon wearing whiskers longer than Lincoln's. Nearly all of the generals of the War Between the States, on both sides, were peering out of whiskers by 1862, and so were their men. Stonewall Jackson grew a mighty beard. Custer grew a unique combination beard and mustache, but it was General Ambrose E. Burnside who gave his name to a special type of whiskers.

The baseball players of the sixties and seventies, as depicted by the careful Currier & Ives,[1] had whiskers. Bankers grew a style all their own. Razors went into the discard, and vendors of quack beard-growers swarmed into the new market. The proper gift to a male was an elegant mustache cup. Manufacturers of soap, patent medicines, and cough drops — notably cough drops — came out with one or more bearded faces on their labels. Whiskers, through some odd turn of the folkways,[2] now were a sign of solid worth, a badge of integrity in every line of endeavor. If the poor barbers thought the end of things had arrived, it is easy to understand why.

As for old Joe Palmer, he was immensely happy, a true prophet who had lived to see his justification. Few prophets have been so fortunate. All over America, Joe Palmer knew, were now full beards, Van Dykes, goatees, galways, dundrearys, mutton chops, burnsides, fringe beards, and millions of stupendous mustaches of the over-Niagara type. Aye, the prophet had come into his own. Yet Joe was no gloater. He seems to have remarked only once on the greatly changed styles of what men wore on their faces. That was when he met the same Reverend Trask who had

so churlishly upbraided him many years before for wearing his beard. Trask himself was now wearing a luxuriant growth. Meeting him on a Fitchburg street one day, Joe stroked his own beard and remarked: "Knowest thou that thy redeemer liveth?"

Joe Palmer died in 1875, when beards were at their fullest, and was thus spared the dreadful sight of their withering and final disappearance. What happened during the thirty-five years following Joe's death would certainly have saddened him.

The whisker debacle of the last quarter of the nineteenth century has engrossed only a few of us minor social historians, but Mr. Lewis Gannett has charted the decline so graphically that little more research needs to be done. He used his alma mater, Harvard University, to demonstrate the mysterious rises and falls of male American hair; and his studies show that graduating classes of the 1860's were hairy as goats. The Class of 1870 had four beards. Two years later a good majority were wearing not beards but mustaches and burnsides. By 1890 beards and burnsides (sideburns are the same thing, only there isn't quite so much to them) were distinctly obsolete, and the mustache was at or nearing its peak.

Decline now followed with tragic speed. The Class of 1900 was without one beard, the first such crowd of sissies since the Mexican War. The last Harvard football mustache appeared in 1901, Mr. Gannett's chart shows, and the last Harvard baseball mustache in 1905. Since then Harvard men — except for a few professors — have been mostly smooth of chin and lip.

The White House witnessed a similar decline of hair. From Lincoln to Wilson, only one man without at least a mustache was elected to the Presidency. Grant had a beard, Hayes was positively hairy. Garfield fairly burgeoned with whiskers. Cleveland had a sizable mustache, Harrison a flowing beard, and both Theodore

---

[1] **Currier & Ives:** an American printing firm noted for detailed and realistic lithographs of American scenes.
[2] **folkways:** customs.

Roosevelt and Taft had mustaches. The lone smooth-shaven President during this entire period was McKinley.

Beginning with Wilson in 1912 and continuing to the present, no President has worn hair on his face. Many thought it was his beard that defeated Hughes,[1] and his was for years the only honest beard to wag on the once heavily whiskered Supreme Court.

Old Joe Palmer, then, died at exactly the right time, and he took some pains to make certain, no matter what styles frivolous men might adopt, that he was not wholly forgotten. In the old cemetery in North Leominster, not far from Fitchburg, is his monument, a rugged square stone as tall as a man; and on its front is an excellent medallion carving of Joe's head, with its noble beard flowing and rippling in white marble. Below the head appears a simple legend: "Persecuted for Wearing the Beard."

Joe Palmer's last home, the celebrated Fruitlands in nearby Harvard, has been restored with loving care as an historical showplace by Clara Endicott Sears — not so much in memory of Palmer as of the Alcotts. In this charming house, however, one may see old Joe's beautiful furniture, and a good photograph of the kindly yet determined old gentleman who wished to be remembered only as the Redeemer of the Beard.

[1] **Hughes:** Charles Evans Hughes, Chief Justice of the Supreme Court, 1930–1941, and candidate for President in 1916.

FOR DISCUSSION

1. Why does the author say that Joseph Palmer was "a man to be reckoned with in any discussion of the Bill of Rights"?

2. Was Joseph Palmer's beard in itself the source of the disturbance? Is it possible that the beard was a mere circumstance — just a trigger of the trouble? If so, what really created the friction? What other things might lead to such incidents? Can you think of other examples in which what is merely *customary* becomes confused with what is *moral?*

3. What was the effect of Joe's letter-writing campaign while in prison? Why do you think the officials became so anxious to free him?

4. Stewart Holbrook has spoken elsewhere of "our own day, when the State everywhere crowds the Man, and the trend is toward regimentation . . ." Do you agree with this observation? Why? Why not? What relevance does this have to Joe Palmer's history?

5. Point out some of the devices of humor that occur in "The Beard of Joseph Palmer." How does the humorous tone contribute to the effectiveness of the essay?

YOUR OWN WRITING

Write a brief essay on eccentricity, using the story of Joe Palmer as a starting point, and adding any other examples that would help illustrate the subject. Begin by checking all the meanings of *eccentric* and *eccentricity* in a dictionary. Observe the roots of the word. Consider the following questions in your essay: How is eccentricity related to character? to individuality? Do you consider eccentricity a good or bad thing? Support your opinion with a thoughtful argument.

THE AUTHOR

STEWART H. HOLBROOK (b. 1893) is a native Vermonter who has lived for a long time in Oregon. He has made an important study of America's Westward Movement and the spread of New England influence in *Yankee Exodus* (1950). His early career was in the logging industry both in the East and in British Columbia. He knows the lumberjacks and logging camps intimately. Two of his many books, *Holy Old Mackinaw* (1938) and *Burning an Empire* (1943), are related to this field, the latter being a dramatic study of forest fires. Among his other works are *Ethan Allen* (1940), *Lost Men of American History* (1946), *The Story of American Railroads* (1947), and *The Age of the Moguls* (1953). His lively narratives and diligent research have made him a highly popular historian-biographer.

DOUGLAS SOUTHALL FREEMAN

Washington Attacks at Trenton

Here is a crucial episode in the career of George Washington, a historic battle that rallied the discouraged, sorely tried colonists to continue the struggle for independence.

RECONSTRUCTING A FAMOUS ACHIEVEMENT. People who read only for surprise, to see how things will come out, risk disappointment in the great American biographies, for they already know the outcome of the important events. Yet thoughtful readers treasure these books, for their great reward is not only finding out the bare facts but following the sequence of events, learning to know intimately the man whose life the book traces, and sharing his difficulties and achievements.

It is hard for us today, knowing so well that the Revolution succeeded, to feel the desperation and discouragement that hung like a pall over that Christmas day when Washington attacked Trenton. But forget for the moment that you know the outcome of the war. Accept the danger and the desperation of this battle. Follow Washington through the action, watching, planning, leading. Then the attack on

Trenton will no longer be just a fact in history books, but a triumph that you feel as keenly as if you had personally battled the icy river and felt the stinging sleet in your own face. Better still, you will know, as those early Americans did, the strength and courage and military leadership of George Washington.

EVERY ounce of courage in the heart of man was needed, because conditions grew worse as night went on. Blocks of ice began to float down the river, which was high and was flowing fast; soon, too, new ice began to form; the wind rose and made the handling of the long, light-draft "Durham" boats difficult even for their crews and for the trained seamen of Glover's Marblehead, Massachusetts, Regiment. The loading of eighteen field cannon on the narrow boats was slow, slow work. At midnight, when Washington had hoped that all his men and guns would be on the Jersey shore, the task was hours from completion. Not until 3 A.M. on the 26th was the last of the artillery pieces out of the boat and safely on Jersey soil, beyond the reach of ice. Another hour was required to put all the regiments at their stations within an arc that Adam Stephen's troops had formed around the landing place.

Four o'clock, nine miles of road to cover, sunrise about 7:23, and light by 7:10 even if the day was dark and tempestuous — in these circumstances Washington reasoned that the advantage of surprise would certainly be lost. He could not hope that the presence of 2,400 men, eighteen cannon, and a considerable number of horses would be unobserved by the Hessians [1] long enough for the columns to reach Trenton. Should the expedition, then, be abandoned? Must the troops be ordered back to the Pennsylvania shore? Washington asked himself the question, but he did not hesitate over the answer: His judgment told him that the loss of the element of surprise scarcely could be worse than the harassment and casualties involved in a retreat across the river in the presence of the enemy. The advance must be made, and the Hessians must be assailed the moment the town was reached.

In that spirit, the Army pressed on. At Birmingham, John Sullivan took about half the troops and cannon and started down the lower or River Road which followed, as its name suggested, the general course of the Delaware. Nathanael Greene, with a like force, filed off to the left and took the upper or Pennington Road.[2] Washington soon joined Greene. As closely as the commanding general could estimate it, the two columns now had nearly the same distance to march — between four and five miles — to the little town of Trenton. He consequently had all the officers set their watches by his, and he gave orders that when either column struck the Hessian outposts, it was to press forward immediately, without waiting to hear from the other column, and was to push into Trenton before the enemy had time to form a line of battle.

A light snow had covered the ground when the army left camp; the wind had risen during the crossing and was roaring angrily down from east northeast. Now, with the approach of dawn, snow began to descend again. With it was mingled sleet or rain that froze and glazed the road. A more difficult time for a march over an unfamiliar route could not have been devised by the devil himself; it was a night when the indifferent soldier would cover his head with his blanket, and the mercenary [3] would hug the fire. Strong and stern would be the discipline that would carry German patrols over roads on which an icy surface was deeper and more slippery every minute. . . .

The Pennington Road now was so heavily covered with sleet and frozen rain that the advance became a slow, treacherous slide and stagger. It was half an hour after daylight when Greene's van [4] was at a point the guides reckoned as one mile from the town. As the enemy's advanced guard was believed to be about half a mile from Trenton, on either road, Washington had now to halt and to prepare himself and his men for the execution within 800 yards, or thereabouts, of the first of the three phases of his plan. This simple design was based on the geographical position of Trenton and on the configuration of its few streets. The town was a poor place of about 100 houses, the greater part of them abandoned temporarily by their owners, and it was located at the point where the Delaware makes a minor turn from southeast to south. Across the lower edge of the town, the Assunpink Creek flowed into the river from the northeast. The depth of the water in this creek varied from time to time and from one part of the stream to

---

[1] **Hessians** (hĕsh'ănz): German soldiers hired by King George III to fight for the British.

[2] See map, page 221, for the movement of both columns.

[3] **mercenary** (mûr'sĕ·nĕr'ĭ): a soldier serving a foreign country for pay.

[4] **van**: the leading unit in a military formation.

another; but, in general, the creek was not safely to be crossed except at the bridge. North from the bridge, Queen Street ran for approximately half a mile to the angle of the road that came down from Pennington, which was to the northwest. King Street, the other principal driveway of the village, was west of Queen, was parallel to it, and had its northern terminus at the same place, the mouth of the Pennington Road. Washington knew that if he could reach and hold the head of these streets, he could sweep [1] them and probably could drive the enemy from them. If, simultaneously, he could seize the bridge across Assunpink, he might be able to trap the Hessians within the half-mile space between the bridge and the Pennington Road. Then a strong thrust from the west, perpendicular to the two streets, might throw the enemy back to the creek. Thus were the strokes to be one, two, three, and as close together as they could be delivered.

Nothing had been heard of General Ewing, who was to cross directly opposite Trenton and was to seize the Assunpink bridge from its southern end; but there was good news and bad from Sullivan's column. It was good in that it brought assurance Sullivan was moving on steadily and without opposition; it was bad in that the New Hampshire general reported his men's muskets wet and unfit for service. Washington's answer was that Sullivan must "advance and charge." The General himself pushed on in Greene's van, through the unrelenting storm, with the men at a "long trot," and about 8 o'clock he left the woods on the Pennington Road at a point about half a mile from the village. Ahead was a cooper's [2] shop which, guides said, the Germans were using as an advanced picket [3] post. In a few

[1] **sweep:** cover with artillery fire.
[2] **cooper:** a maker or repairer of barrels or casks.
[3] **picket:** a guard or sentry.

The plan of the attack: General Washington planned to deliver three successive blows on the town (see arrows). The Hessians would be driven from Trenton and their retreat cut off by the seizure of the bridge across the Assunpink. General Ewing's attack did not materialize.

DOUGLAS SOUTHALL FREEMAN   221

moments, the Americans were challenged; there were shouts and commands; almost a score of Hessians emerged from the building. The Continentals opened fire at once, though the range was overlong; the officer in charge of the post waited until Washington's men were closer. Then, at the word of command, the Germans delivered a volley which went wild in the roaring storm. Without making any pretense of further resistance at their advanced post, the pickets fell back to the eastward across the fields.

Three minutes after the first shot on the Pennington Road, there came from the south the welcome sound of musketry. Sullivan, on the River Road, evidently was as far advanced as Greene and, like him, was rushing the outpost. Even if there was not to be a complete surprise of the enemy, resolution, storm, and circumstance were giving Washington the closest approach to it. Except for the sentinels shot down by Captain Anderson's men during the night, not one German had been encountered on the Pennington Road till the guard at the cooper's shop had been flushed. As far as Washington could ascertain, Sullivan was having equally good fortune. Push forward, then, with all possible speed and in fullest strength; lose not a minute in hurrying the cannon to the head of King and Queen Streets.

As Washington moved down the Pennington Road, he observed something more of the Hessian pickets' withdrawal, and he did not underestimate the skill of it. They could offer slight opposition only, but "for their numbers," he said later, "they behaved very well, keeping up a constant retreating fire from behind houses." This fire of the retiring German outpost did not delay the advance. Half running, half sliding, the Americans continued toward the mouth of the Pennington Road. On closer approach, Washington could see the Germans forming to the right, ahead of

him, in the streets of the town and beyond to the eastward, but he could not ascertain what they were attempting to do. A few minutes more, and Washington was on high ground whence he could view almost the whole of Trenton. He stopped the "long trot" of the infantry and bade them form, in order to give more room to the artillerists of the two leading cannon who were straining to bring the pieces into position. Their comrades with the other advanced guns were scarcely behindhand. From the front of the Second Brigade of Greene's column, three other pieces were being dragged forward as rapidly as the way could be cleared for them. At a time so tense, every movement seemed clumsy and exasperatingly slow; but in reality, the well-drilled and enthusiastic artillerists lost few seconds. Their great moment had come. They knew it. Soon the "b-o-o-m" of the opening gun shook the heavy air. The second shot followed on the instant. Fire itself was triumph, regardless of target, because vigilance and resourcefulness had been required every minute in order to protect the touchholes of the cannon from the wet. The Americans had discovered how this could be done. Soon their round shot would be shrieking down King and Queen Streets.

Visibility was so low at times that Washington probably could see nothing of what was happening at the farther end of those streets, where Sullivan was attacking. It was impossible, as yet, to tell whether Ewing had crossed and now commanded the Assunpink bridge. Nearer at hand, directly west of the buildings that faced east on King Street, Hugh Mercer's men of Greene's command were closing in. Some of them were breaking into houses the enemy held; some were slipping through alleys and walkways and were directing their fire against Germans along the street and beyond it, in the direction of the creek. The Hessians soon undertook to answer the artillery fire by moving cannon into King Street; but these soldiers could be left to the attention of Knox's men and to the care of Stirling's troops, who were eager to dash forward and to take the guns. Washington must keep his eye on the larger moves and must ascertain, if he could, what those confused, though still powerful, mercenaries were going to attempt. For a few minutes it looked as if the enemy might make a bold charge up King Street, but this was broken up easily by the American artillery. Then, as far as Washington could discern, larger numbers of the Hessians gathered on the open ground east of the town and formed their line as if they were going to file off to the American left.

That was the direction of the road from Trenton to Princeton, the only avenue of retreat available to the Hessians if Sullivan or Ewing by this time had occupied the bridge across the Assunpink. Washington had deployed his left in front of a part of the Princeton Road as soon as he reached the head of the streets; he now sent Colonel Hand's veterans and the Philadelphia German Battalion to take position directly across the line of Hessian retreat toward Princeton. The two battalions moved out promptly and with the high spirits that all the Americans were displaying. As soon as the Continentals' bayonets barred the way, Washington thought he saw the Germans halt and then begin to shift again as if they knew it was futile to attempt a retreat up the Princeton Road. They stood now where the sleet from the northeast was flying in their faces, and they were exposing their left flank to a turning movement southward down King and Queen Streets in support of Mercer's men, who continued to fight their way eastward. Stirling's impatient troops were allowed to go forward. If Washington knew at the moment which regiment was in front of the brigade, he doubtless had pride in the fact that the command was the Third Virginia and that the leading

company, the one that undertook to capture the German cannon in King Street, was under a captain of his own surname, William Washington, and a lieutenant, James Monroe, from his native Westmoreland County.

When these Virginians took the German guns and cleared the upper end of King Street, Washington could close the trap on the Germans north of Assunpink Creek, because they were in this desperate plight: their front was blocked; at their back were the cold, deep waters of the creek, which ran, on this stretch, as if it had been set by nature as a snare for molesters. Besides Stirling and Mercer on the enemy's left, Capt. Thomas Forrest was in an advanced position with six guns and was preparing to open fire at shorter range. Washington saw the trap shut. Perhaps, too, he observed an American officer ride out to a parley with the German commanders. Then, presently, up the street spurred a young soldier who drew rein and cried rapturously that German regiments in the field had surrendered.

How numerous they were, Washington did not know; but something the officer said, or else the sound of firing from the vicinity of the bridge led him to believe that Sullivan's column still was fighting. So, wasting neither time nor words, Washington started down King Street, astride his horse, to see for himself what was happening. About halfway to the bridge he came upon some Germans who were assisting a badly wounded officer into a church. Inquiry doubtless brought the explanation that this was Col. Johann Rall, senior officer in the town. At the very moment that the humiliated and suffering Hessian commander was being led away, a prisoner of war, a young American major came up the street as fast as his horse would venture on so slippery a roadway. He was James Wilkinson, who . . . carried the best of news: another Hessian regiment, the last in the town, had grounded arms. Washington's face shone with satisfaction as he listened. He extended his hand in thanks. "Major Wilkinson," he said, "this is a glorious day for our country."

It was victory! In the most desperate hour of the life of the army, less than a week from its virtual disbandment, the Continentals had won their greatest success. Ewing had not been able to cross at Trenton ferry because of the ice; at that hour, nothing had been heard from Cadwalader. The troops who had operated under Washington, and they alone, had defeated a force that consisted, prisoners said, of three German regiments. . . . How the Hessians had permitted themselves to be surprised, nobody was able as yet to explain, otherwise than by saying that wind and rain and sleet had drowned all sounds of firing at the picket posts; but however that might be, American losses had been negligible. Both the young officers, Capt. William Washington and Lieut. James Monroe, had been wounded in leading the charge on the cannon in King Street; one or two privates likewise had been hit, though not fatally so. In the whole engagement from first contact at 8 A.M. to final surrender before 10 o'clock, not one American life had been lost.

FOR DISCUSSION

1. Why was the weather both an enemy and an ally in this operation? Recall specific hardships it imposed on the Americans. What early result of the bad weather seemed to threaten the success of the attack? Why did this threat fail to affect the outcome?

2. Why was this a great victory in terms of casualties and prisoners? What was the even greater strategic importance of the victory?

3. Imagine the effect of the news of this battle on the morale of the colonists. How do you think such news was spread in Washington's day?

FOLLOWING WASHINGTON'S STRATEGY

1. Referring to the map on page 221, describe the military strategy of this battle. Review the plan of the attack, explaining the part each column was assigned in the battle. What movement of the enemy seemed to promise escape? How did Washington meet it?

2. Cite evidence that Washington not only planned his attack carefully but kept up with each development with equal care.

YOUR OWN WRITING

Consider whether the author reveals Washington by telling: (a) what Washington did; (b) what Washington said; (c) what others said about him. Now write a paragraph on the character of Washington as it is revealed by this biographer.

THE AUTHOR

DOUGLAS SOUTHALL FREEMAN (1886–1953) is ranked among the great American biographers for his masterly studies of two fellow Virginians, George Washington and Robert E. Lee. For *Robert E. Lee* he was awarded a Pulitzer prize in 1935.

He won distinction in other fields as well. Although he excelled in formal scholarship — he received his Ph.D. degree from Johns Hopkins University — he chose journalism for his principal career and for thirty-four years was editor of the Richmond *News Leader*. By strictly scheduling his time, he also managed to make daily radio broadcasts, hold a visiting professorship of journalism at Columbia, deliver special lectures at the Army War College, and serve as advisory editor of many historical projects and for institutions as varied as the Library of Congress and the Boy Scouts. Besides his five volumes on Washington and four on Lee, he also wrote the three-volume *Lee's Lieutenants*.

American Art and Artists ➤

Reproduced on the facing page is an oil painting of George Washington by the American artist Thomas Sully (1783–1872).

CARL SANDBURG

Lincoln Speaks at Gettysburg

Here Carl Sandburg, Lincoln's biographer, takes you through the harried days when the President was pondering the speech he was to give at Gettysburg, and describes the day he delivered it.

UNDERSTANDING THE CHARACTER BEHIND THE DEED. In a great biography like Sandburg's *Lincoln,* the printed page carries not merely the events in a man's life but the living spirit of the man himself, as real as flesh and blood. The writer "gets inside his subject" and manages to take his reader with him, so that the thoughts and feelings and motives of the man are as clear as his recorded words and deeds. You can share Sandburg's intimate knowledge of Lincoln if you are sensitive to the details the writer weaves into his narrative.

A PRINTED invitation notified Lincoln that on Thursday, November 19, 1863, exercises would be held for the dedication of a National Soldiers' Ceme-

tery at Gettysburg. The commission of Pennsylvanians had organized a corporation through which Maine, New Hampshire, Vermont, Massachusetts, Rhode Island, Maryland, Connecticut, New York, New Jersey, Pennsylvania, Delaware, West Virginia, Ohio, Indiana, Illinois, Michigan, Wisconsin, and Minnesota were to share the cost of a decent burying ground for the dust and bones of the Union and Confederate dead.

In the helpless onrush of the war, it was known, too many of the fallen had lain as neglected cadavers rotting in the open fields or thrust into so shallow a resting place that a common farm plow caught in their bones. Now, by order of Governor Curtin of Pennsylvania, seventeen acres had been purchased on Cemetery Hill, where the Union center stood its colors on the second and third of July, and plots of soil had been allotted each state for its graves.

The duties of orator of the day had fallen on Edward Everett. Born in 1794, he had been United States Senator, Governor of Massachusetts, member of Congress, Secretary of State under Fillmore, minister to Great Britain, Phi

Beta Kappa poet at Harvard, professor of Greek at Harvard, president of Harvard.

The Union of States was a holy concept to Everett, and the slavery issue secondary, though when president of Harvard from 1846 to 1849, he refused to draw the color line, saying in the case of a Negro applicant, Beverley Williams, that admission to Harvard College depended on examinations. "If this boy passes the examinations, he will be admitted; and if the white students choose to withdraw, all the income of the college will be devoted to his education." Not often was he so provocative. Suave, handsomely venerable in his sixty-ninth year, Everett was a natural choice of the Pennsylvania commissioners. He notified them that he would appear for the Gettysburg dedication November 19.

Lincoln meanwhile, in reply to the printed invitation, sent word to the commissioners that he would be present at the ceremonies. The commissioners then considered whether the President should be asked to deliver an address. Clark E. Carr of Galesburg, Illinois, representing his state on the Board of Commissioners, noted that the decision of the board to invite Lincoln to speak was "an afterthought."

David Wills of Gettysburg, as the special agent for Governor Curtin and also acting for the several states, by letter informed Lincoln, " . . . I am authorized by the Governors of the various States to invite you to be present and participate in these ceremonies . . . It is the desire that after the oration, you, as Chief Executive of the nation, formally set apart these grounds to their sacred use by a few appropriate remarks." "The invitation," wrote Carr, "was not settled upon and sent to Mr. Lincoln until the second of November, more than six weeks after Mr. Everett had been invited to speak, and but little more than two weeks before the exercises were held."

Lamon [1] noted that Lincoln wrote part of his intended Gettysburg address at Washington, covered a sheet of foolscap [2] paper with a memorandum of it, and before taking it out of his hat and reading it to Lamon, he said that it was not at all satisfactory to him. He had been too busy to give it the time he would like to.

Various definite motives besides vague intuitions may have guided Lincoln in his decision to attend and speak even though half his cabinet had sent formal declinations in response to the printed-circular invitations they had all received. Though the Gettysburg dedication was to be under interstate auspices, it had tremendous national significance for Lincoln because on the platform would be the state governors whose co-operation with him was of vast importance. Also a slander and a libel had been widely mouthed and printed that on his visit to the battlefield of Antietam nearly a year before, he had laughed obscenely at his own funny stories and called on Lamon to sing a cheap comic song. Perhaps he might go to Gettysburg and let it be seen how he demeaned himself on a somber landscape of sacrifice.

His personal touch with Gettysburg, by telegraph, mail, courier, and by a throng of associations, made it a place of great realities to him. Just after the battle there, a woman had come to his office, the doorman saying she had been "crying and taking on" for several days trying to see the President. Her husband and three sons were in the army. On part of her husband's pay she had lived for a time, till money from him stopped coming. She was hard put to scrape a living and needed one of her boys to help.

[1] **Lamon:** Ward H. Lamon, a former law partner of Lincoln, who served during these years as the President's personal guard. He later collaborated with a friend to write a biography of Lincoln.

[2] **foolscap:** paper in sheets measuring about 13 by 17 inches.

The President listened to her, standing at a fireplace, hands behind him, head bowed, motionless. The woman finished her plea for one of her three sons in the army. He spoke. Slowly and almost as if talking to himself alone, the words came and only those words:

"I have two, and you have none."

He crossed the room, wrote an order for the military discharge of one of her sons. On a special sheet of paper he wrote full and detailed instructions where to go and what to say in order to get her boy back.

In a few days the doorman told the President that the same woman was again on hand, crying and taking on. "Let her in," was the word. She had found doors opening to her and officials ready to help on seeing the President's written words she carried. She had located her boy, camp, regiment, company. She had found him, yes, wounded at Gettysburg, dying in a hospital, and had followed him to the grave. And, she begged, would the President now give her the next of her boys?

As before he stood at the fireplace, hands behind him, head bent low, motionless. Slowly and almost as if talking to himself alone, the words came and as before only those words:

"I have two, and you have none."

He crossed the room to his desk and began writing. As though nothing else was to do, she followed, stood by his chair as he wrote, put her hand on the President's head, smoothed his thick and disorderly hair with motherly fingers. He signed an order giving her the next of her boys, stood up, put the priceless paper in her hands as he choked out the one word, "There!" and with long, quick steps was gone from the room with her sobs and cries of thanks in his ears.

Thus the Kentuckian, James Speed, gathered the incident and told it. By many strange ways Gettysburg was to Lincoln a fact in crimson mist.

When Lincoln boarded the train for Gettysburg on November 18, his best chum in the world, Tad,[1] lay sick abed, and the doctors were not sure what ailed him. The mother still remembered Willie [2] and was hysterical about Tad. But the President felt imperative duty called him to Gettysburg.

Provost Marshal General James B. Fry as a War Department escort came to the White House, but the President was late in getting into the carriage for the drive to the station. They had no time to lose, Fry remarked. Lincoln said he felt like an Illinois man who was going to be hanged, and as the man passed along the road on the way to the gallows, the crowds kept pushing into the way and blocking passage. The condemned man at last called out, "Boys, you needn't be in such a hurry to get ahead; there won't be any fun till I get there."

Flags and red-white-and-blue bunting decorated the four-car special train. Aboard were the three cabinet members, Nicolay and Hay,[3] army and navy representatives, newspapermen, the French and Italian ministers and attachés. The rear third of the last coach had a drawing room, where from time to time the President talked with nearly everyone aboard as they came and went. Approaching Hanover Junction, he arose and said, "Gentlemen, this is all very pleasant, but the people will expect me to say something to them tomorrow, and I must give the matter some thought." He then returned to the rear room of the car.

At sundown the train pulled into Gettysburg and Lincoln was driven to the Wills residence. A sleepy little country town of 3,500 was overflowing with human pulses again. Private homes were filled with notables and nondescripts. Hundreds slept on the floors of hotels. Military bands blared till late in the

[1] **Tad:** Lincoln's youngest son.
[2] **Willie:** another of Lincoln's sons, who had died in 1862.
[3] **Nicolay and Hay:** John Nicolay and John Hay, Lincoln's private secretaries. Hay later became Secretary of State.

night serenading whomsoever. The weather was mild and the moon up for those who chose to go a-roaming. When serenaders called on the President for the speech, he made again one of those little addresses saying there was nothing to say. "In my position it is sometimes important that I should not say foolish things. [A voice: 'If you can help it.'] It very often happens that the only way to help it is to say nothing at all. Believing that is my present condition this evening, I must beg of you to excuse me from addressing you further."

At dinner in the Wills home that evening, Lincoln met Edward Everett, Governor Curtin, and others. About eleven o'clock, he gathered his sheets of paper and went next door for a half hour with his Secretary of State. Whether Seward made slight or material alterations in the text on the sheets was known only to Lincoln and Seward. It was midnight or later that Lincoln went to sleep. He slept better for having a telegram from Stanton reporting there was no real war news and "On inquiry Mrs. Lincoln informs me that your son is better this evening."

Fifteen thousand, some said thirty thousand or fifty thousand, people were on Cemetery Hill for the exercises next day when the procession from Gettysburg arrived afoot and horseback, members of the United States Government, the army and navy, governors of states, mayors of cities, a regiment of troops, hospital corps, telegraph-company representatives, Knights Templar, Masonic Fraternity, Odd Fellows, and other benevolent associations, the press, fire departments, citizens of Pennsylvania and other states. At ten o'clock, Lincoln, in a black suit, high silk hat, and white gloves, came out of the Wills residence, mounted a horse, and held a reception on horseback. At eleven the parade began to move. Clark E. Carr, just behind the President, believed he noticed that the President sat erect and looked majestic to begin with and then got to

Four score and seven years ago our fathers brought forth on this continent, a new nation, conceived in liberty, and dedicated to the proposition that all men are created equal.

Now we are engaged in a great civil war; testing whether that nation, or any nation so conceived and so dedicated, can long endure. We are met on a great battlefield of that war. We have come to dedicate a portion of that field, as a final resting place for those who here gave their lives that that nation might live. It is altogether fitting and proper that we should do this.

But, in a larger sense, we can not dedicate — we can not consecrate — we can not hallow — this ground. The brave men, living and dead, who struggled here, have consecrated it, far above our poor power to add: or detract. The world will little note, nor long remember what we say here, but it can never forget what they did here. It is for us the living, rather, to be dedicated here to the unfinished work which they who fought here have thus far so nobly advanced. It is rather for us to be here dedicated to the great task remaining before us.

A portion of the Gettysburg Address in Lincoln's own handwriting.

thinking so that his body leaned forward, his arms hung limp, and his head bent far down.

A long telegram from Stanton at ten o'clock had been handed him. Burnside seemed safe though threatened at Knoxville, Grant was starting a big battle at Chattanooga, and "Mrs. Lincoln reports your son's health as a great deal better and he will be out today."

The march began. "Mr. Lincoln was mounted upon a young and beautiful chestnut horse, the largest in the Cumberland Valley," wrote Lieutenant Cochrane. This seemed the first occasion that anyone had looked at the President mounted with a feeling that just the right horse had been picked to match his physical length.

The march was over in fifteen minutes. But Mr. Everett, the orator of the day, had not arrived. Bands played till noon. Mr. Everett arrived.

The United States House chaplain, the Reverend Thomas H. Stockton, offered a prayer while the thousands stood with uncovered heads. Benjamin B. French, officer in charge of buildings in Washington, introduced the Honorable Edward Everett, orator of the day, who rose, bowed low to Lincoln, saying, "Mr. President." Lincoln responded, "Mr. Everett."

The orator of the day then stood in silence before a crowd that stretched to limits that would test his voice. Beyond and around were the wheat fields, the meadows, the peach orchards, long slopes of land, and five and seven miles farther the contemplative blue ridge of a low mountain range. His eyes could sweep all this as he faced the audience. He had taken note of it in his prepared address. "Overlooking these broad fields now reposing from the labors of the waning year, the mighty Alleghenies dimly towering before us, the graves of our brethren beneath our feet, it is with hesitation that I raise my poor voice to break the eloquent silence of God and Nature. . . . As my eye ranges over the fields whose sods were so lately moistened by the blood of gallant and loyal men, I feel, as never before, how truly it was said of old that it is sweet and becoming to die for one's country."

He gave an outline of how the war began, traversed decisive features of the three days' battles at Gettysburg, discussed the doctrine of state sovereignty and denounced it, drew parallels from European history, and came to his peroration quoting Pericles on dead patriots: "The whole earth is the sepulcher of illustrious men." He had spoken for one hour and fifty-seven minutes, some said a trifle over two hours, repeating almost word for word an address that occupied nearly two newspaper pages.

Everett came to his closing sentence without a faltering voice: "Down to the latest period of recorded time, in the glorious annals of our common country, there will be no brighter page than that which relates THE BATTLES OF GETTYSBURG." It was the effort of his life and embodied the perfections of the school of oratory in which he had spent his career. His poise, and chiefly some quality of inside goodheartedness, held most of his audience to him, though the people in the front rows had taken their seats three hours before his oration closed.

The Baltimore Glee Club sang an ode written for the occasion by Benjamin B. French, who had introduced Everett to the audience. The poets Longfellow, Bryant, Whittier, Lowell, George Boker had been requested, but none found time to respond with a piece to be set to music. The two closing verses of the ode by French immediately preceded the introduction of the President to the audience.

Having read Everett's address, Lincoln knew when the moment drew near for him to speak. He took out his own manuscript from a coat pocket, put on his steel-bowed glasses, stirred in his chair, looked over the manuscript, and put it back in his pocket. The Baltimore Glee Club finished singing the ode by French. Ward Hill Lamon introduced the President of the United States. He rose, and, holding in one hand the two sheets of paper at which he occasionally glanced, delivered the address in his high-pitched and clear-carrying voice. The Cincinnati *Commercial* reporter wrote: "The President rises slowly, draws from his pocket a paper, and, when commotion subsides, in a sharp, unmusical treble voice, reads the brief and pithy remarks." Hay wrote in his diary: "The President, in a firm, free way, with more grace than is his wont, said his half-dozen words of consecration." Charles Hale of the Boston *Advertiser*, also officially representing Governor Andrew of Massachusetts, had notebook and pencil in hand, took down the slow-spoken words of the President, as follows: [1]

Fourscore and seven years ago, our fathers brought forth upon this continent a new nation, conceived in liberty and dedicated to the proposition that all men are created equal.

Now we are engaged in a great civil war, testing whether that nation — or any nation, so conceived and so dedicated — can long endure.

We are met on a great battlefield of that war. We are met to dedicate a portion of it as the final resting place of those who have given their lives that that nation might live.

It is altogether fitting and proper that we should do this.

But, in a larger sense, we cannot dedicate, we cannot consecrate, we cannot hallow this ground. The brave men, living and dead, who struggled here, have consecrated it, far above our power to add or detract.

The world will very little note nor long remember what we say here; but it can never forget what they did here.

It is for us, the living, rather, to be dedicated, here, to the unfinished work that they have thus far so nobly carried on. It is rather for us to be here dedicated to the great task remaining before us; that from these honored dead we take increased devotion to that cause for which they here gave the last full measure of devotion; that we here highly resolve that these dead shall not have died in vain; that the nation shall, under God, have a new birth of freedom, and that government of the people, by the people, for the people, shall not perish from the earth.

In the written copy of his speech from which he read, Lincoln used the phrase "our poor power." In other copies of the speech which he wrote out later, he

[1] The speech as here recorded has some slight variations in wording from the standard version, which appears on page 666.

again used the phrase "our poor power." So it was evident that he meant to use the word "poor" when speaking to his audience, but he omitted it. Also in the copy held in his hands while facing the audience, he had not written the words "under God," though he did speak those words and include them in later copies which he wrote. Therefore, the words "under God" were decided upon after he wrote the text the night before at the Wills residence.

The New York *Tribune* and many other newspapers indicated "[Applause]" at five places in the address and "[Long, continued applause]" at the end. The applause, however, according to most of the responsible witnesses, was formal and perfunctory, a tribute to the occasion. Ten sentences had been spoken in less than three minutes.

A photographer had made ready to record a great historic moment, had bustled about with his dry plates, his black box on a tripod, and before he had his head under the hood for an exposure, the President had said "by the people, for the people" and the nick of time was past for a photograph.

The New York *Tribune* man and other like observers merely reported the words of the address, with the one preceding sentence: "The dedicatory remarks were then delivered by the President." These reporters felt no urge to inform their readers about how Lincoln stood; what he did with his hands; how he moved, vocalized; or whether he emphasized or subdued any parts of the address. Strictly, no address as such was on the program for him. He was down for just a few "dedicatory remarks." Lamon wrote that Lincoln told him just after delivering the speech that he had regret over not having prepared it with greater care. "Lamon, that speech won't *scour*. It is a flat failure and the people are disappointed." On the farms where Lincoln grew up as a boy, when wet soil stuck to the moldboard of a plow, they said it didn't "scour."

The nearby *Patriot and Union* of Harrisburg took its fling: "The President succeeded on this occasion because he acted without sense and without constraint in a panorama that was gotten up more for the benefit of his party than for the glory of the nation and the honor of the dead. . . . We pass over the silly remarks of the President; for the credit of the nation, we are willing that the veil of oblivion shall be dropped over them and that they shall no more be repeated or thought of."

Everett's opinion was written to Lincoln the next day: "I should be glad if I could flatter myself that I came as near to the central idea of the occasion in two hours as you did in two minutes." Lincoln's immediate reply was: "In our respective parts yesterday, you could not have been excused to make a short address, nor I a long one. I am pleased to know that, in your judgment, the little I did say was not entirely a failure."

The ride to Washington took until midnight. Lincoln was weary, talked little, stretched out on one of the side seats in the drawing room, and had a wet towel laid across his eyes and forehead.

He had stood that day, the world's foremost spokesman of popular government, saying that democracy was yet worth fighting for. What he meant by "a new birth of freedom" for the nation could have a thousand interpretations. The taller riddles of democracy stood up out of the address. It had the dream touch of vast and furious events epitomized for any foreteller to read what was to come. His cadences sang the ancient song that where there is freedom, men have fought and sacrificed for it, and that freedom is worth men's dying for. For the first time since he became President, he had on a dramatic occasion declaimed, howsoever it might be read, Jefferson's proposition which had been a slogan of the Revolutionary War — "All men are created equal" — leaving no other inference than that he regarded the Negro slave as a man. His outwardly smooth sentences were inside of them gnarled and tough with the enigmas of the American experiment.

Back at Gettysburg the blue haze of the Cumberland Mountains had dimmed till it was a blur in a nocturne. The moon was up and fell with a bland, golden benevolence on the new-made graves of soldiers, on the sepulchers of old settlers, on the horse carcasses of which the onrush of war had not yet permitted removal. The New York *Herald* man walked amid them and ended the story he sent his paper: "The air, the trees, the graves are silent. Even the relic hunters are gone now. And the soldiers here never wake to the sound of reveille."

In many a country cottage over the land, a tall old clock in a quiet corner told time in a ticktock deliberation. Whether the orchard branches hung with pink-spray blossoms or icicles of sleet, whether the outside news was seedtime or harvest, rain or drought, births or deaths, the swing of the pendulum was right and left and right and left in a ticktock deliberation.

The face and dial of the clock had known the eyes of a boy who listened to its ticktock and learned to read its minute and hour hands. And the boy had seen years measured off by the swinging pendulum, and grown to man size, had gone away. And the people in the cottage knew that the clock would stand there and the boy never again come into the room and look at the clock with the query, "What is the time?"

In a row of graves, the unidentified boy would sleep long in the dedicated final resting place at Gettysburg. Why he had gone away and why he would never come back had roots in some mystery of flags and drums, of national fate in which individuals sink as in a deep sea, of men swallowed and vanished in a man-made storm of smoke and steel.

The mystery deepened and moved with ancient music and inviolable con-

A view of present-day Gettysburg. ▶

solation because a solemn Man of Authority had stood at the graves of the unidentified and spoken the words: "We cannot consecrate — we cannot hallow — this ground. The brave men, living and dead, who struggled here, have consecrated it far above our power to add or detract. . . . From these honored dead we take increased devotion to that cause for which they gave their last full measure of devotion."

To the backward and forward pendulum swing of a tall old clock in a quiet corner, they might read those cadenced words, while outside the windows the first flurry of snow blew across the orchard and down over the meadow, the beginnings of winter in a gunmetal gloaming to be later arched with a star-flung sky.

FOR DISCUSSION

1. Review the cares that rested heavily on Lincoln during this period of his life, as revealed by minor parts of this narrative.

2. What situations or incidents suggest that the Presidency was not considered to be as important in 1863 as it is today? Can you recall one occasion when Lincoln thought his presence would be important? How did he make his point?

3. Why does Sandburg report conflicting impressions of witnesses of this event? Which of the contemporary reactions to Lincoln's speech come nearest to the opinion commonly held today? Can you give examples of such contradictory reports on current events?

4. How much would you need to change Lincoln's remarks to make them fit the dedication of any American battlefield cemetery at any time?

5. Compare the style of Lincoln's address with that of Everett's. What did the exchange of notes after the occasion reveal about both men?

6. Point out some of the passages in Sandburg's narrative that reveal most clearly that the writer is a poet as well as a biographer.

UNDERSTANDING THE MAN

1. Cite actions or remarks of Lincoln's to illustrate the chief qualities of the man revealed in this narrative, such as *courtesy* in the exchange of notes with Everett.

2. What is added to your understanding of Lincoln by the story of the woman who had lost her son?

3. Did you notice any occasion when Lincoln seemed aware of purely political responsibilities? How did he respond to them?

4. Which do you think you will remember better a year from now, the circumstances that led up to Lincoln's Gettysburg Address, or Lincoln as a person? Why?

NOTING IMPORTANT DETAILS

Sandburg sketches the picture of Lincoln at Gettysburg so clearly that you should be able to recall without effort details of both sight and sound. Try it.

THE AUTHOR

CARL SANDBURG (b. 1878), a great poet, would have been famous solely for his prose writings. Born in Galesburg, Illinois, of Swedish immigrant parents, he left school at thirteen to work at a wide variety of jobs before volunteering for the Spanish-American War. On his return, he entered Lombard College, working to pay his way and also becoming editor of the literary magazine and captain of the basketball team. Other jobs followed before he settled down on the Chicago *Daily News*.

While on the *Daily News* he published books of poetry (see page 296) and the first two volumes of his great biography of Abraham Lincoln, subtitled *The Prairie Years*. His lifelong devotion to collecting information about Lincoln and his times gave magnificent depth to the background. In 1933 he retired from the *Daily News* to complete the final four volumes of the biography, *The War Years*, for which he was awarded the Pulitzer prize in history in 1940. His other prose works include the novel *Remembrance Rock*, the autobiographical *Always the Young Strangers*, and a one-volume abridgment of *Abraham Lincoln*.

SAMUEL ELIOT MORISON

John Paul Jones: The Battle off Flamborough Head

During the Revolutionary War John Paul Jones (1747–1792) became America's first naval hero. Late in the course of the war, he made a number of raids in English waters, hoping to cripple British shipping and prevent supplies from reaching the British forces in America. He commanded a French frigate, which he called the *Bonhomme Richard* in honor of Benjamin Franklin's *Poor Richard's Almanac.* The French, who were our allies in the war, had sent three ships to support Jones: the *Alliance,* the *Pallas,* and the *Vengeance.*

On the evening of September 23, 1779, off Flamborough Head on the North Sea coast of England, John Paul Jones came upon a large British supply convoy escorted chiefly by the frigate *Serapis,* commanded by Captain Richard Pearson. Unaided by his French allies, one of whom even fired upon the *Bonhomme Richard* in the midst of the fighting, and facing an enemy ship much stronger than his own, Jones nevertheless immediately engaged the *Serapis* in battle. The struggle that followed became one of the great naval battles of history and resulted in a decisive American victory.

"John Paul Jones: The Battle off Flamborough Head" from *John Paul Jones: A Sailor's Biography* by Samuel Eliot Morison. ©, 1959 by Samuel Eliot Morison. Reprinted by permission of Little, Brown & Co.

FOLLOWING DETAILS. One way to increase your enjoyment in reading history is to pay close attention to detail. Samuel Eliot Morison's account of this famous battle is precise and complete. In order fully to understand the events, be sure to follow carefully each new development of the action. The map and charts will help make clear the various maneuvers of the fighting ships. As you read, look for all the exact details that help bring out the color and excitement of this crucial historical event.

The Battle Begins

FLAMBOROUGH HEAD, off which the famous night action was fought, is a broad headline of chalk cliffs rising 450 feet above the sea, cut by deep gullies with tiny beaches at the foot, and honeycombed by numerous caves, which were favorite resorts of smugglers. The tide splits at the Head; half the flood, running from north to south, sweeps seaward off a sand bar called the Smithics; the other half, running between the Smithics and the shore, makes a great "boil" over a reef jutting out from the Head, known as the Flamborough Steel.

chains (or chainwales): devices to support the rigging of the sails.

coehorns: small bronze guns that fire light shells.

fluke: the part of the anchor that hooks in the ground.

fore, main truck, and mizzen: the masts of the ship.

forestay: a large rope used to support a mast.

General Chase: a signal to prepare for battle.

General Quarters: a signal for the men to take their battle stations.

pintle: a large pin supporting a rudder.

"Quarters": a plea for mercy indicating intention to surrender.

rake: sweep with gunfire.

royal yards: spars that support the royals, small sails on the topmost part of the mast.

shotted: loaded.

starboard: the side of a ship on the right of a person facing forward (toward the bow).

struck: lowered. At this time a ship indicated surrender by "striking its colors" (lowering its flag).

studding sails: small sails placed at the sides of the mainsails.

swivels: guns on rotating bases.

tacked: turned.

topgallant sheets: sails near the top of the mast.

transoms: heavy beams or timbers at the stern.

weather (port) quarter: the weather quarter is that part of the ship that faces the wind. The port is the side of a ship on the left of a person facing forward (toward the bow).

Just before low water, a strong inshore current sets northerly, and the ebb current outside the Smithics starts two hours later than the ebb inside. It is dangerous ground for a stranger; the ten-fathom line is about three miles off the Head. At Flamborough Head today, only a lighthouse and a few small cottages on the cliffs alter its 1779 profile, which was the last glimpse that over a hundred brave seamen had of the land to which they hoped to return. And *Bonhomme Richard* in her long career had never looked so beautiful as she did the last full day of her life, when the westering sun gilded her towering pyramid of sail and touched up the high lights on her elaborate quarter galleries and carving.

Captain Pearson was expecting Jones, since the bailiffs [1] of Scarborough had sent out a boat to warn him; but his primary duty was to protect the convoy. Ordering it to sail as close to shore as the merchant captains dared, he stood offshore to cover. Shortly after noon on the 23rd, the convoy, which so far had ignored Pearson's signals, sighted *Richard*, *Alliance*, and *Pallas* and promptly tacked inshore, "letting fly their topgallant sheets and firing guns" as an alarm signal and then turning north to seek refuge under the guns of Scarborough Castle. Light airs were blowing from the southwest. *Serapis* cracked on sail to get between her convoy and the enemy, and succeeded in so doing. "At one o'clock," wrote Pearson in his report, "we got sight of the Enemy's [2] ships from the masthead, and about four we made them plain from the Deck to be three large ships and a brig; upon which I made the *Countess of Scarborough* [3] signal to join me, she being in shore with the Convoy. . . . I then brought to, to let the *Countess of Scarborough* come up, and cleared ship for Action; at half past five she joined me, the Enemy's ships then bearing down upon us with light breeze at SSW; at six Tacked and laid our Head in shore, in order to keep our Ground the better between the Enemy's ships and the Convoy." Brave Pearson did not flinch from engaging an enemy that appeared to be double his strength; and the timid, uncertain maneuvering of the three smaller American ships made him the more brisk to offer battle.

Commodore Jones, who had always

---

[1] **bailiffs:** officials similar to town councilmen.

[2] The original capitalization and spelling in the battle reports have been retained.

[3] *Countess of Scarborough:* a British warship, commanded by Captain Thomas Piercy, which had joined the *Serapis* to help escort the convoy.

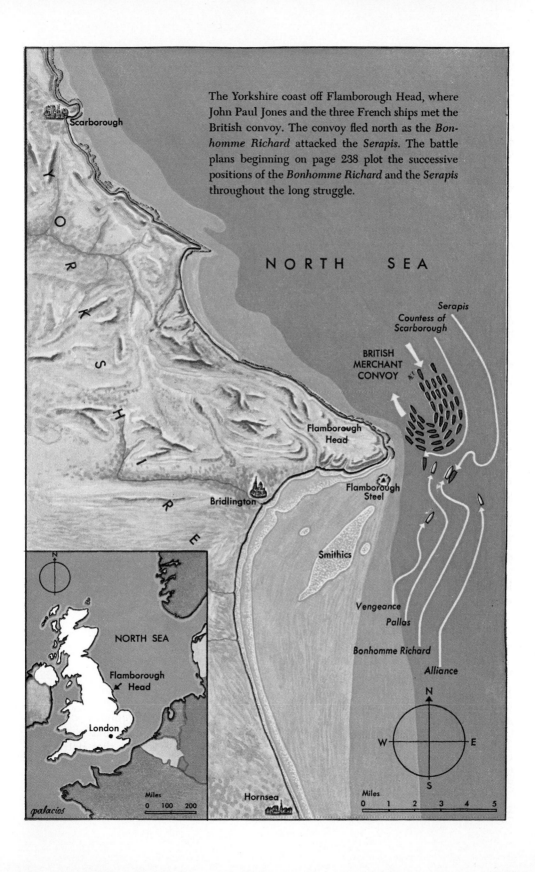

The Yorkshire coast off Flamborough Head, where John Paul Jones and the three French ships met the British convoy. The convoy fled north as the *Bonhomme Richard* attacked the *Serapis*. The battle plans beginning on page 238 plot the successive positions of the *Bonhomme Richard* and the *Serapis* throughout the long struggle.

NORTH SEA

Scarborough

YORKSHIRE

Serapis
Countess of Scarborough

BRITISH MERCHANT CONVOY

Flamborough Head

Flamborough Steel

Bridlington

Smithics

Vengeance
Pallas

Bonhomme Richard

Alliance

NORTH SEA

Flamborough Head

London

Miles
0   100   200

Hornsea

Miles
0   1   2   3   4   5

N
W — E
S

palacios

wanted to break up a Baltic convoy, knowing its importance for supplying the Royal Navy, made every effort to close; but the wind was so light that it took him three and a half hours to cover the ten or eleven miles between himself and *Serapis,* and he realized that he would have to take or sink the two escorts before he could get a crack at the convoy.

At 3:00 P.M. Jones sighted the enemy; at 3:30 *Richard* fired a gun (which Lieutenant Lunt [1] did not hear) to recall the pilot boat, hoisted the signal General Chase, crossed royal yards, and set all three royals. At 4:00 studding sails were set on both sides, and the gunners, seamen, and officers quietly took their assigned stations aloft, on deck and below. At 5:00 the marine drummers marched up and down beating the roll for General Quarters. At 6:00, just as the sun was setting, the Commodore made the agreed signal to "Form Line of Battle" — a blue flag at the fore, blue pendant at the main truck, and blue-and-yellow flag at the mizzen. Nobody paid any attention to it. *Alliance,* in the lead, prudently hauled her wind, leaving *Richard* alone to engage *Serapis; Pallas,* astern of *Richard,* sheered off, but later redeemed herself by engaging *Countess of Scarborough; Vengeance* simply sailed about, looking on.

By 6:30 *Richard* had hauled up her lower courses for better visibility and rounded to on the weather (port) quarter of *Serapis.* Presently the two ships were side by side on the port tack heading west, *Richard* to the southward and windward of *Serapis,* the wind then being southwest by south. Commodore Jones was on the quarterdeck; de Chamillard [2] with about twenty French marines on the poop; Lieutenant Dale

[1] **Lieutenant Lunt:** the American sailor in charge of the pilot boat, a small vessel used as a guide to help large ships maneuver in dangerous waters.
[2] **de Chamillard** (dē shȧ′mē′yȧr).

had charge of the gun deck and the main battery; Lieutenant Stack commanded twenty sailors and marines manning swivels and small arms in the main top; Midshipman Fanning commanded the foretop with fourteen men; and Midshipman Coram the smaller mizzen top with nine men. Midshipman Mayrant stood by the Commodore to act as his aide. The guns were shotted and ready; the gunners of the starboard battery, with lighted match in hand for each piece, were awaiting the word to fire. *Serapis* triced up her gunports, revealing two decks of guns and making a formidable appearance. In Midshipman Fanning's words, "Just as the moon was rising, the weather being clear, the surface of the great deep being perfectly smooth, even as in a millpond," and the two ships being within pistol shot, Captain Pearson hailed, "What ship is that?" Paul Jones, in order to get into close action, was flying British colors. Playing for time, he caused Master Stacey to reply, "The *Princess Royal!*" "Where from?" asked Pearson. The answer, whatever it may have been, was not heard on board *Serapis.* She hailed again, "Answer immediately, or I shall be under the necessity of firing into you." Jones struck his British colors, caused a big red-white-and-blue striped American ensign to be raised, and gave the word to fire his starboard broadside. *Serapis* fired hers almost simultaneously (Battle Plan No. 1). At the first or sec-

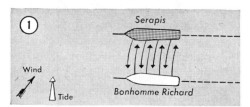

ond salvo, two of Jones's eighteen-pounders burst, killing many gunners and ruining the rest of that battery, as well as blowing up part of the deck above.

"The battle being thus begun," wrote

Jones in his narrative, "was Continued with Unremitting fury." Each captain strove to maneuver his ship across the other's bow or stern, in order to rake. *Serapis*, the faster by reason of her slippery bottom,[1] several times gained an advantageous position "in spite of my best Endeavours to prevent it," admitted Jones. After exchanging two or three broadsides, the Commodore estimated that a gun-to-gun duel would be fatal for him; he must attempt to board and grapple. He backed *Richard's* fore and main topsails, dropped astern on *Serapis'* port quarter, both ships firing furiously at a range of 80 to 100 feet, "filled again, put his helm a-weather" (to port), ran *Richard* up on *Serapis'* starboard quarter, and attempted to board (Plan No. 2). This was a very disadvantageous

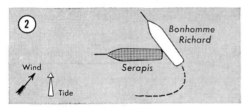

position from which to carry an enemy ship by boarding; it was like attempting an amphibious assault on so narrow a front that the enemy could concentrate his fire on a thin line of men. The English sailors repulsed the boarders, and Jones sheered off.

The next move was Pearson's, an attempt to cross *Richard's* bow to rake her (Plan No. 3); but *Serapis* had not enough

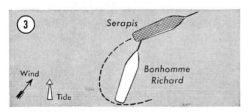

headway to make it; and Jones, following her movements, ran *Richard's* bow into her stern. It was at this juncture —

¹ The *Serapis* was copper-bottomed.

not near the close of the battle as has generally been stated — that Captain Pearson called out, "Has your ship struck?" and Paul Jones made the immortal reply:

"I have not yet begun to fight."

Nor had he. Unable to bring a single cannon to bear on *Serapis* from that position (Plan No. 3), *Richard* backed her topsails to get clear, *Serapis* wore briskly around "on her heel" from a northeasterly to a westerly heading, and *Richard* too pulled away and straightened out (Plan No. 4). *Serapis* being

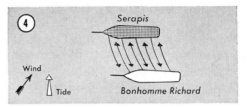

ahead, Pearson backed topsails to check headway and get broadside to *Richard* in order to bring his superior fire power to bear. Jones, divining his intent, ordered Master Stacey "to lay the enemy's ship on board." Taking advantage of a fresh puff of wind, which did not strike *Serapis* because *Richard's* sails blanketed hers, Jones ranged ahead, ordered helm a-weather (to port), and tried the same maneuver that Pearson had attempted on him. He laid *Richard* "athwart hawse" — as the cap of a T — in order to rake his enemy's decks (Plan No. 5).

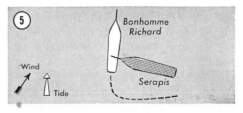

"It did not exactly succeed to my wishes," admitted Jones, because, owing to some of the yards' braces having been shot away, the people could not trim them properly and maneuver quickly enough to clear. The two ships collided, bow to stern; *Serapis* thrust her jib boom (tip end of the bowsprit) right into *Richard's* mizzen shrouds — the rigging that held up her after mast (Plan No. 5). The wind, acting on the sails of both ships, caused them to pivot (Plan No. 6)

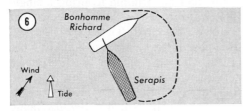

until they were on a north-south axis, bow to stern and stern to bow (Plan No. 7). A fluke of *Serapis'* starboard anchor

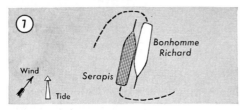

sealed this fatal marriage by hooking the bulwarks of *Richard's* starboard quarter, and the two ships' topsides clapped together so that the muzzles of their guns were touching. Paul Jones, joyfully accepting this new situation, shouted, "Well done, my brave lads, we have got her now; throw on board her the grappling irons, and stand by for boarding!" And while waiting for Master Stacey to rouse out a spare line, the Commodore, with his own hands, seized a forestay of *Serapis* which had parted and fallen across *Richard's* quarterdeck and made it fast to his mizzenmast. At this juncture the master appeared with the line, swearing horribly; the Captain checked him by remarking, "Mr. Stacey, it's no time to be swearing now — you may by the next moment be in eternity; but let us do our duty."

The Deadly Embrace

All this was as pretty a piece of maneuvering as you could see at the start of

a modern yacht race, and the unforeseen clapperclaw[1] was exactly what Jones wanted. He was outgunned even at the start of the action, and he had abandoned his eighteen-pounder battery — his only cannon of the same caliber as the main battery of *Serapis* — suspecting after two blew up, the rest would follow. He knew that his only chance of victory, or even survival, was to disable the rigging of *Serapis* and kill off her crew by musketry and hand grenades, or to take her boarding; and as the British frigate had two covered gun decks, capture by boarding would be very difficult. Captain Pearson, on the contrary, had to shake off *Richard's* deadly hug if he were to bring his superior fire power to bear. To that end he ordered the grappling hooks to be cast off or severed; but *Richard's* sharpshooters picked off the sailors who tried to do that. Pearson then dropped anchor in 15 to 20 fathoms of water, hoping that the wind and tide would swing *Richard* clear. On the contrary, the two ships, spitting fire at each other, pivoted through a half circle, for all the world like one of those macabre dances of death by two skeletons in a medieval engraving. *Serapis*, now held by her anchor, headed south into wind and tide, while *Richard*, still fast grappled to her, pointed north (Plan No. 8).

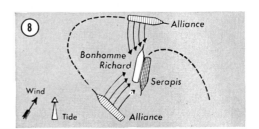

It is now between 8:00 and 8:30; the harvest moon, two days short of full, rises over heavy clouds on the eastern horizon and illuminates the battle. "Flamborough reapers, home-going, pause on the hillside; for what sulfur cloud is

[1] **clapperclaw:** grasping with hands or nails; here, the firm joining of the two ships.

that which defaces the sleek sea; sulfur cloud spitting streaks of fire?" Spectators, attracted from Scarborough and Bridlington [1] by the sound of the opening salvos, flocked to Flamborough Head. They witnessed a naval combat the like of which has never been fought before or since. Here for two long hours, *Bonhomme Richard* and *Serapis* are mortised [2] together, snug as two logs in a woodpile, guns muzzle to muzzle. They are so close that the starboard gun ports of *Serapis,* shut during the first phase of the battle, cannot be opened outboard and have to be blown off by her guns; and the gunners, in order to load and ram their charges home, must thrust their staves into the enemy's gun ports. At one point the sails of both ships are ablaze, and killing is suspended while damage control parties fight the flames; then each ship resumes banging away at the other. The Englishman wants to break off and fight at cannon range but cannot; the American clings desperately to him, knowing that only by maintaining the clinch can he survive. Deprived of his eighteen-pounder battery in the gun room by the bursting of the guns, and of his main battery of twelve-pounders by the blast from *Serapis'* two decks of eighteen-pounders, Commodore Jones has no cannon left except the three nine-pounders on the quarterdeck, one of which he helps to trundle over from the port side and serves with his own hands.

Jones's one advantage, other than his own inflexible determination, is the good marksmanship of the French marine musketeers on deck, and of the polyglot [3] seamen and gunners in the fighting tops. Owing to their fast and accurate shooting with swivels, coehorns, small arms, and tossed grenades, *Sera-* *pis* can keep no man alive on deck, and her open-deck battery of 10 six-pounders is deserted. But her eighteen-pounders, below deck, go on roaring and breaching through *Richard's* topsides, and Jones has no means to counter them. French shipbuilders must have put stout stuff into that old East Indiaman; [4] for when the fight ended, only a few stanchions [5] prevented her quarterdeck from falling into the gun room, or her main deck from crashing into the hold, and her topsides were a mass of fragments and splinters. Jones's tactics of close grappling prevented the English guns from breaking his masts and yards, which continued to support his fighting men in the tops, even when the rest of *Bonhomme Richard* had been reduced to little more than a battered raft.

"During this time," reported Pearson, "from the great Quantity and Variety of Combustible Matters which they threw in upon our Decks, Chains, and in short into every part of the Ship, we were on fire not less than Ten or Twelve times in different parts." It is a scene difficult to imagine, impossible to describe in detail. The yards of *Richard* so far overhang the deck of *Serapis* that her sailors are able to leap into the enemy's tops, throw out the English topmen, and then shoot directly down at her deck and even into the hatches.

Vengeance during the battle maneuvered at a safe distance; the boat commanded by Lunt stood by, not daring to come alongside; *Pallas* hotly engaged *Countess of Scarborough,* and Landais [6] in *Alliance* played the role of a madman. During the early part of the clinch, he raked *Richard,* killing two sailors and driving others from their battle stations. He then sailed close to where the other two ships were fighting, but did nothing

---

[1] **Scarborough and Bridlington:** nearby English towns.
[2] **mortised** (môr′tĭst): closely joined or fastened.
[3] **polyglot** (pŏl′ĭ·glŏt): speaking many languages.

[4] **East Indiaman:** The *Bonhomme Richard* was originally designed for commercial voyages to the East Indies.
[5] **stanchions:** braces or supports.
[6] **Landais** (läɴ·dāz′): the French commander of the *Alliance.*

to help *Pallas*. After that he beat up to windward in very leisurely fashion and, about two hours after his first blast at *Richard,* crossed the axis of the two locked ships (Plan No. 8) to windward of them. Turning downwind, *Alliance* crossed *Richard's* stern, and "while we were hailing her," said Midshipman Mayrant, poured into her port quarter a broadside which holed her between wind and water and even under water. He then passed ahead, returned athwart *Richard's* bows and — despite the Commodore's hailing, "Lay the enemy on board!" the seamen shouting, "Don't fire — you have killed several of our men already!" and Lieutenant Stack calling from his fighting top, "I beg you will not sink us!" — Landais gave *Richard* a third and the most fatal broadside, fired into the forecastle where men driven from the gun deck had gathered. It killed several more, including a chief petty officer.

This cannot have been accidental, as Jones had his night recognition signals burning, the scene was illuminated by moonlight, gun flashes, and fires; *Richard's* topsides were painted black, and those of *Serapis* bright yellow. The evidence is overwhelming that Landais did it on purpose. After the battle he confided to one of the French colonels that his intention was to help *Serapis* sink *Richard,* then board and capture the British frigate, and emerge the hero and victor of the battle. Later he had the impudence to claim that his broadsides forced Captain Pearson to strike; and Pearson himself was not backward in claiming that he succumbed to two frigates, not one. But the testimony collected by Commodore Jones at the Texel [1] is conclusive: *Alliance* was nowhere about in the last half hour of the battle, Landais having fired his last malevolent broadside around 10:00 P.M.

[1] **the Texel:** an island in the North Sea owned by the Netherlands. Jones landed there after the battle and informed the local government of Landais' treachery.

and retired to a safe distance to think up more mischief. His crew suffered not one casualty, and his ship no damage. She was hit only thrice by *Scarborough* at long range; one of the balls stuck in her topsides and the other two bounced off.

The Commodore directed the nine-pounder guns on his quarterdeck and served one of them himself, since Purser Mease, the officer in charge of that one remaining battery, was badly wounded in the head. At one moment Jones became so exhausted that he sat down to rest on a hencoop, when a sailor came up to him and said, "For God's sake, Captain, strike!" Jones paused, then leaped to his feet and said, "No, I will sink, I will never strike!" and resumed his service of the nine-pounder.

His indomitable spirit, and the sharp work of his topmen and marines, were the decisive factors in the battle. They picked off so many British gunners that the boy "powder monkeys" found few people on the gundeck of *Serapis* to receive the powder cartridges being brought up from the magazine, and dropped them on deck. An enterprising seaman of *Richard's* crew, a Scot named William Hamilton, took a basket of hand grenades and a live match out to the end of a yardarm that hung directly above an open hatch of *Serapis* and dropped a grenade right through it, which exploded the powder cartridges that the boys had left lying about. At least twenty men were killed and others frightfully burned. Jones followed up this lucky break by directing the fire of his three nine-pounders, loaded with double-headed shot, against the enemy's mainmast.

Immediately after the big explosion, Captain Pearson was at the point of calling for quarter when three of Jones's petty officers, two of whom had been wounded, put their heads together and decided that *Richard* would sink if she did not strike. The chief gunner, an Englishman named Henry Gardner, ran aft to haul down the ensign; but, finding that a cannon ball had carried away ensign and staff, he began bawling, "Quarters, Quarters, for God's sake!" At this the Commodore, pulling a pistol from his belt, hurled it at the chief and felled him to the deck. Pearson, however, had heard the cry and called over to Jones, "Sir, do you ask for a quarter?" He replied, "No, sir, I haven't as yet *thought* of it, but I'm determined to make *you* strike." Pearson's reply to that was to command, "Boarders Away!" But by the time his boarding party had crossed *Richard's* bulwarks, "They discovered a Superior Number lying under Cover with Pikes in their hands ready to receive them, on which our people" (admitted Pearson) "retreted instantly into our own ship, and returned to their Guns again."

One of the strange things about this part of the action is that neither side attempted to board the other until near the end. The probability is that *Richard's* crew looked like such desperate cutthroats that Pearson did not dare board except as a last expedient; and that Jones, with his keen tactical sense, felt that his men could do more execution with firearms than with boarding pikes and cutlasses. It is also strange that both commanding officers, although in full view on deck throughout the action, and conspicuous by their uniforms, escaped without a scratch. Jones probably ordered his sharpshooters to spare Pearson so that he could have the honor of capturing a captain RN; [1] and Pearson may have given similar orders in the hope of taking the "pirate."

Victory

It was now 10:00 P.M. The battle went on for another thirty minutes, becoming even more bloody and desperate. *Richard's* master-at-arms liberated the prisoners from the hold, to the number of over a hundred, and assured them that they had better man the pumps if they valued their lives. Most of them

[1] RN: Royal Navy.

did so; but one, the master of prize ship *Union,*[2] leaped through an open port of *Serapis,* rushed on deck, and told Captain Pearson that if he could hold out a little longer, Jones would either strike or sink, for there were already five feet of water in the hold.

At this moment — five or ten minutes after ten — the situation of *Bonhomme Richard* seemed hopeless to almost every officer except the Captain. A sinking ship, on fire, all cannon silenced except three nine-pounders while the enemy's eighteens are still blazing away, prisoners at large, officers losing heart, and chiefs bellowing "Quarters!" — all that, which to almost any other commanding officer would have added up to the ultimate in desperate circumstances, failed to break Paul Jones's will to victory. And victory was very near. A few minutes before 10:30, when the mainmast of *Serapis,* which Jones had been pelting with double-headed shot, began to tremble, Captain Pearson lost his nerve. Four of his eighteen-pounders were still firing, but he decided that it was time for him to strike. The Red Ensign, which he had caused to be nailed to its staff, he had to tear down with his own hands since no man near him was able to move.

With the Commodore's permission, Lieutenant Dale now swung himself on board *Serapis* to take possession, followed by a boarding party in which Midshipman Mayrant was wounded by a pike wielded by a British seaman who had not heard that his captain had struck. Nor had the first lieutenant of *Serapis;* he had to have the fact confirmed by Captain Pearson.

Lieutenant Dale now conducts Captain Pearson on board *Richard* and formally introduces him to Commodore Jones. At this point the tottering mainmast of *Serapis* cracks and falls overboard, carrying with it her mizzen topmast. The defeated captain hands his sword to Jones, who promptly returns it

[2] *Union:* a ship captured by Jones in another engagement.

with a few gracious words about his gallant fight, and invites him below into his wrecked cabin to drink a glass of wine. Such were the ceremonial manners of eighteenth-century warfare.

The fight between *Bonhomme Richard* and *Serapis* had lasted between three and three and a half hours. The British frigate was in a deplorable condition; her spars, sails, and rigging were cut away, and dead and dying men lay about her decks. But the state of *Richard* was even more frightful. Her rudder was hanging by one pintle, her stern frames and transoms were almost entirely shot away, the quarterdeck was about to fall into the gun room, at least five feet of water were in the hold, and it was gaining from holes below the waterline (some of them made by *Alliance*), and her topsides were open to the moonlight. The timbers of her lower deck from the mainmast aft, "being greatly decayed with age, were mangled beyond my power of description," observed Jones in his "Narrative" of the battle, "and a person must have been an Eye Witness to form a Just idea of this tremendous scene of Carneg, Wreck and ruin that Every Where appeared. Humanity cannot but recoil from the prospect of such finished horror, and Lament that War should be capable of producing such fatal Consequences."

This last statement was perfectly sincere. Paul Jones, like many of the greatest admirals and generals, loved fighting but hated war. He shared the belief of eighteenth-century philosophers that war was an outmoded and barbarous method of settling international disputes, and hoped that the particular conflict in which he happened to be engaged would be the last. The gods willed otherwise.

FOR DISCUSSION

1. Why was John Paul Jones particularly anxious to break up a Baltic supply convoy?

2. What stratagem did Jones use to get close to the *Serapis* before firing?

3. Why did Jones seek to grapple the *Serapis* as soon as possible?

4. Once the ships were grappled, why did neither side immediately attempt to board?

5. Describe the actions and motives of Captain Landais of the *Alliance*.

6. How did Jones and Pearson behave at the time of surrender? Why do you think they acted as they did?

UNDERSTANDING THE MAN

1. War on land and sea offers many incidents showing how the iron spirit of one man, against all the objective facts in a critical situation, can sometimes produce victory. Explain how this is true in the battle between the *Bonhomme Richard* and the *Serapis*.

2. Comment briefly on the characters of Jones and Pearson, and describe the two men as they are revealed by their words and actions in the fight. Are there any important differences between the two men? If so, did these differences affect the outcome of the battle? Support your opinions by referring to the text.

THE AUTHOR

SAMUEL ELIOT MORISON (b. 1887) is a historian of wide range. His American studies include our colonial era, the history of Harvard (where he has taught American history), and a Pulitzer prize winning biography of Columbus, *Admiral of the Ocean Sea* (1942). He is official U.S. Navy historian of World War II and has produced many volumes on all the theaters of that globe-circling war. *John Paul Jones: A Sailor's Biography* (1959) is the work from which this stirring, accurate battle description comes.

Art and History ➤

This is a detail from "The Encounter of the *Bonhomme Richard* and the *Serapis*," an oil painting by Thomas Mitchell (1735–1790). Does the artist's rendering of the scene agree with Samuel Eliot Morison's description in this selection?

Nonfiction in the Twentieth Century

Nonfiction embraces a variety of literary forms. The basic types, the article, the essay, criticism, reporting, biography, and history, are all represented in the selections you have just read. The following survey of modern nonfiction and the reading list on the next page will lead you further into excellent examples of the varieties of nonfiction.

There is boundless laughter, plus shrewd, satirical wisdom, in the humor of E. B. WHITE, JAMES THURBER, LUDWIG BEMELMANS, and S. J. PERELMAN. You have already read an example of White's nonfiction, and you will enjoy sampling the work of the other three humorists. White and Thurber are masters of fine prose styles; Thurber is noted for his fiction — "The Secret Life of Walter Mitty" is an excellent sample — as well as his nonfiction. Perelman and Bemelmans are famous for witty essays and parodies.

Among women writers, PHYLLIS McGINLEY, who is also noted for her light verse (page 342), is a good informal essayist. CORNELIA OTIS SKINNER and JEAN KERR have written some excellent humorous nonfiction.

VAN WYCK BROOKS is the dean of our literary historians and critics. Other critics and chroniclers of literary history include EDMUND WILSON, F. O. MATTHIESSEN, VERNON PARRINGTON, and ALFRED KAZIN. R. P. BLACKMUR is noted for excellent close examinations of specific works of literature. JOHN CROWE RANSOM, CLEANTH BROOKS, and ROBERT PENN WARREN have dealt primarily with poetry in their critical writings.

Biography continually flourishes as a rewarding and popular field of reading. Among the most skillful twentieth-century biographers are CARL SANDBURG, DOUGLAS SOUTHALL FREEMAN, SAMUEL ELIOT MORISON, and CATHERINE DRINKER BOWEN, all of whom you have met in the preceding pages. MARQUIS JAMES and LOUISE HALL THARP are also fine modern biographers. All of these writers also have claims as historians, along with such formal and informal historians as ALLAN NEVINS, WALTER WEBB, STEWART HOLBROOK, and BRUCE CATTON. LEON EDEL's *Literary Biography* is a fine critical study of biographical and historical writing.

WALTER LIPPMANN, ARTHUR KROCK, JAMES RESTON, JOSEPH HENRY JACKSON, and JOSEPH ALSOP are prominent journalists, distinguished for their perceptive treatments of modern social and political problems.

Such periodicals as *Harper's Magazine*, the *Atlantic Monthly*, and the *American Scholar* offer a continuing flow of fine essays. Many magazines publish collections of their nonfiction. Among such collections are *Gentlemen, Scholars, and Scoundrels* (*Harper's*), *Jubilee* (the *Atlantic*), the *American Scholar Reader*, and *Our Times* (the *Reporter*).

Whatever your interests may be, there are many articles and books from which you may select to increase your knowledge of a particular subject. In addition, an exploration of modern nonfiction can be a pleasant way to discover many new subjects in which you may become interested.

For Further Reading of Nonfiction

GENERAL

Beebe, William, *Adventuring with Beebe* (Duell, Sloan & Pearce, 1955)

Carson, Rachel, *The Sea Around Us* (Oxford Univ. Press, 1951); *The Edge of the Sea* (Houghton Mifflin, 1955)

Devoe, Alan, *This Fascinating Animal World* (McGraw-Hill, 1951)

Kieran, John, *Natural History of New York City* (Houghton Mifflin, 1959)

Krutch, Joseph, *Grand Canyon: Today and All Its Yesterdays* (Sloane, 1958)

Rivers of America Series (Holt, Rinehart & Winston)

Rodman, Selden, *Mexican Journal* (Devin-Adair, 1958)

Teale, Edwin Way, *North with the Spring* (Dodd, Mead, 1951); *Autumn Across America* (Dodd, Mead, 1956)

Stewart, George R., *American Ways of Life* (Doubleday, 1954)

White, E. B., *Here Is New York* (Harper, 1950)

APPRECIATION AND CRITICISM

Bernstein, Leonard, *The Joy of Music* (Simon & Schuster, 1959)

Bethers, Ray, *Art Always Changes* (Hastings, 1958)

Fuller, Edmund, *Man in Modern Fiction* (Random House, 1958)

Gehlmann, John, *The Challenge of Ideas* (Odyssey, 1950)

Morris, Wright, *The Territory Ahead* (Harcourt, Brace & World, 1958)

Wecter, Dixon, *Sam Clemens of Hannibal* (Houghton Mifflin, 1952)

West, Jessamyn, *To See the Dream* (story of the filming of *The Friendly Persuasion*, Harcourt, Brace & World, 1957)

HISTORY AND BIOGRAPHY

Allen, Frederick Lewis, *Only Yesterday* (Harper, 1931); *The Big Change* (Harper, 1952)

*Bowen, Catherine Drinker, *Yankee from Olympus* (Little, Brown, 1943)

*Brooks, Van Wyck, *Helen Keller: Sketch for a Portrait* (Dutton, 1954)

* Included in *Four American Biographies,* edited by Edmund Fuller and O. B. Davis (Harcourt, Brace & World, 1961). Twain's *Autobiography* is abridged.

Buck, Pearl, *My Several Worlds* (John Day, 1954)

Catton, Bruce, *A Stillness at Appomattox* (Pocket Books, 1958)

Cousins, Norman, *Doctor Schweitzer of Lambaréné* (Harper, 1960)

Ferber, Edna, *A Peculiar Treasure* (World Publishing, 1947)

Keller, Helen, *The Story of My Life* (Doubleday, 1947); *Teacher: Anne Sullivan Macy* (Doubleday, 1955)

Kennedy, John F., *Profiles in Courage* (Harper, 1956)

Lindbergh, Charles A., *The Spirit of St. Louis* (Scribner, 1957)

*Sandburg, Carl, *Always the Young Strangers* (Harcourt, Brace & World, 1953); *Abraham Lincoln: The Prairie Years* (Harcourt, Brace & World, 1926)

Stuart, Jesse, *The Thread That Runs So True* (Scribner, 1949)

*Twain, Mark, *Autobiography* (Harper, 1959)

Washington, Booker T., *Up from Slavery* (Oxford Univ. Press, 1945)

Wong, Jade Snow, *Fifth Chinese Daughter* (Harper, 1945)

HUMOR

Benchley, Robert C., *Inside Benchley* (Harper, 1942); *Chips off the Old Benchley* (Harper, 1949)

Gilbreth, Frank B., and Ernestine Gilbreth Carey, *Cheaper by the Dozen* (Crowell, 1948); *Belles on Their Toes* (Crowell, 1950)

Kerr, Jean, *The Snake Has All the Lines* (Doubleday, 1960)

Kimbrough, Emily, and Cornelia Otis Skinner, *Our Hearts Were Young and Gay* (Dodd, Mead, 1942)

Ross, Leonard Q., *The Education of Hyman Kaplan* (Harcourt, Brace & World, 1941)

Thurber, James, *The Thurber Carnival* (Harper, 1945)

White, E. B., *The Second Tree from the Corner,* prose and poetry (Harper, 1954)

FOR LISTENING

Thomas Wolfe's "Circus at Dawn" has been recorded on *Many Voices* 11A.

Modern Poetry

MODERN AMERICAN POETRY is often said to have begun with the founding of *Poetry* magazine in Chicago in 1912. Young, unknown poets were given encouragement by the magazine and began to develop new forms of poetry. Within the next few years, poetry gained more attention than it had received in the entire previous generation. The "new poetry" became a topic of general conversation and the subject of violent likes and dislikes. Yet what seemed revolutionary a few years ago appears now as a return to the best tradition of poetry. Those poets who were once considered extremely radical are today's established artists. At its best, their work illustrates the truth of Ralph Waldo Emerson's statement: "Poetry must be as new as foam, and as old as a rock."

Guide to Reading Poetry

If you want to get full enjoyment from reading poetry, you should make a few adjustments in your usual reading habits.

The first guide to the enjoyment of poetry is: *read each poem slowly*. Thought is compressed in poetry, and must be allowed to expand in the reader's mind. A leisurely first reading, with frequent pauses to insure clear understanding, should be followed by a faster second or even third reading, to grasp the whole poem.

Second, do not be satisfied with a silent reading. Find an opportunity to *read poetry aloud*. Much of the delight of poetry lies in its music, which is only half sensed until the words on the page are translated into sound.

Third, *respond to sensory impressions*. Lend all your senses to the poem. The poet often speaks directly to the senses and the emotions, and the reader should be alert to capture the heightened sensations of true poetry.

Finally, *use your imagination*. The imagination, important in all reading, is vital to poetry. Perhaps no writer is so flattering to his readers as the poet. He often expects one word to suggest whole volumes of meaning. No good poet fills in every detail in precise fashion. He stimulates the reader's imagination to join in perfecting the emotion, the expression, and the thought of the poem.

APPRECIATING THE POET'S ART

The poet works with five elements: thought, tone, imagery, melody, and rhythm. He begins with thought, and his purpose is to re-create that thought or experience in words, rhythms, and melodies. His choice of words must then be precise and economical. Not only are the meanings important, but the relationships, suggestions, and sounds of the words all matter greatly. You can enjoy a poem without paying particular attention to the way the poet blends these various elements, but you can gain additional pleasure by developing your awareness of them. The following list provides a brief outline of the poet's tools.

Imagery: vivid sensory impressions. Images are often visual, but may appeal to the other senses as well:

> Blue waves whitened on a cliff,
> Climbing fire that sways and sings

Simile: a comparison. A simile can be recognized through its use of "like" or "as":

> Far off like floating seeds the ships
> Diverge . . .

Metaphor: another form of comparison. Unlike simile, metaphor does not employ "like" or "as," but makes a direct statement:

> Love is a bird in a fist:

Personification: a special form of metaphor. Personification occurs when something not human — a city, for example — is given human characteristics:

> Stormy, husky, brawling,
> City of the Big Shoulders:

Symbol: a sign that stands for, or refers to, something else. A lion, for instance, is considered a symbol of courage. In the following example, the "two roads" symbolize an important decision in a man's life:

> Two roads diverged in a wood, and I —
> I took the one less traveled by,

Alliteration: the repetition of the beginning sounds of words:

> *B*ooth led *b*oldly with his *b*ig *b*ass drum —

Rhyme: the repetition of the final sounds of words. Rhyming words ordinarily occur at the end of lines of verse:

> The world stands out on either *side*
> No wider than the heart is *wide;*

Internal Rhyme is also used occasionally:

> Here at the *small* field's ending pause
> When the chalk *wall falls* to the foam, and its *tall* ledges . . .

Assonance: the repetition of vowel sounds. Assonance is sometimes used in place of end rhymes, but in most instances it occurs within the line:

> . . . for the l*ea*ping gr*ee*nly spirits of tr*ee*s
> and a blue true dr*ea*m of sky; . . .

Rhythm (or *Meter*): the music or movement of poetry, created through the arrangement of accented and unaccented syllables in a line of verse. Ordinary conversation is rhythmic, since all language contains patterns of accents, but a poem employs much stricter patterns:

> The worst and best are both inclined
> To snap like vixens at the truth;
> But O beware the middle mind
> That purrs and never shows a tooth!

Some basic rhythms will be pointed out as they occur in the following pages. One important point: even though a poem may follow a firm pattern, it should never be read in a sing-song, nursery-rhyme manner. Skillful poets will often introduce slight variations in the meter to avoid this kind of monotony.

ROBERT FROST

ROBERT FROST (b. 1875) is a genuine New Englander by ancestry, though he was born in California and was ten years old when his widowed mother brought her family back home to New Hampshire. Since then his devotion to New England and to poetry has never faltered. After two years of college, Frost worked at editing, teaching, and farming, while trying in vain to win readers for his poems. Discouraged, he sold his farm and went to England, where other poets welcomed the man, and the public welcomed his books, *A Boy's Will* and *North of Boston*. The reputation he won abroad spread to America before his return in 1915. He has since lived on a New England farm, leaving it only to serve various universities as a visiting professor.

In 1924 *New Hampshire* won the first of four Pulitzer prizes that confirm his high place among American poets. As an indication of the esteem in which the poet is held, in 1961 he was granted the high honor of reading one of his poems at the Presidential inauguration. *In the Clearing* (1962) is Frost's most recent collection of poems.

The characters in Frost's poems are close to the soil, and the poems themselves are always rooted in the land and thoroughly realistic. Frost, however, is not a photographic realist. He once commented, "There are two types of realist — the one who offers a good deal of dirt with his potato to show that it is a real one; and the one who is satisfied with the potato brushed clean. I'm inclined to be the second kind . . . To me, the thing that art does for life is to strip it to form."

Of his craft Frost has also written in the preface to his *Collected Poems* (1939) that a poem "begins in delight and ends in wisdom."

The materials of Robert Frost's poetry are the birches and snow and rock walls and apple orchards of New England farms, and the people and animals who live among them. His words are those that might be used by two farmers meeting on a country road. But Frost is far more than a mere recorder of this rural life. He looks on common things and finds in them uncommon meanings: the fork in a road becomes a symbol of the choices men must forever be making; a rock wall is a symbol of more subtle barriers between men. His simple words and beautiful natural rhythms give new life and meaning to conventional verse forms. His poetry pictures both his world and his thoughts with remarkable clarity. The reading of Frost's poems will be easy and smooth on the surface, yet rich in understanding and thought and in delight in the New England countryside.

The Pasture

I'm going out to clean the pasture spring;
I'll only stop to rake the leaves away
(And wait to watch the water clear, I may):
I shan't be gone long — You come too.

I'm going out to fetch the little calf   5
That's standing by the mother. It's so young,
It totters when she licks it with her tongue.
I shan't be gone long — You come too.

The Road Not Taken

Two roads diverged in a yellow wood,
And sorry I could not travel both
And be one traveler, long I stood
And looked down one as far as I could
To where it bent in the undergrowth;   5

Then took the other, as just as fair,
And having perhaps the better claim,
Because it was grassy and wanted wear;
Though as for that the passing there
Had worn them really about the same,   10

And both that morning equally lay
In leaves no step had trodden black.
Oh, I kept the first for another day!
Yet knowing how way leads on to way,
I doubted if I should ever come back.   15

I shall be telling this with a sigh
Somewhere ages and ages hence:
Two roads diverged in a wood, and I —
I took the one less traveled by
And that has made all the difference.   20

Stopping by Woods on a Snowy Evening

Whose woods these are I think I know.
His house is in the village though;
He will not see me stopping here
To watch his woods fill up with snow.

My little horse must think it queer 5
To stop without a farmhouse near
Between the woods and frozen lake
The darkest evening of the year.

He gives his harness bells a shake
To ask if there is some mistake. 10
The only other sound's the sweep
Of easy wind and downy flake.

The woods are lovely, dark, and deep,
But I have promises to keep,
And miles to go before I sleep, 15
And miles to go before I sleep.

Putting in the Seed

You come to fetch me from my work tonight
When supper's on the table, and we'll see
If I can leave off burying the white
Soft petals fallen from the apple tree
(Soft petals, yes, but not so barren quite, 5
Mingled with these, smooth bean and wrinkled pea)
And go along with you ere you lose sight
Of what you came for and become like me,
Slave to a springtime passion for the earth.
How Love burns through the Putting in the Seed 10
On through the watching for that early birth
When, just as the soil tarnishes with weed,

The sturdy seedling with arched body comes
Shouldering its way and shedding the earth crumbs.

"Stopping by Woods on a Snowy Evening" from *You Come Too* by Robert Frost. Copyright 1916, 1921, 1923 by Holt, Rinehart and Winston, Inc. Copyright renewed 1944, 1951 by Robert Frost. Reprinted by permission of Holt, Rinehart and Winston, Inc.
"Putting in the Seed" from *Complete Poems of Robert Frost*. Copyright 1916, 1921, 1923, 1930, 1939, 1947 by Holt, Rinehart and Winston, Inc. Copyright renewed 1944, 1951 by Robert Frost. Reprinted by permission of Holt, Rinehart and Winston, Inc.

As the title indicates, gold is the important symbol in the following poem. Notice that the meaning of the word broadens throughout the poem.

Nothing Gold Can Stay

Nature's first green is gold,
Her hardest hue to hold.
Her early leaf's a flower;
But only so an hour.
Then leaf subsides to leaf.　　　　　　　5
So Eden sank to grief,
So dawn goes down to day.
Nothing gold can stay.

The two following poems, "Fire and Ice" and "It Bids Pretty Fair," center on one theme although they approach it through different symbols. How is the tone of each poem affected by the symbols the poet uses?

Fire and Ice

Some say the world will end in fire,
Some say in ice.
From what I've tasted of desire
I hold with those who favor fire.
But if it had to perish twice,　　　　　　　5
I think I know enough of hate
To say that for destruction ice
Is also great
And would suffice.

It Bids Pretty Fair

The play seems out for an almost infinite run.
Don't mind a little thing like the actors fighting.
The only thing I worry about is the sun.
We'll be all right if nothing goes wrong with the lighting.

"Out, Out —" *

The buzz saw snarled and rattled in the yard
And made dust and dropped stove-length sticks of wood,
Sweet-scented stuff when the breeze drew across it.
And from there those that lifted eyes could count
Five mountain ranges one behind the other   5
Under the sunset far into Vermont.
And the saw snarled and rattled, snarled and rattled,
As it ran light, or had to bear a load.
And nothing happened: day was all but done.
Call it a day, I wish they might have said   10
To please the boy by giving him the half hour
That a boy counts so much when saved from work.
His sister stood beside them in her apron
To tell them "Supper." At the word, the saw,
As if it meant to prove saws knew what supper meant,   15
Leaped out at the boy's hand, or seemed to leap —
He must have given the hand. However it was,
Neither refused the meeting. But the hand!
The boy's first outcry was a rueful laugh,
As he swung toward them holding up the hand   20
Half in appeal, but half as if to keep
The life from spilling. Then the boy saw all —
Since he was old enough to know, big boy
Doing a man's work, though a child at heart —
He saw all spoiled. "Don't let him cut my hand off —   25
The doctor, when he comes. Don't let him, sister!"
So. But the hand was gone already.
The doctor put him in the dark of ether.
He lay and puffed his lips out with his breath.
And then — the watcher at his pulse took fright.   30
No one believed. They listened at his heart.
Little — less — nothing! — and that ended it.
No more to build on there. And they, since they
Were not the one dead, turned to their affairs.

---

* "Out, Out — ": The title is taken from Act V, Scene v of Shakespeare's *Macbeth*. Macbeth speaks after he has been informed of his wife's death.

> Out, out, brief candle!
> Life's but a walking shadow, a poor player,
> That struts and frets his hour upon the stage,
> And then is heard no more.

ROBERT FROST

Mending Wall

Something there is that doesn't love a wall,
That sends the frozen ground swell under it,
And spills the upper boulders in the sun;
And makes gaps even two can pass abreast.
The work of hunters is another thing: 5
I have come after them and made repair
Where they have left not one stone on a stone,
But they would have the rabbit out of hiding,
To please the yelping dogs. The gaps I mean,
No one has seen them made or heard them made,   10
But at spring mending time we find them there.
I let my neighbor know beyond the hill;
And on a day we meet to walk the line
And set the wall between us once again.
We keep the wall between us as we go.   15
To each the boulders that have fallen to each.
And some are loaves and some so nearly balls
We have to use a spell to make them balance:
"Stay where you are until our backs are turned!"
We wear our fingers rough with handling them.   20
Oh, just another kind of outdoor game,
One on a side. It comes to little more:
There where it is we do not need the wall:
He is all pine and I am apple orchard.
My apple trees will never get across   25
And eat the cones under his pines, I tell him.
He only says, "Good fences make good neighbors."
Spring is the mischief in me, and I wonder
If I could put a notion in his head:
"*Why* do they make good neighbors? Isn't it   30
Where there are cows? But here there are no cows.
Before I built a wall I'd ask to know
What I was walling in or walling out,
And to whom I was like to give offense.
Something there is that doesn't love a wall,   35
That wants it down." I could say "Elves" to him,
But it's not elves exactly, and I'd rather
He said it for himself. I see him there
Bringing a stone grasped firmly by the top
In each hand, like an old stone savage armed.   40
He moves in darkness as it seems to me,

"Litchfield Hills," an oil painting by the American artist Ben Foster (1852–1926). ▶

Not of woods only and the shade of trees.
He will not go behind his father's saying,
And he likes having thought of it so well
He says again, "Good fences make good neighbors."   45

Here is a story dramatically revealed through conversation. Even though the talk is quiet in the New England fashion, it probes deeply into human motives and the human spirit.

The Death of the Hired Man

Mary sat musing on the lamp flame at the table,
Waiting for Warren. When she heard his step,
She ran on tiptoe down the darkened passage
To meet him in the doorway with the news
And put him on his guard. "Silas is back."   5
She pushed him outward with her through the door
And shut it after her. "Be kind," she said.
She took the market things from Warren's arms
And set them on the porch, then drew him down
To sit beside her on the wooden steps.   10

"When was I ever anything but kind to him?
But I'll not have the fellow back," he said.
"I told him so last haying, didn't I?
'If he left then,' I said, 'that ended it.'
What good is he? Who else will harbor him   15
At his age for the little he can do?
What help he is there's no depending on.
Off he goes always when I need him most.
He thinks he ought to earn a little pay,
Enough at least to buy tobacco with,   20
So he won't have to 'beg and be beholden.'
'All right,' I say, 'I can't afford to pay
Any fixed wages, though I wish I could.'
'Someone else can.' 'Then someone else will have to.'
I shouldn't mind his bettering himself   25
If that was what it was. You can be certain,
When he begins like that, there's someone at him
Trying to coax him off with pocket money —
In haying time, when any help is scarce.
In winter he comes back to us. I'm done."   30

"Sh! not so loud: he'll hear you," Mary said.

"I want him to: he'll have to soon or late."

"He's worn out. He's asleep beside the stove.
When I came up from Rowe's I found him here,
Huddled against the barn door fast asleep,   35
A miserable sight, and frightening, too —
You needn't smile — I didn't recognize him —
I wasn't looking for him — and he's changed.
Wait till you see."

   "Where did you say he'd been?"

"He didn't say. I dragged him to the house,   40
And gave him tea, and tried to make him smoke.
I tried to make him talk about his travels.
Nothing would do: he just kept nodding off."

"What did he say? Did he say anything?"

"But little."

   "Anything? Mary, confess   45
He said he'd come to ditch the meadow for me."

"Warren!"

  "But did he? I just want to know."

"Of course he did. What would you have him say?
Surely you wouldn't grudge the poor old man
Some humble way to save his self-respect.   50
He added, if you really care to know,
He meant to clear the upper pasture, too.
That sounds like something you have heard before?
Warren, I wish you could have heard the way
He jumbled everything. I stopped to look   55
Two or three times — he made me feel so queer —
To see if he was talking in his sleep.
He ran on Harold Wilson — you remember —
The boy you had in haying four years since.
He's finished school, and teaching in his college.   60
Silas declares you'll have to get him back.
He says they two will make a team for work:
Between them they will lay this farm as smooth!

The way he mixed that in with other things.
He thinks young Wilson a likely lad, though daft   65
On education — you know how they fought
All through July under the blazing sun,
Silas up on the cart to build the load,
Harold along beside to pitch it on."

"Yes, I took care to keep well out of earshot."   70

"Well, those days trouble Silas like a dream.
You wouldn't think they would. How some things linger!
Harold's young college boy's assurance piqued him.
After so many years he still keeps finding
Good arguments he sees he might have used.   75
I sympathize. I know just how it feels
To think of the right thing to say too late.
Harold's associated in his mind with Latin.
He asked me what I thought of Harold's saying
He studied Latin like the violin   80
Because he liked it — that an argument!
He said he couldn't make the boy believe
He could find water with a hazel prong° —
Which showed how much good school had ever done him.
He wanted to go over that. But most of all   85
He thinks if he could have another chance
To teach him how to build a load of hay — "

"I know, that's Silas' one accomplishment.
He bundles every forkful in its place,
And tags and numbers it for future reference,   90
So he can find and easily dislodge it
In the unloading. Silas does that well.
He takes it out in bunches like big birds' nests.
You never see him standing on the hay
He's trying to lift, straining to lift himself."   95

"He thinks if he could teach him that, he'd be
Some good perhaps to someone in the world.
He hates to see a boy the fool of books.

---

83. **find water with a hazel prong**: a common belief that a proper location for a well can be
ascertained by walking around holding in front of one a forked twig of a single season's growth.
The twig is supposed to bend down at the point where water is to be found under the surface.
(Notice the small circle after the word *prong*. This sign is used with poems in this book to call
your attention to each word that is explained in a footnote. The number in the footnote refers
to the line of the poem.)

Poor Silas, so concerned for other folk,
And nothing to look backward to with pride,   100
And nothing to look forward to with hope,
So now and never any different."

Part of a moon was falling down the west,
Dragging the whole sky with it to the hills.
Its light poured softly in her lap. She saw   105
And spread her apron to it. She put out her hand
Among the harplike morning-glory strings,
Taut with the dew from garden bed to eaves,
As if she played unheard the tenderness
That wrought on him beside her in the night.   110
"Warren," she said, "he has come home to die:
You needn't be afraid he'll leave you this time."

"Home," he mocked gently.

                    "Yes, what else but home?
It all depends on what you mean by home.
Of course he's nothing to us, any more   115
Than was the hound that came a stranger to us
Out of the woods, worn out upon the trail."

"Home is the place where, when you have to go there,
They have to take you in."

                    "I should have called it
Something you somehow haven't to deserve."   120

Warren leaned out and took a step or two,
Picked up a little stick, and brought it back
And broke it in his hand and tossed it by.
"Silas has better claim on us, you think,
Than on his brother? Thirteen little miles   125
As the road winds would bring him to his door.
Silas has walked that far no doubt today.
Why didn't he go there? His brother's rich,
A somebody — director in the bank."

"He never told us that."

                    "We know it though."   130

" I think his brother ought to help, of course.
I'll see to that if there is need. He ought of right

To take him in, and might be willing to —
He may be better than appearances.
But have some pity on Silas. Do you think   135
If he'd had any pride in claiming kin
Or anything he looked for from his brother,
He'd keep so still about him all this time?"

"I wonder what's between them."

                              "I can tell you.
Silas is what he is — we wouldn't mind him —   140
But just the kind that kinsfolk can't abide.
He never did a thing so very bad.
He don't know why he isn't quite as good
As anyone. He won't be made ashamed
To please his brother, worthless though he is."   145

"I can't think Si ever hurt anyone."

"No, but he hurt my heart the way he lay
And rolled his old head on that sharp-edged chair back.
He wouldn't let me put him on the lounge.
You must go in and see what you can do.   150
I made the bed up for him there tonight.
You'll be surprised at him — how much he's broken.
His working days are done; I'm sure of it."

"I'd not be in a hurry to say that."

"I haven't been. Go, look, see for yourself.   155
But, Warren, please remember how it is:
He's come to help you ditch the meadow.
He has a plan. You mustn't laugh at him.
He may not speak of it, and then he may.
I'll sit and see if that small sailing cloud   160
Will hit or miss the moon."

                         It hit the moon.
Then there were three, making a dim row,
The moon, the little silver cloud, and she.

Warren returned — too soon, it seemed to her,
Slipped to her side, caught up her hand and waited.   165

"Warren?" she questioned.

                    " Dead," was all he answered.

FOR DISCUSSION

THE SHORT POEMS

1. Review your impressions of the New England countryside and people, gained from reading Frost. Which poems did not touch on the New England background? Do you like them as well as the others? Why, or why not?

2. In "Stopping by Woods on a Snowy Evening," what is the significance behind this simple incident? What is the effect of repeating the last line?

3. Keeping in mind the quotation from Shakespeare, explain the meaning of the title "Out, Out — ." Is the poetic account of the accident with the power saw convincing? Why? Why not?

4. Judging from "Mending Wall," does Frost think that following tradition is always a good thing? Quote lines to support your answer.

THE DEATH OF THE HIRED MAN

1. What do you learn of the characters of Mary and Warren from this conversation? Why did Warren feel that he had no obligation to take Silas back? Why did Mary want to make him welcome?

2. How does the discussion of the rich brother add to your understanding of Silas? What do you think really caused the conflict between Silas and Harold Wilson?

3. What do the passages of description add to the poem? What special significance do you see in the cloud's hitting the moon near the end?

4. How does Warren's behavior when he comes back to Mary prepare you for the news he brings? Does this incident alter your earlier impression of Warren?

UNDERSTANDING SYMBOLS

1. Do "Fire and Ice" and "It Bids Pretty Fair" advance the same general idea or different ideas? Explain.

2. What did you decide the two roads stood for in "The Road Not Taken"? What could they stand for in the mind of a reader applying the symbol to his own life?

3. Interpret the symbolic meaning of the wall in "Mending Wall," of gold in "Nothing Gold Can Stay," and of the play in "It Bids Pretty Fair."

PATTERNS OF POETRY

BLANK VERSE

"Mending Wall" and "The Death of the Hired Man" are written in *blank verse,* an unrhymed form commonly used in most long poems in English. It must not be confused with *free verse,* which follows no regular pattern. Blank verse observes two requirements of pattern — a regular line length of ten syllables, and a rhythm pattern of alternating unaccented and accented syllables, making up a line called *iambic pentameter.* Of course, if every line of a poem were written in this fashion, the result would be monotonous. Thus a great poet like Frost will vary the pattern, often writing lines of only three or four accents, and creating further variations within single lines by shifting the places of the accented syllables. Even with these variations, however, blank verse retains a fairly firm and easily identifiable pattern. Look at the free verse of "Silence" on page 267 and then at the blank verse of "Mending Wall" on page 256. A quick examination will often reveal the difference between the two forms. How does the pattern of each affect the tone? Blank verse usually has a strongly marked rhythm. Could free verse also be called rhythmic?

SONNET

Another important verse form made up of iambic pentameter lines is the *sonnet,* a poem of fourteen lines with a strict rhyme scheme. There are two major types of sonnets. In the *Italian* sonnet, a definite break in thought, mood, or point of view occurs between the first eight and last six lines. In the *Shakespearean* sonnet the thought is more flexible, often with no abrupt change, and the poem concludes with a rhymed couplet, which usually provides a climactic summing up. "Putting in the Seed" (p. 253) is a sonnet that combines elements of both types. Like the Italian sonnet, the poem is clearly divided into two parts, but here the break occurs after the ninth line rather than the eighth; the concluding couplet, which marks the similarity to the Shakespearean sonnet, is set apart for emphasis. What is the situation described in "Putting in the Seed"? What change occurs after the ninth line? How does the sonnet conclude?

EDGAR LEE MASTERS

EDGAR LEE MASTERS (1869–1950) was born in Kansas, grew up in small towns in southern Illinois, spent a short time at Knox College in Galesburg, and prepared for a law career by studying in his father's office. Eventually he became a successful lawyer in Chicago, but he was always equally interested in writing.

Association with the experimental poets contributing to the influential little magazine *Poetry* led him to abandon the conventional verse he had been writing and to try his hand at the "new poetry." His *Spoon River Anthology* quickly won fame. Although he wrote nearly fifty volumes of poetry and fiction, his reputation rests upon this book of some two hundred epitaphs. One, that of Petit the Poet, seems to speak for Masters:

> "Life all around me here in the village:
> Tragedy, comedy, valor, and truth,
> Courage, constancy, heroism, failure —
> All in the loom, and oh, what patterns!"

"Petit the Poet," from *Spoon River Anthology* by Edgar Lee Masters. Published by The Macmillan Company. Reprinted by permission of the Estate of Edgar Lee Masters.

Imagine finding engraved on each tombstone in a village cemetery not the conventional tribute but a plain-spoken account in free verse of all that had been truly significant in the life of the person buried beneath the stone! That is the device on which Spoon River Anthology *is built. The poems tell the experiences of the village life for generations. Good and evil crowd together, joys and hopes are recorded, bitterness and irony stand revealed.*

Flossie Cabanis

From Bindle's opera house in the village
To Broadway is a great step.
But I tried to take it, my ambition fired
When sixteen years of age,
Seeing "East Lynne"° played here in the village   5
By Ralph Barrett, the coming
Romantic actor, who enthralled my soul.
True, I trailed back home, a broken failure,
When Ralph disappeared in New York,
Leaving me alone in the city —   10
But life broke him also.
In all this place of silence
There are no kindred spirits.
How I wish Duse° could stand amid the pathos
Of these quiet fields   15
And read these words.

5. "East Lynne": a melodrama popular in the early years of this century. 14. **Duse** (dōō′zå):
Eleonora Duse (1859–1924), a great Italian actress.

Alfonso Churchill

They laughed at me as "Prof. Moon,"
As a boy in Spoon River, born with the thirst
Of knowing more about the stars.
They jeered when I spoke of the lunar mountains,
And the thrilling heat and cold,   5
And the ebon valleys by silver peaks,
And Spica° quadrillions of miles away,
And the littleness of man.
But now that my grave is honored, friends,
Let it not be because I taught   10
The lore of the stars in Knox College,
But rather for this: that through the stars
I preached the greatness of man,
Who is none the less a part of the scheme of things
For the distance of Spica or the spiral nebulae;°   15
Nor any the less a part of the question
Of what the drama means.

7. **Spica**: a star in the constellation Virgo. 15. **spiral nebulae** (nĕb′ û·lē): cloudy patches in
the sky similar to the Milky Way.

"Flossie Cabanis" and "Alfonso Churchill," from *Spoon River Anthology* by Edgar Lee Masters, published by
The Macmillan Company. Reprinted by permission of Mrs. Edgar Lee Masters.

EDGAR LEE MASTERS   265

Theodore the Poet

As a boy, Theodore, you sat for long hours
On the shore of the turbid Spoon
With deep-set eye staring at the door of the crawfish's burrow,
Waiting for him to appear, pushing ahead,
First his waving antennae, like straws of hay,   5
And soon his body, colored like soapstone,
Gemmed with eyes of jet.
And you wondered in a trance of thought
What he knew, what he desired, and why he lived at all.
But later your vision watched for men and women   10
Hiding in burrows of fate amid great cities,
Looking for the souls of them to come out,
So that you could see
How they lived, and for what,
And why they kept crawling so busily   15
Along the sandy way where water fails
As the summer wanes.

Seth Compton

When I died, the circulating library
Which I built up for Spoon River,
And managed for the good of inquiring minds,
Was sold at auction on the public square,
As if to destroy the last vestige   5
Of my memory and influence.
For those of you who could not see the virtue
Of knowing Volney's *Ruins* ° as well as Butler's *Analogy,*°
And *Faust* ° as well as *Evangeline,*°
Were really the power in the village,   10
And often you asked me,
"What is the use of knowing the evil in the world?"
I am out of your way now, Spoon River,
Choose your own good and call it good.
For I could never make you see   15
That no one knows what is good
Who knows not what is evil;
And no one knows what is true
Who knows not what is false.

8. **Volney's *Ruins:*** a work on the philosophy of history by Constantine Volney (1757–1820), a French writer. **Butler's *Analogy:*** religious writings of an English bishop, Joseph Butler (1692–1752). 9. *Faust* (foust): a drama by the German poet Johann von Goethe (gŭ′tě) (1749–1832). *Evangeline:* a poem by Longfellow (see page 597).

"Theodore the Poet" and "Seth Compton," from *Spoon River Anthology* by Edgar Lee Masters, published by The Macmillan Company. Reprinted by permission of Mrs. Edgar Lee Masters.

Though none of Masters' other books achieved such success as Spoon River
Anthology, *this powerful poem from* Songs and Satires *ranks with his best work.
It presents with dramatic examples a sad and profound truth about human life.*

Silence

I have known the silence of the stars and of the sea,
And the silence of the city when it pauses,
And the silence of a man and a maid,
And the silence for which music alone finds the word,
And the silence of the woods before the winds of spring begin,   5
And the silence of the sick
When their eyes roam about the room.
And I ask: For the depths,
Of what use is language?
A beast of the field moans a few times   10
When death takes its young:
And we are voiceless in the presence of realities —
We cannot speak.

A curious boy asks an old soldier
Sitting in front of the grocery store,   15
"How did you lose your leg?"
And the old soldier is struck with silence,
Or his mind flies away
Because he cannot concentrate it on Gettysburg.
It comes back jocosely   20
And he says, "A bear bit it off."
And the boy wonders, while the old soldier
Dumbly, feebly, lives over
The flashes of guns, the thunder of cannon,
The shrieks of the slain,   25
And himself lying on the ground,
And the hospital surgeons, the knives,
And the long days in bed.
But if he could describe it all
He would be an artist.   30
But if he were an artist, there would be deeper wounds
Which he could not describe.

There is the silence of a great hatred,
And the silence of a great love,
And the silence of a deep peace of mind,   35
And the silence of an embittered friendship.

"Silence" fom *Songs and Satires* by Edgar Lee Masters, published by The Macmillan Company. Reprinted by
permission of Mrs. Edgar Lee Masters.

EDGAR LEE MASTERS   267

There is the silence of a spiritual crisis,
Through which your soul, exquisitely tortured,
Comes with visions not to be uttered
Into a realm of higher life,   40
And the silence of the gods who understand each other without speech.
There is the silence of defeat.
There is the silence of those unjustly punished;
And the silence of the dying whose hand
Suddenly grips yours.   45
There is the silence between father and son,
When the father cannot explain his life,
Even though he be misunderstood for it.

There is the silence that comes between husband and wife,
There is the silence of those who have failed;   50
And the vast silence that covers
Broken nations and vanquished leaders.

There is the silence of Lincoln,
Thinking of the poverty of his youth.
And the silence of Napoleon   55
After Waterloo.
And the silence of Jeanne d'Arc
Saying amid the flames, "Blessèd Jesus"—
Revealing in two words all sorrow, all hope.

And there is the silence of age,   60
Too full of wisdom for the tongue to utter it
In words intelligible to those who have not lived
The great range of life.

And there is the silence of the dead.
If we who are in life cannot speak   65
Of profound experiences,
Why do you marvel that the dead
Do not tell you of death?
Their silence shall be interpreted
As we approach them.   70

FOR DISCUSSION

1. Which of the persons in the Spoon River group represents each of the following: belief in the educational value of contrast and comparison; young ambition betrayed; unquenchable curiosity; interest in man and space?

2. Of all "kindred spirits," why did Flossie Cabanis wish that Duse might read her epitaph?

3. To what does Theodore the Poet compare the crawfish?

4. What was Seth Compton's chief criticism of his townsmen?

5. Of the four Spoon River citizens cele-

brated by these epitaphs, which seems most fulfilled (satisfied by his life and accomplishments)?

6. In "Silence," the poet gives many illustrations of moments of silence. Do you agree that all are beyond ordinary powers of expression? Can you add other moments to the list? What is meant by lines 31–32? What attitude does the poet take toward the "silence of the dead"?

YOUR OWN WRITING

Try writing epitaphs in Masters' style for three of the characters in short stories the class has read; see whether your classmates can fit the appropriate proper name to each.

PATTERNS OF POETRY

FREE VERSE

All the poems by Masters in this book are written in *free verse*, which has neither rhyme nor consistent length nor a regular rhythm pattern. It would be wrong, however, to say that free verse does not have rhythm. It is not prose cut up into lines. Actually, free-verse poets take great pains to achieve rhythmic effects suited to the thought. But the rhythms change with alterations in mood and thought, and are free from a strict pattern. If Masters had used rhymed couplets in "Silence," what effect might have been lost? Can you point out places in the poem where the rhythm changes?

VACHEL LINDSAY

VACHEL LINDSAY (1879–1931) inherited from an artistic mother a love of beauty and from an evangelist grandfather a crusading temperament. After high school in Springfield, Illinois, he attended Hiram College in Ohio and art schools in Chicago and New York, writing poems to explain the meanings of his curious drawings. Unable to succeed as an artist, he returned to his home town, preaching his gospel of beauty, and campaigning against civic wrongs.

He often made long, vagabonding tours afoot, offering his pamphlet, *Rhymes to Be Traded for Bread,* in exchange for lodging and food. After "General William Booth Enters into Heaven" created a sensation, breaking down the barriers between poetry and music, Lindsay made many more tours, chanting his own poems. Intoned in his resonant baritone, the rhythmic sounds of a noisy and exuberant America compelled the attention of great crowds of people. It is probable that exhaustion from this strenuous life was one of the factors in Lindsay's early and tragic death.

The important poems of Vachel Lindsay fall into two groups: those preaching his gospel of beauty and better living for all; and those combining emotionally exciting themes with strong rhythmic effects. One group includes tributes to men Lindsay regarded as heroes in the fight for a fairer, better world. The second group, the rhythmic and exciting poems, is represented here by his imaginative account of heaven's welcome to the Salvation Army leader General William Booth.

The following poem, picturing the head of the Salvation Army marching into heaven followed by his converts, is a prime example of Lindsay's skillful handling of sound. The steady roll of the drum, the blatancy of the trumpets, the uneven tramping of the marchers, with the phrase from the hymn tune running throughout, combine to make the poem a noisy and exciting experience. Only oral reading can do justice to it. As you read the poem aloud, be careful to mold your tone and timing to fit the various musical instruments Lindsay prescribes for the different sections. See the study aid on page 274 for suggestions on a choral reading of the poem.

General William Booth Enters into Heaven

[To be sung to the tune of "The Blood of the Lamb"
with indicated instruments]

I

[*Bass drum beaten loudly*]
Booth led boldly with his big bass drum —
(Are you washed in the blood of the Lamb?)
The Saints smiled gravely and they said, "He's come."
(Are you washed in the blood of the Lamb?)
Walking lepers followed, rank on rank,   5
Lurching bravos from the ditches dank,
Drabs from the alleyways and drug fiends pale —
Minds still passion-ridden, soul powers frail:
Vermin-eaten saints with moldy breath,
Unwashed legions with the ways of Death —   10
(Are you washed in the blood of the Lamb?)

[*Banjos*]
Every slum had sent its half a score
The round world over. (Booth had groaned for more.)
Every banner that the wide world flies
Bloomed with glory and transcendent dyes.   15
Big-voiced lasses made their banjos bang,
Tranced, fanatical, they shrieked and sang:
"Are you washed in the blood of the Lamb?"
Hallelujah! It was queer to see
Bull-necked convicts with that land make free.   20
Loons with trumpets blew a blare, blare, blare
On, on upward thro' the golden air!
(Are you washed in the blood of the Lamb?)

"General William Booth Enters into Heaven" from *Collected Poems* by Vachel Lindsay. Reprinted by permission of The Macmillan Company, publishers.

[Bass drum slower and softer]
Booth died blind and still by faith he trod,
Eyes still dazzled by the ways of God.   25
Booth led boldly, and he looked the chief,
Eagle countenance in sharp relief,
Beard a-flying, air of high command
Unabated in that holy land.

[Sweet flute music]
Jesus came from out the courthouse door,   30
Stretched his hands above the passing poor.
Booth saw not, but led his queer ones there
Round and round the mighty courthouse square.
Yet in an instant all that blear review
Marched on spotless, clad in raiment new.   35
The lame were straightened, withered limbs uncurled,
And blind eyes opened on a new, sweet world.

[Bass drum louder]
Drabs and vixens in a flash made whole!
Gone was the weasel head, the snout, the jowl!
Sages and sibyls° now, and athletes clean,   40
Rulers of empires, and of forests green!

[Grand chorus of all instruments. Tambourines to the foreground]
The hosts were sandaled, and their wings were fire!
(Are you washed in the blood of the Lamb?)
But their noise played havoc with the angel choir.
(Are you washed in the blood of the Lamb?)   45
O, shout Salvation! It was good to see
Kings and princes by the Lamb set free.
The banjos rattled and the tambourines
Jing-jing-jingled in the hands of queens.

[Reverently sung, no instruments]
And when Booth halted by the curb for prayer   50
He saw his Master thro' the flag-filled air.
Christ came gently with a robe and crown
For Booth the soldier, while the throng knelt down.
He saw King Jesus. They were face to face,
And he knelt a-weeping in that holy place.   55
Are you washed in the blood of the Lamb?

40. sibyls (sĭb'ĭlz): fortunetellers.

Lindsay felt a close bond to Abraham Lincoln because he grew up in Lincoln's home town, Springfield, Illinois. The following poem was written during World War I, but, since an assured peace has not yet come to the world, it still bears a significant message.

Abraham Lincoln Walks at Midnight
in Springfield, Illinois

It is portentous, and a thing of state
That here at midnight, in our little town,
A mourning figure walks, and will not rest,
Near the old courthouse pacing up and down,

Or by his homestead, or in shadowed yards   5
He lingers where his children used to play,
Or through the market, on the well-worn stones,
He stalks until the dawn stars burn away.

A bronzed, lank man! His suit of ancient black,
A famous high top hat and plain worn shawl   10
Make him the quaint great figure that men love,
The prairie lawyer, master of us all.

He cannot sleep upon his hillside now.
He is among us — as in times before!
And we who toss and lie awake for long   15
Breathe deep, and start, to see him pass the door.

His head is bowed. He thinks on men and kings.
Yea, when the sick world cries, how can he sleep?
Too many peasants fight, they know not why,
Too many homesteads in black terror weep.   20

The sins of all the war lords burn his heart.
He sees the dreadnoughts° scouring every main.
He carries on his shawl-wrapped shoulders now
The bitterness, the folly, and the pain.

He cannot rest until a spirit dawn   25
Shall come — the shining hope of Europe free:

22. **dreadnoughts** (drĕd'nôts): battleships used by the British in World War I.

"Abraham Lincoln Walks at Midnight" from *Collected Poems* by Vachel Lindsay. Reprinted by permission of The Macmillan Company, publishers.

The league of sober folk, the workers' earth,
Bringing long peace to Cornland, Alp, and Sea.

It breaks his heart that kings must murder still,
That all his hours of travail here for men   30
Seem yet in vain. And who will bring white peace
That he may sleep upon his hill again?

Lindsay was always ready to support causes, or, as in "The Leaden-Eyed," to pro-
test against wrong.

The Leaden-Eyed

Let not young souls be smothered out before
They do quaint deeds and fully flaunt their pride.
It is the world's one crime its babes grow dull,
Its poor are oxlike, limp, and leaden-eyed.

Not that they starve, but starve so dreamlessly,   5
Not that they sow, but that they seldom reap,
Not that they serve, but have no gods to serve,
Not that they die, but that they die like sheep.

A special hero of Lindsay's impressionable youth was John Peter Altgeld, a
governor of Illinois who lived up to his liberal creed in his official decisions, even
though he realized that his actions could cause his political defeat. This poem
records the poet's admiration for Altgeld and his scorn for the followers who
so quickly forgot him.

The Eagle That Is Forgotten

Sleep softly . . . eagle forgotten . . . under the stone.
Time has its way with you there, and the clay has its own.

"We have buried him now," thought your foes, and in secret rejoiced.
They made a brave show of their mourning, their hatred unvoiced.

They had snarled at you, barked at you, foamed at you day after day. 5
Now you were ended. They praised you . . . and laid you away.

The others that mourned you in silence and terror and truth,
The widow bereft of her crust, and the boy without youth,
The mocked and the scorned and the wounded, the lame and the poor
That should have remembered forever . . . remember no more. 10

Where are those lovers of yours, on what name do they call,
The lost, that in armies wept over your funeral pall?
They call on the names of a hundred high-valiant ones,
A hundred white eagles have risen, the sons of your sons,
The zeal in their wings is a zeal that your dreaming began, 15
The valor that wore out your soul in the service of man.

Sleep softly . . . eagle forgotten . . . under the stone.
Time has its way with you there, and the clay has its own.
Sleep on, O brave-hearted, O wise man, that kindled the flame —
To live in mankind is far more than to live in a name, 20
To live in mankind, far, far more . . . than to live in a name.

FOR DISCUSSION

1. Just what is meant by the title "The Leaden-Eyed"? What does Lindsay say is "the world's one crime"? Explain why the physical hardships listed in the second stanza are less terrible than the situations Lindsay describes in the second half of each line.

2. How many of the causes for Lincoln's unrest in "Abraham Lincoln Walks at Midnight" still exist in the world? Give specific instances.

3. In "The Eagle That Is Forgotten," who should have remembered Altgeld most faithfully, according to Lindsay? What consolation does Lindsay find in contemplating Altgeld's fate?

CHORAL READING

You will rarely find better material for choral reading than "General William Booth Enters into Heaven." Sort out from the class deep voices that can best represent the bass drums, medium voices for the banjos, and high, sweet voices for the

flutes. Select a special group with soft, low voices to read the line "Are you washed in the blood of the Lamb?" Let each group practice separately on its parts of the poem. Then, with a leader to direct the groups as a choir, put all the parts together. The whole class should come out strongly on the grand chorus.

THE POET'S ART

ALLITERATION

Along with even bolder sound effects, Lindsay uses *alliteration* freely in "General William Booth Enters into Heaven." It is easy to catch the repeated *b*'s in the first line. Find other examples of alliteration in the rest of the poem.

ONOMATOPOEIA

Poets often choose words that sound like what they mean, a device called *onomatopoeia*. Simple examples of such words are *buzz*, *crunch*, and *pop*. How does Lindsay imitate the sounds of the various musical instruments in "General William Booth Enters into Heaven"?

ELINOR WYLIE

ELINOR WYLIE (1885–1928) was descended from Pennsylvanians who had distinguished themselves in service to their state and their nation. She was reared in a Philadelphia suburb and in Washington, D.C., and educated in private schools. For a time she hesitated between painting and writing as a career, but she had been writing poetry even in her teens, and literature won over art. She had published a number of brilliant and sensitive poems when she met William Rose Benét, poet and member of a distinguished family of writers. As his wife she shared in the literary life of New York.

Although she wrote four prose works — novels with bizarre plots and allegorical overtones — Elinor Wylie's fame rests on her poetry published in *Nets to Catch the Wind, Black Armour, Trivial Breath,* and *Angels and Earthly Creatures.*

All of Elinor Wylie's poems are marked by a distinctive combination of technique, thought, and sentiment. Her lines flow smoothly and musically, yet the melodic rhythm of her poetry never interferes with the meaning. The vivid sensory impressions of her poems indicate the artist's highly developed senses of hearing, touch, and sight. Elinor Wylie's tone ranges widely from the light touch of "Velvet Shoes" to the stern advice in "The Eagle and the Mole."

Velvet Shoes

Let us walk in the white snow
　In a soundless space;
With footsteps quiet and slow,
　At a tranquil pace,
　Under veils of white lace.　　　　5

I shall go shod in silk,
　And you in wool,
White as a white cow's milk,
　More beautiful
　Than the breast of a gull.　　　　10

We shall walk through the still town
　In a windless peace;
We shall step upon white down,
　Upon silver fleece,
　Upon softer than these.　　　　15

We shall walk in velvet shoes:
　Wherever we go
Silence will fall like dews.
　On white silence below.
　We shall walk in the snow.　　　　20

"Breaking Wave," by the American artist Winslow Homer (1836–1910).

Elinor Wylie's fondness for stating her thoughts in symbols or metaphors, as in the next poem, calls for sensitive reading and skill in interpretation.

Sea Lullaby

The old moon is tarnished
With smoke of the flood,
The dead leaves are varnished
With color like blood,

A treacherous smiler   5
With teeth white as milk,
A savage beguiler
In sheathings of silk,

The sea creeps to pillage,
She leaps on her prey;   10
A child of the village
Was murdered today.

She came up to meet him
In a smooth golden cloak,
She choked him and beat him   15
To death, for a joke.

Her bright locks were tangled,
She shouted for joy,
With one hand she strangled
A strong little boy.   20

Now in silence she lingers
Beside him all night
To wash her long fingers
In silvery light.

Pretty Words

Poets make pets of pretty, docile words:
I love smooth words, like gold-enameled fish
Which circle slowly with a silken swish,
And tender ones, like downy-feathered birds:
Words shy and dappled, deep-eyed deer in herds,   5
Come to my hand, and playful if I wish,
Or purring softly at a silver dish,
Blue Persian kittens, fed on cream and curds.

I love bright words, words up and singing early;
Words that are luminous in the dark, and sing;   10
Warm lazy words, white cattle under trees;
I love words opalescent, cool, and pearly,
Like midsummer moths, and honeyed words like bees,
Gilded and sticky, with a little sting.

Nonsense Rhyme

Whatever's good or bad or both
Is surely better than the none;
There's grace in either love or loathe;
Sunlight, or freckles on the sun.

The worst and best are both inclined   5
To snap like vixens at the truth;
But, O, beware the middle mind
That purrs and never shows a tooth!

Beware the smooth ambiguous smile
That never pulls the lips apart;   10
Salt of pure and pepper of vile
Must season the extremer heart.

A pinch of fair, a pinch of foul,
And bad and good make best of all;
Beware the moderated soul   15
That climbs no fractional inch to fall.

Reason's a rabbit in a hutch,
And ecstasy's a werewolf's ghost;
But, O, beware the nothing-much
And welcome madness and the most!   20

The Eagle and the Mole

Avoid the reeking herd,
Shun the polluted flock,
Live like that stoic bird,
The eagle of the rock.

The huddled warmth of crowds   5
Begets and fosters hate;
He keeps, above the clouds,
His cliff inviolate.

When flocks are folded warm,
And herds to shelter run,   10
He sails above the storm,
He stares into the sun.

If in the eagle's track
Your sinews cannot leap,
Avoid the lathered pack,   15
Turn from the steaming sheep.

If you would keep your soul
From spotted sight or sound,
Live like the velvet mole;
Go burrow underground.   20

And there hold intercourse
With roots of trees and stones,
With rivers at their source,
And disembodied bones.

FOR DISCUSSION

1. Select phrases from the poems that show the poet's tendency to introduce an unexpected, even startling, idea. Find other phrases that illustrate Elinor Wylie's appeal to the senses, especially those of sound and sight.

2. Why is the picture of the sea in "Sea Lullaby" more sinister than if the poet had described a destructive storm? How does the ironic title heighten the effect of the poem?

3. Explain the "sense" of "Nonsense Rhyme." Do you agree with the poet's choice between extremes and the middle course? Is the central thought of "The Eagle and the Mole" consistent with this attitude? Explain. What is it that Elinor Wylie dislikes in the general mass of people?

4. Can you point out some examples of alliteration in "Velvet Shoes"? Do you feel that this poetic device is especially effective in this poem?

5. What is the form of "Pretty Words"? Is it a sonnet? If so, how does it differ from Robert Frost's sonnet "Putting in the Seed" on page 253?

6. Can you find examples in "Velvet Shoes" and "Pretty Words" of the vivid sensory impressions that characterize Elinor Wylie's poetry? What do they contribute to the poems?

THE APT WORD

Can you point out some examples of the "pretty words" that the poet professes to love? Find three words in the first stanza of "Velvet Shoes" that help to set the mood for the poem. How do the terms used for the snow contribute to the effect?

THE POET'S ART

PERSONIFICATION. A poetic device that is often used to create fresh and striking images is *personification.* Elinor Wylie uses personification skillfully in "Sea Lullaby." Notice how the sea is spoken of as a person and is vividly described in terms that fit a person, yet picture clearly the real sea. Start off with "creeps to pillage, . . . leaps on her prey." Can you detect the changes in the movement of water along the shore? What pictures of the sea do you get from the following lines?

"teeth white as milk,"
"In a smooth golden cloak,"
"Her bright locks were tangled,"
"To wash her long fingers
  In silvery light."

STEPHEN VINCENT BENÉT

STEPHEN VINCENT BENÉT (1898–1943) is
equally celebrated as a short-story writer and as
a poet. "The Devil and Daniel Webster" ranks
among the all-time favorite American short stories (see page 62). His great poem of the War
Between the States, *John Brown's Body,* quickly
became a best seller, won a Pulitzer prize, and
gains thousands of new readers every year. After
the fashion of the historical novel, this long poem
weaves many strands into a dramatic narrative
of the great struggle: memorable portraits of
Northern and Southern leaders, vivid accounts of
battles, fascinating stories of individuals on both
sides. At the time of his death, Benét had nearly
completed a similar poetic narrative about the
settlement of America, *Western Star,* which won
him a posthumous Pulitzer prize in 1943. A few
years earlier he and his wife Rosemary had collaborated on *A Book of Americans,* a popular

series of light-verse portrayals of famous men. In his last years he wrote radio plays on
patriotic themes to rally support for America's cause in the Second World War. His early
death at the age of forty-five was mourned as a loss to American letters.

*In poetry as in fiction, Stephen Vincent Benét drew his richest inspiration from
America's past. An able craftsman, he varied his rhythms and patterns to fit his
subjects. In "The Mountain Whippoorwill" Benét falls into the swinging
rhythms and easy rhymes of the folk music that the poem describes. His "Portrait
of a Southern Lady," from* John Brown's Body, *is presented with the firm vigor
and occasional satirical flash of the rhymed couplet.*

The Mountain Whippoorwill

(Or, How Hillbilly Jim Won the Great Fiddlers' Prize)

A GEORGIA ROMANCE

Up in the mountains, it's lonesome all the time,
(Sof' win' slewin' thu' the sweet-potato vine).

Up in the mountains, it's lonesome for a child,
(Whippoorwills a-callin' when the sap runs wild).

Up in the mountains, mountains in the fog,   5
Everythin's as lazy as an old houn' dog.

Born in the mountains, never raised a pet,
Don't want nuthin' an' never got it yet.

Born in the mountains, lonesome-born,
Raised runnin' ragged thu' the cockleburrs and corn.   10

Never knew my pappy, mebbe never should.
Think he was a fiddle made of mountain-laurel wood.

Never had a mammy to teach me pretty-please.
Think she was a whippoorwill, a-skitin' thu' the trees.

Never had a brother ner a whole pair of pants,   15
But when I start to fiddle, why, yuh got to start to dance!

Listen to my fiddle — Kingdom Come — Kingdom Come!
Hear the frogs a-chunkin' "Jug o' rum, Jug o' rum!"
Hear that mountain whippoorwill be lonesome in the air,
An' I'll tell yuh how I traveled to the Essex County Fair.   20

Essex County has a mighty pretty fair,
All the smarty fiddlers from the South come there.

Elbows flyin' as they rosin up the bow
For the First Prize Contest in the Georgia Fiddlers' Show.

Old Dan Wheeling, with his whiskers in his ears,   25
Kingpin fiddler for nearly twenty years.

Big Tom Sargent, with his blue walleye,
An' Little Jimmy Weezer that can make a fiddle cry.

All sittin' roun', spittin' high an' struttin' proud,
(Listen, little whippoorwill, yuh better bug yore eyes!)   30
Tun-a-tun-a-tunin' while the jedges told the crowd
Them that got the mostest claps 'd win the bestest prize.

Everybody waitin' for the first tweedledee,
When in comes a-stumblin' — hillbilly me!

Bowed right pretty to the jedges an' the rest,   35
Took a silver dollar from a hole inside my vest,

Plunked it on the table an' said, "There's my callin' card!
An' anyone that licks me — well, he's got to fiddle hard!"

Old Dan Wheeling, he was laughin' fit to holler,
Little Jimmy Weezer said, "There's one dead dollar!"   40

Big Tom Sargent had a yaller-toothy grin,
But I tucked my little whippoorwill spang underneath my chin,
An' petted it an' tuned it till the jedges said, "Begin!"

Big Tom Sargent was the first in line;
He could fiddle all the bugs off a sweet-potato vine.   45
He could fiddle down a possum from a mile-high tree,
He could fiddle up a whale from the bottom of the sea.

Yuh could hear hands spankin' till they spanked each other raw,
When he finished variations on "Turkey in the Straw."

Little Jimmy Weezer was the next to play;   50
He could fiddle all night, he could fiddle all day.

He could fiddle chills, he could fiddle fever,
He could make a fiddle rustle like a lowland river.

He could make a fiddle croon like a lovin' woman,
An' they clapped like thunder when he'd finished strummin'.   55

Then came the ruck of the bobtailed fiddlers,
The let's-go-easies, the fair-to-middlers.

They got their claps an' they lost their bicker,°
An' they all settled back for some more corn licker.

An' the crowd was tired of their no-'count squealing,   60
When out in the center steps Old Dan Wheeling.

He fiddled high and he fiddled low,
(*Listen, little whippoorwill; yuh got to spread yore wings!*)
He fiddled and fiddled with a cherrywood bow.
(*Old Dan Wheeling's got bee honey in his strings.*)   65

He fiddled the wind by the lonesome moon.
He fiddled a most almighty tune.

58. lost their bicker: failed.

STEPHEN VINCENT BENÉT   281

He started fiddling like a ghost.
He ended fiddling like a host.

He fiddled north an' he fiddled south,   70
He fiddled the heart right out of yore mouth.

He fiddled here an' he fiddled there.
He fiddled salvation everywhere.

When he was finished, the crowd cut loose.
(Whippoorwill, they's rain on yore breast.)   75
An' I sat there wonderin' "What's the use?"
(Whippoorwill, fly home to yore nest.)

But I stood up pert an' I took my bow,
An' my fiddle went to my shoulder, so.

An' — they wasn't no crowd to get me fazed° —   80
But I was alone where I was raised.

Up in the mountains, so still it makes yuh skeered.
Where God lies sleepin' in his big white beard.

An' I heard the sound of the squirrel in the pine,
An' I heard the earth a-breathin' thu' the long nighttime.   85

They've fiddled the rose, and they've fiddled the thorn,
But they haven't fiddled the mountain corn.

They've fiddled sinful an' fiddled moral,
But they haven't fiddled the breshwood laurel.

They've fiddled loud, and they've fiddled still,   90
But they haven't fiddled the whippoorwill.

I started off with a *dump-diddle-dump*,
(Oh, hell's broke loose in Georgia!)
Skunk cabbage growin' by the bee-gum stump,
(Whippoorwill, yo're singin' now!)   95

My mother was a whippoorwill pert,
My father, he was lazy,
But I'm hell broke loose in a new store shirt
To fiddle all Georgia crazy.

80. **fazed:** embarrassed.

"Dancing on the Barn Floor," an oil painting by the American artist William Sidney Mount (1807–1868).

Swing yore partners — up an' down the middle!   100
Sashay now — oh, listen to that fiddle!
Flapjacks flippin' on a red-hot griddle,
An' hell broke loose,
Hell broke loose,
Fire on the mountains — snakes in the grass.   105
Satan's here a-bilin' — oh, Lordy, let him pass!
Go down Moses, set my people free;
Pop goes the weasel thu' the old Red Sea!
Jonah sittin' on a hickory bough,
Up jumps a whale — 'an where's yore prophet now?   110
Rabbit in the pea patch, possum in the pot,
Try an' stop my fiddle, now my fiddle's gettin' hot!
Whippoorwill, singin' thu' the mountain hush,
Whippoorwill, shoutin' from the burnin' bush,
Whippoorwill, cryin' in the stable door,   115
Sing tonight as yuh never sang before!
Hell's broke loose like a stompin' mountain shoat,°
Sing till yuh bust the gold in yore throat!
Hell's broke loose for forty miles aroun',
Bound to stop yore music if yuh don't sing it down.   120

117. **shoat** (shōt): a young pig.

STEPHEN VINCENT BENÉT   283

Sing on the mountains, little whippoorwill,
Sing to the valleys, an' slap 'em with a hill,
For I'm struttin' high as an eagle's quill,
An' hell's broke loose,
Hell's broke loose,   125
Hell's broke loose in Georgia!

They wasn't a sound when I stopped bowin',
(*Whippoorwill, yuh can sing no more.*)
But, somewhere or other, the dawn was growin',
(*Oh, mountain whippoorwill!*)   130

An' I thought, "I've fiddled all night an' lost,
Yo're a good hillbilly, but yuh've been bossed."

So I went to congratulate old man Dan,
— But he puts his fiddle into my han' —
An' then the noise of the crowd began!   135

Portrait of a Southern Lady

(FROM *John Brown's Body*)

Mary Lou Wingate, as slightly made
And as hard to break as a rapier blade.
Bristol's daughter and Wingate's bride,
Never well since the last child died
But staring at pain with courteous eyes.   5
When the pain outwits it, the body dies,
Meanwhile the body bears the pain.
She loved her hands and they made her vain,
The tiny hands of her generation
That gathered the reins of the whole plantation;   10
The velvet sheathing the steel demurely
In the trained, light grip that holds so surely.

She was at work by candlelight,
She was at work in the dead of night,
Smoothing out troubles and healing schisms°   15
And doctoring phthisics° and rheumatisms,

15. schisms (sĭz'mz): separations resulting from differences of opinion.   16. phthisics
(tĭz'ĭks) or phthisis (thĭ'sĭs): tuberculosis.

should have could have - put original line numbers

Guiding the cooking and watching the baking,
The sewing, the soap- and candle-making,
The brewing, the darning, the lady-daughters,
The births and deaths in the Negro quarters,   20
Seeing that Suke had some new, strong shoes
And Joe got a week in the calaboose,
While Dicey's Jacob escaped a whipping
And the jelly bag dripped with its proper dripping,
And the shirts and estrangements were neatly mended,   25
And all of the tasks that never ended.

Her manner was gracious but hardly fervent
And she seldom raised her voice to a servant.
She was often mistaken, not often blind;
And she knew the whole duty of womankind,   30
To take the burden and have the power
And seem like the well-protected flower,
To manage a dozen industries
With a casual gesture in scraps of ease,
To hate the sin and to love the sinner   35
And to see that the gentlemen got their dinner
Ready and plenty and piping hot
Whether you wanted to eat or not.
And always, always, to have the charm
That makes the gentlemen take your arm   40
But never the bright, unseemly spell
That makes strange gentlemen love too well,
Once you were married and settled down
With a suitable gentleman of your own.

And when that happened, and you had bred   45
The requisite children, living and dead,
To pity the fool and comfort the weak
And always let the gentlemen speak,
To succor your love from deep-struck roots
When gentlemen went to bed in their boots,   50
And manage a gentleman's whole plantation
In the manner befitting your female station.

This was the creed that her mother taught her
And the creed that she taught to every daughter.
She knew her Bible — and how to flirt   55
With a swansdown fan and a brocade skirt.
For she trusted in God but she liked formalities,
And the world and heaven were both realities.

STEPHEN VINCENT BENÉT   285

— In heaven, of course, we should all be equal,
But, until we came to that golden sequel,   60
Gentility must keep to gentility,
Where God and breeding had made things stable,
While the rest of the cosmos deserved civility
But dined in its boots at the second table.
This view may be reckoned a trifle narrow,   65
But it had the driving force of an arrow,
And it helped Mary Lou to stand up straight,
For she was gentle, but she could hate,
And she hated the North with the hate of Jael°
When the dry hot hands went seeking the nail,   70
The terrible hate of women's ire,
The smoky, the long-consuming fire.
The Yankees were devils, and she could pray
For devils, no doubt, upon Judgment Day,
But now in the world, she would hate them still   75
And send the gentlemen out to kill.

The gentlemen killed and the gentlemen died,
But she was the South's incarnate pride
That mended the broken gentlemen
And sent them out to the war again,   80
That kept the house with the men away
And baked the bricks where there was no clay,
Made courage from terror and bread from bran
And propped the South on a swansdown fan
Through four long years of ruin and stress,   85
The pride — and the deadly bitterness.

69. Jael: a woman of Biblical times who killed the captain of the Canaanites by driving a nail through his forehead while he slept (see Judges 4:15–22).

FOR DISCUSSION

1. Which do you like best about "The Mountain Whippoorwill" — the story, the rhythm, or the imagery? Tell what is good about the other two elements before explaining the special charm of the quality you like best.

2. Point out special idioms, details of nature, and figures of speech that help to create the local color of the hillbilly fiddler and his mountain home.

3. How is suspense over the outcome of the contest built up? Is the outcome more, or less, effective for being indicated so briefly? Why do you think the outcome of the contest is presented in this way?

4. From "Portrait of a Southern Lady," make a list of the duties that filled the days of the mistress of a Southern plantation. Make another list of the beliefs and emotions that guided Mary Lou Wingate's life.

5. Does this portrait fit your previous idea of a Southern lady at the time of the War Between the States? If you have read *Gone with the Wind* or have seen the movie, point out ways in which Mary Lou Wingate and Scarlett O'Hara are alike and unlike.

SARA TEASDALE

SARA TEASDALE (1884–1933) was educated in private schools in St. Louis. After traveling in Europe and the Near East, she returned to St. Louis to begin her career with the publication of delicate, fanciful poems in various magazines. Vachel Lindsay was one of her suitors, but she chose to marry a businessman, and moved with him to New York. Though the marriage was not a success, she continued to live in New York the rest of her life. Her later years were darkened by seclusion and ill health. Of her seven volumes of verse, *Flame and Shadow*, *Dark of the Moon*, and *Strange Victory* contain her most mature work.

In an age when many poets were experimenting with revolutionary new forms and subject matter, Sara Teasdale remained faithful to traditional patterns and themes. She fashioned delicate lyrics to capture the flashes of thought and feeling that traditionally have been regarded as proper material for poetry. They are coins for the memory, such as she describes in the first poem.

The Coin

Into my heart's treasury
I slipped a coin
That time cannot take
Nor a thief purloin —
Oh, better than the minting   5
Of a gold-crowned king
Is the safe-kept memory
Of a lovely thing.

"The Coin" from *Flame and Shadow* by Sara Teasdale. Reprinted by permission of The Macmillan Company, publishers.

Barter

Life has loveliness to sell —
    All beautiful and splendid things,
Blue waves whitened on a cliff,
    Climbing fire that sways and sings,
And children's faces looking up   5
Holding wonder like a cup.

Life has loveliness to sell —
    Music like a curve of gold,
Scent of pine trees in the rain,
    Eyes that love you, arms that hold,   10
And for your spirit's still delight,
Holy thoughts that star the night.

Spend all you have for loveliness,
    Buy it and never count the cost,
For one white singing hour of peace   15
    Count many a year of strife well lost,
And for a breath of ecstasy,
Give all you have been or could be.

"Barter" from *Love Songs* by Sara Teasdale. Reprinted by permission of The Macmillan Company, publishers.

"Christina's World," a tempera painting by the American artist Andrew Wyeth (b. 1917).

The Long Hill

I must have passed the crest a while ago
    And now I am going down —
Strange to have crossed the crest and not to know,
    But the brambles were always catching the hem of my gown.

All the morning I thought how proud I should be   5
    To stand there straight as a queen,
Wrapped in the wind and the sun with the world under me —
    But the air was dull; there was little I could have seen.

It was nearly level along the beaten track
    And the brambles caught in my gown —   10
But it's no use now to think of turning back,
    The rest of the way will be only going down.

The Lamp

If I can bear your love like a lamp before me,
When I go down the long steep Road of Darkness,
I shall not fear the everlasting shadows,
        Nor cry in terror.

If I can find out God, then I shall find Him,   5
If none can find Him, then I shall sleep soundly,
Knowing how well on earth your love sufficed me,
        A lamp in darkness.

"The Long Hill" from *Flame and Shadow* by Sara Teasdale. Reprinted by permission of The Macmillan Company, publishers.
"The Lamp" from *Collected Poems* by Sara Teasdale. Reprinted by permission of The Macmillan Company, publishers.

FOR DISCUSSION

1. What contrasting moods do you find in this group of poems? What great satisfactions in life does the poet voice? Where do you find sadness or wistfulness?

2. In "Barter," does the line "Spend all you have for loveliness" mean to spend money — or something else? Justify your answer from the rest of the poem.

3. How does "The Long Hill" present a human life symbolically? Is the crest the midway point in a life, or the peak of happiness, or the height of success? What do the brambles represent?

4. In "The Lamp," what attitude toward death does the poet take?

PATTERNS OF POETRY

LYRIC STANZAS

Although the term "lyric poetry" loosely covers most poetry that is neither narrative nor dramatic, the word *lyric* is used most often to mean a short, musical poem expressing the poet's thoughts or feelings. Sara Teasdale's poems are good examples of the type. Notice the way she uses a different stanza pattern in each poem. Line length, rhyme scheme, and the number of lines in a stanza are the varying elements of which she builds the patterns. Which poem does not rhyme at all? Is it blank verse? Is it free verse? Explain the reasons for your answer.

SARA TEASDALE   289

ALAN SEEGER

ALAN SEEGER (1888–1916) was born in New York City and attended Harvard University. After graduation he went to France, and at the outbreak of World War I, he joined the French Foreign Legion. From that time until his death in action in 1916, he was almost continuously on the fighting front. His poems are collected in *Juvenilia* and *Last Poems.*

War is an experience that affects people profoundly, and out of each war comes some memorable writing. World War II, for example, affected most of the group you will soon read in "New Voices." Yet few poets of a later time have matched three poets of World War I in personal emotion. Of the three, only Alan Seeger was American. His "I Have a Rendezvous with Death" is often associated with Canadian poet John McCrae's "In Flanders Fields" and English poet Rupert Brooke's "The Soldier."

"The Road, France, 1918," an oil painting by the American artist John Singer Sargent (1856–1925).

I Have a Rendezvous with Death

I have a rendezvous° with Death
At some disputed barricade,
When Spring comes back with rustling shade
And apple blossoms fill the air —
I have a rendezvous with Death   5
When Spring brings back blue days and fair.

It may be he shall take my hand
And lead me into his dark land
And close my eyes and quench my breath —
It may be I shall pass him still.   10
I have a rendezvous with Death
On some scarred slope of battered hill,
When Spring comes round again this year
And the first meadow flowers appear.

God knows 'twere better to be deep   15
Pillowed in silk and scented down,
Where Love throbs out in blissful sleep,
Pulse nigh to pulse and breath to breath,
Where hushed awakenings are dear. . . .
But I've a rendezvous with Death   20
At midnight in some flaming town,
When Spring trips north again this year,
And I to my pledged word am true,
I shall not fail that rendezvous.

1. **rendezvous** (rän′dĕ·vōō): a meeting by appointment.

FOR DISCUSSION

1. Name the three places where Seeger thinks the rendezvous may be kept. What is his attitude toward his part in the war?

2. Why does Seeger emphasize that the rendezvous will take place in spring? In what mood does he approach the meeting?

BUILDING YOUR VOCABULARY

FOREIGN WORDS IN ENGLISH

The key word in this poem, *rendezvous*, came into English from French by a curious double route. In England, French was the language of gallantry and so contributed a number of words and phrases to the lover's vocabulary: *rendezvous*, "an appointed meeting," used especially of lovers' meetings; *tête-à-tête*, literally "head-to-head," for an intimate conversation; and *billet-doux*, "sweet note," for a love letter. But *rendezvous* also came into American English from the French fur trappers who met the American mountain men in the Rockies. It was their term for their annual appointed meeting, far out in the wild country, with fur buyers and traders from St. Louis.

Investigate other words we commonly use that are French in origin: *café*, *restaurant*, *chef*, *entrée*, *fiancé(e)*, *debutante*, *matinee*, *chassis*, *coupé*, *chauffeur*, and others you may think of.

JAMES WELDON JOHNSON

JAMES WELDON JOHNSON (1871–1938) had an unusually varied career. After leaving his native Florida to earn a degree at Atlanta University, he was principal of a high school, studied and practiced law, collaborated with his brother in writing popular songs and light opera, and spent seven years in Venezuela as United States consul. Later, he settled down to a quiet life as professor of creative literature at Fisk University. He met a tragic death in an automobile accident.

Johnson edited collections of spirituals and the poetry of Negro writers. He also published works of fiction, nonfiction, and autobiography in addition to his own poetry. *God's Trombones*, a series of sermons in verse, has had wide appeal.

Much of Johnson's work has its source in the materials of folklore. In his finest poetry, such as "The Creation," he was able to maintain the flavor of these original sources in combination with the style and rhythm of modern free verse.

The Creation

And God stepped out on space,
And He looked around and said,
"I'm lonely —
I'll make me a world."
As far as the eye of God could see   5
Darkness covered everything,
Blacker than a hundred midnights
Down in a cypress swamp.

Then God smiled,
And the light broke,   10
And the darkness rolled up on one side,
And the light stood shining on the other,
And God said, *"That's good!"*

Then God reached out and took the light in His hands,
And God rolled the light around in His hands,   15

Until He made the sun;
And He set that sun a-blazing in the heavens.
And the light that was left from making the sun
God gathered up in a shining ball
And flung against the darkness,   20
Spangling the night with the moon and stars.
Then down between
The darkness and the light
He hurled the world;
And God said, "*That's good!*"   25

Then God Himself stepped down —
And the sun was on His right hand,
And the moon was on His left;
The stars were clustered about His head,
And the earth was under His feet.   30
And God walked, and where He trod
His footsteps hollowed the valleys out
And bulged the mountains up.

Then He stopped and looked and saw
That the earth was hot and barren.   35
So God stepped over to the edge of the world
And He spat out the seven seas;
He batted His eyes and the lightnings flashed;
He clapped His hands and the thunders rolled;
And the waters above the earth came down,   40
The cooling waters came down.

Then the green grass sprouted,
And the little red flowers blossomed,
The pine tree pointed his finger to the sky,
And the oak spread out his arms;   45
The lakes cuddled down in the hollows of the ground,
And the rivers ran down to the sea;
And God smiled again,
And the rainbow appeared,
And curled itself around His shoulder.   50

Then God raised His arm and He waved His hand
Over the sea and over the land,
And He said, "*Bring forth! Bring forth!*"
And quicker than God could drop His hand,
Fishes and fowls   55
And beasts and birds
Swam the rivers and the seas,
Roamed the forests and the woods,

And split the air with their wings,
And God said, *"That's good!"*   60

Then God walked around
And God looked around
On all that He had made,
He looked at His sun,
He looked at His moon,   65
And He looked at His little stars;
He looked on His world
With all its living things,
And God said, *"I'm lonely still."*

Then God sat down   70
On the side of a hill where He could think;
By a deep, wide river He sat down;
With His head in His hands,
God thought and thought,
Till He thought, *"I'll make me a man!"*   75

Up from the bed of the river
God scooped the clay;
And by the bank of the river
He kneeled Him down;
And there the great God Almighty,   80
Who lit the sun and fixed it in the sky,
Who flung the stars to the most far corner of the night,
Who rounded the earth in the middle of His hand —
This Great God,
Like a mother bending over her baby,   85
Kneeled down in the dust
Toiling over a lump of clay
Till he shaped it in His own image;
Then into it He blew the breath of life,
And man became a living soul,   90
Amen. Amen.

FOR DISCUSSION

1. Pick out words and phrases that give an especially poetic quality to this story of the creation. Compare this poem with the first chapter of Genesis to find likenesses and differences.

2. What purely human emotions is God pictured as having? What feeling about God would this sermon foster in those who heard it?

3. Do you think this poem is better in free verse than it would have been in blank verse? Explain why.

4. Point out lines that are especially effective in creating vivid imagery.

◀ *A detail from "The Peaceable Kingdom," an oil painting by the self-taught American artist Edward Hicks (1780–1849).*

CARL SANDBURG

CARL SANDBURG (b. 1878) worked at an amazing variety of jobs — as milk-wagon driver, brickyard helper, stagehand, hotel dishwasher, railroad construction worker, and harvest hand — before he began his writing career. (See page 234 for more about his life and his prose works.) People he knew at work fill his books of poetry: *Chicago Poems; Cornhuskers; Smoke and Steel; Slabs of the Sunburnt West; Good Morning, America;* and *The People, Yes.* His *Complete Poems* won a Pulitzer prize in 1951.

In his youth Sandburg roamed as a hobo, and in later years he has made long tours reading his poems and singing folk songs to his own guitar accompaniment. Picking up more songs and lore along the way, he published a fine collection in *The American Songbag.* He has woven a rich fabric of folk sayings into his poem *The People, Yes.*

The vigor and variety of workaday America pervade the free-verse lines of Carl Sandburg's poetry, written, as he likes to say, "in the American language." In 1916, when Chicago Poems *was published, it stirred an uproar of criticism for its raw, thumping language and its frankness in picturing the city as wicked and brutal. But readers soon found that sympathy and tenderness were as much a part of Sandburg as toughness. You will find lines that pound away like the steel mills and freight trains of Chicago, and others that whisper as softly as waves lapping along a quiet shore.*

Nocturne in a Deserted Brickyard

Stuff of the moon
Runs on the lapping sand
Out to the longest shadows
Under the curving willows,
And round the creep of the wave line,   5
Fluxions° of yellow and dusk on the waters
Make a wide dreaming pansy of an old pond in the night.

      6. **Fluxions** (flŭk'shŭnz): motions.

Fog

The fog comes
on little cat feet.

It sits looking
over harbor and city
on silent haunches
and then moves on.

Grass

Pile the bodies high at Austerlitz ° and Waterloo.°
Shovel them under and let me work —
    I am the grass; I cover all.

And pile them high at Gettysburg
And pile them high at Ypres° and Verdun.°   5
Shovel them under and let me work.
Two years, ten years, and passengers ask the conductor:
    What place is this?
    Where are we now?

    I am the grass.   10
    Let me work.

   1. **Austerlitz, Waterloo**: battles of the Napoleonic Wars. **5. Ypres** (ē'pr', popularly, wĭ'pērz),
Verdun: battles of World War I.

CARL SANDBURG

The following poem, the title piece of Chicago Poems, *was first published in Poetry Magazine. At that time it won an award as "the best poem written by a citizen of the United States during the year."*

Chicago

Hog Butcher for the World,
Toolmaker, Stacker of Wheat,
Player with Railroads and the Nation's Freight Handler;
Stormy, husky, brawling,
City of the Big Shoulders: 5

They tell me you are wicked and I believe them, for I have seen your painted
    women under the gas lamps luring the farm boys.
And they tell me you are crooked and I answer: Yes, it is true I have seen the
    gunman kill and go free to kill again.
And they tell me you are brutal and my reply is: On the faces of women and
    children I have seen the marks of wanton hunger.
And having answered so I turn once more to those who sneer at this my city, and I
    give them back the sneer and say to them:
Come and show me another city with lifted head singing so proud to be alive
    and coarse and strong and cunning.   10
Flinging magnetic curses amid the toil of piling job on job, here is a tall bold
    slugger set vivid against the little soft cities;
Fierce as a dog with tongue lapping for action, cunning as a savage pitted against
    the wilderness,
      Bareheaded,
      Shoveling,
      Wrecking,   15
      Planning,
      Building, breaking, rebuilding,
Under the smoke, dust all over his mouth, laughing with white teeth,
Under the terrible burden of destiny laughing as a young man laughs,
Laughing even as an ignorant fighter laughs who has never lost a battle,   20
Bragging and laughing that under his wrist is the pulse, and under his ribs the
    heart of the people,
        Laughing!
Laughing the stormy, husky, brawling laughter of Youth, half-naked, sweating,
    proud to be Hog Butcher, Toolmaker, Stacker of Wheat, Player with Rail-
    roads and Freight Handler to the Nation.

A view of downtown Chicago ▶

The People Speak

The people, yes, the people,
Until the people are taken care of one way or another,
Until the people are solved somehow for the day and hour,
Until then one hears "Yes but the people what about the people?"
Sometimes as though the people is a child to be pleased or fed   5
Or again a hoodlum you have to be tough with
And seldom as though the people is a caldron and a reservoir
Of the human reserves that shape history. . . .
    Fire, chaos, shadows,
Events trickling from a thin line of flame   10
On into cries and combustions never expected.
The people have the element of surprise. . . .

    "The czar° has eight million men with guns and bayonets.
    Nothing can happen to the czar.
    The czar is the voice of God and shall live forever.   15
    Turn and look at the forest of steel and cannon
    Where the czar is guarded by eight million soldiers.
    Nothing can happen to the czar."
They said that for years and in the summer of 1914 . . .
As a portent and an assurance they said with owl faces: 20
    "Nothing can happen to the czar."
Yet the czar and his bodyguard of eight million vanished
And the czar stood in a cellar before a little firing squad
And the command of fire was given
And the czar stepped into regions of mist and ice;   25
The czar traveled into an ethereal uncharted Siberia
While two kaisers° also vanished from thrones
Ancient and established in blood and iron —
Two kaisers backed by ten million bayonets
Had their crowns in a gutter, their palaces mobbed.   30
    In fire, chaos, shadows,
In hurricanes beyond foretelling of probabilities,
In the shove and whirl of unforeseen combustions
    The people, yes, the people
Move eternally in the elements of surprise,   35
Changing from hammer to bayonet and back to hammer,
The hallelujah chorus forever shifting its star soloists.

    The people learn, unlearn, learn,
    a builder, a wrecker, a builder again,

13. **czar** (or **tsar**): the ruler of Russia until the Revolution of 1917.   27. **kaisers**: rulers of Germany and Austria until 1918.

a juggler of shifting puppets.   40
 In so few eyeblinks
 In transition lightning streaks,
the people project midgets into giants,
the people shrink titans into dwarfs.

 Faiths blow on the winds   45
 and become shibboleths°
 and deep growths
 with men ready to die
for a living word on the tongue,
for a light alive in the bones,   50
for dreams fluttering in the wrists. . . .

Sleep is a suspension midway
and a conundrum° of shadows
lost in meadows of the moon.
 The people sleep.   55
 Ai! ai! the people sleep.
Yet the sleepers toss in sleep
and an end comes of sleep
and the sleepers wake.
 Ai! ai! the sleepers wake! . . .   60

The storm of propaganda blows always.
In every air of today the germs float and hover.
The people have the say-so.
Let the argument go on.
Let the people listen.   65
Tomorrow the people say Yes or No by one question:
 "What else can be done?"
In the drive of faiths on the wind today the people know:
"We have come far and we are going farther yet." . . .

 The people will live on.   70
 The learning and blundering people will live on.
 They will be tricked and sold and again sold
And go back to the nourishing earth for rootholds,
 The people so peculiar in renewal and comeback,
 You can't laugh off their capacity to take it.   75
 The mammoth° rests between his cyclonic dramas. . . .

The people is a tragic and comic two-face:

---

46. shibboleths (shĭb'ô·lĕths): watchwords or party cries. 53. conundrum (kŏ·nŭn'drŭm):
a puzzle. 76. mammoth: a large extinct ancestor of the elephant, distinguished by his woolly
coat and long, curving tusks. Our adjective *mammoth* derives from this animal's name.

hero and hoodlum: phantom and gorilla twisting to moan with a gargoyle° mouth: "They
buy me and sell me . . . it's a game . . .   80
sometime I'll break loose . . ."

Now the steel mill sky is alive.
The fire breaks white and zigzag
shot on a gun-metal gloaming.
Man is a long time coming.   85
Man will yet win.
Brother the earth over may yet line up with brother:

This old anvil — the people, yes —
This old anvil laughs at many broken hammers.
    There are men who can't be bought.   90
    There are women beyond purchase.
    The fireborn are at home in fire.
    The stars make no noise.
    You can't hinder the wind from blowing.
    Time is a great teacher.   95
    Who can live without hope?

In the darkness with a great bundle of grief
    the people march.
In the night, and overhead a shovel of stars for
    keeps, the people march: 100
            "Where to? what next?
            Where to? what next?"

79. **gargoyle** (gär'goil): a grotesque, ugly figure.

Prayers of Steel

Lay me on an anvil, O God.
Beat me and hammer me into a crowbar.
Let me pry loose old walls.
Let me lift and loosen old foundations.

Lay me on an anvil, O God.   5
Beat me and hammer me into a steel spike.
Drive me into the girders that hold a skyscraper together.
Take red-hot rivets and fasten me into the central girders.
Let me be the great nail holding a skyscraper through blue nights into white stars.

"Prayers of Steel" from *Cornhuskers* by Carl Sandburg. Copyright 1918 by Holt, Rinehart and Winston, Inc.
Copyright renewed 1946 by Carl Sandburg. Reprinted by permission of Holt, Rinehart and Winston, Inc.

The Harbor

Passing through huddled and ugly walls
By doorways where women
Looked from their hunger-deep eyes,
Haunted with shadows of hunger-hands,
Out from the huddled and ugly walls,   5
I came sudden, at the city's edge,
On a blue burst of lake,
Long lake waves breaking under the sun
On a spray-flung curve of shore;
And a fluttering storm of gulls,   10
Masses of great gray wings
And flying white bellies
Veering and wheeling free in the open.

FOR DISCUSSION

1. What does Sandburg mean when he speaks of the people as "an old anvil" that "laughs at many broken hammers"? How do the people "Move eternally in the elements of surprise"? What traits of the common run of mankind does the poet most admire? Find lines from "The People Speak" to support your opinion.

2. What was your feeling toward Chicago after reading Sandburg's poem? If Chicago is a "tall bold slugger," what sort of person would best represent Boston? Hollywood? Miami? your own city or town?

3. How do "The Harbor" and "Nocturne in a Deserted Brickyard" show the variety that Sandburg found in the Chicago area? How do they show that the poet was sensitive to beauty? to human struggles and difficulties?

4. Where do you find examples of Sandburg's raw, thumping language? of delicate language? Which do you think he handles better?

SYMBOLISM

Point out examples of Sandburg's use of symbolism in "The Harbor" and in "Grass."

THE POET'S ART

FIGURES OF SPEECH

Much of the vivid imagery that runs through Sandburg's poetry is created by the skillful use of *metaphor, simile,* and *personification.* These figures of speech are all forms of comparison, methods of pointing out similarities between things that are usually considered completely unlike. Sandburg uses a metaphor in "The People Speak" when he writes "the people is a caldron and a reservoir." A good example of simile occurs in "Chicago," where the city is said to be as "fierce as a dog." Notice that a simile is easily recognized because it introduces the comparison by the use of *as* or *like.* The third of these important poetic devices, personification (also discussed on page 278), occurs whenever an inanimate object is described in terms that refer to a human being. Sandburg uses personification in "Chicago" when he writes of the "City of the Big Shoulders," the "tall, bold slugger." Try to pick out some further examples of metaphor, simile, and personification in Sandburg's poetry, and remember to look for these figures of speech in the works of the other poets you will read.

EDNA ST. VINCENT MILLAY

EDNA ST. VINCENT MILLAY (1892–1950) had poems printed in *St. Nicholas Magazine* during her childhood on the coast of Maine, and published her first volume, *Renascence,* the year of her graduation from Vassar. The next five years she lived in the Greenwich Village section of New York City, supporting herself by writing stories under assumed names and acting with the Provincetown Players.

Serious critics condemned as flippant *A Few Figs from Thistles,* but the "gilded youth" of the twenties took it to their hearts. Her next volumes, *Second April, The Harp-Weaver,* and *The Buck in the Snow,* returned to the lyric vein of her earlier work and won wide popularity.

After her marriage she lived on a farm in New England. Her later books of poetry showed increasing concern with current issues but a corresponding decline in lyric appeal.

Flowing melody and an intense delight in the world of nature swept Edna Millay to fame with the poem "Renascence," written when she was only nineteen, and the same qualities mark many of her short lyrics, such as "God's World." In other poems she dwells with equal intensity on the whole gamut of personal emotions, from the delicate wistfulness of "The Spring and the Fall" to the defiant grief of "Dirge Without Music." Although she used a great variety of poetic patterns and also free verse, she achieved her finest expression in simple lyric forms and in the sonnet.

God's World

O world, I cannot hold thee close enough!
   Thy winds, thy wide gray skies!
   Thy mists that roll and rise!
Thy woods, this autumn day, that ache and sag
And all but cry with color! That gaunt crag   5
To crush! To lift the lean of that black bluff!
World, world, I cannot get thee close enough!

Long have I known a glory in it all,
   But never knew I this;

Here such a passion is
As stretcheth me apart. Lord, I do fear
Thou'st made the world too beautiful this year.
My soul is all but out of me — let fall
No burning leaf; prithee, let no bird call.

The Spring and the Fall

In the spring of the year, in the spring of the year,
I walked the road beside my dear.
The trees were black where the bark was wet.
I see them yet, in the spring of the year.
He broke me a bough of the blossoming peach 5
That was out of the way and hard to reach.

In the fall of the year, in the fall of the year,
I walked the road beside my dear.
The rooks went up with a raucous trill.
I hear them still, in the fall of the year. · 10
He laughed at all I dared to praise,
And broke my heart, in little ways.

Year be springing or year be falling,
The bark will drip and the birds be calling.
There's much that's fine to see and hear 15
In the spring of a year, in the fall of a year.
'Tis not love's going hurts my days,
But that it went in little ways.

Lament

Listen, children:
Your father is dead.
From his old coats
I'll make you little jackets;
I'll make you little trousers 5
From his old pants.
There'll be in his pockets
Things he used to put there,
Keys and pennies
Covered with tobacco; 10
Dan shall have the pennies

To save in his bank;
Anne shall have the keys
To make a pretty noise with.
Life must go on, 15
And the dead be forgotten;
Life must go on,
Though good men die;
Anne, eat your breakfast;
Dan, take your medicine; 20
Life must go on;
I forget just why.

Dirge Without Music

I am not resigned to the shutting away of loving hearts in the hard ground.
So it is, and so it will be, for so it has been time out of mind:
Into the darkness they go, the wise and the lovely. Crowned
With lilies and with laurel they go; but I am not resigned.

Lovers and thinkers, into the earth with you,   5
Be one with the dull, the indiscriminate dust.
A fragment of what you felt, of what you knew,
A formula, a phrase remains — but the best is lost.

The answers quick and keen, the honest look, the laughter, the love —
They are gone. They are gone to feed the roses. Elegant and curled   10
Is the blossom. Fragrant is the blossom. I know. But I do not approve.
More precious was the light in your eyes than all the roses of the world.

Down, down, down into the darkness of the grave
Gently they go, the beautiful, the tender, the kind;
Quietly they go, the intelligent, the witty, the brave.   15
I know. But I do not approve. And I am not resigned.

On Hearing a Symphony of Beethoven

Sweet sounds, oh, beautiful music, do not cease!
Reject me not into the world again.
With you alone is excellence and peace,
Mankind made plausible, his purpose plain.
Enchanted in your air benign and shrewd,   5
With limbs asprawl and empty faces pale,
The spiteful and the stingy and the rude
Sleep like the scullions° in the fairy tale.
This moment is the best the world can give:
The tranquil blossom on the tortured stem.   10
Reject me not, sweet sounds! oh, let me live,
Till Doom espy my towers and scatter them,
A city spellbound under the aging sun.
Music my rampart, and my only one.

8. scullions (skŭl'yŭnz): wretches.

In the following poem, watch for the swiftly changing moods that build to the triumphant climax, a "rebirth" of the soul. Be alert to catch the first hint of change from one mood to the next.

Renascence

All I could see from where I stood
Was three long mountains and a wood;
I turned and looked another way,
And saw three islands in a bay.
So with my eyes I traced the line   5
Of the horizon, thin and fine,
Straight around till I was come
Back to where I'd started from;
And all I saw from where I stood
Was three long mountains and a wood.   10
Over these things I could not see;
These were the things that bounded me;
And I could touch them with my hand,
Almost, I thought, from where I stand.

And all at once things seemed so small   15
My breath came short, and scarce at all.
But, sure, the sky is big, I said;
Miles and miles above my head;
So here upon my back I'll lie
And look my fill into the sky.   20
And so I looked, and, after all,
The sky was not so very tall.
The sky, I said, must somewhere stop,
And — sure enough! — I see the top!
The sky, I thought, is not so grand;   25
I 'most could touch it with my hand!
And, reaching up my hand to try,
I screamed to feel it touch the sky.

I screamed, and — lo! — Infinity
Came down and settled over me;   30
Forced back my scream into my chest,
Bent back my arm upon my breast,
And, pressing of the Undefined
The definition on my mind,
Held up before my eyes a glass   35
Through which my shrinking sight did pass
Until it seemed I must behold

"Renascence" from *Collected Poems* by Edna St. Vincent Millay, Harper & Brothers. Copyright 1912–1940 by Edna St. Vincent Millay. Reprinted by permission of Norma Millay Ellis.

EDNA ST. VINCENT MILLAY   307

Immensity made manifold;
Whispered to me a word whose sound
Deafened the air for worlds around,   40
And brought unmuffled to my ears
The gossiping of friendly spheres,
The creaking of the tented sky,
The ticking of Eternity.

I saw and heard, and knew at last   45
The How and Why of all things, past
And present, and forevermore.
The universe, cleft to the core,
Lay open to my probing sense
That, sick'ning, I would fain pluck thence   50
But could not — nay! But needs must suck
At the great wound, and could not pluck
My lips away till I had drawn
All venom out. — Ah, fearful pawn!
For my omniscience° paid I toll   55
In infinite remorse of soul.
All sin was of my sinning, all
Atoning mine, and mine the gall
Of all regret. Mine was the weight
Of every brooded wrong, the hate   60
That stood behind each envious thrust,
Mine every greed, mine every lust.
And all the while for every grief,
Each suffering, I craved relief
With individual desire —   65
Craved all in vain! And felt fierce fire
About a thousand people crawl;
Perished with each — then mourned for all!
A man was starving in Capri;
He moved his eyes and looked at me;   70
I felt his gaze, I heard his moan,
And knew his hunger as my own.
I saw at sea a great fog bank
Between two ships that struck and sank;
A thousand screams the heavens smote;   75
And every scream tore through my throat.
No hurt I did not feel, no death
That was not mine; mine each last breath
That, crying, met an answering cry

55. omniscience (ŏm·nĭsh′ĕns): the ability to know all things.

A detail from "Lake Tahoe" by the American artist Albert Bierstadt (1830–1902).   ▶

From the compassion that was I.   80
All suffering mine, and mine its rod;
Mine, pity like the pity of God.
Ah, awful weight! Infinity
Pressed down upon the finite Me!
My anguished spirit, like a bird,   85
Beating against my lips I heard;
Yet lay the weight so close about
There was no room for it without.
And so beneath the weight lay I
And suffered death, but could not die.   90

Deep in the earth I rested now;
Cool is its hand upon the brow
And soft its breast beneath the head
Of one who is so gladly dead.
And all at once, and over all,   95
The pitying rain began to fall;
I lay and heard each pattering hoof
Upon my lowly, thatchèd roof,
And seemed to love the sound far more
Than ever I had done before.   100
For rain it hath a friendly sound
To one who's six feet underground;
And scarce the friendly voice or face:
A grave is such a quiet place.

The rain, I said, is kind to come   105
And speak to me in my new home.
I would I were alive again
To kiss the fingers of the rain,
To drink into my eyes the shine
Of every slanting silver line,   110
To catch the freshened, fragrant breeze
From drenched and dripping apple trees.
For soon the shower will be done,
And then the broad face of the sun
Will laugh above the rain-soaked earth   115
Until the world with answering mirth
Shakes joyously, and each round drop
Rolls, twinkling, from its grass-blade top.
How can I bear it; buried here,
While overhead the sky grows clear   120
And blue again after the storm?

O, multicolored, multiform
Belovèd beauty over me,

That I shall never, never see
Again! Spring silver, autumn gold,   125
That I shall never more behold!
Sleeping your myriad magics through,
Close sepulchered away from you!
O God, I cried, give me new birth,
And put me back upon the earth!   130
Upset each cloud's gigantic gourd
And let the heavy rain, down poured
In one big torrent, set me free,
Washing my grave away from me!

I ceased; and, through the breathless hush   135
That answered me, the far-off rush
Of herald wings came whispering
Like music down the vibrant string
Of my ascending prayer, and — crash!
Before the wild wind's whistling lash   140
The startled storm clouds reared on high
And plunged in terror down the sky,
And the big rain in one black wave
Fell from the sky and struck my grave.
I know not how such things can be   145
I only know there came to me
A fragrance such as never clings
To aught save happy living things;
A sound as of some joyous elf
Singing sweet songs to please himself,   150
And, through and over everything,
A sense of glad awakening.
The grass, a-tiptoe at my ear,
Whispering to me I could hear;
I felt the rain's cool finger tips   155
Brushed tenderly across my lips,
Laid gently on my sealèd sight,
And all at once the heavy night
Fell from my eyes and I could see —
A drenched and dripping apple tree,   160
A last long line of silver rain,
A sky grown clear and blue again.
And as I looked a quickening gust
Of wind blew up to me and thrust
Into my face a miracle   165
Of orchard breath, and with the smell —
I know not how such things can be! —
I breathed my soul back into me.

Ah! Up then from the ground sprang I
And hailed the earth with such a cry   170
As is not heard save from a man
Who has been dead, and lives again.
About the trees my arms I wound;
Like one gone mad I hugged the ground;
I raised my quivering arms on high;   175
I laughed and laughed into the sky,
Till at my throat a strangling sob
Caught fiercely, and a great heartthrob
Sent instant tears into my eyes;
O God, I cried, no dark disguise   180
Can e'er hereafter hide from me
Thy radiant identity!
Thou canst not move across the grass
But my quick eyes will see Thee pass,
Nor speak, however silently,   185
But my hushed voice will answer Thee.
I know the path that tells Thy way
Through the cool eve of every day;
God, I can push the grass apart
And lay my finger on Thy heart!   190

The world stands out on either side
No wider than the heart is wide;
Above the world is stretched the sky —
No higher than the soul is high.
The heart can push the sea and land   195
Farther away on either hand;
The soul can split the sky in two,
And let the face of God shine through.
But East and West will pinch the heart
That cannot keep them pushed apart;   200
And he whose soul is flat — the sky
Will cave in on him by and by.

FOR DISCUSSION

THE SHORT POEMS

1. How does the attitude toward autumn in "God's World" differ from the attitude in "The Spring and the Fall"?

2. What similarity in theme and mood do you find in "Lament" and in "The Spring and the Fall"? What difference is there? How is the poet's style in these poems varied to fit the different moods? What is the effect of the last two lines of "Lament"?

3. How does "Dirge Without Music" differ from most poems on death? What attitude does the poet take toward death and the possibility of life after death?

4. What two great pleasures does the music give the poet in "On Hearing a Symphony of Beethoven"? Give in your

own words the meaning of the last four lines. What verse form is used in this poem?

RENASCENCE

1. Was the crushing experience of infinity a punishment for touching the sky or for being unaware of the beauty of life? Explain your answer.

2. Compare the response to the outdoor world in the first 28 lines with that in lines 153–62. Is the change great enough to deserve the name of "renascence"?

3. The last twelve lines (a fine passage to memorize) sum up the meaning of the experience. How many links can you find between this passage and the first part of the poem?

4. Why is "God's World" sometimes called " 'Renascence' in miniature"?

E. E. CUMMINGS

EDWARD ESTLIN CUMMINGS was born in 1894 in Cambridge, Massachusetts, the son of a Harvard teacher, and took his B.A. and M.A. degrees at Harvard. During World War I he volunteered as an ambulance driver and spent three months in a French concentration camp. This experience formed the basis for his book *The Enormous Room* (1922). He later served as an infantry private. *EIMI*, the diary of a pilgrimage to the Soviet Union, appeared in 1933. *Tom* (1935) is a ballad scenario; *Him* (1927) and *Santa Claus* (1946) are plays. In 1953 his Charles Eliot Norton lectures, delivered at Harvard, were published as *i: six nonlectures. A Miscellany* (1958) is chiefly essays. Two books, *Poems 1923–1954* and *95 Poems* (1958), comprise all his poetry published in book form. Cummings drew and painted throughout his life:  *CIOPW* reproduces specimens of his work in charcoal, ink, oil, pastel, and water color.

Cummings was an individual and proud of it, and he remained a thorough nonconformist until his death in 1962. He once said, "In an age of standardization, it's almost impossible to express the attitude of an individual. If 180 million people want to be undead, that's their funeral, but I happen to like being alive."

Cummings' unconventional, experimental verse techniques dismay some readers and delight others. For that matter some critics have found fault with Cummings for his freedom in handling such things as punctuation and capitalization. But once the reader has the courage to open a book entitled & or Is 5, the rest of the way can be highly rewarding, for the Cummings poems range from brilliant satire to touching sentiment. They laugh, cry, pray, and wonder, and each has a tune of its own.

Note that, despite a number of variations, the following poem is close to the tradi-tional form of the sonnet.

i thank You God

i thank You God for most this amazing
day:for the leaping greenly spirits of trees
and a blue true dream of sky;and for everything
which is natural which is infinite which is yes

(i who have died am alive again today,   5
and this is the sun's birthday;this is the birth
day of life and of love and wings:and of the gay
great happening illimitably earth)

how should any tasting touching hearing seeing
breathing any — lifted from the no   10
of all nothing — human merely being
doubt unimaginable You?

(now the ears of my ears awake and
now the eyes of my eyes are opened)

sweet spring

"sweet spring is your
time is my time is our
time for springtime is lovetime
and viva sweet love"

(all the merry little birds are   5
flying in the floating in the
very spirits singing in
are winging in the blossoming)

lovers go and lovers come
awandering awondering   10
but any two are perfectly
alone there's nobody else alive

(such a sky and such a sun
i never knew and neither did you

and everybody never breathed   15
quite so many kinds of yes)

not a tree can count his leaves
each herself by opening
but shining who by thousands mean
only one amazing thing   20

(secretly adoring shyly
tiny winging darting floating
merry in the blossoming
always joyful selves are singing)

"sweet spring is your   25
time is my time is our
time for springtime is lovetime
and viva sweet love"

i am a little church(no great cathedral)

i am a little church(no great cathedral)
far from the splendor and squalor of hurrying cities
— i do not worry if briefer days grow briefest,
i am not sorry when sun and rain make april

my life is the life of the reaper and the sower;   5
my prayers are prayers of earth's own clumsily striving
(finding and losing and laughing and crying)children
whose any sadness or joy is my grief or my gladness

around me surges a miracle of unceasing
birth and glory and death and resurrection: 10
over my sleeping self float flaming symbols
of hope,and i wake to a perfect patience of mountains

i am a little church(far from the frantic
world with its rapture and anguish)at peace with nature
— i do not worry if longer nights grow longest;   15
i am not sorry when silence becomes singing

winter by spring,i lift my diminutive spire to
merciful Him Whose only now is forever:
standing erect in the deathless truth of His presence
(welcoming humbly His light and proudly His darkness)   20

FOR DISCUSSION

i thank You God

1. How does the poet support his claim that the day is "amazing"?

2. How do you interpret the line "which is natural which is infinite which is yes"?

3. What or who is described as having been "lifted from the no/ of all nothing"?

4. Rather than using words that rhyme perfectly, Cummings deliberately selects a number of words that simply sound alike. Point out some examples of sound similarities used in place of rhymes. Compare this sonnet to Robert Frost's "Putting in the Seed" on page 253. Are the rhyme schemes similar?

sweet spring

How would you describe the rhythm of this poem? Is the rhythm appropriate to the subject and tone of the poem? Why? Why not?

i am a little church(no great cathedral)

1. What does the poet gain by putting the poem in the first person?

2. What is the purpose in having the little church say what it is not — that is, "no great cathedral"?

3. What attitude toward life does the little church express? Compare this poem to "i thank You God." Are the attitudes expressed in both poems similar or different?

W. H. AUDEN

W. H. (WYSTAN HUGH) AUDEN (b. 1907)
first came to the United States to lecture in 1939.
He has lived in this country almost continuously
since then, and he became a U.S. citizen in 1946.

Auden was born in York, England, and was
educated at Oxford University. Much of his early
work, particularly three poetic dramas on which
he collaborated with a friend, Christopher Isher-
wood, was critical of modern society, dramatizing
the difficulties of the artist torn between conflicting political systems and ideologies.

Look, Stranger (1936) first distinguished Auden
as a lyric poet. Since coming to America, he has
published seven volumes of poetry, one of which,
The Shield of Achilles (1955), won the National
Book Award.

*Some critics have insisted that Auden's work is a poetry of "private parable": a
mystery that only the poet can solve. True, much of Auden's poetry is complex
and difficult, but it can be direct, clear, and forceful as well. Part of Auden's distinction as a poet is his ability to clarify the tensions and difficulties of modern
life without oversimplifying them. Read the following poems carefully to establish
the meaning as clearly as possible. The tone of the poems — ranging from the bitterly satirical to the reverent — is an important element that will become evident
as you read.*

Another Time

For us like any other fugitive,
Like the numberless flowers that cannot number
And all the beasts that need not remember,
It is today in which we live.

So many try to say Not Now,   5
So many have forgotten how
To say I Am, and would be
Lost, if they could, in history.

Bowing, for instance, with such old-world grace
To a proper flag in a proper place,   10
Muttering like ancients as they stump upstairs
Of Mine and His or Ours and Theirs.

Just as if time were what they used to will
When it was gifted with possession still
Just as if they were wrong   15
In no more wishing to belong.

No wonder then so many die of grief,
So many are so lonely as they die;
No one has yet believed or liked a lie,
Another time has other lives to live.   20

"Look, Stranger . . ."

Look, stranger, on this island now
The leaping light for your delight discovers,°
Stand stable here
And silent be,
That through the channels of the ear   5
May wander like a river
The swaying sound of the sea.

Here at the small field's ending pause
When the chalk wall falls to the foam, and its tall ledges
Oppose the pluck   10
And knock of the tide,
And the shingle° scrambles after the suck-
ing surf, and the gull lodges
A moment on its sheer side.

Far off like floating seeds the ships   15
Diverge on urgent voluntary errands;
And the full view
Indeed may enter
And move in memory as now these clouds do,
That pass the harbor mirror   20
And all the summer through the water saunter.

2. **discovers:** here, reveals. 12. **shingle:** gravel.

An oil painting of the composer Ludwig van Beethoven.

The Composer

All the others translate: the painter sketches
A visible world to love or reject;
Rummaging into his living, the poet fetches
The images out that hurt and connect.

From Life to Art by painstaking adaption,   5
Relying on us to cover the rift;
Only your notes are pure contraption,
Only your song is an absolute gift.

Pour out your presence, O delight, cascading
The falls of the knee and the weirs° of the spine,   10
Our climate of silence and doubt invading;

You alone, alone, O imaginary song,
Are unable to say an existence is wrong,
And pour out your forgiveness like a wine.

10. **weirs** (wĕrz): A weir is a small dam; the term is combined with the "falls of the knee" to indicate metaphorically the effect of the music.

W. H. AUDEN   319

Epitaph on a Tyrant

Perfection, of a kind, was what he was after,
And the poetry he invented was easy to understand;
He knew human folly like the back of his hand,
And was greatly interested in armies and fleets;
When he laughed, respectable senators burst with laughter,   5
And when he cried, the little children died in the streets.

FOR DISCUSSION

ANOTHER TIME

1. What is the poet's attitude toward those who "try to say Not Now"? Does Auden feel that it is possible to be "lost in history"? Why or why not?

2. Look up the meanings of "fugitive" in a dictionary. Which definition applies best to the first line of the poem? Keeping this definition in mind, try to express in your own words the thought of the first stanza.

3. What is the "lie" mentioned in the last stanza? What is the meaning of the final line, "Another time has other lives to live"?

4. Compare this poem to "Miniver Cheevy" on page 757. In what ways are the poems similar? How do they differ?

"LOOK, STRANGER . . ."

1. Whom does Auden address as "stranger"? Why do you think he uses this word?

2. Do you think this seascape is on the coast of America? the coast of England? Give evidence from the poem to support your contention.

3. Why does Auden run the word "sucking" from one line to the next?

4. What simile is used to describe the ships? What kind of image does this simile present?

5. Why do you think the poet chose the verb "saunter" to describe the movement of the clouds in the last stanza? There may be more than one reason. Would some other verb have suited you better? Try substituting other verbs that are close in meaning to "saunter," and then read the final line aloud to judge the effect of the substitution.

THE COMPOSER

1. According to the poem, where does the poet seek his material? How does the composer differ from the poet or the painter?

2. What is meant by "the images . . . that hurt and connect"? Why do they hurt? What do they connect?

3. What change in the poem occurs after the eighth line? Glance again at the discussion of the two types of sonnets on page 263. What pattern does "The Composer" more nearly resemble?

4. Whom or what does Auden address in the last six lines?

EPITAPH ON A TYRANT

1. How well does this epitaph fit a tyrant of this century?

2. What sort of perfection does the tyrant seek? What do you think Auden means by "the poetry he invented"?

THE POET'S ART

One of Auden's distinctions is his ability to use all of the varied devices of poetry with skill and judgment. A good example of this skill is the unusual but effective rhyme scheme of "Epitaph on a Tyrant"; another is Auden's use of alliteration in a line like "The swaying sound of the sea." Glance at his poems again to see if you can pick out examples of the following poetic devices: alliteration, metaphor, simile, onomatopoeia, internal rhyme.

ARCHIBALD MacLEISH

ARCHIBALD MacLEISH (b. 1892) has been distinguished as a poet for his concern with the social and political issues of his time. After graduation from Harvard Law School, MacLeish taught and practiced law, then married and lived in France from 1923 to 1928. His studies of a number of modern French and American poets during this period helped him to find his own style in poetry.

Back home again in 1928, MacLeish settled in Connecticut. That year he followed the route of Cortes to Mexico and used the experience as the basis for his Pulitzer prize poem, *Conquistador* (1932). Since then he has served as Librarian of Congress and has taught literature and writing at Harvard.

MacLeish is distinguished for his plays as well as his poetry. His modern version of the Biblical story of Job, *J.B.*, was a Broadway success in 1958.

Like many other modern poets, MacLeish has experimented constantly with new techniques in poetry. Although he occasionally uses the older patterns — the sonnet for example — he usually relies on a less strict form, one that will allow him to catch the flavor and natural rhythm of conversation. The following poems provide a good example of MacLeish's range and mastery of the techniques of modern poetry.

The title of the following poem is symbolic. In a Roman myth, Psyche, a beautiful princess, was loved by Cupid, Venus' son. Psyche's excessive curiosity led to a temporary separation of the lovers.

Psyche with the Candle

Love which is the most difficult mystery
Asking from every young one answers
And most from those most eager and most beautiful —
Love is a bird in a fist:

To hold it hides it, to look at it lets go.   5
It will twist loose if you lift so much as a finger.
It will stay if you cover it — stay but unknown and invisible.
Either you keep it forever with fist closed
Or let it fling
Singing in fervor of sun and in song vanish.   10
There is no answer other to this mystery.

The tone of "Epistle to Be Left in the Earth" is a very important element. Read the poem aloud, if possible, to help establish the tone.

Epistle to Be Left in the Earth

. . . It is colder now,
                    there are many stars,
                                        we are drifting
North by the Great Bear,°
                    the leaves are falling,
The water is stone in the scooped rocks,
                                        to southward

Red sun gray air:
                    the crows are
Slow on their crooked wings,
                                        the jays have left us: 5
Long since we passed the flares of Orion.°
Each man believes in his heart he will die.
Many have written last thoughts and last letters.
None know if our deaths are now or forever:
None know if this wandering earth will be found.   10

We lie down and the snow covers our garments.
I pray you,
            you (if any open this writing)
Make in your mouths the words that were our names.
I will tell you all we have learned,
                                        I will tell you everything:

The earth is round
                    there are springs under the orchards,   15

2. **the Great Bear:** the constellation that includes the North Star. 6. **Orion** (ô·rī′ŏn): a constellation of stars often pictured as a hunter with sword and belt.

"Epistle to Be Left in the Earth" from *Collected Poems of Archibald MacLeish 1917–1952*. Reprinted by permission of and arrangement with Houghton Mifflin Company, the authorized publishers.

The loam cuts with a blunt knife,
$$\qquad\qquad\qquad\text{beware of}$$
Elms in thunder,
$$\qquad\qquad\qquad\text{the lights in the sky are stars —}$$
We think they do not see,
$$\qquad\qquad\qquad\text{we think also}$$
The trees do not know nor the leaves of the grasses
$$\qquad\qquad\qquad\qquad\text{hear us:}$$
The birds too are ignorant.
$$\qquad\qquad\qquad\text{Do not listen.}\qquad\qquad\qquad 20$$
Do not stand at dark in the open windows.
We before you have heard this:
$$\qquad\qquad\qquad\text{they are voices:}$$
They are not words at all but the wind rising.

Also none among us has seen God.
(. . . We have thought often   25
The flaws of sun in the late and driving weather
Pointed to one tree but it was not so.)
As for the nights I warn you the nights are dangerous:
The wind changes at night and the dreams come.

It is very cold,
$$\qquad\qquad\qquad\text{there are strange stars near Arcturus,}°\qquad 30$$

Voices are crying an unknown name in the sky

30. **Arcturus** (ärk·tū′rŭs): a brilliant star in a northern constellation.

As you read the following poem, decide whether the portrait of the boy is convincing. Could this be a description of you at eleven?

Eleven

And summer mornings the mute child, rebellious,
Stupid, hating the words, the meanings, hating
The Think now, Think, the Oh but Think! would leave
On tiptoe the three chairs on the verandah
And crossing tree by tree the empty lawn   5
Push back the shed door and upon the sill
Stand pressing out the sunlight from his eyes
And enter and with outstretched fingers feel

"Eleven" from *Collected Poems of Archibald MacLeish 1917–1952*. Reprinted by permission of and arrangement with Houghton Mifflin Company, the authorized publishers.

ARCHIBALD MacLEISH

The grindstone and behind it the bare wall
And turn and in the corner on the cool   10
Hard earth sit listening. And one by one,
Out of the dazzled shadow in the room,
The shapes would gather, the brown plowshare, spades,
Mattocks,° the polished helves° of picks, a scythe
Hung from the rafters, shovels, slender tines °   15
Glinting across the curve of sickles — shapes
Older than men were, the wise tools, the iron
Friendly with earth. And sit there, quiet, breathing
The harsh dry smell of withered bulbs, the faint
Odor of dung, the silence. And outside   20
Beyond the half-shut door the blind leaves
And the corn moving. And at noon would come,
Up from the garden, his hard crooked hands
Gentle with earth, his knees still earth-stained, smelling
Of sun, of summer, the old gardener, like   25
A priest, like an interpreter, and bend
Over his baskets.
            And they would not speak:
They would say nothing. And the child would sit there
Happy as though he had no name, as though
He had been no one: like a leaf, a stem,   30
Like a root growing —

14. **Mattocks:** tools similar to a pick. **helves:** handles.   15. **tines:** the prongs of a pitchfork.

FOR DISCUSSION

PSYCHE WITH THE CANDLE

What is the metaphorical line about which the rest of the poem centers? Is the metaphor effective? Why? Why not?

EPISTLE TO BE LEFT IN THE EARTH

1. What is the tone of the poem?
2. How do the short, broken lines help to create and sustain the tone?
3. Do you agree or disagree with the writer of the epistle about what man has learned on earth? If not, what would you substitute? What might you add?
4. Do you find any symbols in the poem? If you do, point them out, and explain what you think they represent.

ELEVEN

1. How does the tool shed serve as a haven to the boy?
2. Although the eleven-year-old boy is "mute" and "rebellious," his senses are keen. What sensory experiences are re-created in the poem?

SPECIAL REPORT

"Psyche with the Candle" is based on the myth of Cupid and Psyche, a tale first told by the Roman writer Apuleius. An interested student might enjoy reading the story and presenting a summary of it to the class, pointing out the relationship of the myth to MacLeish's poem. The story can be found in Edith Hamilton's *Mythology* (New American Library).

◄ ". . . the wise tools, the iron / Friendly with earth."

MARK VAN DOREN

MARK VAN DOREN (b. 1894) grew up in Illinois, and after graduating from the University of Illinois, he served in World War I. After the war, he received a traveling fellowship from Columbia University and spent a year in France and England. In 1920 Van Doren received his Ph.D. degree from Columbia, and from that time until his retirement in the spring of 1959, he was a distinguished teacher in Columbia's English Department.

Van Doren's *Collected Poems* won the Pulitzer prize in 1940. Besides his many books of verse, Van Doren has edited anthologies and has written criticism, biography, and children's books.

Van Doren is known as "an inspiring teacher, sympathetic, humorous . . ." As you read the following poems, look for indications of these characteristics.

Wish for the World

Wish for the world that it will never change,
Even if terrible, to total strange.
Even if good, may there be no excess
Beyond this power to think of more, of less,
That is our lone reward for living here.   5
May only what is missing still be clear
On any earth to come, that so can teach
Hell's difference, and heaven's — each from each,
And both from its dear self: the single place
Than which all others have exacter grace,   10
And yet it is the measure. Be it thus
Forever, little world that lengthens us.

Tourist

(AN EPIGRAM)

I passed Olympus° in the night
But had I passed by day,
I still could tell you less of it
Than blind Homer may.

1. **Olympus** (ŏ·lĭm'pŭs): a mountain in Greece, the mythical dwelling place of the gods.

Sweet William's Breath

Sweet William's breath,
Clove pink, clear spice,
Has breathed upon me twice,
Boy and man:
In my gaunt grandmother's garden,   5
Then my own — hot, sweet,
Here it is, and candy good;
Here it is, red, white,
And small and many, like the figures
In her apron long ago.   10
Gaunt she was, and still, and good,
My life ago.

FOR DISCUSSION

1. What is Van Doren's wish for the world? What is our "lone reward for living here"? In the poet's opinion, how does the world "lengthen us"?

2. What is an "epigram"? What does "Tourist" suggest about the understanding of sightseers? What do you know of Homer and his works?

3. In "Sweet William's Breath," what picture are we given of the poet's grandmother? How well does the poem suggest the sight and scent of the flower?

"Eleanor," by the American artist Frank Weston Benson (1862–1951).

New Voices in Modern Poetry

The seven poets included in this section hold well-established places in modern American poetry. Each has been published widely in magazines, and each is represented by a number of books of poetry. Five of these poets have been awarded Pulitzer prizes in recent years. In general, they represent a generation later than that of the poets you have just studied. It is chiefly in this sense that they are "new" voices. No study of modern American poetry would be complete without a consideration of these seven writers. All of them have made distinct contributions to the poetry of our time.

ELIZABETH BISHOP

Elizabeth Bishop (b. 1911) entitled her first volume of poetry *Poems — North and South*, referring to her early life in New England and her later residence in Florida for part of each year. Her effective combination of accurate observation and lively imagination have won her a Guggenheim Fellowship and awards from the American Academy of Arts and Letters and the Shelley Memorial, as well as a Pulitzer prize in 1956. Her present home is in Rio de Janeiro.

The colorful imagery of Elizabeth Bishop's poetry has led many critics to speak of her as "a painter in verse." Is this quality evident in "The Fish"?

The Fish

I caught a tremendous fish
and held him beside the boat
half out of water, with my hook
fast in a corner of his mouth.
He didn't fight.   5
He hadn't fought at all.
He hung a grunting weight,
battered and venerable
and homely. Here and there
his brown skin hung in strips   10
like ancient wallpaper,
and its pattern of darker brown
was like wallpaper:
shapes like full-blown roses
stained and lost through age.   15
He was speckled with barnacles,
fine rosettes of lime,
and infested

"The Fish" from *Poems — North and South: A Cold Spring* by Elizabeth Bishop, published by Houghton Mifflin Company.

with tiny white sea-lice,
and underneath two or three   20
rags of green weed hung down.
While his gills were breathing in
the terrible oxygen
— the frightening gills
fresh and crisp with blood,   25
that can cut so badly —
I thought of the coarse white flesh
packed in like feathers,
the big bones and the little bones,
the dramatic reds and blacks   30
of his shiny entrails,
and the pink swim-bladder
like a big peony.
I looked into his eyes
which were far larger than mine   35
but shallower, and yellowed,
the irises backed and packed
with tarnished tinfoil
seen through the lenses
of old scratched isinglass.   40
They shifted a little, but not
to return my stare.
— It was more like the tipping
of an object toward the light.
I admired his sullen face,   45
the mechanism of his jaw,
and then I saw
that from his lower lip
— if you could call it a lip —
grim, wet, and weaponlike,   50
hung five old pieces of fish-line,
or four and a wire leader
with the swivel still attached,
and with all their five big hooks
grown firmly in his mouth.   55
A green line, frayed at the end
where he broke it, two heavier lines,

and a fine black thread
still crimped from the strain and snap
when it broke and he got away.   60
Like medals with their ribbons
frayed and wavering,
a five-haired beard of wisdom
trailing from his aching jaw.
I stared and stared   65
and victory filled up
the little rented boat,
from the pool of bilge
where oil had spread a rainbow
around the rusted engine   70
to the bailer rusted orange,
and sun-cracked thwarts,°
the oarlocks on their strings,
the gunnels ° — until everything
was rainbow, rainbow, rainbow!   75
And I let the fish go.

72. **thwarts:** the rowers' seats in a boat. 74. **gunnels:** gunwales; on a small boat, the inside rim around the top.

FOR DISCUSSION

1. Elizabeth Bishop uses a number of similes to describe the fish. "His brown skin hung in strips/like ancient wallpaper" is a good example. Can you point out some others?

2. Why does the poet let the fish go?

THEODORE ROETHKE

Theodore Roethke (b. 1908) was educated at the
University of Michigan and Harvard. He insists
that he "hated" school as a boy; nevertheless, he
was a highly successful student, a member of Phi
Beta Kappa, and he later became a teacher. He is
now a professor of English at the University of
Washington. His book *The Waking* won a Pulitzer
prize in 1954; *Words for the Wind* (1958) is his
latest collection of poetry. Some of his best poems
are notable for their humor and their strong sense
of rhythm, qualities that might derive from his
early reading in German and English folklore. He
has said, "I count myself among the happy poets."

*In the following poem Theodore Roethke writes of a night journey west by train
and shapes his poem to the rhythm of the rails. Notice how the poet's use of rhyme
contributes to the feeling of movement.*

Night Journey

Now as the train bears west,
Its rhythm rocks the earth,
And from my Pullman berth
I stare into the night
While others take their rest.　　　　5
Bridges of iron lace,
A suddenness of trees,
A lap of mountain mist
All cross my line of sight,
Then a bleak wasted place,　　　　10
And a lake below my knees.
Full on my neck I feel
The straining at a curve;
My muscles move with steel,

I wake in every nerve.　　　　15
I watch a beacon swing
From dark to blazing bright;
We thunder through ravines
And gullies washed with light.
Beyond the mountain pass　　　　20
Mist deepens on the pane;
We rush into a rain
That rattles double glass.
Wheels shake the roadbed stone,
The pistons jerk and shove,　　　　25
I stay up half the night
To see the land I love.

FOR DISCUSSION

1. How does the poem catch the rhythm
of the train's motion?

2. What lines or phrases reveal the
point of view of the writer in relation to
the landscape?

3. Point out some words or lines that
are effective in creating the impression of
the train's speed and power. The poet uses
rhyme, but it does not follow a definite
pattern. What does this "free" approach to
rhyme add to the poem?

KARL SHAPIRO

Karl Shapiro (b. 1913) was born in Baltimore and educated at Johns Hopkins University. His army service was chiefly in the South Pacific, and while he was there, his Pulitzer prize winning collection, *V-Letter and Other Poems,* was published. In 1950 he was invited to Chicago to edit *Poetry: A Magazine of Verse.* Later he lectured in Austria and in the United States at various universities. In 1953 he traveled to Rome on a Guggenheim Fellowship. In recent years he has been on the faculty of the University of Nebraska, where he teaches and continues to write both poetry and critical essays and to edit a literary magazine, the *Prairie Schooner.*

Karl Shapiro has been called a "coolly satirical" poet, but his poems can be surprisingly tender. "The Interlude, III" provides a good example of this quality.

The Interlude, III

Writing, I crushed an insect with my nail
And thought nothing at all. A bit of wing
Caught my eye then, a gossamer so frail

And exquisite, I saw in it a thing
That scorned the grossness of the thing I wrote.   5
It hung upon my finger like a sting.

A leg I noticed next, fine as a mote,
"And on this frail eyelash he walked," I said,
"And climbed and walked like any mountain goat."

And in this mood I sought the little head,   10
But it was lost; then in my heart a fear
Cried out, "A life — why, beautiful, why dead!"

It was a mite that held itself most dear,
So small I could have drowned it with a tear.

FOR DISCUSSION

1. The poet undergoes an emotional change in "The Interlude, III." How would you describe this change? What causes it?

2. Is there anything unusual about the rhyme scheme of the poem? How is the pattern of this poem similar to that of "Stopping by Woods on a Snowy Evening" on page 253?

"The Interlude, III," copyright 1944 by Karl Shapiro. Reprinted from *Poems 1940–1953,* by Karl Shapiro, by permission of Random House, Inc.

STANLEY KUNITZ

Stanley Kunitz (b. 1905) was born in Worcester, Massachusetts. He was educated at Harvard University, where he received the Garrison Medal for poetry, and graduated with honors. After serving in World War II, he spent a year abroad on a traveling fellowship. He is the editor of *Twentieth Century Authors*, a standard reference work. His book *Selected Poems 1928–1958* won the Pulitzer prize in 1959. In the spring of 1960, he traveled across America giving programs of readings from the prize-winning collection.

The dictionary defines "benediction" as "the act of blessing, a solemn or affectionate invocation of happiness." In other words, a benediction is in the nature of a prayer. Observe, as you read, that the first couplets are devoted to evils from which the poet wishes the loved one protected. Notice how and where the emphasis of the benediction changes.

Benediction

God banish from your house
The fly, the roach, the mouse

That riots in the walls
Until the plaster falls;

Admonish from your door   5
The hypocrite and liar;

No shy, soft, tigrish fear
Permit upon your stair,

Nor agents of your doubt.
God drive them whistling out.   10

Let nothing touched with evil,
Let nothing that can shrivel

Heart's tenderest frond, intrude
Upon your still, deep blood.

Against the drip of night   15

God keep all windows tight,

Protect your mirrors from
Surprise, delirium,

Admit no trailing wind
Into your shuttered mind   20

To plume the lake of sleep
With dreams. If you must weep

God give you tears, but leave
You secrecy to grieve,

And islands for your pride,   25
And love to nest in your side.

God grant that, to the bone,
Yourself may be your own;

God grant that I may be
(My sweet) sweet company.   30

1. What are some of the evils that are to be banished? What words particularly suggest the removal of evils?

2. Several lines of the poem give a feeling of special peace and security. What are those lines? How do they produce the effect?

3. "Benediction" contains a number of subtle metaphors. "Shuttered mind" is one: here, the mind asleep is pictured as a house with shutters drawn over the windows. Can you point out some other metaphors in the poem?

4. What clue do you find to indicate who has received the benediction?

RICHARD EBERHART

Richard Eberhart was born in Minnesota in 1904. After graduation from Dartmouth College, he traveled around the world — as he says, "in search of truth" — and later received his M.A. degree from Cambridge University. He returned to the United States to study at Harvard Graduate School and to teach English. Eberhart served in the navy during World War II. After the war he returned to enter business and become vice-president of an industrial firm. In recent years he has lectured at many universities.

One of Richard Eberhart's hobbies is flying giant kites five to seven feet in height. Perhaps his enjoyment of the sport is related to his enjoyment of poetry, which he has called "a maneuvering of ideas, a spectacular pleasure, achievement and mastery of intractable material . . ." Are these characteristics apparent in the following poem?

On a Squirrel Crossing the Road in Autumn, in New England

It is what he does not know,
Crossing the road under the elm trees,
About the mechanism of my car,
About the Commonwealth of Massachusetts,
About Mozart, India, Arcturus,   5

That wins my praise. I engage
At once in whirling squirrel-praise.

He obeys the orders of nature
Without knowing them.
It is what he does not know   10
That makes him beautiful.
Such a knot of little purposeful nature!

I who can see him as he cannot see himself
Repose in the ignorance that is his blessing.

It is what man does not know of God   15
Composes the visible poem of the world.

                    . . . Just missed him!

FOR DISCUSSION

1. What do you think the poet means when he says that the squirrel "obeys the orders of nature without knowing them"? Why does Eberhart feel that the squirrel's ignorance is what makes him beautiful?

2. What parallel is drawn in the last few lines of the poem? What is "the visible poem of the world"?

3. Why does the poem end with ". . . Just missed him!"?

4. What is the form of this poem? Is it written in free verse? Compare Richard Eberhart's poem to Edgar Lee Masters' "Flossie Cabanis" (page 265) and Carl Sandburg's "Chicago" (page 299). Are the three poems similar in their rhythms? Do the poems differ at all in their use of rhythm? If so, in what ways?

HOWARD NEMEROV

Howard Nemerov (b. 1920) was born and grew up in New York City. He attended Harvard, from which he graduated in 1941. During World War II he was with the Royal Canadian Air Force and the U.S. Army Air Force. He married an English girl and after the war returned to New York City, where he completed his first book of verse, *The Image and the Law* (1947). He has taught at Hamilton College in New York and Bennington College in Vermont. A versatile writer, Nemerov has written poems, short stories, novels, and essays. His fourth and latest book of verse is entitled *Mirrors and Windows*.

In the following poem, observe how particular words and phrases are used to help create the storm effect, as the subject changes from a real to a figurative storm. Notice also the regularity of the rhyme scheme.

Brainstorm

The house was shaken by a rising wind
That rattled window and door. He sat alone
In an upstairs room and heard these things: a blind
Ran up with a bang, a door slammed, a groan
Came from some hidden joist, and a leaky tap,   5
At any silence of the wind, walked like
A blind man through the house. Timber and sap
Revolt, he thought, from washer, baulk,° and spike.
Bent to his book, continued unafraid
Until the crows came down from their loud flight   10
To walk along the rooftree overhead.
Their horny feet, so near but out of sight,
Scratched on the slate; when they were blown away
He heard their wings beat till they came again,
While the wind rose, and the house seemed to sway,   15
And windowpanes began to blind with rain.
The house was talking, not to him, he thought,
But to the crows; the crows were talking back
In their black voices. The secret might be out:

8. **baulk** (often **balk**): a beam or rafter of a house.

Houses are only trees stretched on the rack.   20
And once the crows knew, all nature would know.
Fur, leaf, and feather would invade the form,
Nail rust with rain and shingle warp with snow,
Vine tear the wall, till any straw-borne storm
Could rip both roof and rooftree off and show   25
Naked to nature what they had kept warm.

He came to feel the crows walk on his head
As if he were the house, their crooked feet
Scratched, through the hair, his scalp. He might be dead
It seemed, and all the noises underneath   30
Be but the cooling of the sinews, veins,
Juices, and sodden sacks suddenly let go:
While in his ruins of wiring, his burst mains,
The rainy wind had been set free to blow
Until the green uprising and mob rule   35
That ran the world had taken over him,
Split him like seed, and set him in the school
Where any crutch can learn to be a limb.

Inside his head he heard the stormy crows.

FOR DISCUSSION

1. What words or phrases help create the feeling of a storm?

2. Try to express in your own words the contrast between the first and second stanzas of the poem. Point out some of the lines that help sum up the contrast.

3. What is the house that finally undergoes the storm? What is the effect of the last line of the poem?

RICHARD WILBUR

Richard Wilbur was born in 1921 in New York City. He studied journalism and edited a newspaper while attending Amherst College in Massachusetts, but while serving in World War II, his thoughts turned from journalism to poetry. After his return home he did graduate work at Harvard and began teaching there in 1950. He received the Pulitzer prize in 1950 for *Ceremony and Other Poems*. *Things of This World* (1956), a collection of poems, received another Pulitzer prize and the National Book Award. His latest volume is *Advice to a Prophet and Other Poems* (1961). The following poem, "Year's End," is one of Richard Wilbur's finest.

New Year's Eve can be an occasion for serious emotion as well as gaiety. As you read, observe how the tone of Richard Wilbur's poem changes as it moves from the simple opening description to the thoughtful conclusion.

Year's End

Now winter downs the dying of the year,
And night is all a settlement of snow;
From the soft street the rooms of houses show
A gathered light, a shapen atmosphere,
Like frozen-over lakes whose ice is thin   5
And still allows some stirring down within.

I've known the wind by water banks to shake
The late leaves down, which frozen where they fell
And held in ice as dancers in a spell,
Fluttered all winter long into a lake;   10
Graved on the dark in gestures of descent,
They seemed their own most perfect monument.

There was perfection in the death of ferns
Which laid their fragile cheeks against the stone
A million years. Great mammoths overthrown   15
Composedly have made their long sojourns,
Like palaces of patience, in the gray
And changeless lands of ice. And at Pompeii°

The little dog° lay curled and did not rise
But slept the deeper as the ashes rose   20
And found the people incomplete, and froze
The random hands, the loose unready eyes
Of men expecting yet another sun
To do the shapely thing they had not done.

These sudden ends of time must give us pause.   25
We fray into the future, rarely wrought
Save in the tapestries of afterthought.
More time, more time. Barrages of applause
Come muffled from a buried radio.
The New Year bells are wrangling with the snow.   30

18. **Pompeii** (pŏm·pā′): an ancient city in Italy which was destroyed by the eruption of a volcano, Mount Vesuvius, in A.D. 79. 19. **little dog**: When the ruins of Pompeii were excavated in the nineteenth century, the skeleton of a dog was found in one of the larger buildings.

An Analysis of Richard Wilbur's "Year's End"

A poem must be read and understood as a whole, but a close look at separate lines, even at single words, can often provide an opening to the entire poem. The last line of "Year's End" is a good example:

> The New Year bells are wrangling with
>   the snow.

The choice of the verb seems strange. "Wrangling" means "disputing angrily" or "brawling." Why should the bells "brawl" with the snow? Perhaps we can answer the question by examining the rest of the poem.

The first line announces the theme:

> Now winter downs the dying of the year.

Notice that the poet concentrates on the *death* of the old year, not the *birth* of the new. The title has given us the same clue: "Year's End," not "New Year's Eve." This particular night can be thought of as both an end and a beginning, but the poet has chosen only one aspect, and his choice gives us a hint about what will follow. The first stanza continues to develop the theme by using a number of words that carry suggestions of death or sleep: "winter," "night," "dying." The simile in this stanza extends the suggestion: houses are "like frozen-over lakes," almost "dead" but with some life in them still, "some stirring down within."

In the next stanza the theme is modified slightly. The leaves are caught and held in ice and become "perfect monuments." Unmoving, dead, they nevertheless seem to flutter "all winter long into a lake."

With the mention of the deaths of ferns and mammoths, the third stanza introduces another kind of monumental perfection, one that lasts for centuries. The ferns and mammoths met death with patience and composure, and even now they remain complete and unchanging monuments, caught and held forever in repose.

The fourth stanza marks two crucial changes in the poem. The imagery changes from winter and ice to the picture of sudden volcanic destruction. And the theme changes from patient, unchanging monuments to an end that is quick and agitated. Unlike the ferns, the leaves, the mammoths, the people of Pompeii were not prepared for a sudden end of time.

The theme continues to become more general in the fifth stanza. Man depends on time and is betrayed by time. He "frays'" ("shreds," "unravels") into the future. Unlike the "perfect monuments" of the earlier stanzas, man is "rarely wrought" ("formed," "completed"). His cry is "More time, more time." The final lines should now become clearer:

>   Barrages of applause
> Come muffled from a buried radio.

Like the houses of the first stanza, the radio reveals some life, some "stirring down within," but the stirring is faint, the applause is "muffled."

> The New Year bells are wrangling with
>   the snow.

Snow and ashes bury time, but the bells begin a new year. (Notice that this is the first mention in the poem of the *new* year.) Thus the bells "dispute" with the end of time. They wrangle with the snow.

As you can see, this analysis has grown to a length much greater than the poem itself, and yet we have ignored many elements of "Year's End": rhythm and rhyme, to mention just two. Each of these elements, and many others, could legitimately demand attention and would require still more space for analysis. Like the tapestry of the final stanza, a successful poem like "Year's End" combines many threads into a single whole.

Can you explain why the poet mentions the "little dog" at the beginning of the fourth stanza? How does the dog compare or contrast with the people of Pompeii? (Keep in mind the "perfect monuments" of the earlier stanzas.)

Light Verse

Is poetry a "criticism of life" as Matthew Arnold, an English poet and critic, maintained? Many poets and readers of poetry argue that it is not, yet the definition fits light verse like a glove. Light verse writers sometimes admit that they make lists of life's little irritations and absurdities and use items on the list as their subject matter.

The composer of light verse is an artist in an exacting form. He must have a fine sense of timing and a perfect ear for rhyme. Above all, he must see the funny side of life and take pleasure in making his readers see it too.

There will be no study questions on the following verses. Just sit back, read, and enjoy yourself.

OGDEN NASH

Ogden Nash (b. 1902) has published his light verse in dozens of American magazines. His satirical poetry is uniquely his own because Nash makes his own rules and even more of his own rhymes. Sometimes his poems are pretty much twisted out of shape, but that only adds to the fun. Nash enjoyed a change of pace in 1943 when he collaborated on the lyrics for the successful musical *One Touch of Venus*. He is now said to be one of the most quoted of contemporary American poets.

Ring Out the Old, Ring In the New,
But Don't Get Caught in Between

If there is anything of which American industry has a
    superfluity
It is green lights, know-how, initiative, and ingenuity.
If there is one maxim to American industry unknown
It is, Let well enough alone.
Some people award American industry an encomium°   5
Because it not only paints the lily, it turns it into a two-
    toned job with a forward look and backward fins
    and a calyx° trimmed with chromium.

5. **encomium:** very high praise. 6. **calyx** (kā′lĭks): the leafy portion of a flower.

"Ring Out the Old, Ring In the New" from *You Can't Get There from Here* by Ogden Nash. Copyright, 1956, by Ogden Nash. Reprinted by permission of Little, Brown & Co.

I don't propose to engage in a series of Lincoln-Douglas
    debates,
But take the matter of paper plates.
The future of many a marriage would have been in doubt
But for paper plates, which have imparted tolerability to
    picnics and the maid's day out,   10
But the last paper plates I handled had been improved
    into plastic, and they are so artistic that I couldn't
    throw them away,
And I ended up by washing them against another day.
Look at the automotive industry, how it never relaxes;
It has improved the low-priced three so much that instead
    of a thousand dollars they now cost twenty-
    nine seventy-five, not including Federal and local
    taxes.
Do you know what I think?   15
Ordinary mousetraps will soon be so improved that they
    will be too good for the mice, who will be elbowed
    out by mink.

That low keening you hear is me bemoaning my fate;
I am out of joint, I was born either too early or too late.
As the boll said to the weevil,
Get yourself born before the beginning or after the end,
    but never in the middle of, a technological up-
    heaval.   20
I am adrift, but know not whether I am drifting seaward
    or shoreward,
My neck is stiff from my head trying to turn simultaneously
    backward and forward.
One way I know I am adrift,
My left foot keeps reaching for the clutch when the car
    has an automatic shift.
Another way that I am adrift I know,   25
I'm in a car that I've forgotten has a clutch and I stall it
    when the light says STOP and again when the
    light says GO.
I can no longer enjoy butter on my bread;
Radio and TV have taught me to think of butter as "You
    know what" or "The more expensive spread."
I am on the thin ice of the old order while it melts;
I guess that perhaps in this changing world money   30
    changes less than anything else.
That is one reason money is to me so dear;
I know I can't take it with me, I just want the use of
    some while I am here.

OGDEN NASH   341

PHYLLIS McGINLEY

Phyllis McGinley (b. 1905) has written verse since childhood. She now has to her credit five books of light verse, a book of essays, and a number of delightful stories for children. She has recently earned a reputation as a serious poet with the publication of *Times Three*. She is married, has two daughters, and lives in a New York suburb. She claims it is not true that poets are eccentric. In fact, she cannot think of a single way in which she is eccentric except that she puts sugar in her soup.

Notice the lilting rhythm and unusual rhyme scheme of the following poem.

A Little Night Music

It seems vainglorious and proud
Of Atom-man to boast so loud
   His prowess homicidal,
When one remembers how for years,
With their rude stones and humble spears,   5
Our sires, at wiping out their peers,
   Were almost never idle.

Despite his under-fissioned art
The Hittite° made a splendid start
   Toward smiting lesser nations;   10
While Tamerlane,° it's widely known,
Without a bomb to call his own
   Destroyed whole populations.

Nor did the ancient Persian need
Uranium to kill his Mede,   15
   The Viking earl, his foeman.
The Greeks got excellent results
With swords and engined catapults.
   A chariot served the Roman.

9. **Hittite** (hĭt'īt): an ancient race of people who conquered Asia Minor about 2,000 B.C.
11. **Tamerlane**: a Mongol conqueror (1336?–1405).

Mere cannon garnered quite a yield 20
On Waterloo's tempestuous field.
　　At Hastings and at Flodden°
Stout countrymen, with just a bow
And arrow, laid their thousands low.
　　And Gettysburg was sodden. 25

Though doubtless now our shrewd machines
Can blow the world to smithereens
　　More tidily and so on,
Let's give our ancestors their due.
Their ways were coarse, their weapons few. 30
But ah! how wondrously they slew
　　With what they had to go on.

22. **Hastings** and **Flodden:** Important battles were fought at these locations in England in 1066 and 1513, respectively.

RICHARD ARMOUR

Richard Armour was born in San Pedro, California, in 1906. During World War II he achieved the rank of colonel. He is now professor of English at Scripps College and Claremont Graduate School, Claremont, California. Richard Armour has published scholarly works, several books of prose satire, and several volumes of light verse. He has also written a book entitled *Writing Light Verse.*

Babies

I think that whenever I see one
I'd rather have been than still be one.

Argument

If you convinced me
　　And I convinced you,
Would there not still be
　　Two points of view?

The chances are that only Richard Armour would think of calling cows "inner industrious."

Comment on Cows

Cows
Do nothing but browse
And drowse
And now and then moo.
That's all they do.   5
Yet even while grazing
They aren't lazing.
Even while snacking
They aren't slacking.
If not illustrious,   10
They are inner industrious,
Making milk with all their might
With every bite.
Cream too,
With every chew.   15
I'd like it fine
Could I combine
In such measure
Business with pleasure.

FRANKLIN P. ADAMS

Franklin P. Adams (1881–1960) came from Chicago to New York, where he worked on a number of newspapers, delighting readers with his column, "The Conning Tower." For many years the initials F.P.A. were a well-known trade-mark for humor of high quality.

What do you think F.P.A. is satirizing in this poem?

Those Two Boys

When Bill was a lad he was terribly bad.
    He worried his parents a lot;
He'd lie and he'd swear and pull little girls' hair;
    His boyhood was naught but a blot.

At play and in school he would fracture each rule —   5
    In mischief from autumn to spring;
And the villagers knew when to manhood he grew
    He would never amount to a thing.

When Jim was a child he was not very wild;
    He was known as a good little boy;   10
He was honest and bright and the teachers' delight —
    To his father and mother a joy.

All the neighbors were sure that his virtue'd endure,
    That his life would be free of a spot;
They were certain that Jim had a great head on him   15
    And that Jim would amount to a lot.

And Jim grew to manhood and honor and fame
    And bears a good name;
While Bill is shut up in a dark prison cell —
    You never can tell.   20

"Those Two Boys" from *Tobogganing on Parnassus* by Franklin P. Adams, published by Doubleday & Company, Inc. Reprinted by permission of Mrs. Esther Root Adams.

Poetry in the Twentieth Century

You have now met many of the distinguished American poets of the twentieth century. In addition to these writers, there are some other poets who could not be adequately represented in a general collection but whose work deserves serious consideration. You may enjoy sampling some of their poetry. The reading list on the following page will offer further opportunities to extend your reading of modern poetry.

AMY LOWELL started her poetic career in the years just before World War I, at the same time that ROBERT FROST, CARL SANDBURG, VACHEL LINDSAY, and EDGAR LEE MASTERS were beginning their finest work. Miss Lowell became the leader of the Imagists, a group of poets who, as the name indicates, urged the use of the "hard and clear image" and the "exact word." EZRA POUND, one of the first of the Imagists, became probably the most controversial figure in modern poetry. Although his work is often criticized as being erratic and obscure, he has had a great deal of influence on the poets who have followed him.

Another poet who has been extremely influential is St. Louis-born T. S. ELIOT. Eliot's long poem *The Waste Land* (1922) puzzled and angered many readers on its first appearance but is now widely admired. Eliot became a British subject in 1927. He was awarded the Nobel prize for literature in 1948. The work of ARCHIBALD MacLEISH occasionally shows the influence of Eliot's poetry. HART CRANE was another poet who followed some of the techniques of *The Waste Land*, especially in his long poem, *The Bridge*.

The poetry of WALLACE STEVENS is noted for its remarkable imagery and unusual vocabulary — and also for its complexity. Stevens, like Eliot and Pound, has been a major influence on much of the poetry of our century. "Sunday Morning" is perhaps his finest single poem.

WILLIAM CARLOS WILLIAMS likes to experiment with rhythm in his poetry, often writing a kind of free verse that is close to the rhythm of speech. Another poet who experimented radically with verse rhythms was ROBINSON JEFFERS.

MARIANNE MOORE's poetry is noted for its precise imagery and subtle sense of humor. Both qualities are prominent in "Poetry," her best-known poem. CONRAD AIKEN has written a number of excellent poems; he is also known for his short stories and novels. LOUISE BOGAN is a perceptive critic as well as a fine lyric poet.

During the 1930's a number of Southern writers, many of whom were connected with Vanderbilt University in Tennessee, became known as the Fugitive Group. The outstanding poets of the group included JOHN CROWE RANSOM, ALLEN TATE, and ROBERT PENN WARREN. Ransom's poetry is distinguished by a dry, subtle humor; Tate is noted for his polished, ironic, and often extremely complex verse. Warren, who is also famous as a novelist and short-story writer, has published a number of volumes of impressive poetry. All three poets have written excellent criticism.

The quality of American poetry has shown no indication of decline in recent years. You have already met several "New Voices." Other important poets of a more recent generation include RANDALL JARRELL, PETER VIERECK, ROBERT LOWELL, JOHN CIARDI, MURIEL RUKEYSER, and DELMORE SCHWARTZ. Most of these poets began their careers in the 1940's; by the 1960's all of them had a number of volumes to their credit and had earned significant places in modern poetry.

For Further Reading of Poetry

COLLECTIONS OF POETRY

Auden, W. H., *The Criterion Book of Modern American Verse* (Criterion, 1950)

Brinnin, J. M., and Kimon Friar, *Modern Poetry, American and British* (Appleton-Century-Crofts, 1951)

Ciardi, John, *Mid-Century American Poets* (Twayne, 1950)

Matthiessen, F. O., *The Oxford Book of American Verse* (Oxford, 1950)

Untermeyer, Louis, *Modern American Poetry*, Mid-Century Edition (Harcourt, Brace & World, 1950)

Williams, Oscar, *A Little Treasury of Modern Poetry*, revised ed. (Scribner, 1955); *The New Pocket Anthology of American Verse* (World Publishing, 1955)

BY INDIVIDUAL POETS

Auden, W. H., *Selected Poetry of W. H. Auden* (Modern Library, 1959)

Ciardi, John, *I Marry You* (Rutgers Univ. Press, 1958)

Cummings, E. E. *Poems 1923–1954* (Harcourt, Brace & World, 1954)

Eberhart, Richard, *Great Praises* (Oxford Univ. Press, 1957)

Jarrell, Randall, *Selected Poems* (Knopf, 1955); *Woman at the Washington Zoo* (Atheneum, 1960)

Kunitz, Stanley, *Selected Poems 1928–1958* (Little, Brown, 1958)

Lowell, Robert, *Life Studies*, verse and prose (Farrar, Straus & Cudahy, 1959)

McGinley, Phyllis, *Times Three* (Viking, 1960)

MacLeish, Archibald, *Collected Poems 1917–1952* (Houghton Mifflin, 1952)

Moore, Marianne, *Collected Poems* (Macmillan, 1952)

Nemerov, Howard, *Mirrors and Windows* (Univ. of Chicago Press, 1958)

Ransom, John Crowe, *Selected Poems* (Knopf, 1945)

Roethke, Theodore, *Words for the Wind*, collected verse (Doubleday, 1958)

Shapiro, Karl, *Poems 1940–1953* (Random House, 1953)

Stevens, Wallace, *Poems* (Vintage Books, 1959)

Tate, Allen, *Poems 1922–1947* (Scribner, 1948)

Van Doren, Mark, *Morning Worship* (Harcourt, Brace & World, 1959)

Warren, Robert Penn, *You, Emperors and Others: Poems 1957–1960* (Random House, 1960)

Wilbur, Richard, *Things of This World* (Harcourt, Brace & World, 1956)

Williams, William Carlos, *Collected Later Poems* (New Directions, 1950)

COLLECTIONS OF LIGHT VERSE

Adams, Franklin P., *Innocent Merriment* (McGraw-Hill, 1942)

Wells, Carolyn, *Book of Humorous Verse* (Garden City, 1947)

FOR LISTENING

The following poems have been recorded on *Many Voices* 5A: Frost, "The Death of the Hired Man"; Sandburg, "The People Speak," "Nocturne in a Deserted Brickyard," "Prayers of Steel," "Grass"; Johnson, "The Creation"; Teasdale, "The Long Hill"; Millay, "God's World," "The Spring and the Fall"; Wylie, "Pretty Words," "Sea Lullaby"; Benét, "The Mountain Whippoorwill." On *Many Voices* 11A are: Cummings, "i am a little church(no great cathedral)," "sweet spring"; Auden, "Look, Stranger. . . ," "The Composer," "Epitaph on a Tyrant"; MacLeish, "Eleven"; Van Doren, "Wish for the World"; and all the selections under "New Voices."

Modern Drama

AMERICANS have always been playgoers. Even in Colonial times, regular theaters were established in New York, Philadelphia, Williamsburg, and Charleston. After the Revolution, as settlers pushed into the interior of the continent, traveling companies of actors rode the stagecoaches and canal boats to take their plays to the new settlements. The drama, however, was the last of the forms of literature to come to full flower in America. Though many earlier writers made a career of turning out plays, only in the past forty years have our playwrights made distinguished contributions to American and world literature. Recent American drama has been remarkable for its variety and flexibility. Two playwrights who have contributed much to this brilliant period are Eugene O'Neill and Thornton Wilder. Both are represented in the following pages.

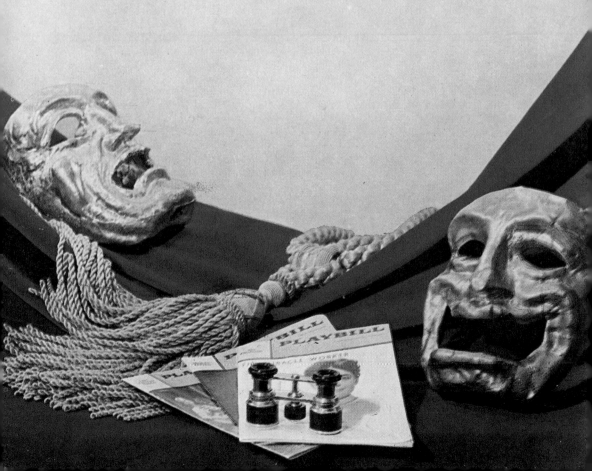

Guide to Reading Drama

Long before men wrote stories, they acted them out. The most primitive form of art was probably a kind of dance pantomime. Dance and acting, then, are older arts than writing. Yet in ancient Greece, where drama first soared to levels of high development, plays were written down in order to preserve them and to insure that the actors would be able to carry out the authors' intentions. Drama, then, is a branch of literature. Unlike most literature, however, the drama is not written simply to be read. It is written for actors to present to a watching and listening audience. When you read a drama, you must be prepared to help bring the play to full life.

USING YOUR IMAGINATION

Shakespeare's play *Henry V* opens with a prologue that calls for the spectators to help with their imaginations:

> For 'tis your thoughts that now must deck our kings,
> Carry them here and there, jumping o'er times,
> Turning the accomplishment of many years
> Into an hourglass.

This is the truest spirit of the theater in all ages. A play takes its power not only from what is written or what is said and done on stage but from the willingness of the audience to enter fully into the play and accept it as real. With drama, as with so much else, you get out of it as much as you put into it.

THE SETTING

In the following pages, you will first try your skill on a careful, completely detailed description of the one scene in Eugene O'Neill's "In the Zone." Your imagination has only to translate the written directions into the specific scene. Next you will have the greater freedom of a play in which there is no scenery at all. Thornton Wilder realizes so well how much the imagination can do to fill in the scene that he has *Our Town* performed on a bare stage, with an unusual character called the Stage Manager taking the audience from place to place with a few words. Some readers prefer the first method, which gives them exact information about the setting; others enjoy the greater challenge of the second method and find satisfaction in creating their own version of the scene. In either case, the one essential is the same — the reader's imagination.

THE CHARACTERS

The imaginative skill that visualizes a scene also helps to picture the characters. Here, both the eye and the ear must work together. You not only see the character, expanding the brief descriptive phrases to picture the whole person, but you also hear his manner of speech and the tone of his voice. Does the character speak in a loud, shrill voice, or a quiet, subdued one? Is his voice confident or hesitant? To hear the living speech, your imagination must get inside the character and share the feelings or motives that lie behind each spoken word.

READING DIALOGUE

The distinctive characteristic of drama — the telling of a story almost entirely through dialogue — calls for still another ability, a specific skill in understanding the special uses of dramatic dialogue. '

From the opening directions of the play you learn the setting; against the setting you visualize the cast of characters. Then the dialogue sweeps you into the story, and you find yourself in the midst of a group of unfamiliar people. You watch and listen to them to find out what sort of people they are, and what they are doing. In a similar situation in real life, you might wait for some time before you learn what is going on, but in a play the nonessentials are trimmed away, and every word of dialogue counts.

First, the dialogue *identifies the characters* for you. The first few speeches made by a character — or made about him — give you important clues to his nature.

Second, dialogue reveals the *relationship of the characters* to one another. It is this relationship that usually reveals the situation on which the play is based. The characters want something, or fear something, or in some other way conflict with one another. Whatever the exact nature of the situation, you feel a certain tension; a conflict exists and must be resolved before the play ends.

Third, dialogue *moves the plot.* You will usually have no difficulty in following the course of action, but if you do, pause a moment to ask yourself: Who is trying to achieve a definite purpose? What is that purpose? What opposition is he meeting? What other characters are in conflict with him? If you answer these questions yourself, you will be prepared for the decisive moments of the plot when the course of action is suddenly changed or resolved.

The fourth special function of dialogue is to *create an emotional response* in the audience. The dialogue of a play helps to set its tone. Since the dramatist cannot address his audience directly, his characters must express for him whatever feelings or ideas he wishes to convey. Look for speeches that establish the tone of the play and seem to express its theme.

YOUR PART IN THE PLAY

As you read the O'Neill and Wilder plays that follow, let your mind, as Shakespeare's Prologue urged, "deck" the persons and places. Set up a theater in your own mind, complete with whatever cast and costumes, lights and scenery, sound effects and actions the playwright describes. When you read a play, you are producer, director, and actor all in one.

EUGENE O'NEILL

In the Zone

Eugene O'Neill is considered by common consent to be the greatest of American dramatists. Few men have possessed his insight into character and his knowledge of men's motives. He knew well the part that fear can play in forcing men to act irrationally and tragically. "In the Zone" concentrates on a group of seamen under extreme tension as their blacked-out merchant ship moves through submarine waters.

UNDERSTANDING DIALOGUE. O'Neill's specific description of the scene of this short play and his frequent guidance as to the tone in which remarks are made will aid your imagination in bringing the happenings to life. Turn your keenest attention to getting the full value of the dialogue. Keep in mind the four purposes that dialogue serves: identifying characters, revealing the situation, advancing the action, and intensifying an emotional response. You will sense at least one of these purposes in each speech you read. Then the story will unfold clearly and powerfully, advancing steadily to a strong climax.

Characters

All are seamen on the British tramp steamer Glencairn.

SMITTY	IVAN
DAVIS	PAUL
SWANSON	JACK
SCOTTY	DRISCOLL
COCKY	

SCENE: *The seamen's forecastle. On the right above the bunks, three or four portholes covered with black cloth can be seen. On the floor near the doorway is a pail with a tin dipper. A lantern in the middle of the floor, turned down very low, throws a dim light around the place. Five men,* SCOTTY, IVAN, SWANSON, SMITTY, *and* PAUL, *are in their bunks apparently asleep. It is about ten minutes of twelve on a night in the fall of the year 1915.*[1]

SMITTY *turns slowly in his bunk and, leaning out over the side, looks from one to another of the men as if to assure himself that they are asleep. Then he climbs carefully out of his bunk and stands in the middle of the forecastle fully dressed, but in his stocking feet,*

[1] **1915**: at the peak of German submarine attacks in World War I.

glancing around him suspiciously. Reassured, he leans down and cautiously pulls out a suitcase from under the bunks in front of him.

Just at this moment DAVIS appears in the doorway, carrying a large steaming coffeepot in his hand. He stops short when he sees SMITTY. A puzzled expression comes over his face, followed by one of suspicion, and he retreats farther back in the alleyway, where he can watch SMITTY without being seen.

All the latter's movements indicate a fear of discovery. He takes out a small bunch of keys and unlocks the suitcase, making a slight noise as he does so. SCOTTY wakes up and peers at him over the side of the bunk. SMITTY opens the suitcase and takes out a small black tin box, carefully places this under his mattress, shoves the suitcase back under the bunk, climbs into his bunk again, closes his eyes, and begins to snore loudly.

DAVIS enters the forecastle, places the coffeepot beside the lantern, and goes from one to the other of the sleepers and shakes them vigorously, saying to each in a low voice: Near eight bells, Scotty. Arise and shine, Swanson. Eight bells, Ivan. SMITTY yawns loudly with a great pretense of having been dead asleep. All of the rest of the men tumble out of their bunks, stretching and gaping, and commence to pull on their shoes. They go one by one to the cupboard near the open door, take out their cups and spoons, and sit down together on the benches. The coffeepot is passed around. They munch their biscuits and sip their coffee in dull silence.

DAVIS (suddenly jumping to his feet — nervously). Where's that air comin' from?

[All are startled and look at him wonderingly.]

SWANSON (a squat, surly-faced Swede — grumpily). What air? I don't feel nothing.

DAVIS (excitedly). I kin feel it — a draft. (He stands on the bench and looks around — suddenly exploding.) Squarehead! (He leans over the upper bunk in which PAUL is sleeping and slams the porthole shut.) I got a good notion to report him. Serve him bloody well right! What's the use o' blindin' the ports when that thickhead goes an' leaves 'em open?

SWANSON (yawning — too sleepy to be aroused by anything — carelessly). Dey don't see what little light go out yust one port.

SCOTTY (protestingly). Dinna be a loon, Swanson! D'ye no ken the dangerr o' showin' a licht wi' a pack o' submarines lyin' aboot?

IVAN (shaking his shaggy oxlike head in an emphatic affirmative). Dot's right, Scotty. I don' li-ike blow up, no, by devil!

SMITTY (his manner slightly contemptuous). I don't think there's much danger of meeting any of their submarines, not until we get into the war zone, at any rate.

DAVIS. (He and SCOTTY look at SMITTY suspiciously — harshly.) You don't, eh? (He lowers his voice and speaks slowly.) Well, we're in the war zone right this minit if you wants to know.

[The effect of this speech is instantaneous. All sit bolt upright on their benches and stare at DAVIS.]

SMITTY. How do you know, Davis?

DAVIS (angrily). 'Cos Drisc heard the First [1] send the Third below to wake the skipper when we fetched the zone — 'bout five bells, it was. Now whata y' got to say?

SMITTY (conciliatingly [2]). Oh, I wasn't doubting your word, Davis; but you know they're not pasting up bulletins to let the crew know when the zone

[1] the First: the first mate, the deck officer ranking just below the captain.
[2] conciliatingly (kŏn·sĭl'ĭ·āt'ĭng·lĭ): trying to win over to a friendly attitude.

is reached — especially on ammunition ships like this.

IVAN (*decidedly*). I don't li-ike dees voyage. Next time I ship on windjammer Boston to River Plate, load with wood only so it float, by golly!

SWANSON (*fretfully*). I hope British navy blow 'em to hell, those submarines, py damn!

SCOTTY (*looking at* SMITTY, *who is staring at the doorway in a dream, his chin on his hands — meaningly*). It is no the submarrines only we've to fear, I'm thinkin'.

DAVIS (*assenting eagerly*). That's no lie, Scotty.

SWANSON. You mean the mines?

SCOTTY. I wasna thinkin' o' mines, eitherr.

DAVIS. There's many a good ship blown up and at the bottom of the sea, what never hit no mine or torpedo.

SCOTTY. Did ye neverr read of the Germman spies and the dirrty work they're doin' all the war?

[*He and* DAVIS *both glance at* SMITTY, *who is deep in thought and is not listening to the conversation.*]

DAVIS. An' the clever way they fool you!

SWANSON. Sure; I read it in paper many time.

DAVIS. Well — (*He is about to speak but hesitates and finishes lamely.*) you got to watch out, that's all I says.

IVAN (*drinking the last of his coffee and slamming his fist on the bench explosively*). I tell you dis rotten coffee give me bellyache, yes! (*They all look at him in amused disgust.*)

SCOTTY (*sardonically*). Dinna fret about it, Ivan. If we blow up ye'll no be mindin' the pain in your middle.

[JACK *enters. He is a young American with a tough, good-natured face. He wears dungarees and a heavy jersey.*]

JACK. Eight bells, fellers.

IVAN (*stupidly*). I don' hear bell ring.

JACK. No, and yuh won't hear any ring, yuh boob — (*Lowering his voice unconsciously*) now we're in the war zone.

SWANSON (*anxiously*). Is the boats all ready?

JACK. Sure; we can lower 'em in a second.

DAVIS. A lot o' good the boats'll do, with us loaded deep with all kinds o' dynamite and stuff the like o' that! If a torpedo hits this hooker we'll all be in hell b'fore you could wink your eye.

JACK. They ain't goin' to hit us, see? That's my dope. Whose wheel is it?

IVAN (*sullenly*). My wheel. (*He lumbers out.*)

JACK. And whose lookout?

SWANSON. Mine, I tink. (*He follows* IVAN.)

JACK (*scornfully*). A lot of use keepin' a lookout! We couldn't run away or fight if we wanted to. (*To* SCOTTY *and* SMITTY) Better look up the bo'sun or the Fourth,[1] you two, and let 'em see you're awake. (SCOTTY *goes to the doorway and turns to wait for* SMITTY, *who is still in the same position, head on hands, seemingly unconscious of everything.* JACK *slaps him roughly on the shoulder and he comes to with a start.*) Aft and report, Duke! What's the matter with yuh — in a dope dream? (SMITTY *goes out after* SCOTTY *without answering.* JACK *looks after him with a frown.*) He's a queer guy. I can't figger him out.

DAVIS. Nor no one else. (*Lowering his voice — meaningly*) An' he's liable to turn out queerer than any of us think if we ain't careful.

JACK (*suspiciously*). What d'yuh mean?

[*They are interrupted by the entrance of* DRISCOLL *and* COCKY.]

COCKY (*protestingly*). Blimey if I don't fink I'll put this 'ere watch ahtside on deck. (*He and* DRISCOLL *go over and*

---

[1] bo'sun or the Fourth: petty officer or the officer (fourth mate) in charge of the watch.

get their cups.) I down't want to be caught in this 'ole if they 'its us. (*He pours out coffee.*)

DRISCOLL (*pouring his.*) Divil a bit ut wud matther where ye arre. Ye'd be blown to smithereens b'fore ye cud say your name. (*He sits down, overturning as he does so the untouched cup of coffee which* SMITTY *had forgotten and left on the bench. They all jump nervously as the tin cup hits the floor with a bang.* DRISCOLL *flies into an unreasoning rage.*) Who's the swab left this cup where a man 'ud sit on ut?

DAVIS. It's Smitty's.

DRISCOLL (*kicking the cup across the forecastle*). Does he think he's too much av a bloody gentleman to put his own away loike the rist av us? If he does I'm the bye'll beat that noshun out av his head.

COCKY. Be the airs 'e puts on you'd think 'e was the Prince of Wales. Wot's 'e doin' on a ship I arsks yer? 'E ain't now good as a sailor, is 'e? — dawdlin' abaht on deck like a chicken wiv 'is 'ead cut orf!

JACK (*good-naturedly*). Aw, the Duke's all right. S'posin' he did ferget his cup — what's the dif? (*He picks up the cup and puts it away — with a grin.*) This war zone stuff's got yer goat, Drisc — and yours too, Cocky — and I ain't cheerin' much fur it myself, neither.

COCKY (*with a sigh*). Blimey, it ain't no bleedin' joke, yer first trip, to know as there's a ship full of shells li'ble to go orf in under your bloomin' feet, as you might say, if we gets 'it be a torpedo or mine. (*With sudden savagery*) Calls theyselves 'uman bein's, too! Blarsted 'Uns!

DRISCOLL (*gloomily*). 'Tis me last trip in the bloody zone, God help me. The divil take their twenty-foive per cent bonus — and be drowned like a rat in a trap in the bargain, maybe.

DAVIS. Wouldn't be so bad if she wasn't carryin' ammunition. Them's the kind the subs is layin' for.

DRISCOLL (*irritably*). Fur the love av hivin' don't be talkin' about ut. I'm sick wid thinkin' and jumpin' at iviry bit av a noise.

[*There is a pause, during which they all stare gloomily at the floor.*]

JACK. Hey, Davis, what was you sayin' about Smitty when they come in?

DAVIS (*with a great air of mystery*). I'll tell you in a minit. I want to wait an' see if he's comin' back. (*Impressively*) You won't be callin' him all right when you hears what I seen with my own eyes. (*He adds with an air of satisfaction*) An' you won't be feelin' no safer, neither.

[*They all look at him with puzzled glances full of a vague apprehension.* DRISCOLL *fills his pipe and lights it. The others, with an air of remembering something they had forgotten, do the same.* SCOTTY *enters.*]

SCOTTY (*in awed tones*). Mon, but it's clear outside the nicht! Like day.

DAVIS (*in low tones*). Where's Smitty, Scotty?

SCOTTY. Out on the hatch starin' at the moon like a mon half-daft.

DAVIS. Kin you see him from the doorway?

SCOTTY (*goes to doorway and carefully peeks out*). Aye, he's still there.

DAVIS. Keep your eyes on him for a moment. I've got something I wants to tell the boys, and I don't want him walkin' in in the middle of it. Give a shout if he starts this way.

SCOTTY (*with suppressed excitement*). Aye, I'll watch him. And I've somethin' myself to tell aboot his Lordship.

DRISCOLL (*impatiently*). Out wid ut! You're talkin' more than a pair av auld women wud be standin' in the road, and gittin' no further along.

DAVIS. Listen! You 'member when I went to git the coffee, Jack?

JACK. Sure, I do.

DAVIS. Well, I brings it down here

same as usual and got as far as the door there when I sees him.

JACK. Smitty?

DAVIS. Yes, Smitty! He was standin' in the middle of the fo'c's'tle there (*Pointing*) lookin' around sneakin'-like at Ivan and Swanson and the rest 's if he wants to make certain they're asleep.

[*He pauses significantly, looking from one to the other of his listeners.* SCOTTY *is nervously dividing his attention between* SMITTY *on the hatch outside and* DAVIS' *story, fairly bursting to break in with his own revelations.*]

JACK (*impatiently*). What of it?

DAVIS. Listen! He was standin' right there — (*Pointing again*) in his stockin' feet — no shoes on, mind, so he wouldn't make no noise!

JACK. (*spitting disgustedly*). Aw!

DAVIS (*not heeding the interruption*). I seen right away somethin' on the queer was up so I slides back into the alleyway where I kin see him but he can't see me. After he makes sure they're all asleep he goes in under the bunks there — bein' careful not to raise a noise, mind! — an' takes out his bag there. (*By this time, everyone,* JACK *included, is listening breathlessly to his story.*) Then he fishes in his pocket an' takes out a bunch o' keys an' kneels down beside the bag an' opens it.

SCOTTY (*unable to keep silent longer*). Mon, didn't I see him do that same thing wi' these two eyes. 'Twas just that moment I woke and spied him.

DAVIS (*surprised, and a bit nettled to have to share his story with anyone*). Oh, you seen him, too, eh? (*To the others*) Then Scotty kin tell you if I'm lyin' or not.

DRISCOLL. An' what did he do whin he'd the bag opened?

DAVIS. He bends down and reaches out his hand sort o' scared-like, like it was somethin' dang'rous he was after, an' feels round in under his duds, hidden in under his duds an' wrapped up in 'em, it was, an' he brings out a black iron box!

COCKY (*looking around him with a frightened glance*). Blimey!

[*The others likewise betray their uneasiness, shuffling their feet nervously.*]

DAVIS. Ain't that right, Scotty?

SCOTTY. Right as rain, I'm tellin' ye!

DAVIS (*to the others with an air of satisfaction*). There you are! (*Lowering his voice*) An' then what d'you suppose he did? Sneaks to his bunk an' slips the black box in under his mattress — in under his mattress, mind! —

JACK. And it's there now?

DAVIS. Course it is!

[JACK *starts toward* SMITTY'S *bunk.* DRISCOLL *grabs him by the arm.*]

DRISCOLL. Don't be touchin' ut, Jack!

JACK. Yuh needn't worry. I ain't goin' to touch it. (*He pulls up* SMITTY'S *mattress and looks down. The others stare at him, holding their breaths. He turns to them, trying hard to assume a careless tone.*) It's there, aw right.

COCKY (*miserably upset*). I'm gointer 'op it aht on deck. (*He gets up, but* DRISCOLL *pulls him down again.* COCKY *protests.*) It fair guvs me the trembles sittin' still in 'ere.

DRISCOLL (*scornfully*). Are ye frightened, ye toad? 'Tis a foin thing fur grown men to be shiverin' loike childer at a bit av a black box. (*Scratching his head in uneasy perplexity*) Still, ut's queer, the looks av ut.

DAVIS (*sarcastically*). A bit of a black box, eh? How big d'you think them — (*He hesitates*) — things has to be — big as this fo'c's'tle?

JACK (*in a voice meant to be reassuring*). Aw, I'll bet it ain't nothin' but some coin he's saved he's got locked up in there.

DAVIS (*scornfully*). That's likely, ain't it? Then why does he act so s'picious? He's been on ship near two year, ain't he? He knows there ain't no thiefs in this fo'c's'tle, don't he? An' you know 's well 's I do he didn't have no money when he came on board an' he ain't saved none since. Don't you? (JACK *doesn't answer.*) Listen! D'you know what he done after he put that thing in under his mattress? — an' Scotty'll tell you if I ain't speakin' truth. He looks round to see if anyone's woke up —

SCOTTY. I clapped my eyes shut when he turned round.

DAVIS. An' then he crawls into his bunk an' shuts his eyes, an' starts in *snorin', pretendin'* he was asleep, mind!

SCOTTY. Aye, I could hear him.

DAVIS. An' when I goes to call him I don't even shake him. I just says, "Eight bells, Smitty," in a'most a whisper-like, an' up he gets yawnin' and stretchin' fit to kill hisself 's if he'd been dead asleep.

COCKY. Blimey!

DRISCOLL (*shaking his head*). Ut looks bad, divil a doubt av ut.

DAVIS (*excitedly*). An' now I come to think of it, there's the porthole. How'd it come to git open, tell me that? I know'd well Paul never opened it. Ain't he grumblin' about bein' cold all the time?

SCOTTY. The mon that opened it meant no good to this ship, whoever he was.

JACK (*sourly*). What porthole? What're you talkin' about?

DAVIS (*pointing over* PAUL's *bunk*). There. It was open when I come in. I felt the cold air on me neck an' shut it. It would'a been clear's a lighthouse to any sub that was watchin'— an' we s'posed to have all the ports blinded! Who'd do a dirty trick like that? It wasn't none of us, nor Scotty here, nor Swanson, nor Ivan. Who would it be, then?

COCKY (*angrily*). Must'a been 'is bloody Lordship.

DAVIS. For all's we know he might'a been signalin' with it. They does it like that by winkin' a light. Ain't you read how they gets caught doin' it in London an' on the coast?

COCKY (*firmly convinced now*). An' wots 'e doin' aht alone on the 'atch —

keepin' 'isself clear of us like 'e was afraid?

DRISCOLL. Kape your eye on him, Scotty.

SCOTTY. There's no a move oot o' him.

JACK (*in irritated perplexity*). Ain't he an Englishman? What'd he wanta —

DAVIS. English? How d'we know he's English? Cos he talks it? That ain't no proof. Ain't you read in the papers how all them German spies they been catchin' in England has been livin' there for ten, often as not twenty years, an' talks English as good's anyone? An' look here, ain't you noticed he don't talk natural? He talks it too good, that's what I mean. He don't talk exactly like a toff,[1] does he, Cocky?

COCKY. Not like any toff as I ever met up wiv.

DAVIS. No, an' he don't talk it like us, that's certain. An' he don't look English. An' what d'we know about him when you come to look at it? Nothin'! He ain't ever said where he comes from or why. All we knows is he ships on here in London 'bout a year b'fore the war starts, as an A.B.[2] — stole his papers most lik'ly — when he don't know how to box the compass,[3] hardly. Ain't that queer in itself? An' was he ever open with us like a good shipmate? No, he's always had that sly air about him 's if he was hidin' somethin'.

DRISCOLL (*slapping his thigh — angrily*). Divil take me if I don't think ye have the truth av ut, Davis.

COCKY (*scornfully*). Lettin' on be 'is silly airs, and all, 'e's the son of a blarsted earl or somethink!

DAVIS. An' the name he calls hisself — Smith! I'd risk a quid[4] of my next pay-

---

[1] **toff:** British slang for a dandy, a snob.
[2] **A.B.:** "able-bodied seaman," a term used for a skilled, experienced seaman, in contrast to the less skilled "ordinary seaman."
[3] **box the compass:** name the thirty-two points of the compass in their order.
[4] **quid:** British slang for a sovereign, or pound sterling. At the time of the play, the pound was worth about five dollars; today the rate of exchange is about $2.80.

day that his real name is Schmidt, if the truth was known.

JACK (*evidently fighting against his own conviction*). Aw, say, you guys give me a pain! What'd they want puttin' a spy on this old tub for?

DAVIS (*shaking his head sagely*). They're deep ones, an' there's a lot o' things a sailor'll see in the ports he puts in ought to be useful to 'em. An' if he kin signal to 'em an' they blows us up it's one ship less, ain't it? (*Lowering his voice and indicating* SMITTY's *bunk*) Or if he blows us up hisself.

SCOTTY (*in alarmed tones*). Hush, mon! Here he comes!

[SCOTTY *hurries over to a bench and sits down. A thick silence settles over the forecastle. The men look from one to another with uneasy glances.* SMITTY *enters and sits down beside his bunk. He is seemingly unaware of the dark glances of suspicion directed at him from all sides. He slides his hand back stealthily over his mattress and his fingers move, evidently feeling to make sure the box is still there. The others follow this movement carefully with quick looks out of the corners of their eyes. Their attitudes grow tense as if they were about to spring at him. Satisfied the box is safe,* SMITTY *draws his hand away slowly and utters a sigh of relief.*]

SMITTY (*in a casual tone which to them sounds sinister*). It's a good light night for the subs if there's any about.

[*For a moment he sits staring in front of him. Finally he seems to sense the hostile atmosphere of the forecastle and looks from one to the other of the men in surprise. All of them avoid his eyes. He sighs with a puzzled expression and gets up and walks out of the doorway. There is silence for a moment after his departure and then a storm of excited talk breaks loose.*]

DAVIS. Did you see him feelin' if it was there?

COCKY. 'E ain't 'arf a sly one wiv 'is talk of submarines!

SCOTTY. Did ye see the sneakin' looks he gave us?

DRISCOLL. If ivir I saw black shame on a man's face 'twas on his whin he sat there!

JACK (*thoroughly convinced at last*). He looked bad to me. He's a crook, aw right.

DAVIS (*excitedly*). What'll we do? We gotter do somethin' quick or —

[*He is interrupted by the sound of something hitting against the port side of the forecastle with a dull, heavy thud. The men start to their feet in wild-eyed terror and turn as if they were going to rush for the deck. They stand that way for a strained moment, scarcely breathing and listening intently.*]

JACK (*with a sickly smile*). It's on'y a piece of driftwood or a floatin' log. (*He sits down again.*)

DAVIS (*sarcastically*). Or a mine that didn't go off — that time — or a piece o' wreckage from some ship they've sent to Davy Jones.

COCKY (*mopping his brow with a trembling hand*). Blimey! (*He sinks back weakly on a bench.*)

DRISCOLL (*furiously*). Blarst ut! No man at all cud be puttin' up wid the loike av this — an' I'm not wan to be fearin' anything or any man in the worrld'll stand up to me face to face; but this divil's trickery in the darrk — (*He starts for* SMITTY's *bunk.*) I'll throw ut out wan av the portholes an' be done wid ut. (*He reaches toward the mattress.*)

SCOTTY (*grabbing his arm — wildly*). Arre ye daft, mon?

DAVIS. Don't monkey with it, Drisc. I knows what to do. Bring the bucket o' water here, Jack, will you? (JACK *gets it and brings it over to* DAVIS.) An' you, Scotty, see if he's back on the hatch.

SCOTTY (*cautiously peering out*). Aye, he's sittin' there the noo.[1]

DAVIS. Sing out if he makes a move. Lift up the mattress, Drisc — careful now! (DRISCOLL *does so with infinite caution.*) Take it out, Jack — careful — don't shake it now. Here — put it in the water — easy! There, that's fixed it! (*They all sit down with great sighs of relief.*) The water'll git in and spoil it.

DRISCOLL (*slapping* DAVIS *on the back*). Good wurrk for ye, Davis. (*He spits on his hands aggressively.*) An' now what's to be done wid that black-hearted thraitor?

COCKY (*belligerently*). Guv 'im a shove in the marf[2] and 'eave 'im over the side!

DAVIS. An' serve him right!

JACK. Aw, say, give him a chance. Yuh can't prove nothin' till yuh find out what's in there.

DRISCOLL (*heatedly*). Is ut more proof ye'd be needin' afther what we've seen an' heard? Then listen to me — an' ut's Driscoll talkin' — if there's divilmint in that box an' we see plain 'twas his plan to murrdher his own shipmates that have served him fair — (*He raises his fist.*) I'll choke his rotten hearrt out wid me own hands, an' over the side wid him, and one man missin' in the mornin'.

DAVIS. An' no one the wiser. He's the balmy kind what commits suicide.

COCKY. They 'angs spies ashore.

JACK (*resentfully*). If he's done what yuh think I'll croak him myself. Is that good enough for yuh?

DRISCOLL (*looking down at the box*). How'll we be openin' this, I wonder?

SCOTTY (*from the doorway — warningly*). He's standin' up.

DAVIS. We'll take his keys away from him when he comes in. Quick, Drisc! You an' Jack get beside the door and grab him. (*They get on either side of the door.* DAVIS *snatches a small coil of rope from one of the upper bunks.*)

[1] the noo: now.
[2] marf: mouth.

This'll do for me an' Scotty to tie him.

SCOTTY. He's turnin' this way — he's comin'! (*He moves away from door.*)

DAVIS. Stand by to lend a hand, Cocky.

COCKY. Righto.

[*As* SMITTY *enters the forecastle he is seized roughly from both sides and his arms pinned behind him. At first he struggles fiercely, but seeing the uselessness of this, he finally stands calmly and allows* DAVIS *and* SCOTTY *to tie up his arms.*]

SMITTY (*when they have finished — with cold contempt*). If this is your idea of a joke I'll have to confess it's a bit too thick for me to enjoy.

COCKY (*angrily*). Shut yer marf, 'ear!

DRISCOLL (*roughly*). Ye'll find ut's no joke, me bucko, b'fore we're done wid you. (*To* SCOTTY) Kape your eye peeled, Scotty, and sing out if anyone's comin'.

[SCOTTY *resumes his post at the door.*]

SMITTY (*with the same icy contempt*). If you'd be good enough to explain —

DRISCOLL (*furiously*). Explain, is ut? 'Tis you'll do the explainin' — an' quick, or we'll know the reason why. (*To* JACK *and* DAVIS) Bring him here, now. (*They push* SMITTY *over to the bucket.*) Look here, ye murrdherin' swab. D'you see ut?

[SMITTY *looks down with an expression of amazement which rapidly changes to one of anguish.*]

DAVIS (*with a sneer*). Look at him! S'prised, ain't you? If you wants to try your dirty spyin' tricks on us you've got-ter git up earlier in the mornin'.

COCKY. Thorght yer weren't 'arf a fox, didn't yer?

SMITTY (*trying to restrain his growing rage*). What — what do you mean? That's only — How dare — What are you doing with my private belongings?

COCKY (*sarcastically*). Ho yus! Private b'longings!

DRISCOLL (*shouting*). What is ut, ye swine? Will you tell us to our faces? What's in ut?

SMITTY (*biting his lips— holding himself in check with a great effort*). Nothing but — That's my business. You'll please attend to your own.

DRISCOLL. Oho, ut is, is ut? (*Shaking his fist in* SMITTY'S *face*) Talk aisy now if ye know what's best for you. Your business, indade! Then we'll be makin' ut ours, I'm thinkin'. (*To* JACK *and* DAVIS) Take his keys away from him an' we'll see if there's one'll open ut, maybe. (*They start in searching* SMITTY, *who tries to resist and kicks out at the bucket.* DRISCOLL *leaps forward and helps them push him away.*) Try to kick ut over, wud ye? Did ye see him then? Tryin' to murrdher us all! Take that pail out av his way, Cocky.

[SMITTY *struggles with all of his strength and keeps them busy for a few seconds. As* COCKY *grabs the pail,* SMITTY *makes a final effort and, lunging forward, kicks again at the bucket but only succeeds in hitting* COCKY *on the shin.* COCKY *immediately sets down the pail with a bang and, clutching his knee in both hands, starts hopping around the forecastle, groaning and swearing.*]

COCKY. Ooow! Kicked me, 'e did! Bloody, bleedin', rotten Dutch 'og! (*Approaching* SMITTY, *who has given up the fight and is pushed back against the wall near the doorway, with* JACK *and* DAVIS *holding him on either side — wrathfully, at the top of his lungs.*) Kick me, will yer? I'll show yer what for, yer bleedin' sneak! (*He draws back his fist.* DRISCOLL *pushes him to one side.*)

DRISCOLL. Shut your mouth! D'you want to wake the whole ship? (*COCKY grumbles and retires to a bench, nursing his sore shin.*)

JACK (*taking a small bunch of keys from* SMITTY'S *pocket*). Here yuh are, Drisc.

DRISCOLL (*taking them.*) We'll soon be knowin'.

[*He takes the pail and sits down, placing it on the floor between his feet.* SMITTY *again tries to break loose but he is too tired and is easily held back against the wall.*]

SMITTY (*breathing heavily and very pale*). Cowards!

JACK (*with a growl*). Nix on the rough talk, see. That don't git yuh nothin'.

DRISCOLL (*looking at the lock on the box in the water and then scrutinizing the keys in his hand*). This'll be ut, I'm thinkin'. (*He selects one and gingerly reaches his hand in the water.*)

SMITTY (*his face grown livid — chokingly*). Don't you open that box, Driscoll. If you do, so help me, I'll kill you if I have to hang for it.

DRISCOLL (*pausing — his hand in the water*). Whin I open this box I'll not be the wan to be kilt, me sonny bye! I'm no dirty spy.

SMITTY (*his voice trembling with rage; his eyes are fixed on* DRISCOLL'S *hand*). Spy? What are you talking about? I only put that box there so I could get it quick in case we were torpedoed. Are you all mad? Do you think I'm — (*Chokingly*) You stupid curs! You cowardly dolts!

[DAVIS *claps his hand over* SMITTY'S *mouth.*]

DAVIS. That'll be enough from you!

[DRISCOLL *takes the dripping box from the water and starts to fit in the key.* SMITTY *springs forward furiously, almost escaping from their grasp, and drags them after him halfway across the forecastle.*]

DRISCOLL. Hold him, ye divils!

[*He puts the box back in the water and jumps to their aid.* COCKY *hovers on the outskirts of the battle, mindful of the kick he received.*]

SMITTY (*raging*). Cowards! Rotten curs! (*He is thrown to the floor and held there.*) Cowards! Cowards!

DRISCOLL. I'll shut your dirty mouth for you.

[*He goes to his bunk and pulls out a big wad of waste and comes back to* SMITTY.]

SMITTY. Cowards! Cowards!

DRISCOLL (*with no gentle hand slaps the waste over* SMITTY's *mouth*). That'll teach you to be misnamin' a man, ye sneak. Have ye a handkerchief, Jack? (JACK *hands him one and he ties it tightly around* SMITTY's *head over the waste.*) That'll fix your gab. Stand him up, now, and tie his feet, too, so he'll not be movin'. (*They do so and leave him with his back against the wall near* SCOTTY. *Then they all sit down beside* DRISCOLL, *who again lifts the box out of the water and sets it carefully on his knees. He picks out the key, then hesitates, looking from one to the other uncertainly.*) We'd best be takin' this to the skipper, d'you think, maybe?

JACK (*irritably*). This is our game and we c'n play it without no help.

COCKY. Now bleedin' horficers, I says!

DAVIS. They'd only be takin' all the credit and makin' heroes of theyselves.

DRISCOLL (*boldly*). Here goes, thin! (*He slowly turns the key in the lock. The others instinctively turn away. He carefully pushes the cover back on its hinges and looks at what he sees inside with an expression of puzzled astonishment. The others crowd up close. Even* SCOTTY *leaves his post to take a look.*) What is ut, Davis?

DAVIS (*mystified*). Looks funny, don't it? Somethin' square tied up in a rubber bag. Maybe it's dynamite — or somethin' — you can't never tell.

JACK. Aw, it ain't got no works so it ain't no bomb, I'll bet.

DAVIS (*dubiously*). They makes them all kinds, they do.

JACK. Open it up, Drisc.

DAVIS. Careful now!

[DRISCOLL *takes a black rubber bag resembling a large tobacco pouch from the box and unties the string which is wound tightly around the top. He opens it and takes out a small packet of letters also tied up with string. He turns these over in his hands and looks at the others questioningly.*]

JACK (*with a broad grin*). On'y letters! (*Slapping* DAVIS *on the back*) Yuh're a fine Sherlock Holmes, ain't yuh? Letters from his best girl, too, I'll bet. Let's turn the Duke loose, what d'yuh say? (*He starts to get up.*)

DAVIS (*fixing him with a withering look*). Don't be so smart, Jack. Letters, you says, 's if there never was no harm in 'em. How d'you s'pose spies gets their orders and sends back what they finds out if it ain't by letters and such things? There's many a letter is worser'n any bomb.

COCKY. Righto! They ain't as innercent as they looks, I'll take me oath, when you read 'em. (*Pointing at* SMITTY) Not 'is Lordship's letters, not be no means!

JACK (*sitting down again*). Well, read 'em and find out.

[DRISCOLL *commences untying the packet. There is a muffled groan of rage and protest from* SMITTY.]

DAVIS (*triumphantly*). There! Listen to him! Look at him tryin' to git loose! Ain't that proof enough? He knows well we're findin' him out. Listen to me! Love letters, you says, Jack, 's if they couldn't harm nothin'. Listen! I was readin' in some magazine in New York on'y two weeks back how some German spy in Paris was writin' love letters to some woman spy in Switzerland who sent 'em on to Berlin, Germany. To read 'em you wouldn't s'pect nothin' — just mush and all. (*Impressively*) But they had a way o' doin' it — a sneakin' way. They had a piece o' plain paper with pieces cut out of it an' when they puts it on top o' the letter they sees on'y the words what tells them what they wants to know. An' the Frenchies gets beat in a fight all on account o' that letter.

COCKY (awed). Blimey! They ain't 'arf smart bleeders!

DAVIS (seeing his audience is again all with him). 'An even if these letters of his do sound all right they may have what they calls a code. You can't never tell. (To DRISCOLL, who has finished untying the packet) Read one of 'em, Drisc. My eyes is weak.

DRISCOLL (takes the first one out of its envelope and bends down to the lantern with it; he turns up the wick to give him a better light). I'm no hand to be readin' but I'll try ut.

[Again there is a muffled groan from SMITTY as he strains at his bonds.]

DAVIS (gloatingly). Listen to him! He knows. Go ahead, Drisc!

DRISCOLL (his brow furrowed with concentration). Ut begins: Dearest Man — (His eyes travel down the page.) An' thin there's a lot av blarney tellin' him how much she misses him now she's gone away to singin' school — an' how she hopes he'll settle down to rale worrk an' not be skylarkin' around now that she's away loike he used to before she met up wid him — and ut ends: "I love you betther than anythin' in the worrld. You know that, don't you, dear? But b'fore I can agree to live out my life wid you, you must prove to me that the black shadow — I won't menshun uts hateful name but you know what I mean — which might wreck both our lives, does not exist for you. You can do that, can't you, dear? Don't you see you must for my sake?" (He pauses for a moment — then adds gruffly) Ut's signed: "Edith."

[At the sound of the name, SMITTY, who has stood tensely with his eyes shut as if he were undergoing torture during the reading, makes a muffled sound like a sob and half turns his face to the wall.]

JACK (sympathetically). What's the use of readin' that stuff even if —

DAVIS (interrupting him sharply). Wait! Where's that letter from, Drisc?

DRISCOLL. There's no address on the top av ut.

DAVIS (meaningly). What'd I tell you? Look at the postmark, Drisc — on the envelope.

DRISCOLL. The name that's written is Sidney Davidson, wan hundred an' —

DAVIS. Never mind that. O' course it's a false name. Look at the postmark.

DRISCOLL. There's a furrin' stamp on ut by the looks av ut. The mark's blurred so it's hard to read. (He spells it out laboriously.) B-e-r — the nixt is an l, I think — i — an' an n.

DAVIS (excitedly). Berlin! What did I tell you? I knew them letters was from Germany.

COCKY (shaking his fist in SMITTY's direction). Rotten 'ound!

[The others look at SMITTY as if this last fact had utterly condemned him in their eyes.]

DAVIS. Give me the letter, Drisc. Maybe I kin make somethin' out of it. (DRISCOLL hands the letter to him.) You go through the others, Drisc, and sing out if you sees anythin' queer.

[He bends over the first letter as if he were determined to figure out its secret meaning. JACK, COCKY, and SCOTTY look over his shoulder with eager curiosity. DRISCOLL takes out some of the other letters, running his eyes quickly down the pages. He looks curiously over at SMITTY from time to time, and sighs frequently with a puzzled frown.]

DAVIS (disappointedly). I gotter give it up. It's too deep for me, but we'll turn 'em over to the perlice when we docks at Liverpool to look through. This one I got was written a year before the war started, anyway. Find anythin' in yours, Drisc?

DRISCOLL. They're all the same as the first — lovin' blarney, an' how her singin' is doin', and the great things the Dutch teacher says about her voice, an' how glad she is that her Sidney bye is worrkin' harrd an' makin' a man av himself for her sake.

[SMITTY *turns his face completely to the wall.*]

DAVIS (*disgustedly*). If we on'y had the code!

DRISCOLL (*taking up the bottom letter*). Hullo! Here's wan addressed to this ship — S.S. *Glencairn*, ut says — whin we was in Cape Town sivin months ago — (*Looking at the postmark*) Ut's from London.

DAVIS (*eagerly*). Read it!

[*There is another choking groan from* SMITTY.]

DRISCOLL (*reads slowly — his voice becomes lower and lower as he goes on*). Ut begins wid simply the name Sidney Davidson — no dearest or sweetheart to this wan. "Ut is only from your chance meetin' wid Harry — whin you were drunk — that I happen to know where to reach you. So you have run away to sea loike the coward you are because you knew I had found out the truth — the truth you have covered over with your mean little lies all the time I was away in Berlin and blindly trusted you. Very well, you have chosen. You have shown that your drunkenness means more to you than any love or faith av mine. I am sorry — for I loved you, Sidney Davidson — but this is the end. I lave you — the mem'ries; an' if ut is any satisfaction to you I lave you the real-i-zation that you have wrecked my loife as you have wrecked your own. My one remainin' hope is that nivir in God's worrld will I ivir see your face again. Goodby. Edith."

[*As he finishes there is a deep silence, broken only by* SMITTY's *muffled sobbing. The men cannot look at each other.* DRISCOLL *holds the rubber bag limply in his hand and some small white object falls out of it and drops noiselessly on the floor. Mechanically* DRISCOLL *leans over and picks it up, and looks at it wonderingly.*]

DAVIS (*in a dull voice*). What's that?

DRISCOLL (*slowly*). A bit av a dried-up flower — a rose, maybe.

[*He drops it into the bag and gathers up the letters and puts them back. He replaces the bag in the box and locks it up and puts it back under* SMITTY's *mattress. The others follow him with their eyes. He steps softly over to* SMITTY *and cuts the ropes about his arms and ankles with his sheath knife, and unties the handkerchief over the gag.* SMITTY *does not turn around but covers his face with his hands and leans his head against the wall. His shoulders continue to heave spasmodically but he makes no further sound.*]

DRISCOLL. (*Stalks back to the others — there is a moment of silence, in which each man is in agony with the hopelessness of finding a word he can say — then* DRISCOLL *explodes.*) Are we never goin' to turn in fur a wink av sleep?

[*They all start as if awakening from a bad dream and gratefully crawl into their bunks, shoes and all, turning their faces to the wall, and pulling their blankets up over their shoulders.* SCOTTY *tiptoes past* SMITTY *out into the darkness . . .* DRISCOLL *turns down the light and crawls into his bunk as*

[THE CURTAIN FALLS]

FOR DISCUSSION

1. Sketch the circumstances that aroused the suspicions of the crew. Which do you think was the more powerful factor in arousing suspicion — Smitty's actions or the general fear of a submarine attack? Explain your answer.

2. Which of the seamen scoffed at the fears of the others? Do you think he was braver, or only more sensible? Why would the play have been less effective without this character?

3. How did Smitty's behavior on seeing the crew handle his box affect your own belief in his guilt or innocence? When were the men convinced that their suspicions were unfounded?

4. Were you satisfied that the story revealed by the letters could account for Smitty's behavior? What do you think the future holds for Smitty?

5. O'Neill rarely tells a story without special significance. What thoughts do you discover in this one about the influence of fear on human behavior? about the attitude of a group toward a member who is "different"? about being too ready to suspect other people's motives?

UNDERSTANDING DIALOGUE

1. Find in the first two pages of "In the Zone" speeches that illustrate each of the four uses of dialogue (see page 350). Which of these uses are most important in this part of the play?

2. Explain how the first two or three remarks made by each of the seamen help to establish his identity and prepare you for the part he will take in the action later in the play. Why do you think O'Neill used so many different accents in this small group?

3. What is the chief emotional effect created in the early part of the play? Read aloud bits of dialogue that build up this effect. What other emotions are stirred by the last part of the play? Find lines that make them especially effective.

As the Artist Sees It

Reproduced on page 363 is an interpretation of the final scene of Eugene O'Neill's "In the Zone." This charcoal sketch is by Harvey Dinnerstein. In the sketch Smitty can easily be identified, while the man holding the pail is probably Cocky. With the help of Eugene O'Neill's stage directions, can you name the three remaining characters? Has the artist succeeded in making the characters distinct individuals?

THE AUTHOR

EUGENE O'NEILL (1888–1953) gained familiarity with the stage from his father, a successful actor. O'Neill attended Princeton for one year and spent two more in rough-and-ready life at sea and along waterfronts. While recovering from tuberculosis, he decided to become a dramatist and later entered a playwriting course at Harvard University. In 1916 he became associated with the Provincetown Players in Massachusetts, who produced many of his one-act plays.

Eugene O'Neill's power as a dramatic writer was apparent from the beginning of his career. He first wrote one-act plays based largely on his experiences at sea, the most distinguished short plays yet seen in America. In 1920 he reached Broadway with *Beyond the Horizon*, winning the first of his three Pulitzer prizes. This play is constructed in the familiar three-act pattern, but in succeeding plays O'Neill developed an unconventional technique, telling the story in a series of short scenes and displaying the impressionistic methods that mark all his major dramas. Most of his plays dwell on somber themes, but in 1932 he revealed a vein of gentle comedy in *Ah, Wilderness!* Among his most famous works are *The Emperor Jones* (1920), which has been made into an opera; *Anna Christie* (1921); *Strange Interlude* (1928); *Mourning Becomes Electra* (1931), a modern treatment of a Greek tragedy; and the posthumous plays, *Long Day's Journey into Night* and *A Touch of the Poet*. He received the Nobel prize for literature in 1936.

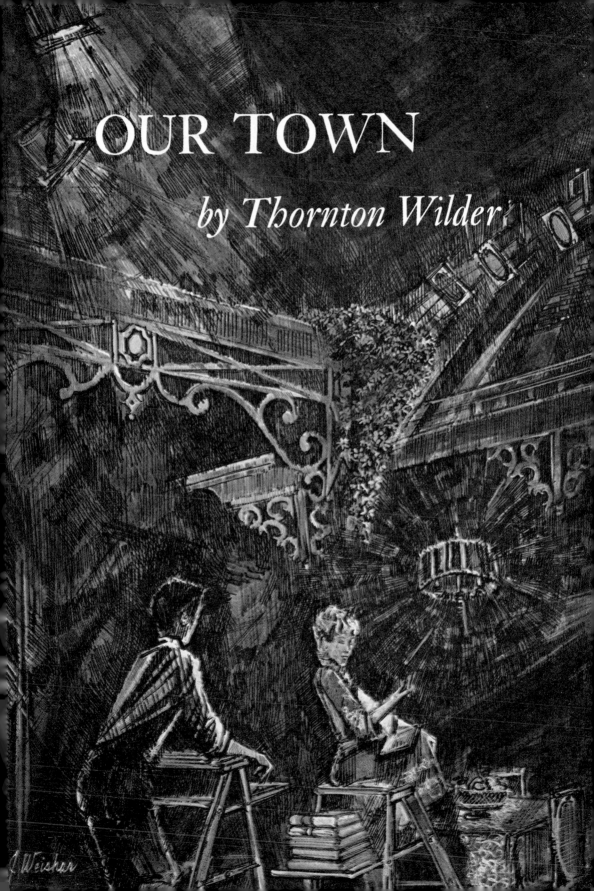

OUR TOWN

by Thornton Wilder

A REALISTIC PLAY. It is easier to write about uncommon events than common ones; about unhappy events rather than happy ones; about violence rather than peace. Novelty, shock, or any other strong sensations do the author's work for him to some extent. To move us by presenting the commonplace aspects of life that we all share, the writer must see more than we have seen and give us deeper insights into experiences that we have taken for granted. Thornton Wilder has met this challenge superbly in *Our Town*. He will make you laugh, and possibly weep; and more, he will make you think. He has described the play as "an attempt to find a value above all price for the smallest events in our daily life." Thousands of theatergoers and readers, in many countries, have agreed that Wilder has succeeded. *Our Town* is both new and old, local and universal. It is the best-loved play of the modern American stage.

THE FORM OF THE PLAY. *Our Town* moves freely in time and space, unbound by rigid chronology or fixed scenery. To many people this seems new: actually it is a return to the oldest practices of the theater. The Stage Manager, moving about and arranging the stage before our eyes, is borrowed from the Chinese theater. Wilder has made him a drawling New Englander and used him to tie together the loose elements of the play and to interpret much of its meaning for us. The Stage Manager gives the play unity, no matter how much it skips about, and he even steps in and out of the action in small roles from time to time. He makes the play intensely real by calling upon each of us to supply the details of reality out of our own lives as we recognize how much we have in common with all that happens. *Our Town* is enriched by what *our* imaginations bring to it.

Characters

STAGE MANAGER
DR. GIBBS
JOE CROWELL, JR.
HOWIE NEWSOME
MRS. GIBBS
MRS. WEBB
GEORGE GIBBS
REBECCA GIBBS
WALLY WEBB
EMILY WEBB
PROFESSOR WILLARD
MR. WEBB
WOMAN IN THE BALCONY
TALL MAN AT BACK OF AUDITORIUM
LADY IN A BOX
SIMON STIMSON
MRS. SOAMES
CONSTABLE WARREN
SI CROWELL
SAM CRAIG
JOE STODDARD
PEOPLE OF THE TOWN

The entire play takes place in Grover's Corners, New Hampshire, 1901 to 1913.

Act I

No curtain. No scenery. The audience, arriving, sees an empty stage in half-light.

Presently the STAGE MANAGER, *hat on and pipe in mouth, enters and begins placing a table and several chairs downstage left, and a table and chairs downstage right. "Left" and "right" are from the point of view of the actor facing the audience. "Up" is toward the back wall.*

As the house lights go down, he has finished setting the stage and, leaning against the right proscenium[1] *pillar, watches the late arrivals in the audience. When the auditorium is in complete darkness, he speaks.*

[1] **proscenium** (prŏ·sē′nĭ·ŭm): the small area on a stage in front of the curtain, where action takes place when the curtain is closed.

STAGE MANAGER. This play is called *Our Town*. It was written by Thornton Wilder; produced and directed by A_____ [or: produced by A_____; directed by B_____]. In it you will see Miss C_____, Miss D_____, Miss E_____, and Mr. F_____, Mr. G_____, Mr. H_____, and many others.

The name of the town is Grover's Corners, New Hampshire — just across the Massachusetts line: longitude forty-two degrees, forty minutes; latitude seventy degrees, thirty-seven minutes.

The first act shows a day in our town. The day is May 7, 1901. The time is just before dawn.

[*A rooster crows.*]

The sky is beginning to show some streaks of light over in the east there, behind our mount'in. The morning star always gets wonderful bright the minute before it has to go. (*He stares at it for a moment, then goes upstage.*)

Well, I'd better show you how our town lies. Up here (*That is, parallel with the back wall*) is Main Street. Way back there is the railway station; tracks go that way. Polish Town's across the tracks and some Canuck [1] families. (*Toward the left*) Over there is the Congregational Church; across the street's the Presbyterian. Methodist and Unitarian are over there. Baptist is down in the holla by the river. Catholic Church is over beyond the tracks.

Here's the Town Hall and Post Office combined; jail's in the basement. Bryan [2] once made a speech from these steps here. Along here's a row of stores. Hitching posts and horse blocks in front of them. First automobile's going to come along in about five years — belonged to Banker Cartwright, our richest citizen . . . lives in the big white house up on the hill.

[1] Canuck: French-Canadian.
[2] Bryan: William Jennings Bryan (1860–1925), Democratic Presidential nominee in 1896, 1900, and 1908.

Here's the grocery store and here's Mr. Morgan's drugstore. Most everybody in town manages to look into those two stores once a day. Public school's over yonder. High school's still farther over. Quarter of nine mornings, noontimes, and three o'clock afternoons, the hull town can hear the yelling and screaming from those schoolyards. (*He approaches the table and chairs downstage right.*)

This is our doctor's house — Doc Gibbs's. This is the back door.

[*Two arched trellises are pushed out, one by each proscenium pillar.*]

There's some scenery for those who think they have to have scenery. There's a garden here. Corn . . . peas . . . beans . . . hollyhocks . . . heliotrope . . . and a lot of burdock. (*Crosses the stage.*)

In those days our newspaper come out twice a week — the Grover's Corners *Sentinel* — and this is Editor Webb's house. And this is Mrs. Webb's garden. Just like Mrs. Gibbs's, only it's got a lot of sunflowers, too. Right here — big butternut tree.

[*He returns to his place by the right proscenium pillar and looks at the audience for a minute.*]

Nice town, y'know what I mean? Nobody very remarkable ever come out of it — s'far as we know. The earliest tombstones in the cemetery up there on the mountain say 1670, 1680 — they're Grovers and Cartwrights and Gibbses and Herseys — same names as are around here now.

Well, as I said, it's about dawn. The only lights on in town are in a cottage over by the tracks where a Polish mother's just had twins. And in the Joe Crowell house, where Joe Jr.'s getting up so as to deliver the paper. And in the depot, where Shorty Hawkins is gettin' ready to flag the five forty-five for Boston.

[*A train whistle is heard. The* STAGE MANAGER *takes out his watch and nods.*]

Naturally, out in the country — all around — they've been lights on for some time, what with milkin's and so on. But town people sleep late.

So — another day's begun. There's Doc Gibbs comin' down Main Street now, comin' back from that baby case. And here's his wife comin' downstairs to get breakfast. Doc Gibbs died in 1930. The new hospital's named after him. Mrs. Gibbs died first — long time ago, in fact. She went out to visit her daughter, Rebecca, who married an insurance man in Canton, Ohio, and died there — pneumonia — but her body was brought back here. She's up in the cemetery there now, in with a whole mess of Gibbses and Herseys — she was Julia Hersey 'fore she married Doc Gibbs in the Congregational Church over there.

In our town we like to know the facts about everybody. . . . That's Doc Gibbs. And there comes Joe Crowell, Jr., delivering Mr. Webb's *Sentinel.*

[DR. GIBBS *has been coming along Main Street from the left. At the point where he would turn to approach his house, he stops, sets down his — imaginary — black bag, takes off his hat, and rubs his face with fatigue, using an enormous handkerchief.* MRS. GIBBS *has entered her kitchen, gone through the motions of putting wood into a stove, lighting it, and preparing breakfast. Suddenly,* JOE CROWELL, JR., *starts down Main Street from the right, hurling imaginary newspapers into doorways.*]

JOE CROWELL, JR. Morning, Doc Gibbs.
DR. GIBBS. Morning, Joe.
JOE CROWELL, JR. Somebody been sick, Doc?
DR. GIBBS. No. Just some twins born over in Polish Town.
JOE CROWELL, JR. Do you want your paper now?

DR. GIBBS. Yes, I'll take it. Anything serious goin' on in the world since Wednesday?
JOE CROWELL, JR. Yessir. My schoolteacher, Miss Foster, 's getting married to a fella over in Concord.
DR. GIBBS. I declare. How do you boys feel about that?
JOE CROWELL, JR. Well, of course, it's none of my business — but I think if a person starts out to be a teacher, she ought to stay one.
DR. GIBBS. How's your knee, Joe?
JOE CROWELL, JR. Fine, Doc. I never think about it at all. Only like you said, it always tells me when it's going to rain.
DR. GIBBS. What's it telling you today? Goin' to rain?
JOE CROWELL, JR. No, sir.
DR. GIBBS. Sure?
JOE CROWELL, JR. Yessir.
DR. GIBBS. Knee ever make a mistake?
JOE CROWELL, JR. No, sir.

[JOE *goes off.* DR. GIBBS *stands reading his paper.*]

STAGE MANAGER. Here comes Howie Newsome delivering the milk.

[HOWIE NEWSOME *comes along Main Street, passes* DR. GIBBS, *comes down the center of the stage, leaves some bottles at* MRS. WEBB's *back door, and crosses the stage to* MRS. GIBBS's.]

HOWIE NEWSOME. Git-ap, Bessie. What's the matter with you? . . . Morning, Doc.
DR. GIBBS. Morning, Howie.
HOWIE NEWSOME. Somebody sick?
DR. GIBBS. Pair of twins over to Mrs. Goruslawski's.
HOWIE NEWSOME. Twins, eh? This town's gettin' bigger every year.
DR. GIBBS. Going to rain, Howie?
HOWIE NEWSOME. No, no. Fine day — that'll burn through. Come on, Bessie.
DR. GIBBS. Hello, Bessie. (*He strokes her.*) How old is she, Howie?
HOWIE NEWSOME. Going on seventeen. Bessie's all mixed up about the route ever since the Lockharts stopped

takin' their quart of milk every day. She wants to leave 'em a quart just the same — keeps scolding me the hull trip.

[*He reaches* MRS. GIBBS's *back door. She is waiting for him.*]

MRS. GIBBS. Good morning, Howie.

HOWIE NEWSOME. Morning, Mrs. Gibbs. Doc's just comin' down the street.

MRS. GIBBS. Is he? Seems like you're late today.

HOWIE NEWSOME. Yes. Somep'n went wrong with the separator.[1] Don't know what 'twas.

[*He goes back to Main Street, clucks for Bessie, and goes off right.* DR. GIBBS *reaches his home and goes in.*]

MRS. GIBBS. Everything all right?

DR. GIBBS. Yes. I declare — easy as kittens.

MRS. GIBBS. Bacon'll be ready in a minute. Set down and drink your coffee. Child-*run!* Child-*run!* Time to get up. George! Rebecca! . . . You can catch a couple hours' sleep this morning, can't you?

DR. GIBBS. Hm! . . . Mrs. Wentworth's coming at eleven. Guess I know what it's about, too. Her stummick ain't what it ought to be.

MRS. GIBBS. All told, you won't get more'n three hours' sleep. Frank Gibbs, I don't know what's goin' to become of you. I do wish I could get you to go away some place and take a rest. I think it would do you good.

MRS. WEBB. Emileeee! Time to get up! Wally! Seven o'clock!

MRS. GIBBS. I declare, you got to speak to George. Seems like something's come over him lately. He's no help to me at all. I can't even get him to cut me some wood.

DR. GIBBS. Is he sassy to you?

MRS. GIBBS. No. He just whines! All he thinks about is that baseball — George! Rebecca! You'll be late for school.

[1] separator: a machine that separates cream from milk.

DR. GIBBS. M-m-m. . . .

MRS. GIBBS. George!

DR. GIBBS. George, look sharp!

GEORGE'S VOICE. Yes, Pa!

DR. GIBBS (*as he goes off the stage*). Don't you hear your mother calling you?

MRS. WEBB. Walleee! Emileee! You'll be late for school! Walleee! You wash yourself good or I'll come up and do it myself.

REBECCA GIBBS's VOICE. Ma! What dress shall I wear?

MRS. GIBBS. Don't make a noise. Your father's been out all night and needs his sleep. I washed and ironed the blue gingham for you special.

REBECCA. Ma, I hate that dress.

MRS. GIBBS. Oh, hush up with you.

REBECCA. Every day I go to school dressed like a sick turkey.

MRS. GIBBS. Now, Rebecca, don't be impossible. You always look *very* nice.

REBECCA. Mamma, George's throwing soap at me.

MRS. GIBBS. I'll come up and slap the both of you — that's what I'll do.

[*A factory whistle sounds. The children enter and take their places at the breakfast tables:* EMILY *and* WALLY WEBB; GEORGE *and* REBECCA GIBBS.]

STAGE MANAGER. We've got a factory in our town too — hear it? Makes blankets. Cartwrights own it and it brung 'em a fortune.

MRS. WEBB. Children! Now I won't have it. Breakfast is just as good as any other meal and I won't have you gobbling like wolves. It'll stunt your growth — that's a fact. Put away your book, Wally.

WALLY. Aw, Ma!

MRS. WEBB. You know the rule's well as I do — no books at table. As for me, I'd rather have my children healthy than bright!

EMILY. I'm both, Mamma; you know I am. I'm the brightest girl in school for my age. I have a wonderful memory.

MRS. WEBB. Eat your breakfast.

WALLY. I'm bright, too, when I'm

looking at my stamp collection.

MRS. GIBBS. I'll speak to your father about it when he's rested. Seems to me twenty-five cents a week's enough for a boy your age. I declare I don't know how you spend it all.

GEORGE. Aw, Ma — I gotta lotta things to buy.

MRS. GIBBS. Strawberry phosphates — that's what you spend it on.

GEORGE. I don't see how Rebecca comes to have so much money. She has more'n a dollar.

REBECCA (spoon in mouth, dreamily). I've been saving it up gradual.

MRS. GIBBS. Well, dear, I think it's a good thing every now and then to spend some.

REBECCA. Mamma, do you know what I love most in the world — do you? Money!

MRS. GIBBS. Eat your breakfast.

[The school bell is heard.]

CHILDREN. Mamma, there's first bell. . . . I gotta hurry. . . . I don't want any more.

MRS. WEBB. Walk fast, but you don't have to run. Wally, pull up your pants at the knee. Stand up straight, Emily.

MRS. GIBBS. Tell Miss Foster I send her my best congratulations. Can you remember that?

REBECCA. Yes, Ma.

MRS. GIBBS. You look real nice, Rebecca. Pick up your feet.

ALL. Good-by.

[The children from the two houses join at the center of the stage and go up to Main Street, then off left. MRS. GIBBS fills her apron with food for the chickens and comes down to the footlights.]

MRS. GIBBS. Here, chick, chick, chick, . . . No, go away, you. Go away. . . . Here, chick, chick, chick. What's the matter with you? Fight, fight, fight — that's all you do. Hm . . . you don't belong to me. Where'd you come from?

(She shakes her apron.) Oh, don't be so scared. Nobody's going to hurt you.

[MRS. WEBB is sitting by her trellis, stringing beans.]

Good morning, Myrtle. How's your cold?

MRS. WEBB. Well, it's better; but I told Charles I didn't know as I'd go to choir practice tonight. Wouldn't be any use.

MRS. GIBBS. Just the same, you come to choir practice, Myrtle, and try it.

MRS. WEBB. Well, if I don't feel any worse than I do now I probably will. While I'm resting myself, I thought I'd string some of these beans.

MRS. GIBBS (rolling up her sleeves as she crosses the stage for a chat). Let me help you. Beans have been good this year.

MRS. WEBB. I've decided to put up forty quarts if it kills me. The children say they hate 'em, but I notice they're able to get 'em down all winter. (Pause)

MRS. GIBBS. Now, Myrtle. I've got to tell you something, because if I don't tell somebody I'll burst.

MRS. WEBB. Why, Julia Gibbs!

MRS. GIBBS. Here, give me some more of those beans. Myrtle, did one of those secondhand furniture men from Boston come to see you last Friday?

MRS. WEBB. No-o.

MRS. GIBBS. Well, he called on me. First I thought he was a patient wantin' to see Dr. Gibbs. 'N he wormed his way into my parlor, and, Myrtle Webb, he offered me three hundred and fifty dollars for Grandmother Wentworth's highboy, as I'm sitting here!

MRS. WEBB. Why, Julia Gibbs!

MRS. GIBBS. He did! That old thing! Why, it was so big I didn't know where to put it, and I almost give it to Cousin Hester Wilcox.

MRS. WEBB. Well, you're going to take it, aren't you?

MRS. GIBBS. I don't know.

MRS. WEBB. You don't know — three

hundred and fifty dollars! What's come over you?

MRS. GIBBS. Well, if I could get the Doctor to take the money and go away some place on a real trip, I'd sell it like that. Myrtle, ever since I was *that* high I've had the thought that I'd like to see Paris, France. I suppose I'm crazy.

MRS. WEBB. Oh, I know what you mean. How does the Doctor feel about it?

MRS. GIBBS. Well, I did beat about the bush a little and said that if I got a leg-acy — that's the way I put it — I'd make him take me somewhere.

MRS. WEBB. M-m-m. . . . What did he say?

MRS. GIBBS. You know how he is. I haven't heard a serious word out of him ever since I've known him. No, he said, it might make him discontented with Grover's Corners to go traipsin' about Europe; better let well enough alone, he says. Every two years he makes a trip to the battlefields of the Civil War; and that's enough treat for anybody, he says.

MRS. WEBB. Well, Mr. Webb just *admires* the way Dr. Gibbs knows everything about the Civil War. Mr. Webb's a good mind to give up Napoleon and move over to the Civil War, only Dr. Gibbs being one of the greatest experts in the country just makes him despair.

MRS. GIBBS. It's a fact! Dr. Gibbs is never so happy as when he's at Antietam or Gettysburg. The times I've walked over those hills, Myrtle, stopping at every bush and pacing it all out, like we was going to buy it.

MRS. WEBB. Well, if that secondhand man's really serious about buyin' it, Julia, you sell it. And then you'll get to see Paris, all right.

MRS. GIBBS. Oh, I'm sorry I mentioned it. Only it seems to me that once in your life before you die you ought to see a country where they don't talk and think in English and don't even want to.

[*The* STAGE MANAGER *returns to the center of the stage.*]

STAGE MANAGER. That'll do. That'll do. Thank you very much, ladies.

[MRS. GIBBS *and* MRS. WEBB *gather up their things, return into their homes, and disappear.*]

Now we're going to skip a few hours in the day at Grover's Corners. But before we go on, I want you to know some more things about the town — all kinds of things. So I've asked Professor Willard of our State University to come down here and sketch in a few details of our past history — kind of scientific account, you might say. Is Professor Willard here?

[PROFESSOR WILLARD, *a rural savant,*[1] *pince-nez*[2] *on a wide satin ribbon, enters from the right with some notes in his hand.*]

May I introduce Professor Willard of our university. A few brief notes, thank you, Professor — unfortunately our time is limited.

PROFESSOR WILLARD. Grover's Corners . . . let me see . . . Grover's Corners lies on the old Archeozoic[3] granite of the Appalachian range. I may say it's some of the oldest land in the world. We're very proud of that. A shelf of Devonian basalt[4] crosses it with vestiges of Mesozoic shale,[5] and some sandstone outcroppings; but that's all more recent: two hundred, three hundred million years old. Some highly interesting fossils have been found — I may say unique fossils — two miles out of town, in Silas Peckham's cow pasture. They

---

[1] **savant** (să·vän'): scholar.

[2] **pince-nez** (păns'nā'): an old-fashioned pair of eyeglasses that are clipped to the nose with a spring.

[3] **Archeozoic** (är'kē·ō·zō'ĭk): formed in the earliest era of geological history.

[4] **Devonian basalt** (dē·vō'nĭ·ăn bà·sôlt'): rock of volcanic origin formed in a later geological period.

[5] **Mesozoic shale** (mĕs'ō·zō'ĭk shāl): another type of rock formed early in the world's history.

can be seen at the museum in our university at any time. . . . Did you wish the meteorological conditions?

STAGE MANAGER. Thank you. We would.

PROFESSOR WILLARD. The mean precipitation is forty inches. The mean annual temperature is forty-three degrees, ranging between one hundred two degrees in the shade and thirty-eight degrees below zero in winter. The . . . the . . . uh . . .

STAGE MANAGER. Thank you, Professor. And have you Professor Gruber's notes on the history of human life here?

PROFESSOR WILLARD. Hm . . . yes . . . anthropological data. Early Amerindian [1] stock. Cotahatchee [2] tribes . . . no evidence before the tenth century of this era . . . hm . . . now entirely disappeared . . . possible traces in three families. Migration toward the end of the seventeenth century of English brachycephalic [3] blue-eyed stock . . . for the most part. Since then some influx of Slav and Mediterranean types. . . .

STAGE MANAGER. And the population, Professor Willard?

PROFESSOR WILLARD. Within the town limits, 2,640. The postal district brings in 507 more. Mortality and birth rates are constant; by MacPherson's gauge, 6.032.

STAGE MANAGER. Thank you *very* much, Professor. We're all very much obliged to you, I'm sure.

PROFESSOR WILLARD. Not at all, sir; not at all.

STAGE MANAGER. This way, Professor, and thank you again.

[*Exit* PROFESSOR WILLARD.]

Now the political and social report: Editor Webb. . . . Oh, Mr. Webb?

[MRS. WEBB *appears at her back door.*]

MRS. WEBB. He'll be here in a minute. . . . He just cut his hand while he was eatin' an apple.

STAGE MANAGER. Thank you, Mrs. Webb.

MRS. WEBB. Charles! Everybody's waitin'. (*Exit*)

STAGE MANAGER. Mr. Webb is publisher and editor of the Grover's Corners *Sentinel*. That's our local paper, y'know.

[MR. WEBB *enters from his house, pulling on his coat. His finger is bound in a handkerchief.*]

MR. WEBB. Hm. . . . I don't have to tell you that we're run here by a board of selectmen. [4] All males vote at the age of twenty-one. Women vote indirect. We're lower middle class, sprinkling of professional men . . . ten per cent illiterate laborers. Politically, we're eighty-six per cent Republicans; six per cent Democrats; four per cent Socialists; rest, indifferent. Religiously, we're eighty-five per cent Protestants; twelve per cent Catholics; rest, indifferent. Do you want the poverty and insanity statistics?

STAGE MANAGER. Thank you, no. Have you any comments, Mr. Webb?

MR. WEBB. Very ordinary town, if you ask me. Little better behaved than most. Probably a lot duller. But our young people here seem to like it well enough: ninety per cent of 'em graduating from high school settle down right here to live — even when they've been away to college.

STAGE MANAGER. Thank you, Mr. Webb. Now, is there anyone in the audience who would like to ask Editor Webb anything about the town?

WOMAN IN THE BALCONY. Is there much drinking in Grover's Corners?

MR. WEBB. Well, ma'am, I wouldn't know what you'd call *much*. Satiddy nights the farm hands meet down in Ellery Greenough's stable and holler some. Fourth of July I've been known to taste

---

[1] **Amerindian**: pertaining to the American Indian.

[2] **Cotahatchee** (kô·tà·hǎ′chē).

[3] **brachycephalic** (brăk′ĭ·sĕ·făl′ĭk): short-headed, or broad-headed.

[4] **board of selectmen**: a board of officers elected annually.

a drop myself — and Decoration Day, of course. We've got one or two town drunks, but they're always having remorses every time an evangelist comes to town. No, ma'am, I'd say likker ain't a regular thing in the home here, except in the medicine chest. Right good for snake bite, y'know — always was.

TALL MAN AT BACK OF AUDITORIUM. Is there no one in town aware of —

STAGE MANAGER. Come forward, will you, where we can all hear you — what were you saying?

TALL MAN. Is there no one in town aware of social injustice and industrial inequality?

MR. WEBB. Oh, yes, everybody is — somethin' terrible. Seems like they spend most of their time talking about who's rich and who's poor.

TALL MAN. Then why don't they do something about it?

MR. WEBB. Well, we're ready to listen to everybody's suggestion as to how you can see that the diligent and sensible'll rise to the top and the lazy and quarrelsome sink to the bottom. We'll listen to anybody. Meantime, until that's settled, we try to take care of those that can't help themselves, and those that can we leave alone. Are there any more questions?

LADY IN A BOX. Oh, Mr. Webb? Mr. Webb, is there any culture or love of beauty in Grover's Corners?

MR. WEBB. Well, ma'am, there ain't much — not in the sense you mean. Come to think of it, there's some girls that play the piano at high school commencement; but they ain't happy about it. Yes, and I see where my daughter's been made to read *The Merchant of Venice* over to the school. Seems all pretty remote to 'em, y'know what I mean. No, ma'am, there isn't much culture; but maybe this is the place to tell you that we've got a lot of pleasures of a kind here: we like the sun comin' up over the mountain in the morning, and we all notice a good deal about the birds. We pay a lot of attention to them,

and trees and plants. And we watch the change of the seasons: yes, everybody knows about them. But those other things — you're right, ma'am — there ain't much. *Robinson Crusoe* and the Bible; and Handel's "Largo," we all know that; and Whistler's "Mother" — those are just about as far as we go.

LADY IN A BOX. So I thought. Thank you, Mr. Webb.

STAGE MANAGER. All right! All right! Thank you, everybody.

[MR. WEBB *retires.*]

We'll go back to the town now. It's middle of the afternoon. All 2,642 have had their dinners, and all the dishes have been washed. There's an early-afternoon calm in our town: a buzzin' and a hummin' from the school buildings; only a few buggies on Main Street — the horses dozing at the hitching posts; you all remember what it's like. Doc Gibbs is in his office, tapping people and making them say "Ah." Mr. Webb's cuttin' his lawn over there; one man in ten thinks it's a privilege to push his own lawn mower.

No, Sir. It's later than I thought. There are the children coming home from school already.

[EMILY WEBB *comes sedately down Main Street, carrying some schoolbooks. There are some signs that she is imagining herself to be a lady of striking elegance. Her father's movements to and fro with the lawn mower bring him into her vicinity.*]

EMILY. I *can't,* Lois. I've got to go home and help my mother. I *promised.*

MR. WEBB. Emily, walk simply. Who do you think you are today?

EMILY. Papa, you're terrible. One minute you tell me to stand up straight, and the next minute you call me names. I just don't listen to you. (*She gives him an abrupt kiss.*)

MR. WEBB. Golly, I never got a kiss from such a great lady before.

[*He goes out of sight.* EMILY *leans over and picks some flowers by the gate of her house.* GEORGE GIBBS *comes careening down Main Street. He is throwing a ball up to dizzy heights and waiting to catch it again. This sometimes requires his taking six steps backward.*]

GEORGE. Excuse me, Mrs. Forrest.

STAGE MANAGER (*as* MRS. FORREST). Go out and play in the fields, young man. You got no business playing baseball on Main Street.

GEORGE. Awfully sorry, Mrs. Forrest. . . . Hello, Emily.

EMILY. H'lo.

GEORGE. You made a fine speech in class.

EMILY. Well . . . I was really ready to make a speech about the Monroe Doctrine, but at the last minute Miss Corcoran made me talk about the Louisiana Purchase instead. I worked an awful long time on both of them.

GEORGE. Gee, it's funny, Emily. From my window up there I can just see your head nights when you're doing your homework over in your room.

EMILY. Why, can you?

GEORGE. You certainly do stick to it, Emily. I don't see how you can sit still that long. I guess you like school.

EMILY. Well, I always feel it's something you have to go through.

GEORGE. Yeah.

EMILY. I don't mind it really. It passes the time.

GEORGE. Yeah. . . . Emily, what do you think? We might work out a kinda telegraph from there to there; and once in a while you could give me a kinda hint or two about one of those algebra problems. I don't mean the answers, Emily, of course not . . . just some little hint. . . .

EMILY. Oh, I think *hints* are allowed. So — ah — if you get stuck, George, you whistle to me; and I'll give you some hints.

GEORGE. Emily, you're just naturally bright, I guess.

EMILY. I figure that it's just the way a person's born.

GEORGE. Yeah. But, you see, I want to be a farmer, and my Uncle Luke says whenever I'm ready I can come over and work on his farm, and if I'm any good I can just gradually have it.

EMILY. You mean the house and everything?

[*Enter* MRS. WEBB.]

GEORGE. Yeah. Well, thanks. . . . I better be getting out to the baseball field. Thanks for the talk, Emily. . . . Good afternoon, Mrs. Webb.

MRS. WEBB. Good afternoon, George.

GEORGE. So long, Emily.

EMILY. So long, George.

MRS. WEBB. Emily, come and help me string these beans for the winter. George Gibbs let himself have a real conversation, didn't he? Why, he's growing up. How old would George be?

EMILY. I don't know.

MRS. WEBB. Let's see. He must be almost sixteen.

EMILY. Mamma, I made a speech in class today, and I was very good.

MRS. WEBB. You must recite it to your father at supper. What was it about?

EMILY. The Louisiana Purchase. It was like silk off a spool. I'm going to make speeches all my life. . . . Mamma, are these big enough?

MRS. WEBB. Try and get them a little bigger if you can.

EMILY. Mamma, will you answer me a question, serious?

MRS. WEBB. Seriously dear — not serious.

EMILY. Seriously. Will you?

MRS. WEBB. Of course, I will.

EMILY. Mamma, am I good-looking?

MRS. WEBB. Yes, of course you are. All my children have got good features; I'd be ashamed if they hadn't.

EMILY. Oh, Mamma, that's not what I mean. What I mean is: Am I *pretty*?

MRS. WEBB. I've already told you, yes.

Now, that's enough of that. You have a nice, young, pretty face. I never heard of such foolishness.

EMILY. Oh, Mamma, you never tell us the truth about anything.

MRS. WEBB. I *am* telling you the truth.

EMILY. Mamma, were *you* pretty?

MRS. WEBB. Yes, I was, if I do say it. I was the prettiest girl in town next to Mamie Cartwright.

EMILY. But, Mamma, you've got to say *some*thing about me. Am I pretty enough . . . to get anybody . . . to get people interested in me?

MRS. WEBB. Emily, you make me tired. Now stop it. You're pretty enough for all normal purposes. Come along now and bring that bowl with you.

EMILY. But, Mamma, you're no help at all.

STAGE MANAGER. Thank you. Thank you! That'll do. We'll have to interrupt again here. Thank you, Mrs. Webb; thank you, Emily.

[MRS. WEBB *and* EMILY *withdraw.*]

There are some more things we've got to explore about this town. This time we're going to go about it in another way: we're going to look back on it from the future. I'm not going to tell you what became of these two families we're seeing most of, because the rest of the play will tell you about them. But take some of these others.

Take Joe Crowell, Jr. Joe was a very bright fellow. He graduated with honors and got a scholarship to Boston Tech — M.I.T., that is. But the war broke out, and Joe died in France. All that education for nothing.

Howie Newsome's still delivering milk at Grover's Corners. He's an old man now, has a lot of help; but he still delivers it himself. Says he gets the feel of the town that way. Carries all the accounts in his head; never has to write down a word.

Mr. Morgan's drugstore ain't the same — it's all citified. Mr. Morgan retired and went to live in San Diego,

California, where his daughter married a real-estate man, name of Kerby. Mr. Morgan died there in 1935 and was buried in a lot of palm trees. Kinda lost his religion at the end and took up New Thought or something. They read some newfangled poetry over him and cremated him. The New Hampshire in him sort of broke down in that climate, seems like.

The Cartwrights got richer and richer. The house is closed most of the year. They're off eating big dinners in hotels now — in Virginia Hot Springs and Miami Beach. They say the winters are cold here. I see where they've become 'Piscopalians.

The Cartwright interests have just begun building a new bank in Grover's Corners — had to go to Vermont for the marble, sorry to say. And they've asked a friend of mine what they should put in the cornerstone for people to dig up a thousand years from now. Of course, they've put in a copy of the New York *Times* and a copy of Mr. Webb's *Sentinel*. We're kind of interested in this, because some scientific fellas have found a way of painting all that reading matter with a kind of glue — silicate glue — that'll make it keep a thousand, two thousand, years. We're putting in a Bible . . . and the Constitution of the United States and a copy of William Shakespeare's plays. What do you say, folks? What do you think? Y'know — Babylon once had two million people in it, and all we know about 'em is the names of the kings and some copies of wheat contracts and . . . the sales of slaves. Yes, every night all those families sat down to supper, and the father came home from his work, and the smoke went up the chimney — same as here. And even in Greece and Rome all we know about the real life of the people is what we can piece together out of the joking poems and the comedies they wrote for the theater back then. So I'm going to have a copy of this play put in the cornerstone and the people a thousand years from now'll know a few simple facts about us — more than the Treaty of Versailles and the Lindbergh flight. See what I mean?

Well — you people a thousand years from now — in the provinces north of New York at the beginning of the twentieth century, people et three times a day: soon after sunrise, at noon, and at sunset. Every seventh day, by law and by religion, was a day of rest, and all work came to a stop. The religion at that time was Christianity. I guess you have some other records about Christianity. The domestic setup was marriage: a binding relation between a male and one female that lasted for life. Christianity strictly forbade killing, but you were allowed to kill animals, and you were allowed to kill human beings in war and government punishings. I guess we don't have to tell you about the government and business forms, because that's the kind of thing people seem to hand down first of all. Let me see now if there's anything else. Oh, yes — at death people were buried in the ground just as they are.

So, friends, this is the way we were in our growing up and in our marrying and in our doctoring and in our living and in our dying. Now we'll return to our day in Grover's Corners: A lot of time has gone by. It's evening. You can hear choir practice going on in the Congregational Church. All the children are at home doing their schoolwork. The day is running down like a tired clock.

[*A choir partially concealed in the orchestra pit has begun singing "Blest Be the Tie That Binds."* SIMON STIMSON *stands directing them. Two ladders have been pushed onto the stage; they serve as indication of the second story in the Gibbs and Webb houses.* GEORGE *and* EMILY *mount them, and apply themselves to their schoolwork.* DR. GIBBS *has entered and is seated in his kitchen, reading.*]

SIMON STIMSON. Now look here, everybody. Music come into the world to give pleasure. Softer! Softer! Get it out of your heads that music's only good when it's loud. You leave loudness to the Methodists. You couldn't beat 'em, even if you wanted to. Now again. Tenors!

GEORGE. Hssst! Emily!

EMILY. Hello.

GEORGE. Hello.

EMILY. I can't work at all. The moonlight's so *terrible.*

GEORGE. Emily, did you get the third problem?

EMILY. Which?

GEORGE. The *third?*

EMILY. Why, yes, George — that's the easiest of them all.

GEORGE. I don't see it. Emily, can you give me a hint?

EMILY. I'll tell you one thing: the answer's in yards.

GEORGE. In yards! How do you mean?

EMILY. In *square* yards.

GEORGE. Oh . . . in square yards.

EMILY. Yes, George, don't you see?

GEORGE. Yeah.

EMILY. In square yards of *wallpaper.*

GEORGE. Wallpaper — oh, I see. Thanks a lot, Emily.

EMILY. You're welcome. My, isn't the moonlight *terrible?* And choir practice going on. I think if you hold your breath you can hear the train all the way to Contookuck. Hear it?

GEORGE. M-m-m. What do you know!

EMILY. Well, I guess I better go back and try to work.

GEORGE. Good night, Emily. And thanks.

EMILY. Good night, George.

SIMON STIMSON. Before I forget it: How many of you will be able to come in Tuesday afternoon and sing at Fred Hersey's wedding? Show your hands. That'll be fine; that'll be right nice. We'll do the same music we did for Jane Trowbridge's last month. . . . Now we'll do "Art thou weary; art thou languid?" It's a question, ladies and gentlemen; make it talk. Ready.

DR. GIBBS. Oh, George, can you come down a minute?

GEORGE. Yes, Pa. (*He descends the ladder.*)

DR. GIBBS. Make yourself comfortable, George; I'll only keep you a minute. George, how old are you?

GEORGE. I? I'm sixteen, almost seventeen.

DR. GIBBS. What do you want to do after school's over?

GEORGE. Why, you know, Pa, I want to be a farmer on Uncle Luke's farm.

DR. GIBBS. You'll be willing, will you, to get up early and milk and feed the stock . . . and you'll be able to hoe and hay all day?

GEORGE. Sure, I will. What are you . . . what do you mean, Pa?

DR. GIBBS. Well, George, while I was in my office today I heard a funny sound. . . . And what do you think it was? It was your mother chopping wood. There you see your mother — getting up early, cooking meals all day long, washing and ironing; and still she has to go out in the back yard and chop wood. I suppose she just got tired of asking you. She just gave up and decided it was easier to do it herself. And you eat her meals and put on the clothes she keeps nice for you, and you run off and play baseball — like she's some hired girl we keep around the house but that we don't like very much. Well, I knew all I had to do was call your attention to it. Here's a handkerchief, son. George, I've decided to raise your spending money twenty-five cents a week. Not, of course, for chopping wood for your mother, because that's a present you give her, but because you're getting older — and I imagine there are lots of things you must find to do with it.

GEORGE. Thanks, Pa.

DR. GIBBS. Let's see — tomorrow's payday. You can count on it. Hmm. Probably Rebecca'll feel she ought to have some more too. Wonder what could have happened to your mother. Choir practice never was as late as this before.

GEORGE. It's only half-past eight, Pa.

DR. GIBBS. I don't know why she's in that old choir. She hasn't any more voice than an old crow. . . . Traipsin' around the streets at this hour of the night. . . . Just about time you retired, don't you think?

GEORGE. Yes, Pa.

[GEORGE *mounts to his place on the ladder. Laughter and good nights can be heard on stage left, and presently* MRS. GIBBS, MRS. SOAMES, *and* MRS. WEBB *come down Main Street. When they arrive at the center of the stage, they stop.*]

MRS. SOAMES. Good night, Martha. Good night, Mr. Foster.

MRS. WEBB. I'll tell Mr. Webb; I *know* he'll want to put it in the paper.

MRS. GIBBS. My, it's late!

MRS. SOAMES. Good night, Irma.

MRS. GIBBS. Real nice choir practice, wa'n't it? Myrtle Webb! Look at that moon, will you! Tsk-tsk-tsk. Potato weather, for sure.

MRS. SOAMES. Naturally I didn't want to say a word about it in front of those others, but now we're alone — really, it's the worst scandal that ever was in this town!

MRS. GIBBS. What?

MRS. SOAMES. Simon Stimson!

MRS. GIBBS. Now, Louella!

MRS. SOAMES. But, Julia! To have the organist of a church drink and drink year after year. You know he was drunk tonight.

MRS. GIBBS. Now, Louella. We all know about Mr. Stimson, and we all know about the troubles he's been through, and Dr. Ferguson knows too; and if Dr. Ferguson keeps him on there in his job, the only thing the rest of us can do is just not to notice it.

MRS. SOAMES. Not to notice it! But it's getting worse.

MRS. WEBB. No, it isn't, Louella. It's getting better. I've been in that choir twice as long as you have. It doesn't happen anywhere near so often. . . . My, I hate to go to bed on a night like this. I better hurry. Those children'll be sitting up till all hours. Good night, Louella. (*She hurries downstage, enters her house, and disappears.*)

MRS. GIBBS. Can you get home safe, Louella?

MRS. SOAMES. It's as bright as day. I can see Mr. Soames scowling at the window now. You'd think we'd been to a dance the way the menfolk carry on.

[*Repeated good nights.* MRS. GIBBS *arrives at her home.*]

MRS. GIBBS. Well, we had a real good time.

DR. GIBBS. You're late enough.

MRS. GIBBS. Why, Frank, it ain't any later 'n usual.

DR. GIBBS. And you stopping at the corner to gossip with a lot of hens.

MRS. GIBBS. Now, Frank, don't be grouchy. Come out and smell my heliotrope in the moonlight. (*They stroll out arm in arm along the footlights.*) Isn't that wonderful? What did you do all the time I was away?

DR. GIBBS. Oh, I read — as usual. What were the girls gossiping about tonight?

MRS. GIBBS. Well, believe me, Frank — there is something to gossip about.

DR. GIBBS. Hmm! Simon Stimson far gone, was he?

MRS. GIBBS. Worst I've ever seen him. How'll that end, Frank? Dr. Ferguson can't forgive him forever.

DR. GIBBS. I guess I know more about Simon Stimson's affairs than anybody in this town. Some people ain't made for small-town life. I don't know how that'll end; but there's nothing we can do but just leave it alone. Come, get in.

MRS. GIBBS. No, not yet. . . . Oh, Frank, I'm worried about you.

DR. GIBBS. What are you worried about?

MRS. GIBBS. I think it's my duty to make plans for you to get a real rest and change. And if I get that legacy,

well, I'm going to insist on it.

DR. GIBBS. Now, Julia, there's no sense in going over that again.

MRS. GIBBS. Frank, you're just *unreasonable!*

DR. GIBBS. Come on, Julia, it's getting late. First thing you know you'll catch cold. I gave George a piece of my mind tonight. I reckon you'll have your wood chopped for a while anyway. No, no, start getting upstairs.

MRS. GIBBS. Oh, dear. There's always so many things to pick up, seems like. You know, Frank, Mrs. Fairchild always locks her front door every night. All those people up that part of town do.

DR. GIBBS. They're all getting citified, that's the trouble with them. They haven't got nothing fit to burgle and everybody knows it.

[*They disappear.* REBECCA *climbs up the ladder beside* GEORGE.]

GEORGE. Get out, Rebecca. There's only room for one at this window. You're always spoiling everything.

REBECCA. Well, let me just look a minute.

GEORGE. Use your own window.

REBECCA. I did; but there's no moon there. . . . George, do you know what I think, do you? I think maybe the moon's getting nearer and nearer and there'll be a big 'splosion.

GEORGE. Rebecca, you don't know anything. If the moon were getting nearer, the guys that sit up all night with telescopes would see it first and they'd tell about it, and it'd be in all the newspapers.

REBECCA. George, is the moon shining on South America, Canada, and half the whole world?

GEORGE. Well — prob'ly is.

[*The* STAGE MANAGER *strolls on.*]

STAGE MANAGER. Nine-thirty. Most of the lights are out. No, there's Constable Warren trying a few doors on Main Street. And here comes Editor Webb, after putting his newspaper to bed.

MR. WEBB. Good evening, Bill.

CONSTABLE WARREN. Evenin', Mr. Webb.

MR. WEBB. Quite a moon!

CONSTABLE WARREN. Yep.

MR. WEBB. All quiet tonight?

CONSTABLE WARREN. Simon Stimson is rollin' around a little. Just saw his wife movin' out to hunt for him, so I looked the other way — there he is now.

[SIMON STIMSON *comes down Main Street from the left, only a trace of unsteadiness in his walk.*]

MR. WEBB. Good evening, Simon. . . . Town seems to have settled down for the night pretty well. . . .

[SIMON STIMSON *comes up to him and pauses a moment.*]

Good evening. . . . Yes, most of the town's settled down for the night, Simon. . . . I guess we better do the same. Can I walk along a ways with you?

[SIMON STIMSON *continues on his way without a word and disappears at the right.*]

Good night.

CONSTABLE WARREN. I don't know how that's goin' to end, Mr. Webb.

MR. WEBB. Well, he's seen a peck of trouble, one thing after another. . . . Oh, Bill . . . if you see my boy smoking cigarettes, just give him a word, will you? He thinks a lot of you, Bill.

CONSTABLE WARREN. I don't think he smokes no cigarettes, Mr. Webb. Leastways, not more'n two or three a year. He don't belong to that crowd that hangs out down by the gully.

MR. WEBB. Mm. . . . I hope not. Well, good night, Bill.

CONSTABLE WARREN. Good night, Mr. Webb. (*Exit*)

MR. WEBB. Who's that up there? Is that you, Myrtle?

EMILY. No, it's me, Papa.

MR. WEBB. Why aren't you in bed?

EMILY. I don't know. I just can't sleep yet, Papa. The moonlight's so *won* der ful. And the smell of Mrs. Gibbs's heliotrope. Can you smell it?

MR. WEBB. Hm. . . . Yes. Haven't any troubles on your mind, have you, Emily?

EMILY. *Troubles,* Papa? *No.*

MR. WEBB. Well, enjoy yourself, but don't let your mother catch you. Good night, Emily.

EMILY. Good night, Papa.

[MR. WEBB *crosses into the house, whistling "Blest Be the Tie That Binds," and disappears.*]

REBECCA. I never told you about that letter Jane Crofut got from her minister when she was sick. The minister of her church in the town she was in before she came here. He wrote Jane a letter and on the envelope the address was like this. It said: Jane Crofut, The Crofut Farm, Grover's Corners, Sutton County, New Hampshire, United States of America.

GEORGE. What's funny about that?

REBECCA. But listen, it's not finished: the United States of America, Continent of North America, Western Hemisphere, the Earth. the Solar System, the Universe, the Mind of God — that's what it said on the envelope.

GEORGE. What do you know!

REBECCA. And the postman brought it just the same.

GEORGE. What do you know!

STAGE MANAGER. That's the end of the first act, friends. You can go and smoke now, those that smoke.

FOR DISCUSSION

1. How soon do you realize that the Stage Manager is not an ordinary character in a play? Is he even an ordinary human being? What is the first hint that he intends to take liberties with time?

2. Find the speech in which the Stage

Manager explains one of the purposes of the play. Does the first act achieve this purpose? What sort of happenings fill this act? What appeal do they have for an audience?

3. Does the admission that Grover's Corners pays little attention to social justice, or to culture and beauty, affect your attitude toward the town? Recall the evidences of "culture" Editor Webb offers as typical of his town. Are they familiar to you? Do you think Wilder means that this is enough? Why do you think Wilder introduces this point?

4. Drama consists partly in the unfolding of action. Although Act I seems simply to picture the life of the town, it presents several situations that hold promise of future action. Identify these situations and tell what future developments could arise from each of them.

5. What does Emily mean when she twice says, "the moonlight's so *terrible*"?

6. In the course of his talk with George about chopping wood, why does Dr. Gibbs say, "Here's a handkerchief, son"?

7. In a play, the end of an act usually has special significance. Why does the author choose Rebecca's story about the peculiarly addressed letter to end Act I?

Act II

The tables and chairs of the two kitchens are still on the stage. The ladders have been withdrawn. The STAGE MANAGER *has been at his accustomed place, watching the audience return to its seats.*

STAGE MANAGER. Three years have gone by. Yes, the sun's come up over a thousand times. Summers and winters have cracked the mountains a little bit more, and the rains have brought down some of the dirt. Some babies that weren't even born before have begun talking regular sentences already; and a number of people who thought they were right young and spry have noticed that they can't bound up a flight of stairs like they used to, without their heart fluttering a little. Some older sons are sitting at the head of the table, and some people I know are having their meat cut up for them.

All that can happen in a thousand days. Nature's been pushing and contriving in other ways, too: a number of young people fell in love and got married. Yes, the mountain got bit away a few fractions of an inch, millions of gallons of water went by the mill, and here and there a new home was set up under a roof. Almost everybody in the world gets married. You know what I mean? In our town there aren't hardly any exceptions. Most everybody in the world climbs into their graves married.

The first act was called "The Daily Life." This act is called "Love and Marriage." There's another act coming after this; I reckon you can guess what that's about.

So it's three years later. It's 1904. It's July 7, just after high school commencement. That's the time most of our young people jump up and get married. Soon as they've passed their last examinations in solid geometry and Cicero's [1] orations, looks like they suddenly feel themselves fit to be married.

It's early morning. Only this time it's been raining. It's been pouring and thundering. Mrs. Gibbs's garden, and Mrs. Webb's here — drenched. All those bean poles and pea vines — drenched. All yesterday over there on Main Street the rain looked like curtains being blown along. Hm . . . it may begin again any minute.

There! You can hear the five-forty-five for Boston. And here comes Howie Newsome delivering the milk. And there's Si Crowell delivering the papers like his brother before him. You remember about his brother — all that education he's going to get and that'll be wasted? And there's Mrs. Gibbs and Mrs. Webb come down to make breakfast, just as though it were an ordinary day. I don't have to point out to the women in my audience that those ladies they see before them, both those ladies cooked three meals a day — one of 'em for twenty years, the other for forty — and no summer vacation. They brought up two children apiece, washed, cleaned the house — and never a nervous breakdown. Never thought themselves hard-used, either.

It's like what one of those Middle West poets said: You've got to love life to have life, and you've got to have life to love life. [2] . . . It's what they call a vicious circle.

[SI CROWELL *has entered, hurling imaginary newspapers into doorways.* HOWIE NEWSOME *has come along Main Street with* BESSIE.]

HOWIE NEWSOME. Git-ap, Bessie.

SI CROWELL. Morning, Howie.

HOWIE NEWSOME. Morning, Si. Anything in the papers I ought to know?

SI CROWELL. Nothing much, except we're losing about the best baseball pitcher Grover's Corners ever had.

HOWIE NEWSOME. Reckon he was. He's been standing off the whole of south New Hampshire singlehanded, looks like.

SI CROWELL. He could hit and run bases, too.

HOWIE NEWSOME. Yep. Mighty fine ballplayer. . . . Bessie! I guess I can stop and talk if I've a mind to!

SI CROWELL. I don't see how he could give up a thing like that just to get married. Would you, Howie?

HOWIE NEWSOME. Can't tell, Si. Never had no talent that way.

[CONSTABLE WARREN *enters. They exchange good mornings.*]

You're up early, Bill.

CONSTABLE WARREN. Seein' if there's anything I can do to prevent a flood. River's been risin' all night.

HOWIE NEWSOME. Si Crowell's all worked up here about George Gibbs's retiring from baseball.

CONSTABLE WARREN. Yes, sir; that's the way it goes. Back in eighty-four we had a player, Si — even George Gibbs

---

[1] **Cicero:** a Roman statesman and orator, 106–43 B.C. His speeches are often studied in advanced Latin classes.

[2] The lines, an approximate quotation, are from "Lucinda Matlock" in Edgar Lee Masters' *Spoon River Anthology.*

couldn't touch him. Name of Hank Todd. Went down to Maine and become a parson. Wonderful ballplayer. . . . Howie, how did the weather look to you?

HOWIE NEWSOME. No, 'tain't bad. Think maybe it'll clear up for good.

[CONSTABLE WARREN *and* SI CROWELL *continue on their way.* HOWIE NEWSOME *brings the milk first to* MRS. GIBBS's *house. She meets him by the trellis.*]

MRS. GIBBS. Good morning, Howie. Do you think it's going to rain again?

HOWIE NEWSOME. Morning, Mrs. Gibbs. It rained so heavy, I think maybe it'll clear up.

MRS. GIBBS. Certainly hope it will.

HOWIE NEWSOME. How much did you want today?

MRS. GIBBS. I guess I'll need three-a-milk and two-a-cream, Howie. I'm going to have a house full of relations.

HOWIE NEWSOME. My wife says to tell you we both hope they'll be very happy, Mrs. Gibbs. Know they *will*.

MRS. GIBBS. Thanks a lot, Howie. Tell your wife I hope she gits there to the wedding.

HOWIE NEWSOME. Yes, she'll be there; she'll be there if she kin. (*He crosses to* MRS. WEBB's *house*.) Morning, Mrs. Webb.

MRS. WEBB. Oh, good morning, Mr. Newsome. I told you four quarts of milk, but I hope you can spare me another.

HOWIE NEWSOME. Yes'm . . . and the two of cream.

MRS. WEBB. Will it rain all day, Mr. Newsome?

HOWIE NEWSOME. No'm. Just sayin' to Mrs. Gibbs as how it may lighten up. Mrs. Newsome told me to tell you as how we hope they'll both be very happy, Mrs. Webb. Know they *will*.

MRS. WEBB. Thank you, and thank Mrs. Newsome; and we hope to see you all at the wedding.

HOWIE NEWSOME. Yes, Mrs. Webb.

We hope to git there. Couldn't miss that. Chck! Bessie!

[*Exit* HOWIE NEWSOME. DR. GIBBS *descends in his shirt sleeves, and sits down at his breakfast table.*]

DR. GIBBS. Well, Ma, the day has come. You're losin' one of your chicks.

MRS. GIBBS. Frank Gibbs, don't you say another word. I feel like crying every minute. Sit down and drink your coffee.

DR. GIBBS. The groom's up shaving himself. Whistling and singing, like he's glad to leave us. Every now and then he says "I do" to the mirror, but it don't sound convincing to me.

MRS. GIBBS. I declare I don't know how he'll get along. I've arranged his clothes and seen to it he's put warm things on — Frank, they're too young! Emily won't think of such things. He'll catch his death of cold within a week. . . . Here's something I made for you.

DR. GIBBS. Why, Julia Hersey! French toast!

MRS. GIBBS. 'Tain't hard to make, and I had to do something.

DR. GIBBS. I remember my wedding morning, Julia.

MRS. GIBBS. Now, don't start that, Frank Gibbs. I tell you I can't stand it.

DR. GIBBS. I was the scaredest young fella in the State of New Hampshire. I thought I'd made a mistake for sure. And when I saw you comin' down that aisle I thought you were the prettiest girl I'd ever seen, but the only trouble was that I'd never seen you before. There I was in the Congregational Church marryin' a total stranger.

MRS. GIBBS. And how do you think I felt! . . . Did you hear Rebecca stirring about upstairs?

DR. GIBBS. Only morning in the year she hasn't been managing everybody's business. She's shut up in her room. I got the impression that maybe she's crying.

MRS. GIBBS. Good Lord! This has got

to stop. . . . Rebecca! Rebecca! Everything's getting cold down here.

[GEORGE *comes rattling down the stairs, very brisk.*]

GEORGE. Good morning, everybody. Only five more hours to live. (*Makes the gesture of cutting his throat.*)

MRS. GIBBS. Where are you going?

GEORGE. Just stepping across the grass to see my girl.

MRS. GIBBS. Now, George! You take an umbrella, or I won't let you out of this house.

GEORGE. Aw, Ma. It's just a *step!*

MRS. GIBBS. From tomorrow on you can kill yourself in all weathers; but while you're in my house you live wisely, thank you. There are your overshoes right there in the hall. And here's an umbrella.

GEORGE. Aw, Ma!

MRS. GIBBS. Maybe Mrs. Webb isn't used to callers at seven in the morning. Take a cup-a-coffee first.

GEORGE. Be back in a minute. (*He crosses the stage, leaping over the puddles.*) Good morning, Mother Webb.

MRS. WEBB. Goodness! You frightened me! Now, George, you can come in a minute out of the wet, but you know I can't ask you in.

GEORGE. Why not?

MRS. WEBB. George, you know's well as I do: the groom can't see his bride on his wedding day, not until he sees her in church.

GEORGE. Aw! That's just a superstition.

[*Enter* MR. WEBB.]

MR. WEBB. Good morning, George.

GEORGE. Mr. Webb, you don't believe in that superstition, do you?

MR. WEBB. There's a lot of common sense in some superstitions, George.

MRS. WEBB. Millions have folla'd it, George, and you don't want to be the first to fly in the face of custom.

GEORGE. How is Emily?

MRS. WEBB. She hasn't waked up yet.

I haven't heard a sound out of her.

GEORGE. Emily's *asleep!*

MRS. WEBB. No wonder! We were up till all hours, sewing and packing. I'll tell you what I'll do; you set down here a minute with Mr. Webb and drink this cup of coffee, and I'll go upstairs and see she doesn't come down and surprise you. There's some bacon, too; but don't be long about it.

[*Exit* MRS. WEBB. *Embarrassed silence.*]

MR. WEBB. Well, George, how are you?

GEORGE. Oh, fine. I'm fine. (*Pause*) Mr. Webb, what sense could there be in a superstition like that?

MR. WEBB. Well, you see, on her wedding morning a girl's head's apt to be full of . . . clothes and things like that. Don't you think that's probably it?

GEORGE. Ye-e-s. I never thought of that.

MR. WEBB. A girl's apt to be a mite nervous on her wedding day. (*Pause*)

GEORGE. I wish a fellow could get married without all that marching up and down.

MR. WEBB. Well, every man that's ever lived has felt that way about it, George; but it hasn't done much good. It's the women that have built up weddings, my boy. From now on they have it pretty much as they like. . . . All those good women standing shoulder to shoulder making sure that the knot's tied in a mighty public way.

GEORGE. But . . . you *believe* in it, don't you, Mr. Webb?

MR. WEBB. Oh, yes; oh, yes. Don't you misunderstand me, my boy. Marriage is a wonderful thing — wonderful thing. And don't you forget that, George.

GEORGE. No, sir. Mr. Webb, how old were you when you got married?

MR. WEBB. Well, you see, I'd been to college and I'd taken a little time to get settled. But Mrs. Webb — she wasn't much older than what Emily is. Oh, age hasn't much to do with it, George — not compared to other things.

GEORGE. What were you going to say, Mr. Webb?

MR. WEBB. Oh, I don't know — was I going to say something? (*Pause*) George, I was thinking the other night of some advice my father gave me when I got married. Charles, he said, Charles, start out early showing who's boss, he said. Best thing to do is to give an order, even if it don't make sense; just so she'll learn to obey. And he said: If anything about your wife irritates you — her conversation, or anything — just get up and leave the house. That'll make it clear to her, he said. And, ah, yes! he said never, *never* let your wife know how much money you have, never.

GEORGE. Well, Mr. Webb . . . I don't think I could. . . .

MR. WEBB. So I took the opposite of my father's advice and I've been happy ever since. And let that be a lesson to you, George, never to ask advice on personal matters. . . . George, are you going to raise chickens on your farm?

GEORGE. What?

MR. WEBB. Are you going to raise chickens on your farm?

GEORGE. Uncle Luke's never been much interested, but I thought —

MR. WEBB. A book came into my office the other day, George, on the Philo System of raising chickens. I want you to read it. I'm thinking of beginning in a small way in the back yard, and I'm going to put an incubator in the cellar —

[*Enter* MRS. WEBB.]

MRS. WEBB. Charles, are you talking about that old incubator again? I thought you two'd be talking about things worthwhile.

MR. WEBB. Well, Myrtle, if you want to give the boy some good advice, I'll go upstairs and leave you alone with him.

MRS. WEBB. Now, George, I'm sorry, but I've got to send you away so that Emily can come down and get some breakfast. She told me to tell you that she sends you her love, but that she doesn't want to lay eyes on you. So good-by, George.

[GEORGE *crosses the stage to his own home and disappears.*]

MR. WEBB. Myrtle, I guess you don't know about that older superstition.

MRS. WEBB. What do you mean, Charles?

MR. WEBB. Since the cave men: the groom shouldn't be left alone with his father-in-law on the day of the wedding, or near it. Now don't forget that!

STAGE MANAGER. Thank you. Thank you, everybody. Now I have to interrupt again here. You see, we want to know how all this began — this wedding, this plan to spend a lifetime together. I'm awfully interested in how big things like that begin. You know how it is. You're twenty-one or twenty-two, and you make some decisions; then whisssh! you're seventy. You've been a lawyer for fifty years, and that white-haired lady at your side has eaten over fifty thousand meals with you. How do such things begin?

George and Emily are going to show you now the conversation they had when they first knew that . . . that . . . as the saying goes . . . they were meant for one another. But before they do it I want you to try and remember what it was like when you were young, when you were fifteen or sixteen. For some reason it is very hard to do: those days when even the little things in life could be almost too exciting to bear. And particularly the days when you were first in love; when you were like a person sleepwalking, and you didn't quite see the street you were in and didn't quite hear everything that was said to you. You're just a little bit crazy. Will you remember that, please?

Now they'll be coming out of high school at three o'clock. George has just been elected president of the junior class; and, as it's June, that means he'll be president of the senior class all next year. And Emily's just been elected secretary and treasurer. I don't have to tell you how important that is. (*He places a board across the backs of two chairs, parallel to the footlights, and places two high stools behind it. This is the counter of* MR. MORGAN's *drugstore.*) All ready!

[EMILY, *carrying an armful of imaginary schoolbooks, comes along Main Street from the left.*]

EMILY. I can't, Louise. I've got to go home. Good-by. . . . Oh, Earnestine! Earnestine! Can you come over tonight and do algebra? I did the first and third in study hall. No, they're not hard. But, Earnestine, that Caesar's awful hard. I don't see why we have to do a thing like that. Come over about seven. Tell your mother you *have* to. G'by. . . . G'by, Helen. G'by, Fred.

[GEORGE, *also carrying books, catches up with her.*]

GEORGE. Can I carry your books home for you, Emily?

EMILY (*coldly*). Thank you. (*She gives them to him.*)

GEORGE. Excuse me a minute, Emily. . . . Say, Bob, get everything ready. I'll be there in a quarter of an hour. If I'm a little late, start practice anyway. And give Herb some long high ones. His eye needs a lot of practice. Seeya later.

EMILY. Good-by, Lizzy.

GEORGE. Good-by, Lizzy. . . . I'm awfully glad you were elected, too, Emily.

EMILY. Thank you.

[*They have been standing on Main Street, almost against the back wall.* GEORGE *is about to take the first steps toward the audience when he stops again.*]

GEORGE. Emily, why are you mad at me?

EMILY. I'm not mad at you.

GEORGE. You . . . you treat me so funny.

EMILY. Well, I might as well say it right out, George. I don't like the whole change that's come over you in the last year. I'm sorry if that hurts your feelings, but I've just got to tell the truth and shame the devil.

GEORGE. I'm awfully sorry, Emily. Wha-a-what do you mean?

EMILY. Well, up to a year ago I used to like you a lot. And I used to watch you as you did everything . . . because we'd been friends so long . . . and then you began spending all your time at baseball . . . and you never even spoke to anybody any more; not even to your own family you didn't . . . and, George, it's a fact, you've got awful conceited and stuck-up, and all the girls say so. They may not say so to your face, but that's what they say about you behind your back; and it hurts me to hear them say it, but I've got to agree with them a little. I'm sorry if it hurts your feelings . . . but I can't be sorry I said it.

GEORGE. I . . . I'm glad you said it, Emily. I never thought that such a thing was happening to me. I guess it's hard for a fella not to have faults creep into his character.

[*They take a step or two in silence, then stand still in misery.*]

EMILY. I always expect a man to be perfect, and I think he should be.

GEORGE. Oh . . . I don't think it's possible to be perfect, Emily.

EMILY. Well, my father is and, as far as I can see, your father is. There's no reason on earth why you shouldn't be, too.

GEORGE. Well, Emily . . . I feel it's the other way round. That men aren't naturally good, but girls are. Like you and your mother and my mother.

EMILY. Well, you might as well know right now that I'm not perfect. It's not as easy for a girl to be perfect as a man, because we girls are more nervous.

Now I'm sorry I said all that about you. I don't know what made me say it.

GEORGE. No, no — I guess if it's the truth you ought to say it. You stick to it, Emily.

EMILY. I don't know if it's the truth or not. And I suddenly feel that it isn't important at all.

GEORGE. Emily, would you like an ice-cream soda, or something, before you go home?

EMILY. Well, thank you. . . . I would.

[*They come into the drugstore and seat themselves on the stools.*]

STAGE MANAGER (*as* MR. MORGAN). Hello, George. Hello, Emily. What'll you have? Why, Emily Webb, what've you been crying about?

GEORGE (*groping for an explanation*). She . . . she just got an awful scare, Mr. Morgan. She almost got run over by that hardware-store wagon. Everybody always says that Tom Huckins drives like a crazy man.

STAGE MANAGER. Here, take a drink of water, Emily. You look all shook up. . . . There! Now, what'll you have?

EMILY. I'll have a strawberry phosphate, thank you, Mr. Morgan.

GEORGE. No, no. You go and have an ice-cream soda with me, Emily. Two strawberry ice-cream sodas, Mr. Morgan.

STAGE MANAGER (*working the faucets*). Yes, sir. I tell you, you've got to look both ways before you cross Main Street these days. Gets worse every year. There are a hundred and twenty-five horses in Grover's Corners this minute I'm talking to you. State inspector was in here yesterday. And now they're bringing in these auto-mobiles, the best thing to do is to just stay home. Why, I can remember the time when a dog could lie down all day in the middle of Main Street and nothing would come to disturb him. . . . Yes, Miss Ellis; be with you in a minute. . . . Here are your sodas. Enjoy 'em. (*He goes off.*)

EMILY. They're so expensive.

GEORGE. No, no — don't you think of that. We're celebrating. First, we're celebrating our election. And then do you know what else I'm celebrating?

EMILY. No.

GEORGE. I'm celebrating because I've got a friend who tells me all the things that ought to be told me.

EMILY. George, *please* don't think of that. I don't know why I said it. It's not true. You're —

GEORGE. No, you stick to it, Emily. I'm glad you spoke to me like you did. But you'll see: I'm going to change so quick — you bet I'm going to change. And, Emily, I want to ask you a favor.

EMILY. What?

GEORGE. Emily, if I go away to State Agriculture College next year, will you write me a letter once in a while?

EMILY. I certainly will. I certainly will, George. (*Pause*) It certainly seems like being away three years you'd get out of touch with things.

GEORGE. No, no. I mustn't do that. You see, I'm not only going to be just a farmer. After a while, maybe, I'll run for something to get elected. So your letters'll be very important to me; you know, telling me what's going on here and everything. . . .

EMILY. Just the same, three years is a long time. Maybe letters from Grover's Corners wouldn't be so interesting after a while. Grover's Corners isn't a very important place when you think of all New Hampshire; but I think it's a very nice town.

GEORGE. The day wouldn't come when I wouldn't want to know everything that's happening here. I know *that's* true, Emily.

EMILY. Well, I'll try to make my letters interesting. (*Pause*)

GEORGE. Y'know, Emily, whenever I meet a farmer, I ask him if he thinks it's important to go to agricultural school to be a good farmer.

EMILY. Why, George —

GEORGE. Yeah, and some of them say

that it's even a waste of time. You can get all those things, anyway, out of the pamphlets the government sends out. And Uncle Luke's getting old — he's about ready for me to start in taking over his farm tomorrow, if I could.

EMILY. My!

GEORGE. And, like you say, being gone all that time . . . in other places and meeting other people. . . . If anything like that can happen, I don't want to go away. I guess new people aren't any better than old ones. I'll bet they almost never are. Emily, I feel that you're as good a friend as I've got. I don't need to go and meet the people in other towns.

EMILY. But, George, maybe it's very important for you to go and learn all that about cattle judging and soils and those things. And if you're going into politics, maybe you ought to meet people from other parts of the state . . . of course, I don't know.

GEORGE (after a pause). Emily, I'm going to make up my mind right now. I won't go. I'll tell Pa about it tonight.

EMILY. Why, George, I don't see why you have to decide right now. It's a whole year away.

GEORGE. Emily, I'm glad you spoke to me about that . . . that fault in my character. And what you said was right; but there was *one* thing wrong in it, and that was when you said that for a year I wasn't noticing people, and . . . you, for instance. Listen, Emily . . . you say you were watching me when I did everything. . . . Why, I was doing the same about you all the time. Why, sure — I always thought about you as one of the chief people I thought about. I always made sure where you were sitting on the bleachers, and who you were with. And we've always had lots of talks . . . and joking, in the halls; and they always meant a lot to me. Of course, they weren't as good as the talk we're having now. Lately I'd been noticing that you'd been acting kind of funny to me; and for three days I've been trying to walk home with you, but

something's always got in the way. Yesterday I was standing over against the wall waiting for you, and you walked home with Miss Corcoran.

EMILY. George! . . . Life's awful funny! How could I have known that? Why, I thought —

GEORGE. Listen, Emily, I'm going to tell you why I'm not going to agricultural school. I think that once you've found a person that you're very fond of . . . I mean a person who's fond of you, too — at least enough to be interested in your character. . . . Well, I think that's just as important as college is, and even more so. That's what I think.

EMILY. I think it's awfully important, too.

GEORGE. Emily.

EMILY. Yes, George.

GEORGE. Emily, if I improve and make a big change . . . would you be . . . I mean, *could* you be . . .

EMILY. I . . . I am now; I always have been. (*Pause*)

GEORGE. So I guess this is an important talk we've been having.

EMILY. Yes.

GEORGE (*taking a deep breath and straightening his back*). Wait just a minute and I'll take you home. (*He rises and goes to the* STAGE MANAGER, *who appears and comes toward him.*) Mr. Morgan, I'll have to go home and get the money to pay you for this. It'll only take a minute.

STAGE MANAGER. What's that? George Gibbs, do you mean to tell me —

GEORGE. Yes, but I had reasons, Mr. Morgan. Look, here's my gold watch to keep until I come back with the money.

STAGE MANAGER. That's all right. Keep your watch. I'll trust you.

GEORGE. I'll be back in five minutes.

STAGE MANAGER, I'll trust you ten years, George — not a day more. . . . Got all over your shock, Emily?

EMILY. Yes, thank you, Mr. Morgan. It was nothing.

GEORGE (*taking up the books from the counter*). I'm ready.

THORNTON WILDER   387

[*They walk in grave silence down the stage, turn, and pass through the trellis at the Webb's back door and disappear.*]

STAGE MANAGER. Thank you, Emily. Thank you, George. . . . Now before we go on to the wedding, there are still some more things we ought to know about this — about this marriage. I want to know some more about how the parents took it; but what I want to know most of all is — oh, you know what I mean — what Grover's Corners thought about marriage, anyway. You know's well as I do: people are never able to say right out what they think of money, or death, or fame, or marriage. You've got to catch it between the lines; you've got to *overhear* it.

Oh, Doctor! Mrs. Gibbs!

[*They appear at their side of the stage and exchange a glance of understanding with him. The* STAGE MANAGER *lays across two chairs the same plank that served as a drugstore counter, and it has now become* MRS. GIBBS's *ironing board.* DR. GIBBS *sits down in a rocker and smokes.* MRS. GIBBS *irons a moment in silence, then goes to the foot of the stairs.*]

MRS. GIBBS (*calling*). Rebecca! It's time you turned out your light and went to sleep. George, you'd better get some sleep, too.

REBECCA'S VOICE. Ma, I haven't finished my English.

MRS. GIBBS. What? Well, I bet you haven't been working, Rebecca. You've been reading that Sears Roebuck catalogue, that's what you've been doing. All right, I'll give you ten more minutes. If you haven't finished by then, you'll just have to fail the course and be a disgrace to your father and me. . . . George, what are you doing?

GEORGE'S VOICE (*hurt*). I'm doing history.

MRS. GIBBS. Well, you'd better go to bed. You're probably sleeping at the desk as it is. (*She casts an amused eye at her husband and returns to her ironing.*)

DR. GIBBS. I had a long talk with the boy today.

MRS. GIBBS. Did you?

DR. GIBBS. I tell you, Mrs. G., there's nothing so terrifying in the world as a son. The relation of a father to a son is the confounded awkwardest — I always come away feeling like a soggy sponge of hypocrisy.

MRS. GIBBS. Well, a mother and a daughter's no picnic, let me tell you.

DR. GIBBS. George is set on it: he wants to marry Emily soon as school's out and take her right on to the farm. (*Pause*) He says he can sit up nights and learn agriculture from government pamphlets, without going to college for it.

MRS. GIBBS. He always was crazy about farming. Gets that from my people.

DR. GIBBS. At a pinch I guess he could start in farming, but I swear I think he's too young to get married. Julia, he's just a green, half-grown kid. He isn't ready to be a family man.

MRS. GIBBS. No, he ain't. You're right. But he's a good boy and I wouldn't like to think of him being alone out there . . . coming into town Satiddy nights, like any old farm hand, tuckered out from work and looking for excitement. He might get into bad ways. It wouldn't be enough fun for him to come and sit by our stove, and holding hands with Emily for a year mightn't be enough either. He might lose interest in her.

DR. GIBBS. Hm.

MRS. GIBBS. Frank, I been watching her. George is a lucky boy when you think of all the silly girls in the world.

DR. GIBBS. But, Julia, George *married*. That great, gangling, selfish nincompoop.

MRS. GIBBS. Yes, I know. (*She takes up a collar and examines it.*) Frank, what do you do to your collars? Do you gnaw 'em? I never saw such a man for collars.

DR. GIBBS. Julia, when I married you,

do you know what one of my terrors was in getting married?

MRS. GIBBS. Pshaw! Go on with you!

DR. GIBBS. I was afraid we weren't going to have material for conversation more'n'd last us a few weeks. I was afraid we'd run out and eat our meals in silence. That's a fact. You and I've been conversing for twenty years now without any noticeable barren spells.

MRS. GIBBS. Well, good weather, bad weather, 'tain't very choice, but I always manage to find something to say. (*Pause*)

DR. GIBBS. What do you think? What do you think, Julia? Shall we tell the boy he can go ahead and get married?

MRS. GIBBS. Seems like it's up to us to decide. Myrtle and Charles Webb are willing. They think it's a good idea to throw the young people into the sea and let 'em sink or swim, as soon as they're ready.

DR. GIBBS. What does that mean? Must we decide right now? This minute?

MRS. GIBBS. There you go putting the responsibility on me!

DR. GIBBS. Here it is, almost April. . . . I'll go up and say a word to him right now before he goes to bed. (*He rises.*) You're sure, Julia? You've nothing more to add?

MRS. GIBBS (*stops ironing a moment*). I don't know what to say. Seems like it's too much to ask, for a big outdoor boy like that to go and get shut up in classrooms for three years. And once he's on the farm, he might just as well have a companion, seeing he's found a fine girl like Emily. . . . People are meant to live two-by-two in this world. . . . Yes, Frank, go up and tell him it's all right.

[DR. GIBBS *crosses and is about to call when* MRS. GIBBS, *her hands on her cheeks, staring into the audience, speaks in sharp alarm.*]

Wait a minute! Wait a minute! (*Then, resuming her ironing*) No — go and tell him.

DR. GIBBS. Why did you stop then, Julia?

MRS. GIBBS. Oh, you know: I thought of all those times we went through in the first years when George and Rebecca were babies — you walking up and down with them at three in the morning, the whooping cough, the time George fell off the porch. You and I were twenty-five years old, and more. It's wonderful how one forgets one's troubles like that. . . . Yes, Frank, go upstairs and tell him. It's worth it.

DR. GIBBS. Yes, they'll have a lot of troubles, but that's none of our business. Let'm. Everybody has a right to his own troubles. You ought to be present, Julia — important occasion like that. I'll call him. . . . George! Oh, George!

GEORGE'S VOICE. Yes, Pa.

DR. GIBBS. Can you come down a minute? Your mother and I want to speak to you.

GEORGE. Yeah, sure.

MRS. GIBBS (*putting her arm through her husband's*). Lord, what a fool I am; I'm trembling all over. There's nothing to tremble about.

STAGE MANAGER. Thank you! Thank you! . . . Now we're ready to go on with the wedding.

[*While he talks, the actors remove the chairs and tables and trellises from the Gibbs and Webb homes. They arrange the pews for the church in the back of the stage. The congregation will sit facing the back wall. The aisle of the church is in the middle of the scene. A small platform is placed against the back wall; on this the* STAGE MANAGER, *as minister, can stand.*]

There are a lot of things to be said about a wedding; there are a lot of thoughts that go on during a wedding. We can't get them all into one wedding, naturally, and especially not into a wedding at Grover's Corners, where they're awfully plain and short. In this wedding I play the minister. That gives me the right to say a few more things about it.

For a while now, the play gets pretty serious. Y'see, some churches say that marriage is a sacrament. I don't quite know what that means, but I can guess. Like Mrs. Gibbs said a few minutes ago: People were made to live two-by-two. This is a good wedding, but people are so put together that even at a good wedding there's a lot of confusion way down deep in people's minds; and we thought that that ought to be in our play, too.

The real hero of this scene isn't on the stage at all, and you know who that is. It's like what one of those European fellas said: Every child born into the world is nature's attempt to make a perfect human being. Well, we've seen nature pushing and contriving for some time now. We all know that nature's interested in quantity; but I think she's interested in quality, too — that's why I'm in the ministry. Maybe she's trying to make another good governor for New Hampshire. And don't forget the other witnesses at this wedding — the ancestors. Millions of them. Most of them set out to live two-by-two, also. Millions of them.

Well, that's all my sermon. 'Twan't very long, anyway.

[*The organ starts playing Handel's "Largo." The congregation streams into the church and sits in silence.* MRS. WEBB, *on the way to her place, turns back and speaks to the audience.*]

MRS. WEBB. I don't know why on earth I should be crying. I suppose there's nothing to cry about. It came over me at breakfast this morning; there was Emily eating her breakfast as she's done for seventeen years, and now she's going off to eat it in someone else's house. I suppose that's it. And Emily! She suddenly said: I can't eat another mouthful, and she put her head down on the table and *she* cried.

[*The choir starts singing "Love Divine, All Love Excelling."* GEORGE, *coming through the audience, has reached the stage. He stares at the congregation a moment, then takes a few steps of withdrawal toward the right proscenium pillar.*]

GEORGE (*darkly, to himself*). I wish I were back at school. . . . I don't want to get married.

[*His mother has left her seat and come toward him. She stops, looking at him anxiously.*]

MRS. GIBBS. George, what's the matter?

GEORGE. Ma, I don't want to grow *old*. Why's everybody pushing me so?

MRS. GIBBS. Why, George . . . you wanted it.

GEORGE. Why do I have to get married at all? Listen, Ma, for the last time I ask you —

MRS. GIBBS. No, no, George . . . you're a man now.

GEORGE. Listen, Ma, you never listen to me. All I want to do is to be a fella. Why do —

MRS. GIBBS. George! If anyone should hear you! Now stop. Why, I'm ashamed of you!

GEORGE (*passing his hand over his forehead*). What's the matter? I've been dreaming. Where's Emily?

MRS. GIBBS. Gracious! You gave me such a turn.

GEORGE. Cheer up, Ma. What are you looking so funny for? Cheer up; I'm getting married.

MRS. GIBBS. Let me catch my breath a minute.

GEORGE. Now, Ma, you save Thursday nights. Emily and I are coming over to dinner every Thursday night . . . you'll see. Ma, what are you crying for? Come on, we've got to get ready for this.

[*In the meantime* EMILY, *in white and wearing her wedding veil, has come through the audience and mounted onto the stage. She, too, draws back when she sees the congregation in the church. The choir begins "Blest Be the Tie That Binds."*]

EMILY. I never felt so alone in my whole life. And George over there, looking so . . . I *hate* him, I wish I were dead. Papa! Papa!

MR. WEBB (*leaving his seat in the pews and coming toward her anxiously*). Emily! Emily! Now don't get upset.

EMILY. But, Papa, I don't want to get married.

MR. WEBB. Sh-sh — Emily. Everything's all right.

EMILY. Why can't I stay for a while just as I am? Let's go away.

MR. WEBB. No, no, Emily. Now stop and think.

EMILY. Don't you remember that you used to say — all the time you used to say that I was *your* girl. There must be lots of places we can go to. Let's go away. I'll work for you. I could keep house.

MR. WEBB. Sh. . . . You mustn't think of such things. You're just nervous, Emily. Now, now — you're marrying the best young fellow in the world. George is a fine fellow.

EMILY. But, Papa —

MR. WEBB. George! George!

[MRS. GIBBS *returns to her seat.* GEORGE *hears* MR. WEBB *and looks up.* MR. WEBB *beckons to him. They move to the center of the stage.*]

I'm giving away my daughter, George. Do you think you can take care of her?

GEORGE. Mr. Webb, I want to . . . I want to try. Emily, I'm going to do my best. I love you, Emily. I need you.

EMILY. Well, if you love me, help me. All I want is someone to love me.

GEORGE. I will, Emily.

EMILY. If ever I'm sick or in trouble, that's what I mean.

GEORGE. Emily, I'll try. I'll try.

EMILY. And I mean for ever. Do you hear? For ever and ever.

[*They fall into each other's arms. The March from Lohengrin is heard.*]

MR. WEBB. Come, they're waiting for us. Now you know it'll be all right. Come, quick.

[GEORGE *slips away and takes his place beside the* STAGE MANAGER-CLERGYMAN. EMILY *proceeds up the aisle on her father's arm.*]

STAGE MANAGER. Do you, George, take this woman, Emily, to be your wedded wife, to have . . .

[MRS. SOAMES *has been sitting in the last row of the congregation. She now turns to her neighbors and speaks in a shrill voice.*]

MRS. SOAMES. Perfectly lovely wedding! Loveliest wedding I ever saw. Oh, I do love a good wedding, don't you? Doesn't she make a lovely bride?

GEORGE. I do.

STAGE MANAGER. Do you, Emily, take this man, George, to be your wedded husband . . .

MRS. SOAMES. Don't know *when* I've seen such a lovely wedding. But I always cry. Don't know why it is, but I always cry. I just like to see young people happy, don't you? Oh, I think it's lovely.

[*The ring. The kiss. The stage is suddenly arrested into silent tableau.*]

STAGE MANAGER (*his eyes on the distance, says to the audience*). I've married two hundred couples in my day. Do I believe in it? I don't know. M—— marries N——. Millions of them. The cottage, the gocart, the Sunday afternoon drives in the Ford, the first rheumatism, the grandchildren, the second rheumatism, the deathbed, the reading of the will — Once in a thousand times it's interesting. Well, let's have Mendelssohn's "Wedding March"!

[*The organ picks up the march. The bride and groom come down the aisle, radiant but trying to be very dignified.*]

MRS. SOAMES. Aren't they a lovely couple? Oh, I've never been to such a nice wedding. I'm sure they'll be happy. I always say *happiness*, that's the great thing! The important thing is to be happy.

[*The bride and groom reach the steps leading into the audience. A bright light is thrown upon them. They descend into the auditorium and run up the aisle joyously.*]

STAGE MANAGER. That's all the second act. Ten minutes' intermission, folks.

FOR DISCUSSION

1. What effect is achieved by having the second act open with the same people and the same activities as the first?

2. How does the rainy wedding day fit the shifting mood of the characters?

3. Does the conversation between Emily and George after school help you to understand "how all this began," as the Stage Manager says? Why had Emily resented George's absorption in baseball? Do they seem to realize what a serious step they are approaching? Find lines that show they do, and others that make them sound young and inexperienced.

4. Why do both the parents and the young people have spells of reluctance to go on with the wedding? What had been Dr. Gibbs's fear about getting married? Explain his statement that "everybody has a right to his own troubles."

5. The Stage Manager says this is a "good" wedding. Do you agree? Why does he add, ". . . there's a lot of confusion way down deep in people's minds; . . . that ought to be in our play, too"?

Act III

During the intermission the audience has seen the actors arranging the stage. On the right-hand side, a little right of the center, ten or twelve ordinary chairs have been placed in three openly spaced rows facing the audience. These are graves in the cemetery.

Toward the end of the intermission the actors enter and take their places. The front row contains, toward the center of the stage, an empty chair; then MRS. GIBBS *and* SIMON STIMSON. *The second row contains, among others,* MRS. SOAMES. *The third row has* WALLY WEBB. *The dead sit in a quiet without stiffness and in a patience without listlessness.*

The STAGE MANAGER *takes his accustomed place and waits for the house lights to go down.*

STAGE MANAGER. This time nine years have gone by, friends — summer, 1913. Gradual changes in Grover's Corners. Horses are getting rarer. Farmers coming into town in Fords. Chief difference is in the young people, far as I can see. They want to go to the moving pictures all the time. They want to wear clothes like they see there . . . want to be citified. Everybody locks their house doors now at night. Ain't seen any burglars in town yet, but everybody's heard about 'em. But you'd be surprised, though — on the whole, things don't change much at Grover's Corners.

Guess you want to know what all these chairs are here fur. Smarter ones have guessed it already. I don't know how you feel about such things, but this certainly is a beautiful place. It's on a hilltop — a windy hilltop — lots of sky, lots of clouds, often lots of sun and moon and stars. You come up here on a fine afternoon and you can see range on range of hills — awful blue they are — up there by Lake Sunapee and Lake Winnipesaukee . . . and way up, if you've got a glass, you can see the White Mountains and Mt. Washington — where North Conway and Conway is. And, of course, our favorite mountain, Mt. Monadnock's right here — and all around it lie these towns — Jaffrey, 'n East Jaffrey, 'n Peterborough, 'n Dublin; and (*Then, pointing down in the audience*) there, quite a ways down, is Grover's Corners.

Yes, beautiful spot up here. Mountain laurel and li-lacks. I often wonder why people like to be buried in Woodlawn and Brooklyn when they might pass the same time up here in New Hampshire. Over in that corner (*Pointing to stage left*) are the old stones — 1670, 1680. Strong-minded people that come a long way to be independent. Summer people walk around there laughing at the funny words on the tombstones . . . it don't do any harm. And genealogists come up from Boston — get paid by city people for looking up their ancestors. They want to make sure they're Daughters of the American Revolution and of the *Mayflower*. . . . Well, I guess that don't do any harm, either. Wherever you come near the human race, there's layers and layers of nonsense.

Over there are some Civil War veterans too. Iron flags on their graves. . . . New Hampshire boys . . . had a notion that the Union ought to be kept together, though they'd never seen more than fifty miles of it themselves. All they knew was the name, friends — the United States of America. The United States of America. And they went and died about it.

This here is the new part of the cemetery. Here's your friend Mrs. Gibbs. 'N let me see — Here's Mr. Stimson, organist at the Congregational Church. And over there's Mrs. Soames, who enjoyed the wedding so — you remember? Oh, and a lot of others. And Editor Webb's boy Wallace, whose appendix burst while he was on a Boy Scout trip to Crawford Notch. Yes, an awful lot of sorrow has sort of quieted down up here. People just wild with grief have brought their relatives up to this hill. We all know how it is. And then time . . . and sunny days . . . and rainy days . . . 'n snow . . . tz-tz-tz. We're all glad they're in a beautiful place, and we're coming up here ourselves when our fit's over. This certainly is an important part of Grover's Corners. A lot of thoughts come up here, night and day, but there's no post office.

Now I'm going to tell you some things you know already. You know'm as well as I do, but you don't take'm out and look at'm very often. I don't care what they say with their mouths — everybody knows that *something* is eternal. And it ain't houses, and it ain't names, and it ain't earth, and it ain't even the stars . . . everybody knows in their bones that *something* is eternal, and that something has to do with human beings. All the greatest people ever lived have been telling us that for five thousand years, and yet you'd be surprised how people are always losing hold of it. There's something way down deep that's eternal about every human being. (*Pause*) You know as well as I do that the dead don't stay interested in us living people for very long. Gradually, gradually, they lose hold of the earth . . . and the ambitions they had . . . and the pleasures they had . . . and the things they suffered . . . and the people they loved. They get weaned away from earth. That's the way I put it — weaned away. Yes, they stay here while the earth part of 'em burns away, burns out; and all that time they slowly get indifferent to what's goin' on in Grover's Corners.

They're waitin'. They're waitin' for something that they feel is comin'. Something important and great. Aren't they waitin' for the eternal part in them to come out clear? Some of the things they're going to say maybe'll hurt your feelings — but that's the way it is: mother 'n daughter . . . husband 'n wife . . . enemy 'n enemy . . . money 'n miser — all those terribly important things kind of grow pale around here. And what's left? What's left when memory's gone, and your identity, Mrs. Smith? (*He looks at the audience a minute, then turns to the stage.*)

Well! There are some *living* people. There's Joe Stoddard, our undertaker, supervising a new-made grave. And here comes a Grover's Corners boy that left town to go out West.

[JOE STODDARD *has hovered about in the background.* SAM CRAIG *enters left, wiping his forehead from the exertion. He carries an umbrella and strolls front.*]

SAM CRAIG. Good afternoon, Joe Stoddard.

JOE STODDARD. Good afternoon, good afternoon. Let me see now: Do I know you?

SAM CRAIG. I'm Sam Craig.

JOE STODDARD. Gracious sakes' alive! Of all people! I should'a knowed you'd be back for the funeral. You've been away a long time, Sam.

SAM CRAIG. Yes, I've been away over twelve years. I'm in business out in Buffalo now, Joe. But I was in the East when I got news of my cousin's death, so I thought I'd combine things a little and come and see the old home. You look well.

JOE STODDARD. Yes, yes, can't complain. Very sad, our journey today, Samuel.

SAM CRAIG. Yes.

JOE STODDARD. Yes, yes. I always say I hate to supervise when a young person is taken. I see you brought your umbrella. It's going to rain and make it sadder still, seems like. They'll be here in a few minutes now. I had to come here early today — my son's supervisin' at the home.

SAM CRAIG (*reading stones*). Old Farmer McCarty. I used to do chores for him — after school. He had the lumbago.

JOE STODDARD. Yes, we brought Farmer McCarty here a number of years ago now.

SAM CRAIG (*staring at* MRS. GIBBS's *knees*). Why, this is my Aunt Julia. . . . I'd forgotten that she'd . . . of course, of course.

JOE STODDARD. Yes, Doc Gibbs lost his wife two, three years ago . . . about this time. And today's another pretty bad blow for him, too.

MRS. GIBBS. (*to* SIMON STIMSON, *in an even voice*). That's my sister Carrie's boy, Sam — Sam Craig.

SIMON STIMSON. I'm always uncomfortable when *they're* around.

MRS. GIBBS. Simon.

SIMON STIMSON. They and their nonsense and their idiotic glee at being alive.

MRS. GIBBS. Simon, be patient.

SAM CRAIG. Do they choose their own verses much, Joe?

JOE STODDARD. No . . . not usual. Mostly the bereaved pick a verse.

SAM CRAIG. Doesn't sound like Aunt Julia. There aren't many of those Hersey sisters left now. Let me see. Where are — I wanted to look at my father's and mother's . . .

JOE STODDARD. Over there with the Craigs. . . . Avenue F.

SAM CRAIG (reading SIMON STIMSON's epitaph). He was organist at church, wasn't he? Hm, drank a lot, we used to say.

JOE STODDARD. Nobody was supposed to know about it. He'd seen a peck of trouble. Those musical fellas ain't like the rest of us, I reckon. (Behind his hand) Took his own life, y'know?

SAM CRAIG. Oh, did he?

JOE STODDARD. Hung himself in the attic. They tried to hush it up, but of course it got around. His wife's just married Senator Barstow. Many a time I've seen her, eleven o'clock at night, goin' around the streets huntin' for her husband. Think o' that! Now she's married to Senator Barstow over at Manchester. He chose his own epy-taph. You can see it there. It ain't a verse exactly.

SAM CRAIG. Why, it's just some notes of music! What is it?

JOE STODDARD. Oh, I wouldn't know. It was wrote up in the Boston papers at the time.

SAM CRAIG. Joe, what did she die of?

JOE STODDARD. Who?

SAM CRAIG. My cousin.

JOE STODDARD Oh, didn't you know? Had some trouble bringing a baby into the world. Let's see, today's Friday — 'twas almost a week ago now.

SAM CRAIG (putting up his umbrella). Did the baby live?

JOE STODDARD (raising his coat collar). No. 'Twas her second, though. There's a little boy 'bout four years old.

SAM CRAIG. The grave's going to be over there?

JOE STODDARD. Yes, there ain't much more room over here among the Gibbses, so they're opening up a whole new Gibbs section over by Avenue B. You'll excuse me now. I see they're comin'.

THE DEAD (not lugubrious, and strongly New England in accent). Rain'll do a lot of good. . . . Yes, reckon things were gettin' downright parched. Don't look like it's goin' to last long, tho'. . . . Lemuel, you remember the flood of seventy-nine? Carried away all the bridges but one.

[From left to right, at the back of the stage, comes a procession. Four men carry a casket, invisible to us. All the rest are under umbrellas. One can vaguely see DR. GIBBS, GEORGE, the WEBBS, etc. They gather about a grave in the back center of the stage, a little to the left of center.]

MRS. SOAMES. Who is it, Julia?

MRS. GIBBS (without raising her eyes). My daughter-in-law, Emily Webb.

MRS. SOAMES (a little surprised, but no emotion). Well, I declare! The road up here must have been awful muddy. What did she die of, Julia?

MRS. GIBBS. In childbirth.

MRS. SOAMES. Childbirth. (Almost with a laugh) I'd forgotten all about that! My, wasn't life awful — (With a sigh) and wonderful.

SIMON STIMSON (with a sideways glance). Wonderful, was it?

MRS. GIBBS. Simon! Now, remember!

MRS. SOAMES. I remember Emily's wedding. Wasn't it a lovely wedding! And I remember her reading the class poem at graduation exercises. Emily was one of the brightest girls ever graduated from high school. I've heard Principal Wilkins say so time after time. I called on them at their new farm just before I died. Perfectly beautiful farm.

A WOMAN FROM AMONG THE DEAD. It's on the same road we lived on.

A MAN AMONG THE DEAD. Yes, just near the Elks's picnic grounds. Remember, Joe? By the lake where we always used to go Fourth of July? Right smart farm.

[*They subside. The group by the grave starts singing "Blest Be the Tie That Binds."*]

A WOMAN AMONG THE DEAD. I always liked that hymn. I was hopin' they'd sing a hymn.

A MAN AMONG THE DEAD. My wife — my second wife — knows all the verses of about every hymn there is. It just beats the Dutch — she can go through them all by heart.

[*Pause. Suddenly* EMILY *appears from among the umbrellas. She is wearing a white dress. Her hair is down her back and tied by a white ribbon like a little girl's. She comes slowly, gazing wonderingly at* THE DEAD, *a little dazed. She stops halfway and smiles faintly.*]

EMILY. Hello.

VOICES AMONG THE DEAD. Hello, Emily. H'lo, M's. Gibbs.

EMILY. Hello, Mother Gibbs.

MRS. GIBBS. Emily.

EMILY. Hello. (*The hymn continues.* EMILY *looks back at the funeral. She says dreamily*) It's raining.

MRS. GIBBS. Yes. . . . They'll be gone soon, dear. Just rest yourself.

[EMILY *sits down in the empty chair by* MRS. GIBBS.]

EMILY. It seems thousands and thousands of years since I . . . How stupid they all look. They don't have to look like that!

MRS. GIBBS. Don't look at them now, dear. They'll be gone soon.

EMILY. Oh, I wish I'd been here a long time. I don't like being new here. . . . How do you do, Mr. Stimson?

SIMON STIMSON. How do you do, Emily.

[EMILY *continues to look about her with a wan and wondering smile, but for a moment her eyes do not return to the funeral group. As though to shut out from her mind the thought of that group, she starts speaking to* MRS. GIBBS *with a touch of nervousness.*]

EMILY. Mother Gibbs, George and I have made that farm into just the best place you ever saw. We thought of you all the time. We wanted to show you the new barn and a great long ce-ment drinking fountain for the stock. We bought that out of the money you left us.

MRS. GIBBS. I did?

EMILY. Don't you remember, Mother Gibbs — the legacy you left us? Why, it was over three hundred and fifty dollars.

MRS. GIBBS. Yes, yes, Emily.

EMILY. Well, there's a patent device on this drinking fountain so that it never overflows, Mother Gibbs, and it never sinks below a certain mark they have there. It's fine. (*Her voice trails off, and her eyes return to the funeral group.*) It won't be the same to George without me, but it's a lovely farm. (*Suddenly she looks directly at* MRS. GIBBS.) Live people don't understand, do they?

MRS. GIBBS. No, dear — not very much.

EMILY. They're sort of shut up in little boxes, aren't they? I feel as though I knew them last a thousand years ago. . . . My boy is spending the day at Mrs. Carter's. (*She sees* MR. CARTER *among* THE DEAD.) Oh, Mr. Carter, my little boy is spending the day at your house.

MR. CARTER. Is he?

EMILY. Yes, he loves it there. . . . Mother Gibbs, we have a Ford, too. Never gives any trouble. I don't drive, though. Mother Gibbs, when does this feeling go away? Of being . . . one of *them*? How long does it . . .

MRS. GIBBS. Sh! dear. Just wait and be patient.

EMILY (*with a sigh*). I know. . . . Look, they're finished. They're going.

MRS. GIBBS. Sh. . . .

[*The umbrellas leave the stage.* DR.

GIBBS *comes over to his wife's grave and stands before it a moment.* EMILY *looks up at his face.* MRS. GIBBS *does not raise her eyes.*]

EMILY. Look! Father Gibbs is bringing some of my flowers to you. He looks just like George, doesn't he? Oh, Mother Gibbs, I never realized before how troubled and how . . . how in the dark live persons are. From morning till night that's all they are — troubled.

[DR. GIBBS *goes off.*]

THE DEAD. Little cooler than it was. . . . Yes, that rain cooled it off a little. Those northeast winds always do the same thing, don't they? If it isn't a rain, it's a three-day blow. . . . Reckon it may clear up before night; often does.

[*A patient calm falls on the stage. The* STAGE MANAGER *appears at his proscenium pillar, smoking.* EMILY *sits up abruptly, with an idea.*]

EMILY. But, Mother Gibbs, one can go back; one can go back there again . . . into living. I feel it. I know it. Why, just then for a moment I was thinking about . . . about the farm . . . and for a minute I *was* there, and my baby was on my lap as plain as day.

MRS. GIBBS. Yes, of course you can.

EMILY. I can go back there and live all those days over again . . . why not?

MRS. GIBBS. All I can say is, Emily, *don't.*

EMILY (*taking a few steps toward the* STAGE MANAGER). But it's true, isn't it? I can go and live . . . back there . . . again.

STAGE MANAGER. Yes, some have tried — but they soon come back here.

MRS. GIBBS. Don't do it, Emily.

MRS. SOAMES. Emily, don't. It's not what you think it'd be.

EMILY. But I won't live over a sad day. I'll choose a happy one — I'll choose the day I first knew that I loved George. Why should that be painful?

[*They are silent. Her question turns to the* STAGE MANAGER.]

STAGE MANAGER. You not only live it, but you watch yourself living it.

EMILY. Yes?

STAGE MANAGER. And as you watch it, you see the thing that they — down there — never know. You see the future. You know what's going to happen afterward.

EMILY. But is that — painful? Why?

MRS. GIBBS. That's not the only reason why you shouldn't do it, Emily. When you've been here longer, you'll see that our life here is our hope that soon we'll forget all that, and think only of what's ahead, and be ready for what's ahead. When you've been here longer, you'll understand.

EMILY (*softly*). But, Mother Gibbs, how can I ever forget that life? It's all I know. It's all I had.

[MRS. GIBBS *does not answer.*]

Mr. Stimson, did you go back?

SIMON STIMSON (*sharply*). No.

EMILY. Did you, Mrs. Soames?

MRS. SOAMES. Oh, Emily. It isn't wise. Really, it isn't. All we can do is just warn you. It won't be what you expect.

EMILY (*slowly*). But it's a thing I must know for myself. I'll choose a happy day, anyway.

MRS. GIBBS. No. At least choose an unimportant day. Choose the least important day in your life. It will be important enough.

EMILY (*to the* STAGE MANAGER). Then it can't be since I was married, or since the baby was born. I can choose a birthday at least, can't I? . . . I choose my twelfth birthday.

STAGE MANAGER. All right. February 11, 1899. A Tuesday. . . . Do you want any special time of day?

EMILY. Oh, I want the whole day.

STAGE MANAGER. We'll begin at dawn. You remember it had been snowing for several days; but it had stopped the night before, and they had begun clearing the roads. The sun's coming up.

EMILY (*with a cry*). There's Main Street. . . . Why, that's Mr. Morgan's drugstore before he changed it! . . . And there's the livery stable. (*She walks toward the back of the stage.*)

STAGE MANAGER. Yes, it's 1899. This is fourteen years ago.

EMILY. Oh, that's the town I knew as a little girl. And, look, there's the old white fence that used to be around our house. Oh, I'd forgotten that! Oh, I love it so! Are *they* inside?

STAGE MANAGER. Yes, your mother'll be coming downstairs in a minute to make breakfast.

EMILY (*softly*). Will she?

STAGE MANAGER. And you remember: your father had been away for several days; he came back on the early-morning train.

EMILY. No . . .

STAGE MANAGER. He'd been back to his college to make a speech — in western New York, at Clinton.

EMILY. Look! There's Howie Newsome. There's our policeman. But he's *dead;* he *died.*

[*The* STAGE MANAGER *retires to his corner. The voices of* HOWIE NEWSOME, CONSTABLE WARREN, *and* JOE CROWELL, JR., *are heard at the left of the stage.*]

HOWIE NEWSOME. Whoa, Bessie! Bessie! . . . Morning, Bill.

CONSTABLE WARREN. Morning, Howie.

HOWIE NEWSOME. You're up early.

CONSTABLE WARREN. Been rescuin' a party; darn near froze to death, down by Polish Town thar. Got drunk and lay out in the snowdrifts. Thought he was in bed when I shook'm.

EMILY. Why, there's Joe Crowell.

JOE CROWELL, JR. Good morning, Mr. Warren. Morning, Howie.

[MRS. WEBB *has appeared in her kitchen, but* EMILY *does not see her until she calls.*]

MRS. WEBB. Chil-*dren!* Wally! Emily! . . . Time to get up.

EMILY. Mamma, here I am! Oh, how young Mamma looks! I didn't know Mamma was ever that young. Oh!

MRS. WEBB. You can come and dress by the kitchen fire, if you like; but hurry.

[HOWIE NEWSOME *has entered along Main Street and brings the milk to* MRS. WEBB'S *door.*]

Good morning, Mr. Newsome. Whhhh — it's cold.

HOWIE NEWSOME. Ten below by my barn, Mrs. Webb.

MRS. WEBB. Think of it. Keep yourself wrapped up. (*She takes her bottles in, shuddering.*)

EMILY (*with an effort*). Mamma, I can't find my blue hair ribbon anywhere.

MRS. WEBB. Just open your eyes, dear, that's all. I laid it out for you special — on the dresser, there. If it were a snake, it would bite you.

EMILY. Yes, yes. . . . (*She puts her hand on her heart.*)

[MR. WEBB *comes along Main Street, where he meets* CONSTABLE WARREN.]

MR. WEBB. Good morning, Bill.

CONSTABLE WARREN. Good morning, Mr. Webb. You're up early.

MR. WEBB. Yes, just been back to my old college in New York State. Been any trouble here?

CONSTABLE WARREN. Well, I was called up this mornin' to rescue a Polish fella — darn near froze to death he was.

MR. WEBB. We must get it in the paper.

CONSTABLE WARREN. 'Twan't much.

EMILY (*whispers*). Papa.

[MR. WEBB *shakes the snow off his feet and enters his house.*]

MR. WEBB. Good morning, Mother.

MRS. WEBB. How did it go, Charles?

MR. WEBB. Oh, fine, I guess. I told'm a few things.

MRS. WEBB. Did you sit up on the train all night?

MR. WEBB. Yes. Never could sleep on a Pullman anyway.

MRS. WEBB. Charles, seems to me — we're rich enough so that you could sleep in a train once in a while.

MR. WEBB. Everything all right here?

MRS. WEBB. Yes — can't think of anything that's happened, special. Been right cold. Howie Newsome says it's ten below over to his barn.

MR. WEBB. Yes? Well, it's colder than that at Hamilton College. Students' ears are falling off. It ain't Christian. . . . Paper have any mistakes in it?

MRS. WEBB. None that I noticed. Coffee's ready when you want it.

[*He starts upstairs.*]

Charles! Don't forget; it's Emily's birthday. Did you remember to get her something?

MR. WEBB (*patting his pocket*). Yes, I've got something here.

MRS. WEBB. Goodness sakes! I hope she likes what I got for her. I hunted hard enough for it. Chil*dren!* Hurry up! Hurry up!

MR. WEBB. Where's my girl? Where's my birthday girl? (*He goes off left.*)

MRS. WEBB. Don't interrupt her now, Charles. You can see her at breakfast. She's slow enough as it is. Hurry up, children! It's seven o'clock. Now, I don't want to call you again.

EMILY (*softly, more in wonder than in grief*). I can't bear it. They're so young and beautiful. Why did they ever have to get old? Mamma, I'm here. I'm grown up. I love you all, everything. . . . I can't look at everything hard enough. There's the butternut tree. (*She wanders up Main Street.*) There's Mr. Morgan's drugstore. And there's the high school, for ever and ever and ever. And there's the Congregational Church where I got married. Oh, dear. Oh, dear. Oh, dear!

[*The* STAGE MANAGER *beckons partially to her. He points to the house. She says a breathless "yes" and goes to the house.*]

Good morning, Mamma.

MRS. WEBB (*at the foot of the stairs, kissing her in a matter-of-fact way*). Well, now, dear, a very happy birthday to my girl and many happy returns. There are some surprises waiting for you on the kitchen table.

EMILY. Oh, Mamma, you *shouldn't* have. (*She throws an anguished glance at the* STAGE MANAGER.) I can't — I can't.

MRS. WEBB (*facing the audience, over her stove*). But birthday or no birthday, I want you to eat your breakfast good and slow. I want you to grow up and be a good strong girl. (*She goes to the stairs and calls.*) Wally! Wally, wash yourself good. Everything's getting cold down here. (*She returns to the stove with her back to* EMILY.)

[EMILY *opens her parcels.*]

That in the blue paper is from your Aunt Carrie, and I reckon you can guess who brought the post-card album. I found it on the doorstep when I brought in the milk. George Gibbs must have come over in the cold pretty early . . . right nice of him.

EMILY (*to herself*). Oh, George! I'd forgotten that.

MRS. WEBB. Chew that bacon slow. It'll help keep you warm on a cold day.

EMILY (*beginning softly but urgently*). Oh, Mamma, just look at me one minute as though you really saw me. Mamma, fourteen years have gone by. I'm dead. You're a grandmother, Mamma. I married George Gibbs, Mamma. Wally's dead, too. Mamma, his appendix burst on a camping trip to North Conway. We felt just terrible about it — don't you remember? But, just for a moment now we're all together. Mamma, just for a moment we're happy. Let's look at one another.

MRS. WEBB. That in the yellow paper is something I found in the attic among your grandmother's things. You're old enough to wear it now, and I thought you'd like it.

EMILY. And this is from you. Why,

Mamma, it's just lovely and it's just what I wanted. It's beautiful! (*She flings her arms around her mother's neck.*)

[*Her mother goes on with her cooking, but is pleased.*]

MRS. WEBB. Well, I hoped you'd like it. Hunted all over. Your Aunt Norah couldn't find one in Concord, so I had to send all the way to Boston. (*Laughingly*) Wally has something for you, too. He made it at manual-training class, and he's very proud of it. Be sure you make a big fuss about it. Your father has a surprise for you, too; don't know what it is myself. Sh — here he comes.

MR. WEBB (*offstage*). Where's my girl? Where's my birthday girl?

EMILY (*in a loud voice to the* STAGE MANAGER). I can't. I can't go on. Oh! Oh. It goes so fast. We don't have time to look at one another. (*She breaks down, sobbing.*)

[*At a gesture from the* STAGE MANAGER, MRS. WEBB *disappears.*]

I didn't realize. So all that was going on and we never noticed. Take me back — up the hill — to my grave. But first — wait! One more look. Good-by, good-by, world. Good-by, Grover's Corners . . . Mamma and Papa. Good-by to clocks ticking . . . and Mamma's sunflowers. And food and coffee. And new-ironed dresses and hot baths . . . and sleeping and waking up. Oh, earth, you're too wonderful for anybody to realize you. (*She looks toward the* STAGE MANAGER *and asks, abruptly, through her tears*) Do any human beings ever realize life while they live it — every, every minute?

STAGE MANAGER. No. (*Pause*) The saints and poets, maybe — they do some.

EMILY. I'm ready to go back. (*She returns to her chair beside* MRS. GIBBS.) Mother Gibbs, I should have listened to you. Now I want to be quiet for a while. . . . Oh, Mother Gibbs, I saw it all. I saw your garden.

MRS. GIBBS. Did you, dear?

EMILY. That's all human beings are! Just blind people.

MRS. GIBBS. Look, it's clearing up. The stars are coming out.

EMILY. Oh, Mr. Stimson, I should have listened to them.

SIMON STIMSON (*with mounting violence; bitingly*). Yes, now you know. Now you know! That's what it was to be alive. To move about in a cloud of ignorance, to go up and down trampling on the feelings of those . . . of those about you. To spend and waste time as though you had a million years. To be always at the mercy of one self-centered passion or another. Now you know — that's the happy existence you wanted to go back and see. Did you shout to 'em? Did you call to 'em?

EMILY. Yes, I did.

SIMON STIMSON. Now you know them as they are: in ignorance and blindness.

MRS. GIBBS (*spiritedly*). Simon Stimson, that ain't the whole truth, and you know it.

[THE DEAD *have begun to stir.*]

THE DEAD. Lemuel, wind's coming up, seems like. . . . Oh, dear, I keep remembering things tonight. . . . It's right cold for June, ain't it?

MRS. GIBBS. Look what you've done, you and your rebellious spirit stirring us up here. . . . Emily, look at that star. I forget its name.

THE DEAD. I'm getting to know them all, but I don't know their names. My boy, Joel, was a sailor — knew 'em all. He'd set on the porch evenings and tell 'em all by name. Yes, sir, it was wonderful. A star's mighty good company. Yes, yes. Yes, 'tis.

SIMON STIMSON. Here's one of *them* coming.

THE DEAD. That's funny. 'Tain't no time for one of them to be here. Goodness sakes.

EMILY. Mother Gibbs, it's George.

MRS. GIBBS. Sh, dear. You just rest yourself.

EMILY. It's George.

[GEORGE *enters from the left and slowly comes toward them.*]

A MAN FROM AMONG THE DEAD. And my boy, Joel, who knew the stars — he used to say it took millions of years for that speck o' light to git to the earth. Don't seem like a body could believe it, but that's what he used to say — millions of years.

ANOTHER. That's what they say.

[GEORGE *flings himself on* EMILY's *grave.*]

THE DEAD. Goodness! That ain't no way to behave! He ought to be home.

EMILY. Mother Gibbs?

MRS. GIBBS. Yes, Emily?

EMILY. They don't understand much, do they?

MRS. GIBBS. No, dear, not very much.

[*The* STAGE MANAGER *appears at the right, one hand on a dark curtain, which he slowly draws across the scene. In the distance a clock is heard striking the hour very faintly.*]

STAGE MANAGER. Most everybody's asleep in Grover's Corners. There are a few lights on. Shorty Hawkins, down at the depot, has just watched the Albany train go by. And at the livery stable somebody's setting up late and talking. . . . Yes, it's clearing up. There are the stars — doing their old, old crisscross journeys in the sky. Scholars haven't settled the matter yet, but they seem to think there are no living beings up there. They're just chalk . . . or fire. Only this one is straining away, straining away all the time to make something of itself. The strain's so bad that every sixteen hours everybody lies down and gets a rest. (*He winds his watch.*) Hm. . . . Eleven o'clock in Grover's Corners. . . . You get a good rest, too. Good night.

[THE END]

FOR DISCUSSION

1. Now that you have read Act III, what title would you give it? As you think back to the opening of the play, what significance do you see in the case the doctor had been attending?

2. In the description of the setting of Act III, the reader is told the significance of the people sitting in rows of chairs. What is the first explanation a theater audience would get? Why is this representation of a cemetery easier to accept in Act III than it would have been in the opening scene of the play?

3. Discuss the line "Wherever you come near the human race, there's layers and layers of nonsense." What do you think it means? When the Stage Manager says this, he refers to people's concern with their ancestry, but can you apply the remark to other practices and situations?

4. Mrs. Gibbs left $350 to George and Emily when she died. Where had we heard about that sum before? Where did it come from and what other use had been planned for it? George and Emily may have used the money well, but why is there something sad about the mention of it?

5. Discuss Emily's attempt to relive her twelfth birthday. This scene is similar to the opening scenes of the play. Why does it have so much greater impact than the earlier scenes? What does Wilder seem to say about "important" and "unimportant" days? Do you think others among the dead had tried to go back? Who definitely had not? Why?

6. Discuss the meaning of Emily's lines, "Oh, Mamma, just look at me one minute as though you really saw me" and "It goes so fast. We don't have time to look at one another." Consider, too, her question of the Stage Manager: "Do any human beings ever realize life while they live it — every, every minute?" What is his answer? What does the Stage Manager imply about the nature of saints and poets?

REVIEWING THE PLAY

1. Why has Wilder limited the play to simple happenings that occur frequently? Why would extraordinary or melodramatic incidents conflict with the basic theme of the play?

2. In the course of a full-length play, the chief characters usually undergo some change in attitude or thinking. What changes did you notice in Emily and George? in other characters? What caused the changes? Is there any change in the Stage Manager? Why or why not?

3. How does the tone of the dialogue fit the scene and subject of the play? Recall some remarks in the play that you have heard many times.

4. The speech and behavior of the characters is highly realistic. Does this clash with the fantasy of the cemetery scene? Does the realistic dialogue conflict with the lack of realistic scenery and props? Do you think the play is better without props and scenery? Why or why not? Has the unusual form of this play taught you anything about the nature of drama? What?

5. There are many simple sentiments expressed in this play, yet in each act certain lines markedly draw us away from an excessively sentimental tone. Find such lines in each act and discuss how they prevent sentimentality.

YOUR OWN WRITING

Several composition subjects follow. Those that may not be assigned for writing can be treated in discussion.

1. Read carefully the long speech of the Stage Manager in Act I about the contents for a cornerstone. Write a theme on what this speech tells us about the values and purposes of literature in general. Consider also what this passage tells us about Wilder's purpose in writing *Our Town*. Use quotations from the play to support your opinions.

2. Grover's Corners, New Hampshire, is a specific place, and the beginning of this century is a specific time. Time passes and people and places change, but what can this play about *there* and *then* say to you about your life *here* and *now?* In an essay, indicate what meaning the events of *Our Town* can have for the present. Quote from the play to support your opinions.

3. Consider Mrs. Soames's line "My, wasn't life awful — and wonderful." Simon Stimson reacts bitterly to this. Consider his harsh speech after the funeral and Mrs. Gibbs's rebuke to him. Write a theme

about the attitudes of these three characters. Which attitude does Wilder seem to accept? Which of the three statements best expresses the theme of *Our Town?*

THE AUTHOR

THORNTON WILDER (b. 1897) traveled widely in his youth. Born in Madison, Wisconsin, he started his schooling in California and continued it in China, where his father was stationed for eight years in government service. He attended college at Oberlin, Yale, and Princeton. After graduate study in Rome and a few years of teaching, he turned his attention to writing.

With a series of experimental short plays and a remarkable novel, *The Bridge of San Luis Rey*, Wilder established a reputation for originality. This novel won a Pulitzer prize in 1928, and when *Our Town* duplicated the triumph ten years later, Wilder became the first writer to win the coveted honor in both fields. *The Skin of Our Teeth* won Wilder his third Pulitzer prize in 1943 and was revived with great success in 1955, just as his new comedy, *The Matchmaker*, was appearing on Broadway. His other novels are *The Cabala, The Woman of Andros, Heaven's My Destination*, and *The Ides of March*. Wilder returned to serious drama in 1962 with three one-act plays of two projected seven-play cycles based on the seven ages of man and the seven deadly sins.

Our Town ➤

Reproduced on the facing page is a re-creation of Grover's Corners prepared especially for this book by Aldren Watson. The homes of Dr. Gibbs and Editor Webb are shown in the lower left-hand corner of the picture. Can you identify other important buildings and landmarks? The artist is a native of New England. Do you feel that he has captured the flavor of Grover's Corners, New Hampshire?

The drawings that open each act of *Our Town* (pages 365, 380, 392) are by the contemporary stage designer Joseph Weishar.

The photograph on page 405 was taken during the 1959–60 production of *Our Town* by the Circle in the Square Theater, New York.

Our Town: An Afterword

Thornton Wilder has said that in *Our Town* he sought to "find a value above all price for the smallest events in our daily life." Throughout the play we can see how he has directed our attention to precious trifles, from the humor of Howie Newsome's old horse still wanting to leave a quart of milk for a family that has moved away to the piercing sadness of Emily's good-by to Grover's Corners and the world:

> Good-by to clocks ticking . . . and Mamma's sunflowers. And food and coffee. And new-ironed dresses and hot baths . . . and sleeping and waking up.

The play reveals a loving concern for simple, everyday matters, yet "the smallest events in our daily life" are shown against the perspective of nothing less than the universe. This perspective is seen at the end of Act One, when Rebecca tells about the unusual address on the letter received by Jane Crofut. Jane, and the Crofut Farm, are successively located in "the Earth, the Solar System, the Universe, the Mind of God."

The large is measured against the small in many ways throughout the play. Professor Willard, speaking of the geological history of Grover's Corners, says of some sandstone outcroppings, "that's all more recent: two hundred, three hundred million years old." Again, something as remote and impersonal as ancient fossils is brought close to us by being pinpointed in "Silas Peckham's cow pasture." The large perspective of *Our Town* is emphasized in a number of subtle ways. For example, Wilder has remarked: "The recurrent words in this play (few have noticed it) are 'hundreds,' 'thousands,' and 'millions.'"

It is clear that time also interests Wilder in *Our Town*. The play moves about quite freely through that mysterious stream. The three acts treat of three phases of life, and the Stage Manager points our way forward or backward in time as the development of the play requires. In a significant first-act speech by the Stage Manager, we find the future, the past, and the present — in that order — combined in one sentence:

> First automobile's going to come along in about five years — belonged to Banker Cartwright, our richest citizen . . . lives in the big white house up on the hill.

The play's concern with a specific spot on the map grows into an awareness of the entire universe. In the same way, out of the interest in time arises the awareness of eternity. Introducing Act Three, the Stage Manager says:

> Now I'm going to tell you some things you know already. You know'm as well as I do, but you don't take'm out and look at'm very often. I don't care

Our Town: Act II

what they say with their mouths — everybody knows that *something* is eternal . . . everybody knows in their bones that *something* is eternal, and that something has to do with human beings.

The Stage Manager also expresses an interest in beginnings — not only the geological beginnings of the earth but the emotional beginnings of human relationships. He wants to know how *this* came out of *that*. He traces the history of the bond between Emily and George before he lets their wedding proceed.

> Now I have to interrupt again here. You see, we want to know how all this began — this wedding, this plan to spend a lifetime together. I'm awfully interested in how big things like that begin. You know how it is. You're twenty-one or twenty-two, and you make some decisions; then whisssh! you're seventy. You've been a lawyer for fifty years, and that white-haired lady at your side has eaten over fifty thousand meals with you. How do such things begin?

As to the value of life — the fruits of all such beginnings — Wilder offers a series of counterbalanced comments. Some characters lean more toward one point of view than the other, but it is clear which one *Our Town* rests on. In the graveyard scene the bitter Simon Stimson, whose sorrows have often been mentioned, sums up one point of view:

> That's what it was to be alive. To move about in a cloud of ignorance . . . To spend and waste time as though you had a million years. To be always at the mercy of one self-centered passion or another.

Mrs. Gibbs rebuffs him:

> Simon Stimson, that ain't the whole truth, and you know it.

Earlier, Mrs. Soames had said:

> My, wasn't life awful — and wonderful.

And Emily ends her good-by speech with,

> Oh, earth, you're too wonderful for anybody to realize you.

Yet Emily's realization of the wonder of earth has come at the end of a shattering experience — the act of returning, against the advice of the others, to watch herself live over a fairly ordinary day. In the course of that day — which Emily can bear for only a few minutes — we understand why "the smallest events in our daily life" have "a value above all price." Emily was warned not to choose an "important" day. The impact of even an unimportant day proved unendurably sharp and piercing. We learn from the Stage Manager's answer to Emily's question that no one ever fully realizes life while he lives it — every minute. Only, "the saints and poets, maybe — they do some."

Drama in the Twentieth Century

It is in this century, and indeed essentially in the years since 1920, that American drama has shown its greatest vigor. The influence of modern American playwrights has been felt on the stages of all the world. There are a number of excellent anthologies available to anyone who is interested in reading American drama. Some of these collections are listed on the next page, along with listings of the works of individual authors.

EUGENE O'NEILL ranks as our greatest dramatist. He experimented boldly with stage techniques, in plays varying from one short act to those requiring four to five hours for performance. Knowledge of O'Neill's work is a foundation for knowledge of modern American drama. THORNTON WILDER, another versatile innovator, has written some excellent plays that vary widely from the manner of *Our Town*.

It is hard to single out a few figures from the long roster of American playwrights. SIDNEY HOWARD and SIDNEY KINGSLEY are chiefly realistic dramatists concerned with social and psychological problems. ROBERT E. SHERWOOD ranged from the subtle characterizations of *The Petrified Forest* to the bolder strokes of *Abe Lincoln in Illinois*. GEORGE S. KAUFMAN and MOSS HART collaborated to give the theater some hilarious comedies. MAXWELL ANDERSON has created a number of impressive verse tragedies. Other important dramatists include PHILIP BARRY, S. N. BEHRMAN, CLIFFORD ODETS, and LILLIAN HELLMAN.

Among the writers of the younger generation, ARTHUR MILLER has gained an important place with his powerful *Death of a Salesman*, a portrait of a man ruined by pinning his faith on shallow values. If MARY CHASE had written no more than the one play, we would always be grateful for the warm and wildly imaginative humor of *Harvey*.

In this survey of modern American drama, we should not overlook that highly popular type of play, the musical. Our twentieth-century theater has seen some great musical plays. JEROME KERN's *Show Boat* was based on the novel of that name by EDNA FERBER. The greatest of American folk operas is *Porgy and Bess*, a colorful story of Charleston, for which DUBOSE HEYWARD wrote the libretto and GEORGE GERSHWIN provided the music. RICHARD RODGERS and LORENZ HART created a series of sparkling musical comedies. Rodgers later collaborated with OSCAR HAMMERSTEIN, JR., on such highly popular shows as *Oklahoma!*, *South Pacific*, and *The King and I*. A later team, ALAN JAY LERNER and FREDERICK LOEWE, gained fame with *My Fair Lady* and *Camelot*. Composer LEONARD BERNSTEIN collaborated with lyricist STEPHEN SONDHEIM to create the widely acclaimed *West Side Story;* earlier, Bernstein had worked with LILLIAN HELLMAN and RICHARD WILBUR on *Candide*.

Although television sometimes seems to neglect its fullest potential, it is a field that offers many opportunities to the dramatic writer. Playwrights such as PADDY CHAYEFSKY, HORTON FOOTE, REGINALD ROSE, ROD SERLING, and TAD MOSEL have made significant contributions to this newest type of drama.

For Further Reading of Drama

COLLECTIONS (OLDER AND MODERN PLAYS)

A   Cerf, Bennett, and V. H. Cartmell, S. R. O. The Most Successful Plays in the History of the American Stage (Doubleday, 1944)

B   Clark, B. H., Favorite American Plays of the 19th Century (Princeton Univ. Press, 1943)

C   Halline, A. G., American Plays (American Book, 1935)

D   Moses, M. J., Representative Plays by American Dramatists, 3 vols. (Dutton, 1925, 1926)

E   Moses, M. J., Representative American Dramas (Little, Brown, 1941)

F   Quinn, A. H., Representative American Plays (Appleton-Century-Crofts, 1953)

COLLECTIONS (MODERN PLAYS ONLY)

G   Cerf, Bennett, and V. H. Cartmell, Sixteen Famous American Plays (Garden City, 1946)

H   Clark, B. H., and W. H. Davenport, Nine Modern American Plays (Appleton-Century-Crofts, 1951)

I   Coe, Kathryn, and W. H. Cordell, Pulitzer Prize Plays, 1918–1934 (Random House, 1940)

J   Cordell, R. A., Representative Modern Plays (Nelson, 1929)

K   Gassner, John, Twenty-five Best Plays of the Modern American Theatre, revised ed. (Crown, 1949)

L   Gassner, John, Best Plays of the Modern American Theatre, second series (Crown, 1947)

M   Hatcher, Harlan H., Modern American Drama, revised ed. (Harcourt, Brace & World, 1949)

N   Nagelberg, M. M., Drama in Our Time (Harcourt, Brace & World, 1948)

O   Sper, Felix, Living American Plays (Globe, 1954)

INDIVIDUAL PLAYS

(Capital letters after the titles refer to collections listed above, in which the plays may be found.)

Anderson, Maxwell, High Tor, I; Winterset, F, M

Barry, Philip, Holiday, E; The Philadelphia Story, L; You and I, C

Connelly, Marc, The Green Pastures, D, G, I

Davis, Owen, Icebound, C, J

Gibson, William, The Miracle Worker (Knopf, 1957)

Glaspell, Susan, Alison's House, J

Green, Paul, In Abraham's Bosom, J

Hart, Moss, and G. S. Kaufman, You Can't Take It with You, O; The Man Who Came to Dinner, G, L

Howard, Sidney, The Late Christopher Bean, O; The Silver Cord, F; with Paul de Kruif, Yellow Jack, N

Kelly, George, The Show-Off, E

Kesselring, Joseph, Arsenic and Old Lace, A, L

Kingsley, Sidney, Dead End, G; Men in White, I; The Patriots, L

Lindsay, Howard, and Russel Crouse, Life with Father, G

MacLeish, Archibald, J.B. (Houghton Mifflin, 1958)

O'Neill, Eugene, Beyond the Horizon, F, I; The Hairy Ape, H, K

Rice, Elmer, The Adding Machine, E; Street Scene, J, I, K

Saroyan, William, The Time of Your Life, G, L, M

Sherwood, Robert, Abe Lincoln in Illinois, H, K, N; The Petrified Forest, G

Thurber, James, and Elliott Nugent, The Male Animal, L

Van Druten, John, I Remember Mama, L

COLLECTIONS OF SHORT PLAYS

Griffith, F. J., and J. Mersand, Modern One-Act Plays (Harcourt, Brace & World, 1950)

Mayorga, Margaret, The Best Short Plays of 1937, etc., series continues annually (Beacon)

COLLECTIONS OF TELEVISION PLAYS

Chayefsky, Paddy, Television Plays (Simon & Schuster, 1955)

Foote, Horton, Harrison, Texas (Harcourt, Brace & World, 1956)

Mosel, Tad, Other People's Houses (Simon & Schuster, 1956)

Rose, Reginald, Six Television Plays (Simon & Schuster, 1956)

Serling, Rod, Patterns; Four TV Plays (Simon & Schuster, 1957)

Part 2

The Growth
of American
Literature

THE COLONIAL TIME

THE MAKING OF A NATION

THE AMERICAN IMAGINATION AWAKENS

NEW ENGLAND'S GOLDEN YEARS

GROWTH AND CONFLICT

TIME OF CHANGE

The Colonial Time

A T THE BEGINNING of the seventeenth century, the vast continental area that was to become the United States had been probed only slightly by English and European explorers. The great hoards of gold and the elaborate civilizations that had been found earlier in the tragic conquests of Mexico and Peru were not to be discovered on this continent. The treasures of the north were not immense quantities of gold and silver. They were rather the lasting wealth of abundant good lands, to be won more by drudgery than by arms. Valor was needed, but not solely of a military brand; endurance was needed, but of hardships other than war. Men had to come to terms with the New World--with the land, the rivers and lakes, the forests and prairies and mountains, and with the Indians. Everything was new and strange, and men had to adjust to drastic changes in their way of life.

Early Narratives and Chronicles

The settling of this continent north of Florida occurred surprisingly late. Almost a hundred years earlier the Caribbean Islands, Mexico, and other parts of Central and South America had been occupied by the Spanish. At last, early in the seventeenth century, the English settlements in Virginia and Massachusetts began the main stream of what we recognize as our own national history. The first writings that we call American were the narratives and journals of these settlements.

From the beginning the important events of American history have been recorded in literature. Few nations have enjoyed such good fortune. The kinds of records that for older nations were lost in dim ages of prehistory, or exist only in myth and legend, are in our own history fully preserved on the printed page and in authentic drawings and paintings.

The explanation of this good fortune is simple. Our own country is the first great nation to come into being after the invention of the printing press. Equally important is the fact that the discovery and exploration of America were part of that larger discovery and exploration that we call the Renaissance, the rebirth of learning in Europe. The nations that contributed most to the opening up of the New World were affected by the rebirth of learning, and the men who made America — explorers, warriors, and settlers — not only had something to say but were able to say it well and give it permanence in print.

It was a stirring, hazardous life these first Americans led, and our earliest writers pictured it so well that later Americans can still share the adventure. The early chronicles record with admirable directness all manner of hardships and perils on sea and land. Starvation, storm, cold, and disease mowed down many. We see in these accounts the precarious relations with the Indians. Colorful Indian figures such as Squanto and Massasoit stalk through the pages. Bloody war, savage on both sides, breaks out with the Pequot tribe. Miles Standish, of later romantic legend, leads Pilgrim fighting men against the Indians. The chronicles capture happier moments, too, such as the celebration of the first Thanksgiving.

THE FIRST AMERICAN WRITER

Less than a year after the planting of the Jamestown colony in 1607, there were dissatisfactions among the members. One of them returned to England with complaints. By the next vessel Captain John Smith, one of the leaders of the colony, sent a letter to the Virginia Company in London, defending the handling of the settlement and proclaiming the merits of the new land. The greater part of this letter was published in 1608, under the title *A True Relation of Such Occurrences and Accidents of Note as Hath Happened in Virginia Since the First Planting of That Colony.*

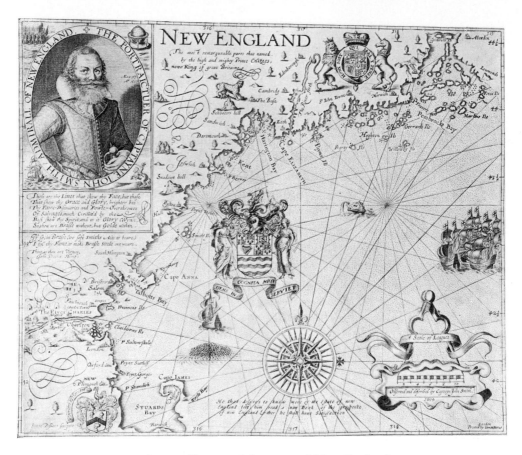

John Smith's map of the coast of New England.

Thus Captain John Smith became our first American writer. The little book was read eagerly by many and made a reputation for its author. Smith enjoyed this taste of fame and determined to maintain his reputation. His next book was *A Map of Virginia; with a Description of the Country* (1612). Like many similar accounts of the period, the book was a guide to the country and an invitation to the bold spirits needed to enlarge and strengthen the English plantations in the new land.

Smith published eight works in all, some of them dealing with New England, the coast of which he explored and mapped after his fortune faded with the Virginia Company. He sought a post as guide to the Pilgrims but, though they made use of his publications and maps, they did not want the man. He had too much color and flamboyance for sober Puritan tastes; moreover, he was suspected of having less than complete regard for the exact truth. His *General History of Virginia* (1624) contains his most famous tale of how the Indian princess Pocahontas saved him from the wrath of her father Powhatan by laying her head upon Smith's when the Indians were about "to beat out his brains." This pleasing story, alas, is not credited by anyone. While the rescue was probably not genuine, the girl was, although even her name is wrongly reported (Matoaka was her real name). Nevertheless, through Smith's book, she has remained "Pocahontas" in legend and history. She later married John Rolfe, one of the Jamestown settlers, and went back to England with him.

Captain Smith may not have been a modest man, but it is clear that he contributed more to the survival of the Jamestown colony than did anyone else. He tirelessly explored the rivers and bays around the Chesapeake region. And he saw from the beginning what was eventually to be a basic principle of American history, the need of "workers"

A portrait of Pocahontas as she appeared while living in England.

instead of "gentlemen" for the tough job of planting colonies and pushing the frontiers westward. He wrote to London:

> When you send again, I entreat you, rather send but thirty carpenters, husbandmen, gardeners, fishermen, blacksmiths, masons, and diggers up of trees' roots, well provided, than a thousand such as we have . . .

Early New England Literature

Although the literature of Virginia and the South displayed little variety in the colonial time, New England had from the beginning a literature of ideas: theological, moral, historical, political. The Puritans had come to New England for the sake of religious freedom, while Virginia had been planted mainly as a commercial venture. Southern society was almost completely rural, interested primarily in the development of a tobacco economy. Because of the lack of schools in the South, well-to-do planters sent their sons to England to be educated, or relied on tutors or the local rector of the Anglican church. With some exceptions, to the Virginians literature was largely a leisure pastime, while with New Englanders it was usually a high and serious undertaking.

The Puritans in New England embraced hardships (though not all could survive them), together with the discipline of a harsh church. The first intention in Massachusetts was to found a theocracy — a society in which God would govern through the church. The church thus became the supreme political body. The ideal may have been inspiring, but because of the imperfections of the human material, in practice theocracy often led to injustice and intolerance.

Whatever the faults of these Puritans, they still had toughness, purpose, and character. They grappled strongly with the challenges they set themselves. This is the reason for the boast by William Stoughton, one of the later Puritans, that "God hath sifted a nation that he might send choice grain into this wilderness." Choice grain is used as seed grain, and Stoughton's claim was proved true in what developed from this original planting.

WILLIAM BRADFORD AND JOHN WINTHROP

William Bradford, first governor of Plymouth, and John Winthrop, who held the same post at Boston, were men superior to even the remarkable qualities that distinguished many of their associates. Each has left us a priceless gift: Bradford, *The History of Plymouth Plantation;* Winthrop, *The History of New England.* Though these works were known and used in manuscript by other writers, Winthrop's text was not printed in full until 1826, and Bradford's not until 1856.

Bradford wrote much of his *History* in the midst of the events he describes. He started it in 1630, ten years after the Mayflower voyage, beginning his story with an account of the small group of Puritans who migrated from England to Amsterdam and then to the New World. The simplicity and earnestness of the book, with its direct reporting, make it readable and moving. In addition to the *History,* Bradford left us a wealth of letters, other prose writings about the colony, and even a narrative poem.

Shortly before his death in 1657, he wrote a summation of his life of faith in simple verses, beginning:

> From my years young in days of youth,
> God did make known to me His Truth,
> And call'd me from my native place
> For to enjoy the Means of Grace.
> In wilderness He did me guide,
> And in strange lands for me provide.

In this same poem he identifies himself with the name by which the whole band has been remembered:

> As Pilgrim passed I to and fro.

He was perhaps the greatest of them. The New England colonies mourned him, in words written later by Cotton Mather, as "a common blessing and father to them all."

John Winthrop was a man of the same caliber. In England he had been a lawyer and lord of a manor. He was elected governor of the Massachusetts Bay group before their sailing, and in spite of disputes within the settlement, he was its foremost leader throughout the remaining nineteen years of his life. During these years he was either the governor or deputy-governor of the colony.

John Winthrop began to keep a journal on the Bay Colonists' voyage to Massachusetts aboard the ship *Arbella* in 1630. He maintained this practice for the rest of his life. Parts of his *Journal* were first published in 1790. The complete work was at last printed in 1826 under the title *The History of New England*. This name is less appropriate than "journal," for the work has not the scope and order of a history. Other Winthrop papers exist, but the *Journal* remains his chief work. Like Bradford's book, Winthrop's is notable for its candid simplicity and honesty, though the Plymouth governor is the better writer. Each book is the most valuable kind of historical source — an account of events by a man who has been a major figure of his time. Both accounts were written,

John Winthrop

not from literary ambition, but from a sense of the need to record important events in permanent form. Yet, through a direct and vigorous prose style, each account attained literary excellence. *[handwritten annotations]*

[handwritten annotations]

OTHER INTERESTING CHRONICLES

There were other chronicles, earlier in publication. *Mourt's Relation* (1622) is the first published book about the Plymouth venture. George Morton, the author, published it under the name of "G. Mourt." It contains the story of the Mayflower voyage and includes the substance of the Plymouth compact, of which Bradford gives the complete text. Most opinion holds that the little book was pieced together from journal entries of Bradford and Edward Winslow.

Winslow, slightly younger than Bradford, was aboard the *Mayflower* and also served the colony as governor three times. In 1624 he returned to England on colony business and there published *Good News from New England*. It was a progress report and recruitment propaganda, somewhat similar in purpose to John Smith's *True Relation*. For all its valiantly cheerful title, the book warns against "too great lightness" in taking up the life of a colonist.

Of quite a different order is the book of Edward Johnson, by trade a shipwright and also a captain of militia. In 1654 he published it anonymously under the not very suitable title *A History of New England*. Its quality and spirit are much better captured in the subtitle by which the book became generally known: *Wonder-Working Providence of Sion's Saviour in New England*. In enthusiastic prose, intermixed with verse, with true Puritan vision Johnson sees all the events in New England as the design and direct work of God. To him the settlers were Christian soldiers crusading against the heathen in strange lands. Unlike most of the earlier writers, Johnson was an ordinary citizen and not a leader in colonial affairs. The chief contribution of his book is its detailed picture of daily life and events in colonial Massachusetts.

THE FIRST AMERICAN PUBLICATION

Most of these early American chronicles were published originally in England. The first printing of any kind in the colonies was done on Stephen Daye's press in 1639, and he produced the earliest book to be made on these shores, the famous *Bay Psalm Book*, a year later in 1640.

THE IMPORTANCE OF THE EARLY CHRONICLES

The value of the early chronicles is manifold. In addition to preserving a vivid picture of the life of the first settlers, they record events of lasting importance and reveal the conflicts that beset the struggling settlements.

Once the first settlements were lastingly rooted in the land, new kinds of literary concerns followed the early chronicles. Yet these first histories, journals, and records, and the men who made them, hold permanent places of honor in our literature.

Puritan Thought

We have used the word "Puritan" frequently. Now we must move from their outward actions of settling a land to consider the beliefs and ideas that inspired them and greatly influenced our history. To do this, we shall have to ask just what "Puritan" means.

As the word itself hints, Puritans wanted to make *pure* their religious beliefs and practices. The Puritan was a "would-be purifier." The word was coined by the opponents of the group and was applied to them in scorn; it was intended to ridicule them as persons who thought themselves holier or better than others. The term is used in this sense in one of Shakespeare's plays. The undaunted Puritans claimed the name for themselves, adopting it as a badge of honor.

The Puritans wished to restore simplicity to church services and the authority of the Bible to theology. They felt that the Church of England was too close to the Church of Rome in doctrine, form of worship, and organization of authority. Another point of controversy was that the Church of England was the established church, that is, the official church of the state, and the most extreme Puritans, among them the Plymouth Plantation group, felt that the influences of politics and the court had led to corruption within the church. These Puritans were "Separatists" — that is, they wished to break free from the Church of England. The Massachusetts Bay group, on the other hand, wished to reform the church but remain a part of it. Yet once they were settled in this land, they too moved gradually toward complete separation.

Puritans included people from the humblest to the loftiest ranks of English society, both educated and uneducated, poor and rich. Their faults were those common to persons who hold extreme opinions. The Puritans looked upon themselves as a chosen people, and it followed logically that anyone who challenged their way of life was opposing God's will and was not to be accepted. They were thus zealous in defense of their own beliefs but often intolerant of the beliefs of others. They drove out of their settlements all whose opinions seemed dangerous to them, and history has criticized them for their actions. Yet in the persecution of what they considered error, the Puritans were no worse than many other movements in history — religious, political, or scientific.

Puritan opposition to pleasure and the arts has sometimes been exaggerated, but it is true that their lives were disciplined and hard. Puritans tended to suspect joy and laughter as symptoms of sin: a Puritan woman was once threatened with banishment for smiling in church. The Puritans made laws about private morality as well as public behavior. Yet this very attempt to suppress all sin seemed to produce outbreaks of misbehavior, as if in reaction to the strictness.

Puritan religious teaching tended to emphasize the image of a wrathful God and to forget His mercy. From this harsh side of Puritan thought comes the picture of what Nathaniel Hawthorne called the "stern and black-browed Puritans." This was indeed one of their aspects, but only one. Governor Bradford and Governor Winthrop were men of character, courage, and noble spirit. We must not lose sight of what Roger Williams called the Puritans' "holy affections, and upright aims, and great self-denial, to enjoy more of God in this wilderness . . ."

The best way to learn more of the colonial Puritan mind is to meet two important figures, John Cotton and the man just quoted, Roger Williams.

Two Puritan Leaders

JOHN COTTON

The first major intellectual spokesman of the Massachusetts Bay Colony was John Cotton, sometimes called "the Patriarch of New England." From the time he came to Boston in 1633, he was the "teacher" (that is, spiritual leader) of the community, and its guiding influence toward the ideal of theocracy (a state ruled by the church). Despite his strong views and forceful manner in debate, he was a gentleman of gracious courtesy. He was also the finest scholar who so far had come to this land. Cotton Mather, his grandson, wrote of him: "Twelve hours in a day he commonly studied, and would call that a *scholar's* day."

John Cotton wrote several books of hard-hitting Puritan argument, but his primary influence was through the pulpit. The people of Massachusetts delighted to hear him preach, and some of his listeners were convinced that he could make no mistake, for "God would not suffer Mr. Cotton to err." Yet err he did, great and good man that he was. Practical circumstances allied him with much less noble spirits than his own in suppressing differences of opinion. In a dispute over whether "errors" in religious opinion could be tolerated, he found himself acting against two of his fellow Puritans, Mistress Anne Hutchinson and Roger Williams, for both of whom he felt personal affection and regard.

Through John Cotton we can see an important characteristic of the Puritans. They were much more concerned with authority than with democracy. Noting the possible dangers of rule by a king, Cotton once wrote:

> Owing therefore to the vices or defects of men, it is safer and more tolerable when several bear rule, that they may thus mutually assist, instruct, and admonish each other, and should any be disposed to go too far, the others are censors and masters to curb his excess.

Nevertheless, there was no question in his mind of going beyond the aristocratic rule of qualified men.

> Democracy I do not conceive that ever God did ordain as a fit government either for church or commonwealth. If the people be governors, who shall be governed?

Whatever faults and limitations he may have had, John Cotton's firmness and devotion to his beliefs always demanded respect. Cotton was partly responsible for Roger Williams' exile from Massachusetts; yet nineteen years after John Cotton's death, Williams wrote of "the love and honor which I have always shown (in speech and writing) to that excellently learned and holy man . . ."

ROGER WILLIAMS

Roger Williams had been educated in law at Cambridge University. Instead of following that calling, he entered the church and was caught up in the Puritan tide. When he came to the Massachusetts colonies in 1631, he was more democratic in his view of church government than the leaders of any of the settlements. As a result he was soon in disagreement with them, which eventually led to his exile to what is now Rhode Island.

With Williams begins the history of religious toleration in America, and with him, too, the history of the separation of church and state. In him we have a balance to John Cotton. Williams was distinctly a Puritan. What he regarded as the incorrect beliefs of the Quakers who later came to Rhode Island shocked him deeply. Nevertheless, he would not persecute them as did the leaders of Massachusetts. Williams' toleration did not stem from a lack of religious convictions. Instead, it sprang from the idea that simply to be virtuous in conduct and devout in belief did not give anyone the right to force belief on others. He felt that oaths in the name of God should not be administered to unbelievers because such an oath is a form of religious affirmation. He also felt that no political order or church system could identify itself directly with God.

On all of these issues, Roger Williams clashed with the prevailing ideas of the Bay Colony. The Puritan leaders, including John Cotton, saw no solution but his banishment. Partly on the friendly advice of Governor Winthrop, Williams made his way to the shores of Narragansett Bay in midwinter, "sorely tried for fourteen weeks in a bitter winter season, not knowing what bread nor bed did mean." He founded a community which he called Providence, because of "God's merciful providence to him in his distress."

Like John Eliot, who translated the Bible into the Indian tongue, Roger Williams was interested in the Indian language. One of his works was *A Key into the Language of America; Or, an Help to the Language of the Natives in That Part of America Called New England*. In the book we can find such exchanges as:

Chénock wonck cuppeeyeâumen?   *When will you be here again?*
Nétop tattà.   *My friend, I cannot tell.*

Williams is as important for his political views as for his religious beliefs. One of his statements shows him to have been far closer to the ideas that would eventually prevail in this land than to the Puritan view of government expressed by John Cotton. Williams wrote:

> . . . the sovereign, original, and foundation of civil power lies in the people . . . It is evident that such governments as are by them erected and established have no more power, nor for any longer time, than the civil power or people consenting and agreeing shall entrust them with.

This earnest "seeker," as he called himself, meaning one who is never content to rest on his present wisdom, was one of our great men. Perhaps he wrote no single thought sharper or more typical of his ideals than "Persecution of men's bodies seldom or never does these men's souls good."

TWO PURITAN POETS

Many Puritans wrote verse, sometimes using that form for their narratives of actual events. Most Puritan verse was decidedly plodding, but the work of two writers, Anne Bradstreet and Edward Taylor, rose to the level of real poetry.

Anne Dudley Bradstreet is one of the most interesting of the early poets. Both her father and her husband were governors of Massachusetts, and all came here on the first voyage of the *Arbella* in June 1630. Anne Bradstreet's extensive literary production was managed along with the task of being a wilderness wife and the mother of eight children. We could hardly say that she wrote in her leisure time.

Her first published work appeared in London. It was taken there without her knowledge by her brother-in-law, who put the work into the hands of a publisher. She was perhaps too shy to offer it herself. The title of this collection of poems complimented her, in classical allusion, as *The Tenth Muse Lately Sprung Up in America*. (In Greek mythology the Muses were nine daughters of Zeus. Each was the patron of a particular art such as poetry, dance, music, etc.) Some of Anne Bradstreet's poetic ventures were overambitious, but she wrote well when she dealt with the simple events of her daily life. The note of piety, gently sounded, was in her work:

I heard the merry grasshopper then sing,
The black-clad cricket bear a second part;
They kept one tune and played on the same string
Seeming to glory in their little art.
Small creatures abject thus their voices raise,
And in their kind resound their Maker's praise,
Whilst I, as mute, can warble forth no higher lays?

The best of the Puritan poets was Edward Taylor, who came from England as a young man and attended Harvard, later entering the major profession of the time, the ministry. He is the most accomplished poetic craftsman of our early years. His work followed the style and forms of the leading English poets of the mid-seventeenth century, and although Taylor was not the match of the best of these, he showed an authentic poetic ability. Most of Taylor's work treated religious themes, with many poems based directly on the Psalms. Some striking images appear in his work, as when, in a passage about the earth, he speaks of the sky and clouds and employs a surprising figure of speech:

Who spread its canopy? Or curtains spun?
Who in this bowling alley bowled the sun?

Taylor did not publish any of his work. His poems were found in manuscript in 1937, more than two hundred years after his death. This discovery brought Taylor to immediate prominence in our colonial literary history, and enriched our poetic heritage. A complete edition of Taylor's poems appeared in 1960.

A PURITAN SATIRIST

Nathaniel Ward was an admirer of Anne Bradstreet's poetry. He wrote verses of praise to stand as prefaces to some of her poems. Though he came here at the age of fifty-six and remained only thirteen years before returning to England, Ward left his mark on the colonies with *The Body of Liberties*, the first code of laws for Massachusetts. Puritan though he was, the style of his book *The Simple Cobbler of Aggawam* had a touch of the hearty Elizabethan literature. The work, published on his return to England in 1647, was a somewhat violent satire against toleration of the sort that Roger Williams practiced.

Later Prominent Puritans

THE MATHERS OF MASSACHUSETTS

The Mather family left a strong stamp upon colonial New England and quite a body of written works — though these are now read chiefly by scholars. Richard Mather, a Puritan minister, came to the colony in 1635. He was one of the authors of the *Bay Psalm Book*. Today he is primarily remembered as the founder of a remarkable family. His son Increase (a good Puritan name) and his grandson Cotton (John Cotton being his maternal grandfather) represent something most

significant: the first and second generations of learned men born and educated
in this land. Almost everyone else whom
we have met thus far had been born
and schooled in England.

Increase Mather was a graduate of
Harvard College, which had been
founded in 1636, only six years after the
Massachusetts Bay Colony was begun.
In time Increase served as the president
of Harvard, and he did much to advance scientific learning in and out of
the college. Unfortunately, along with
a sense of the best scientific thinking,
both he and his son Cotton Mather had
a touch of the worst superstitions of
their age.

Increase Mather.

In 1692, in Salem, a fearful outbreak of hysteria occurred over supposed cases
of witchcraft. Before a year had run its course, there had been nineteen hangings
of accused witches, and one man had been pressed to death with stones. (Though
the term "witch burning" is often heard, no one was burned in Salem.) More than
a hundred other accused witches were put in prison, and many were tortured to
force confessions. When the madness had finally subsided, some prominent people repented and repudiated their part in the proceeding. It must be said in justice
that this was no unique fault of New England, or of Puritanism. It was a sign of a
barbarous superstition that was still widespread. Equal atrocities were dreadfully
common in England and all over Europe, where many so-called witches were
burned. The Mathers had helped to inflame the dread of witchcraft, even though
they eventually criticized, and recoiled from, the gross injustices in the conduct
of the Salem trials.

Yet this father and son understood and admired the two greatest English
scientists of the time, Isaac Newton and Robert Boyle. The Mathers also held
advanced views on the disputed subject of inoculation for smallpox, a fearful
killer in colonial times. Cotton Mather so courageously advocated inoculation, in
opposition to ignorant, frightened public opinion, that a crude bomb, fortunately
a dud, was thrown into his window with the message: "Cotton Mather — you
dog — I'll inoculate you with this — with a pox to you."

Cotton Mather is not an appealing figure. He was often vain and violent in dealing with others. He wanted to be president of Harvard, but failed, and the disappointment embittered him. The course of events had changed, and Mather's influence had declined. Yet his major work, among an enormous total output, still
has value. The *Magnalia Christi Americana: or, The Ecclesiastical History of New
England,* is rich with information on its time.

Contemporary with the Mathers was Judge Samuel Sewall. He left a variety of writings, but by far the most important was his *Diary* of forty-seven years. It is a candid, detailed reflection of events and people in Boston between 1674 and 1729, except for an eight-year gap. Sewall has much to say about the Mathers, including a surprisingly out-of-character event: "Dr. C. Mather, fishing in Spy Pond, falls into the water, the boat being ticklish, but receives no hurt." Sewall was also a close friend of the poet Edward Taylor. More than a hundred years after Sewall's death, another poet, John Greenleaf Whittier, described him as

> Samuel Sewall, the good and wise.
> His face with lines of firmness wrought,
> He wears the look of a man unbought . . .

JONATHAN EDWARDS

Jonathan Edwards was one of the finest intellects of the entire colonial period. He was born in Connecticut in the early years of the eighteenth century — an era that was to be dramatically laden with the destiny of this nation. He began writing at ten ("On the Nature of the Soul"), and at twelve wrote "The Habits of Spiders." You will read on pages 435–36 a portion of his famous sermon "Sinners in the Hands of an Angry God." A reference in the sermon to a spider dangled over a flame suggests a possible source in Edward's boyhood essay.

His chief work, *The Freedom of the Will*, was the finest piece of philosophical writing that had yet appeared in this country. In this book, and in other writings, Edwards anticipated some of the important developments in English and European philosophy.

Edwards fell into disagreement with the people of the large church he held in Northampton, Massachusetts, and they dismissed him. He then went to what was relative wilderness in the Housatonic Valley of Connecticut, at Stockbridge, as a missionary to the Indians. It was not his natural field of labor. The happiest event of his life drew him away from there to be president of the college that was to become Princeton University. Sadly, Edwards died only a few months after the appointment.

THE END OF THE PURITAN ERA

The day of the Puritan passed. Jonathan Edwards' career is a good example of the changing temper of the times. Had this remarkable Puritan been born fifty years earlier, he would probably have become a power throughout the colonies. As it was, he never wielded significant influence. People of all levels of birth, of all manner of beliefs and opinions, were coming to the land. Even with the slow travel of the day, they were mingling and observing — and changing rapidly. The Puritan way could not prevail forever, even in its original strongholds. The emphasis in our literature shifted away from the disputes of the theocrats.

Yet Puritan prose was a manly prose, vigorous and purposeful, confident and filled with faith, firm to assert conviction, and eloquent in its statements. One of the early colonial travelers was a Maryland physician, Dr. Alexander Hamilton (no kin to the later statesman of that name). He heard a sermon in Boston, and wrote of its "solid sense, strong connected reasoning, and good language." This sums up the best qualities of Puritan letters. They are qualities that are worth preserving.

Colonial Travelers

Early voices quite unlike the Puritans' in tone were those of certain travelers and observers who were moved to set down, generally without intention of publication, what they had experienced and seen. The first of these travelers was a spirited gentlewoman, Sarah Kemble Knight, often called simply Madam Knight. She was a Boston schoolteacher who is said to have taught the young Benjamin Franklin. Be that as it may, a year or so before that remarkable man was born, Madam Knight, on family business, journeyed on horseback from Boston to New York and back. She followed the coastline in the dead of winter, 1704–05, and kept a lively journal of the trip.

In Virginia William Byrd was a planter of varied abilities and interests. On his lands and by his initiative, the city of Richmond was established. In 1728 Byrd carried out the task of surveying the boundary between Virginia and North Caro-

Colonists about to embark for America: from an engraving done in 1732.

lina. He kept a journal of this enterprise, which was published more than a hundred years later as *The History of the Dividing Line.* This and Byrd's other writings, all set down for his own pleasure, regard life with an amused and worldly relaxation much removed from the Puritan outlook.

The same relaxed tone that characterizes William Byrd's writings appears in the *Itinerarium,* the journal of the Annapolis physician Dr. Alexander Hamilton, mentioned earlier. In 1744 Dr. Hamilton journeyed from Annapolis to New Hampshire for his health. The trip was leisurely. Dr. Hamilton traveled slowly through Maryland, Pennsylvania, New York, and Massachusetts, buying books, seeing sights, and hearing sermons. His journal is an engaging chronicle, revealing a man of taste and culture.

We could class as travelers the Philadelphia Quakers John Bartram and his son William. They were the first of a long line of distinguished American naturalists. Both father and son published journals containing extensive descriptions of plant and animal life in the New World. Either together or separately, the Bartrams covered an extraordinary amount of territory. The title of one of John's journals speaks of travels through much of the eastern part of the country, while William's most famous book is called *Travels Through North and South Carolina, Georgia, East and West Florida* . . . ; its long title continuing with a list of the Indian tribes in those regions.

In many ways the greatest of the colonial travelers was another Quaker, the gentle John Woolman. While still in his twenties, he began a career as a traveling preacher. For the rest of his life, with few exceptions he made at least one long trip a year, sometimes being away from his home for as much as four months. His *Journal,* first published in 1774, is regarded as one of the great humane documents in our literature. The *Journal* is the first eloquent American witness against slavery, which in Woolman's time was equally current in both the North and the South, with the trade centered in the North. Woolman sounded a remarkably prophetic note:

> . . . while our buying captives taken in war animates those parties to push on the war and increase desolation amongst them, we too are putting upon our shoulders a burdensome stone, a burden that will grow heavier and heavier till times change in a way disagreeable to us.

The poet John Greenleaf Whittier said that Woolman's writings had a "sweetness as of violets," and the English writer Charles Lamb recommended that people "get the writings of John Woolman by heart." Perhaps the purest example of Woolman's gentle spirit is a passage from one of his essays:

> There is a principle, which is pure, placed in the human mind, which in different places and ages hath had different names. It is, however, pure and proceeds from God. It is deep, and inward, confined to no forms of religion, nor excluded from any, where the heart stands in perfect sincerity. In whomsoever this takes root, and grows, they become brethren.

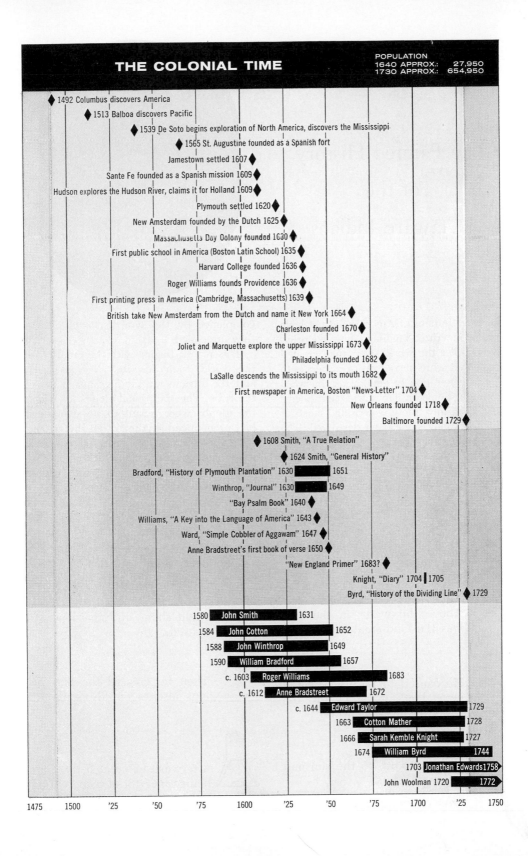

The Painted History
of the
Delaware Indians

The early Indians of America did not have a phonetic written language, but, like primitive peoples the world over, they created poems that were passed on from person to person, generation to generation, by word of mouth. Some Indian stories and poems were cast into picture writing, most of which has long since been destroyed. The most ambitious "literary" product of the Indians of the United States is the *Walam Olum* of the Delaware Indians. The text, apparently taken down by dictation, is ac-companied by 184 symbols, or glyphs, as they are called.

This record begins with the creation of the world, then describes a great flood, and the various wanderings and wars of the tribe. The traditional chants, of which the glyphs were meant to be reminders, had pronounced rhythm, often rhyme, and were undoubtedly accompanied by primitive dances. These qualities, together with its imaginative ideas, justify calling the painted history a form of poetry.

On the Creation

 At first sea water covered all the land.

 Above the water in the mist was the God-creator.

 He caused to be much water, great land, many clouds, the wide sky.

 He caused to be the sun and moon and stars.

 Winds blew hard, clearing the deep water and making it run off.

 Light shone and an island appeared.

 Then he created the first beings, also angels, also souls.

 Afterward he created the man-being, ancestor of man.

He gave to man the first mother of men.

 Fishes he gave to man, and turtles and beasts and birds.

 But an evil spirit created bad beings, black snakes, and monsters.

 At first all beings were friends together.

 But then, while secretly on earth, the snake-god led men to worship evil.

 Wickedness, crime, unhappiness, thus came to the world.

FOR DISCUSSION

1. The glyphs are supposed to have some connection with a gesture language used by the Indians. Which of those given here strongly suggest a gesture to be made with hands or arms? Which symbols best suggest the beings or things referred to in the text?

2. How many points of similarity can you find between the Indian account of the creation and the account in the Bible?

SPECIAL REPORT

Let one student read the story of the creation in Genesis, another that in Greek mythology, another that in Norse mythology, and report to the class the points of likeness and difference to the painted history.

The earliest settlements in America and the locations of the major Indian tribes. ▶

WILLIAM
BRADFORD
1590–1657

. The Landing at Plymouth

A man of high character, firm, discreet, tactful, wise, and fair, Bradford was the natural leader of Plymouth Colony. With the exception of five years when he begged to be relieved, he was annually elected governor by the colonists. Something of that same vote of confidence can be given his reliable *History of Plymouth Plantation*, from which the following account of the landing of the Pilgrims at Plymouth in 1620 is taken.

September 6. Those troubles [caused by the unseaworthiness of their ships] being blown over, and now all being compact together in one ship, they put to sea again with a prosperous wind, which continued divers [1] days together, which was some encouragement unto them; yet, according to the usual manner, many were afflicted with seasickness. And I may not omit here a special work of God's providence. There was a proud and very profane young man, one of the seamen, of a lusty, able body, which made him the more haughty; he would always be contemning the poor people in their sickness and cursing them daily with griev-

ous execrations,[2] and did not let [3] to tell them that he hoped to help to cast half of them overboard before they came to their journey's end, and to make merry with what they had; and if he were by any gently reproved, he would curse and swear most bitterly. But it pleased God, before they came half seas over, to smite this young man with a grievous disease, of which he died in a desperate manner, and so was himself the first that was thrown overboard. Thus his curses light on his own head, and it was an astonishment to all his fellows for they noted it to be the just hand of God upon him.

After they had enjoyed fair winds and weather for a season, they were encountered many times with cross winds and met with many fierce storms with which the ship was shroudly [4] shaken, and her upper works made very leaky; and one of the main beams in the midships was bowed and cracked, which put them in some fear that the ship could not be able to perform the

[1] **divers** (dī′vẽrz): several.

[2] **execrations** (ĕksê·krā′shŭnz): curses.
[3] **let:** omit, leave undone.
[4] **shroudly:** so that great strain was put upon the shrouds (ropes giving lateral support to the masts).

voyage. So some of the chief of the company, perceiving the mariners to fear the sufficiency of the ship, as appeared by their mutterings, they entered into serious consultation with the master and other officers of the ship, to consider in time of the danger, and rather to return than to cast themselves into a desperate and inevitable peril. And truly there was great distraction and difference of opinion amongst the mariners themselves; fain would they do what could be done for their wages' sake (being now near half the seas over) and on the other hand they were loath to hazard their lives too desperately. But in examining of all opinions, the master and others affirmed they knew the ship to be strong and firm under water; and for the buckling of the main beam, there was a great iron screw the passengers brought out of Holland, which would raise the beam into its place; the which being done, the carpenter and master affirmed that with a post put under it, set firm in the lower deck and otherways bound, he would make it sufficient. And as for the decks and upper works, they would caulk them as well as they could, and though with the working of the ship they would not long keep staunch, yet there would otherwise be no great danger, if they did not overpress her with sails. So they committed themselves to the will of God and resolved to proceed.

In sundry of these storms the winds were so fierce and the seas so high, as they could not bear a knot of sail, but were forced to hull for divers days together. And in one of them, as they thus lay at hull in a mighty storm, a lusty young man called John Howland, coming upon some occasions above the gratings, was, with a roll of the ship, thrown into sea; but it pleased God that he caught hold of the topsail halyards which hung overboard and ran out at length. Yet he held his hold (though he was sundry fathoms under water) till he was hauled up by the same rope to the brim of the water, and then with a boat hook and other means got into the ship again and his life saved. And though he was something ill with it, yet he lived many years after and became a profitable member both in church and commonwealth. In all this voyage there died but one of the passengers, which was William Butten, a youth, servant to Samuel Fuller, when they drew near the coast.

But to omit other things (that I may be brief), after long beating at sea they fell with that land which is called Cape Cod; the which being made and certainly known to be it, they were not a little joyful. After some deliberation had amongst themselves and with the master of the ship, they tacked about and resolved to stand for the southward (the wind and weather being fair) to find some place about Hudson's River for their habitation. But after they had sailed that course about half the day, they were amongst dangerous shoals and roaring breakers, and they were so far entangled therewith as they conceived themselves in great danger; and the wind shrinking upon them withal they resolved to bear up again for the Cape and thought themselves happy to get out of those dangers before night overtook them, as by God's good providence they did. And the next day they got into the Cape Harbor where they rid in safety. . . .

Being thus arrived in a good harbor, and brought safe to land, they fell upon their knees and blessed the God of heaven who had brought them over the vast and furious ocean, and delivered them from all the perils and miseries thereof, again to set their feet on the firm and stable earth, their proper element. And no marvel if they were thus joyful, seeing wise Seneca [1] was so affected with sailing a few miles on the coast of his own Italy, as he affirmed, that he had rather remain twenty years

[1] Seneca: a Roman statesman (4? B.C.– A.D. 65).

on his way by land than pass by sea to any place in a short time, so tedious and dreadful was the same unto him.

But here I cannot but stay and make a pause, and stand half amazed at this poor people's present condition; and so I think will the reader, too, when he well considers the same. Being thus past the vast ocean, and a sea of troubles before in their preparation (as may be remembered by that which went before), they had now no friends to welcome them nor inns to entertain or refresh their weather-beaten bodies; no houses or much less towns to repair to, to seek for succor. It is recorded in Scripture as a mercy to the Apostle and his shipwrecked company, that the barbarians showed them no small kindness in refreshing them, but these savage barbarians, when they met with them (as after will appear) were readier to fill their sides full of arrows than otherwise. And for the season it was winter, and they that know the winters of that country know them to be sharp and violent, and subject to cruel and fierce storms, dangerous to travel to known places, much more to search an unknown coast. Besides, what could they see but a hideous and desolate wilderness, full of wild beasts and wild men — and what multitudes there might be of them they knew not. Neither could they, as it were, go up to the top of Pisgah [1] to view from this wilderness a more goodly country to feed their hopes; for which way soever they turned their eyes (save upward to the heavens) they could have little solace or content in respect of any outward objects. For summer being done, all things stand upon them with a weather-beaten face, and the whole country, full of woods and thickets, represented a wild and savage hue. If they looked behind them, there was the mighty ocean which they had passed and was now as

¹ **Pisgah:** a mountain in Jordan from which Moses viewed the Promised Land.

a main bar and gulf to separate them from all the civil parts of the world. . . .

What could now sustain them but the Spirit of God and His grace? May not and ought not the children of these fathers rightly say: "Our fathers were Englishmen which came over this great ocean, and were ready to perish in this wilderness; but they cried unto the Lord, and He heard their voice and looked on their adversity. Let them therefore praise the Lord, because He is good: and His mercies endure forever."

FOR DISCUSSION

1. Point out some passages which show that Bradford succeeded in his intention to write his record in a "plain style, with a singular regard for the simple truth in all things."
2. In what instances does Bradford reveal his Puritan faith?
3. What characteristics of the Pilgrims have come to be considered typical of modern Americans?
4. Can you point out passages that show Bradford as a man of firm and fair character? Are there any indications in his writing of his qualities of leadership?
5. Can you find evidence in Bradford's writing of the Puritan belief that everything, whether good or bad, was the specific result of God's direct intervention in men's affairs?

American Art and Artists ➤

Reproduced on the facing page are two oil paintings depicting the Pilgrims' first voyage to the New World. At the top is "Embarkation of the Pilgrims at Dufthaven," by the American artist Robert Weir (1803–1889). At the bottom is "The Landing of the Pilgrims," painted by the Italian-born American artist Michael Corné (c. 1752–1845). Both paintings represent the interest in historical scenes and subjects that characterized much nineteenth-century art.

The Bay Psalm Book

The so-called *Bay Psalm Book* is famous as the first book to be printed in America (1640). One of eleven copies known today sold at auction in 1947 for $151,000. Its authors knew that they were not writing poetry. They wanted to fit the meaning of the Psalms to hymn tunes. What was lost you can note by comparing the King James version of Psalm 1 with that of the *Bay* version.

The Bay Psalm Book

O Blessed man, that in th' advice of
    wicked doeth not walk;
nor stand in sinners way, nor sit in
    chayre of scornfull folk,

But in the law of Jehovah,   5
    is his longing delight:
and in his law doth meditate, by day
    and eke by night.

And he shall be like to a tree
    planted by water rivers: 10
that in his season yields his fruit,
    and his leaf never withers.

And all he doth, shall prosper well,
    the wicked are not so:
but they are like unto the chaffe,   15
    which winde drives to and fro.

Therefore shall not ungodly men,
    rise to stand in the doome,
nor shall the sinners with the just,
    in their assemblie come.   20

For of the righteous men, the Lord
    acknowledgeth the way:
but the way of ungodly men,
    shall utterly decay.

The King James Bible

1. Blessed is the man that walketh not in the counsel of the ungodly, nor standeth in the way of sinners, nor sitteth in the seat of the scornful.

2. But his delight is in the law of the Lord; and in his law doth he meditate day and night.

3. And he shall be like a tree planted by the rivers of water, that bringeth forth his fruit in his season; his leaf also shall not wither; and whatsoever he doeth shall prosper.

4. The ungodly are not so: but are like the chaff which the wind driveth away.

5. Therefore the ungodly shall not stand in the judgment, nor sinners in the congregation of the righteous.

6. For the Lord knoweth the way of the righteous: but the way of the ungodly shall perish.

The New England Primer

The "reader" of Puritan children was *The New England Primer*, the most celebrated pre-Revolutionary American textbook. Although it was probably published as early as 1683, the earliest whole edition known is that of 1727. Among the *Primer's* staple ingredients were the Lord's Prayer; the catechism; a dialogue among Christ, Youth, and the Devil; and the rhymed alphabet with illustrations. These rhymes were memorized and chanted in unison by the students.

A In *Adam's* Fall
We Sinned all.

B Thy Life to Mend
This *Book* Attend.

C The *Cat* doth play
And after flay.

D A *Dog* will bite
A Thief at night.

E An *Eagles* flight
Is out of fight.

FOR DISCUSSION

1. What are the major differences between the *Bay Psalm Book* version of Psalm I and the King James version? What changes in wording decrease the literary effectiveness of the former? Why? *The Bay Psalm Book* has rhyme but loses some pleasant alliteration. Point out examples.

2. In your opinion, which of the moral maxims in *The New England Primer* best illustrates the spirit of Puritanism?

3. Recall the Biblical story or suggested incident for as many of the *Primer's* maxims as you can.

4. In what words do you find examples of the characteristic seventeenth-century similarity of the letters *f* and *s* in printing? Does the modern letter *s* occur at all? Do you see any pattern in the use of these symbols?

SPECIAL REPORT

What other famous American schoolbooks besides *The New England Primer* can you name? Make a report to the class on the McGuffey's *Readers*, by William Holmes McGuffey, which were particularly influential.

EDWARD TAYLOR

1646?–1729

Meditation Six

Educated at Harvard for the ministry, in 1671 Taylor accepted a call to the settlement of Westfield, Massachusetts. Here he lived and worked as pastor and physician for the rest of his life. But somehow he kept in touch with what the better English poets of his day were doing. His own poetry shows that he followed their techniques, often rising above imitation.

THE CONCEIT. In Taylor's day poets delighted in the use of the *conceit,* a rather artificial comparison carried out in great detail. In the following poem (modernized in spelling) Taylor uses the figure of a mint in which God coins His image. Note how the conceit is employed consistently throughout the poem. (Taylor also uses a pun: the "angel" was an English gold coin, which showed the archangel Michael slaying the dragon.)

Canticles II: 1: I am . . . the lily of the valleys.

Am I thy gold? Or Purse, Lord, for thy
    Wealth;
    Whether in mine or mint refined for
    thee?

"Meditation Six" from *The Poetical Works of Edward Taylor,* edited by Thomas H. Johnson. Copyright 1939, Rocklands Editions. Copyright 1943, Princeton University Press.

I'm counted so, but count me o'er thy-
    self,
    Lest gold-washed face, and brass in
    Heart I be.
    I Fear my Touchstone touches when
    I try   5
Me and my Counted Gold too overly.

Am I new minted by thy Stamp in-
    deed?
    Mine Eyes are dim; I cannot clearly
    see.
Be thou my Spectacles that I may read
    Thine Image and Inscription stamped
    on me.   10
    If thy bright Image do upon me
    stand,
I am a Golden Angel in thy hand.

Lord, make my Soul thy Plate: thine
    Image bright
    Within the Circle of the same enfoil.°
And on its brims in golden Letters
    write   15
    Thy Superscription in an Holy style.
    Then I shall be thy Money, thou my
    Hoard:
    Let me thy Angel be, be thou my
    Lord.

14. **enfoil:** enfold.

1. Be sure you understand Edward Taylor's use of the *conceit* — an elaborate and extended figure of speech. How are the expressions "gold-washed face" and "brass in Heart" appropriate to the conceit?

2. Show how the poet uses the same word with slightly different meanings; for example, line 3 — *counted . . . count.* What is the pun on *o'er?* Look up the following terms of coinage, and then work out the double meanings: *face, touchstone, stamp, plate.*

JONATHAN EDWARDS

1703–1758

FROM

Sinners in the Hands of an Angry God

A local historian reports that when Jonathan Edwards, the last great Puritan minister, delivered the sermon from which this excerpt was taken, "there was heard such a breathing of distress and weeping, that the preacher was obliged to speak to the people and desire silence that he might be heard." Edwards' delivery is said to have been forceful but not violent. His other writings show him to have been of a somewhat more gentle nature.

THIS that you have heard is the case of every one of you that are out of Christ. That world of misery, that lake of burning brimstone, is extended abroad under you. There is the dreadful pit of the glowing flames of the wrath of God; there is hell's wide gaping mouth open; and you have nothing to stand upon, nor any thing to take hold of; there is nothing between you and hell but the air; it is only the power and mere pleasure of God that holds you up. . . .

There are black clouds of God's wrath now hanging directly over your heads, full of the dreadful storm, and big with thunder; and were it not for the restraining hand of God, it would immediately burst forth upon you. The sovereign pleasure of God, for the present, stays His rough wind; otherwise it would come with fury, and your destruction would come like a whirlwind, and you would be like the chaff [1] of the summer threshing floor. . . .

The God that holds you over the pit of hell, much as one holds a spider, or some loathsome insect over the fire, abhors you, and is dreadfully provoked: His wrath toward you burns like fire; He looks upon you as worthy

[1] chaff: the waste product remaining after grain has been threshed.

of nothing else, but to be cast into the fire; He is of purer eyes than to bear to have you in His sight; you are ten thousand times more abominable in His eyes, than the most hateful venomous serpent is in ours. You have offended Him infinitely more than ever a stubborn rebel did his prince; and yet it is nothing but His hand that holds you from falling into the fire every moment. It is to be ascribed to nothing else, that you did not go to hell the last night; that you were suffered to awake again in this world, after you closed your eyes to sleep. And there is no other reason to be given, why you have not dropped into hell since you arose in the morning, but that God's hand has held you up. There is no other reason to be given why you have not gone to hell, since you have sat here in the house of God, provoking His pure eyes by your sinful wicked manner of attending His solemn worship. Yea, there is nothing else that is to be given as a reason why you do not this very moment drop down into hell.

O sinner! Consider the fearful danger you are in: it is a great furnace of wrath, a wide and bottomless pit, full of the fire of wrath, that you are held over in the hand of that God, whose wrath is provoked and incensed as much against you as against many of the damned in hell. You hang by a slender thread, with the flames of divine wrath flashing about it, and ready every moment to singe it and burn it asunder; and you have no interest in any Mediator, and nothing to lay hold of to save yourself, nothing to keep off the flames of wrath, nothing of your own, nothing that you ever have done, nothing that you can do, to induce God to spare you one moment. . . .

It is *everlasting* wrath. It would be dreadful to suffer this fierceness and wrath of Almighty God one moment; but you must suffer it to all eternity. There will be no end to this exquisite [1]

[1] exquisite: here, intense.

horrible misery. When you look forward, you shall see a long forever, a boundless duration before you, which will swallow up your thoughts, and amaze your soul; and you will absolutely despair of ever having any deliverance, any end, any mitigation, any rest at all. You will know certainly that you must wear out long ages, millions of millions of ages, in wrestling and conflicting with this almighty merciless vengeance; and then when you have so done, when so many ages have actually been spent by you in this manner, you will know that all is but a point to what remains. So that your punishment will indeed be infinite. Oh, who can express what the state of a soul in such circumstances is! All that we can possibly say about it, gives but a very feeble, faint representation of it; it is inexpressible and inconceivable: For "who knows the power of God's anger?"

How dreadful is the state of those that are daily and hourly in the danger of this great wrath and infinite misery! But this is the dismal case of every soul in this congregation that has not been born again, however moral and strict, sober and religious, they may otherwise be. . . .

FOR DISCUSSION

1. Select an appropriate adjective to describe the tone of the sermon. How does the tone suit the purpose of the sermon?

2. Choose some examples to show how Edwards' grammar differs from modern usage.

American Art and Architecture ➤

Reproduced on the facing page is the oil painting "Church at Old Lyme," by the American artist Childe Hassam (1859–1935). This Connecticut church is typical of the New England architecture of Jonathan Edwards' day.

SARAH KEMBLE KNIGHT
1666–1727

FROM HER Journal

In 1704, on horseback — not by stagecoach — a woman made the rugged round trip between Boston and New York. That woman was the energetic and capable Sarah Kemble Knight, Boston shopkeeper, schoolmistress, household head, and, in later life, innkeeper. Presumably her business in settling estates required her presence in New York. She left Boston in October 1704, and returned in March 1705.

She must have been an engaging and alert person. Her *Journal* on this trip is a healthy, refreshing account of practical matters and of ordinary people. Now let Sarah Kemble Knight herself entertain you with her observations in her own original spelling and the quaint capitalization of the time.

STRANGE CUSTOMS OF CONNECTICUT

Saturday, Oct. 7th, wee sett out early in the Morning, and being something unacquainted with the way, having ask't it of some wee mett, they told us wee must Ride a mile or two and turne down a Lane on the Right hand; and by their Direction wee Rode on but not Yet comeing to the turning, wee mett a Young fellow and ask't him how farr it was to the Lane which turn'd down towards Guilford. Hee said wee must

Ride a little further, and turn down by the Corner of uncle Sams Lott. My Guide vented his Spleen [1] at the Lubber [2]; and we soon after came into the Rhode, [3] and keeping still on, without any thing further Remarkebell, about two a clock afternoon we arrived at New Haven, where I was received with all Posible Respects and civility. Here I discharged Mr. Wheeler with a reward to his satisfaction, and took some time to rest after so long and toilsome a Journey; And I inform'd myselfe of the manners and customs of the place, and at the same time employed myselfe in the afair I went there upon.

They are Govern'd by the same Laws as wee in Boston (or little differing) thr'out this whole Colony of Connecticot, And much the same way of Church Government, and many of them good, Sociable people, and I hope Religious too: but a little too much Independant in their principalls, and, as I have been told, were formerly in their Zeal very Riggid in their Administrations towards such as their Lawes made Offenders, even to a harmless Kiss or Innocent

---

[1] **Spleen:** anger.
[2] **Lubber:** lazy fellow.
[3] **Rhode:** road.

merriment among Young People. Whipping being a frequent and counted an easy Punishment, about which, as other Crimes, the Judges were absolute in their Sentances. . . .

There are every where in the Towns as I passed, a Number of Indians, the Natives of the Country, and are the most salvage of all the salvages of that kind that I had ever Seen: little or no care taken (as I heard upon enquiry) to make them otherwise. They have in some places Landes of their owne, and Govern'd by Law's of their own making; — they marry many wives and at pleasure put them away, and on the least dislike or fickle humor, on either side, saying *stand away* to one another is a sufficient Divorce. And indeed those uncomely *Stand aways* are too much in Vougue among the English in this Indulgent Colony as their Records plentifully prove, and that on very trivial matters, of which some have been told me, but are not proper to be Related by a Female pen, tho some of that foolish sex have had too large a share in the story. . . .

They give the title of merchant to every trader; who Rate their Goods according to the time and spetia [1] they pay in: viz. Pay, mony, Pay as mony, and trusting. *Pay* is Grain, Pork, Beef, &c. at prices sett by the General Court that Year; *mony* is pieces of Eight, Ryalls,[2] or Boston or Bay shillings (as they call them,) or Good hard money, as sometimes silver coin is termed by them; also Wampon, vizt. Indian beads which serves for change. *Pay as mony* is provisions, as aforesaid one Third cheaper then as the Assembly or General Court sets it; and *Trust* as they and the merchant agree for time.

Now, when the buyer comes to ask for a comodity, sometimes before the merchant answers that he has it, he sais, *is Your pay redy?* Perhaps the Chap Reply's Yes: what do You pay in? say's the merchant. The buyer having answered, then the price is set; as suppose he wants a sixpenny knife, in pay it is 12d — in pay as money eight pence, and hard money its own price, viz. 6d. It seems a very Intricate way of trade and what Lex Mercatoria [3] had not thought of.

Being at a merchants house, in come a tall country fellow, with his alfogeos [4] full of Tobacco; for they seldom Loose their Cudd, but keep Chewing and Spitting as long as they're eyes are open, — he advanc't to the midle of the Room, makes an Awkward Nodd, and spitting a Large deal of Aromatick Tincture, he gave a scrape with his shovel-like shoo, leaving a small shovel full of dirt on the floor, made a full stop, Hugging his own pretty Body with his hands under his arms, Stood staring rown'd him, like a Catt let out of a Baskett. At last, like the creature Balamm Rode on,[5] he opened his mouth and said: have You any Ribinen for Hatbands to sell I pray? The Questions and Answers about the pay being past, the Ribin is bro't and opened. Bumpkin Simpers, cryes its confounded Gay I vow; and beckning to the door, in comes Jone Tawdry [6] dropping about 50 curtsees, and stands by him: hee shows her the Ribin. *Law You* sais shee, *its right Gent,[7] do You take it, tis dreadfully pretty.* Then she enquires, *have you any hood silk I pray?* Which being brought and bought, *Have*

[1] spetia: specie; coin.
[2] pieces of Eight: Spanish dollars containing eight reals (Ryalls). Each real was then worth twelve cents.
[3] Lex Mercatoria (mûr·ká·tō′rĭ·á): the law of merchants.
[4] alfogeos (ăl·fō′jĭ·ōs): Spanish saddlebags; here used humorously for cheeks.
[5] creature Balamm Rode on: a famous ass in the Bible that was given the power of speech to rebuke its owner, Balaam (Num. 22:21–33).
[6] Jone Tawdry: humorous name for a country girl.
[7] Gent: a rustic abbreviation for genteel or elegant.

You any thred silk to sew it with says shee, which being accommodated with they Departed. They Generaly stand after they come in a great while speachless, and sometimes dont say a word till they are askt what they want, which I impute to the Awe they stand in of the merchants, who they are constantly almost Indebted too; and must take what they bring without Liberty to choose for themselves; but they serve them as well, making the merchants stay long enough for their pay.

We may observe here the great necessity and bennifitt both of Education and Conversation; for these people have as Large a portion of mother witt, and sometimes a Larger, than those who have bin brought up in Citties; But for want of emprovements, Render themselves almost Ridiculos, as above. I should be glad if they would leave such follies, and am sure all that Love Clean Houses (at least) would be glad on't too.

They are generaly very plain in their dress, throuout all the Colony, as I saw, and follow one another in their modes; that You may know where they belong especially the women, meet them where you will.

Their Chief Red Letter day is St. Election,[1] which is annually Observed according to Charter, to choose their Governor: a blessing [2] they can never be thankfull enough for, as they will find, if ever it be their hard fortune to loose it. . . .

HARDSHIPS OF TRAVEL

Decr. 6th. Being by this time well Recruited and rested after my Journy, my business lying unfinished by some concerns at New York depending thereupon, my Kinsman, Mr. Thomas Trowbridge of New Haven, must needs take a Journy there before it could be accomplished, I resolved to go there in company with him, and a man of the town which I engaged to wait on me there. Accordingly, Dec. 6th we set out from New Haven, and about 11 the same morning came to Stratford ferry; which crossing, about two miles on the other side Baited our horses and would have eat a morsell ourselves, But the Pumpkin and Indian mixt Bred had such an Aspect, and the Barelegg'd Punch so awkerd or rather Awful a sound, that we left both, and proceeded forward, and about seven at night come to Fairfield, where we met with good entertainment and Lodg'd; and early next morning set forward to Norowalk, from its halfe Indian name *Northwalk*, when about 12 at noon we arrived, and Had a Dinner of Fryed Venison, very savoury. Landlady wanting some pepper in the seasoning, bid the Girl hand her the spice in the little *Gay* cupp on the shelfe. From hence we Hasted towards Rye, walking and Leading our Horses neer a mile together, up a prodigios [3] high Hill; and so Riding till about nine at night, and there arrived and took up our Lodgings at an ordinary,[4] which a French family kept. Here being very hungry, I desired a fricasee which the Frenchman undertakeing, managed so contrary to my notion of Cookery, that I hastned to Bed superless; And being shewd the way up a pair of stairs which had such a narrow passage that I had almost stopt by the Bulk of my Body; But arriving at my apartment found it to be a little Lento [5] Chamber furnisht

---

[1] **St. Election:** a humorous way of indicating that an election was as religiously observed as a saint's day in a Catholic country.
[2] **blessing:** In Massachusetts the governor was appointed by the king, to the great dissatisfaction of that colony.

[3] **prodigios** (modern spelling *prodigious*): here, very; remarkably.
[4] **ordinary:** inn.
[5] **Lento:** a lean-to room, or one under a low, sloping roof.

Cambridge, Massachusetts: from an engraving made in 1725. ▶

amongst other Rubbish with a High Bedd and a Low one, a Long Table, a Bench and a Bottomless chair, — Little Miss went to scratch up my Kennell [1] which Russelled as if shee'd bin in the Barn amongst the Husks, and supose such was the contents of the tickin — nevertheless being exceedingly weary, down I laid my poor Carkes [2] (never more tired) and found my Covering as scanty as my Bed was hard. Annon I heard another Russelling noise in The Room — called to know the matter — Little miss said shee was making a bed for the men; who, when they were in Bed, complained their leggs lay out of it by reason of its shortness — my poor bones complained bitterly not being used to such Lodgings, and so did the man who was with us; and poor I made but one Grone, which was from the time I went to bed to the time I Riss, which was about three in the morning, Setting up by the Fire till light, and having discharged our ordinary [3] which was as dear as if we had had far Better fare — wee took our leave of Monsieur and about seven in the morn come to New Rochell a french town, where we had a good Breakfast. And in the strength of that about an how'r before sunsett got to York. [4]

[1] **scratch up my Kennell:** humorous for shake up my mattress.
[2] **Carkes:** carcass.
[3] **discharged our ordinary:** paid the bill.
[4] **York:** New York.

FOR DISCUSSION

1. Point out details that indicate that Dame Knight had a sense of humor.
2. What evidence is there that Connecticut seemed to her a foreign country? In what ways was she tolerant or intolerant of these "foreigners"? To what extent was her intolerance justified?
3. What were the difficulties of travel in 1704? What were the difficulties of business dealings?

SPELLING IN COLONIAL DAYS — AND NOW

You could scarcely read the psalm from *The Bay Psalm Book* and the selection from Dame Knight's *Journal* without being impressed by the difference between seventeenth-century and modern spelling. *Chayre, winde, chaffe, shoo, bennifitt, farr, midle* are only a few of the many words that look queer to us. Point out other differences in spelling.

Spelling had not yet become standardized in the colonial days. Noah Webster's *American Spelling Book* did not appear until 1783. Are there any advantages in having one standard way to spell a word? Can you explain why not all our words are spelled phonetically (the way they sound)?

On the whole, do you think modern spelling is an improvement? How would you judge whether spelling has improved? What makes one spelling preferable to another? Which spelling in each of the following groups do you prefer, and why: *catalog, catalogue; color, colour; gray, grey; night, nite; plough, plow; program, programme; shew, show; tho, though; traveler, traveller?* What is meant by "spelling reform"? What are the advantages and disadvantages of "reformed spelling"? In this connection someone may wish to look up the famous playwright G. B. Shaw's views on the subject and the bequest in his will to assist spelling reform.

Colonial New England

Reproduced on page 441 is a detail from a line engraving entitled "A Prospect of the Colleges in Cambridge, in New England." A smaller detail from this work appears on page 438. The engraving was made in 1725 by the American artist William Burges, a contemporary of Sarah Kemble Knight.

While travel was often difficult during colonial times, the quality of life in and around Boston had begun to take on a certain elegance during Madam Knight's day. The coach and the clothing shown in the engraving form a strong contrast to the Puritan simplicity of fifty years earlier.

COLONEL
WILLIAM BYRD
1674–1744

FROM
A History
of the Dividing Line

Colonel Byrd, whose most important literary work is represented here, did not think of himself as a man of letters but as a man of affairs. His books were tossed off as by-products of public duties. In 1728 he helped run the boundary line between Virginia and North Carolina, and for his own amusement recorded his experiences in a journal, later expanded into a "history," from which the following selection is taken. Byrd's aristocratic background and wide reading contributed to his style — a style more polished than that displayed by most other colonial keepers of journals.

CAMP LIFE

March 12 [1728]. . . . . Our landlord [1] had a tolerable good house and clean furniture, and yet we could not be tempted to lodge in it. We chose rather to lie in the open field, for fear of growing too tender. A clear sky, spangled with stars, was our canopy which, being the last thing we saw before we fell asleep, gave us magnificent dreams. The truth of it is, we took so much pleasure in that natural kind of lodging that I think at the foot of the account

[1] landlord: a plantation owner named Ballance.

mankind are great losers by the luxury of feather beds and warm apartments.

The curiosity of beholding so new and withal so sweet a method of encamping brought one of the senators of North Carolina to make us a midnight visit. But he was so very clamorous in his commendations of it that the sentinel, not seeing his quality, either through his habit [2] or behavior, had like to have treated him roughly.

After excusing the unseasonableness of his visit, and letting us know he was a Parliament man, he swore he was so taken with our lodging that he would set fire to his house as soon as he got home and teach his wife and children to lie, like us, in the open field.

THE DISMAL SWAMP

March 14. Before nine of the clock this morning, the provisions, bedding, and other necessaries were made up into packs for the men to carry on their shoulders into the Dismal. They were victualed for eight days at full allowance, nobody doubting but that would be abundantly sufficient to carry them through that inhospitable place; nor in-

[2] habit: dress.

deed was it possible for the poor fellows to stagger under more. As it was, their loads weighed from sixty to seventy pounds, in just proportion to the strength of those who were to bear them.

'Twould have been unconscionable [1] to have saddled them with burthens heavier than that, when they were to lug them through a filthy bog which was hardly practicable with no burthen at all. Besides this luggage at their backs, they were obliged to measure the distance, mark the trees, and clear the way for the surveyors every step they went. It was really a pleasure to see with how much cheerfulness they undertook, and with how much spirit they went through all this drudgery. For their greater safety, the commissioners took care to furnish them with Peruvian bark,[2] rhubarb, and hipocoacanah,[3] in case they might happen, in that wet journey, to be taken with fevers or fluxes.

Although there was no need of example to inflame persons already so cheerful, yet to enter [4] the people with better grace, the author and two more of the commissioners accompanied them half a mile into the Dismal. The skirts of it were thinly planted with dwarf reeds and gall bushes but, when we got into the Dismal itself, we found the reeds grew there much taller and closer and, to mend the matter, was so interlaced with bamboo briers that there was no scuffling through them without the help of pioneers. At the same time, we found the ground moist and trembling under our feet like a quagmire, insomuch that it was an easy matter to run a ten-foot pole up to the head in it, without exerting any uncommon strength to do it.

Two of the men, whose burthens were the least cumbersome, had orders

to march before with their tomahawks and clear the way, in order to make an opening for the surveyors. By their assistance we made a shift to push the line half a mile in three hours, and then reached a small piece of firm land about one hundred yards wide standing up above the rest like an island. Here the people were glad to lay down their loads and take a little refreshment, while the happy man whose lot it was to carry the jug of rum began already, like Aesop's bread-carrier,[5] to find it grow a good deal lighter.

After reposing about an hour, the commissioners recommended vigor and constancy to their fellow travelers, by whom they were answered with three cheerful huzzas in token of obedience. This ceremony was no sooner over but they took up their burthens and attended the motion of the surveyors who, though they worked with all their might, could reach but one mile farther, the same obstacles still attending them which they had met with in the morning.

However small this distance may seem to such as are used to travel at their ease, yet our poor men, who were obliged to work with an unwieldy load at their backs, had reason to think it a long way; especially in a bog where they had no firm footing, but every step made a deep impression, which was instantly filled with water. At the same time they were laboring with their hands to cut down the reeds, which were ten feet high, their legs were hampered with the briers. Besides, the weather happened to be very warm, and the tallness of the reeds kept off every friendly breeze from coming to refresh them. And, indeed, it was a little provoking to hear the wind whistling among the branches of the white ce-

---

[1] **unconscionable** (ŭn·kŏn'shŭn·à·b'l): unjust.

[2] **Peruvian bark:** quinine.

[3] **hipocoacanah:** a medicinal herb now known as ipecac.

[4] **enter:** start off.

[5] **Aesop's bread-carrier:** According to the fable, the man who wanted the lightest burden on the journey was laughed at for choosing the bread, which was the heaviest; but by night the bread had all been distributed and he had only the empty basket to carry.

dars, which grew here and there amongst the reeds, and at the same time not have the comfort to feel the least breath of it.

In the meantime the three commissioners returned out of the Dismal the same way they went in and, having joined their brethren, proceeded that night as far as Mr. Wilson's.

This worthy person lives within sight of the Dismal, in the skirts whereof his stocks range and maintain themselves all the winter, and yet he knew as little of it as he did of *Terra Australis Incognita*.[1] He told us a Canterbury tale [2] of a North Briton whose curiosity spurred him a long way into this great desert, as he called it, near twenty years ago, but he, having no compass, nor seeing the sun for several days together, wandered about till he was almost famished; but at last he bethought himself of a secret his countrymen make use of to pilot themselves in a dark day.

He took a fat louse out of his collar and exposed it to the open day on a piece of white paper which he brought along with him for his journal. The poor insect, having no eyelids, turned himself about till he found the darkest part of the heavens, and so made the best of his way toward the north. By this direction he steered himself safe out, and gave such a frightful account of the monsters he saw and the distresses he underwent, that no mortal since has been hardy enough to go upon the like dangerous discovery.

[1] *Terra Australis Incognita*: unknown southern land.
[2] **Canterbury tale**: here, an incredible tale. The *Canterbury Tales* are famous old stories recounted in verse by the first great English poet, Chaucer.

The Old Bruton Parish Church in Virginia.

March 25. . . . In the meantime, we who stayed behind had nothing to do but make the best observations we could upon that part of the country. The soil of our landlord's plantation, though none of the best, seemed more fertile than any thereabouts, where the ground is near as sandy as the deserts of Africa, and consequently barren. The road leading from thence to Edenton, being in distance about twenty-seven miles, lies upon a ridge called Sandy Ridge, which is so wretchedly poor that it will not bring potatoes.

The pines in this part of the country are of a different species from those that grow in Virginia: their bearded leaves are much longer and their cones much larger. Each cell contains a seed of the size and figure of a black-eyed pea, which, shedding in November, is very good mast [1] for hogs, and fattens them in a short time.

The smallest of these pines are full of cones, which are eight or nine inches long, and each affords commonly sixty or seventy seeds. This kind of mast has the advantage of all other by being more constant, and less liable to be nipped by the frost or eaten by the caterpillars. The trees also abound more with turpentine, and consequently yield more tar than either the yellow or the white pine; and for the same reason make more durable timber for building. The inhabitants hereabouts pick up knots of lightwood in abundance, which they burn into tar, and then carry it to Norfolk or Nansimond for a market. The tar made in this method is the less valuable because it is said to burn the cordage, though it is full as good for all other uses as that made in Sweden and Muscovy. [2]

Surely there is no place in the world where the inhabitants live with less labor than in North Carolina. It approaches nearer to the description of Lubberland [3] than any other, by the great felicity of the climate, the easiness of raising provisions, and the slothfulness of the people.

Indian corn is of so great increase that a little pains will subsist [4] a very large family with bread, and then they may have meat without any pains at all, by the help of low grounds, and the great variety of mast that grows on the high land. The men for their parts, just like the Indians, impose all the work upon the poor women. They make their wives rise out of their beds early in the morning, at the same time that they lie and snore till the sun has run one third of his course and dispersed all the unwholesome damps. Then, after stretching and yawning for half an hour, they light their pipes, and, under the protection of a cloud of smoke, venture out into the open air; though, if it happens to be never so little cold, they quickly return shivering into the chimney corner. When the weather is mild, they stand leaning with both their arms upon the cornfield fence, and gravely consider whether they had best go and take a small heat at the hoe: but generally find reasons to put it off till another time.

Thus they loiter away their lives, like Solomon's sluggard [5] with their arms across, and at the winding up of the year scarcely have bread to eat.

To speak the truth, 'tis a thorough aversion to labor that makes people file off to North Carolina, where plenty and warm sun confirm them in their disposition to laziness for their whole lives.

---

[1] mast: nuts, acorns, seeds, etc.; used as feed for hogs.

[2] Muscovy: Russia.

[3] Lubberland: a paradise for lazy fellows. The following comments on the natives show the antipathy between the aristocratic Virginians and the small farmers of North Carolina, who were largely former servants.

[4] subsist: here, provide.

[5] Solomon's sluggard: King Solomon said, "Go to the ant, thou sluggard; consider her ways, and be wise." (Proverbs, 6:6)

FOR DISCUSSION

1. Find evidences of Byrd's energy, his sense of humor, his London education.

2. What passage shows most clearly how much his own life had been changed by pioneer conditions?

3. Would he have been satisfied with an easier way of life? How did he feel about those who looked for the easy way?

4. Can you find evidence in Byrd's writing of his qualities as a leader and of his sense of fair play? Point out lines in the text that indicate the presence (or absence) of both characteristics. Do you think that conditions in the New World were at least partially responsible for some of the attitudes Byrd expresses?

FURTHER READING

Rear Admiral Richard E. Byrd, the explorer, was a descendant of William Byrd. A committee may wish to read one or more of the following books by Richard Byrd and report on the similarities they find in the personalities of the two men. Richard Byrd's writings include: *Skyward, Little America, Discovery,* and *Alone* (Putnam).

American Art and Architecture

Reproduced on page 445 is an oil painting entitled "The Old Bruton Church in Virginia." The painting is the work of the American artist Alfred Wordsworth Thompson (1840–1896). The church, which dates from the early eighteenth century, is located in Williamsburg, Virginia, and is considered a fairly typical specimen of colonial architecture.

It has been said that it was architecture, rather than any of the other arts, that first expressed visually the character of the American colonies. In the early years of the first settlements, little time could be given to developing native forms of architecture, but by the 1720's and 30's colonial architects (many of them self-taught) had begun to arrive at their own styles and techniques. The churches they built, in both the North and the South, are fine examples of early American design. (See page 437.)

READING ON THE COLONIAL TIME

Adams, James T., *Provincial Society* (Macmillan, 1927)

American Heritage Jr. Library, *The Story of Yankee Whaling* (American Heritage, 1959)

Andrews, C. M., *Colonial Folkways* (Yale Univ. Press, 1919); *Fathers of New England* (Yale Univ. Press, 1919)

Bailey, C. S., *Pioneer Art in America* (Viking, 1944)

Benét, R. and S. V., *Western Star* (Holt, Rinehart & Winston, 1943)

Bridenbaugh, Carl, *Cities in the Wilderness* (Ronald, 1938)

Chitwood, O. P., *History of Colonial America* (Harper, 1948)

Coleman, R. V., *The First Frontier* (Scribner, 1948)

Earle, Alice M., *Child Life in Colonial Days* (Macmillan, 1899); *Home Life in Colonial Days* (Macmillan, 1898)

Eaton, J., *Lone Journey* (Roger Williams) (Harcourt, Brace & World, 1944)

Gibler, E., *The Plymouth Adventure: A Chronicle of the Voyage of the Mayflower* (Doubleday, 1950)

Gray, E. J., *Penn* (Viking, 1938)

Inglis, F., *Roanoke Hundred* (Bobbs-Merrill, 1948)

Langdon, W. C., *Everyday Things in American Life,* 2 vols. (Scribner, 1937–1941)

Leach, Douglas E., *Flintlock and Tomahawk: New England in King Philip's War* (Macmillan, 1958)

Morison, S. E., *Christopher Columbus, Mariner* (Little, Brown, 1955)

Rowse, Alfred L., *Elizabethans and America* (Harper, 1959)

Singmaster, E., *I Heard of a River* (Winston, 1948)

Smith, B., *Captain John Smith* (Lippincott, 1953).

Tunis, Edwin, *Colonial Lives* (World Publishing, 1957)

Wertenbaker, T. J., *The Golden Age of Colonial Culture* (New York Univ. Press, 1942)

Wright, L. B., *Atlantic Frontier* (Knopf, 1947)

FOR LISTENING

Edward Taylor's "Meditation Six" has been recorded on *Many Voices* 11B.

The Making of
a Nation

A S WE HAVE SEEN, theology dominated the Puritan phase of American writing. Politics was the next great subject to command the attention of our best minds. Since ideas, in the written or spoken word, inspire and direct men's actions, our writers held vitally important places in the movement for American independence. Freedom was won as much by the fiery rhetoric of Thomas Paine's *Common Sense* and the eloquence of the Declaration of Independence as by the weapons of Washington or Lafayette. Without the writings of Thomas Paine, there might have been no army for Washington to lead; without the writings of Thomas Jefferson, France might never have aided our cause. Other nations were hammered together on the anvil of war, but the thirteen original American states were persuaded to become a single nation by the arguments of statesmen and men of letters.

Vigorous, Restless Colonies

By the mid-eighteenth century colonial America was no longer a group of scattered, struggling settlements. It was a series of neighboring, flourishing colonies with rapidly expanding, mixed populations. The word "state," which suggests an independent government, was beginning to replace "colony" in the people's thinking — an important sign of the political trend. The people of these states were vigorous, the natural resources were rich and plentiful, and native industries were sprouting everywhere. Literary activities were growing at the same time. Boston remained a major center of thought, but Philadelphia, New York, and the state of Virginia emerged as equal sources of political and literary talent.

Our growth, particularly our industrial growth, led to intense strain with England. The British government did not want colonial industries competing with those in England. The British wanted the colonies to remain politically and economically dependent on the mother country. They took a series of measures to insure this dependence. They hampered colonial economy by requiring Americans to ship raw materials abroad and to import finished goods at prices higher than the cost of making them in this country. Politically, the British government forced dependence by ruling the colonies from overseas and by taxing the colonies without giving them representation in Parliament.

The restless, growing American states could not accept this design for their future. If they had been given real liberty to order their own lives and develop their economic growth, Americans might have been willing to remain loosely associated with the mother country. However, shortsighted British policies continued to stir colonial unrest. Impatience mounted at what the Declaration of Independence later called "a long train of abuses . . . an absolute tyranny . . . an unwarrantable jurisdiction . . ." Politics became the concern of the day, the concern of every man. A nation was being shaped.

ST. JOHN DE CRÈVECŒUR

What was it about the new land that made Englishmen and Europeans suddenly become *Americans* when they made their homes here? It is hard for us, more than two hundred years later, to capture the sense of this change. It is caught for us in the words of a Frenchman, St. John de Crèvecœur (dē krĕv′kûr′), who settled with his family in New York shortly after the French and Indian War. De Crèvecœur wrote a book called *Letters from an American Farmer*, which is notable for its description of the American life and spirit (see page 1). He wrote:

A European, when he first arrives, seems limited in his intentions, as well as in his views; but . . . he no sooner breathes our air than he forms new schemes, and embarks in designs he never would have thought of in his own country . . . Here individuals of all nations are melted into a new race of men, whose labors and posterity will one day cause great changes in the world.

BENJAMIN FRANKLIN

The great changes began faster than De Crèvecœur had expected. Among the men most responsible for bringing them about was Benjamin Franklin. His earliest political writings aimed at creating harmony between England and the colonies. Later, as the situation grew worse, Franklin wrote two sharp satires against British policies, entitled "An Edict by the King of Prussia," and "Rules by Which a Great Empire May Be Reduced to a Small One." The latter included such satiric counsel as: "In laying . . . taxes, never regard the heavy burdens those remote people already undergo . . . Remember to make your arbitrary tax more grievous . . . by public declarations . . . that your power of taxing them has no limits . . . Send armies into their country under pretence of protecting the inhabitants; but, instead of garrisoning the forts of their frontiers with those troops . . . order the troops into the heart of the country, that the savages may be encouraged to attack the frontiers, and that the troops may be protected by the inhabitants . . ." (A sketch of Franklin's life appears on page 454.)

THOMAS JEFFERSON

Of Franklin's associates in the struggle for freedom, Thomas Jefferson was perhaps the most distinguished. Gifted and versatile, this tall, gangling, red-haired young man from the Virginia frontier put his many talents to good use. He served his country as a member of the Continental Congress, as a representative in the Virginia House of Burgesses, as Governor of Virginia, as Minister to France, as first Secretary of State, as Vice-President, and as President.

His contributions were not only political. Jefferson planned a system of free public education for Virginia and founded the University of Virginia. He was a skilled architect, scientist, and inventor. He was responsible for the decimal system of American coinage. He never thought of himself as an author, but his essays, letters, and public papers, when finally collected, may fill fifty volumes. It is his great state papers, lofty and eloquent, that are important to us today. In the Declaration of Independence and the First Inaugural Address, Thomas Jefferson expressed the democratic principles that have become a part of America's political creed.

THOMAS PAINE

The first blunt call for outright independence was a pamphlet called *Common Sense*. It was published anonymously, for it was too revolutionary to bear its author's name. In three months, more than 100,000 copies of the pamphlet were sold. The author cried, "I challenge the warmest advocate for reconciliation to show a single advantage that this country can reap by being connected with Great Britain . . . The republican form of government is the best because it is founded on the most natural principles." Rather overconfidently, the writer assured the timid that "our present numbers are sufficient to repel the force of all the world."

The author of this forceful, extreme pamphlet was Thomas Paine. His writings helped prepare the public mood for the great Declaration of Independence that followed six months after the publication of *Common Sense*. Paine was a man of many talents. Interested in science like his friend Benjamin Franklin, he was an inventor of designs for iron bridges, and he developed plans for a steamboat. As a pamphleteer he was without equal. His was the most powerful single voice of propaganda on behalf of the Revolution. His power is seen in his passionate, inspiring series of sixteen *Crisis* papers. Many of these were written "on a drumhead" while Paine himself was a soldier in some of the darkest moments of the war between 1776 and 1783.

PATRICK HENRY

Great words originally written to be spoken can belong to literature as well as those written solely to be read. In March of 1775, Patrick Henry delivered a speech before the House of Burgesses of Virginia. This rafter-ringing speech ended with the much-quoted words, "I know not what course others may take; but as for me, give me liberty or give me death." It was an emotion that more and more Americans were coming to share.

THE DECLARATION OF INDEPENDENCE

North and south the colonies were aflame with the spirit of liberty. In the early summer of 1776 the first major document of our nation was prepared by a committee of the Continental Congress, meeting in Philadelphia. Thomas Jefferson, our third President, wrote the Declaration; Benjamin Franklin and John Adams, our second President, helped to revise and polish it. On July 3, the day before the Declaration of Independence was proclaimed, Adams wrote to his wife Abigail:

> Yesterday the greatest question was decided which ever was debated in America, and a greater, perhaps, never was nor will be decided among men . . . You will think me transported with enthusiasm, but I am not. I am well aware of the toil and blood and treasure that it will cost us to maintain this declaration, and support and defend these States. Yet, through all the gloom, I can see rays of ravishing light and glory. I can see that the end is more than worth all the means, and that posterity will triumph in that day's transaction, even though we should rue it, which I trust in God we shall not.

THE DEBATES ON THE CONSTITUTION

The men whose spoken and written words expressed the aims of the struggle for independence include George Washington himself and many others who filled the high offices of the young nation. These men engaged in a series of crucial debates on the Constitution after the war had been won. Thomas Jefferson and Alexander Hamilton, the first Secretary of the Treasury, were especially prominent in these debates.

While the Constitution was being written, there was conflict between Jefferson's group, which favored a loosely structured government with most power concentrated in the separate states, and Hamilton's party, which was in favor of a strong central, or federal, government. After the Constitution itself, perhaps the richest single collection of American political thought is the series of *Federalist* essays that grew out of this conflict. The essays were aimed to win public support for ratification of the Constitution. Most of the *Federalist* papers were written by Hamilton, and his influence is noticeable throughout all of them. Other essays were by James Madison, our fourth President, and by John Jay, who became the first Chief Justice of the Supreme Court.

THE POWER OF THE WORD

This is the last period of our literature to be so intensely wrapped up in historical events, though literature is never wholly removed from its historical background. As you read the selections from this period of the founding of our nation, you will see something of the extent to which words shape the destinies of men. The American leaders had forceful and honest minds. They gloried in grappling with ideas and in driving to the heart of a great argument. Perhaps the greatest tribute ever paid them was spoken on the floor of the very body they attacked most vigorously, the British Parliament. Lord Chatham said there:

> When your Lordships look at the papers transmitted to us from America; when you consider their decency, firmness, and wisdom, you cannot but respect their cause and wish to make it your own. . . . For solidity of reasoning, force of sagacity, and wisdom of conclusion, under such a difficult body of circumstances, no nation or body of men can stand in preference to the general congress at Philadelphia.

As you read the following selections, tune your ear to them. Let the sounds of this eloquent language ring in your ears, and it may stamp your thought in some lasting way. Hear the tone of Patrick Henry's mighty climax: "Forbid it, Almighty God!" Mark the strong simplicity of Thomas Paine's "These are the times that try men's souls." It is a sentence of eight simple monosyllables — but it has memorable rhythm and force. Try expressing the thought in other ways, and you will begin to appreciate Paine's skill in language. And you will listen long to hear a nobler note than the closing words of the Declaration of Independence:

> And for the support of this declaration, with a firm reliance on the protection of Divine Providence, we mutually pledge to each other our lives, our fortunes, and our sacred honor.

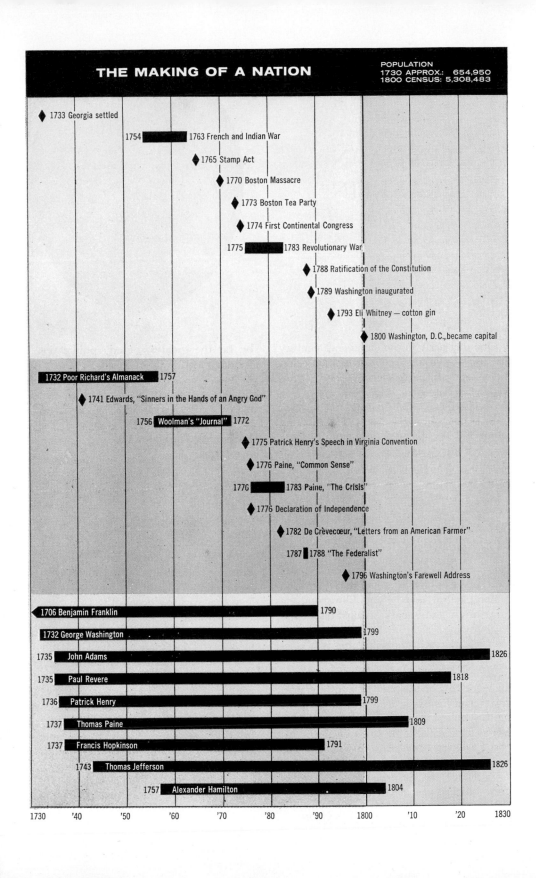

THE MAKING OF A NATION

POPULATION
1730 APPROX.: 654,950
1800 CENSUS: 5,308,483

◆ 1733 Georgia settled

1754 ▮▮▮ 1763 French and Indian War

◆ 1765 Stamp Act

◆ 1770 Boston Massacre

◆ 1773 Boston Tea Party

◆ 1774 First Continental Congress

1775 ▮▮▮ 1783 Revolutionary War

◆ 1788 Ratification of the Constitution

◆ 1789 Washington inaugurated

◆ 1793 Eli Whitney — cotton gin

◆ 1800 Washington, D.C., became capital

1732 Poor Richard's Almanack ▮▮ 1757

◆ 1741 Edwards, "Sinners in the Hands of an Angry God"

1756 Woolman's "Journal" 1772

◆ 1775 Patrick Henry's Speech in Virginia Convention

◆ 1776 Paine, "Common Sense"

1776 ▮▮▮ 1783 Paine, "The Crisis"

◆ 1776 Declaration of Independence

◆ 1782 De Crèvecœur, "Letters from an American Farmer"

1787 ▮ 1788 "The Federalist"

◆ 1796 Washington's Farewell Address

1706 Benjamin Franklin ▮▮▮▮▮▮ 1790

1732 George Washington ▮▮▮▮▮▮ 1799

1735 John Adams ▮▮▮▮▮▮▮▮ 1826

1735 Paul Revere ▮▮▮▮▮▮▮ 1818

1736 Patrick Henry ▮▮▮▮▮▮ 1799

1737 Thomas Paine ▮▮▮▮▮▮▮ 1809

1737 Francis Hopkinson ▮▮▮▮ 1791

1743 Thomas Jefferson ▮▮▮▮▮▮▮▮ 1826

1757 Alexander Hamilton ▮▮▮▮▮ 1804

1730 '40 '50 '60 '70 '80 '90 1800 '10 '20 1830

BENJAMIN
FRANKLIN
1706–1790

One day early in the eighteenth century an observer beside a pond in Boston could have seen a strange sight. A boy, swimming, had fastened to his wrist the string of a kite. The kite, soaring in the sky, pulled him through the water. Writing about it later, the boy told how his kite "carried me quite over without the least fatigue, and with the greatest pleasure imaginable."

The resourceful swimmer was Benjamin Franklin. A few years later he invented flippers for hands and feet, anticipating modern frogman equipment. And the kite he used in Boston was a forerunner of the famous one he flew in Philadelphia, years later, in a thunderstorm. On that day, from a metal key attached to the kite string, he drew bright static sparks against his knuckles, proving for the first time what a few men had guessed, that lightning was electricity.

Born in Boston in 1706, Benjamin Franklin went to Philadelphia as a young man and began his career as a printer. Some of John Woolman's writings (see page 424) were among the first to issue from his press. Success came early to Franklin. His weekly newspaper, the Pennsylvania *Gazette* (later the *Saturday Evening Post*) grew quickly to a circulation of 10,000 —

by far the greatest of any publication in America at that time. From 1732 to 1758, he wrote and published his famous *Poor Richard's Almanac,* an annual collection of proverbs. It soon became the most popular book of its kind, largely because of Franklin's shrewd humor, and first spread his reputation.

Business enterprise alone could hardly absorb Franklin's energies. While still a young man, he founded the Junto, a club for informal discussion of scientific, economic, and political ideas. The club was also responsible for a number of practical civic improvements. In Philadelphia, Franklin established America's first circulating library. Later he founded the college that was to become the University of Pennsylvania.

Benjamin Franklin's scientific achievements won international acclaim, and he was elected to learned societies in England and France. His energy and versatility were remarkable. His many inventions, besides the lightning rod, included the Franklin stove, bifocal glasses, a miniature printing press, and even a strange musical instrument called an "armonica," which employed combinations of tuned glasses. He contributed to the theories of electricity and first applied the terms "positive" and "negative" to electrical charges. He was also one of the first men to study and map the Gulf Stream.

Successful in business, renowned in science, this most modern-spirited of early Americans also served his nation brilliantly. He developed and improved the postal system, making it run at a profit after years of losses. As a representative of the Colonies, he tried in vain to counsel the British toward policies that would let America grow and flourish in association with England. When this aim became hopeless, he supported the cause of independence, served in the Continental Congress, and aided Jefferson in writing the Declaration of Independence. He conducted the difficult negotiations with France that brought financial and military support for America in the war. In 1787 he was a delegate to the convention that wrote our Constitution.

It is easy to forget, in the glory of his public achievements, that Franklin was our first major writer. If he had never been a scientist or a statesman, he would still command respect in the field of literature. His own statements about the art of writing reveal some of the qualities that make his work valuable:

> The words used should be the most expressive that the language affords, provided that they are the most generally understood. Nothing should be expressed in two words that can be expressed in one . . . The whole should be smooth, clear, and short, for the contrary qualities are displeasing.

In the following pages you will read selections from Franklin's most famous works, his *Autobiography* and *Poor Richard's Almanac*. Among his other important writings are two satirical essays, "An Edict by the King of Prussia" and "Rules by Which a Great Empire May Be Reduced to a Small One."

When Franklin died in 1790, at the age of eighty-four, he was an honored figure, mourned by many nations. One of his fellow Americans said, "His shadow lies heavier than any other man's on this young nation." Over fifty years after Franklin's death, Henry David Thoreau, the famous New England essayist, had some interesting thoughts about myths and Benjamin Franklin. Thoreau wrote:

> Mythology, far from being false or fabulous . . . contains only enduring and essential truth. We moderns . . . collect only the raw materials of biography and history . . . which itself is but materials to serve for a mythology . . . And Franklin — there may be a line for him in the future classical dictionary, recording what that demigod did, and referring him to some new genealogy, "Son of _____ and _____. He aided the Americans to gain their independence, instructed mankind in economy, and drew down lightning from the clouds."

FROM HIS Autobiography

Franklin's *Autobiography,* an account of his life up to 1757, portrays his weakness frankly and his strength without false modesty. The first section, written in the form of a letter to his son, is especially direct, simple, and interesting. It shows clearly the difference between Franklin, the great disciple of common sense, and his Puritan forebears. The devout New Englanders of earlier generations searched the Scriptures and listened anxiously to long sermons in the attempt to discover whether they were among the chosen of God. But Franklin calmly decided for himself what virtues were desirable and, with the coolest practical judgment, laid out a daily course of action that would develop those qualities in himself.

Entrance into Philadelphia

I HAVE been the more particular in this description of my journey, and shall be so of my first entry into that city, that you may in your mind compare such unlikely beginnings with the figure I have since made there. I was in my working dress, my best clothes being to come round by sea. I was dirty from my journey; my pockets were stuff'd out with shirts and stockings, and I knew no soul nor where to look for lodging. I was fatigued with traveling, rowing, and want of rest; I was very hungry; and my whole stock of cash consisted of a Dutch dollar and about a shilling in copper. The latter I gave the people of the boat for my passage, who at first refus'd it, on account of my rowing; but I insisted on their taking it. A man being sometimes more generous when he has but a little money than when he has plenty, perhaps thro' fear of being thought to have but little.

Then I walked up the street, gazing about till near the market house I met a boy with bread. I had made many a meal on bread, and, inquiring where he got it, I went immediately to the baker's he directed me to, in Second-street, and ask'd for bisket, intending such as we had in Boston; but they, it

seems, were not made in Philadelphia. Then I asked for a three-penny loaf, and was told they had none such. So not considering or knowing the difference of money, and the greater cheapness nor the names of his bread, I bade him give me three-penny worth of any sort. He gave me, accordingly, three great puffy rolls. I was surpriz'd at the quantity, but took it, and, having no room in my pockets, walk'd off with a roll under each arm, and eating the other. Thus I went up Market-street as far as Fourth-street, passing by the door of Mr. Read, my future wife's father; when she, standing at the door, saw me, and thought I made, as I certainly did, a most awkward, ridiculous appearance. Then I turned and went down Chestnut-street and part of Walnut-street, eating my roll all the way, and, coming round, found myself again at Market-street wharf, near the boat I came in, to which I went for a draught of the river water; and, being filled with one of my rolls, gave the other two to a woman and her child that came down the river in the boat with us, and were waiting to go farther.

Thus refreshed, I walked again up the street, which by this time had many clean-dressed people in it, who were all walking the same way. I joined them, and thereby was led into the

A view of Philadelphia, drawn about 1720 by Peter Cooper.

great meeting house of the Quakers near the market. I sat down among them, and, after looking round awhile and hearing nothing said, being very drowsy thro' labor and want of rest the preceding night, I fell fast asleep, and continued so till the meeting broke up, when one was kind enough to rouse me. This was, therefore, the first house I was in or slept in, in Philadelphia.

Project of Arriving at Moral Perfection

It was about this time I conceived the bold and arduous project of arriving at moral perfection. I wished to live without committing any fault at any time; I would conquer all that either natural inclination, custom, or company might lead me into. As I knew, or thought I knew, what was right and wrong, I did not see why I might not always do the one and avoid the other. But I soon found I had undertaken a task of more difficulty than I had imagined. While my care was employed in guarding against one fault, I was often surprised by another; habit took the advantage of inattention; inclination was sometimes too strong for reason. I concluded, at length, that the mere speculative conviction that it was our interest to be completely virtuous was not sufficient to prevent our slipping; and

that the contrary habits must be broken, and good ones acquired and established, before we can have any dependence on a steady, uniform rectitude of conduct. For this purpose I therefore contrived the following method.

In the various enumerations of the moral virtues I had met with in my reading, I found the catalogue more or less numerous, as different writers included more or fewer ideas under the same name. Temperance, for example, was by some confined to eating and drinking, while by others it was extended to mean the moderating every other pleasure, appetite, inclination, or passion, bodily or mental, even to our avarice and ambition. I proposed to myself, for the sake of clearness, to use rather more names, with fewer ideas annexed to each, than a few names with more ideas; and I included under thirteen names of virtues all that at that time occurred to me as necessary or desirable, and annexed to each a short precept, which fully expressed the extent I gave to its meaning.

These names of virtues, with their precepts, were:

1. TEMPERANCE

Eat not to dullness; drink not to elevation.

BENJAMIN FRANKLIN   457

2. SILENCE

Speak not but what may benefit others or yourself; avoid trifling conversation.

3. ORDER

Let all your things have their places; let each part of your business have its time.

4. RESOLUTION

Resolve to perform what you ought; perform without fail what you resolve.

5. FRUGALITY

Make no expense but to do good to others or yourself; i.e., waste nothing.

6. INDUSTRY

Lose no time; be always employed in something useful; cut off all unnecessary actions.

7. SINCERITY

Use no hurtful deceit; think innocently and justly; and, if you speak, speak accordingly.

8. JUSTICE

Wrong none by doing injuries, or omitting the benefits that are your duty.

9. MODERATION

Avoid extremes; forbear resenting injuries so much as you think they deserve.

10. CLEANLINESS

Tolerate no uncleanliness in body, clothes, or habitation.

11. TRANQUILLITY

Be not disturbed at trifles, or at accidents common or unavoidable.

12. CHASTITY

13. HUMILITY

Imitate Jesus and Socrates.

My intention being to acquire the *habitude* of all these virtues, I judged it would be well not to distract my attention by attempting the whole at once, but to fix it on one of them at a time; and, when I should be master of that, then to proceed to another, and so on, till I should have gone through the thirteen; and as the previous acquisition of some might facilitate the acquisition of certain others, I arranged them with that view, as they stand above. Temperance first, as it tends to procure that coolness and clearness of head, which is so necessary where constant vigilance was to be kept up, and guard maintained against the unremitting attraction of ancient habits and the force of perpetual temptations. This being acquired and established, Silence would be more easy; and my desire being to gain knowledge at the same time that I improved in virtue, and considering that in conversation it was obtained rather by the use of the ears than of the tongue, and therefore wishing to break a habit I was getting into of prattling, punning, and joking, which only made me acceptable to trifling company, I gave Silence the second place. This and the next, Order, I expected would allow me more time for attending to my project and my studies. Resolution, once become habitual, would keep me firm in my endeavors to obtain all the subsequent virtues; Frugality and Industry, freeing me from my remaining debt and producing affluence and independence, would make more easy the practice of Sincerity and Justice, etc., etc. Conceiving then, that, agreeably to the advice of Pythagoras[1] in his Golden Verses, daily examination would be necessary, I contrived the following method for conducting that examination.

I made a little book, in which I allotted a page for each of the virtues. I ruled each page with red ink, so as to have seven columns, one for each day

[1] Pythagoras: (pĭ·thăg'ō·răs): a famous Greek philosopher of the sixth century B.C.

of the week, marking each column with a letter for the day. I crossed these columns with thirteen red lines, marking the beginning of each line with the first letter of one of the virtues, on which line, and in its proper column, I might mark, by a little black spot, every fault I found upon examination to have been committed respecting that virtue upon that day.

I determined to give a week's strict attention to each of the virtues successively. Thus, in the first week, my great guard was to avoid even the least offense against Temperance, leaving the other virtues to their ordinary chance, only marking every evening the faults of the day. Thus, if in the first week I could keep my first line, marked T, clear of spots, I supposed the habit of that virtue so much strengthened, and its opposite weakened, that I might venture extending my attention to include the next, and for the following week keep both lines clear of spots. Proceeding thus to the last, I could go through a course complete in thirteen weeks, and four courses in a year. And like him who, having a garden to weed, does not attempt to eradicate all the bad herbs at once, which would exceed his reach and his strength, but works on one of the beds at a time, and, having accomplished the first, proceeds to a second, so I should have, I hoped, the encouraging pleasure of seeing on my pages the progress I made in virtue, by clearing successively my lines of their spots, till in the end, by a number of courses, I should be happy in viewing a clean book, after a thirteen weeks' daily examination. . . .

The precept of Order requiring that *every part of my business should have its allotted time*, one page in my little book contained the following scheme of employment for the twenty-four hours of a natural day.

THE MORNING	5	Rise, wash, and address *Powerful Goodness!* Contrive day's business, and take the resolution of the day; prosecute the present study, and breakfast.
	6	
Question. What good shall I do this day?		
	7	
	8	
	9	Work.
	10	
	11	
NOON	12	Read, or overlook my accounts, and dine.
	1	
	2	
	3	
	4	Work.
	5	
EVENING	6	Put things in their places. Supper. Music or diversion, or conversation. Examination of the day.
	7	
Question. What good have I done today?	8	
	9	
	10	
	11	
	12	
NIGHT	1	Sleep.
	2	
	3	
	4	

I entered upon the execution of this plan for self-examination, and continued it with occasional intermissions for some time. I was surprised to find myself so much fuller of faults than I had imagined; but I had the satisfaction of seeing them diminish. To avoid the trouble of renewing now and then my little book, which, by scraping out the marks on the paper of old faults to make room for new ones in a new course, became full of holes, I transferred my tables and precepts to the ivory leaves of a memorandum book, on which the lines were drawn with red ink, that made a durable stain, and on those lines I marked my faults with a black lead pencil, which marks I could easily wipe out with a wet sponge. After a while I went through one course only in a year, and afterward only one in several years, till at length I omitted them entirely, being employed in voyages and business abroad, with a multiplicity of affairs that interfered; but I always carried my little book with me.

My scheme of Order gave me the most trouble; and I found that, though it might be practicable where a man's business was such as to leave him the disposition [1] of his time, that of a journeyman printer, for instance, it was not possible to be exactly observed by a master, who must mix with the world, and often receive people of business at their own hours. Order, too, with regard to places for things, papers, etc., I found extremely difficult to acquire. I had not been early accustomed to it, and, having an exceeding good memory, I was not so sensible of the inconvenience attending want of method. This article, therefore, cost me so much painful attention, and my faults in it vexed me so much, and I made so little progress in amendment, and had such frequent relapses, that I was almost ready to give up the attempt, and content myself with a faulty character in that respect, like the man who, in buying an ax of a smith, my neighbor, desired to have the whole of its surface as bright as the edge. The smith consented to grind it bright for him if he would turn the wheel; he turned, while the smith pressed the broad face of the ax hard and heavily on the stone, which made the turning of it very fatiguing. The man came every now and then from the wheel to see how the work went on, and at length would take his ax as it was, without further grinding. "No," said the smith, "turn on, turn on; we shall have it bright by and by; as yet, it is only speckled." "Yes," says the man, "*but I think I like a speckled ax best*."

And I believe this may have been the case with many, who, having, for want of some such means as I employed, found the difficulty of obtaining good and breaking bad habits in other points of vice and virtue, have given up the struggle, and concluded that "*a speckled ax was best*"; for something that pretended to be reason was every now and then suggesting to me that such extreme nicety as I exacted for myself might be a kind of foppery [2] in morals, which, if it were known, would make me ridiculous; that a perfect character might be attended with the inconvenience of being envied and hated; and that a benevolent man should allow a few faults in himself, to keep his friends in countenance.

In truth, I found myself incorrigible with respect to Order; and now I am grown old, and my memory bad, I feel very sensibly the want of it. But, on the whole, though I never arrived at the perfection I had been so ambitious of obtaining, but fell far short of it, yet I was, by the endeavor, a better and a happier man than I otherwise should have been if I had not attempted it; as those who aim at perfect writing by

---

[1] **disposition:** here, management.

[2] **foppery:** foolishness.

imitating the engraved copies, though they never reach the wished-for excellence of those copies, their hand is mended by the endeavor.

It may be well my posterity should be informed that to this little artifice, with the blessing of God, their ancestor owed the constant felicity of his life, down to his seventy-ninth year, in which this is written. What reverses may attend the remainder is in the hand of Providence; but, if they arrive, the reflection on past happiness enjoyed ought to help his bearing them with more resignation. To Temperance he ascribes his long-continued health, and what is still left to him of a good constitution; to Industry and Frugality, the early easiness of his circumstances and acquisition of his fortune, with all that knowledge that enabled him to be a useful citizen, and obtained for him some degree of reputation among the learned; to Sincerity and Justice, the confidence of his country, and the honorable employs it conferred upon him; and to the joint influence of the whole mass of the virtues, even in the imperfect state he was able to acquire them, all that evenness of temper, and that cheerfulness in conversation, which makes his company still sought for, and agreeable even to his younger acquaintance. I hope, therefore, that some of my descendants may follow the example and reap the benefit.

It will be remarked that, though my scheme was not wholly without religion, there was in it no mark of any of the distinguishing tenets of any particular sect. I had purposely avoided them; for, being fully persuaded of the utility and excellency of my method, and that it might be serviceable to people in all religions, and intending some time or other to publish it, I would not have anything in it that should prejudice anyone, of any sect, against it. I purposed writing a little comment on each virtue, in which I would have shown the advantages of possessing it, and the mis-

chiefs attending its opposite vice; and I should have called my book *The Art of Virtue*, because it would have shown the means and manner of obtaining virtue, which would have distinguished it from mere exhortation to be good, that does not instruct and indicate the means, but is like the apostle's man of verbal charity, who, without showing to the naked and hungry how or where they might get clothes or victuals, only exhorted them to be fed and clothed.— James 2:15–16.

But it so happened that my intention of writing and publishing this comment was never fulfilled. I did, indeed, from time to time, put down short hints of the sentiments, reasonings, etc., to be made use of in it, some of which I have still by me; but the necessary close attention to private business in the earlier part of my life, and public business since, have occasioned my postponing it; for, it being connected in my mind with *a great and extensive project* that required the whole man to execute, and which an unforseen succession of employs prevented my attending to, it has hitherto remained unfinished.

In this piece it was my design to explain and enforce this doctrine, that vicious actions are not hurtful because they are forbidden, but forbidden because they are hurtful, the nature of man alone considered; that it was, therefore, everyone's interest to be virtuous who wished to be happy even in this world; and I should, from this circumstance (there being always in the world a number of rich merchants, nobility, states, and princes, who have need of honest instruments for the management of their affairs, and such being so rare), have endeavored to convince young persons that no qualities were so likely to make a poor man's fortune as those of probity and integrity.

My list of virtues contained at first but twelve; but a Quaker friend having kindly informed me that I was generally thought proud; that my pride showed itself frequently in conversation; that I was not content with being in the right when discussing any point, but was overbearing and rather insolent, of which he convinced me by mentioning several instances; I determined endeavoring to cure myself, if I could, of this vice or folly among the rest, and I added Humility to my list.

I cannot boast of much success in acquiring the *reality* of this virtue, but I had a good deal with regard to the *appearance* of it. I made it a rule to forbear all direct contradiction to the sentiments of others, and all positive assertion of my own. I even forbade myself, agreeably to the old law of our Junto,[1] the use of every word or expression in the language that imported a fixed opinion, such as *certainly, undoubtedly,* etc., and I adopted, instead of them, *I conceive, I apprehend,* or *I imagine* a thing to be so or so; or *it so appears to me at present.* When another asserted

something that I thought an error, I denied myself the pleasure of contradicting him abruptly, and of showing immediately some absurdity in his proposition; and in answering I began by observing that in certain cases or circumstances his opinion would be right, but in the present case there *appeared* or *seemed* to me some differences, etc. I soon found the advantage of this change in my manner; the conversations I engaged in went on more pleasantly. The modest way in which I proposed my opinions procured them a readier reception and less contradiction; I had less mortification when I was found to be in the wrong, and I more easily prevailed with others to give up their mistakes and join with me when I happened to be in the right.

And this mode,[2] which I at first put on with some violence to natural inclination, became at length so easy and so habitual to me that perhaps for these fifty years past no one has ever heard a dogmatical expression escape me. And to this habit (after my character of integrity) I think it principally owing that I had early so much weight with my fellow citizens when I proposed new institutions, or alterations in the old, and so much influence in public councils when I became a member; for I was but a bad speaker, never eloquent, subject to much hesitation in my choice of words, hardly correct in language, and yet I generally carried my points.

In reality, there is, perhaps, no one of our natural passions so hard to subdue as *pride.* Disguise it, struggle with it, beat it down, stifle it, mortify it as much as one pleases, it is still alive, and will every now and then peep out and show itself; you will see it, perhaps, often in this history; for, even if I could conceive that I had completely overcome it, I should probably be proud of my humility.

---

[1] **Junto:** the name of the debating society organized by Franklin.

[2] **mode:** manner.

Sayings
of Poor Richard

A standard way for a colonial printer to eke out his income was to publish an almanac, a descriptive calendar of the year, giving information about such matters as the times of sunrise and sunset, movements of tides, and eclipses. All this information was much the same in any almanac. But a difference existed in the little "fillers" with which the editor rounded out the pages. Franklin's "fillers" in *Poor Richard's Almanack* were memorable "sayings" and bits of practical advice that made his almanac a household favorite for twenty-five years and made Poor Richard immortal.

INTENSIVE READING. Franklin borrowed freely from the wisdom of the ages, but often he rephrased the maxims, using homely metaphors rich in meaning for his readers. Few men have used figures of speech to better advantage. As you read these sayings, be sure you get the underlying meaning in such figures as "A small leak will sink a great ship."

1. Experience keeps a dear school, but a fool will learn in no other.

2. Hunger is the best pickle.

3. Love your neighbor; yet don't pull down your hedge.

4. If a man empties his purse into his head, no man can take it away from him. An investment in knowledge always pays the best interest.

5. Three may keep a secret if two of them are dead.

6. Tart words make no friends; a spoonful of honey will catch more flies than a gallon of vinegar.

7. Glass, china, and reputation are easily cracked and never well mended.

8. Fish and visitors smell in three days.

9. One today is worth two tomorrows.

10. A truly great man will neither trample on a worm nor sneak to an emperor.

11. He that riseth late must trot all day, and shall scarce overtake his business at night; while laziness travels so slowly that poverty soon overtakes him. Drive thy business. Let it not drive thee.

12. A little neglect may breed mischief; for want of a nail the shoe was lost; for want of a shoe the horse was lost; for want of a horse the rider was lost; for want of the rider the battle was lost.

Poor Richard, 1733.

A N

Almanack

For the Year of Chrift

1733,

Being the Firft after LEAP YEAR.

And makes fince the Creation Years
By the Account of the Eaftern *Greeks* 7241
By the Latin Church, when ☉ ent. ♈ 6932
By the Computation of *W.W.* 5742
By the *Roman* Chronology 5682
By the *Jewifh* Rabbies. 5494

Wherein is contained

The Lunations, Eclipfes, Judgment of the Weather, Spring Tides, Planets Motions & mutual Afpects, Sun and Moon's Rifing and Setting, Length of Days, Time of High Water, Fairs, Courts, and obfervable Days.

Fitted to the Latitude of Forty Degrees, and a Meridian of Five Hours Weft from *London,* but may without fenfible Error, ferve all the adjacent Places, even from *Newfoundland* to *South-Carolina.*

By RICHARD SAUNDERS, Philom.

PHILADELPHIA:
Printed and fold by *B. FRANKLIN,* at the New Printing-Office near the Market

13. If you would know the value of money, go and try to borrow some; he that goes a-borrowing goes a-sorrowing.

14. He that composes himself is wiser than he that composes books.

15. He that is of the opinion that money will do everything may well be suspected of doing everything for money.

16. If a man could have half his wishes, he would double his troubles.

17. Creditors have better memories than debtors.

18. 'Tis hard for an empty bag to stand upright.

19. A lie stands on one leg, truth on two.

20. The sleeping fox catches no poultry.

21. A plowman on his legs is higher than a gentleman on his knees.

22. When the well's dry, we know the worth of water.

23. A small leak will sink a great ship.

24. 'Tis easier to build two chimneys than to keep one in fuel.

25. Now that I have a sheep and a cow, everybody bids me good morrow.

26. Silks and satins, scarlet and velvet, put out the kitchen fire.

27. To err is human, to repent divine; to persist devilish.

28. The use of money is all the advantage there is in having money.

29. Keep thy shop and thy shop will keep thee.

30. Tho' modesty is a virtue, bashfulness is a vice.

FOR DISCUSSION

AUTOBIOGRAPHY

1. What sort of man does this selection reveal Franklin to be?
2. According to Franklin, what is the best way to establish a new habit? Do you feel that this is an effective method?
3. Franklin found a number of definitions for "Temperance." Why did he decide to use only one meaning? Where do the other definitions appear in his list?
4. In what way do you feel that Franklin's attempt to acquire humility contributed to his career as a statesman?
5. Select any American you have studied in "The Colonial Time": Taylor, Edwards, Knight, Byrd. In what way would a list of virtues made by this writer differ from Franklin's list?

SAYINGS OF POOR RICHARD

1. List the virtues suggested by these sayings. How do they compare with Franklin's list of thirteen virtues?
2. Which sayings do you prefer? Learn them.
3. Try inventing from three to six "Maxims for Moderns."

INTENSIVE READING: METAPHOR

Poets are not the only writers who make use of metaphors. Good prose writers will often use such figures of speech to add color and directness to their writing. Choose some examples of metaphors from the "Sayings of Poor Richard," and restate them in your own words. Which versions are clearer — yours or Franklin's? Which are longer? Can you think of some other reasons why Franklin employed metaphors in these sayings?

Franklin in Art ➤

Throughout his life Franklin was a favorite subject of painters. At the top of the next page is "Benjamin Franklin Before the Privy Council," by the French-born American artist Christian Schussele. The oval portrait is by the French artist Joseph Duplessis. The portrait at the right is by the American artist Charles Willson Peale.

Above: *Christian Schussele's painting shows Franklin in his pre-Revolutionary role as a representative of the discontented Colonies.* Below right: *Peale's portrait symbolizes Franklin's political and scientific achievements.*

Above: *The Duplessis portrait shows Franklin late in life, as he appeared when he was the American Minister to France.*

PATRICK HENRY

1736–1799

Speech in the Virginia Convention

Patrick Henry was one of the Virginians who were convinced that the colonists must resort to armed resistance. On March 23, 1775, he delivered the following speech before the House of Burgesses. This body had reassembled after having been dissolved by the royal governor, and a resolution had been proposed that "Virginia be immediately put into a posture of defense." The opposition within the House was strong and influential, for the rich planters feared a popular uprising even more than they feared oppression from the crown.

Imagine yourself one of the men torn between the momentous choices that confronted the burgesses at this fateful session. Picture the rawboned, six-foot lawyer from the western foothills rising to make his impassioned appeal.

Mr. President:

No man thinks more highly than I do of the patriotism, as well as abilities, of the very worthy gentlemen who have just addressed the house. But different men often see the same subject in different lights; and, therefore, I hope it will not be thought disrespectful to those gentlemen, if, entertaining as I

do opinions of a character very opposite to theirs, I shall speak forth my sentiments freely and without reserve. This is no time for ceremony. The question before the house is one of awful moment to this country. For my own part, I consider it as nothing less than a question of freedom or slavery. And in proportion to the magnitude of the subject ought to be the freedom of the debate. It is only in this way that we can hope to arrive at truth and fulfill the great responsibility which we hold to God and our country. Should I keep back my opinions at such a time, through fear of giving offense, I should consider myself as guilty of treason toward my country, and of an act of disloyalty toward the Majesty of Heaven, which I revere above all earthly kings.

Mr. President, it is natural to man to indulge in the illusions of hope. We are apt to shut our eyes against a painful truth and listen to the song of that siren till she transforms us into beasts. Is this the part of wise men, engaged in a great and arduous struggle for liberty? Are we disposed to be of the number of those who having eyes see not, and having ears hear not, the things which so nearly concern their temporal salvation? For my part, whatever anguish of spirit it may cost, I am willing to know the whole truth; to know the worst and to provide for it.

I have but one lamp by which my feet are guided, and that is the lamp of experience. I know of no way of judging of the future but by the past. And judging by the past, I wish to know what there has been in the conduct of the British ministry for the last ten years to justify those hopes with which gentlemen have been pleased to solace themselves and the house? Is it that insidious smile with which our petition has been lately received? Trust it not, sir; it will prove a snare to your feet. Suffer not yourselves to be betrayed with a kiss. Ask yourselves how this gracious reception of our petition comports with those warlike preparations which cover our waters and darken our land. Are fleets and armies necessary to a work of love and reconciliation? Have we shown ourselves so unwilling to be reconciled that force must be called in to win back our love? Let us not deceive ourselves, sir. These are the implements of war and subjugation — the last arguments to which kings resort.

I ask gentlemen, sir, what means this martial array, if its purpose be not to force us to submission? Can gentlemen assign any other possible motive for it? Has Great Britain any enemy in this quarter of the world, to call for all this accumulation of navies and armies? No, sir, she has none. They are meant for us: they can be meant for no other. They are sent over to bind and rivet upon us those chains which the British ministry have been so long forging.

And what have we to oppose to them? Shall we try argument? Sir, we have been trying that for the last ten years. Have we anything new to offer upon the subject? Nothing. We have held the subject up in every light of which it is capable; but it has been all in vain.

Shall we resort to entreaty and humble supplication? What terms shall we find which have not been already exhausted? Let us not, I beseech you, sir, deceive ourselves longer.

Sir, we have done everything that could be done to avert the storm which is now coming on. We have petitioned; we have remonstrated; we have supplicated; we have prostrated ourselves before the throne and have implored its interposition [1] to arrest the tyrannical hands of the ministry and Parliament. Our petitions have been slighted, our remonstrances have produced additional violence and insult; our supplications have been disregarded; and we have been spurned with contempt from the foot of the throne! In vain, after these things, may we indulge the fond [2] hope of peace and reconciliation. There is no longer any room for hope. If we wish to be free, if we mean to preserve inviolate those inestimable privileges for which we have been so long contending, if we mean not basely to abandon the noble struggle in which we have been so long engaged, and which we have pledged ourselves never to abandon until the glorious object of our contest shall be obtained — we must fight! I repeat it, sir, we must fight! An appeal to arms and to the God of Hosts is all that is left us!

They tell us, sir, that we are weak — unable to cope with so formidable an adversary. But when shall we be stronger? Will it be the next week, or the next year? Will it be when we are totally disarmed, and when a British guard shall be stationed in every house? Shall we gather strength by irresolution and inaction? Shall we acquire the means of effectual resistance by lying supinely [3] on our backs and hugging the delusive phantom of hope until our enemies

[1] **interposition:** intervention; entrance into the problem.
[2] **fond:** foolish.
[3] **supinely** (sú·pīn′lĭ): sluggishly.

shall have bound us hand and foot? Sir, we are not weak, if we make a proper use of those means which the God of nature hath placed in our power. Three millions of people, armed in the holy cause of liberty, and in such a country as that which we possess, are invincible by any force which our enemy can send against us. Besides, sir, we shall not fight our battles alone. There is a just God who presides over the destinies of nations and who will raise up friends to fight our battles for us. The battle, sir, is not to the strong alone; it is to the vigilant, the active, the brave. Besides, sir, we have no election.[1] If we were base enough to desire it, it is now too late to retire from the contest. There is no retreat but in sub-

[1] election: choice.

mission and slavery! Our chains are forged! Their clanging may be heard on the plains of Boston! The war is inevitable — and let it come! I repeat it, sir, let it come!

It is in vain, sir, to extenuate the matter. Gentlemen may cry, Peace, Peace — but there is no peace. The war is actually begun! The next gale that sweeps from the north will bring to our ears the clash of resounding arms! Our brethren are already in the field! Why stand we here idle? What is it that gentlemen wish? What would they have? Is life so dear, or peace so sweet, as to be purchased at the price of chains and slavery? Forbid it, Almighty God! I know not what course others may take; but as for me, give me liberty or give me death!

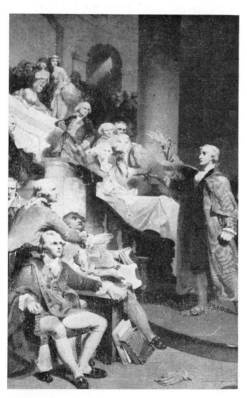

A nineteenth-century engraving showing Patrick Henry addressing the Virginia House of Burgesses.

FOR DISCUSSION

1. In this speech are a number of important general statements, such as, "And in proportion to the magnitude of the subject ought to be the freedom of the debate." Make a list of these general statements, and decide whether or not they are still valid today.

2. Does this speech begin and end in the same tone? Why? Why not?

DRAMATIZING HISTORY

Re-create the Virginia Convention, with students assigned to prepare speeches of reluctant burgesses, to whom Patrick Henry may reply. The objectors should not forget to mention the usual internal results of revolution. Conclude with a vote on the resolution.

UNDERSTANDING ALLUSIONS

To what does Patrick Henry refer when he says, "Suffer not yourselves to be betrayed with a kiss"? Many members of the House of Burgesses were opposed to war. In the light of that opposition, do you think that this is an effective allusion? Why? Why not?

THOMAS
PAINE
1737–1809

FROM The Crisis

The Revolutionary War came, and with it some black hours of discouragement for Americans. In December 1776, Thomas Paine fortified men's spirits with the first of a series of articles called *The Crisis*.

THESE are the times that try men's souls. The summer soldier and the sunshine patriot will, in this crisis, shrink from the service of their country; but he that stands it *now*, deserves the love and thanks of man and woman. Tyranny, like hell, is not easily conquered; yet we have this consolation with us, that the harder the conflict, the more glorious the triumph. What we obtain too cheap, we esteem too lightly: it is dearness only that gives everything its value. Heaven knows how to put a proper price upon its goods, and it would be strange indeed if so celestial an article as *freedom* should not be highly rated. Britain, with an army to enforce her tyranny, has declared that she has a right, not only to *tax*, but "to *bind* us in *all cases whatsoever*"; and if being bound in that manner is not slavery, then there is not such a thing as slavery upon earth. Even the expression is impious,[1] for so unlimited a power can belong only to God.

I have as little superstition in me as any man living, but my secret opinion has ever been, and still is, that God Almighty will not give up a people to military destruction or leave them unsupportedly to perish, who have so earnestly and so repeatedly sought to avoid the calamities of war by every decent method which wisdom could invent. Neither have I so much of the infidel in me as to suppose that He has relinquished the government of the world and given us up to the care of devils; and, as I do not, I cannot see on what grounds the king of Britain can look up to heaven for help against us.

I once felt all that kind of anger which a man ought to feel against the mean principles that are held by the Tories. A noted one, who kept a tavern at Amboy, was standing at his door, with as pretty a child in his hand, about eight or nine years old, as ever I saw, and after speaking his mind as freely as he thought was prudent, finished with this unfatherly expression, "Well! give me peace in my day." Not a man lives

---

[1] impious (ĭm′pĭ·ŭs): profane.

on the continent [1] but fully believes that a separation must some time or other finally take place, and a generous parent should have said, "If there must be trouble, let it be in my day, that my child may have peace"; and this single reflection, well applied, is sufficient to awaken every man to duty. Not a place upon earth might be so happy as America. Her situation is remote from all the wrangling world, and she has nothing to do but to trade with them. A man can distinguish himself between temper and principle, and I am as confident as I am that God governs the world, that America will never be happy till she gets clear of foreign dominion. Wars, without ceasing, will break out till that period arrives, and the continent must in the end be conqueror; for though the flame of liberty may sometimes cease to shine, the coal can never expire.

The heart that feels not now, is dead; the blood of his children will curse his cowardice who shrinks back at a time when a little might have saved the whole and made them happy. I love the man that can smile in trouble, that can gather strength from distress and grow brave by reflection. 'Tis the business of little minds to shrink; but he whose heart is firm, and whose conscience approves his conduct, will pursue his principles unto death. My own line of reasoning is to myself as straight and clear as a ray of light. Not all the treasures of the world, so far as I believe, could have induced me to support an offensive war, for I think it murder; but if a thief breaks into my house, burns and destroys my property, and kills or threatens to kill me or those that are in it, and to "bind me in all cases whatsoever" to his absolute will, am I to suffer it? What signifies it to me, whether he who does it is a king or a common man; my countryman or not my countryman; whether it be done by an indi-

[1] **the continent:** here Paine refers to the North American continent.

vidual villain or an army of them? If we reason to the root of things, we shall find no difference; neither can any just cause be assigned why we should punish in the one case and pardon in the other.

FOR DISCUSSION

1. What does Paine mean by the "summer soldier and the sunshine patriot"?
2. What statement by the British government does he consider a clear example of tyranny?
3. What answer does Paine have for the timid person who is afraid of England's might? for the one who says, "Give me peace in my day"? for the one who believes all war is wrong?
4. If you had been an undecided citizen of that day, which would have moved you more strongly to action — Patrick Henry or Thomas Paine? Why?

Revolutionary Art →

During the years just before the outbreak of the Revolutionary War, expressions of anti-British sentiment were not confined to speeches and pamphlets. Reproduced on the facing page is a potent piece of Revolutionary propaganda, Paul Revere's engraving of the Boston Massacre.

The Boston Massacre occurred on the night of March 5, 1770, when a Boston mob provoked troops from the British garrison into firing on them. The Bostonians were probably as much at fault as the British (in fact, John Adams defended the troops successfully at their trial), but the patriots quickly seized on the incident as a means of gaining sympathy and recruits for their cause.

This "broadside," as such single-sheet publications were called, was entirely the work of Paul Revere (1735–1818). Today, Revere is known primarily as the trusted express rider for Boston's Sons of Liberty, but his famous "midnight ride" unfortunately tends to overshadow his many other accomplishments. Acknowledged as the finest silversmith of his day, this versatile craftsman was also a bellmaker, goldsmith, dentist, printer, engraver, and inventor.

The BLOODY MASSACRE perpetrated in King — t — Street BOSTON on March 5th 1770 by a party of the 29th REGt.

unhappyBoston! see thy Sons deplore,
ny hallow'd Walks besmear'd with guiltless Gore:
hile faithless P——n and his savage Bands,
ith murd'rous Rancour stretch their bloody Hands,
ike fierce Barbarians grinning o'er their Prey,
pprove the Carnage,and enjoy the Day.

If scalding drops fromRage from Anguish Wrung
If speechless Sorrows lab'ring for a Tongue
Or if a weeping World can ought appease
The plaintive Ghosts of Victims such as these:
The Patriot's copious Tears for each are shed.
A glorious Tribute which embalms the Dead.

But know,Fate summons to that awful Goal,
Where Justice strips the Murd'rer of his Soul:
Should venal C——ts the scandal of the Land,
Snatch the relentless Villain from her Hand,
Keen Execrations on this Plate inscrib'd,
Shall reach a Judge who never can be brib'd.

The unhappy Sufferers were Messs. Samr GRAY, Saml MAVERICK, Jamr CALDWELL, CRISPUS ATTUCKS & Patr CARR
Killed. Six wounded; two of them (CHRISTr MONK & JOHN CLARK) Mortally

THOMAS
JEFFERSON

1743–1826

The epitaph Jefferson wrote for himself is significant:

HERE WAS BURIED
THOMAS JEFFERSON,
AUTHOR OF THE DECLARATION
OF INDEPENDENCE,
OF THE STATUTE OF VIRGINIA FOR
RELIGIOUS FREEDOM, AND FATHER
OF THE UNIVERSITY OF VIRGINIA

Jefferson believed that political freedom was closely entwined with freedom of worship and freedom of thought. Therefore he valued most these three contributions — political freedom for America, religious freedom for his state, and intellectual freedom for those who would seek it. Each of the following selections from his writing gives us a measure of this versatile and brilliant man.

The Declaration of Independence

In June 1776, a committee of the Second Continental Congress, consisting of Thomas Jefferson, John Adams, Benjamin Franklin, Roger Sherman, and Robert R. Livingston, was appointed to draft a declaration of independence. At the request of this committee, Thomas Jefferson wrote the text, which, after a few changes by the committee, was presented to Congress on June 28. After several days of debate, the Declaration of Independence was formally adopted on July 4, 1776. This document is remarkable for the clarity, dignity, and beauty of its language.

INTENSIVE READING. Do not let the grandeur and the elevated style of this great document blind you to its profound meaning. Use your glossary, and if necessary a dictionary, to grasp the thought of each sentence and phrase.

W HEN, in the course of human events, it becomes necessary for one people to dissolve the political bands which have connected them with another, and to assume among the powers of the earth the separate and equal station to which the laws of nature and of nature's God entitle them, a decent respect to the opinions of mankind requires that they should declare the causes which impel them to the separation.

We hold these truths to be self-evident: that all men are created equal, that they are endowed by their Creator with certain unalienable rights, that among these are life, liberty, and the pursuit of happiness. That to secure these rights, governments are instituted among men, deriving their just powers from the consent of the governed. That whenever any form of government becomes destructive of these ends, it is the right of the people to alter or abolish it, and to institute a new government, laying its foundation on such principles, and organizing its powers in such form, as to them shall seem most likely to effect their safety and happiness. Prudence, indeed, will dictate that governments long established should not be changed for light and transient causes; and accordingly all experience hath shown that mankind are more disposed to suffer, while evils are sufferable, than to right themselves by abolishing the forms to which they are accustomed. But when a long train of abuses and usurpations, pursuing invariably the same object, evinces a design to reduce them under absolute despotism, it is their right, it is their duty, to throw off such government, and to provide new guards for their future security. Such has been the patient sufferance of these colonies; and such is now the necessity which constrains them to alter their former systems of government. The history of the present King of Great Britain is a history of repeated injuries and usurpations, all having in direct object the establishment of an absolute tyranny over these states. To prove this, let facts be submitted to a candid world.

[At this point the document contains a long list of injustices suffered by the Colonies.]

In every stage of these oppressions we have petitioned for redress in the most humble terms: Our repeated petitions have been answered only by repeated injuries.

A prince whose character is thus marked by every act which may define a tyrant, is unfit to be the ruler of a free people.

Nor have we been wanting in attentions to our British brethren. We have warned them from time to time of attempts by their legislature to extend an unwarrantable jurisdiction over us. We have reminded them of the circumstances of our emigration and settlement here. We have appealed to their native justice and magnanimity and we have conjured [1] them by the ties of our common kindred to disavow these usurpations which would inevitably interrupt our connection and correspondence. They too have been deaf to the voice of justice and of consanguinity.[2] We must, therefore, acquiesce in the necessity which denounces [3] our separation and hold them, as we hold the rest of mankind, enemies in war, in peace, friends.

We, therefore, the representatives of the United States of America, in General Congress assembled, appealing to the Supreme Judge of the world for the rectitude of our intentions, do, in the name, and by the authority of the good people of these Colonies, solemnly publish and declare that these United Colonies are and of right ought to be free and independent States; that they are absolved from all allegiance to the British Crown, and that all political connection between them and the State of Great Britain is and ought to be totally dissolved; and that as free and independent States, they have full power to

[1] **conjured** (kŏn·jōōrd′): here, appealed to; begged.
[2] **consanguinity** (kŏn′săng·gwĭn′ĭ·tĭ): blood relationship.
[3] **denounces**: here, makes known in a solemn or official manner.

THOMAS JEFFERSON   473

levy war, conclude peace, contract alliances, establish commerce, and to do all other acts and things which independent States may of right do.

And for the support of this declaration, with a firm reliance on the protection of Divine Providence, we mutually pledge to each other our lives, our fortunes, and our sacred honor.

FROM The
First Inaugural Address

The Presidential campaign of 1800 had been intensely fought. There was bitter strife between the Federalists and the party organized by Jefferson, who, in the election, proved to be the choice of the people. Jefferson's "First Inaugural Address" was a brilliant exposition of his political principles as well as a strong plea "to bind up the nation's wounds" inflicted in party strife. You will read the section of Jefferson's speech that summarizes his "essential principles" of government.

March 4, 1801

. . . About to enter, fellow citizens, on the exercise of duties which comprehend everything dear and valuable to you, it is proper you should understand what I deem the essential principles of this government, and consequently those which ought to shape its administration. I will compress them in the narrowest compass they will bear, stating the general principle but not all its limitations:

Equal and exact justice to all men of whatever state or persuasion, religious or political;

Peace, commerce, and honest friendship with all nations; entangling alliances with none;

The support of the state governments in all their rights, as the most competent administrations for our domestic concerns and the surest bulwarks against antirepublican tendencies;

The preservation of the general government in its whole constitutional vigor, as the sheet anchor of our peace at home and safety abroad;

A jealous care of the right of election by the people — a mild and safe corrective of abuses which are lopped by the sword of revolution where peaceable remedies are unprovided;

Absolute acquiescence in the decisions of the majority, the vital principle of republics, from which is no appeal but to force, the vital principle and immediate parent of despotism;

A well-disciplined militia, our best reliance in peace and for the first moments of war, till regulars may relieve them;

The supremacy of the civil over the military authority;

Economy in the public expense, that labor may be lightly burdened;

The honest payment of our debts and sacred preservation of the public faith;

Encouragement of agriculture and of commerce as its handmaid;

The diffusion of information and arraignment of all abuses at the bar of public reason;

Freedom of religion, freedom of the press, and freedom of person under the protection of the habeas corpus;

And trial by juries impartially selected.

These principles form the bright constellation which has gone before us and guided our steps through an age of revolution and reformation. The wisdom of our sages and the blood of our heroes have been devoted to their attainment. They should be the creed of our political faith, the text of civic instruction, the touchstone by which to try the services of those we trust; and should we wander from them in moments of error or of alarm, let us hasten to retrace our steps and to regain the road which alone leads to peace, liberty, and safety.

Portrait of Washington

Washington's eight years as President concluded the critical period of the birth of the American republic. Jefferson had worked closely with Washington as Secretary of State from 1789 to 1793, the year he resigned. We may be grateful to Jefferson for preserving his impression of a man as great in peace as in war. Jefferson wrote the portrait at the age of seventy, while enjoying an active retirement at Monticello.

Monticello, January 2, 1814

. . . I think I knew General Washington intimately and thoroughly; and were I called on to delineate [1] his character, it should be in terms like these.

His mind was great and powerful, without being of the very first order; his penetration strong, though not so acute as that of Newton, Bacon, or Locke; [2] and as far as he saw, no judgment was ever sounder. It was slow in operation, being little aided by invention or imagination, but sure in conclusion. Hence the common remark of his officers, of the advantage he derived from councils of war, where hearing all suggestions, he selected whatever was best; and certainly no general ever planned his battle more judiciously. But if deranged [3] during the course of the action, if any member of his plan was dislocated by sudden circumstances, he was slow in readjustment. The consequence was that he often failed in the field, and rarely against an enemy in station, as at

---

[1] delineate (dḗ·lĭn′ḗ·āt): sketch.
[2] Newton, Bacon, Locke: English philosophers and scientists of the seventeenth and eighteenth centuries. Newton discovered the law of gravitation, Bacon developed the inductive method of scientific study, and Locke published studies of human psychology and of political science.
[3] deranged (dḗ·rānjd′): disordered.

Boston and York. He was incapable of fear, meeting personal dangers with the calmest unconcern. Perhaps the strongest feature in his character was prudence, never acting until every circumstance, every consideration, was maturely weighed; refraining if he saw a doubt, but, when once decided, going through with his purpose, whatever obstacles opposed. His integrity was most pure, his justice the most inflexible I have ever known, no motives of interest or consanguinity, of friendship or hatred being able to bias his decision. He was, indeed, in every sense of the words, a wise, a good, and a great man. His temper was naturally high-toned; but reflection and resolution had obtained a firm and habitual ascendancy over it. If ever, however, it broke its bonds, he was most tremendous in his wrath. In his expenses he was honorable, but exact; liberal in contributions to whatever promised utility; but frowning and unyielding on all visionary [4] projects and all unworthy calls on his charity. His heart was not warm in its affections; but he exactly calculated every man's value, and gave him a solid esteem proportioned to it. His person, you know, was fine, his stature exactly what one would wish, his deportment easy, erect and noble; the best horseman of his age, and the most graceful figure that could be seen on horseback. Although in the circle of his friends, where he might be unreserved with safety, he took a free share in conversation, his colloquial talents were not above mediocrity, possessing neither copiousness [5] of ideas, nor fluency of words. In public, when called on for a sudden opinion, he was unready, short, and embarrassed. Yet he wrote readily, rather diffusely, in an easy and correct style. This he had acquired by conversation with the world, for his education was merely reading, writing, and common arithmetic, to

---

[4] visionary: overly idealistic; impractical.
[5] copiousness (kō′pĭ-*us*·nĕs): abundance.

THOMAS JEFFERSON 475

which he added surveying at a later day. His time was employed in action chiefly, reading little, and that only in agriculture and English history. His correspondence became necessarily extensive, and, with journalizing his agricultural proceedings, occupied most of his leisure hours within doors. On the whole, his character was, in its mass, perfect, in nothing bad, in few points indifferent; and it may truly be said, that never did nature and fortune combine more perfectly to make a man great, and to place him in the same constellation with whatever worthies have merited from man an everlasting remembrance. For his was the singular destiny and merit, of leading the armies of his country successfully through an arduous war, for the establishment of its independence; of conducting its councils through the birth of a government, new in its forms and principles, until it had settled down into a quiet and orderly train; and of scrupulously obeying the laws through the whole of his career, civil and military, of which the history of the world furnishes no other example.

FOR DISCUSSION

THE DECLARATION OF INDEPENDENCE

1. What often quoted phrases do you find here? In the popular mind the Declaration of Independence and the Constitution of the United States are sometimes confused. Do you find any phrases here that you had supposed were in the Constitution?

2. To what extent does the Declaration of Independence maintain that "all men are created equal"?

3. What attitude is shown toward the British people? What attitude is shown toward the king?

4. What are some of the problems confronting the world today that have a direct connection with the "self-evident" truths expressed in the second paragraph of the Declaration?

THE FIRST INAUGURAL ADDRESS

1. Which of Jefferson's principles of government do you think most important? Which do not exist in undemocratic countries? Which ones have been incorporated into our American democracy?

PORTRAIT OF WASHINGTON

1. What facts not given here can you offer in support of the view that Washington's character was remarkable?

2. According to Jefferson, in what ways did "nature" and in what ways did "fortune" combine to make Washington a great man?

FURTHER READING

Two books that you will enjoy reading are: *Thomas Jefferson: Father of Democracy* by Vincent Sheean (Random House, 1953), a short, entertaining biography; and Sidney Kingsley's play *The Patriots*, in J. Gassner, *Best Plays of the Modern American Theatre* (Crown, 1947), in which both Jefferson and Hamilton appear as leading characters.

Thomas Jefferson's Home ➤

On the facing page are two views of Thomas Jefferson's home, Monticello, located near Charlottesville, Virginia. The name Jefferson chose refers to the location of the home on a hilltop (*monticello* in Italian means "little mountain").

Monticello was begun in 1767 and completed about thirty years later. Jefferson designed the thirty-five-room home, supervised the construction, landscaped the grounds, and even designed the furniture and curtains. Like Benjamin Franklin, Jefferson had a talent for invention, and he devised a number of ingenious gadgets for the home, including a compass and wind indicator mounted in the ceiling of the parlor, and a clock that told the day of the week as well as the time. The drawing room of Monticello boasted the first parquet floor (inlaid wood, arranged in patterns) in America.

Today Jefferson's elegant home is a national shrine, visited yearly by thousands of Americans.

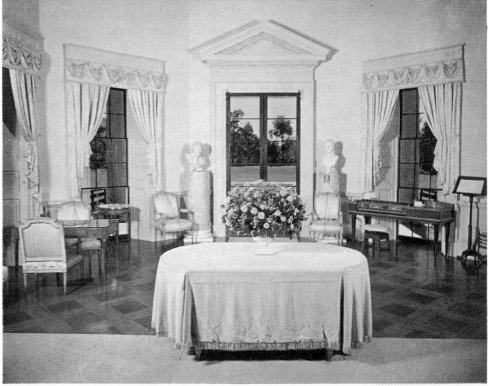

FRANCIS HOPKINSON

1737–1791

The Battle of the Kegs

Hopkinson used satire to ridicule the British. This lawyer, musician, and composer had signed the Declaration of Independence and had helped to draft the Articles of Confederation. His mirth in this selection was occasioned by an actual incident of the war, the sending of kegs of gunpowder down the Delaware River to annoy British shipping at Philadelphia.

Gallants, attend, and hear a friend
  Trill forth harmonious ditty:
Strange things I'll tell, which late befell
  In Philadelphia city.

'Twas early day, as poets say,   5
  Just when the sun was rising,
A soldier stood on a log of wood
  And saw a thing surprising.

As in amaze he stood to gaze,
  The truth can't be denied, sir,   10
He spied a score of kegs or more
  Come floating down the tide, sir.

A sailor, too, in jerkin blue,
  This strange appearance viewing,
First damned his eyes, in great surprise,   15
  Then said, "Some mischief's brewing:

"These kegs, I'm told, the rebels hold,
  Packed up like pickled herring;
And they're come down to attack the town,
  In this new way of ferrying."   20

The soldier flew, the sailor too,
  And scared almost to death, sir,
Wore out their shoes to spread the news,
  And ran till out of breath, sir.

Now up and down throughout the town
  Most frantic scenes were acted;   26
And some ran here and others there,
  Like men almost distracted.

Some fire cried, which some denied,
  But said the earth had quakèd;   30
And girls and boys, with hideous noise,
  Ran through the streets half naked.

Sir William,° he, snug as a flea,
  Lay all this time a-snoring,
Nor dreamed of harm, as he lay warm,
  [The Yankees quite ignoring].   36

Now in a fright he starts upright,
  Awaked by such a clatter;
He rubs his eyes and boldly cries,
  "For God's sake, what's the matter?"

At his bedside he then espied   41
  Sir Erskine at command, sir:
Upon one foot he had one boot,
  An' t'other in his hand, sir.

"Arise, arise!" Sir Erskine cries;   45
  "The rebels, more's the pity,
Without a boat are all afloat
  And ranged before the city.

"The motley crew, in vessels new,
  With Satan for their guide, sir,   50
Packed up in bags, or wooden kegs,
  Come driving down the tide, sir.

"Therefore prepare for bloody war:
  These kegs must all be routed
Or surely we despised shall be,   55
  And British courage doubted."

33. **Sir William:** Sir William Howe, the commander-in-chief of the British forces in America.

The royal band now ready stand,
  All ranged in dread array, sir,
With stomachs stout, to see it out,
  And make a bloody day, sir.   60

The cannons roar from shore to shore,
  The small arms make a rattle;
Since wars began, I'm sure no man
  E'er saw so strange a battle.

The rebel dales, the rebel vales,   65
  With rebel trees surrounded,
The distant woods, the hills and floods,
  With rebel echoes sounded.

The fish below swam to and fro,
  Attacked from every quarter: 70
"Why, sure," thought they, "the devil's
    to pay
  'Mongst folks above the water."

The kegs, 'tis said, though strongly
    made
  Of rebel staves and hoops, sir,   74
Could not oppose their powerful foes,
  The conquering British troops, sir.

From morn till night these men of
    might
  Displayed amazing courage,
And when the sun was fairly down
  Retired to sup their porridge.   80

An hundred men, with each a pen,
  Or more, upon my word, sir,
It is most true would be too few
  Their valor to record, sir.

Such feats did they perform that day
  Against those wicked kegs, sir,   86
That years to come, if they get home,
  They'll make their boasts and brags,
    sir.

FOR DISCUSSION

1. Do you feel that satire of this sort is an effective weapon? Is there any trace of bitterness in Hopkinson's satire?

2. Compare Hopkinson's poem with the speeches and writings of Patrick Henry and Thomas Paine. Which do you think had greater effect on the colonists?

YOUR OWN WRITING

Write a bit of satire, in prose if you prefer, attacking something which you consider ridiculous.

SPECIAL REPORT

An interested student may look up information and report to the class on Francis Hopkinson as a musician and song writer.

ALEXANDER HAMILTON

1757–1804

Speech in Defense of the Constitution

On June 21, 1788, sixty-five legislators of New York state met to consider ratifying the Constitution. Forty-six were Anti-Federalists: they favored keeping a separate government for New York rather than joining with other states under a United States government. Some feared that under the proposed Constitution the rich or the well-educated might gain complete control of the federal government. Hamilton's speech allayed their fears. The result? The Constitution was ratified by a majority of three.

RECOGNIZING THE AUTHOR'S IDEAS. As you read this selection, see if you can recognize in what ways Hamilton's view of government differs, if at all, from that of Jefferson.

S IR, we hear constantly a great deal which is rather calculated to awake our passions and create prejudices, than to conduct us to the truth and teach us our real interests. I do not suppose this to be the design of the gentlemen. Why, then, are we told so often of an aristocracy? For my part, I hardly know the meaning of this word, as it is applied.

If all we hear be true, this government is really a very bad one. But who are the aristocracy among us? Where do we find men elevated to a perpetual rank above their fellow citizens, and possessing powers entirely independent of them? The arguments of the gentlemen only go to prove that there are men who are rich, men who are poor, some who are wise, and others who are not; that, indeed, every distinguished man is an aristocrat. This reminds me of a description of the aristocrats I have seen in a late publication styled the *Federal Farmer*. The author reckons in the aristocracy all governors of states, members of Congress, chief magistrates, and all officers of the militia. This description, I presume to say, is ridiculous. The image is a phantom. Does the new government render a rich man more eligible than a poor one? No. It requires no such qualification. It is bottomed on the broad and equal principle of your state constitution.

Sir, if the people have it in their option to elect their most meritorious men, is this to be considered as an objection? Shall the Constitution oppose their wishes and abridge their most invaluable privilege? While property continues to be pretty equally divided, and a considerable share of information pervades the community, the tendency of the people's suffrages will be to elevate merit even from obscurity. As riches increase and accumulate in few hands, as luxury prevails in society, virtue will be in a greater degree considered as only a graceful appendage of wealth, and the tendency of things will be to depart from the republican standard. This is the real disposition of human nature: it is what neither the honorable member nor myself can correct; it is a common misfortune, that awaits our state constitution as well as all others.

There is an advantage incident to large districts of election, which perhaps the gentlemen, amidst all their apprehensions of influence and bribery, have not adverted to. In large districts, the corruption of the electors is much more difficult; combinations for the purposes of intrigue are less easily formed; factions [1] and cabals [2] are little known. In a small district, wealth will have a more complete influence, because the people in the vicinity of a great man are more immediately his dependents and because this influence has fewer objects to act upon. It has been remarked that it would be disagreeable to the middle class of men to go to the seat of the new government. If this be so, the difficulty will be enhanced by the gentleman's proposal. If his argument be true, it proves that the larger the representation is, the less will be your chance of having it filled. But it appears to me frivolous to bring forward such arguments as these. It has answered no other purpose than to induce me, by way of reply, to enter into discussion, which I consider as useless, and not applicable to our subject.

It is a harsh doctrine that men grow wicked in proportion as they improve and enlighten their minds. Experience has by no means justified us in the supposition that there is more virtue in one class of men than in another. Look through the rich and the poor of the community, the learned and the ignorant. Where does virtue predominate? The difference indeed consists, not in the quantity, but kind, of vices which are incident to various classes; and here the advantage of character belongs to the wealthy. Their vices are probably more favorable to the prosperity of the state than those of the indigent, and partake less of moral depravity.

After all, sir, we must submit to this idea, that the true principle of a republic is that the people should choose whom they please to govern them. Representation is imperfect in proportion as the current of popular favor is checked. This great source of free government, popular election, should be perfectly pure and the most unbounded liberty allowed. Where this principle is adhered to; where, in the organization of the government, the legislative, executive, and judicial branches are rendered distinct; where, again, the legislature is divided into separate houses, and the operations of each are controlled by various checks and balances, and, above all, by the vigilance and weight of the state government — to talk of tyranny and the subversion of our liberties is to speak the language of enthusiasm.[3] This balance between the national and state governments ought to be dwelt on with peculiar [4] attention, as it is of the utmost importance. It forms a double security to the people. If one encroaches on their rights, they will find a powerful protection in the other. Indeed, they will both be prevented from overpassing their constitutional limits, by a certain rivalship, which will ever subsist between

---

[1] factions: an organization or party within a state, usually characterized by dissension and opposition to the public good.
[2] cabals (kȧ·bȧlz′): a group of persons united in secret designs or plots.

[3] enthusiasm: here, an overriding emotional zeal.
[4] peculiar: here, particular.

them. I am persuaded that a firm union is as necessary to perpetuate our liberties as it is to make us respectable; and experience will probably prove that the national government will be as natural a guardian of our freedom as the state legislatures themselves.

FOR DISCUSSION

1. With what parts of Hamilton's argument do you agree? With what parts do you disagree?

2. What two prophecies does Hamilton make in this speech? Have they come to pass?

3. What does Hamilton think is the great advantage of a balance between the national and state governments? How does our form of government provide for "checks and balances"?

RECOGNIZING THE AUTHOR'S IDEAS

Contrast the political philosophies of Hamilton and Jefferson. Which is more nearly embodied in the United States Constitution? Toward which has been the trend of the amendments?

THE PREAMBLE TO THE CONSTITUTION

The Preamble to the Constitution is well worth memorizing: "We, the people of the United States, in order to form a more perfect Union, establish justice, insure domestic tranquillity, provide for the common defense, promote the general welfare, and secure the blessings of liberty to ourselves and our posterity, do ordain and establish this Constitution for the United States of America."

GEORGE WASHINGTON

1732–1799

FROM THE Farewell Address

The First Citizen of his day could not reach his friends and fellow citizens by radio or television when he wanted to convey to them his decision not to run for a third term. He published his resolution in a Philadelphia newspaper. This great document from the pen of the Virginia planter, soldier, military leader, and Presi-

dent has often been quoted throughout our nation's history. In our own times Congressmen turn to it for advice and precedent. Every American should know and understand Washington's ideas.

The editors have culled selected passages and have inserted headings to help you get the main points. You may have to consult the glossary for the meanings of some of the words, but first see whether you can understand the meaning from the context.

PRESERVE LIBERTY

INTERWOVEN as is the love of liberty with every ligament of your hearts, no recommendation of mine is necessary to fortify or confirm the attachment.

PROTECT NATIONAL UNITY

The unity of government, which constitutes you one people, is a main pillar of your real independence, the support of your tranquillity at home, your peace abroad; of your safety; of your prosperity; of that very liberty which you so highly prize. The name of America, which belongs to you, in your national capacity, must always exalt the just pride of patriotism, more than any appellation derived from local discriminations. One of the expedients of party to acquire influence, within particular districts, is to misrepresent the opinions and aims of other districts. You cannot shield yourselves too much against the jealousies and heartburnings which spring from these misrepresentations.

OBEY THE LAW

The basis of our political systems is the right of the people to make and to alter their constitutions of government. But the constitution which at any time exists, till changed by an explicit and authentic act of the whole people, is sacredly obligatory upon all. The very idea of the power and the right of the people to establish government presupposes the duty of every individual to obey the established government.

BEWARE OF EASY CHANGES IN GOVERNMENT

Toward the preservation of your government, and the permanency of your present happy state, it is requisite, not only that you steadily discountenance irregular opposition to its acknowledged authority, but also that you resist with care the spirit of innovation upon its principles, however specious the pretexts. Remember that facility in changes, upon the credit of mere hypothesis and opinion, exposes to perpetual change, from the endless variety of hypothesis and opinion; and remember, especially, that, for the efficient management of your common interests, in a country so extensive as ours, a government of as much vigor as is consistent with the perfect security of liberty is indispensable. Liberty itself will find in such a government, with powers properly distributed and adjusted, its surest guardian.

BEWARE OF POLITICAL PARTY SPIRIT

Let me warn you in the most solemn manner against the baneful effects of the spirit of party generally. The alternate domination of one faction over another, sharpened by the spirit of revenge natural to party dissension, is in itself a frightful despotism. The disorders and miseries which result gradually incline the minds of men to seek security and repose in the absolute power of an individual; and sooner or later the chief of some prevailing faction, more able or more fortunate than his competitors, turns his disposition to the purposes of his own elevation, on the ruins of public liberty.

PRESERVE THE SYSTEM OF CHECKS AND BALANCES

The necessity of reciprocal checks in the exercise of political power, by dividing and distributing it into different depositories, and constituting each the guardian of the public weal against invasions by the others, has been evinced by experiments ancient and modern, some of them in our country and under our own eyes. To preserve them must be as necessary as to institute them. If, in the opinion of the people, the distribution or modification of the constitutional powers be in any particular wrong, let it be corrected by an amendment in the way which the Constitution designates. But let there be no change by usurpation.

CHERISH RELIGION AND MORALITY

Of all the dispositions and habits which lead to political prosperity, religion and morality are indispensable supports.

PROMOTE EDUCATION

Promote, as an object of primary importance, institutions for the general diffusion of knowledge. In proportion as the structure of a government gives force to public opinion, it is essential that public opinion should be enlightened.

CHERISH PUBLIC CREDIT

As a very important source of strength and security, cherish public credit.

AVOID PERMANENT ALLIANCES

Observe good faith and justice toward all nations; cultivate peace and harmony with all. The nation which indulges toward another an habitual hatred or an habitual fondness is in some degree a slave. It is a slave to its animosity or to its affection, either of which is sufficient to lead it astray from its duty and its interest.

The great rule of conduct for us, in regard to foreign nations, is, in extending our commercial relations, to have with them as little political connection as possible. Europe has a set of primary interests, which to us have none, or a remote relation. Hence she must be engaged in frequent controversies, the causes of which are essentially foreign to our concerns. Hence, therefore, it must be unwise in us to implicate ourselves by artificial ties, in the ordinary vicissitudes of her politics or the ordinary combinations and collisions of her friendships and enmities. Our detached and distant situation invites and

enables us to pursue a different course. Why forego the advantages of so peculiar a situation? It is our true policy to steer clear of permanent alliances with any portion of the foreign world. Even our commercial policy should hold an equal and impartial hand; neither seeking nor granting exclusive favors or preferences, constantly keeping in view that it is folly in one nation to look for disinterested favors from any other; that it must pay with a portion of its independence for whatever it may accept under that character.

Letter to the Hebrew Congregation in Newport, Rhode Island

This letter from President Washington gave to the Jewish residents of Newport reassurance of safety and reminded their Christian neighbors that religious freedom is a basic principle of our republic.

August 21, 1790

Gentlemen,

While I receive, with much satisfaction, your Address replete [1] with expressions of affection and esteem, I rejoice in the opportunity of assuring you that I shall always retain a grateful remembrance of the cordial welcome I experienced in my visit to Newport, from all classes of Citizens.

The reflection on the days of difficulty and danger which are past is rendered the more sweet from a consciousness that they are succeeded by days of uncommon prosperity and security. If we have wisdom to make the best use of the advantages with which

---

[1] **replete** (rê·plēt'): filled.

"Letter to the Hebrew Congregation in Newport, Rhode Island" by George Washington. Reprinted by permission of the Society of Friends of Touro Synagogue.

we are now favored, we cannot fail, under the just administration of a good Government, to become a great and a happy people.

The Citizens of the United States of America have a right to applaud themselves for having given to mankind examples of an enlarged and liberal policy worthy of imitation. All possess alike liberty of conscience and immunities of citizenship. It is now no more that toleration is spoken of, as if it was by the indulgence of one class of people that another enjoyed the exercise of their inherent national rights. For happily the Government of the United States, which gives to bigotry no sanction, to persecution no assistance, requires only that they who live under its protection should demean[1] themselves as good citizens, in giving it on all occasions their effectual support.

It would be inconsistent with the frankness of my character not to avow that I am pleased with your favorable opinion of my administration and fervent wishes for my felicity. May the children of the stock of Abraham who dwell in this land continue to merit and enjoy the good will of the other inhabitants while every one shall sit in safety under his own vine and fig tree, and there shall be none to make him afraid. May the father of all mercies scatter light and not darkness in our paths, and make us all in our several vocations useful here, and in his own due time and way everlastingly happy.

G. Washington

[1] demean (dė·mēn'): behave.

FOR DISCUSSION

1. The body of the "Farewell Address" falls into two main parts: advice on national affairs and advice on foreign affairs. Make an outline of the points under each.

2. Washington forewarns emphatically against the dangers of long alliances or en-mity between nations. Give some striking examples from world history.

3. Do you think that all of Washington's advice still applies today? What probably does? What may not?

4. Which passages in the "Farewell Address" illustrate characteristics pointed out by Jefferson in his portrait of Washington (see page 475)?

5. Compare the style of Washington's "Farewell Address" to the style of Patrick Henry's speech. How is the style of an address intended for oral delivery likely to differ from the style of one intended to be read?

6. In speaking of religious freedom in America, in his "Letter to the Hebrew Congregation in Newport, Rhode Island," why does Washington refer to the word *toleration* as an inadequate word?

GETTING THE MEANING FROM CONTEXT

Do we today expect political leaders to "talk down" to us? Or do we admire the statesman who has a genuine command of the language? Washington respected the intelligence of his audience and did not hesitate to use the precise word even if it were difficult. In the light of the context, tell what each of the following italicized words means.

1. your *tranquillity* at home
2. more than any *appellation*
3. one of the *expedients*
4. by an *explicit* . . . act
5. *subvert* the power
6. sacredly *obligatory* upon all
7. it is *requisite*
8. that you steadily *discountenance* irregular opposition
9. the spirit of *innovation*
10. however *specious* the pretexts
11. credit of mere *hypothesis*
12. against the *baneful* effects
13. is in itself a frightful *despotism*
14. necessity of *reciprocal* checks
15. guardian of the public *weal*
16. no change by *usurpation*
17. a slave to its *animosity*
18. in the ordinary *vicissitudes* of her politics
19. for *disinterested* favors
20. *indispensable* supports

← American Art and Artists

On the facing page is reproduced a portrait of George Washington by the American artist Charles Willson Peale (1741–1827). The oil painting, completed in 1779, symbolizes Washington's victories at Trenton and Princeton (see the captured Hessian flag at the right and the college buildings at the left rear). Peale himself served in both campaigns, commanding a group of about eighty volunteers.

Charles Willson Peale was one of the most productive of the early American portrait painters. In all, he completed seven portraits of George Washington, and he also painted many other famous figures of the Revolutionary period. His portraits reproduced in this book include John Adams on page 201, John Paul Jones on page 235, Benjamin Franklin on page 465, and Alexander Hamilton on page 480.

Peale is also remarkable as the founder of a large and talented family. Many of his seventeen children rose to distinction in either the arts or the sciences. Rembrandt Peale, one of the older sons, painted the portrait of Thomas Jefferson on page 472. Another son, Franklin, was a gifted mechanical engineer. A niece, Sarah Miriam, became the first professional woman portraitist in the United States. A younger son, Titian R. Peale II (1799–1885) began a fine career as a naturalist, but in later years he took up a new, experimental art — photography.

READING ON
THE MAKING OF A NATION

Alden, John R., *The American Revolution* (Harper, 1954)

American Heritage Jr. Library, *Thomas Jefferson and His World* (American Heritage, 1960)

Becker, Carl, *The Eve of the Revolution* (Yale Univ. Press, 1915)

Commager, H. S., and A. Nevins, *Heritage of America* (Little, Brown, 1943)

Lawson, Robert, *Watchwords of Liberty* (Little, Brown, rev., 1957)

Miller, J. C., *Origins of the American Revolution* (Little, Brown, 1943)

Street, James H., *The Revolutionary War* (Dial, 1954)

Van Doren, C. C., *The Great Rehearsal* (Viking, 1948)

BIOGRAPHY

JOHN ADAMS. Bowen, Catherine D., *John Adams* (Little, Brown, 1950)

ETHAN ALLEN. Holbrook, S. H., *America's Ethan Allen*, illus. by Lynd Ward (Houghton Mifflin, 1949)

GEORGE ROGERS CLARK, Havighurst, Walter, *George Rogers Clark, Soldier in the West* (McGraw-Hill, 1952); Nolan, J. C., *George Rogers Clark, Soldier and Hero* (Messner, 1954)

BENJAMIN FRANKLIN. Daugherty, James, *Poor Richard* (Viking, 1941); Goodman, Nathan, ed., *The Ingenious Dr. Franklin* (Univ. of Pennsylvania Press, 1956); Meadowcroft, E. L., *The Story of Benjamin Franklin* (Grosset & Dunlap, 1952)

ALEXANDER HAMILTON. Desmond, Alice C., *Alexander Hamilton's Wife* (Dodd, Mead, 1952); Schachner, Nathan, *Alexander Hamilton* (Yoseloff, 1957)

THOMAS JEFFERSON. Bowers, Claude G., *Young Jefferson, 1743–1789* (Houghton Mifflin, 1945); Malone, Dumas, *Jefferson, the Virginian* (Little, Brown, 1948); Sheean, Vincent, *Thomas Jefferson, Father of Democracy* (Random House, 1953)

JOHN PAUL JONES. Ellsberg, Edward, *I Have Just Begin to Fight: The Story of John Paul Jones*, illus. (Dodd, Mead, 1942); Johnson, G. W. *First Captain* (Coward-McCann, 1947); Morison, S. E., *John Paul Jones: A Sailor's Biography* (Little, Brown, 1959)

LAFAYETTE. Criss, Mildred, *Lafayette on the Heights of Freedom* (Dodd, Mead, 1954)

PAUL REVERE. Forbes, Esther, *America's Paul Revere* (Houghton Mifflin, 1946)

GEORGE WASHINGTON. Eaton, Jeanette, *Leader by Destiny* (Harcourt, Brace & World, 1938); Freeman, Douglas S., *George Washington* (Scribner, 1948)

FOR LISTENING

The selections by Patrick Henry and Thomas Paine have been recorded on *Many Voices* 11B.

The American Imagination Awakens

WHILE the Revolutionary War made the United States independent of England, the War of 1812 made the United States independent of Europe. The young country proved its strength and determination. The generation that grew up after 1815 could take independence for granted because it had never known any other condition. From 1815 to the end of the century, the United States was to be free of military involvements with Europe. The time was now ripe for the springing up of imaginative literature on a national scale. The country was free to grow in its own way, to explore its own character, to express its own ideals, and to draw upon the inspirations and literary resources of the vast, undeveloped continent. American writers now began to develop American themes.

A Changing America

In colonial America the Frenchman De Crèvecœur (page 449) had defined the changes that came over settlers when they arrived in this land. Now, in the brand-new United States of America, cities were flourishing, streams of newcomers were pouring in, and frontiers were being pushed forward rapidly. Another French observer, Alexis de Tocqueville (dē tôk'vēl'), described what we were becoming. His *Democracy in America* (1838) is a tribute to the reality of the great political experiment that had been launched by the Revolution. De Tocqueville traveled from the coastal cities to the wilderness outposts and testified:

> If there is a country in the world where the doctrine of the sovereignty of the people can be fairly appreciated, where it can be studied in its application to the affairs of society, and where its dangers and its advantages may be judged, that country is assuredly America.

As the character of the country changed and developed, so did the literature.

Three Literary Influences

Three different elements existed side by side in this period of our literature. They were a growing spirit of nationalism, a renewed interest in our European heritage, and romanticism. During these years all three elements often could be found in the works of the same writer.

NATIONALISM

The spirit of nationalism took pride in the newborn nation and held an unwavering belief in its virtues. Writers also began to pay more attention to the country's past, and this eventually led to a fresh awareness of the Indian. Influences from the lives and traditions of these first inhabitants soon entered our stories, poems, and dramas. Nationalism in literature also meant such varied things as Noah Webster's *American Dictionary* (1828) and patriotic songs like "America" and "The Star-Spangled Banner."

OUR EUROPEAN HERITAGE

With nationalism came a renewal of interest in English language and literature. Americans felt a richer appreciation of their cultural ties with the mother country once their independence was assured. Political frictions began to sink into the past. Old affections came to the foreground. American interests extended even farther, to embrace the cultural influences of all Europe and of the classical Greek and Roman world. Our architecture entered a period known as the "Greek revival." For generations, many of our buildings were fashioned after the temples and public structures of Athens and Rome.

ROMANTICISM

The words "romantic" and "romanticism" have a variety of meanings in the literary field. When the words are applied to our early national literature, they generally refer to four characteristics: idealism, an interest in distant times and places, an interest in the supernatural or mysterious, and a love of nature.

The whole background of the young country tended to promote idealism. Literary idealism saw the man of the New World as a person of heroic proportions, a bit larger than life. His strength, manly virtues, and integrity were contrasted to the weaker, corrupted, selfish qualities of the man of the Old World. This is the point of the title of our first American comic play, *The Contrast* by Royall Tyler, produced in 1787. In the play, Tyler sets the sterling American Colonel Manly in contrast to the soft English ladies' man Dimple. The contrast is carried through to the servants of the leading men. Dimple's Jessamy is as false and trifling as his master, while Manly's Jonathan is a homespun, comic good fellow. Jonathan is the first of a type, ignorant of worldly ways but possessing country shrewdness, which developed into a popular comic character known as the "stage Yankee."

In its second aspect, the romantic spirit looked to the past. It colored Dutch history in the Hudson Valley through the eyes of Washington Irving. Romanticism also looked back with affection on the old scenes of England and Europe, as in parts of Irving's *Sketch Book, Bracebridge Hall,* and *The Alhambra.* (Irving's life and writings are treated in detail on page 494.) The figure of the Indian was clothed with romance in James Fenimore Cooper's novels and Henry Wadsworth Longfellow's *Hiawatha.* The South found a romantic voice in the novels of John Pendleton Kennedy and William Gilmore Simms. Distant, exotic places also appealed to the romantic spirit. Herman Melville romanticized the South Sea Islanders in his early novels, *Typee* and *Omoo.*

The third, and the strangest, face of romanticism was the so-called "Gothic" imagination. The word is derived from the Middle Ages: Gothic tales, like the gargoyles on Gothic cathedrals, are often grotesque and terrifying. Gothic tales deal with mystery, horror, fear, and the supernatural. *Wieland* (1798) and other novels by Charles Brockden Brown, sometimes called America's first "professional" author, pioneered the Gothic tale in this country, but this strange style found its finest dark blooming in the poems and stories of Edgar Allan Poe. (See page 513 for details on Poe's life and writings.)

Finally, writers like Irving, Cooper, and the poet William Cullen Bryant expressed romanticism through their love of nature. In many of the romantic writers, the love of nature became an almost mystical adoration. Thus, Bryant's poems often express the feeling that thinking of nature is much like religious thought. (See page 506 for more details about Bryant.)

"Washington Irving and His Literary Friends," an oil painting by Christian Schussele (1826–1879). Irving is shown dressed in black, seated in the red chair. The other writers include Hawthorne and Longfellow (fifth and sixth from left), Emerson and Bryant (fifth and fourth from right), and Cooper (second from right).

Romanticism was a powerful force in English and European literature as well as American. William Wordsworth, Samuel Taylor Coleridge, Sir Walter Scott, Lord Byron, Percy Bysshe Shelley, and John Keats were important writers in the movement in England. The novels of Scott — especially *Waverly, Ivanhoe,* and *Quentin Durward* — greatly influenced American writers, who responded to Scott's visions of romantic chivalry and high honor.

Romanticism is in part a rejection of ordinary life. In the Gothic fantasy the reader escapes from reality in search of thrilling sensations. Sometimes romanticism expresses the idea that things were better in earlier days, or would be better in some wild new setting unspoiled by civilization. Of course, the life of colorful, remote places does not really have the glow that romance casts upon it. Before our Revolution the French writer Rousseau had advanced the appealing idea of primitive virtue — the "noble savage" or innocent child of nature. Later romantic writers often re-created this picture. Yet the life of primitive man can be very different from the way it appears in the writings of the romantics. In truth, both savage and civilized men, in their different ways, are complex beings.

Life requires a delicate balance between the "romantic" vision and its opposite, which is often called the "realistic" view. If either view prevails without the modifying influence of the other, a nation and its literature can become warped in spirit. At its best, our early literature kept a sane balance between these two contrasting visions of life.

Our Earliest Imaginative Writers

Before going on to consider in detail the major writers of this period — Cooper, Irving, Bryant, Poe, Hawthorne, and Melville — a few earlier figures in our literature deserve mention.

There were literary stirrings at the time of the Revolution and in the years immediately following that war. Philip Freneau was one of our first true poets. Only a few of his poems, such as "To the Memory of the Brave Americans" (which commemorates soldiers killed in the Revolutionary War) and "The Indian Burying Ground," are really fine, but they are enough to gain him a lasting place in our literature.

In Connecticut, centering around Hartford, a group of writers became known as "The Hartford Wits," or "The Connecticut Wits." The best known of them were John Trumbull and Joel Barlow. Trumbull's *M'Fingal* (1782) was an anti-British parody. Barlow, who served the country ably as a diplomat, was a friend of Thomas Paine and of Robert Fulton, the inventor of the steamboat. Barlow attempted an epic poem, *The Columbiad* (1807), but his best work is the earlier mock epic *The Hasty Pudding* (1796), a poem full of pleasant images of Connecticut life.

A word is due to the good-hearted Episcopal minister and traveling bookseller Mason Locke Weems, often called Parson Weems. He wrote several popular biographies of American heroes. Most famous of them is *The Life and Memorable Actions of George Washington* (about 1800). The book is the source of the famous cherry-tree myth.

There were many active playwrights during the years following the war. No play of this time reached the level of great drama, yet some were highly popular. *The Contrast* has been mentioned. Its author, Royall Tyler, became Chief Justice of the Supreme Court of Vermont. William Dunlap was an important figure both as a writer and a manager in the theater of those years. Dunlap's *André* (1798) was an effective play about the brave British major who was captured as a spy in the Benedict Arnold treason plot. Anna Cora Mowatt's *Fashion* (1845) is a comedy that has been presented again in recent years. Another early playwright, Robert Montgomery Bird, also wrote a novel called *Nick of the Woods; or, The Jibbenainosay [Devil]* (1837). The book lasted for years as a popular seller and still makes interesting reading.

JAMES FENIMORE COOPER

The first important American novelist began his literary career on a dare. James Fenimore Cooper was reading a boring English novel when he said to his wife that he could write a better one himself. His wife challenged him to make good his boast; so at the age of thirty, Cooper began a career that would bring him wealth and world-wide fame. His first novel was a failure, but Cooper tried again, and this time he was successful. *The Spy* (1821) was a rousing tale about espionage against the British during the Revolutionary War. It was inspired by stories that Cooper had heard from his father's friend John Jay, who was the first Chief Justice of the Supreme Court.

Born in New Jersey in 1789, the year the Constitution was adopted, Cooper was taken as an infant to the shores of Lake Otsego, in New York state, where his father established the community of Cooperstown.

Cooper launched two kinds of immensely popular stories: the sea adventure tale, and the frontier saga. The best of his many sea romances was *The Pilot* (1823). The hero of the novel represents John Paul Jones, the great naval fighter of the Revolutionary War. Cooper's knowledge of the sea rested on his earlier three years' service as a midshipman. Later in his career, in 1839, he wrote the first official history of the U.S. Navy.

Cooper's enduring fame rests on his frontier stories, especially the five novels that comprise the *Leatherstocking Tales* (1823 to 1841). In their order of events (not the order in which they were written), the novels are *The Deerslayer, The Last of the Mohicans, The Pathfinder, The Pioneers,* and *The Prairie*. A modern American historian, Allan Nevins, who has edited a one-volume version of the series, calls these five novels "the nearest approach yet to an American epic." (See page 188 for a review of Nevins' edition.)

Cooper had his faults. Mark Twain, in an amusing essay called "Fenimore Cooper's Literary Offenses," poked fun at the inconsistencies and improbabilities in the novels. Yet Cooper cannot be judged as though he were a realistic novelist. As some of Twain's own works show, a rousing story and a cast of colorful characters will cover a multitude of flaws.

The central figure in the novels, Natty Bumppo, goes by the various names of Leatherstocking, Deerslayer, Pathfinder, and Hawkeye. He captured the imagination of readers around the world. Close after him in romantic appeal come the two noble red men, the Mohican Chief Chingachgook and his son, Uncas. With these and with a vast group of supporting characters, virtuous or villainous, Cooper made the American conscious of his past, and made the European conscious of America.

The unimaginably great American forests did not last long under the American ax, which was both a builder and a destroyer. Cooper captured and preserved the forest for us in his vivid, imaginative landscapes. He captured and preserved, too, the men who roamed that forest.

In 1820, a British writer, Sydney Smith, asked contemptuously, "Who reads an American book?" This was the year in which Irving's *Sketch Book* appeared, the year Cooper took a literary dare from his wife. Three years earlier, Bryant had published his first poem. Just seven years later, Poe published his first volume of poetry. Together, these four writers answered Smith's question. Who reads an American book? Almost anyone who reads at all.

WASHINGTON
IRVING
1783–1859

The first major literary figure to appear on the American scene – the first to be honored solely as an imaginative writer – was Washington Irving. He was born into a prosperous merchant family in New York in 1783. As a young man he studied law but never seriously pursued that profession. Threatened with tuberculosis at twenty-one, Irving went abroad for two years, traveling in England, France, and Italy. After his return to New York, he collaborated with his brothers and several friends to write the *Salmagundi* papers (1807–1808). These were light satires on New York society, modeled in part on the famous English *Spectator* series.

In 1809 Irving published a book with a long title, mocking a literary fashion of his time. In full, the title was:

A History of New York from the Beginning of the World to the End of the Dutch Dynasty, containing, among many surprising and curious matters, the unutterable ponderings of Walter the Doubter, the disastrous projects of William the Testy, and the chivalric achievements of Peter the Headstrong; the Three Dutch Governors of New Amsterdam; Being the Only Authentic History of the Times That Ever Hath Been or Ever Will Be Published.

The book pretended to be the work of an eccentric and slightly mysterious little historian named Diedrich Knickerbocker. Fortunately, Irving's elaborate title is usually shortened to *Knickerbocker's History of New York*.

Many residents of New York knew nothing about the city's early days as New Amsterdam under Dutch rule. Irving sketched in the outlines of that past in *Knickerbocker's History*, but, of course, as a humorist and storyteller he was quite free with some of the facts.

Writing at first had simply been a pastime for Irving, but the failure of the family business forced him to make literature his means of living. Fortunately, he flourished at it. Returning to England, Irving became a friend of Sir Walter Scott, whose historical novels inspired him to try to give the New World some of the sense of a romantic past that Europe possessed. Irving remained in Europe for seventeen years, returning to this country in 1832. Out of this long stay came *Bracebridge Hall, Tales of a Traveler,* and *The Alhambra*. Late in his life, Irving went back to Europe as the American Minister to Spain.

Even though his heart lay much with the past, Irving did not forget the immediate drama unfolding in this country. He journeyed to the West and wrote *A Tour* on the Prairies (1835), describing the Arkansas River region and the Pawnee Indians who lived in that area. *The Adventures of Captain Bonneville, U.S.A.* (1837) was an account of the exploration of the Rockies. Another interesting book was *Astoria* (1836), the first account of the great American fur trade that was opening the land along the Columbia River. Irving's last work was a biography of George Washington in five volumes.

None of his many books equaled the popularity of the collection of stories and essays he called *The Sketch Book*. It was published in installments in 1819–20 in America and later published in book form in England. *The Sketch Book* contains many English scenes, including memorable descriptions of Christmas in England, but its undoubted masterpieces are the two Hudson Valley tales, "The Legend of Sleepy Hollow" (with Ichabod Crane), and "Rip Van Winkle." These two stories form an imperishable part of our literature and our folklore.

Edgar Allan Poe, in a critical article, called Irving "the most deservedly eminent among all the pioneers of American literature." The praise was well merited. Irving was the first American writer to draw international attention to our literature. He was a genial writer of the best informal prose that had been developed in this country up to his time.

The Devil and Tom Walker

Imagine yourself a guest at Sunnyside, Irving's home at Tarrytown on the Hudson. Dinner is finished. Lean back in an easy chair before a crackling log fire, and let your host tell you one of his famous stories. Irving begins; he weaves the tale with the artistic touch of a master storyteller.

A FEW miles from Boston in Massachusetts, there is a deep inlet, winding several miles into the interior of the country from Charles Bay, and terminating in a thickly wooded swamp or morass. On one side of this inlet is a beautiful dark grove; on the opposite side the land rises abruptly from the water's edge into a high ridge, on which grow a few scattered oaks of great age and immense size. Under one of these gigantic trees, according to old stories, there was a great amount of treasure buried by Kidd the pirate. The inlet allowed a facility to bring the money in a boat secretly and at night to the very foot of the hill; the elevation of the place permitted a good lookout to be kept that no one was at hand; while the remarkable trees formed good landmarks by which the place might easily be found again. The old stories add, moreover, that the Devil presided at the hiding of the money, and took it under his guardianship; but this, it is well known, he always does with buried treasure, particularly when it has been ill-gotten. Be that as it may, Kidd never returned to recover his wealth; being shortly after seized at Boston, sent out to England, and there hanged for a pirate.

About the year 1727, just at the time that earthquakes were prevalent in New England, and shook many tall sinners down upon their knees, there lived near this place a meager, miserly fellow, of the name of Tom Walker. He had a wife as miserly as himself: they were so miserly that they even conspired to cheat each other. Whatever the woman could lay hands on she hid away; a hen could not cackle but she was on the alert to secure the new-laid egg. Her husband was continually prying about to detect her secret hoards, and many and fierce were the conflicts that took place about what ought to have been common property. They lived in a forlorn-looking house that stood alone, and had an air of starvation. A few straggling savin [1] trees, emblems of sterility, grew near it; no smoke ever curled from its chimney; no traveler stopped at its door. A miserable horse, whose ribs were as articulate as the bars of a gridiron, stalked about a field where a thin carpet of moss, scarcely covering the ragged beds of pudding stone, tantalized and balked his hunger; and sometimes he would lean his head over the fence, look piteously at the passer-by, and seem to petition deliverance from this land of famine.

The house and its inmates had altogether a bad name. Tom's wife was a tall termagant,[2] fierce of temper, loud of tongue, and strong of arm. Her voice was often heard in wordy warfare with her husband; and his face sometimes showed signs that their conflicts were not confined to words. No one ventured, however, to interfere between them. The lonely wayfarer shrunk within himself at the horrid clamor and clapper-clawing, eyed the den of discord askance, and hurried on his way, rejoicing, if a bachelor, in his celibacy.

One day that Tom Walker had been to a distant part of the neighborhood, he took what he considered a short cut homeward, through the swamp. Like most short cuts, it was an ill-chosen route. The swamp was thickly grown with great gloomy pines and hemlocks, some of them ninety feet high, which made it dark at noonday, and a retreat for all the owls of the neighborhood. It was full of pits and quagmires, partly covered with weeds and mosses, where the green surface often betrayed the traveler into a gulf of black, smothering mud; there were also dark and stagnant pools, the abodes of the tadpole, the bullfrog, and the water snake, where

the trunks of pines and hemlocks lay half drowned, half rotting, looking like alligators sleeping in the mire.

Tom had long been picking his way cautiously through this treacherous forest; stepping from tuft to tuft of rushes and roots, which afforded precarious footholds among deep sloughs; or pacing carefully, like a cat, along the prostrate trunks of trees; startled now and then by the sudden screaming of the bittern, or the quacking of a wild duck rising on the wing from some solitary pool. At length he arrived at a firm piece of ground, which ran out like a peninsula into the deep bosom of the swamp. It had been one of the strongholds of the Indians during their wars with the first colonists. Here they had thrown up a kind of fort, which they had looked upon as almost impregnable, and had used as a place of refuge for their squaws and children. Nothing remained of the old Indian fort but a few embankments, gradually sinking to the level of the surrounding earth, and already overgrown in part by oaks and other forest trees, the foliage of which formed a contrast to the dark pines and hemlocks of the swamp.

It was late in the dusk of evening when Tom Walker reached the old fort, and he paused there awhile to rest himself. Anyone but he would have felt unwilling to linger in this lonely, melancholy place, for the common people had a bad opinion of it from the stories handed down from the time of the Indian wars, when it was asserted that the savages held incantations here, and made sacrifices to the evil spirit.

Tom Walker, however, was not a man to be troubled with any fears of the kind. He reposed himself for some time on the trunk of a fallen hemlock, listening to the boding cry of the tree toad, and delving with his walking staff into a mound of black mold at his feet. As he turned up the soil unconsciously, his staff struck against something hard. He raked it out of the vegetable mold

---

[1] savin (săv'ĭn): a North American juniper or red cedar.
[2] termagant (tûr'má·gănt): a boisterous, scolding woman.

and lo! a cloven skull, with an Indian tomahawk buried deep in it, lay before him. The rust on the weapon showed the time that had elapsed since this deathblow had been given. It was a dreary memento of the fierce struggle that had taken place in this last foothold of the Indian warriors.

"Humph!" said Tom Walker, as he gave it a kick to shake the dirt from it.

"Let that skull alone!" said a gruff voice. Tom lifted up his eyes, and beheld a great black man seated directly opposite him, on the stump of a tree. He was exceedingly surprised, having neither heard nor seen anyone approach; and he was still more perplexed on observing, as well as the gathering gloom would permit, that the stranger was neither Negro nor Indian. It is true he was dressed in a rude half-Indian garb, and had a red belt or sash swathed round his body; but his face was neither black nor copper color, but swarthy and dingy, and begrimed with soot, as if he had been accustomed to toil among fires and forges. He had a shock of coarse black hair that stood out from his head in all directions, and bore an ax on his shoulder.

He scowled for a moment at Tom with a pair of great red eyes.

"What are you doing on my grounds?" said the black man, with a hoarse, growling voice.

"Your grounds!" said Tom, with a sneer, "No more your grounds than mine; they belong to Deacon Peabody."

"Deacon Peabody be d——d," said the stranger, "as I flatter myself he will be, if he does not look more to his own sins and less to those of his neighbors. Look yonder, and see how Deacon Peabody is faring."

Tom looked in the direction that the stranger pointed, and beheld one of the great trees, fair and flourishing without, but rotten at the core, and saw that it had been nearly hewn through, so that the first high wind was likely to blow it down. On the bark of the tree

was scored the name of Deacon Peabody, an eminent man, who had waxed wealthy by driving shrewd bargains with the Indians. He now looked around, and found most of the tall trees marked with the name of some great man of the colony, and all more or less scored by the ax. The one on which he had been seated, and which had evidently just been hewn down, bore the name of Crowninshield; and he recollected a mighty rich man of that name, who made a vulgar display of wealth, which it was whispered he had acquired by buccaneering.

"He's just ready for burning!" said the black man, with a growl of triumph. "You see, I am likely to have a good stock of firewood for winter."

"But what right have you," said Tom, "to cut down Deacon Peabody's timber?"

"The right of a prior claim," said the other. "This woodland belonged to me long before one of your white-faced race put foot upon the soil."

"And pray, who are you, if I may be so bold?" said Tom.

"Oh, I go by various names. I am the wild huntsman in some countries; the black miner in others. In this neighborhood I am known by the name of the black woodsman. I am he to whom the red men consecrated this spot, and in honor of whom they now and then roasted a white man, by way of sweet-smelling sacrifice. Since the red men have been exterminated by you white savages, I amuse myself by presiding at the persecutions of Quakers and Anabaptists;[1] I am the great patron and prompter of slave dealers, and the grand master of the Salem witches."

"The upshot of all which is that, if I mistake not," said Tom, sturdily, "you

---

[1] **Anabaptists:** a religious sect that arose in Switzerland in 1523. Its members were subject to persecution because of their opposition to infant baptism. **Quakers** were persecuted in England in 1689 because of their pacifism and their refusal to take oaths.

are he commonly called Old Scratch."

"The same, at your service!" replied the black man, with a half-civil nod.

Such was the opening of this interview, according to the old story; though it has almost too familiar an air to be credited. One would think that to meet with such a singular personage, in this wild, lonely place, would have shaken any man's nerves; but Tom was a hard-minded fellow, not easily daunted, and he had lived so long with a termagant wife that he did not even fear the Devil.

It is said that after this commencement they had a long and earnest conversation together, as Tom returned homeward. The black man told him of great sums of money buried by Kidd the pirate, under the oak trees on the high ridge, not far from the morass. All these were under his command, and protected by his power, so that none could find them but such as propitiated his favor. These he offered to place within Tom Walker's reach, having conceived an especial kindness for him; but they were to be had only on certain conditions. What these conditions were may be easily surmised, though Tom never disclosed them publicly. They must have been very hard, for he required time to think of them, and he was not a man to stick at trifles when money was in view. When they had reached the edge of the swamp, the stranger paused. "What proof have I that all you have been telling me is true?" said Tom. "There's my signature," said the black man, pressing his finger on Tom's forehead. So saying, he turned off among the thickets of the swamp, and seemed, as Tom said, to go down, down, down, into the earth, until nothing but his head and shoulders could be seen, and so on, until he totally disappeared.

When Tom reached home, he found the black print of a finger burnt, as it were, into his forehead, which nothing could obliterate. The first news his wife had to tell him was the sudden death of Absalom Crowninshield, the rich buc-

caneer. It was announced in the papers with the usual flourish, that "a great man had fallen in Israel."

Tom recollected the tree which his black friend had just hewn down, and which was ready for burning. "Let the freebooter roast," said Tom; "who cares!" He now felt convinced that all he had heard and seen was no illusion.

He was not prone to let his wife into his confidence; but as this was an uneasy secret, he willingly shared it with her. All her avarice was awakened at the mention of hidden gold, and she urged her husband to comply with the black man's terms, and secure what would make them wealthy for life. However Tom might have felt disposed to sell himself to the Devil, he was determined not to do so to oblige his wife; so he flatly refused, out of the mere spirit of contradiction. Many and bitter were the quarrels they had on the subject; but the more she talked, the more resolute was Tom not to be damned to please her.

At length she determined to drive the bargain on her own account and, if she succeeded, to keep all the gain to herself. Being of the same fearless temper as her husband, she set off for the old Indian fort toward the close of a summer's day. She was many hours absent. When she came back, she was reserved and sullen in her replies. She spoke something of a black man whom she had met about twilight hewing at the root of a tall tree. He was sulky, however, and would not come to terms: she was to go again with a propitiatory [1] offering, but what it was she forbore to say.

The next evening she set off for the swamp, with her apron heavily laden. Tom waited and waited for her, but in vain; midnight came, but she did not make her appearance: morning, noon, night returned, but still she did not come. Tom now grew uneasy for her

[1] propitiatory (prō·pĭsh′ĭ·á·tō′rĭ): for the purpose of gaining favor.

safety, especially as he found she had carried off in her apron the silver tea-pot and spoons, and every portable article of value. Another night elapsed, another morning came, but no wife. In a word, she was never heard of more.

What was her real fate nobody knows, in consequence of so many pretending to know. It is one of those facts which have become confounded by a variety of historians. Some asserted that she lost her way among the tangled mazes of the swamp, and sank into some pit or slough; others, more uncharitable, hinted that she had eloped with the household booty, and made off to some other province; while others surmised that the tempter had decoyed her into a dismal quagmire, on the top of which her hat was found lying. In confirmation of this, it was said a great black man, with an ax on his shoulder, was seen late that very evening coming out of the swamp, carrying a bundle tied in a checked apron, with an air of surly triumph.

The most current and probable story, however, observes that Tom Walker grew so anxious about the fate of his wife and his property that he set out at length to seek them both at the Indian fort. During a long summer's afternoon he searched about the gloomy place, but no wife was to be seen. He called her name repeatedly, but she was nowhere to be heard. The bittern alone responded to his voice, as he flew screaming by; or the bullfrog croaked dolefully from a neighboring pool. At length, it is said, just in the brown hour of twilight, when the owls began to hoot, and the bats to flit about, his attention was attracted by the clamor of carrion crows hovering about a cypress tree. He looked up, and beheld a bundle tied in a checked apron and hanging in the branches of the tree, with a great vulture perched hard by, as if keeping watch upon it. He leaped with joy; for he recognized his wife's apron, and supposed it to contain the household valuables.

"Let us get hold of the property," said he consolingly to himself, "and we will endeavor to do without the woman."

As he scrambled up the tree, the vulture spread its wide wings, and sailed off, screaming, into the deep shadows of the forest. Tom seized the checked apron, but woeful sight! found nothing but a heart and liver tied up in it!

Such, according to this most authentic old story, was all that was to be found of Tom's wife. She had probably attempted to deal with the black man as she had been accustomed to deal with her husband; but though a female scold is generally considered a match for the Devil, yet in this instance she appears to have had the worst of it. She must have died game, however; for it is said Tom noticed many prints of cloven feet deeply stamped about the tree, and found handfuls of hair, that looked as if they had been plucked from the coarse black shock of the woodman. Tom knew his wife's prowess by experience. He shrugged his shoulders, as he looked at the signs of a fierce clap-perclawing. "Egad," said he to himself, "Old Scratch must have had a tough time of it!"

Tom consoled himself for the loss of his property with the loss of his wife, for he was a man of fortitude. He even felt something like gratitude toward the black woodman, who, he considered, had done him a kindness. He sought, therefore, to cultivate a further acquaintance with him, but for some time without success; the old blacklegs played shy, for, whatever people may think, he is not always to be had for calling for; he knows how to play his cards when pretty sure of his game.

At length, it is said, when delay had whetted Tom's eagerness to the quick, and prepared him to agree to anything rather than not gain the promised treasure, he met the black man one evening in his usual woodman's dress, with his ax on his shoulder, sauntering along the swamp, and humming a tune. He affected to receive Tom's advances with great indifference, made brief replies, and went on humming his tune.

By degrees, however, Tom brought him to business, and they began to haggle about the terms on which the former was to have the pirate's treasure. There was one condition which need not be mentioned, being generally understood in all cases where the Devil grants favors; but there were others about which, though of less importance, he was inflexibly obstinate. He insisted that the money found through his means should be employed in his service. He proposed, therefore, that Tom should employ it in the black traffic; that is to say, that he should fit out a slave ship. This, however, Tom resolutely refused; he was bad enough in all conscience; but the Devil himself could not tempt him to turn slave trader.

Finding Tom so squeamish on this point, he did not insist upon it, but proposed, instead, that he should turn usurer;[1] the Devil being extremely anxious for the increase of usurers, looking upon them as his peculiar[2] people.

To this no objections were made, for it was just to Tom's taste.

"You shall open a broker's shop in Boston next month," said the black man.

"I'll do it tomorrow, if you wish," said Tom Walker.

"You shall lend money at two per cent a month."

"Egad, I'll charge four!" replied Tom Walker.

"You shall extort bonds, foreclose mortgages, drive the merchants to bankruptcy — "

"I'll drive them to the devil," cried Tom Walker.

"You are the usurer for my money!" said blacklegs with delight. "When will you want rhino?"[3]

"This very night."

"Done!" said the Devil.

"Done!" said Tom Walker.

So they shook hands and struck a bargain.

A few days' time saw Tom Walker seated behind his desk in a counting-house in Boston.

His reputation for a ready-moneyed man, who would lend money out for a good consideration, soon spread abroad. Everybody remembers the time of Governor Belcher,[4] when money was particularly scarce. It was a time of paper credit. The country had been deluged with government bills; the famous Land Bank[5] had been established; there had been a rage for speculating; the people had run mad with schemes for new settlements, for building cities in the wilderness; land jobbers went about with maps of grants, and townships, and El Dorados,[6] lying nobody knew where, but which everybody was ready to purchase. In a word, the great speculating fever which breaks out every now and then in the country had raged to an alarming degree, and everybody was dreaming of making sudden fortunes from nothing. As usual the fever had subsided; the dream had gone off, and the imaginary fortunes with it; the patients were left in doleful plight, and the whole country resounded with the consequent cry of "hard times."

At this propitious time of public distress did Tom Walker set up as usurer in Boston. His door was soon thronged by customers. The needy and adventurous, the gambling speculator, the dreaming land jobber, the thriftless tradesman, the merchant with cracked credit, in short, everyone driven to raise money by desperate means and desper-

[1] usurer (ū′zhŏŏ·rẽr): one who lends money at excessive rates of interest.
[2] peculiar: here, special or particular.
[3] rhino: slang for money.

[4] Belcher: Jonathan Belcher was governor of Massachusetts from 1730 to 1741.
[5] Land Bank: a loan system by which the province advanced money on mortgages on land.
[6] El Dorados (dô·rä′dōz): Spanish, literally, "the golden"; hence, places of fabulous riches.

ate sacrifices hurried to Tom Walker.

Thus Tom was the universal friend of the needy, and acted like a "friend in need"; that is to say, he always exacted good pay and good security. In proportion to the distress of the applicant was the highness of his terms. He accumulated bonds and mortgages, gradually squeezed his customers closer and closer, and sent them at length, dry as a sponge, from his door.

In this way he made money hand over hand, became a rich and mighty man, and exalted his cocked hat upon 'Change.[1] He built himself, as usual, a vast house, out of ostentation; but left the greater part of it unfinished and unfurnished, out of parsimony. He even set up a carriage in the fullness of his vainglory, though he nearly starved the horses which drew it; and as the ungreased wheels groaned and screeched on the axletrees, you would have thought you heard the souls of the poor debtors he was squeezing.

As Tom waxed old, however, he grew thoughtful. Having secured the good things of this world, he began to feel anxious about those of the next. He thought with regret on the bargain he had made with his black friend, and set his wits to work to cheat him out of the conditions. He became, therefore, all of a sudden, a violent churchgoer. He prayed loudly and strenuously, as if heaven were to be taken by force of lungs. Indeed, one might always tell when he had sinned most during the week, by the clamor of his Sunday devotion. The quiet Christians who had been modestly and steadfastly traveling Zionward were struck with self-reproach at seeing themselves so suddenly outstripped in their career by this new-made convert. Tom was as rigid in religious as in money matters; he was a stern supervisor and censurer of his neighbors, and seemed to think every

[1] 'Change: Exchange, the place where merchants, brokers, bankers, etc., meet to do business.

sin entered up to their account became a credit on his own side of the page. He even talked of the expediency of reviving the persecution of Quakers and Anabaptists. In a word, Tom's zeal became as notorious as his riches.

Still, in spite of all this strenuous attention to forms, Tom had a lurking dread that the Devil, after all, would have his due. That he might not be taken unawares, therefore, it is said he always carried a small Bible in his coat pocket. He had also a great folio Bible on his countinghouse desk, and would frequently be found reading it when people called on business; on such occasions he would lay his green spectacles in the book, to mark the place, while he turned round to drive some usurious bargain.

Some say that Tom grew a little crackbrained in his old days, and that, fancying his end approaching, he had his horse new shod, saddled and bridled, and buried with his feet uppermost; because he supposed that at the last day the world would be turned upside down; in which case he should find his horse standing ready for mounting, and he was determined at the worst to give his old friend a run for it. This, however, is probably a mere old wives' fable. If he really did take such a precaution, it was totally superfluous; at least so says the authentic old legend, which closes this story in the following manner.

One hot summer afternoon in the dog days, just as a terrible black thundergust was coming up, Tom sat in his countinghouse, in his white linen cap and India silk morning gown. He was on the point of foreclosing a mortgage, by which he would complete the ruin of an unlucky land speculator for whom he had professed the greatest friendship. The poor land jobber begged him to grant a few months' indulgence. Tom had grown testy and irritated, and refused another day.

"My family will be ruined, and

brought upon the parish," said the land jobber.

"Charity begins at home," replied Tom; "I must take care of myself in these hard times."

"You have made so much money out of me," said the speculator.

Tom lost his patience and his piety. "The devil take me," said he, "if I have made a farthing!"

Just then there were three loud knocks at the street door. He stepped out to see who was there. A black man was holding a black horse, which neighed and stamped with impatience. "Tom, you're come for," said the black fellow, gruffly. Tom shrank back, but too late. He had left his little Bible at the bottom of his coat pocket, and his big Bible on the desk buried under the mortgage he was about to foreclose: never was sinner taken more unawares. The black man whisked him like a child into the saddle, gave the horse the lash, and away he galloped, with Tom on his back, in the midst of the thunderstorm. The clerks stuck their pens behind their ears, and stared after him from the windows. Away went Tom Walker, dashing down the streets; his white cap bobbing up and down; his morning gown fluttering in the wind, and his steed striking fire out of the pavement at every bound. When the clerks turned to look for the black man, he had disappeared.

Tom Walker never returned to foreclose the mortgage. A countryman, who lived on the border of the swamp, reported that in the height of the thunder-gust he had heard a great clattering of hoofs and a howling along the road, and running to the window caught sight of a figure, such as I have described, on a horse that galloped like mad across the fields, over the hills, and down into the black hemlock swamp toward the old Indian fort; and that shortly after, a thunderbolt falling in that direction seemed to set the whole forest in a blaze.

The good people of Boston shook their heads and shrugged their shoulders, but had been so much accustomed to witches and goblins, and tricks of the Devil, in all kinds of shapes, from the first settlement of the colony, that they were not so much horror-struck as might have been expected. Trustees were appointed to take charge of Tom's effects. There was nothing, however, to administer upon. On searching his coffers, all his bonds and mortgages were found reduced to cinders. In place of gold and silver, his iron chest was filled with chips and shavings; two skeletons lay in his stable instead of his half-starved horses, and the very next day his great house took fire and was burnt to the ground.

Such was the end of Tom Walker and his ill-gotten wealth. Let all griping money brokers lay this story to heart. The truth of it is not to be doubted. The very hole under the oak trees, whence he dug Kidd's money, is to be seen to this day; and the neighboring swamp and old Indian fort are often haunted in stormy nights by a figure on horseback, in morning gown and white cap, which is doubtless the troubled spirit of the usurer. In fact, the story has resolved itself into a proverb, and is the origin of that popular saying, so prevalent throughout New England, of "The Devil and Tom Walker."

A Republic of Prairie Dogs

After seventeen years abroad, Irving returned to America in 1832, eager to know his own country — especially the Far West. *A Tour on the Prairies,* his account of the expedition he made at that time through Indian territory, is the finest extant description of frontier life in the 1830's. The book combines thrilling, dangerous adventure and vivid description. The chapter entitled "A Republic of Prairie Dogs" is also notable for its whimsical humor.

O N RETURNING from our expedition in quest of the young Count, I learned that a burrow, or village, as it is termed, of prairie dogs had been discovered on the level summit of a hill, about one mile from the camp. Having heard much of the habits and peculiarities of these little animals, I determined to pay a visit to the community. The prairie dog is, in fact, one of the curiosities of the Far West, about which travelers delight to tell marvelous tales, endowing him at times with something of the politic and social habits of a rational being, and giving him systems of civil government and domestic economy almost equal to what they used to bestow upon the beaver.

The prairie dog is an animal of the coney [1] kind, and about the size of a rabbit. He is of a sprightly, mercurial nature; quick, sensitive, and somewhat petulant. He is very gregarious, living in large communities, sometimes of several acres in extent, where innumerable little heaps of earth show the entrances to the subterranean cells of the inhabitants, and the well-beaten tracks, like lanes and streets, show their mobility and restlessness. According to the accounts given of them, they would seem to be continually full of sport, business, and public affairs; whisking about hither and thither, as if on gossiping visits to each other's houses, or congregating in the cool of the evening, or after a shower, and gamboling together in the open air. Sometimes, especially when the moon shines, they pass half the night in revelry, barking or yelping with short, quick, yet weak tones, like those of very young puppies. While in the height of their playfulness and clamor, however, should there be the least alarm, they all vanish into their cells in an instant, and the village remains blank and silent. In case they are hard pressed by their pursuers, without any hope of escape, they will assume a pugnacious air, and a most whimsical look of impotent wrath and defiance.

The prairie dogs are not permitted to remain sole and undisturbed inhabitants of their own homes. Owls and rattlesnakes are said to take up their abodes with them; but whether as invited guests or unwelcome intruders is a matter of controversy. The owls are of a peculiar kind, and would seem to partake of the character of the hawk; for they are taller and more erect on their legs, more alert in their looks and rapid in their flight than ordinary owls, and do not confine their excursions to the night, but sally forth in broad day.

Some say that they only inhabit cells which the prairie dogs have deserted, and suffered to go to ruin, in consequence of the death in them of some relative; for they would make out this little animal to be endowed with keen sensibilities that will not permit it to remain in the dwelling where it has witnessed the death of a friend. Other fanciful speculators represent the owl as a kind of housekeeper to the prairie dog; and, from having a note very similar, insinuate that it acts, in a manner, as family preceptor, and teaches the young litter to bark.

As to the rattlesnake, nothing satisfactory has been ascertained of the part he plays in this most interesting household; though he is considered as little better than a sycophant [2] and sharper, that winds himself into the concerns of the honest, credulous little dog, and takes him in most sadly. Certain it is, if he acts as toad-eater, he occasionally solaces himself with more than the usual perquisites [3] of his order; as he is now and then detected with one of the

[1] coney (kō′nĭ): the European rabbit.

[2] sycophant (sĭk′ȯ-fănt): flatterer.
[3] perquisites (pûr′kwĭ-zĭtz): income.

younger members of the family in his maw.

Such are a few of the particulars that I could gather about the domestic economy of this little inhabitant of the prairies, who, with his pigmy republic, appears to be a subject of much whimsical speculation and burlesque remarks, among the hunters of the Far West.

It was toward evening that I set out with a companion to visit the village in question. Unluckily, it had been invaded in the course of the day by some of the rangers, who had shot two or three of its inhabitants, and thrown the whole sensitive community in confusion. As we approached, we could perceive numbers of the inhabitants seated at the entrances of their cells, while sentinels seemed to have been posted on the outskirts, to keep a lookout. At sight of us, the picket guards scampered in and gave the alarm; whereupon every inhabitant gave a short yelp, or bark, and dived into his hole, his heels twinkling in the air as if he had thrown a somersault.

We traversed the whole village, or republic, which covered an area of about thirty acres; but not a whisker of an inhabitant was to be seen. We probed their cells as far as the ramrods of our rifles would reach, but could unearth neither dog, nor owl, nor rattlesnake. Moving quietly to a little distance, we lay down upon the ground, and watched for a long time, silent and motionless. By and by, a cautious old burgher would slowly put forth the end of his nose, but instantly draw it in again. Another, at a greater distance, would emerge entirely; but, catching a glance at us, would throw a somersault, and plunge back again into his hole. At length, some who resided on the opposite side of the village, taking courage from the continued stillness, would steal forth, and hurry off to a distant hole, the residence possibly of some family connection, or gossiping friend, about whose safety they were solicitous, or with whom they wished to compare notes about the late occurrences.

Others, still more bold, assembled in little knots, in the street and public places, as if to discuss the recent outrages offered to the commonwealth, and the atrocious murders of their fellow burghers.

We rose from the ground and moved forward, to take a nearer view of these public proceedings, when, yelp! yelp! yelp! — there was a shrill alarm passed from mouth to mouth; the meetings suddenly dispersed; feet twinkled in the air in every direction; and in an instant all had vanished into the earth.

The dusk of the evening put an end to our observations, but the train of whimsical comparisons produced in my brain by the moral attributes which I had heard given to these little politic animals still continued after my return to camp; and late in the night, as I lay awake after all the camp was asleep, and heard in the stillness of the hour a faint clamor of shrill voices from the distant village, I could not help picturing to myself the inhabitants gathered together in noisy assemblage, and windy debate, to devise plans for the public safety, and to vindicate the invaded rights and insulted dignity of the republic.

FOR DISCUSSION

THE DEVIL AND TOM WALKER

1. What parts of "The Devil and Tom Walker" were most amusing to you? How would you characterize Irving's humor? Give some examples to illustrate your answer.

2. What would be your reply to someone who criticized the story "because it is so impossible and could never have happened"?

Some characters from Irving's Knickerbocker's History. *(See page 494.)* ▶

3. Point out some familiar expressions that Irving has made concrete in this story, such as "The Devil would have his due."

4. What colors are dominant in the story? Do these have any special significance?

5. Compare this story to "The Devil and Daniel Webster" (p. 62).

A REPUBLIC OF PRAIRIE DOGS

From Irving's style you might know at once that this account is not that of a scientist. What qualities characteristic of Irving's other writing are apparent in his observations on prairie dogs?

AN AUTHOR'S TECHNIQUE

Although Irving's pace is leisurely, he is able to characterize persons and things with startling economy. Find, for example, near the beginning of "The Devil and Tom Walker," a single sentence characterizing Tom's house; one describing his horse; one describing his wife. Can you, in words of your own, achieve the same effect in each case without using many more words?

SPECIAL REPORT

Bargaining with the Devil is a familiar theme in world literature. A committee might report on the similarity of Irving's story to Marlowe's play *The Tragedy of Dr. Faustus,* Goethe's verse drama and Gounod's opera *Faust.*

FURTHER READING

You may be interested in reading a recent edition of *A Tour on the Prairies,* edited by John F. McDermott (Univ. of Oklahoma Press, 1956, paperback.)

WILLIAM CULLEN BRYANT
1794–1878

In 1817, the stately poem called "Thanatopsis" (Greek, meaning "view of death") introduced the best poet to appear in America up to that time. William Cullen Bryant had written this remarkable poem seven years earlier at the age of sixteen. (The author later added lines at both the beginning and end of the poem. This final version of "Thanatopsis" is the one you will read on page 507.)

Coming to New York City from his native Massachusetts, Bryant began working on the New York *Review,* and a few years later became an editor with the New York *Evening Post.* He was to remain with the latter newspaper for fifty years, during most of that time as editor-in-chief and part owner. Apart from his fame as a poet, Bryant merits a reputation as one of the great editors of American journalism. He supported such causes as free speech, free trade, and the abolition of slavery. When Abraham Lincoln came to New York in 1860 to make his famous Cooper Union speech, which greatly increased his chances for the Presidential nomination, Bryant presided at the meeting and introduced the Illinois politician, who was then little known to the New York public.

Greater poets than Bryant were to follow, but none possessed more of the quality of serene and noble imaginative power. "To a Waterfowl" is perhaps the peak of his work. Matthew Arnold, the eminent English critic and poet, called it the "most perfect brief poem in the language."

The finest of Bryant's poems were written in his youth, before Bryant felt the pressures of his career in journalism. Nevertheless, he continued to write poetry throughout much of his life, publishing a number of volumes. Among his most important later works are his translations of the *Iliad* and the *Odyssey* into English blank verse. As Irving had shown that American prose had come of age, so Bryant demonstrated to European readers that American poetry was ready to demand serious attention. He was the first American to gain the stature of a major poet.

"Thanatopsis," a poem that Bryant wrote in his teens, was perhaps the first great poem written in America. The dignity of its blank verse and the power of its expression are truly remarkable for so young a writer.

BLANK VERSE. You will remember that blank verse has lines of equal syllabic length but no rhyme (see page 263). The thought of one line frequently spills over into the next, perhaps ending in the middle of another. Punctuation is a guide to units of thought. Do not hesitate at the end of a line unless you find a punctuation mark there. Taking a whole sentence at a time is the best way to get the meaning. If, even then, you are puzzled, look for the subject of the sentence; it may not be at the beginning.

Thanatopsis *

To him who in the love of Nature holds
Communion with her visible forms, she speaks
A various language; for his gayer hours
She has a voice of gladness, and a smile
And eloquence of beauty, and she glides   5
Into his darker musings, with a mild
And healing sympathy, that steals away
Their sharpness, ere he is aware. When thoughts
Of the last bitter hour come like a blight
Over thy spirit, and sad images   10
Of the stern agony, and shroud, and pall,
And breathless darkness, and the narrow house,
Make thee to shudder and grow sick at heart —
Go forth, under the open sky, and list
To Nature's teachings, while from all around —   15

* Thanatopsis (thăn-à-tŏp′sĭs).

Earth and her waters, and the depths of air —
Comes a still voice — Yet a few days,° and thee
The all-beholding sun shall see no more
In all his course; nor yet in the cold ground,
Where thy pale form was laid, with many tears,   20
Nor in the embrace of ocean, shall exist
Thy image. Earth, that nourished thee, shall claim
Thy growth, to be resolved to earth again,
And, lost each human trace, surrendering up
Thine individual being, shalt thou go   25
To mix forever with the elements,
To be a brother to the insensible rock
And to the sluggish clod, which the rude swain
Turns with his share,° and treads upon. The oak
Shall send his roots abroad, and pierce thy mold.   30

    Yet not to thine eternal resting place
Shalt thou retire alone, nor couldst thou wish
Couch more magnificent. Thou shalt lie down
With patriarchs of the infant world — with kings,
The powerful of the earth — the wise, the good,   35
Fair forms, and hoary seers of ages past,
All in one mighty sepulcher. The hills
Rock-ribbed and ancient as the sun — the vales
Stretching in pensive quietness between;
The venerable woods — rivers that move   40
In majesty, and the complaining brooks
That make the meadows green; and, poured round all,
Old Ocean's gray and melancholy waste —
Are but the solemn decorations all
Of the great tomb of man. The golden sun,   45
The planets, all the infinite host of heaven,
Are shining on the sad abodes of death,
Through the still lapse of ages. All that tread
The globe are but a handful to the tribes
That slumber in its bosom. Take the wings   50
Of morning,° pierce the Barcan° wilderness,

---

17. **Yet a few days:** This is the first line to be retained from the original poem. The opening couplets of the earlier version were dropped. 29. **share:** plowshare. 50–51. **Take . . . morning:** from the Old Testament Psalm 139:9. 51. **Barcan:** pertaining to Barca, a district in North Africa on the Mediterranean coast.

"Kindred Spirits," an oil painting by the American artist Asher Durand (1796–1886). ▶
Shown in the painting are William Cullen Bryant (hatless) and his friend,
the painter Thomas Cole.

   THE AMERICAN IMAGINATION AWAKENS

Or lose thyself in the continuous woods
Where rolls the Oregon,° and hears no sound,
Save his own dashings — yet the dead are there;
And millions in those solitudes, since first   55
The flight of years began, have laid them down
In their last sleep — the dead reign there alone.
So shalt thou rest, and what if thou withdraw
In silence from the living, and no friend
Take note of thy departure? All that breathe   60
Will share thy destiny. The gay will laugh
When thou art gone, the solemn brood of care
Plod on, and each one as before will chase
His favorite phantom; yet all these shall leave
Their mirth and their employments, and shall come   65
And make their bed with thee.° As the long train
Of ages glides away, the sons of men,
The youth in life's green spring, and he who goes
In the full strength of years, matron and maid,
The speechless babe, and the gray-headed man —   70
Shall one by one be gathered to thy side,
By those who in their turn shall follow them.

    So live, that when thy summons comes to join
The innumerable caravan, which moves
To that mysterious realm where each shall take   75
His chamber in the silent halls of death,
Thou go not, like the quarry slave at night,
Scourged to his dungeon, but, sustained and soothed
By an unfaltering trust, approach thy grave,
Like one who wraps the drapery of his couch   80
About him, and lies down to pleasant dreams.

---

53. **Oregon**: now known as the Columbia River, between Oregon and Washington. 66. **And make their bed with thee**: This was the end of the original poem as Bryant had written it in 1810 at the age of sixteen.

When, as a young man, Bryant was licensed to practice law, he was confronted by the problem of where to begin his career. One December afternoon, tramping over the hills to consider the town of Plainfield, Massachusetts, he felt particularly depressed by the uncertainty of his future. Then he happened to see a solitary bird flying south along the sunset afterglow. As his biographer, John Bigelow, describes the incident, "He watched the lone wanderer until it was lost in the distance. He then went on with new strength and courage. When he reached the house where he was to stop for the night, he immediately sat down and wrote the lines 'To a Waterfowl,' the concluding verse of which will perpetuate to future ages the lesson in faith which the scene had impressed on him."

Bryant addresses the poem to the bird, as he sees it pass between him and the setting sun. As you read, notice the change in tone from depression to "new strength and courage." Many readers memorize the last stanza of the poem.

To a Waterfowl

Whither, midst falling dew,
While glow the heavens with the last steps of day,
Far, through their rosy depths, dost thou pursue
    Thy solitary way?

Vainly the fowler's eye   5
Might mark thy distant flight to do thee wrong,
As, darkly seen against the crimson sky,
    Thy figure floats along.

Seek'st thou the plashy brink
Of weedy lake, or marge of river wide,   10
Or where the rocking billows rise and sink
    On the chafed oceanside?

There is a Power whose care
Teaches thy way along the pathless coast —
The desert and illimitable air —   15
    Lone wandering, but not lost.

All day thy wings have fanned,
At that far height, the cold, thin atmosphere,
Yet stoop not, weary, to the welcome land,
    Though the dark night is near.   20

And soon that toil shall end;
Soon shalt thou find a summer home, and rest,
And scream among thy fellows; reeds shall bend,
    Soon, o'er thy sheltered nest.

Thou'rt gone, the abyss of heaven   25
Hath swallowed up thy form; yet, on my heart
Deeply hath sunk the lesson thou hast given,
    And shall not soon depart.

He who, from zone to zone,
Guides through the boundless sky thy certain flight,   30
In the long way that I must tread alone,
    Will lead my steps aright.

WILLIAM CULLEN BRYANT   511

In 1815 Bryant "broke the spell" that bound him to poetry and tried to devote himself to the practice of law. But the "witchery of song" proved to be irresistible, and in 1824, giving up the law, he entered upon the period of his greatest poetic productivity. In the following brief lyric you will find the reasons for both of these changes in Bryant's attitude toward poetry.

I Broke the Spell That Held Me Long

I broke the spell that held me long,
The dear, dear witchery of song.
I said, the poet's idle lore
Shall waste my prime of years no more,
For Poetry, though heavenly born,   5
Consorts with poverty and scorn.

I broke the spell — nor deemed its power
Could fetter me another hour.
Ah, thoughtless! how could I forget
Its causes were around me yet?   10
For wheresoe'er I looked, the while,
Was Nature's everlasting smile.

Still came and lingered on my sight
Of flowers and streams the bloom and light,
And glory of the stars and sun;   15
And these and poetry are one.
They, ere the world had held me long,
Recalled me to the love of song.

FOR DISCUSSION

THANATOPSIS

1. Does this poem in any way reveal that it is the work of a teen-age youth? Explain.

2. According to the opening lines, what different messages does nature give us?

3. Contrast the two views of death in lines 17–30 and 31–72. What consolation is there in the two facts presented in lines 31–33?

4. How is earth the "great tomb of man"? What are its "decorations"? Why should acceptance of the universal fact of death be a natural thing?

5. According to the poet, in what spirit should one approach death?

TO A WATERFOWL

1. Point out the stanzas that make up each of the three parts of this poem: the picture seen by the poet, his meditation about the bird, and his application of these thoughts to his own life.

2. Why do many persons find comfort in the last stanza? What faith does it express?

I BROKE THE SPELL THAT HELD ME LONG

1. What was Bryant's attitude toward poetry before he stopped writing it? What was his attitude before he began writing it again?

2. What finally caused Bryant to resume writing poetry?

EDGAR ALLAN POE
1809–1849

Edgar Allan Poe was born in Boston in 1809, the child of struggling traveling actors. Both of his parents died within two years of his birth. Edgar was taken into the home of John Allan, a merchant of Richmond, Virginia, whose name Poe later added to his own.

For a brief period Poe was happy with the Allan family, but friction soon began to develop between the boy and his foster father. Poe entered the University of Virginia, but left a short time later because he would not enter the profession of law as Allan wished. After a brief enlistment in the army, Poe accepted an appointment to West Point, which Allan had helped to arrange. Poe was discharged less than a year later, in 1831, for reasons that are still not completely clear. The episode marked the final break between Poe and the Allans.

For a time he lived in Baltimore with his father's sister, Mrs. Maria Clemm, and her daughter Virginia. He had already published two volumes of poems at his own expense, but had made no money and little reputation from them. When he won a contest with his story "Ms. Found in a Bottle" in 1833, the Southern novelist John Pendleton Kennedy helped him get a job as editor with the *Southern Literary Messenger* in Richmond. Poe lost the position because of excessive drinking and an inability to meet deadlines, but he managed to regain the job in 1835. Confident of a secure position and a steady income, Poe then married his young cousin, Virginia Clemm.

In his post on the *Messenger,* Poe showed his true talents as an editor, a poet, a literary critic, and a writer of fiction. He remained for over two years, improving the magazine and building its circulation enormously. Then he quit suddenly in 1837, partly because he felt that his salary was far too low. With his family he set out to try his luck in New York and Philadelphia.

For several years he drifted. He was an editor at various times of *Graham's Magazine,* two newspapers, and *Burton's Gentleman's Magazine* (where "The Fall of the House of Usher" first appeared). The years from 1837 to 1845 were hard, yet in spite of shifting jobs and chronic poverty, Poe managed to write some of his most famous stories during this period. His first collection of short stories, *Tales of the Grotesque and Arabesque,* appeared in 1840. "The Raven" was published in 1845 as the title poem of a collection. Through his essays and reviews, Poe had also gained stature as a literary critic. Yet none of his successes brought him security. Misfortune spoiled every opportunity and frustrated his dream of starting his own magazine.

Ironically, while Poe was struggling in America, his work was commanding more and more praise in Europe, where he was hailed as a pioneer in poetic and fictional techniques. His influence was especially strong on many French writers.

His European fame was of little benefit to Poe. Poverty remained his typical condition. After an agonizingly slow decline, his young wife Virginia died of tuberculosis in the winter of 1847, in their bare cottage in New York City. Four years later, at forty, Poe himself was dead. Like so much else about the man, many of the circumstances surrounding his death remain a mystery. He had traveled to Richmond to make arrangements for his marriage to a widow, Mrs. A. B. Shelton. On the return trip to New York, he stopped in Baltimore to visit some friends. A common theory is that, arriving in the city on election day, he fell into the hands of political hoodlums who got him drunk and used him as a voter in dishonest election practices. Whatever had occurred, on October 3 Poe was found in a tavern in a drunken and desperately ill condition. He died four days later.

In the following pages you will learn something about Poe's literary theories and read some of his prose and poetry. This man, despite his tragic and disordered life, holds a unique and honored place in our literature. The list of his accomplishments is impressive. He was our first literary critic. With his stories "The Gold Bug" and "The Murders in the Rue Morgue," he founded the school of the detective story. His poetry has had international influence for over a century. And, almost alone, he was responsible for the short story as a form of fiction.

One of Poe's biographers — the novelist Hervey Allen — called his life of Poe *Israfel*. This is also the title of one of Poe's most beautiful poems. The reference is from the *Koran,* the sacred book of Mohammedanism. Poe's introduction to the poem speaks of "the angel Israfel, whose heartstrings are a lute, and who has the sweetest voice of all God's creatures." The final stanza of the poem shows why Poe's biographer went to it for a title. The lines could be Poe's own epitaph, his sad commentary on what he might have been:

If I could dwell
  Where Israfel
  Hath dwelt, and he where I,
He might not sing so wildly well
  A mortal melody,
While a bolder note than this might swell
  From my lyre within the sky.

Poe's Poems

THEORY OF POETRY. In the brief preface to a collection of his poems, Poe said, "Under happier circumstances [poetry alone] would have been the field of my choice. With me poetry has not been a purpose, but a passion; and the passion should be held in reverence." Poe went on to say that he thought of his poems as "excitements" of the spirit, excitements that neither should nor could be stimulated by money or praise.

Poe felt that a poem should be relatively short — a reading time of a half hour he considered an absolute maximum — because the excitement of a poem cannot be sustained for a longer period. He considered an epic poem, such as Milton's *Paradise Lost* or Homer's *Iliad,* to be simply a series of short poems with inevitable lapses of interest between the passages of excitement and elevation.

Poe argued that a poem is not a sermon. It should never appeal primarily to man's moral sense or to his reason. Instead, it should appeal to his sense of the beautiful. The effect of a poem should be a glimpse of unattainable beauty. Meter, rhythm, and rhyme — the music of poetry — help to create the emotional effect of the poem, the instant of "shivering delight."

A detail from an Athenian tombstone, carved during the fourth century B.C. The classic restraint of the sculpture is echoed in the following poem.

"To Helen" is one of the earliest poems by Poe, inspired by his youthful admiration for the beautiful Mrs. Stanard, the mother of one of his school friends. He later identified her as "the first purely ideal love of my soul." Lines 9–10 of this poem are very famous and are frequently quoted.

To Helen

Helen, thy beauty is to me
  Like those Nicaean° barks of yore,
That gently, o'er a perfumed sea,
  The weary, wayworn wanderer bore
  To his own native shore.   5

On desperate seas long wont to roam,
  Thy hyacinth° hair, thy classic face,
Thy naiad° airs have brought me home
  To the glory that was Greece
  And the grandeur that was Rome.   10

Lo! in yon brilliant window niche
  How statuelike I see thee stand,
The agate lamp within thy hand!
  Ah, Psyche,° from the regions which
  Are Holy Land!   15

2. **Nicaean** (nī·sē′ăn): pertaining to Nicaea, a town of Asia Minor. 7. **hyacinth:** A favorite adjective for hair in the old Greek epics was "hyacinthine," usually meaning beautiful and curling. 8. **naiad** (nā′ăd): in Greek mythology, a water nymph. 14. **Psyche** (sī′kė): the Greek word for "soul" or "mind," derived from the myth of the Greek maiden beloved of Cupid.

LISTENING FOR MELODY. All of Poe's verse is remarkably melodious, but "The Bells" approaches magic. It is probably the purest "sound" poem in the English language. Here Poe reproduces the tonal effects of the bells, largely by a choice of words that approximate their actual sound. This device is called *onomatopoeia* (ŏn'ô·măt'ô·pē'yà), the use of a word whose sound suggests its meaning.

Any poem is best read aloud, but this one *must* be. The rolling *l*'s and *r*'s and the resonant *m*'s and *n*'s, linked with the vowel sounds that imitate the timbre of the various metals, set the bells to ringing as you speak the words.

The Bells

I

Hear the sledges with the bells,
    Silver bells!
What a world of merriment their melody foretells!
    How they tinkle, tinkle, tinkle,
      In the icy air of night!   5
    While the stars, that oversprinkle
    All the heavens, seem to twinkle
      With a crystalline delight;
    Keeping time, time, time,
    In a sort of runic° rhyme,   10
To the tintinnabulation that so musically wells
    From the bells, bells, bells, bells,
      Bells, bells, bells —
  From the jingling and the tinkling of the bells.

II

Hear the mellow wedding bells,   15
    Golden bells!
What a world of happiness their harmony foretells!
    Through the balmy air of night
    How they ring out their delight!
      From the molten-golden notes,   20
      And all in tune,
    What a liquid ditty floats
To the turtledove that listens, while she gloats
      On the moon!
    Oh, from out the sounding cells,   25
What a gush of euphony° voluminously wells!
    How it swells!
    How it dwells
On the future! how it tells

10. **runic** (rōo'nĭk): pertaining to runes, letters in an ancient alphabet, used in the writing of ancient Teutonic poetry; hence, strange, magical. 26. **euphony** (ū'fô·nĭ): pleasant sounds.

Of the rapture that impels   30
  To the swinging and the ringing
    Of the bells, bells, bells,
  Of the bells, bells, bells, bells,
     Bells, bells, bells —
To the rhyming and the chiming of the bells!   35

III

   Hear the loud alarum bells,
     Brazen bells!
What a tale of terror, now, their turbulency tells!
    In the startled ear of night
    How they scream out their affright!   40
     Too much horrified to speak,
     They can only shriek, shriek,
      Out of tune,
In a clamorous appealing to the mercy of the fire,
In a mad expostulation with the deaf and frantic fire,   45
    Leaping higher, higher, higher,
    With a desperate desire,
   And a resolute endeavor
   Now — now to sit or never,
By the side of the pale-faced moon.   50
    Oh, the bells, bells, bells!
    What a tale their terror tells
     Of despair!
   How they clang, and clash, and roar!
   What a horror they outpour   55
On the bosom of the palpitating air!
    Yet the ear, it fully knows,
     By the twanging
     And the clanging,
    How the danger ebbs and flows;   60
   Yet the ear distinctly tells,
     In the jangling
     And the wrangling,
   How the danger sinks and swells —
By the sinking or the swelling in the anger of the bells,   65
    Of the bells,
  Of the bells, bells, bells, bells,
    Bells, bells, bells —
In the clamor and the clangor of the bells!

IV

   Hear the tolling of the bells,   70
    Iron bells!

EDGAR ALLAN POE   517

What a world of solemn thought their monody° compels!
    In the silence of the night
    How we shiver with affright
At the melancholy menace of their tone!   75
    For every sound that floats
    From the rust within their throats
       Is a groan.
    And the people — ah, the people,
    They that dwell up in the steeple,   80
      All alone,
    And who tolling, tolling, tolling
     In that muffled monotone,
    Feel a glory in so rolling
      On the human heart a stone —   85
They are neither man nor woman,
They are neither brute nor human,
     They are ghouls:°
    And their king it is who tolls;
    And he rolls, rolls, rolls,   90
      Rolls
    A paean° from the bells;
And his merry bosom swells
    With the paean of the bells,
    And he dances, and he yells: 95
Keeping time, time, time,
In a sort of runic rhyme,
    To the paean of the bells,
     Of the bells:
Keeping time, time, time,   100
In a sort of runic rhyme,
    To the throbbing of the bells,
Of the bells, bells, bells —
    To the sobbing of the bells;
Keeping time, time, time,   105
    As he knells, knells, knells,
In a happy runic rhyme,
    To the rolling of the bells,
Of the bells, bells, bells:
    To the tolling of the bells,   110
Of the bells, bells, bells, bells,
    Bells, bells, bells —
To the moaning and the groaning of the bells.

---

72. **monody** (mŏn′ô·dĭ): a type of music carried by one voice. In ancient Greek times a monody was sung as a dirge or funeral song; hence, the word suggests sorrow and tragedy. 88. **ghouls** (go͞olz): imaginary evil creatures reputed to rob graves and eat the corpses. 91. **paean** (pē′ăn): a hymn of joy or praise.

LISTENING FOR MOOD. Poe had very definite views on the nature of poetry — that its essence should be beauty of sound, and that sadness is the mood most in keeping with beautiful music. Therefore, he said, there is no subject more fitting for poetry than the death of a beautiful woman.

"The Raven" does not reflect Poe's personal sorrow for the death of his wife (which came two years *after* the poem was published). In reality, the "lost Lenore" was created by Poe's imagination to supply the mood of sadness needed to create poetic beauty. Notice again Poe's almost uncanny power over the sounds of words. Here he uses *internal* rhyme (a chiming of words at the middle and end of the same line) and the repetition of phrases particularly well.

The Raven

Once upon a midnight dreary, while I pondered, weak and weary,
Over many a quaint and curious volume of forgotten lore —
While I nodded, nearly napping, suddenly there came a tapping,
As of someone gently rapping, rapping at my chamber door.
" 'Tis some visitor," I muttered, "tapping at my chamber door: 5
    Only this and nothing more."

Ah, distinctly I remember it was in the bleak December,
And each separate dying ember wrought its ghost upon the floor.
Eagerly I wished the morrow; — vainly I had sought to borrow
From my books surcease of sorrow — sorrow for the lost Lenore,   10
For the rare and radiant maiden whom the angels name Lenore:
    Nameless here forevermore.

And the silken sad uncertain rustling of each purple curtain
Thrilled me — filled me with fantastic terrors never felt before;
So that now, to still the beating of my heart, I stood repeating,   15
" 'Tis some visitor entreating entrance at my chamber door,
Some late visitor entreating entrance at my chamber door:
    This it is and nothing more."

Presently my soul grew stronger; hesitating then no longer,
"Sir," said I, "or Madam, truly your forgiveness I implore;   20

But the fact is I was napping, and so gently you came rapping,
And so faintly you came tapping, tapping at my chamber door,
That I scarce was sure I heard you" — here I opened wide the door —
    Darkness there and nothing more.

Deep into that darkness peering, long I stood there wondering, fearing,   25
Doubting, dreaming dreams no mortal ever dared to dream before;
But the silence was unbroken, and the stillness gave no token,
And the only word there spoken was the whispered word "Lenore!"
This I whispered, and an echo murmured back the word "Lenore":
    Merely this and nothing more.   30

Back into the chamber turning, all my soul within me burning,
Soon again I heard a tapping somewhat louder than before.
"Surely," said I, "surely that is something at my window lattice;
Let me see, then, what thereat is, and this mystery explore:
Let my heart be still a moment and this mystery explore: 35
    'Tis the wind and nothing more."

Open here I flung the shutter, when, with many a flirt and flutter,
In there stepped a stately Raven of the saintly days of yore.
Not the least obeisance° made he; not a minute stopped or stayed he;
But, with mien of lord or lady, perched above my chamber door,   40
Perched upon a bust of Pallas° just above my chamber door:
    Perched, and sat, and nothing more.

Then this ebony bird beguiling my sad fancy into smiling
By the grave and stern decorum of the countenance it wore —
"Though thy crest be shorn and shaven, thou," I said, "art sure no craven,   45
Ghastly grim and ancient Raven wandering from the nightly shore:
Tell me what thy lordly name is on the night's Plutonian° shore!"
    Quoth the Raven, "Nevermore."

Much I marveled this ungainly fowl to hear discourse so plainly,
Though its answer little meaning — little relevancy bore;   50
For we cannot help agreeing that no living human being
Ever yet was blessed with seeing bird above his chamber door,
Bird or beast upon the sculptured bust above his chamber door,
    With such name as "Nevermore."

But the Raven, sitting lonely on the placid bust, spoke only   55
That one word, as if his soul in that one word he did outpour.
Nothing further then he uttered, not a feather then he fluttered,

    39. **obeisance** (ô·bā′săns): a gesture of respect. 41. **Pallas** (păl′ăs): Pallas Athene, Greek goddess of wisdom, called Minerva by the Romans. 47. **Plutonian** (ploō·tō′nĭ·ăn): referring to Pluto, the god who in Greek mythology presided over the regions of the dead.

Till I scarcely more than muttered — "Other friends have flown before;
On the morrow *he* will leave me, as my hopes have flown before."
    Then the bird said, "Nevermore."   60

Startled at the stillness broken by reply so aptly spoken,
"Doubtless," said I, "what it utters is its only stock and store,
Caught from some unhappy master whom unmerciful disaster
Followed fast and followed faster till his songs one burden bore:
Till the dirges of his hope that melancholy burden bore   65
    Of 'Never — nevermore.'"

But the Raven still beguiling all my fancy into smiling,
Straight I wheeled a cushioned seat in front of bird and bust and door;
Then, upon the velvet sinking, I betook myself to linking
Fancy unto fancy, thinking what this ominous bird of yore,   70
What this grim, ungainly, ghastly, gaunt, and ominous bird of yore
    Meant in croaking "Nevermore."

This I sat engaged in guessing, but no syllable expressing
To the fowl whose fiery eyes now burned into my bosom's core;
This and more I sat divining, with my head at ease reclining   75
On the cushion's velvet lining that the lamplight gloated o'er,
But whose velvet violet lining with the lamplight gloating o'er
    She shall press, ah, nevermore!

Then, methought, the air grew denser, perfumed from an unseen censer
Swung by seraphim whose footfalls tinkled on the tufted floor.   80
"Wretch," I cried, "thy God hath lent thee — by these angels he hath sent thee
Respite — respite and nepenthe° from thy memories of Lenore!
Quaff, oh quaff this kind nepenthe, and forget this lost Lenore!"
    Quoth the Raven, "Nevermore."

"Prophet!" said I, "thing of evil — prophet still, if bird or devil!   85
Whether tempter sent, or whether tempest tossed thee here ashore,
Desolate yet all undaunted, on this desert land enchanted —
On this home by horror haunted — tell me truly, I implore:
Is there — *is* there balm in Gilead?° — tell me — tell me, I implore!"
    Quoth the Raven, "Nevermore."   90

"Prophet!" said I, "thing of evil — prophet still, if bird or devil!
By that heaven that bends above us, by that God we both adore,
Tell this soul with sorrow laden if, within the distant Aidenn,°

---

    82. **nepenthe** (nė·pĕn'thė): a drug that destroys pain and brings forgetfulness. 89. **balm in Gilead** (gĭl'ė·ăd): a healing lotion made in Gilead, a part of ancient Palestine (see Jer. 8:22); therefore, relief from affliction. 93. **Aidenn** (ā'dĕn): from the Arabic for Eden.

It shall clasp a sainted maiden whom the angels name Lenore:
Clasp a rare and radiant maiden whom the angels name Lenore!"   95
      Quoth the Raven, "Nevermore."

"Be that word our sign of parting, bird or fiend!" I shrieked, upstarting:
"Get thee back into the tempest and the night's Plutonian shore!
Leave no black plume as a token of that lie thy soul hath spoken!
Leave my loneliness unbroken! quit the bust above my door!   100
Take thy beak from out my heart, and take thy form from off my door!"
      Quoth the Raven, "Nevermore."

And the Raven, never flitting, still is sitting, still is sitting
On the pallid bust of Pallas just above my chamber door;
And his eyes have all the seeming of a demon's that is dreaming,   105
And the lamplight o'er him streaming throws his shadow on the floor:
And my soul from out that shadow that lies floating on the floor
      Shall be lifted — nevermore!

FOR DISCUSSION

TO HELEN

1. How does the poet show the distance — the emotional distance — between himself and Helen? Why do you think he used the name "Helen"?

2. Is the mood of the poem simple or complex?

SOUND-VALUES IN THE BELLS

Observe carefully the use of the liquid consonants — *l, m, n*. What other consonants appear with notable frequency? What difference can you note in the use of vowels for the various metals? How does this selection of vowels and consonants affect the general mood and sound of the four different sections?

Find good examples of onomatopoetic words. What definition for *tintinnabulation* can you give? What is the dictionary definition? Find examples of alliteration and repetition.

ATMOSPHERE IN THE RAVEN

1. What atmosphere and mood are established at the very beginning of the po-

em? From the few, but effective, details given, picture to yourself the room that is the setting for the poem.

2. What in the raven's manner makes the poem unusually weird and depressing? What do you think the raven symbolizes?

3. Find examples of internal rhyme, alliteration, and repetition of phrases.

CHORAL READING

Poe's poems lend themselves particularly well to choral reading by the class or part of the class. If you wish to try this, here are a few simple directions: Divide into groups according to high, medium, and low voices, somewhat as in a singing choir. Vary the effects of the reading by having certain passages read by a single voice or a single range of voices in contrast to passages read by the entire group. "The Bells" is a good poem to begin with, as the differences are so obvious, beginning with the high voices and dropping to the low voices. Vary the volume as well as the pitch. Some passages may be read lightly; others, with the emphasis of the entire chorus.

A lithograph by the French artist Edouard Manet (1832–1883), ▶
used as an illustration in a French edition of "The Raven."
Another Manet lithograph from the same edition appears on page 519.

The Fall of the House of Usher

Poe excelled in writing tales of mystery and the supernatural. "The Fall of the House of Usher" was, and is, one of the most popular of his stories, and the reasons for its success are clear. From the opening paragraph, the tale is dominated by an atmosphere of mystery and foreboding. Because the narrator (the "I" of the story) is an observant and, above all, a sane man, his suspicions and fears are transferred to the mind of the reader, growing and developing as the story reaches its horrifying climax. Because of Poe's masterful handling of the tale, and the skill with which he employs even the most minor details to help create the impressive climax, the story exerts a strange fascination. Like "The Raven," "The Fall of the House of Usher" casts it own spell of unearthly beauty.

POE'S SHORT–STORY THEORY. Just as Poe believed that in order to be effective a poem must be short enough to be read at one sitting, he also felt that a story should be short enough to produce a single emotional effect. If the story stretches to such length that the reader must put it down and come back to it later, Poe felt that this effect would be lost. Of course, Poe maintained that the short-story writer must decide exactly what emotional effect he wishes to create, and then he must choose every character, every incident, indeed, every word, to contribute to that effect. Many writers have disagreed with Poe's theories, but it is clear that he followed his own rules closely. Notice, in the following story, how every incident and every word is chosen to achieve the emotional effect Poe desired.

> Son cœur est un luth suspendu;
> Sitôt qu'on le touche il résonne.[1]
> —De Béranger

DURING the whole of a dull, dark, and soundless day in the autumn of the year, when the clouds hung oppressively low in the heavens, I had been passing alone, on horseback, through a singularly dreary tract of country, and at length found myself, as the shades of the evening drew on, within view of the melancholy House of Usher. I know not how it was — but, with the first glimpse of the building, a sense of insufferable gloom pervaded my spirit. I say insufferable; for the feeling was unrelieved by any of that half-pleasurable, because poetic, sentiment with which the mind usually receives even the sternest natural images of the desolate or terrible. I looked upon the scene before me — upon the mere house, and the simple landscape features of the domain — upon the bleak walls — upon the vacant eyelike windows — upon a few rank sedges [2] — and upon a few white trunks of decayed trees — with an utter depression of soul which I can compare to no earthly sensation more properly than to the after-dream of the reveler upon opium — the bitter lapse into everyday life — the hideous dropping off of the veil. There was an iciness, a sinking, a sickening of the heart — an unredeemed dreariness of thought which no goading of the imagination could torture into aught of the sublime. What was it — I paused to think — what was it that so unnerved me in the contemplation of the House of Usher? It was a mystery all insoluble; nor could I grapple with the shadowy fancies that crowded upon me

---

[1] "His heart is a suspended lute;/Touch it and the strings resound." From the poem "Le Refus" by Pierre Jean de Béranger (1780–1857).

[2] sedges: grasslike plants.

as I pondered. I was forced to fall back upon the unsatisfactory conclusion that while, beyond doubt, there *are* combinations of very simple natural objects which have the power of thus affecting us, still the analysis of this power lies among considerations beyond our depth. It was possible, I reflected, that a mere different arrangement of the particulars of the scene, of the details of the picture, would be sufficient to modify, or perhaps to annihilate its capacity for sorrowful impression; and, acting upon this idea, I reined my horse to the precipitous brink of a black and lurid tarn [1] that lay in unruffled luster by the dwelling, and gazed down — but with a shudder even more thrilling than before — upon the remodeled and inverted images of the gray sedge, and the ghastly tree stems, and the vacant and eyelike windows.

Nevertheless, in this mansion of gloom, I now proposed to myself a sojourn of some weeks. Its proprietor, Roderick Usher, had been one of my boon companions in boyhood; but many years had elapsed since our last meeting. A letter, however, had lately reached me in a distant part of the country — a letter from him — which, in its wildly importunate nature, had admitted of no other than a personal reply. The MS.[2] gave evidence of nervous agitation. The writer spoke of acute bodily illness — of a mental disorder which oppressed him — and of an earnest desire to see me, as his best and indeed his only personal friend, with a view of attempting, by the cheerfulness of my society, some alleviation of his malady. It was the manner in which all this, and much more, was said — it was the apparent *heart* that went with his request — which allowed me no room for hesitation; and I accordingly obeyed forthwith what I still considered a very singular summons.

Although, as boys, we had been even intimate associates, yet I really knew little of my friend. His reserve had been always excessive and habitual. I was aware, however, that his very ancient family had been noted, time out of mind, for a peculiar sensibility of temperament, displaying itself, through long ages, in many works of exalted art, and manifested, of late, in repeated deeds of munificent yet unobtrusive charity, as well as in a passionate devotion to the intricacies, perhaps even more than to the orthodox and easily recognizable beauties, of musical science. I had learned, too, the very remarkable fact that the stem of the Usher race, all time-honored as it was, had put forth, at no period, any enduring branch; in other words, that the entire family lay in the direct line of descent, and had always, with very trifling and very temporary variation, so lain. It was this deficiency, I considered, while running over in thought the perfect keeping of the character of the premises with the accredited character of the people, and while speculating upon the possible influence which the one, in the long lapse of centuries, might have exercised upon the other — it was this deficiency, perhaps, of collateral [3] issue, and patrimony [4] with the name, which had, at length, so identified the two as to merge the original title of the estate in the quaint and equivocal appellation of the "House of Usher" — an appellation which seemed to include, in the minds of the peasantry who used it, both the family and the family mansion.

I have said that the sole effect of my somewhat childish experiment — that of looking down within the tarn — had been to deepen the first singular impression. There can be no doubt that the consciousness of the rapid increase of my superstition — for why should I not

---

[1] **tarn**: a small lake or pool.
[2] **MS.**: manuscript.
[3] **collateral**: related, but not in a direct line of descent.
[4] **patrimony** (păt′rĭ·mō′nĭ): inheritance.

so term it? — served mainly to accelerate the increase itself. Such, I have long known, is the paradoxical law of all sentiments having terror as a basis. And it might have been for this reason only, that, when I again uplifted my eyes to the house itself, from its image in the pool, there grew in my mind a strange fancy — a fancy so ridiculous, indeed, that I but mention it to show the vivid force of the sensations which oppressed me. I had so worked upon my imagination as really to believe that about the whole mansion and domain there hung an atmosphere peculiar to themselves and their immediate vicinity — an atmosphere which had no affinity with the air of heaven, but which had reeked up from the decayed trees, and the gray wall, and the silent tarn — a pestilent and mystic vapor, dull, sluggish, faintly discernible, and leaden-hued.

Shaking off from my spirit what *must* have been a dream, I scanned more narrowly the real aspect of the building. Its principal feature seemed to be that of an excessive antiquity. The discoloration of ages had been great. Minute fungi overspread the whole exterior, hanging in a fine tangled webwork from the eaves. Yet all this was apart from any extraordinary dilapidation. No portion of the masonry had fallen; and there appeared to be a wild inconsistency between its still perfect adaptation of parts, and the crumbling condition of the individual stones. In this there was much that reminded me of the specious totality of old woodwork which has rotted for long years in some neglected vault, with no disturbance from the breath of the external air. Beyond this indication of extensive decay, however, the fabric gave little token of instability. Perhaps the eye of a scrutinizing observer might have discovered a barely perceptible fissure, which, extending from the roof of the building in front, made its way down the wall in a zigzag direction, until it became lost in the sullen waters of the tarn.

Noticing these things, I rode over a short causeway to the house. A servant in waiting took my horse, and I entered the Gothic archway of the hall. A valet, of stealthy step, thence conducted me, in silence, through many dark and intricate passages in my progress to the studio of his master. Much that I encountered on the way contributed, I know not how, to heighten the vague sentiments of which I have already spoken. While the objects around me — while the carvings of the ceilings, the somber tapestries of the walls, the ebon blackness of the floors, and the phantasmagoric [1] armorial trophies which rattled as I strode, were but matters to which, or to such as which, I had been accustomed from my infancy — while I hesitated not to acknowledge how familiar was all this — I still wondered to find how unfamiliar were the fancies which ordinary images were stirring up. On one of the staircases, I met the physician of the family. His countenance, I thought, wore a mingled expression of low cunning and perplexity. He accosted me with trepidation and passed on. The valet now threw open a door and ushered me into the presence of his master.

The room in which I found myself was very large and lofty. The windows were long, narrow, and pointed, and at so vast a distance from the black oaken floor as to be altogether inaccessible from within. Feeble gleams of encrimsoned light made their way through the trellised panes and served to render sufficiently distinct the more prominent objects around; the eye, however, struggled in vain to reach the remoter angles of the chamber, or the recesses of the vaulted and fretted [2] ceiling. Dark draperies hung upon the walls. The general furniture was profuse, comfortless, antique, and tattered. Many books and musical instruments lay scattered about, but failed to give any vitality to the

[1] phantasmagoric (făn·tăz′má·gŏr′ĭk), deceptive, fantastic.
[2] fretted: carved in patterns.

scene. I felt that I breathed an atmosphere of sorrow. An air of stern, deep, and irredeemable gloom hung over and pervaded all.

Upon my entrance, Usher arose from a sofa on which he had been lying at full length, and greeted me with a vivacious warmth which had much in it, I at first thought, of an overdone cordiality — of the constrained effort of the *ennuyé*[1] man of the world. A glance, however, at his countenance convinced me of his perfect sincerity. We sat down; and for some moments, while he spoke not, I gazed upon him with a feeling half of pity, half of awe. Surely, man had never before so terribly altered, in so brief a period, as had Roderick Usher! It was with difficulty that I could bring myself to admit the identity of the wan being before me with the companion of my early boyhood. Yet the character of his face had been at all times remarkable. A cadaverousness[2] of complexion; an eye large, liquid, and luminous beyond comparison; lips somewhat thin and very pallid, but of surpassingly beautiful curve; a nose of a delicate Hebrew model, but with a breadth of nostril unusual in similar formations; a finely molded chin, speaking, in its want of prominence, of a want of moral energy; hair of a more than weblike softness and tenuity;[3] these features, with an inordinate expansion above the regions of the temple, made up altogether a countenance not easily to be forgotten. And now in the mere exaggeration of the prevailing character of these features, and of the expression they were wont to convey, lay so much of change that I doubted to whom I spoke. The now ghastly pallor of the skin, and the now miraculous luster of the eye, above all things startled and even awed me. The silken hair, too, had been suffered to grow all unheeded, and as, in its wild gossamer texture, it floated rather than fell about the face, I could not, even with effort, connect its Arabesque[4] expression with any idea of simple humanity.

In the manner of my friend I was at once struck with an incoherence — an inconsistency; and I soon found this to arise from a series of feeble and futile struggles to overcome an habitual trepidancy — an excessive nervous agitation. For something of this nature I had indeed been prepared, no less by his letter, than by reminiscences of certain boyish traits, and by conclusions deduced from his peculiar physical conformation and temperament. His action was alternately vivacious and sullen. His voice varied rapidly from a tremulous indecision (when the animal spirits seemed utterly in abeyance[5]) to that species of energetic concision — that abrupt, weighty, unhurried, and hollow-sounding enunciation — that leaden, self-balanced, and perfectly modulated guttural[6] utterance, which may be observed in the lost drunkard, or the irreclaimable eater of opium, during the periods of his most intense excitement.

It was thus that he spoke of the object of my visit, of his earnest desire to see me, and of the solace he expected me to afford him. He entered, at some length, into what he conceived to be the nature of his malady. It was, he said, a constitutional and a family evil, and one for which he despaired to find a remedy — a mere nervous affection,[7] he immediately added, which would undoubtedly soon pass off. It displayed itself in a host of unnatural sensations. Some of these, as he detailed them, interested and bewildered me; although, perhaps, the terms and the general manner of their narration had their weight. He

---

[1] *ennuyé* (än′nwē′yā′): bored (French).
[2] cadaverousness (ká·dăv′ēr·ŭs·nĕs): corpselike quality.
[3] tenuity (tĕn·ū′ĭ·tĭ): thinness.

[4] **Arabesque** (ăr′á·bĕsk): fantastic.
[5] **in abeyance** (á·bā′ăns): suppressed.
[6] **guttural** (gŭt′ēr·ăl): throaty.
[7] **affection**: here, affliction.

suffered much from a morbid acuteness of the senses; the most insipid food was alone endurable; he could wear only garments of certain texture; the odors of all flowers were oppressive; his eyes were tortured by even a faint light; and there were but peculiar sounds, and these from stringed instruments, which did not inspire him with horror.

To an anomalous species of terror I found him a bounden slave. "I shall perish," said he, "I *must* perish in this deplorable folly. Thus, thus, and not otherwise, shall I be lost. I dread the events of the future, not in themselves, but in their results. I shudder at the thought of any, even the most trivial, incident, which may operate upon this intolerable agitation of soul. I have, indeed, no abhorrence of danger, except in its absolute effect — in terror. In this unnerved, in this pitiable, condition, I feel that the period will sooner or later arrive when I must abandon life and reason together, in some struggle with the grim phantasm,[1] FEAR."

I learned, moreover, at intervals, and through broken and equivocal hints, another singular feature of his mental condition. He was enchained by certain superstitious impressions in regard to the dwelling which he tenanted, and whence, for many years, he had never ventured forth — in regard to an influence whose supposititious force was conveyed in terms too shadowy here to be restated — an influence which some peculiarities in the mere form and substance of his family mansion had, by dint of long sufferance, he said, obtained over his spirit — an effect which the physique of the gray walls and turrets, and of the dim tarn into which they all looked down, had, at length, brought about upon the morale of his existence.

He admitted, however, although with hesitation, that much of the peculiar gloom which thus afflicted him could be traced to a more natural and far more palpable origin — to the severe and long-continued illness — indeed to the evidently approaching dissolution — of a tenderly beloved sister, his sole companion for long years, his last and only relative on earth. "Her decease," he said, with a bitterness which I can never forget, "would leave him (him, the hopeless and the frail) the last of the ancient race of the Ushers." While he spoke, the lady Madeline (for so was she called) passed through a remote portion of the apartment, and, without having noticed my presence, disappeared. I regarded her with an utter astonishment not unmingled with dread; and yet I found it impossible to account for such feelings. A sensation of stupor oppressed me as my eyes followed her retreating steps. When a door, at length, closed upon her, my glance sought instinctively and eagerly the countenance of the brother; but he had buried his face in his hands, and I could only perceive that a far more than ordinary wanness had overspread the emaciated fingers through which trickled many passionate tears.

The disease of the lady Madeline had long baffled the skill of her physicians. A settled apathy, a gradual wasting away of the person, and frequent although transient affections of a partially cataleptical[2] character were the unusual diagnosis. Hitherto she had steadily borne up against the pressure of her malady, and had not betaken herself finally to bed; but on the closing in of the evening of my arrival at the house, she succumbed (as her brother told me at night with inexpressible agitation) to the prostrating power of the destroyer; and I learned that the glimpse I had obtained of her person would thus probably be the last I should obtain — that the lady, at least while living, would be seen by me no more.

[1] **phantasm** (făn'tăz'm): a figment of the imagination; an illusion.

[2] **cataleptical** (kăt'*á*·lĕp'tĭk'l): pertaining to a stroke characterized by a deathlike rigidity.

For several days ensuing, her name was unmentioned by either Usher or myself; and during this period I was busied in earnest endeavors to alleviate the melancholy of my friend. We painted and read together, or I listened, as if in a dream, to the wild improvisations of his speaking guitar. And thus, as a closer and still closer intimacy admitted me more unreservedly into the recesses of his spirit, the more bitterly did I perceive the futility of all attempt at cheering a mind from which darkness, as if an inherent positive quality, poured forth upon all objects of the moral and physical universe in one unceasing radiation of gloom.

I shall ever bear about me a memory of the many solemn hours I thus spent alone with the master of the House of Usher. Yet I should fail in any attempt to convey an idea of the exact character of the studies, or of the occupations, in which he involved me, or led me the way. An excited and highly distempered ideality [1] threw a sulfureous [2] luster over all. His long improvised dirges will ring forever in my ears. Among other things, I hold painfully in mind a certain singular perversion and amplification of the wild air of the last waltz of von Weber.[3] From the paintings over which his elaborate fancy brooded, and which grew, touch by touch, into vaguenesses at which I shuddered the more thrillingly, because I shuddered knowing not why — from these paintings (vivid as their images now are before me) I would in vain endeavor to educe [4] more than a small portion which should lie within the compass of merely written words. By the utter simplicity, by the nakedness of his designs, he arrested and overawed attention. If ever mortal painted an idea, that mortal was Roderick Usher. For me at least, in the cir-

cumstances then surrounding me, there arose out of the pure abstractions which the hypochondriac contrived to throw upon his canvas, an intensity of intolerable awe, no shadow of which felt I ever yet in the contemplation of the certainly glowing yet too concrete reveries of Fuseli.[5]

One of the phantasmagoric conceptions of my friend, partaking not so rigidly of the spirit of abstraction, may be shadowed forth, although feebly, in words. A small picture presented the interior of an immensely long and rectangular vault or tunnel, with low walls, smooth, white, and without interruption or device. Certain accessory points of the design served well to convey the idea that this excavation lay at an exceeding depth below the surface of the earth. No outlet was observed in any portion of its vast extent, and no torch or other artificial source of light was discernible; yet a flood of intense rays rolled throughout, and bathed the whole in a ghastly and inappropriate splendor.

I have just spoken of that morbid condition of the auditory nerve which rendered all music intolerable to the sufferer, with the exception of certain effects of stringed instruments. It was, perhaps, the narrow limits to which he thus confined himself upon the guitar which gave birth, in great measure, to the fantastic character of his performances. But the fervid facility of his impromptus could not be so accounted for. They must have been, and were, in the notes, as well as in the words of his wild fantasias (for he not unfrequently accompanied himself with rhymed verbal improvisations), the result of that intense mental collectedness and concentration to which I have previously alluded as observable only in particular moments of the highest artificial excitement. The words of one of

[1] **distempered ideality:** feverish obsession.
[2] **sulfureous** (sŭl·fū′rė·ŭs): fiery.
[3] **von Weber** (fôn vā′bēr): Carl Maria von Weber (1786–1826) a German composer.
[4] **educe** (ė·dūs′): bring forth, reveal.

[5] **Fuseli:** Johann Heinrich Fuseli (or Füssli) (1742–1825), a Swiss painter who lived in England.

these rhapsodies I have easily remembered. I was, perhaps, the more forcibly impressed with it as he gave it, because, in the under or mystic current of its meaning, I fancied that I perceived, and for the first time, a full consciousness on the part of Usher of the tottering of his lofty reason upon her throne. The verses, which were entitled "The Haunted Palace," ran very nearly, if not accurately thus:

I

In the greenest of our valleys,
    By good angels tenanted,
Once a fair and stately palace —
    Radiant palace — reared its head.
In the monarch Thought's dominion —
    It stood there!
Never seraph spread a pinion
    Over fabric half so fair.

II

Banners yellow, glorious, golden,
    On its roof did float and flow
(This — all this — was in the olden
    Time long ago);
And every gentle air that dallied,
    In that sweet day,
Along the ramparts plumed and pallid,
    A wingèd odor went away.

III

Wanderers in that happy valley
    Through two luminous windows saw
Spirits moving musically
    To a lute's well-tunèd law;
Round about a throne, where sitting
    (Porphyrogene!) [1]
In state his glory well befitting,
    The ruler of the realm was seen.

IV

And all with pearl and ruby glowing,
    Was the fair palace door,
Through which came flowing, flowing,
    flowing
  And sparkling evermore,

A troop of Echoes whose sweet duty
    Was but to sing,
In voices of surpassing beauty,
    The wit and wisdom of their king.

V

But evil things, in robes of sorrow,
    Assailed the monarch's high estate;
(Ah, let us mourn, for never morrow
    Shall dawn upon him, desolate!)
And, round about his home, the glory
    That blushed and bloomed
Is but a dim-remembered story
    Of the old time entombed.

VI

And travelers now within that valley,
    Through the red-litten [2] windows see
Vast forms that move fantastically
    To a discordant melody;
While, like a rapid ghastly river,
    Through the pale door,
A hideous throng rush out forever,
    And laugh — but smile no more.

I well remembered that suggestions arising from this ballad led us into a train of thought wherein there became manifest an opinion of Usher's, which I mention not so much on account of its novelty (for other men have thought thus), as on account of the pertinacity with which he maintained it. This opinion, in its general form, was that of the sentience [3] of all vegetable things. But in his disordered fancy, the idea had assumed a more daring character, and trespassed, under certain conditions, upon the kingdom of inorganization. [4] I lack words to express the full extent, or the earnest *abandon* of his persuasion. The belief, however, was connected (as I have previously hinted) with the gray stones of the home of his forefathers. The conditions of the sentence had been here, he imagined, fulfilled in the method of collocation of these stones

[1] **Porphyrogene** (pôr'fĭ·rŏ·jēn'): pertaining to royalty or "the purple." The word comes from porphyry, a dark-red or purple rock.

[2] **litten:** poetic for lighted.
[3] **sentience** (sĕn'shĭ·ĕns): consciousness.
[4] **kingdom of inorganization:** the world of inanimate objects.

— in the order of their arrangement, as well as in that of the many fungi which overspread them, and of the decayed trees which stood around — above all, in the long undisturbed endurance of this arrangement, and in its reduplication in the still waters of the tarn. Its evidence—the evidence of the sentience — was to be seen, he said (and I here started as he spoke), in the gradual yet certain condensation of an atmosphere of their own about the waters and the walls. The result was discoverable, he added, in that silent yet importunate and terrible influence which for centuries had molded the destinies of his family, and which made *him* what I now saw him — what he was. Such opinions need no comment, and I will make none.

Our books — the books which, for years, had formed no small portion of the mental existence of the invalid — were, as might be supposed, in strict keeping with this character of phantasm. We pored together over such works as the *Ververt et Chartreuse* [1] of Gresset; the *Belphegor* of Machiavelli; the *Heaven and Hell* of Swedenborg; the *Subterranean Voyage of Nicholas Klimm* by Holberg; the *Chiromancy* of Robert Flud, of Jean D'Indaginé, and of De la Chambre; the *Journey into the Blue Distance* of Tieck; and the *City of the Sun* of Campanella. One favorite volume was a small octave edition of the *Directorium Inquisitorium*, by the Dominican Eymeric de Gironne; and there were passages in Pomponius Mela, about the old African Satyrs and Ægipans, over which Usher would sit dreaming for hours. His chief delight, however, was found in the perusal of an exceedingly rare and curious book in quarto Gothic — the manual of a forgotten church — the *Vigiliæ Mortuorum Secundum Chorum Ecclesiæ Maguntinæ.*

[1] *Ververt et Chartreuse,* etc.: All of the books listed are works of mysticism or magic.

I could not help thinking of the wild ritual of this work, and of its probable influence upon the hypochondriac, when, one evening, having informed me abruptly that the lady Madeline was no more, he stated his intention of preserving her corpse for a fortnight (previously to its final interment), in one of the numerous vaults within the main walls of the building. The worldly reason, however, assigned for this singular proceeding, was one which I did not feel at liberty to dispute. The brother had been led to his resolution (so he told me) by consideration of the unusual character of the malady of the deceased, of certain obtrusive and eager inquiries on the part of her medical men, and of the remote and exposed situation of the burial ground of the family. I will not deny that when I called to mind the sinister countenance of the person whom I met upon the staircase, on the day of my arrival at the house, I had no desire to oppose what I regarded as at best but a harmless, and by no means an unnatural precaution.

At the request of Usher, I personally aided him in the arrangements for the temporary entombment. The body having been encoffined, we two alone bore it to its rest. The vault in which we placed it (and which had been so long unopened that our torches, half smothered in its oppressive atmosphere, gave us little opportunity for investigation) was small, damp, and entirely without means of admission for light; lying, at great depth, immediately beneath that portion of the building in which was my own sleeping apartment. It had been used, apparently, in remote feudal times, for the worst purposes of a donjon-keep,[2] and, in later days, as a place of deposit for powder, or some other highly combustible substance, as a portion of its floor, and the whole interior of a long archway through which we

[2] **donjon-keep:** dungeon.

reached it, were carefully sheathed with copper. The door, of massive iron, had been, also, similarly protected. Its immense weight caused an unusually sharp, grating sound, as it moved upon its hinges.

Having deposited our mournful burden upon trestles within this region of horror, we partially turned aside the yet unscrewed lid of the coffin, and looked upon the face of the tenant. A striking similitude between the brother and sister now first arrested my attention; and Usher, divining, perhaps, my thoughts, murmured out some few words from which I learned that the deceased and himself had been twins, and that sympathies of a scarcely intelligible nature had always existed between them. Our glances, however, rested not long upon the dead — for we could not regard her unawed. The disease which had thus entombed the lady in the maturity of youth, had left, as usual in all maladies of a strictly cataleptical character, the mockery of a faint blush upon the bosom and the face, and that suspiciously lingering smile upon the lip which is so terrible in death. We replaced and screwed down the lid, and, having secured the door of iron, made our way, with toil, into the scarcely less gloomy apartments of the upper portion of the house.

And now, some days of bitter grief having elapsed, an observable change came over the features of the mental disorder of my friend. His ordinary manner had vanished. His ordinary occupations were neglected or forgotten. He roamed from chamber to chamber with hurried, unequal, and objectless step. The pallor of his countenance had assumed, if possible, a more ghastly hue — but the luminousness of his eye had utterly gone out. The once occasional huskiness of his tone was heard no more; and a tremulous quaver, as if of extreme terror, habitually characterized his utterance. There were times,

indeed, when I thought his unceasingly agitated mind was laboring with some oppressive secret, to divulge which he struggled for the necessary courage. At times, again, I was obliged to resolve all into the mere inexplicable vagaries [1] of madness, for I beheld him gazing upon vacancy for long hours, in an attitude of the profoundest attention, as if listening to some imaginary sound. It was no wonder that his condition terrified — that it infected me. I felt creeping upon me, by slow yet certain degrees, the wild influences of his own fantastic yet impressive superstitions.

It was, especially, upon retiring to bed late in the night of the seventh or eighth day after the placing of the lady Madeline within the donjon, that I experienced the full power of such feelings. Sleep came not near my couch — while the hours waned and waned away, I struggled to reason off the nervousness which had dominion over me. I endeavored to believe that much, if not all, of what I felt, was due to the bewildering influence of the gloomy furniture of the room — of the dark and tattered draperies, which, tortured into motion by the breath of a rising tempest, swayed fitfully to and fro upon the walls, and rustled uneasily about the decorations of the bed. But my efforts were fruitless. An irrepressible tremor gradually pervaded my frame; and, at length, there sat upon my very heart an incubus [2] of utterly causeless alarm. Shaking this off with a gasp and a struggle, I uplifted myself upon the pillows, and peering earnestly within the intense darkness of the chamber, hearkened — I know not why, except that an instinctive spirit prompted me — to certain low and indefinite sounds which came, through the pauses of the storm, at long intervals, I knew not whence. Overpowered by an intense sentiment of horror, unaccountable yet

[1] vagaries (vȧ·gâr′ĭz): whims.
[2] incubus (ĭn′kû·bŭs): a burden, an oppressive spirit.

unendurable. I threw on my clothes with haste (for I felt I should sleep no more during the night), and endeavored to arouse myself from the pitiable condition into which I had fallen, by pacing to and fro through the apartment.

I had taken but few turns in this manner, when a light step on an adjoining staircase arrested my attention. I presently recognized it as that of Usher. In an instant afterward he rapped, with a gentle touch, at my door, and entered, bearing a lamp. His countenance was, as usual, cadaverously wan — but, moreover, there was a species of mad hilarity in his eyes — an evidently restrained hysteria in his whole demeanor. His air appalled me — but anything was preferable to the solitude which I had so long endured, and I even welcomed his presence as a relief.

"And you have not seen it?" he said abruptly, after having stared about him for some moments in silence — "you have not then seen it? — but, stay! you shall." Thus speaking, and having carefully shaded his lamp, he hurried to one of the casements, and threw it freely open to the storm.

The impetuous fury of the entering gust nearly lifted us from our feet. It was, indeed, a tempestuous yet sternly beautiful night, and one wildly singular in its terror and its beauty. A whirlwind had apparently collected its force in our vicinity; for there were frequent and violent alterations in the direction of the wind; and the exceeding density of the clouds (which hung so low as to press upon the turrets of the house) did not prevent our perceiving the lifelike velocity with which they flew careering from all points against each other, without passing away into the distance. I say that even their exceeding density did not prevent our perceiving this — yet we had no glimpse of the moon or stars, nor was there any flashing forth of the lightning. But the under surfaces of the huge masses of agitated vapor, as well as all terrestrial objects immediate-

ly around us, were glowing in the unnatural light of a faintly luminous and distinctly visible gaseous exhalation which hung about and enshrouded the mansion.

"You must not — you shall not behold this!" said I, shuddering, to Usher, as I led him, with a gentle violence, from the window to a seat. "These appearances, which bewilder you, are merely electrical phenomena not uncommon — or it may be that they have their ghastly origin in the rank miasma [1] of the tarn. Let us close this casement; the air is chilling and dangerous to your frame. Here is one of your favorite romances. I will read, and you shall listen: and so we will pass away this terrible night together."

The antique volume which I had taken up was the *Mad Trist* of Sir Launcelot Canning; [2] but I had called it a favorite of Usher's more in sad jest than in earnest; for, in truth, there is little in its uncouth and unimaginative prolixity [3] which could have had interest for the lofty and spiritual ideality of my friend. It was, however, the only book immediately at hand; and I indulged a vague hope that the excitement which now agitated the hypochondriac might find relief (for the history of mental disorder is full of similar anomalies) even in the extremeness of the folly which I should read. Could I have judged, indeed, by the wild overstrained air of vivacity with which he hearkened, or apparently hearkened, to the words of the tale, I might well have congratulated myself upon the success of my design.

I had arrived at that well-known portion of the story where Ethelred, the hero of the Trist, having sought in vain for peaceable admission into the dwelling of the hermit, proceeds to make

[1] rank miasma (mĭ-ăz′mà): thick, harmful atmosphere.
[2] *Mad Trist* of Sir Launcelot Canning: The book and the author were Poe's inventions.
[3] prolixity (prŏ-lĭk′sĭ-tĭ): wordiness.

good an entrance by force. Here, it will be remembered, the words of the narrative run thus:

"And Ethelred, who was by nature of a doughty heart, and who was now mighty withal, on account of the powerfulness of the wine which he had drunken, waited no longer to hold parley with the hermit, who, in sooth, was of an obstinate and maliceful turn, but, feeling the rain upon his shoulders, and fearing the rising of the tempest, uplifted his mace [1] outright, and, with blows, made quickly room in the plankings of the door for his gauntleted hand; and now pulling therewith sturdily, he so cracked, and ripped, and tore all asunder, that the noise of the dry and hollow-sounding wood alarumed and reverberated throughout the forest."

At the termination of this sentence, I started and, for a moment, paused; for it appeared to me (although I at once concluded that my excited fancy had deceived me) — it appeared to me that, from some very remote portion of the mansion, there came, indistinctly, to my ears, what might have been, in its exact similarity of character, the echo (but a stifled and dull one certainly) of the very cracking and ripping sound which Sir Launcelot had so particularly described. It was, beyond doubt, the coincidence alone which had arrested my attention; for, amid the rattling of the sashes of the casements, and the ordinary commingled noises of the still increasing storm, the sound, in itself, had nothing, surely, which should have interested or disturbed me. I continued the story:

"But the good champion Ethelred, now entering within the door, was sore enraged and amazed to perceive no signal of the maliceful hermit; but, in the stead thereof, a dragon of a scaly and prodigious demeanor, and of a fiery tongue, which sate in guard before a palace of gold, with a floor of silver; and upon the wall there

¹ mace: club.

hung a shield of shining brass with this legend enwritten —

> Who entereth herein, a conqueror hath bin;
> Who slayeth the dragon, the shield he shall win.

And Ethelred uplifted his mace, and struck upon the head of the dragon, which fell before him, and gave up his pesty breath, with a shriek so horrid and harsh and withal so piercing, that Ethelred had fain to close his ears with his hands against the dreadful noise of it, the like whereof was never before heard."

Here again I paused abruptly, and now with a feeling of wild amazement, I did actually hear (although from what direction it proceeded I found it impossible to say) a low and apparently distant, but harsh, protracted, and most unusual screaming or grating sound — the exact counterpart of what my fancy had already conjured up for the dragon's unnatural shriek as described by the romancer.

Oppressed, as I certainly was, upon the occurrence of this second and most extraordinary coincidence, by a thousand conflicting sensations, in which wonder and extreme terror were predominant, I still retained sufficient presence of mind to avoid exciting, by any observation, the sensitive nervousness of my companion. I was by no means certain that he had noticed the sounds in question; although, assuredly, a strange alteration had, during the last few minutes, taken place in his demeanor. From a position fronting my own, he had gradually brought round his chair, so as to sit with his face to the door of the chamber; and thus I could but partially perceive his features, although I saw that his lips trembled as if he were murmuring inaudibly. His head had dropped upon his breast — yet I knew that he was not asleep, from the wide and rigid opening of the eye as I caught a glance of it in profile. The motion of his body, too, was at variance with this idea — for he rocked from side to side with a gentle yet constant and uniform sway. Having rapidly taken notice of all this, I resumed the narrative of Sir Launcelot, which thus proceeded:

"And now, the champion, having escaped from the terrible fury of the dragon, bethinking himself of the brazen shield, and of the breaking up of the enchantment which was upon it, removed the carcass from out of the way before him, and approached valorously over the silver pavement of the castle to where the shield was upon the wall; which in sooth tarried not for his full coming, but fell down at his feet upon the silver floor, with a mighty great and terrible ringing sound."

No sooner had these syllables passed my lips, than — as if a shield of brass had indeed, at the moment, fallen heavily upon a floor of silver — I became aware of a distinct, hollow, metallic, and clangorous, yet apparently muffled, reverberation. Completely unnerved, I leaped to my feet; but the measured rocking movement of Usher was undisturbed. I rushed to the chair in which he sat. His eyes were bent fixedly before him, and throughout his whole countenance there reigned a stony rigidity. But, as I placed my hand upon his shoulder, there came a strong shudder over his whole person; a sickly smile quivered about his lips; and I saw that he spoke in a low, hurried, and gibbering murmur, as if unconscious of my presence. Bending closely over him, I at length drank in the hideous import of his words.

"Not hear it? — yes, I hear it, and *have* heard it. Long — long — long — many minutes, many hours, many days, have I heard it — yet I dared not — oh, pity me, miserable wretch that I am! — I dared not — I *dared* not speak! *We have put her living in the tomb!* Said I not that my senses were acute? I *now* tell you that I heard her first feeble movements in the hollow coffin. I heard them — many, many days ago — yet I dared not — *I dared not speak!* And now — tonight — Ethelred — ha! ha! — the breaking of the hermit's door, and the death-cry of the dragon, and the clangor of the shield — say, rather, the rending of her coffin, and the grating of the iron hinges of her prison, and her struggles within the coppered archway of the vault! Oh! whither shall I fly? Will she not be here anon [1]? Is she not hurrying to upbraid me for my haste? Have I not heard her footstep on the stair? Do I not distinguish that heavy and horrible beating of her heart? Madman!" — here he sprang furiously to his feet, and shrieked out his syllables, as if in the effort he were giving up his soul — *"Madman! I tell you that she now stands without the door!"*

As if in the superhuman energy of his utterance there had been found the potency of a spell, the huge antique panels to which the speaker pointed threw slowly back, upon the instant, their ponderous and ebony jaws. It was the work of the rushing gust — but then without those doors there *did* stand the lofty and enshrouded figure of the lady Madeline of Usher. There was blood upon her white robes, and the evidence of some bitter struggle upon every portion of her emaciated frame. For a moment she remained trembling and reeling to and fro upon the threshold — then, with a low moaning cry, fell heavily inward upon the person of her brother, and in her violent and now final death-agonies, bore him to the floor a corpse, and a victim to the terrors he had anticipated.

From that chamber, and from that mansion, I fled aghast. The storm was still abroad in all its wrath as I found myself crossing the old causeway. Suddenly there shot along the path a wild light, and I turned to see whence a gleam so unusual could have issued; for the vast house and its shadows were

[1] anon (á·nŏn'): soon.

alone behind me. The radiance was that of the full, setting, and blood-red moon, which now shone vividly through that once barely discernible fissure, of which I have before spoken as extending from the roof of the building, in a zigzag direction, to the base. While I gazed, this fissure rapidly widened — there came a fierce breath of the whirlwind — the entire orb of the satellite burst at once upon my sight — my brain reeled as I saw the mighty walls rushing asunder — there was a long tumultuous shouting sound like the voice of a thousand waters — and the deep and dank tarn at my feet closed sullenly and silently over the fragments of the *House of Usher.*

FOR DISCUSSION

1. What may have been Poe's purpose in having the term "The House of Usher" stand both for Roderick Usher's mansion and for the remaining members of his family?

2. On page 526 Poe states that no portion of the masonry of the mansion had fallen, yet the individual stones appeared to be crumbling. Does this statement suggest more than it actually says? Explain.

3. In Roderick Usher's ballad, "The Haunted Palace," what does the haunted palace symbolize?

4. Why did Usher decide to keep the corpse of his sister in a vault beneath the house for two weeks before the final interment?

5. What purpose might Poe have had in telling the reader that the lady Madeline's tomb was in former times a "donjon-keep"?

6. How does the narrator's oral reading of the romance (paralleling as it does the sounds in the donjon-keep) contribute to the mood of the story?

7. What may have been Poe's purpose in revealing that Roderick and Madeline Usher were twins?

8. How does the final incident of the story support Poe's theory of composition?

9. What clues given early in the story make the last happening believable?

SETTING THE TONE

Note the words in the first sentence that set the tone of the story:

"During the whole of a *dull, dark, soundless* day in . . . *autumn* . . . when clouds hung *oppressively low* . . . , I had been passing *alone* . . . through a *singularly dreary* tract of country, and at length found myself, as the *shades* of the *evening* drew on, within view of the *melancholy* House of Usher."

YOUR OWN WRITING

Decide on a single emotional effect you would like to create in the mind of your reader. The effect may be fear, joy, horror, suspicion, pity, calm, or some other emotion that occurs to you. Do not try to tell a whole story: try to create a mood in a single paragraph. Choose every sentence, every word with care. Remember that precise words that appeal to the senses and that re-create a sensory experience will serve you best. Do not write "moved" if a character "crawled." Do not say a band "played" if it "blared" or "boomed." When you have finished your paragraph, write on the back of your paper the emotional effect you have tried to produce.

FURTHER READING

To see other sides of Poe's skill, read a tale based on deduction and reasoning, such as "The Gold Bug" or "The Purloined Letter." Other Poe stories of strange, uncanny beauty are "The Masque of the Red Death" and "Ligeia." His masterpieces depicting mental unbalance are "The Cask of Amontillado," "The Black Cat," and "The Tell-Tale Heart."

As the Artist Sees It

On page 536 Robert Shore has depicted the final scene of Edgar Allan Poe's "The Fall of the House of Usher." Notice how the artist has tried to bring out the mood of Poe's grim story through the use of color. The entire scene is bathed in a red glow, as the house stands poised for a moment before its complete destruction. Do you find a feeling of impending disaster in the painting?

Two Major Novelists

We have watched full-fledged literary figures such as Irving, Cooper, Poe, and Bryant appear on our national scene and succeed in capturing the respect not only of America but of England and Europe as well. Yet thus far the stature of these men has been based on the combined effect of all their works. We have not yet seen the appearance of a single American book powerful enough to stand by itself and earn unquestioned right to the word "great." Now, in two successive years, appear two such books: American novels that are engrossing as stories and profound in moral and philosophical depth, written by men who happened to be good friends. The novels were *The Scarlet Letter* (1850) by Nathaniel Hawthorne, and *Moby Dick* (1851) by Herman Melville.

NATHANIEL HAWTHORNE:
". . . The Largest Brain with the Largest Heart . . ."

Visitors to Salem, Massachusetts, can see a fascinating old gray house with all the characteristics, inside and out, of early Puritan architecture. Its interest is heightened by certain mysterious panels and hidden passages. It is called "The House of the Seven Gables," and it is the traditional site of Hawthorne's famous, mystery-haunted novel of that name.

The House of the Seven Gables deals with the effects of a curse, and though the tale itself is fiction, the germ of the story sprang from the author's family history. One of Nathaniel Hawthorne's ancestors was Judge Hathorne, who presided at the notorious Salem witch trials and was put under a curse by the husband of one of the convicted witches. (The ghost of Judge Hathorne presides over the trial in "The Devil and Daniel Webster," page 62.) The spelling of the family name remained Hathorne until young Nathaniel inserted the "w."

Nathaniel Hawthorne was born in Salem in 1804. In his youth the town was a port whose glory had departed. There had been an era when the ship lanes had linked Salem with every remote and romantic place on earth; when spices, silks, ivories, teas, and other precious stuffs were piled on its wharves; when the face of almost every race of man could be seen in its narrow streets. Now in the shifts of wealth and commerce, Boston and other ports had surpassed Salem. Its trade dwindled to a trickle and finally stopped altogether. Hawthorne, in "The Custom House," the introductory chapter to *The Scarlet Letter,* described the old employees of the shipping office rocking in rows of chairs, mostly idle now in a town where once there had been a scurrying hustle.

Hawthorne's father, a sea captain, had died of yellow fever in Dutch Guiana, when the boy was a mere four years old. When the news came of his father's death, Hawthorne's mother withdrew into her upstairs bedroom, coming out only rarely during the remaining forty years of her life. The boy and his two sisters lived in almost complete isolation from her and from each other. In a few years

Hawthorne left Salem and entered Bowdoin College, in Maine. Among his college friends were Henry Wadsworth Longfellow and Franklin Pierce, who became the fourteenth President of the United States.

From Bowdoin Hawthorne returned to Salem. For nearly twelve years, from 1825 to 1836, he lived in virtual solitude in this idle town. Unlike his friend Herman Melville, who traveled widely and observed much in his youth, there was little in his own actual experiences as yet to serve as literary material. Hawthorne gathered his material by observing and listening to others. He roamed around the town, moving among old sailors on the docks, farmers from the country, men clustered in taverns, and the old wives of the town at the market. He listened to all of them. Their talk was filled with New England lore, legend, and superstition. He made annual excursions into Vermont and New Hampshire and absorbed hints for many stories on these jaunts. He also read the annals and chronicles of the Puritan world. He filled his notebooks and his thoughts with these scraps of impressions and memories, and after a few years began pouring them out as marvelously wrought tales.

During this period in Salem, Hawthorne had harvested the richness of his background. Then a sound instinct made him leave the town where his ancestors had dwelt for two centuries. In "The Custom House" he remarks, "Human nature will not flourish any more than a potato, if it be planted and replanted, for too long a series of generations, in the same worn-out soil." In this chapter, too, he reveals the depth of his concern with the dark side of Puritanism, the harshness and the persecutions. He says of his ancestors, especially Judge Hathorne, "I . . . hereby take shame upon myself for their sakes, and pray that any curse incurred by them . . . may be now and henceforth removed."

For a time in the 1830's, he edited a magazine in Boston, and afterward worked at the customs office. Then he lived for a few months in 1841 at Brook Farm, one of the famous New England experiments in communal living, where some of the region's most remarkable, if somewhat impractical, people gathered. Hawthorne was essentially of a solitary nature, and group life was not for him, but the experience provided the material for his later novel *The Blithedale Romance* (1852). In 1841 he married Sophia Peabody, of a prominent Salem family. For some three years Hawthorne and Sophia lived in the house called the Old Manse, in Concord. It was there that he wrote the splendid stories in the volume called *Mosses from an Old Manse* (1846).

Besides the customs office position in Boston, he accepted two other political appointments. He was Surveyor of the Port of Salem for three years, until a change of administration liberated him to write *The Scarlet Letter*. When his college friend Franklin Pierce became President, he appointed Hawthorne to a consular position in Liverpool. Hawthorne eventually went on to Rome, where he found the inspiration for his novel *The Marble Faun* (1860).

Hawthorne's unique gift was for the creation of strongly symbolic stories which touch the deepest roots of man's moral nature. The finest example is the re-

Nathaniel Hawthorne

creation of Puritan Boston, *The Scarlet Letter*. In this novel each word, image, and event works toward a single effect. It is a complex story of guilt, its effects upon various persons, and how deliverance is obtained for some of them.

His ability to create vivid and symbolic images that embody great moral questions appears strongly in his short stories. In "Ethan Brand" a marble heart stands for pride and isolation from one's fellow men. "Young Goodman Brown" uses the background of witchcraft to explore uncertainties of belief that trouble a man's heart and mind. "Dr. Heidegger's Experiment" and "The Ambitious Guest," which you will read, have symbolic and legendary qualities. "The Great Stone Face" is another of his allegorical stories.

It was Hawthorne's ability to make a story exist in its own right but at the same time appear as a moral symbol that most influenced the work of Herman Melville. Melville called his friend "the largest brain with the largest heart" in American literature. Hawthorne shares with Edgar Allan Poe the distinction of advancing the art of the short story, giving to the form qualities that are uniquely American. Like Poe he often used grotesque or fantastic events, but Hawthorne's work is broader in range and has more depth of thought. Poe was concerned with the immediate emotional effects of literature and often seemed indifferent to investigations of value or morality. To Hawthorne and Melville, however, the telling of a tale was a way of inquiring into the meaning of life.

HERMAN MELVILLE
"The Man Who Lived Among Cannibals"

Around 1920, the American literary world rediscovered an almost forgotten book and suddenly became aware of a major American writer. The book was *Moby Dick*, a tremendous chronicle of a whaling voyage in pursuit of a seemingly supernatural white whale. This monster and the figure of Captain Ahab, who is obsessed with the chase, seized the imaginations of modern readers. The book is steeped in symbolism, another strong appeal to readers of this century. In the brief span of time since the rediscovery of *Moby Dick*, a great deal of Melville study has sprung up. Complete editions of his works with scholarly notes are available, along with many biographical and critical commentaries, some perceptive and valuable and some far-fetched, about the man and his work.

Melville's youth was like a young man's dream of romance, and many of his experiences were the direct sources of his earliest books. He was born in New York in 1819. His family was poor, times were hard, and the boy received no formal education after the age of fifteen — a considerable contrast to the background of many of the other writers we have met. A whaling ship, he said, was "my Yale College and my Harvard." Yet Melville owed a debt to his reading, too. Cooper's novels were among the books that had stirred him as a boy.

Restless and venturesome by temperament, Melville shipped as a cabin boy on a merchant vessel to England in 1839, when he was twenty. At twenty-two he signed for a voyage on the whaler *Acushnet*, thoroughly ignorant of the grim hardships that could accompany such a venture. The voyage did not prosper, and conditions were harsh. After a year and a half at sea, the young man, with another youth named Tobias Greene, deserted the ship in the remote Pacific islands of the Marquesas group, below the equator, northeast of Tahiti.

The two deserters ventured into a valley on the island of Nukahiva and found themselves among the Typees, a Polynesian tribe reputed to be cannibals. Happily for Melville and for American literature, the Typees did not devour the two men but held them four months in good-natured imprisonment. They were allowed to share freely in the life of the tribe. They escaped separately, Melville being picked up by an Australian whaler that took him to Tahiti. After short cruises on this ship and another American whaler, Melville signed as a seaman on a naval vessel, the frigate *United States*, and returned home in 1844.

His adventures led to his literary career. *Typee* (1846) was a romanticized account of his stay among the Polynesians. The book was basically factual but was no doubt elaborated somewhat and built up from Melville's reading as well as his experience. It was an immediate popular success, and Melville soon became known as the "man who lived among cannibals." Equally successful was a sequel, *Omoo* (1847), about his adventures on Tahiti and other islands. Later Melville based *Redburn* (1849) on his first voyage to England, and *White-Jacket* (1850) on his brief career in the navy. He drew upon his naval experiences again for *Billy Budd* (1891).

Living for some thirteen years on a farm called Arrowhead near Pittsfield, Massachusetts, he made the acquaintance of his neighbor Hawthorne. It was

Herman Melville

at Arrowhead that Melville wrote *Moby Dick*. Melville was not content simply to narrate adventures. Deep questions and a restlessness of spirit were stirring in him. These forces, together with the combined influences of his reading of Shakespeare and his association with Hawthorne (to whom the book is dedicated) helped *Moby Dick* to escape the romantic travel-tale mold of Melville's earlier works and to become a unique and enduring work. Ironically, this masterpiece, the cornerstone of Melville's modern fame, seemed a complete failure at the time. The public was not ready for its brooding, sometimes frightening speculations about man and God and the universe. They wanted the simple, romantic narratives of the *Typee* and *Omoo* sort. Critics in general also failed to see the qualities of *Moby Dick*. Hawthorne was one of the few who recognized it as a work of genius.

Melville himself said in *Moby Dick*, "to write a mighty book you must have a mighty theme." Here he had it — the rebellious struggle of Captain Ahab against the overwhelming, mysterious vastness of the universe and its awesome, sometimes merciless forces. The fitting symbol for his theme was the "gliding great demon of the seas of life," the white whale. Ahab's ship, the *Pequod*, was like a world in miniature, with characters ranging from the observer and narrator Ishmael to the savage harpooners and the motley crew.

Had Melville described romantically the "whaling voyage by one Ishmael" in the manner of his popular books, *Moby Dick* would probably have been received with enthusiasm. What baffled its early readers was the book's wild extravagances of mood and language, its effect of what the modern critic Van Wyck Brooks calls "a shredded Shakespearean play." Melville confided to Hawthorne that it had been "broiled in hell-fire," referring to the turbulence of his own spirit from which the book sprang. *Moby Dick* was too powerful for the readers of its time. Two other philosophical novels, *Mardi,* two years earlier than *Moby Dick,* and *Pierre,* one year later, are interesting but are not of the same stature as Melville's masterpiece. Hawthorne said of *Mardi* that it had "depths here and there that compel a man to swim for his life." The comment was immeasurably more true of the story of the white whale.

Melville wrote a good deal more: some able short stories such as "Bartleby the Scrivener," quite a bit of poetry, which is now arousing increased respect, and two celebrated short novels, *Benito Cereno* and *Billy Budd.* The latter, his last and one of his most interesting works, has been made into a fine play in our time. With flashes of Melville's best fire, *Billy Budd*, like *Moby Dick,* uses a ship as a symbol of society and searchingly examines the problems of good and evil.

Melville passed the last twenty years or so of his life in almost total obscurity, withdrawn from literary circles. Back in New York, for nineteen years he was a clerk in a customhouse. His long-agitated spirit finally seemed calm. He had withdrawn himself from a world about whose values he was so often skeptical. His death went unnoticed by the public in 1891, but his literary reputation was born again in this century and will last as long as our literature.

NATHANIEL HAWTHORNE

1804–1864

Dr. Heidegger's Experiment

Everyone at one time or another asks himself: "If I had my life to live over, how would I change it? Would I profit by experience?" It's a fascinating question, and in this story, a fantasy built around the idea of the Fountain of Youth, Hawthorne provides logical but surprising answers. This story appeared in *Twice-told Tales,* and, interestingly enough, it was in a critical review of this book that Poe stated his own philosophy of short-story writing. Poe wrote of the Tales, "We know of few compositions which the critic can more honestly commend."

HAWTHORNE'S IDEAS. In your reading you can readily observe some of the ideas with which Hawthorne is concerned. There is the idea of scientific experiment, which took strong hold of popular fancy in a century of marvelous scientific discovery. There is also the problem of the effect of sin in its various forms upon human nature. You can easily see that in contrast to Poe, who sometimes appeared to be interested more in artistic effects than in moral problems, Hawthorne dealt with right and wrong in human conduct. Much of the excitement of his stories comes from his informal, natural way of treating such basic problems.

THAT very singular man, old Dr. Heidegger, once invited four venerable friends to meet him in his study. There were three white-bearded gentlemen, Mr. Medbourne, Colonel Killigrew, and Mr. Gascoigne, and a withered gentlewoman, whose name was the Widow Wycherly. They were all melancholy old creatures, who had been unfortunate in life, and whose greatest misfortune it was that they were not long ago in their graves. Mr. Medbourne, in the vigor of his age, had been a prosperous merchant, but had lost his all by a frantic speculation, and was now little better than a mendicant.[1] Colonel Killigrew had wasted his best years, and his health and substance, in the pursuit of sinful pleasures, which had given birth to a brood of pains, such as the gout, and divers other torments of soul and body. Mr. Gascoigne was a ruined politician, a man of evil fame, or at least had been so till time had buried him from the knowledge of the present generation, and made him obscure instead of infamous. As for the Widow Wycherly, tradition tells us that she was a great beauty in her day; but, for

[1] **mendicant** (měn′dĭ·kănt): a beggar.

a long while past, she had lived in deep seclusion, on account of certain scandalous stories which had prejudiced the gentry of the town against her. It is a circumstance worth mentioning that each of these three old gentlemen, Mr. Medbourne, Colonel Killigrew, and Mr. Gascoigne, were early lovers of the Widow Wycherly, and had once been on the point of cutting each other's throats for her sake. And, before proceeding further, I will merely hint that Dr. Heidegger and all his four guests were sometimes thought to be a little beside themselves — as is not unfrequently the case with old people, when worried either by present troubles or woeful recollections.

"My dear old friends," said Dr. Heidegger, motioning them to be seated, "I am desirous of your assistance in one of those little experiments with which I amuse myself here in my study."

If all stories were true, Dr. Heidegger's study must have been a very curious place. It was a dim, old-fashioned chamber, festooned with cobwebs, and besprinkled with antique dust. Around the walls stood several oaken bookcases, the lower shelves of which were filled with rows of gigantic folios [1] and black-letter quartos,[2] and the upper with little parchment-covered duodecimos.[3] Over the central bookcase was a bronze bust of Hippocrates,[4] with which, according to some authorities, Dr. Heidegger was accustomed to hold consultations in all difficult cases of his practice. In the obscurest corner of the room stood a tall and narrow oaken closet, with its door ajar, within which doubtfully appeared a skeleton. Between two of the bookcases hung a looking glass, presenting its high and dusty plate within a tar-

nished gilt frame. Among many wonderful stories related of this mirror, it was fabled that the spirit of all the doctor's deceased patients dwelt within its verge, and would stare him in the face whenever he looked thitherward. The opposite side of the chamber was ornamented with the full-length portrait of a young lady, arrayed in the faded magnificence of silk, satin, and brocade, and with a visage as faded as her dress. Above half a century ago, Dr. Heidegger had been on the point of marriage with this young lady; but being affected with some slight disorder, she had swallowed one of her lover's prescriptions, and died on the bridal evening. The greatest curiosity of the study remains to be mentioned; it was a ponderous folio volume, bound in black leather, with massive silver clasps. There were no letters on the back, and nobody could tell the title of the book. But it was well known to be a book of magic; and once, when a chambermaid had lifted it, merely to brush away the dust, the skeleton had rattled in its closet, the picture of the young lady had stepped one foot upon the floor, and several ghastly faces had peeped forth from the mirror; while the brazen head of Hippocrates frowned and said, "Forbear!"

Such was Dr. Heidegger's study. On the summer afternoon of our tale, a small round table, as black as ebony, stood in the center of the room, sustaining a cut-glass vase of beautiful form and elaborate workmanship. The sunshine came through the window, between the heavy festoons of two faded damask curtains, and fell directly across this vase; so that a mild splendor was reflected from it on the ashen visages of the five old people who sat around. Four champagne glasses were also on the table.

"My dear old friends," repeated Dr. Heidegger, "may I reckon on your aid in performing an exceedingly curious experiment?"

[1] folios: books from twelve to twenty inches in height.
[2] quartos: books about nine and one-half by twelve and one-half inches.
[3] duodecimos (dū′ō·dĕs′ĭ·mōz): small volumes, about five by eight inches.
[4] Hippocrates (hĭ·pŏk′rá·tēz): (460?–377? B.C.) a Greek physician.

Now Dr. Heidegger was a very strange old gentleman, whose eccentricity had become the nucleus for a thousand fantastic stories. Some of these fables, to my shame be it spoken, might possibly be traced back to my own veracious self; and if any passages of the present tale should startle the reader's faith, I must be content to bear the stigma of a fictionmonger.

When the doctor's four guests heard him talk of his proposed experiment, they anticipated nothing more wonderful than the murder of a mouse in an air pump, or the examination of a cobweb by the microscope, or some similar nonsense, with which he was constantly in the habit of pestering his intimates. But, without waiting for a reply, Dr. Heidegger hobbled across the chamber and returned with the same ponderous folio, bound in black leather, which common report affirmed to be a book of magic. Undoing the silver clasps, he opened the volume and took from among its black-letter pages a rose, or what was once a rose, though now the green leaves and crimson petals had assumed one brownish hue, and the ancient flower seemed ready to crumble to dust in the doctor's hands.

"This rose," said Dr. Heidegger, with a sigh, "this same withered and crumbling flower, blossomed five and fifty years ago. It was given me by Sylvia Ward, whose portrait hangs yonder; and I meant to wear it in my bosom at our wedding. Five and fifty years it has been treasured between the leaves of this old volume. Now, would you deem it possible that this rose of half a century could ever bloom again?"

"Nonsense!" said the Widow Wycherly, with a peevish toss of her head. "You might as well ask whether an old woman's wrinkled face could ever bloom again."

"See!" answered Dr. Heidegger.

He uncovered the vase and threw the faded rose into the water which it contained. At first, it lay lightly on the surface of the fluid, appearing to imbibe none of its moisture. Soon, however, a singular change began to be visible. The crushed and dried petals stirred and assumed a deepening tinge of crimson, as if the flower were reviving from a deathlike slumber; the slender stalk and twigs of foliage became green; and there was the rose of half a century, looking as fresh as when Sylvia Ward had first given it to her lover. It was scarcely full blown; for some of its delicate red leaves curled modestly around its moist bosom, within which two or three dewdrops were sparkling.

"That is certainly a very pretty deception," said the doctor's friends; carelessly, however, for they had witnessed greater miracles at a conjurer's show; "pray how was it effected?"

"Did you never hear of the 'Fountain of Youth'?" asked Dr. Heidegger, "which Ponce de Leon,[1] the Spanish adventurer, went in search of two or three centuries ago?"

"But did Ponce de Leon ever find it?" said the Widow Wycherly.

"No," answered Dr. Heidegger, "for he never sought it in the right place. The famous Fountain of Youth, if I am rightly informed, is situated in the southern part of the Floridian peninsula, not far from Lake Macaco. Its source is overshadowed by several gigantic magnolias, which, though numberless centuries old, have been kept as fresh as violets by the virtues of this wonderful water. An acquaintance of mine, knowing my curiosity in such matters, has sent me what you see in the vase."

"Ahem!" said Colonel Killigrew, who believed not a word of the doctor's story; "and what may be the effect of this fluid on the human frame?"

"You shall judge for yourself, my dear colonel," replied Dr. Heidegger; "and all of you, my respected friends, are welcome to so much of this admirable fluid as may restore to you the

[1] Ponce de Leon (pŏns' dē lē'ŭn): (1460?–1521) Spanish discoverer of Florida.

NATHANIEL HAWTHORNE   545

bloom of youth. For my own part, having had much trouble in growing old, I am in no hurry to grow young again. With your permission, therefore, I will merely watch the progress of the experiment."

While he spoke, Dr. Heidegger had been filling the four champagne glasses with the water of the Fountain of Youth. It was apparently impregnated with an effervescent gas, for little bubbles were continually ascending from the depths of the glasses, and bursting in silvery spray at the surface. As the liquor diffused a pleasant perfume, the old people doubted not that it possessed cordial and comfortable properties; and though utter skeptics as to its rejuvenescent power, they were inclined to swallow it at once. But Dr. Heidegger besought them to stay a moment.

"Before you drink, my respectable old friends," said he, "it would be well that, with the experience of a lifetime to direct you, you should draw up a few general rules for your guidance, in passing a second time through the perils of youth. Think what a sin and shame it would be, if, with your peculiar advantages, you should not become patterns of virtue and wisdom to all the young people of the age!"

The doctor's four venerable friends made him no answer, except by a feeble and tremulous laugh; so very ridiculous was the idea that, knowing how closely repentance treads behind the steps of error, they should ever go astray again.

"Drink, then," said the doctor, bowing. "I rejoice that I have so well selected the subjects of my experiment."

With palsied hands, they raised the glasses to their lips. The liquor, if it really possessed such virtues as Dr. Heidegger imputed to it, could not have been bestowed on four human beings who needed it more woefully. They looked as if they had never known what youth or pleasure was, but had been the offspring of Nature's dotage, and always the gray, decrepit, sapless, miserable creatures who now sat stooping round the doctor's table, without life enough in their souls or bodies to be animated even by the prospect of growing young again. They drank off the water, and replaced their glasses on the table.

Assuredly there was an almost immediate improvement in the aspect of the party, not unlike what might have been produced by a glass of generous wine, together with a sudden glow of cheerful sunshine brightening over all their visages at once. There was a healthful suffusion on their cheeks, instead of the ashen hue that had made them look so corpselike. They gazed at one another and fancied that some magic power had really begun to smooth away the deep and sad inscriptions which Father Time had been so long engraving on their brows. The Widow Wycherly adjusted her cap, for she felt almost like a woman again.

"Give us more of this wondrous water!" cried they, eagerly. "We are younger — but we are still too old! Quick — give us more!"

"Patience, patience!" quoth Dr. Heidegger, who sat watching the experiment with philosophic coolness. "You have been a long time growing old. Surely, you might be content to grow young in half an hour! But the water is at your service."

Again he filled their glasses with the liquor of youth, enough of which still remained in the vase to turn half the old people in the city to the age of their own grandchildren. While the bubbles were yet sparkling on the brim, the doctor's four guests snatched their glasses from the table, and swallowed the contents at a single gulp. Was it delusion? Even while the draught was passing down their throats, it seemed to have wrought a change on their whole systems. Their eyes grew clear and bright; a dark shade deepened among their silvery locks, they sat around the table, three gentlemen of middle age, and a woman, hardly beyond her buxom prime.

"My dear widow, you are charming!" cried Colonel Killigrew, whose eyes had been fixed upon her face, while the shadows of age were flitting from it like darkness from the crimson daybreak.

The fair widow knew, of old, that Colonel Killigrew's compliments were not always measured by sober truth; so she started up and ran to the mirror, still dreading that the ugly visage of an old woman would meet her gaze. Meanwhile, the three gentlemen behaved in such a manner as proved that the water of the Fountain of Youth possessed some intoxicating qualities; unless, indeed, their exhilaration of spirits were merely a lightsome dizziness caused by the sudden removal of the weight of years. Mr. Gascoigne's mind seemed to run on political topics, but whether relating to the past, present, or future could not easily be determined, since the same ideas and phrases have been in vogue these fifty years. Now he rattled forth full-throated sentences about patriotism, national glory, and the people's right; now he muttered some perilous stuff or other, in a sly and doubtful whisper, so cautiously that even his own conscience could scarcely catch the secret; and now, again, he spoke in measured accents, and a deeply deferential tone, as if a royal ear were listening to his well-turned periods. Colonel Killigrew all this time had been trolling forth a jolly bottle song, and ringing his glass in symphony with the chorus, while his eyes wandered toward the buxom figure of the Widow Wycherly. On the other side of the table, Mr. Medbourne was involved in a calculation of dollars and cents, with which was strangely intermingled a project for supplying the East Indies with ice, by harnessing a team of whales to the polar icebergs.

As for the Widow Wycherly, she stood before the mirror curtsying and simpering to her own image, and greeting it as the friend whom she loved better than all the world beside. She thrust her face close to the glass, to see whether some long-remembered wrinkle or crow's-foot had indeed vanished. She examined whether the snow had so entirely melted from her hair that the venerable cap could be safely thrown aside. At last, turning briskly away, she came with a sort of dancing step to the table.

"My dear old doctor," cried she, "pray favor me with another glass!"

"Certainly, my dear madam, certainly!" replied the complaisant[1] doctor; "See! I have already filled the glasses."

There, in fact, stood the four glasses, brimful of this wonderful water, the delicate spray of which, as it effervesced from the surface, resembled the tremulous glitter of diamonds. It was now so nearly sunset that the chamber had grown duskier than ever; but a mild and moonlike splendor gleamed from within the vase, and rested alike on the four guests and on the doctor's venerable figure. He sat in a high-backed, elaborately carved oaken armchair, with a gray dignity of aspect that might have well befitted that very Father Time, whose power had never been disputed, save by this fortunate company. Even while quaffing the third draught of the Fountain of Youth, they were almost awed by the expression of his mysterious visage.

But, the next moment, the exhilarating gush of young life shot through their veins. They were now in the happy prime of youth. Age, with its miserable train of cares and sorrows and diseases, was remembered only as the trouble of a dream, from which they had joyously awaked. The fresh gloss of the soul, so early lost, and without which the world's successive scenes had been but a gallery of faded pictures,

[1] complaisant (kŏm·plā′zănt): obliging.

again threw its enchantment over all their prospects. They felt like new-created beings in a new-created universe.

"We are young! We are young!" they cried exultingly.

Youth, like the extremity of age, had effaced the strongly marked characteristics of middle life, and mutually assimilated them all. They were a group of merry youngsters, almost maddened with the exuberant frolicsomeness of their years. The most singular effect of their gaiety was an impulse to mock the infirmity and decrepitude of which they had so lately been the victims. They laughed loudly at their old-fashioned attire, the wide-skirted coats and flapped waistcoats of the young men, and the ancient cap and gown of the blooming girl. One limped across the floor like a gouty grandfather; one set a pair of spectacles astride of his nose, and pretended to pore over the black-letter pages of the book of magic; a third seated himself in an armchair, and strove to imitate the venerable dignity of Dr. Heidegger. Then all shouted mirthfully, and leaped about the room. The Widow Wycherly — if so fresh a damsel could be called a widow — tripped up to the doctor's chair, with a mischievous merriment in her rosy face.

"Doctor, you dear old soul," cried she, "get up and dance with me!" And then the four young people laughed louder than ever, to think what a queer figure the poor old doctor would cut.

"Pray excuse me," answered the doctor quietly. "I am old and rheumatic, and my dancing days were over long ago. But either of these gay young gentlemen will be glad of so pretty a partner."

"Dance with me, Clara!" cried Colonel Killigrew.

"No, no, I will be her partner!" shouted Mr. Gascoigne.

"She promised me her hand, fifty years ago!" exclaimed Mr. Medbourne.

They all gathered round her. One caught both her hands in his passionate grasp — another threw his arm about her waist — the third buried his hand among the glossy curls that clustered beneath the widow's cap. Blushing, panting, struggling, chiding, laughing, her warm breath fanning each of their faces by turns, she strove to disengage herself, yet still remained in their triple embrace. Never was there a livelier picture of youthful rivalship, with bewitching beauty for the prize. Yet, by a strange deception, owing to the duskiness of the chamber, and the antique dresses which they still wore, the tall mirror is said to have reflected the figures of the three old, gray, withered grandsires ridiculously contending for the skinny ugliness of a shriveled grandam.

But they were young: their burning passions proved them so. Inflamed to madness by the coquetry of the girl-widow, who neither granted nor quite withheld her favors, the three rivals began to interchange threatening glances. Still keeping hold of the fair prize, they grappled fiercely at one another's throats. As they struggled to and fro, the table was overturned, and the vase dashed into a thousand fragments. The precious Water of Youth flowed in a bright stream across the floor, moistening the wings of a butterfly, which, grown old in the decline of summer, had alighted there to die. The insect fluttered lightly through the chamber, and settled on the snowy head of Dr. Heidegger.

"Come, come, gentlemen! — come, Madam Wycherly," exclaimed the doctor, "I really must protest against this riot."

They stood still and shivered; for it seemed as if gray Time were calling them back from their sunny youth, far down into the chill and darksome vale of years. They looked at old Dr. Heidegger, who sat in his carved armchair, holding the rose of half a century, which he had rescued from among the fragments of the shattered vase. At the motion of his hand, the four rioters resumed their seats; the more readily, because their violent exertions had wearied them, youthful though they were.

"My poor Sylvia's rose!" ejaculated Dr. Heidegger, holding it in the light of the sunset clouds; "it appears to be fading again."

And so it was. Even while the party were looking at it, the flower continued to shrivel up, till it became as dry and fragile as when the doctor had first thrown it into the vase. He shook off the few drops of moisture which clung to its petals.

"I love it as well thus as in its dewy freshness," observed he, pressing the withered rose to his withered lips. While he spoke, the butterfly fluttered down from the doctor's snowy head, and fell upon the floor.

His guests shivered again. A strange chillness, whether of the body or spirit they could not tell, was creeping gradually over them all. They gazed at one another, and fancied that each fleeting moment snatched away a charm, and left a deepening furrow where none had been before. Was it an illusion?

Had the changes of a lifetime been crowded into so brief a space, and were they now four aged people, sitting with their old friend Dr. Heidegger?

"Are we grown old again, so soon?" cried they, dolefully.

In truth they had. The Water of Youth possessed merely a virtue more transient than that of wine. The delirium which it created had effervesced away. Yes! they were old again. With a shuddering impulse, that showed her a woman still, the widow clasped her skinny hands before her face, and wished that the coffin lid were over it, since it could be no longer beautiful.

"Yes, friends, ye are old again," said Dr. Heidegger, "and lo! the Water of Youth is all lavished on the ground. Well — I bemoan it not; for if the fountain gushed at my very doorstep, I would not stoop to bathe my lips in it — no, though its delirium were for years instead of moments. Such is the lesson ye have taught me!"

But the doctor's four friends had taught no such lesson to themselves. They resolved forthwith to make a pilgrimage to Florida, and quaff at morning, noon, and night, from the Fountain of Youth.

The Ambitious Guest

Hawthorne here uses an actual incident, giving it deeper meaning by the philosophical ideas he adds to it. He had read the account of the avalanche and the strange fate of the escaping family in *His-* *torical Relics of the White Mountains* by J. H. Spaulding. The characters were Hawthorne's own creation. Their ambitions, their fears, and their fancies add poignancy to the tale's climax.

NATHANIEL HAWTHORNE   549

ONE September night a family had gathered round their hearth, and piled it high with the driftwood of mountain streams, the dry cones of the pine, and the splintered ruins of great trees that had come crashing down the precipice. Up the chimney roared the fire, and brightened the room with its broad blaze. The faces of the father and mother had a sober gladness; the children laughed; the eldest daughter was the image of Happiness at seventeen; and the aged grandmother, who sat knitting in the warmest place, was the image of Happiness grown old. They had found the "herb, heart's-ease," in the bleakest spot of all New England. This family was situated in the Notch of the White Hills, where the wind was sharp throughout the year, and pitilessly cold in the winter — giving their cottage all its fresh inclemency before it descended on the valley of the Saco. They dwelt in a cold spot and a dangerous one; for a mountain towered above their heads, so steep that the stones would often rumble down its sides and startle them at midnight.

The daughter had just uttered some simple jest that filled them all with mirth, when the wind came through the Notch and seemed to pause before their cottage — rattling the door, with a sound of wailing and lamentation, before it passed into the valley. For a moment it saddened them, though there was nothing unusual in the tones. But the family were glad again when they perceived that the latch was lifted by some traveler, whose footsteps had been unheard amid the dreary blast which heralded his approach, and wailed as he was entering, and went moaning away from the door.

Though they dwelt in such a solitude, these people held daily converse with the world. The romantic pass of the Notch is a great artery, through which the lifeblood of internal commerce is continually throbbing between Maine, on one side, and the Green Mountains and the shores of the St. Lawrence, on the other. The stagecoach always drew up before the door of the cottage. The wayfarer, with no companion but his staff, paused here to exchange a word, that the sense of loneliness might not utterly overcome him ere he could pass through the cleft of the mountain, or reach the first house in the valley. And here the teamster, on his way to Portland market, would put up for the night, and, if a bachelor, might sit an hour beyond the usual bedtime, and steal a kiss from the mountain maid at parting. It was one of those primitive taverns where the traveler pays only for food and lodging, but meets with a homely kindness beyond all price. When the footsteps were heard, therefore, between the outer door and the inner one, the whole family rose up, grandmother, children, and all, as if about to welcome someone who belonged to them, and whose fate was linked with theirs.

The door was opened by a young man. His face at first wore the melancholy expression, almost despondency, of one who travels a wild and bleak road, at nightfall and alone, but soon brightened up when he saw the kindly warmth of his reception. He felt his heart spring forward to meet them all, from the old woman, who wiped a chair with her apron, to the little child that held out its arms to him. One glance and smile placed the stranger on a footing of innocent familiarity with the eldest daughter.

"Ah, this fire is the right thing!" cried he; "especially when there is such a pleasant circle round it. I am quite benumbed; for the Notch is just like the pipe of a great pair of bellows; it has blown a terrible blast in my face all the way from Bartlett."

"Then you are going toward Vermont?" said the master of the house, as he helped to take a light knapsack off the young man's shoulders.

"Yes; to Burlington, and far enough beyond," replied he. "I meant to have been at Ethan Crawford's tonight; but a pedestrian lingers along such a road as this. It is no matter; for, when I saw this good fire, and all your cheerful faces, I felt as if you had kindled it on purpose for me, and were waiting my arrival. So I shall sit down among you, and make myself at home."

The frank-hearted stranger had just drawn his chair to the fire when something like a heavy footstep was heard without, rushing down the steep side of the mountain, as with long and rapid strides, and taking such a leap in passing the cottage as to strike the opposite precipice. The family held their breath, because they knew the sound, and their guest held his by instinct.

"The old mountain has thrown a stone at us, for fear we should forget him," said the landlord, recovering himself. "He sometimes nods his head and threatens to come down; but we are old neighbors, and agree together pretty well on the whole. Besides, we have a sure place of refuge hard by if he should be coming in good earnest."

Let us now suppose the stranger to have finished his supper of bear's meat; and, by his natural felicity of manner, to have placed himself on a footing of kindness with the whole family, so that they talked as freely together as if he belonged to their mountain brood. He was of a proud, yet gentle spirit — haughty and reserved among the rich and great; but ever ready to stoop his head to the lowly cottage door, and be like a brother or a son at the poor man's fireside. In the household of the Notch he found warmth and simplicity of feeling, the pervading intelligence of New England, and a poetry of native growth, which they had gathered when they little thought of it from the mountain peaks and chasms, and at the very threshold of their romantic and dangerous abode. He had traveled far and

alone; his whole life, indeed, had been a solitary path; for, with the lofty caution of his nature, he had kept himself apart from those who might otherwise have been his companions. The family, too, though so kind and hospitable, had that consciousness of unity among themselves, and separation from the world at large which, in every domestic circle, should still keep a holy place where no stranger may intrude. But this evening a prophetic sympathy impelled the refined and educated youth to pour out his heart before the simple mountaineers, and constrained them to answer him with the same free confidence. And thus it should have been. Is not the kindred of a common fate a closer tie than that of birth?

The secret of the young man's character was a high and abstracted [1] ambition. He could have borne to live an undistinguished life, but not to be forgotten in the grave. Yearning desire had been transformed to hope: and hope, long cherished, had become like certainty, that, obscurely as he journeyed now, a glory was to beam on all his pathway — though not, perhaps, while he was treading it. But when posterity should gaze back into the gloom of what was now the present, they would trace the brightness of his footsteps, brightening as meaner glories faded, and confess that a gifted one had passed from his cradle to his tomb with none to recognize him.

"As yet," cried the stranger — his cheek glowing and his eye flashing with enthusiasm — "as yet, I have done nothing. Were I to vanish from the earth tomorrow, none would know so much of me as you; that a nameless youth came up at nightfall from the valley of Saco, and opened his heart to you in the evening, and passed through the Notch by sunrise, and was seen no more. Not a soul would ask, 'Who was he? Whither did the wanderer go?' But

[1] abstracted: here, idealistic; not concerned with practical matters.

I cannot die till I have achieved my destiny. Then let death come! I shall have built my monument!"

There was a continual flow of natural emotion, gushing forth amid abstracted reverie, which enabled the family to understand this young man's sentiments, though so foreign from their own. With quick sensibility of the ludicrous, he blushed at the ardor into which he had been betrayed.

"You laugh at me," said he, taking the eldest daughter's hand, and laughing himself. "You think my ambition as nonsensical as if I were to freeze myself to death on the top of Mount Washington, only that people might spy at me from the country round about. And, truly, that would be a noble pedestal for a man's statue!"

"It is better to sit here by this fire," answered the girl, blushing, "and be comfortable and contented, though nobody thinks about us."

"I suppose," said her father, after a fit of musing, "there is something natural in what the young man says; and if my mind had been turned that way, I might have felt just the same. It is strange, Wife, how his talk has set my head running on things that are pretty certain never to come to pass."

"Perhaps they may," observed the wife. "Is the man thinking what he will do when he is widower?"

"No, no!" cried he, repelling the idea with reproachful kindness. "When I think of your death, Esther, I think of mine too. But I was wishing we had a good farm in Bartlett, or Bethlehem, or Littleton, or some other township round the White Mountains; but not where they could tumble on our heads. I should want to stand well with my neighbors and be called Squire, and sent to General Court for a term or two; for a plain, honest man may do as much good there as a lawyer. And when I should be grown quite an old man, and you an old woman, so as not to be long apart, I might die happy enough in my bed, and leave you all crying around me. A slate gravestone would suit me as well as a marble one — with just my name and age, and a verse of a hymn, and something to let people know that I lived an honest man and died a Christian."

"There, now!" exclaimed the stranger; "it is our nature to desire a monument, be it slate or marble, or a pillar of granite, or a glorious memory in the universal heart of man."

"We're in a strange way tonight," said the wife, with tears in her eyes. "They say it's a sign of something, when folks' minds go a-wandering so. Hark to the children!"

They listened accordingly. The younger children had been put to bed in another room, but with an open door between, so that they could be heard talking busily among themselves. One and all seemed to have caught the infection from the fireside circle, and were outvying each other in wild wishes, and childish projects of what they would do when they came to be men and women. At length a little boy, instead of addressing his brothers and sisters, called out to his mother.

"I'll tell you what I wish, Mother," cried he. "I want you and Father and Grandma'm, and all of us, and the stranger, too, to start right away, and go and take a drink out of the basin of the Flume!"

Nobody could help laughing at the child's notion of leaving a warm bed, and dragging them from a cheerful fire, to visit the basin of the Flume — a brook which tumbles over the precipice, deep within the Notch. The boy had hardly spoken when a wagon rattled along the road, and stopped a moment before the door. It appeared to contain two or three men who were cheering their hearts with the rough chorus of a song, which resounded in broken notes between the cliffs, while the singers hesitated whether to continue their journey or put up here for the night.

"Father," said the girl, "they are calling you by name."

But the good man doubted whether they had really called him, and was unwilling to show himself too solicitous of gain by inviting people to patronize his house. He therefore did not hurry to the door; and the lash being soon applied, the travelers plunged into the Notch, still singing and laughing, though their music and mirth came back drearily from the heart of the mountain.

"There, Mother!" cried the boy, again. "They'd have given us a ride to the Flume."

Again they laughed at the child's pertinacious [1] fancy for a night ramble. But it happened that a light cloud passed over the daughter's spirit; she looked gravely into the fire, and drew a breath that was almost a sigh. It forced its way, in spite of a little struggle to repress it. Then starting and blushing, she looked quickly round the circle, as if they had caught a glimpse into her bosom. The stranger asked what she had been thinking of.

'Nothing," answered she, with a downcast smile. "Only I felt lonesome just then."

"Oh, I have always had a gift of

---

¹ pertinacious (pûr'tĭ-nā'shŭs): stubborn.

feeling what is in other people's hearts," said he, half seriously. "Shall I tell the secrets of yours? For I know what to think when a young girl shivers by a warm hearth, and complains of lonesomeness at her mother's side. Shall I put these feelings into words?"

"They would not be a girl's feelings any longer if they could be put into words," replied the mountain nymph, laughing, but avoiding his eye.

All this was said apart. Perhaps a germ of love was springing in their hearts, so pure that it might blossom in Paradise, since it could not be matured on earth; for women worship such gentle dignity as his; and the proud, contemplative, yet kindly soul is oftenest captivated by simplicity like hers. But while they spoke softly, and he was watching the happy sadness, the lightsome shadows, the shy yearnings of a maiden's nature, the wind through the Notch took a deeper and drearier sound. It seemed, as the fanciful stranger said, like the choral strain of the spirits of the blast, who in old Indian times had their dwelling among these mountains, and made their heights and recesses a sacred region. There was a wail along the road, as if a funeral were passing. To chase away the gloom, the family threw pine branches on their fire, till the dry leaves crackled and the flame arose, discovering once again a scene of peace and humble happiness. The light hovered about them fondly, and caressed them all. There were the little faces of the children, peeping from their beds apart, and here the father's frame of strength, the mother's subdued and careful mien, the highbrowed youth, the budding girl, and the good old grandam, still knitting in the warmest place. The aged woman looked up from her task, and with fingers ever busy, was the next to speak.

"Old folks have their notions," said she, "as well as young ones. You've been wishing and planning, and letting your heads run on one thing and another, till you've set my mind a-wandering too. Now what should an old woman wish for, when she can go but a step or two before she comes to her grave? Children, it will haunt me night and day till I tell you."

"What is it, Mother?" cried the husband and wife at once.

Then the old woman, with an air of mystery which drew the circle closer round the fire, informed them that she had provided her graveclothes some years before — a nice linen shroud, a cap with a muslin ruff, and everything of a finer sort than she had worn since her wedding day. But this evening an old superstition had strangely recurred to her. It used to be said, in her younger days, that if anything were amiss with a corpse, if only the ruff were not smooth, or the cap did not set right, the corpse in the coffin and beneath the clods would strive to put up its cold hands and arrange it. The bare thought made her nervous.

"Don't talk so, Grandmother!" said the girl, shuddering.

"Now," continued the old woman, with singular earnestness, yet smiling strangely at her own folly, "I want one of you to hold a looking glass over my face. Who knows but I may take a glimpse at myself, and see whether all's right?"

"Old and young, we dream of graves and monuments," murmured the stranger youth. "I wonder how mariners feel when the ship is sinking, and they, unknown and undistinguished, are to be buried together in the ocean — that wide and nameless sepulcher?"

For a moment, the old woman's ghastly conception so engrossed the minds of her hearers that a sound abroad in the night, rising like the roar of a blast, had grown broad, deep, and terrible, before the fated group were conscious of it. The house and all within it trembled; the foundations of the earth seemed to be shaken, as if this awful sound were the peal of the last

trump.[1] Young and old exchanged one wild glance, and remained an instant, pale, affrighted, without utterance, or power to move. Then the same shriek burst simultaneously from all their lips.

"The slide! The slide!"

The simplest words must intimate, but not portray, the unutterable horror of the catastrophe. The victims rushed from their cottage, and sought refuge in what they deemed a safer spot — where, in contemplation of such an emergency, a sort of barrier had been reared. Alas! they had quitted their security, and fled right into the pathway of destruction. Down came the whole side of the mountain, in a cataract [2] of ruin. Just before it reached the house, the stream broke into two branches — shivered not a window there, but overwhelmed the whole vicinity, blocked up the road, and annihilated everything in its dreadful course. Long ere the thunder of the great slide had ceased to roar among the mountains, the mortal agony had been endured, and the victims were at peace. Their bodies were never found.

The next morning, the light smoke was seen stealing from the cottage chimney up the mountainside. Within, the fire was yet smoldering on the hearth, and the chairs in a circle round it, as if the inhabitants had but gone forth to view the devastation of the slide, and would shortly return, to thank Heaven for their miraculous escape. All had left separate tokens, by which those who had known the family were made to shed a tear for each. Who has not heard their name? The story has been told far and wide, and will forever be a legend of these mountains. Poets have sung their fate.

There were circumstances which led some to suppose that a stranger had been received into the cottage on this

---

[1] **trump:** used poetically for trumpet.
[2] **cataract:** a waterfall; used figuratively here.

awful night, and had shared the catastrophe of all its inmates. Others denied that there were sufficient grounds for such a conjecture. Woe for the high-souled youth, with his dream of earthly immortality! His name and person utterly unknown; his history, his way of life, his plans, a mystery never to be solved, his death and his existence equally a doubt! Whose was the agony of that death moment?

FOR DISCUSSION

DR. HEIDEGGER'S EXPERIMENT

1. Why did the characters have to be the kind that one could not admire?

2. Did their actions after drinking the magic liquid impress you as funny or sad?

3. What is Hawthorne's answer to the question on which the story hinges: would we live our lives differently if we could live them over? Do you agree with his conclusion? What value is there in speculating on a situation that could not happen in actual life?

4. What is the function of the mirror in the story? Do you feel that this manipulation adds to or detracts from the effectiveness of the story as a whole? What is the symbolic significance of the rose?

5. Which elements in this story are romantic? Which are realistic?

THE AMBITIOUS GUEST

1. This story is marked by strong contrasts. Point out those between the interior and exterior, between the family and the stranger, the nature of their conversation and the fate that overtook them.

2. Do the ambitions of the stranger seem natural ones to you? How do they affect the other members of the family? In your judgment, has the youth accomplished anything? The last paragraph in the story is worth careful consideration.

3. What terrible irony is there in the final fate of the family? Find evidences of Hawthorne's preparing us for the tragedy.

4. How many questions on the meaning and value of human life can you find involved in this story? What is the significance of the title?

STORY IDEAS FROM HAWTHORNE'S "AMERICAN NOTEBOOKS"

For a number of years, Hawthorne kept notebooks in which he jotted down ideas for stories. Here are a few of his entries:

"The print in blood of a naked foot to be traced through the street of a town."

"In an old house, a mysterious knocking might be heard on the wall, where had formerly been a doorway, now bricked up."

"Follow out the fantasy of a man taking his life in installments, instead of at one payment — say ten years of life alternately with ten years of suspended animation."

"The semblance of a human face to be formed on the side of a mountain or in the fracture of a small stone by a *lusus naturae* [a trick of nature]. The face is an object of curiosity for years or centuries, and by and by a boy is born whose features gradually assume the aspect of that portrait. At some critical juncture, the resemblance is found to be perfect. A prophecy may be connected."

Here is an idea Hawthorne passed on to Longfellow. Do you recognize it?

"H. L. C. heard from a French Canadian a story of a young couple in Acadie. On their marriage day, all the men of the Province were summoned to assemble in the church to hear a proclamation. When assembled, they were all seized and shipped off to be distributed through New England, among them the new bridegroom. His bride set off in search of him, — wandered about New England all her lifetime, and at last when she was old, she found her bridegroom on his deathbed. The shock was so great that it killed her likewise."

Art and Literature

Reproduced on pages 556–557 are three paintings of scenes that form the background for some of Nathaniel Hawthorne's most important writings.

Above is "The Trial of George Jacobs," one of the Salem witchcraft trials, presided over by Judge Hathorne, Nathaniel Hawthorne's ancestor. The painting is by the American artist T. H. Matteson. At the right is "Brook Farm" (the background for Hawthorne's The Blithedale Romance), painted by the nineteenth-century American artist John Wolcott. Below is a painting of Crowninshield Wharf in Salem by the early nineteenth-century American artist George Ropes. Here Hawthorne gathered ideas for many of his works, including The House of the Seven Gables and The Scarlet Letter.

HERMAN MELVILLE

1819–1891

Captain Ahab

FROM *Moby Dick*

Moby Dick is the story of the fateful voyage of the *Pequod*, a whaling ship commanded by the compelling, mysterious figure Captain Ahab, magnificent in his strengths and his weaknesses. Throughout the novel Captain Ahab relentlessly pursues the white whale that has years before taken off his leg and made a "poor pegging lubber" of him. In the following selection from Chapters 28 and 36 of the book, Melville introduces Captain Ahab to the reader and relates the incident in which the captain stirs up the crew to be on the alert for his enemy.

A strange collection of interesting characters are the officers of the *Pequod*: Starbuck, the first mate; Stubb, the second mate; Flask, the third mate. Even stranger are the harpooners: Tashtego, an Indian from Gay Head on Martha's Vineyard; Daggoo, a Negro of gigantic size and strength; and Queequeg, "a native of Kokovoko, an island far away to the West and South." ("It is not shown on any map," Melville says; "true places never are.") The teller of the story is a young sailor who joins the crew on this final voyage. At the start he says, "Call me Ishmael," a name symbolizing the "wanderer," since it is the name of the outcast son of Abraham in the Bible.

From this short selection you may not feel the epic sweep of *Moby Dick*, but you will sense the book's excitement and the poetic beauty of Melville's style.

For several days after leaving Nantucket, nothing above hatches was seen of Captain Ahab. The mates regularly relieved each other at the watches, and for aught that could be seen to the contrary, they seemed to be the only commanders of the ship; only they sometimes issued from the cabin with orders so sudden and peremptory, that after all it was plain they but commanded vicariously.[1] Yet, their supreme lord and dictator was there, though hitherto unseen by any eyes not permitted to penetrate into the now sacred retreat of the cabin.

Every time I ascended to the deck from my watches below, I instantly gazed aft to mark if any strange face was visible; for my first vague disquietude [2] touching the unknown captain,

[1] **vicariously** (vĭ·kâr'ĭ·ŭs·lĭ): not directly; through something or someone else.
[2] **disquietude** (dĭs·kwī'ĕ·tūd): uneasiness.

now in the seclusion of the sea, became almost a perturbation. . . . Now, it being Christmas when the ship shot from out her harbor, for a space we had biting polar weather, though all the time running away from it to the southward; and by every degree and minute of latitude which we sailed, gradually leaving that merciless winter and all its intolerable weather behind us. It was one of those less lowering,[1] but still gray and gloomy enough mornings of the transition, when with a fair wind the ship was rushing through the water with a vindictive sort of leaping and melancholy rapidity, that as I mounted to the deck at the call of the forenoon watch, so soon as I leveled my glance toward the taffrail,[2] foreboding shivers ran over me. Reality outran apprehension; Captain Ahab stood upon his quarter-deck.

There seemed no sign of common bodily illness about him, nor of the recovery from any. He looked like a man cut away from the stake, when the fire has overrunningly wasted all the limbs without consuming them, or taking away one particle from their compacted aged robustness. His whole high, broad form seemed made of solid bronze, and shaped in an unalterable mold, like Cellini's cast Perseus.[3] Threading its way out from among his gray hairs, and continuing right down one side of his tawny, scorched face and neck, till it disappeared in his clothing, you saw a slender rodlike mark, lividly whitish. It resembled that perpendicular seam sometimes made in the straight, lofty trunk of a great tree, when the upper lightning tearingly darts down it, and without wrenching a single twig, peels and grooves out the bark from top to bottom ere running off into the soil, leaving the tree still greenly alive, but branded. Whether that mark was born with him, or whether it was the scar left by some desperate wound, no one could certainly say. By some tacit consent, throughout the voyage little or no allusion was made to it, especially by the mates. But once an old Gay Head Indian among the crew superstitiously asserted that not till he was full forty years old did Ahab become that way branded, and then it came upon him, not in the fury of any mortal fray, but in an elemental strife at sea. . . .

So powerfully did the whole grim aspect of Ahab affect me, and the livid brand which streaked it, that for the first few moments I hardly noted that not a little of this overbearing grimness was owing to the barbaric white leg upon which he partly stood. It had previously come to me that this ivory leg had at sea been fashioned from the polished bone of the sperm whale's jaw. "Aye, he was dismasted off Japan," said the old Gay Head Indian once; "but like his dismasted craft, he shipped[4] another mast without coming home for it. He has a quiver of 'em."

I was struck with the singular posture he maintained. Upon each side of the *Pequod's* quarter-deck, and pretty close to the mizzen shrouds, there was an auger hole, bored about half an inch or so, into the plank. His bone leg steadied in that hole, one arm elevated, and holding by a shroud, Captain Ahab stood erect, looking straight out beyond the ship's ever-pitching prow. There was an infinity of firmest fortitude, a determinate, unsurrenderable willfulness, in the fixed and fearless, forward dedication of that glance. Not a word he spoke; nor did his officers say aught to him; though by all their minutest gestures and expressions, they plainly

---

[1] **lowering** (lou'ẽr·ĭng): darkening, threatening a storm.

[2] **taffrail:** the upper portion of a ship's stern, or the rail around the stern.

[3] **Cellini's cast Perseus:** a famous statue of Perseus holding the Gorgon's head, by Benvenuto Cellini (băn·vå·nōō'tồ chĕ·lē'nĕ) (1500–1571).

[4] **shipped:** took aboard, obtained.

showed the uneasy, if not painful, consciousness of being under a troubled master-eye. And not only that, but moody, stricken Ahab stood before them with a crucifixion in his face, in all the nameless, regal, overbearing dignity of some mighty woe.

Ere long, from his first visit in the air, he withdrew into his cabin. But after that morning, he was every day visible to the crew, either standing in his pivot-hole, or seated upon an ivory stool he had, or heavily walking the deck. As the sky grew less gloomy, indeed, began to grow a little genial, he became still less and less a recluse; as if, when the ship had sailed from home, nothing but the dead wintry bleakness of the sea had then kept him so secluded. And, by and by, it came to pass, that he was almost continually in the air; but, as yet, for all that he said, or perceptibly did, on the at last sunny deck, he seemed as unnecessary there as another mast. But the *Pequod* was only making a passage now, not regularly cruising; nearly all whaling preparatives needing supervision the mates were fully competent to, so that there was little or nothing, out of himself, to employ or excite Ahab now, and thus chase away, for that one interval, the clouds that layer upon layer were piled upon his brow, as ever all clouds choose the loftiest peaks to pile themselves upon.

Nevertheless, ere long, the warm, warbling persuasiveness of the pleasant holiday weather we came to seemed gradually to charm him from his mood. For, as when the red-cheeked dancing girls April and May trip home to the wintry, misanthropic[1] woods, even the barest, ruggedest, most thunder-cloven old oak will at least send forth some few green sprouts to welcome such gladhearted visitants; so Ahab did, in the end, a little respond to the playful allurings of that girlish air. More than once did he put forth the faint blossom of a look, which, in any other man, would have soon flowered out in a smile.

One morning shortly after breakfast, Ahab, as was his wont,[2] ascended the cabin-gangway to the deck. There most sea captains usually walk at that hour, as country gentlemen, after the same meal, take a few turns in the garden.

Soon his steady, ivory stride was heard, as to and fro he paced his old rounds, upon planks so familiar to his tread that they were all over dented, like geological stones, with the peculiar mark of his walk. Did you fixedly gaze, too, upon that ribbed and dented brow, there also, you would see still stranger footprints — the footprints of his one unsleeping, ever-pacing thought.

But on the occasion in question, those dents looked deeper, even as his nervous step that morning left a deeper mark. And, so full of his thought was Ahab that at every uniform turn that he made, now at the mainmast and now at the binnacle, you could almost see that thought turn in him as he turned, and pace in him as he paced; so completely possessing him, indeed, that it all but seemed the inward mold of every outer movement.

"D'ye mark him, Flask?" whispered Stubb; "the chick that's in him pecks the shell. 'Twill soon be out."

The hours wore on — Ahab now shut up within his cabin; anon, pacing the deck, with the same intense bigotry of purpose[3] in his aspect.

It drew near the close of day. Suddenly he came to a halt by the bulwarks, and inserting his bone leg into the auger hole there, and with one hand grasping a shroud, he ordered Starbuck to send everybody aft.

"Sir!" said the mate, astonished at

[1] misanthropic (mĭs·ăn·thrŏp'ĭk): hating mankind.

[2] wont (wŭnt): custom.

[3] bigotry (bĭg'ŭt·rĭ) of purpose: almost frenzied singlemindedness; bigotry means exclusion of other beliefs or ideas.

"Cachalot Fishery," a colored aquatint of an oil painting. Herman Melville called this painting one of the finest representations of whaling that he had ever seen.

an order seldom or never given on shipboard, except in some extraordinary case.

"Send everybody aft," repeated Ahab. "Mastheads, there! come down!"

When the entire ship's company were assembled, and with curious and not wholly unapprehensive faces, were eyeing him, for he looked not unlike the weather horizon when a storm is coming up, Ahab, after rapidly glancing over the bulwarks, and then darting his eyes among the crew, started from his standpoint, and as though not a soul were nigh him, resumed his heavy turns upon the deck. With bent head and half-slouched hat he continued to pace, unmindful of the wondering whispering among the men; till Stubb cautiously whispered to Flask that Ahab must have summoned them there for the purpose of witnessing a pedestrian feat. But this did not last long. Vehemently pausing, he cried:

"What do ye do when ye see a whale, men?"

"Sing out for him!" was the impulsive rejoinder from a score of clubbed voices.

"Good!" cried Ahab, with a wild approval in his tones, observing the hearty animation into which his unexpected question had so magnetically thrown them.

"And what do ye next, men?"

"Lower away, and after him!"

"And what tune is it ye pull to, men?"

"A dead whale or a stove [1] boat!"

More and more strangely and fiercely glad and approving grew the countenance of the old man at every shout, while the mariners began to gaze curiously at each other, as if marveling how it was that they themselves became so

[1] stove: with a hole broken in. *Stove* is a variation of the past participle of *stave*.

excited at such seemingly purposeless questions.

But they were all eagerness again as Ahab, now half-revolving in his pivot-hole with one hand reaching high up a shroud and tightly, almost convulsively, grasping it, addressed them thus:

"All ye mastheaders have before now heard me give orders about a white whale. Look ye! d'ye see this Spanish ounce of gold?" holding up a broad bright coin to the sun — "it is a sixteen-dollar piece, men. D'ye see it? Mr. Starbuck, hand me yon top maul."

While the mate was getting the hammer, Ahab, without speaking, was slowly rubbing the gold piece against the skirts of his jacket, as if to heighten its luster, and without using any words, was meanwhile lowly humming to himself, producing a sound so strangely muffled and inarticulate that it seemed the mechanical humming of the wheels of his vitality in him.

Receiving the top maul from Starbuck, he advanced toward the mainmast with the hammer uplifted in one hand, exhibiting the gold with the other, and with a high, raised voice exclaiming: "Whosoever of ye raises me a white-headed whale with a wrinkled brow and a crooked jaw; whosoever of ye raises me that white-headed whale, with three holes punctured in his starboard fluke [1] — look ye, whosoever of ye raises me that same white whale, he shall have this gold ounce, my boys!"

"Huzza! huzza!" cried the seamen, as with swinging tarpaulins they hailed the act of nailing the gold to the mast.

"It's a white whale, I say," resumed Ahab, as he threw down the top maul: "a white whale. Skin your eyes for him, men; look sharp for white water; if ye see but a bubble, sing out."

All this while Tashtego, Daggoo, and Queequeg had looked on with even more intense interest and surprise than the rest, and at the mention of the wrinkled brow and crooked jaw they had started as if each was separately touched by some specific recollection.

"Captain Ahab," said Tashtego, "that white whale must be the same that some call Moby Dick."

"Moby Dick?" shouted Ahab. "Do ye know the white whale then, Tash?"

"Does he fantail a little curious, sir, before he goes down?" said the Gay Header deliberately.

"And has he a curious spout, too," said Daggoo, "very bushy, even for a parmacety,[2] and mighty quick, Captain Ahab?"

"And he have one, two, tree — oh! good many iron in him hide, too, Captain," cried Queequeg disjointedly, "all twiske-tee be-twisk, like him — him — " faltering hard for a word, and screwing his hand round and round as though uncorking a bottle — "like him — him — "

"Corkscrew!" cried Ahab, "aye, Queequeg, the harpoons lie all twisted and wrenched in him; aye, Daggoo, his spout is a big one, like a whole shock of wheat, and white as a pile of our Nantucket wool after the great annual sheep-shearing; aye, Tashtego, and he fantails like a split jib in a squall. Death and devils! men, it is Moby Dick ye have seen — Moby Dick — Moby Dick!"

"Captain Ahab," said Starbuck, who, with Stubb and Flask, had thus far been eyeing his superior with increasing surprise, but at last seemed struck with a thought which somewhat explained all the wonder, "Captain Ahab, I have heard of Moby Dick — but it was not Moby Dick that took off thy leg?"

"Who told thee that?" cried Ahab; then pausing, "Aye, Starbuck; aye, my hearties all round; it was Moby Dick that dismasted me; Moby Dick that brought me to this dead stump I stand on now. Aye, aye," he shouted with a

[1] fluke: one of the lobes of a whale's tail.

[2] parmacety (pär′má·sē′tĭ): dialect for a whale that produces spermaceti, a waxy solid used in making candles.

terrific, loud, animal sob, like that of a heart-stricken moose; "Aye, aye! it was that accursed white whale that razed me; made a poor pegging lubber of me forever and a day!" Then tossing both arms, with measureless imprecations [1] he shouted out: "Aye, aye! and I'll chase him round Good Hope, and round the Horn, and round the Norway Maelstrom, and round perdition's flames before I give him up. And this is what ye have shipped for, men! to chase that white whale on both sides of land, and over all sides of earth, till he spouts black blood and rolls fin out. What say ye, men, will ye splice hands on it, now? I think ye do look brave."

"Aye, aye!" shouted the harpooners and seamen, running closer to the excited old man: "A sharp eye for the white whale; a sharp lance for Moby Dick!"

"God bless ye," he seemed to half sob and half shout. "God bless ye, men."

---

[1] imprecations (ĭm′prē·kā′shŭns): curses.

FOR DISCUSSION

1. In what two ways is Captain Ahab compared to a tree? How does Melville describe the marks of the peg leg on the deck? Point out other passages that contain striking figures of speech.

2. In what specific ways does Ahab play upon the crew's emotions to make them eager for the capture of Moby Dick? What do you think of the psychology he employs?

3. Look again at the description of Moby Dick. What details and comparisons seem particularly effective? How do you know that capture of the white whale has become an obsession with Captain Ahab?

4. Many critics believe this story is a great allegory. Some feel that Ahab represents evil, and Moby Dick represents good, or truth. Some give exactly the opposite interpretation. Which of these two points of view seems the more reasonable to you? Perhaps you can give a third interpretation.

FURTHER READING

You may want to read the whole of *Moby Dick,* or the abridgment in *Four American Novels,* edited by Edmund Fuller and Olga Achtenhagen (Harcourt, Brace & World, 1959), as well as Melville's adventure stories *Typee* and *Omoo.* A good book on whaling is Georges Blond's *Great Story of Whales* (Hanover, 1955), dedicated to Melville.

READING ON THE AMERICAN IMAGINATION AWAKENS

BOOKS ABOUT THE PERIOD

Brooks, Van Wyck, *The World of Washington Irving* (Dutton, 1944)
Miller, P., *The Raven and the Whale* (Harcourt, Brace & World, paperback, 1962)

ON INDIVIDUAL AUTHORS

IRVING. Benét, Laura, *Washington Irving, Explorer of American Legend* (Dodd, Mead, 1944)
COOPER. Grossman, James, *James Fenimore Cooper* (Sloane, 1949)
POE. Allen, Hervey, *Israfel* (Holt, Rinehart & Winston, 1949); Benét, Laura, *Young Edgar Allan Poe* (Dodd, Mead, 1941); Fagin, Nathan B., *The Histrionic Mr. Poe* (Johns Hopkins Press, 1949); Quinn, A. H., *Edgar Allan Poe* (Appleton-Century-Crofts, 1941); Winwar, Frances, *The Haunted Palace, a Life of Edgar Allan Poe* (Harper, 1959)
HAWTHORNE. Hawthorne, Hildegarde, *A Romantic Rebel* (Appleton-Century-Crofts, 1932); Tharp, Louise Hall, *The Peabody Sisters of Salem* (Little, Brown, 1950); Van Doren, Mark, *Nathaniel Hawthorne* (Sloane, 1950)
MELVILLE. Arvin, Newton, *Herman Melville* (Sloane, 1950); Howard, Leon, *Herman Melville: A Biography* (Univ. of California Press, 1951; 2nd ed., paperback, 1958); Leyda, Jay, *The Melville Log,* a source book of Melville material (Harcourt, Brace & World, 1951)

FOR LISTENING

Bryant's "To a Waterfowl" and Poe's "To Helen" and "The Bells" have been recorded on *Many Voices* 5B.

New England's Golden Years

D URING THE PERIOD in which Hawthorne and Melville were doing their most productive work, all of New England experienced a remarkable intellectual and literary flowering. An astonishing array of varied talents and vivid personalities suddenly appeared. Three towns within a few miles of each other—Boston, Cambridge (with Harvard College), and Concord—were the chief centers of literary activity in this productive time. New England was a seedbed of ideas. Preachers, educators, jurists, orators, scientists, and historians contributed to its intellectual leadership. Its scholars made Harvard the most distinguished of American colleges. Boston's painters, philosophers, and poets were known to the whole world. Emerson, Longfellow, Whittier, Holmes, Thoreau, and Lowell were born within a few years and a few miles of each other. These were truly New England's Golden Years.

"The Hub of the Universe"

The rapidly expanding city of Boston outstripped its smaller neighbor, Salem, as a shipping center. In Boston a world trade was developing. Its wealthy homes possessed the fabrics and porcelains of the East, the ivories of Africa, and the books of Europe. Gaudy peacocks strutted in some Boston gardens. Education and culture were thriving. The Boston and Roxbury Latin Schools, like Harvard College, dated back to the earliest years of settlement. The Boston Athenaeum, established in 1805, contained one of our first fine libraries and helped to nourish the minds of generations of writers and thinkers. A number of publishing houses were founded in Boston during these years, and as the century advanced, a series of important literary magazines appeared. The *North American Review* was begun in 1815 and lasted until 1939. Though William Cullen Bryant was not one of the Boston literary group, it was in the pages of the *Review* that his "Thanatopsis" and "To a Waterfowl" first appeared. Some years later came the *Atlantic Monthly*, which still flourishes.

Though New England made its major contributions to literature, the other arts were not neglected during this period. The Handel and Haydn Society advanced musical taste. Boston was the home of the portrait painter Gilbert Stuart, renowned for his paintings of George Washington (see page 482). The architect Charles Bulfinch built the State House and many other buildings, private and public, that still adorn the city. His son, Thomas, wrote the volumes that became known as *Bulfinch's Mythology*, the first popular collection in this country of the ancient classical stories. All in all, this was the lively Boston that Oliver Wendell Holmes buoyantly dubbed "the hub of the solar system." A later variation was even less modest: "the hub of the universe."

Transcendentalism

In the Boston-Cambridge-Concord triangle there arose, during the 1840's, an intellectual movement with the formidable name of *Transcendentalism.* Taken apart, the word is not too difficult. The verb "to transcend" means "to go beyond" something. For the Transcendentalists, the term meant simply that there are truths that go beyond, or transcend, proof. These are the truths known to the heart rather than to the mind, the truths that are felt emotionally even though they cannot be proved logically. For example, a doctor can tell scientifically whether a man is alive or not, but he cannot tell scientifically whether or not it is good to be alive. The Transcendentalists held that most of what we call "values" lie outside the limits of reason and belong rather to the realm of instinct or intuition. They are matters of private experience, faith, and conviction.

Transcendentalism represented a whole outside world of thought and speculation that moved into the New England consciousness and took on characteristic shapes there. Many influences from different places and times mingled in the movement. A German philosopher, Immanuel Kant, gave Transcendentalism its name. He, with other German thinkers, influenced the views of some important English writers, the poet-critics Samuel Taylor Coleridge and William Wordsworth, and the Scottish philosopher-historian Thomas Carlyle. These three, especially Carlyle, exchanged ideas with Ralph Waldo Emerson of Concord. It was Emerson who was responsible for bringing the movement to New England and nurturing its growth in this country.

Much of the spirit of New England Transcendentalism is caught for us in Emerson's words:

> Great men are they who see that spiritual is stronger than any material force, that thoughts rule the world.

Mixed in with the other elements of Transcendentalism was a revived interest in the Greek philosopher Plato, and in the thought of the Orient, especially as found in Confucius and Buddha. All this was rich and strange to conservative, one-time Puritan Boston. It was many years before most people finally came to accept Emerson's thought and to distinguish him with the title the "Sage of Concord." (See page 569 for a sketch of Emerson's life.)

THE TRANSCENDENTAL CLUB

A group that came to be called informally the Transcendental Club met sometimes at Emerson's home in Concord. The most important member of the group, after Emerson himself, was Henry David Thoreau. For many years considered merely an eccentric minor disciple of Emerson, Thoreau has recently taken his place as an original, influential thinker. His life is treated in detail on page 583.

Among the other members of the club were Bronson Alcott, schoolmaster and visionary, and Margaret Fuller, one of the most talented women of her day, who is partly the source of a character in Hawthorne's *The Blithedale Romance*. The Transcendental Club established a magazine, the *Dial*, which Margaret Fuller and Emerson each edited at different times.

SOCIAL EXPERIMENTS

Among the interesting by-products of the Transcendental movement were two co-operative farm colonies devoted to an ideal of communal living. All work, privileges, and pay were to be shared alike, with leisure time spent on educational and cultural activities. The first of these communities was Brook Farm, which lasted for six years. Nathaniel Hawthorne dwelt there for a time. Later, Bronson Alcott founded a similar venture called Fruitlands, which survived for less than a year. Joseph Palmer, whose difficulties over his beard are described in a selection beginning on page 213, was an active member of that experiment, and he bought the farm when the others gave up the idea.

Bronson Alcott held original ideas on schooling, leading in the direction of what later came to be called "progressive education." His emphasis was on free expression for the individual child. Hawthorne's sister-in-law, Elizabeth Peabody, was Alcott's assistant at the Temple School, which he established in Boston. Though he wrote much, Bronson Alcott is better remembered as a conversationalist and a personality. He visited Thomas Carlyle in Scotland, who later called Alcott "a venerable Don Quixote whom nobody can laugh at without loving."

The Alcott name is perhaps best known through Bronson's daughter Louisa. She grew up in the large, often poor, but generally happy family, stimulated by the host of learned and creative friends of her father's circle. Her "Transcendental Wild Oats" is a sharp satire on her father's Fruitlands venture. The best of her many successful novels, beloved by generations of readers, is *Little Women* (1868).

The New England Historians

Not all of the important writers of this period were connected with the Transcendental movement. Among these other writers were several notable historians. One of them, George Bancroft, had a distinguished career in public life as Secretary of both the Army and Navy, one of the founders of the Naval Academy at Annapolis, and Ambassador to England. His *History of the United States* (1834) was the first large-scale study of our nation.

John Lothrop Motley concentrated on the history of the Netherlands. Of his several works on that subject, the first, which established his reputation, was *The Rise of the Dutch Republic* (1856). Motley was noted for his ability to narrate the facts of history accurately and dramatically.

Greatest of all the Massachusetts historians, and the most unusual in one of the circumstances of his life, was William Hickling Prescott. In a scuffle as a boy, he was struck in the eyes by a hard bread crust and was almost totally blind as a result of this freakish accident. In spite of this drastic handicap to research, Prescott plunged into the study of history and literature. Spain was his primary field, and his first major work was *The Reign of Ferdinand and Isabella* (1838), a study of the monarchs who had financed Columbus' voyages.

Prescott's masterpiece was a triumph of pure research in an almost unknown field, *The History of the Conquest of Mexico* (1843). Washington Irving had contemplated such a book but graciously dropped the project in favor of the younger man's work. Imaginations everywhere were roused by Prescott's account of the adventure that brought the European into contact with the strange, sometimes terrifying, civilization of the Aztecs, and brought face to face two extraordinary men, Cortes and Montezuma. Though modern scholarship has learned more details, no book has displaced Prescott's as a comprehensive account of these events. Prescott's other major work is *The History of the Conquest of Peru* (1847).

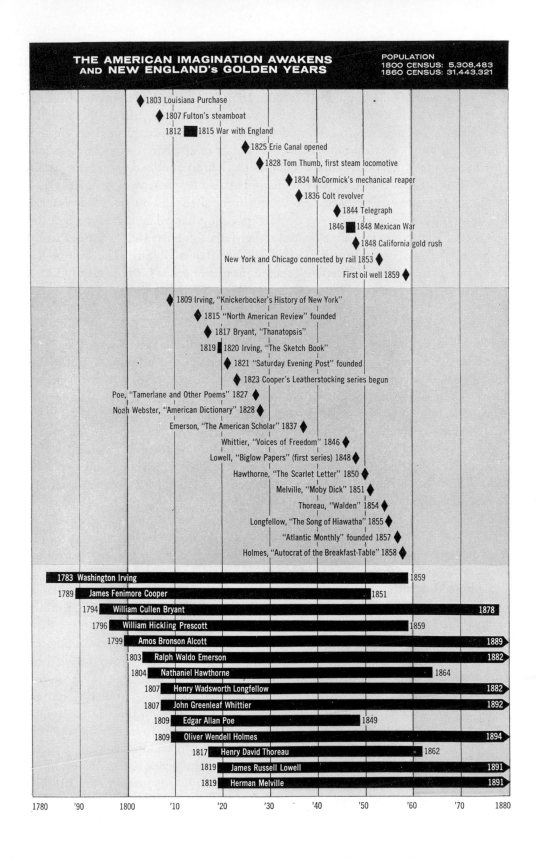

THE AMERICAN IMAGINATION AWAKENS
AND NEW ENGLAND's GOLDEN YEARS

POPULATION
1800 CENSUS: 5,308,483
1860 CENSUS: 31,443,321

1803 Louisiana Purchase
1807 Fulton's steamboat
1812 ■ 1815 War with England
1825 Erie Canal opened
1828 Tom Thumb, first steam locomotive
1834 McCormick's mechanical reaper
1836 Colt revolver
1844 Telegraph
1846 ■ 1848 Mexican War
1848 California gold rush
New York and Chicago connected by rail 1853
First oil well 1859

1809 Irving, "Knickerbocker's History of New York"
1815 "North American Review" founded
1817 Bryant, "Thanatopsis"
1819 ▮ 1820 Irving, "The Sketch Book"
1821 "Saturday Evening Post" founded
1823 Cooper's Leatherstocking series begun
Poe, "Tamerlane and Other Poems" 1827
Noah Webster, "American Dictionary" 1828
Emerson, "The American Scholar" 1837
Whittier, "Voices of Freedom" 1846
Lowell, "Biglow Papers" (first series) 1848
Hawthorne, "The Scarlet Letter" 1850
Melville, "Moby Dick" 1851
Thoreau, "Walden" 1854
Longfellow, "The Song of Hiawatha" 1855
"Atlantic Monthly" founded 1857
Holmes, "Autocrat of the Breakfast-Table" 1858

1783 Washington Irving — 1859
1789 James Fenimore Cooper — 1851
1794 William Cullen Bryant — 1878
1796 William Hickling Prescott — 1859
1799 Amos Bronson Alcott — 1889
1803 Ralph Waldo Emerson — 1882
1804 Nathaniel Hawthorne — 1864
1807 Henry Wadsworth Longfellow — 1882
1807 John Greenleaf Whittier — 1892
1809 Edgar Allan Poe — 1849
1809 Oliver Wendell Holmes — 1894
1817 Henry David Thoreau — 1862
1819 James Russell Lowell — 1891
1819 Herman Melville — 1891

1780   '90   1800   '10   '20   '30   '40   '50   '60   '70   1880

RALPH
WALDO
EMERSON

1803–1882

Ralph Waldo Emerson was responsible for bringing Transcendentalism to New England, and he was recognized throughout his life as the leader of the movement, yet he never applied the term "Transcendentalist" to himself or to his beliefs and ideas.

Like many original minds, he was often several jumps ahead of what his followers thought was his position or philosophy. He was one of the most influential of American thinkers, yet he had no elaborate, formal system of thought and he never attempted to create one.

Emerson believed above all in individualism, independence of mind, and self-reliance:

> There is a time in every man's education when he arrives at the conviction that envy is ignorance; that imitation is suicide; that he must take himself for better, for worse, as his portion . . . Trust thyself: every heart vibrates to that iron string.

> Whoso would be a man must be a nonconformist.

He admired courage:

> It was a high counsel that I once heard given to a young person, "Always do what you are afraid to do."

He was not afraid of changing or clashing ideas:

> A foolish consistency is the hobgoblin of little minds . . . With consistency a great soul has simply nothing to do.

It is not surprising that Emerson's followers often failed to keep up with his agile mind.

Emerson was born in Boston in 1803. He graduated from Harvard, taught school for a short time, then became pastor of the Second Church of Boston in 1829. He resigned this position two years later and began his literary life. He traveled to Europe, spending most of his time in Italy and England. He met many of the important writers of his time. One of them, the Scottish writer Thomas Carlyle, was to remain a lifelong friend and an important influence on much of Emerson's work.

On his return to this country, Emerson published his first book, *Nature* (1836), which met with a mild reception. However, two speeches in the next two years, "The American Scholar" and "The Divinity School Address," made him famous. Emerson then embarked on a series of lecture tours in England and America. Many of his lectures were later distilled into his famous *Essays* and other books. Among his most important works are *Representative Men* (1850) and *English Traits* (1856). His *Poems* appeared in 1847.

Emerson's poetry is uneven in quality, but always highly individual, and some of it is excellent. He felt that:

> The poet knows that he speaks adequately . . . only when he speaks somewhat wildly, or "with the flower of the mind."

His own poetry often displays these characteristics. In his day, Emerson's poems were criticized for their lack of form and polish. In recent years, however, his poetry has received high praise. His harsh rhythms and striking images appeal to many modern readers as artful techniques.

Emerson's prose style was sometimes as highly individual as his poetry. Many of his essays were put together from his journal entries, speeches, and random notes, and they are often somewhat disorganized. Yet his skill in polishing each sentence into a striking thought makes his writing memorable. When you read his prose in the following pages, keep in mind that his unit of thought is generally the sentence rather than the paragraph. The results can be rewarding. Emerson's prose, at its best, ranks with the finest American literature can offer.

One of his great statements was in "The American Scholar." That title is now carried by one of the finest magazines in America. Oliver Wendell Holmes called the speech "our intellectual Declaration of Independence." In the address, Emerson defined the scholar's obligations for all ages:

> Action is with the scholar subordinate, but it is essential. Without it he is not yet man. Without it thought can never ripen into truth . . . Inaction is cowardice, but there can be no scholar without the heroic mind . . . The true scholar grudges every opportunity of action passed by as a loss of power.
>
> He is the world's eye. He is the world's heart . . . These being his functions, it becomes him to feel all confidence in himself, and to defer never to the popular cry . . . Let him not quit his belief that a popgun is a popgun, though the ancient and honorable of the earth affirm it to be the crack of doom . . . In self-trust all the virtues are comprehended. Free should be the scholar — free and brave.

Another of his famous statements indicates how deeply Emerson believed and practiced his own principles of scholarship and intellectual self-reliance:

> I gain my point, gain all points, whenever I can reach a young man with any statement which teaches him his own worth.

Emerson wrote two short poems and one long essay (page 578) on the subject of compensation. The idea of balance in human life — night and day, good and evil, action and repose — was a favorite of his.

Compensation

Why should I keep holiday
    When other men have none?
Why but because, when these are gay,
    I sit and mourn alone?

And why, when mirth unseals all tongues,   5
    Should mine alone be dumb?
Ah! late I spoke to silent throngs,
    And now their hour is come.

To understand all the kinds of "forbearance" Emerson advocates, you may need to read this poem several times.

Forbearance

Hast thou named all the birds without a gun?
Loved the wood rose, and left it on its stalk?
At rich men's tables eaten bread and pulse?°
Unarmed, faced danger with a heart of trust?

And loved so well a high behavior,   5
In man or maid, that thou from speech refrained,
Nobility more nobly to repay?
O, be my friend, and teach me to be thine!

3. **pulse:** the seeds of peas, beans, or similar vegetables.

Today at Concord you can see a graceful bridge, and near it, through the trees, a famous bronze statue of the Minute Man. On its base is carved the first stanza of "The Concord Hymn." At the other end of the bridge stands a second monument commemorating the Battle of Concord, which opened the American Revolution.

Emerson and his Concord neighbors were determined that the battle of 1775 should be remembered "when, like our sires, our sons are gone." Emerson's poem turned the trick; the "shot heard round the world" is indeed immortal.

The Concord Hymn

By the rude bridge that arched the flood,
　Their flag to April's breeze unfurled,
Here once the embattled farmers stood,
　And fired the shot heard round the world.

The foe long since in silence slept;   5
　Alike the conqueror silent sleeps;
And Time the ruined bridge has swept
　Down the dark stream which seaward creeps.

On this green bank, by this soft stream,
　We set today a votive stone;   10
That memory may their deed redeem,
　When, like our sires, our sons are gone.

Spirit, that made those heroes dare
　To die and leave their children free,
Bid Time and Nature gently spare   15
　The shaft we raise to them and thee.

The long poem "Voluntaries" contains five disconnected stanzas, each treating of some act of the will in relation to the struggles of life. The third of these stanzas is the best known. Look for four lines that are frequently quoted.

Voluntaries III

In an age of fops and toys,
Wanting wisdom, void of right,
Who shall nerve heroic boys
To hazard all in Freedom's fight —
Break sharply off their jolly games,   5
Forsake their comrades gay
And quit proud homes and youthful dames
For famine, toil, and fray?
Yet on the nimble air benign
Speed nimbler messages,   10
That waft the breath of grace divine
To hearts in sloth and ease.
So nigh is grandeur to our dust,
So near is God to man,
When duty whispers low, *Thou must,*   15
The youth replies, *I can.*

FOR DISCUSSION

1. As you observe your own life and the lives of others, do you find compensation such as Emerson describes in his poem? What other kinds of compensation do you find?

2. Why do you think Emerson admired a person who displayed the qualities found in "Forbearance"? Are these the qualities you yourself would seek in a friend? If not, make your own list of qualities.

3. In "The Concord Hymn," what is meant by "the shot heard round the world"? What appeal is made in the last stanza? Why is *hymn* a suitable word to describe this poem?

4. What does "Voluntaries III" show of Emerson's attitude toward youth? Can you think of some examples to show how modern youth has responded to duty?

5. Compare Emerson's poems to Bryant's and Poe's. In general, how do the three poets differ? Do they display any similar characteristics? If so, point out the similarities. What evidence can you find in these poems that Emerson, as well as Bryant, was a lover of nature?

YOUR OWN WRITING

For each poem, write one or two short sentences to show the main point Emerson makes.

SPECIAL REPORT

Compare "The Concord Hymn" with Lincoln's Gettysburg Address (see pages 231 and 666). What similarities and differences were there in the occasions of the poem and the speech? in the appeals made at the end of each?

A view of Emerson's study. ▶

Emerson's Essays

You have seen that Emerson's poems resemble little essays in verse, because he is usually trying to convey compactly an idea or a bit of philosophy. His essays themselves deal with his search for an interpretation of life and his concern with moral problems. A glance at the titles will show this: "Nature," "Manners," "Friendship," "Compensation," "Self-Reliance." Each treats of some quality of human life with a sincerity, perception, and wisdom that have won for their author such titles as seer, prophet, and sage.

In the essay "Gifts" Emerson attempts to influence the reader to "high thinking" on the matter of giving and receiving gifts.

EMERSON'S UNIT OF THOUGHT. The organization of an Emerson essay may seem loose. Remember that these essays were composed from the *Journals* that Emerson started to keep as a young man. He jotted down his random reflections, and over the years these many volumes became a treasury of carefully worded ideas. The result is that Emerson's essays contain striking sentences one after another, each highly polished in style and in itself containing a whole idea. It will help you in reading Emerson to remember that his unit of thought is generally the sentence — not the paragraph. Read slowly to get the complete meaning of *each* sentence.

GIFTS

Gifts of one who loved me —
'Twas high time they came;
When he ceased to love me,
Time they stopped for shame.

IT IS said that the world is in a state of bankruptcy, that the world owes the world more than the world can pay, and ought to go into chancery,[1] and be sold. I do not think this general insolvency, which involves in some sort all the population, to be the reason of the difficulty experienced at Christmas and New Year, and other times, in bestowing gifts; since it is always so pleasant to be generous, though very vexatious to pay debts. But the impediment lies in the choosing. If, at any time, it comes into my head that a present is due from me to somebody, I am puzzled what to give, until the opportunity is gone. Flowers and fruits are always fit presents — flowers, because they are a proud assertion that a ray of beauty outvalues all the utilities of the world. These gay natures contrast with the somewhat stern countenance of ordinary nature; they are like music heard out of a workhouse. Nature does not cocker[2] us; we are children, not pets; she is not fond;[3] everything is dealt to us without fear or favor, after severe universal laws. Yet these delicate flowers look like the frolic and interference of love and beauty. Men used to tell us that we love flattery, even though we are not deceived by it, because it shows that we are of importance enough to be courted. Something like that pleasure, the flowers give us: what am I to whom these sweet hints are addressed? Fruits are acceptable gifts, because they are the flower of commodities, and admit of fantastic values being attached to them. If a man should send to me to come a hundred miles to visit him, and should set before me a basket of fine summer fruit, I should think there was some proportion between the labor and the reward.

For common gifts, necessity makes pertinences and beauty every day, and

---

[1] **chancery** (chăn'sĕr-ĭ): a court of law that handles matters pertaining to estates and finances.

[2] **cocker:** spoil, coddle.

[3] **fond:** here, foolishly tender or weakly indulgent.

one is glad when an imperative leaves him no option, since if the man at the door has no shoes, you have not to consider whether you could procure him a paintbox. And as it is always pleasing to see a man eat bread, drink water, in the house or out of doors, so it is always a great satisfaction to supply these first wants. Necessity does everything well. In our condition of universal dependence, it seems heroic to let the petitioner be the judge of his necessity, and to give all that is asked, though at great inconvenience. If it be a fantastic desire, it is better to leave to others the office of punishing him. I can think of many parts I should prefer playing to that of the Furies.[1]

Next to things of necessity, the rule for a gift, which one of my friends prescribed, is that we might convey to some person that which properly belonged to his character, and was easily associated with him in thought. But our tokens of compliment and love are for the most part barbarous. Rings and other jewels are not gifts, but apologies for gifts. The only gift is a portion of thyself. Thou must bleed for me. Therefore the poet brings his poem; the shepherd, his lamb; the farmer, corn; the miner, a gem; the sailor, coral and shells; the painter, his picture; the girl, a handkerchief of her own sewing. This is right and pleasing, for it restores society in so far to its primary basis, when a man's biography is conveyed in his gift, and every man's wealth is an index of his merit. But it is a cold, lifeless business when you go to the shops to buy me something which does not represent your life and talent, but a goldsmith's. This is fit for kings, and rich men who represent kings, and a false state of property, to make presents of gold and silver stuffs, as a kind of symbolical sin-offering, or payment of blackmail.

---

[1] Furies: in Greek mythology, beings who punished the wicked.

The law of benefits is a difficult channel, which requires careful sailing, or rude boats. It is not the office of a man to receive gifts. How dare you give them? We wish to be self-sustained. We do not quite forgive a giver. The hand that feeds us is in some danger of being bitten. We can receive anything from love, for that is a way of receiving it from ourselves; but not from anyone who assumes to bestow. We sometimes hate the meat which we eat, because there seems something of degrading dependence in living by it.

Brother, if Jove to thee a present make,
Take heed that from his hands thou nothing take.

We ask the whole. Nothing less will content us. We arraign society, if it do not give us, besides earth and fire and water, opportunity, love, reverence, and objects of veneration.

He is a good man who can receive a gift well. We are either glad or sorry at a gift, and both emotions are unbecoming. Some violence, I think, is done, some degradation borne, when I rejoice or grieve at a gift. I am sorry when my independence is invaded, or when a gift comes from such as do not know my spirit, and so the act is not supported; and if the gift pleases me overmuch, then I should be ashamed that the donor should read my heart, and see that I love his commodity and not him. The gift, to be true, must be the flowing of the giver unto me, correspondent to my flowing unto him. When the waters are at a level, then my goods pass to him, and his to me. All his are mine, all mine his. I say to him, "How can you give me this pot of oil, or this flagon of wine, when all your oil and wine is mine?" Which belief of mine this gift seems to deny. Hence the fitness of beautiful, not useful things for gifts. This giving is flat usurpation, and therefore when the beneficiary is ungrateful, as all beneficiaries hate all

Timons,[1] not at all considering the value of the gift, but looking back to the greater store it was taken from, I rather sympathize with the beneficiary than with the anger of my lord Timon. For the expectation of gratitude is mean, and is continually punished by the total insensibility of the obliged person. It is a great happiness to get off without injury and heartburning from one who had had the ill luck to be served by you. It is a very onerous [2] business, this of being served, and the debtor naturally wishes to give you a slap. A golden text for these gentlemen is that which I so admire in the Buddhist, who never thanks, and who says, "Do not flatter your benefactors."

The reason of these discords I conceive to be that there is no commensurability [3] between a man and any gift. You cannot give anything to a magnanimous person. After you have served him, he at once puts you in debt by his magnanimity. The service a man renders his friend is trivial and selfish, compared with the service he knows his friend stood in readiness to yield him, alike before he had begun to serve his friend, and now also. Compared with that good will I bear my friend, the benefit it is in my power to render him seems small. Besides, our action on each other, good as well as evil, is so incidental and at random, that we can seldom hear the acknowledgments of any person who would thank us for a benefit without some shame and humiliation. We can rarely strike a direct stroke, but must be content with an oblique one; we seldom have the satisfaction of yielding a direct benefit, which is directly received. But recti-

tude scatters favors on every side without knowing it, and receives with wonder the thanks of all people.

I fear to breathe any treason against the majesty of love, which is the genius and god of gifts, and to whom we must not affect to prescribe. Let him give kingdoms or flower leaves indifferently. There are persons from whom we always expect fairy tokens; let us not cease to expect them. This is prerogative, and not to be limited by our municipal rules. For the rest, I like to see that we cannot be bought and sold. The best of hospitality and of generosity is also not in the will, but in fate. I find that I am not much to you; you do not need me; you do not feel me; then am I thrust out of doors, though you proffer me house and lands. No services are of any value, but only likeness. When I have attempted to join myself to others by services, it proved an intellectual trick — no more. They eat your service like apples, and leave you out. But love them, and they feel you, and delight in you all the time.

Selections from Other Emerson Essays

Because Emerson's unit of thought is the sentence and not the paragraph, and because he illuminates his ideas by illustration after illustration, the reader can gain from selected passages some notion of Emerson's point of view and a clear impression of his thought.

FROM NATURE

IT SEEMS as if the day was not wholly profane in which we have given heed to some natural object. The fall of snowflakes in a still air, preserving to each crystal its perfect form; the blowing of sleet over a wide sheet of water, and over plains; the waving rye field;

---

[1] Timons (tī'mĕnz): Timon, the leading character in Shakespeare's play *Timon of Athens*, spent his entire fortune on lavish gifts and was then spurned by those who had flattered him and had received his gifts.

[2] onerous (ŏn'ẽr·ŭs): oppressive.

[3] commensurability (kŏ·mĕn'shoo·rá·bǐl'ĭ-tǐ): proportion.

the mimic waving of acres of houstonia,[1] whose innumerable florets whiten and ripple before the eye; the reflections of trees and flowers in glassy lakes; the musical, steaming, odorous south wind, which converts all trees to wind harps; the crackling and spurting of hemlock in the flames; or of pine logs, which yield glory to the walls and faces in the sitting room — these are the music and pictures of the most ancient religion. . . We can find these enchantments without visiting the Como Lake, or the Madeira Islands. . . . In every landscape, the point of astonishment is the meeting of the sky and the earth, and that is seen from the first hillock as well as from the top of the Alleghenies. The stars at night stoop down over the brownest, homeliest common with all the spiritual magnificence which they shed on the Campagna,[2] or on the marble deserts of Egypt. . . . The difference between landscape and landscape is small, but there is great difference in the beholders. . . . Nature cannot be surprised in undress. Beauty breaks in everywhere.

from MANNERS

THE gentleman is a man of truth, lord of his own actions, and expressing that lordship in his behavior, not in any manner dependent and servile either on persons, or opinions, or possessions. Beyond this fact of truth and real force, the word denotes good nature or benevolence; manhood first and then gentleness. The popular notion certainly adds a condition of ease and fortune; but that is a natural result of personal force and love, that they should possess and dispense the goods of the world. In times of violence every eminent person must fall in with many opportunities to approve[3] his stoutness and worth; therefore every man's name that emerged at all from the mass in the feudal ages rattles in our ear like a flourish of trumpets. But personal force never goes out of fashion. That is still paramount today, and in the moving crowd of good society, the men of valor and reality are known, and rise to their natural place. The competition is transferred from war to politics and trade, but the personal force appears readily enough in these new arenas. . . . My gentleman gives the law where he is; he will outpray saints in chapel, outgeneral veterans in the field, and outshine all courtesy in the hall. He is good company for pirates, and good with academicians.[4]

from FRIENDSHIP

A FRIEND is a person with whom I may be sincere. Before him I may think aloud. I am arrived at last in the presence of a man so real and equal that I may drop even those undermost garments of dissimulation,[5] courtesy, and second thought, which men never put off, and may deal with him with the simplicity and wholeness with which one chemical atom meets another. Sincerity is the luxury allowed, like diadems and authority, only to the highest rank, *that* being permitted to speak truth, as having none above it to court or conform unto. Every man alone is sincere. At the entrance of a second person, hypocrisy begins. We parry and fend the approach of our fellow man by compliments, by gossip, by amusements, by affairs. We cover up our thought from him under a hundred folds. . . . Almost every man we meet requires some civility, requires to be

---

[1] houstonia (hōōs·tō′nĭ·á): a low, slender plant named for Dr. William Houston, an English naturalist.

[2] Campagna (käm·pä′nyä): the countryside surrounding Rome.

[3] approve: prove.

[4] academicians (á·kăd′ĕ·mĭsh′ănz): members of learned academies; scholars.

[5] dissimulation (dĭ·sĭm′ú·lā′shŭn): pretense.

humored — he has some fame, some talent, some whim of religion or philanthropy in his head that is not to be questioned, and which spoils all conversation with him. But a friend is a sane man who exercises not my ingenuity but me. My friend gives me entertainment without requiring me to stoop, or to lisp, or to mask myself. A friend therefore is a sort of paradox in nature. I who alone am, I who see nothing in nature whose existence I can affirm with equal evidence to my own, behold now the semblance of my being, in all its height, variety, and curiosity, reiterated in a foreign form; so that a friend may well be reckoned the masterpiece of nature.

FROM COMPENSATION

. . . IN THE animal kingdom, the physiologist has observed that no creatures are favorites, but a certain compensation balances every gift and every defect. . . .

The same dualism underlies the nature and condition of man. Every excess causes a defect; every defect an excess. Every sweet hath its sour; every evil its good. Every faculty which is a receiver of pleasure has an equal penalty for its abuse. It is to answer for its moderation with its life. For every grain of wit there is a grain of folly. For everything you have missed, you have gained something else; and for everything you gain, you lose something. If riches increase, they are increased that use them. If the gatherer gathers too much, nature takes out of the man what she puts into his chest; swells the estate, but kills the owner. Nature hates monopolies and exceptions. The waves of the sea do not more speedily seek a level from their loftiest tossing than the varieties of condition tend to equalize themselves. There is always some leveling circumstance that puts down the overbearing, the strong, the rich, the fortunate, substantially on the same ground with all others. . . .

The farmer imagines power and place are fine things. But the President has paid dear for his White House. It has commonly cost him all his peace, and the best of his manly attributes. To preserve for a short time so conspicuous an appearance before the world, he is content to eat dust before the real masters who stand erect behind the throne. Or do men desire the more substantial and permanent grandeur of genius? Neither has this an immunity. He who by force of will or of thought is great and overlooks [1] thousands has the responsibility of overlooking. With every influx of light comes new danger. Has he light? He must bear witness to the light, and always outrun that sympathy which gives him such keen satisfaction, by his fidelity to new revelations of the incessant soul.

FROM SELF–RELIANCE

THERE is a time in every man's education when he arrives at the conviction that envy is ignorance; that imitation is suicide; that he must take himself for better, for worse, as his portion; that though the wide universe is full of good, no kernel of nourishing corn can come to him but through his toil bestowed on that plot of ground which is given him to till. The power which resides in him is new in nature, and none but he knows what he can do, nor does he know until he has tried. . . .

Society everywhere is in conspiracy against the manhood of every one of its members. Society is a joint stock company, in which the members agree, for the better securing of his bread to each shareholder, to surrender the liberty and culture of the eater. The virtue in most request is conformity. Self-reliance is its aversion. It loves not realities and creators but names and customs.

Whoso would be a man must be a nonconformist. He who would gather

[1] overlooks: here, supervises.

immortal palms must not be hindered by the name of goodness, but must explore if it be goodness. Nothing is at last sacred but the integrity of your own mind. . . .

A foolish consistency is the hobgoblin of little minds, adored by little statesmen and philosophers and divines. With consistency a great soul has simply nothing to do. He may as well concern himself with his shadow on the wall. Speak what you think now in hard words, and tomorrow speak what tomorrow thinks in hard words again, though it contradict everything you said today. "Ah, so you shall be sure to be misunderstood." Is it so bad, then, to be misunderstood? Pythagoras was misunderstood, and Socrates, and Jesus, and Luther, and Copernicus,[1] and Galileo, and Newton, and every pure and wise spirit that ever took flesh. To be great is to be misunderstood. . . .

The civilized man has built a coach, but has lost the use of his feet. He is supported on crutches, but lacks so much support of muscle. He has got a fine Geneva watch, but he has lost the skill to tell the hour by the sun. A Greenwich nautical almanac he has, and so, being sure of the information when he wants it, the man in the street does not know a star in the sky. The solstice [2] he does not observe; the equinox [3] he knows as little; and the whole bright calendar of the year is without a dial in his mind. His notebooks impair his memory; his libraries overload his wit; the insurance office increases the number of accidents; and it may be a question whether machinery does not encumber; whether we have not lost by refinement some energy, by a Chris-

tianity entrenched in establishments and forms some vigor of wild virtue. For every Stoic was a Stoic; but in Christendom, where is the Christian?

from CHARACTER

THERE is this eternal advantage to morals, that, in the question between truth and goodness, the moral cause of the world lies behind all else in the mind. It was for good, it is to good, that all works. Surely it is not to prove or show the truth of things — that sounds a little cold and scholastic — no, it is for benefit that all subsists. As we say in our modern politics, catching at last the language of morals, that the object of the State is the greatest good for the greatest number — so, the reason we must give for the existence of the world is that it is for the benefit of all being.

Morals implies freedom and will. The will constitutes the man. He has his life in Nature, like a beast: but choice is born in him; here is he that chooses; here is the Declaration of Independence, the July Fourth, of zoology and astronomy. He chooses — as the rest of the creation does not. But will, pure and perceiving, is not willfulness. When a man, through stubbornness, insists to do this or that, something absurd or whimsical, only because he will, he is weak, he blows with his lips against the tempest, he dams the incoming ocean with his cane. It were an unspeakable calamity if anyone should think he had the right to impose a private will on others. That is the part of a striker, an assassin. All violence, all that is dreary and repels, is not power but the absence of power.

Morals is the direction of the will on universal ends. He is immoral who is acting to any private end. He is moral — we say it with Marcus Aurelius [4] and

---

[1] **Copernicus** (kṓ·pûr′nĭ·kŭs): (1473–1543) a Prussian-Polish astronomer.

[2] **solstice** (sŏl′stĭs): the time when the sun is farthest from the equator and closest to either the north or south pole.

[3] **equinox** (ē′kwĭ·nŏks): the time when the equator crosses the sun's center, and day and night are of equal length.

[4] **Marcus Aurelius** (ô·rē′lĭ·ŭs): a Roman emperor and philosopher (121–180).

with Kant [1]— whose aim or motive may become a universal rule, binding on all intelligent beings; and with Vauvenargues,[2] "the mercenary sacrifice of the public good to a private interest is the eternal stamp of vice."

All the virtues are special directions of this motive; justice is the application of this good of the whole to the affairs of each one; courage is contempt of danger in the determination to see this good of the whole enacted; love is delight in the preference of that benefit redounding to another over the securing of our own share; humility is a sentiment of our insignificance when the benefit of the universe is considered.

FROM Emerson's Journals

RELATING WHAT YOU READ. Like Franklin, Emerson has contributed many wise sayings that have passed into our common stock of quotations. But the essential difference between the two men can be seen when one rereads the sayings of Poor Richard (page 463) and then turns immediately to the following.

Greatness is a property for which no man gets credit too soon; it must be possessed long before it is acknowledged. — 1822

I see no reason why I should bow my head to man, or cringe in my demeanor. — 1824

Faith is a telescope. — 1824

I confess I am a little cynical on some topics, and when a whole nation is roaring Patriotism at the top of its voice, I am fain to explore the cleanness of its hands and purity of its heart. I have generally found the gravest and most useful citizens are not the easiest provoked to swell the noise, though they may be punctual at the polls. — 1824

I am always made uneasy when the conversation turns in my presence upon popular ignorance and the duty of adapting our public harangues and writings to the mind of the people. 'Tis all pedantry [3] and ignorance. The people know as much and reason as well as we do. None so quick as they to discern brilliant genius or solid parts. And I observe that all those who use this cant most are such as do not rise above mediocrity of understanding. — 1828

But the only evil I find in idleness is unhappiness. — 1828

The effect of a fanciful word misplaced is like that of a horn of exquisite polish growing on a human head. — 1831

Don't trust children with edge tools. Don't trust man, great God, with more power than he has, until he has learned to use that little better. What a hell should we make of the world if we could do what we would! Put a button on the foil till the young fencers have learned not to put each other's eyes out. — 1832

The maker of a sentence, like the other artist, launches out into the infinite and builds a road into Chaos and old Night, and is followed by those who hear him with something of wild, creative delight. — 1834

Poetry must be as new as foam, and as old as the rock. — 1844

Life consists in what a man is thinking of all day. — 1847

[1] **Kant** (kănt): Immanuel Kant (1724–1804), a German philosopher.
[2] **Vauvenargues** (vōv·närg'): the Marquis de Vauvenargues (1715–1747), a French moralist.
[3] **pedantry** (pĕd'ănt·rĭ): the pretentious display of knowledge.

A painting of the Railroad Jubilee on Boston Common, held in 1851. ▶

GIFTS

1. Why does Emerson think that flowers and fruits are always fit presents? Does he approve of giving necessities? jewelry? handkerchiefs? Under what circumstances do you think he would approve or disapprove of the following gifts: a check, winter underwear, a gold bracelet, a photograph, embroidered table linen, a corsage, a book of poetry, a necktie?

2. What difficulties does he see in receiving gifts? In the light of this essay, what criticisms can you make of some of our common practices in Christmas giving? Do you disagree with Emerson on any point? If so, how?

3. What do you think Emerson means when he says, "We do not quite forgive a giver"?

4. What does he say about love? How does he relate this subject to the notion of gifts?

5. Would Emerson think that Americans should expect gratitude from nations to whom America has given great amounts of money?

NATURE

1. Summarize in one sentence the meaning of this selection.

2. What, if any, "transcendental" elements are present?

MANNERS

1. Name two or three persons prominent in public life today who could be called gentlemen according to Emerson's definition.

2. Does Emerson demand of his "gentleman" any qualities of which you would disapprove? On what grounds would you disapprove?

FRIENDSHIP

1. What difference is there between a friend as Emerson defines one and a friend in the common use of the word?

2. To what extent do your friendships stand the test of Emerson's definition?

COMPENSATION

1. Would you agree with Emerson that there are *always* compensations in life? Give illustrations to prove your point.

2. See if you cannot, as you think about Emerson's essay, discern a weakness in his concept.

SELF-RELIANCE

1. By what kind of people is Emerson's message of self-reliance most needed? Do you feel that it is needed in your high school? Is it needed generally in the country today? Support your points by examples.

2. From what you know of Emerson, do you think he would approve of lawbreaking? Why or why not?

3. To Emerson, what are the enemies of self-reliance? Just what part do you think intuition plays in achieving self-reliance?

CHARACTER

1. According to Emerson, what is the difference between morality and immorality?

2. How does Emerson distinguish between "will" and "willfulness"?

3. Do you agree with Emerson's definitions of justice, courage, love, and humility as given in the last paragraph of the selection? Why? Why not?

4. Compare the selection from "Character" with that from "Self-Reliance." Do Emerson's statements in "Character" conflict with his attitudes toward self-reliance? If so, do you feel that the conflict can be explained?

SPECIAL REPORT

Look up the lives of the great men mentioned in the selection from "Self-Reliance" to find out in what ways they were misunderstood.

YOUR OWN WRITING

In an expository paragraph of your own, support or argue against any one of the definitions Emerson gives in the last paragraph of the selection from "Character."

American Art and Artists

Reproduced on page 581 is a detail from "The Railroad Jubilee on Boston Common, 1851." This oil painting of Emerson's Boston was done by the nineteenth-century American artist William Sharp.

HENRY DAVID THOREAU

1817–1862

FROM *Walden*

Emerson's truest disciple, the man who put into practice many of Emerson's theories, was Henry David Thoreau. Thoreau was born in Concord in 1817. He was educated at Harvard, graduating in 1837, the year of Emerson's famous address, "The American Scholar." Coming under Emerson's influence (Thoreau had once walked eighteen miles to Boston to hear him lecture), Thoreau lived for more than a year in Emerson's house, doing chores and serving as a general handyman, and most important of all, absorbing many of the older man's ideas.

In 1845 Thoreau began a two-year residence at Walden Pond. "I went to the woods," he wrote, "because I wished to live deliberately, to front only the essential facts of life . . ." He lived at Walden in a hut built by his own hands. He shied away from all kinds of social organization, though he had no intention of living the life of a hermit. He received some visitors and now and then returned to Concord to see his friends.

In *Walden* (1854), the superb book that came out of this two-year experiment, Thoreau explained many of the beliefs that led him to try this kind of life. He thought it better for a man to work one day a week and rest six, rather than the other way

around — not from laziness but because he felt that man's simple necessities could be met on that ratio and the rest of the time could be devoted to thought. Thoreau maintained that this was a private purpose, not a program for society. For Thoreau, as for Emerson, self-reliance and independence of mind ranked above all:

> I would not have anyone adopt my mode of living, each should find out his own way, not his neighbor's or his parents'.

In the same spirit he wrote:

> If a man does not keep pace with his companions, perhaps it is because he hears a different drummer. Let him step to the music which he hears, however measured or far away.

Thoreau's sensitive harmony with all of nature was extraordinary. Birds would perch on him, all animals trusted him, and it is even said that the fish in Walden Pond would let themselves be handled by him. In *Walden,* he remarks:

> I frequently tramped eight or ten miles through the deepest snow to keep an appointment with a beech tree or a yellow birch, or an old acquaintance among the pines.

In 1847, Thoreau left Walden Pond, not because the experiment was a failure, but because it was complete. Thoreau had fresher experiences to discover:

I left the woods for as good a reason as I went there. Perhaps it seemed to me that I had several more lives to live and could not spare any more time for that one.

In 1846, while still at Walden Pond, Thoreau was arrested for failure to pay a trifling sum in taxes. He spent a night in Concord jail. He had refused the payment deliberately because he disapproved of slavery and of the government's conduct of the Mexican War. From this experience came his famous essay, "Civil Disobedience" (1849), which states Thoreau's belief that no man should violate his conscience at the command of a government. When Emerson saw him in prison and asked, "Henry, what are you doing in there?" Thoreau replied sternly, "What are you doing *out there?*"

Henry David Thoreau was only forty-five when he died. He had spent all his life in or near Concord, with only a few short trips to Maine or Cape Cod, and one longer journey to Canada. Yet he had no sense of being confined by the narrow geographical limits of his life. "I have traveled a good deal," he wrote, "in Concord."

FROM Walden

The world we live in pulls hard for *things*. Every newspaper or magazine we open, every lull on the radio and on television, tempts us with new gadgets and luxuries. Man's struggle to get possession of material comforts to make life easier and pleasanter is as old as the human race. The struggle to keep *things* from swamping him is almost as old. Great writers down through the ages have warned us that the surest way to have an empty life is to fill it with *things*. When you are young and have many wants, this warning is not so impressive. It is only when the edge is worn off the delight of possession and the possessions themselves take up more and more of your time and attention that you begin to see the charms of the simple life.

Walden is one of the greatest accounts in literature of an experiment with the simple life. It was only an experiment. Thoreau was no hermit. He learned what he wanted to know — What is real living? — and went back to his usual village life, wiser and happier.

The following selection from the chapter "Where I Lived and What I Lived For" presents in short compass the core of Thoreau's reflection about life, things, time, and hurry. You will have to think through some of Thoreau's statements, but if his thinking becomes a part of you, you may achieve a happy compromise and never be hedged in by material possessions. Or, fifteen or twenty years from now, if you find *things* closing in on you, some reflection of Thoreau's can bring balance and sanity back into your life.

I WENT to the woods because I wished to live deliberately, to front only the essential facts of life, and see if I could not learn what it had to teach, and not, when I came to die, discover that I had not lived. I did not wish to live what was not life, living is so dear; nor did I wish to practice resignation, unless it was quite necessary.

I wanted to live deep and suck out all the marrow of life, to live so sturdily and Spartanlike as to put to rout all that was not life, to cut a broad swath and shave close, to drive life into a corner, and reduce it to its lowest terms, and, if it proved to be mean, why then to get the whole and genuine meanness of it, and publish its meanness to the world; or if it were sublime, to know it by experience, and be able to give a true account of it in my next excursion. For most men, it appears to me, are in a strange uncertainty about it, whether it is of the devil or of God, and have *somewhat hastily* concluded that it is the chief end of man here to "glorify God [1] and enjoy Him forever."

Still we live meanly, like ants; though the fable tells us that we were long ago changed into men; like pygmies we fight with cranes; it is error upon error, and clout upon clout, and our best virtue has for its occasion a superfluous and evitable [2] wretchedness.

Our life is frittered away by detail. An honest man has hardly need to count more than his ten fingers, or in extreme cases he may add his ten toes, and lump the rest. Simplicity, simplicity, simplicity! I say, let your affairs be as two or three, and not a hundred or a thousand; instead of a million count half a dozen, and keep your accounts on your thumbnail.

In the midst of this chopping sea of civilized life, such are the clouds and storms and quicksands and thousand-and-one items to be allowed for, that a man has to live, if he would not founder and go to the bottom and not make his port at all, by dead reckoning, and he must be a great calculator indeed who succeeds. Simplify, simplify. Instead of three meals a day, if it be necessary, eat but one; instead of a hundred dishes, five; and reduce other things in proportion.

Our life is like a German Confederacy,[3] made up of petty states, with its

[1] "glorify God, etc.": the answer to the first question in the Westminster Shorter Catechism (Presbyterian).

[2] evitable: avoidable.

[3] German Confederacy: Germany from 1815–1866 was a loose union of 38 independent states with no king, no capital, and no common government.

boundary forever fluctuating, so that even a German cannot tell you how it is bounded at any moment. The nation itself, with all its so-called internal improvements, which, by the way, are all external and superficial, is just such an unwieldy and overgrown establishment, cluttered with furniture and tripped up by its own traps, ruined by luxury and heedless expense, by want of calculation and a worthy aim, as the million households in the land; and the only cure for it, as for them, is in a rigid economy, a stern and more than Spartan simplicity of life and elevation of purpose. It lives too fast. . . .

Why should we live with such hurry and waste of life? We are determined to be starved before we are hungry. Men say that a stitch in time saves nine, and so they take a thousand stitches today to save nine tomorrow. . . .

Hardly a man takes a half-hour's nap after dinner, but when he wakes he holds up his head and asks, "What's the news?" as if the rest of mankind had stood his sentinels. Some give directions to be waked every half-hour, doubtless for no other purpose; and then, to pay for it, they tell what they have dreamed. After a night's sleep the news is as indispensable as the breakfast. "Pray tell me anything new that has happened to a man anywhere on this globe"; and he reads it over his coffee and rolls, that a man has had his eyes gouged out this morning on the Wachito River; never dreaming the while that he lives in the dark, unfathomed mammoth cave of this world, and has but the rudiment of an eye himself.

For my part, I could easily do without the post office. I think that there are very few important communications made through it. To speak critically, I never received more than one or two letters in my life — I wrote this some years ago — that were worth the postage. The penny-post is, commonly, an institution through which you seriously offer a man that penny for his thoughts which is so often safely offered in jest. And I am sure that I never read any memorable news in a newspaper. If we read of one man robbed, or murdered, or killed by accident, or one house burned, or one vessel wrecked, or one steamboat blown up, or one cow run over on the Western Railroad, or one mad dog killed, or one lot of grass-hoppers in the winter — we never need read of another. One is enough. If you are acquainted with the principle, what do you care for a myriad instances and applications?

To a philosopher all *news*, as it is called, is gossip, and they who edit and read it are old women over their tea. Yet not a few are greedy after this gossip. There was such a rush, as I hear, the other day at one of the offices to learn the foreign news by the last arrival, that several large squares of plate glass belonging to the establishment were broken by the pressure — news which I seriously think a ready wit might write a twelvemonth, or twelve years, beforehand with sufficient accuracy. . . .

What news! how much more important to know what that is which was never old! Kieou-he-yu (great dignitary of the state of Wei) sent a man to Khoung-tseu to know his news. Khoung-tseu caused the messenger to be seated near him, and questioned him in these terms: "What is your master doing?" The messenger answered with respect: "My master desires to diminish the number of his faults, but he cannot come to the end of them." The messenger being gone, the philosopher remarked: "What a worthy messenger! What a worthy messenger!" . . .

Shams and delusions are esteemed for soundest truths, while reality is fabulous. If men would steadily observe realities only, and not allow themselves to be deluded, life, to compare it with such things as we know, would be like a fairy tale and the Arabian Nights' En-

tertainments. If we respected only what is inevitable and has a right to be, music and poetry would resound along the streets. When we are unhurried and wise, we perceive that only great and worthy things have any permanent and absolute existence, that petty fears and petty pleasures are but the shadow of the reality. This is always exhilarating and sublime. By closing the eyes and slumbering, and consenting to be deceived by shows, men establish and confirm their daily life of routine and habit everywhere, which still is built on purely illusory foundations. Children, who play life, discern its true law and relations more clearly than men, who fail to live it worthily, but who think that they are wiser by experience, that is, by failure. . . .

Let us spend one day as deliberately as nature, and not be thrown off the track by every nutshell and mosquito's wing that falls on the rails. Let us rise early and fast, or break fast, gently and without perturbation; let company come and let company go, let the bells ring and the children cry — determined to make a day of it. Why should we knock under and go with the stream? Let us not be upset and overwhelmed in that terrible rapid and whirlpool called a dinner, situated in the meridian shallows. Weather this danger and you are safe, for the rest of the way is downhill. With unrelaxed nerves, with morning vigor, sail by it, looking another way, tied to the mast like Ulysses.[1] If the engine whistles, let it whistle till it is hoarse for its pain. If the bell rings, why should we run? We will consider what kind of music they are like. Let us settle ourselves, and work and wedge our feet downward through the mud and slush of opinion, and prejudice, and tradition, and delusion, and ap-

[1] **tied to the mast like Ulysses:** According to Homer's *Odyssey*, Ulysses had his men lash him to a mast so that he could not succumb to the sirens' song and be shipwrecked on the rocks.

pearance, that alluvion [1] which covers the globe, through Paris and London, through New York and Boston and Concord, through Church and State, through poetry and philosophy and religion, till we come to a hard bottom and rocks in place, which we can call *reality,* and say, "This is, and no mistake"; and then begin, having a *point d'appui,* [2] below freshet and frost and fire, a place where you might found a wall or a state, or set a lamppost safely, or perhaps a gauge, not a Nilometer, but a Realometer, that future ages might know how deep a freshet of shams and appearances had gathered from time to time. If you stand right fronting and face to face to a fact, you will see the sun glimmer on both its surfaces, as if it were a cimeter, [3] and feel its sweet edge dividing you through the heart and marrow, and so you will happily conclude your mortal career. Be it life or death, we crave only reality. If we are really dying, let us hear the rattle in our throats and feel cold in the extremities; if we are alive, let us go about our business.

Time is but the stream I go a-fishing in. I drink at it; but while I drink I see the sandy bottom and detect how shallow it is. Its thin current slides away, but eternity remains. I would drink deeper; fish in the sky, whose bottom is pebbly with stars. I cannot count one. I know not the first letter of the alphabet. I have always been regretting that I was not as wise as the day I was born. The intellect is a cleaver; it discerns and rifts [4] its way into the secret of things. I do not wish to be any more busy with my hands than is necessary. My head is hands and feet. I feel all my best faculties concentrated in it. My

instinct tells me that my head is an organ for burrowing, as some creatures use their snout and forepaws, and with it I would mine and burrow my way through these hills. I think that the richest vein is somewhere hereabouts; so by the divining rod [5] and thin rising vapors I judge; and here I will begin to mine.

[5] **divining rod:** a forked stick that is supposed to indicate the presence of water or metal underground.

FOR DISCUSSION

1. Why did Thoreau go to the woods to live? Answer in your own words.

2. What does Thoreau mean by the statement that "a man has to live . . . by dead reckoning"? Why, therefore, must man simplify his life?

3. What criticisms does he make of our national life? With which of these criticisms do you agree or disagree? What is the solution to some of these shortcomings? In the last analysis, who, according to Thoreau, are to blame for a nation's shortcomings?

4. What are some of Thoreau's objections to the way most people live? What reason does he usually give for his objection? Can you imagine reaching a stage in life when you would agree with Thoreau on his points? For example, think of your own favorite ways of passing time away. Which ones involve growth in understanding and enjoyment of life?

5. How does Thoreau evaluate the daily news? Formulate some opinion as to Thoreau's regard for the human being.

6. Come to grips with Thoreau's notion of facing reality, and be able to state your understanding in your own words. What does he mean by a "Realometer"?

7. What self-portrait do you feel Thoreau draws of himself within the compass of this selection?

[1] **alluvion:** soil, sand, or similar material deposited by running water.

[2] *point d'appui* (pwăn' dá'pwē'): a French phrase meaning "a point of support."

[3] **cimeter** (sĭm'ĭ-tĕr): a saber with a curved blade; usually spelled scimitar.

[4] **rifts:** here, cuts.

YOUR OWN WRITING

Keep a journal of your own, making it a record of your observations and thoughts from day to day, rather than a mere calendar of events.

Four New England Poets

The surge of literary activity in New England brought forth some excellent poetry. Three neighbors on the elm-shaded, quiet streets of Cambridge around Harvard Square were sometimes called the Cambridge poets. They were Henry Wadsworth Longfellow, James Russell Lowell, and Oliver Wendell Holmes. Not far away, in Haverhill, was the birthplace and family homestead of the Quaker poet John Greenleaf Whittier.

The Cambridge poets were a lively, versatile group. Highly productive in the art of verse, they also engaged in many other activities. Longfellow was a distinguished professor of modern languages at Harvard. Lowell later succeeded him in that position. Holmes, who was a physician as well as a man of letters, taught anatomy in the Harvard medical school. The fame of the Cambridge poets and Whittier soon spread out across the world — the world, as Holmes claimed, that had Boston as its hub.

HENRY WADSWORTH LONGFELLOW

This Bowdoin classmate of Hawthorne loomed largest of all as a poet among the New England writers. Longfellow traveled widely in Europe. He knew the languages and literature of France, Spain, Italy, Germany, and some of the Scandinavian lands. He studied the *Kalevala*, the ancient epic of Finland, and used its rhythmic patterns in his famous *Hiawatha*.

Longfellow came to Harvard in 1836 as professor of French and Spanish. A youthful, dashing, cloaked figure, he was altogether the romantic image of the poet. (The flowing beard that is so often associated with him came much later. It was grown to cover the scar tissue from severe burns suffered when he tried to save his wife from a fire that took her life.)

His students at Harvard were spellbound by his vast store of tales and legends from foreign lands. Longfellow taught with distinction for eighteen years, but he left Harvard in 1854, for he said that the responsibilities of teaching were "a great hand laid on all the strings of my lyre, stopping their vibration."

Longfellow's work became enormously popular, both at home and abroad. His knowledge of the literatures of other lands spurred his ambition to help launch a national literature in America. *The Spanish Student* (1843) and many of his *Tales of a Wayside Inn* (1886) are set against European backgrounds, but the most characteristic of his long narrative poems are those he drew from the American scene. Paul Revere's ride was immortalized in the first poem of the *Wayside Inn* series. *The Courtship of Miles Standish* (1858) was a gentle recollection of the early Puritans. *Evangeline* (1847) won many hearts with its tale of lovers separated when they were driven out of Acadia (Nova Scotia) during the French and Indian War. Perhaps best of all was *Hiawatha* (1855), woven from legends of the Great Lakes Indians.

Longfellow's study in Cambridge.

Whether they were Puritans or Indians or Revolutionary heroes, Longfellow placed his characters squarely in the stream of American tradition. This quality, plus the romantic nature of his stories, appealed strongly to the readers of his day. His optimistic vision of life also helped earn him his enormous popularity.

His popularity encountered a few dissenting voices. Poe, in particular, attacked him. He felt that Longfellow had borrowed too much from European literature, and he also considered Longfellow overpraised. Lowell, in his *Fable for Critics*, chided Poe:

> You mustn't fling mudballs at Longfellow so,
> Does it make a man worse that his character's such
> As to make his friends love him (as you think) too much?

Yet Poe was quite generous with his praise of what he considered Longfellow's best work, especially his poems of the sea.

Basically, Longfellow's voice was a gentle and hopeful one. He did not enter much into the great, rising conflicts of his day, though he did write a few anti-slavery poems. They are effective, but are not characteristic of his best work.

Longfellow's reputation as a poet suffered a great decline in this century.

Poetry, and tastes in poetry, had become more complex and sophisticated. The concluding "moral tag" that summed up the lesson of a poem, was a feature of much of Longfellow's poetry. It was a fashion of his times, but many later readers found the direct moralizing difficult to accept. Nevertheless, the first critical reaction against Longfellow's poetry was often unfair. In the past few years, many critics have been willing to take a long second look at Longfellow's work. They are reaching a balance between the exaggerated praise of Longfellow's day and the unfair attacks of the 1920's and 1930's. In the words of a present-day critic, passages of Longfellow's poetry touch upon "tragedy and greatness" and "have a claim to be considered the equal of the best in nineteenth-century poetry."

JAMES RUSSELL LOWELL

Lowell, who succeeded Longfellow as professor of modern languages at Harvard, was a man of many interests — perhaps too many. He was never able to concentrate on a single activity, but spread his talents over a variety of fields. A poet of considerable technical skill, he was far less dedicated to his art than Longfellow was. By the time Lowell turned to teaching, he was ready to let the "strings of his lyre" be silenced.

As a young man he studied law, but decided it was not for him. Maria White, whom he married, drew him into the antislavery movement. The first important phase of his long career in journalism was as editor of the *National Antislavery Standard*. It was during this early period in his life — the years from 1845 to 1850 — that Lowell wrote the main body of his poetry.

After Poe, Lowell was our second important literary critic. His most pungent criticism was not in essays, but in the gay, modern-sounding jingles of his poem, *A Fable for Critics* (1848). You will read some typical passages from the poem on page 602. There, eight of the writers we have met are discussed, including Lowell himself. The self-criticism was shrewd and accurate, and also partly a tactic of concealment, for the *Fable* was published anonymously. Lowell acknowledged it only after several other persons boasted that it was theirs.

Poe (according to the *Fable*, "Three fifths of him genius and two fifths sheer fudge") struck back in a sharp review that ended by saying that Lowell had "lowered himself at least fifty per cent in the literary public opinion." Yet these drastically dissimilar men greatly advanced the art of criticism in America. Lowell, only a year earlier than the *Fable*, had written a generous biographical-critical article on Poe for *Graham's Magazine*. Despite their verbal battles there was a great deal of respect between the two poet-critics.

Unlike Longfellow, Lowell was very much a topical poet, that is, he wrote much about events and people of his time. Among his best-known works are *The Biglow Papers* (1848 and 1867). In the first series of these, Lowell created the figure of Hosea Biglow, a Yankee farmer (a direct descendent of "Jonathan" in Tyler's *The Contrast*, page 492). Through the salty observations of Hosea, Lowell expressed sharp criticism of United States policy in the Mexican War. The second series of the papers supported the Northern side in the War Between the States.

The Biglow Papers are deliberate doggerel verse, and most of their interest has declined, as often happens with topical writing that is unsupported by some enduring additional quality. Yet some of Hosea Biglow's comments on life remain lively as folklore and local color. A good example is "The Courtin'."

Among his serious poems, some of Lowell's best lines are seen in The Vision of Sir Launfal and "The First Snowfall."

After the great struggles over slavery and union were ended, Lowell settled into the conservative outlook that characterized the later years of his life. Toward the end of his career, he served his country ably as a diplomat. Like Irving before him, Lowell was appointed Ambassador to Spain.

OLIVER WENDELL HOLMES

There's Holmes, who is matchless among you for wit,
A Leyden jar always full-charged, from which flit
The electrical tingles of hit after hit . . .
His are just the fine hands, too, to weave you a lyric
Full of fancy, fun, feeling, or spiced with satiric . . .

Thus the little Cambridge doctor was sketched in Lowell's Fable. Holmes summed himself up when a friend remarked, "Holmes, you are intellectually the most alive man I ever knew." Holmes answered joyously, "I am, I am! From the crown of my head to the sole of my foot, I'm alive, I'm alive!"

It would be hard to find someone capable of carrying on more activities at one time. After graduation from Harvard, Holmes studied medicine in Edinburgh and Paris, returning to practice in Cambridge and Boston. He was successful in his career as a doctor. He wrote several important medical papers, and became professor of anatomy at Harvard and dean of the medical school.

In the midst of so demanding a profession, Holmes found time to be a steadily productive writer and one of the most accomplished conversationalists in a transcendently talkative town. "Old Ironsides," written in impulsive indignation in his youth to save the honored frigate Constitution from being scrapped, made him abruptly famous. His reputation flourished with The Autocrat of the Breakfast-Table (1858) which, in delightful character sketches and anecdotes, detailed his observations as a dweller in a boardinghouse. All America seemed to find itself reflected in his pages. The book was enormously popular, and Holmes followed it with two more breakfast-table collections, The Poet and The Professor.

The Autocrat, apart from its table talk, included several of his poems, among them two that represent the opposite poles of his poetic talents. "The Deacon's Masterpiece; or The Wonderful 'One-Hoss Shay' " is an example of his satirical humorous verse. The poem is about the decline of Puritanism; the idea is embodied in the image of a carriage that is built carefully to last forever, each part of which disintegrates simultaneously at the end of a hundred years. In contrast,

"The Chambered Nautilus," a serious poem, is the most perfectly fashioned thing Holmes ever wrote. Read it for its musical lines and its fine development of a philosophical idea.

The little physician also wrote two biographies and several novels. Probably the best of his novels was *Elsie Venner* (1861). Holmes was active in Boston and Cambridge life almost to the end of the nineteenth century. His son, Oliver Wendell, Jr., as tall and reserved as his father was short and talkative, had a great career as a judge, concluding his career as justice of the Supreme Court.

JOHN GREENLEAF WHITTIER

Whittier was not a member of the Cambridge circle, though he knew the other three poets quite well. Born in Haverhill, Massachusetts, in the Merrimac Valley that Thoreau also loved, Whittier worked for some years in Boston as a journalist. However, he preferred the life of a small town, and he eventually returned to his birthplace. Unlike the writers of the Harvard group, he was largely self-educated, chiefly through the Bible and other religious reading, and especially, as Benjamin Franklin could testify, through the constant education that must accompany work in journalism.

A Quaker, earnest in spirit, Whittier detested slavery, and much of his poetry, particularly his early work, was concerned with the subject. His Quaker love of peace had no quality of timidity in it. He flamed with the intensity of his convictions, and both as a writer and a speaker his was a strong voice in the Abolition movement. He bravely faced angry, heckling mobs of slavery sympathizers. The office of the *Pennsylvania Freeman,* which he published for two years, was burned, but Whittier continued his personal crusade against slavery. Whittier himself felt that he had sacrificed literature to reform, but much of his antislavery poetry was of excellent quality. Nor did his Abolitionist activities interfere with his second great interest — the life of rural New England.

In this second phase of his poetic career, Whittier wrote of simple, homely subjects — the beauty and peace of farm life, and the old traditions and legends of New England. Whittier knew the old traditions well, for his roots in New England went back to 1640. Like Longfellow, he often drew upon the old tales in his poetry, as in "Skipper Ireson's Ride," a ballad about a sea captain who was attacked by the angry women of Marblehead for abandoning his ship. "Barbara Frietchie" is one of the best-known ballads and legends about the War Between the States. "Maud Muller" and "The Barefoot Boy" were other favorites of his wide audience, but the best loved of all his works is the long "Winter Idyll" *Snow-Bound* (1866). The poem is a memorable picture of New England farm life, drawn from Whittier's recollections of his own youth.

The late years of Whittier's life were peaceful compared to the days of Abolitionist struggles. His chief problem had become his remarkable popularity, which was so great that he sometimes complained of being besieged by his many admirers at his home in Essex County, Massachusetts.

HENRY
WADSWORTH
LONGFELLOW
1807–1882

In the summer of 1843, while on his wedding journey, Longfellow visited the United States Arsenal in Springfield, Massachusetts. Upon seeing the shining guns stacked from floor to ceiling, Mrs. Longfellow remarked, "How like an organ!" and she urged her husband to write a poem on peace. Written some months after the visit to the arsenal, the following poem bears a timely message for the modern world. It is an impressive plea for peace.

The Arsenal at Springfield

This is the Arsenal. From the floor to ceiling,
   Like a huge organ, rise the burnished arms;
But from their silent pipes no anthem pealing
   Startles the villages with strange alarms.

Ah! what a sound will rise, how wild and dreary,   5
   When the death angel touches those swift keys!
What loud lament and dismal Miserere°
   Will mingle with their awful symphonies!

I hear even now the infinite fierce chorus,
   The cries of agony, the endless groan,   10
Which, through the ages that have gone before us,
   In long reverberations reach our own.

7. **Miserere** (mĭz′ĕ·rē′rè): the first word in the Latin version of the psalm beginning "Have mercy upon me, O Lord!"

On helm and harness rings the Saxon hammer,
    Through Cimbric ° forest roars the Norseman's song,
And loud, amid the universal clamor,   15
    O'er distant deserts sounds the Tatar ° gong.

I hear the Florentine,° who from his palace
    Wheels out his battle bell with dreadful din,
And Aztec ° priests upon their teocallis °
    Beat the wild war drums made of serpent's skin;   20

The tumult of each sacked and burning village;
    The shout that every prayer for mercy drowns;
The soldiers' revels in the midst of pillage;
    The wail of famine in beleaguered ° towns;

The bursting shell, the gateway wrenched asunder,   25
    The rattling musketry, the clashing blade;
And ever and anon, in tones of thunder,
    The diapason ° of the cannonade.

Is it, O man, with such discordant noises,
    With such accursèd instruments as these,   30
Thou drownest Nature's sweet and kindly voices,
    And jarrest the celestial harmonies?

Were half the power, that fills the world with terror,
    Were half the wealth, bestowed on camps and courts,
Given to redeem the human mind from error,   35
    There were no need of arsenals nor forts:

The warrior's name would be a name abhorrèd!
    And every nation, that should lift again
Its hands against a brother, on its forehead
    Would wear forevermore the curse of Cain! °   40

Down the dark future, through long generations,
    The echoing sounds grow fainter and then cease;

---

14. **Cimbric** (sĭm'brĭk): referring to the Cimbri, a tribe of Norsemen destroyed by the Romans. 16. **Tatar** (tä'tēr): The Tatars (commonly spelled Tartar), a race of savage Orientals, swept over Asia and most of Europe in the thirteenth century. 17. **Florentine** (flŏr'ĕn·tēn): The soldiers of Florence, Italy, in medieval times actually wheeled a great bell out into the battlefield. 19. **Aztec**: a native race of Mexicans, found and later practically exterminated by the Spaniards. **teocallis** (tē'ō·kăl'ĭz): flat-topped pyramids of worship. 24. **beleaguered**: blockaded. 28. **diapason** (dī'á·pā'zŭn): in music, the entire range of tones of an instrument. 40. **Cain**: a son of Adam and Eve, who was cursed because he slew his brother Abel (Genesis 4).

And like a bell, with solemn, sweet vibrations,
  I hear once more the voice of Christ say, "Peace!"

Peace! and no longer from its brazen portals   45
  The blast of War's great organ shakes the skies!
But beautiful as songs of the immortals,
  The holy melodies of love arise.

The closing lines of "The Building of the Ship" have become part of the body of America's patriotic literature that should be familiar to all Americans. In a long poem the author describes the careful building of a great sailing vessel, which is to be named the *Union*, because on the day of its completion, the old master builder will give his daughter in marriage to a young craftsman. The conclusion of the poem, which is given here, addresses the country itself as the Ship of State.

In 1849, when the poem was published, the Union of States had already been threatened by dissension between the North and the South. There is still significance for our own generation in this solemn dedication to the Union.

The Ship of State

Thou, too, sail on, O Ship of State!
Sail on, O *Union*, strong and great!
Humanity with all its fears,
With all the hopes of future years,
Is hanging breathless on thy fate!   5
We know what Master laid thy keel,
What Workmen wrought thy ribs of steel,
Who made each mast, and sail, and rope,
What anvils rang, what hammers beat,
In what a forge, and what a heat   10
Were shaped the anchors of thy hope!
Fear not each sudden sound and shock,
'Tis of the wave and not the rock;
'Tis but the flapping of the sail,
And not a rent made by the gale!   15
In spite of rock and tempest's roar,
In spite of false lights on the shore,
Sail on, nor fear to breast the sea!
Our hearts, our hopes, are all with thee,
Our hearts, our hopes, our prayers, our tears,   20
Our faith triumphant o'er our fears,
Are all with thee — are all with thee!

HENRY WADSWORTH LONGFELLOW   595

Although Longfellow is best known and perhaps best loved for his simple poems in simple patterns, he was master of elaborate verse forms and of a stately manner befitting solemn subjects. The next poem, published in *Voices of the Night* four years after the death of the poet's first wife, displays both qualities. Emotional restraint, rhythm, and imagery combine to make "Hymn to the Night" a memorable poem.

Hymn to the Night

'Ασπασίη, τρίλλιστος*

I heard the trailing garments of the Night
    Sweep through her marble halls!
I saw her sable skirts all fringed with light
    From the celestial walls!

I felt her presence, by its spell of might,   5
    Stoop o'er me from above;
The calm, majestic presence of the Night,
    As of the one I love.

I heard the sounds of sorrow and delight,
    The manifold, soft chimes,   10
That fill the haunted chambers of the Night,
    Like some old poet's rhymes.

From the cool cisterns of the midnight air
    My spirit drank repose;
The fountain of perpetual peace flows there —   15
    From those deep cisterns flows.

O holy Night; from thee I learn to bear
    What man has borne before!
Thou layest thy finger on the lips of Care,
    And they complain no more.   20

Peace! Peace! Orestes-like° I breathe this prayer!
    Descend with broad-winged flight,
The welcome, the thrice-prayed for, the most fair,
    The best-beloved Night!

* 'Ασπασίη, τρίλλιστος (ăs′pá·zē′ă, trĭl′ĭs·tŏs): "Welcome, thrice prayed for . . ." *Iliad*, Book viii. 21. **Orestes-like:** Orestes (ŏ·rĕs′tēz) was a youth in Greek literature who prayed to Athena for peace from the pursuit of the Furies.

One of the elements that brings vividness to Longfellow's narrative of Evangeline's quest for her beloved Gabriel is the interspersing of brief descriptions of actual scenes that, interestingly enough, Longfellow had not always seen with his own eyes. The following passage depicts the West, at a time when that part of our country was romantically glamorized.

For the background of *Evangeline*, and for Longfellow's source for the story, see the excerpt from Hawthorne's *American Notebooks* on page 555.

The Western Land

FROM *Evangeline IV*

Far in the West there lies a desert land, where the mountains
Lift, through perpetual snows, their lofty and luminous summits.
Down from their jagged, deep ravines, where the gorge, like a gateway,
Opens a passage rude to the wheels of the emigrant's wagon,
Westward the Oregon flows and the Walloway and Owyhee.   5
Eastward, with devious course, among the Wind River Mountains,
Through the Sweetwater Valley precipitate leaps the Nebraska;
And to the south, from Fontaine-qui-bout and the Spanish Sierras,
Fretted with sands and rocks, and swept by the wind of the desert,
Numberless torrents, with ceaseless sound, descend to the ocean,   10
Like the great chords of a harp, in loud and solemn vibrations.
Spreading between these streams are the wondrous, beautiful prairies;
Billowy bays of grass ever rolling in shadow and sunshine,
Bright with luxuriant clusters of roses and purple amorphas.°
Over them wandered the buffalo herds, and the elk and the roebuck;   15
Over them wandered the wolves, and herds of riderless horses;
Fires that blast and blight, and winds that are weary with travel;
Over them wander the scattered tribes of Ishmael's children,
Staining the desert with blood; and above their terrible war-trails
Circles and sails aloft, on pinions majestic, the vulture,   20
Like the implacable soul of a chieftain slaughtered in battle,
By invisible stairs ascending and scaling the heavens.
Here and there rise smokes from the camps of these savage marauders;
Here and there rise groves from the margins of swift-running rivers;
And the grim, taciturn bear, the anchorite° monk of the desert,   25
Climbs down their dark ravines to dig for roots by the brookside,
And over all is the sky, the clear and crystalline heaven,
Like the protecting hand of God inverted above them.

14. amorphas (*à·môr′făz*): a small flowering shrub. 25. anchorite: one who lives in seclusion; a hermit.

HENRY WADSWORTH LONGFELLOW   597

Longfellow was the first of several American poets to excel in writing sonnets. The one that follows was part of the poet's introduction to his translation of the great Italian epic, Dante's *Divine Comedy*. He had undertaken this monumental task as a refuge from grief when his second wife was burned to death.

THE SONNET FORM. The sonnet form has fourteen lines; and in the Italian sonnet there is a distinct division of thought between the first eight lines and the last six. Watch for the division between the two parts of this sonnet, and notice that the picture in the first part is carried over as a figure of speech in the second.

Divina Commedia I

Oft have I seen at some cathedral door
A laborer, pausing in the dust and heat,
Lay down his burden, and with reverent feet
Enter, and cross himself, and on the floor
Kneel to repeat his paternoster° o'er;   5
Far off the noises of the world retreat;
The loud vociferations of the street
Become an undistinguishable roar.

So, as I enter here from day to day,
And leave my burden at this minster° gate   10
Kneeling in prayer, and not ashamed to pray,
The tumult of the time disconsolate,
To inarticulate murmurs dies away,
While the eternal ages watch and wait.

5. paternoster (pä′tĕr·nŏs′tĕr): the Lord's Prayer. 10. minster: church; here used figuratively for Dante's *Divine Comedy*.

From boyhood Longfellow loved the sea. In the next poem you will feel the long swing of the tides and hear the wash of waves. Part of the fascination of the sea is its mystery, and appropriately Longfellow weaves into the poem the shadowy outline of a story that leaves questions in your mind.

The Tide Rises, the Tide Falls

The tide rises, the tide falls,
The twilight darkens, the curlew° calls;
Along the sea sands damp and brown
The traveler hastens toward the town,
   And the tide rises, the tide falls.   5

2. curlew (kûr′lū): a large bird found in Europe and North America.

Darkness settles on roofs and walls,
But the sea, the sea in the darkness calls;
The little waves, with their soft white hands,
Efface the footprints in the sands,
    And the tide rises, the tide falls.   10

The morning breaks; the steeds in their stalls
Stamp and neigh as the hostler calls;
The day returns, but nevermore
Returns the traveler to the shore,
    And the tide rises, the tide falls.   15

FOR DISCUSSION

THE ARSENAL AT SPRINGFIELD

1. Show how an impression of sound or music is carried throughout the poem. In what two ways is the organ a fitting instrument with which to compare the arsenal?

2. What different ages and parts of the world are brought into the survey of war sounds? How does this review of other times and other places strengthen Longfellow's point? What great plea does he make for peace?

THE SHIP OF STATE

1. In "The Ship of State," explain what you think is meant by the Master and the Workmen.

2. Give some examples from American history of what the poet might have had in mind to represent the anvils, hammers, forge, and so on. What events just prior to 1849, when the poem was published, might have been referred to in "sudden sound and shock," "rock and tempest's roar," "false lights on the shore"?

3. The entire passage from "The Ship of State" is a fine example of *analogy*. Explain the meaning of this word by specific reference to the passage.

4. Compare the dedication at the end with that at the conclusion of Lincoln's Gettysburg Address (pages 231 and 666). The entire stanza deserves memorizing.

HYMN TO THE NIGHT

1. Point out words or lines in "Hymn to the Night" that refer to the poet's re-

cent bereavement; cite others that have a soothing effect upon the spirit.

2. What personification does Longfellow employ here? Comment on its effectiveness.

3. Examine the rhyme scheme of the poem. How many stanzas employ a rhyme on "night"?

THE WESTERN LAND

1. What notion of the West do you gain from this brief excerpt? Do you find inaccuracies in the reporting? In spite of any of these, do you feel the description remains convincing?

2. Is it necessary for an author to experience or see firsthand all the scenes he incorporates in his fictions?

DIVINA COMMEDIA I

1. Summarize the thought of "Divina Commedia I" in two sentences, one for the octave (first eight lines) and one for the sestet (last six lines). Point out two phrases in the sestet that hint at the sorrow in the poet's life.

2. Some of the characteristics of the sonnet form have been listed on page 598. Does Longfellow's sonnet reveal these characteristics? Why may the sonnet pattern be a greater challenge to a poet than the form of a long narrative poem?

THE TIDE RISES, THE TIDE FALLS

1. What picture of the sea is suggested by the rhythm of the opening lines and by the refrain of the poem?

2. Describe the mood of the poem. What narrative is suggested?

JAMES
RUSSELL
LOWELL

1819–1891

Lowell created Hosea Biglow, an illiterate but shrewd New England farmer, to voice his feelings on the Mexican War situation in 1848. The *Biglow Papers* have immortalized the Yankee dialect. From the first series, "The Courtin'" is a favorite.

The Courtin'

Zekle crep' up quite unbeknown,
  An' peeked in thru the winder,
An' there sot Huldy all alone,
  'Ith no one nigh to hender.

Agin' the chimbly crooknecks hung, 5
  An' in amongst 'em rusted
The ole queen's-arm° thet gran'ther
    Young
  Fetched back from Concord busted.

The wannut logs shot sparkles out
  Toward the pootiest, bless her! 10
An' leetle fires danced all about
  The chiny on the dresser.

The very room, coz she wuz in,
  Looked warm frum floor to ceilin',
An' she looked full ez rosy agin 15
  Ez th' apples she wuz peelin'.

She heerd a foot an' knowed it, tu,
  A-raspin' on the scraper —

7. ole queen's-arm: old musket.

All ways to once her feelin's flew
  Like sparks in burnt-up paper. 20

He kin' o' l'itered on the mat,
  Some doutfle o' the sekle;
His heart kep' goin' pitypat,
  But hern went pity Zekle.

An' yit she gin her cheer a jerk 25
  Ez though she wished him furder,
An' on her apples kep' to work,
  Parin' away like murder.

"You want to see my Pa, I s'pose?"
  "Wal, no; I come designin' — " 30
"To see my Ma? She's sprinklin' clo'es
  Agin tomorrer's i'nin'."

He stood a spell on one foot fust,
  Then stood a spell on t'other.
An' on which one he felt the wust 35
  He couldn't ha' told ye, nuther.

Sez he, "I'd better call agin";
  Sez she, "Think likely, *Mister*";

The last word pricked him like a pin,
  An' — wal, he up an' kist her.　　40

When Ma bimeby upon 'em slips,
  Huldy sot pale ez ashes,
All kind o' smily round the lips
  An' teary round the lashes.

Her blood riz quick, though, like the
  tide　　45
Down to the Bay o' Fundy.
An' all I know is they wuz cried°
  In meetin', come nex' Sunday.

47. they wuz cried: The announcement of
their marriage was read in church.

"The First Snowfall" begins as if it were merely a description of winter's first snow; but
as it progresses, it reveals the poet's sorrow for a personal loss.

The First Snowfall

The snow had begun in the gloaming,
  And busily all the night
Had been heaping field and highway
  With a silence deep and white.

Every pine and fir and hemlock　　5
  Wore ermine too dear for an earl,
And the poorest twig on the elm tree
  Was ridged inch deep with pearl.

From sheds new-roofed with Carrara°
  Came Chanticleer's muffled crow,　10
The stiff rails softened to swan's-down,
  And still fluttered down the snow.

I stood and watched by the window
  The noiseless work of the sky,
And the sudden flurries of snowbirds,
  Like brown leaves whirling by.　　16

I thought of a mound in sweet Auburn
  Where a little headstone stood;
How the flakes were folding it gently,
  As did robins the babes in the wood.

Up spoke our own little Mabel,　　21
  Saying, "Father, who makes it snow?"
And I told of the good All-Father
  Who cares for us here below.

Again I looked at the snowfall,　　25
  And thought of the leaden sky
That arched o'er our first great sorrow,

9. Carrara (kȧ·kär'ȧ): white marble from
the city of that name in Italy.

When that mound was heaped so
  high.

I remembered the gradual patience
  That fell from that cloud like snow,
Flake by flake, healing and hiding　31
  The scar that renewed our woe.

And again to the child I whispered,
  "The snow that husheth all,
Darling, the merciful Father　　35
  Alone can make it fall!"

Then, with eyes that saw not, I kissed
  her;
  And she, kissing back, could not
  know　　38
That *my* kiss was given to her sister,
  Folded close under deepening snow.

Lowell was one of the most respected literary critics of his day, turning out essays on both American and foreign books and authors. Yet he most interestingly shows his talent for detecting the strength and weakness in writers of his own day not in an essay, but in a poem that was published anonymously in his twenty-ninth year.

A *Fable for Critics* is a long poem of over one thousand lines in rhymed couplets, addressed — as was the fashion — to Apollo, the god of poetry and art. In the selection that follows, Lowell wittily describes a number of writers who are represented in this book, even pointing out his own weaknesses. You have already read selections by most of the authors he describes and can compare your impressions with his.

AN AUTHOR'S TECHNIQUE. Watch for the various ways in which Lowell achieves humor in this good-natured criticism of his contemporaries.

A Fable for Critics

[*Emerson*] There comes Emerson first, whose rich words, every one,
Are like gold nails in temples to hang trophies on,
Whose prose is grand verse, while his verse, the Lord knows,
Is some of it pr——. No, 'tis not even prose;
I'm speaking of meters; some poems have welled   5
From those rare depths of soul that have ne'er been excelled.
They're not epics, but that doesn't matter a pin,
In creating, the only hard thing's to begin;
A grass blade's no easier to make than an oak,
If you've once found the way, you've achieved the grand stroke. . . .   10

[*Bryant*] There is Bryant, as quiet, as cool, and as dignified,
As a smooth silent iceberg, that never is ignified,
Save when by reflection 'tis kindled o' nights
With a semblance of flame by the chill northern lights.
He may rank (Griswold ° says so) first bard of your nation,   15
(There's no doubt that he stands in supreme iceolation)
Your topmost Parnassus ° he may set his heel on,
But no warm applauses come, peal following peal on —
He's too smooth and too polished to hang any zeal on. . . .
If he stir you at all, it is just, on my soul,   20
Like being stirred up with the very North Pole. . . .

[*Whittier*] There is Whittier, whose swelling and vehement heart
Strains the strait-breasted drab of the Quaker apart,
And reveals the live man, still supreme and erect,
Underneath the bemummying ° wrappers of sect;   25
There was ne'er a man born who had more of the swing
Of the true lyric bard and all that kind of thing;

---

15. **Griswold:** American critic and editor of Lowell's day, represented in the poem as leading the poets up to Apollo. 17. **Parnassus** (pär·năs′ŭs): mountain in Greece, sacred to Apollo and the Muses. 25. **bemummying** (bē·mŭm′ĭ·ing): stifling.

And his failures arise (though he seems not to know it)
From the very same cause that has made him a poet —
A fervor of mind which knows no separation   30
'Twixt simple excitement and pure inspiration. . . .
Then his grammar's not always correct, nor his rhymes,
And he's prone to repeat his own lyrics sometimes,
Not his best, though, for those are struck off at white heats
When the heart in his breast like a trip hammer beats,   35
And can ne'er be repeated again any more
Than they could have been carefully plotted before. . . .

[*Hawthorne*] There is Hawthorne, with genius so shrinking and rare
That you hardly at first see the strength that is there;
A frame so robust, with a nature so sweet,   40
So earnest, so graceful, so solid, so fleet,
Is worth a descent from Olympus ° to meet;
'Tis as if a rough oak that for ages had stood,
With his gnarled bony branches like ribs of the wood,
Should bloom after cycles of struggle and scathe,°   45
With a single anemone ° trembly and rathe.°. . .
When Nature was shaping him, clay was not granted
For making so full-sized a man as she wanted,
So, to fill out her model, a little she spared
From some finer-grained stuff for a woman prepared,   50
And she could not have hit a more excellent plan
For making him fully and perfectly man. . . .

[*Poe and Longfellow*] There comes Poe, with his raven, like Barnaby Rudge,°
Three fifths of him genius and two fifths sheer fudge,
Who talks like a book of iambs and pentameters,°   55
In a way to make people of common sense damn meters,
Who has written some things quite the best of their kind,
But the heart somehow seems all squeezed out by the mind,
Who — but heyday! What's this? Messieurs Mathews ° and Poe,
You mustn't fling mud balls at Longfellow so,   60
Does it make a man worse that his character's such
As to make his friends love him (as you think) too much?
Why, there is not a bard at this moment alive
More willing than he that his fellows should thrive;
While you are abusing him thus, even now   65
He would help either one of you out of a slough;

42. Olympus: mountain in Greece, home of the gods. 45. scathe: misfortune. 46. anemone
(ȧ·nĕm′ô·nê): a flowering herb. rathe: early in the season. 53. Barnaby Rudge: a crazed youth
in Dickens' novel of that name, who had a pet raven; Poe had his poem "The Raven." 55. iambs
and pentameters: metrical terms. The *iamb* is a foot consisting of a short syllable followed by a
long one; *pentameter* is a line having five metrical feet. 59. **Mathews:** an editor and critic of
the time who, like Poe, wrote severe criticism of Longfellow.

You may say that he's smooth and all that till you're hoarse,
But remember that elegance also is force;
After polishing granite as much as you will,
The heart keeps its tough old persistency still;   70
Deduct all you can, *that* still keeps you at bay;
Why, he'll live till men weary of Collins and Gray.°. . .

[*Holmes*] There's Holmes, who is matchless among you for wit,
A Leyden jar ° always full charged, from which flit
The electrical tingles of hit after hit;   75
In long poems 'tis painful sometimes, and invites
A thought of the way the new telegraph writes,
Which pricks down its little sharp sentences spitefully,
As if you'd got more than you'd title to rightfully,
And you find yourself hoping its wild father lightning   80
Would flame in for a second and give you a fright'ning. . . .

[*Lowell*] There is Lowell, who's striving Parnassus to climb
With a whole bale of *isms* tied together with rhyme; . . .
His lyre has some chords that would ring pretty well,
But he'd rather by half make a drum of the shell,   85
And rattle away till he's old as Methusalem,°
At the head of a march to the last new Jerusalem.

72. **Collins and Gray:** well-known English poets of the eighteenth century. 74. **Leyden** (lī'dĕn) **jar:** an electricity condenser that can give strong shocks. 86. **Methusalem** (mê·thū'-zĕ·lĕm): Methuselah, oldest man in the Bible (Gen. 5:27).

The Vision of Sir Launfal, Lowell's long romantic narrative, tells of a young knight's lifelong search for the Holy Grail, and of his finding it at last in the cup he shared with a beggar. The following stanzas are favorites.

FROM *The Vision of Sir Launfal*

Earth gets its price for what Earth gives us;
   The beggar is taxed for a corner to die in,
The priest hath his fee who comes and shrives us,
   We bargain for the graves we lie in;
At the devil's booth are all things sold,   5
Each ounce of dross costs its ounce of gold;
   For a cap and bells our lives we pay,
Bubbles we buy with a whole soul's tasking:
   'Tis heaven alone that is given away,
   'Tis only God may be had for the asking;   10
No price is set on the lavish summer;
   June may be had by the poorest comer.

And what is so rare as a day in June?
    Then, if ever, come perfect days;
Then Heaven tries earth if it be in tune,   15
    And over it softly her warm ear lays;
Whether we look or whether we listen,
We hear life murmur, or see it glisten;
Every clod feels a stir of might,
    An instinct within it that reaches and towers,   20
And groping blindly above it for light,
    Climbs to a soul in grass and flowers.

Even as a young man Lowell was not afraid to be in the minority if he felt that his stand upheld the principles of freedom and democracy for which our forefathers had fought. Here, then, is a young man's admonition to be on the alert and to think as a citizen about a public issue.

FROM *Stanzas on Freedom*

Men! whose boast it is that ye
Come of fathers brave and free,
If there breathe on earth a slave,
Are ye truly free and brave?
If ye do not feel the chain,   5
When it works a brother's pain,
Are you not base slaves indeed,
Slaves unworthy to be freed? . . .

Is true freedom but to break
Fetters for our own dear sake,   10
And, with leathern hearts, forget
That we owe mankind a debt?
No! true freedom is to share
All the chains our brothers wear,
And, with heart and hand, to be   15
Earnest to make others free!

They are slaves who fear to speak
For the fallen and the weak;
They are slaves who will not choose
Hatred, scoffing, and abuse,   20
Rather than in silence shrink
From the truth they needs must think;
They are slaves who dare not be
In the right with two or three.

JAMES RUSSELL LOWELL   605

FOR DISCUSSION

THE COURTIN'

1. Be sure that you understand the dialect. Any words or phrases that are not clear should be restated in standard English. What does a dialect poem lose when translated into standard English?
2. Point out details in the poem that seem to be typical of an old-fashioned New England kitchen.
3. Point out bits of humor either in the actions of the characters or in the poet's choice of words. Does Lowell depend only upon dialect for his humorous effect? What is Lowell's attitude, seemingly, toward his characters?

THE FIRST SNOWFALL

1. Point out concrete details that help you to visualize the setting. What do you think of such a figure of speech as "From sheds new-roofed with Carrara" or "As did robins the babes in the wood"?
2. What feeling does the last stanza arouse in you? Does the tone of the poem change in the last stanza? If so, has Lowell prepared the reader for such a change, or does it come as a surprise?

A FABLE FOR CRITICS

1. The most natural way to study *A Fable for Critics* is to discuss whether Lowell's comments seem justified from what you have read by these authors. If you disagree with his impression of any of them, try to discover whether he was wrong or whether you have not read enough by that author to judge his work as a whole.
2. Are the authors on the whole treated sympathetically or satirically? Which of these men, if any, would have been justified in feeling angry at Lowell's comments on them?
3. Think of two good reasons Lowell could have had for including himself in the poem.

THE VISION OF SIR LAUNFAL

1. In what ways do these lines reveal an entirely different aspect of Lowell as a poet?
2. What things must we pay for in one way or another in this life? What things are given away?

STANZAS ON FREEDOM

Define Lowell's concept of freedom. With what kind of people would Lowell have no patience? To what extent do you agree with him? If you disagree, defend your stand.

AN AUTHOR'S TECHNIQUE

Find examples of intentional misspellings, of forced rhymes, of idiomatic speech, of puns, and of clever figures of speech used by Lowell for the purpose of humor.

You may find it interesting to compare Lowell in these respects with the modern poet Ogden Nash (page 340). What may Nash perhaps owe to Lowell?

SPECIAL REPORT

A class member may look up the expanded version of "The Courtin'" and prepare a short, clear report about the differences between the two editions, indicating his personal preference.

YOUR OWN WRITING

The manner of "A Fable for Critics" is not hard to imitate. Try writing "A Fable for Teachers," "A Fable for Students," or another poem of humorous, brief comments on familiar persons or types.

FURTHER READING

If you are a good reader, you might enjoy reading all of *The Vision of Sir Launfal*. Other poems from the *Biglow Papers* that you may enjoy include "A Letter from Ezekiel Biglow," "What Mr. Robinson Thinks," and "Sunthin' in the Pastoral Line." Lowell's "Ode Recited at the Harvard Commemoration" (in honor of the Harvard men who had given their lives during the War Between the States) is generally considered his greatest serious poem.

OLIVER WENDELL HOLMES

1809–1894

Youth smiles at age in "My Aunt," first published when Holmes was twenty-two.

My Aunt

My aunt! my dear unmarried aunt!
    Long years have o'er her flown;
Yet still she strains the aching clasp
    That binds her virgin zone;
I know it hurts her — though she looks
    As cheerful as she can;   6
Her waist is ampler than her life,
    For life is but a span.

My aunt! my poor deluded aunt!
    Her hair is almost gray;   10
Why will she train that winter curl
    In such a springlike way?
How can she lay her glasses down,
    And say she reads as well,
When through a double convex lens
    She just makes out to spell?   16

Her father — grandpapa! forgive
    This erring lip its smiles—
Vowed she should make the finest girl
    Within a hundred miles;   20
He sent her to a stylish school;
    'Twas in her thirteenth June;
And with her, as the rules required,
    "Two towels and a spoon."

They braced my aunt against a board,
    To make her straight and tall;   26

They laced her up, they starved her
    down,
    To make her light and small;
They pinched her feet, they singed her
    hair,
    They screwed it up with pins —   30
O never mortal suffered more
    In penance for her sins.

But when my precious aunt was done,
    My grandsire brought her back
(By daylight, lest some rabid youth   35
    Might follow on the track);
"Ah!" said my grandsire, as he shook
    Some powder in his pan,°
"What could this lovely creature do
    Against a desperate man!"   40

Alas! not chariot, nor barouche,°
    Nor bandit cavalcade,
Tore from the trembling father's arms
    His all-accomplished maid.
For her how happy had it been!   45
    And Heaven had spared to me
To see one sad, ungathered rose
    On my ancestral tree.

38. **powder in his pan:** gunpowder in the hollow lock by which old guns were primed. 41. **barouche** (bà·rōōsh'): four-wheeled carriage.

"*The* Constitution *and the* Guerrière," *an oil painting by the American artist Thomas Birch (1779–1851).*

The following poem is a vigorous protest against the destruction of the frigate *Constitution,* which had defeated the *Guerrière* in the War of 1812. First published in the Boston *Advertiser,* it was copied in newspapers and scattered on broadsides all over the country. Such indignation was aroused that the ship was saved as a national memorial. The poem was written when Holmes was twenty-one, and it made him famous almost overnight.

Old Ironsides

Ay, tear her tattered ensign down!
  Long has it waved on high,
And many an eye has danced to see
  That banner in the sky;
Beneath it rung the battle shout,   5
  And burst the cannon's roar —
The meteor of the ocean air
  Shall sweep the clouds no more.

Her decks, once red with heroes' blood,
  Where knelt the vanquished foe,   10
When winds were hurrying o'er the
    flood,
  And waves were white below,

No more shall feel the victor's tread,
  Or know the conquered knee —
The harpies of the shore shall pluck   15
  The eagle of the sea!

Oh, better that her shattered hulk
  Should sink beneath the wave;
Her thunders shook the mighty
    deep,
  And there should be her grave;   20
Nail to the mast her holy flag,
  Set every threadbare sail,
And give her to the god of storms,
  The lightning and the gale!

Holmes was interested in the compartmented shell of the nautilus, of which he had several specimens. The name "nautilus," meaning sailor, grew out of the old belief that the little creature sailed by the gauzy wings that are really its tentacles.

The Chambered Nautilus

This is the ship of pearl, which, poets feign,
   Sails the unshadowed main —
   The venturous bark that flings
On the sweet summer wind its purpled wings
In gulfs enchanted, where the Siren° sings,   5
   And coral reefs lie bare,
Where the cold sea-maids rise to sun their streaming hair.

Its webs of living gauze no more unfurl;
   Wrecked is the ship of pearl!
   And every chambered cell,   10
Where its dim dreaming life was wont to dwell,
As the frail tenant shaped his growing shell,
   Before thee lies revealed —
Its irised ceiling rent, its sunless crypt unsealed!

Year after year beheld the silent toil   15
   That spread his lustrous coil;
   Still, as the spiral grew,
He left the past year's dwelling for the new,
Stole with soft step its shining archway through,
   Built up its idle door,   20
Stretched in his last-found home, and knew the old no more.

Thanks for the heavenly message brought by thee,
   Child of the wandering sea,
   Cast from her lap, forlorn!
From thy dead lips a clearer note is born   25
Than ever Triton° blew from wreathèd horn!
   While on mine ears it rings,
Through the deep caves of thought I hear a voice that sings:

Build thee more stately mansions, O my soul,
   As the swift seasons roll!   30
   Leave thy low-vaulted past!
Let each new temple, nobler than the last,
Shut thee from heaven with a dome more vast,
   Till thou at length art free,
Leaving thine outgrown shell by life's unresting sea!   35

5. **Siren:** In classical mythology the sirens were sea nymphs near the west coast of Italy who lured mariners to their deaths by singing enchanting songs. 26. **Triton** (trī′tŏn): ancient sea god whose lower part resembled a fish. He is usually represented as blowing a trumpet made of a sea shell.

OLIVER WENDELL HOLMES

"Contentment" first appeared in *The Autocrat of the Breakfast-Table*, where the Autocrat introduced it to his fellow boarders in the following manner: "Should you like to hear what moderate wishes life brings one to at last? I used to be very ambitious — wasteful, extravagant, and luxurious in all my fancies. Read too much in the *Arabian Nights*. Must have the lamp — couldn't do without the ring. Exercise every morning on the brazen horse. Plump down into castles as full of little milk-white princesses as a nest is of young sparrows. All love me dearly at once. Charming idea of life, but too high-colored for the reality. I have outgrown all this; my tastes have become exceedingly primitive — almost, perhaps, ascetic. . . . I think you will be willing to hear some lines which embody the subdued and limited desires of my maturity."

Contentment

Little I ask; my wants are few;
   I only wish a hut of stone
(A *very plain* brown stone will do)
   That I may call my own;
And close at hand is such a one,   5
In yonder street that fronts the sun.

Plain food is quite enough for me;
   Three courses are as good as ten;
If nature can subsist on three,
   Thank Heaven for three. Amen!   10
I always thought cold victual nice;
My *choice* would be vanilla ice.

I care not much for gold or land;
   Give me a mortgage here and there,
Some good bank-stock, some note of
      hand,   15
   Or trifling railroad share —
I only ask that Fortune send
A *little* more than I shall spend.

Honors are silly toys, I know,
   And titles are but empty names;   20
I would, *perhaps*, be Plenipo,°
   But only near St. James°;
I'm very sure I should not care
To fill our Gubernator's° chair.

Jewels are baubles; 'tis a sin   25
   To care for such unfruitful things;
One good-sized diamond in a pin,

   Some, *not so large*, in rings,
A ruby, and a pearl, or so,
Will do for me; I laugh at show.   30

My dame should dress in cheap attire;
   (Good heavy silks are never dear);
I own perhaps I *might* desire
   Some shawls of true Cashmere,
Some marrowy crapes of China silk,   35
Like wrinkled skins on scalded milk.

I would not have the horse I drive
   So fast that folks must stop and stare;
An easy gait — two forty-five —
   Suits me; I do not care;   40
Perhaps, for just a *single spurt*,
Some seconds less would do no hurt.

Of pictures, I should like to own
   Titians and Raphaels three or four,
I love so much their style and tone;   45
   One Turner, and no more,
(A landscape — foreground golden
    dirt —
The sunshine painted with a squirt.)

Of books but few — some fifty score
   For daily use, and bound for wear;
The rest upon an upper floor;   51
   Some *little* luxury *there*
Of red morocco's° gilded gleam
And vellum° rich as country cream.

21. **Plenipo:** Ambassador Plenipotentiary (with full powers). 22. **St. James:** the Court of St. James's in London. 24. **Gubernator:** governor.

53. **morocco:** a fine grade of leather. 54. **vellum:** either a rich calfskin binding or an expensive grade of paper; probably the former.

Busts, cameos, gems — such things as
   these,   55
   Which others often show for pride,
I value for their power to please,
   And selfish churls° deride;
One Stradivarius, I confess,
Two Meerschaums, I would fain pos-
   sess.   60

Wealth's wasteful tricks I will not learn,
   Nor ape the glittering upstart fool;
Shall not carved tables serve my turn,

58. churls: surly fellows.

But *all* must be of buhl?°
Give grasping pomp its double share,
I ask but *one* recumbent chair.   66

Thus humble let me live and die,
   Nor long for Midas' golden touch;
If Heaven more generous gifts deny,
   I shall not miss them *much* —   70
Too grateful for the blessing lent
Of simple tastes and mind content!

64. buhl (bōōl): decoration in which tor-
toise shell, yellow metal, white metal, etc., are
inlaid in furniture, making scrolls and other
designs.

FOR DISCUSSION

MY AUNT

1. What clearly indicates that this was
written in Holmes's youth? Does the poem
seem disrespectful? What thoughts on the
relations between youth and age do they
awaken in you?
2. How did the education of Holmes's
aunt differ from that of a girl today? What
changes have come about in the position
of, and attitudes toward, unmarried wom-
en since Holmes's day?
3. What melodramatic elements does
Holmes use to get across his implied message?
4. Compare and contrast the nature of
the humor in "Contentment" and "My
Aunt."

OLD IRONSIDES

1. Do you recall why the nickname
"Old Ironsides" was given to the *Constitution?* Who are called the "harpies of
the shore"? What were three possible fates
for the vessel? Which did Holmes advocate? Which came about finally?
2. Why should an old, useless, outdated
ship be kept? What objects of historical
interest are there in your community?
Would you be willing that they be destroyed? Should the community make an
effort to preserve them? Why?

THE CHAMBERED NAUTILUS

1. Holmes is largely a poet of ideas.
Does he present those ideas more effec-

tively by humor, by satire, or by idealism?
2. Express in your own words the comparison made by the poet between the
shell and man's life. What "moral" does
Holmes get across?

CONTENTMENT

1. What kind of person would ask for
the things asked for in this poem? What
would be his set of values?
2. Do you think that Thoreau would
agree with Holmes's satire on these notions of contentment?
3. What part does contentment play in
our lives? Can it work in both a positive
and negative direction? What is the difference between contentment and satisfaction?

SPECIAL REPORT

Look up and report on the history of the
Constitution, especially its fight with the
Guerrière.

UNDERSTANDING ALLUSIONS

Holmes's poem "Contentment" contains a number of allusions that enrich the
meaning for the reader who knows the
connotations of the words. What can you
find in your library about *Titian, Raphael,
Turner, Stradivarius, Meerschaum?*

OLIVER WENDELL HOLMES   611

JOHN
GREENLEAF
WHITTIER
1807–1892

The following poem prefaced the collected edition of Whittier's poems that appeared in 1849, and it still gives us our best introduction to Whittier as a man and a poet. "Proem" means a preface or introduction.

Proem

I love the old melodious lays
Which softly melt the ages through,
  The songs of Spenser's° golden days,
  Arcadian Sidney's° silvery phrase,
Sprinkling our noon of time with freshest morning dew.   5

  Yet, vainly in my quiet hours
To breathe their marvelous notes I try;
  I feel them, as the leaves and flowers
  In silence feel the dewy showers,
And drink with glad still lips the blessing of the sky.   10

  The rigor of a frozen clime,
The harshness of an untaught ear,
  The jarring words of one whose rhyme
  Beat often Labor's hurried time,
Or Duty's rugged march through storm and strife, are here.   15

  Of mystic beauty, dreamy grace,
No rounded art the lack supplies;
  Unskilled the subtle lines to trace,

---

3. **Spenser's:** Edmund Spenser (1552?–1599), a major English poet, author of *The Faerie Queene*. 4. **Sidney's:** Sir Philip Sidney (1554–1586), author of *Arcadia*, a pastoral romance.

Or softer shades of Nature's face,
I view her common forms with unanointed eyes.   20

Nor mine the seerlike power to show
The secrets of the heart and mind;
   To drop the plummet line below
   Our common world of joy and woe,
A more intense despair or brighter hope to find.   25

Yet here at least an earnest sense
Of human right and weal is shown;
   A hate of tyranny intense,
   And hearty in its vehemence,
As if my brother's pain and sorrow were my own.   30

O Freedom! if to me belong
Nor mighty Milton's° gift divine,
   Nor Marvell's° wit and graceful song,
   Still with a love as deep and strong
As theirs, I lay, like them, my best gifts on thy shrine!   35

32. **Milton's:** John Milton (1608–1674), English Puritan poet, author of *Paradise Lost.*
33. **Marvell's:** Andrew Marvell (1621–1678), English Puritan poet and political satirist.

With the question of slavery settled and the war closed, Whittier turned to thoughts of home. Being a bachelor, he had lived in closer touch with the family of his boyhood than he might otherwise have done. These ties had been broken by the death of his mother and elder sister and recently of his younger sister Elizabeth. Only his brother and he were left.

The Whittier family home had been built in 1688 and had come to symbolize for Whittier strong personal relationships. What could be more natural than that he should write a memorial poem describing the old household?

Snow-Bound, published in 1866, was immediately hailed as the greatest American pastoral poem. Told in simple, direct English, it is, according to the scholar and critic G. F. Whicher, a remarkable "integration of precisely remembered detail and tender devotion." The poem is printed here in a shortened version.

FROM *Snow-Bound*

A WINTER IDYLL*

The sun that brief December day
Rose cheerless over hills of gray,
And, darkly circled, gave at noon
A sadder light than waning moon.

* **Idyll:** a poem or story that is a "little picture" of some pastoral, or country, scene.

Slow tracing down the thickening sky
Its mute and ominous prophecy,   6
A portent seeming less than threat,
It sank from sight before it set.
A chill no coat, however stout,
Of homespun stuff could quite shut out,
A hard, dull bitterness of cold,   11
That checked, mid-vein, the circling race

Of lifeblood in the sharpened face,
The coming of the snowstorm told.
The wind blew east: we heard the roar
Of Ocean on his wintry shore,   16
And felt the strong pulse throbbing there
Beat with low rhythm our inland air.

Meanwhile we did our nightly chores —
Brought in the wood from out of doors,
Littered the stalls, and from the mows
Raked down the herd's-grass for the cows;   22
Heard the horse whinnying for his corn;
And, sharply clashing horn on horn,
Impatient down the stanchion rows   25
The cattle shake their walnut bows;
While, peering from his early perch
Upon the scaffold's pole of birch,
The cock his crested helmet bent
And down his querulous challenge sent.

Unwarmed by any sunset light   31
The gray day darkened into night,
A night made hoary with the swarm
And whirl-dance of the blinding storm,
As zigzag, wavering to and fro,   35
Crossed and recrossed the winged snow:
And ere the early bedtime came,
The white drift piled the window frame,
And through the glass the clothesline posts   39
Looked in like tall and sheeted ghosts.

So all night long the storm roared on:
The morning broke without a sun;
In tiny spherule° traced with lines
Of Nature's geometric signs,
In starry flake and pellicle,°   45
All day the hoary meteor fell;
And, when the second morning shone,
We looked upon a world unknown,
On nothing we could call our own.
Around the glistening wonder bent   50
The blue walls of the firmament,
No cloud above, no earth below—

43. spherule: a little sphere. 45. pellicle
(pĕl′ĭ-k'l): a thin film.

A universe of sky and snow!
The old familiar sights of ours
Took marvelous shapes; strange domes and towers   55
Rose up where sty or corncrib stood,
Or garden wall, or belt of wood;
A smooth white mound the brush pile showed,
A fenceless drift what once was road;
The bridle post an old man sat   60
With loose-flung coat and high cocked hat;
The wellcurb had a Chinese roof;°
And even the long sweep, high aloof,
In its slant splendor, seemed to tell
Of Pisa's leaning miracle.°   65

A prompt, decisive man, no breath
Our father wasted: "Boys, a path!"
Well pleased (for when did farmer boy
Count such a summons less than joy?)
Our buskins° on our feet we drew;   70
With mittened hands, and caps drawn low,
To guard our necks and ears from snow,
We cut the solid whiteness through.
And, where the drift was deepest, made
A tunnel walled and overlaid   75
With dazzling crystal: we had read
Of rare Aladdin's° wondrous cave,
And to our own his name we gave,
With many a wish the luck were ours
To test his lamp's supernal° powers. 80
We reached the barn with merry din,
And roused the prisoned brutes within.
The old horse thrust his long head out,
And grave with wonder gazed about;
The cock his lusty greeting said,   85

62. wellcurb had a Chinese roof: When asked how this could be, Whittier explained that a board had been placed across the curb to hold the bucket and that this gave the roof effect. 65. Pisa's (pē′zȧz) leaning miracle: a famous slanting tower in Pisa, Italy. 70. buskins: a name for heavy boots derived from the high-heeled boots worn by ancient Greek actors. 77. Aladdin: the youth in the *Arabian Nights* who discovered great treasure in a cave through the power of a magical lamp. 80. supernal (sȧ·pûr′năl): superior to earthly qualities.

And forth his speckled harem led;
The oxen lashed their tails, and hooked,
And mild reproach of hunger looked;
The hornèd patriarch of the sheep,   89
Like Egypt's Amun° roused from sleep,
Shook his sage head with gesture mute,
And emphasized with stamp of foot.

All day the gusty north wind bore
The loosening drift its breath before;
Low circling round its southern zone,
The sun through dazzling snow-mist
    shone.   96
No church bell lent its Christian tone
To the savage air, no social smoke
Curled over woods of snow-hung oak.
A solitude made more intense   100
By dreary-voicèd elements,
The shrieking of the mindless wind,
The moaning tree boughs swaying
    blind,
And on the glass the unmeaning beat
Of ghostly finger tips of sleet.   105
Beyond the circle of our hearth
No welcome sound of toil or mirth
Unbound the spell, and testified
Of human life and thought outside.
We minded that the sharpest ear   110
The buried brooklet could not hear,
The music of whose liquid lip
Had been to us companionship,
And, in our lonely life, had grown
To have an almost human tone.   115

As night drew on, and, from the crest
Of wooded knolls that ridged the west,
The sun, a snow-blown traveler, sank
From sight beneath the smothering
    bank,   119
We piled with care our nightly stack
Of wood against the chimney back —
The oaken log, green, huge, and thick,
And on its top the stout backstick;
The knotty forestick laid apart,   124
And filled between with curious art
The ragged brush; then, hovering near,
We watched the first red blaze appear,

Heard the sharp crackle, caught the
    gleam
On whitewashed wall and sagging
    beam,
Until the old, rude-furnished room   130
Burst, flowerlike, into rosy bloom;
While radiant with a mimic flame
Outside the sparkling drift became,
And through the bare-boughed lilac
    tree
Our own warm hearth seemed blazing
    free.   135
The crane and pendent trammels°
    showed,
The Turks' heads° on the andirons
    glowed;
While childish fancy, prompt to tell
The meaning of the miracle,
Whispered the old rhyme: *"Under the
    tree*   140
When fire outdoors burns merrily,
There the witches are making tea."

The moon above the eastern wood
Shone at its full; the hill range stood
Transfigured in the silver flood,   145
Its blown snows flashing cold and keen,
Dead white, save where some sharp ra-
    vine
Took shadow, or the somber green
Of hemlocks turned to pitchy black
Against the whiteness at their back.
For such a world and such a night   151
Most fitting that unwarming light,
Which only seemed where'er it fell
To make the coldness visible.
Shut in from all the world without,   155
We sat the clean-winged hearth° about,
Content to let the north wind roar
In baffled rage at pane and door,
While the red logs before us beat
The frost line back with tropic heat;
And ever, when a louder blast   161
Shook beam and rafter as it passed,

90. **Egypt's Amun:** an Egyptian god frequently represented with a ram's head; usually spelled Amon or Ammon.

136. **crane and pendent trammels:** Trammels are adjustable pothooks that are hung
on a swinging arm (crane) attached to the
hearth. 137. **Turks' heads:** The design of the
top of the andiron resembled a Turkish cap.
156. **clean-winged hearth:** a turkey wing was
used for a hearth broom.

The merrier up its roaring draft
The great throat of the chimney
    laughed;
The house dog on his paws outspread
Laid to the fire his drowsy head,   166
The cat's dark silhouette on the wall
A couchant° tiger's seemed to fall;
And, for the winter fireside meet,
Between the andirons' straddling feet,
The mug of cider simmered slow,   171
The apples sputtered in a row,
And, close at hand, the basket stood
With nuts from brown October's wood.

What matter how the night behaved?
What matter how the north wind
    raved?   176
Blow high, blow low, not all its snow
Could quench our hearthfire's ruddy
    glow. . . .
We sped the time with stories old,   179
Wrought puzzles out, and riddles told,
Or stammered from our schoolbook lore
"The Chief of Gambia's golden
    shore."°. . .

THE FATHER

Our father rode again his ride
On Memphremagog's° wooded side;
Sat down again to moose and
    samp°   185
In trapper's hut and Indian camp. . . .
We shared the fishing off Boar's Head,°
The chowder on the sand beach made,
Dipped by the hungry, steaming hot,
With spoons of clamshell from the
    pot.   190
We heard the tales of witchcraft old,
And dream and sign and marvel told
To sleepy listeners as they lay
Stretched idly on the salted hay,
Adrift along the winding shores,   195

---

168. couchant: lying down. 182. "The Chief of Gambia's golden shore": a line from a popular poem of the day called "The African Chief." This shows the interest in antislavery in Whittier's boyhood. 184. Memphremagog (mĕm'frĕ·mā'gŏg): a lake between Vermont and Canada. 185. samp: boiled Indian corn. 187. Boar's Head: a point on the coast north of Salisbury, Massachusetts.

When favoring breezes deigned to blow
The square sail of the gundalow,°
And idle lay the useless oars.

THE MOTHER

Our mother, while she turned her wheel
Or ran the new-knit stocking heel,   200
Told how the Indian hordes came
    down
At midnight on Cocheco° town,
And how her own great-uncle bore
His cruel scalp-mark to fourscore.
Recalling, in her fitting phrase   205
So rich and picturesque and free,
(The common unrhymed poetry
Of simple life and country ways),
The story of her early days —   209
She made us welcome to her home;
Old hearths grew wide to give us room;
We stole with her a frightened look
At the gray wizard's conjuring-book,
The fame whereof went far and wide
Through all the simple countryside; 215
We heard the hawks at twilight play,
The boat horn on Piscataqua,°
The loon's weird laughter far away;
We fished her little trout brook, knew
What flowers in wood and meadow
    grew,   220
What sunny hillsides autumn-brown
She climbed to shake the ripe nuts
    down,
Saw where in sheltered cove and bay
The duck's black squadron anchored
    lay,   224
And heard the wild geese calling loud
Beneath the gray November cloud. . . .

THE UNCLE

Our uncle,° innocent of books,
Was rich in lore of fields and brooks,
The ancient teachers never dumb

---

197. gundalow: a variant of gondola, a heavy, flat-bottomed barge or boat. 202. Cocheco (kŏ·chē'kō): Indian name for Dover, New Hampshire. 217. Piscataqua (pĭs·kăt'à-kwô): a river between Maine and New Hampshire. The rhyme shows that Whittier gave it a rustic pronunciation. 227. Our uncle: Moses, the bachelor brother of Whittier's father.

Of Nature's unhoused lyceum.°   230
In moons and tides and weather wise,
He read the clouds as prophecies,
And foul or fair could well divine,
By many an occult hint and sign,
Holding the cunning-warded keys° 235
To all the woodcraft mysteries;
Himself to Nature's heart so near
That all her voices in his ear
Of beast or bird had meanings clear.
A simple, guileless, childlike man,   240
Content to live where life began;
Strong only on his native grounds,
The little world of sights and sounds
Whose girdle was the parish
     bounds. . . .

THE AUNT

Next, the dear aunt,° whose smile of
     cheer   245
And voice in dreams I see and hear —
The sweetest woman ever Fate
Perverse denied a household mate,
Who, lonely, homeless, not the less
Found peace in love's unselfishness,
And welcome wheresoe'er she went,
A calm and gracious element,   252
Whose presence seemed the sweet in-
     come
And womanly atmosphere of home —
Called up her girlhood memories,   255
The huskings and the apple bees,
The sleigh rides and the summer sails,
Weaving through all the poor details
And homespun warp° of circumstance
A golden woof-thread of romance. . . .

THE ELDER SISTER

There, too, our elder sister° plied   261
Her evening task the stand beside;

230. **lyceum:** originally an area in which
the Greek philosopher Aristotle lectured, now
ordinarily used to indicate any lecture hall.
235. **cunning-warded keys:** keys with notches
nicely adjusted to fit different locks. 245. **the
dear aunt:** Aunt Mercy, his mother's sister,
who always made her home with the Whit-
tiers. 259–260. **warp:** the threads lengthwise
in a loom, crossed by the **weft** or **woof**, the
filling thread carried by the shuttle. 261. **elder
sister:** Mary, who died five years before the
poem was written.

A full, rich nature, free to trust,
Truthful and almost sternly just,
Impulsive, earnest, prompt to act,   265
And make her generous thought a fact,
Keeping with many a light disguise
The secret of self-sacrifice.
A heart sore tried! thou hast the best
That Heaven itself could give thee —
     rest,   270
Rest from all bitter thoughts and things!
     How many a poor one's blessing went
     With thee beneath the low green tent
Whose curtain never outward swings!

THE YOUNGER SISTER

As one who held herself a part   275
Of all she saw, and let her heart
     Against the household bosom lean,
Upon the motley-braided mat
Our youngest° and our dearest sat. . . .
The chill weight of the winter snow 280
     For months upon her grave has lain;
And now, when summer south winds
     blow
     And brier and harebell bloom again,
I tread the pleasant paths we trod,
I see the violet-sprinkled sod   285
Whereon she leaned, too frail and weak
The hillside flowers she loved to seek,
Yet following me where'er I went
With dark eyes full of love's content.
The birds are glad; the brier rose fills
The air with sweetness; all the hills   291
Stretch green to June's unclouded sky;
But still I wait with ear and eye
For something gone which should be
     nigh,
A loss in all familiar things,   295
In flower that blooms, and bird that
     sings. . . .

THE SCHOOLMASTER

Brisk wielder of the birch and rule,
The master of the district school

279. **Our youngest:** Elizabeth, the unmarried sister, who kept house for Whittier until
she died about a year before the poem was
written. As she too possessed some poetic gift,
the brother and sister were most congenial,
and the poet's mourning for her is feelingly
expressed.

JOHN GREENLEAF WHITTIER

Held at the fire his favored place;
Its warm glow lit a laughing face 300
Fresh-hued and fair, where scarce ap-
    peared
The uncertain prophecy of beard.
He teased the mitten-blinded cat,
Played cross pins on my uncle's hat,
Sang songs, and told us what be-
    falls 305
In classic Dartmouth's college halls.

Born the wild Northern hills among,
From whence his yeoman father wrung
By patient toil subsistence scant,
Not competence and yet not want, 310
He early gained the power to pay
His cheerful, self-reliant way;
Could doff at ease his scholar's gown
To peddle wares from town to town;
Or through the long vacation's reach
In lonely lowland districts teach, 316
Where all the droll experience found
At stranger hearths in boarding round,
The moonlit skater's keen delight,
The sleigh drive through the frosty
    night, 320
The rustic party, with its rough
Accompaniment of blindman's buff,
And whirling plate, and forfeits paid,
His winter task a pastime made.
Happy the snow-locked homes wherein
He tuned his merry violin, 326
Or played the athlete in the barn,
Or held the good dame's winding yarn,
Or mirth-provoking versions told
Of classic legends rare and old, 330
Wherein the scenes of Greece and
    Rome
Had all the commonplace of home,
And little seemed at best the odds
'Twixt Yankee peddlers and old gods.

. . .

At last the great logs, crumbling low,
Sent out a dull and duller glow, 336
The bull's-eye watch that hung in view,
Ticking its weary circuit through,
Pointed with mutely warning sign
Its black hand to the hour of nine. 340
That sign the pleasant circle broke:

My uncle ceased his pipe to smoke,
Knocked from its bowl the refuse gray
And laid it tenderly away;
Then roused himself to safely cover 345
The dull red brands with ashes over.
And while, with care, our mother laid
The work aside, her steps she stayed
One moment, seeking to express
Her grateful sense of happiness 350
For food and shelter, warmth and
    health,
And love's contentment more than
    wealth,
With simple wishes (not the weak,
Vain prayers which no fulfillment seek,
But such as warm the generous heart,
O'erprompt to do with Heaven its
    part) 356
That none might lack, that bitter night,
For bread and clothing, warmth and
    light.

Within our beds awhile we heard
The wind that round the gables roared,
With now and then a ruder shock, 361
Which made our very bedsteads rock.
We heard the loosened clapboards
    tossed,
The board nails snapping in the frost;
And on us, through the unplastered
    wall, 365
Felt the light-sifted snowflakes fall.
But sleep stole on, as sleep will do
When hearts are light and life is new;
Faint and more faint the murmurs
    grew,
Till in the summerland of dreams 370
They softened to the sound of streams,
Low stir of leaves, and dip of oars,
And lapsing waves on quiet shores.

Next morn we wakened with the shout
Of merry voices high and clear; 375
And saw the teamsters drawing near
To break the drifted highways out.
Down the long hillside treading slow
We saw the half-buried oxen go, 379
Shaking the snow from heads uptossed,
Their straining nostrils white with frost.
Before our door the straggling train

Drew up, an added team to gain.
The elders threshed their hands a-cold,
  Passed, with the cider mug, their
    jokes   385
  From lip to lip; the younger folks
Down the loose snowbanks, wrestling,
    rolled,
Then toiled again the cavalcade
  O'er windy hill, through clogged ra-
    vine,
  And woodland paths that wound be-
    tween   390
Low dropping pine boughs winter-
    weighed.
From every barn a team afoot,
At every house a new recruit,
Where, drawn by Nature's subtlest law,
Haply the watchful young men saw 395
Sweet doorway pictures of the curls
And curious eyes of merry girls,
Lifting their hands in mock defense
Against the snowball's compliments,
And reading in each missive tossed 400
The charm with Eden never lost.

We heard once more the sleigh bells'
    sound;
  And, following where the teamsters
    led,
The wise old Doctor went his round,
Just pausing at our door to say,   405
In the brief autocratic way
Of one who, prompt at Duty's call,
Was free to urge her claim on all,   408
  That some poor neighbor sick abed
At night our mother's aid would need.
For, one in generous thought and deed,
  What mattered in the sufferer's sight
  The Quaker matron's inward light,
The Doctor's mail of Calvin's creed?°
All hearts confess the saints elect   415
  Who, twain in faith, in love agree,
And melt not in an acid sect
  The Christian pearl of charity!

  So days went on: a week had passed
Since the great world was heard from
    last.   420

414. **Calvin's creed:** The doctor was a follower of Calvin, a Swiss religious reformer.

The Almanac we studied o'er,
Read and reread our little store
Of books and pamphlets, scarce a score;
One harmless novel, mostly hid
From younger eyes, a book forbid, 425
And poetry (or good or bad,
A single book was all we had). . . .
At last the floundering carrier bore
The village paper to our door.   429
Lo! broadening outward as we read,
To warmer zones the horizon spread;
In panoramic length unrolled
We saw the marvels that it told. . . .

Welcome to us its week-old news,
Its corner for the rustic Muse,   435
  Its monthly gauge of snow and rain,
Its record, mingling in a breath
The wedding bell and dirge of death;
Jest, anecdote, and lovelorn tale,
The latest culprit sent to jail;   440
Its hue and cry of stolen and lost,
Its vendue° sales and goods at cost,
  And traffic calling loud for gain.
We felt the stir of hall and street,
The pulse of life that round us beat;
The chill embargo of the snow   446
Was melted in the genial glow;
Wide swung again our ice-locked door,
And all the world was ours once more!

442. **vendue** (věn'dū): auction.

"The Eternal Goodness," somewhat shortened here, is generally considered the finest of Whittier's religious verses. Simplicity, sincerity, and human kindness are evident throughout.

The Eternal Goodness

O friends! with whom my feet have
    trod
The quiet aisles of prayer,
Glad witness to your zeal for God
    And love of man I bear.

I trace your lines of argument;   5
    Your logic linked and strong
I weigh as one who dreads dissent,
    And fears a doubt as wrong.

But still my human hands are weak
    To hold your iron creeds:°   10
Against the words ye bid me speak
    My heart within me pleads.

Who fathoms the Eternal Thought?
    Who talks of scheme and plan?
The Lord is God! He needeth not   15
    The poor device of man.

I walk with bare, hushed feet the ground
    Ye tread with boldness shod;
I dare not fix with mete and bound°
    The love and power of God.   20

Ye praise His justice; even such
    His pitying love I deem:
Ye seek a king; I fain would touch
    The robe that hath no seam.°

Ye see the curse which overbroods   25
    A world of pain and loss;
I hear our Lord's Beatitudes
    And prayer upon the cross.

More than your schoolmen teach, with-
    in
    Myself, alas! I know: 30

10. iron creeds: beliefs of the Puritans, the "friends" of the first line. 19. mete and bound: definite boundaries (legal term). 24. the robe . . . no seam: the robe worn by Christ before His crucifixion.

Too dark ye cannot paint the sin,
    Too small the merit show.

I bow my forehead to the dust,
    I veil mine eyes for shame,
And urge, in trembling self-distrust,   35
    A prayer without a claim.

I see the wrong that round me lies,
    I feel the guilt within;
I hear, with groan and travail-cries,
    The world confess its sin.   40

Yet, in the maddening maze of things,
    And tossed by storm and flood,
To one fixed trust my spirit clings;
    I know that God is good!

Not mine to look where cherubim   45
    And seraphs may not see,
But nothing can be good in Him
    Which evil is in me.

The wrong that pains my soul below
    I dare not throne above;   50
I know not of His hate — I know
    His goodness and His love. . . .

I long for household voices gone,
    For vanished smiles I long,
But God hath led my dear ones on,   55
    And He can do no wrong.

I know not what the future hath
    Of marvel or surprise,
Assured alone that life and death
    His mercy underlies. . . .   60

I know not where His islands lift
    Their fronded palms in air;
I only know I cannot drift
    Beyond His love and care. . . .

FOR DISCUSSION

PROEM

1. Whittier thinks of himself as a very different kind of poet from the Elizabethans Spenser and Sidney. How does the third stanza account for his different approach to poetry?

2. The last two stanzas express the strong feelings that motivate his writing. What are these feelings?

3. Why has "Proem," since its first appearance in 1849, invariably served as a preface to each collected edition of Whittier's poems?

SNOW-BOUND

1. Describe the various members of the group around the fire. Each character may be described by a different student. Select the character best liked by the class. Which ones do you think Whittier describes most sympathetically?

2. Compare the amusements of the evening with those which would probably entertain a modern family. How does the reading matter compare with that in your home?

3. What similarities do you find to the situation in "The Ambitious Guest" (page 549)? Are the two families alike or different? Prove by details.

THE ETERNAL GOODNESS

1. Sum up in a few sentences the main thought of this poem. In what way does it show that Whittier was a Quaker?

2. What contrast is there between the thinking of Whittier and that of the "friends" addressed?

3. Compare Whittier's Quaker thinking with the Puritan thinking of Edwards (page 435).

4. This poem was written in 1865 at the close of the war. What relation has this fact to its earning popularity?

READING ALOUD

As Snow-Bound is written in simple language, its oral reading is an enjoyable classroom activity. As you read it aloud, point out some of the details that make the forecast of snow and the storm itself especially vivid. Select figures of speech that seem to enhance the description.

DRAMATIZING "SNOW-BOUND"

Put the conversation around the fire into dramatic form that may be acted in class. For contrast, the conversation of a modern family group may be dramatized as part of the same program.

FURTHER READING

Find other poems on snow and frost, such as "The Snowstorm," by Emerson; "A Snowstorm," by Henry Van Dyke; "Snow Shower," by Bryant; "Snow Song," by Lucy Larcom; "To a Snowflake," by Francis Thompson; "Snow Flakes," by Longfellow; "The Frost Spirit," by Whittier. How do these compare with Snow-Bound in quality and effectiveness of description?

READING ON NEW ENGLAND'S GOLDEN YEARS

ON INDIVIDUAL AUTHORS

EMERSON. Brooks, Van Wyck, The Life of Emerson (Literary Guild, 1932); Whicher, S. E., Freedom and Fate: An Inner Life of Ralph Waldo Emerson (Univ. of Pennsylvania Press, 1953)

THOREAU. Canby, H. S., Thoreau (Houghton Mifflin, 1943); Kane, Henry B., Thoreau's Walden (Knopf, 1946); Norman, Charles, To a Different Drum (Harper, 1954); Whicher, G. F., Walden Revisited (Hendricks, 1945)

LONGFELLOW. Wagenknecht, Edward, Longfellow, A Full-Length Portrait (Longmans, 1955)

LOWELL. Howard, Leon, Victorian Knight-Errant (Univ. of California Press, 1952)

HOLMES. Bowen, Catherine, Yankee from Olympus, on Holmes's son, but contains good background material (Little, Brown, 1944); Tilton, Eleanor M., The Amiable Autocrat (Abelard, 1947)

FOR LISTENING

Longfellow's "The Tide Rises, the Tide Falls" and "Hymn to the Night," and Lowell's "The Courtin'" have been recorded on Many Voices 5B; Emerson's "Forbearance," "Voluntaries III," and "Compensation" have been recorded on Many Voices 11B.

Growth and Conflict

GREAT OPEN SPACES of land always exert a powerful pull on the human tide. The vast American West, much of it land of the most desirable kind despite desert stretches and hazards from Indians, drew a steady flow of men from the eastern coastal states. "Westward the course of empire takes its way" became the American motto. The movement was irresistible—the wonder of all who observed it. By mid-century the boundaries of the nation extended to the Rio Grande on the south, to Puget Sound on the north, and to the Pacific Ocean on the west. At the same time, the center of literature shifted from New England and moved across the Appalachians and out to the Mississippi Valley, and beyond. Americans, and American literature, moved westward.

The Advancing Frontier

The word "frontier" had two meanings in the early nineteenth century. In Europe it meant the border between one nation and another. In expanding young America, it meant something very different. Here, "frontier" referred to the ever-shifting, hard-to-measure line between settlement and sheer wilderness. It is the place where the pioneer comes up against wilderness; where society starts over again. It is more than a location, it is a stage of culture. The American frontier, over many years, was pushed westward until the land was mastered from sea to sea. After that, the remaining task was one of development.

The movement west was slow getting started, for all the rivers flowed eastward into the Atlantic, there were no roads to the interior, and the giant Appalachians created a massive barrier from Canada to Georgia. Once across the Appalachians, there came a plunge into the vast, primeval forests, oppressing and frightening to many. Yet pioneers began to follow the Indian trails through the mountains, and soon there were roads connecting the eastward-flowing rivers with those that flowed to the west — to the Ohio and down the Mississippi to the Gulf of Mexico. Then, in 1825, the Erie canal was opened and a new surge of population flooded along the canal and on the waters of the Great Lakes out onto the plains.

There were several waves of migration and several periods of development. First came the woodsmen — "woodsies" some called them — men who felt restless and cramped if there were another settler within miles of them. Game was their food, and fur was their trade. When others followed, they pushed on. Behind this first wave came those who settled down to the serious clearing of the land, the creating of fields where forest had been. After the fields came the growth of towns, some of which were the beginnings of great cities.

Thomas Carlyle, Emerson's Scottish friend, wrote to the Concord sage in 1849:

> How beautiful to think of lean, tough Yankee settlers . . . steering over the Western Mountains to annihilate the jungle . . .

Putting aside the inaccuracy of "jungle," it is an apt comment on an extraordinary migration. It is difficult to explain exactly what caused the movement. "Why do you climb Mt. Everest?" someone asked the English mountaineer Mallory, who later lost his life on its heights. "Because it is there," was his answer. In the same way, it must be that those Americans who felt the tug of the open land to the west could not resist what they called simply the "strong bent of their spirits to remove thither."

The woods and the great rivers are not the whole story of the westward movement. Prairie, desert, and mountain each has its own drama. The covered wagon, or "prairie schooner," is an epic symbol in itself. Before the wagons rolled, Lewis and Clark had worked their way along the rugged route that became the famed Oregon Trail, opening the door to the Pacific Northwest. Other parties struck for California on the Santa Fe and Old Spanish trails. This was an era that saw human and animal bones left along thousands of miles of desolate land. It saw tragedies such as that of the ill-fated Donner party, which perished in blizzards on the mountain passes (see page 207). Yet no matter what hardships they had to face, some always made their way through.

PIONEER READING

Wilderness frontiers were crude and rough, but not all that came from them was crudeness: consider Mark Twain and Abraham Lincoln. Books were precious to the pioneers, as the youthful Lincoln's hunger for reading demonstrates. The Bible was in many cabins. Two of the earliest observers of the wilderness, the French visitor De Tocqueville (page 489) and the ornithologist (student of bird life) John James Audubon, testified to finding the Bible and volumes of Shakespeare's works in lonely settlements. These books, together with *The Pilgrim's Progress* by the seventeenth-century English writer John Bunyan, helped mold frontier styles in speech and writing.

FOLKLORE OF THE FRONTIER

The drama of the westward thrust generated legendary tales. Certain names sprang into prominence and were talked about by the pioneers. It was the kind of talk that breeds legends.

Several real persons became entwined in folklore. One of the first, and by far the gentlest, was Jonathan Chapman, who passed into the American tradition as "Johnny Appleseed." In the first half of the nineteenth century, Johnny wandered the wilderness regions that became Ohio and Indiana. With his seed-laden knapsacks he established countless orchards. The seeds, and religious books — seeds of another sort — were all he carried. He was respected and loved by all; unharmed by wild creatures, and never molested by Indians even in times of war.

Daniel Boone and Davy Crockett were real figures whose images soon grew to legendary proportions. Crockett was elected to Congress. Political writers produced a supposed autobiography, *A Narrative of the Life of Colonel Crockett, of the State of Tennessee* (1834), and other books that were attributed to him. It is unlikely that Crockett had much to do with writing the books, but they passed with their subject into American folk literature. Crockett met, in the Alamo, a heroic death that was worthy of his legend. Along the Mississippi and Ohio were the brawling rivermen — Mike Fink was characteristic of them — each ready to tell all comers that he was "half horse, half alligator, a little touched with the snapping turtle; can wade the Mississippi, leap the Ohio, ride upon a streak of lightning, and slip without a scratch down a honey locust; can whip my weight in

"Road West Through the Alleghenies," an aquatint made from a sketch by the Swiss artist Karl Bodmer (1805–1893).

wildcats — and, if any gentleman pleases, for a ten-dollar bill, he may throw in a panther." All these legends found their way into books as writers like Mark Twain, whose boyhood and youth were spent along the Mississippi River, began to publish their knowledge of the frontier and its robust life.

FRONTIER AND INDIAN RECORDS

The ornithologist John James Audubon both painted and wrote about the wilderness scene. Many other pioneers kept journals and diaries, wrote letters, and preserved their written records. There are recollections of the perilous trek across the desert, like that of Sarah Eleanor Royce, mother of a famous Harvard philosopher, Josiah Royce.

Earliest of all western literature was, of course, the Indian's. Except for the Cherokees of the southeastern states, the Indians had no written literature, but many of the most civilized tribes had a large and elaborate oral literature. Some of their poetry of oral tradition has recently been recorded by students of folklore.

Two Major Writers

The finest early contributions to the record of westward expansion were made by two New England writers. Francis Parkman told the story of a land route west, and Richard Henry Dana, Jr., described the journey by sea to California and back.

In his youth Francis Parkman did not seem likely to travel in the rugged West, nor to have much prospect of a literary career. He was a frail, sheltered child

Francis Parkman

from a well-to-do Boston family. Like most young men of such origins, he went to Harvard, where, in common with many of our literary men, he studied law, which he was never to practice.

Much of Parkman's life was spent as an invalid. His eyes were also weak, so weak that it was almost impossible for him to read. Parkman's handicap was similar to that of his fellow historian Prescott. Parkman's frailties angered him; his energetic, bold nature refused to submit to confinement. At twenty-three, in 1846, Parkman went west to explore the frontier, assuming that the wild country would either strengthen or kill him.

He and another young Bostonian, Quincy Adams Shaw, plunged as tenderfeet into a strange, new world. A modern novelist of the west, A. B. Guthrie, has remarked that they were lucky. The year of their travels was a quiet one among the Indians. These novices also gained security by having as a guide Henry Chatillon, an experienced mountain man who was married to a chief's daughter. Their rambling, casual trip would have been impossible a year or so later, since Indian hostility was on the rise. At the time, however, what Parkman calls the Dakotas (the Sioux), and the Pawnees, both formidable tribes, received them peaceably, and Parkman gives us an excellent picture of their life and ways. Determined and venturesome, though at times he was so ill he could not ride, Parkman worked his way most of the length of the Oregon Trail, then turned south and made his return to the Mississippi along the Santa Fe Trail.

Parkman's physical weakness was not cured by his trip. Indeed, he suffered a severe breakdown after his return. Yet his vigorous determination flourished. He dictated his record of the experience to his friend Shaw. The book, entitled *The Oregon Trail* (1849), became popular immediately, and it remains an American classic. Not as important as his great histories that were to follow, it is still Parkman's most widely read work.

Dependent on others for help, seldom able to read or write more than a few lines a day, this remarkable historian nevertheless produced a massive history of the French in the New World. The seven volumes of this work stretched from the days of the Jesuit explorers through the French and Indian War, which determined who would control the destiny of North America. Parkman concluded the work in 1892, a year before his death. A modern critic has said, "There seems to be little doubt that Francis Parkman was America's greatest narrative historian."

RICHARD HENRY DANA, JR.

Another young writer whose career was affected by eye trouble was Richard Henry Dana, Jr. During his days as a Harvard undergraduate, Dana was forced to drop his studies because of failing eyesight. He was more fortunate than Prescott or Parkman, for he managed to recover from the condition. To help relieve his eyes from the strain of reading, in 1834 Dana signed as a common seaman for a voyage to California on the brig *Pilgrim*. He returned on another vessel.

In 1840 he published the account of his adventures, *Two Years Before the Mast*. It has held its place ever since as a stirring, realistic description of life at sea that has influenced all later writing of sea tales. The book received the finest tribute it could have: it was widely read by sailors, who testified that this was indeed an accurate picture of life on shipboard. Dana included some hair-raising accounts of shipboard dangers, such as his being sent aloft into the rigging of a wildly plunging ship. He depicted, too, the brutality of discipline in the merchant marine, and the book aroused indignation at the injustices suffered by sailors.

The book adds to the picture of a growing, restless America. Dana's voyage around the Horn to California was a common route to the West, especially in the later Gold Rush years. Dana gives a vivid picture of Spanish-ruled California and of the crude shack settlement that was San Francisco.

Back at Harvard, his eyes strengthened, Dana completed his study of law. He stayed in that profession rather than continuing a career in literature. He was actively concerned in gaining justice for sailors, and they often sought his help in legal problems. Though he wrote a little more, he produced nothing else that lives beside his first fine book. The fame of *Two Years Before the Mast* lost its savor for Dana in later years. He once said, "My life has been a failure compared with what I might and ought to have done . . . My great success — my book — was a boy's work . . ." Dana's destiny would have surprised him. He had a solid, if not brilliant, career in law, but his "boy's work" is what we remember him for.

Richard Henry Dana, Jr.

INDIAN
FOLK
LITERATURE

Though Cooper had idealized the individual Indian, and Longfellow had romanticized him in his *Hiawatha*, it was not until the twentieth century that Americans became interested in Indian folk literature. With the aid of the phonograph, this body of oral tradition could now be studied and translated.

Indian culture was varied: some tribes led a desperate hand-to-mouth existence little better than that of the animals around them; but others, in particular the proud, mounted Indians of the plains and the pueblo dwellers of the Southwest, found time to develop legends and songs rich in imagery.

Lament of a Young Man for His Son

TRANSLATED FROM THE PAIUTE * BY MARY AUSTIN

Son, my son!
I will go up to the mountain
And there I will light a fire
To the feet of my son's spirit,
And there I will lament him;   5
Saying,
O my son,
What is life to me, now you are departed?

Son, my son,
In the deep earth   10
We softly laid thee
In a chief's robe,
In a warrior's gear.
Surely there,
In the spirit land   15
Thy deeds attend thee!

* **Paiute** (pī·ūt'): a tribe of Shoshonean Indians who lived in the American Southwest.

"Lament of a Young Man for His Son," translated by Mary Austin. Reprinted by permission of and arrangement with Houghton Mifflin Company, the authorized publishers.

Surely,
The corn comes to the ear again!
But I, here,
I am the stalk that the seed-gatherers   20
Descrying° empty, afar, left standing.
Son, my son!
What is my life to me, now you are departed?

21. Descrying: observing.

In the settled life of the Pueblo Indians of the Southwest, weaving was a highly developed art. Weaving terms often figured in their speech. To the Tewa Indians, for instance, the light desert rain characteristic of that part of the country, with its showers visibly threading their way downward, looked like the loom on which they wove their blankets. They called such showers the "sky loom." Any rain was a blessing in their parched land. This song is a prayer for one of the desert rains.

Song of the Sky Loom

TEWA INDIAN SONG

O our Mother the Earth, O our Father the Sky,
Your children are we, and with tired backs
We bring you the gifts you love.
Then weave for us a garment of brightness;
May the warp be the white light of morning,   5
May the weft be the red light of evening,
May the fringes be the falling rain,
May the border be the standing rainbow.
Thus weave for us a garment of brightness,
That we may walk fittingly where birds sing,   10
That we may walk fittingly where grass is green,
O our Mother the Earth, O our Father the Sky.

FOR DISCUSSION

LAMENT OF A YOUNG MAN FOR HIS SON

What is the deep feeling conveyed in these lines? To what extent does this lament meet your standards for poetry?

SONG OF THE SKY LOOM

Why do you think the Pueblos regard the earth as their mother, the sky as their father? How is the picture of a loom developed by various images in the poem?

FURTHER READING

You can read more Indian songs in *The Winged Serpent* (John Day, 1946), edited by Margot Astrov, and narratives in *Indian Tales of the Desert People* by W. D. Hayes (McKay, 1957).

INDIAN HUMOR

The American Indian, with his poetic love of natural beauty, was not always solemn. Here is a little song translated by James Powell:

> The poor little bee
> That lives in the tree,
> The poor little bee
> That lives in the tree
> Has only one arrow
> In his quiver.

STANLEY
VESTAL

1887–1957

John Colter's Race for Life

The first of the westward-pushing Americans to come in contact with the Indians were the trappers and fur traders. Courage, quickwittedness, and stamina were demanded of these men on that outer fringe of the frontier. One of the most famous encounters of the trappers was John Colter's foot race with the Blackfeet.

J OHN COLTER caused the mountain men more trouble than any other one man living. For hostile Injuns gave the trappers more trouble than all other things combined, and of all the hostiles on the Missouri, the Blackfeet were the worst. That is why Colter may be said to have caused the mountain men so much trouble. He it was who made the Blackfeet hostile!

It happened in this way: Manuel Lisa, that old fox of the fur trade, was burning up with eagerness to trade with the Blackfeet. All traders were, for that matter, because the Blackfeet had a magnificent range, rich in fur and game of all kinds, and utterly unspoiled — since they allowed no white

trappers in their country. Lisa had talked with some Blackfeet at his fort at the mouth of the Big Horn, and had found them friendly. He rubbed his greedy hands, and made up his mind to send a man to the Three Forks of the Missouri to fix things up with the chiefs.

John Colter was the best man Lisa had. John Colter was the man to go. And because old Lisa was so greedy, he sent Colter also to the camps of the Crow Nation — then on the Upper Wind River, near Jackson's Hole.

It was five hundred miles to the Crow camp. But Colter, a veteran of the Lewis and Clark expedition who had already spent several winters trapping on the Upper Missouri, simply filled his shot pouch and powder horn, slung a thirty-pound pack on his shoulders, picked up his long rifle, and hit the trail alone. Five hundred miles was nothing to John Colter. Before he was through, he walked five thousand.

He found the Crows on Wind River and informed them that Lisa was coming to trade. Then he asked the chiefs to send a man to guide him over the mountains to the headwaters of the Missouri. No white man had ever gone that way before.

That request made the chiefs grunt and stare. They knew that no Crow living was bold enough to venture alone into the country of the hostile Blackfeet. For ages those two tribes had been deadly enemies. Old Lisa's packs couldn't hold enough vermilion,[1] gunpowder, or butcher knives to pay for a risk like that. They didn't like to admit that, but it was true. And so they merely stared and grunted.

But Colter insisted, and at last, after conferring among themselves, the chiefs agreed to guide him through.

"Good," said Colter. "Who will go with me?"

The oldest chief grinned at the fearless white man. "We *all* go," he said grimly.

Then Colter and a heap of Crows headed west through that wild, rugged country, crossed the Wind River Mountains by Togwotee Pass, and the Teton[2] Range by Teton Pass. That brought them to the Teton Basin, known in old times as Pierre's Hole.

That lovely valley was dangerous country — a battleground of warring tribes. The Blackfeet and their allies, the Gros Ventres[3] of the prairies, claimed the Hole as their hunting grounds. No spot in the mountains held more peril for the mountain men.

One afternoon, as the colorful cavalcade strung down into the broad valley, Colter suddenly halted. Up ahead, behind a clump of sagebrush, he had seen somebody moving. But now that he had halted he saw nothing. There was not a sound to be heard.

Then, suddenly, a man sprang up and tossed a double handful of dust into the air, as an angry buffalo bull paws up the earth before he charges. The wind caught the dust and spread it into a broad, tawny banner — the

Injun call to battle. At the same moment the war whoop chattered in Colter's ears, raising prickles along his spine: *Wah-ah-ah-ah-ah!*

"Blackfeet!" yelled the Crow chief, pulling the buckskin cover from his fusil.[4]

Blackfeet — or Gros Ventres — they certainly were, and on the warpath! A hundred of them suddenly rose from the ground like magic, and came plunging pell-mell out of the ravine and across the open. On they came at the dead run on their spotted ponies, with motley ornaments and arms, splendid war bonnets of lustrous black-and-white eagle feathers swinging about their heads, half-naked, painted, yelling at the top of their lungs, brandishing their bows and lances.

The Crow chief rode back and forth, yelling at his men. They were all in confusion, stripping off their buffalo robes, jerking the covers from their shields, unlimbering their bows, yelling and singing war songs to make their hearts strong. Looking at them, Colter almost wished he had come alone.

He sat still in his saddle. He had no wish to fight the Crows' battles. He had come there to smoke with the Blackfeet.

But already the battle had been joined. The foremost Blackfeet were upon the Crows, charging them confidently with all the advantage of superior numbers, surprise, and the fierce momentum of attack. They circled along the Crow front, waging a hit-and-run warfare, pushing the disorganized Crows back. Every moment the Crows gave ground. Colter found himself out in front, alone.

The Blackfeet charged past him like swallows or swooping hawks. The first to pass tapped him smartly over the head with his bow. The second stung his left leg with an arrow, which passed through, pinning him to his pony's ribs.

[1] **vermilion** (vẽr·mĭl′yŭn): a red pigment used for war paint.

[2] **Teton** (tē′tŏn).

[3] **Gros Ventres** (grō väɴ′tr′): French for "big stomachs," from their greediness.

[4] **fusil** (fū′zĭl): a flintlock musket.

The horse reared and shook his head, fighting the bit, as the third Injun dashed up and tried to split Colter's skull with a hatchet.

Then Colter went into action. His rifle lay across the pommel of his saddle. Without raising it, he yanked back the hammer, pulled the trigger, and dropped the nearest of his enemies. Then he swung his rifle in one hand and knocked the second from his saddle. The third he caught by his long hair, pulled him backward across his own horse, and stabbed him in the ear.

That was enough for the Blackfeet. The others sheered off from Colter, and gave him time to gain control of his plunging horse, cut off the shaft of the arrow through his leg, dismount, and reload.

Then the Crows, seeing their lone ally victorious, rallied. And as they swarmed back toward him, Colter threw himself prone, leveled his rifle, and picked off another painted enemy. His third shot killed the Blackfoot chief's horse. At that, the Blackfeet galloped away out of range, the chief hanging on to the tail of one of the Blackfoot ponies.

From that safe distance they made insulting gestures at the Crows and called to them in the Blackfoot language, which Colter understood well enough. "The white man saved you," they jeered. "Wait!" they yelled. "We have friends with guns, too. Stay where you are, and tomorrow we will rub you out to the last man."

The Crows skirmished with the Blackfeet until sundown. Then the Blackfeet rode away.

Colter dressed his wounded leg as best he could. His leg was sore; but his heart was sorer than his leg, for he knew that this chance fight had made his mission a failure. The Blackfeet had seen him, knew him for a white man, blamed their defeat upon him. Probably they would recognize him if they saw him again. He dared not venture farther into their country after that. His only consolation was that it wasn't his fault.

That night the Crows did not make camp in the Hole. They hit the trail for their camp on Wind River.

Colter protested, but the Crows covered their ears. Their chief said blandly, "You asked us to bring you over the mountains. We have done it. Now we go home." And away they went.

Colter refused to go with them. He remained in the Hole with his wounded leg. But not for long. He mounted, rode on the trail of the Crows until he found a place where he could diverge from it and cover his trail. Then he struck into the pines and rode for Lisa's fort at the mouth of the Big Horn. That unexplored route took him across what is now Yellowstone Park. It was the summer of 1807.

Thus Colter was the first white man to behold the wonders of the Yellowstone, to see the Three Tetons, Pierre's Hole, and the headwaters of Snake River. At last he got back to the fort, where he passed the winter. His leg healed nicely, and he had little to do but grow a beard.

Old Lisa was deeply disappointed. But he could not give up his dream of trade with the Blackfeet. In the spring he ordered Colter to go and visit them again! This time a man named Potts went along.

The two of them made headquarters on the Jefferson Fork of the Missouri and set their traps, waiting for Injuns to show up. They had not long to wait.

Neither of these men was very eager to meet the Blackfeet. They set their traps by night, and took them up again before sunrise. One morning very early the two of them were paddling silently up a small creek on the Jefferson Fork, examining their traps from their canoe. All at once they heard a great noise, as of a herd of horses or buffalo. The banks of the little stream were too high for them to see what caused the racket.

Colter whispered to his comrade, "Injuns. Let's cache!"

"You must be scairt, for sartain," Potts sneered. "Them's buffaloes."

Colter might have argued the matter. But before he could say anything, the Indians came in sight, hundreds of them — and on both sides of the creek. They signaled the white men to come ashore.

The trappers had no choice. They paddled to the bank. The moment the canoe touched the bank, the nearest Indian grabbed Potts's rifle. But Colter, who was a big man and as strong as he was brave, wrested it from the redskin and handed it back to Potts. Colter stepped ashore. But Potts, now thoroughly frightened, stayed in the canoe and shoved off into the water.

That move ended all pretense of friendship. One of the Indians shot an arrow at Potts. The man in the canoe called out, "Colter, I'm wounded!"

"Come on back, you fool!" Colter yelled. "You cain't get away now."

But Potts, losing his head again, raised his rifle, took aim at the mass of Indians, and fired. One of the redskins dropped, dead as a nail. Immediately the air was filled with arrows; and Potts collapsed in the canoe, stuck full of feathered shafts. As Colter said, "He was made a riddle of."

The folly of Potts had put poor Colter in terrible jeopardy. The Indians grabbed him, tore off his clothing, held him fast. Then they began to talk and gesture, arguing as to the method by which he should be put to death. He waited, helpless, naked as a jay bird, while his executioners coolly discussed the method of his slaying.

Most of them favored setting him up as a target for their arrows. But one of the chiefs, wishing to show his authority, differed from the rest. Going up to Colter, he took hold of him by his shoulders, shook him, and demanded to know how fast he could run.

During his stay with the Crows, Colter had made it a point to learn some Blackfoot words. Their language was commonly understood by their neighbors. Colter knew what the chief was saying. He knew that he had a chance to make "the Injun run."

The trapper was a swift runner, and he infinitely preferred a run for his life to being tied up and slowly tortured to death with arrows. Therefore, he cunningly replied that he was a very bad runner. "No good," he answered. "Heap no good."

The chief grinned grimly. Taking Colter from his captors, he led him out on the prairie some three hundred yards from the horde of redskins. Then, turning the white man loose, he said, "Run, then, and save yourself, if you *can!*"

The chief beckoned to his followers. They yelped the war whoop. Colter sprang forward, and ran so fast that he surprised himself.

Before him stretched the open prairie. Beyond it, six miles away, lay the Jefferson Fork. He ran for that, and for three miles he did not look back.

No wonder. The plain was thick with prickly pear, and Colter's feet were bare. Soon the soles of his feet were filled with the spines of the cactus. But Colter did not let that slow him down. He preferred cactus spines to arrows in his body. He ran like a deer. And when he did look back over his shoulder, he took courage. Most of the Indians were far behind. Only one — a long-legged fellow armed with a lance — was nearer than a hundred yards.

For the first time Colter began to hope that he might escape. He put everything he had into the race, and sprinted so hard that a torrent of blood burst from his nostrils and covered his chest and belly. That almost finished him, but he labored on, though he knew that the man with the lance was gaining.

The river was only a mile off now. But suddenly he heard the thud of his enemy's feet coming up behind. Every moment he expected to feel the spear-head strike his naked back. He looked over his shoulder — the warrior was not twenty paces back! He knew that it would not be long now.

Colter was a fighter; he had no intention of being stabbed from behind without a struggle. And so, unarmed, bleeding, and naked as he was, he suddenly stopped, faced about, and spread out his arms.

The warrior, startled at this sudden move and at Colter's body all covered with blood, tried to stop, and raised his lance to strike the white man. But he was tired also, and stumbled as he threw the lance. The point struck the earth and lodged there; the shaft broke in his hand. The Blackfoot went down.

Colter snatched up the lance head, stabbed the redskin before he could get up. Then he ran on. When the foremost Indians reached their dying comrade, they halted; and all at once began to wail and yell.

But Colter, gasping and exhausted as he was, never faltered. He plunged on to the river bottoms, rushed through the fringe of stately cottonwoods, and plunged into the cool waters of the river. The current swept him down, half-fainting.

Not far below lay an island; and about it a great clutter of drift timber had piled up, making a sort of raft above the island. Colter dived under these interlocked logs and, coming to the surface, bumped his head several times upon them. Finally, when his lungs were ready to burst, he managed to find a space among the trunks above water — and rested there, drawing deep breaths in the darkness. His hiding place was covered with small drift, leaves, and sticks — a layer several feet deep.

From that refuge he heard the Blackfeet come running down the bank, screeching like so many devils. All that day they poked about the pile of driftwood. Sometimes he could see them

through the chinks of his hiding place. But whenever he thought they might see him, he pulled himself entirely under water. He began to think he had saved his life, until it came to his mind that they might set the wood on fire.

So he remained, torn with anxiety, until at last night came. Then, hearing nothing of the Blackfeet, he dived out from under the ruck of logs, and floated down river until he thought all danger of discovery was ended. Then he swam ashore, and hurried overland toward Lisa's fort all night.

He was fully seven days' journey from the fort. He was starving, and had no means of killing meat. He was naked and exposed to the rays of the summer sun. His feet were full of spines, swollen and sore. But it was the season when the tipsin ripens, and Colter fed himself on this root as he went along. Somehow or other he reached the fort at last.

Such was John Colter.

FOR DISCUSSION

1. What incident shows Colter to be cooler in judgment than the other trappers? How does his endurance compare with that developed by modern athletes? Which of his actions show unusual courage?

2. This narrative, like many others about the period, shows that chance played a large part in determining whether the Indians were to be friends or enemies. What piece of bad luck turned the tide against Colter on two different occasions?

3. Discuss whether or not the events in this story seem true or exaggerated, convincing or unconvincing. Point out some specific examples.

4. Note that Old Lisa has a certain power over John Colter. Why, do you feel, does Colter obey Lisa's orders so willingly? What does your answer to this question contribute to your interpretation of the closing sentence: "Such was John Colter"?

SARAH ELEANOR ROYCE

1819– ?

Peril on the Western Trail

FROM *A Frontier Lady*

Among the famous forty-niners seeking fortune in the California gold rush was the Josiah Royce family. Mrs. Royce's diary, unpublished until 1932, gives a personal account of the hazards of crossing the desert in a covered wagon drawn by oxen.

W<small>E</small> WERE traveling parallel with a placid river on our right, beyond which were trees; and from us to the water's edge, the ground sloped so gently it appeared absurd not to turn aside to its brink and refresh ourselves and our oxen.

But as day dawned, these beautiful sights disappeared, and we began to look anxiously for the depression in the ground and the holes dug which we were told would mark the Sink of the Humboldt. But it was nearly noonday before we came to them. There was still some passable water in the holes, but not fit to drink clear; so we contrived to gather enough sticks of sage to boil some, made a little coffee, ate our lunch, and thus refreshed, we hastened to find

"Peril on the Western Trail" from *A Frontier Lady* by Sarah Royce. Reprinted by permission of Yale University Press.

the forking road. Our director had told us that within about two or three miles beyond the Sink we might look for the road to the left, and we did look, and kept looking and going on drearily till the sun got lower and lower and night was fast approaching. Then the conviction which had long been gaining ground in my mind took possession of the whole party. We had passed the forks of the road before daylight that morning and were now miles out on the desert without a mouthful of food for the cattle and only two or three quarts of water in a little cask.

What could be done? Halt we must, for the oxen were nearly worn out and night was coming on. The animals must at least rest, if they could not be fed; and that they might rest, they were chained securely to the wagon, for, hungry and thirsty as they were, they would, if loose, start off frantically in search of water and food and soon drop down exhausted. Having fastened them in such a way that they could lie down, we took a few mouthfuls of food, and then, we in our wagon and the men not far off upon the sand, fell wearily to sleep — a forlorn little company wrecked upon the desert.

The first question in the morning was,

"How can the oxen be kept from starving?" A happy thought occurred. We had thus far on our journey managed to keep something in the shape of a bed to sleep on. It was a mattress tick, and just before leaving Salt Lake, we had put into it some fresh hay — not very much, for our load must be as light as possible; but the old gentleman traveling with us had also a small straw mattress; the two together might keep the poor things from starving for a few hours. At once a small portion was dealt out to them, and for the present they were saved. For ourselves we had food which we believed would about last us till we reached the gold mines if we could go right on; if we were much delayed anywhere, it was doubtful. The two or three quarts of water in our little cask would last only a few hours, to give moderate drinks to each of the party. For myself I inwardly determined I should scarcely take any of it, as I had found throughout the journey that I could do with less drink than most land travelers. Some of the men, however, easily suffered with thirst, and as to my little girl, it is well known a child cannot do long without either water or milk. Everything looked rather dark and dubious.

Should we try to go on? But there were miles of desert before us, in which we knew neither grass or water could be found. . . . Here we were without water and with only a few mouthfuls of poor feed, while our animals were already tired out and very hungry and thirsty. No, it would be madness to go farther out in the desert under such conditions. Should we then turn back and try to reach the meadows with their wells? But as near as we could calculate, it could not be less than twelve or fifteen miles to them. Would it be possible for our poor cattle to reach there? Their only food would be that pitiful mess still left in our mattresses. It might be divided into two portions, giving them each a few mouthfuls more at noon, and then, if they kept on their feet long enough to reach the holes at the Sink, we might possibly find enough water to give them each a little drink, which with the remainder of the fodder might keep them up till the meadows were reached. It was a forlorn hope, but it was all we had.

The morning was wearing away while these things were talked over. Precious time was being wasted, but the truth was the situation was so new and unexpected that it seemed for a while to confuse — almost to stupefy — most of the little party; and those least affected in this way felt so deeply the responsibility of the next move that they dared not decide upon it hastily. . . . But this would never do. So the more hopeful ones proposed that we should all eat something and as soon as the noon heat abated, prepare for a move. So we took some lunch, and soon the men were lying upon the sand at short distances from each other, fast asleep. Soon some of the party awoke and after a little talk concluded that two of them would walk to a bald ridge that rose out of the flat waste about a mile and a half distant and take a view from thence in the faint hope that we might yet be mistaken and the forking road and the meadows might still be in advance. My husband said he would go, and the best of the two young men went with him, while the other two wandered listlessly off again. I made no opposition; I felt no inclination to oppose, though I knew the helplessness and loneliness of the position would thus be greatly increased. But that calm strength, that certainty of One near and all-sufficient, hushed and cheered me. Only a woman who has been alone upon a desert with her helpless child can have any adequate idea of my experience for the next hour or two. But that consciousness of an unseen Presence still sustained me.

When the explorers returned from

their walk to the ridge, it was only to report no discovery, nothing to be seen on all sides but sand and scattered sagebrush interspersed with the carcasses of dead cattle. So there was nothing to be done but to turn back and try to find the meadows. Turn back! What a chill the words sent through one. Turn back, on a journey like that, in which every mile had been gained by most earnest labor, growing more and more intense until of late it had seemed that the certainty of advance with every step was all that made the next step possible. And now for miles we were to go back. In all that long journey no steps ever seemed so heavy, so hard to take, as those with which I turned my back to the sun that afternoon of October 4, 1849.

We had not been long on the move when we saw dust rising in the road at a distance and soon perceived we were about to meet a little caravan of wagons. Then a bright gleam of hope stole in. They had doubtless stopped at the meadow and were supplied with grass and water. Might it not be possible that they would have enough to spare for us? Then we could go on with them. My heart bounded at the thought. But the hope was short-lived. We met, and some of the men gathered round our wagon with eager inquiries, while those who could not leave their teams stood looking with wonder at a solitary wagon headed the wrong way.

Our story was soon told. It turned out that they were camping in the meadows at the very time we passed the forking road without seeing it, the morning we so ambitiously started soon after midnight. Ah, we certainly got up too early that day! If we had only seen that road and taken it, we might now have been with this company, provided for the desert, and no longer alone. But when the question was asked whether they could spare sufficient grass and water to get our team over the desert, they shook their heads and unanimous-

ly agreed that it was out of the question. Their own cattle, they said, were weak from long travel and too often scant supplies. They had only been able to load up barely enough to get to the Carson River. The season was far advanced, and the clouds hanging of late round the mountaintops looked threatening. It would be like throwing away their own lives without any certainty of saving ours, for, once out in the desert without food, we would all be helpless together. One of the men had his family with him, a wife and two or three children; and while they talked the woman was seen coming toward us. She had not, when they first halted, understood that any but men were with the lone wagon. As soon as she heard to the contrary and what were the circumstances, she hastened, with countenance full of concern, to condole with me; and I think, had the decision depended alone upon her, she would have insisted upon our turning back with them and sharing their feed and water to the last.

But fortunately for them, probably for us all, other counsel prevailed, and we resumed our depressing backward march. . . .

I had now become so impressed with the danger of the cattle giving out that I refused to ride except for occasional brief rests. So, soon after losing sight of the dust of the envied little caravan, I left the wagon and walked the remainder of the day. For a good while I kept near the wagon, but by and by, being very weary, I fell behind. The sun had set before we reached the Sink, and the light was fading fast when the wagon disappeared from my sight behind a slight elevation; and as the others had gone on in advance some time before, I was all alone on the barren waste. However, as I recognized the features of the neighborhood and knew we were quite near the Sink, I felt no particular apprehension, only a feeling that it was a weird and dreary scene,

so slowly and I was so preternaturally [1]
stimulated by anxiety to get forward
that before I was aware of it I would
be some rods ahead of the cattle, straining my gaze as if expecting to see a
land of promise, long before I had any
rational hope of the kind. My imagination acted intensely. I seemed to see
Hagar [2] in the wilderness walking wearily away from her fainting child among
the dried-up bushes and seating herself
in the hot sand. I seemed to become
Hagar myself, and when my little one
from the wagon behind me called out,
"Mamma, I want a drink," I stopped,
gave her some, noted that there were
but a few swallows left, then mechanically pressed onward again, alone, repeating over and over the words, "Let
me not see the death of the child." [3]

Wearily passed the hottest noonday
hour, with many an anxious look at the
horned heads which seemed to me to
bow lower and lower, while the poor
tired hoofs almost refused to move. The
two young men had been out of sight
for some time when all at once we
heard a shout and saw, a few hundred
yards in advance, a couple of hats
thrown into the air and four hands
waving triumphantly. As soon as we got
near enough, we heard them call out,
"Grass and water! Grass and water!"
and shortly we were at the meadows.

On Monday morning we loaded up,
but did not hurry, for the cattle had
not rested any too long; another day
would have been better, but we dared
not linger. So, giving them time that
morning thoroughly to satisfy themselves with grass and water, we once
more set forward toward the formidable desert and, at that late season,
with our equipment, and the scarcely

and instinctively urged forward my
lagging footsteps in hope of regaining
sight of the wagon.

The next morning we resumed our
backward march after feeding out the
last mouthful of fodder. The water in
the little cask was nearly used up in
making coffee for supper and breakfast,
but if only each one would be moderate in taking a share when thirst impelled him, we might yet reach the
walls before anyone suffered seriously.
We had lately had but few chances for
cooking, and only a little boiled rice
with dried fruit and a few bits of biscuit remained after we had done breakfast. If we could only reach the meadows by noon! But that we could hardly
hope for; the animals were so weak and
tired. There was no alternative, however; the only thing to be done was to
go steadily on, determined to do and
endure to the utmost.

I found no difficulty this morning in
keeping up with the team. They went

[1] **preternaturally** (prē′tẽr·năt′ụ·ră·lĭ): ab-
normally.
[2] **Hagar** (hā′gär): bondwoman of Sarah
and Abraham in the Bible (Genesis, 21).
With her son Ishmael she was an outcast.
[3] "**Let . . . child.**": Hagar speaks these
words in the wilderness.

less formidable Sierras. The feeling that we were once more going forward instead of backward gave an animation to every step which we could never have felt but by contrast. By night we were again at the Sink, where we once more camped; but we durst [1] not, the following morning, launch out upon the desert with the whole day before us, for though it was now the 9th of October, the sun was still powerful for some hours daily, and the arid sand doubled its heat. Not much after noon, however, we ventured out upon the sea of sand, this time to cross or die. . . .

Morning was now approaching, and we hoped, when full daylight came, to see some signs of the river. But for two or three weary hours after sunrise nothing of the kind appeared. The last of the water had been given to the cattle before daylight. When the sun was up we gave them the remainder of their hay, took a little breakfast, and pressed forward. For a long time not a word was spoken save occasionally to the cattle. I had again unconsciously got in advance, my eyes scanning the horizon to catch the first glimpse of any change, though I had no definite idea in my mind what first to expect. But now there was surely something. Was it a cloud? It was very low at first, and I feared it might evaporate as the sun warmed it. But it became rather more distinct and a little higher. I paused and stood till the team came up. Then, walking beside it, I asked my husband what he thought that low dark line could be. "I think," he said, "it must be the timber on Carson River." Again we were silent, and for a while I watched anxiously the heads of the two leading cattle. They were rather unusually fine animals, often showing considerable intelligence, and so faithful had they been, through so many trying scenes, I could not help feeling a sort of attachment to them; and I pitied them as I observed how low their heads

[1] durst: a form of dare.

drooped as they pressed their shoulders so resolutely and yet so wearily against the bows. Another glance at the horizon. Surely there was now visible a little unevenness in the top of that dark line, as though it might indeed be trees. "How far off do you think that is now?" I said. "About five or six miles, I guess," was the reply. At that moment the white-faced leader raised his head, stretched forward his nose, and uttered a low moo-o-oo. I was startled, fearing it was the sign for him to fall, exhausted. "What is the matter with him?" I said. "I think he smells the water," was the answer. "How can he at such a distance?" As I spoke, the other leader raised his head, stretched out his nose, and uttered the same sound. The hinder cattle seemed to catch the idea, whatever it was; they all somewhat increased their pace and from that time showed renewed animation.

But we had yet many weary steps to take, and noon had passed before we stood in the shade of those longed-for trees beside the Carson River. As soon as the yokes were removed, the oxen walked into the stream and stood a few moments, apparently enjoying its coolness, then drank as they chose, came out, and soon found feed that satisfied them for the present, though at this point it was not abundant. The remainder of that day was spent in much-needed rest. . . . We had conquered the desert.

FOR DISCUSSION

1. What practical problems confronted the party? In what way were these different from problems that a party traveling over the same area now might meet?

2. What is the character of the group? of Mrs. Royce?

3. What spiritual outlook is evident in this account?

4. Do you know of any lands within our national boundaries that remain unexplored today?

SARAH ELEANOR ROYCE   639

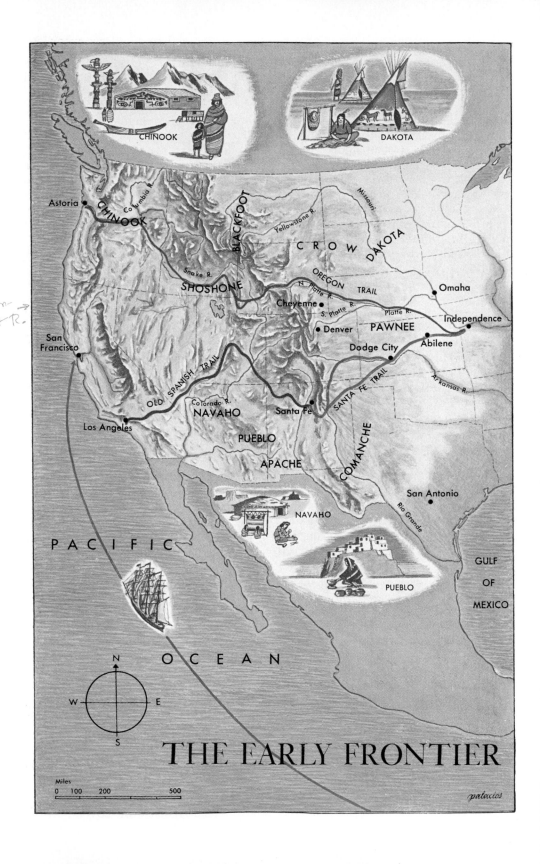

Hum-
bolt R.

THE EARLY FRONTIER

FRANCIS PARKMAN

1823–1893

The Ogillallah Village

FROM *The Oregon Trail*

Most early writing about the Indians was colored either by the hostility of those who fought them on the frontier or by the romantic notions of those who lived at a safe distance. Parkman eluded both exaggerations. Soon after finishing college, he followed the Oregon Trail on horseback — some 1,700 miles. He spent most of the summer of 1846 with a Sioux tribe, studying firsthand the Indian mind and character. His famous account of this adventurous expedition is *The Oregon Trail*, published in 1849, from which the following selection is taken.

THIS is hardly the place for portraying the mental features of the Indians. The same picture, slightly changed in shade and coloring, would serve with very few exceptions for all the tribes north of the Mexican territories. But with this similarity in their modes of thought, the tribes of the lake and ocean shores, of the forests and of the plains, differ greatly in their manner of life. Having been domesticated for several weeks among one of the wildest of the hordes that roam over the remote prairies, I had unusual opportunities of

observing them and flatter myself that a sketch of the scenes that passed daily before my eyes may not be devoid of interest. They were thorough savages. Neither their manners nor their ideas were in the slightest degree modified by contact with civilization. They knew nothing of the power and real character of the white men, and their children would scream in terror when they saw me. Their religion, superstitions, and prejudices were the same handed down to them from immemorial time. They fought with the weapons that their fathers fought with, and wore the same garments of skins. They were living representatives of the "stone age"; for though their lances and arrows were tipped with iron procured from the traders, they still used the rude stone mallet of the primeval world.

Great changes are at hand in that region. With the stream of emigration to Oregon and California, the buffalo will dwindle away, and the large wandering communities who depend on them for support must be broken and scattered. The Indians will soon be abased by whisky and overawed by military posts; so that within a few years the traveler may pass in tolerable security through their country. Its danger and its charm will have disappeared together.

As soon as Raymond and I discovered the village from the gap in the hills, we were seen in our turn; keen eyes were constantly on the watch. As we rode down upon the plain, the side of the village nearest us was darkened with a crowd of naked figures. Several men came forward to meet us. I could distinguish among them the green blanket of the Frenchman Reynal. When we came up, the ceremony of shaking hands had to be gone through in due form; and then all were eager to know what had become of the rest of my party. I satisfied them on this point, and we all moved together toward the village.

"You've missed it," said Reynal; "if you'd been here day before yesterday, you'd have found the whole prairie over yonder black with buffalo as far as you could see. There were no cows, though; nothing but bulls. We made a 'surround' every day till yesterday. See the village there; don't that look like good living?"

In fact, I could see, even at that distance, long cords stretched from lodge to lodge, over which the meat, cut by the squaws into thin sheets, was hanging to dry in the sun. I noticed, too, that the village was somewhat smaller than when I had last seen it, and I asked Reynal the cause. He said that old Le Borgne had felt too weak to pass over the mountains, and so had remained behind with all his relations, including Mahto-Tatonka and his brothers. The Whirlwind, too, had been unwilling to come so far, because, as Reynal said, he was afraid. Only half a dozen lodges had adhered to him, the main body of the village setting their chief's authority at naught and taking the course most agreeable to their inclinations.

"What chiefs are there in the village now?" asked I.

"Well," said Reynal, "there's old Red Water, and the Eagle Feather, and the Big Crow, and the Mad Wolf, and the Panther, and the White Shield, and — what's his name? — the half-breed Shienne." [1]

By this time we were close to the village, and I observed that, while the greater part of the lodges were very large and neat in their appearance, there was at one side a cluster of squalid, miserable huts. I looked toward them, and made some remark about their wretched appearance. But I was touching upon delicate ground.

"My squaw's relations live in those lodges," said Reynal, very warmly; "and there isn't a better set in the whole village."

"Are there any chiefs among them?"

"Chiefs?" said Reynal. "Yes, plenty!"

"What are their names?"

"Their names? Why, there's the Arrow-Head. If he isn't a chief, he ought to be one. And there's the Hail-Storm. He's nothing but a boy, to be sure; but he's bound to be a chief one of these days."

Just then we passed between two of the lodges, and entered the great area of the village. Superb naked figures stood silently gazing on us.

"Where's the Bad Wound's lodge?" said I to Reynal.

"There you've missed it again! The Bad Wound is away with the Whirlwind. If you could have found him here, and gone to live in his lodge, he would have treated you better than any man in the village. But there's the Big Crow's lodge yonder, next to old Red Water's. He's a good Indian for the whites, and I advise you to go and live with him."

"Are there many squaws and children in his lodge?" said I.

"No; only one squaw and two or three children. He keeps the rest in a separate lodge by themselves."

So, still followed by a crowd of Indians, Raymond and I rode up to the

[1] **Shienne** (shī-ĕn'): Parkman's spelling of Cheyenne.

entrance of Big Crow's lodge. A squaw came out immediately and took our horses. I put aside the leather flap that covered the low opening and, stooping, entered the Big Crow's dwelling. There I could see the chief in the dim light, seated at one side on a pile of buffalo robes. He greeted me with a guttural "How, Colà!" I requested Reynal to tell him that Raymond and I were come to live with him. The Big Crow gave another low exclamation. The announcement may seem intrusive, but, in fact, every Indian in the village would have deemed himself honored that white men should give such preference to his hospitality.

The squaw spread a buffalo robe for us in the guest's place at the head of the lodge. Our saddles were brought in, and scarcely were we seated upon them before the place was thronged with Indians, crowding to see us. The Big Crow produced his pipe and filled it with a mixture of tobacco and *shongsasha*, or red willow bark. Round and round it passed, and a lively conversation went forward. Meanwhile a squaw placed before the two guests a wooden bowl of boiled buffalo meat; but unhappily this was not the only banquet destined to be inflicted on us. One after another, boys and young squaws thrust their heads in at the opening, to invite us to various feasts in different parts of the village. For half an hour or more we were actively engaged in passing from lodge to lodge, in each tasting of the bowl of meat set before us and inhaling a whiff or two from our entertainer's pipe. A thunderstorm that had been threatening for some time now began in good earnest. We crossed over to Reynal's lodge, though it hardly deserved the name, for it consisted only of a few old buffalo robes, supported on poles, and was quite open on one side. Here we sat down, and the Indians gathered round us.

"What is it," said I, "that makes the thunder?"

"It's my belief," said Reynal, "that it's a big stone rolling over the sky."

"Very likely," I replied; "but I want to know what the Indians think about it."

So he interpreted my question, which produced some debate. There was a difference of opinion. At last old Mene-Seela, or Red Water, who sat by himself at one side, looked up with his withered face and said he had always known what the thunder was. It was a great black bird; and once he had seen it, in a dream, swooping down from the Black Hills, with its loud, roaring wings; and when it flapped them over a lake, they struck lightning from the water.

"The thunder is bad," said another old man, who sat muffled in his buffalo robe; "he killed my brother last summer."

Reynal, at my request, asked for an explanation; but the old man remained doggedly silent and would not look up. Some time after, I learned how the accident occurred. The man who was killed belonged to an association which, among other mystic functions, claimed the exclusive power and privilege of fighting the thunder. Whenever a storm which they wished to avert was threatening, the thunder fighters would take their bows and arrows, their guns, their magic drum, and a sort of whistle made out of the wing bone of the war eagle, and, thus equipped, run out and fire at the rising cloud—whooping, yelling, whistling, and beating their drum, to frighten it down again. One afternoon, a heavy black cloud was coming up; and they repaired to the top of a hill, where they brought all their magic artillery into play against it. But the undaunted thunder, refusing to be terrified, darted out a bright flash, which struck one of the party dead as he was in the very act of shaking his long iron-pointed lance against it. The rest scattered and ran yelling in an ecstasy of superstitious terror back to their lodges.

The lodge of my host, Kongra-Tonga, or the Big Crow, presented a picturesque spectacle that evening. A score or more of Indians were seated around it in a circle, their dark naked forms just visible by the dull light of the smoldering fire in the middle. The pipe glowed brightly in the gloom as it passed from hand to hand. Then a squaw would drop a piece of buffalo fat on the dull embers. Instantly a bright flame would leap up, darting its light to the very apex of the tall conical structure, where the tops of the slender poles that supported the covering of hide were gathered together. It gilded the features of the Indians, as with animated gestures they sat around it, telling their endless stories of war and hunting, and displayed rude garments of skins that hung around the lodge; the bow, quiver, and lance, suspended over the resting place of the chief, and the rifles and powder horns of the two white guests. For a moment all would be bright as day; then the flames would die out, fitful flashes from the embers would illumine the lodge and then leave it in darkness. Then the light would wholly fade, and the lodge and all within it be involved again in obscurity.

As I left the lodge next morning, I was saluted by howling and yelping all around the village; and half its canine population rushed forth to the attack. Being as cowardly as they were clamorous, they kept jumping about me at the distance of a few yards, only one little cur, about ten inches long, having spirit enough to make a direct assault. He dashed valiantly at the leather tassel which in the Dahcotah fashion was trailing behind the heel of my moccasin, and kept his hold, growling and snarling all the while, though every step I made almost jerked him over on his back. As I knew that the eyes of the whole village were on the watch to see if I showed any sign of fear, I walked forward without looking to the right or left, surrounded wherever I went by

this magic circle of dogs. When I came to Reynal's lodge I sat down by it, on which the dogs dispersed, growling, to their respective quarters. Only one large white one remained, running about before me and showing his teeth. I called him, but he only growled the more. I looked at him well. He was fat and sleek; just such a dog as I wanted. "My friend," thought I, "you shall pay for this! I will have you eaten this very morning!"

I intended that day to give the Indians a feast, by way of conveying a favorable impression of my character and dignity; and a white dog is the dish which the customs of the Dahcotah prescribe for all occasions of formality and importance. I consulted Reynal; he soon discovered that an old woman in the next lodge was owner of the white dog. I took a gaudy cotton handkerchief, and, laying it on the ground, arranged some vermilion, beads, and other trinkets upon it. Then the old squaw was summoned. I pointed to the dog and to the handkerchief. She gave a scream of delight, snatched up the prize, and vanished with it into her lodge. For a few more trifles I engaged the services of two other squaws, each of whom took the white dog by one of his paws and led him away behind the lodges. Having killed him, they threw him into a fire to singe; then chopped him up and put him into two large kettles to boil. Meanwhile I told Raymond to fry in buffalo fat what little flour we had left, and also to make a kettle of tea as an additional luxury.

The Big Crow's squaw was briskly at work sweeping out the lodge for the approaching festivity. I confided to my host himself the task of inviting the guests, thinking that I might thereby shift from my own shoulders the odium of neglect and oversight.

When feasting is in question, one hour of the day serves an Indian as well as another. My entertainment came off at about eleven o'clock. At that hour

"The Dog Feast," an oil painting by the American artist George Catlin (1796–1872). Catlin specialized in painting the American Indian, and it is said that Daniel Webster, when he saw some of the painter's work, cried "I was blind to all this red majesty and beauty and mystery that we are trampling down."

Reynal and Raymond walked across the area of the village, to the admiration of the inhabitants, carrying the two kettles of dog meat slung on a pole between them. These they placed in the center of the lodge, and then went back for the bread and the tea. Meanwhile I had put on a pair of brilliant moccasins, and substituted for my old buckskin frock a coat which I had brought with me in view of such public occasions. I also made careful use of the razor, an operation which no man will neglect who desires to gain the good opinion of Indians. Thus attired, I seated myself between Reynal and Raymond at the head of the lodge. Only a few minutes elapsed before all the guests had come in and were seated on the ground, wedged together in a close circle. Each

brought with him a wooden bowl to hold his share of the repast. When all were assembled, two of the officials called "soldiers" by the white men came forward with ladles made of the horn of the Rocky Mountain sheep and began to distribute the feast, assigning a double share to old men and chiefs. The dog vanished with astonishing celerity, and each guest turned his dish bottom upward to show that all was gone. Then the bread was distributed in its turn, and finally the tea. As the "soldiers" poured it out into the same wooden bowls that had served for the substantial part of the meal, I thought it had a particularly curious and uninviting color.

"Oh," said Reynal, "there was not tea enough, so I stirred some soot in the kettle to make it look strong."

Fortunately an Indian's palate is not very discriminating. The tea was well sweetened, and that was all they cared for.

Now, the feast being over, the time for speechmaking was come. The Big Crow produced a flat piece of wood on which he cut up tobacco and *shong-sasha,* and mixed them in due proportions. The pipes were filled and passed from hand to hand around the company. Then I began my speech, each sentence being interpreted by Reynal as I went on, and echoed by the whole audience with the usual exclamations of assent and approval. As nearly as I can recollect, it was as follows:

"I had come," I told them, "from a country so far distant that, at the rate they travel, they could not reach it in a year."

"How! how!"

"There the Meneaska [1] were more numerous than the blades of grass on the prairie. The squaws were far more beautiful than any they had ever seen, and all the men were brave warriors."

"How! how! how!"

I was assailed by twinges of conscience as I uttered these last words. But I recovered myself and began again.

"While I was living in the Meneaska lodges, I had heard of the Ogillallah, how great and brave a nation they were, how they loved the whites, and how well they could hunt the buffalo and strike their enemies. I resolved to come and see if all that I heard was true."

"How! how! how! how!"

"As I had come on horseback through the mountains, I had been able to bring them only a very few presents."

"How!"

"But I had enough tobacco to give them all a small piece. They might

[1] **Meneaska** (mē-nē-ăs′kà): an Indian name for white men.

smoke it and see how much better it was than the tobacco which they got from the traders."

"How! how! how!"

"I had plenty of powder, lead, knives, and tobacco at Fort Laramie. These I was anxious to give them; and if any of them should come to the fort before I went away, I would make them handsome presents."

"How! how! how! how!"

Raymond then cut up and distributed among them two or three pounds of tobacco, and old Mene-Seela began to make a reply. It was long, but the following was the pith of it:

"He had always loved the whites. They were the wisest people on earth. He believed they could do anything, and he was always glad when any of them came to live in Ogillallah lodges. It was true I had not made them many presents, but the reason of it was plain. It was clear that I liked them, or I never should have come so far to find their village."

Several other speeches of similar import followed, and then, this more serious matter being disposed of, there was an interval of smoking, laughing, and conversation. Old Mene-Seela suddenly interrupted it with a loud voice:

"Now is a good time," he said, "when all the old men and chiefs are here together, to decide what the people shall do. We came over the mountains to make our lodges for next year. Our old ones are good for nothing; they are rotten and worn out. But we have been disappointed. We have killed buffalo bulls enough, but we have found no herds of cows, and the skins of bulls are too thick and heavy for our squaws to make lodges of. There must be plenty of cows about the Medicine Bow Mountain. We ought to go there. To be sure, it is farther westward than we have ever been before; and perhaps the Snakes will attack us, for those hunting grounds belong to them. But we must have new lodges at any rate; our old ones will not serve for another year. We ought not to be afraid of the Snakes. Our warriors are brave, and they are all ready for war. Besides, we have three white men with their rifles to help us!"

This speech produced a good deal of debate. As Reynal did not interpret what was said, I could only judge of the meaning by the features and gestures of the speakers. At the end of it, however, the greater number seemed to have fallen in with Mene-Seela's opinion. A short silence followed; and then the old man struck up a discordant chant, which I was told was a song of thanks for the entertainment I had given them.

"Now," said he, "let us go and give the white men a chance to breathe."

So the company all dispersed into the open air; and for some time the old chief was walking round the village, singing his song in praise of the feast, after the custom of the nation.

At last the day drew to a close; and as the sun went down, the horses came trooping from the surrounding plains to be picketed before the dwellings of the respective masters. Soon within the great circle of lodges appeared another concentric circle of restless horses; and here and there fires glowed and flickered amid the gloom, on the dusky figures around them. I went over and sat by the lodge of Reynal. The Eagle Feather, who was a son of Mene-Seela and brother of my host, the Big Crow, was seated there already; and I asked him if the village would move in the morning. He shook his head, and said that nobody could tell; for since old Mahto-Tatonka had died, the people had been like children that did not know their own minds. They were no better than a body without a head. So I, as well as the Indians themselves, fell asleep that night without knowing whether we should set out in the morning toward the country of the Snakes.

FOR DISCUSSION

1. What characteristics of the Indian do you discover in this account? What previous notions about the Indian have you revised after reading Parkman?
2. What other Indian superstitions besides the one about thunder do you know?
3. What details show that Parkman thoroughly understood the Indians whose guest he was?
4. To what extent do you think the white man was justified in taking the American continent from the Indian?
5. Point out ways in which Parkman's style is a good example of exposition.

FURTHER READING

Look up the excellent one-volume representation of Parkman's writings, *The Parkman Reader*, edited by Samuel Eliot Morison (Little, Brown, 1955). *The Battle for North America* (Doubleday, 1948) is a good condensation by John Tebbel of Parkman's six-volume masterpiece, *France and England in North America*.

Two novels by A. B. Guthrie, Jr., *The Big Sky* and *The Way West*, give absorbing pictures of the Oregon Trail country during the settling of the West.

Howard Doughty's *Francis Parkman* (Macmillan, 1962) is an excellent study of the historian's life and work.

American Art and Artists

Reproduced on page 645 is "The Dog Feast," an oil painting by the American artist George Catlin (1796–1872). A detail from this painting appears on page 641.

Like Francis Parkman, George Catlin saw the West when it was still unknown to most Americans, and he traveled over the country with little regard to personal danger. Early in life Catlin set himself a mission — to record the vanishing American Indian and his way of life.

Catlin's art had freshness and power, but during his own day much of his work was ignored. In recent years, however, his paintings have received renewed interest, and he is now considered one of the finest American painters of his time.

RICHARD
HENRY
DANA, JR.

1815–1882

From the Forecastle

FROM *Two Years Before the Mast*

While trappers and explorers were opening the overland way across the continent, Yankee ships were making the hard voyage to reach the Pacific coast by sea. Richard Henry Dana, Jr., obliged to leave Harvard because of failing eyesight, shipped as an ordinary sailor on a vessel bound from Boston around Cape Horn to California and back. Dana learned firsthand the tyranny and brutal treatment that sailors had to endure. His book, *Two Years Before the Mast,* exerted an important influence on maritime legislation, and it also became one of the best-loved adventure stories America has produced.

Friday, July 1.[1] We were now nearly up to the latitude of Cape Horn; and having over forty degrees of easting to make, we squared away the yards before a strong westerly gale, shook a reef out of the fore topsail, and stood on our way, east by south, with the prospect of being up with the Cape in a week or ten days. As for myself, I had had no sleep for forty-eight hours; and the want of rest, together with constant

[1] The year is 1835. Dana's voyage began in August, 1834.

wet and cold, had increased the swelling, so that my face was nearly as large as two, and I found it impossible to get my mouth open wide enough to eat. In this state the steward applied to the captain for some rice to boil for me, but he only got a "No! d—— you! Tell him to eat salt junk and hard bread, like the rest of them." This was, in truth, what I expected. However, I did not starve; for Mr. Brown, who was a man as well as a sailor and had always been a good friend to me, smuggled a pan of rice into the galley, and told the cook to boil it for me, and not let the "old man" see it. Had it been fine weather, or in port, I should have gone below and lain by until my face got well; but in such weather as this, and shorthanded as we were, it was not for me to desert my post; so I kept on deck, and stood my watch and did my duty as well as I could.

Monday, July 4. This was Independence Day in Boston. What firing of guns, and ringing of bells, and rejoicings of all sorts, in every part of our country! The ladies (who have not gone down to Nahant for a breath of cool air and sight of the ocean) walking the streets with parasols over their heads, and the dandies in their white pantaloons and silk stockings! What quantities of ice cream have been eaten, and how many loads of ice brought into the city from a distance and sold out by the lump and the pound!

The smallest of the islands which we saw today would have made the fortune of poor Jack,[1] if he had had it in Boston; and I dare say he would have had no objection to being there with it. This, to be sure, was no place to keep the Fourth of July. To keep ourselves warm, and the ship out of the ice, was as much as we could do. Yet no one forgot the day; and many were the wishes and conjectures and comparisons, both serious and ludicrous, which were made among all hands. The sun shone bright as long as it was up, only that a scud of black clouds was ever and anon driving across it. At noon we were in latitude 54° 27′ S., and longitude 85° 5′ W., having made a good deal of easting, but having lost in our latitude by the heading off of the wind. Between daylight and dark — that is between nine o'clock and three — we saw thirty-four ice islands of various sizes; some no bigger than the hull of our vessel, and others apparently nearly as large as the one that we first saw.

At 4:00 P.M. (it was then quite dark) all hands were called, and sent aloft, in a violent squall of hail and rain, to take in sail. We had now all got on our "Cape Horn rig," thick boots, southwesters coming down over our necks and ears, thick trousers and jackets, and some with oilcloth suits over all. Mittens, too, we wore on deck; but it would not do to go aloft with them, as, being wet and stiff, they might let a man slip overboard, for all the hold he could get upon a rope: so we were obliged to work with bare hands, which, as well as our faces, were often cut with

[1] Jack: "Jack Tar" was a general name for a common sailor.

the hailstones, which fell thick and large. Our ship was now all cased with ice — hull, spars, and standing rigging; and the running rigging so stiff that we could hardly bend it so as to belay it, or, still less, take a knot with it; and the sails frozen. One at a time (for it was a long piece of work and required many hands) we furled the courses, mizzen topsail, and fore-topmast staysail; and close-reefed the fore and main topsails; and hove the ship to under the fore, with the main hauled up by the clewlines and buntlines and ready to be sheeted home if we found it necessary to make sail to get to windward of an ice island. A regular lookout was then set, and kept by each night. It blew hard the whole time, and there was an almost constant driving of either rain, hail, or snow. In addition to this, it was "as thick as muck" and the ice was all about us.

The captain was on deck nearly the whole night, and kept the cook in the galley, with a roaring fire, to make coffee for him, which he took every few hours, and once or twice gave a little to his officers; but not a drop of anything was there for the crew. The captain, who sleeps all the daytime and comes and goes at night as he chooses, can have his brandy and water in the cabin, and his hot coffee at the galley; while Jack, who has to stand through everything and work in wet and cold, can have nothing to wet his lips or warm his stomach. This was a "temperance ship," by her articles, and, like too many such ships, the temperance was all in the forecastle. The sailor, who only takes his one glass as it is dealt out to him, is in danger of being drunk; while the captain, upon whose self-possession and cool judgment the lives of all depend, may be trusted with any amount to drink at his will.

But this is not doubling Cape Horn. Eight hours of the night our watch was on deck, and during the whole of that time we kept a bright lookout: one man on each bow, another in the bunt of the foreyard, the third mate on the scuttle, one man on each quarter, and another always standing by the wheel. The chief mate was everywhere, and commanded the ship when the captain was below. When a large piece of ice was seen in our way, or drifting near us, the word was passed along, and the ship's head turned one way and another; and sometimes the yards squared or braced up. There was little else to do than to look out, and we had the sharpest eyes in the ship on the forecastle. The only variety was the monotonous voice of the lookout forward — "Another island!" — "Ice ahead!" — "Ice on the lee bow!" — "Hard up the helm!" — "Keep her off a little!" — "Stead-y!"

In the meantime the wet and cold had brought my face into such a state that I could neither eat nor sleep; and though I stood it out all night, yet, when it became light, I was in such a state that all hands told me I must go below, and lie by for a day or two, or I should be laid up for a long time. When the watch was changed I went into the steerage, and took off my hat and comforter, and showed my face to the mate, who told me to go below at once, and stay in my berth until the swelling went down, and gave the cook orders to make a poultice for me, and said he would speak to the captain.

I went below and turned in, covering myself over with blankets and jackets, and lay in my berth nearly twenty-four hours, half asleep and half awake, stupid from the dull pain.

It was a dreadful night for those on deck. A watch of eighteen hours, with wet and cold and constant anxiety, nearly wore them out; and when they came below at nine o'clock for breakfast, they almost dropped asleep on their chests, and some of them were so stiff that they could with difficulty sit down. Not a drop of anything had been given them during the whole time (though the captain, as on the night that I was on deck, had his coffee every four hours), except that the mate stole a potful of coffee for two men to drink behind the galley, while he kept a lookout for the captain. Every man had his station and was not allowed to leave it; and nothing happened to break the monotony of the night, except once setting the main topsail to run clear of a large island to leeward which they were drifting fast upon. Some of the boys got so sleepy and stupefied that they actually fell asleep at their posts; and the young third mate, Mr. Hatch, whose post was the exposed one of standing on the fore scuttle, was so stiff, when he was relieved, that he could not bend his knees to get down. By a constant lookout and a quick shifting of the helm, as the islands and pieces came in sight, the ship went clear of everything but a few small pieces, though daylight showed the ocean covered for miles.

At daybreak it fell a dead calm; and with the sun the fog cleared a little and a breeze sprang up from the westward, which soon grew into a gale. We had now a fair wind, daylight, and comparatively clear weather; yet, to the surprise of everyone, the ship continued hove-to. "Why does not he run?" "What is the captain about?" was asked by everyone; and from questions it soon grew into complaints and murmurings. When the daylight was so short, it was too bad to lose it, and a fair wind too, which everyone had been praying for. As hour followed hour, and the captain showed no sign of making sail, the crew became impatient, and there was a good deal of talking and consultation together on the forecastle. They had been beaten out with the exposure and hardship, and impatient to get out of it; and this unaccountable delay was more than they could bear in quietness, in their excited and restless state. Some said the captain was frightened — completely cowed by the dangers and difficulties that surrounded us, and was afraid to make sail — while others said that in his anxiety and suspense he had made a free use of brandy and opium, and was unfit for his duty.

The carpenter, who was an intelligent man, and a thorough seaman, and had great influence with the crew, came down into the forecastle and tried to induce them to go aft and ask the captain why he did not run, or request him, in the name of all hands, to make sail. This appeared to be a very reasonable request, and the crew agreed that if he did not make sail before noon, they would go aft. Noon came, and no sail was made. A consultation was held again; and it was proposed to take the ship from the captain and give the command of her to the mate, who had been heard to say that if he could have his way, the ship would have been half the distance to the Cape before night — ice or no ice. And so irritated and impatient had the crew become that even this proposition, which was open mutiny, was entertained; and the carpenter went to his berth, leaving it tacitly understood that something serious would be done if things remained as they were many hours longer. When the carpenter left, we talked it all over and I gave my advice strongly against it. Another of the men, too, who had known something of the kind attempted in another ship by a crew who were dissatisfied with their captain, and which was followed with serious consequences, was opposed to it. Stimson, who soon came down, joined us, and we determined to have nothing to do with it. By these means the crew were soon induced to give it up for the present, though they said they would not lie where they were much longer without knowing the reason.

I still remained in my berth, fast recovering, yet not well enough to go safely on deck. And I should have been perfectly useless; for, from having eaten nothing for nearly a week, except a little rice which I forced into my mouth the last day or two, I was as weak as an infant. To be sick in a forecastle is miserable indeed. It is the worst part of a dog's life, especially in bad weather. The forecastle, shut up tight to keep out the water and cold air; the watch either on deck or asleep in their berths; no one to speak to; the pale light of the single lamp, swinging to and fro from the beam, so dim that one can scarcely see, much less read, by it; the water dropping from the beams and carlines and running down the sides, and the forecastle so wet and dark and cheerless, and so lumbered up with chests and wet clothes, that sitting up is worse than lying in the berth. These are some of the evils. Fortunately I needed no help from anyone, and no medicine; and if I had needed help, I don't know where I should have found it. Sailors are willing enough; but it is true, as is often said, no one ships for nurse on board a vessel. Our merchant ships are always undermanned; and if one man is lost by sickness, they cannot spare another to take care of him. A sailor is always presumed to be well, and if he's sick he's a poor dog. One has to stand his wheel, and another his lookout; and the sooner he gets on deck again the better.

Accordingly, as soon as I could possibly go back to my duty, I put on my thick clothes and boots and southwester and made my appearance on deck. I had been but a few days below, yet everything looked strangely enough. The ship was cased in ice — decks, sides, masts, yards, and rigging. Two close-reefed topsails were all the sail she had on, and every sail and rope was frozen so stiff in its place that it seemed as though it would be impossible to start anything. Reduced, too, to her topmasts, she had altogether a most forlorn and crippled appearance. The sun had come up brightly; the snow was swept off the decks and ashes thrown upon them so that we could walk, for they had been as slippery as glass. It was, of course, too cold to carry on any ship's work, and we had only to walk the deck and keep ourselves warm. The wind was still ahead, and the whole ocean, to the eastward, covered with islands and field ice.

At four bells the order was given to square away the yards, and the man who came from the helm said that the captain had kept her off to N.N.E. What could this mean? The wildest rumors got adrift. Some said that he was going to run out of the ice and cross the Pacific, and go home round the Cape of Good Hope. Soon, however, it leaked out, and we found that we were running for the Straits of Magellan. The news soon spread through the ship, and all tongues were at work talking about it. No one on board had been through the straits; but I had in my chest an account of the passage of the ship *A. J. Donelson*, of New York, through those straits a few years before. The account was given by the captain, and the representation was as favorable as possible. It was soon read by everyone on board, and various opinions pronounced. The determination of our captain had at least this good effect: it gave us something to think and talk about, made a break in our life, and diverted our minds from the monotonous dreariness of the prospect before us. Having made a fair wind of it, we were going off at a good rate and leaving the thickest of the ice behind us. This, at least, was something.

Having been long enough below to get my hands well warmed and softened, the first handling of the ropes was rather tough; but a few days hardened them. And as soon as I got my mouth open wide enough to take in a piece of salt beef and hard bread, I was all right again.

FOR DISCUSSION

1. What evidence does Dana cite to prove that the distinction between the

captain and the crew was unfair?

2. How does Dana make you feel keenly the bitter cold in which the sailors worked? Why does he include the description of a usual Fourth of July in Boston?

3. What in Dana's writing gives you confidence in the truth of his report?

INTERPRETING SAILING TERMS

Review the terms *latitude* and *longitude*. Then proceed to the nautical phrases found in the very opening paragraph of this selection: "squared away the yards" and "shook a reef out of the fore topsail"; and the later phrase, "the running rigging so stiff that . . ." And here's one for the sailing enthusiast to explain to the class: "We furled the courses, mizzen topsail, and the fore-topmast staysail; and close-reefed the fore and main topsails; and hove the ship to under the fore. . . ."

SPECIAL REPORT

Compare shipboard working conditions today with Dana's description. What safeguards now exist for merchant sailors?

FURTHER READING

For more information about the actual life of a sailor, you may wish to read all of Dana's *Two Years Before the Mast.* Two short novels by Herman Melville, *Redburn* and *Billy Budd,* also picture life at sea in the nineteenth century.

A Yankee Clipper ➤

This is a detail from "The American Bark *Zephyr*," an oil painting by the American artist William Bygrave. The painting, completed in 1860, shows the ship in the port of Messina, Sicily.

Clippers like the *Zephyr* were the fastest ships of their time, and they dominated trade routes from about 1830 to 1870, when they could no longer meet the competition from the steamship. The Gold Rush probably marked the height of the clipper's prestige: in one year, clippers carried 90,000 passengers around the Horn to California, following the route Dana had taken in the 1830's.

JOHN
JAMES
AUDUBON
1785–1851

Off the Gannet Rocks

FROM *Labrador Journal*

Known primarily as the great artist and ornithologist who devoted a lifetime to the study of America's birds, Audubon was also a writer. Roaming and painting and keeping notes, he prepared a separate text to accompany the 435 engraved plates in his *Birds of America*. On his journey to Labrador in 1833, he kept the journal from which this selection is taken.

Although an excellent marksman, Audubon became sensitive to the enormous and senseless waste of bird life. The gannet, about which he writes here, is a great white sea fowl with black webbed feet and a wingspread as wide as a man is tall. The guillemot (gil′ĕ·mŏt) is a narrow-billed auk of the northern seas.

June 14, off the Gannet Rocks

OUR ANCHOR was raised, and our pilot, a Mr. Godwin from Nova Scotia, put the vessel toward what he called "the Bird Rocks," where he told us that gannets (*Sula bassana*) bred in great numbers. For several days past we have met with an increased number of

"June 14, off the Gannet Rocks" from *Audubon's America* by Donald Culross Peattie. Reprinted by permission of, and arrangement with, Houghton Mifflin Company, the authorized publishers.

gannets, and as we sailed this morning, we observed long and numerous files, all flying in the direction of the rocks. Their flight now was low above the water, forming easy undulations, flapping thirty or forty times, and sailing about the same distance; these were all returning from fishing, and were gorged with food for their mates or young. About ten a speck rose on the horizon, which I was told was the Rock; we sailed well, the breeze increased fast, and we neared this object apace. At eleven I could distinguish its top plainly from the deck, and thought it covered with snow to the depth of several feet; this appearance existed on every portion of the flat, projecting shelves. Godwin said, with the coolness of a man who had visited this rock for ten successive seasons, that what we saw was not snow — but gannets!

I rubbed my eyes, took my spyglass, and in an instant the strangest picture stood before me. They were birds we saw — a mass of birds of such a size as I never before cast my eyes on. The whole of my party stood astounded and amazed, and all came to the conclusion that such a sight was of itself sufficient to invite anyone to come across the Gulf to view it at this season. The nearer we approached, the greater our surprise at the enormous number of these birds, all calmly seated on their eggs or newly hatched brood, their heads all turned to windward, and toward us. The air above for a hundred yards, and for some distance around the whole rock, was filled with gannets on the wing, which from our position made it appear as if a heavy fall of snow was directly above us.

Our pilot told us the wind was too high to permit us to land, and I felt sadly grieved at this unwelcome news. Anxious as we all were, we decided to make the attempt; our whaleboat was overboard, the pilot, two sailors, Tom Lincoln, and John[1] pushed off with guns and clubs. Our vessel was brought to, but at that instant the wind increased, and heavy rain began to fall. Our boat neared the rock, and went to the lee of it, and was absent nearly an hour, but could not land. The air was filled with gannets, but no difference could we perceive on the surface of the rock. The birds, which we now could distinctly see, sat almost touching each other and in regular lines, seated on their nests quite unconcerned. The discharge of the guns had no effect on those that were not touched by the shot, for the noise of the gulls, guillemots, etc., deadened the sound of the gun; but where the shot took effect, the birds scrambled and flew off in such multitudes, and in such confusion, that whilst some eight or ten were falling into the water either dead or wounded, others pushed off their eggs, and these fell into the sea by hundreds in all directions. The sea now becoming very rough, the boat was obliged to return, with some birds and some eggs; but the crew had not climbed the rock, a great disappointment to me.

Godwin tells me the top of the rock is about a quarter of a mile wide, north

[1] **Tom Lincoln and John:** Audubon took with him on this trip four young men interested in science, and his own son John.

and south, and a little narrower east and west; its elevation above the sea between three and four hundred feet. The sea beats round it with great violence, except after long calms, and it is extremely difficult to land upon it, and much more so to climb to the top of it, which is a platform; it is only on the southeast shore that a landing can be made, and the moment a boat touches, it must be hauled up on the rocks. The whole surface is perfectly covered with nests, placed about two feet apart, in such regular order that you may look through the lines as you would look through those of a planted patch of sweet potatoes or cabbage. The fishermen who kill these birds, to get their flesh for codfish bait, ascend in parties of six or eight, armed with clubs; sometimes, indeed, the party comprises the crews of several vessels. As they reach the top, the birds, alarmed, rise with a noise like thunder, and fly off in such hurried, fearful confusion as to throw each other down, often falling on each other till there is a bank of them many feet high. The men strike them down and kill them until fatigued or satisfied. Five hundred and forty have been thus murdered in one hour by six men. The birds are skinned with little care, and the flesh cut off in chunks; it will keep fresh about a fortnight.

The nests are made by scratching down a few inches, and the edges surrounded with seaweeds. The eggs are pure white, and as large as those of a goose. By the 20th of May, the rock is already covered with birds and eggs; about the 20th of June, they begin to hatch. So great is the destruction of these birds annually that their flesh supplies the bait for upwards of forty fishing boats, which lie close to the Byron Island each season. When the young are hatched, they are black, and for a fortnight or more the skin looks like that of the dogfish. They become gradually downy and white, and when two months old, look much like young

lambs. Even while shooting at these birds, hundreds passed us carrying great masses of weeds to their nests. The birds were thick above our heads, and I shot at one to judge of the effect of the report of the gun; it had none. . . .

The breeze was now so stiff that the waves ran high; so much so that the boat was perched on the comb of the wave one minute, the next in the trough. John steered, and he told me afterward he was nearly exhausted. The boat was very cleverly hauled on deck by a single effort. The stench from the rock is insufferable, as it is covered with the remains of putrid fish, rotten eggs, and dead birds, old and young. No man who has not seen what we have this day can form the least idea of the impression the sight made on our minds.

FOR DISCUSSION

1. What hardships did Audubon and his party endure in order to observe the gannets? What was Audubon's purpose?

2. What are some of the admirable characteristics of gannets? What are their weaknesses? What evidence do you find that Audubon tries to personify the gannets?

3. How were the gannets being destroyed? What other birds and animals of our continent have suffered similar wasteful destruction? Do you know of any birds or animals native to North America that have become extinct since Audubon's day?

FURTHER READING

Your library may not have the large folio of Audubon's *The Birds of America*, but it is likely to have the one-volume Macmillan edition. You will probably also enjoy reading *Audubon's America*, edited by Donald Culross Peattie (Houghton Mifflin, 1940), or Constance Rourke's biography, *Audubon* (Harcourt, Brace & World, 1936).

American Art and Artists

Reproduced above is "The Gannet," an oil painting by John James Audubon for his book *The Birds of America*. The portrait of Audubon that appears on page 654 was painted by his son.

The War Between the States

The most tragic and dramatic era of our history was that which had its terrible, stirring climax in the War Between the States. This event has seized the imaginations of generations of Americans. Even now, an ever-swelling flood of books about the war continues to accumulate long after the din of battle, the roar of cannon, the songs and the speeches have ceased. The war is rooted in the memories of countless American families. It re-established, at great price, the founding fathers' concept of a Federal union.

The war was a conflict of brothers, a great rift within a family — often in a literal sense. Many times brothers or other blood kin were found on opposing sides. Conviction and courage, gallantry and honor, were found on each side. Wisdom and folly were shared alike. On each side, too, were found notable abilities and strong leadership, as seen clearly in the figures of Abraham Lincoln and Robert E. Lee. Each of these men approached his tragic role with a heavy heart but firm in determination to follow conscience and duty; each was to command both respect and affection from the generations that followed.

The conflict grew from complicated, swiftly developing differences. The North was becoming an industrial region, with new kinds of economic and manpower needs. The South remained chiefly an agricultural economy, where slave labor was an important factor, especially in the cotton fields. There were differences in political philosophy, too. The North, in general, looked with favor on an increasing strength of the central government. In the South, political opinion preferred the independence of each state with a minimum of Federal control. These views ultimately collided in the debate as to whether the Union could, or could not, be dissolved at the will of any of the states.

Yet no brief statement can capture the complex causes of the war. Talk of secession was not confined to the South. In the North, radical Abolitionists like William Lloyd Garrison were quite ready to dissolve the Union if they could not have their way about slavery. Fugitive slave cases in the Supreme Court and in state courts, North and South, led to bitter disagreements, whichever way the decisions went.

The voices of eloquent men rang in the halls of Congress. Daniel Webster, Henry Clay, and John C. Calhoun sometimes pressed regional demands, sometimes sought for compromise. Yet all events seemed to move toward armed conflict. As a symptom, in 1859, two years before the war, a fanatical Abolitionist named John Brown raided the U.S. Arsenal at Harper's Ferry, Virginia. Brown hoped to capture arms and equip a general insurrection of slaves. Colonel Robert E. Lee commanded the Federal troops that crushed Brown's plan and captured him in a brief fight. Brown was tried and hanged, but in death he became a symbol to the antislavery ranks. His name was kept alive in the song "John Brown's Body," which became a marching tune for Union troops when the war kindled into general flame in 1861.

When the mortal storm of war subsided after four anguished years, some half million lives, South and North, had been lost. The Union still existed. Some four million slaves were free, though many were to suffer in their uprooted condition more than they had in their former bondage. A tragic convulsion had wrenched the nation; a long, slow healing had to follow.

THE LITERATURE OF THE CONFLICT

In 1852, in the North, a famous book fanned the sparks of the approaching war. A New England woman, Harriet Beecher Stowe, published *Uncle Tom's Cabin.* The book created a popular emotional image of slavery as it was thought of by Abolitionists. It so agitated northern opinion that President Lincoln once addressed Mrs. Stowe, with some exaggeration, as "the little woman who wrote the book that made this great war." The novel was not entirely biased: it portrayed some Southern characters sympathetically, and the villain, Simon Legree, was from Vermont.

In the early years of the war, Julia Ward Howe wrote "The Battle Hymn of the Republic." This and "Dixie" became the great marches of the war. Humorists Artemus Ward and Petroleum V. Nasby, who were to share lecture platforms with Mark Twain in later years, wrote political satires that were essentially friendly to Abraham Lincoln and his policies. Writing of a high literary quality, however, did not exist during these years.

Literature does not flourish in the midst of war; it is resumed in the silence and ruin afterward. Some writers whom we have met were involved in the struggle. Doubtless, many who would have been writers died in battle before their voices had been heard. James Russell Lowell lost a nephew in the war. Oliver Wendell Holmes's son, the younger Oliver who was to become a great judge in the Supreme Court, was wounded three times.

Louisa May Alcott was a field nurse. The poet Walt Whitman tended the wounded on battlefields and in Washington hospitals. The southern poets Paul Hamilton Hayne, Henry Timrod, and Sidney Lanier all fought and suffered in the conflict. Timrod commemorated the martyrs of the war in his beautiful "Ode on the Confederate Dead."

LATER LITERATURE OF THE WAR

The vast flood of writing about the War Between the States includes one of the greatest of American novels, Stephen Crane's *The Red Badge of Courage* (1895), and Stephen Vincent Benét's stirring narrative poem, *John Brown's Body* (1928).

Lincoln and Lee

The War Between the States gave Americans two of our country's greatest heroes: Lincoln and Lee. Each was a man of singular nobility of character, and each wrote and spoke at certain moments with great vision and power.

ABRAHAM LINCOLN

Lincoln has become a legend. When he died, Secretary of War Stanton — who once had called him a "gorilla" — pronounced the classic epitaph, "Now he belongs to the Ages." At the time of deepest crisis, Lincoln came forth to save the Union. He grew up on a rude frontier. He spoke the language of the common man, pithy, salty, homely, yet with deep currents of feeling. He seemed to take upon himself all the burdens of the earth.

Lincoln was an incomparable storyteller, with an inexhaustible fund of stories and pithy sayings. "Don't swap horses in the middle of the stream," he admonished in his wartime campaign for re-election. When asked how he liked being President, he recalled the remark of the man who had been tarred and feathered and ridden on a rail: "If it weren't for the honor of the thing, I'd rather walk."

The actual body of Lincoln's writing is quite small — you can put most of the important material within the covers of a single volume. It is a rich volume. Among his letters are some masterpieces: the letter to Mrs. Bixby, for example, consoling her on the loss of her sons; the letter to Horace Greeley, "I would save the Union"; the letter to James Conkling after the fall of Vicksburg, "The signs look better . . . The Father of Waters goes again unvexed to the sea."

The greatest of Lincoln's literary contributions were speeches: the Peoria speech of 1854, the "House Divided" speech of 1858, the famous debates with Senator Douglas, the Second Inaugural Address, and the most nearly perfect thing he ever wrote, the Gettysburg Address.

ROBERT E. LEE

Many Confederate officers wrote memoirs after the war. Lee did not. He preferred to let his record speak for itself, a record not only of unsurpassed military brilliance, but of dignity, austerity, and courage. Lee was not only the prop and pillar of a state; he was its spirit and symbol as well.

The volume of Lee's writing is not large, but it is characterized by a clear, vigorous style, and at times by a moving eloquence. His personal letters reveal an old-fashioned graciousness, a quiet humor, and a high sense of duty and rectitude; his official papers are clear, succinct, and dignified. In a letter he explains why, for all his disapproval of secession, he must nevertheless go along with his state of Virginia in the conflict. His speeches are quietly moving: his Farewell to the Army of Northern Virginia after the surrender at Appomattox reveals his greatness and generous spirit.

If writing *by* Lee is meager, writing *about* Lee is monumental. Many of his fellow officers wrote about him. We have scores of pen pictures: Lee watching the bloody repulse of the Yankees at Fredericksburg, "It is well war is so terrible, else we might grow too fond of it"; Lee leading a desperate counterattack, and the shouts from the ranks, "Lee to the rear, Lee to the rear," before his soldiers would charge; Lee bidding farewell to his beloved Army of Northern Virginia, and admonishing his people to "bury contention with the war."

SPIRITUALS

Part of America's wealth of song includes the Negro spirituals. Together with western cowboy ballads, these spirituals constitute the most important folk literature developed in America.

You can best appreciate the beauty of these songs by listening to recordings. But as you read the words, picture the scenes that gave rise to the spirituals: men and women picking cotton in the fields; men loading heavy bales on barges, with one rich voice singing out the varying lines and the whole company joining in the refrain.

Nobody Knows de Trouble I See

No - bod - y knows de trou-ble I see, No - bod - y knows but Je - sus— No - bod- y knows de trou-ble I see, Glo - ry, hal - le - lu - jah! Oh, No - bod - y knows de trou - ble I see, No - bod - y knows but Je - sus— No - bod - y knows de trou - ble I see,

Glo-ry, hal-le-lu-jah! Sometimes I'm up Some-times I'm down,

Oh, yes, Lord; Some-times I'm al-mos' to de groun'___

Oh, yes, Lord. Al-tho' you see me goin' 'long so,

Oh, yes, Lord: I have my tri-als here be-low___

Oh, yes, Lord. Oh! No-bod-y knows de trou-ble I see,

No-bod-y knows but Je-sus___ No-bod-y knows de

trou-ble I see, Glo-ry, hal-le-lu-jah!

Deep River *

Deep river, my home is over Jordan;
Deep river, Lord; I want to cross over into campground.

O don't you want to go
To that gospel feas',
That Promised Land
Where all is peace?

O deep river, my home is over Jordan;
Deep river, Lord; I want to cross over into campground.

* Other versions exist; commonly *Canaan* is substituted for *campground.*

Let My People Go!

When Is-rael was in E-gypt's land Let my peo-ple go, Oppressed so hard they could not stand, Let my peo-ple go.
Go down Mos-es, 'Way down in E-gypt's land,——
Tell— ole— Pha - raoh To let my peo-ple
go. O let my peo-ple go.——

2. Thus said the Lord, bold Moses said,
   Let my people go!
   If not I'll smite your first-born dead;
   Let my people go!

3. No more shall they in bondage toil,
   Let my people go!
   Let them come out with Egypt's spoil,
   Let my people go!

"Let My People Go" from *The American Book of Negro Spirituals* by James Weldon Johnson. Copyright 1925 by The Viking Press, Inc., 1953 by Grace Nail Johnson, J. Rosamond Johnson and Lawrence Brown. Reprinted by permission of The Viking Press, Inc.

FOR DISCUSSION

1. Your first impression is no doubt one of mood. Words and music work together to achieve mood. What seems to be characteristically the dominant mood? Do you know any spirituals that express other moods?

2. What evidence is there of the deep religious faith of the people who composed and developed spirituals as a unique contribution to the world's music?

RECORDINGS OF SPIRITUALS

Spirituals have been recorded by such singers as Marian Anderson, Dorothy Maynor, and Mahalia Jackson. Listen also to recordings by vocal quartets and choirs to appreciate the harmony.

DANIEL
WEBSTER

1782–1852

Liberty and Union

In the heated controversy over slavery and in the ensuing argument of states' rights versus national sovereignty, John C. Calhoun was the great spokesman for the South and Daniel Webster for the North. As students of literature, we need not concern ourselves with the constitutional questions involved in this debate, but the conclusion of Webster's famous "Reply to Hayne" in January 1830 should be familiar to every American.

CAREFUL READING. As you read this speech, be sure that you do not miss any of the main ideas that Webster develops. Note especially the central thought in the concluding portion of the speech.

I PROFESS in my career hitherto to have kept steadily in view the prosperity and honor of the whole country, and the preservation of our Federal Union. It is to that Union we owe our safety at home, and our consideration and dignity abroad. It is to that Union that we are chiefly indebted for whatever makes us most proud of our country. That Union we reached only by the discipline of our virtues in the severe school of adversity. It had its origin in the necessities of disordered finance, prostrate commerce, and ruined credit. Under its benign influences, these great interests immediately awoke as from the dead, and sprang forth with newness of life. Every year of its duration has teemed with fresh proofs of its utility and its blessings; and although our territory has stretched out wider and wider, and our population spread farther and farther, they have not outrun its protection or its benefits. It has been to us all a copious fountain of national, social, and personal happiness.

I have not allowed myself to look beyond the Union to see what might lie hidden in the dark recess behind. I have not coolly weighed the chances of preserving liberty, when the bonds that unite us together shall be broken asunder. I have not accustomed myself to hang over the precipice of disunion, to see whether, with my short sight, I can fathom the depth of the abyss below; nor could I regard him as a safe counselor in the affairs of this government, whose thoughts should be mainly bent on considering, not how the Union should be best preserved, but how tolerable might be the condition of the people when it should be broken up and destroyed. While the Union lasts, we have high, exciting, gratifying prospects spread out before us — for us and our children. Beyond that, I seek not to penetrate the veil. God grant that, in my day, at least, that curtain may not rise! God grant that on my vision never may be opened what lies behind! When my eyes shall be turned to behold for the last time the sun in heaven, may I not see him shining on the broken and dishonored fragments of a once glorious Union; on states dissevered, discordant, belligerent; on a land rent with civil feuds, or drenched, it may be, in fraternal blood! Let their last feeble and lingering glance rather behold the gorgeous ensign of the Republic, now known and honored throughout the earth, still full high advanced, its arms and trophies streaming in their original luster, not a stripe erased or polluted, nor a single star obscured; bearing for its motto no such miserable interrogatory as "What is all this worth?" nor those other words of delusion and folly, "Liberty first, and Union afterward"; but everywhere, spread all over in characters of living light, blazing on all its ample folds, as they float over the sea and over the land and in every wind under the whole heavens, that other sentiment, dear to every true American heart — Liberty *and* Union, now and forever, one and inseparable!

FOR DISCUSSION

1. Point out some of the words and phrases that Webster repeats throughout "Liberty and Union." How does repetition add to the effectiveness of this speech?

2. Behind the fervor that undeniably comes through, what real conviction impresses itself upon the reader?

3. Is the question of states' rights versus national sovereignty still being debated today?

CAREFUL READING

Try to state briefly each of the main ideas of this speech. What is the climax?

THE 7TH OF MARCH SPEECH

It was in 1850, twenty years after his "Reply to Hayne," that Daniel Webster made his momentous 7th of March speech. It lost him many staunch friends in the North, for he argued that no issue was great enough to justify sacrificing the Union. Even the mild Quaker Whittier denounced him in his poem "Ichabod":

So fallen! so lost! the light withdrawn
Which once he wore!
The glory from his gray hairs gone
Forevermore!

Whittier later wrote a short preface to "Ichabod" in which he said ". . . my admiration of the splendid personality and intellectual power of the great senator was never stronger than when I laid down his speech and, in one of the saddest moments of my life, penned my protest . . . But death softens all resentments, and the consciousness of a common inheritance of frailty and weakness modifies the severity of judgment. Years after, in 'The Lost Occasion,' I gave utterance to an almost universal regret that the great statesman did not live to . . . make his last days glorious in defense of 'Liberty and Union, one and inseparable.'"

In 1852 Webster died, a discouraged man. Yet modern historians rate this speech as his last great service to the nation. His final words to the Senate are his epitaph: "No man can suffer too much, and no man can fall too soon, if he suffer or if he fall in defense of the liberties and Constitution of his country."

American Art and Artists ➤

Reproduced on the facing page is a portrait in oils of Daniel Webster, painted by the American artist George P. A. Healy (1813–1894). Healy also painted the portrait of Abraham Lincoln that is reproduced on page 669. The third portrait in this section, that of Robert E. Lee (page 673), is by the nineteenth-century American artist John A. Elder.

ABRAHAM
LINCOLN

1809–1865

It was Lincoln who set down in simple words the truest statement America has of the trials and griefs and triumphant faiths of the time. These brief selections from his speeches and letters show his gift for speaking and writing simply and honestly, yet with the profound wisdom and nobility of a truly great nature.

THE Gettysburg Address

Look back at Carl Sandburg's account (page 226) of the circumstances under which this address was delivered.

November 19, 1863

FOUR SCORE and seven years ago our fathers brought forth on this continent a new nation, conceived in liberty, and dedicated to the proposition that all men are created equal.

Now we are engaged in a great civil war, testing whether that nation, or any nation so conceived and so dedicated, can long endure. We are met on a great battlefield of that war. We have come to dedicate a portion of that field as a final resting place for those who here gave their lives that that nation might live. It is altogether fitting and proper that we should do this.

But in a larger sense we cannot dedicate, we cannot consecrate, we cannot hallow this ground. The brave men, living and dead, who struggled here, have consecrated it far above our poor power to add or detract. The world will little note nor long remember what we say here, but it can never forget what they did here. It is for us, the living, rather, to be dedicated here to the unfinished work which they who fought here have thus far so nobly advanced. It is rather for us to be here dedicated to the great task remaining before us — that from these honored dead we take increased devotion to that cause for which they gave the last full measure of devotion; that we here highly resolve that these dead shall not have died in vain; that this nation, under God, shall have a new birth of freedom; and that government of the people, by the people, for the people, shall not perish from the earth.

Letter to Mrs. Bixby

It is characteristic of Lincoln that he found time amid his cares and responsibilities to write this personal letter to a mother mourning her sons lost for the cause of the Union. Characteristic, too, is the fact that he expressed in the letter feelings many people had experienced, but few had found words for.

Washington, November 21, 1864

Dear Madam:

I have been shown in the files of the War Department a statement of the Adjutant General of Massachusetts that you are the mother of five sons who have died gloriously on the field of battle. I feel how weak and fruitless must be any words of mine which should attempt to beguile you from the grief of a loss so overwhelming. But I cannot refrain from tendering to you the consolation that may be found in the thanks of the Republic they died to save. I pray that our heavenly Father may assuage the anguish of your bereavement, and leave you only the cherished memory of the loved and lost, and the solemn pride that must be yours to have laid so costly a sacrifice upon the altar of freedom. *Yours, very sincerely and respectfully,*

Abraham Lincoln

To Mrs. Bixby,
Boston, Massachusetts

Second Inaugural Address

The morning of Lincoln's second inauguration was cold and stormy, but at noon the sun came out as the procession moved with dignity from the White House. Numbers of wounded soldiers were conspicuous in the great throng. The following comment upon the address was made by the London *Spectator* after the President's death: "We cannot read it without a renewed conviction that it is the noblest political document known to history, and should have for the nation and the statesmen he left behind him something of a sacred and almost prophetic character." The last paragraph of this speech and the Gettysburg Address are inscribed on opposite walls of the beautiful Lincoln Memorial in Washington, D.C.

March 4, 1865

FELLOW COUNTRYMEN: At this second appearing to take the oath of the Presidential office, there is less occasion for an extended address than there was at the first. Then a statement, somewhat in detail, of a course to be pursued, seemed fitting and proper. Now, at the expiration of four years, during which public declarations have been constantly called forth on every point and phase of the great contest which still absorbs the attention and engrosses the energies of the nation, little that is new could be presented. The progress of our arms, upon which all else chiefly depends, is as well known to the public as to myself; and it is, I trust, reasonably satisfactory and encouraging to all. With high hope for the future, no prediction in regard to it is ventured.

On the occasion corresponding to this four years ago, all thoughts were anxiously directed to an impending civil war. All dreaded it — all sought to avert it. While the inaugural address was being delivered from this place, devoted altogether to saving the Union without war, insurgent agents were in the city seeking to destroy it without war — seeking to dissolve the Union, and divide effects, by negotiation. Both parties deprecated war; but one of them would make war rather than let the nation survive; and the other would accept war rather than let it perish. And the war came.

One-eighth of the whole population were colored slaves, not distributed generally over the Union, but localized in the southern part of it. These slaves constituted a peculiar and powerful interest. All knew that this interest was, somehow, the cause of the war. To strengthen, perpetuate, and extend this interest was the object for which the insurgents would rend the Union, even by war; while the government claimed no right to do more than to restrict the territorial enlargement of it.

Neither party expected for the war the magnitude or the duration which it has already attained. Neither anticipated that the cause of the conflict might cease with, or even before, the conflict itself should cease. Each looked for an easier triumph and a result less fundamental and astounding. Both read the same Bible, and pray to the same God; and each invokes His aid against the other. It may seem strange that any men should dare to ask a just God's assistance in wringing their bread from the sweat of other men's faces; but let us judge not, that we be not judged.[1] The prayers of both could not be answered — that of neither has been answered fully.

The Almighty has his own purposes. "Woe unto the world because of offenses! for it must needs be that offenses come; but woe to that man by whom the offense cometh." [2] If we shall suppose that American slavery is one of those offenses which, in the province of God, must needs come, but which, having continued through His appointed time, He now wills to remove, and that He gives to both North and South this terrible war, as the woe due to those by whom the offense came, shall we discern therein any departure from those divine attributes which the believers in a living God always ascribe to Him? Fondly do we hope — fervently do we pray — that this mighty scourge

of war may speedily pass away. Yet, if God wills that it continue until all the wealth piled by the bondman's two hundred and fifty years of unrequited toil shall be sunk, and until every drop of blood drawn with the lash shall be paid by another drawn with the sword, as was said three thousand years ago, still it must be said, "The judgments of the Lord are true and righteous altogether." [3]

With malice toward none; with charity for all; with firmness in the right, as God gives us to see the right, let us strive on to finish the work we are in; to bind up the nation's wounds; to care for him who shall have borne the battle, and for his widow and his orphan — to do all which may achieve and cherish a just and lasting peace among ourselves, and with all nations.

[3] **The judgments . . . altogether:** Psalms 19:9.

FOR DISCUSSION

1. Many qualities of Lincoln are reflected in this series of brief utterances. Find passages that show his humility, his consideration of others, his insistence on the right, his devoutness, his heavy sense of responsibility as commander in chief.

2. As an independent inquirer into human freedom and responsibility, what are some of Lincoln's findings?

3. One of Lincoln's gifts was the ability to put into simple words the profound feelings that often defeat attempts at expression. Find passages that have become part of the creed of our nation.

4. It is now recognized that Lincoln's death was an even greater loss to the South than to the North. What course would he have taken with the defeated Confederacy?

5. With the possible exception of Napoleon, more books have been written about Lincoln than any other human figure. Can you think of several reasons why this should be so? What makes Lincoln a complicated subject?

[1] **judge not . . . judged:** Matthew 7:1.
[2] **Woe . . . cometh:** Matthew 18:7.

The George Healy portrait of Abraham Lincoln ▶

ROBERT E. LEE

1807–1870

Among our greatest heroes is Robert E. Lee — gentleman, daringly brave soldier, resourceful leader, and humanitarian. Defeat could not down him, and throughout his life he inspired remarkable devotion.

Most of his writing consists of letters and military papers. But these reveal his strength of character, his strong loyalties, and his deep concern for his country.

Letter to His Son

In this letter to his son, Lee reveals that he is greatly disturbed over the possibility of a rupture in the Union.

I RECEIVED Everett's *Life of Washington* which you sent me, and enjoyed its perusal. How his spirit would be grieved could he see the wreck of his mighty labors! I will not, however, permit myself to believe, until all ground of hope is gone, that the fruit of his noble deeds will be destroyed, and that his precious advice and virtuous example will so soon be forgotten by his countrymen. As far as I can judge by the papers, we are between a state of anarchy and civil war. May God avert both of these evils from us! I fear that mankind will not for years be sufficiently Christianized to bear the absence of restraint and force. I see that four states [1] have declared themselves out of the Union; four more will apparently follow their example. Then, if the border states are brought into the gulf of revolution, one half of the country will be arrayed against the other. I must try and be patient and await the end, for I can do nothing to hasten or retard it.

The South, in my opinion, has been aggrieved by the acts of the North, as you say. I feel the aggression and am willing to take every proper step for redress. It is the principle I contend for, not individual or private benefit. As an American citizen, I take great pride in my country, her prosperity and institutions, and would defend any state if her rights were invaded. But I can anticipate no greater calamity for the country than a dissolution of the Union. It would be an accumulation of all the evils we complain of, and I am willing to sacrifice everything but honor for its preservation. I hope, therefore, that all

[1] South Carolina, Mississippi, Florida, Alabama.

constitutional means will be exhausted before there is a resort to force. Secession is nothing but revolution. The framers of our Constitution never exhausted so much labor, wisdom, and forbearance in its formation, and surrounded it with so many guards and securities, if it was intended to be broken by every member of the Confederacy at will. It was intended for "perpetual union," so expressed in the preamble, and for the establishment of a government, not a compact, which can only be dissolved by revolution or the consent of all the people in convention assembled. It is idle to talk of secession. Anarchy would have been established, and not a government, by Washington, Hamilton, Jefferson, Madison, and the other patriots of the Revolution. . . . Still, a Union that can only be maintained by swords and bayonets, and in which strife and civil war are to take the place of brotherly love and kindness, has no charm for me. I shall mourn for my country and for the welfare and progress of mankind. If the Union is dissolved, and the government disrupted, I shall return to my native state and share the miseries of my people; and, save in defense, will draw my sword on none.

Letter to General Scott

Only four months after his letter to his son, Lee submitted his resignation from the regular army. A principled restraint and firm but human tone come through the letter.

Arlington, Virginia
April 20, 1861

General: Since my interview with you on the 18th inst., I have felt that I ought no longer to retain my commission in the army. I therefore tender my resignation, which I request you will recommend for acceptance. It would

have been presented at once but for the struggle it has cost me to separate myself from a service to which I have devoted the best years of my life, and all the ability I possessed.

During the whole of that time — more than a quarter of a century — I have experienced nothing but kindness from my superiors and a most cordial friendship from my comrades. To no one, General, have I been as much indebted as to yourself for uniform kindness and consideration, and it has always been my ardent desire to merit your approbation. I shall carry to the grave the most grateful recollections of your kind consideration, and your name and fame shall always be dear to me.

Save in defense of my native state, I never desire again to draw my sword.

Be pleased to accept my most earnest wishes for the continuance of your happiness and prosperity, and believe me, most truly yours,

R. E. Lee

Farewell to the Army of Northern Virginia

Lee's last order to his loyal men shows the qualities that inspired their devotion.

Headquarters
Army of Northern Virginia
April 10, 1865

After four years of arduous service, marked by unsurpassed courage and fortitude, the Army of Northern Virginia has been compelled to yield to overwhelming numbers and resources.

I need not tell the survivors of so many hard-fought battles who have remained steadfast to the last that I have consented to this result from no distrust of them; but feeling that valor and devotion could accomplish nothing that would compensate for the loss that must have attended the continuance of the contest, I determined to avoid the useless sacrifice of those whose past services have endeared them to their countrymen. By the terms of the agreement, officers and men can return to their homes and remain until exchanged.

You may take with you the satisfaction that proceeds from the consciousness of duty faithfully performed, and I earnestly pray that a merciful God will extend to you His blessing and protection.

With an unceasing admiration of your constancy and devotion to your country, and a grateful remembrance of your kind and generous consideration of myself, I bid you all an affectionate farewell.

R. E. Lee, General

FOR DISCUSSION

1. What beliefs did Lee hold about secession? Judging from his letter to his son, what were his reasons for deciding finally to uphold the secessionists? What passages show his devotion to his native state?
2. What does Lee's letter to General Scott reveal to us about Lee, the man?
3. Why is Lee's farewell to his army considered a great document in American history? Discuss how it is possible for a man to be great though apparently he has failed. What can we learn from Lee in the hour of his defeat?
4. How does Lee reveal his greatness in his adjustment to the situation confronting him at the end of the war?
5. Do you find any points of resemblance between Lee and Lincoln? What was the greatest difference between them?

HENRY TIMROD

1828–1867

The following tribute to the southern dead by one of the South's most gifted poets was pronounced, like Lincoln's Gettysburg Address, above the graves of those it honored.

Ode on the Confederate Dead

Sung at the occasion of decorating the graves of the Confederate dead at Magnolia Cemetery, Charleston, S.C., 1867

Sleep sweetly in your humble graves,
  Sleep, martyrs of a fallen cause;
Though yet no marble column craves
  The pilgrim here to pause.

In seeds of laurel in the earth   5
  The blossom of your fame is blown,
And somewhere, waiting for its birth,
  The shaft is in the stone!

Meanwhile, behalf the tardy years
  Which keep in trust your storied
    tombs,   10

Behold! your sisters bring their tears,
  And these memorial blooms.

Small tributes! but your shades will
    smile
  More proudly on these wreaths
    today,
Than when some cannon-molded pile
  Shall overlook this bay.   16

Stoop, angels, hither from the skies!
  There is no holier spot of ground
Than where defeated valor lies,
  By mourning beauty crowned!   20

FOR DISCUSSION

Two emotions mark this poem. Is bitterness over the defeat one? Is there any echo of the issues for which the war was fought?

A portrait of Robert E. Lee by John A. Elder. ▶

The Postwar West

After the War Between the States, attention shifted again to the West as the great arena of American adventure. As we have seen, the epic events that occurred in the West during the first stages of exploration and expansion had kindled imaginations and beckoned travelers. The tragic war had interrupted western development, but with the war over, eyes turned westward again. Now the object was to develop, to settle, to civilize the land. The task would not be easy. The land was wild, dangerous, and crude. Yet it was potentially rich, especially in mineral resources; its dangers were a challenge; and along with its wildness it offered an awesome beauty and a mood of expansiveness for the human spirit.

Legends of the Late Frontier

Some of the country's figures took on mythical proportions. The West had its dragon slayers and giant killers, its Hercules and Achilles. The West produced, in the persons of the outlaw and the lawman, the standard American types of hero and villain. These types, and their many followers, still haunt the television screen in the decayed end of the tradition — the "Horse Opera." Cooper's "noble red men" of the eastern forests, Chingachgook and Uncas, had disappeared; in their place came their western counterparts. In the fierce Indian wars of the plains and mountains, such figures as Cochise, Sitting Bull, and Geronimo were sometimes cast as the great-hearted adversaries of the pioneers.

Even the "bad man" had a cloak of glamour thrown over him for a time. Jesse James and William Quantrill were outlaws, train and bank robbers, whose activities as guerilla fighters in the war were continued as private lawlessness after the fighting was over. Jesse James, in particular, became a legendary figure. Probably the most famous of the individual bad men, and one of the youngest, was Billy the Kid — he became the center of a somewhat sentimental myth, but was in truth no more than a hoodlum.

The "bad man" tradition, of course, carried with it the opposite figure of the "lawman," the local sheriff or the U.S. Marshal. The most famous of these daredevils of the fast draw were Wild Bill Hickok and Wyatt Earp.

The cowboy, the gambler, the old prospector, the miner — all were part of the great gallery of the West. They were bound to find their place in song and legend. Folk ballads and tall tales plucked the heart strings or stretched the imagination. Pecos Bill was a southwestern Hercules; raised by coyotes, he long thought himself to be one because, like other coyotes, he had fleas and howled all night. He could kill a deer by running him to exhaustion. He could hug a bear to death. He once rode a cyclone to Texas when the country needed rain. He was said to have invented the lariat. Many of these tall tales were more exaggerated versions of the earlier Davy Crockett and Mike Fink legends.

The Hercules of the lumberjacks in the Northwest was the mighty Paul Bunyan. With the help of Babe, the Blue Ox, he cut down trees by the quarter section, drained lakes, and changed the flow of great rivers. It was Paul who hauled good white snow from China across the frozen Pacific in the Year of the Blue Snow. The cookstove in his logging camp covered an acre. He once swam straight up a column of rain and turned it off.

Down South was John Henry, the steel-driving man of the railroad construction gangs. He worked himself to death winning a stone-drilling contest against a steam drill, and he stands as a symbol of human muscle and determination resisting the coming of the machine. Though such supermen still live in folk tradition, the legend of the West also flourished in less exaggerated figures. Buffalo Bill Cody, Kit Carson, Calamity Jane, Annie Oakley, and General George Armstrong Custer were popular during these years. They, or characters modeled on them, were the stock-in-trade of many popular Wild West Shows of the time.

All of these legends began as word of mouth, but they rapidly found a place in the written word. Around 1860 a man named Erastus Beadle, an eastern printer located, appropriately, in Cooperstown, New York, where the creator of the Deerslayer had lived, began to publish "dime novels." He was not alone in this trade. As popular reading material, dime novels flourished for years.

There were writers of quality, too, who had gone West and were working there, drawing material from the land and the people. They began to create a formal literature. In time, out of this background came writers like Harte and Twain.

BRET HARTE

Bret Harte was an easterner, born and raised in Albany, New York, who went to seek his fortune in California in 1854, when he was eighteen years old. He tried his luck in the mines, but like many others, including Mark Twain, he found more profit in print than in rocks. It was as a writer and editor that Harte built his fame. San Francisco had two publications to which Harte contributed: the *Golden Era* and the *Californian*. Later Harte became the editor of a new literary magazine, the *Overland Monthly*, California's challenge to the *Atlantic Monthly*. For this magazine Harte wrote a series of stories, sketches, and poems that caught the popular fancy. By 1870 such famous tales as "The Luck of Roaring Camp," "The Outcasts of Poker Flat," "Tennessee's Partner," and his famous poem, "Plain Language from

Bret Harte

Truthful James," had made Bret Harte internationally famous as the first literary voice of the American West.

He drew vivid pictures of the western scene he knew so well. He put odd place names on eastern lips: Poker Flat, One Horse Gulch, Sandy Bar, and Red Dog. This was local color, and Harte, in a way, is the father of the local-color school of writing. True, there had been local color before — Irving's Hudson River stories or Whittier's *Snow-Bound*, for example — but Harte was the first to exploit the setting for its own sake and to subordinate characters and events to that setting.

Harte's characters had sentimental appeal, especially such types as the sinful or flawed man or woman who revealed a heart of gold when the chips were down. The New England schoolmarm bringing the spark of learning to the raw West was another of his favorites. This gallery rapidly became the stock types, the thread-bare characters of all later "westerns," but they were fresh in costume, place, and language when Harte first drew them. He is, in a sense, the fountainhead of all the western stories that were to follow him, and he is better than most of his successors, for, at least in the early stories, he revealed an artist's touch.

As Bret Harte's literary powers dwindled and his fame at home declined, he began a career in diplomacy. He went to Prussia and then to Scotland in consular posts. Harte finally settled in London, where he remained until his death in 1902.

MARK TWAIN

As an editor and counselor to other writers, Harte's influence was large. Mark Twain, cutting his own literary teeth in San Francisco during these years, testified later that "Bret Harte trimmed and trained and schooled me patiently."

Twain started his own literary career with a local-color story, "The Celebrated Jumping Frog of Calaveras County," but there were signs even in this first tale that Twain would quickly surpass the skill of his teacher. The story had much more in it than mere local color; it had, too, the kind of humor that had characterized much of the literature of the frontier South and West for a generation.

Yet Mark Twain was far more than a western writer or a humorist. He was the most American of writers, the most national, the most genuinely democratic. Ranging over the country and the world, Twain's writings sum up one of the most colorful eras in American history. (A biographical sketch of Mark Twain appears on page 698.)

The Fading of the Old West

The railroads brought an end to the Old West. The ribbons of steel carried the iron horse across plain, desert, and mountain from sea to sea. The old frontier was gone. The speed and means of travel were revolutionized, and the economy of the region was altered. The cattle kingdom replaced the mining kingdom, and after the cowboy came the farmer. It was the railroad that brought him, for the railroad made it possible to ship wheat and corn to market.

As the Old West faded, the transcontinental railroad added a last chapter to

A nineteenth-century lithograph showing a railroad bridge over the Humboldt River in Nevada.

the epic. The railheads crept out from East and West, simultaneously, to wind over mountains or drill through them, until the lines met and were joined at Promontory Point in Utah. The transcontinental railroad was a remarkable chronicle of engineering achievement, politics, and finance.

The course of the rails made the destinies of some great cities. Chicago became the rail gateway to the West, leading to Dodge City, Abilene, Omaha, Cheyenne, and Denver. In the Far West, up and down the Pacific Coast, the magic combination of railways eastward and sea lanes westward promised greatness to San Francisco, Los Angeles, Portland, and Seattle. The crude San Francisco of 1840 that Dana had described in *Two Years Before the Mast* became, twenty years later, the city of Harte and Twain, where a new literature was beginning. The city has flourished ever since as one of the nation's cultural centers.

The Last Frontier

In the heart of the West, during the later years of this period, a writer was at work on a book that had no relationship to his time and place. The writer was the territorial governor of New Mexico, General Lew Wallace, a veteran of both the Mexican War and the War Between the States. In his official residence at Santa Fe, the governor pursued his literary work at night, behind closed shutters, for

Billy the Kid had sworn that he would kill him. The book in progress was *Ben-Hur* (1880). It became one of the best-selling novels of all time and remains in print in several editions and in many languages. It was long popular as a play and has twice been made into lavish motion pictures. Wallace wrote other successful novels including *The Fair God*, a story of the conquest of Mexico.

OKLAHOMA LAND

Among the last western lands to be opened for free settlement were certain portions of Oklahoma Territory. Originally, these lands had been set apart for the use of several Indian tribes: the Seminoles, Cherokees, Creeks, Osages, and others. As a result of the constant pressure of white settlers, much of this land was repurchased or simply withdrawn from the Indians. From 1889 through 1893, portions of the so-called Cherokee Strip and other parts of the territory were thrown open for settlement in dramatic fashion.

All those who wished to race for claims, sometimes as many as 20,000, were marshaled along a line, miles long, and at the discharge of starting guns, they dashed into the territory to stake out what land they could. Some evaded the watchful Federal troops, entered the territory sooner than was lawful, and staked their claims in advance. Such people were called "sooners."

Edna Ferber made one of these land dashes the focus of a popular novel, *Cimarron* (1930). Marquis James, a Pulitzer prize winning biographer, described another of these scrambles for land in his autobiographical book *The Cherokee Strip* (1945). With the settlement of the last of the Oklahoma free lands, an era of the West finally closed.

THE NORTHERN PLAINS

One of the compelling events of the late West is the settling of the northern plains by Danish, Norwegian, and Swedish immigrants. The most impressive chronicler of this era was a man from Norway, Ole Rölvaag, who wrote powerfully of the pioneering thrust of his fellow Norwegians into that prairie region. While the clearing of trees had been the problem of the Ohio and Indiana settlers, the absence of trees afflicted the early plainsmen. Their dwellings were built of sod; storm and wind swept unchecked upon them; the sun beat without mercy. Prairie fires menaced the settlers, and sometimes when crops were good, a plague of locusts would wipe out the yield.

Rölvaag belongs to this century and to the tide of realism that was stirring in Europe and America in the early 1900's. He came to America in 1896, at the age of twenty. He studied at St. Olaf College in Minnesota and remained there to teach Norwegian. All his books were written originally in that language. His fame rests on a sequence of three novels, the most famous of which is the first, *Giants in the Earth* (1927), a powerful story of the plains settlements. The other volumes are *Peder Victorious* and *Their Fathers' God*, completed shortly before Rölvaag's death in 1931.

WESTERN SONGS
AND BALLADS

In *The American Songbag* Carl Sandburg printed this ballad about the typical pioneer home on the prairies with an explanatory introduction:

"A little girl from western Nebraska, home again after a trip to the East, was asked, 'What is the East?' She answered, 'The East is where trees come between you and the sky.' Early settlers noticed log cabins were scarcer as timberland thinned out going farther west. On the windy, open prairies of the Great Plains, the best house to be had in short order was of sod. A cellar was dug first; long slices of turf were piled around the cellar lines; wooden crosspoles held the sod roof. Ceilings went high or low: tall men put roofs farther from the ground than short men did. In timber country farther east they sang 'The Little Old Log Cabin in the Lane'; its tune was familiar to the lonely 'sod-buster' who made this song about his dwelling — in a region where rivers are sometimes a half mile wide and a half inch deep."

The Little Old Sod Shanty
Pioneer Ballad

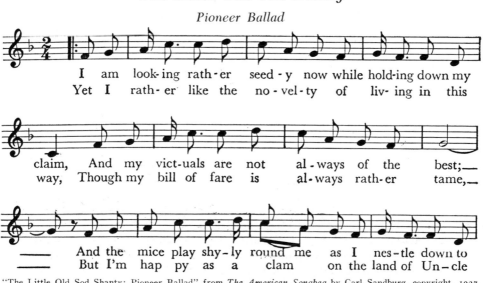

I am look-ing rath-er seed-y now while hold-ing down my
Yet I rath-er like the no-vel-ty of liv-ing in this

claim, And my vict-uals are not al-ways of the best;__
way, Though my bill of fare is al-ways rath-er tame,__

____ And the mice play shy-ly round me as I nes-tle down to
____ But I'm hap py as a clam on the land of Un-cle

"The Little Old Sod Shanty: Pioneer Ballad" from *The American Songbag* by Carl Sandburg, copyright, 1927, by Harcourt, Brace and Company, Inc. Reprinted by permission of Harcourt, Brace & World, Inc.

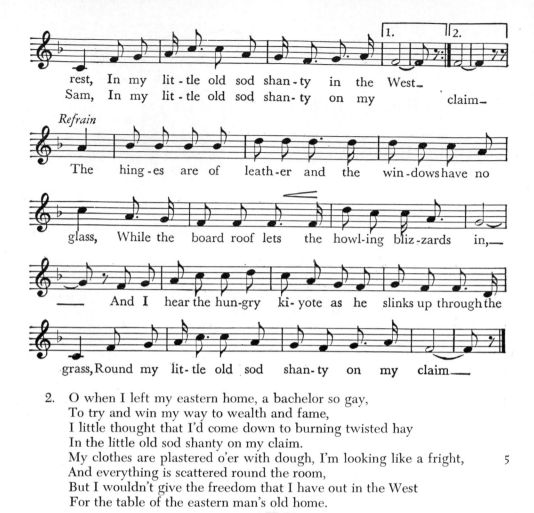

rest, In my lit-tle old sod shan-ty in the West—
Sam, In my lit-tle old sod shan-ty on my claim—

Refrain

The hing-es are of leath-er and the win-dows have no glass, While the board roof lets the howl-ing bliz-zards in,— —— And I hear the hun-gry ki-yote as he slinks up through the grass, Round my lit-tle old sod shan-ty on my claim——

2. O when I left my eastern home, a bachelor so gay,
   To try and win my way to wealth and fame,
   I little thought that I'd come down to burning twisted hay
   In the little old sod shanty on my claim.
   My clothes are plastered o'er with dough, I'm looking like a fright,   5
   And everything is scattered round the room,
   But I wouldn't give the freedom that I have out in the West
   For the table of the eastern man's old home.

3. Still I wish that some kindhearted girl would pity on me take,
   And relieve me from the mess that I am in;   10
   The angel, how I'd bless her if this her home she'd make
   In the little old sod shanty on my claim.
   And we would make our fortunes on the prairies of the West,
   Just as happy as two lovers we'd remain;
   We'd forget the trials and troubles we endured at the first,   15
   In the little old sod shanty on our claim.

4. And if kindly fate should bless us with now and then an heir,
   To cheer our hearts with honest pride of fame,
   O then we'd be contented for the toil that we had spent
   In the little old sod shanty on our claim.   20
   When time enough had lapsed and all of those little brats
   To noble man- and womanhood had grown,
   It wouldn't seem half so lonely as around us we should look,
   And see the little old sod shanty on our claim.

"The Cowboy" by the American artist Frederic Remington ▶

Cowboys built up a body of songs second in number only to the Negro spirituals. The cowboy had two reasons for singing. He sang to pass the time away, in camp with his fellows, or riding herd, or covering his range alone. He also found that singing helped with his work. Wistful songs of homes far away were useful on night herd duty, because slow, sad tunes quieted the cattle.

All Day on the Prairie

TEXAS COWBOY SONG ARRANGED BY DAVID GUION

All day on the prairie in the saddle I ride,
Not even a dog, boys, to trot by my side.
My fire I must kindle with chips° gathered round,
And boil my own coffee without being ground.

I wash in a pool, dry on a toesack;°   5
I carry my wardrobe all on my back;
For want of an oven I cook in a pot,
And sleep on the ground for want of a cot.

And then, if my cooking is not so complete,
You cannot blame me for wanting to eat,   10
But show me a man, boys, that sleeps more profound
Than this big cowpuncher who sleeps on the ground.

My ceiling's the sky, boys, my floor is the grass,
My music's the lowing of herds as they pass;
My books are the rivers, my sermons the stones,   15
My parson's a wolf on his pulpit of bones.

3. **chips:** pieces of dried dung, the only fuel available on the treeless prairies. 5. **toesack:** a coarse sack such as those used for grain, made of jute or hemp fiber.

FOR DISCUSSION

THE LITTLE OLD SOD SHANTY

What is the settler's one wish? Do you think he will get it? Will he be happy if he does?

ALL DAY ON THE PRAIRIE

1. Does the cowboy seem to complain about the comforts that he lacks, or is he proud of getting along without them?

2. Literary quotations often crop up in cowboy songs, because reading aloud was a favorite pastime around the campfire or in the bunkhouse at night. Find lines that contain an echo of Shakespeare's lines in *As You Like It* (Act II, Sc. i, ll. 15–17):

And this our life exempt from public haunt
Finds tongues in trees, books in the running brooks,
Sermons in stones, and good in everything.

JAMES
STEVENS

1892–

An American Hercules

The old and the new Northwest lumber camps have given American folklore that fabulous hero of tall tales, Paul Bunyan. James Stevens worked for many months in lumber camps in Washington, Oregon, and Idaho before retelling the best stories about the giant logger in his book *Paul Bunyan*. In "An American Hercules" Mr. Stevens has written especially for *Adventures in American Literature* an account of the way the Paul Bunyan legend developed, giving as an example of the stories a hitherto unrecorded yarn of typical flavor.

Picture the proper setting for the tale, as Mr. Stevens describes it in the introduction to his book:

" A Paul Bunyan bunkhouse service is a glory to hear, when it is spontaneous and in a proper setting, preferably around a big heated stove in the winter, when the wind is howling through crackling boughs outside and the pungent smell of steaming wool drifts down from the drying lines above the stove. When a vasty spirit of the woods really moves the meeting, a noble and expansive ecstasy of the soul is exhibited."

"An American Hercules" by James Stevens. Reprinted by permission of the author.

P AUL BUNYAN, the mythical hero of the lumberjacks, is the supreme figure of American folklore. Paul was a Herculean logger who combed his beard with a young pine tree; who skidded his timber with Babe the Blue Ox, a creature so vast that he measured forty-two ax handles and a plug of chewing tobacco between the horns; who operated a camp cookhouse where the flapjack griddle was greased by twenty-four Arabs — imported from the Sahara Desert because they could stand the heat — skating to and fro with slabs of bacon strapped to their feet; who tamed the Mississippi when it was young and wild by building river corrals and driving the river through their gates (the Great Lakes remain as evidence of this feat); who ruled the American country in the period when it was only a timberland. This epoch, according to the best authorities, began with the Winter of the Blue Snow and ended with the Spring the Rain Came Up from China.

Here, indeed, is a full-bodied myth. The Paul Bunyan stories have been told in American logging camps since 1840. They are unquestionably of Canadian origin. There was a Paul Bunyan who won fame in the Papineau Rebellion of 1837. There is no evidence that the beginnings of the stories are beyond him. The other materials and characters of the myth were developed out of the magic of bunkhouse nights; when the workday in the woods, or on the iced road, or on the drive, was done; when the camp men, isolated from all life but that of the woods, had no other outlet for their fancies than the creation of romances about their own life.

Thus Paul Bunyan; Babe the Blue Ox; Johnny Inkslinger, the timekeeper who figured with a fountain pen fed by hose lines from twenty-four barrels of ink; Hels Helson, the Big Swede and bull of the woods, who muddied the Missouri River forever with one spring bath; and many smaller characters — such as Hot Biscuit Slim, the cook; Shanty Boy, the bard; and Big Ole, the blacksmith — have been celebrated in logging camps from Bangor, Maine, to Portland, Oregon. The tall tale, the "whopper," is not confined, of course, to the lumber camps. It appears with the earliest accounts of the Appalachian pioneers. It is forever present in the best writings of Mark Twain. Other mythical heroes have won a certain fame, such as Tony Beaver of the Virginia mountains and Pecos Bill, the southwestern *vaquero*[1] who once straddled a cyclone and rode it to a finish. But the myth of Paul Bunyan stands alone, possessing, as it does, its own time, place, and people.

The stories are told in this manner:

Supper is over in the logging camp, and the after-supper period of smoking and quiet is also done. A murmur of talk about the day's work rises from the gang around the heating stove. There is a strong smell of steaming wool from the drying lines. Blue pipe smoke drifts through the mellow light of the Rochester burners. A gust of frosty air

blows in whenever the bunkhouse door is opened. Some logger ventures the opinion that this will be the hardest winter this part of the country has ever known. Weather talk runs on until someone states solemnly that "the weather ain't what she used to be. Gettin' old now, the weather is. Take the Year of the Two Winters, in Paul Bunyan's time. Yes, sir. Then. That year two winters come all at once. . . ."

Then there is a contest to see who can tell the tallest tale about cold weather in the day of Paul Bunyan.

Or it is a summer night, and the loggers are circling a smudge fire outside the bunkhouse. Mosquitoes swarm up from the swamp below camp. So mosquito stories are in order. Any man is free to invent new Paul Bunyan yarns himself, or he can repeat the stories heard from other bards. Occasionally some bard is so inspired that his creation is never forgotten, and becomes a permanent addition to the Paul Bunyan myth. Such is the story of the mammoth mosquitoes and their amazing experiences with Bum and Bill, Paul Bunyan's battling bees.

Here is the story.

It was in the Year of the Dry Summer that Paul Bunyan's loggers first encountered mosquitoes. That was the season Paul Bunyan invented thunder. Day after day, week after week, month after month, the great hero-leader of the loggers toiled through experiments with all the sounds he could imagine. Just as cows, pigs, dogs, hens, and ducks could be called, so could clouds be called, thought Paul Bunyan. Seventeen thousand various kinds of calls the great logger tried that summer before he hit on the sound of thunder. Then his labors were rewarded. Paul Bunyan had not thundered once before a stray cloud rolled up from the west. He thundered on, and by midnight so many clouds had gathered that the Dry Summer ended in a downpour that

---

[1] *vaquero* (vä·kâr′ô): cowboy (Spanish).

was a deluge instead of a rain. Ever since that parched season the weather has used the thunder which Paul Bunyan invented for it.

But Paul Bunyan had other troubles during this wretched summer. Time and again he had to quit his important labor of trying out sounds that would call up clouds, and attend to small bothers, plagues, and worries. The most troublesome of all these troubles was the invasion of mosquitoes.

The mammoth mosquitoes came from the Tall Wolf country. There the tribe had experienced a devastating famine. For the larger it grew, the smaller became the tribe of tall wolves, the mammoth mosquitoes' natural prey. Eventually the last tall wolf was gone, and only a small company of female mosquitoes was left from the once vast and powerful insect tribe. These females were forced by hunger into migration. They were ready to fall and perish from exhaustion when they reached Paul Bunyan's loggers, who, stripped to the waist, were at work even on this, the hottest of the Dry Summer's days.

Paul Bunyan was afar from his loggers at the moment, pondering deeply on the problem of calling up the clouds. He failed to notice when the ring of axes and the drone of saws were hushed. Not until agonizing yells arose from his loggers did the hero-leader realize that a new trouble had come to camp. Then he saw that his men were struggling for their lives all through the timber five miles away. Two strides and one leap, and Paul Bunyan was on the scene of battle.

Many of his loggers were already white and faint from loss of blood, and the others were hacking desperately with their axes at the dodging, diving mosquitoes. Two of the mammoth winged females were sprawled lifelessly over some pine logs. Others had paused in the fight to bind up their split bills. The battle raged on.

Paul Bunyan was so stirred with wrath at the sight that he unloosed a yell of astonishment and anger. The loggers, of course, were all lifted off their feet and then hurled to the ground by the force of that cyclonic voice; and the mammoth mosquitoes instantly took advantage of this and plunged on the loggers with bloodthirsty hums. Each one held down seven or more men at once and prepared to feast.

For a moment Paul Bunyan was in a panic. He thought of smashing the mosquitoes with smacks of his hand but that would have crushed the loggers underneath. With a mighty effort, the great logger collected his wits. He had to think fast, and he did. Paul Bunyan was that kind of man. And at once he acted.

What he did was to call for Babe the Blue Ox, whose ears were so far from his muzzle that he couldn't hear himself snort. As he approached, Babe saw what was needed for the emergency. He did not wait for orders. Without even a glance at Paul, the Blue Ox did a squads rightabout, halted, straightened out his tail, and began to flirt the mosquitoes off the prone loggers with swishes of his huge tail brush. In one minute every frustrated mosquito was humming angrily in the air, and the saved loggers were galloping for the protection of the bunkhouses. There they remained. All night the ravenous mammoth mosquitoes maintained a deafening and ominous hum over the bunkhouses. Paul Bunyan listened. He figured and planned, the ideas for sounds to call clouds forgotten for the moment. At dawn Paul Bunyan had a satisfying idea. He called for Johnny Inkslinger, his timekeeper and man of science.

"Johnny," said Paul, "you need a vacation."

"Yes, sir, Mr. Bunyan," said Johnny, but not very enthusiastically; for if there was anything he hated it was to leave his figures, his grand fountain pen, and ink barrels.

"A vacation," Paul Bunyan repeated firmly. "So a vacation you shall take. A hunting vacation, Johnny. I'm going to send you bee hunting."

"Mr. Bunyan," said Johnny Inkslinger, "I am a good hunter and I like to hunt. Why, once I found a moose who had died of old age, found his moldering bones, I did, and I tracked him to his birthplace, How's that for hunting, Mr. Bunyan?" said Johnny proudly. But then he looked doubtful. "I dont' know about hunting bees, though, Mr. Bunyan."

"You must not only hunt bees, Johnny. You must trap 'em and tame 'em."

"Now, Mr. Bunyan, that's asking a lot," protested Johnny Inkslinger. "I never did claim to be a bee trapper, or a bee tamer, either. Why pick on me, Mr. Bunyan?"

"Don't question orders, Johnny," said Paul Bunyan, kindly but sternly. "You pack up now for a vacation in the Mastodonic [1] Clover country. Once there, hunt, trap, and tame the two fighting-est, savagest, irritablest, cantankerous-est bees you can find. Then trot 'em home to camp."

"Trot 'em, Mr. Bunyan?"

"Trot 'em, Johnny. Trot the bees."

"Yes, sir," said Johnny; and with a will, for he was sentimental about obeying orders.

When Johnny Inkslinger was sent by Paul Bunyan to do anything, he did it. So he wasn't a day in the Mastodonic Clover country until he had hunted down, trapped, and tamed — as nearly as two such fighting, savage, irritable, and cantankerous bees could be tamed — the two famous battling bees, Bum and Bill. Johnny tamed the two bees so that they allowed him to chain their wings to their bodies. They also trusted him with their stingers, which he put in his knapsack. Then Johnny Inkslinger put calked boots on the bees' hind

---

[1] **Mastodonic**: from "mastodon," an extinct elephantlike animal.

feet, trotted them out of the clover country, trotted them on over hill and dale, trotted them all the way to camp, just as Paul Bunyan had ordered.

Paul Bunyan had a great hive ready for the two warriors. When their wings were unchained, Bum and Bill took off their calked boots, stretched their legs, ate a hearty meal of lump sugar, and turned in for a refreshing sleep. The next morning they buzzed for their stingers at sunup and showed in other ways that they were eager for battle. Paul Bunyan himself led them to the woods, for Johnny Inkslinger insisted on getting back to his figures at once.

Logging had been continued under the tail of Babe the Blue Ox. For three days he had been swishing the ravenous mammoth mosquitoes away from the loggers. He was so tail-weary that he welcomed Bum and Bill, the battling bees, with a joyful moo that shivered the timber for miles. The bees answered with buzzes of rage, and it required all of Paul Bunyan's bee-taming art to convince the fighting bees that Babe was a friend and not the enemy. Bum and Bill were still buzzing suspicion when they sighted the actual foe. Then, with a battle cry that sounded like the rasping roar of a band saw, Bum and Bill lit out in a beeline and charged in an irresistible attack. In seventeen seconds the bodies of seventeen mammoth mosquitoes crashed down into the timber, shattering scores of great pines into splinters. A thunderous hum of fear sounded from the survivors. They flew off in a panic. Pursued and pursuers vanished in the haze of the Dry Summer, which smothered the forest. Soon the hums of fear and the buzzes of rage were only faint murmurs among the far trees. Paul Bunyan's teeth shone through his beard in a smile of triumph.

"Yay, Babe!" he commanded the Blue Ox.

The logging went on.

Paul Bunyan brushed his hands and praised the saints that this mosquito trouble had been so easily ended. Then he returned to his great task of trying out sounds which would call up clouds. The labor engrossed the great logger to such a degree that the mosquito invasion vanished from his thoughts. He also forgot the two big battling bees who had driven the invaders from the logging camp. But Johnny Inkslinger did not forget. Often he raised his head from his books and held his fountain pen poised in the air, while the hose lines from the ink barrels gushed an inky flood to the office floor. This Johnny Inkslinger did not notice in such moments, for he was remembering his grand success as a bee hunter, a bee trapper, and a bee tamer. It was one of the proudest memories of his life.

And often Johnny Inkslinger wondered what had become of the bees he had tamed, what had happened to the female mammoth mosquitoes Bum and Bill had driven from the camp. Weeks had passed, and still there was not a hum from the mosquitoes or a buzz from the bees.

Then, during such a moment of wondering and remembering, Johnny Inkslinger heard a sound from the distance that was nothing but a buzz-hum. He ran out of the office and peered into the heat haze. A small, dark cloud seemed to be moving toward the camp. Johnny watched and waited. The cloud grew larger. As it approached the loggers in the woods, Johnny saw that the cloud was a vast swarm of giant insects. They hovered over the loggers for an instant, then dived without circling. And again agonizing yells rolled up from the timber and smote Paul Bunyan's ears.

"What's happened down there?" Paul Bunyan shouted.

"The mosquitoes have come back!" said Johnny Inkslinger.

"It's a new kind, then," said Paul Bunyan, coming on the run and calling Babe the Blue Ox. "Look at 'em. They're bees!"

"They're mosquitoes," said Johnny. "Look at their bills!"

"But look at their stingers!"

"Sure enough," said Johnny Inkslinger, almost dumb with astonishment. "Why — why — Mr. Bunyan — they — "

"Look at 'em!" yelled Paul Bunyan. "Why, they got bills in front and stingers behind, and they're getting the loggers going and coming! You know what's happened? Those two bees have married the mosquitoes, that's what! And these are the offspring! Bills in front and stingers behind! Yay, Babe!"

And on Paul galloped with Babe the Blue Ox, who soon got his tail brush to working and let the loggers escape to the bunkhouses. But these mammoth insects which were half mosquito and half bee wouldn't be denied. They attacked the bunkhouses. One would stick his bill under one side of a shake on a bunkhouse roof, and his stinger under the other side; and then he would flap his wings until he had ripped off the shake; and the loggers would have to stand guard with pike poles and peavies [1] to keep the savage insects from coming at them through the ripped roofs. Paul Bunyan saw that he needed to act quick. So he spent another night in figuring and planning. And, just as usual, he had a grand idea at daylight. He called for Johnny Inkslinger.

"Johnny," said Paul Bunyan, "we are going to carry sugar."

"Yes, Mr. Bunyan."

"We are going to throw some rafts together, Johnny, and then we are going to load the rafts with all the sugar in camp. After that we are going to rope the rafts together and have Babe the Blue Ox tow the whole raft fleet out into the middle of Lake Michigan."

Johnny Inkslinger never batted an eye. He knew the great logger too well to think that any of his ideas were foolish. So Johnny went to work without a

[1] **peavies:** poles with iron points and movable iron hooks.

word; and by noon the rafts were built, loaded, and roped together. Paul hitched Babe to the head raft of the fleet.

"Yay, Babe," he commanded.

And the Blue Ox bowed his neck, lumbered off, and straight to the center of Lake Michigan he towed the raft-loads of sugar. Johnny Inkslinger stayed on shore. He watched and waited. Soon he saw all the mosquito-bees flying out over the lake after the rafts. Then Johnny Inkslinger realized what Paul Bunyan was up to.

"Oh, ain't he got a brain, though?" said Johnny Inkslinger worshipfully. "Oh, but ain't Paul Bunyan got a brain?"

And a brain Paul Bunyan certainly had. For he had figured that the bee blood in the hybrid insects would send them after the sugar. And he had figured that their mosquito blood would make them fill their stomachs till they were stuffed. And Paul Bunyan knew the weight of sugar. . . .

Sure enough, the mosquito-bees glutted themselves on sugar till they could hardly fly. Then Paul Bunyan started Babe on a run for the shore. The stuffed insects tried to follow. But lower and lower they flew; and soon, with anguished buzz-hums, they all sank into the waters of the great lake; and that was the last of them.

The camp of Paul Bunyan was never again troubled by mammoth mosquitoes, or by mammoth mosquito-bees, either. Bum and Bill at last returned to camp, and gave every appearance of being ashamed of themselves. Paul Bunyan did not reproach them, but gave them a home in a furnished hive; and thereafter Bum and Bill occupied themselves solely with making honey for the loggers' flapjacks. Their fighting days were done.

History does not state the fate of the female mammoth mosquitoes. Some authorities advance the idea that they flew to Asia. They point to the elephant to prove their contention. The elephant, they assert, is descended from the mammoth mosquito of Paul Bunyan's time. Other authorities ridicule this idea, asserting that the elephant is too small to be a descendant of the mammoth mosquito.

All such ideas and contentions are guesswork, however. And guesswork has no place in the history of Paul Bunyan.

FOR DISCUSSION

1. Can you understand why life on the frontier made tall tales especially popular there? If you know about other folk heroes like Pecos Bill and John Henry, compare their exploits with Paul Bunyan's. Who among them seems to you the most representative American hero? How does the hero of your choice compare with such Greek heroes as Hercules and Odysseus?

2. Even with the fun and exaggeration, you can learn something about logging camps and how they operated from tales of Paul Bunyan. What information did you pick up?

3. Why is it difficult to dramatize a tall tale? Which medium (screen, radio, television, puppet, marionette) would be the most effective?

YOUR OWN WRITING

Telling tall tales has always been a favorite American diversion. Your own neighborhood has its pet "whoppers." Write out one of them — or make up a fresh one of your own.

FURTHER READING

You will enjoy reading James Stevens' *Paul Bunyan*, J. C. Bowman's *Pecos Bill*, or Margaret Prescott Montague's *Tony Beaver* for one of your outside reading assignments. If you prefer reading short stories, try Mark Twain's great yarn, "The Celebrated Jumping Frog of Calaveras County."

BRET HARTE

1836–1902

The Outcasts of Poker Flat

Bret Harte's skill with plot and suspense would have made his stories popular in any day. But to understand the way they swept the country during the 1860's and 1870's, imagine yourself an easterner hungry with curiosity about the wild, rough life of the West. Then you will observe how he fills his stories with the sort of details in setting and in characterization that build up "local color."

As MR. JOHN OAKHURST, gambler, stepped into the main street of Poker Flat on the morning of the twenty-third of November, 1850, he was conscious of a change in its moral atmosphere since the preceding night. Two or three men, conversing earnestly together, ceased as he approached, and exchanged significant glances. There was a Sabbath lull in the air, which, in a settlement unused to Sabbath influences, looked ominous.

Mr. Oakhurst's calm, handsome face betrayed small concern in these indications. Whether he was conscious of any predisposing cause was another ques-

"The Outcasts of Poker Flat" by Bret Harte. Reprinted by permission of Houghton Mifflin Company.

tion. "I reckon they're after somebody," he reflected; "likely it's me." He returned to his pocket the handkerchief with which he had been whipping away the red dust of Poker Flat from his neat boots, and quietly discharged his mind of any further conjecture.

In point of fact, Poker Flat was "after somebody." It had lately suffered the loss of several thousand dollars, two valuable horses, and a prominent citizen. It was experiencing a spasm of virtuous reactions, quite as lawless and ungovernable as any of the acts that had provoked it. A secret committee had determined to rid the town of all improper persons. This was done permanently in regard to two men who were then hanging from the boughs of a sycamore in the gulch, and temporarily in the banishment of certain other objectionable characters. I regret to say that some of these were ladies. It is but due to the sex, however, to state that their impropriety was professional, and it was only in such easily established standards of evil that Poker Flat ventured to sit in judgment.

Mr. Oakhurst was right in supposing that he was included in this category. A few of the committee had urged hanging him as a possible example and a sure method of reimbursing themselves from his pockets of the sums he had won from them. "It's agin justice," said Jim Wheeler, "to let this yer young man from Roaring Camp — an entire stranger — carry away our money." But a crude sentiment of equity residing in the breasts of those who had been fortunate enough to win from Mr. Oakhurst overruled this narrower local prejudice.

Mr. Oakhurst received his sentence with philosophic calmness, none the less coolly that he was aware of the hesitation of his judges. He was too much of a gambler not to accept fate. With him life was at best an uncertain game, and he recognized the usual percentage in favor of the dealer.

A body of armed men accompanied the deported wickedness of Poker Flat to the outskirts of the settlement. Besides Mr. Oakhurst, who was known to be a coolly desperate man, and for whose intimidation the armed escort was intended, the expatriated [1] party consisted of a young woman familiarly known as "The Duchess"; another who had won the title of "Mother Shipton"; and "Uncle Billy," a suspected sluice robber and confirmed drunkard. The cavalcade provoked no comments from the spectators, nor was any word uttered by the escort. Only when the gulch which marked the uttermost limit of Poker Flat was reached, the leader spoke briefly and to the point. The exiles were forbidden to return at the peril of their lives.

As the escort disappeared, their pent-up feelings found vent in a few hysterical tears from the Duchess, some bad language from Mother Shipton, and a Parthian [2] volley of expletives from Uncle Billy. The philosophic Oakhurst alone remained silent. He listened calmly to Mother Shipton's desire to cut somebody's heart out, to the repeated statements of the Duchess that she would die in the road, and to the alarming oaths that seemed to be bumped out of Uncle Billy as he rode forward. With the easy good humor characteristic of his class, he insisted upon exchanging his own riding horse, "Five-Spot," for the sorry mule which the Duchess rode. But even this act did not draw the party into any closer sympathy. The young woman adjusted her somewhat draggled plumes with a feeble, faded coquetry; [3] Mother Shipton eyed the possessor of Five-Spot with malevolence, and Uncle Billy included the whole party in one sweeping anathema. [4]

The road to Sandy Bar — a camp that, not having as yet experienced the regenerating influences of Poker Flat, consequently seemed to offer some invitation to the emigrants — lay over a steep mountain range. It was distant a day's severe travel. In that advanced season the party soon passed out of the moist, temperate regions of the foothills into the dry, cold, bracing air of the Sierras. The trail was narrow and difficult. At noon the Duchess, rolling out of her saddle upon the ground, declared her intention of going no farther, and the party halted.

The spot was singularly wild and impressive. A wooded amphitheater, surrounded on three sides by precipitous cliffs of naked granite, sloped gently toward the crest of another precipice that overlooked the valley. It was, undoubtedly, the most suitable spot for a camp, had camping been advisable. But Mr. Oakhurst knew that scarcely half the journey to Sandy Bar was accomplished, and the party were not equipped or provisioned for delay. This fact he pointed out to his companions

[1] **expatriated** (ĕks·pā'trĭ·āt'd): exiled.
[2] **Parthian:** The Parthians were an ancient people who, when retreating during a battle, were supposed to have turned around to shoot their arrows at the enemy.

[3] **coquetry** (kō'kĕ·trĭ): flirtation.
[4] **anathema** (à·năth'ê·mà): a curse.

curtly, with a philosophic commentary on the folly of "throwing up their hand before the game was played out." But they were furnished with liquor, which in this emergency stood them in place of food, fuel, rest, and prescience.[1] In spite of his remonstrances, it was not long before they were more or less under its influence. Uncle Billy passed rapidly from a bellicose[2] state into one of stupor, the Duchess became maudlin, and Mother Shipton snored. Mr. Oakhurst alone remained erect, leaning against a rock, calmly surveying them.

Mr. Oakhurst did not drink. It interfered with a profession which required coolness, impassiveness, and presence of mind, and, in his own language, he "couldn't afford it." As he gazed at his recumbent fellow exiles, the loneliness begotten of his pariah[3] trade, his habits of life, his very vices, for the first time seriously oppressed him. He bestirred himself in dusting his black clothes, washing his hands and face, and other acts characteristic of his studiously neat habits, and for a moment forgot his annoyance. The thought of deserting his weaker and more pitiable companions never perhaps occurred to him. Yet he could not help feeling the want of that excitement which, singularly enough, was most conducive to that calm equanimity for which he was notorious. He looked at the gloomy walls that rose a thousand feet sheer above the circling pines around him, at the sky ominously clouded, at the valley below, already deepening into shadow; and, doing so, suddenly he heard his own name called.

A horseman slowly ascended the trail. In the fresh, open face of the newcomer Mr. Oakhurst recognized Tom Simson, otherwise known as "The Innocent," of Sandy Bar. He had met him sometime before over a "little game,"

[1] prescience (prē'shĭ-ĕns): foresight.
[2] bellicose (bĕl'ĭ-kōs): hostile.
[3] pariah (pȧ-rī'ȧ): outcast.

and had, with perfect equanimity, won the entire fortune — amounting to some forty dollars — of that guileless youth. After the game was finished, Mr. Oakhurst drew the youthful speculator behind the door and thus addressed him: "Tommy, you're a good little man, but you can't gamble worth a cent. Don't try it over again." He then handed him his money back, pushed him gently from the room, and so made a devoted slave of Tom Simson.

There was a remembrance of this in his boyish and enthusiastic greeting of Mr. Oakhurst. He had started, he said, to go to Poker Flat to seek his fortune. "Alone?" No, not exactly alone; in fact (a giggle), he had run away with Piney Woods. Didn't Mr. Oakhurst remember Piney? She that used to wait on the table at the Temperance House? They had been engaged a long time, but old Jake Woods had objected, and so they had run away, and were going to Poker Flat to be married, and here they were. And they were tired out, and how lucky it was they had found a place to camp, and company. All this the Innocent delivered rapidly, while Piney, a stout, comely damsel of fifteen, emerged from behind the pine tree, where she had been blushing unseen, and rode to the side of her lover.

Mr. Oakhurst seldom troubled himself with sentiment, still less with propriety; but he had a vague idea that the situation was not fortunate. He retained, however, his presence of mind sufficiently to kick Uncle Billy, who was about to say something, and Uncle Billy was sober enough to recognize in Mr. Oakhurst's kick a superior power that would not bear trifling. He then endeavored to dissuade Tom Simson from delaying further, but in vain. He even pointed out the fact that there was no provision, nor means of making a camp. But, unluckily, the Innocent met this objection by assuring the party that he was provided with an extra mule loaded with provisions, and by the discov-

inward scorn, as he surveyed the sylvan group, the glancing firelight, and the tethered animals in the foreground. Suddenly an idea mingled with the alcoholic fumes that disturbed his brain. It was apparently of a jocular nature, for he felt impelled to slap his leg again and cram his fist into his mouth.

As the shadows crept slowly up the mountain, a slight breeze rocked the tops of the pine trees and moaned through their long and gloomy aisles. The ruined cabin, patched and covered with pine boughs, was set apart for the ladies. As the lovers parted, they unaffectedly exchanged a kiss, so honest and sincere that it might have been heard above the swaying pines. The frail Duchess and the malevolent Mother Shipton were probably too stunned to remark upon this last evidence of simplicity, and so turned without a word to the hut. The fire was replenished, the men lay down before the door, and in a few minutes were asleep.

Mr. Oakhurst was a light sleeper. Toward morning he awoke benumbed and cold. As he stirred the dying fire, the wind, which was now blowing strongly, brought to his cheek that which caused the blood to leave it — snow!

He started to his feet with the intention of awakening the sleepers, for there was no time to lose. But, turning to where Uncle Billy had been lying, he found him gone. A suspicion leaped to his brain, and a curse to his lips. He ran to the spot where the mules had been tethered — they were no longer there. The tracks were already rapidly disappearing in the snow.

The momentary excitement brought Mr. Oakhurst back to the fire with his usual calm. He did not waken the sleepers. The Innocent slumbered peacefully, with a smile on his good-humored, freckled face; the virgin Piney slept beside her frailer sisters as sweetly as though attended by celestial guardians; and Mr. Oakhurst, drawing his blanket over his shoulders, stroked his mus-

ery of a rude attempt at a log house near the trail. "Piney can stay with Mrs. Oakhurst," said the Innocent, pointing to the Duchess, "and I can shift for myself."

Nothing but Mr. Oakhurst's admonishing foot saved Uncle Billy from bursting into a roar of laughter. As it was, he felt compelled to retire up the canyon until he could recover his gravity. There he confided the joke to the tall pine trees, with many slaps of his leg, contortions of his face, and the usual profanity. But when he returned to the party, he found them seated by a fire — for the air had grown strangely chill and the sky overcast — in apparently amicable conversation. Piney was actually talking in an impulsive girlish fashion to the Duchess, who was listening with an interest and animation she had not shown for many days. The Innocent was holding forth, apparently with equal effect, to Mr. Oakhurst and Mother Shipton, who was actually relaxing into amiability. "Is this yer a d——d picnic?" said Uncle Billy, with taches and waited for the dawn. It came slowly in a whirly mist of snow-flakes that dazzled and confused the eye. What could be seen of the landscape appeared magically changed. He looked over the valley, and summed up the present and future in two words, "Snowed in!"

A careful inventory of the provisions, which, fortunately for the party, had been stored within the hut, and so escaped the felonious fingers of Uncle Billy, disclosed the fact that with care and prudence, they might last ten days longer. "That is," said Mr. Oakhurst *sotto voce* [1] to the Innocent, "if you're willing to board us. If you ain't — and perhaps you'd better not — you can wait till Uncle Billy gets back with provisions." For some occult [2] reason, Mr. Oakhurst could not bring himself to disclose Uncle Billy's rascality, and so offered the hypothesis that he had wandered from the camp and had accidentally stampeded the animals. He dropped a warning to the Duchess and Mother Shipton, who of course knew the facts of their associate's defection. "They'll find out the truth about us *all* when they find out anything," he added significantly, "and there's no good frightening them now."

Tom Simson not only put all his worldly store at the disposal of Mr. Oakhurst, but seemed to enjoy the prospect of their enforced seclusion. "We'll have a good camp for a week, and then the snow'll melt, and we'll all go back together." The cheerful gaiety of the young man and Mr. Oakhurst's calm infected the others. The Innocent, with the aid of pine boughs, extemporized a thatch for the roofless cabin, and the Duchess directed Piney in the rearrangement of the interior with a taste and tact that opened the blue eyes of that provincial maiden to their fullest

extent. "I reckon now you're used to fine things at Poker Flat," said Piney. The Duchess turned away sharply to conceal something that reddened her cheeks through their professional tint, and Mother Shipton requested Piney not to "chatter." But when Mr. Oakhurst returned from a weary search for the trail, he heard the sound of happy laughter echoed from the rocks. He stopped in some alarm, and his thoughts first naturally reverted to the whisky, which he had prudently cached. "And yet it don't somehow sound like whisky," said the gambler. It was not until he caught sight of the blazing fire through the still blind storm, and the group around it, that he settled to the conviction that it was "square fun."

Whether Mr. Oakhurst had cached his cards with the whisky as something debarred the free access of the community, I cannot say. It was certain that, in Mother Shipton's words, he "didn't say 'cards' once" during that evening. Haply the time was beguiled by an accordion, produced somewhat ostentatiously by Tom Simson from his pack. Notwithstanding some difficulties attending the manipulation of this instrument, Piney Woods managed to pluck several reluctant melodies from its keys, to an accompaniment by the Innocent on a pair of bone castanets. But the crowning festivity of the evening was reached in a rude camp-meeting hymn, which the lovers, joining hands, sang with great earnestness and vociferation. I fear that a certain defiant tone and Covenanters' [3] swing to its chorus, rather than any devotional quality, caused it speedily to infect the others, who at last joined in the refrain:

"I'm proud to live in the service of the Lord,
And I'm bound to die in His army."

---

[1] *sotto voce* (sôt'tô vō'chä): in an undertone (Italian).

[2] **occult** (ŏ·kŭlt'): hidden, mysterious.

[3] **Covenanters:** in seventeenth-century Scotland, adherents of the Presbyterian Covenant to resist the rule of the Anglican churches.

The pines rocked, the storm eddied and whirled above the miserable group, and the flames of their altar leaped heavenward, as if in token of the vow.

At midnight the storm abated, the rolling clouds parted, and the stars glittered keenly above the sleeping camp. Mr. Oakhurst, whose professional habits had enabled him to live on the smallest possible amount of sleep, in dividing the watch with Tom Simson, somehow managed to take upon himself the greater part of that duty. He excused himself to the Innocent by saying that he had "often been a week without sleep." "Doing what?" asked Tom. "Poker!" replied Oakhurst sententiously. "When a man gets a streak of luck, he don't get tired. The luck gives in first. Luck," continued the gambler reflectively, "is a mighty queer thing. All you know about it for certain is that it's bound to change. And it's finding out when it's going to change that makes you. We've had a streak of bad luck since we left Poker Flat — you come along, and slap, you get into it, too. If you can hold your cards right along, you're all right. For," added the gambler, with cheerful irrelevance,

"I'm proud to live in the service of the Lord,
And I'm bound to die in His army."

The third day came, and the sun, looking through the white-curtained valley, saw the outcasts dividing their slowly decreasing store of provisions for the morning meal. It was one of the peculiarities of that mountain climate that its rays diffused a kindly warmth over the wintry landscape, as if in regretful commiseration of the past. But it revealed drift on drift of snow piled high around the hut — a hopeless, uncharted, trackless sea of white lying below the rocky shores to which the castaways still clung. Through the marvelously clear air the smoke of the pastoral village of Poker Flat rose miles away. Mother Shipton saw it, and from a re-

mote pinnacle of her rocky fastness hurled in that direction a final malediction. It was her last vituperative attempt, and perhaps for that reason was invested with a certain degree of sublimity. It did her good, she privately informed the Duchess. "Just you go out there and cuss, and see." She then set herself to the task of amusing "the child," as she and the Duchess were pleased to call Piney. Piney was no chicken, but it was a soothing and original theory of the pair thus to account for the fact that she didn't swear and wasn't improper.

When night crept up again through the gorges, the reedy notes of the accordion rose and fell in fitful spasms and long-drawn gasps by the flickering campfire. But music failed to fill entirely the aching void left by insufficient food, and a new diversion was proposed by Piney — storytelling. Neither Mr. Oakhurst nor his female companions caring to relate their personal experiences, this plan would have failed too, but for the Innocent. Some months before he had chanced upon a stray copy of Mr. Pope's [1] ingenious translation of the *Iliad*. He now proposed to narrate the principal incidents of that poem — having thoroughly mastered the argument and fairly forgotten the words — in the current vernacular of Sandy Bar. And so, for the rest of that night, the Homeric demigods again walked the earth. Trojan bully and wily Greek wrestled in the winds, and the great pines in the canyon seemed to bow to the wrath of the son of Peleus. [2] Mr. Oakhurst listened with great satisfaction. Most especially was he interested in the fate of "Ashheels," as the Innocent persisted in denominating the "swift-footed Achilles."

So, with small food and much of Homer and the accordion, a week passed

[1] **Mr. Pope's:** Alexander Pope, an English poet (1688–1744).
[2] **son of Peleus** (pē'lūs): Achilles (á·kǐl'-ēz), a character in *Iliad*.

over the heads of the outcasts. The sun again forsook them, and again from leaden skies the snowflakes were sifted over the land. Day by day closer around them drew the snowy circle, until at last they looked from their prison over drifted walls of dazzling white, that towered twenty feet above their heads. It became more and more difficult to replenish their fires, even from the fallen trees beside them, now half-hidden in the drifts. And yet no one complained. The lovers turned from the dreary prospect and looked into each other's eyes, and were happy. Mr. Oakhurst settled himself coolly to the losing game before him. The Duchess, more cheerful than she had been, assumed the care of Piney. Only Mother Shipton — once the strongest of the party — seemed to sicken and fade. At midnight on the tenth day, she called Oakhurst to her side. "I'm going," she said, in a voice of querulous weakness, "but don't say anything about it. Don't waken the kids. Take the bundle from under my head, and open it." Mr. Oakhurst did so. It contained Mother Shipton's rations for the last week, untouched. "Give 'em to the child," she said, pointing to the sleeping Piney. "You've starved yourself," said the gambler. "That's what they call it," said the woman querulously, as she lay down again, and, turning her face to the wall, passed quietly away.

The accordion and the bones were put aside that day, and Homer was forgotten. When the body of Mother Shipton had been committed to the snow, Mr. Oakhurst took the Innocent aside, and showed him a pair of snowshoes, which he had fashioned from the old packsaddle. "There's one chance in a hundred to save her yet," he said, pointing to Piney: "but it's there," he added, pointing toward Poker Flat. "If you can reach there in two days, she's safe." "And you?" asked Tom Simson. "I'll stay here," was the curt reply.

The lovers parted with a long embrace. "You are not going, too?" said the Duchess, as she saw Mr. Oakhurst apparently waiting to accompany him. "As far as the canyon," he replied. He turned suddenly and kissed the Duchess, leaving her pallid face aflame, and her trembling limbs rigid with amazement.

Night came, but not Mr. Oakhurst. It brought the storm again and the whirling snow. Then the Duchess, feeding the fire, found someone had quietly piled beside the hut enough fuel to last a few days longer. The tears rose to her eyes, but she hid them from Piney.

The women slept but little. In the morning, looking into each other's faces, they read their fate. Neither spoke, but Piney, accepting the position of the stronger, drew near and placed her arm around the Duchess' waist. They kept this attitude for the rest of the day. That night the storm reached its greatest fury, and, rending asunder the protecting vines, invaded the very hut.

Toward morning they found themselves unable to feed the fire, which gradually died away. As the embers slowly blackened, the Duchess crept closer to Piney, and broke the silence of many hours: "Piney, can you pray?" "No, dear," said Piney simply. The Duchess, without knowing exactly why, felt relieved, and, putting her head upon Piney's shoulder, spoke no more. And so reclining, the younger and purer pillowing the head of her soiled sister upon her virgin breast, they fell asleep.

The wind lulled as if it feared to waken them. Feathery drifts of snow, shaken from the long pine boughs, flew like white-winged birds, and settled about them as they slept. The moon through the rifted clouds looked down upon what had been the camp. But all human stain, all trace of earthly travail, was hidden beneath the spotless mantle mercifully flung from above.

They slept all that day and the next, nor did they waken when voices and footsteps broke the silence of the camp. And when pitying fingers brushed the snow from their wan faces, you could scarcely have told from the equal peace that dwelt upon them which was she that had sinned. Even the law of Poker Flat recognized this, and turned away, leaving them still locked in each other's arms.

But at the head of the gulch, on one of the largest pine trees, they found the deuce of clubs pinned to the bark with a bowie knife. It bore the following, written in pencil in a firm hand:

> BENEATH THIS TREE
> LIES THE BODY
> OF
> ## JOHN OAKHURST,
> WHO STRUCK A STREAK OF BAD LUCK
> ON THE 23D OF NOVEMBER, 1850,
> AND
> HANDED IN HIS CHECKS
> ON THE 7TH DECEMBER, 1850.

And pulseless and cold, with a Derringer by his side and a bullet in his heart, though still calm as in life, beneath the snow lay he who was at once the strongest and yet the weakest of the outcasts of Poker Flat.

FOR DISCUSSION

1. What typically western circumstances form the basis of this story? Why had the citizens' committee suddenly decided to clean up Poker Flat? What was the argument for merely banishing Oakhurst instead of hanging him?

2. Which characters do you consider realistic? How was Oakhurst different from the typical mining-camp gambler? Why did he not drink? Is this detail realistic or romantic? Can you detect any instances of exaggeration in this story for the sake of building up its western atmosphere, its local color? What characters, if any, seem to you to possess a contradictory combination of traits?

3. Explain the last statement in the story, that Oakhurst "was at once the strongest and yet the weakest of the outcasts of Poker Flat."

4. There is evidence of humor in this tale, although it is one of Harte's more serious stories. Which characters furnish most of the humor?

AN AUTHOR'S TECHNIQUE

Bret Harte's diction contributes much to the characterization of the outcasts; for example, "the *felonious* fingers of Uncle Billy"; "the loneliness begotten of [Oakhurst's] *pariah* trade," the "*malevolence*" of Mother Shipton. What does the author's choice of words add, in each case, to your understanding of the character? Find other examples.

The outcasts take their expulsion in different ways, and Harte also uses some choice words to describe their reactions. One of the party is *bellicose* (how does this differ from *belligerent?*). Another is *maudlin*, a state often associated, as in this case, with drunkenness. Only one of the characters meets the crisis with *equanimity*. Think about the meaning of each word and, without looking back to the text, see if you can recall which character's reaction it described.

FURTHER READING

For comparison of this story with one about a genuine western desperado and the vigilantes' handling of him, read Chapter 11 of Mark Twain's *Roughing It.*

Bret Harte's San Francisco →

This is a detail from a lithograph made from an original sketch of San Francisco by the English artist S. F. Marryat. The lithograph was printed in London in 1851.

San Francisco was claimed for the United States in 1848, during the war with Mexico. A few months later, the city began to feel the effects of the Gold Rush. The population soared from 800 in 1848 to 25,000 in 1850; many of the new inhabitants lived in tents or temporary dwellings. When gold production began to decline after 1855, the city came into its own as the West Coast's major port.

MARK
TWAIN
1835–1910

Samuel Langhorne Clemens took his famous pen name from the cry of the leadsmen on Mississippi River steamboats, "by the mark, twain," meaning a depth of two fathoms. As "Mark Twain," Sam Clemens became a symbol of American literature to the whole world. His fame and popularity were so great that when he found himself bankrupt at the age of almost sixty, he paid off all his debts and re-established his fortune by a world-circling lecture tour.

Mark Twain was born in 1835. He spent his boyhood in Hannibal, Missouri, a small town on the Mississippi River, and he was to return to that scene again and again in his finest books. Late in his life he wrote:

> I can call back the solemn twilight and the mystery of the deep woods, the earthy smells, the faint odors of the wild flowers . . . I can call it all back and make it as real as it ever was, and as blessed. I can call back the prairie and its loneliness and peace, and a vast hawk hanging motionless in the sky.

Yet he also said:

> If I confine myself to boy life at times, it is because that life had a peculiar charm for me, and not because I was unfamiliar with other phases of life.

Mark Twain had enough careers to provide materials for a hundred books.

He began as a printer in Hannibal, then traveled east to New York, practicing the printing trade. Returning to the Mississippi in the 1850's, he became a river pilot, and spent some of the happiest years of his life on the steamboats. In 1861, when the War Between the States interrupted river traffic, Twain spent a short time in the Confederate army, then went to the Far West. He did some prospecting, dealt in mining stock, and finally got into journalistic work in California and Nevada. From that time on, Mark Twain was a writer.

In San Francisco, in 1865, he published a sketch that tickled the public and started the spread of his reputation. It was "The Celebrated Jumping Frog of Calaveras County," and it clearly showed the talent for characterization and frontier humor that continued in such later, famous tales as "Baker's Bluejay Yarn" and "His Grandfather's Old Ram."

Twain showed us many faces of America and many aspects of American life. In *Roughing It* (1872) he takes us to the heart of the Far West. His boyhood in Hannibal is seen in *Tom Sawyer* (1876), and the boy's viewpoint is carried into the larger vision of Twain's masterpiece, *Huckleberry Finn* (1884). *Life on the Mississippi* (1883) is the greatest of all documents about the mighty river, preserving the lore and the glamour of Mississippi steamboat days in the 1850's.

Twain's subjects ranged far from his memories of boyhood. In *The Gilded Age*, he collaborated with Charles Dudley Warner to satirize political and social events of the 1870's. In his travel books, *The Innocents Abroad* and *A Tramp Abroad*, Twain showed the sights of Europe and the Holy Land to his contemporaries. *A Connecticut Yankee in King Arthur's Court* satirizes the traditions of knighthood and chivalry. Characteristically, however, Twain was skeptical of both "progress" and "tradition."

Although Twain often viewed life sentimentally, he could regard it pessimistically as well. His pessimism was deep and abiding, fed by his observation of human folly. Two books published after his death, *The Mysterious Stranger* (1916) and his *Autobiography* (1924), show the untrained philosopher struggling with his long, troubled thoughts about life, death, God, and eternity.

This beloved American writer, who made millions laugh but refused to call himself a humorist, was a complex and often difficult man. Yet one of his closest friends, the novelist and critic William Dean Howells, said "One could not know him well without realizing him the most serious, the most humane, the most conscientious of men." These are the qualities that make Twain's writing memorable.

Across the Plains by Stagecoach

In this selection we go with Twain on his journey to Nevada in 1861 with his older brother, the newly appointed secretary of that territory. The statutes and the unabridged dictionary that are so troublesome in the stagecoach are the new secretary's equipment for his office. In *Roughing It*, from which this selection is taken, Mark Twain gives a rich account of his experiences in the Far West.

B Y EIGHT O'CLOCK everything was ready, and we were on the other side of the river.[1] We jumped into the stage, the driver cracked his whip, and we bowled away and left "the States" behind us. It was a superb summer morning, and all the landscape was brilliant with sunshine. There was a freshness and breeziness, too, and an exhilarating sense of emancipation from all sorts of

[1] river: the Missouri. The fact that at this time the land west of the state of Missouri had not yet been admitted to statehood explains the next sentence.

"Across the Plains by Stagecoach" from *Roughing It* by Mark Twain. Reprinted by permission of Harper & Brothers.

cares and responsibilities, that almost made us feel that the years we had spent in the close, hot city, toiling and slaving, had been wasted and thrown away. We were spinning along through Kansas, and in the course of an hour and a half, we were fairly abroad on the Great Plains. Just here the land was rolling — a grand sweep of regular elevations and depressions as far as the eye could reach — like the stately heave and swell of the ocean's bosom after a storm. And everywhere were cornfields, accenting with squares of deeper green this limitless expanse of grassy land. But presently this sea upon dry ground was to lose its "rolling" character and stretch away for seven hundred miles as level as a floor!

Our coach was a great swaying and swinging stage, of the most sumptuous description — an imposing cradle on wheels. It was drawn by six handsome horses, and by the side of the driver sat the "conductor," the legitimate captain of the craft; for it was his business to take charge and care of the mails, baggage, express matter, and passengers. We three were the only passengers this trip. We sat on the back seat, inside. About all the rest of the coach was full of mailbags — for we had three days' delayed mails with us. Almost touching our knees, a perpendicular wall of mail matter rose up to the roof. There was a great pile of it strapped on top of the stage, and both the fore and hind boots [1] were full. We had twenty-seven hundred pounds of it aboard, the driver said — "a little for Brigham, and Carson, and 'Frisco, but the heft of it for the Injuns, which is powerful troublesome 'thout they get plenty of truck to read." But as he just then got up a fearful convulsion of his countenance which was suggestive of a wink being swallowed by an earthquake, we guessed that his remark was intended to be facetious, and to mean that we would unload the most of our mail matter somewhere on the Plains and leave it to the Indians, or whosoever wanted it.

We changed horses every ten miles, all day long, and fairly flew over the hard, level road. We jumped out and stretched our legs every time the coach stopped, and so the night found us still vivacious and unfatigued. . . .

About an hour and a half before daylight we were bowling along smoothly over the road — so smoothly that our cradle only rocked in a gentle, lulling way that was gradually soothing us to sleep, and dulling our consciousness — when something gave way under us. We were dimly aware of it, but indifferent to it. The coach stopped. We heard the driver and conductor talking together outside, and rummaging for a lantern, and swearing because they could not find it — but we had no interest in whatever had happened, and it only added to our comfort to think of those people out there at work in the murky night, and we snug in our nest with the curtains drawn. But presently, by the sounds, there seemed to be an examination going on, and then the driver's voice said:

"By George, the thorough brace is broke! "

This startled me broad awake — as an undefined sense of calamity is always apt to do. I said to myself: "Now, a thorough brace is probably part of a horse; and doubtless a vital part, too, from the dismay in the driver's voice. Leg, maybe, and yet how could he break his leg waltzing along such a road as this? No, it can't be his leg. That is impossible unless he was reaching for the driver. Now, what can be the thorough brace of a horse, I wonder? Well, whatever comes, I shall not air my ignorance in this crowd, anyway."

Just then the conductor's face appeared at a lifted curtain, and his lantern glared in on us and our wall of mail matter. He said:

"Gents, you'll have to turn out a spell. Thorough brace is broke."

We climbed out into a chill drizzle, and felt ever so homeless and dreary. When I found that the thing they called a "thorough brace" was the massive combination of belts and springs which the coach rocks itself in, I said to the driver:

"I never saw a thorough brace used up like that before, that I can remember. How did it happen?"

"Why, it happened by trying to make one coach carry three days' mail — that's how it happened," said he. "And right here is the very direction [2] which is wrote on all the newspaper bags which was to be put out for the Injuns for to keep 'em quiet. It's most uncommon lucky becuz it's so nation [3] dark I should 'a' gone by unbeknowns if that air thorough brace hadn't broke."

I knew that he was in labor with another of those winks of his, though I could not see his face, because he was

---

[1] **boots:** leather compartments for baggage.

[2] **direction:** address.
[3] **nation:** tarnation (slang).

bent down at work; and wishing him a safe delivery, I turned to and helped the rest get out the mail sacks. It made a great pyramid by the roadside when it was all out. When they had mended the thorough brace, we filled the two boots again, but put no mail on top, and only half as much inside as there was before. The conductor bent all the seat backs down, and then filled the coach just half full of mailbags from end to end. We objected loudly to this for it left us no seats. But the conductor was wiser than we, and said a bed was better than seats, and moreover this plan would protect his thorough braces. We never wanted any seats after that. The lazy bed was infinitely preferable. I had many an exciting day, subsequently, lying on it, reading the statutes and the dictionary, and wondering how the characters would turn out.

The conductor said he would send back a guard from the next station to take charge of the abandoned mailbags, and we drove on.

It was now just dawn; and as we stretched our cramped legs full length on the mail sacks, and gazed out through the windows across the wide wastes of greensward clad in cool powdery mist to where there was an expectant look in the eastern horizon, our perfect enjoyment took the form of a tranquil and contented ecstasy. The stage whirled along at a spanking gait, the breeze flapping curtains and suspended coats in a most exhilarating way; the cradle swayed and swung luxuriously, the pattering of the horses' hoofs, the cracking of the driver's whip, and his "Hi-yi! g'lang!" were music; the spinning ground and the waltzing trees appeared to give us a mute hurrah as we went by, and then slack up and look after us with interest, or envy, or something; and as we lay and smoked the pipe of peace and compared all this luxury with the years of tiresome city life that had gone before it, we felt that there was only one complete and satis-

fying happiness in the world and we had found it.

After breakfast, at some station whose name I have forgotten, we three climbed up on the seat behind the driver, and let the conductor have our bed for a nap. And by and by, when the sun made me drowsy, I lay down on my face on top of the coach, grasping the slender iron railing and slept for an hour or more. That will give one an appreciable idea of those matchless roads. Instinct will make a sleeping man grip a fast hold of the railing when the stage jolts, but when it only swings and sways, no grip is necessary. Overland drivers and conductors used to sit in their places and sleep thirty or forty minutes at a time, on good roads, while spinning along at the rate of eight or ten miles an hour. I saw them do it, often. There was no danger about it; a sleeping man *will* seize the irons in time when the coach jolts. These men were hard worked, and it was not possible for them to stay awake all the time. . . .

As the sun went down and the evening chill came on, we made preparation for bed. We stirred up the hard leather letter sacks, and the knotty canvas bags of printed matter (knotty and uneven because of projecting ends and corners of magazines, boxes, and books). We stirred them up and redisposed them in such a way as to make our bed as level as possible. And we *did* improve it, too, though after all our work it had an upheaved and billowy look about it, like a little piece of a stormy sea. Next we hunted up our boots from odd nooks among the mailbags where they had settled, and put them on. Then we got down our coats, vests, pantaloons, and heavy woolen shirts, from the arm loops where they had been swinging all day, and clothed ourselves in them — for there being no ladies either at the stations or in the coach, and the weather being hot, we had looked to our comfort by stripping to our underclothing, at nine o'clock in the morning.

All things being ready now, we stowed the uneasy dictionary where it would lie as quiet as possible, and placed the water canteens and pistols where we could find them in the dark. Then we smoked a final pipe, and swapped a final yarn; after which we put the pipes, tobacco, and bag of coins in snug holes and caves among the mail-bags, and then fastened down the coach curtains all around and made the place as "dark as the inside of a cow," as the conductor phrased it in his picturesque way. It was certainly as dark as any place could be — nothing was even dim-ly visible in it. And finally we rolled ourselves up like silkworms, each per-son in his own blanket, and sank peace-fully to sleep.

Whenever the stage stopped to change horses, we would wake up, and try to recollect where we were — and succeed — and in a minute or two the stage would be off again, and we like-wise. We began to get into country, now, threaded here and there with lit-tle streams. These had high, steep banks on each side, and every time we flew down one bank and scrambled up the other, our party inside got mixed some-what. First we would all be down in a pile at the forward end of the stage, nearly in a sitting posture, and in a sec-ond we would shoot to the other end, and stand on our heads. And we would sprawl and kick, too, and ward off cor-ners and ends of mailbags that came lumbering over us and about us; and as the dust arose from the tumult, we would all sneeze in chorus, and the ma-jority of us would grumble and prob-ably say some hasty thing like: "Take your elbow out of my ribs! — Can't you quit crowding?"

Every time we avalanched from one end of the stage to the other, the un-abridged dictionary would come too; and every time it came it damaged somebody. One trip it "barked" the Secretary's elbow; the next trip it hurt me in the stomach, and the third it tilted Bemis' nose up till he could look down his nostrils — he said. The pistols and coin soon settled to the bottom, but the pipes, pipestems, tobacco, and can-teens clattered and floundered after the dictionary every time it made an assault upon us, and aided and abetted the book by spilling tobacco in our eyes, and water down our backs.

Still, all things considered, it was a very comfortable night. It wore gradu-ally away, and when at last a cold gray light was visible through the puckers and chinks in the curtains, we yawned and stretched with satisfaction, shed our cocoons, and felt that we had slept as much as was necessary. By and by as the sun rose up and warmed the world, we pulled off our clothes and got ready for breakfast. We were just pleasantly in time, for five minutes afterward the driver sent the weird music of his bugle winding over the grassy solitudes, and presently we detected a low hut or two in the distance. Then the rattling of the coach, the clatter of our six horses' hoofs, and the driver's crisp commands awoke to a louder and stronger empha-sis, and we went sweeping down on the station at our smartest speed. It was fascinating — that old overland stage-coaching.

THE PONY EXPRESS

In a little while all interest was taken up with stretching our necks and watch-ing for the "pony-rider" — the fleet mes-senger who sped across the continent from St. Joe to Sacramento, carrying letters nineteen hundred miles in eight days! Think of that for perishable horse and human flesh and blood to do! The pony-rider was usually a little bit of a man, brimful of spirit and endurance. No matter what time of the day or night his watch came on, and no matter whether it was winter, or summer, rain-ing, snowing, hailing, or sleeting, or whether his "beat" was a level, straight road or a crazy trail over mountain crags and precipices, or whether it led through peaceful regions or regions that swarmed with hostile Indians, he must be always ready to leap into the saddle and be off like the wind! There was no idling-time for a pony-rider on duty. He rode fifty miles without stopping, by daylight, moonlight, starlight, or through the blackness of darkness, just as it happened. He rode a splendid horse that was born for a racer and fed and lodged like a gentleman, kept him at his utmost speed for ten miles, and then as he came crashing up to the station where stood two men holding fast a fresh, impatient steed, the transfer of rider and mailbag was made in the twinkling of an eye, and away flew the eager pair and were out of sight before the spectator could get hardly the ghost of a look.

Both rider and horse went "flying light." The rider's dress was thin, and fitted close; he wore a "roundabout"[1] and a skullcap, and tucked his pantaloons into his boot tops like a race-rider. He carried no arms — he carried nothing that was not absolutely necessary, for even the postage of his literary freight was worth *five dollars a letter.* He got but little frivolous correspondence to carry — his bag had business letters in it, mostly. His horse was stripped of all unnecessary weight, too. He wore a little wafer of a racing saddle, and no visible blanket. He wore light shoes, or none at all. The little flat mail pockets strapped under the rider's thighs would each hold about the bulk of a child's primer. They held many and many an important business chapter and newspaper letter, but these were written on paper as airy and thin as gold leaf, nearly, and thus bulk and weight were economized. The stagecoach traveled about a hundred to a hundred and twenty-five miles a day (twenty-four hours), the pony-rider about two hundred and fifty. There

[1] "roundabout": a short, tight jacket.

were about eighty pony-riders in the saddle all the time, night and day, stretching in a long scattering procession from Missouri to California, forty flying eastward, and forty toward the west, and among them making four hundred gallant horses earn a stirring livelihood and see a deal of scenery every single day in the year.

We had had a consuming desire from the beginning to see a pony-rider, but somehow or other all that passed us and all that met us managed to sneak by in the night, and so we heard only a whiz and a hail, and the swift phantom of the desert was gone before we could get our heads out of the windows. But now we were expecting one along every moment, and would see him in broad daylight. Presently the driver exclaims: *"Here he comes!"*

Every neck is stretched further, and every eye strained wider. Away across the endless dead level of the prairie a black speck appears against the sky, and it is clear that it moves. Well, I should think so! In a second or two it becomes a horse and rider, rising and falling, rising and falling — sweeping toward us nearer and nearer — growing more and more distinct, more and more sharply defined — nearer and still nearer, and the flutter of the hoofs comes faintly to the ear — another instant a whoop and a hurrah from our upper deck, a wave of the rider's hand, but no reply, and man and horse burst past our excited faces and go swinging away like a belated fragment of a storm!

So sudden is it all, and so like a flash of unreal fancy, that but for the flake of white foam left quivering and perishing on a mail sack after the vision had flashed by and disappeared, we might have doubted whether we had seen any actual horse and man at all.

American Art and Artists

On pages 704–705 are paintings of three scenes from the West of Mark Twain's day.

Mark Twain's West

These scenes are typical of the kind Twain saw in the West during the 1860's. The painting above is "On the Road, 1860," by the nineteenth-century American artist Thomas P. Otter. On the left is "The Coming and Going of the Pony Express," by the American Frederic Remington (1861–1909). Below is "Held Up," by the American artist N. H. Trotter (1827–1898).

I Find
Fool Gold

There is something about a gold strike — or a uranium strike, for that matter — that heats a man's blood like a fever. Mark Twain had a strong strain of the prospector in his nature. Enjoy this anecdote, also from *Roughing It.*

After leaving the Sink, we traveled along the Humboldt River a little way. People accustomed to the monster mile-wide Mississippi grow accustomed to associating the term "river" with a high degree of watery grandeur. Consequently, such people feel rather disappointed when they stand on the shores of the Humboldt or the Carson and find that a "river" in Nevada is a sickly rivulet which is just the counterpart of the Erie canal in all respects save that the canal is twice as long and four times as deep. One of the pleasantest and most invigorating exercises one can

contrive is to run and jump across the Humboldt River till he is overheated, and then drink it dry.

On the fifteenth day we completed our march of two hundred miles and entered Unionville, Humboldt County, in the midst of a driving snowstorm. Unionville consisted of eleven cabins and a liberty pole. Six of the cabins were strung along one side of a deep canyon, and the other five faced them. The rest of the landscape was made up of bleak mountain walls that rose so high into the sky from both sides of the canyon that the village was left, as it were, far down in the bottom of a crevice. It was always daylight on the mountaintops a long time before the darkness lifted and revealed Unionville.

We built a small, rude cabin in the side of the crevice and roofed it with canvas, leaving a corner open to serve as a chimney, through which the cattle used to tumble occasionally, at night, and mash our furniture and interrupt our sleep. It was very cold weather and fuel was scarce. Indians brought brush

"I Find Fool Gold" from *Roughing It* by Mark Twain. Reprinted by permission of Harper & Brothers.

and bushes several miles on their backs; and when we could catch a laden Indian, it was well — and when we could not (which was the rule, not the exception), we shivered and bore it.

I confess, without shame, that I expected to find masses of silver lying all about the ground. I expected to see it glittering in the sun on the mountain summits. I said nothing about this, for some instinct told me that I might possibly have an exaggerated idea about it, and so, if I betrayed my thought, I might bring derision upon myself. Yet I was as perfectly satisfied in my own mind as I could be of anything that I was going to gather up, in a day or two, or at furthest a week or two, silver enough to make me satisfactorily wealthy — and so my fancy was already busy with plans for spending this money. The first opportunity that offered, I sauntered carelessly away from the cabin, keeping an eye on the other boys, and stopping and contemplating the sky when they seemed to be observing me; but as soon as the coast was manifestly clear, I fled away as guiltily as a thief might have done and never halted till I was far beyond sight and call. Then I began my search with a feverish excitement that was brimful of expectation — almost, of certainty.

I crawled about the ground, seizing and examining bits of stone, blowing the dust from them or rubbing them on my clothes, and then peering at them with anxious hope. Presently I found a bright fragment and my heart bounded! I hid behind a boulder and polished it and scrutinized it with a nervous eagerness and a delight that was more pronounced than absolute certainty itself could have afforded. The more I examined the fragment the more I was convinced that I had found the door to fortune. I marked the spot and carried away my specimen. Up and down the rugged mountainside I searched, with always increasing interest and always augmenting gratitude that I had come to Humboldt and come in time. Of all the experiences of my life, this secret search among the hidden treasures of silver-land was the nearest to unmarred ecstasy. It was a delirious revel. By and by, in the bed of a shallow rivulet, I found a deposit of shining yellow scales, and my breath almost forsook me! A gold mine, and in my simplicity I had been content with vulgar silver! I was so excited that I half believed my overwrought imagination was deceiving me. Then a fear came upon me that people might be observing me and would guess my secret. Moved by this thought, I made a circuit of the place, and ascended a knoll to reconnoiter. Solitude. No creature was near. Then I returned to my mine, fortifying myself against possible disappointment, but my fears were groundless — the shining scales were still there. I set about scooping them out, and for an hour I toiled down the windings of the stream and robbed its bed. But at last the descending sun warned me to give up the quest, and I turned homeward laden with wealth. As I walked along I could not help smiling at the thought of my being so excited over my fragment of silver when a nobler metal was almost under my nose. In this little time the former had so fallen in my estimation that once or twice I was on the point of throwing it away.

The boys were as hungry as usual, but I could eat nothing. Neither could I talk. I was full of dreams and far away. Their conversation interrupted the flow of my fancy somewhat, and annoyed me a little, too. I despised the sordid and commonplace things they talked about. But as they proceeded, it began to amuse me. It grew to be rare fun to hear them planning their poor little economies and sighing over possible privations and distresses when a gold mine, all our own, lay within sight of the cabin, and I could point it out at any moment. Smothered hilarity began to oppress me, presently. It was hard to resist the impulse to burst out with exultation and reveal everything; but I did resist. I said within myself that I would filter the great news through my lips calmly and be serene as a summer morning while I watched its effect in their faces. I said:

"Where have you all been?"

"Prospecting."

"What did you find?"

"Nothing."

"Nothing? What do you think of the country?"

"Can't tell, yet," said Mr. Ballou, who was an old gold-miner, and had likewise had considerable experience among the silver mines.

"Well, haven't you formed any sort of opinion?"

"Yes, a sort of a one. It's fair enough here, maybe, but overrated. Seven-thousand-dollar ledges are scarce, though. That Sheba may be rich enough, but we don't own it; and, besides, the rock is so full of base metals that all the science in the world can't work it. We'll not starve here, but we'll not get rich, I'm afraid."

"So you think the prospect is pretty poor?"

"No name for it!"

"Well, we'd better go back, hadn't we?"

"Oh, not yet — of course not. We'll try it a riffle first."

"Suppose, now — this is merely a supposition, you know — suppose you could find a ledge that would yield, say, a hundred and fifty dollars a ton — would that satisfy you?"

"Try us once!" from the whole party.

"Or suppose — merely a supposition, of course — suppose you were to find a ledge that would yield two thousand dollars a ton — would *that* satisfy you?"

"Here — what do you mean? What are you coming at? Is there some mystery behind all this?"

"Never mind. I am not saying anything. You know perfectly well there

are no rich mines here — of course you do. Because you have been around and examined for yourselves. Anybody would know that, that had been around. But just for the sake of argument, suppose — in a kind of general way — suppose some person were to tell you that two-thousand-dollar ledges were simply contemptible — contemptible, understand — and that right yonder, in sight of this very cabin, there were piles of pure gold and pure silver — oceans of it — enough to make you all rich in twenty-four hours! Come!"

"I should say he was as crazy as a loon!" said old Ballou, but wild with excitement, nevertheless.

"Gentlemen," said I, "I don't say anything — I haven't been around, you know, and of course don't know anything — but all I ask of you is to cast your eye on *that*, for instance, and tell me what you think of it!" and I tossed my treasure before them.

There was an eager scrabble for it, and a closing of heads together over it under the candlelight. Then old Ballou said:

"Think of it? I think it is nothing but a lot of granite rubbish and nasty glittering mica that isn't worth ten cents an acre!"

So vanished my dreams. So melted my wealth away. So toppled my airy castle to the earth and left me stricken and forlorn.

Moralizing, I observed, then, that "all that glitters is not gold."

Mr. Ballou said I could go further than that, and lay it up among my treasures of knowledge that *nothing* that glitters is gold. So I learned then, once for all, that gold in its native state is but dull, unornamental stuff, and that only low-born metals excite the admiration of the ignorant with an ostentatious glitter. However, like the rest of the world, I still go on underrating men of gold and glorifying men of mica. Commonplace human nature cannot rise above that.

Mark Twain
and the Public Reading

"His Grandfather's Old Ram"

FROM *His Autobiography*

In a sense Christmas came early to Mark Twain one December day in 1867. On that day he had his first glimpse of the girl he later married, "Livy," Miss Olivia Langdon, sister of one of his best friends, Charley Langdon; and on that day he heard the great English novelist Charles Dickens give a public reading. Twain promptly fell in love with the girl and stored up memories of the Dickens performance, memories that he activated in 1884, when for the first time he attempted public readings on his own. At that time Twain hired a manager and a helper. He was in business! How different Twain's public readings were from those that had given him the idea you can guess from this selection.

"His Grandfather's Old Ram" from Chapter 35 of *The Autobiography of Mark Twain*, edited by Charles Neider. Copyright © 1959 by The Mark Twain Company. Reprinted by permission of Harper & Brothers.

Here Twain explains how he adapted from his book *Roughing It* his famous story of "His Grandfather's Old Ram" and practiced re-creating the story orally until his platform storytelling skill made him known the world over. The "Old Ram" story is one of Twain's best, and it will teach you a good deal about the art of the storyteller.

WHAT is called a "reading," as a public platform entertainment, was first essayed by Charles Dickens, I think. He had made it very popular at home, and he made it so acceptable and so popular in America that his houses were crowded everywhere, and in a single season he earned two hundred thousand dollars. I heard him once during that season; it was in Steinway Hall, in

December, and it made the fortune of my life — not in dollars, I am not thinking of dollars; it made the real fortune of my life in that it made the happiness of my life; on that day I called at the St. Nicholas Hotel to see my Quaker City Excursion shipmate, Charley Langdon, and was introduced to a sweet and timid and lovely young girl, his sister. The family went to the Dickens reading and I accompanied them. It was forty years ago; from that day to this, the sister has never been out of my mind nor heart.

Mr. Dickens read scenes from his printed books. From my distance he was a small and slender figure, rather fancifully dressed, and striking and picturesque in appearance. He wore a black velvet coat with a large and glaring red flower in the buttonhole. He stood under a red upholstered shed, behind whose slant was a row of strong lights — just such an arrangement as artists use to concentrate a strong light upon a great picture. Dickens' audience sat in a pleasant twilight, while he performed in the powerful light cast upon him from the concealed lamps. He read with great force and animation, in the lively passages, and with stirring effect. It will be understood that he did not merely read but also acted.

I had never tried reading as a trade, and I wanted to try it. It was ghastly! At least in the beginning. I had selected my readings well enough but had not studied them. I supposed it would only be necessary to do like Dickens — get out on the platform and read from the book. I did that and made a botch of it. Written things are not for speech; their form is literary; they are stiff, inflexible, and will not lend themselves to happy and effective delivery with the tongue — where their purpose is to merely entertain, not instruct; they have to be limbered up, broken up, colloquialized, and turned into the common forms of unpremeditated talk — otherwise they will bore the house, not entertain it. After a week's experience with the book, I laid it aside and never carried it to the platform again; but meantime I had memorized those pieces, and in delivering them from the platform, they soon transformed themselves into flexible talk, with all their obstructing preciseness and formalities gone out of them for good.

One of the readings which I used was part of an extravagant chapter in dialect from *Roughing It* which I entitled "His Grandfather's Old Ram." After I had memorized it, it began to undergo changes on the platform, and it continued to edit and revise itself night after night until, by and by, from dreading to begin on it before an audience, I came to like it and enjoy it. I never knew how considerable the changes had been when I finished the season's work; I never knew until ten or eleven years later, when I took up that book in a parlor in New York one night to read that chapter to a dozen friends, of the two sexes, who had asked for it. It *wouldn't read* — that is, it wouldn't read aloud. I struggled along with it for five minutes and then gave it up and said I should have to tell the tale as best I might from memory. It turned out that my memory was equal to the emergency; it reproduced the platform form of the story pretty faithfully after that interval of years. I still remember that form of it, I think, and I wish to recite it here, so that the reader may compare it with the story as told in *Roughing It,* if he pleases, and note how different the spoken version is from the written and printed version.

The idea of the tale is to exhibit certain bad effects of a good memory: the sort of memory which is too good, which remembers everything and forgets nothing, which has no sense of proportion and can't tell an important event from an unimportant one but preserves them all, states them all, and thus retards the progress of a narrative, at the same time making a tangled, inextricable[1] confusion of it and intolerably wearisome to the listener. The historian of "His Grandfather's Old Ram" had that kind of a memory. He often tried to communicate that history to his comrades, the other surface miners, but he could never complete it because his memory defeated his every attempt to march a straight course; it persistently threw remembered details in his way that had nothing to do with the tale; these unrelated details would interest him and sidetrack him; if he came across a name or a family or any other thing that had nothing to do with his tale, he would diverge from his course to tell about the person who owned that name or explain all about that family — with the result that as he plodded on, he always got further and further from his grandfather's memorable adventure with the ram, and finally went to sleep before he got to the end of the story, and so did his comrades. Once he did manage to approach so nearly to the end, apparently, that the boys were filled with an eager hope; they believed that at last they were going to find out all about the grandfather's adventure and what it was that had happened. After the usual preliminaries, the historian said:

"Well, as I was a-sayin', he bought that old ram from a feller up in Siskiyou County and fetched him home and turned him loose in the medder, and next morning he went down to have a look at him, and accident'ly dropped a ten-cent piece in the grass and stooped down — so — and was a-fumblin' around in the grass to git it, and the ram he was a-standin' up the slope taking notice; but my grandfather wasn't taking notice, because he had his back to the ram and was int'rested about the dime. Well, there he was, as I was a-sayin', down at the foot of the slope a-bendin'

over — so — fumblin' in the grass, and the ram he was up there at the top of the slope, and Smith — Smith was a-standin' there — no, not jest there, a little further away — fifteen foot perhaps — well, my grandfather was a-stoopin' way down — so — and the ram was up there observing, you know, and Smith he . . . (musing) . . . the ram he bent his head down, so . . . Smith of Calaveras . . . no, no it couldn't ben Smith of Calaveras — I remember now that he — b'George it was Smith of Tulare County — 'course it was, I remember it now perfectly plain.

"Well, Smith he stood just there, and my grandfather he stood just here, you know, and he was a-bendin' down just so, fumblin' in the grass, and when the old ram see'd him in that attitude, he took it fur an invitation — and here he come! down the slope thirty mile an hour and his eye full of business. You see, my grandfather's back being to him, and him stooping down like that, of course he — why sho! it warn't Smith of Tulare at all, it was Smith of Sacramento — my goodness, how did I ever come to get them Smiths mixed like that — why, Smith of Tulare was jest a nobody, but Smith of Sacramento — why the Smiths of Sacramento come of the best southern blood in the United States; there warn't ever any better blood south of the line than the Sacramento Smiths. Why look here, one of them married a Whitaker! I reckon that gives you an idea of the kind of society the Sacramento Smiths could 'sociate around in; there ain't no better blood than that Whitaker blood; I reckon anybody'll tell you that.

"Look at Mariar Whitaker — there was a girl for you! Little? Why yes, she was little, but what of that? Look at the heart of her — had a heart like a bullock — just as good and sweet and lovely and generous as the day is long; if she had a thing and you wanted it, you could have it — have it and welcome.

[1] inextricable (ĭn·ĕks'trĭ·ká·b'l): impossible to untie or untangle.

She had a glass eye, and she used to lend it to Flora Ann Baxter that hadn't any, to receive company with; well she was pretty large, and it didn't fit; it was a number seven, and she was excavated for a fourteen, and so that eye wouldn't lay still; every time she winked, it would turn over. It was a beautiful eye and set her off admirable, because it was a lovely pale blue on the front side — the side you look out of — and it was gilded on the back side; didn't match the other eye, which was one of them browny-yellery eyes and tranquil and quiet, you know, the way that kind of eyes are; but that warn't any matter — they worked together all right and plenty picturesque. When Flora Ann winked, that blue-and-gilt eye would whirl over, and the other one stand still, and as soon as she begun to get excited, that handmade eye would give a whirl and then go on a-whirlin' faster and faster, and a-flashin' first blue and then yaller and then blue and then yaller, and when it got to whizzing and flashing like that, the oldest man in the world couldn't keep up with the expression on that side of her face. Flora Ann Baxter married a Hogadorn. I reckon that lets you understand what kind of blood she was — old Maryland Eastern Shore blood; not a better family in the United States than the Hogadorns.

"Sally — that's Sally Hogadorn — Sally married a missionary, and they went off carrying the good news to the cannibals out in one of them way-off islands round the world in the middle of the ocean somers, and they et her; et him too, which was irregular; it warn't the custom to eat the missionary, but only the family, and when they see what they had done, they was dreadful sorry about it, and when the relations sent down there to fetch away the things, they said so — said so right out — said they was sorry, and 'pologized, and said it shouldn't happen again; said 'twas an accident.

"Accident! now that's foolishness; there ain't no such thing as an accident; there ain't nothing happens in the world but what's ordered just so by a wiser Power than us, and it's always fur a good purpose; we don't know what the good purpose was, sometimes — and it was the same with the families that was short a missionary and his wife. But that ain't no matter, and it ain't any of our business; all that concerns us is that it was a special providence and it had a good intention. No, sir, there ain't no such thing as an accident. Whenever a thing happens that you think is an accident, you make up your mind it ain't no accident at all — it's a special providence.

"You look at my Uncle Lem — what do you say to that? That's all I ask you — you just look at my Uncle Lem and talk to me about accidents! It was like this: one day my Uncle Lem and his dog was downtown, and he was a-leanin' up against a scaffolding — sick, or drunk, or somethin' — and there was an Irishman with a hod of bricks up the ladder along about the third story, and his foot slipped and down he come, bricks and all, and hit a stranger fair and square and knocked the everlasting aspirations out of him; he was ready for the coroner in two minutes. Now then, people said it was an accident.

"Accident! there warn't no accident about it; 'twas a special providence, and had a mysterious, noble intention back of it. The idea was to save that Irishman. If the stranger hadn't been there, that Irishman would have been killed. The people said 'special providence — sho! the dog was there — why didn't the Irishman fall on the dog? Why warn't the dog app'inted?' Fer a mighty good reason — the dog would 'a' seen him a-comin'; you can't depend on no dog to carry out a special providence. You couldn't hit a dog with an Irishman because — lemme see, what was that dog's name . . . (musing) . . . oh, yes, Jasper — and a mighty good dog too; he wa'n't no common dog, he wa'n't no mongrel; he was a composite. A composite dog is a dog that's made up of all the valuable qualities that's in the dog breed — kind of a syndicate; and a mongrel is made up of the riffraff that's left over. That Jasper was one of the most wonderful dogs you ever see. Uncle Lem got him of the Wheelers. I reckon you've heard of the Wheelers; ain't no better blood south of the line than the Wheelers.

"Well, one day Wheeler was a-meditating and dreaming around in the carpet factory, and the machinery made a snatch at him, and first you know he was a-meandering all over that factory, from the garret to the cellar, and everywhere, at such another gait as — why, you couldn't even see him; you could only hear him whiz when he went by. Well, you know a person can't go through an experience like that and arrive back home the way he was when he went. No, Wheeler got wove up into thirty-nine yards of best three-ply carpeting. The widder was sorry, she was uncommon sorry, and loved him and done the best she could fur him in the circumstances, which was unusual. She took the whole piece — thirty-nine yards — and she wanted to give him proper and honorable burial, but she couldn't bear to roll him up; she took and spread him out full length and said she wouldn't have it any other way. She wanted to buy a tunnel for him, but there wasn't any tunnel for sale, so she boxed him in a beautiful box and stood it on the hill on a pedestal twenty-one foot high, and so it was monument and grave together, and economical — sixty foot high — you could see it from everywhere — and she painted on it, 'To the loving memory of thirty-nine yards best three-ply carpeting containing the mortal remainders of Millington G. Wheeler go thou and do likewise.'"

At this point the historian's voice began to wobble and his eyelids to droop with weariness and he fell asleep; and so from that day to this, we are still in ignorance; we don't know whether the old grandfather ever got the ten-cent piece out of the grass; we haven't any idea what it was that happened or whether anything happened at all.

Upon comparing the above with the original in *Roughing It*, I find myself unable to clearly and definitely explain why tho one can be effectively *recited* before an audience and the other can't; there is a reason, but it is too subtle for adequate conveyance by the lumbering vehicle of words; I sense it but cannot express it; it is as elusive as an odor, pungent, pervasive,[1] but defying analysis. I give it up. I merely know that the one version will recite and the other won't.

By reciting I mean, of course, delivery from memory; neither version can be read effectively from the book. There are plenty of good reasons why this should be so, but there is one reason which is sufficient by itself, perhaps: in reading from the book you are telling another person's tale at second hand; you are a mimic and not the person involved; you are an artificiality, not a reality; whereas in telling the tale without the book, you absorb the character and presently become the man himself, just as is the case with the actor.

The greatest actor would not be able to carry his audience by storm with a book in his hand; reading from the book renders the nicest shadings of delivery impossible. I mean those studied fictions which seem to be the impulse of the moment and which are so effective; such as, for instance, fictitious hesitancies for the right word, fictitious unconscious pauses, fictitious unconscious side remarks, fictitious unconscious embarrassments, fictitious uncon-

[1] **pervasive:** capable of spreading over a large area.

scious emphases placed upon the wrong word with a deep intention back of it — these and all the other artful fictive [1] shades which give to a recited tale the captivating naturalness of an impromptu narration can be attempted by a book reader and are attempted, but they are easily detectable as artifice, and although the audience may admire their cleverness and their ingenuity as artifice, they only get at the intellect of the house, they don't get at its heart; and so the reader's success lacks a good deal of being complete.

When a man is reading from a book on the platform, he soon realizes that there is one powerful gun in his battery of artifice that he can't work with an effect proportionate to its caliber; that is the *pause* — that impressive silence, that eloquent silence, that geometrically progressive silence which often achieves a desired effect where no combination of words howsoever felicitous could accomplish it. The pause is not of much use to the man who is reading from a book because he cannot know what the exact length of it ought to be; he is not the one to determine the measurement — the audience must do that for him. He must perceive by their faces when the pause has reached the proper length, but his eyes are not on the faces, they are on the book; therefore he must determine the proper length of the pause by guess; he cannot guess with exactness, and nothing but exactness, absolute exactness, will answer.

The man who recites without the book has all the advantage; when he comes to an old familiar remark in his tale which he has uttered nightly for a hundred nights — a remark preceded or followed by a pause — the faces of the audience tell him when to end the pause. For one audience the pause will be short, for another a little longer, for

another a shade longer still; the performer must vary the length of the pause to suit the shades of difference between audiences. These variations of measurement are so slight, so delicate, that they may almost be compared with the shadings achieved by Pratt and Whitney's ingenious machine which measures the five-millionth part of an inch. An audience is that machine's twin; it can measure a pause down to that vanishing fraction.

In "His Grandfather's Old Ram" a pause has place; it follows a certain remark, and Mrs. Clemens and Clara, when we were on our way around the world, would afflict themselves with my whole performance every night when there was no sort of necessity for it in order that they might watch the house when that pause came; they believed that by the effect they could accurately measure the high or low intelligence of the audience. I knew better, but it was not in my interest to say so. When the pause was right, the effect was sure; when the pause was wrong in length, by the five-millionth of an inch, the laughter was only mild, never a crash. That passage occurs in "His Grandfather's Old Ram" where the question under discussion is whether the falling of the Irishman on the stranger was an accident or was a special providence. If it was a special providence and if the sole purpose of it was to save the Irishman, why was it necessary to sacrifice the stranger? "The dog was there. Why didn't he fall on the dog? Why warn't the dog app'inted? Becuz *the dog would 'a' seen him a-comin'*." That last remark was the one the family waited for. A pause *after* the remark was absolutely necessary with any and all audiences because no man, howsoever intelligent he may be, can instantly adjust his mind to a new and unfamiliar, and yet for a moment or two apparently plausible, logic, which recognizes in a dog an instrument too indifferent to pious restraint and too alert in looking out for his own personal interest to be safely depended upon in an emergency requiring self-sacrifice for the benefit of another, even when the command comes from on high.

FOR DISCUSSION

ACROSS THE PLAINS BY STAGECOACH

1. Describe the stagecoach in which the brothers made their trip, and the system of shifting horses and drivers. What was the "conductor's" job?

2. What were the chief hazards of the trip? How does the author make them amusing?

3. What details of the pony-express rider's costume and equipment were designed for speed? Explain how the pony-express system operated.

4. By what devices does Mark Twain create suspense?

I FIND FOOL GOLD

1. What picture does this selection give us of prospecting?

2. How does this account hold up as storytelling? Compare and contrast this selection with the stories by Poe and Hawthorne.

3. In what way is Twain the crackerbox philosopher in this story?

MARK TWAIN AND THE PUBLIC READING

1. Why did Twain find his first public reading experiences "ghastly"?

2. Explain how the story of "His Grandfather's Old Ram" happens to have so many characters.

3. According to the narrator of the ram story, how was a "composite dog" different from a mongrel?

4. In your opinion, why did Twain feel it so important to emphasize that the story of the ram is a better public performance when told and not read?

5. What techniques of the actor must the public reader master if he is to be successful?

6. Why was it essential to pause after the remark, "Becuz the dog would 'a' seen him a-comin' "?

IN REVIEW

1. What attitudes toward life does Twain present in these selections? In what sense was Mark Twain a moralist?

2. Can Mark Twain be considered typically American as a writer? What impression might foreign readers gain of American life from reading Twain's books?

AN AUTHOR'S TECHNIQUE: FIGURATIVE LANGUAGE

Any stagecoach trip in the West during the 1860's was probably lively, and so was any trip with Mark Twain for a traveling companion. Few writers, however, can equal Twain in getting the effect of the action and color over to the reader. In "Across the Plains by Stagecoach," one way Twain gives the reader the feeling of color and movement is through the figurative use of verbs. The lantern brought to the door of the stagecoach *glared* in on the passengers. Two features of the landscape viewed from the moving stagecoach were the *spinning* ground and the *waltzing* trees. What made the trees seem to *waltz?* When they crossed streams with steep banks, the passengers *avalanched* from one end of the stage to the other.

Mark Twain also creates a vivid picture of the journey through his use of metaphor and simile. The Great Plains are "like the stately heave and swell of the ocean's bosom after a storm." At night the passengers rolled up in their blankets "like silkworms." Mark Twain uses figurative language throughout the three selections included in this book. Can you point out some other examples of simile and metaphor, and of Twain's figurative use of verbs?

FURTHER READING

If you have never read *The Adventures of Tom Sawyer* or *The Adventures of Huckleberry Finn,* you should delay no longer. They are a part of American culture. If you have read them, you might discuss which of the two you remember better. How do the two novels differ as to narrative power, richness of insight, characterization, and plot development? How do these two books differ from other writings of Mark Twain?

OLE E. RÖLVAAG

1876–1931

Prairie Doom

<small>FROM</small> *Giants in the Earth*

Ole Rölvaag [1] came as a young man from Norway to join his uncle on a farm in South Dakota, where he heard tales of the early struggles of the pioneer settlers. Later he put these tales into the novel *Giants in the Earth* and its sequel, *Peder Victorious*. The family in the novel consists of Per Hansa, the father; Beret,[2] the mother; and their four children. At this point in the story, they have completed their long journey from the East and are settled in a sod house in Dakota. But the great wave of settlers is constantly coming on from the East, and passing them for points farther west. Hardship and tragedy often ride with the caravans. Neighborliness and generosity are frequently called upon to help exhausted travelers. In those days every man's house had to be an inn. Along with independence and individualism, the pioneers had to develop the spirit of co-operation. Otherwise they could not have survived. Rölvaag has given us the most faithful picture we have of the pioneers who settled the vast prairie lands of the Northwest.

[1] **Ole Rölvaag** (ō'lĕ rûl'vôg).
[2] **Per Hansa** (pĕr hän'sȧ); **Beret** (bĕr'ĕt).

THAT summer many land seekers passed through the settlement on their way west. The arrival of a caravan was always an event of the greatest importance. How exciting they were, those little ships of the Great Plain! The prairie schooners, rigged with canvas tops which gleamed whitely in the shimmering light, first became visible as tiny specks against the eastern sky; one might almost imagine them to be sea gulls perched far, far away on an endless green meadow; but as one continued to watch, the white dots grew; they came drifting across the prairie like the day; after long waiting, they gradually floated out of the haze, distinct and clear; then, as they drew near, they proved to be veritable wagons, with horses hitched ahead, with folk and all their possessions inside, and a whole herd of cattle following behind.

The caravan would crawl slowly into the settlement and come to anchor in front of one of the sod houses; the moment it halted, people would swarm down and stretch themselves and begin to look after the teams; cattle would bellow; sheep would bleat as they ran about. Many queer races and costumes were to be seen in these caravans, and a babble of strange tongues shattered the air. Nut-brown youngsters, dressed only in a shirt and a pair of pants, would fly around between the huts, looking for other youngsters; an infant, its mother crooning softly to it, would sit securely perched in the fold of her arm; white-haired old men and women, who should have been living quietly at home, preparing for a different journey, were also to be seen in the group, running about like youngsters; the daily jogging from sky line to sky line had brightened their eyes and quickened their tongues. All were busy; each had a thousand questions to ask; every last one of them was in high spirits, though they knew no other home than the wagon and the blue skies above. . . .[1] The Lord only could tell whence all these people had come and whither they were going! . . .

The caravan usually intended to stop only long enough for the womenfolk to boil coffee and get a fresh supply of water; but the starting was always delayed, for the men had so many questions to ask. Once in a while during these halts, a fiddler would bring out his fiddle and play a tune or two, and then there would be dancing. Such instances were rare, but good cheer and excitement invariably accompanied these visits.

Why not settle right here? the Spring Creek folk would ask the west movers. . . . There's plenty of good land left — nothing better to be found between here and the Pacific Ocean!

No, not yet. They weren't quite ready to settle; these parts looked fairly crowded. . . . The farther west, the better. . . . They guessed they would have to go on a way, though this really looked pretty good! . . .

And so the caravans would roll onward into the green stillness of the West. How strange — they vanished faster than they had appeared! The white sails grew smaller and smaller in the glow of the afternoon, until they had dwindled to nothing; the eye might seek them out there in the waning day, and search till it grew blurred, but all in vain — they were gone, and had left no trace! . . .

Foggy weather had now been hanging over the prairie for three whole days; a warm mist of rain mizzled continuously out of the low sky. Toward evening of the third day, the fog lifted and clear sky again appeared; the setting sun burst through the cloud banks rolling up above the western horizon, and transformed them into marvelous fairy castles. . . . While this was going on, over to the northeast of the Solum boys' place, a lonely wagon had crept into sight; it had almost reached the creek before anyone had noticed it, for the Solum boys were visiting among the Sognings, where there were many young people. But as Beret sat out in the yard, milking, the wagon crossed her view. When she brought in the milk, she remarked in her quiet manner that they were going to have company, at which tidings the rest of the family had to run out and see who might be coming at this time of day.

There was only one wagon, with two cows following behind; on the left side walked a brown-whiskered, stooping man — he was doing the driving; close behind him came a half-grown boy, dragging his feet heavily. The wagon at last crawled up the hill and came to a stop in Per Hansa's yard, where the whole family stood waiting.

"I don't suppose there are any Norwegians in this settlement? No, that would be too much to expect," said the man in a husky, worn-out voice.

"If you're looking for Norwegians, you have found the right place, all right! We sift the people as they pass

---

[1] In this selection the dots do not represent something omitted, but are used by the author, as often in poetry, to suggest a thoughtful pause and produce a slow-moving, meditative style.

through here — keep our own, and let the others go!" . . . Per Hansa wanted to run on, for he felt in high spirits; but he checked himself, observing that the man looked as if he stood on the very brink of the grave.

Was there any chance of putting up here for the night?

"Certainly! certainly!" cried Per Hansa briskly, "provided they were willing to take things as they were."

The man didn't answer but walked, instead, to the wagon and spoke to someone inside.

"Kari,[1] now you must brace up and come down. Here we have found Norwegians at last!" As if fearing a contradiction, he added, "Ya, they are real Norwegians. I've talked with them."

On top of his words, there came out of the wagon, first a puny boy with a hungry face, somewhat smaller than the other boy; then a girl of about the same size, but looking much older. She helped to get down another boy, about six years old, who evidently had been sleeping and looked cross and tired. That seemed to be all.

The man stepped closer to the wagon. "Aren't you coming, Kari?"

A groan sounded within the canvas. The girl grabbed hold of her father's arm. "You must untie the rope! Can't you remember *anything?*" she whispered angrily.

"Ya, that's right! Wait a minute till I come and help you."

An irresistible curiosity took hold of Per Hansa; in two jumps he stood on the tongue of the wagon. The sight that met his eyes sent chills running down his spine. Inside sat a woman on a pile of clothes with her back against a large immigrant chest; around her wrists and leading to the handles of the chest a strong rope was tied; her face was drawn and unnatural. Per Hansa trembled so violently that he had to catch hold of the wagon box, but inwardly

[1] Kari (kăr′ĭ).

he was swearing a steady stream. To him it looked as if the woman was crucified.

"For God's sake, man! . . ."

The stranger paid no attention; he was pottering about and pleading, "Come down now, Kari. . . . Ya, all right, I'll help you! Everything's going to be all right — I know it will! . . . Can you manage to get up?" He had untied the rope, and the woman had risen to her knees.

"O God!" she sighed, putting her hands to her head.

"Please come. That's right; I'll help you!" pleaded the man, as if he were trying to persuade a child.

She came down unsteadily. "Is this the place, Jacob?" she asked in a bewildered way.

But now Beret ran up and put her arm around her; the women looked into each other's eyes, and instantly a bond of understanding had been established. "You come with me!" urged Beret. . . .

"O God! This isn't the place, either!" wailed the woman; but she followed Beret submissively into the house.

"Well, well!" sighed the man as he began to unhitch the horses. "Life isn't easy — no, it certainly isn't." . . .

Per Hansa watched him anxiously, hardly knowing what to do. Both the boys kept close to him. Then an idea flashed through his mind: "You boys run over to Hans Olsa's and tell him not to go to bed until I come. . . . No, I don't want him here. And you two stay over there tonight. Now run along!"

Turning to the man, he asked, "Aren't there any more in your party?"

"No, not now. We were five, you see, to begin with — five in all — but the others had to go on. . . . Haven't they been by here yet? Well, they must be somewhere over to the westward. . . . No, life isn't easy." . . . The man wandered on in his monotonous, blurred tone; he sounded all the time as if he were half sobbing.

"Where do you come from?" Per Hansa demanded gruffly.

The man didn't give a direct answer, but continued to ramble on in the same mournful way, stretching his story out interminably. . . . They had been wandering over the prairie for nearly six weeks. . . . Ya, it was a hard life. When they had started from Houston County, Minnesota, there had been five wagons in all. Strange that the others hadn't turned up here. Where could they be? It seemed to him as if he had traveled far enough to reach the ends of the earth! . . . Good God, what a nightmare life was! If he had only — only known! . . .

"Did the others go away and *leave you?*" Per Hansa hadn't intended to ask that question, but it had slipped out before he realized what he was saying. He wondered if there could be anything seriously wrong. . . .

"They couldn't possibly wait for us — couldn't have been expected to. Everything went wrong, you see, and I didn't know when I would be able to start again. . . . Turn the horses loose, John," he said to the boy. "Take the pail, and see if you can squeeze some milk out of the cows. Poor beasts, they don't give much now!" Then he turned to Per Hansa again. "I don't know what would have become of us if we hadn't reached this place tonight! We'd have been in a bad hole, that I assure you! Womenfolk can't bear up." . . . The man stopped and blew his nose.

Per Hansa dreaded what might be coming next. "You must have got off your course, since you are coming down from the north?"

The man shook his head helplessly. "To tell the truth, I don't know where we've been these last few days. We couldn't see the sun."

"Haven't you got a compass?"

"Compass? No! I tried to steer with a rope but the one I had wasn't long enough."

"You didn't!" exclaimed Per Hansa excitedly, full of a sudden new interest.

"Ya, I tried that rope idea — hitched it to the back of the wagon, and let it drag in the wet grass. But it didn't work — I couldn't steer straight with it. The rope was so short, and kept kinking around so much, that it didn't leave any wake."

"Uh-huh!" nodded Per Hansa wisely. "You must be a seafaring man, to have tried that trick!"

"No, I'm no sailor. But fisherfolk out here have told me that it's possible to steer by a rope. . . . I had to try *something.*"

"Where did you cross the Sioux?"

"How do I know where I crossed it? We came to a river a long way to the east of here — that must have been the Sioux. We hunted and hunted before we could find a place shallow enough to cross. . . . God! this has certainly been a wandering in the desert for me! . . . But if Kari only gets better, I won't complain — though I never dreamed that life could be so hard." . . .

"Is she — is she *sick,* that woman of yours?"

The man did not answer this question immediately; he wiped his face with the sleeve of his shirt. When he spoke again, his voice had grown even more blurred and indistinct. "Physically she seems to be as well as ever — as far as I can see. She certainly hasn't overworked since we've been traveling. I hope there's nothing wrong with her. . . . But certain things are hard to bear — I suppose it's worse for the mother, too — though the Lord knows it hasn't been easy for me, either! . . . You see, we had to leave our youngest boy out there on the prairie." . . .

"*Leave* him?" . . . These were the only two words that came to Per Hansa's mind.

"Ya, there he lies, our little boy! . . . I never saw a more promising man — you know what I mean — when he grew up. . . . But now — oh, well." . . .

Per Hansa felt faint in the pit of his

stomach; his throat grew dry; his voice became as husky as that of the other; he came close up to him. "Tell me — how did this happen?"

The man shook his head again, in a sort of dumb despair. Then he cleared his throat and continued with great effort. "I can't tell how it happened! Fate just willed it so. Such things are not to be explained. . . . The boy had been ailing for some time — we knew that, but didn't pay much attention. We had other things to think of. . . . Then he began to fail fast. We were only one day's journey this side of Jackson; so we went back. That was the time when the others left us. I don't blame them much — it was uncertain when we could go on. . . . The doctor we found wasn't a capable man — I realize it now. He spoke only English and couldn't understand what I was saying. He had no idea what was wrong with the boy — I could see that plainly enough. . . . Ya, well — so we started again. . . . It isn't any use to fight against fate; that's an old saying, and a true one, too, I guess. . . . Before long we saw that the boy wasn't going to recover. So we hurried on, day and night, trying to catch our neighbors. . . . Well, that's about all of it. One night he was gone — just as if you had blown out a candle. Ya, let me see — that was five nights ago."

"Have you got him there in the wagon?" demanded Per Hansa, grabbing the man by the arm.

"No, no," he muttered huskily. "We buried him out there by a big stone — no coffin or anything. But Kari took the best skirt she had and wrapped it all around him — we had to do *something*, you know. . . . But," he continued, suddenly straightening up, "Paul cannot lie there! As soon as I find my neighbors, I'll go and get him. Otherwise Kari . . ." The man paused between the sobs that threatened to choke him. "I have had to tie her up the last few days. She insisted on getting out and

going back to Paul. I don't think she has had a wink of sleep for over a week. . . . It's just as I was saying — some people can't stand things." . . .

Per Hansa leaned heavily against the wagon. "Has she gone crazy?" he asked hoarsely.

"She isn't much worse than the rest of us. I don't believe . . . Kari is really a well-balanced woman . . . but you can imagine how it feels, to leave a child *that* way." . . .

The boy, John, had finished milking. He had put the pail down and was standing a little way off, listening to his father's story; suddenly, he threw himself on the ground, sobbing as if in convulsions.

"John! John!" admonished the father. "Aren't you ashamed of yourself — a grown-up man like you! Take the milk and carry it into the house!"

"That's right!" echoed Per Hansa, pulling himself together. "We'd better all go in. There's shelter here, and plenty to eat."

Beret was bustling around the room when they entered; she had put the woman to bed, and now was tending her. "Where are the boys?" she asked.

Per Hansa told her that he had sent them to Hans Olsa's for the night.

"That was hardly necessary; we could have made room here somehow." Beret's voice carried a note of keen reproach.

The man had paused at the door; now he came over to the bed, took the limp hand, and muttered, "Poor soul! . . . Why, I believe she's asleep already!"

Beret came up and pushed him gently aside. "Be careful! Don't wake her. She needs the rest."

"Ya, I don't doubt it — not I! She hasn't slept for a week, you see — the poor soul!" With a loud sniff, he turned and left the room.

When suppertime came, the woman seemed to be engulfed in a stupefying sleep. Beret did not join the others at the supper table, but busied herself, in-

"In Search of the Land of Milk and Honey," an oil painting by the American artist Harvey Dunn (1884–1952).

stead, by trying to make the woman more comfortable; she loosened her clothes, took off her shoes, and washed her face in warm water; during all this the stranger never stirred. That done, Beret began to fix up sleeping quarters for the strangers—in the barn. She carried in fresh hay and brought out all the bedding she had; she herself would take care of the woman, in case she awoke and needed attention. Beret did little talking, but she went about these arrangements with a firmness and confidence that surprised her husband.

Per Hansa came in from the barn, after helping the strangers settle themselves for the night. Beret was sitting on the edge of the bed, dressing the baby for the night; she had put And-Ongen[1] to bed beside the distracted woman.

"Did she tell you much?" he asked in a low voice.

Beret glanced toward the other bed before she answered.

[1] **And-Ongen:** Beret's little daughter.

"Only that she had had to leave one of her children on the way. She wasn't able to talk connectedly."

"It's a terrible thing!" he said, looking away from his wife. "I think I'll go over to Hans Olsa's for a minute. I want to talk this matter over with him."

"Talk it over with him?" she repeated coldly. "I don't suppose Hans Olsa knows everything!"

"No, of course not. But these people have got to be helped, and we can't do it all alone." He hesitated for a minute, as if waiting for her consent. "Well, I won't be gone long," he said as he went out of the door.

When he returned, an hour later, she was still sitting on the edge of the bed, with the baby asleep on her lap. They sat in silence for a long while; at last he began to undress. She waited until he was in bed, then turned the lamp low and lay down herself, but without undressing. . . . The lamp shed only a faint light. It was so quiet in the room that one could hear the breathing of all the others. Beret lay there listening;

though the room was still, it seemed alive to her with strange movements; she forced herself to open her eyes and look around. Noticing that Per Hansa wasn't asleep either, she asked:

"Did you look after the boys?"

"Nothing the matter with them! They were fast asleep in Sofie's bed."

"You told them everything, at Hans Olsa's?"

"Of course!"

"What did they think of it?"

Per Hansa raised himself on his elbows and glanced at the broken creature lying in the bed back of theirs. The woman, apparently, had not stirred a muscle. "It's a bad business," he said. "We must try to get together a coffin and find the boy. We can't let him lie out there — that way." . . . As Beret made no answer, he briefly narrated the story that the man had told him. "The fellow is a good-for-nothing, stupid fool, I'm sure of that," concluded Per Hansa.

She listened to him in silence. For some time she brooded over her thoughts; then in a bitter tone she suddenly burst out, "Now you can see that this kind of a life is impossible! It's beyond human endurance."

He had not the power to read her thoughts; he did not want to know them; tonight every nerve in his body was taut with apprehension and dismay. But he tried to say, reassuringly, "Hans Olsa and I will both go with the man, as soon as the day breaks. If we only had something to make the coffin of! The few pieces of board that I've got here will hardly be enough. . . . Now let's go to sleep. Be sure and call me if you need anything!"

He turned over resolutely, as if determined to sleep; but she noticed that he was a long time doing it. . . . I wonder what's going through his mind? she thought. She was glad to have him awake, just the same; tonight there were strange things abroad in the room. . . .

[Perhaps you would like to know what happened later to these unfortunate travelers. During the night the crazed woman, Kari, thinking she must search for the body of her little boy, seized And-Ongen, Beret's child, and carried her out on the prairie. When their absence was discovered, Per Hansa rushed out in pursuit and was able to bring them back before any harm was done except for the terror suffered by Per and Beret. The next day the neighbors made a little coffin, and two of the men started out with the strangers to try to find the child's body. After four days they returned with the little coffin still empty. Then the strangers started out again on their westward trek, and this is the last we hear of them in the story. The whole incident, however, is a foreshadowing of the mental darkness that settled over Beret toward the end of the novel.]

FOR DISCUSSION

1. Which hardships of pioneer days are more emphasized in this selection, the physical or the mental? What brighter side of the picture is given? Discuss the life of pioneers from all these viewpoints. How does the drama of life pictured here differ from that of the miner or cattleman?

2. How many different nationalities can you name that had a prominent part in the settlement of the West? Why were the Scandinavians particularly suited to build up the Northwest? How many of their characteristics can you gather from this selection?

3. Make a list, either individually or as a class, of all the books you have read or the movies you have seen that picture the covered-wagon days. Discuss the impressions of prairie life you have gained from these in comparison with the selection from *Giants in the Earth*.

YOUR OWN WRITING

Where in our modern world have large-scale migrations taken place? Have most of these been voluntary or forced? Investigate one of these, and write an incident of a migrating family; use vivid details to make the characters come alive.

MARQUIS
JAMES
1891–1955

The Run for
the Cherokee Strip

In 1893 a section of Indian land in what is now Oklahoma was opened to white settlement. James's father rode in that "run" to stake out his claim, and that is the event recounted here.

Marquis James began his writing career as a small-town newspaperman. He was twice awarded the Pulitzer prize for his biographies *The Raven: A Biography of Sam Houston* and *Andrew Jackson: Portrait of a President.*

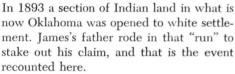ROM my mother I learned of Papa's own part in the race. It was the kind of story that Mama, with her love of horses, would tell with relish.

Especially for the Run, Papa had bought a race horse in El Reno. It was wind-broken but otherwise a sound and strong animal, capable of carrying my father's more than two hundred pounds.

"In his young days your father was a real fancy rider," Mama would say. "And, for a man of his size, very easy on a horse."

This was no small tribute. My mother was about as accomplished a judge of riding as any woman in our part of the country.

The Run was a young man's undertaking. My father was crowding forty-nine, a good twenty years older than the average man who entered the race on horseback with serious intentions of reaching Enid in time to stake anything. A year and a half of law practice in Old Oklahoma and the Indian nations had made him fairly used to the saddle again. Nevertheless, he took three weeks to condition himself and to find out what he and his horse could do. He knew the ropes well enough to get himself the best possible place on the starting line — smack on the Chisholm Trail, just north of Hennessey, in Old Oklahoma.

You could begin your race anywhere you could get to on one of the four borders of the Strip, which was about a hundred and sixty-five miles east and west by fifty-eight miles north and south. Papa picked the Hennessey section because it lay closest Enid, which he figured would be *the* town of the Strip. There was also the Trail to follow. It made for easier riding and led straight to the desired townsite. On a prairie, experience is necessary to preserve a sense of direction.

Mama's understanding was that Papa spent about three days and nights on the line, holding his place. The wonder is the wait wasn't longer, considering the premium on places in the neighborhood of the Trail. I have heard men tell of spending three weeks on the line. Probably they were with covered-wagon outfits, but, unless close to water, they must have got pretty tired of it. The sheets of some of the wagons were scrawled with notices of intention such as "Oklahoma or Bust." Substituting "Texas" or "Oregon," the phrase had been western usage for a good fifty years.

The line was patrolled by soldiers to prevent anyone from crossing over before the opening gun. The country had been evacuated by the cattle outfits which formerly leased it from the Indians. Excepting land-office and post-office staffs and soldiers on the site of each county seat, the Strip was depopulated. That was the theory, and it came tolerably close to being the fact. Nobody knows how many sooners did manage to hide out in the promised land before the opening gun was fired, but probably not more than you would find trying to obtain their ends by illegal means in any collection of a hundred thousand persons. . . .

After a man had staked a claim, he had to "file" at the nearest land office. In order to file he was required to exhibit an evidence of registration permitting him to make the Run in the first place. Registration slips were issued from booths along the line. It was in no way difficult for a prospective sooner who knew the country to register a week before the Run and sneak up a draw through the thinly patrolled line. He could camp in the blackjacks west of Enid, for instance, and ride out with the first honest comers — as Mr. Wilcox suspected the man in light-blue overalls

had done. A cavalry troop encamped on the Enid site had reconnoitered the surrounding country for three weeks. Though the lieutenant in command was sure a number of sooners had eluded him, they must have formed a minute proportion of the whole body of settlers.

The Hennessey stretch of the line broke five minutes before the official gun. Somebody may have discharged a firearm by accident. My father was in the saddle and ready. Waiting only to see that there was no turning back the tide, he, too, set off, keeping to the Chisholm Trail and reining his horse to a pace it could maintain for fifteen or sixteen miles and have a spurt left for an emergency.

The Chisholm Trail was the name cowmen gave to the Oklahoma section of the Abilene Trail, greatest of the southwestern cattle thoroughfares. It ran from San Antonio, Texas, to the railway terminus at Abilene, Kansas, a distance of eight hundred miles. Though little used for cattle drives since the completion of the Rock Island Railroad through the Cherokee Strip in 1889, the famous prairie road was still distinct. Like a carelessly laid ribbon, which your eye would lose in the dips and pick up in the rises of the undulating plain, the Oklahoma part stretched almost due north. On level places it was like several ribbons side by side. These markings were the Trail's core, made by the wheels of chuck wagons, calf wagons, freighters, and stages. When wheels and hoofs wore through the sod, creating a "high center," teamsters would start a new road alongside the old. For two or three hundred yards on either side of these ruts, the grass had been beaten down by the feet of the cattle. This on level stretches. To ford a stream or cross a draw, the Trail narrowed.

The race was going well for my father. At first many riders and some drivers passed him; but this he had counted on. In the fullness of time, without increasing the pace of his horse, he began to pass them. When Papa calculated that he had gone about fifteen miles, he was feeling the strain, and his horse was feeling it. Ahead of him were perhaps fifty riders in sight whom he doubted his ability to pass. (Fifty out of fifteen thousand starters from Hennessey.)

Glancing to the east, my father saw the top of a distant string of trees. That meant a stream, an asset of great value to a claim: also an asset of great value to my father, who liked trees. They were the thing he missed most on the plains. Turning his horse from the Trail, he crossed the Rock Island track and the bed of a dry creek. He urged his tiring mount up the rise. On the other side he saw only a shallow draw, its naked sides exposing coarse sandy soil tinted from red to orange. Was this a wild-goose chase? Holding a northeast course, he made for the next rise. He was traveling over short-grass prairie, knobby-surfaced and with washes of bare red soil: a good place for a horse, especially a tired, wind-broken horse, its breath coming in rasps, to stumble; and no good to grow anything. The crest of this second rise brought a welcome sight into view: the trees he had seen from the Trail; and beyond them more trees.

Watering the roots of the first trees was a disappointing stream, hardly more than a yard wide. (This was the driest season of the year.) But better trees were beyond; indeed, what seemed a veritable forest, in terms of the plains, with a noble green mass — surely the granddaddy of all the trees in the Cherokee Strip — dominating the whole. The first of these trees were soon reached. The creek was wider there: ten or twelve feet across. The illusion of a grove had been caused by the way the creek curved in the shape of an S. Papa followed the course of the stream in the direction of the Big Tree. He crossed the creek once and found

that, to reach the Big Tree, he must cross again or double a loop. He started to double the loop and came upon a steep ravine. The ravine wouldn't have been much to head, but Papa didn't take the time. Precious minutes had been lost feeling his way toward the trees. On the next fold of the prairie to the south, other riders were in sight. Unseen riders might be coming up the draws. Papa wanted that creek, flowing in the shape of an S with good bottom land in the loops; and he wanted the Big Tree. His horse barely made the steep yonder side of the ravine. A few rods farther, at the high point on our pasture, luxuriant in red top, Papa dismounted and set his stake on what proved to be the Southeast Quarter of Section 17, Township 22, Range 6 West of the Indian Meridian.

It was 12:53 P.M., September 16, 1893. As the Hennessey line had broken at 11:55, my father had ridden seventeen miles in fifty-eight minutes without injuring his horse. A note of pride would touch Mama's tone as she spoke the last four words. Walter Cook covered eighteen miles in fifty to fifty-five minutes — he carried no watch and no one seems to have timed him exactly.

Something else my father had had to watch out for during the last part of his ride were the markers, designating section and certain quarter-section corners. Twenty years before, surveyors had checkerboarded the Strip with these little monuments. Where there were any, roughly cut sandstones sticking six or eight inches above the ground were used; elsewhere, "pits and mounds." A pit-and-mounds marker consisted of a hole about three feet deep, surrounded by four piles of earth and sod indicating the points of the compass. Virgin prairie sod is thick and durable. Except where beaten down by cattle, these mounds could still be picked up by a person who knew what to look for easier than the stones hidden by grass.

An actual photograph of the Run for the Cherokee Strip in 1893.

Before the Run much of the Strip had been burned over. I have heard this laid to sooners, in an effort to drive off rightful homesteaders. It appears, however, to have been the work of the troops — with the object of rendering markers more readily visible, of preventing prairie fires with possible serious consequences during the chaotic first days of settlement, and of smoking out sooners. The fires had been set too late. In areas, they were burning on the day of the Run, and for some time after. I have heard men tell of riding through lines of flame, and of droves of rabbits, coyotes, and snakes fleeing the fires. Near North Town a woman was burned to death trying to save her team.

Streams, arid gulches, green bottom-land grass, and so on stopped the fires in places. Where my father was had not been burned at all. Stone and pit-and-mounds markers were mixed in together, and all hard to see. Later examination disclosed the three designated corners of his quarter to be marked with stones — in all likelihood not visible more than a few yards away. As there was no time to search out these markers before he staked, my father had to estimate his boundaries by eye — while in motion on horseback, taking his bearings from the last marker he had seen. In the matter of acquiring title to the Big Tree, luck was with him, too. Only three corners of any quarter section were marked. Lines had to be run to determine the fourth. When they were run on our place, the Big Tree was found to be less than a hundred yards from the Utsler boundary. Of course my father could have tried to make sure of the tree by setting his stake right under it. But he would have sacrificed the advantage of observation — for claim-jumpers and sooners — which his commanding position in the pasture afforded.

Having driven his stake, Papa set up a pup tent to which he affixed an American flag. I would like to know who gave him that flag. . . . From the tent he could see almost the entire claim, barring the East Draw and where the bluff hid the creek. He removed his saddle and, leading his horse so it would cool off gradually, began a tour of his estimated boundaries — probably looking for the markers. In the East Bottom he found a man preparing to set his stake. Cases of lead poisoning developed from a number of such meetings that day. But this man was no sooner or intentional claim-jumper. He rode with Papa to higher ground and took a look at the tent and the flag.

"You beat me out, stranger," said the man. "I'll strike eastward a piece."

Papa wished him luck, and never saw the man again.

FOR DISCUSSION

1. What specific information do you gain from this selection about staking a claim in the Old West?

2. What were some of the perennial problems that claimers had to cope with?

3. Does this method of handling territorial claims seem fair? Can you think of a better way?

4. See if you can find evidence in this selection that the Old West — the more romanticized, storybook one — was already disappearing by 1893.

FOR YOUR VOCABULARY

In reading the literature of the West, you encountered many words and phrases that denote something typical of life in that part of the country. How many of the following words or phrases can you explain clearly, without consulting the context or a dictionary?

bar (special meaning)   prairie schooners
boots (special meaning)   prickly pears
chips (special meaning)   sluice robber
flat   sod shanty
gulch   toesack
holding down a claim   trapper
lead poisoning   victuals
pantaloons   whopper

READING ON GROWTH AND CONFLICT

INFORMAL HISTORY

Adams, Andy, *The Log of a Cowboy* (Houghton Mifflin, 1931)

Baumann, John, *Idaho Sprout* (Morrow, 1950)

Brooks, Van Wyck, *The Confident Years: 1885–1915* (Dutton, 1952)

Dobie, J. Frank, *Apache Gold and Yaqui Silver* (Little, Brown, 1939)

Eaton, Frank, *Pistol Pete, Veteran of the Old West* (Little, Brown, 1952)

Sandoz, Mari, *Cheyenne Autumn* (Mc-Graw-Hill, 1953)

Vestal, Stanley, *Sitting Bull, Champion of the Sioux* (Univ. of Oklahoma Press, 1957)

FICTION

Cable, G. W., *Old Creole Days* (Heritage, 1943)

Ferber, Edna, *Show Boat* (Grosset & Dunlap, 1926); *Cimarron* (Grosset & Dunlap, 1943)

Guthrie, A. B., *The Big Sky* (Sloane, 1949); *The Way West* (Sloane, 1950)

Hough, Emerson, *North of '36* (Grosset & Dunlap, 1941)

Lane, R. W., *Let the Hurricane Roar* (Longmans, 1933)

Richter, Conrad, *The Sea of Grass* (Grosset & Dunlap, 1943); *Light in the Forest* (Knopf, 1953)

Schaefer, Jack, *Shane* (Houghton Mifflin, 1949)

NARRATIVE POEMS

Altrocchi, Julia, *Snow-covered Wagons; A Pioneer Epic; The Donner Party Expedition* (Macmillan, 1936)

Benét, Stephen Vincent, *John Brown's Body* (Oxford Univ. Press, 1944)

Neihardt, J. G., *A Cycle of the West* (Macmillan, 1949)

FOLKLORE

Bowman, J. C., *Pecos Bill* (Whitman, 1937)

Lomax, John A., *Cowboy Songs* (Macmillan, 1938)

Price, Robert, *Johnny Appleseed, Man and Myth* (Indiana Univ. Press, 1954)

BIOGRAPHY

Cook, J. H., *Fifty Years on the Old Frontier as a Cowboy, Hunter, Guide, and Ranchman* (Univ. of Oklahoma Press, 1957)

Dobie, J. Frank, *A Vaquero of the Brush Country* (Little, Brown, 1943)

Havighurst, Walter, *Annie Oakley of the Wild West* (Macmillan, 1954)

Rourke, Constance, *Davy Crockett* (Harcourt, Brace & World, 1955)

Siringo, Charles A., *A Texas Cowboy* (Sloane, 1950)

Vestal, Stanley, *Kit Carson* (Houghton Mifflin, 1931); *Jim Bridger, Mountain Man* (Morrow, 1946)

FOR LISTENING

Lincoln's Gettysburg Address and Lee's Farewell to the Army of Northern Virginia have been recorded on *Many Voices* 5B; "Mark Twain and the Public Reading" and "The Pony Express" have been recorded on *Many Voices* 11B.

Time of Change

BY THE 1890's the frontier was gone, and with it the Old West. With the end of the land rush, the process of expansion changed from that of pushing into new territory to that of settling and developing the once-open spaces. American society and American experience were changing rapidly. Railroads were girdling the nation and binding its regions closer together. Science, invention, and the discovery of iron and oil were hastening the shift from farming to industry. The telegraph was changing the whole tempo of communications. Our mobility and our sense of physical unity were increasing a thousandfold. We could no longer think in purely regional terms. We began to develop a heightened national sense. Our writers began to speak for the whole country rather than for any part of it.

CINCINNATI CENTENNIAL EXPOSITION OF THE OHIO VALLEY

JULY 4 to OCT. 27.

UNEQUALLED DISPLAY IN EVERY DEPARTMENT.

REDUCED RATES FROM ALL POINTS

GRAND JUBILEE. 100 DAYS & NIGHTS

Industrialization

The great development that changed the face of the modern world, the Industrial Revolution, now struck this country with full force. Small business suddenly became big business. The age of the factory, the age of heavy industry, the age of steel and of mass production burst upon us. These were the years when the United States rose to world power, and these were the years, too, of a sharp increase in all activities of government. Cities grew at great pace, and their growth brought a host of new problems of government, housing, and education. The nation became conscious of the corruption and slums that were a part of the reality of cities. There was "progress" — a word that some almost worshiped — and beside it there was often misery.

Realism in Literature

Growth and corruption, progress and poverty — all were bound to find reflection in our literature. For a long time the prevailing moods in American writing had been essentially romantic and optimistic. When the sorrows and evils of life were shown, they were modified by sentimental treatment, or else they were depicted as occurring in distant times and places.

A literary transition was coming. A new mood was felt in the literature of Europe, England, and America. The literary change had a basis in the changing society. The new mood brought new ways of looking at the world. Mark Twain, who belonged partly to the earlier romantic era, felt the change; his attacks on injustice grew sharper in his later years.

The most common name for the new phase in our literature is *realism*. Realistic writers were attempting to show life as it actually was. The new realistic spirit was to look upon all of life; if the writers found good, they were to acknowledge it; but if they found harshness, ugliness, cruelty, and injustice, these too must be revealed without concealment and without apology.

The new spirit was felt in all fields of writing. Poets found fresh things to write about and original forms in which to write. The writer of fiction and the dramatist dealt with varied situations. Characters and scenes that had never been treated by our earlier writers now began to appear in our plays, novels, and short stories. The new mood extended far beyond fiction. The essayist, the historian, and the philosopher began to probe and challenge our behavior and our values in new and disturbing ways.

New Directions in Poetry

In 1855 a poet published a volume of poetry that contained the startling line:

I sound my barbaric yawp over the roofs of the world.

Could the voice of a poet be so brash? What were his poetic materials? They were not the sigh of the lover; not the celebration of flowers and sunsets and chivalry; not classical references and images. Instead, the twelve poems in the book contained a multitude of common things that were seen freshly, as if with new eyes:

The blab of the pave, tires of carts, sluff of boot soles, talk of the promenaders . . .
The peddler sweats with his pack on his back (the purchaser higgling about the
    odd cent) . . .

I believe a leaf of grass is no less perfect than the journeywork of the stars . . .
And the running blackberry would adorn the parlors of heaven,
And the narrowest hinge in my hand puts to scorn all machinery,
And the cow crunching with depress'd head surpasses any statue . . .

These were unusual materials for poetry, and the poems themselves were even more unusual. They did not look like poems at all, with their long, sprawling sentences, their lack of rhyme, and their disregard of traditional rhythms. There was something new here, a new vision, a new rush and tumult of rhythm, an irregular, compelling pulsation. This was the voice of Walt Whitman in *Leaves of Grass*.

It was obvious that such a poet either had to be swept away and forgotten, or else, if he gained a place, he would change the patterns of poetry. Whitman could not be swept away; he surprised some readers and outraged others, but he commanded attention. Whitman's choice of new forms was quite deliberate. He broke away from conventional forms and patterns, from the odes and sonnets of the past. He rejected the older notions of what was beautiful and what was the proper material for poetry. The new poetry, ushered in by Whitman, found beauty in the commonplaces of existence, in the everyday experiences of ordinary men and women. Whitman's poetry affirmed what the greatest poets have always shown, that all of life, not just a part, is the proper material for art. He said, "Everything comes out of the people, the everyday people, the people as you find them and leave them . . . just people!" Whitman found beauty even in ugliness, even in the perversities and follies of human beings. "Life, coarse and rank," Whitman asserted, was the stuff of poetry.

Whitman cast off the old shackles of formality to experiment freely with changing rhythms and variations in the lengths of lines. In his poems a line might stretch until it threatened to become a paragraph, or it might shorten to a syllable or two. Rhythm was present, but its patterns were irregular. The new style was called "free verse" by some poets and critics. To some, this seemed to mean "anything goes," but that was not quite right. There was form of a certain kind in the most "free" of Whitman's verse, but the form grew naturally out of the theme and mood of the poem, rather than following traditional patterns. Whitman's new rhythms, however, did have at least one significant forerunner. There are characteristics of "free verse" in some of the flowing rhythms of the King James Bible, and this influence can often be felt in Whitman's poetry. (See page 732 for more information on Whitman's life and writings.)

The Other Major Poets

Not all of the new poets wrote free, unrhymed verse. Free verse did not supplant the other styles; it simply became one more means of expression. All the major poets of this time, however, did experiment widely in new styles and subjects.

Sidney Lanier (see page 743 for a biographical sketch) expressed a predominantly romantic view of life, and his work is permeated by music, especially "The Marshes of Glynn," with its melodious lines and intricate images. Yet Lanier was a transitional figure as well, for scattered through his poems are notes of realism, shown most clearly in his awareness of the impact of industrialism.

Emily Dickinson was born earlier than Mark Twain or Sidney Lanier, but in many ways she seems a more modern figure. Most of her poems were first published long after her death. Because she was writing for herself alone, she wrote in her own way, with little regard for the traditional poetic conventions. Her half-rhymes, her irregular rhythms, and her experiments in verse forms anticipated much that we consider characteristic of modern poetry. A sketch of her life appears on page 750.

Edwin Arlington Robinson (see page 755 for a biographical sketch) was the most distinguished poet of the early years of the twentieth century. At times, he was also one of the most difficult poets. His was a subtle mind, acute in probing into the causes of behavior. Like the novelist Henry James, Robinson was a keen psychologist, examining in his poems every phrase, every gesture of his characters.

Stephen Crane, who is also famous for his fiction, began writing poetry after he was introduced to some of Emily Dickinson's work. His poems are terse and compact, and often symbolic. He tells capsule stories in a quiet conversational tone and gains strong effects through his deliberately casual manner. A biographical sketch of Crane appears on pages 806–07.

The work of each of these poets was distinctively individual. Each had something original to say. Each expressed new moods and themes in his work. Each contributed new forms and methods to poetry. Yet all of them shared the new spirit that Whitman had first expressed in *Leaves of Grass*. All of them have ranges of method, subject, speculation, and experience that mark a "new direction" and carry us to the threshold of modern poetry.

WALT
WHITMAN

1819–1892

Walt Whitman's first volume of poetry was called *Leaves of Grass.* He clung to this name for all succeeding editions even when the book had expanded from the original twelve poems to more than four hundred. The first edition contained the long poem, "Song of Myself," which is Whitman's poetic autobiography and the supreme statement of his spirit. Whitman sent a copy of the book to Emerson, whose philosophy had influenced his thinking, especially in drawing Whitman's attention to nature. Emerson, acknowledging the gift, wrote:

> I find it the most extraordinary piece of wit and wisdom that America has yet contributed . . . I give you joy of your free and brave thought. I find incomparable things said, incomparably well. I greet you at the beginning of a great career . . .

Thoreau called the book a "trumpet note ringing through the American camp." In one of his rare trips, he journeyed from Concord to see the new poet, and came away saying, "He is Democracy." Not everyone agreed with Thoreau's complimentary spirit. The poems were too frank for some readers, and many critics denounced Whitman's work as chaotic.

Whitman was born in 1819 on Long Island, and spent his early life in Brooklyn and New York. He often went to Coney Island, "at that time, a long, bare, unfrequented shore, which I had all to myself, and where I loved, after bathing, to race up and down the hard sand, and declaim Homer and Shakespeare to the surf and sea gulls by the hour." Whitman attended public schools, and he read constantly during his leisure time. In the 1840's he worked for various newspapers, including the Brooklyn *Daily Eagle,* which he edited for two years.

During these years, Whitman had been writing some poetry, but the poems were all weak imitations of the styles that were then popular in England. After a trip to New Orleans and Chicago, however, Whitman's entire personality seemed to be transformed. "Walter" Whitman became "Walt." The well-dressed young newspaperman began wearing rough workman's clothing, a battered hat, an open collar, and an untrimmed beard. And the poetry also changed drastically. Whitman discarded most of the common poetic devices of the time and wrote instead in a loose, rolling rhythm, with no rhymes. What caused this sudden change is still a mystery. Some experience in New Orleans may have affected him. As far as the poetry is concerned, it must have owed something to Whitman's reading of the King James Bible. There were perhaps other influences, too, but it is clear that Whitman had, in effect, created a new kind of poetry.

The author and his work were large and hearty and full of vigor. Whitman was a man who liked to walk, to observe the ways of the country and the life of the city; to talk to the farmer or the workman; to stand on docks or ride the ferryboats and see the varied action of the river and the harbor. He traveled over the face of the land he loved and ceaselessly celebrated. The American democracy had found no more passionate publicist.

During the War Between the States Whitman tended the wounded in hospitals and on the battlefields. The poems in *Drum-Taps* (later incorporated into *Leaves of Grass*) showed the face of war. Whitman's laments for Lincoln, in "O Captain! My Captain" and "When Lilacs Last in the Dooryard Bloom'd," gave voice to a mourning nation.

In his poetry, Whitman tried to embrace all of America, perhaps an impossible task for a poet. Yet Whitman came closer to this goal than any other American writer. Whitman, in sum, has helped us to understand our nation, its destiny, and the vigor of its life. And he helped to expand the vision of his art in a way that influenced many of the poets that followed him.

For a long time, Whitman's admirers in America were only a handful. His genius, like Poe's, was recognized abroad more swiftly than at home. In the late years of his life, however, his countrymen came to recognize his worth. They knew at last that he was one of our great poets.

"Song of Myself," only part of which is given here, forms the core of *Leaves of Grass*. After many revisions in different editions, it now stands as Whitman's declaration of independence of man as an individual. The poem is not easy reading, but it will amply repay thoughtful rereading.

FROM *Song of Myself*

I celebrate myself, and sing myself,
And what I assume you shall assume,
For every atom belonging to me as good belongs to you.
I loaf and invite my soul,
I lean and loaf at my ease observing a spear of summer grass. . . .   5

The smoke of my own breath,
My respiration and inspiration, the beating of my heart, the passing of blood and
    air through my lungs,
The sniff of green leaves and dry leaves, and of the shore and dark-color'd sea-
    rocks, and of hay in the barn,
The play of shine and shade on the trees as the supple boughs wag,
The delight alone or in the rush of the streets, or along the fields and hillsides,   10
The feeling of health, the full-noon trill, the song of me rising from bed and
    meeting the sun. . . .

Excerpt from "Song of Myself" from *Leaves of Grass*, by Walt Whitman. Copyright 1924 by Doubleday & Company, Inc.

Stop this day and night with me and you shall possess the origin of all poems,
You shall possess the good of the earth and sun (there are millions of suns left),
You shall no longer take things at second or third hand, nor look through the eyes
     of the dead, nor feed on the specters in books,
You shall not look through my eyes either, nor take things from me,   15
You shall listen to all sides and filter them from your self. . . .

I am of old and young, of the foolish as much as the wise,
Regardless of others, ever regardful of others,
Maternal as well as paternal, a child as well as a man,
Stuff'd with the stuff that is coarse and stuff'd with the stuff that is fine,   20
One of the Nation of many nations, the smallest the same and the largest the same,
A Southerner soon as a Northerner, a planter nonchalant and hospitable down
     by the Oconee° I live,
A Yankee bound my own way ready for trade, my joints the limberest joints on
     earth and the sternest joints on earth,
A Kentuckian walking the vale of the Elkhorn in my deerskin leggings, a
     Louisianian or Georgian,
A boatman over lakes or bays or along coasts, a Hoosier, Badger, Buckeye;   25
At home on Kanadian snowshoes or up in the bush, or with fishermen off New-
     foundland,
At home in the fleet of iceboats, sailing with the rest and tacking,
At home on the hills of Vermont or in the woods of Maine, or the Texan ranch,
Comrade of Californians, comrade of free Northwesterners, . . .
Comrade of raftsmen and coalmen, comrade of all who shake hands and welcome
     to drink and meat,   30
A learner with the simplest, a teacher of the thoughtfulest,
A novice beginning yet experient° of myriads of seasons,
Of every hue and caste am I, of every rank and religion. . . .

I am the poet of the Body and I am the poet of the Soul,
The pleasures of heaven are with me and the pains of hell are with me,   35
The first I graft and increase upon myself, the latter I translate into a new
     tongue. . . .
Smile O voluptuous cool-breath'd earth!
Earth of the slumbering and liquid trees!
Earth of departed sunset — earth of the mountains misty-topt!
Earth of the vitreous° pour of the full moon just tinged with blue!   40
Earth of shine and dark mottling the tide of the river!
Earth of the limpid gray of clouds brighter and clearer for my sake!
Far-swooping elbow'd earth — rich apple-blossom'd earth!
Smile, for your lover comes. . . .

Agonies are one of my changes of garments, . . .   45
I take part, I see and hear the whole,
The cries, curses, roar, the plaudits for well-aim'd shots,
The ambulanza slowly passing trailing its red drip,
Workmen searching after damages, making indispensable repairs,

    22. **Oconee** (ô·kō′nê): a river in central Georgia. 32. **experient:** having experienced. 40. **vitreous** (vĭt′rê·ŭs); glasslike in color or luster.

The fall of grenades through the rent roof, the fan-shaped explosion,   50
The whizz of limbs, heads, stone, wood, iron, high in the air. . . .

All forces have been steadily employ'd to complete and delight me,
Now on this spot I stand with my robust soul. . . .

I tramp a perpetual journey (come listen all!)
My signs are a rainproof coat, good shoes, and a staff cut from the woods,   55
No friend of mine takes his ease in my chair,
I have no chair, no church, no philosophy,
I lead no man to a dinner table, library, exchange,
But each man and each woman of you I lead upon a knoll,
My left hand hooking you round the waist,   60
My right hand pointing to landscapes of continents and the public road.
Not I, not anyone else can travel that road for you,
You must travel it for yourself. . . .
The spotted hawk swoops by and accuses me, he complains of my gab and my
          loitering.
I too am not a bit tamed, I too am untranslatable,   65
I sound my barbaric yawp over the roofs of the world. . . .

I bequeath myself to the dirt to grow from the grass I love,
If you want me again, look for me under your boot soles.
You will hardly know who I am or what I mean,
But I shall be good health to you nevertheless,   70
And filter and fiber your blood.
Failing to fetch me at first, keep encouraged,
Missing me one place, search another,
I stop somewhere waiting for you.

I Hear America Singing

I hear America singing, the varied carols I hear,
Those of mechanics, each one singing his as it should be blithe and strong,
The carpenter singing his as he measures his plank or beam,
The mason singing his as he makes ready for work, or leaves off work,
The boatman singing what belongs to him in his boat, the deck hand singing on the
          steamboat deck,   5
The shoemaker singing as he sits on his bench, the hatter singing as he stands,
The woodcutter's song, the plowboy's on his way in the morning, or at noon in-
          termission or at sundown,
The delicious singing of the mother, or of the young wife at work, or of the girl
          sewing or washing,
Each singing what belongs to him or her and to none else,
The day what belongs to the day — at night the party of young fellows, robust,
          friendly.   10
Singing with open mouths their strong melodious songs.

WALT WHITMAN   735

Manhattan as it appeared in Whitman's day: from a nineteenth-century lithograph.

Whitman loved the old Indian names. His native Long Island he preferred to call Pauma-nok, and his exuberant affection for his city, New York, needed *Mannahatta* to express it. The name is, of course, perpetuated in Manhattan Island, which is the heart of the city today. Before you begin the poem, read or reread Carl Sandburg's "Chicago" on page 299. How does Whitman's treatment of New York compare to Sandburg's treatment of Chicago?

Mannahatta

I was asking for something specific and perfect for my city,
Whereupon lo! upsprang the aboriginal° name.

Now I see what there is in a name,° a word, liquid, sane, unruly, musical, self-
    sufficient,
I see that the word of my city is that word from of old,
Because I see that word nested in nests of water bays, superb,   5
Rich, hemmed thick all around with sailships and steamships, an island sixteen
    miles long, solid-founded,
Numberless crowded streets, high growths of iron, slender, strong, light, splendidly
    uprising toward clear skies,
Tides swift and ample, well loved by me, toward sundown,
The flowing sea-currents, the little islands, larger adjoining islands, the heights,
    the villas,
The countless masts, the white shore-steamers, the lighters, the ferryboats, the
    black sea-steamers well modeled,   10
The downtown streets, the jobbers' houses of business, the houses of business of
    the ship merchants and money brokers, the river streets,
Immigrants arriving, fifteen or twenty thousand in a week.
The carts hauling goods, the manly race of drivers of horses, the brown-faced
    sailors.
The summer air, the bright sun shining, and the sailing clouds aloft,
The winter snows, the sleigh bells, the broken ice in the river, passing along up or
    down with the flood tide or ebb tide,   15
The mechanics of the city, the masters, well formed, beautiful-faced, looking you
    straight in the eyes,
Trottoirs° thronged, vehicles, Broadway, the women, the shops and shows,
A million people — manners free and superb — open voices — hospitality — the
    most courageous and friendly young men,
City of hurried and sparkling waters! city of spires and masts!
City nested in bays! my city!   20

2. aboriginal (ăb′ŏ·rĭj′ĭ·năl): first. 3. what . . . name: Whitman here comments playfully on the famous lines in Shakespeare's *Romeo and Juliet* (Act II, Scene ii):

        Oh, be some other name!
    What's in a name? That which we call a rose
    By any other name would smell as sweet.

17. trottoirs (trŏ·twär′): sidewalks (French).

No part of human life and no part of the natural world can seem commonplace to one who shares the vision Whitman expresses in the next poem.

Miracles

Why, who makes much of a miracle?
As to me I know of nothing else but miracles,
Whether I walk the streets of Manhattan
Or dart my sight over the roofs of houses toward the sky,
Or wade with naked feet along the beach just in the edge of the water,   5
Or stand under trees in the woods,
Or talk by day with anyone I love,
Or sit at table at dinner with the rest,
Or look at strangers opposite me riding in the car,
Or watch honeybees busy around the hive of a summer forenoon,   10
Or animals feeding in the fields,
Or birds, or the wonderfulness of insects in the air,
Or the wonderfulness of the sundown, or of stars shining so quiet and bright,
Or the exquisite delicate curve of the new moon in spring;
These with the rest, one and all, are to me miracles,   15
The whole referring, yet each distinct and in its place.

To me every hour of the night and dark is a miracle,
Every cubic inch of space is a miracle,
Every square yard of the surface of the earth is spread with the same,
Every foot of the interior swarms with the same.   20

To me the sea is a continual miracle,
The fishes that swim — the rocks — the motion of the waves — the ships with men
          in them,
What stranger miracles are there?

A Noiseless Patient Spider

A noiseless patient spider,
I marked where on a little promontory it stood isolated,
Marked how to explore the vacant vast surrounding,
It launched forth filament, filament, filament, out of itself,
Ever unreeling them, ever tirelessly speeding them.   5

And you O my soul where you stand,
Surrounded, detached, in measureless oceans of space,
Ceaselessly musing, venturing, throwing, seeking the spheres to connect them,
Till the bridge you will need be formed, till the ductile° anchor hold,
Till the gossamer thread you fling catch somewhere, O my soul.   10

          9. ductile (dŭk′tĭl): capable of being drawn or hammered thin.

The next poem comments on the limitations of science and the scientific mind. The experience Whitman shares is a common one, that of attending a lecture by a famous authority in his field.

When I Heard the Learn'd Astronomer

When I heard the learn'd astronomer,
When the proofs, the figures, were ranged in columns before me,
When I was shown the charts and diagrams, to add, divide, and measure them,
When I sitting heard the astronomer where he lectured with much applause in the
    lecture room,
How soon unaccountable I became tired and sick,   5
Till rising and gliding out I wandered off by myself,
In the mystical moist air, and from time to time,
Looked up in perfect silence at the stars.

The upheaval that war brings into civilian life has rarely been more sharply etched than in the following poem. An irregular rhythm serves to emphasize the chaos.

Beat! Beat! Drums!

Beat! beat! drums! — blow! bugles! blow!
Through the windows — through doors — burst like a ruthless force,
Into the solemn church, and scatter the congregation,
Into the school where the scholar is studying;
Leave not the bridegroom quiet — no happiness must he have now with his bride,
Nor the peaceful farmer any peace, plowing his field or gathering his grain,   6
So fierce you whir and pound, you drums — so shrill you bugles blow.

Beat! beat! drums — blow! bugles! blow!
Over the traffic of cities — over the rumble of wheels in the streets;
Are beds prepared for sleepers at night in the houses? no sleepers must sleep in
    those beds,   10
No bargainers' bargains by day — no brokers or speculators — would they continue?
Would the talkers be talking? would the singer attempt to sing?
Would the lawyer rise in the court to state his case before the judge?
Then rattle quicker, heavier drums — you bugles wilder blow.

Beat! beat! drums! — blow! bugles! blow!   15
Make no parley — stop for no expostulation,
Mind not the timid — mind not the weeper or prayer,
Mind not the old man beseeching the young man,
Let not the child's voice be heard, nor the mother's entreaties,
Make even the trestles to shake the dead where they lie awaiting the hearses,   20
So strong you thump, O terrible drums — so loud you bugles blow.

"When I Heard the Learn'd Astronomer" and "Beat! Beat! Drums!" from *Leaves of Grass* by Walt Whitman, copyright, 1924. Reprinted by permission of Doubleday & Company, Inc.

WALT WHITMAN

Of all the poets who have paid tribute to Lincoln, none has sounded more feelingly than Whitman the note of personal grief at the President's death. When news of the assassination came to the poet, he was at home with his mother. He tells us, "Not a mouthful was eaten all day by either of us. We each drank half a cup of coffee; that was all. Little was said. We got every newspaper, morning and evening, and the frequent extras of that period, and passed them silently to each other."

Whitman gave full expression to his grief in "When Lilacs Last in the Dooryard Bloom'd." In this long poem he skillfully weaves together three themes: the fact of Lincoln's assassination, his own sense of personal loss and a triumphant comment on death. The following carol occurs near the end of the poem.

The Carol of Death

Come lovely and soothing death,
Undulate round the world, serenely arriving, arriving,
In the day, in the night, to all, to each,
Sooner or later delicate death.

Praised be the fathomless universe,   5
For life and joy, and for object and knowledge curious,
And for love, sweet love — but praise! praise! praise!
For the sure-enwinding arms of cool-enfolding death.

Dark mother always gliding near with soft feet,
Have none chanted for thee a chant of fullest welcome?   10
Then I chant it for thee, I glorify thee above all,
I bring thee a song that when thou must indeed come, come unfalteringly.

Approach strong deliveress,
When it is so, when thou hast taken them I joyously sing the dead,
Lost in the loving floating ocean of thee,   15
Laved° in the flood of thy bliss O death.

From me to thee glad serenades,
Dances for thee I propose saluting thee, adornments and feastings for thee,
And the sights of the open landscape and the high-spread sky are fitting,
And life and the fields, and the huge and thoughtful night. 20

The night in silence under many a star,
The ocean shore and the husky whispering wave whose voice I know,
And the soul turning to thee O vast and well-veiled death,
And the body gratefully nestling close to thee.

Over the treetops I float thee a song,   25
Over the rising and sinking waves, over the myriad fields and the prairies wide,
Over the dense-packed cities all and the teeming wharves and ways,
I float this carol with joy, with joy to thee O death.

16. **Laved**: bathed.

Written by invitation to be read at the Dartmouth College commencement in 1872, the following poem largely restates the poet's nationalistic ideas and feelings, thoughts presented earlier in his prose work *Democratic Vistas*.

FROM *Thou Mother with Thy Equal Brood*

Sail, sail thy best, ship of Democracy,
Of value is thy freight, 'tis not the Present only,
The Past is also stored in thee,
Thou holdest not the venture of thyself alone, not of the Western continent alone,
Earth's *résumé*° entire floats on thy keel O ship, is steadied by thy spars,   5
With thee Time voyages in trust, the antecedent° nations sink or swim with thee,
With all their ancient struggles, martyrs, heroes, epics, wars, thou bear'st the other
    continents,
Theirs, theirs as much as thine, the destination-port triumphant;
Steer them with good strong hand and wary eye, O helmsman, thou carriest great
    companions,
Venerable priestly Asia sails this day with thee,   10
And royal feudal Europe sails with thee.

5. *résumé* (rā′zû·mā′): a summing up. 6. **antecedent** (ăn′tê·sēd′ĕnt): going before in time.

FOR DISCUSSION

SONG OF MYSELF

1. You may have noted some obvious contradictions in this excerpt. Whitman was quite aware of these. How do contradictions become a necessary part of Whitman's inclusiveness — his attempt to absorb all of mankind?

2. Point out examples of a positive kind of beauty and examples of a harsher kind of realism. Would you say that in general Whitman is realistic? What elements might be termed romantic?

3. Find support for Whitman's fundamental joy in life. How does he employ the senses to communicate this joy?

4. Point out lines or passages in which Whitman regards himself as part of nature; as part of the history of mankind; as part of the present experience of man; as an independent being. What in this poem do you think would have pleased Emerson? What might have displeased the other New England poets? Does this poem bring you a new understanding and appreciation of human values? If so, how?

I HEAR AMERICA SINGING

1. What does this poem have to say, directly or indirectly, about happiness?

2. How does this poem show Whitman's democratic interest in all types of people? Where does he describe them objectively, and where does he identify himself more fully with their lives? Are all these types of people still in America?

MANNAHATTA

Compare Whitman's picture of New York with cities you know. What details give a definite "city" effect and would not be true of a small town?

MIRACLES

What attitude toward life is presented here? In what way is this poem a healthful antidote to a purely scientific attitude toward life?

A NOISELESS PATIENT SPIDER

1. How might you define or explain Whitman's concept of the soul's yearnings?

2. Much pleasure in this poem may be gained from noting its parallelism. Examine the structure carefully, and point out the line-for-line parallels from stanza to stanza.

WHEN I HEARD THE LEARN'D ASTRONOMER

1. What ironical meaning does "learn'd" have in this poem?

2. In what sense does Whitman become "tired and sick"? Can you recall reading any other poem that parallels somewhat the mood described here?

3. Is this poem relevant today? Why or why not?

BEAT! BEAT! DRUMS!

1. In what way is the rhythm of "Beat! Beat! Drums!" appropriate to the theme of this poem? Illustrate your answer with references to specific lines. What is the prevailing tone?

2. What effects of war upon civilian life are especially emphasized? Which of the effects mentioned seem to you the most devastating?

THE CAROL OF DEATH

1. Is the tone of "The Carol of Death" prevailingly mournful or consoling? Contrast this tone with that of the preceding poem.

2. How does this picture of death compare with those given by Bryant in "Thanatopsis" (page 507) and with other poems on death you have read?

THOU MOTHER WITH THY EQUAL BROOD

1. What genuine hope does Whitman have for democracy? What real responsibilities must it bear?

2. Find lines that show that Whitman is both laudatory and critical of democracy. Point out how Whitman is both nationalistic and world-minded.

IN REVIEW

1. What subjects primarily interested Whitman? List them in your own words. Which of the interests did he share with Longfellow, Lowell, and Whittier? Which ones were new in American poetry?

2. Considering both theme and poetic style, what is your own reaction to Whitman's poetry? Do you feel that his poetry is, or eventually will become, a poetry for the people?

3. In what ways does Whitman's use of meter and line and stanza patterns differ from that of more conventional poets? What connection do you see between his poetic style and the usual themes or subjects of his poetry? Find evidence of a loose sort of pattern based on parallels and repetitions.

4. Why do you think Whitman is often called "the poet of democracy"? Point out evidence from these poems of his democratic beliefs. In this respect, what modern poets does he remind you of?

6. One of Whitman's special attractions is his gift for magnificent short descriptive phrases. Collect a series of such phrases from these poems, dealing with a sufficient variety of subjects to give an accurate impression of his interests.

RELATING WHAT YOU READ

Read or reread Sandburg's *The People Speak* (page 300). How does it compare with what you have read from Whitman?

YOUR OWN WRITING

1. Look back at "I Hear America Singing." What other types of people would you add to bring the picture up to date? Try to write lines about them that fit into the general pattern of the poem.

2. Notice, in "Mannahatta," how Whitman likes to list or "catalogue" details. Then think of the characteristics of your own community, and try writing a similar picture of it in rhythmic free verse.

FURTHER READING

Read all of "When Lilacs Last in the Dooryard Bloom'd," from which "The Carol of Death" is taken, and reread "O Captain, My Captain!" — which you doubtless already know. In comparing these two poems, what marked differences do you find in the whole treatment of the death of Lincoln?

SIDNEY
LANIER

1842–1881

Both Walt Whitman and Sidney Lanier have great bridges named for them, appropriate memorials for poets who were bridges between two great eras of poetry. Whitman's bridge is across the Delaware River, not far from Camden, New Jersey, where the poet's last years were spent. The Lanier bridge is a soaring arch over the lovely Georgia sea marshes that the poet celebrated in his most famous poem, "The Marshes of Glynn."

Sidney Lanier grew up in Macon, Georgia, graduated from Oglethorpe College, and enlisted in the Confederate army at the outbreak of the War Between the States. He was captured and spent the last five months of the war in a Federal prison. The imprisonment drastically weakened his already fragile health. At thirty-nine, he died of tuberculosis. Before his death, however, Lanier gave voice to a new generation of the South and proclaimed its place in our literature. Lanier, the first important postwar Southern writer, was a spokesman not of regional but of national vision. His early long poem "Corn" celebrated all America, taking the farm as the symbol of the nation. "Corn," "Psalm of the West," "The Symphony," and "Song of the Chattahoochee," rank with "The Marshes of Glynn" as Lanier's major poems. In addition, he wrote a novel, *Tiger Lilies* (1867), and a popular retelling of the Arthurian legend for young readers.

Lanier was a gifted musician as well as a brilliant poet, and his musical talents led to his experiments with new forms of verse. He attempted to draw the arts of music and poetry closer together, not by setting words to music in traditional ways, but by seeking to bring the structure of entire poems closer to the forms of music. He outlined his methods in *The Science of English Verse,* a highly original study of poetic techniques.

Lanier's early death cut short a career of great promise. Had he lived, he might have done even more to relate the arts of poetry and music. Yet there is much to admire in the few poems he left us.

Lanier's two great loves were for music and for the outdoor scenes of his native Georgia. He combines the two in the following poem, "Song of the Chattahoochee," as he describes the swift course of a river with rhythms that echo the movement of the water. All the devices that make for melody in poetry — alliteration, rhyme, repetition — share in creating the music of this poem.

Song of the Chattahoochee

Out of the hills of Habersham,°
    Down the valleys of Hall,°
I hurry amain° to reach the plain,
Run the rapid and leap the fall,
Split at the rock and together again,   5
Accept my bed, or narrow or wide,
And flee from folly on every side
With a lover's pain to attain the plain
Far from the hills of Habersham,
    Far from the valleys of Hall.   10

    All down the hills of Habersham,
    All through the valleys of Hall,
The rushes cried, *Abide, abide,*
The willful waterweeds held me thrall,°
The laving laurel turned my tide,   15
The ferns and the fondling grass said *Stay,*
The dewberry dipped for to work delay,
And the little reeds sighed, *Abide, abide,*
    Here in the hills of Habersham,
    Here in the valleys of Hall.   20

    High o'er the hills of Habersham,
    Veiling the valleys of Hall,
The hickory told me manifold°
Fair tales of shade, the poplar tall
Wrought me her shadowy self to hold,   25
The chestnut, the oak, the walnut, the pine,
Overleaning, with flickering meaning and sign,
Said, *Pass not, so cold, these manifold*
    Deep shades of the hills of Habersham,
    These glades in the valleys of Hall.   30

    And oft in the hills of Habersham,
    And oft in the valleys of Hall,
The white quartz shone, and the smooth brook-stone
Did bar me of passage with friendly brawl,
And many a luminous jewel lone   35
— Crystals clear or a-cloud with mist,
Ruby, garnet, and amethyst —
Made lures with the lights of streaming stone
    In the clefts of the hills of Habersham,
    In the beds of the valleys of Hall.   40

1–2. **Habersham** and **Hall**: counties in Lanier's native state of Georgia. 3. **amain** (*á·mān'*): at full speed. 14. **thrall** (thrôl): enslaved. 23. **manifold**: plentiful and varied, as in "our *manifold* benefits."

"Song of the Chattahoochee" by Sidney Lanier. Reprinted by permission of Charles Scribner's Sons.

But oh, not the hills of Habersham,
And oh, not the valleys of Hall
Avail: I am fain° for to water the plain.
Downward the voices of Duty call —
Downward, to toil and be mixed with the main;°   45
The dry fields burn, and the mills are to turn,
And a mryiad flowers mortally yearn,
And the lordly main from beyond the plain
   Calls o'er the hills of Habersham,
   Calls through the valleys of Hall.   50

43. **I am fain:** poetic for "I desire" or "I wish." 45. **main:** poetic for the sea.

Strong religious feeling appears in many of Lanier's poems. "A Ballad of Trees and the Master" is a striking and original conception of Christ's experience in the Garden of Gethsemane, the scene of His agony and arrest. Vividly and memorably the poet's imagination makes us see the Biblical story in a new light. The poem has several musical settings and is often sung by church choirs.

A Ballad of Trees and the Master

Into the woods my Master went,
Clean forspent, forspent.°
Into the woods my Master came,
Forspent with love and shame.
But the olives they were not blind to Him,   5
The little gray leaves were kind to Him:
The thorn tree had a mind° to Him
When into the woods He came.

Out of the woods my Master went,
And He was well content.   10
Out of the woods my Master came,
Content with death and shame.°
When Death and Shame would woo Him last,
From under the trees they drew Him last:
'Twas on a tree they slew him — last   15
When out of the woods He came.

2. **clean forspent:** wholly exhausted. 7. **had a mind:** probably, regarded him kindly. 12. **Content . . . shame:** In other words, He was now willing to accept death on the cross.

"A Ballad of Trees and the Master" by Sidney Lanier. Reprinted by permission of Charles Scribner's Sons.

A glance will reveal that "The Marshes of Glynn" is not a poem of regular lines and set pattern. The poetry Lanier created to express the beauty of the seaside marshes is not the neat melody of a song but the flowing sweep of a symphony. A song composed of short, regular lines might portray a carefully laid out garden, but not the wild magnificence of the marshes.

Long descriptive passages preface each statement of the feelings the marshes stir in the poet. To help you follow the thought, marginal notes guide you to the main point of each section. Using these notes to keep the thought development clear, you can enjoy fully the imagery and melody of each descriptive passage and share the moods that lead the poet from weariness and doubt to serene confidence.

This is not an easy poem, but it is a great one. Read it slowly the first time to understand it. Then read it again more rapidly, preferably aloud, to blend music and imagery, mood and thought, into one splendid poetic experience.

The Marshes of Glynn

The poet addresses the deep tangled shadows amid the live oaks, seeing in them a retreat for lovers,

Glooms of the live oaks, beautiful-braided and woven
With intricate shades of the vines that myriad-cloven°
Chamber the forks of the multiform boughs —
    Emerald twilights —
    Virginal shy lights,   5
Wrought of the leaves to allure to the whisper of vows,
When lovers pace timidly down through the green colonnades°
Of the dim sweet woods, of the dear dark woods,
    Of the heavenly woods and glades,
That run to the radiant marginal sand beach within   10
    The wide sea-marshes of Glynn —

and seeing in them a quiet retreat for prayer and solitary thought.

Beautiful glooms, soft dusks in the noonday fire —
Wildwood privacies, closets of lone desire,
Chamber from chamber parted with wavering arras° of leaves —
Cells° for the passionate pleasure of prayer for the soul that
    grieves,   15
Pure with a sense of the passing of saints through the wood,
Cool for the dutiful weighing of ill with good —

Through the heat of a June day, he has relaxed in the shadows.

O braided dusks of the oak and woven shades of the vine,
While the riotous noonday sun of the June day long did shine
Ye held me fast in your heart and I held you fast in mine;   20
But now when the noon is no more, and riot is rest,
And the sun is await at the ponderous gate of the West,

2. **myriad-cloven:** divided into a great number of parts. 7. **colonnades** (kŏl'ŏ-nādz'): lines of columns placed at regular intervals; the term is often used metaphorically, as it is here, to describe the appearance of a wood. 14. **arras** (ăr'ăs): tapestry. 15. **cells:** small rooms in monasteries or convents.

At evening he is rested from the cares of the world and strong against fear, no longer weary and afraid of great spaces.

And the slant yellow beam down the wood aisle doth seem
Like a lane into heaven that leads from a dream —
Ay, now, when my soul all day hath drunken the soul of the oak,
And my heart is at ease from men, and the wearisome sound of
    the stroke   26
    Of the scythe of time, and the trowel of trade is low,
    And belief overmasters doubt, and I know that I know,
    And my spirit is grown to a lordly great compass within,
That the length and the breadth and the sweep of the marshes of
    Glynn   30
Will work me no fear like the fear they have wrought me of yore
When length was fatigue, and when breadth was but bitterness
    sore,
And when terror and shrinking and dreary unnamable pain
Drew over me out of the merciless miles of the plain —

So he steps out confidently from the protecting woods to the open sweep of the marshes.

Oh, now, unafraid, I am fain to face   35
    The vast sweet visage of space.
To the edge of the wood I am drawn, I am drawn,
Where the gray beach glimmering runs, as a belt of the dawn,
    For a mete° and a mark
    To the forest dark —   40
        So:
Affable live oak, bending low —
Thus — with your favor — soft, with a reverent hand,
(Not lightly touching your person, Lord of the land!)
Bending your beauty aside, with a step I stand   45
On the firm-packed sand,
      Free
By a world of marsh that borders a world of sea.

He rejoices in the wide panorama of curving marshes and sea.

    Sinuous southward and sinuous northward the shimmering
      band
    Of the sand beach fastens the fringe of the marsh to the folds
      of the land.   50
Inward and outward to northward and southward the beach lines
    linger and curl
As a silver-wrought garment that clings to and follows the firm
    sweet limbs of a girl.
Vanishing, swerving, evermore curving again into sight,
Softly the sand beach wavers away to a dim gray looping of light.
And what if behind me to westward the wall of the woods stands
    high?   55
The world lies east: how ample, the marsh and the sea and the
    sky!
A league and a league of marsh grass, waist-high, broad in the
    blade,
Green, and all of a height, and unflecked with a light or a shade,
Stretch leisurely off, in a pleasant plain,
To the terminal° blue of the main.   60

    39. mete: boundary. 60. terminal: here, forming a boundary.

SIDNEY LANIER   747

Oh, what is abroad in the marsh and the terminal sea?
       Somehow my soul seems suddenly free

His soul is freed
of its care by the
sweeping views.

From the weighing of fate and the sad discussion of sin,
By the length and the breadth and the sweep of the marshes of
     Glynn.

The marshes
seem open, serene
and confident,
like a man who
has won greatness
of soul after
suffering and is
in harmony with
God.

Ye marshes, how candid and simple and nothing withholding and
     free   65
Ye publish yourselves to the sky and offer yourselves to the sea!
Tolerant plains, that suffer the sea and the rains and the sun,
Ye spread and span like the catholic° man who hath mightily won
God out of knowledge and good out of infinite pain
And sight out of blindness and purity out of a stain.   70

The poet resolves
to find refuge
and strength in
the greatness of
God, which he
senses in the
greatness of the
marshes.

As the marsh hen secretly builds on the watery sod,
Behold I will build me a nest on the greatness of God:
I will fly in the greatness of God as the marsh hen flies
In the freedom that fills all the space 'twixt the marsh and the
     skies:
By so many roots as the marsh grass sends in the sod   75
I will heartily lay me ahold on the greatness of God:
Oh, like to the greatness of God is the greatness within
The range of the marshes, the liberal marshes of Glynn.

The sea comes
in with the rising
tide, and the sun
goes down.

And the sea lends large, as the marsh: lo, out of his plenty the sea
Pours fast: full soon the time of the flood tide must be: 80
Look how the grace of the sea doth go
About and about through the intricate channels that flow
       Here and there,
           Everywhere,
Till his waters have flooded the uttermost creeks and the low-lying
     lanes,
                                                                  85
And the marsh is meshed with a million veins,
That like as with rosy and silvery essences flow
       In the rose-and-silver evening glow.
           Farewell, my lord Sun!
The creeks overflow: a thousand rivulets run   90
'Twixt the roots of the sod; the blades of the marsh grass stir;
Passeth a hurrying sound of wings that westward whir,
Passeth, and all is still; and the currents cease to run;
And the sea and the marsh are one.

How still the plains of the waters be!   95
The tide is in his ecstasy;
The tide is at his highest height;
       And it is night.

68. **catholic:** universal.

And now from the Vast of the Lord will the waters of sleep
Roll in on the souls of men,   100
But who will reveal to our waking ken°
The forms that swim and the shapes that creep
    Under the waters of sleep?
And I would I could know what swimmeth below when the tide
    comes in   104
On the length and the breadth of the marvelous marshes of Glynn.

101. **ken:** understanding.

FOR DISCUSSION

SONG OF THE CHATTAHOOCHEE

1. Observe how neatly this poem is organized, with the second, third, and fourth stanzas each offering a different kind of temptation to linger. Point out the topic of each stanza.

2. Why must the river rush on to the plain? No direct moral is expressed, but the last stanza suggests a comparison with man's life. What is it?

3. The rhythm and music recall what other American poet whose work you have read? Is a mood evoked? If so, how would you describe it?

A BALLAD OF TREES AND THE MASTER

Why was Christ "forspent" when He went into the woods? Why was He "content with death and shame" when He came out of the woods? How is the repeated mention of trees brought to a climax at the end?

THE MARSHES OF GLYNN

1. What are your chief impressions of the wooded parts of the marshes? What mood did they create in the poet? Can you find any clues to the source of the weariness and fear from which he fled to the woods?

2. State your dominant impression of the grassy plain beyond the woods. What pictures remain in your mind? What resolve formed in the poet's mind as he looked over the wide stretches?

3. Describe the coming in of the tide. How is sleep like a tide sweeping over the souls of men? What do you think the poet means by the following lines?

The forms that swim and the shapes that creep
    Under the waters of sleep

4. Find passages that have a particularly musical sound. Give examples of internal rhyme and alliteration that contribute to the music.

PATTERNS OF POETRY

Make a chart of the rhymed words in one stanza of "Song of the Chattahoochee" to show how intricate the pattern is. Be sure to show the internal rhymes (a word in the center of a line rhyming with the end word). Do all the stanzas follow the same pattern? Find examples of alliteration. What are the slight variations in the refrain at the end of each stanza? Why is this variation more effective than identical refrains would be?

FURTHER READING

Read Alfred Tennyson's "The Brook," with which "Song of the Chattahoochee" is often compared. How are the poems alike? How different? Which rhythm do you prefer? Which thought?

POETIC NAMES

Place names of Indian origin, like "Chattahoochee," are often flowing and musical. Are there any in your state that would fit into poems? Try putting several of them together to make musical lines. In this connection, you will enjoy reading Stephen Vincent Benét's poem "American Names."

SIDNEY LANIER   749

EMILY DICKINSON

1830–1886

This shy New England woman, at the opposite extreme of temperament from Walt Whitman, shares with him the distinction of being a major forerunner of modern poetry. Unlike Whitman, who rejoiced to sound his "barbaric yawp," Emily Dickinson is a prime example of the poet of privacy. To borrow some of her own words, she is the soul that

>. . . Selects her own society
>Then shuts the door . . .

Her poems were not written to court fame, to proclaim herself to the world. Nor, in the ordinary sense, were her poems written to share herself with others.

>How dreary to be somebody!
> How public like a frog
>To tell your name the livelong day
> To an admiring bog!

The poems are the direct expressions of her mind and heart, communicated to herself in a long solitude of reflection. The result is an extremely personal body of work, which, except for four early poems, was published only after her death.

The details of her life are as elusive as the meaning of some of her poems. Some facts are clear enough. She was born in 1830, and grew up in an imposing house that still stands in Amherst, Massachusetts. Her father, Edward Dickinson, was a prominent lawyer, wealthy, with a formidable bearing and a temperament that reflected the stern side of the Puritan heritage. Emily was dominated by him, yet it is clear that she loved him. Her life was ordered, even rigidly formal, but Emily had friends and lived much like any other young woman of her time. Despite her somber surroundings, she was a lively, fun-loving girl. She received an excellent education at Amherst Academy and Mount Holyoke College. While still a young woman, however, Emily Dickinson became a recluse.

For whatever reasons — the question has been debated often, and many theories have been offered — in her early twenties Emily began to withdraw from ordinary contacts with the world. For the remaining thirty years of her life, she was seldom seen outside the large house in Amherst, unless glimpsed in the evening walking in the garden. Precisely what caused her withdrawal is still a mystery. The problem preoccupied biographers and led to an intense study not only of the poems but also of her many letters. Every scrap of evidence and testimony was examined and discussed. The evidence led to much speculation, most of it unsound and romantic, but dramatic enough to make her life the source of three modern plays and a number of biographical studies.

In the upper rooms which she made her own, she was not idle. She occupied her long hours with extensive correspondence with several friends, and with the writing of a large number of remarkable poems. The poetry is uneven in quality, occasionally marred by carelessness, and sometimes almost too cryptic to communicate to the reader. Many poems are simply fragments, never meant to be published. The majority of the poems are so fine, however, that Emily Dickinson's place as a major poet is firm. Several modern critics have called her the greatest woman poet in our language.

Some of her poems were shown to members of her family, or were sent in letters to her friends. Most of them, however, were found in bundles in her rooms after her death — over 1,200 poems in all. As early as 1890 the first selection was published, but not until 1955 did a supposedly complete edition appear.

Emily Dickinson's personality can be as mystifying as the details of her life. Shut off from much of life, she was nevertheless a playful humorist and a daring thinker. Though the voice in her poems is soft, the thought is strong. Though the life of the poet was solitary, her vision penetrated the patterns of existence. Her mind played freshly with ideas. Her skill in packing her lines with cryptic meanings appeals strongly to modern readers. She loved to return to the same subjects, taking a playful second or third look and often finding a humorous contradiction. It is sometimes interesting to set one poem against another, such as "I Never Saw a Moor," which is a strong affirmation, and "Faith Is a Fine Invention," which contains a wry reservation. The contrast is typical.

It is difficult to guess how directly the fabric of Emily Dickinson's life is woven into her poetry. It is clear that we cannot explain either her poems or her life in terms of a single emotional crisis, as many biographers have tried to do. Like all great poets, Emily Dickinson drew on her imagination and vision, as well as her personal experiences, in creating her poems.

Images, impressions of the senses expressed through words, are the very heart of poetry. Emily Dickinson was a master of the fresh, startling image. It is through this quality, and through the compression and the unusual rhythmic patterns of her poetry, that Emily Dickinson takes her place as a poet of "new directions." Hers is clearly a modern voice.

I Never Saw a Moor

I never saw a moor,
   I never saw the sea;
Yet know I how the heather looks,
   And what a wave must be.

I never spoke with God,   5
   Nor visited in heaven;
Yet certain am I of the spot
   As if the chart were given.

"I Never Saw a Moor" by Emily Dickinson. Reprinted by permission of Little, Brown and Company.

How Happy Is the Little Stone

How happy is the little stone
That rambles in the road alone,
And doesn't care about careers,
And exigencies° never fears;
Whose coat of elemental brown   5
A passing universe put on;
And independent as the sun,
Associates or glows alone,
Fulfilling absolute decree
In casual simplicity.   10

4. **exigencies** (ĕk′sĭ·jĕn·sĭz): needs or requirements.

My Life Closed Twice

My life closed twice before its close;
   It yet remains to see
If Immortality unveil
   A third event to me,

So huge, so hopeless to conceive, 5
   As these that twice befell.
Parting is all we know of heaven,
   And all we need of hell.

I'm Nobody

I'm nobody! Who are you?
   Are you nobody, too?
Then there's a pair of us — don't tell!
   They'd banish us, you know.

How dreary to be somebody!   5
   How public like a frog
To tell your name the livelong day
   To an admiring bog!

The Sky Is Low

The sky is low, the clouds are mean,
A traveling flake of snow
Across a barn or through a rut
Debates if it will go.

A narrow wind complains all day   5
How someone treated him.
Nature, like us, is sometimes caught
Without her diadem.

Success Is Counted Sweetest

Success is counted sweetest
By those who ne'er succeed.
To comprehend a nectar
Requires sorest need.

Not one of all the purple host   5
Who took the flag today
Can tell the definition,
So clear, of victory,

As he, defeated, dying,
On whose forbidden ear   10
The distant strains of triumph
Break, agonized and clear.

A Word

A word is dead
When it is said,
    Some say.
I say it just
Begins to live
    That day. `

Faith Is a Fine Invention

Faith is a fine invention
For gentlemen who see;
But microscopes are prudent
In an emergency!

There Is No Frigate like a Book

There is no frigate like a book
  To take us lands away,
Nor any coursers° like a page
  Of prancing poetry.
This traverse may the poorest take   5
  Without oppress of toll;
How frugal is the chariot
  That bears a human soul!

3. coursers (kōr′sẽrz): swift horses.

The Bustle in a House

The bustle in a house
The morning after death
Is solemnest of industries
Enacted upon earth —

The sweeping up the heart,   5
And putting love away
We shall not want to use again
Until eternity.

"Success Is Counted Sweetest," "A Word," "Faith Is a Fine Invention," "There Is No Frigate like a Book," and "The Bustle in a House" from *Poems by Emily Dickinson*, edited by Martha Dickinson Bianchi and Alfred Leete Hampson. Reprinted by permission of Little, Brown and Company.

EMILY DICKINSON   753

Some Keep the Sabbath

Some keep the Sabbath going to
    church;
  I keep it staying at home,
With a bobolink for a chorister,
  And an orchard for a dome.

Some keep the Sabbath in surplice;°   5
  I just wear my wings;
And instead of tolling the bell for
    church,
  Our little sexton sings.

God preaches — a noted clergyman —
  And the sermon is never long;   10
So instead of getting to heaven at last,
  I'm going all along!

5. surplice (sûr′plĭs): a white vestment worn by Roman Catholic and Anglican clergymen.

If I Can Stop One Heart from Breaking

If I can stop one heart from breaking,
I shall not live in vain;
If I can ease one life the aching,
Or cool one pain,
Or help one fainting robin   5
Unto his nest again,
I shall not live in vain.

"Some Keep the Sabbath" and "If I Can Stop One Heart from Breaking" from *Poems by Emily Dickinson,* edited by Martha Dickinson Bianchi and Alfred Leete Hampson. Reprinted by permission of Little, Brown and Company.

FOR DISCUSSION

1. For each poem, interpret the meaning in a sentence or two. Do you find the poems hard or easy to understand? Do members of the class disagree about the meaning of any?

2. From these poems, how much can you learn of Emily Dickinson's attitude toward society? religion? nature? Do her attitudes seem consistent, or are they sometimes contradictory?

3. Select some phrases that seem especially original. Study the last line of each poem. What characteristic do they all have in common?

4. Her use of figures of speech is particularly interesting. How many can you find in this group of short poems? Interpret four or five of the best ones.

5. What attention does the poet pay to adjectives? Does she use few or many? Point out examples of the vivid use of verbs and nouns.

6. Compare Emily Dickinson's poetry to Walt Whitman's. There are many obvious contrasts, but can you find some ways in which the two poets are similar?

THE CLEAR, SHARP WORD

One of the goals of a group of American poets called the Imagists was to search for the sharp, clear word or phrase that might do the work of a sentence.

Emily Dickinson has sometimes been called the first of the Imagists. Her economy of words has influenced many moderns. In addition, she often packs a surprise punch into a word or phrase. From her "I'm Nobody," recall the line "How public like a frog." Is the association an appropriate one? a novel one? Are you able to restate this notion easily in your own words? Try it. Is your version longer? Is it clearer?

In the lyric "The Bustle in a House," notice how much is said by the word *industries.* The reader comes upon the word unexpectedly. How does the poet continue the imagery? Find other examples of Emily Dickinson's use of the right, the original, the meaningful word.

FURTHER READING

1. Since Emily Dickinson's poems have no titles except part or all of their first lines, the best way to recommend further reading of her work is simply to say, "Get a volume of her poems, and go on an exploring expedition."

2. An excellent biography of the poet is *Emily Dickinson, An Interpretive Biography,* by Thomas H. Johnson (Harvard Univ. Press, 1955).

EDWIN
ARLINGTON
ROBINSON

1869–1935

One of the most productive of the new poets grew up in Gardiner, Maine, in the late years of the nineteenth century. Gardiner later became "Tilbury Town," the title of an early collection of Robinson's poetry, and the background for a series of vivid character sketches in verse.

Edwin Arlington Robinson was born in 1869 in the village of Head Tide, Maine. He graduated from high school in Gardiner, entered Harvard, then left two years later to devote his life to poetry.

Robinson began his career as a poet in bleakness and poverty. He lived in difficult circumstances in New York City, working at various odd jobs. Some time around 1904 one of his early books, *Captain Craig,* came to the attention of President Theodore Roosevelt. The President, learning of the poet's difficulties, in 1905 gave Robinson a clerk's job in the customhouse in New York. It was a position similar to the one that Herman Melville had held just a few years earlier. The position was not a particularly high-paying one, but the new job had the desired effect of allowing Robinson to devote much more of his time to poetry.

In the following years, Robinson's powerful, realistic poems continued to impress a growing audience. By 1910 he was able to devote himself completely to writing. He produced a large body of work, became one of our most widely read poets, and was honored with the Pulitzer prize in 1922, 1925, and 1928.

Robinson's approach to characterization, and his diction and themes, reflect the new movements in poetry. "Richard Cory" and "Miniver Cheevy" are good examples of his realistic attitudes. Among his later poems, one of the finest is a brilliant commentary on Shakespeare's character called "Ben Jonson Entertains a Man from Stratford." Robinson was also interested in the Arthurian legends, and in his long works *Merlin, Lancelot,* and *Tristram,* he wrote the most extensive poems based on these stories since Tennyson. While the English poet dwelt mainly on the pageantry and romance of King Arthur's court, Robinson typically explored the dark, hidden faults in human character that led to the decline and fall of the Round Table.

Robinson's poems sometimes appear to be simple, yet the surface simplicity often serves to conceal an intricacy and subtlety of thought. Like Robert Frost, Robinson was also noted for his use of a dry, sometimes biting, New England humor. Robinson's skill as a poet has continued to earn even greater praise in recent years.

Here in the formal structure of a sonnet, Edwin Arlington Robinson criticizes the poets of his own age, "these little sonnet-men," unfeeling, assembly-line writers.

Oh for a Poet

Oh for a poet — for a beacon bright
To rift this changeless glimmer of dead gray;
To spirit back the Muses, long astray,
And flush Parnassus with a newer light;
To put these little sonnet-men to flight   5
Who fashion, in a shrewd mechanic way,
Songs without souls, that flicker for a day,
To vanish in irrevocable night.

What does it mean, this barren age of ours?
Here are the men, the women, and the flowers,   10
The seasons, and the sunset, as before.
What does it mean? Shall there not one arise
To wrench one banner from the western skies,
And mark it with his name forevermore?

In his exploration of human character, Robinson found many puzzles and contradictions, as he does in "Richard Cory."

Richard Cory

Whenever Richard Cory went downtown,
   We people on the pavement looked at him:
He was a gentleman from sole to crown,
   Clean-favored, and imperially slim.

And he was always quietly arrayed,   5
   And he was always human when he talked;
But still he fluttered pulses when he said,
   "Good morning," and he glittered when he walked.

And he was rich — yes, richer than a king —
   And admirably schooled in every grace: 10
In fine, we thought that he was everything
   To make us wish that we were in his place.

So on we worked, and waited for the light,
   And went without the meat, and cursed the bread;
And Richard Cory, one calm summer night,   15
   Went home and put a bullet through his head.

"Oh for a Poet" from *The Children of the Night* by Edwin Arlington Robinson. Reprinted by permission of Charles Scribner's Sons.
"Richard Cory" by Edwin Arlington Robinson. Reprinted by permission of Charles Scribner's Sons.

Miniver Cheevy is a very different person from Richard Cory. Don't miss the humor in this devastating portrait of a man who would be a hero as of old!

Miniver Cheevy

Miniver Cheevy, child of scorn,
　Grew lean while he assailed the sea-
　　sons;
He wept that he was ever born,
　And he had reasons.

Miniver loved the days of old　　5
　When swords were bright and steeds
　　were prancing;
The vision of a warrior bold
　Would set him dancing.

Miniver sighed for what was not,
　And dreamed, and rested from his
　　labors;　　　　　　　　　　10
He dreamed of Thebes° and Camelot,°
　And Priam's° neighbors.

Miniver mourned the ripe renown
　That made so many a name so frag-
　　rant;
He mourned Romance, now on the
　town,　　　　　　　　　　　15

And Art, a vagrant.

Miniver loved the Medici,°
　Albeit° he had never seen one;
He would have sinned incessantly
　Could he have been one.　　　20

Miniver cursed the commonplace
　And eyed a khaki suit with loathing;
He missed the medieval grace
　Of iron clothing.

Miniver scorned the gold he sought,　25
　But sore annoyed was he without it;
Miniver thought, and thought, and
　　thought,
　And thought about it.

Miniver Cheevy, born too late,
　Scratched his head and kept on think-
　　ing;　　　　　　　　　　　30
Miniver coughed, and called it fate,
　And kept on drinking.

11. **Thebes** (thēbz): a famous city of ancient Greece. **Camelot** (kăm'ĕ·lŏt): the city of King Arthur and the Knights of the Round Table. 12. **Priam** (prī'ăm): the king of Troy during the time the Greeks were besieging it.

17. **Medici** (mĕd'ê·chê): a highly cultivated but often unprincipled family of Florence, Italy, that flourished during the fifteenth and sixteenth centuries. 18. **Albeit** (ôl·bē'ĭt): although.

"An Old Story" describes a relationship between two persons. Why do you think the poet chose this title for the poem?

An Old Story

Strange that I did not know him then,
　That friend of mine!
I did not even show him then
　One friendly sign;

But cursed him for the ways he had　5
　To make me see

My envy of the praise he had
　For praising me.

I would have rid the earth of him
　Once in my pride! . . .　　　　10
I never knew the worth of him
　Until he died.

"Miniver Cheevy" by Edwin Arlington Robinson. Reprinted by permission of Charles Scribner's Sons. "An Old Story" from *The Children of the Night* by Edwin Arlington Robinson. Reprinted by permission of Charles Scribner's Sons.

EDWIN ARLINGTON ROBINSON

It is hard for us to realize today that few great men have been more hated and ridiculed than Abraham Lincoln was during his lifetime. See what opinion of Lincoln the poet has given the speaker in the next poem. If you need help with the mythological allusions, consult the study aid on page 759.

The Master

A flying word from here and there
Had sown the name at which we
    sneered,
But soon the name was everywhere,
To be reviled and then revered:
A presence to be loved and feared — 5
We cannot hide it, or deny
That we, the gentlemen who jeered,
May be forgotten by and by.

He came when days were perilous
And hearts of men were sore be-
    guiled;   10
And having made his note of us,
He pondered and was reconciled.
Was ever master yet so mild
As he, and so untamable?
We doubted, even when he smiled, 15
Not knowing what he knew so well.

He knew that undeceiving fate
Would shame us whom he served un-
    fought;   20
He knew that he must wince and wait —
The jest of those for whom he
    fought;   20
He knew devoutly what he thought
Of us and of our ridicule;
He knew that we must all be taught
Like little children in a school.

We gave a glamour to the task   25
That he encountered and saw through,
But little of us did he ask,
And little did we ever do.
And what appears if we review
The season when we railed and
    chaffed?   30
It is the face of one who knew
That we were learning while we
    laughed.

The face that in our vision feels
Again the venom that we flung,
Transfigured to the world reveals 35
The vigilance to which we clung.
Shrewd, hallowed, harassed, and among
The mysteries that are untold,
The face we see was never young,
Nor could it wholly have been old. 40

For he, to whom we had applied
Our shopman's test of age and worth,
Was elemental when he died,
As he was ancient at his birth:
The saddest among kings of earth, 45
Bowed with a galling crown, this man
Met rancor with a cryptic mirth,
Laconic — and Olympian.

The love, the grandeur, and the fame
Are bounded by the world alone; 50
The calm, the smoldering, and the
    flame
Of awful patience were his own:
With him they are forever flown
Past all our fond self-shadowings,
Wherewith we cumber° the Un-
    known   55
As with inept Icarian wings.

For we were not as other men:
'Twas ours to soar and his to see;
But we are coming down again,
And we shall come down pleasantly; 60
Nor shall we longer disagree
On what it is to be sublime,
But flourish in our perigee°
And have one Titan at a time.

55. **cumber:** burden. 63. **perigee** (pĕr'ĭ·jē): that point in the orbit of the moon nearest to the earth; here, metaphorically, lowness or baseness.

FOR DISCUSSION

OH FOR A POET

1. What is Robinson's criticism of the writers of his age? Is his criticism still applicable to our own time?

2. The poem is written in sonnet form. How does this fact add to the irony?

RICHARD CORY

1. What are possible causes for Richard's suicide? Why do you suppose Robinson did not himself supply the reason for Cory's desperate act?

2. What bit of philosophy about life does this poem suggest to your mind? What does Richard Cory's fate suggest about people's inner and outer lives?

3. Give in your own words the meaning of the first two lines of the last stanza.

MINIVER CHEEVY

1. Point out the lines in this poem that you found particularly amusing. How does the rhyme pattern add to the playful tone of the poem?

2. What is the real trouble with Miniver? What kinds of people do you know who spend their energies longing for "the good old days"? Discuss whether or not romance and adventure are to be found only in the past.

3. What conditions in modern life tend to produce men like Richard Cory and Miniver Cheevy?

AN OLD STORY

1. What is the significance of the title?

2. Explain in your own words the reason for the speaker's jealousy. Try to put into exact language your reasons for disliking someone. Discuss whether your reasons reveal something about you yourself as well as something about the object of your dislike.

THE MASTER

1. What picture of Lincoln — the outer and inner man — emerges from this poem? Cite evidence that Robinson has shown genuine insight in depicting him.

2. The poem is written as a mono-

logue. What did Robinson gain by using this device? What kind of a person is the speaker?

3. What is the nature of your emotional response to this poem?

4. What tragic drama is inherent in the situation as depicted? Does this poem remind you of any of Emerson's essays?

UNDERSTANDING ALLUSIONS

"The Master" gains much of its effect through the use of allusions. Here are explanations for those that occur in the poem. **Laconic** (lȧ·kŏn'ĭk): sparing of words, like the Lacedaemonians of ancient Greece. **Olympian:** like the Greek gods who dwelt on Mount Olympus; grand, imposing. **Icarian** (ī·kâr'ĭ·ăn) from Icarus (ĭk'ȧ·rŭs): soaring too high for safety. In mythology, Icarus, whose father, Daedalus, made him waxen wings, flew too near the sun; the wax melted and the boy fell into the sea. **Titan** (tī'tăn): a giant. The Titans, in Greek mythology, were the earliest of the gods.

RELATING WHAT YOU READ

Compare "The Master" with Vachel Lindsay's "Abraham Lincoln Walks at Midnight" (p. 272). Then read or reread Carl Sandburg's "Lincoln at Gettysburg" on page 226. Do you feel that Robinson and Sandburg share similar attitudes toward Lincoln? Do both writers emphasize the same character traits in speaking of the man?

SYMBOLS

A symbol is something that stands for something else. *Meat* and *bread*, for example, are often used as symbols for food in general. In "Richard Cory" *meat* stands for the more desirable things of life; *bread* stands for the bare necessities. This use of symbols is one of the factors that make poetry richer, denser, more compact than prose.

In the same poem, what does Robinson mean by "the people on the pavement"? Can you find some other symbols in Robinson's poems?

STEPHEN CRANE

1871–1900

Stephen Crane is known primarily as a novelist and short-story writer. (A sketch of his life introduces his short story "The Bride Comes to Yellow Sky" on page 807.) It is important, however, to recognize Crane's accomplishments as a poet. In 1895, reviewing Stephen Crane's first volume of poetry, *The Black Riders,* a critic in the *Nation* said the poems were "Whitman condensed and Dickinson expanded." In general, the remark was accurate. Like Whitman's and Dickinson's, Crane's poetic style was unorthodox and his meaning often obscure and difficult. Like Whitman, Crane seldom used rhyme, and he often seemed to avoid conventional rhythms and the use of words that anyone could possibly label "poetic." However, although Crane occasionally catalogues as Whitman did,

Rumbling wheels, hoof-beats, bells,
Welcomes, farewells, love-calls, final moans,

he seems closer in style to Emily Dickinson. His lines, like hers, are short, and condensed in meaning; the poems are miniature parables. Finally, like the two earlier poets, Crane was far in advance of his time, and his poems foreshadow some of the techniques that were to be used by American poets of the twentieth century.

Crane's poems often resemble his short stories, both in structure and mood. They make a statement, followed by a contradiction, a turning, and a thrust of irony. Are these characteristics apparent in the following poem?

The Book of Wisdom

I met a seer.
He held in his hands
The book of wisdom.
"Sir," I addressed him,
"Let me read."   5
"Child — " he began.
"Sir," I said,
"Think not that I am a child,
For already I know much
Of that which you hold;   10
Aye, much."

He smiled.
Then he opened the book
And held it before me.
Strange that I should have grown so suddenly blind.   15

Think as I Think

"Think as I think," said a man,
"Or you are abominably wicked;
You are a toad."
And after I had thought of it,
I said, "I will, then, be a toad."

There Were Many

There were many who went in huddled
    procession
They knew not whither;
But, at any rate, success or calamity
Would attend all in equality.
There was one who sought a new
    road.   5
He went into direful thickets,
And ultimately he died thus, alone;
But they said he had courage.

Tell Brave Deeds

"Tell brave deeds of war."

Then they recounted tales —
"There were stern stands
And bitter runs for glory."

Ah, I think there were braver deeds.

I Saw a Man

I saw a man pursuing the horizon;
Round and round they sped.
I was disturbed at this;
I accosted the man.
"It is futile," I said,   5
"You can never —"
"You lie," he cried,
And ran on.

"Think as I Think," "There Were Many," "Tell Brave Deeds," "I Saw a Man," reprinted from *The Collected Poems of Stephen Crane* by Stephen Crane, by permission of Alfred A. Knopf, Inc. Copyright 1930 by Alfred A. Knopf, Inc.

The Wayfarer

The wayfarer,
Perceiving the pathway to truth,
Was struck with astonishment.
It was thickly grown with weeds.
"Ha," he said,   5
"I see that none has passed here
In a long time."
Later he saw that each weed
Was a singular knife.
"Well," he mumbled at last,   10
"Doubtless there are other roads."

"The Wayfarer," reprinted from *The Collected Poems of Stephen Crane* by Stephen Crane, by permission of Alfred A. Knopf, Inc. Copyright 1930 by Alfred A. Knopf, Inc.

FOR DISCUSSION

THE BOOK OF WISDOM

1. What is a "seer"?
2. What line marks the turning point of the poem?

THINK AS I THINK

This poem involves a decision on the part of the narrator. Do you approve or disapprove of his decision?

THERE WERE MANY

"But they said he had courage." Is this last line of the poem sincere praise of the man who sought a new road, or is it satirical?

TELL BRAVE DEEDS

What deeds of war may be braver than "stern stands and bitter runs for glory"?

I SAW A MAN

Is the theme of this poem one of hope or despair?

THE WAYFARER

As you read the poem, do you feel that the wayfarer will be successful in finding other roads to truth?

Other Poets in a Time of Change

While Whitman, Dickinson, Robinson, and Crane were radically changing the themes and techniques of poetry, many other poets continued to work in the more traditional forms. In general, such poets as James Whitcomb Riley, Eugene Field, and Edwin Markham were not innovators or leaders in the "New Directions" movement, but their work was extremely popular for many years, and some of their best poems are still read today.

JAMES WHITCOMB RILEY

1849–1916

Like Mark Twain, James Whitcomb Riley, "the Hoosier poet," made a national reputation as a public platform performer — reading from his own verse, interspersed with wit and wisdom. His prosperous father's profession of law was not for him. He "graduated as a house, sign, and ornamental painter," tried acting, and eventually became a country newspaperman, moving on to the Indianapolis *Journal.* That city and its environs became his locale. From early boyhood in Greenfield, Indiana, Riley had a keen ear for the speech of Indiana country people, especially the more eccentric ones among the population. He liked children too, "the rough and tumble kind." These became the material for his famous Hoosier dialect poems, which Riley first claimed were written by a simple and uneducated farmer, a certain "Benj. F. Johnson of Boone, the Hoosier poet." Riley printed letters from "Johnson" to prove that the poems were authentic. "When the Frost Is on the Punkin," one of Riley's best-known poems, needs no introduction. Enjoy it again.

When the Frost Is on the Punkin

When the frost is on the punkin and the fodder's in the shock,
And you hear the kyouck and gobble of the struttin' turkey cock,
And the clackin' of the guineys, and the cluckin' of the hens,
And the rooster's hallylooyer as he tiptocs on the fence;
O, it's then's the time a feller is a-feelin' at his best,   5
With the risin' sun to greet him from a night of peaceful rest,
As he leaves the house, bareheaded, and goes out to feed the stock,
When the frost is on the punkin and the fodder's in the shock.

They's something kindo' harty-like about the atmusfere
When the heat of summer's over and the coolin' fall is here —   10
Of course we miss the flowers, and the blossums on the trees,
And the mumble of the hummin'birds and buzzin' of the bees;
But the air's so appetizin'; and the landscape through the haze
Of a crisp and sunny morning of the airly autumn days
Is a pictur' that no painter has the colorin' to mock —   15
When the frost is on the punkin and the fodder's in the shock.

The husky, rusty russel of the tossels of the corn,
And the raspin' of the tangled leaves, as golden as the morn;
The stubble in the furries — kindo' lonesomelike, but still
A-preachin' sermuns to us of the barns they growed to fill;   20
The strawstack in the medder, and the reaper in the shed;
The hosses in theyr stalls below — the clover overhead! —
O, it sets my hart a-clickin' like the tickin' of a clock,
When the frost is on the punkin and the fodder's in the shock!

Then your apples all is gethered, and the ones a feller keeps   25
Is poured around the celler floor in red and yeller heaps;
And your cider makin's over, and your wimmern folks is through
With theyr mince and apple butter, and theyr souse and sausage, too!
I don't know how to tell it — but ef sich a thing could be
As the Angels wantin' boardin', and they'd call around on *me* —   30
I'd want to 'commodate 'em — all the whole indurin' flock —
When the frost is on the punkin and the fodder's in the shock!

FOR DISCUSSION

1. Be sure you can interpret Riley's dialect to get the meaning, especially in words like "hallylooyer," "furries," "medder."

2. See page 600 for Lowell's use of the New England dialect. How does Riley resemble him? Can you point out examples in Riley of words that are misspelled yet are pronounced as though correctly spelled?

3. Find examples of the poet's appealing to each of the five senses, and of his use of onomatopoeia.

FURTHER READING

Old favorites from Riley include "The Old Man and Jim," "Knee-deep in June," "Wet-Weather Talk," "An Old Sweetheart of Mine," "A Life Lesson," "Out to Old Aunt Mary's," "Little Orphant Annie," "The Raggedy Man."

JAMES WHITCOMB RILEY

EUGENE FIELD

1850–1895

Field has been called the "poet laureate of childhood." He was a witty, eccentric newspaper columnist, and most of his poems were first published in newspapers. His newspaper connections were in St. Louis (his birthplace), Denver, and Chicago. Sentiment and tenderness are apparent in his series of lullabies of all nations and in his best-known poem of childhood, "Little Boy Blue."

Little Boy Blue

The little toy dog is covered with dust,
   But sturdy and staunch he stands;
The little toy soldier is red with rust,
   And his musket molds in his hands.
Time was when the little toy dog was new   5
   And the soldier was passing fair;
And that was the time when our Little Boy Blue
   Kissed them and put them there.

"Now don't you go till I come," he said,
   "And don't you make any noise!"   10
So toddling off to his trundle bed,
   He dreamt of the pretty toys;
And, as he was dreaming, an angel song
   Awakened our Little Boy Blue —
Oh! the years are many, the years are long,   15
   But the little toy friends are true!

Ay, faithful to Little Boy Blue they stand,
   Each in the same old place,
Awaiting the touch of a little hand,
   The smile of a little face;   20
And they wonder, as waiting the long years through,
   In the dust of that little chair,
What has become of our Little Boy Blue
   Since he kissed them and put them there.

FOR DISCUSSION

1. Though "Little Boy Blue" is about a child, why is it definitely a poem for adults rather than children? Notice carefully just how little description of the child Eugene Field has given us. Why did he do this? How do you picture the Little Boy Blue?

2. Compare "Little Boy Blue" to Robert Frost's "Out, Out . . ." (page 255). In what ways do the poems differ? How are they alike? Which poem do you prefer?

EDWIN MARKHAM

1852–1940

During his varied life as farmer, ranch hand, and teacher in Oregon and California, Edwin Markham wrote many poems which won only moderate success up to the time he was forty-seven years old. Then he published "The Man with the Hoe." Coming at a time when there was a great wave of concern about common workers and their hard lot, the poem stirred tremendous interest and made Markham suddenly famous. It has continued to hold a firm place among American poems.

The subtitle explains the origin of the poem. In Millet's (mĭ·lā′) painting, Markham saw the figure of "the landless, the soul-blighted workman of the world; the dumb creature that has no time to rest, no time to think, no time for hopes that make us men." You will find a detail from Millet's painting on page 767.

The Man with the Hoe

Written after Seeing Millet's World-famous Painting
of a Brutalized Toiler in the Deep Abyss of Labor

God made man in His own image; in the image of God made He him. — Genesis.

Bowed by the weight of centuries he leans
Upon his hoe and gazes on the ground,
The emptiness of ages in his face,
And on his back the burden of the world.
Who made him dead to rapture and despair,　　　　　　　　　5
A thing that grieves not and that never hopes,
Stolid and stunned, a brother to the ox?
Who loosened and let down this brutal jaw?
Whose was the hand that slanted back this brow?
Whose breath blew out the light within this brain?　　　　　10

Is this the thing the Lord God made and gave
To have dominion over sea and land;
To trace the stars and search the heavens for power;
To feel the passion of eternity?
Is this the dream He dreamed who shaped the suns　　　　　15
And marked their ways upon the ancient deep?
Down all the caverns of hell to their last gulf

There is no shape more terrible than this —
More tongued with cries against the world's blind greed —
More filled with signs and portents° for the soul —   20
More packed with danger to the universe.

What gulfs between him and the seraphim°!
Slave of the wheel of labor, what to him
Are Plato and the swing of Pleiades°?
What the long reaches of the peaks of song,   25
The rift of dawn, the reddening of the rose?
Through this dread shape the suffering ages look;
Time's tragedy is in that aching stoop;
Through this dread shape humanity betrayed,
Plundered, profaned, and disinherited,   30
Cries protest to the Powers that made the world,
A protest that is also prophecy.

O masters, lords and rulers in all lands,
Is this the handiwork you give to God,
This monstrous thing distorted and soul-quenched?   35
How will you ever straighten up this shape;
Touch it again with immortality;
Give back the upward looking and the light;
Rebuild in it the music and the dream;
Make right the immemorial infamies,   40
Perfidious° wrongs, immedicable° woes?

O masters, lords and rulers in all lands,
How will the future reckon with this man?
How answer his brute question in that hour
When whirlwinds of rebellion shake all shores?   45
How will it be with kingdoms and with kings —
With those who shaped him to the thing he is —
When this dumb Terror shall rise to judge the world,
After the silence of the centuries?

20. **portents** (pōr′těnts): forewarnings. 22. **seraphim** (sěr′ȧ·fĭm): the highest order of angels. 24. **Pleiades** (plē′yȧ·dēz): a group of stars near the constellation Orion. In a Greek myth, the Pleiades were seven daughters of Atlas who were transformed into stars, six of which can be detected with the naked eye. 41. **perfidious** (pẽr·fĭd′ĭ·ŭs): treacherous. **immedicable** (ĭm·měd′ĭ·kȧ·b'l): incurable.

FOR DISCUSSION

1. Point out physical features that create the impression of a crushed being, hardly human. What are some of the things in your own life that this man has never had time or opportunity to enjoy?

2. With what questions does the poem close? To whom are they addressed?

3. Some critics have said that Millet never intended to portray such a hopeless creature, but simply an honest workman resting. Study the copy of the picture, and decide which interpretation you prefer.

4. What relation does this poem bear to our mechanistic civilization? Would you say that the prophecy in it has been fulfilled?

A detail from "The Man with the Hoe," by Jean François Millet (1814–1875).

New Directions in Prose

The great social changes caused by the Industrial Revolution and the growth of our cities drastically altered, for better and worse, many phases of American life. Great changes produce sharp responses. In the new realistic mood of American prose, writers examined our changing society and found much to criticize. Their tone was often biting, and their protests were sharp. The literature of self-criticism, of dissent from popular attitudes, of protest against the way some things were going, was proof that the original spirit of the nation was very much alive. The new mood in literature was a healthy sign, and in many cases it helped contribute to reforms and developments that we now take for granted.

Realism brought new kinds of subject matter, scenes, and characters into literature. The realistic writers dealt with factories and slums, workmen, bosses, corrupt politicians, petty criminals, and social outcasts. They wrote about reformers, political agitators, shopkeepers, businessmen, the rising middle class, and slum dwellers. They examined routine daily experiences and a host of other common concerns. Ordinary people and events began to appear prominently in a literature that had once been dominated by romantic lovers, soldiers, adventurers, men and women of high social standing, or quaint, folksy rural characters. The realists offered stark descriptions of the hardships and poverty that were often a part of farm life. It was impossible to write about the changing age without dealing with all of these new subjects. They were here to stay as a part of the whole range of life that forms the writer's material.

The trend toward realism gathered momentum slowly. Not all those who approached writing with new attitudes were alike. Some were considered radical, while others remained essentially conservative. Yet in all its variations of theme and technique, realism was a widespread development that gained in force and importance throughout the late nineteenth century. While there is no single writer who illustrates all the aspects of the new realism, William Dean Howells is perhaps more representative than anyone else.

WILLIAM DEAN HOWELLS

Howells was not the greatest of our writers, but few writers ever dominated a generation as he did. William Dean Howells was self-educated, beginning with what he learned in his father's printing shop in Ohio, and in the small library in his home. From printing shop to newspaper was a natural step, and Howells, like Franklin, Whittier, Whitman, and Twain, sharpened his literary skills as a journalist. In 1860, after writing a campaign biography of Abraham Lincoln, Howells received a consular post in Venice. The experience opened the world of European languages and literature to him, as similar travel had done for earlier American writers. When he returned to the United States in 1865, he was drawn to Boston by its literary fame. There he joined the staff of the *Atlantic Monthly*. He served as chief editor of the magazine for the years 1871–81.

Howells published a great many novels, travel books, and poems, but his work as a pioneer of realism began in 1882 with the novel *A Modern Instance*. This book was followed in a few years by his greatest novel, *The Rise of Silas Lapham* (1885), a story of a clash between old Boston families and a member of the newly wealthy group of industrialists. Howells' sympathy is with Silas, the man of the new age. The novel pictures a rapidly changing social situation which was bringing new classes to the American scene.

Howells felt that the literary center was shifting from Boston to New York; so in 1885 he went to New York to continue his own writing and to begin an

William Dean Howells

association with *Harper's* Magazine. The New York scene appeared in his next major novel, *A Hazard of New Fortunes* (1890). His three major novels, together with his many other writings, form the most faithful picture in our literature of the middle-class America of Howells' time.

Howells was the leading critic of his day, and, for many years, the chief literary influence in the country. He was a kindly encourager of new writers, with a sharp eye for talent wherever it might be found. He praised and supported the work of such younger men as Stephen Crane, Frank Norris, and Hamlin Garland. Only two years younger than Mark Twain, Howells came to be one of the closest friends of that great writer. His *My Mark Twain*, written in 1910 after Twain's death, is an intimate memoir, providing insight into both men.

SARAH ORNE JEWETT

The Maine coast was the scene of Sarah Orne Jewett's prose sketches and stories. She was the daughter of a rural doctor, and she often rode with her father on his calls. For a perceptive girl there was no better way to gain knowledge of the people and the region. Like the earlier Hawthorne, she was impressed by the decay that struck the coastal towns when their days as active seaports were ended. The effects of this change form one of her major subjects.

Howells was one of the first to hail Miss Jewett's work. She is best remembered for the volume of stories called *The Country of the Pointed Firs* (1896). Her work had a great influence on a young woman far away in Nebraska, Willa Cather (see page 50), who, in a few years, was to become an even more distinguished writer.

Wisconsin born, Hamlin Garland grew up in the prairie regions of Iowa and the Dakotas during the late years of the nineteenth century. He went East to study, and when he came back to the West, he saw prairie life in a fresh light:

> All the gilding of farm life melted away. The hard and bitter realities came back on me in a flood. Nature was as beautiful as ever . . . but no splendor of cloud, no grace of sunset, could conceal the poverty of these people. I perceived life without its glamour.

His short stories, collected in *Main-traveled Roads* (1891), dealt with the harsh farm life of the prairie region which he called the "Middle Border." Garland wrote several novels and various works of nonfiction, many of them concerned with the plight of the farmer. One of his finest books, and one of the best pictures we have of the late West, is his autobiography, *A Son of the Middle Border* (1917).

HENRY JAMES

Henry James was one of the most important writers of his age, and his reputation has continued to grow in this century. Born in New York City in 1843, James was educated both in the United States and in Europe. In 1877, when his career as a writer was just beginning, James chose to make England his permanent home. He continued to make occasional trips to the Continent, and he revisited the United States three or four times during the remaining years of his life. He became a British subject in 1915, one year before his death.

Henry James.

James was a versatile and productive writer. His essays on Hawthorne and Emerson are good examples of thoughtful literary criticism. His shorter fiction, such as *The Turn of the Screw* or *Daisy Miller*, often shows him at his best. His reputation, however, rests chiefly on his longer novels, some of the most important of which are *The Portrait of a Lady* (1881), *Washington Square* (1881), *The Wings of the Dove* (1902), and *The Ambassadors* (1903).

James began as a writer of what he called the "international novel." In his early books the central characters are usually Americans who travel to Europe and in some way come into conflict with the sophisticated European culture. James valued much of what Europe had to offer, but he valued even more highly the moral idealism of America. Significantly, his American characters are often shown as superior to a somewhat tarnished European society. In his later novels James concentrated more and more on relations between individuals, exploring minutely the consciousness of a few central characters, and recording their reactions to one another or to a particular situation. His later novels were sometimes criticized as being unnecessarily involved, yet relations between civilized human beings often are extremely complex, and no one has surpassed James's treatment of such relations.

Henry Adams.

PHILOSOPHERS AND SOCIAL CRITICS

Henry Adams came of a distinguished family; his grandfather and his great-grandfather had been Presidents of the United States, and his father was a congressman and diplomat. He himself was both a novelist and a historian. His best-known book is *The Education of Henry Adams* (1918), an unusual autobiography, written in the third person, which contains many thoughtful comments on the rapidly changing America of the late nineteenth century. His other works include a novel, *Democracy*, and a philosophical history, *Mont-Saint-Michel and Chartres*.

Thorstein Veblen, Gustavus Myers, and Henry George were important political, economic, and social commentators who challenged popular attitudes of their day. One of the most imaginative social critics was Edward Bellamy. His novel *Looking Backward* (1888) expressed Bellamy's ideas of reform by the "time travel" device of leaping forward to the year 2000 and describing the improvements that had occurred by then. *Looking Backward* is probably the finest American example of Utopian literature — the attempt to describe an ideal society — a type of writing that takes its name from an early English book, *Utopia*, by Sir Thomas More. William James, brother of the novelist Henry James, was a distinguished philosopher and pioneer psychologist. His *Varieties of Religious Experience* (1902) is a significant discussion of religious values.

One group of zealous reformers dug so deeply into scandals at the beginning of this century that President Theodore Roosevelt angrily called them "muckrakers." Prominent among such writers were the journalists Ida Tarbell and Lincoln Steffens. Steffens' book *The Shame of the Cities* (1904) is an angry exposure of crime and political corruption in a number of large American cities.

The Changing South

No section of the country changed more rapidly than the South in the years after the war. Two changes were of basic importance. First, the Negro was free and began to take his place in the economy and culture of the section. Negro colleges were training leaders for teaching and the professions. Only fifty years after slavery there were more Negro students in college than there were students in all the colleges and universities of Britain. Their representative in these postwar years was Booker T. Washington, head of Tuskegee Institute, whose *Up from Slavery* is one of the most readable of American autobiographies. The second major change in the South was a rapid industrialization which within a generation transformed this region from a cotton and tobacco economy to one of diversified farming and industry.

Out of these changes came new ideas and new writing. Much of this writing was of the "local-color" variety, but before long a school of realists made an appearance in the South as elsewhere. Its most distinguished spokesman was George Washington Cable of Louisiana. Like Sidney Lanier, Cable had served in the Confederate army and known hardship and sorrow after the war. His work took him into the old records of New Orleans, and there he found material for a long series of stories and novels about Creole Louisiana. His best-known book is the collection of short stories entitled *Old Creole Days* (1879).

In a Lighter Vein

Finley Peter Dunne, a Chicago journalist, published several volumes of humorous monologues by a genial Irishman named Mr. Dooley. Mr. Dooley's witty, satirical opinions became widely popular during the early years of this century. Dunne was the forerunner of a number of newspaper and magazine writers who have used humor for social criticism — men like Will Rogers and, in more recent years, James Thurber and E. B. White.

William Sydney Porter was born in North Carolina and spent a great deal of time in Texas, but through his short stories about "Bagdad-on-the-Subway," he became closely identified with New York City. Under the pen name of O. Henry, he turned out hundreds of short stories and became perhaps the best-liked writer of the early twentieth century. The typical O. Henry story involved laughter, a great deal of sentiment, and a surprise twist at the end. This formula was his trade-mark, and has often been imitated since.

Ambrose Bierce was a journalist and short-story writer with a taste for satirical humor. His *Devil's Dictionary* and *Fantastic Fables* are full of sharp thrusts at human foibles and follies. His short stories, like Poe's, are often concerned with the grim and the mysterious. One of the best examples of his fiction is "An Occurrence at Owl Creek Bridge," from the collection called *In the Midst of Life; Tales of Soldiers and Civilians* (1891).

The Later Realists

The climax of the nineteenth-century realistic movement carried over into our own time. It came with a group of five powerful writers, some of whom had received early encouragement from William Dean Howells.

The life of Stephen Crane, a brilliant writer of both poetry and prose, is discussed in greater detail on pages 806–07. Crane died at twenty-eight, before his talents had come to full flower, yet he probably contributed as much to the realistic movement as any other writer of his time.

Frank Norris (1870–1902), died, like Stephen Crane, before reaching the height of his powers. In his youth, as an art student in Paris, he began writing some undistinguished poetry. It was the great French realist, Émile Zola, who inspired Norris to become a novelist. In common with many of the realistic writers of this time, Norris did some news reporting, including coverage of the Boer War in South Africa and the Spanish-American War. The best of Norris' novels are *McTeague* (1899), a story of poverty in San Francisco; *The Octopus* (1901), about the struggle between California wheat growers and the railroads; and *The Pit* (1903), which deals with high finance and speculation on the wheat exchange in Chicago.

Jack London (1876–1916) had a turbulent, colorful life, and his writings partly reflect his active existence. His realism dealt more with raw, elemental nature than with political or economic events. London's boyhood was harsh, his later youth homeless and sometimes lawless. His experiences included time spent as a seal hunter, as a prospector in the Klondike gold rush, and as a war correspondent both in the Russo-Japanese War and during our own expedition against Pancho Villa in Mexico in 1916. He died shortly after this last assignment. His most popular novels are *The Call of the Wild* (1903), *The Sea-Wolf* (1904), and *Martin Eden* (1909).

Theodore Dreiser (1871–1945) lived to mature his talents. His works extend into the modern period of our literature. His early novels, *Sister Carrie* (1900) and *Jennie Gerhardt* (1911), were both concerned with the role of women in our society. Some of the details of these stories seemed shocking to the readers of the time. His later novel, *An American Tragedy* (1925), dealt with similar subjects but received no such criticism — an interesting indication of how great a change had occurred in reading tastes in just a few years. This last book is considered Dreiser's finest novel.

Upton Sinclair (b. 1878) is another writer who has lived into our era; but his best work belongs to an earlier period. His novels are elaborate expressions of his social ideas. The most famous of them is *The Jungle* (1906), which deals with the harsh lot of immigrant workers in the stockyards and meat-packing plants of Chicago. The book led directly to President Theodore Roosevelt's investigation of meat-packing conditions, a study that resulted in the first Federal Pure-Food legislation.

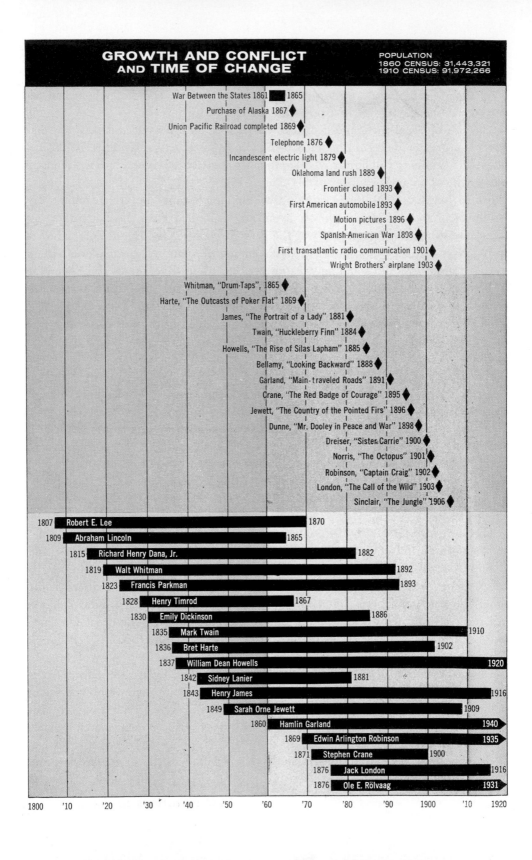

GROWTH AND CONFLICT
AND TIME OF CHANGE

POPULATION
1860 CENSUS: 31,443,321
1910 CENSUS: 91,972,266

War Between the States 1861 ■ 1865
Purchase of Alaska 1867 ◆
Union Pacific Railroad completed 1869 ◆
Telephone 1876 ◆
Incandescent electric light 1879 ◆
Oklahoma land rush 1889 ◆
Frontier closed 1893 ◆
First American automobile 1893 ◆
Motion pictures 1896 ◆
Spanish-American War 1898 ◆
First transatlantic radio communication 1901 ◆
Wright Brothers' airplane 1903 ◆

Whitman, "Drum-Taps", 1865 ◆
Harte, "The Outcasts of Poker Flat" 1869 ◆
James, "The Portrait of a Lady" 1881 ◆
Twain, "Huckleberry Finn" 1884 ◆
Howells, "The Rise of Silas Lapham" 1885 ◆
Bellamy, "Looking Backward" 1888 ◆
Garland, "Main-traveled Roads" 1891 ◆
Crane, "The Red Badge of Courage" 1895 ◆
Jewett, "The Country of the Pointed Firs" 1896 ◆
Dunne, "Mr. Dooley in Peace and War" 1898 ◆
Dreiser, "Sister Carrie" 1900 ◆
Norris, "The Octopus" 1901 ◆
Robinson, "Captain Craig" 1902 ◆
London, "The Call of the Wild" 1903 ◆
Sinclair, "The Jungle" 1906 ◆

1807 Robert E. Lee 1870
1809 Abraham Lincoln 1865
1815 Richard Henry Dana, Jr. 1882
1819 Walt Whitman 1892
1823 Francis Parkman 1893
1828 Henry Timrod 1867
1830 Emily Dickinson 1886
1835 Mark Twain 1910
1836 Bret Harte 1902
1837 William Dean Howells 1920
1842 Sidney Lanier 1881
1843 Henry James 1916
1849 Sarah Orne Jewett 1909
1860 Hamlin Garland 1940
1869 Edwin Arlington Robinson 1935
1871 Stephen Crane 1900
1876 Jack London 1916
1876 Ole E. Rölvaag 1931

1800   '10   '20   '30   '40   '50   '60   '70   '80   '90   1900   '10   1920

SARAH ORNE JEWETT

1849–1903

A White Heron

Miss Jewett's father was a country doctor and a local historian. Driving with him about the countryside, she had time to observe the life of the quiet towns and weathered farms of New England. She saw stories all about her, and some of her finest work grew from her observation of the simple lives of her Maine neighbors. In the best of her realistic stories, Miss Jewett captured the New England speech as only a native could. Though she never dealt with the startling incidents and situations of high adventure, Miss Jewett recognized the drama and the conflict that can occur in even the simplest lives. She knew that what seems to be a trivial event can often have a far-reaching effect. In "A White Heron" she tells of such an event.

THE WOODS were already filled with shadows one June evening, just before eight o'clock, though a bright sunset still glimmered faintly among the trunks of the trees. A little girl was driving home her cow, a plodding, dilatory,[1] provoking creature in her behavior, but

[1] dilatory: slow, delaying.

a valued companion for all that. They were going away from the western light, and striking deep into the dark woods, but their feet were familiar with the path, and it was no matter whether their eyes could see it or not.

There was hardly a night the summer through when the old cow could be found waiting at the pasture bars; on the contrary, it was her greatest pleasure to hide herself away among the huckleberry bushes, and though she wore a loud bell, she had made the discovery that if one stood perfectly still, it would not ring. So Sylvia had to hunt for her until she found her, and call Co'! Co'! with never an answering Moo, until her childish patience was quite spent. If the creature had not given good milk and plenty of it, the case would have seemed very different to her owners. Besides, Sylvia had all the time there was, and very little use to make of it. Sometimes in pleasant weather it was a consolation to look upon the cow's pranks as an intelligent attempt to play hide-and-seek, and as the child had no playmates, she lent herself to this amusement with a good deal of zest. Though this chase had been so long that the wary animal herself had given an unusual signal of her whereabouts, Sylvia had only laughed when she came upon Mistress Moolly at the swamp-side, and urged her affectionately homeward with a twig of birch leaves. The old cow was not inclined to wander farther; she even turned in the right direction for once as they left the pasture, and stepped along the road at a good pace. She was quite ready to be milked now, and seldom stopped to browse. Sylvia wondered what her grandmother would say because they were so late. It was a great while since she had left home at half-past five o'clock, but everybody knew the difficulty of making this errand a short one. Mrs. Tilley had chased the hornèd torment too many summer evenings herself to blame anyone else for lingering, and was only thankful as she waited that she had Sylvia, nowadays, to give such valuable assistance. The good woman suspected that Sylvia loitered occasionally on her own account; there never was such a child for straying about out of doors since the world was made! Everybody said that it was a good change for a little maid who had tried to grow for eight years in a crowded manufacturing town, but, as for Sylvia herself, it seemed as if she never had been alive at all before she came to live at the farm. She thought often with a wistful compassion of a wretched dry geranium that belonged to a town neighbor.

" 'Afraid of folks,' " old Mrs. Tilley said to herself, with a smile, after she had made the unlikely choice of Sylvia from her daughter's houseful of children, and was returning to the farm. " 'Afraid of folks,' they said! I guess she won't be troubled no great with 'em up to the old place!" When they reached the door of the lonely house and stopped to unlock it, and the cat came to purr loudly and rub against them, a deserted pussy, indeed, but fat with young robins, Sylvia whispered that this was a beautiful place to live in, and she never should wish to go home.

II

The companions followed the shady wood-road, the cow taking slow steps, and the child very fast ones. The cow stopped long at the brook to drink, as if the pasture were not half a swamp, and Sylvia stood still and waited, letting her bare feet cool themselves in the shoal water, while the great twilight moths struck softly against her. She waded on through the brook as the cow moved away, and listened to the thrushes with a heart that beat fast with pleasure. There was a stirring in the great boughs overhead. They were full of little birds and beasts that seemed to be wide awake, and going about their world, or else saying good night to each other in sleepy twitters. Sylvia herself felt sleepy as she walked along. However, it was not much farther to the house, and the air was soft and sweet. She was not often in the woods so late as this, and it made her feel as if she were a part of the gray shadows and the moving leaves. She was just thinking how long it seemed since she first came to the farm a year ago, and wondering if everything went on in the noisy town just the same as when she was there; the thought of the great red-faced boy who used to chase and frighten her made her hurry along the path to escape from the shadow of the trees.

Suddenly this little woods girl is horror-stricken to hear a clear whistle not very far away. Not a bird's whistle, which would have a sort of friendliness, but a boy's whistle, determined, and somewhat aggressive. Sylvia left the cow to whatever sad fate might await her, and stepped discreetly aside into the bushes, but she was just too late. The enemy had discovered her, and called out in a very cheerful and persuasive tone, "Halloa, little girl, how far is it to the road?" and trembling Sylvia answered almost inaudibly, "A good ways."

She did not dare to look boldly at the tall young man, who carried a gun over his shoulder, but she came out of her bush and again followed the cow, while he walked alongside.

"I have been hunting for some birds," the stranger said kindly, "and I have lost my way, and need a friend very much. Don't be afraid," he added gallantly. "Speak up and tell me what your name is, and whether you think I can spend the night at your house, and go out gunning early in the morning."

Sylvia was more alarmed than before. Would not her grandmother consider her much to blame? But who could have foreseen such an accident as this? It did not appear to be her fault, and she hung her head as if the stem of it were broken, but managed to answer "Sylvy," with much effort when her companion again asked her name.

Mrs. Tilley was standing in the doorway when the trio came into view. The cow gave a loud moo by way of explanation.

"Yes, you'd better speak up for yourself, you old trial! Where'd she tuck herself away this time, Sylvy?" But Sylvia kept an awed silence; she knew by instinct that her grandmother did not comprehend the gravity of the situation. She must be mistaking the stranger for one of the farmer lads of the region.

The young man stood his gun beside the door, and dropped a heavy game-bag beside it; then he bade Mrs. Tilley good evening, and repeated his wayfarer's story, and asked if he could have a night's lodging.

"Put me anywhere you like," he said. "I must be off early in the morning, before day; but I am very hungry, indeed. You can give me some milk at any rate, that's plain."

"Dear sakes, yes," responded the hostess, whose long-slumbering hospitality seemed to be easily awakened. "You

might fare better if you went out on the main road a mile or so, but you're welcome to what we've got. I'll milk right off, and you make yourself at home. You can sleep on husks or feathers," she proffered graciously. "I raised them all myself. There's good pasturing for geese just below here toward the ma'sh. Now step round and set a plate for the gentleman, Sylvy!" And Sylvia promptly stepped. She was glad to have something to do, and she was hungry herself.

It was a surprise to find so clean and comfortable a little dwelling in this New England wilderness. The young man had known the horrors of its most primitive housekeeping, and the dreary squalor of that level of society which does not rebel at the companionship of hens. This was the best thrift of an old-fashioned farmstead, though on such a small scale that it seemed like a hermitage. He listened eagerly to the old woman's quaint talk, he watched Sylvia's pale face and shining gray eyes with ever-growing enthusiasm, and insisted that this was the best supper he had eaten for a month; then afterward the new-made friends sat down in the doorway together while the moon came up.

Soon it would be berry time, and Sylvia was a great help at picking. The cow was a good milker, though a plaguy thing to keep track of, the hostess gossiped frankly, adding presently that she had buried four children, so that Sylvia's mother, and a son (who might be dead) in California were all the children she had left. "Dan, my boy, was a great hand to go gunning," she explained sadly. "I never wanted for pa'-tridges or gray squer'ls while he was to home. He's been a great wand'rer, I expect, and he's no hand to write letters. There, I don't blame him, I'd ha' seen the world myself if it had been so I could."

"Sylvy takes after him," the grandmother continued affectionately, after a minute's pause. "There ain't a foot o' ground she don't know her way over, and the wild creatur's counts her one o' themselves. Squer'ls she'll tame to come an' feed right out o' her hands, and all sorts o' birds. Last winter she got the jay birds to bangeing [1] here, and I believe she'd a' scanted herself of her own meals to have plenty to throw out amongst 'em, if I hadn't kep' watch. Anything but crows, I tell her, I'm willin' to help support — though Dan he went an' tamed one o' them that did seem to have reason same as folks. It was round here a good spell after he went away. Dan an' his father they didn't hitch — but he never held up his head ag'in after Dan had dared him

[1] bangeing: colloquial for gathering.

an' gone off."

The guest did not notice this hint of family sorrows in his eager interest in something else.

"So Sylvy knows all about birds, does she?" he exclaimed, as he looked around at the little girl who sat, very demure but increasingly sleepy, in the moonlight. "I am making a collection of birds myself. I have been at it ever since I was a boy." (Mrs. Tilley smiled.) "There are two or three very rare ones I have been hunting for these five years. I mean to get them on my own ground if they can be found."

"Do you cage 'em up?" asked Mrs. Tilley doubtfully, in response to this enthusiastic announcement.

"Oh no, they're stuffed and preserved, dozens and dozens of them," said the ornithologist, "and I have shot or snared every one myself. I caught a glimpse of a white heron three miles from here on Saturday, and I have followed it in this direction. They have never been found in this district at all. The little white heron, it is," and he turned again to look at Sylvia with the hope of discovering that the rare bird was one of her acquaintances.

But Sylvia was watching a hoptoad in the narrow footpath.

"You would know the heron if you saw it," the stranger continued eagerly. "A queer tall white bird with soft feathers and long thin legs. And it would have a nest perhaps in the top of a high tree, made of sticks, something like a hawk's nest."

Sylvia's heart gave a wild beat; she knew that strange white bird, and had once stolen softly near where it stood in some bright-green swamp grass, away over at the other side of the woods. There was an open place where the sunshine always seemed strangely yellow and hot, where tall, nodding rushes grew, and her grandmother had warned her that she might sink in the soft black mud underneath and never be heard of more. Not far beyond were the salt marshes, and beyond those was the sea, the sea which Sylvia wondered and dreamed about, but never had looked upon, though its great voice could often be heard above the noise of the woods on stormy nights.

"I can't think of anything I should like so much as to find that heron's nest," the handsome stranger was saying. "I would give ten dollars to anybody who could show it to me," he added desperately, "and I mean to spend my whole vacation hunting for it if need be. Perhaps it was only migrating, or had been chased out of its own region by some bird of prey."

Mrs. Tilley gave amazed attention to all this, but Sylvia still watched the toad, not divining, as she might have done at some calmer time, that the creature wished to get to its hole under the doorstep, and was much hindered by the unusual spectators at that hour of the evening. No amount of thought, that night, could decide how many wished-for treasures the ten dollars, so lightly spoken of, would buy.

The next day the young sportsman hovered about the woods, and Sylvia kept him company, having lost her first fear of the friendly lad, who proved to be most kind and sympathetic. He told her many things about the birds and what they knew and where they lived and what they did with themselves. And he gave her a jackknife, which she thought as great a treasure as if she were a desert-islander. All day long he did not once make her troubled or afraid except when he brought down some unsuspecting singing creature from its bough. Sylvia would have liked him vastly better without his gun; she could not understand why he killed the very birds he seemed to like so much. But as the day waned, Sylvia still watched the young man with loving admiration. She had never seen anybody so charming and delightful; the woman's heart, asleep in the child, was vaguely thrilled by a dream of love.

Some premonition of that great power stirred and swayed these young creatures who traversed the solemn woodlands with soft-footed silent care. They stopped to listen to a bird's song; they pressed forward again eagerly, parting the branches — speaking to each other rarely and in whispers; the young man going first and Sylvia following, fascinated, a few steps behind, with her gray eyes dark with excitement.

She grieved because the longed-for white heron was elusive, but she did not lead the guest, she only followed, and there was no such thing as speaking first. The sound of her own unquestioned voice would have terrified her — it was hard enough to answer yes or no when there was need of that. At last evening began to fall, and they drove the cow home together, and Sylvia smiled with pleasure when they came to the place where she heard the whistle and was afraid only the night before.

III

Half a mile from home, at the farther edge of the woods, where the land was highest, a great pine tree stood, the last of its generation. Whether it was left for a boundary mark, or for what reason, no one could say; the woodchoppers who had felled its mates were dead and gone long ago, and a whole forest of sturdy trees, pines and oaks and maples, had grown again. But the stately head of this old pine towered above them all and made a landmark for sea and shore miles away. Sylvia knew it well. She had always believed that whoever climbed to the top of it could see the ocean; and the little girl had often laid her hand on the great rough trunk and looked up wistfully at those dark boughs that the wind always stirred, no matter how hot and still the air might be below. Now she thought of the tree with a new excitement, for why, if one climbed it at break of day, could not one see all the world, and easily dis-

cover from whence the white heron flew, and mark the place, and find the hidden nest?

What a spirit of adventure, what wild ambition! What fancied triumph and delight and glory for the later morning when she could make known the secret! It was almost too real and too great for the childish heart to bear.

All night the door of the little house stood open and the whippoorwills came and sang upon the very step. The young sportsman and his old hostess were sound asleep, but Sylvia's great design kept her broad awake and watching. She forgot to think of sleep. The short summer night seemed as long as the winter darkness, and at last when the whippoorwills ceased, and she was afraid the morning would after all come too soon, she stole out of the house and followed the pasture path through the woods, hastening toward the open

ground beyond, listening with a sense of comfort and companionship to the drowsy twitter of a half-awakened bird, whose perch she had jarred in passing. Alas, if the great wave of human interest which flooded for the first time this dull little life should sweep away the satisfactions of an existence heart to heart with nature and the dumb life of the forest!

There was the huge tree asleep yet in the paling moonlight, and small and hopeful Sylvia began with utmost bravery to mount to the top of it, with tingling, eager blood coursing the channels of her whole frame, with her bare feet and fingers that pinched and held like bird's claws to the monstrous ladder reaching up, up, almost to the sky itself. First she must mount the white oak tree that grew alongside, where she was almost lost among the dark branches and the green leaves heavy and wet with dew; a bird fluttered off its nest, and a red squirrel ran to and fro and scolded pettishly at the harmless housebreaker. Sylvia felt her way easily. She had often climbed there, and knew that higher still one of the oak's upper branches chafed against the pine trunk just where its lower boughs were set close together. There, when she made the dangerous pass from one tree to the other, the great enterprise would really begin.

She crept out along the swaying oak limb at last, and took the daring step across into the old pine tree. The way was harder than she thought; she must reach far and hold fast, the sharp dry twigs caught and held her and scratched her like angry talons, the pitch made her thin little fingers clumsy and stiff as she went round the tree's great stem, higher and higher upward. The sparrows and robins in the woods below were beginning to wake and twitter to the dawn, yet it seemed much lighter there aloft in the pine tree, and the child knew she must hurry if her project were to be of any use.

The tree seemed to lengthen itself out as she went up, and to reach farther and farther upward. It was like a great mainmast to the voyaging earth; it must truly have been amazed that morning through all its ponderous frame as it felt this determined spark of human spirit wending its way from higher branch to branch. Who knows how steadily the least twigs held themselves to advantage this light, weak creature on her way! The old pine must have loved his new dependent. More than all the hawks and bats, and moths, and even the sweet-voiced thrushes, was the brave, beating heart of the solitary gray-eyed child. And the tree stood still and frowned away the winds that June morning while the dawn grew bright in the east.

Sylvia's face was like a pale star, if one had seen it from the ground, when the last thorny bough was past, and she stood trembling and tired but wholly triumphant, high in the treetop. Yes, there was the sea with the dawning sun making a golden dazzle over it, and toward that glorious east flew two hawks with slow-moving pinions. How low they looked in the air from that height when before one had only seen them far up, and dark against the blue sky. Their gray feathers were as soft as moths; they seemed only a little way from the tree, and Sylvia felt as if she too could go flying away among the clouds. Westward, the woodlands and farms reached miles and miles into the distance; here and there were church steeples, and white villages; truly it was a vast and awesome world!

The birds sang louder and louder. At last the sun came up bewilderingly bright. Sylvia could see the white sails of ships out at sea, and the clouds that were purple and rose-colored and yellow at first began to fade away. Where was the white heron's nest in the sea of green branches, and was this wonderful sight and pageant of the world the only reward for having climbed to such a giddy height? Now look down again, Sylvia, where the green marsh is set among the shining birches and dark hemlocks; there where you saw the white heron once, you will see him again; look, look! a white spot of him like a single floating feather comes up from the dead hemlock and grows larger, and rises, and comes close at last, and goes by the landmark pine with steady sweep of wing and outstretched slender neck and crested head. And wait! wait! do not move a foot or a finger, little girl, do not send an arrow of light and consciousness from your two eager eyes, for the heron has perched on a pine bough not far beyond yours, and cries back to his mate on the nest, and plumes his feathers for the new day!

The child gives a long sigh a minute later when a company of shouting catbirds comes also to the tree, and vexed by their fluttering and lawlessness, the solemn heron goes away. She knows his secret now, the wild, light, slender bird that floats and wavers, and goes back like an arrow presently to his home in the green world beneath. Then Sylvia, well satisfied, makes her perilous way down again, not daring to look far below the branch she stands on, ready to cry sometimes because her fingers ache and her lamed feet slip. Wondering over and over again what the stranger would say to her, and what he would think when she told him how to find his way straight to the heron's nest.

"Sylvy, Sylvy!" called the busy old grandmother again and again, but nobody answered, and the small husk bed was empty, and Sylvia had disappeared.

The guest waked from a dream, and remembering his day's pleasure, hurried to dress himself that it might sooner begin. He was sure from the way the shy little girl looked once or twice yesterday that she had at least seen the white heron, and now she must really be made to tell. Here she comes now, paler than ever, and her worn old frock is torn and tattered, and smeared with pine pitch. The grandmother and the sportsman stand in the door together and question her, and the splendid moment has come to speak of the dead hemlock tree by the green marsh.

But Sylvia does not speak after all, though the old grandmother fretfully rebukes her, and the young man's kind, appealing eyes are looking straight in her own. He can make them rich with money; he has promised it, and they are poor now. He is so well worth making happy, and he waits to hear the story she can tell.

No, she must keep silence! What is it that suddenly forbids her and makes her dumb? Has she been nine years growing and now, when the great world for the first time puts out a hand to her, must she thrust it aside for a bird's sake? The murmur of the pine's green branches is in her ears, she remembers how the white heron came flying through the golden air and how they watched the sea and the morning together, and Sylvia cannot speak; she cannot tell the heron's secret and give its life away.

Dear loyalty, that suffered a sharp pang as the guest went away disappointed later in the day, that could have served and followed him and loved him as a dog loves! Many a night Sylvia heard the echo of his whistle haunting the pasture path as she came home with the loitering cow. She forgot even her sorrow at the sharp report of his gun and the piteous sight of the thrushes and sparrows dropping silent to the ground, their songs hushed and their pretty feathers stained and wet with blood. Were the birds better friends than their hunter might have been — who can tell? Whatever treasures were lost to her, woodlands and summertime, remember! Bring your gifts and graces, and tell your secrets to this lonely country child!

FOR DISCUSSION

1. Explain what is meant by the statement, "as for Sylvia herself, it seemed as if she never had been alive at all before she came to live at the farm."

2. In paragraph five of the story, Miss Jewett suddenly changes to the present tense for just one sentence. What may be her reason for doing so?

3. Can you explain Mrs. Tilley's choice of Sylvia — a choice the story calls "unlikely" — from her daughter's houseful of children?

4. Why did Mrs. Tilley smile when the stranger said he had been collecting birds ever since he was a boy?

5. When Sylvia climbed the tall pine and discovered the secret of the white heron's nest, did she mean to tell the stranger?

6. Why does the author describe in detail Sylvia's climbing of the tree instead of her descent, which may have been even more dangerous and more frightening?

7. Does the conclusion of the story seem logical to you? Why? Why not? Can you compare the story to any you have ever read in which a child or an adult is offered money to reveal a secret?

8. The last paragraph of the story begins, "Dear loyalty . . ." Sylvia feels conflicting loyalties in the story. Explain what they are.

PERSONIFICATION

The paragraph on page 781 beginning "The tree seemed to lengthen itself . . ." is a fine example of personification. What is the effect of this figure of speech?

American Art and Artists ➤

Reproduced on the facing page is a detail from "The Home of the Heron," an oil painting by the American artist George Inness (1825–1894). Inness was one of the last members of the Hudson River school, a group of nineteenth-century American landscape painters who found inspiration in the rugged scenery along the Hudson River and in the Catskill Mountains of New York state. George Inness is generally considered to be the finest artist of this school.

HAMLIN
GARLAND

1860–1940

Under the Lion's Paw

Before Garland's day those who wrote about farm life usually saw the country through the romantic eyes of the city dweller, the summer visitor, or the auction-sale hunter. With the publication of *Main-traveled Roads* (1890), a volume of short stories, the voice of an actual farmer was heard in literature. Garland wrote realistically about life on the Middle Border, the prairie region of Minnesota, Wisconsin, Nebraska, and the Dakotas.

As western lands were taken up, the true frontier came to its end. Instead of staking a claim to a free government homestead, the new settler had to deal with the men who already held the land. That is the situation in this story. In this instance Garland forces the reader to form his own impression. "This is what happened," he says, in effect. "It's up to you to decide what it means."

IT WAS the last of autumn and first day of winter coming together. All day long the plowmen on their prairie farms had moved to and fro in their wide, level

fields through the falling snow, which melted as it fell, wetting them to the skin — all day, notwithstanding the frequent squalls of snow, the dripping, desolate clouds, and the muck of the furrows, black and tenacious as tar.

Under their dripping harness the horses swung to and fro silently, with that marvelous uncomplaining patience which marks the horse. All day the wild geese, honking wildly, as they sprawled sidewise down the wind, seemed to be fleeing from an enemy behind, and with neck outthrust and wings extended, sailed down the wind, soon lost to sight.

Yet the plowman behind his plow, though the snow lay on his ragged greatcoat, and the cold, clinging mud rose on his heavy boots, fettering him like gyves,[1] whistled in the very beard of the gale. As day passed, the snow, ceasing to melt, lay along the plowed land, and lodged in the depth of the stubble, till on each slow round the last furrow stood out black and shining as jet between the plowed land and the gray stubble.

When night began to fall, and the geese, flying low, began to alight invisibly in the near cornfield, Stephen

"Under the Lion's Paw" from *Main-traveled Roads* by Hamlin Garland, published by Harper & Brothers. Reprinted by permission of Constance Garland Doyle and Isabel Garland Lord.

[1] **gyves** (jīvs): shackles, chains.

Council was still at work "finishing a land." He rode on his sulky plow when going with the wind, but walked when facing it. Sitting bent and cold but cheery under his slouch hat, he talked encouragingly to his four-in-hand.

"Come round there, boys! — Round agin! We got t' finish this land. Come in there, Dan! *Stiddy,* Kate — stiddy! None o' y'r tantrums, Kittie. It's purty tuff, but got a be did. *Tchk! tchk!* Step along, Pete! Don't let Katy git y'r single-tree [1] on the wheel. *Once* more!"

They seemed to know what he meant, and that this was the last round, for they worked with greater vigor than before.

"Once more, boys, an' then, sez I, oats an' a nice warm stall, an' sleep f'r all."

By the time the last furrow was turned on the land, it was too dark to see the house, and the snow was changing to rain again. The tired and hungry man could see the light from the kitchen shining through the leafless hedge, and he lifted a great shout, "Supper f'r a half a dozen!"

It was nearly eight o'clock by the time he had finished his chores and started for supper. He was picking his way carefully through the mud, when the tall form of a man loomed up before him with a premonitory cough.

"Waddy ye want?" was the rather startled question of the farmer.

"Well, ye see," began the stranger, in a deprecating tone, "we'd like t' git in f'r the night. We've tried every house f'r the last two miles, but they hadn't any room f'r us. My wife's jest about sick, 'n' the children are cold and hungry —"

"Oh, y' want 'o stay all night, eh?"

"Yes, sir; it 'ud be a great accom —"

"Waal, I don't make it a practice t' turn anybuddy 'way hungry, not on sech nights as this. Drive right in. We ain't got much, but sech as it is —"

---

[1] **singletree:** the swinging bar to which the harness is attached.

But the stranger had disappeared. And soon his steaming, weary team, with drooping heads and swinging singletrees, moved past the well to the block beside the path. Council stood at the side of the "schooner" and helped the children out — two little half-sleeping children — and then a small woman with a babe in her arms.

"There ye go!" he shouted jovially, to the children. "*Now* we're all right! Run right along to the house there, an' tell Ma'm Council you wants sumpthin' t' eat. Right this way, Mis' — keep right off t' the right there. I'll go an' git a lantern. Come," he said to the dazed and silent group at his side.

"Mother," he shouted, as he neared the fragrant and warmly lighted kitchen, "here are some wayfarers an' folks who need sumpthin' t' eat an' a place t' snooze." He ended by pushing them all in.

Mrs. Council, a large, jolly, rather coarse-looking woman, took the children in her arms. "Come right in, you little rabbits. 'Most asleep, hey? Now here's a drink o' milk f'r each o' ye. I'll have s'm tea in a minute. Take off y'r things and step up t' the fire."

While she set the children to drinking milk, Council got out his lantern and went out to the barn to help the stranger about his team, where his loud, hearty voice could be heard as it came and went between the haymow and the stalls.

The woman came to light as a small, timid, and discouraged-looking woman, but still pretty, in a thin and sorrowful way.

"Land sakes! An' you've traveled all the way from Clear Lake t'day in this mud! Waal! waal! No wonder you're all tired out. Don't wait f'r the men, Mis' —" She hesitated, waiting for the name.

"Haskins."

"Mis' Haskins, set right up to the table an' take a good swig o' tea whilst I make y' s'm toast. It's green tea, an' it's good. I tell Council as I git older I don't seem to enjoy Young Hyson n'r Gunpowder. I want the reel green tea, jest as it comes off'n the vines. Seems t' have more heart in it, some way. Don't s'pose it has. Council says it's all in m' eye."

Going on in this easy way, she soon had the children filled with bread and milk and the woman thoroughly at home, eating some toast and sweet-melon pickles, and sipping the tea.

"See the little rats!" she laughed at the children. "They're full as they can stick now, and they want to go to bed. Now, don't git up, Mis' Haskins; set right where you are an' let me look after 'em. I know all about young ones, though I'm all alone now. Jane went an' married last fall. But, as I tell Council, it's lucky we keep our health. Set right there, Mis' Haskins; I won't have you stir a finger."

It was an unmeasured pleasure to sit there in the warm, homely kitchen, the jovial chatter of the housewife driving out and holding at bay the growl of the impotent, cheated wind.

The little woman's eyes filled with tears which fell down upon the sleeping baby in her arms. The world was not so desolate and cold and hopeless, after all.

"Now I hope Council won't stop out there and talk politics all night. He's the greatest man to talk politics an' read the *Tribune* — How old is it?"

She broke off and peered down at the face of the babe.

"Two months 'n' five days," said the mother, with a mother's exactness.

"Ye don't say! I want 'o know! The dear little pudzy-wudzy!" she went on, stirring it up in the neighborhood of the ribs with her fat forefinger.

"Pooty tough on 'oo to go gallivant'n' 'cross lots this way — "

"Yes, that's so; a man can't lift a mountain," said Council, entering the door. "Mother, this is Mr. Haskins, from Kansas. He's been eat up 'n' drove out by grasshoppers."

"Glad t' see yeh! — Pa, empty that washbasin 'n' give him a chance t' wash."

Haskins was a tall man, with a thin, gloomy face. His hair was a reddish brown, like his coat, and seemed equally faded by the wind and sun, and his sallow face, though hard and set, was pathetic somehow. You would have felt that he had suffered much by the line of his mouth showing under his thin, yellow mustache.

"Hain't Ike got home yet, Sairy?"

"Hain't seen 'im."

"W-a-a-l, set right up, Mr. Haskins; wade right into what we've got; 'tain't much, but we manage to live on it — she gits fat on it," laughed Council, pointing his thumb at his wife.

After supper, while the women put the children to bed, Haskins and Council talked on, seated near the huge cooking stove, the steam rising from their wet clothing. In the Western fashion Council told as much of his own life as he drew from his guest. He asked but few questions, but by and by the story of Haskins' struggles and defeat came out. The story was a terrible one, but he told it quietly, seated with his elbows on his knees, gazing most of the time at the hearth.

"I didn't like the looks of the country anyhow," Haskins said, partly rising and glancing at his wife. "I was ust t' northern Ingyannie, where we have lots o' timber 'n' lots o' rain, 'n' I didn't like the looks o' that dry prairie. What galled me the worst was goin' s' far away acrosst so much fine land layin' all through here vacant."

"And the 'hoppers eat ye four years, hand runnin', did they?"

"Eat! They wiped us out. They chawed everything that was green. They jest set around waitin' f'r us to die t' eat us, too. My God! I ust t' dream of 'em sittin' 'round on the bedpost, six feet long, workin' their jaws. They eat the fork handles. They got worse 'n' worse till they jest rolled on one another, piled up like snow in winter. Well, it ain't no use. If I was t' talk all winter I couldn't tell nawthin'. But all the while I couldn't help thinkin' of all that land back here that nobuddy was usin' that I ought o' had' stead o' bein' out there in that cussed country."

"Waal, why didn't ye stop an' settle here?" asked Ike, who had come in and was eating his supper.

"Fer the simple reason that you fellers wantid ten 'r fifteen dollars an acre fer the bare land, and I hadn't no money fer that kind o' thing."

"Yes, I do my own work," Mrs. Council was heard to say in the pause which followed. "I'm a gettin' purty heavy t' be on m' laigs all day, but we can't afford t' hire, so I keep rackin' around somehow, like a foundered horse. S' lame — I tell Council he can't tell how lame I am, f'r I'm jest as lame in one laig as t' other." And the good soul laughed at the joke on herself as she took a handful of flour and dusted the biscuit board to keep the dough from sticking.

"Well, I hain't *never* been very strong," said Mrs. Haskins. "Our folks was Canadians an' small-boned, and then since my last child I hain't got up again fairly. I don't like t' complain. Tim has about all he can bear now — but they was days this week when I jest wanted to lay right down an' die."

"Waal, now, I'll tell ye," said Council, from his side of the stove, silencing everybody with his good-natured roar, "I'd go down and *see* Butler, *anyway,* if I was you. I guess he'd let you have his place purty cheap; the farm's all run down. He's ben anxious t' let t' somebuddy next year. It 'ud be a good chance fer you. Anyhow, you go to bed and sleep like a babe. I've got some plowing t' do, anyhow, an' we'll see if somethin' can't be done about your case. Ike, you go out an' see if the horses is all right, an' I'll show the folks t' bed."

When the tired husband and wife

were lying under the generous quilts of the square bed, Haskins listened a moment to the wind in the eaves, and then said, with a slow and solemn tone, "There are people in this world who are good enough t' be angels, an' only haff t' die to *be* angels."

II

Jim Butler was one of those men called in the West "land-poor." Early in the history of Rock River, he had come into the town and started in the grocery business in a small way, occupying a small building in a mean part of the town. At this period of his life, he earned all he got, and was up early and late sorting beans, working over butter, and carting his goods to and from the station. But a change came over him at the end of the second year, when he sold a lot of land for four times what he paid for it. From that time forward he believed in land speculation as the surest way of getting rich. Every cent he could save or spare from his trade he put into land at forced sale, or mortgages on land, which were "just as good as the wheat," he was accustomed to say.

Farm after farm fell into his hands, until he was recognized as one of the leading landowners of the county. His mortgages were scattered all over Cedar County, and as they slowly but surely fell in, he sought usually to retain the former owner as tenant.

He was not ready to foreclose; indeed, he had the name of being one of the "easiest" men in the town. He let the debtor off again and again, extending the time whenever possible.

"I don't want y'r land," he said. "All I'm after is the int'rest on my money — that's all. Now, if y' want 'o stay on the farm, why, I'll give y' a good chance. I can't have the land layin' vacant." And in many cases the owner remained as tenant.

In the meantime he had sold his store; he couldn't spend time in it; he was mainly occupied now with sitting around town on rainy days smoking and "gassin' with the boys," or in riding to and from his farms. In fishing time he fished a good deal. Doc Grimes, Ben Ashley, and Cal Cheatham were his cronies on these fishing excursions or hunting trips in the time of chickens or partridges. In winter they went to northern Wisconsin to shoot deer.

In spite of all these signs of easy life, Butler persisted in saying he "hadn't enough money to pay taxes on his land," and was careful to convey the impression that he was poor in spite of his twenty farms. At one time he was said to be worth fifty thousand dollars, but land had been a little slow of sale of late, so that he was not worth so much.

A fine farm, known as the Higley place, had fallen into his hands in the usual way the previous year, and he had not been able to find a tenant for it. Poor Higley, after working himself nearly to death on it in the attempt to lift the mortgage, had gone off to Dakota, leaving the farm and his curse to Butler.

This was the farm which Council advised Haskins to apply for; and the next day Council hitched up his team and drove down to see Butler.

"You jest let *me* do the talkin'," he said. "We'll find him wearin' out his pants on some salt barrel somew'ers; and if he thought you *wanted* a place, he'd sock it to you hot and heavy. You jest keep quiet; I'll fix 'im."

Butler was seated in Ben Ashley's store telling fish yarns when Council sauntered in casually.

"Hello, But; lyin' agin, hey?"

"Hello, Steve! How goes it?"

"Oh, so-so. Too dang much rain these days. I thought it was goin' t' freeze up f'r good last night. Tight squeak if I get m' plowin' done. How's farmin' with *you* these days?"

"Bad. Plowin ain't half done."

"It 'ud be a religious idee f'r you t' go out an' take a hand y'rself."

"I don't haff to," said Butler, with a wink.

"Got anybody on the Higley place?"

"No. Know of anybody?"

"Waal, no; not eggsackly. I've got a relation back t' Michigan who's ben hot an' cold on the idee o' comin' West f'r some time. *Might* come if he could get a good layout. What do you talk on the farm?"

"Well, I d' know. I'll rent it on shares or I'll rent it money rent."

"Waal, how much money, say?"

"Well, say ten per cent, on the price — two-fifty."

"Waal, that ain't bad. Wait on 'im till 'e thrashes?" [1]

Haskins listened eagerly to this important question, but Council was cooly eating a dried apple which he had speared out of a barrel with his knife. Butler studied him carefully.

"Well, knocks me out of twenty-five dollars interest."

"My relation'll need all he's got t' git his crops in," said Council, in the same, indifferent way.

"Well, all right; *say* wait," concluded Butler.

"All right; this is the man. Haskins, this is Mr. Butler — no relation to Ben — the hardest-working man in Cedar County."

On the way home Haskins said: "I ain't much better off. I'd like that farm; it's a good farm, but it's all run down, an' so 'm I. I could make a good farm of it if I had half a show. But I can't stock it n'r seed it."

"Waal, now, don't you worry," roared Council in his ear. "We'll pull y' through somehow till next harvest. He's agreed t' hire it plowed, an' you can earn a hundred dollars plowin' an' y' c'n git the seed o' me, an' pay me back when y' can."

Haskins was silent with emotion, but

[1] "Wait on 'im till 'e thrashes?": Wait for payment until the first crop of wheat is threshed?

at last he said, "I ain't got nothin' t' live on."

"Now, don't you worry 'bout that. You jest make your headquarters at ol' Steve Council's. Mother'll take a pile o' comfort in havin' y'r wife an' children 'round. Y' see, Jane's married off lately, an' Ike's away a good 'eal, so we'll be darn glad 't have y' stop with us this winter. Nex' spring we'll see if y' can't git a start agin." And he chirruped to the team, which sprang forward with the rumbling, clattering wagon.

"Say, looky here, Council, you can't do this. I never saw — " shouted Haskins in his neighbor's ear.

Council moved about uneasily in his seat and stopped his stammering gratitude by saying: "Hold on, now; don't make such a fuss over a little thing. When I see a man down, an' things all on top of 'm, I jest like t' kick 'em off an' help 'm up. That's the kind of religion I got, an' it's about the *only* kind."

They rode the rest of the way home in silence. And when the red light of the lamp shone out into the darkness of the cold and windy night, and he thought of this refuge for his children and wife, Haskins could have put his arm around the neck of his burly companion and squeezed him like a lover. But he contented himself with saying, "Steve Council, you'll git y'r pay fr this some day."

"Don't want any pay. My religion ain't run on such business principles."

The wind was growing colder, and the ground was covered with a white frost, as they turned into the gate of the Council farm, and the children came rushing out, shouting, "Papa's come!" They hardly looked like the same children who had sat at the table the night before. Their torpidity,[1] under the influence of sunshine and Mother Council, had given way to a sort of spasmodic cheerfulness, as insects in winter revive when laid on the hearth.

_____
[1] **torpidity**: lack of energy.

III

Haskins worked like a fiend, and his wife, like the heroic woman that she was, bore also uncomplainingly the most terrible burdens. They rose early and toiled without intermission till the darkness fell on the plain, then tumbled into bed, every bone and muscle aching with fatigue, to rise with the sun next morning to the same round of the same ferocity of labor.

The eldest boy drove a team all through the spring, plowing and seeding, milked the cows, and did chores innumerable, in most ways taking the place of a man.

An infinitely pathetic but common figure — this boy on the American farm, where there is no law against child labor. To see him in his coarse clothing, his huge boots, and his ragged cap, as he staggered with a pail of water from the well, or trudged in the cold and cheerless dawn out into the frosty field behind his team, gave the city-bred visitor a sharp pang of sympathetic pain. Yet Haskins loved his boy, and would have saved him from this if he could, but he could not.

By June the first year the result of such herculean toil began to show on the farm. The yard was cleaned up and sown to grass, the garden plowed and planted, and the house mended.

Council had given them four of his cows.

"Take 'em an' run 'em on shares. I don't want 'o milk s' many. Ike's away s' much now, Sat'd'ys an' Sund'ys, I can't stand the bother anyhow."

Other men, seeing the confidence of Council in the newcomer, had sold him tools on time; and as he was really an able farmer, he soon had round him many evidences of his care and thrift. At the advice of Council, he had taken the farm for three years, with the privilege of rerenting or buying at the end of the term.

"It's a good bargain, an' y' want 'o nail it," said Council. "If you have any kind ov a crop, you c'n pay y'r debts, an' keep seed an' bread."

The new hope which now sprang up in the heart of Haskins and his wife grew almost as a pain by the time the wide field of wheat began to wave and rustle and swirl in the winds of July. Day after day he would snatch a few moments after supper to go and look at it.

"Have ye seen the wheat t'day, Nettie?" he asked one night as he rose from supper.

"No, Tim, I ain't had time."

"Well, take time now. Le's go look at it."

She threw an old hat on her head — Tommy's hat — and looking almost pretty in her thin, sad way, went out with her husband to the hedge.

"Ain't it grand, Nettie? Just look at it."

It was grand. Level, russet here and there, heavy-headed, wide as a lake, and full of multitudinous whispers and gleams of wealth, it stretched away before the gazers like the fabled field of the cloth of gold.

"Oh, I think — I *hope* we'll have a good crop, Tim; and oh, how good the people have been to us!"

"Yes; I don't know where we'd be t'day if it hadn't been f'r Council and his wife."

"They're the best people in the world," said the little woman, with a great sob of gratitude.

"We'll be in the field on Monday sure," said Haskins, gripping the rail of the fences as if already at the work of the harvest.

The harvest came, bounteous, glorious, but the winds came and blew it into tangles, and the rain matted it here and there close to the ground, increasing the work of gathering it threefold.

Oh, how they toiled in those glorious days! Clothing dripping with sweat, arms aching, filled with briers, fingers raw and bleeding, backs broken with the weight of heavy bundles, Haskins

and his man toiled on. Tommy drove the harvester, while his father and a hired man bound on the machine. In this way they cut ten acres every day, and almost every night after supper, when the hand went to bed, Haskins returned to the field shocking the bound grain in the light of the moon. Many a night he worked till his anxious wife came out at ten o'clock to call him in to rest and lunch.

At the same time she cooked for the men, took care of the children, washed and ironed, milked the cows at night, made the butter, and sometimes fed the horses and watered them while her husband kept at the shocking.

No slave in the Roman galleys could have toiled so frightfully and lived, for this man thought himself a free man and that he was working for his wife and babes.

When he sank into his bed with a deep groan of relief, too tired to change his grimy, dripping clothing, he felt that he was getting nearer and nearer to a home of his own, and pushing the wolf of want a little farther from his door.

There is no despair so deep as the despair of a homeless man or woman. To roam the roads of the country or the streets of the city, to feel there is no rood of ground on which the feet can rest, to halt weary and hungry outside lighted windows and hear laughter and song within — these are the hungers and rebellions that drive men to crime and women to shame.

It was the memory of this homelessness, and the fear of its coming again, that spurred Timothy Haskins and Nettie, his wife, to such ferocious labor during that first year.

IV

" 'M, yes; 'm, yes; first-rate," said Butler, as his eye took in the neat garden, the pigpen, and the well-filled barnyard. "You're gitt'n' quite a stock around yeh. Done well, eh?"

Haskins was showing Butler around

the place. He had not seen it for a year, having spent the year in Washington and Boston with Ashley, his brother-in-law, who had been elected to Congress.

"Yes, I've laid out a good deal of money durin' the last three years. I've paid out three hundred dollars f'r fencin'."

"Um — h'm! I see, I see," said Butler, while Haskins went on:

"The kitchen there cost two hundred; the barn ain't cost much in money, but I've put a lot o' time on it. I've dug a new well, and I — "

"Yes, yes, I see. You've done well. Stock worth a thousand dollars," said Butler, picking his teeth with a straw.

"About that," said Haskins, modestly. "We begin to feel's if we was gitt'n' a home f'r ourselves; but we've worked hard. I tell you we begin to feel it, Mr. Butler, and we're goin' t' begin to ease up purty soon. We've been kind o' plannin' a trip back t' *her* folks after the fall plowin's done."

"*Eggs-actly!*" said Butler, who was evidently thinking of something else. "I suppose you've kind o' calc'lated on stayin' here three years more?"

"Well, yes. Fact is, I think I c'n buy the farm this fall, if you'll give me a reasonable show."

"Um — m! What do you call a reasonable show?"

"Well, say a quarter down and three years' time."

Butler looked at the huge stacks of wheat, which filled the yard, over which the chickens were fluttering and crawling, catching grasshoppers, and out of which the crickets were singing innumerably. He smiled in a peculiar way as he said, "Oh, I won't be hard on yeh. But what did you expect to pay f'r the place?"

"Why, about what you offered it for before, two thousand five hundred, or *possibly* three thousand dollars," he added quickly, as he saw the owner shake his head.

"This farm is worth five thousand and five hundred dollars," said Butler, in a careless and decided voice.

"*What!*" almost shrieked the astounded Haskins. "What's that? Five thousand? Why, that's double what you offered it for three years ago."

"Of course, and it's worth it. It was all run down then; now it's in good shape. You've laid out fifteen hundred dollars in improvements, according to your own story."

"But *you* had nothin' t' do about that. It's my work an' my money."

"You bet it was; but it's my land."

"But what's to pay me for all my — "

"Ain't you had the use of 'em?" replied Butler, smiling calmly into his face.

Haskins was like a man struck on the head with a sandbag; he couldn't think; he stammered as he tried to say: "But — I never'd git the use — You'd rob me! More'n that: you agreed — you promised that I could buy or rent at the end of three years at — "

"That's all right. But I didn't say I'd let you carry off the improvements, nor that I'd go on renting the farm at two-fifty. The land is doubled in value, it don't matter how; it don't enter into the question; an' now you can pay me five hundred dollars a year rent, or take it on your own terms at fifty-five hundred, or — git out."

He was turning away when Haskins, the sweat pouring from his face, fronted him, saying again:

"But *you've* done nothing to make it so. You hain't added a cent. I put it all there myself, expectin' to buy. I worked an' sweat to improve it. I was workin' for myself an' babes — "

"Well, why didn't you buy when I offered to sell? What y' kickin' about?"

"I'm kickin' about payin' you twice f'r my own things — my own fences, my own kitchen, my own garden."

Butler laughed. "You're too green t' eat, young feller. *Your* improvements! The law will sing another tune."

"But I trusted your word."

"Never trust anybody, my friend. Besides, I didn't promise not to do this thing. Why, man, don't look at me like that. Don't take me for a thief. It's the law. The reg'lar thing. Everybody does it."

"I don't care if they do. It's stealin' jest the same. You take three thousand dollars of my money — the work o' my hands and my wife's." He broke down at this point. He was not a strong man mentally. He could face hardship, ceaseless toil, but he could not face the cold and sneering face of Butler.

"But I don't take it," said Butler, coolly. "All you've got to do is to go on jest as you've been a-doin', or give me a thousand dollars down, and a mortgage at ten per cent on the rest."

Haskins sat down blindly on a bundle of oats nearby, and with staring eyes and drooping head went over the situation. He was under the lion's paw. He felt a horrible numbness in his heart and limbs. He was hid in a mist, and there was no path out.

Butler walked about, looking at the huge stacks of grain, and pulling now and again a few handfuls out, shelling the heads in his hands and blowing the chaff away. He hummed a little tune as he did so. He had an accommodating air of waiting.

Haskins was in the midst of the terrible toil of the last year. He was walking again in the rain and the mud behind his plow; he felt the dust and dirt of the threshing. The ferocious husking-time, with its cutting wind and biting, clinging snows, lay hard upon him. Then he thought of his wife, how she had cheerfully cooked and baked, without holiday and without rest.

"Well, what do you think of it?" inquired the cool, mocking, insinuating voice of Butler.

"I think you're a thief and a liar!" shouted Haskins, leaping up. "A blackhearted houn'!" Butler's smile maddened him; with a sudden leap he caught a fork in his hands, and whirled

it in the air. "You'll never rob another man, damn ye!" he grated through his teeth, a look of pitiless ferocity in his accusing eyes.

Butler shrank and quivered, expecting the blow; stood, held hypnotized by the eyes of the man he had a moment before despised — a man transformed into an avenging demon. But in the deadly hush between the lift of the weapon and its fall, there came a gush of faint, childish laughter, and then across the range of his vision, far away and dim, he saw the sun-bright head of his baby girl, as, with the pretty, tottering run of a two year old, she moved across the grass of the dooryard. His hands relaxed; the fork fell to the ground; his head lowered.

"Make out y'r deed an' mor'gage, an' git off'n my land, an' don't ye never cross my line again; if y' do, I'll kill ye."

Butler backed away from the man in wild haste, and climbing into his buggy with trembling limbs, drove off down the road, leaving Haskins seated dumbly on the sunny pile of sheaves, his head sunk into his hands.

FOR DISCUSSION

1. The first section of this story pictures two important elements of life on the Middle Border. Identify each of them.

2. How did Mrs. Council put the weary travelers at ease as she welcomed them to her kitchen? Do you detect a definite purpose in her chattering on and on?

3. In his fight to make a good life for himself and his family, Haskins had to struggle against distinctly different kinds of obstacles. What were they? Are these enemies still arrayed against farmers?

4. In what different ways did Council help Haskins? Recall passages that prove that Haskins appreciated his kindness. What did Council mean by saying, "My religion ain't run on . . . business principles"?

5. Describe the life of the Haskins family while they were trying to get re-estab-

lished. What did Garland think about child labor on the Border farms? How do you know that even a prosperous farmer had to work hard?

6. What did Butler do that was unfair in making his final trade with Haskins? Was Butler within his legal rights? Give arguments for and against the law involved.

7. Explain the significance of the title. How does the phrase occur in the story? Do you feel in the end that Haskins has really freed himself from the lion's paw? Is Butler still as much of a "lion" as he was earlier?

8. Contrast the characters of Council and Butler. Discuss whether Butler should be considered a producer or a nonproducer in society. Did he fulfill a necessary function in the early Midwest? Would he today? How important in American life today is the ideal for which Haskins fought?

9. To appreciate literary realism, compare this story with "The Outcasts of Poker Flat" (page 689) as to plot and characterization. What special satisfaction does each type of story offer? Which type do you prefer?

American Art and Artists

Reproduced below is the oil painting "Buffalo Bones Are Plowed Under," by the American artist Harvey Dunn (1884–1952). Dunn also painted the picture on page 721, entitled "In Search of the Land of Milk and Honey."

Like Hamlin Garland and Ole Rölvaag, Harvey Dunn knew well the rugged life of the Middle Border. Dunn's parents moved into Dakota territory in 1881, at a time when Sitting Bull was still a menace in the area and when the typical plains home was a sod house or in some cases merely a dugout in a hillside. Dunn eventually went East and opened a famous art school in New Jersey. He never forgot his frontier childhood, however, and his best paintings return to that subject, capturing a sense of the rugged pioneer qualities needed on the late frontier.

JACK
LONDON

1876–1916

To Build a Fire

Jack London's own adventures rivaled those of his heroes. A street waif, he played and fought on the water front at Oakland, California. At seventeen he joined the crew of a sailing vessel. At eighteen he became a hobo, roaming over the United States and Canada. Jailed for vagrancy in Niagara, London decided that his life was going wrong and could be righted only by education. He spent three months in high school, followed by a few more months of intensive private study. He then enrolled at the University of California, but after a few months departed to seek his fortune in Alaska.

The gold rush to the Klondike was at its height, but fortune did not materialize for Jack London. After a year he sailed back to San Francisco — nineteen hundred miles in an open boat. There followed several years of struggle to make ends meet, until the novels and stories he had been working on all this time began to pay. At thirty, he built a schooner, the *Snark,* in which he and his wife sailed the South Seas during much of the remaining decade of his life. Jack London lived dangerously and furiously, but when he died at forty,

he had written forty-eight volumes in less than twenty years.

It was in Hawaii that London wrote "To Build a Fire," considered by many his greatest story. It was obviously based on his experience in Alaska. "To Build a Fire" will strike you as quite different from any of the stories you have read. There is only one human being in it. But what an opponent he takes on! You meet the opponent even before you meet the man; but, like the man, you do not at once realize the terrific power of that enemy.

D AY had broken cold and gray, exceedingly cold and gray, when the man turned aside from the main Yukon trail and climbed the high earth bank, where a dim and little-traveled trail led eastward through the fat spruce timberland. It was a steep bank, and he paused for breath at the top, excusing the act to himself by looking at his watch. It was nine o'clock. There was no sun or hint of sun, though there was not a cloud in the sky. It was a clear day, and yet there seemed an intangible pall over the face of things, a subtle gloom that made the day dark, and that was due to the ab-

"To Build a Fire," from *Lost Faces,* by Jack London. Reprinted by permission of The Macmillan Company, publishers.

sence of sun. This fact did not worry the man. He was used to the lack of sun. It had been days since he had seen the sun, and he knew that a few more days must pass before that cheerful orb, due south, would just peep above the sky line and dip immediately from view.

The man flung a look back along the way he had come. The Yukon lay a mile wide and hidden under three feet of ice. On top of this ice were as many feet of snow. It was all pure white, rolling in gentle undulations where the ice jams of the freeze-up had formed. North and south, as far as his eye could see, it was unbroken white, save for a dark hairline that curved and twisted from around the spruce-covered island to the south, and that curved and twisted away into the north, where it disappeared behind another spruce-covered island. This dark hairline was the trail — the main trail — that led south five hundred miles to the Chilkoot Pass, Dyea, and salt water; and that led north seventy miles to Dawson, and still on to the north a thousand miles to Nulato, and finally to St. Michael on Bering Sea, a thousand miles and half a thousand more.

But all this — the mysterious, far-reaching hairline trail, the absence of sun from the sky, the tremendous cold, and the strangeness and weirdness of it all — made no impression on the man. It was not because he was long used to it. He was a newcomer in the land, a cheechako, and this was his first winter. The trouble with him was that he was without imagination. He was quick and alert in the things of life, but only in the things, and not in the significances. Fifty degrees below zero meant eighty-odd degrees of frost. Such fact impressed him as being cold and uncomfortable, and that was all. It did not lead him to meditate upon his frailty as a creature of temperature, and upon man's frailty in general, able only to live within certain narrow limits of heat and cold, and from there on it did not lead him to the conjectural field of immortal-

ity and man's place in the universe. Fifty degrees below zero stood for a bite of frost that hurt and that must be guarded against by the use of mittens, ear flaps, warm moccasins, and thick socks. Fifty degrees below zero was to him just precisely fifty degrees below zero. That there should be anything more to it than that was a thought that never entered his head.

As he turned to go on, he spat speculatively. There was a sharp, explosive crackle that startled him. He spat again. And again, in the air, before it could fall to the snow, the spittle crackled. He knew that at fifty below, spittle crackled on the snow, but his spittle had crackled in the air. Undoubtedly it was colder than fifty below — how much colder he did not know. But the temperature did not matter. He was bound for the old claim on the left fork of Henderson Creek, where the boys were already. They had come over across the divide from the Indian Creek country, while he had come the roundabout way to take a look at the possibilities of getting out logs in the spring from the islands in the Yukon. He would be into camp by six o'clock; a bit after dark, it was true, but the boys would be there, a fire would be going, and a hot supper would be ready. As for lunch, he pressed his hand against the protruding bundle under his jacket. It was also under his shirt, wrapped up in a handkerchief and lying against the naked skin. It was the only way to keep the biscuits from freezing. He smiled agreeably to himself as he thought of those biscuits, each cut open and sopped in bacon grease, and each enclosing a generous slice of fried bacon.

He plunged in among the big spruce trees. The trail was faint. A foot of snow had fallen since the last sled had passed over, and he was glad he was without a sled, traveling light. In fact, he carried nothing but the lunch wrapped in the handkerchief. He was surprised, however, at the cold. It certainly was cold, he concluded, as he rubbed his numb nose and cheekbones with his mittened hand. He was a warm-whiskered man, but the hair on his face did not protect the high cheekbones and the eager nose that thrust itself aggressively into the frosty air.

At the man's heels trotted a dog, a big native husky, the proper wolf dog, gray-coated and without any visible or temperamental difference from its brother, the wild wolf. The animal was depressed by the tremendous cold. It knew that it was no time for traveling. Its instinct told it a truer tale than was told to the man by the man's judgment. In reality, it was not merely colder than fifty below zero; it was colder than sixty below, than seventy below. It was seventy-five below zero. Since the freezing point is thirty-two above zero; it meant that one hundred and seven degrees of frost obtained. The dog did not know anything about thermometers. Possibly in its brain there was no sharp consciousness of a condition of very cold such as was in the man's brain. But the brute had its instinct. It experienced a vague but menacing apprehension that subdued it and made it slink along at the man's heels and that made it question eagerly every unwonted movement of the man, as if expecting him to go into camp or to seek shelter somewhere and build a fire. The dog had learned fire, and it wanted fire, or else to burrow under the snow and cuddle its warmth away from the air.

The frozen moisture of its breathing had settled on its fur in a fine powder of frost, and especially were its jowls, muzzle, and eyelashes whitened by its crystaled breath. The man's red beard and mustache were likewise frosted, but more· solidly, the deposit taking the form of ice and increasing with every warm, moist breath he exhaled. Also, the man was chewing tobacco, and the muzzle of ice held his lips so rigidly that he was unable to clear his chin when he expelled the juice. The result

was that a crystal beard of the color and solidity of amber was increasing its length on his chin. If he fell down it would shatter itself, like glass, into brittle fragments. But he did not mind the appendage. It was the penalty all tobacco chewers paid in that country, and he had been out before in two cold snaps. They had not been so cold as this, he knew, but by the spirit thermometer at Sixty Mile he knew they had been registered at fifty below and at fifty-five.

He held on through the level stretch of woods for several miles, crossed a wide flat, and dropped down a bank to the frozen bed of a small stream. This was Henderson Creek, and he knew he was ten miles from the forks. He looked at his watch. It was ten o'clock. He was making four miles an hour, and he calculated that he would arrive at the forks at half-past twelve. He decided to celebrate that event by eating his lunch there.

The dog dropped in again at his heels, with a tail drooping discouragement, as the man swung along the creek bed. The furrow of the old sled trail was plainly visible, but a dozen inches of snow covered the marks of the last runners. In a month no man had come up or down that silent creek. The man held steadily on. He was not much given to thinking, and just then particularly he had nothing to think about save that he would eat lunch at the forks and that at six o'clock he would be in camp with the boys. There was nobody to talk to; and, had there been, speech would have been impossible because of the ice muzzle on his mouth. So he continued monotonously to chew tobacco and to increase the length of his amber beard.

Once in a while the thought reiterated itself that it was very cold and that he had never experienced such cold. As he walked along he rubbed his cheekbones and nose with the back of his mittened hand. He did this automatically, now and again changing hands. But rub as he would, the instant he stopped his cheekbones went numb, and the following instant the end of his nose went numb. He was sure to frost his cheeks; he knew that, and experienced a pang of regret that he had not devised a nose strap of the sort Bud wore in cold snaps. Such a strap passed across the cheeks, as well, and saved them. But it didn't matter much, after all. What were frosted cheeks? A bit painful, that was all; they were never serious.

Empty as the man's mind was of thought, he was keenly observant, and he noticed the changes in the creek, the curves and bends and timber jams, and always he sharply noted where he placed his feet. Once, coming around a bend, he shied abruptly, like a startled horse, curved away from the place where he had been walking, and retreated several paces back along the trail. The creek, he knew, was frozen clear to the bottom — no creek could contain water in that arctic winter — but he knew also that there were springs that bubbled out from the hillsides and ran along under the snow and on top of the ice of the creek. He knew that the coldest snaps never froze these springs, and he knew likewise their danger. They were traps. They hid pools of water under the snow that might be three inches deep, or three feet. Sometimes a skin of ice half an inch thick covered them, and in turn was covered by the snow. Sometimes there were alternate layers of water and ice skin, so that when one broke through he kept on breaking through for a while, sometimes wetting himself to the waist.

That was why he had shied in such panic. He had felt the give under his feet and heard the crackle of a snow-hidden ice skin. And to get his feet wet in such a temperature meant trouble and danger. At the very least it meant delay, for he would be forced to stop and build a fire, and under its protection to bare his feet while he dried his socks and moccasins. He stood and studied the creek bed and its banks, and decided that the flow of water came from the right. He reflected a while, rubbing his nose and cheeks, then skirted to the left stepping gingerly and testing the footing for each step. Once clear of the danger, he took a fresh chew of tobacco and swung along at his four-mile gait.

In the course of the next two hours he came upon several similar traps. Usually the snow above the hidden pools had a sunken, candied appearance that advertised the danger. Once again, however, he had a close call; and once, suspecting danger, he compelled the dog to go on in front. The dog did not want to go. It hung back until the man shoved it forward, and then it went quickly across the white, unbroken surface. Suddenly it broke through, floundered to one side; and got away to firmer footing. It had wet its forefeet and legs, and almost immediately the water that clung to it turned to ice. It made quick efforts to lick the ice off its legs, then dropped down in the snow and began to bite out the ice that had formed between the toes. This was a matter of instinct. To permit the ice to remain would mean sore feet. It did not know this. It merely obeyed the mysterious prompting that arose from the deep crypts of its being. But the man knew, having achieved a judgment on the subject, and he removed the mitten from his right hand and helped tear out the ice particles. He did not expose his fingers more than a minute, and was astonished at the swift numbness that smote them. It certainly was cold. He pulled on the mitten hastily, and beat the hand savagely across his chest.

At twelve o'clock the day was at its brightest. Yet the sun was too far south on its winter journey to clear the horizon. The bulge of the earth intervened between it and Henderson Creek, where the man walked under a clear sky at noon and cast no shadow. At half-past twelve, to the minute, he arrived at the forks of the creek. He was pleased at the speed he had made. If he kept it up, he would certainly be with the boys by six. He unbuttoned his jacket and shirt and drew forth his lunch. The action consumed no more than a quarter of a minute, yet in that brief moment the numbness laid hold of the exposed fingers. He did not put the mitten on, but, instead, struck the fingers a dozen sharp smashes against his leg. Then he sat down on a snow-covered log to eat. The sting that followed upon the striking of his fingers against his leg ceased so quickly that he was startled. He had had no chance to take a bite of biscuit. He struck the fingers repeatedly and returned them to the mitten, baring the other hand for the purpose of eating. He tried to take a mouthful, but the ice muzzle prevented. He had forgotten to build a fire and thaw out. He chuckled at his foolishness, and as he chuckled he noted the numbness creeping into the exposed fingers. Also he noted that the stinging which had first come to his toes when he sat down was already passing away. He wondered whether the toes were warm or numb. He moved them inside the moccasins and decided that they were numb.

He pulled the mitten on hurriedly and stood up. He was a bit frightened. He stamped up and down until the stinging returned into the feet. It certainly was cold, was his thought. That man from Sulfur Creek had spoken the truth when telling how cold it sometimes got in the country. And he had laughed at him at the time! That showed one must not be too sure of things. There was no mistake about it, it *was* cold. He strode up and down, stamping his feet and threshing his arms, until reassured by the returning warmth. Then he got out matches and proceeded to make a fire. From the undergrowth, where high water of the previous spring had lodged a supply of seasoned twigs, he got his firewood. Working carefully from a small beginning, he soon had a roaring fire, over which he thawed the ice from

his face and in the protection of which he ate his biscuits. For the moment the cold of space was outwitted. The dog took satisfaction in the fire, stretching out close enough for warmth and far enough away to escape being singed.

When the man had finished, he filled his pipe and took his comfortable time over a smoke. Then he pulled on his mittens, settled the ear flaps of his cap firmly about his ears, and took the creek trail up the left fork. The dog was disappointed and yearned back toward the fire. This man did not know cold. Possibly all the generations of his ancestry had been ignorant of cold, of real cold, of cold one hundred and seven degrees below freezing point. But the dog knew; all its ancestry knew, and it had inherited the knowledge. And it knew that it was not good to walk abroad in such fearful cold. It was the time to lie snug in a hole in the snow and wait for a curtain of cloud to be drawn across the face of outer space whence this cold came. On the other hand, there was no keen intimacy between the dog and the man. The one was the toil-slave of the other, and the only caresses it had ever received were the caresses of the whiplash and of harsh and menacing throat sounds that threatened the whiplash. So the dog made no effort to communicate its apprehension to the man. It was not concerned in the welfare of the man; it was for its own sake that it yearned back toward the fire. But the man whistled, and spoke to it with the sound of whiplashes, and the dog swung in at the man's heels and followed after.

The man took a chew of tobacco and proceeded to start a new amber beard. Also, his moist breath quickly powdered with white his mustache, eyebrows, and lashes. There did not seem to be so many springs on the left fork of the Henderson, and for half an hour the man saw no signs of any. And then it happened. At a place where there were no signs, where the soft, unbroken snow seemed to advertise solidity beneath, the man broke through. It was not deep. He wet himself halfway to the knees before he floundered out to the firm crust.

He was angry, and cursed his luck aloud. He had hoped to get into camp with the boys at six o'clock, and this would delay him an hour, for he would have to build a fire and dry out his footgear. This was imperative at that low temperature — he knew that much; and he turned aside to the bank, which he climbed. On top, tangled in the underbrush about the trunks of several small spruce trees, was a high-water deposit of dry firewood — sticks and twigs, principally, but also larger portions of seasoned branches and fine, dry, last year's grasses. He threw down several large pieces on top of the snow. This served for a foundation and prevented the young flame from drowning itself in the snow it otherwise would melt. The flame he got by touching a match to a small shred of birch bark that he took from his pocket. This burned even more readily than paper. Placing it on the foundation, he fed the young flame with wisps of dry grass and with the tiniest dry twigs.

He worked slowly and carefully, keenly aware of his danger. Gradually, as the flame grew stronger, he increased the size of the twigs with which he fed it. He squatted in the snow, pulling the twigs out from their entanglement in the brush and feeding directly to the flame. He knew there must be no failure. When it is seventy-five below zero, a man must not fail in his first attempt to build a fire — that is, if his feet are wet. If his feet are dry, and he fails, he can run along the trail for half a mile and restore his circulation. But the circulation of wet and freezing feet cannot be restored by running when it is seventy-five below. No matter how fast he runs, the wet feet will freeze the harder.

All this the man knew. The old-timer on Sulfur Creek had told him about it the previous fall, and now he was appreciating the advice. Already all sensation had gone out of his feet. To build the fire, he had been forced to remove his mittens, and the fingers had quickly gone numb. His pace of four miles an hour had kept his heart pumping blood to the surface of his body and to all the extremities. But the instant he stopped, the action of the pump eased down. The cold of space smote the unprotected tip of the planet, and he, being on that unprotected tip, received the full force of the blow. The blood of his body recoiled before it. The blood was alive, like the dog, and like the dog it wanted to hide away and cover itself up from the fearful cold. So long as he walked four miles an hour, he pumped that blood, willy-nilly, to the surface; but now it ebbed away and sank down into the recesses of his body. The extremities were the first to feel its absence. His wet feet froze the faster, and his exposed fingers numbed the faster, though they had not yet begun to freeze. Nose and cheeks were already freezing, while the skin of all his body chilled as it lost its blood.

But he was safe. Toes and nose and cheeks would be only touched by the frost, for the fire was beginning to burn with strength. He was feeding it with twigs the size of his finger. In another minute he would be able to feed it with branches the size of his wrist, and then he could remove his wet footgear, and, while it dried, he could keep his naked feet warm by the fire, rubbing them at first, of course, with snow. The fire was a success. He was safe. He remembered the advice of the old-timer on Sulfur Creek, and smiled. The old-timer had been very serious in laying down the law that no man must travel alone in the Klondike after fifty below. Well, here he was; he had had the accident; he was alone; and he had saved himself. Those old-timers were rather womanish, some of them, he thought. All a man had to do was to keep his head,

JACK LONDON 799

and he was all right. Any man who was a man could travel alone. But it was surprising the rapidity with which his cheeks and nose were freezing. And he had not thought his fingers could go lifeless in so short a time. Lifeless they were, for he could scarcely make them move together to grip a twig, and they seemed remote from his body and from him. When he touched a twig he had to look and see whether or not he had hold of it. The wires were pretty well down between him and his finger ends.

All of which counted for little. There was the fire, snapping and crackling and promising life with every dancing flame. He started to untie his moccasins. They were coated with ice; the thick German socks were like sheaths of iron halfway to the knees; and the moccasin strings were like rods of steel all twisted and knotted as by some conflagration. For a moment he tugged with his numb fingers, then, realizing the folly of it, he drew his sheath knife.

But before he could cut the strings it happened. It was his own fault, or, rather, his mistake. He should not have built the fire under the spruce tree. He should have built it in the open. But it had been easier to pull the twigs from the bush and drop them directly on the fire. Now the tree under which he had done this carried a weight of snow on its boughs. No wind had blown for weeks, and each bough was fully freighted. Each time he had pulled a twig he had communicated a slight agitation to the tree — an imperceptible agitation, so far as he was concerned, but an agitation sufficient to bring about the disaster. High up in the tree one bough capsized its load of snow. This fell on the boughs beneath, capsizing them. This process continued, spreading out and involving the whole tree. It grew like an avalanche, and it descended without warning upon the man and the fire, and the fire was blotted out! Where it had burned was a mantle of fresh and disordered snow.

The man was shocked. It was as though he had just heard his own sentence of death. For a moment he sat and stared at the spot where the fire had been. Then he grew very calm. Perhaps the old-timer on Sulfur Creek was right. If he had only had a trailmate, he would have been in no danger now. The trailmate could have built the fire. Well, it was up to him to build the fire over again, and this second time there must be no failure. Even if he succeeded, he would most likely lose some toes. His feet must be badly frozen by now, and there would be some time before the second fire was ready.

Such were his thoughts, but he did not sit and think them. He was busy all the time they were passing through his mind. He made a new foundation for a fire, this time in the open, where no treacherous tree could blot it out. Next he gathered dry grasses and tiny twigs from the high-water flotsam. He could not bring his fingers together to pull them out, but he was able to gather them by the handful. In this way he got many rotten twigs and bits of green moss that were undesirable, but it was the best he could do. He worked methodically, even collecting an armful of the larger branches to be used later when the fire gathered strength. And all the while the dog sat and watched him, a certain yearning wistfulness in its eyes, for it looked upon him as the fire provider, and the fire was slow in coming.

When all was ready, the man reached in his pocket for a second piece of birch bark. He knew the bark was there, and, though he could not feel it with his fingers, he could hear its crisp rustling as he fumbled for it. Try as he would, he could not clutch hold of it. And all the time, in his consciousness, was the knowledge that each instant his feet were freezing. This thought tended to put him in a panic, but he fought against it and kept calm. He pulled on his mittens with his teeth, and threshed his arms back and forth, beating his hands with all his might against his sides. He did this sitting down, and he stood up to do it; and all the while the dog sat in the snow, its wolf brush of a tail curled around warmly over its forefeet, its sharp wolf ears pricked forward intently as it watched the man. And the man, as he beat and threshed with his arms and hands, felt a great surge of envy as he regarded the creature that was warm and secure in its natural covering.

After a time he was aware of the first faraway signals of sensation in his beaten fingers. The faint tingling grew stronger till it evolved into a stinging ache that was excruciating, but which the man hailed with satisfaction. He stripped the mitten from his right hand and fetched forth the birch bark. The exposed fingers were quickly going numb again. Next he brought out his bunch of sulfur matches. But the tremendous cold had already driven the life out of his fingers. In his effort to separate one match from the others, the whole bunch fell in the snow. He tried to pick it out of the snow, but failed. The dead fingers could neither touch nor clutch. He was very careful. He drove the thought of his freezing feet, and nose, and cheeks, out of his mind, devoting his whole soul to the matches. He watched, using the sense of vision in place of that of touch, and when he saw his fingers on each side of the bunch, he closed them — that is, he willed to close them, for the wires were down, and the fingers did not obey. He pulled the mitten on the right hand, and beat it fiercely against his knee. Then, with both mittened hands, he scooped the bunch of matches, along with much snow, into his lap. Yet he was no better off.

After some manipulation he managed to get the bunch between the heels of his mittened hands. In this fashion he carried it to his mouth. The ice crackled and snapped when by a violent effort he opened his mouth. He drew the lower jaw in, curled the upper lip out of the way, and scraped the bunch with his upper teeth in order to separate a match. He succeeded in getting one, which he dropped on his lap. He was no better off. He could not pick it up. Then he devised a way. He picked it up in his teeth and scratched it on his leg. Twenty times he scratched before he succeeded in lighting it. As it flamed he held it with his teeth to the birch bark. But the burning brimstone went up his nostrils and into his lungs, causing him to cough spasmodically. The match fell into the snow and went out.

The old-timer on Sulfur Creek was right, he thought in the moment of controlled despair that ensued: after fifty below, a man should travel with a partner. He beat his hands, but failed in exciting any sensation. Suddenly he bared both hands, removing the mittens with his teeth. He caught the whole bunch between the heels of his hands. His arm muscles, not being frozen, enabled him to press the hand heels tightly against the matches. Then he scratched the bunch along his leg. It flared into flame, seventy sulfur matches at once! There was no wind to blow them out. He kept his head to one side to escape the strangling fumes, and held the blazing bunch to the birch bark. As he so held it, he became aware of sensation in his hand. His flesh was burning. He could smell it. Deep down below the surface he could feel it. The sensation developed into pain that grew acute. And still he endured it, holding the flame of the matches clumsily to the bark that would not light readily because his own burning hands were in the way, absorbing most of the flame.

At last, when he could endure no more, he jerked his hands apart. The blazing matches fell sizzling into the snow, but the birch bark was alight. He began laying dry grasses and the tiniest twigs on the flame. He could not pick and choose, for he had to lift the fuel between the heels of his hands. Small pieces of rotten wood and green moss clung to the twigs, and he bit them off as well as he could with his teeth. He cherished the flame carefully and awkwardly. It meant life, and it must not perish. The withdrawal of blood from the surface of his body now made him begin to shiver, and he grew more awkward. A large piece of green moss fell squarely on the little fire. He tried to poke it out with his fingers, but his shivering frame made him poke too far, and he disrupted the nucleus of the little fire, the burning grasses and tiny twigs separating and scattering. He tried to poke them together again, but, in spite of the tenseness of the effort, his shivering got away with him, and the twigs were hopelessly scattered. Each twig gushed a puff of smoke and went out. The fire provider had failed. As he looked apathetically about him, his eyes chanced on the dog, sitting across the ruins of the fire from him, in the snow, making restless, hunching movements, slightly lifting one forefoot and then the other, shifting its weight back and forth on them with wistful eagerness.

The sight of the dog put a wild idea into his head. He remembered the tale of the man, caught in a blizzard, who killed a steer and crawled inside the carcass, and so was saved. He would kill the dog and bury his hands in the warm body until the numbness went out of them. Then he could build another fire. He spoke to the dog, calling it to him; but in his voice was a strange note of fear that frightened the animal, who had never known the man to speak in such a way before. Something was the matter, and its suspicious nature sensed danger — it knew not what danger, but somewhere, somehow, in its brain arose an apprehension of the man. It flattened its ears down at the sound of the man's voice, and its restless, hunching movements and the liftings and shiftings of its forefeet became more pronounced; but it would not come to the man. He

got on his hands and knees and crawled toward the dog. This unusual posture again excited suspicion, and the animal sidled mincingly away.

The man sat up in the snow for a moment and struggled for calmness. Then he pulled on his mittens, by means of his teeth, and got up on his feet. He glanced down at first in order to assure himself that he was really standing up, for the absence of sensation in his feet left him unrelated to the earth. His erect position in itself started to drive the webs of suspicion from the dog's mind; and when he spoke peremptorily with the sound of whiplashes in his voice, the dog rendered its customary allegiance and came to him. As it came within reaching distance, the man lost his control. His arms flashed out to the dog, and he experienced genuine surprise when he discovered that his hands could not clutch, that there was neither bend nor feeling in the fingers. He had forgotten for the moment that they were frozen and that they were freezing more and more. All this happened quickly, and before the animal could get away, he encircled its body with his arms. He sat down in the snow, and in this fashion held the dog, while it snarled and whined and struggled.

But it was all he could do, hold its body encircled in his arms and sit there. He realized that he could not kill the dog. There was no way to do it. With his helpless hands he could neither draw nor hold his sheath knife nor throttle the animal. He released it, and it plunged wildly away, with tail between its legs, and still snarling. It halted forty feet away and surveyed him curiously, with ears sharply pricked forward. The man looked down at his hands in order to locate them, and found them hanging on the ends of his arms. It struck him as curious that one should have to use his eyes in order to find out where his hands were. He began threshing his arms back and forth, beating the mittened hands against his sides. He did this for five minutes, violently, and his heart pumped enough blood up to the surface to put a stop to his shivering. But no sensation was aroused in the hands. He had an impression that they hung like weights on the ends of his arms, but when he tried to run the impression down, he could not find it.

A certain fear of death, dull and oppressive, came to him. This fear quickly became poignant as he realized that it was no longer a mere matter of freezing his fingers and toes, or of losing his hands and feet, but that it was a matter of life and death, with the chances against him. This threw him into a panic, and he turned and ran up the creek bed along the old dim trail. The dog joined in behind and kept up with him. He ran blindly, without intention, in fear such as he had never known in his life. Slowly, as he plowed and floundered through the snow, he began to see things again — the banks of the creek, the old timber jams, the leafless aspens, and the sky. The running made him feel better. He did not shiver. Maybe, if he ran on, his feet would thaw out; and, anyway, if he ran far enough, he would reach the camp and the boys. Without doubt he would lose some fingers and toes and some of his face; but the boys would take care of him, and save the rest of him when he got there. And at the same time there was another thought in his mind that said he would never get to the camp and the boys; that it was too many miles away, that the freezing had too great a start on him, and that he would soon be stiff and dead. This thought he kept in the background and refused to consider. Sometimes it pushed itself forward and demanded to be heard, but he thrust it back and strove to think of other things.

It struck him as curious that he could run at all on feet so frozen that he could not feel them when they struck the earth and took the weight of his body. He seemed to himself to skim along above the surface, and to have no connection with the earth. Somewhere he had once seen a winged Mercury, and he wondered if Mercury felt as he felt when skimming over the earth.

His theory of running until he reached camp and the boys had one flaw in it: he lacked the endurance. Several times he stumbled, and finally he tottered, crumpled up, and fell. When he tried to rise, he failed. He must sit and rest, he decided, and next time he would merely walk and keep on going. As he sat and regained his breath, he noted that he was feeling quite warm and comfortable. He was not shivering, and it even seemed that a warm glow had come to his chest and trunk. And yet, when he touched his nose or cheeks, there was no sensation. Running would not thaw them out. Nor would it thaw out his hands and feet. Then the thought came to him that the frozen portions of his body must be extending. He tried to keep this thought down, to forget it, to think of something else; he was aware of the panicky feeling that it caused, and he was afraid of the panic. But the thought asserted itself, and persisted, until it produced a vision of his body totally frozen. This was too much, and he made another wild run along the trail. Once he slowed down to a walk, but the thought of the freezing extending itself made him run again.

And all the time the dog ran with him, at his heels. When he fell down a second time, it curled its tail over its forefeet and sat in front of him, facing him, curiously eager and intent. The warmth and security of the animal angered him, and he cursed it till it flattened down its ears appeasingly. This time the shivering came more quickly upon the man. He was losing in his battle with the frost. It was creeping into his body from all sides. The thought of it drove him on, but he ran no more than a hundred feet, when he staggered and pitched headlong. It was his last panic. When he had recovered his breath and control, he sat up and entertained in his mind the conception of meeting death with dignity. However, the conception did not come to him in such terms. His idea of it was that he had been making a fool of himself, running around like a chicken with its head cut off — such was the simile that occurred to him. Well, he was bound to freeze anyway, and he might as well take it decently. With this new-found peace of mind came the first glimmerings of drowsiness. A good idea, he thought, to sleep off to death. It was like taking an anesthetic. Freezing was not so bad as people thought. There were lots worse ways to die.

He pictured the boys finding his body next day. Suddenly he found himself with them, coming along the trail and looking for himself. And, still with them, he came around a turn in the trail and found himself lying in the snow. He did not belong with himself any more, for even then he was out of himself standing with the boys and looking at himself in the snow. It certainly was cold, was his thought. When he got back to the States, he could tell the folks what real cold was. He drifted on from this to a vision of the old-timer on Sulfur Creek. He could see him quite clearly, warm and comfortable, and smoking a pipe.

"You were right, old hoss; you were right," the man mumbled to the old-timer of Sulfur Creek.

Then the man drowsed off into what seemed to him the most comfortable and satisfying sleep he had ever known. The dog sat facing him and waiting. The brief day drew to a close in a long, slow twilight. There were no signs of a fire to be made, and, besides, never in the dog's experience had it known a man to sit like that in the snow and make no fire. As the twilight drew on, its eager yearning for the fire mastered it, and with a great lifting and shifting of forefeet, it whined softly, then flattened its ears down in anticipation of being chidden by the man. But the man remained silent. Later, the dog whined loudly. And still later it crept close to the man and caught the scent of death. This made the animal bristle and back away. A little longer it delayed, howling under the stars that leaped and danced and shone brightly in the cold sky. Then it turned and trotted up the trail in the direction of the camp it knew, where were the other food providers and fire providers.

FOR DISCUSSION

1. Very little is said about "the man" in this story; you are not even told his name. Yet the few pieces of information revealed about him are very important. Illustrate this with specific passages from the story. What criticism of human beings does London make in this story?

2. Is the man's lack of imagination a help or hindrance to him in his particular situation? Discuss whether a literal, matter-of-fact mind stands a person in better stead during a crisis than an imaginative, far-roving mind.

3. The dog stands midway between the man and impersonal nature. How does the author use the dog to increase your sense of danger? What does the story suggest about animal instinct as opposed to human instinct? Do you think this conclusion is scientifically sound? Describe the relationship between the dog and the man. Had the dog trusted the man more, would the story have ended differently?

4. Struggle against cold is a particularly dramatic and dangerous part of human existence. How does this story suggest that cold makes a man his own enemy?

5. How would the quality of the story have been affected had the man been rescued?

As the Artist Sees It ➤

Here Robert Shore has pictured the climax of Jack London's "To Build a Fire." Notice how the artist has emphasized the sense of desperation in the man's last attempt to save himself. Is extreme cold evident in the colors of the painting?

STEPHEN
CRANE

1871–1900

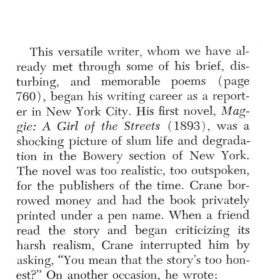

This versatile writer, whom we have already met through some of his brief, disturbing, and memorable poems (page 760), began his writing career as a reporter in New York City. His first novel, *Maggie: A Girl of the Streets* (1893), was a shocking picture of slum life and degradation in the Bowery section of New York. The novel was too realistic, too outspoken, for the publishers of the time. Crane borrowed money and had the book privately printed under a pen name. When a friend read the story and began criticizing its harsh realism, Crane interrupted him by asking, "You mean that the story's too honest?" On another occasion, he wrote:

. . . I understand that a man is born into the world with his own pair of eyes, and he is not at all responsible for his vision — he is merely responsible for his quality of personal honesty. To keep close to this personal honesty is my supreme ambition . . .

Crane never forgot this ideal. All of his work is distinguished by his honest realism. Another outstanding characteristic of Crane's writing, and one that does not appear too often in the literature of this period, is a subtle and satiric sense of humor.

Stephen Crane was born in Newark, New Jersey, in 1871. The son of a Methodist minister, Crane was one of a family of fourteen. He attended preparatory school and then spent one year at Lafayette College, where it is said he shocked his English professor by a violent criticism of Tennyson's poetry. He spent another year at Syracuse University, where he played shortstop on the varsity baseball team. During these years, Crane had been reading some of the important French and Russian realistic novelists. Influenced by them, and determined to devote his life to writing, Crane left school and began working as a journalist.

His career as a newspaperman gave him a series of opportunities for firsthand observation. He saw slum life in the New York Bowery. He traveled through Texas and Mexico, reporting for a newspaper syndicate. He went on a short expedition to Cuba, then journeyed to Greece to report on the Greco-Turkish War. Returning to the United States, Crane married, and he and his wife sailed for England. While in that country, Crane became a close friend of the novelist Joseph Conrad, who later wrote an introduction to Crane's biography.

During these years of travel and journalism, Crane had been writing a number of short stories. "The Open Boat" is based on one of his actual experiences. The story, an account of a desperate struggle for survival after the sinking of a ship, has been called "one of the short masterpieces of modern American prose." His other stories range over a variety of scenes in the United States. "An Experiment in Misery" takes place in New York. "The Monster" is set in upper New York state. Two of his finest tales take place in the West. They are "The Blue Hotel" and "The Bride Comes to Yellow Sky."

His short stories alone would have earned Crane an honorable place in our literature, but standing above everything else is his masterpiece, *The Red Badge of Courage* (1895). This novel of the War Between the States stands with *The Scarlet Letter*, *Moby Dick*, and *Huckleberry Finn* as one of the four finest American novels of the nineteenth century. When he wrote the novel, Crane had not seen war at first hand, but after his experiences in Greece and later in Cuba during the Spanish-American War, he said to a friend, "*The Red Badge* is all right." The work of his imagination had been proved accurate.

While reporting on the Spanish-American War in Cuba for the New York *World,* Crane earned a reputation for bravery under fire. However, the experience severely injured his health. He died of tuberculosis on June 5, 1900, five months before his twenty-ninth birthday. His early death was a tragic loss to our literature.

The Bride Comes to Yellow Sky

A modern magazine of "westerns," advertising its short-story needs, specifies that each story should have "a strong central character resolving a tough situation or a famous situation from a new angle. Hero or villain may be lead character." As you read this story, decide whether the editors of the magazine would have bought it.

T HE GREAT Pullman was whirling onward with such dignity of motion that a glance from the window seemed simply to prove that the plains of Texas were pouring eastward. Vast flats of green grass, dull-hued spaces of mesquite and cactus, little groups of frame houses, woods of light and tender trees, all were sweeping into the east, sweeping over the horizon, a precipice.

A newly married pair had boarded this coach at San Antonio. The man's face was reddened from many days in the wind and sun, and a direct result

"The Bride Comes to Yellow Sky" reprinted from *Stephen Crane: An Omnibus* by Stephen Crane, by permission of Alfred A. Knopf, Inc. Copyright, 1952, by Alfred A. Knopf, Inc.

of his new black clothes was that his brick-colored hands were constantly performing in a most conscious fashion. From time to time he looked down respectfully at his attire. He sat with a hand on each knee, like a man waiting in a barber's shop. The glances he devoted to other passengers were furtive and shy.

The bride was not pretty, nor was she very young. She wore a dress of blue cashmere, with small reservations of velvet here and there, and with steel buttons abounding. She continually twisted her head to regard her puff sleeves, very stiff, straight, and high. They embarrassed her. It was quite apparent that she had cooked, and that she expected to cook, dutifully. The blushes caused by the careless scrutiny of some passengers as she had entered the car were strange to see upon this plain, under-class countenance, which was drawn in placid, almost emotionless lines.

They were evidently very happy. "Ever been in a parlor car before?" he asked, smiling with delight.

"No," she answered, "I never was. It's fine, ain't it?"

"Great! And then after a while we'll go forward to the diner, and get a big layout. Finest meal in the world. Charge a dollar."

"Oh, do they?" cried the bride. "Charge a dollar? Why, that's too much — for us — ain't it, Jack?"

"Not this trip, anyhow," he answered bravely. "We're going to go the whole thing."

Later he explained to her about the trains. "You see, it's a thousand miles from one end of Texas to the other; and this train runs right across it, and never stops but four times." He had the pride of an owner. He pointed out to her the dazzling fittings of the coach; and in truth her eyes opened wider as she contemplated the sea-green figured velvet, the shining brass, silver, and glass, the wood that gleamed as darkly brilliant as the surface of a pool of oil. At one end a bronze figure sturdily held a support for a separated chamber, and at convenient places on the ceiling were frescoes [1] in olive and silver.

To the minds of the pair, their surroundings reflected the glory of their marriage that morning in San Antonio; this was the environment of their new estate; and the man's face in particular beamed with an elation that made him appear ridiculous to the Negro porter. This individual at times surveyed them from afar with an amused and superior grin. On other occasions he bullied them with skill in ways that did not make it exactly plain to them that they were being bullied. He subtly used all the manners of the most unconquerable kind of snobbery. He oppressed them; but of this oppression they had small knowledge, and they speedily forgot that infrequently a number of travelers covered them with stares of derisive enjoyment. Historically there was sup-

posed to be something infinitely humorous in their situation.

"We are due in Yellow Sky at 3:42," he said, looking tenderly into her eyes.

"Oh, are we?" she said, as if she had not been aware of it. To evince surprise at her husband's statement was part of her wifely amiability. She took from a pocket a little silver watch; and as she held it before her, and stared at it with a frown of attention, the new husband's face shone.

"I bought it in San Anton' from a friend of mine," he told her gleefully.

"It's seventeen minutes past twelve," she said, looking up at him with a kind of shy and clumsy coquetry. A passenger, noting this play, grew excessively sardonic, and winked at himself in one of the numerous mirrors.

At last they went to the dining car. Two rows of Negro waiters, in glowing white suits, surveyed their entrance with the interest, and also the equanimity, of men who had been forewarned. The pair fell to the lot of a waiter who happened to feel pleasure in steering them through their meal. He viewed them with the manner of a fatherly pilot, his countenance radiant with benevolence. The patronage, entwined with the ordinary deference, was not plain to them. And yet, as they returned to their coach, they showed in their faces a sense of escape.

To the left, miles down a long purple slope, was a little ribbon of mist where moved the keening [2] Rio Grande. The train was approaching it at an angle, and the apex was Yellow Sky. Presently it was apparent that, as the distance from Yellow Sky grew shorter, the husband became commensurately restless. His brick-red hands were more insistent in their prominence. Occasionally he was even rather absent-minded and faraway when the bride leaned forward and addressed him.

[1] frescoes (frĕs′kōz): paintings made on fresh plaster before it dries.

[2] keening: lamenting; moaning. Used here figuratively to indicate the sound of the river.

As a matter of truth, Jack Potter was beginning to find the shadow of a deed weigh upon him like a leaden slab. He, the town marshal of Yellow Sky, a man known, liked, and feared in his corner, a prominent person, had gone to San Antonio to meet a girl he believed he loved, and there, after the usual prayers, had actually induced her to marry him, without consulting Yellow Sky for any part of the transaction. He was now bringing his bride before an innocent and unsuspecting community.

Of course, people in Yellow Sky married as it pleased them, in accordance with a general custom; but such was Potter's thought of his duty to his friends, or of their idea of his duty, or of an unspoken form which does not control men in these matters, that he felt he was heinous. He had committed an extraordinary crime. Face to face with his girl in San Antonio, and spurred by his sharp impulse, he had gone headlong over all the social hedges. At San Antonio he was like a man hidden in the dark. A knife to sever any friendly duty, any form, was easy to his hand in that remote city. But the hour of Yellow Sky — the hour of daylight — was approaching.

He knew full well that his marriage was an important thing to his town. It could only be exceeded by the burning of the new hotel. His friends could not forgive him. Frequently he had reflected on the advisability of telling them by telegraph, but a new cowardice had been upon him. He feared to do it. And now the train was hurrying him toward a scene of amazement, glee, and reproach. He glanced out of the window at the line of haze swinging slowly in toward the train.

Yellow Sky had a kind of brass band, which played painfully, to the delight of the populace. He laughed without heart as he thought of it. If the citizens could dream of his prospective arrival with his bride, they would parade the band at the station and escort them,

amid cheers and laughing congratulations, to his adobe home.

He resolved that he would use all the devices of speed and plainscraft in making the journey from the station to his house. Once within the safe citadel, he could issue some sort of vocal bulletin, and then not go among the citizens until they had time to wear off a little of their enthusiasm.

The bride looked anxiously at him. "What's worrying you, Jack?"

He laughed again. "I'm not worrying, girl; I'm only thinking of Yellow Sky."

She flushed in comprehension.

A sense of mutual guilt invaded their minds and developed a finer tenderness. They looked at each other with eyes softly aglow. But Potter often laughed the same nervous laugh; the flush upon the bride's face seemed quite permanent.

The traitor to the feelings of Yellow Sky narrowly watched the speeding landscape. "We're nearly there," he said.

STEPHEN CRANE 809

Presently the porter came and announced the proximity of Potter's home. He held a brush in his hand, and, with all his airy superiority gone, he brushed Potter's new clothes as the latter slowly turned this way and that way. Potter fumbled out a coin and gave it to the porter, as he had seen others do. It was a heavy and muscle-bound business, as that of a man shoeing his first horse.

The porter took their bag, and as the train began to slow, they moved forward to the hooded platform of the car. Presently the two engines and their long string of coaches rushed into the station of Yellow Sky.

"They have to take water here," said Potter, from a constricted throat and in mournful cadence, as one announcing death. Before the train stopped, his eye had swept the length of the platform, and he was glad and astonished to see there was none upon it but the station agent, who, with a slightly hurried and anxious air, was walking toward the water tanks. When the train had halted, the porter alighted first, and placed in position a little temporary step.

"Come on, girl," said Potter, hoarsely. As he helped her down, they each laughed on a false note. He took the bag from the Negro, and bade his wife cling to his arm. As they slunk rapidly away, his hangdog glance perceived that they were unloading the two trunks, and also that the station agent, far ahead near the baggage car, had turned and was running toward him, making gestures. He laughed, and groaned as he laughed, when he noted the first effect of his marital bliss upon Yellow Sky. He gripped his wife's arm firmly to his side, and they fled. Behind them the porter stood, chuckling fatuously.

II

The California express on the Southern Railway was due at Yellow Sky in twenty-one minutes. There were six men at the bar of the Weary Gentleman saloon. One was a drummer [1] who talked a great deal and rapidly; three were Texans who did not care to talk at that time; and two were Mexican sheepherders, who did not talk as a general practice in the Weary Gentleman saloon. The barkeeper's dog lay on the boardwalk that crossed in front of the door. His head was on his paws, and he glanced drowsily here and there with the constant vigilance of a dog that is kicked on occasion. Across the sandy street were some vivid green grass-plots, so wonderful in appearance, amid the sands that burned near them in a blazing sun, that they caused a doubt in the mind. They exactly resembled the grass mats used to represent lawns on the stage. At the cooler end of the railway station, a man without a coat sat in a tilted chair and smoked his pipe. The fresh-cut bank of the Rio Grande circled near the town, and there could be seen beyond it a great plum-colored plain of mesquite.

Save for the busy drummer and his companions in the saloon, Yellow Sky was dozing. The newcomer leaned gracefully upon the bar, and recited many tales with the confidence of a bard who has come upon a new field.

"— and at the moment that the old man fell downstairs with the bureau in his arms, the old woman was coming up with two scuttles of coal, and of course — "

The drummer's tale was interrupted by a young man who suddenly appeared in the open door. He cried: "Scratchy Wilson's drunk, and has turned loose with both hands." The two Mexicans at once set down their glasses and faded out of the rear entrance of the saloon.

The drummer, innocent and jocular, answered: "All right, old man. S'pose he has? Come in and have a drink, anyhow."

But the information had made such an obvious cleft in every skull in the

[1] **drummer:** a traveling salesman.

room that the drummer was obliged to see its importance. All had become instantly solemn. "Say," said he, mystified, "what is this?" His three companions made the introductory gesture of eloquent speech; but the young man at the door forestalled them.

"It means, my friend," he answered, as he came into the saloon, "that for the next two hours this town won't be a health resort."

The barkeeper went to the door, and locked and barred it; reaching out of the window, he pulled in heavy wooden shutters, and barred them. Immediately a solemn, chapel-like gloom was upon the place. The drummer was looking from one to another.

"But say," he cried, "what is this, anyhow? You don't mean there is going to be a gun fight?"

"Don't know whether there'll be a fight or not," answered one man, grimly, "but there'll be some shootin' — some good shootin'."

The young man who had warned them waved his hand. "Oh, there'll be a fight fast enough, if anyone wants it. Anybody can get a fight out there in the street. There's a fight just waiting."

The drummer seemed to be swayed between the interest of a foreigner and a perception of personal danger.

"What did you say his name was?" he asked.

"Scratchy Wilson," they answered in chorus.

"And will he kill anybody? What are you going to do? Does this happen often? Does he rampage around like this once a week or so? Can he break in that door?"

"No, he can't break down that door," replied the barkeeper. "He's tried it three times. But when he comes you'd better lay down on the floor, stranger. He's dead sure to shoot at it, and a bullet may come through."

Thereafter the drummer kept a strict eye upon the door. The time had not yet been called for him to hug the floor, but, as a minor precaution, he sidled near to the wall. "Will he kill anybody?" he said again.

The men laughed low and scornfully at the question.

"He's out to shoot, and he's out for trouble. Don't see any good in experimentin' with him."

"But what do you do in a case like this? What do you do?"

A man responded: "Why, he and Jack Potter — "

"But," in chorus the other men interrupted, "Jack Potter's in San Anton'."

"Well, who is he? What's he got to do with it?"

"Oh, he's the town marshal. He goes out and fights Scratchy when he gets on one of these tears."

"Wow!" said the drummer, mopping his brow. "Nice job he's got."

The voices had toned away to mere whisperings. The drummer wished to ask further questions, which were born of an increasing anxiety and bewilderment; but when he attempted them, the men merely looked at him in irritation and motioned him to remain silent. A tense, waiting hush was upon them. In the deep shadows of the room, their eyes shone as they listened for sounds from the street. One man made three gestures at the barkeeper; and the latter, moving like a ghost, handed him a glass and a bottle. The man poured a full glass of whisky, and set down the bottle noiselessly. He gulped the whisky in a swallow, and turned again toward the door in immovable silence. The drummer saw that the barkeeper, without a sound, had taken a Winchester from beneath the bar. Later he saw this individual beckoning to him, so he tiptoed across the room.

"You better come with me back of the bar."

"No, thanks," said the drummer, perspiring; "I'd rather be where I can make a break for the back door."

Whereupon the man of bottles made a kindly but peremptory gesture. The drummer obeyed it, and, finding himself seated on a box with his head below the level of the bar, balm was laid upon his soul at sight of various zinc and copper fittings that bore a resemblance to armor plate. The barkeeper took a seat comfortably upon an adjacent box.

"You see," he whispered, "this here Scratchy Wilson is a wonder with a gun — a perfect wonder; and when he goes on the war-trail, we hunt our holes — naturally. He's about the last one of the old gang that used to hang out along the river here. He's a terror when he's drunk. When he's sober he's all right — kind of simple — wouldn't hurt a fly — nicest fellow in town. But when he's drunk — whoo!"

There were periods of stillness. "I wish Jack Potter was back from San Anton'," said the barkeeper. "He shot Wilson up once — in the leg — and he would sail in and pull out the kinks in this thing."

Presently they heard from a distance the sound of a shot, followed by three wild yowls. It instantly removed a bond from the men in the darkened saloon. There was a shuffling of feet. They looked at each other. "Here he comes," they said.

III

A man in a maroon-colored flannel shirt, which had been purchased for purposes of decoration, and made principally by some Jewish women on the East Side of New York, rounded a corner and walked into the middle of the main street of Yellow Sky. In either hand the man held a long, heavy, blue-black revolver. Often he yelled, and these cries rang through a semblance of a deserted village, shrilly flying over the roofs in a volume that seemed to have no relation to the ordinary vocal strength of a man. It was as if the surrounding stillness formed the arch of a tomb over him. These cries of ferocious challenge rang against walls of silence.

And his boots had red tops with gilded imprints, of the kind beloved in winter by little sledding boys on the hillsides of New England.

The man's face flamed in a rage begot of whisky. His eyes, rolling, and yet keen for ambush, hunted the still doorways and windows. He walked with the creeping movement of the midnight cat. As it occurred to him, he roared menacing information. The long revolvers in his hands were as easy as straws; they were moved with an electric swiftness. The little fingers of each hand played sometimes in a musician's way. Plain from the low collar of the shirt, the cords of his neck straightened and sank, straightened and sank, as passion moved him. The only sounds were his terrible invitations. The calm adobes preserved their demeanor at the passing of this small thing in the middle of the street.

There was no offer of fight — no offer of fight. The man called to the sky. There were no attractions. He bellowed and fumed and swayed his revolvers here and everywhere.

The dog of the barkeeper of the Weary Gentleman saloon had not appreciated the advance of events. He yet lay dozing in front of his master's door. At sight of the dog, the man paused and raised his revolver humorously. At sight of the man, the dog sprang up and walked diagonally away, with a sullen head, and growling. The man yelled, and the dog broke into a gallop. As it was about to enter an alley, there was a loud noise, a whistling, and something spat the ground directly before it. The dog screamed, and, wheeling in terror, galloped headlong in a new direction. Again there was a noise, a whistling, and sand was kicked viciously before it. Fear-stricken, the dog turned and flurried like an animal in a pen. The man stood laughing, his weapons at his hips.

Ultimately the man was attracted by the closed door of the Weary Gentleman saloon. He went to it and, hammering with a revolver, demanded drink.

The door remaining imperturbable, he picked a bit of paper from the walk, and nailed it to the framework with a knife. He then turned his back contemptuously upon this popular resort and, walking to the opposite side of the street and spinning there on his heel quickly and lithely, fired at the bit of paper. He missed it by a half inch. He swore at himself, and went away. Later he comfortably fusilladed the windows of his most intimate friend. The man was playing with this town; it was a toy for him.

But still there was no offer of fight. The name of Jack Potter, his ancient antagonist, entered his mind, and he concluded that it would be a glad thing if he should go to Potter's house, and by bombardment induce him to come out and fight. He moved in the direction of his desire, chanting Apache scalp-music.

When he arrived at it, Potter's house presented the same still front as had the other adobes. Taking up a strategic position, the man howled a challenge. But this house regarded him as might a great stone god. It gave no sign. After a decent wait, the man howled further challenges, mingling with them wonderful epithets.

Presently there came the spectacle of a man churning himself into deepest rage over the immobility of a house. He fumed at it as the winter wind attacks a prairie cabin in the North. To the distance there should have gone the sound of a tumult like the fighting of two hundred Mexicans. As necessity bade him, he paused for breath or to reload his revolvers.

IV

Potter and his bride walked sheepishly and with speed. Sometimes they laughed together shamefacedly and low.

"Next corner, dear," he said finally.

They put forth the efforts of a pair walking bowed against a strong wind.

Potter was about to raise a finger to point the first appearance of the new home when, as they circled the corner, they came face to face with a man in a maroon-colored shirt, who was feverishly pushing cartridges into a large revolver. Upon the instant the man dropped his revolver to the ground and, like lightning, whipped another from its holster. The second weapon was aimed at the bridegroom's chest.

There was a silence. Potter's mouth seemed to be merely a grave for his tongue. He exhibited an instinct to at once loosen his arm from the woman's grip, and he dropped the bag to the sand. As for the bride, her face had gone as yellow as old cloth. She was a slave to hideous rites, gazing at the apparitional snake.

The two men faced each other at a distance of three paces. He of the revolver smiled with a new and quiet ferocity.

"Tried to sneak up on me," he said. "Tried to sneak up on me!" His eyes grew more baleful. As Potter made a slight movement, the man thrust his revolver venomously forward. "No, don't you do it, Jack Potter. Don't you move a finger toward a gun just yet. Don't you move an eyelash. The time has come for me to settle with you, and I'm goin' to do it my own way, and loaf along with no interferin'. So if you don't want a gun bent on you, just mind what I tell you."

Potter looked at his enemy. "I ain't got a gun on me, Scratchy," he said. "Honest, I ain't." He was stiffening and steadying, but yet somewhere at the back of his mind a vision of the Pullman floated: the sea-green figured velvet, the shining brass, silver, and glass, the wood that gleamed as darkly brilliant as the surface of a pool of oil — all the glory of the marriage, the environment of the new estate. "You know I fight when it comes to fighting, Scratchy Wilson; but I ain't got a gun on me. You'll have to do all the shootin' yourself."

His enemy's face went livid. He stepped forward, and lashed his weapon to and fro before Potter's chest. "Don't you tell me you ain't got no gun on you, you whelp. Don't tell me no lie like that. There ain't a man in Texas ever seen you without no gun. Don't take me for no kid." His eyes blazed with light, and his throat worked like a pump.

"I ain't takin' you for no kid," answered Potter. His heels had not moved an inch backward. "I'm takin' you for a fool. I tell you I ain't got a gun, and I ain't. If you're goin' to shoot me up, you better begin now; you'll never get a chance like this again."

So much enforced reasoning had told on Wilson's rage; he was calmer. "If you ain't got a gun, why ain't you got a gun?" he sneered. "Been to Sunday school?"

"I ain't got a gun because I've just come from San Anton' with my wife. I'm married," said Potter. "And if I'd thought there was going to be any galoots like you prowling around when I brought my wife home, I'd had a gun, and don't you forget it."

"Married!" said Scratchy, not at all comprehending.

"Yes, married. I'm married," said Potter, distinctly.

"Married?" said Scratchy. Seemingly for the first time, he saw the drooping, drowning woman at the other man's side. "No!" he said. He was like a creature allowed a glimpse of another world. He moved a pace backward, and his arm, with the revolver, dropped to his side. "Is this the lady?" he asked.

"Yes, this is the lady," answered Potter.

There was another period of silence.

"Well," said Wilson at last, slowly, "I s'pose it's all off now."

"It's all off if you say so, Scratchy. You know I didn't make the trouble." Potter lifted his valise.

"Well, I 'low it's off, Jack," said Wilson. He was looking at the ground. "Married!" He was not a student of chivalry; it was merely that in the presence of this foreign condition he was a simple child of the earlier plains. He picked up his starboard revolver, and, placing both weapons in their holsters, he went away. His feet made funnel-shaped tracks in the heavy sand.

FOR DISCUSSION

1. What words do you find in the first paragraph of the story that give the feeling of the train's movement?

2. Why do you think Crane emphasized the man's "brick-colored hands," his "new black clothes"?

3. Why had the marshal, Jack Potter, not told his friends of his marriage?

4. How does the marshal show his delight in the elegance of the parlor car?

5. How is the drummer (and the reader) made aware of the danger of Scratchy Wilson on the "war-trail"?

6. Is the description of Scratchy Wilson convincing? Why does Scratchy laugh when the dog shows fear?

7. Find examples of humor in the story.

8. How is the suspense of the story created? maintained?

9. Explain the metaphor: "Potter's mouth seemed to be merely a grave for his tongue."

10. How does the bride reveal her terror of Scratchy Wilson?

11. What finally caused Scratchy to back down and go away without harming Potter?

12. Compare "The Bride Comes to Yellow Sky" with any story of the West that you have read or seen dramatized on television. Is Crane's story more or less convincing? Why?

FURTHER READING

Stephen Crane's *The Red Badge of Courage* is considered one of the greatest American novels. If you have not yet read it, you may want to do so now. The complete book is included in *Four American Novels*, edited by Edmund Fuller and Olga Achtenhagen (Harcourt, Brace & World, 1959).

O. HENRY

1862–1910

The Cop and the Anthem

O. Henry put his peculiar stamp upon the short story. An O. Henry story never lacks a plot, each detail being carefully planned. But the surprise ending was the trick that O. Henry made his special trade-mark. His use of conversation, often humorous or slangy and sometimes exaggerated, is also typical.

O. Henry's real name was William Sydney Porter. Before settling down to newspaper work and writing, he worked as a drugstore clerk, went to a Texas ranch for his health, and became a teller in a bank in Austin, where he was charged with embezzlement. He protested his innocence, but becoming panicky, he fled trial. His wife's illness caused him to return, stand trial, and take the punishment — three years in a Federal prison. There he wrote some of his stories. From his own life he drew the material for his accounts of the everyday people, the hard-luck souls that he describes with a warmth of human understanding and sympathy.

AN AUTHOR'S TECHNIQUE. Early in the story you will recognize the author's *tone*. Tone is a quality you readily recognize in spoken words, for it usually reveals the speaker's true feeling or attitude and slants the total meaning. You can recognize tone in a short story by the choice of words and details.

O n his bench in Madison Square, Soapy moved uneasily. When wild geese honk high of nights, and when women without sealskin coats grow kind to their husbands, and when Soapy moves uneasily on his bench in the park, you may know that winter is near at hand.

A dead leaf fell in Soapy's lap. That was Jack Frost's card. Jack is kind to the regular denizens [1] of Madison Square and gives fair warning of his annual call. At the corners of four streets, he hands his pasteboards to the North Wind, footman of the mansion of All Outdoors, so that the inhabitants thereof may make ready.

Soapy's mind became cognizant of the fact that the time had come for him to resolve himself into a singular Committee of Ways and Means to provide against the coming rigor. And therefore he moved uneasily on his bench.

[1] **denizens:** inhabitants.

"The Cop and the Anthem" from *The Four Million*, by O. Henry. Copyright 1904 by Doubleday & Company, Inc. Reprinted by permission of the publishers.

The hibernatorial [1] ambitions of Soapy were not of the highest. In them there were no considerations of Mediterranean cruises, of soporific [2] Southern skies, or drifting in the Vesuvian Bay. Three months on the Island [3] was what his soul craved. Three months of assured board and bed and congenial company, safe from Boreas [4] and bluecoats, seemed to Soapy the essence of things desirable.

For years the hospitable Blackwell's had been his winter quarters. Just as his more fortunate fellow New Yorkers had bought their tickets to Palm Beach and the Riviera each winter, so Soapy had made his humble arrangements for his annual hegira [5] to the island. And now the time was come. On the previous night three Sabbath newspapers, distributed beneath his coat, about his ankles, and over his lap, had failed to repulse the cold as he slept on his bench near the spurting fountain in the ancient square. So the Island loomed big and timely in Soapy's mind. He scorned the provisions made in the name of charity for the city's dependents. In Soapy's opinion the Law was more benign than Philanthropy. There was an endless round of institutions, municipal and eleemosynary,[6] on which he might set out and receive lodging and food accordant with the simple life. But to one of Soapy's proud spirit the gifts of charity are encumbered. If not in coin you must pay in humiliation of spirit for every benefit received at the hands of philanthropy. As Caesar had his Brutus, every bed of charity must have its

toll of a bath, every loaf of bread its compensation of a private and personal inquisition. Wherefore it is better to be a guest of the law which, though conducted by rules, does not meddle unduly with a gentleman's private affairs.

Soapy, having decided to go to the Island, at once set about accomplishing his desire. There were many easy ways of doing this. The pleasantest was to dine luxuriously at some expensive restaurant; and then, after declaring insolvency, be handed over quietly and without uproar to a policeman. An accommodating magistrate would do the rest.

Soapy left his bench and strolled out of the square and across the level sea of asphalt, where Broadway and Fifth Avenue flow together. Up Broadway he turned, and halted at a glittering café, where are gathered together nightly the choicest products of the grape, the silkworm, and the protoplasm.[7]

Soapy had confidence in himself from the lowest button of his vest upward. He was shaven, and his coat was decent and his neat, black, ready-tied four-in-hand had been presented to him by a lady missionary on Thanksgiving Day. If he could reach a table in the restaurant unsuspected, success would be his. The portion of him that would show above the table would raise no doubt in the waiter's mind. A roasted mallard duck, thought Soapy, would be about the thing — with a bottle of Chablis,[8] and then Camembert,[9] a demitasse [10] and a cigar. One dollar for the cigar would be enough. The total would not be so high as to call forth any supreme manifestation of revenge from the café management; and yet the meat would leave him filled and happy for

---

[1] **hibernatorial** (hī′bẽr·na̍·tō′rĭ-ăl): pertaining to hibernation, wintering in close quarters.
[2] **soporific**: causing sleep.
[3] **the Island**: Blackwell's Island in the East River was once the site of a workhouse. It is now called Welfare Island.
[4] **Boreas**: the north wind.
[5] **hegira** (hē·jī′ra̍): the flight of Mohammed from Mecca; used here to indicate any similar flight.
[6] **eleemosynary** (ĕl′ê·mŏs′ĭ-nĕr′ĭ): charitable.

[7] **protoplasm**: the substance of animal and plant cells; here, generally, flesh and blood.
[8] **Chablis** (shä′blĕ′): a white French wine.
[9] **Camembert** (kăm′ĕm·bâr′): a soft cheese originally made in France.
[10] **demitasse** (dĕm′ĭ·tăs′): a small cup of black coffee.

the journey to his winter refuge.

But as Soapy set foot inside the restaurant door the head waiter's eye fell upon his frayed trousers and decadent shoes. Strong and ready hands turned him about and conveyed him in silence and haste to the sidewalk and averted the ignoble fate of the menaced mallard.

Soapy turned off Broadway. It seemed that his route to the coveted island was not to be an epicurean one. Some other way of entering limbo must be thought of.

At a corner of Sixth Avenue, electric lights and cunningly displayed wares behind plate glass made a shop window conspicuous. Soapy took a cobblestone and dashed it through the glass. People came running around the corner, a policeman in the lead. Soapy stood still, with his hands in his pockets, and smiled at the sight of brass buttons.

"Where's the man that done that?" inquired the officer excitedly.

"Don't you figure out that I might have had something to do with it?" said Soapy, not without sarcasm, but friendly, as one greets good fortune.

The policeman's mind refused to accept Soapy even as a clue. Men who smash windows do not remain to parley with the law's minions. They take to their heels. The policeman saw a man halfway down the block running to catch a car. With drawn club he joined in the pursuit. Soapy, with disgust in his heart, loafed along, twice unsuccessful.

On the opposite side of the street was a restaurant of no great pretensions. It catered to large appetites and modest purses. Its crockery and atmosphere were thick; its soup and napery thin. Into this place Soapy took his accusive [1] shoes and telltale trousers without challenge. At a table he sat and consumed beefsteak, flapjacks, doughnuts, and pie. And then to the waiter he betrayed the

---

¹ accusive: tending to accuse. The word was coined by O. Henry.

---

fact that the minutest coin and himself were strangers.

"Now, get busy and call a cop," said Soapy. "And don't keep a gentleman waiting."

"No cop for youse," said the waiter, with a voice like butter cakes and an eye like the cherry in a Manhattan cocktail. "Hey, Con!"

Neatly upon his left ear on the callous pavement two waiters pitched Soapy. He arose, joint by joint, as a carpenter's rule opens, and beat the dust from his clothes. Arrest seemed but a rosy dream. The Island seemed very far away. A policeman who stood before a drugstore two doors away laughed and walked down the street.

Five blocks Soapy traveled before his courage permitted him to woo capture again. This time the opportunity presented what he fatuously termed to himself a "cinch." A young woman of a modest and pleasing guise was standing before a show window gazing with sprightly interest at its display of shaving mugs and inkstands, and two yards from the window a large policeman of severe demeanor leaned against a water plug.

It was Soapy's design to assume the role of the despicable and execrated "masher." The refined and elegant appearance of his victim and the contiguity of the conscientious cop encouraged him to believe that he would soon feel the pleasant official clutch upon his arm that would insure his winter quarters on the right little, tight little isle.

Soapy straightened the lady missionary's ready-made tie, dragged his shrinking cuffs into the open, set his hat at a killing cant, and sidled toward the young woman. He made eyes at her, was taken with sudden coughs and "hems," smiled, smirked, and went brazenly through the impudent and contemptible litany of the "masher." With half an eye Soapy saw that the policeman was watching him fixedly.

The young woman moved away a few steps, and again bestowed her absorbed attention upon the shaving mugs. Soapy followed, boldly stepping to her side, raised his hat and said:

"Ah there, Bedelia! Don't you want to come and play in my yard?"

The policeman was still looking. The persecuted young woman had but to beckon a finger and Soapy would be practically en route for his insular haven. Already he imagined he could feel the cozy warmth of the station house. The young woman faced him and, stretching out a hand, caught Soapy's coat sleeve.

"Sure, Mike," she said joyfully, "if you'll blow me to a pail of suds. I'd have spoke to you sooner, but the cop was watching."

With the young woman playing the clinging ivy to his oak, Soapy walked past the policeman overcome with gloom. He seemed doomed to liberty.

At the next corner he shook off his companion and ran. He halted in the district where by night are found the lightest streets, hearts, vows, and librettos. Women in furs and men in greatcoats moved gaily in the wintry air. A sudden fear seized Soapy that some dreadful enchantment had rendered him immune to arrest. The thought brought a little panic upon it, and when he came upon another policeman lounging grandly in front of a transplendent[1] theater, he caught at the immediate straw of "disorderly conduct."

On the sidewalk Soapy began to yell drunken gibberish at the top of his harsh voice. He danced, howled, raved, and otherwise disturbed the welkin.[2]

The policeman twirled his club, turned his back to Soapy and remarked to a citizen:

"'Tis one of them Yale lads celebratin' the goose egg they give to the Hart-

ford College. Noisy; but no harm. We've instructions to lave them be."

Disconsolate, Soapy ceased his unavailing racket. Would never a policeman lay hands on him? In his fancy the Island seemed an unattainable Arcadia.[3] He buttoned his thin coat against the chilling wind.

In a cigar store he saw a well-dressed man lighting a cigar at a swinging light. His silk umbrella he had set by the door on entering. Soapy stepped inside, secured the umbrella, and sauntered off with it slowly. The man at the cigar light followed hastily.

"My umbrella," he said, sternly.

"Oh, is it?" sneered Soapy, adding insult to petit larceny. "Well, why don't you call a policeman? I took it. Your umbrella! Why don't you call a cop? There stands one on the corner."

The umbrella owner slowed his steps. Soapy did likewise, with a presentiment that luck would again run against him. The policeman looked at the two curiously.

"Of course," said the umbrella man — "that is — well, you know how these mistakes occur — I — if it's your umbrella, I hope you'll excuse me — I picked it up this morning in a restaurant — if you recognize it as yours, why — I hope you'll — "

"Of course it's mine," said Soapy, viciously.

The ex-umbrella man retreated. The policeman hurried to assist a tall blonde in an opera cloak across the street in front of a streetcar that was approaching two blocks away.

Soapy walked eastward through a street damaged by improvements. He hurled the umbrella wrathfully into an excavation. He muttered against the men who wear helmets and carry clubs. Because he wanted to fall into their clutches, they seemed to regard him as a king who could do no wrong.

At length Soapy reached one of the

---

[1] transplendent: brilliantly luxurious; another O. Henry coinage.

[2] welkin: sky; air.

[3] Arcadia: an imaginary ideal place.

avenues to the east where the glitter and turmoil was but faint. He set his face down this toward Madison Square, for the homing instinct survives even when the home is a park bench.

But on an unusually quiet corner Soapy came to a standstill. Here was an old church, quaint and rambling and gabled. Through one violet-stained window a soft light glowed, where, no doubt, the organist loitered over the keys, making sure of his mastery of the coming Sabbath anthem. For there drifted out to Soapy's ears sweet music that caught and held him transfixed against the convolutions of the iron fence.

The moon was above, lustrous and serene; vehicles and pedestrians were few; sparrows twittered sleepily in the eaves — for a little while the scene might have been a country churchyard. And the anthem that the organist played cemented Soapy to the iron fence, for he had known it well in the days when his life contained such things as mothers and roses and ambitions and friends and immaculate thoughts and collars.

The conjunction of Soapy's receptive state of mind and the influences about the old church wrought a sudden and wonderful change in his soul. He viewed with swift horror the pit into which he had tumbled, the degraded days, unworthy desires, dead hopes, wrecked faculties, and base motives that made up his existence.

And also in a moment his heart responded thrillingly to this novel mood. An instantaneous and strong impulse moved him to battle with his desperate fate. He would pull himself out of the mire; he would make a man of himself again; he would conquer the evil that had taken possession of him. There was time; he was comparatively young yet; he would resurrect his old eager ambitions and pursue them without faltering. Those solemn but sweet organ notes had set up a revolution in him.

Tomorrow he would go into the roaring downtown district and find work. A fur importer had once offered him a place as driver. He would find him tomorrow and ask for the position. He would be somebody in the world. He would —

Soapy felt a hand laid on his arm. He looked quickly around into the broad face of a policeman.

"What are you doin' here?" asked the officer.

"Nothin'," said Soapy.

"Then come along," said the policeman.

"Three months on the Island," said the Magistrate in the Police Court the next morning.

FOR DISCUSSION

1. Like many other O. Henry stories, this one illustrates the "irony of life." Explain how.

2. How successful was the surprise ending? There are two tests of a good surprise ending: (a) you should not be able to see it coming; (b) you should be obliged to admit, on looking back over the story, that all the necessary clues were there. Point out the clues that O. Henry gave to prepare the reader for the ending.

3. What details show that O. Henry was familiar with the New York setting he used in this story?

4. What are the two opposing forces in the plot of this story? What is the final effect?

5. Does the character Soapy strike you as a believable human being or a composite character based on several real counterparts? What details prove that Soapy was not ignorant? Do you think Soapy would have carried out his good resolutions? Why? Why not?

6. In such a story as this, why must the author take care not to develop characterization too fully?

YOUR OWN WRITING

Your own experience may offer some examples of the "irony of life." Select one, and relate it in a short composition.

O. HENRY   819

FINLEY
PETER
DUNNE
1867–1936

Mr. Dooley on Machinery

Not all the writing about the rapid rise of industry in America was solemn and serious. One of the most popular and influential commentators between 1898 and 1910 was Finley Peter Dunne, Chicago newspaperman. His Mr. Dooley, an Irish saloonkeeper who commented amusingly to his friend Hennessy on what he read in the papers, became such a favorite that nine "Mr. Dooley" books were published between 1898 and 1911.

Dunne followed no political party and spoke his mind freely, applying humor and good common sense to widely discussed issues of his day. He had courage, too, for he often championed unpopular figures in the news, and during the muckraking era he criticized reformers as well as the bosses of political machines.

In the following piece, Mr. Dooley "debunks" the popular worship of machines and exaggerated faith in mechanical progress. You will find ideas here worth a second thought in this day when machines threaten to destroy the men who made them.

READING DIALECT. Dialect is easier to understand when read aloud. You'll enjoy trying it now, with Mr. Dooley's comments.

"Mr. Dooley on Machinery" from *Observations of Mr. Dooley* by Finley Peter Dunne. Reprinted by permission of Harper & Brothers.

$\mathbf{M}$R. DOOLEY was reading from a paper. "'We live,' he says, 'in an age iv wondhers. Niver befure in th' histhry iv th' wurruld has such pro-gress been made.'

"Thrue wurruds an' often spoken. Even in me time things has changed. Whin I was a la-ad Long Jawn Wintworth [1] cud lean his elbows on th' highest buildin' in this town. It took two months to come here fr'm Pittsburgh on a limited raft an' a stagecoach that run fr'm La Salle to Mrs. Murphy's hotel. They wasn't anny tillygraft that I can raymimber an' th' sthreetcar was pulled be a mule an' dhruv be an engineer be th' name iv Mulligan. We thought we was a pro-grissive people. Ye bet we did. But look at us today. I go be Casey's house tonight an' there it is a fine story-an'-a-half frame house with Casey settin' on th' dure shtep dhrinkin' out iv a pail. I go be Casey's house tomorrah an' it's a hole in th' groun'. I rayturn to Casey's house on Thursday an' it's a fifty-eight-story buildin' with a morgedge onto it an' they're thinkin' iv takin' it down an' replacin' it with a modhren sthructure. Th' shoes that Corrigan th' cobbler wanst wurruked on f'r

---

[1] **Long Jawn Wintworth:** John Wentworth, a mayor of Chicago.

a week, hammerin' away like a wood-pecker, is now tossed out be th' dozens fr'm th' mouth iv a masheen. A cow goes lowin' softly in to Armour's an' comes out glue, beef, gelatin, fertylizer, celooloid, joolry, sofy cushions, hair restorer, washin' sody, soap, lithrachoor, an' bed-springs so quick that while aft she's still cow, for'ard she may be anything fr'm buttons to Pannyma hats. I can go fr'm Chicago to New York in twenty hours; but I don't have to, thank th' Lord. Thir-ty years ago we thought 'twas marvel-ous to be able to tillygraft a man in Saint Joe an' get an answer that night. Now, be wireless tillygraft ye can get an answer befure ye sind th' tillygram if they ain't careful. Me friend Macroni [1] has done that. Be manes iv his wondher iv science a man on a ship in mid-ocean can sind a tillygram to a man on shore, if he has a confid'rate on board. That's all he needs. Be mechanical science an' thrust in th' op'rator annywan can set on th' shore iv Noofoundland an' chat with a frind in th' County Kerry.[2]

"Yes, sir, mechanical science has made gr-reat sthrides. Whin I was a young man we used to think Hor'ce Greeley was th' gr-reatest livin' Ameri-can. He was a gran' man, a gran' man with feathers beneath his chin an' specs on his nose like th' windows in a diver's hemlet. His pollyticks an' mine cudden't live in th' same neighborhood, but he was a gran' man all th' same. We used to take th' Cleveland *Plain Dealer* in thim days f'r raycreation an' th' New York *Thrybune* f'r exercise. 'Twas con-sidhered a test iv a good-natured Dim-mycrat if he cud read an article in th' *Thrybune* without havin' to do th' sta-tions iv th' cross[3] afterward f'r what

[1] Macroni: Of course he means Marconi (1874–1937), the Italian inventor who put wireless telegraphy on a commercial basis.

[2] County Kerry: in southwest Ireland.

[3] do th' stations iv th' cross: say a prayer before each of the fourteen pictures placed in a Catholic church, representing stages of Christ's progress with the cross on the way to His crucifixion.

he said. I almost did wanst, but they was a line at th' end about a frind iv mine be th' name iv Andhrew Jackson an' I wint out an' broke up a Methodist prayer meetin'. He was th' boy that cud put it to ye so that if ye voted th' Dim-mycrat tickit it was jus' th' same as de-mandin' a place in purgatory. Th' farm-ers wud plant annything fr'm a rutybaga to a Congressman on his advice. He niv-er had money enough to buy a hat, but he cud go to th' Sicrety iv th' Threasury an' tell him who's pitcher to put on th' useful valentines we thrade f'r gro-ceries.

"But if Hor'ce Greeley was alive to-day, where'd he be? Settin' on three inches iv th' edge iv a chair in th' out-side office iv me frind Pierpont Mor-gan[4] waitin' f'r his turn. In th' line is th' Imp'ror iv Germany, th' new cook, th' prisidint iv a railroad, th' cap'n iv th' yacht, Rimbrandt[5] th' painther, Jawn W. Grates,[6] an' Hor'ce. Afther a while th' boy at th' dure says, 'Ye're next, ol' party. Shtep lively, f'r th' boss has had a Weehawken Peerooginy[7] sawed off on him this mornin' an' he mustn't be kep' waitin'.' An' th' iditor goes in. 'Who ar-re ye? says th' gr-reat man, givin' him wan iv thim piercin' looks that whin a man gets it he has to be sewed up at wanst. 'I'm ye'er iditor,' says Hor'ce. 'Which wan?' says Pierpont. 'Number two hundhred an' eight.' 'What's ye'er spishilty?' 'Tahriff an' th' improvemint iv th' wurruld,' says Hor'ce. 'See Per-kins,' says Pierpont, an' th' intherview is

[4] Morgan: John Pierpont Morgan, Sr. (1837–1913), American financier.

[5] Rimbrandt: Rembrandt van Rijn (vän rīn') (1606–1669), famous Dutch painter, in-cluded humorously because Morgan was a great collector of art.

[6] Jawn W. Grates: misspelling of John W. Gates, a famous speculator.

[7] Weehawken Peerooginy: Perugino (1446–1523) was a famous Italian painter. Weehaw-ken is a town in New Jersey. The combina-tion suggests that Morgan has been cheated in supposing he had purchased an original old master that proved to be only a copy.

over. Now what's made th' change? Mechanical science, Hinnissy. Somewan made a masheen that puts steel billets within th' reach iv all. Hince Charlie Schwab.[1]

"What's it done f'r th' wurruld? says ye. It's done ivrything. It's give us fast ships an' an autymatic hist f'r th' hod, an' small flats an' a taste iv solder in th' peaches. If annybody says th' wurruld ain't betther off thin it was, tell him that a masheen has been invinted that makes honey out iv pethrolyum. If he asts ye why they ain't anny Shakesperes today, say, 'No, but we no longer make sausages be hand.'

" 'Tis pro-gress. We live in a cinchry iv pro-gress an' I thank th' Lord I've seen most iv it. Man an' boy I've lived pretty near through this wondherful age. If I was proud I cud say I seen more thin Julyus Caesar iver see or cared to. An' here I am, I'll not say how old, still pushin' th' malt acrost th' counther at me thirsty counthrymen. All around me is th' refinemints iv mechanical janius. Instead iv broachin'[2] th' beer kag with a club an' dhrawin' th' beer through a fassit as me Puritan forefathers done, I have that wondher iv invintive science th' beer pump. I cheat mesilf with a cash raygisther. I cut off th' end iv me good cigar with an injanyous device an' pull th' cork out iv a bottle with a conthrivance that wud've made that frind that Hogan boasts about, that ol' boy Archy Meeds,[3] think they was witchcraft in th' house. Science has been a gr-reat blessin' to me. But amidst all these granjoors here am I th' same ol' antiquated combination iv bellows an' pump I always was. Not so good. Time has worn me out. Th' years like little boys with jackknives has

carved their names in me top. Ivry day I have to write off something f'r deprecyation. 'Tis about time f'r whoiver owns me to wurruk me off on a thrust. Mechanical science has done ivrything f'r me but help me. I suppose I ought to feel supeeryor to me father. He niver see a high buildin' but he didn't want to. He cudden't come here in five days but he was a wise man an' if he cud've come in three he'd have stayed in th' County Roscommon.[4]

"Th' pa-pers tells me that midical science has kept pace with th' hop-skip-an'-a-jump iv mechanical inginooty. Th' doctors has found th'mikrobe iv ivrything fr'm lumbago to love an' fr'm jandice to jealousy, but if a brick bounces on me head I'm crated up th' same as iv yore an' put away. Rockyfellar can make a pianny out iv a bar'l iv crude ile, but no wan has been able to make a blade iv hair grow on Rockyfellar. They was a doctor over in France that discovered a kind iv a thing that if t'was pumped into ye wud make ye live till people got so tired iv seein' ye around they cud scream. He died th' nex' year iv premachure ol' age. They was another doctor cud insure whether th' nex wan wud be a boy or a girl. All ye had to do was to decide wud it be Arthur or Ethel an' lave him know. He left a fam'ly iv unmarredgeable daughters.

"I sometimes wondher whether progress is anny more thin a kind iv a shift. It's like a merry-go-round. We get up on a speckled wooden horse an' th' mechanical pianny plays a chune an' away we go, hollerin'. We think we're thravelin' like th' divvle but th' man that doesn't care about merry-go-rounds knows that we will come back where we were. We get out dizzy an' sick an' lay on th' grass an' gasp, 'Where am I? Is this th' meelin-yum?'[5] An' he says,

---

[1] **Charlie Schwab:** Charles M. Schwab (1862–1939), president of two steel corporations and other industrial corporations.

[2] broachin': opening.

[3] **Archy Meeds:** Archimedes (är′kĭ-mē′dēz), a Greek mathematician and inventor (287?– 212 B.C.).

[4] **County Roscommon** (rŏs·kŏm′ŭn): in central Ireland.

[5] **meelin-yum:** millennium, the thousand years during which, according to the Book of Revelation, Christ will return to rule on earth.

'No, 'tis Ar-rchey Road.' Father Kelly says th' Agyptians done things we cudden't do an' th' Romans put up skyscrapers an' aven th' Chinks had tillyphones an' phonygrafts.

"I've been up to th' top iv th' very highest buildin' in town, Hinnissy, an' I wasn't anny nearer Hivin thin if I was in th' sthreet. Th' stars was as far away as iver. An' down beneath is a lot iv us runnin' an' lapin' an' jumpin' about, pushin' each other over, haulin' little sthrips iv ir'n to pile up in little buildin's that ar're called skyscrapers but not be th' sky; wurrukin' night an' day to make a masheen that'll carry us fr'm wan jack-rabbit colony to another an' yellin', 'Pro-gress!' Pro-gress, oho! I can see th' stars winkin' at each other an' sayin', 'Ain't they funny! Don't they think they're playin' the divil!'

"No, sir, masheens ain't done much fr man. I can't get up anny kind iv fam'ly inthrest fr a steam dredge or a hydraulic hist. I want to see skyscrapin' men. But I won't. We're about th' same hight as we always was, th' same hight an' build, composed iv th' same inflamable an' perishyable mateeryal, an exthra hazardous risk, unimproved an' li'ble to collapse. We do make progress, but it's th' same kind Julyus Caesar made an' ivry wan has made befure or since an' in this age iv masheenery we're still burrid be hand."

"What d'ye think iv th' man down in Pinnsylvania who says th' Lord an' him is partners in a coal mine?" asked Mr. Hennessy, who wanted to change the subject.

"Has he divided th' profits?" asked Mr. Dooley.

FOR DISCUSSION

1. What kinds of machines does Mr. Dooley mention? Have we any still more astonishing machines today? What is automation?

2. What is Dooley's conclusion about the importance of machinery? Do you agree with him? How would you relate his ideas to those of Thoreau?

3. Is the Irish dialect effective? What does it contribute to the effect of the article?

READING ON TIME OF CHANGE

ON INDIVIDUAL AUTHORS

CRANE. Linson, Corwin K., *My Stephen Crane* (Syracuse Univ. Press, 1958)

DICKINSON. Bingham, Millicent T., *Emily Dickinson* (Harper, 1954)

O. HENRY. Nolan, Jeanette C., *O. Henry: The Story of William Sydney Porter* (Messner, 1944)

WHITMAN. Brooks, Van Wyck, *The Times of Melville and Whitman* (Dutton, 1947); Deutsch, Babette, *Walt Whitman, Builder of America* (Messner, 1941)

BY INDIVIDUAL AUTHORS

Bellamy, Edward, *Looking Backward: 2000–1887*

Bierce, Ambrose, "An Occurrence at Owl Creek Bridge"

Crane, Stephen, "The Open Boat"; "The Blue Hotel"; "An Episode of War"

Dickinson, Emily, *Complete Poems* (Little, Brown, 1960)

Garland, Hamlin, *Main-traveled Roads, A Son of the Middle Border* (autobiography)

Howells, William Dean, *The Rise of Silas Lapham; A Modern Instance; A Hazard of New Fortunes*

James, Henry, *Roderick Hudson; The American; Daisy Miller; The Portrait of a Lady*

Jewett, Sarah Orne, *The Country of the Pointed Firs*

London, Jack, *White Fang; Martin Eden; The Call of the Wild*

Norris, Frank, *The Octopus*

FOR LISTENING

The selection from Walt Whitman's "Song of Myself" and his shorter poems "A Noiseless Patient Spider" and "I Hear America Singing," as well as Lanier's "The Marshes of Glynn" and Dunne's "Mr. Dooley on Machinery," have been recorded on *Many Voices* 5B.

The Twentieth Century

You have followed the outline of this country's history, shown as the background and source of a developing American literature. You have observed how our literature not only reflects the history of our country, but how, through its influence on thought and action, it has helped to create that history. The literature of the Revolutionary period provides one example of the ways in which the written or spoken word can directly affect men's lives.

In Part One of this book, there are many selections from the best writers of our own day, grouped by literary types. Comments on these modern writers have been placed with their stories, articles, poems, or plays. In addition, a short survey of twentieth-century writers follows each of the modern sections (the short story, page 123; the novel, pages 125–29; nonfiction, page 246; poetry, pages 346–47; and drama, page 407). Therefore it will not be necessary to discuss the rich American literature of the twentieth century as fully as we have discussed the literature of the earlier centuries. However, it may help your understanding of modern American literature if we sketch the historical events of this century and point out some of the ways in which modern writing is related to those events.

The American Achievement

The American of the early twentieth century stood on the threshold of a new era. Before this time, most Americans had lived and worked on farms. Men, women, and even children had labored long hours the year round, in some cases making a barely adequate living. Life had been relatively simple, centered in the home, in the church, in the small town. Throughout most of the nineteenth century, the nation itself had been more concerned with its own development than with the affairs of the rest of the world.

Now the situation was changing rapidly. People were moving to cities. The nation was becoming increasingly industrialized. Women were entering business and industry. The average American was about to enjoy a standard of living higher than he had ever known before. The country was attempting to educate all its people. America began to exert a cultural as well as a political leadership among the nations of the world.

Americans could look back upon their past with pride. In less than a century and a half since the establishment of the nation — a brief span in history — they had made remarkable progress toward those goals to which their nation's founders had pledged themselves. They had achieved a more perfect union. They had largely established justice, insured domestic tranquility, provided for the common defense, promoted the general welfare, and secured the blessings of liberty for themselves and — it was to be hoped — for their posterity. They had lifted the burdens from the shoulders of millions of men, given a second chance to immigrants from the Old World, maintained freedom at home and supported it abroad, advanced equality, enlarged material well-being, and championed the causes of peace.

In addition Americans had created a culture of their own — a literature, education, art, science, and technology that compared favorably with the culture enjoyed by the older nations of the West. Europeans were now reading American writers, studying in American universities, subscribing to American newspapers and magazines. They were applauding American plays and swarming to see American movies.

Americans had inherited all of the past — the past of Greece and Rome and Judea, of Italy, France, and above all of England. Nature, too, had provided them with rich resources. To their goodly heritage and rich environment Americans themselves had added, over the years, industry, resourcefulness, courage, intelligence, and vision.

Crisis and Trial

America's position as a world power was soon tested. From 1914 to 1918 there occurred a war on a scale so large, involving so many countries, that it was called the World War, although western Europe was its decisive battleground. The United States entered the war in 1917, responding to the call to "keep the world safe for democracy." After months of bitter fighting, America, England, and France defeated Germany and its allies.

After the war, America entered one of its periods of greatest prosperity. Not all Americans shared in the benefits of the economic boom, but, in general, wages were high and goods were plentiful. Throughout the 1920's the country grew in financial power. There seemed to be no limit to the boom, but suddenly in 1929 the bottom dropped out of the stock market, and the country entered a period of economic depression. Now came years of hard times, with millions of men out of work, with banks and businesses closing their doors, with industry grinding to a standstill. The country began to take steps to remedy the mistakes of the past, to restore and conserve natural resources, and to prevent the recurrence of a similar crisis.

Literary Trends

During the two decades following World War I, much of our literature reflected the attitudes and methods that had been developed by the earlier realists. During the 1920's in particular, some of our writers became increasingly critical of American society. Of course, all writers did not share this mood: many continued to treat traditional themes in traditional ways. The romantic historical novel gained in popularity during these years. A number of writers, however, became deeply embittered. A few of them turned their backs on the country and went to Europe to live and write. The impact of the war had been enormous, turning upside down the beliefs and values of many. Some writers began to refer to themselves as a "lost generation," meaning a generation that had somehow lost touch with its traditions and ideals.

Then, during the period of depression, some significant changes occurred in our literature. Many of our novelists, poets, and dramatists began to rediscover America. The economic and social crisis led to an awakening of interest in our heritage, as our writers went back to the past to find again the hopes, the ideals, and the values that had inspired the founders of our country. The revival of pride in the American achievement was timely, for the nation was shortly to be confronted with two crucial challenges.

World Conflicts

After the first World War, the great dream had been that such a war could not happen again, that nations would somehow find means to preserve peace. Only a little more than twenty years passed before we were awakened from the dream. We in America, who for many years had seemed independent of the rest of the world, were caught in the swift current of world-wide events. Beginning in 1939, war flamed over the globe. In Europe Adolf Hitler hurled his mighty armies on Poland, The Netherlands, Belgium, and France, on Scandinavia, and eventually on Russia. In Africa Mussolini ruthlessly crushed the natives who would not accept his rule. In Asia Japanese war lords seized vast areas of China and aimed for rule of the entire Orient and the Pacific as well. The global aggressions soon began to threaten America. With the Japanese attack on Pearl Harbor on December 7, 1941, the United States was plunged into war. After four years of fighting, Germany, Italy, and Japan surrendered unconditionally to America and its allies.

In the years following World War II, the United States, as the major democratic power, confronted the formidable challenge of the Communist world of Russia and Red China. Despite renewed visions of peace and hope, a state of "cold war" existed with no end in sight. Under the pressures of the tense world situation, the cold war sometimes erupted into open fighting. In the early 1950's Communism and democracy clashed in a grueling war in Korea. Through the late 1950's and early 1960's, trouble continued to break out in a number of critical areas of the world. In the midst of this struggle between democracy and Communism, attention focused on the startling scientific acceleration of our time. The race in science took on crucial importance as the United States prepared to face the gravest crisis in its history.

Literature Today

The pressures of our time have had an enormous effect on our writers, including those who began their careers in the 1920's or 1930's, but especially the writers of the generation that grew to adulthood during World War II. Like all literature, recent writing is deeply involved in the events of its time. Our writers are not wholly joyless or despairing today, but they are definitely somber, and aware of their grave responsibilities. As the rest of the free world looks to the United States for leadership, the writer becomes increasingly important in helping transmit American beliefs, ideals, and culture throughout the globe.

In establishing a nation, subduing a continent, creating a democracy, spreading material well-being, diffusing education, and maintaining freedom at home and abroad, Americans had created a proud heritage. Yet it was clear that, as the country entered the 1960's, it stood not at the end of an era but on the threshold of history.

The poet W. H. Auden has called our time "The Age of Anxiety." While it may be this, it is an age of challenge as well. If we meet the challenge of our time with courage and dedication, we can move into a new era of boundless opportunity. In this age, therefore, lie potential themes for great literature.

GENERAL REFERENCE BOOKS ON AMERICAN LITERATURE

Blair, Walter, *Native American Humor* (Chandler, paperback, 1960)

Brooks, Van Wyck, *Makers and Finders: A History of the Writer in America, 1800–1915*, 5 vols. (Dutton, Everyman's Library)

Brooks, Van Wyck, and Otto L. Bettmann, *Our Literary Heritage: A Pictorial History of the Writer in America* (Dutton, 1956)

W. P. Trent and others, eds., *Cambridge History of American Literature*, 3 vols. in 1 (Macmillan, 1954)

Chase, R., *The American Novel and Its Tradition* (Doubleday, paperback, 1957)

Cowie, Alexander, *The Rise of the American Novel* (American Book, 1948)

Deutsch, Babette, *Poetry in Our Time* (Columbia Univ. Press, 1956)

Gregory, Horace, and Marya Zaturenska, *A History of American Poetry, 1900–1940* (Harcourt, Brace & World, 1946)

Hart, James D., *Oxford Companion to American Literature*, revised ed. (Oxford Univ. Press, 1956)

Kazin, Alfred, *On Native Grounds* (Harcourt, Brace & World, 1942)

Matthiessen, F. O., *American Renaissance: Art and Expression in the Age of Emerson and Whitman* (Oxford Univ. Press, 1941)

Mott, Frank L., *Golden Multitudes: The Story of Best Sellers in the United States* (R. R. Bowker, 1960)

Parrington, V. L., *Main Currents in American Thought* (Harcourt, Brace & World, 1939)

Quinn, Arthur Hobson, ed., *The Literature of the American People* (Appleton-Century-Crofts, 1951)

Spiller, Robert E., *The Cycle of American Literature* (Macmillan, 1955)

Spiller, Robert E., and others, eds., *Literary History of the United States*, revised ed. (Macmillan, 1953)

Thorp, Willard, *American Writing in the Twentieth Century* (Harvard Univ. Press, 1960)

Van Doren, Carl, *The American Novel, 1879–1939* (Macmillan, 1940)

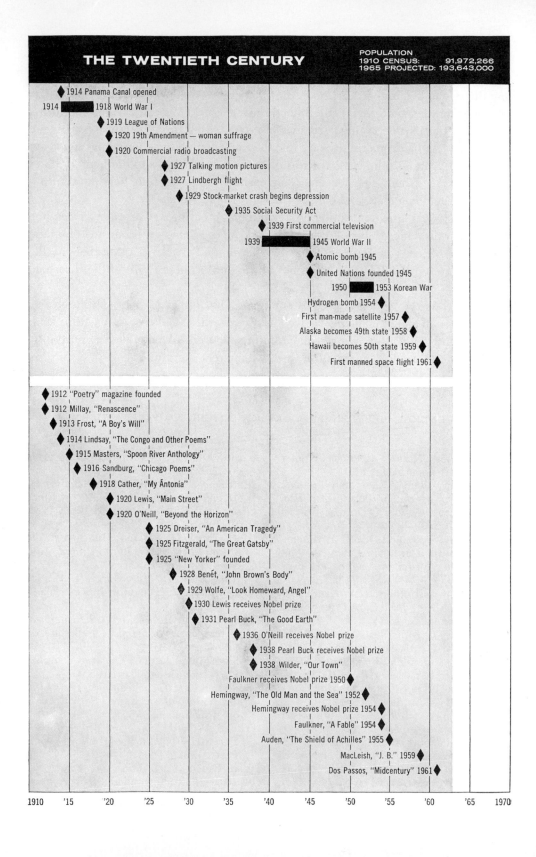

THE TWENTIETH CENTURY

POPULATION
1910 CENSUS: 91,972,266
1965 PROJECTED: 193,643,000

1914 Panama Canal opened
1914 ■■■ 1918 World War I
1919 League of Nations
1920 19th Amendment — woman suffrage
1920 Commercial radio broadcasting
1927 Talking motion pictures
1927 Lindbergh flight
1929 Stock-market crash begins depression
1935 Social Security Act
1939 First commercial television
1939 ■■■ 1945 World War II
Atomic bomb 1945
United Nations founded 1945
1950 ■■■ 1953 Korean War
Hydrogen bomb 1954
First man-made satellite 1957
Alaska becomes 49th state 1958
Hawaii becomes 50th state 1959
First manned space flight 1961

1912 "Poetry" magazine founded
1912 Millay, "Renascence"
1913 Frost, "A Boy's Will"
1914 Lindsay, "The Congo and Other Poems"
1915 Masters, "Spoon River Anthology"
1916 Sandburg, "Chicago Poems"
1918 Cather, "My Ántonia"
1920 Lewis, "Main Street"
1920 O'Neill, "Beyond the Horizon"
1925 Dreiser, "An American Tragedy"
1925 Fitzgerald, "The Great Gatsby"
1925 "New Yorker" founded
1928 Benét, "John Brown's Body"
1929 Wolfe, "Look Homeward, Angel"
1930 Lewis receives Nobel prize
1931 Pearl Buck, "The Good Earth"
1936 O'Neill receives Nobel prize
1938 Pearl Buck receives Nobel prize
1938 Wilder, "Our Town"
Faulkner receives Nobel prize 1950
Hemingway, "The Old Man and the Sea" 1952
Hemingway receives Nobel prize 1954
Faulkner, "A Fable" 1954
Auden, "The Shield of Achilles" 1955
MacLeish, "J. B." 1959
Dos Passos, "Midcentury" 1961

1910   '15   '20   '25   '30   '35   '40   '45   '50   '55   '60   '65   1970

Glossary

A

abase (*a*·bās′). To degrade; to lower in rank

abash (*a*·băsh′). To confuse; to confound.

abet (*a*·bet′). To encourage or support.

abide (*a*·bīd′). To stay; to continue.

abridge (*a*·brĭj′). To shorten; to condense.

absolve (ăb·sŏlv′). To set free from guilt or blame.

acclaim (*ă*·klām′). To applaud; to praise.

acquisition (ăk′wĭ·zĭsh′ŭn). 1. The act of getting. 2. The thing acquired.

acrid (ăk′rĭd). Bitterly irritating; sharp to the taste.

actuality (ăk′tŭ·ăl′ĭ·tĭ). Reality.

adduce (*ă*·dūs′). To advance arguments; to cite.

adenoidal (ăd′ê·noi′dăl). Describing a condition which obstructs breathing through the nose.

adhere (ăd·hēr′). 1. To cling; to be attached. 2. To be devoted to.

adjacent (*ă*·jā′sĕnt). Lying near; bordering.

adobe (*a*·dō′bĭ). Brick or clay dried in the sun; a structure made from such brick.

adornment (*a*·dôrn′mĕnt). Decoration.

adversity (ăd·vûr′sĭ·tĭ). A condition of affliction; misfortune.

advisable (ăd·vīz′*a*·b′l). Prudent; proper to be done. **advisability.** The wisdom or prudence of doing something; as "he considered the *advisability* of leaving."

aesthetic (ĕs·thĕt′ĭk). Concerned with the beautiful in art or nature, especially as contrasted to the useful.

afflict (*ă*·flĭkt′). To cause pain or distress.

aggrieved (*ă*·grēvd′). Distressed.

agile (ăj′ĭl). Quick; easy in moving.

alight (*a*·līt′). To dismount; to descend. **alit** (*a*·lĭt′). *past and past participle.*

alleviation (*ă*·lē′vĭ·ā′shŭn). Relief; lessening. **alleviate** *v.*

allusion (*ă*·lū′zhŭn). Indirect reference. **allude** *v.*

ambiguity (ăm′bĭ·gū′ĭ·tĭ). Something capable of being understood in two or more senses. **ambiguous.** Doubtful; inexplicable.

amicable (ăm′ĭ·ka·b′l). Friendly; neighborly.

anarchy (ăn′*ar*·kĭ). State of confusion or disorder.

animation (ăn′ĭ·mā′shŭn). 1. State of being alive. 2. Vigor, liveliness, spirit.

annal (ăn′ăl). Record of an event or year. **annals** *n. pl.* Historical records; chronicles.

annex (*ă*·nĕks′). To add or attach. **annex** *n.* Something attached.

annihilate (*ă*·nī′ĭ·lāt). To reduce to nothing; to destroy completely.

anomaly (*a*·nŏm′*a*·lĭ). Something out of the ordinary; an irregularity. **anomalous.** Abnormal.

antagonistic (ăn·tăg′ŏ·nĭs′tĭk). Hostile; opposed.

antiquarian (ăn′tĭ·kwâr′ĭ·ăn) (or **antiquary**). One who studies the past through relics; a collector of relics. **antiquarian** *adj.* Pertaining to such studies.

apathy (ăp′*a*·thĭ). 1. Lack of feeling. 2. Indifference. **apathetic.** Lacking interest; indifferent.

apex (ā′pĕks). 1. The point of climax. 2. The tip or summit.

apparatus (ăp′*a*·rā′tŭs). Materials; any complex instrument.

apparitional (ăp′*a*·rĭsh′ŭn′l). Ghostlike. **apparition.** A phantom; an unexpected appearance.

appellation (ăp′ĕ·lā′shŭn). A name.

appendage (*ă*·pĕn′dĭj). Something added to a greater thing; a limb (finger, arm, etc.).

appreciable (*ă*·prē′shĭ·*a*·b′l). Enough in amount to be recognized; capable of being perceived or measured.

appropriate (*ă*·prō′prĭ·āt). 1. To take complete possession. 2. To divide equally.

ardent (är′dĕnt). Warm; eager.

ardor (är′dēr). Warmth of emotion.

arduous (är′dŭ·ŭs). 1. Difficult. 2. Strenuous.

arid (ăr′ĭd). 1. dry; barren. 2. Lacking in interest.

arraign (*ă*·rān′). 1. To charge, to accuse. 2. To call a prisoner before a court.

artifice (är′tĭ·fĭs). 1. An ingenious device; a skillful contriving. 2. Trickery.

ascendency (*ă*·sĕn′dăn·sĭ). Controlling influence; supremacy.

asperity (ăs·pĕr′ĭ tĭ). Harshness; sharpness of temper.

aspiration (ăs′pĭ·rā′shŭn). Longing; ambition.

assail (*ă*·sāl′). To attack; to assault.

assay (*ă*·sā′). 1. To evaluate; to analyze. 2. To try; to attempt.

āpe, chāotic, bâre, ăt, ăttend, ärt, flăsk, *a*top; ēke, mẽrely, ĕlect, ĕcho, prudĕnt, doêr; ītem, ĭnn, rarĭty; ōde, ŏpaque, fôr, dŏt, lŏft, cŏnfide; sōon, tŏŏk; sour, toil; tūbe, ûnique, tûrn, sŭp, ŭntil. bar; church; dog; ardůous; fat; go; hear; jail; key; lame; meat; not; ring; pay; ran; see; shell; ten; there, thick; pastůre; vast; wind; yes; zoo, zh = z in azure.

assent (ă·sĕnt'). To give consent; to admit the truth of something.

assess (ă·sĕs'). 1. To fix an amount, as to *assess* damages or *assess* a tax. 2. To appraise; to estimate.

asunder (ă·sŭn'dĕr). Into parts or pieces, as to burst *asunder*.

attribute (ăt'rĭ·būt) *n*. A quality or characteristic.

attribute (ă·trĭb'ût) *v*. To assign; to credit someone or something, as they *attribute* honesty to him.

audacity (ô·dăs'ĭ·tĭ). Boldness; fearlessness.

augment (ôg·mĕnt'). To increase; to enlarge.

auspice (ôs'pĭs). 1. Sign; omen (usually favorable). 2. Usually plural, protection, as under the *auspices* of the president. **auspicious.** Favorable.

authenticate (ô·thĕn'tĭ·kāt). To prove genuine.

auxiliary (ôg·zĭl'yȧ·rĭ). Additional; supplementary.

avarice (ăv'ȧ·rĭs). Excessive desire for wealth. **avaricious.** Greedy.

aversion (ȧ·vûr'zhŭn). 1. Dislike. 2. Act of avoiding or rejection.

avow (ȧ·vou'). To declare openly.

awesome (ô'sŭm). Causing terror or awe.

axis (ăk'sĭs). A straight line (real or imaginary) passing through the center of a body.

B

ballad (băl'ȧd). 1. A song. 2. A short narrative poem, usually in four-line stanzas.

beguile (bē·gīl'). 1. To deceive. 2. To charm.

benign (bē·nīn'). 1. Gentle. 2. Favorable.

benumb (bē·nŭm'). To deprive of sensation; to numb or deaden.

bereavement (bē·rēv'mĕnt). Deprivation. **bereave.** To deprive.

beseech (bē·sēch'). To beg or plead.

bias (bī'ȧs). Prejudice.

bigotry (bĭg'ŭt·rĭ). Intolerance; an obstinate devotion to one's own opinions.

bizarre (bĭ·zär'). Very odd; eccentric; fantastic.

blight (blīt). 1. A plant disease causing withering or death. 2. Anything that causes death or destruction.

boisterous (bois'tēr·ŭs). Noisy and unrestrained.

bounteous (boun'tē·ŭs). Liberal; generous.

bovine (bō'vīn). Pertaining to the ox or cow.

brazen (brā'z'n). 1. Made of brass. 2. Shameless.

bulwark (bŏŏl'wẽrk). A defense or support.

C

cadaver (kȧ·dăv'ẽr). A corpse.

callous (kăl'ŭs). Hardened in feelings; unfeeling; unsympathetic.

cannonade (kăn'ŭn·ād'). To attack with cannon. **cannonade** *n*. Act of shooting cannon.

cantankerous (kăn·tang'kẽr·ŭs). Ill-natured.

capricious (kȧ·prĭsh'ŭs). Inclined to change suddenly; inconstant.

carp (kärp). To complain; to find fault.

celibacy (sĕl'ĭ·bȧ·sĭ). Single life, especially that of one who has taken vows not to marry.

censurer (sĕn'shẽr·ẽr). A fault-finder; a hostile critic.

chary (châr'ĭ). Cautious.

chasten (chās''n). 1. To punish. 2. To refine by eliminating faults or errors.

chestnut (chĕs'nŭt). 1. A nut from a tree of the beech family. 2. An old tale or joke.

chide (chīd). To scold; reprove. **chidden** *past participle*.

chiseled (chĭz''ld). Clear-cut.

chronicler (krŏn'ĭ·klẽr). One who records events.

churlishness (chûr'lĭsh·nĭs). Roughness; unmanageability.

cipher (sī'fẽr). Code.

circumstantial (sûr'kŭm·stăn'shăl). 1. Depending on or pertaining to circumstances. 2. Incidental, not essential. 3. Fully detailed.

claimant (klām'ȧnt). One who demands title to something.

clamorous (klăm'ẽr·ŭs). Noisy.

cloven (klō'vĕn). Divided into two or more parts, as in *cloven-footed*.

cognizant (kog'nĭ·zȧnt). Aware of by observation; understanding.

combustible (kŏm·bŭs'tĭ·b'l). Inflammable. **combustible** *n*. Anything inflammable.

comely (kŭm'lĭ). Pleasing to the sight.

commensurate (kŏ·mĕn'shŏŏ·rĭt). Equal to; corresponding.

commiserate (kŏ·mĭz'ẽr·āt). To sympathize.

compact (kŏm'păkt). An agreement or contract. **compact** (kŏm·păkt'). *adj*. Closely united; brief.

compass (kŭm'pȧs). 1. To enclose or surround. 2. To accomplish.

complement (kŏm'plē·mĕnt). That which completes; full quantity. **complement** *v*. To supply something that was lacking.

comportment (kŏm·pōrt'mĕnt). Behavior.

conceive (kŏn·sēv'). To think; to imagine.

concentric (kŏn·sĕn'trĭk). Possessing a common center, as a series of circles within one another.

āpe, chãotic, bâre, ăt, ȧttend, ärt, flásk, ȧtop; ēke, mẽrely, ĕlect, ĕcho, prudĕnt, doẽr; ītem, ĭnn, rarĭty; ōde, ŏpaque, fôr, dŏt, lŏft, cŏnfide; sōōn, tŏŏk; sour, toil; tūbe, ūnique, tûrn, sŭp, ŭntil.

concession (kŏn·sĕsh′ŭn). The act of conceding; acknowledgment.

condole (kŏn·dōl′). To express sympathy.

conducive (kŏn·dū′sĭv). Helpfu .

configuration (kŏn·fĭg′ū·rā′shŭn). Form; pattern; disposition of parts.

congeniality (kŏn·jē′nĭ·ăl′ĭ·tĭ). Suitability; ability to agree.

conjectural (kŏn·jĕk′tûr·ăl). Based on a guess, or on slight evidence. **conjecture** *n.* A guess, an inference from slight evidence. *v.* To guess; to infer.

connotation (kŏn′ō·tā′shŭn). The suggestions or implications of a word apart from its recognized meaning (its *denotation*).

consecrate (kŏn′sē·krāt). To render holy or sacred.

constancy (kŏn′stăn·sĭ). Steadfastness; fidelity.

constrain (kŏn·strān′). To force; restrain.

constraint (kŏn·strānt′). 1. Restraint. 2. Embarrassment.

contemporary (kŏn·tĕm′pō·rĕr′ĭ). 1. One who lives at the same time as another. 2. One of the same age as another.

contiguity (kŏn′tĭ·gū′ĭ·tĭ). Nearness.

contingent (kŏn·tĭn′jĕnt). 1. Dependent. 2. Possible. **contingent** *n.* Group; party.

convolution (kŏn′vō·lū′shŭn). 1. A fold or coil. 2. Winding or coiled formation.

cope (kōp). To struggle successfully with something; to meet on equal terms.

copious (kō′pĭ·ŭs). 1. Plentiful. 2. Wordy.

corpulent (kôr′pū·lĕnt). Fat.

corroborate (kŏ·rŏb′ō·rāt). To confirm; to establish.

countenance (koun′tē·nǎns). The face. **countenance** *v.* To aid, to favor.

cow (kou). To intimidate.

craven (krā′vĕn). Afraid; cowardly.

credibility (krĕd′ĭ·bĭl′ĭ·tĭ). Reliability.

credulous (krĕd′ū·lŭs). Inclined to believe on little evidence.

crevice (krĕv′ĭs). A narrow opening.

criterion (krī·tēr′ĭ·ŭn). A standard of judgment; a test.

crypt (krĭpt). An underground vault or tomb.

cryptic (krĭp′tĭk). Secret; mysterious.

culmination (kŭl′mĭ·nā′shŭn). 1. Full development; the summit. 2. The act of reaching full development.

cumbersome (kŭm′bēr·sŭm). Clumsy; heavy.

curate (kū′rāt). 1. A clergyman. 2. The assistant of a rector or vicar.

cynical (sĭn′ĭ·kǎl). Distrustful of human motives.

D

daub (dôb). To apply paint, plaster, etc. to a surface, usually unskillfully; hence, smear.

debacle (dē·bä′k′l). Violent disturbance; sudden collapse.

debar (dē·bär′). Exclude.

decadent (dē·kā′dĕnt). Characterizing decline or deterioration.

decipher (dē·sī′fēr). To decode.

declaim (dē·klām′). To speak or state, usually rhetorically.

declination (dĕk′lĭ·nā′shŭn). 1. A deviation. 2. A decline. 3. A polite refusal.

decorum (dē·kō′rŭm). 1. Formality in behavior. 2. Orderliness.

decrepitude (dē·krĕp′ĭ·tūd). State of being broken down with age.

decry (dē·krī′). To condemn; to criticize hostilely and openly.

deem (dēm). To think; to judge.

deference (dĕf′ēr·ĕns). Courteous respect.

deftness (dĕft′nĭs). Skill.

degenerate (dē·jĕn′ēr·āt). To deteriorate; to lower in quality. **degenerate** (dē·jĕn′ēr·ĭt). *adj.* Degraded; debased.

delectable (dē·lĕk′tá·b′l). Pleasing; delightful.

delete (dē·lēt′). To erase.

delusion (dē·lū′zhǔn). 1. A false belief. 2. Something that misleads the mind. **delusive** *adj.*

delve (dĕlv). To dig; to seek.

demean (dē·mēn′). 1. To conduct oneself. 2. To degrade.

demeanor (dē·mēn′ēr). Behavior.

demoniacal (dē′mō·nī′á·kǎl). Devilish.

demonstrative (dē·mŏn′strá·tĭv). 1. Making clearly evident. 2. Displaying feeling.

demure (dē·mūr′). Prim; modest, usually as a pretense.

denominate (dē·nŏm′ĭ·nāt). To name; to call.

denunciation (dē·nŭn′sĭ·ā′shŭn). 1. A forewarning of evil. 2. An accusation, a condemnation.

deplorable (dē·plōr′á·b′l). Grievous; sad.

deploy (dē·ploi′). To spread out; to extend the front of a military formation.

depopulate (dē·pŏp′ū·lāt). To deprive a land of its inhabitants, usually through war or disease.

deprecate (dĕp′rē·kāt). To indicate disapproval of something.

derision (dē·rĭzh′ŭn). Scorn; contempt.

derisive (dē·rī′sĭv). Indicating scorn or contempt.

---

bar; church; dog; ardŭous; fat; go; hear; jail; key; lame; meat; not; ring; pay; ran; see; shell; ten; there, thick; pastūre; vast; wind; yes; zoo, zh = z in azure.

despicable (dĕs'pǐ·ka·b'l). Deserving contempt.

diadem (dī'a·dĕm). A crown.

diffident (dǐf'ǐ·dĕnt). Shy; lacking confidence.

diffuse (dǐ·fūz'). 1. To spread out. 2. To spread wastefully. **diffuse** (dǐ·fūs'). *adj.* 1. Widespread. 2. Wordy.

disavow (dǐs'a·vou'). 1. To refuse to acknowledge. 2. To deny responsibility for.

discern (dǐ·zûrn'). To see; to observe.

discipline (dǐs'ǐ·plǐn). 1. Training. 2. Punishment. 3. That which is taught; hence, a subject of study.

discomfiture (dǐs·kŭm'fǐ·tûr). Uneasiness; frustration.

disconsolate (dǐs·kŏn'sō·lǐt). Dejected; sad.

discordant (dǐs·kôr'dănt). Disagreeing; jarring.

discreet (dǐs·krēt'). Showing good judgment; prudent.

disdainful (dǐs·dān'fŏŏl). Scornful.

disparage (dǐs·păr'ǐj). To belittle; to speak scornfully of.

dissension (dǐ·sĕn'shŭn). Disagreement; discord.

dissever (dǐ·sĕv'ēr). To break apart; to disunite.

dissipation (dǐs'ǐ·pā'shŭn). 1. Wasteful spending. 2. An idle, harmful way of life.

dissolution (dǐs'ō·lū'shŭn). Breaking up; disintegration.

dissonance (dǐs'ō·năns). Lack of agreement; discord.

dissuade (dǐ·swād'). 1. To advise someone against something. 2. To turn someone from his purpose.

distaste (dǐs·tāst'). Dislike.

distemper (dǐs·tĕm'pēr). To disturb.

distillation (dǐs'tǐ·lā'shŭn). The act of distilling, that is, freeing a substance of impurities; hence, the essence of something.

distraught (dǐs·trôt). Distracted; crazed.

divine (dǐ·vīn'). To foresee; to prophesy.

document (dŏk'ŭ·mĕnt). 1. To provide evidence for something. 2. To furnish with documents.

doddering (dŏd'ēr·ǐng). Trembling or shaking from frailty or extreme age; foolish.

dogged (dŏg'ed). Obstinate; determined.

dominion (dō·mǐn'yŭn). 1. The supreme authority. 2. The territory governed by such an authority.

dotage (dōt'ǐj). Feeble-mindedness in old age.

drayman (drā'măn). One whose work is carting or driving a wagon.

dualism (dū'ăl·ǐz'm). Any system employing a double principle; a twofold distinction.

dubious (dū'bǐ·ŭs). Doubtful; not clear.

durable (dū'ra·b'l). Lasting; enduring.

E

ebb (ĕb). To decline; to flow back; to recede.

eccentricity (ĕk'sĕn·trǐs'ǐ·tǐ). Unusual trait; oddity.

eddy (ĕd'ǐ). To move in a whirlpool or in a circular direction.

effectual (ĕ·fĕk'tū·ăl). Adequate; effective.

effervescent (ĕf'ēr·vĕs'ĕnt). Lively; bubbly.

elation (ē·lā'shŭn). Lifted or elevated spirits; joy; delight.

eloquence (ĕl'ō·kwĕns). Vivid or graceful use of language; forceful or persuasive talk.

emaciated (ē·mā'shǐ·āt'd). Extremely thin.

emanate (ĕm'a·nāt). To come forth; to flow.

embodiment (ĕm'bŏd'ǐ·mĕnt). The act of giving body or concrete expression to something, as a knight is the *embodiment* of chivalry. **embody** (ĕm·bŏd'ǐ). To give body to; to make something concrete.

emergence (ē·mûr'jĕns). Coming into view; issuing forth.

emigrant (ĕm'ǐ·grănt). One who leaves his country to settle permanently in another.

encroach (ĕn·krōch'). To intrude; to trespass on another's rights or possessions.

encrust (ĕn·krŭst'). To cover with a hard coat or crust.

encumber (ĕn·kŭm'bēr). To obstruct or interfere with by placing a burden on. **encumbrance.** Burden.

endearment (ĕn·dēr'mĕnt). A sign of affection.

endow (ĕn·dou'). To furnish a permanent fund for support; to enrich in some way.

engross (ĕn·grōs'). To absorb fully; to take the whole of something.

engulf (ĕn·gŭlf'). To swallow up.

enigma (ē·nǐg'ma). Anything perplexing; a mystery or riddle.

ensnare (ĕn·snâr'). To catch; to entrap.

entreaty (ĕn·trēt'ǐ). A plea; a request.

entwine (ĕn·twīn'). To coil or wrap together or around.

enumeration (ē·nū'mēr·ā'shŭn). The act of counting, numbering, or listing.

eon (ē'ŏn). An immeasurably long time period.

ephemeral (ĕ·fĕm'ēr·ăl). Short-lived; fleeting.

epicurean (ĕp'ǐ·kū·rē'ăn). Luxurious in eating or drinking tastes and habits.

epithet (ĕp'ǐ·thĕt). A descriptive word or phrase, generally accompanying a noun.

epitomize (ē·pǐt'ō·mīz). To summarize.

āpe, chăotic, bâre, ăt, ăttend, ärt, flăsk, atop; ēke, mērely, ĕlect, ĕcho, prudĕnt, doēr; ītem, ǐnn; rarǐty; ōde, ŏpaque, fôr, dŏt, lŏft, cŏnfide; sōon, tŏŏk; sour, toil; tūbe, ūnique, tûrn, sŭp, ŭntil.

epoch (ĕp′ŏk). A period of time characterized by an important discovery or a distinctive development.

equanimity (ē′kwà·nĭm′ĭ·tĭ). Calmness; evenness of temper.

equatorial (ē′kwà·tō′rĭ·ăl). Pertaining to the equator.

equidistant (ē′kwĭ·dĭs′tănt). Equally distant.

equity (ĕk′wĭ·tĭ). Fairness.

equivocal (ē·kwĭv′ō·kăl). Having two or more interpretations; uncertain; doubtful.

eradicate (ē·răd′ĭ·kāt). To drive out; to erase completely.

erode (ē·rōd′). 1. To wear away. 2. To be worn away.

essay (ĕ·sā′). To test, try out; to attempt.

ethereal (ē·thēr′ē·ăl). Spiritlike; airy.

eulogy (ū′lō·jĭ). A speech in praise of a deceased person; more commonly, any kind of praise.

evacuate (ē·văk′û·āt). 1. To remove; to withdraw. 2. To empty.

evince (ē·vĭns′). To show; to make evident.

exasperate (ĕg·zăs′pēr·āt). To irritate; to anger.

excruciating (ĕks·kroo′shĭ·āt′ĭng). Extremely painful; torturing.

execrate (ĕk′sē·krāt). 1. To curse someone. 2. To detest.

exhort (ĕg·zôrt′). To advise; to urge.

expedient (ĕks·pē′dĭ·ĕnt). Suitable; advantageous.

expeditionary (ĕks′pē·dĭsh′ŭn·ĕr·ĭ). Referring to an expedition, a journey for a specific purpose.

expiration (ĕk·spĭ·rā′shŭn). 1. An end; the conclusion of a matter. 2. Death.

expletive (ĕks′plē·tĭv). 1. Something, usually a word, added merely as a filling. 2. An oath or exclamation.

explicitness (ĕks·plĭs′ĭt·nĭs). Clarity; distinctness of meaning.

extant (ĕks′tănt). Existing; not lost or destroyed.

extemporize (ĕks·tĕm′pō·rīz). To do or speak without prior study or preparation; to improvise.

extenuate (ĕks·tĕn′û·āt). 1. To excuse. 2. To diminish; to underestimate.

extol (ĕks·tŏl′). To praise; to elevate through praise.

extort (ĕks·tôrt′). To take by force or illegally.

extremity (ĕks·trĕm′ĭ·tĭ). 1. The utmost limit. 2. The limb of a body.

extricate (ĕks′trĭ·kāt). To free.

exultant (ĕg·zŭl′tănt). Expressing joy or triumph.

F

facetious (fà·sē′shŭs). Causing laughter, usually inappropriate; witty.

facilitate (fà·sĭl′ĭ·tāt). To make easy.

faculty (făk′ŭl·tĭ). 1. The ability to do something or to act. 2. Physical function, as the *faculty* of seeing. 3. The governing body of a college or university.

famish (făm′ĭsh). To starve or suffer extreme hunger.

fanatic (fà·năt′ĭk). Overly enthusiastic. *n.* An excessively enthusiastic person.

fatuous (făt′û·ŭs). Foolish.

fauna (fô′nà). Animals or animal life (distinguished from *flora*, plant life).

feasible (fē′zĭ·b′l). Possible; capable of being handled successfully.

felicitous (fē·lĭs′ĭ·tŭs). Happily or gracefully expressed; fit.

felicity (fē·lĭs′ĭ·tĭ). Happiness; success.

felonious (fē·lō′nĭ·ŭs). Criminal; villainous.

ferment (fēr·mĕnt′). To be agitated. *n.* A state of agitation or unrest.

ferocious (fē·rō′shŭs). Fierce; violent.

ferret (fĕr′ĕt). An animal of the weasel family, noted for its shrewd habits in hunting.

fervor (fûr′vēr). Intense feeling; passion.

fetter (fĕt′ēr). 1. A foot shackle. 2. Anything restraining. *v.* To restrain or confine.

filial (fĭl′ĭ·ăl). Relating to a son or daughter.

filigree (fĭl′ĭ·grē). Ornamental openwork of delicate design, usually of fine wire or metal.

finicky (fĭn′ĭ·kĭ). Excessively particular; too precise.

fissure (fĭsh′ēr). A narrow opening.

flagon (flăg′ŭn). A container for liquid, usually with a spout and handle.

flounder (floun′dēr). To struggle; to move clumsily.

fluctuate (flŭk′tû·āt). To waver; to vary; to change constantly.

foal (fōl). The young (colt or filly) of the horse family. *v.* To bring forth a colt or filly.

forbear (fôr·bâr′). To refrain from doing something; to control oneself. **forbearance.** Restraint; patience.

freight (frāt). 1. To place a load or burden on. 2. To transport.

frivolous (frĭv′ō·lŭs). 1. Of little importance; slight. 2. Given to trifling; flippant.

fulsome (fŏŏl′sŭm). Offensive because of insincerity.

furtive (fûr′tĭv). Secret; sly.

fuse (fūz). To unite; to combine.

fusillade (fū′zĭ·lād′). A rapid or simultaneous discharge of guns. *v.* To shoot rapidly or simultaneously.

---

bar; church; dog; ardûous; fat; go; hear; jail; key; lame; meat; not; ring; pay; ran; see; shell; ten; there, thick; pastûre; vast; wind; yes; zoo, zh = z in azure.

G

gait (gāt). Manner of walking.

gangling (găng′glĭng). Loose in build; lanky.

geometric (gē′ō·mĕt′rĭk). **1.** Pertaining to geometry. **2.** Using geometric designs such as triangles, bands, etc. for patterns.

gibberish (jĭb′ēr·ĭsh). Loud and foolish talk.

gild (gĭld). To overlay with a gold covering.

gloaming (glōm·ĭng). Twilight.

gnarled (närld). Full of knots; twisted; rugged.

gout (gout). A disease involving the painful inflammation of the joints.

grizzled (griz″ld). Streaked with gray.

guile (gīl). Cunning; treachery.

guise (gīz). **1.** Behavior. **2.** Appearance; aspect. **3.** Mask.

gusto (gŭs′tō). Taste; great appreciation.

H

haggard (hăg′ērd). Wild-eyed; gaunt.

hallow (hăl′ō). To make sacred.

harangue (há·răng′). A speech, often noisy and ranting.

harass (hăr′ás). To tire; to make weary. **harassment** (hăr′as·mĕnt). Wearying; exhausting.

heinous (hā′nŭs). Outrageous; hateful; atrocious.

herculean (hûr·kū′lē·ăn). Having superhuman strength or size.

hermitage (hûr′mĭ·tĭj). A secluded home; the residence of a hermit.

hirsute (hûr′sūt). Hairy; shaggy.

hobble (hŏb″l). **1.** To walk unevenly; to limp. **2.** To fetter or shackle in order to prevent movement (used especially of horses).

hypochondria (hī′pō·kŏn′drĭ·á). **1.** The state of believing in imaginary ailments. **2.** Emotional depression. **hypochondriac.** One who imagines himself to be diseased.

I

ignoble (ĭg·nō′b′l). Not honorable; base.

illimitable (ĭl·lĭm′ĭt·á·b′l). Not capable of being limited; impossible to measure.

imbibe (ĭm·bīb′). To drink in; to absorb.

immemorial (ĭm′mĕ·mō′rĭ·ăl). Beyond the reach of memory or history; ancient.

immigrant (ĭm′ĭ·grănt). One who settles in a new country.

immune (ĭ·mūn′). Exempt; protected.

impede (ĭm·pēd′). To stop; to obstruct.

impediment (ĭm·pĕd′ĭ·mĕnt). Obstacle; hindrance.

imperative (ĭm·pĕr′á·tĭv). In the nature of a command; authoritative; compulsory.

imperceptible (ĭm·pēr·sĕp′tĭ·b′l). Not capable of being perceived by the senses; unnoticeable.

imperious (ĭm·pēr′ĭ·ŭs). **1.** Arrogant; lordly. **2.** Urgent.

imperturbable (ĭm′pēr·tûr′bá·b′l). Impossible to disturb; calm; cool.

impetuous (ĭm·pĕt′û·ŭs). Rash; hasty; impulsive.

implacable (ĭm·plā′ká·b′l). Not able to be calmed or pacified; unwilling to forgive; relentless.

implement (ĭm′plĕ·mĕnt). To accomplish; to carry out.

implicate (ĭm′plĭ·kāt). **1.** To imply. **2.** To involve.

importunate (ĭm·pôr′tû·nĭt). Troublesomely demanding; too eager in requesting.

impotent (ĭm′pō·tĕnt). Lacking power or vigor.

impregnable (ĭm·prĕg′ná·b′l). Unconquerable; able to withstand attack.

impromptu (ĭm·prŏmp′tū). Offhand; done without previous preparation.

impropriety (ĭm′prō·prī′ĕ·ti). An improper or unbecoming act.

improvisation (ĭm′prō·vĭ·zā′shŭn). The composition or performance of art, music, etc., without previous preparation.

improvise (ĭm′prō·vīz). To paint, compose, etc., without previous preparation.

impunity (ĭm·pū′nĭ·tĭ). Freedom from punishment or harm; safety.

inalienable (in·āl′yĕn·á·b′l). Incapable of being given up or transferred to another.

inanimate (ĭn·ăn′ĭ·māt). **1.** Not possessing life. **2.** Dead; lifeless; spiritless.

inaudible (ĭn·ô′dĭ·b′l). Unable to be heard.

inauspicious (ĭn′ôs·pĭsh′ŭs). Unlucky; unfavorable.

incantation (ĭn′kăn·tā′shŭn). The use of spells or verbal charms in magic; magic; sorcery.

incense (ĭn·sĕns′). To inflame with anger; to incite.

incessant (ĭn·sĕs′ănt). Unceasing; continual.

inconclusiveness (ĭn′kŏn·klōō′sĭv·nĭs). Indecisiveness; not leading to a definite conclusion or result.

incorrigible (ĭn·kŏr′ĭ·jĭ·b′l). Incapable of being reformed; unruly.

indispensible (ĭn′dĭs·pĕn′sá·b′l). Essential.

indolence (ĭn′dō·lĕns). Laziness; sloth.

indomitable (ĭn·dŏm′ĭ·tá·b′l). Impossible to subdue or conquer.

induce (ĭn·dūs′). **1.** To persuade. **2.** To bring about.

āpe, chǎotic, bâre, ǎt, ǎttend, ärt, flǎsk, átop; ēke, mẽrely, ĕlect, ĕcho, prudĕnt, doẽr; ītem, ĭnn, rarĭty; ōde, ŏpaque, fôr, dŏt, lŏft, cŏnfide; sōon, tŏŏk; sour, toil; tūbe, ûnique, tûrn, sŭp, ŭntil.

ineptitude (ĭn·ĕpt′ĭ·tūd). Awkwardness; clumsiness.

infelicity (ĭn′fê·lĭs′ĭ·tĭ). Inappropriateness; clumsiness or awkwardness of expression.

infirmity (ĭn·fûr′mĭ·tĭ). **1.** Feebleness; frailty. **2.** A disease; a personal failing or defect.

influx (ĭn′flŭks). A flowing in; a pouring in.

ingratiating (ĭn·grā′shĭ·āt′ĭng). Winning favor or approval.

inherent (ĭn·hēr′ĕnt). Belonging by nature; firmly fixed; essential.

injunction (ĭn·jŭngk′shŭn). **1.** An act prohibiting or directing. **2.** An order requiring the performance of something.

innate (ĭn′nāt). Inborn; natural; part of the essential nature.

inordinate (ĭn·ôr′dĭ·nĭt). Excessive; unrestrained.

inquisition (ĭn′kwĭ·zĭsh′ŭn). **1.** Inquiry; search for information. **2.** A tribunal formed for the purpose of discovering and punishing heresy.

inscrutable (ĭn·skrōō′ta·b'l). Mysterious; incomprehensible.

insinuating (ĭn·sĭn′û·āt′ĭng). **1.** Hinting indirectly. **2.** Introducing artfully; instilling. **3.** Winning or trying to win confidence through subtle methods.

insolent (ĭn′sô·lĕnt). Disrespectful; haughty; overbearing.

insoluble (ĭn·sŏl′û·b'l). **1.** Not dissolvable. **2.** Impossible to explain or solve.

insolvency (ĭn·sŏl′vĕn·sĭ). State of being unable to pay one's debts; poverty.

instancy (ĭn′stăn·sĭ). Urgency; instantaneousness; speed.

insular (ĭn′sû·lēr). **1.** Pertaining to an island. **2.** Isolated. **3.** Narrow of mind; not liberal.

intangible (ĭn·tăn′jĭ·b'l). Incapable of being perceived by the senses; untouchable.

interglacial (ĭn′tēr·glā′shăl). Occurring between two glacial periods.

intermediary (ĭn′tēr·mē′dĭ·ĕr′ĭ). **1.** Intermediate. **2.** Acting as an agent between two parties. *n.* A mediator; one who acts as an agent between two parties.

interminable (ĭn·tûr′mĭ·na·b'l). Endless.

interwoven (ĭn′tēr·wō′vĕn). Woven or mingled together.

intimate (ĭn′tĭ·mĭt). Very personal; private; familiar. (–māt) *v.* To hint, or to suggest.

intrusive (ĭn·trōō′sĭv). Intruding; entering without right or by force.

invincible (ĭn·vĭn′sĭ·b'l). Incapable of being conquered.

inviolable (ĭn·vī′ô·la·b'l). Incapable of being harmed, destroyed, or corrupted.

irascibility (ĭ·răs′ĭ·bĭl′ĭ·tĭ). Quickness to anger; touchiness.

irrelevance (ĭr·rĕl′ê·văns). That which is not applicable, pertinent, or necessary.

irrepressible (ĭr′rê·prĕs′ĭ·b'l). Uncontrollable; incapable of being restrained.

J

jocular (jŏk′û·lēr). Merry; sportive; witty.

jubilant (jōō′bĭ·lănt). Joyful; rejoicing.

judicial (jōō·dĭsh′ăl). **1.** Pertaining to the courts. **2.** Disposed to form judgment; critical; exercising judgment.

jurist (jōōr′ĭst). One who knows the law or practices it.

juxtaposition (jŭks′ta·pô·zĭsh′ŭn). A placing side by side.

K

keel (kēl). The bottom timbers or plates of a vessel.

knavery (nāv′ēr·ĭ). Petty villainy; fraud.

knowledgeable (nŏl′ĕj·a·b'l). Possessing or showing knowledge.

L

lament (la·mĕnt′). To express or feel grief; to mourn.

legacy (lĕg′a·sĭ). **1.** Any inheritance. **2.** A gift of property by will.

libel (lī′bĕl). A defaming or harmfully intended statement. *v.* To make or publish a defaming statement.

libretto (lĭ·brĕt′ō). The text or words of any choral or musical composition.

ligament (lĭg′a·mĕnt). **1.** A band of tissues connecting bones or supporting organs. **2.** Anything that connects one thing to another; a bond.

limbo (lĭm′bō). A place of confinement or neglect, especially of those forgotten.

litany (lĭt′a·nĭ). A form of prayer consisting of alternate responses from clergy and congregation.

livid (lĭv′ĭd). **1.** Discolored. **2.** Ash gray.

loiter (loi′tēr). To lag behind; to delay.

ludicrous (lū′dĭ·krŭs). Ridiculous; laughable.

lurch (lûrch). To roll or sway suddenly; to stagger.

lurid (lū′rĭd). **1.** Dismal; ghastly. **2.** Violently passionate.

luster (lŭs′tēr). **1.** Shine; brightness. **2.** Splendor; radiance. **lustrous.** Radiant, bright.

luxuriant (lŭks·û′rĭ·ănt). **1.** Abundant in growth. **2.** Profuse; lavish.

---

bar; church; dog; ardŭous; fat; go; hear; jail; key; lame; meat; not; ring; pay; ran; see; shell; ten; there, thick; pastŭre; vast; wind; yes; zoo, zh = z in azure.

M

macabre (má·kä′b′r). Gruesome; ghastly.

magnanimity (măg′ná·nĭm′ĭ·tĭ). Nobility of soul; honor; elevation of mind above what is low or unworthy.

maladjustment (măl′ă·jŭst′mĕnt). Poor or inadequate adjustment or adaptation.

malediction (măl′ĕ·dĭk′shŭn). A curse; a slander.

malevolence (má·lĕv′ō·lĕns). The state or act of wishing evil; malice.

manifest (măn′ĭ·fĕst). Evident; capable of being perceived; not obscure.

manifestation (măn′ĭ·fĕs·tā′shŭn). A display; a disclosure.

marital (măr′ĭ·tăl). Pertaining to a husband or marriage.

marshal (mär′shăl). 1. To arrange in order, esp. military order. 2. To guide or lead.

mastiff (más′tĭf). A large, smooth-coated hunting dog.

mayhem (mā′hĕm). The maiming or disfiguring of a person.

medallion (mē·dăl′yŭn). A medal, usually large.

medieval (mē′dĭ·ē′văl). Pertaining to the Middle Ages.

mediocrity (mē·dĭ·ŏk′rĭ·tĭ). Quality of only moderate skill or ability; ordinariness.

medium (mē′dĭ·ŭm). 1. That through which anything is accomplished. 2. A substance through which an effect is transmitted. **mediums** or **media** *plural.*

mercenary (mûr′sĕ·nĕr′ĭ). Acting merely for pay or reward of some sort. *n.* A soldier who serves in a foreign country's army for pay.

meticulous (mē·tĭk′u·lŭs). Excessively careful of small details.

militant (mĭl′ĭ·tănt). Engaged in war; aggressive.

mincing (mĭn′sĭng). To walk or talk in an affected manner.

minion (mĭn′yŭn). A dependent or inferior servant or agent.

mitigation (mĭt·ĭ·gā′shŭn). The act of becoming less severe; relief. **mitigate.** To make less harsh or severe; to relieve.

molder (mōl′dẽr). To crumble; to decay.

monger (mŭng′gẽr). A trader or dealer, usually implying discredit, as in *rumormonger.*

monotone (mŏn′ō·tōn). 1. Succession of sounds on one key or pitch. 2. Sameness of style or tone.

mortify (môr′tĭ·fī). 1. To vex; to humiliate. 2. To deaden or humble oneself through strict discipline. 3. To destroy the vigor or strength of someone.

mosaic (mō·zā′ĭk). A picture or design made by the inlay of small pieces of glass, stone, etc.

motif (mō·tēf′). The theme or dominant feature of a work of fine art or literature.

multiplicity (mŭl′tĭ·plĭs′ĭ·tĭ). 1. Quality of being multiple or various. 2. A great number.

multitudinous (mŭl′tĭ·tū′dĭn·ŭs). 1. Forming a great multitude. 2. Issuing from or resembling a vast number of persons.

munificent (mû·nĭf′ĭ·sĕnt). Liberal; lavish.

mural (mū′răl). A wall painting.

muse (mūz). 1. The goddess who inspires a poet. 2. [Cap.] In Greek mythology, one of the nine goddesses who were patrons of the arts and sciences. *v.* To ponder; to think carefully.

mystic (mĭs′tĭk). 1. Having the characteristics of mystery. 2. Pertaining to mysticism or other such beliefs. *n.* One who follows a mystical way of life.

N

negligible (nĕg′lĭ·jĭ·b′l). Unimportant; something that can be neglected or discarded.

niche (nĭch). 1. A wall recess. 2. A place or condition suited to the abilities of a person or the qualities of a thing.

nondescript (nŏn′dē·skrĭpt). 1. Not easily described. 2. A person of no particular class or distinction.

nostalgic (nŏs·tăl′jĭk). Homesick.

O

oasis (ō·ā′sĭs). A fertile spot in a desert or waste land.

oblique (ŏb·lēk′). 1. Slanting; inclined. 2. Not straightforward; underhanded.

organic (ôr·găn′ĭk). 1. Pertaining to living organisms, animal or vegetable. 2. Organized; systematically co-ordinated.

orgy (ôr′gĭ). Excessive indulgence; revelry.

ostentation (ŏs′tĕn·tā′shŭn). Unnecessary show; pretention. **ostentatious.** Showy; fond of excessive display.

P

pallid (păl′ĭd). Lacking color; pale.

palpable (păl′pá·b′l). 1. Capable of being touched or felt. 2. Plain; obvious.

pandemonium (păn′dē·mō′nĭ·ŭm). A wild din or outburst; tumult.

paradox (păr′á·dŏks). A self-contradictory or apparently false statement that may contain some truth.

āpe, chãotic, bâre, ăt, ăttend, ärt, flásk, átop; ēke, mẹrely, ĕlect, ĕcho, prudĕnt, doẽr; ītem, ĭnn, rarĭty; ōde, ọpaque, fôr, dŏt, lôft, cŏnfide; sōon, tŏŏk; sour, toil; tūbe, ûnique, tûrn, sŭp, ŭntil.

paramount (păr'a·mount). Highest in rank; supreme.

paraphernalia *pl.* (păr'a·fēr·nā'lǐ·a). Personal belongings; furnishings; apparatus.

parley (pär'lǐ). **1.** Mutual conversation. **2.** A talk with an enemy, usually a conversation regarding a truce or an exchange of prisoners.

parsimony (pär'sǐ·mō'nǐ). Stinginess; excessive frugality.

patronage (pā'trŭn·ǐj). **1.** Support or encouragement from a patron. **2.** Condescension; expressing an air of superiority; snobbery.

peat (pēt). A piece of turf used for fuel.

peremptory (pēr·ĕmp'tō·rǐ). Decisive; commanding; leaving no chance for refusal.

perennial (pēr·ĕn'ǐ·ăl). **1.** Lasting through the year. **2.** Unceasing; never-failing; continual.

perfunctory (pēr·fŭngk'tō·rǐ). **1.** Done mechanically and carelessly. **2.** Indifferent.

peroration (pĕr·ō·rā'shŭn). The final summing up of an argument; conclusion.

perspective (pēr·spĕk'tǐv). **1.** A scene, usually one giving an impression of distance. **2.** A view of something from a particular standpoint.

pertinacity (pûr·tǐ·năs'ǐ·tǐ). Unyielding persistence; obstinacy.

pertinence (pûr'tǐ·nĕns). Relevancy; something related to the matter at hand; anything significant.

perturbation (pûr'tēr·bā'shŭn). State of great alarm or agitation.

perusal (pē·rōōz'ăl). A reading, usually a careful one.

pestilent (pĕs'tǐ·lĕnt). Deadly; poisonous; injurious.

pettish (pĕt'ǐsh). Peevish; ill-tempered.

petulant (pĕt'ū·lănt). Fretful; inclined to find fault or complain.

phenomenon (fē·nŏm'ē·nŏn). **1.** A fact or event. **2.** An exceptional thing or person. **phenomena** *plural.*

philanthropy (fǐl·ăn'thrō·pǐ). Love for mankind; good will.

piety (pī'ĕ·tǐ). **1.** Loyalty; devotion. **2.** Dutifulness and devoutness in religious matters.

pinion (pǐn'yŭn). **1.** To bind or hold fast. **2.** Confine. *n.* A feather.

pithy (pǐth'ǐ). Having substance and point; concise.

placid (plăs'ǐd). Calm; quiet; peaceful.

plaintive (plān'tǐv). Sorrowful or melancholy.

plausible (plô'zǐ·b'l). Reasonable; credible; believable, sometimes with a hint of possible deception.

plowshare (plou'shâr'). The part of the plow which cuts the furrow.

poignant (poin'yănt). **1.** Piercing; keen. **2.** Moving; touching.

pollute (pŏ·lūt'). To make unclean; to contaminate.

pompous (pŏmp'ŭs). Self-important; showy.

ponderous (pŏn'dēr·ŭs). Extremely heavy; lacking lightness or spirit.

posterity (pŏs·tĕr'ǐ·tǐ). **1.** Offspring or descendants. **2.** All future generations.

postulate (pŏs'·tūlāt). **1.** To demand; to claim. **2.** To assume as true or real; to put forth as necessary or required.

potency (pō'tĕn·sǐ). **1.** The ability to effect a result. **2.** Potentiality; capability of developing naturally.

poultice (pōl'tǐs). A soft, heated composition applied to a sore part of the body.

preamble (prē'ăm'b'l). An introductory portion; a preface.

preceptor (prē·sĕp'tēr). A teacher; a principal or headmaster of a school.

precipice (prĕs'ǐ·pǐs). A steep or overhanging place; a cliff.

precipitous (prē·sǐp'ǐ·tŭs). **1.** Steep. **2.** Hasty; abrupt.

precursor (prē·kûr'sēr). One that precedes; forerunner.

predatory (prĕd'a·tō'rǐ). **1.** Pertaining to plundering. **2.** Living by preying on other animals.

predispose (prē'dǐs·pōz'). To incline beforehand, usually favorably; to give a favorable tendency or bias to something.

premonition (prē'mō·nǐsh'ŭn). A forewarning; a foreboding.

premonitory (prē·mŏn'ǐ·tō·rǐ). Giving previous warning.

prerogative (prē·rŏg'a·tǐv). **1.** A right or privilege. **2.** Of first importance.

presentiment (prē·zĕn'tǐ·mĕnt). A feeling that something will happen; a premonition or foreboding.

presuppose (prē'sŭ·pōz'). **1.** To suppose beforehand; to take for granted. **2.** To require or depend upon something preceding, as an argument *presupposes* a difference of opinion.

pretension (prē·tĕn'shŭn). **1.** An excuse; a false explanation. **2.** A claim to invite admiration.

pretext (prē'tĕkst). An excuse; an apology or explanation designed to hide the real reason for an act.

primeval (prī·mē'văl). Belonging to the earliest ages; primitive.

privation (prī·vā'shŭn). **1.** A depriving. **2.** A want of a necessity; a lack.

proffer (prŏf'ēr). To offer.

---

bar; church; dog; arduous; fat; go; hear; jail; key; lame; meat; not; ring; pay; ran; see; shell; ten; there, thick; pasture; vast; wind; yes; zoo, zh = z in azure.

prompt (prŏmpt). **1.** To move; to incite. **2.** To remind; to suggest.

proprietary (prō·prī'ĕ·tĕr'ĭ). Pertaining to a property; indicating ownership or exclusive control.

propriety (prō·prī'ĕ·tĭ). **1.** Suitability; fitness. **2.** Code or observance of standards; politeness; decorum.

prostrate (prŏs'trāt). **1.** Lying prone on the ground. **2.** Thrown down; overthrown.

provocative (prō·vŏk'ȧ·tĭv). Serving to provoke, stimulate, or incense; arousing to action.

provoke (prō·vōk'). To arouse; to incite.

proximity (prŏks·ĭm'ĭ·tĭ). State of being next or very close to.

prudent (prōo'dĕnt). Highly sensible; cautious; not rash.

pugnacious (pŭg·nā'shŭs). Disposed to fight; combative; extremely aggressive.

pungent (pŭn'jĕnt). **1.** Causing a sharp sensation; acrid. **2.** Sharply painful; piercing.

Q

quack (kwăk). **1.** Someone who pretends to medical knowledge. **2.** One who falsely claims any kind of knowledge. *adj.* Characterized by unfounded claims; false.

quaff (kwȧf). To drink.

quagmire (kwăg'mīr'). **1.** A swamp or bog. **2.** A difficult or treacherous position.

quail (kwāl). To lose heart; to shrink, cower, or recoil.

quell (kwĕl). **1.** To subdue; to suppress. **2.** To quiet; to pacify.

quench (kwĕnch). **1.** To extinguish. **2.** To subdue or suppress. **3.** To cool.

R

radiance (rā'dĭ·ȧns). Brilliance; vivid glow.

rakish (rāk'ĭsh). Sporty; jauntily careless.

ramification (răm'ĭ·fĭ·kā'shŭn). **1.** Offshoot; outgrowth. **2.** Result; consequence.

rampage (răm'pāj). To storm or rush about wildly. *n.* Violent, riotous actions.

rampart (răm'pärt). A protective barrier; a fortification.

rapt (răpt). Transported with emotion; intent; engrossed; completely absorbed in thought or emotion.

ravenous (răv'ĕn·ŭs). **1.** Covetous; grasping. **2.** Eager for food or satisfaction.

rebuff (rē·bŭf'). **1.** To snub. **2.** To drive back. *n.* A sharp check; a rejection or refusal; a repulse.

rebuke (rē·būk'). To reprimand; to reprove. *n.* A reprimand; a reproof.

recluse (rē·klōos'). One who lives in seclusion; a hermit. *adj.* Solitary; hidden away.

reconnoiter (rĕk'ŏ·noi'tĕr). To survey; to examine a region.

recount (rē·kount'). To narrate; to tell in detail. **recounter** (rē·kount'r'). Narrator; storyteller.

rectitude (rĕk'tĭ·tūd'). **1.** Uprightness; strict following of moral standards. **2.** Correctness of judgment.

redound (rē·dound'). To come as a result; to flow back.

referendum (rĕf'ēr·ĕn'dŭm). **1.** The referring of a measure to voters for approval or rejection. **2.** A vote on proposed legislation.

reflective (rē·flĕk'tĭv). Thoughtful; deliberative.

reimburse (rē'ĭm·bûrs'). To repay.

reiterate (rē·ĭt'ēr·āt). To repeat.

remnant (rĕm'nȧnt). **1.** Residue; remainder. **2.** A fragment.

remonstrance (rē·mŏn'strȧns). Protest; objection.

replenish (rē·plĕn'ĭsh). To fill again; to restock.

repose (rē·pōz'). To lie at rest. *n.* A state of calm, of quiet dignity.

repulse (rē·pŭls'). **1.** To repel; to beat back. **2.** To reject.

resilient (rē·zĭl'ĭ·ĕnt). Returning to the original position or shape; elastic; flexible.

resonant (rĕz'ŏ·nȧnt). **1.** Re-echoing. **2.** Intensified and enriched through additional echoes or vibrations.

reticent (rĕt'ĭ·sĕnt). Inclined to silence; uncommunicative; reserved.

retraction (rē·trăk'shŭn). **1.** Act of withdrawing a statement, promise or accusation; revocation; apology. **2.** A drawing back.

revel (rĕv'ĕl). **1.** To be festive in a riotous manner. **2.** To take great delight in. *n.* Merry-making; noisy celebration.

revile (rē·vīl'). To abuse; to rail at; to reproach angrily.

rite (rīt). Ceremony; ritual.

ritualistic (rĭt'ū·ȧl·ĭs'tĭk). **1.** Pertaining to a rite or ritual. **2.** Observance of a ritual.

rivulet (rĭv'ū·lĕt). A small stream; a creek.

rotund (rō·tŭnd'). Round; spherical.

rudiment (rōo'dĭ·mĕnt). **1.** First principle or step; something undeveloped. **2.** In biology, an organ that is just beginning to develop or one that was arrested in an early stage of development.

S

salable (sāl'ȧ·b'l). Capable of being marketed or sold.

āpe, chāotic, bâre, ăt, ăttend, ärt, flăsk, ȧtop; ēke, mẹrely, ĕlect, ĕcho, prudĕnt, doēr; ītem, ĭnn, rarĭty; ōde, ŏpaque, fôr, dŏt, lŏft, cŏnfide; sōon, tŏŏk; sour, toil; tūbe, ŭnique, tûrn, sŭp, ŭntil.

sanction (săngk'shŭn). Confirmation; approval. *v.* To approve; to ratify.

sardonic (sär·dŏn'ĭk). Bitterly scornful; disdainful; sneering.

scenty (sĕnt'ĭ). Fragrant.

scrupulous (skrōō'pū·lŭs). Careful; upright; exact.

scrutinize (skrōō'tĭ·nīz). To examine closely; to inspect. **scrutiny.** A detailed examination; a close inspection.

sculptural (skŭlp'tūr·ăl). Describing that which is carved, engraved or sculptured, or that which has characteristics of a sculpture; statuelike; chiseled; majestic.

sear (sēr). 1. To wither; to dry up. 2. To burn; to scorch.

sediment (sĕd'ĭ·mĕnt). The matter which settles to the bottom; dregs or remains.

seer 1. (sē'ẽr). One who sees. 2. (sēr) One who can foresee events; a prophet.

semblance (sĕm'blăns). 1. Outward appearance. 2. Aspect; image. 3. Similarity; seeming, especially a false seeming or appearance.

sententious (sĕn·tĕn'shŭs). Pompous; marked by excessive formality.

sepulcher (sĕp'ŭl·kẽr). A tomb; burial vault.

serene (sē·rēn'). Tranquil; calm.

serpentine (sûr'pĕn·tēn). 1. Like a serpent; wily. 2. Turning one way and another; winding; twisting.

sever (sĕv'ẽr). To divide; to cut; to separate.

shale (shāl). A kind of rock.

sham (shăm). A substitute; a counterfeit; an imitation claiming to be the real thing.

sheepish (shēp'ĭsh). Sheeplike in meekness, stupidity or timidity; bashful, shy.

sibilant (sĭb'ĭ·lănt). Hissing in sound.

sidle (sī'd'l). 1. To move sidewise. 2. To advance furtively; to creep up slyly.

silt (sĭlt). 1. Loose, tiny rock particles suspended in water. 2. A deposit of such material as by a river.

simper (sĭm'pẽr). To smile affectedly, in a silly way. *n.* A silly smile.

slander (slăn'dẽr). A false report tending to injure the reputation of another. *v.* To issue such a false report; to defame.

sloth (slōth). Laziness; indolence.

smite (smīt). 1. To strike; to drive; to hammer. 2. To destroy the life or vigor of someone or something.

sojourn (sō·jûrn'). A temporary stay or visit. *v.* To dwell temporarily.

solace (sŏl'ĭs). Alleviation of grief or anxiety; a source of consolation or comfort. *v.* To console; to give comfort in grief.

solicitude (sō·lĭs'ĭ·tūd). Anxiety; care or attention; also excessive attention.

sonorous (sō·nō'rŭs). 1. Resonant; full in sound. 2. Impressive in sound.

speculative (spĕk'ū·lā'tĭv). 1. Contemplative; meditative; thoughtful. 2. Pertaining to a business venture involving financial risk.

sporadic (spō·răd'ĭk). Infrequent; occurring in scattered instances.

squalor (skwŏl'ẽr). Miserable and unkempt conditions; filth, especially as resulting from neglect or extreme poverty.

stagnant (stăg'nănt). 1. Foul. 2. Not active; dull.

stark (stärk). 1. Harsh; barren. 2. Unadorned; bare.

staunch (stônch). To stop or check the flow — variant of **stanch.** *adj.* 1. Loyal; steadfast; trustworthy. 2. Strong; firm.

steerage (stēr'ĭj). 1. Direction; guidance; management. 2. In a passenger vessel, the section for passengers paying the cheapest fares and receiving poorer accommodations.

sterile (stĕr'ĭl). Barren; not fertile.

stigma (stĭg'mà). 1. A blemish; a brand. 2. Any mark of infamy or disgrace.

stipulate (stĭp'ū·lāt). To agree; to bargain; to specify something as a condition of agreement.

strew (strōō). To spread by scattering; to cover by scattering or spreading over. **strewn** *past participle.*

strychnine (strĭk'nĭn). A poison.

stupefaction (stū'pē·făk'shŭn). Insensibility of mind or feeling; extreme astonishment or confusion.

stupefy (stū'pē·fī). To make dull or stupid; to deprive of sensibility.

subjugation (sŭb'jōō·gā'shŭn). Conquest; the act of being brought under power; servitude or slavery.

sublime (sŭb·līm'). 1. Elevated; exalted. 2. Splendid; emotionally uplifting.

submissive (sŭb·mĭs'ĭv). Inclined to submit; yielding; meek.

subside (sŭb·sīd'). 1. To sink or settle to the bottom. 2. To become quiet; to diminish in force or intensity.

subsist (sŭb·sĭst'). 1. To exist; to have existence. 2. To abide; to remain in the present state. 3. To live.

succulence (sŭk'ū·lĕns). 1. Juiciness. 2. Vitality; freshness.

suffrage (sŭf'rĭj). 1. A prayer; a plea. 2. The right of voting. 3. Assent; vote.

sultry (sŭl'trĭ). 1. Very hot and moist; oppressive; sweltering. 2. Warm with passion or anger.

sumptuous (sŭmp'tū·ŭs). Costly; luxurious; splendid.

---

bar; church; dog; ardũous; fat; go; hear; jail; key; lame; meat; not; ring; pay; ran; see; shell; ten; there, thick; pastũre; vast; wind; yes; zoo, zh = z in azure.

sundry (sŭn′drĭ). Several; various; miscellaneous.

superficial (sū′pēr·fĭsh′ăl). 1. Lacking in depth; shallow. 2. Not significant.

superfluous (sŭ·pûr′flŏŏ·ŭs). 1. In excess of what is required; unnecessary; creating an overflow or surplus. 2. Extravagant; wasteful.

supplication (sŭp′lĭ·kā′shŭn). An entreaty; a humble plea or petition.

supposition (sŭp′ō·zĭsh′ŭn). A theory; an assumption. **supposititious** (sŭ·pŏz′ĭ·tĭsh′ŭs). 1. Counterfeit; false; fraudulent. 2. Theoretical; assumed; supposed.

sustain (sŭs·tān′). 1. To maintain; to continue. 2. To support; to hold up something. 3. To endure; to suffer or undergo.

swoon (swŏŏn). To faint.

syndicate (sĭn′dĭ·kăt). To manage. *n.* A corporation; an association of persons formed to carry out a project.

T

tableau (tăb′lō). A picture; a representation of a scene made by grouping persons who remain silent and motionless.

tack (tăk). In nautical usage, to change the direction of a vessel by shifting sails; to follow a zigzag course. *n.* The direction of a vessel.

tally (tăl′ĭ). Reckoning; score; count. *v.* To count; to score.

talon (tăl′ŭn). The claw of a bird.

tangible (tăn′jĭ·b′l). 1. Capable of being touched; perceptible. 2. Capable of being grasped by the mind.

tantalize (tăn′tȧ·līz). To tease by keeping something out of reach.

tart (tärt). 1. Sharp to the taste; sour. 2. Pungent; keen.

tauten (tôt′n). To make tightly drawn.

tawny (tô′nĭ). 1. A red-brown or yellow-brown color. 2. Dusky; tanned.

tempestuous (tĕm·pĕs′tū·ŭs). Having a violent nature; turbulent.

tenable (tĕn′ȧ·b′l). Capable of being held or defended.

tenacious (tē·nā′shŭs). 1. Holding fast; capable of retaining. 2. Sticking; adhesive.

tender (tĕn′dẽr). To offer; to present something for acceptance.

tentative (tĕn′tȧ·tĭv). Experimental; of the nature of a test.

terrestrial (tĕ·rĕs′trĭ·ăl). Earthly; belonging to the land.

tether (tĕth′ẽr). To confine by a rope.

timorous (tĭm′ẽr·ŭs). Full of fear; timid.

tincture (tĭngk′tûr). 1. Something that colors or stains. 2. A trace; a slight mark. *v.* To stain; to give to something a new quality, color, flavor, etc.

tolerable (tŏl′ẽr·ȧ·b′l). 1. Capable of being endured. 2. Moderately good; satisfactory.

torrential (tŏ·rĕn′shăl). Flowing rapidly and violently.

torrid (tŏr′ĭd). 1. Hot; parched. 2. Scorching; burning.

touchstone (tŭch′stōn′). A test of quality; a standard.

tousle (tou′z′l) (colloq.). To rumple; to dishevel.

transient (trăn′shĕnt). 1. Passing quickly; short-lived. 2. Changeable; unsettled.

transition (trăn·zĭsh′ŭn). A passage or crossing from one place, state, etc., to another; change.

translucent (trăns·lū′sĕnt). 1. Shining. 2. Partly but not completely transparent.

traverse (trăv′ẽrs). 1. To pass across or through. 2. To survey or examine carefully. *n.* A passage or journey; a route.

trepidation (trĕp′ĭ·dā′shŭn). 1. A trembling. 2. State of alarm; fear.

tumultuous (tū·mŭl′tū·ŭs). Full of commotion and agitation; turbulent; violent.

turbulent (tûr′bū·lĕnt). Characterized by unrest, disturbance, or violent agitation; tempestuous.

U

unalloyed (ŭn′ȧ·loid′). Unmixed; pure.

unavailing (ŭn′ȧ·vāl′ĭng). Useless; not advantageous or profitable.

undulate (ŭn′dū·lāt). To move in waves; to surge. **undulated.** Having a wavy surface.

unduly (ŭn·dū′lĭ). Excessively; beyond the proper degree.

unencumber (ŭn′ĕn·cŭm′bẽr). Not to impede; to take a burden off.

unfathomed (ŭn·făth′ĕm′d). Unmeasured; uncomprehensible.

unkempt (ŭn·kĕmpt′). Uncombed; rough; unpolished.

unpremeditated (ŭn′prē·mĕd′ĭ·tāt′ĕd). Not planned or contrived beforehand.

unpretentious (ŭn′prē·tĕn′shŭs). Not showy; not ambitious; modest.

unremitting (ŭn′rē·mĭt′ĭng). Incessant; persevering; unceasing.

unrequited (ŭn′rē·kwīt′ĕd). Not returned.

unvarnished (ŭn·vär′nĕsht). Not embellished or distorted.

unwonted (ŭn·wŭn′tĕd). 1. Unaccustomed. 2. Uncommon; unusual.

āpe, chăotic, bâre, ăt, ăttend, ärt, flásk, ȧtop; ēke, mẹrely, ĕlect, ĕcho, prudĕnt, doẽr; ĭtem, ĭnn; rarĭty; ōde, ọpaque, fôr, dŏt, lŏft, cŏnfide; sŏŏn, tŏŏk; sour, toil; tūbe, ûnique, tûrn, sŭp, ŭntil.

urban (ûr′băn). Pertaining to, or characteristic of, a city.

usurpation (ū′zēr·pā′shŭn). Act of illegally seizing or taking over power.

V

vacuous (văk′ū·ŭs). 1. Empty. 2. Stupid; dull.

vagary (vá·gâr′ĭ). An eccentricity; an odd action, notion, etc.

vagrancy (vā′grăn·sĭ). The condition of one who has no settled home or residence.

vagrant. A wanderer or vagabond.

vainglorious (vān′glō′rĭ·ŭs). Vain; boastful; proud.

venerable (věn′ēɪ·á·b'l). Worthy of respect, especially because of advanced age.

veneration (věn′ēr·ā′shŭn). 1. Respect; awe. 2. Worship.

venomous (věn′ŭm·ŭs). Full of poison; spiteful; malignant.

verbose (vûr·bōs′). Tending to be wordy.

veritable (věr′ĭ·tá·b'l). Actual; real; true.

vindictive (vĭn·dĭk′tĭv). Desiring revenge; vengeful.

visage (vĭz′ĭj). 1. Face, countenance, or look. 2. Appearance.

vituperative (vī·tū′pēr·ā′tĭv). Abusive in words; berating; scolding.

vivacious (vī·vā′shŭs). Lively in temper or conduct.

vociferation (vō·sĭf′ēr·ā′shŭn). A loud outcry; a clamor.

W

waif (wāf). Anything found or anything without an owner; a stray article or person; a homeless child.

wan (wŏn). Pale; sickly in appearance.

wane (wān). 1. To diminish; to decrease. 2. To become dim or faint.

wary (wâr′ĭ). 1. Cautious; careful. 2. Guarded.

weal (wēl). 1. *Archaic.* A sound, prosperous state; health; prosperity. 2. *Archaic.* The state.

wile (wīl). 1. A trick; a sly device. 2. Trickery.

wither (wĭth′ēr). 1. To dry; to lose freshness or vigor. 2. To wrinkle; to decay; to shrink.

witticism (wĭt′ĭ·sĭz′m). A witty saying or phrase; a jest.

wont (wŭnt). 1. Custom; habit. *adj.* Accustomed.

wraith (rāth). A ghost; a likeness of a living person, supposedly seen just before his death.

writhe (rīth). To twist violently; to become distorted.

wrought (rôt). 1. Fashioned; formed. 2. Manufactured; beaten into shape, as metal.

---

bar; church; dog; ardŭous; fat; go; hear; jail; key; lame; meat; not; ring; pay; ran; see; shell; ten; there, thick; pastūre; vast; wind; yes; zoo, zh = z in azure.

Special Indexes

SPECIAL STUDY MATERIAL ON THE TYPES OF LITERATURE

The Guides to Reading:

READING SKILL STUDY AIDS, listed here according to subject, appear on the following pages.

VOCABULARY EXERCISES appear on the following pages: 48, 72, 191, 278, 291, 485, 652, 727, 754

SUGGESTIONS FOR COMPOSITION are presented on the following pages: 12, 60, 86, 99, 122, 172, 218, 224, 269, 339, 402, 479, 537, 572, 582, 587, 606, 688, 722, 742, 819

ART REPRODUCTIONS IN THE TEXT include works by the following artists:

Birch, Thomas (American, 1779–1851), p. 608

Bodmer, Karl (Swiss, 1805–1893), p. 625

Burges, William (American, active 1715–1731), pp. 438, 442

Bygrave, William (American, 19th Century), p. 653

Catlin, George (American, 1796–1872), pp. 641, 645

Corné, Michael (American, c. 1752–1845), p. 430

Delacroix, Ferdinand (French, 1799–1863), p. 73

Dunn, Harvey (American, 1884–1952), pp. 721, 793

Duplessis, Joseph (French, 1725–1802), p. 464

Durand, Asher (American, 1796–1886), p. 509

Elder, John A. (American, 1833–1895), p. 673

Foster, Ben (American, 1852–1926), p. 257

Halsall, William (American, 19th Century), p. 428

Hassam, Childe (American, 1859–1935), p. 436

Healy, George P. A. (American, 1813–1894), pp. 663, 665, 669

Hesselius, Gustavus (American, 1682–1755), p. 426

Hicks, Edward (American, 1780–1849), p. 295

Homer, Winslow (American, 1836–1910), p. 276

Huntington, Daniel (American 1816–1906), p. 506

Inness, George (American, 1825–1894), p. 782

Jones, A. (American, 19th Century), p. 468

Julio, E. B. F. (American, 19th Century), p. 670

Kneller, Sir Godfrey (English, 1646–1723), p. 443

Manet, Edouard (French, 1832–1883), pp. 519, 523

Marryat, S. F. (English, 19th Century), p. 697

Matteson, Tompkins H. (American, 1813–1884), p. 556

Millet, Jean François (French, 1814–1875), p. 767

Mitchell, Thomas (English, 1735–1790), p. 245

Mount, William Sidney (American, 1807–1868), p. 283

Osgood, Samuel (American, 1808–1885), p. 513

Otis, Bass (American, 1784–1861), p. 469

Otter, Thomas P. (American, 19th Century), pp. 704–05

Peale, Charles Willson (American, 1741–1827), pp. 201, 235, 465, 480, 486

Peale, Rembrandt (American, 1778–1860), p. 472

Perry, Lilla Cabot (American, 20th Century), p. 755

Quidor, John (American, 1802–1881), p. 73

Remington, Frederic (American, 1861–1909), pp. 87, 149, 155, 679, 704

Revere, Paul (American, 1735–1818), p. 470

Rhead, Louis (English, 19th Century), p. 73

Ropes, George (American, 19th Century), pp. 556–57

Rowse, A. W. (American, 19th Century), p. 583

Sargent, John Singer (American, 1856–1925), pp. 290, 770

Schussele, Christian (American, 1826–1879), pp. 464, 491

Sharp, William (American, 1802–?), p. 581

Stuart, Gilbert (American, 1755–1828), p. 482

Sully, Thomas (American, 1783–1872), pp. 225, 466

Thompson, Alfred Wordsworth (American, 1840–1896), p. 445

Trotter, N. H. (American, 1827–1898), p. 704

Weir, Robert (American, 1803–1889), p. 430

Wolcott, John (American, 19th Century), p. 557

Wyeth, Andrew (American, b. 1917), p. 288

General Index

ACKNOWLEDGMENTS

ART WORK DONE SPECIFICALLY FOR THIS EDITION

Paintings and drawings by Robert Shore: pp. 9, 13, 94, 98, 329, 536, 794, 805.

Pastels and drawings by Harvey Dinnerstein: pp. 14, 26, 30, 37, 43, 44, 62, 69, 351, 363, 619, 716, 723, 784, 820.

Watercolors and drawings by Marilyn Miller: pp. 50, 53, 57, 61, 100, 105, 689, 692, 775, 777, 780, 809.

Watercolors and drawings by Lawrence Bjorklund: pp. 74, 80, 88, 93, 188, 191, 193, 505, 601, 630, 635, 638, 706, 709.

Watercolors and drawings by Donald Bolognese: pp. 112, 115, 119, 344, 479, 543, 549, 552, 683, 815.

Stage design by Joseph Weishar: pp. 365, 380, 392.

Pastel by Aldren Watson: p. 403.

Maps and charts by Raphael Palacios: pp. 170, 209, 221, 237, 238–240, 427, 640.

STILL LIFES

Still life, p. 6: Swords, courtesy of Spanish Tourist Bureau; Chess set, courtesy of Georg Jensen.
Still life, p. 248: Chair, courtesy of Herman Miller.

TEXT PHOTOGRAPHS

p. 25, Photo Researchers; p. 29, upper left, center left, upper right, Photo Researchers; bottom, Magnum; p. 48, Pix; p. 60, Knopf; p. 73, top, courtesy, Kennedy Galleries; bottom left, Bettmann; bottom right, courtesy, NYPL, Print Room; p. 87, courtesy, The Sterling and Francine Clark Art Institute; p. 99, Random House; p. 111, Shostal; p. 125, Harbrace Photo; pp. 135, 138, Harbrace Photo, Stanley Rice; p. 139, Free-Lance Photographers Guild; p. 143, Shostal; p. 144, Ray Atkeson; p. 148, Bettmann; p. 155, courtesy, Museum of Fine Arts of Houston, Hogg Brothers Collection; pp. 156, 161, Black Star; p. 162, Harper & Bros.; p. 163, Black Star; p. 173, Monkmeyer; pp. 174, 183, Friedman-Abels; p. 184, Culver; p. 195, Susan McCartney; p. 196, Scribner's; p. 197, Susan McCartney; p. 201, courtesy, Independence National Historical Park; p. 205, Susan McCartney; p. 207, NYPL; p. 219, Brown Brothers; p. 225, courtesy, The Union League of Philadelphia; p. 226, Culver; p. 229, Bettmann; p. 233, Free-Lance Photographers Guild; p. 235, courtesy, Independence National Historical Park; p. 245, courtesy, United States Naval Academy Museum; p. 251, Pix; p. 257, courtesy, The Art Institute of Chicago; p. 264, top, Pix; bottom, Alan Newman; p. 269, Bettmann; p. 275, Knopf; p. 276, courtesy, Museum of Fine Arts, Boston; p. 279, Culver; p. 283, courtesy, Melville Collection, Suffolk Museum at Stony Brook; p. 287, Brown Brothers; p. 288, Collection, The Museum of Modern Art, New York; p. 290, bottom, courtesy, Museum of Fine Arts, Boston; p. 292, Viking Press; p. 294, courtesy, Abby Aldrich Rockefeller Folk Art Collection, Williamsburg; p. 296, top, Harbrace Photo; bottom, Standard Oil Co., (N.J.); p. 299, Photo Researchers; p. 304, Bettmann; p. 309, courtesy, Museum of Fine Arts, Boston; p. 313, Harbrace Photo; p. 315, Photo Researchers; p. 317, Pix; p. 319, Brown Brothers; p. 321, Houghton Mifflin; p. 324, Susan McCartney; p. 326, Harbrace Photo; p. 327, courtesy, Museum of Fine Arts, Boston; p. 328, Farrar, Straus & Cudahy; p. 330, Black Star; p. 331, Imogene Cunningham; p. 332, Random House; p. 333, Little, Brown; p. 334, top, Washington Post; p. 335, Monkmeyer; p. 336, The University of Chicago Press; p. 337, Harbrace Photo; p. 340, Brown Brothers; p. 342, Lippincott; p. 343, McGraw-Hill; p. 345, Funk and Wagnalls;

p. 364, Bettmann; p. 405, Martha Swope; p. 412, courtesy, NYPL, Print Room; p. 413, courtesy, National Gallery of Art, Mellon Collection; p. 415, courtesy, State House, Boston; p. 421, courtesy, Massachusetts Historical Society; p. 423, NYPL, Rare Book Room; p. 426, courtesy, The Historical Society of Pennsylvania; pp. 428, 431, courtesy, Pilgrim Hall; p. 433, courtesy, NYPL, Rare Book Room; p. 434, NYPL; p. 435, Library of Congress; p. 437, courtesy, The Parrish Art Museum; pp. 438, 441, courtesy, NYPL, Print Room; p. 443, Bettmann; pp. 445, 454, courtesy, The Metropolitan Museum of Art; pp. 456–457, courtesy, The Library Company of Philadelphia; p. 461, Harbrace Photo; p. 463, Bettmann; p. 465, top, courtesy, Henry E. Huntington Library and Art Gallery; bottom left, courtesy, The New York Historical Society; bottom right, courtesy, The Historical Society of Pennsylvania; pp. 466, 469, courtesy, Independence National Historical Park; p. 468, Bettmann; p. 471, courtesy, The Metropolitan Museum of Art; p. 472, courtesy, The New York Historical Society; p. 477, top, Shostal; bottom, Photo Researchers; p. 480, courtesy, Independence National Historical Park; p. 482, courtesy, The Metropolitan Museum of Art; p. 486, courtesy, Colonial Williamsburg; p. 491, courtesy, Sleepy Hollow Restorations; p. 494, courtesy, The Pierpont Morgan Library; p. 506, courtesy, The Brooklyn Museum Collection; p. 509, courtesy, NYPL; p. 513, courtesy, The New York Historical Society; p. 515, Max Hirmer Verlag; pp. 519, 523, courtesy, NYPL, Print Room; p. 540, courtesy, The Essex Institute; p. 541, courtesy, The Berkshire Athenaeum; pp. 556–557, top left, courtesy, The Essex Institute; top right, courtesy, Mrs. Robert Blake Watson; bottom, courtesy, Peabody Museum; pp. 558, 561, courtesy, Shelburne Museum; pp. 569, 573, courtesy, Emerson House, Susan McCartney; p. 581, courtesy, The Museum of Fine Arts, Boston, M. & M. Karolik Collection, and American Heritage Publishing Company; p. 583, courtesy, Concord Free Public Library; p. 589, courtesy, Longfellow House, Susan McCartney; pp. 593, 600, 607, Library of Congress; p. 608, courtesy, Department of the Navy; p. 612, Culver; p. 625, courtesy, NYPL, Rare Book Room; pp. 626, 627, Bettmann; p. 628, courtesy, Georgia Historical Commission; pp. 641 and 645, courtesy, Kennedy Galleries, and American Heritage Publishing Company; p. 648, John Morrell & Co.; p. 653, courtesy, The Mariners Museum; p. 654, courtesy, The American Museum of Natural History; p. 656, courtesy, National Audubon Society; pp. 660, 663, Bettmann; p. 665, courtesy, The Newberry Library; p. 666, Brown Brothers; p. 669, courtesy, The Corcoran Gallery of Art; p. 670, Bettmann; p. 673, courtesy, The Corcoran Gallery of Art; p. 675, Bettmann; p. 677, courtesy, Columbia University, Special Collections; p. 679, NYPL; p. 681, courtesy, The Amon Carter Museum of Western Art; p. 697, courtesy, The New York Historical Society; p. 698, Bettmann; pp. 704–705, top, courtesy, Nelson-Atkins Museum; lower left, courtesy, Gilcrease Institute of American History and Art; lower right, courtesy, Smithsonian Institute; p. 721, courtesy, City Library, De Smet, South Dakota; p. 726, courtesy, Oklahoma Historical Society; p. 732, courtesy, The Metropolitan Museum of Art; p. 736, courtesy, NYPL, Stokes Collection; p. 743, Library of Congress; p. 750, Harper & Bros.; p. 755, Macmillan; p. 762, Ewing Galloway; p. 767, from the collection of the late Mr. and Mrs. William Crocker; p. 769, Bettmann; p. 770, courtesy, National Portrait Gallery, London; p. 771, Brown Brothers; p. 783, courtesy, The Art Institute of Chicago; p. 793, courtesy, South Dakota State University; p. 806, Bettmann.

H
I
J
K